W9-BZE-535

CONTENTS

COMPANY HISTORIES

DEDICATION

To my family who believes in me,
My friends who inspire me,
My teachers and students who challenge me,
And the toy collectors who've taught me that you're never too old or
too young to appreciate a good toy.

ACKNOWLEDGMENTS: LATE NIGHTS AND LOUD MUSIC

Compiling this 11th edition involved a lot of late nights, loud music, and amazing quantities of Diet Coke. Taking on a project this size would be an overwhelming task for one person and I am very grateful for the outpouring of assistance I've received.

Building on the tradition established by Richard O'Brien more than 25 years ago was no small challenge. This book would not have been possible without the dedication of new and continuing contributors. Their expertise, patience, and generous counsel led to the numerous improvements you will discover in this text.

Contributors include, Capt. Perry R. Eichor, Franc Isla, Ron Smith, Judith Izen, the late Bill Bertoia, Bertoia Auctions, Leo Rishty, Jim Buskirk, John Fawcett, John K. Snyder, Marcie Tubbs, Kate Bossen, John J. Murray, Charles W. Best, Randy Welch, Keith Kaonis, Stan Alekna, Richard Leach, Scott Smiles, Darryll R. Jones, Jeff Hubbard, Randy Prasse, Mark Rich (thanks for all of your encouragement and those enjoyable toy talks!), and Jim and Judy Sneed. Several sections were unaltered from the 10th edition and the contributions of those individuals are acknowledged at the beginnings of those sections. I look forward to working with all of you on the 12th Edition.

The talented staff of Krause Publications deserves big thanks—Clay Miller designed the book's front cover, Brian Brogaard designed the back cover and gorgeous color section, Wendy Wendt was responsible for the book's delightful interior design, Ethel Thulien and Sally Olson helped with the interior pages, Patsy Howell provided last-minute design help (a.k.a. damage control), Sandi Morrison ran the data patterns with a smile, and the patient members of our scanning departments handled all the last-minute additions the editor couldn't resist. Special thanks to everyone who pitched in to get this book safely to the printer.

Editorial thanks go to Merry Dudley, editor of *Toy Cars & Models* magazine, for volunteering hours of data entry and proofreading countless pages (and for getting me out of the building to see *Lord of the Rings: The Return of the King*). Additional thanks to book editors Kris Manty and Tracy Schmidt who typed and corrected the chapter introductions and provided moral support.

Thanks also to the toy collectors and dealers who have made this hobby such a joy throughout my life. Your generosity and willingness to share information is much appreciated. This book is for you and I hope you enjoy it.

Last but certainly not least, I also owe a debt of thanks to my family and friends for their enduring patience and endless support through the struggle to bring this edition to life. You're the best!

Karen O'Brien
January 2004

INTRODUCTION

A Successful Toy Show

How do you determine whether or not a toy show was a success? If you're a collector, does it involve finding a great bargain on an elusive treasure? If you're a dealer, does it involve the financial benefit of selling everything on your table? Or as participants in the toy hobby, are there less tangible and even more rewarding factors that could lead to a successful toy show experience? For me, the answer is yes.

When leaving a recent toy show, I passed a fellow patron who was in the process of telling his buddy that the show wasn't worth his time and he'd think twice before coming back. He wasn't walking away empty-handed, however, and I resisted the urge to stop the fellow and ask exactly why he thought this particular show was a failure. I had just finished writing my monthly column for *Toy Shop* magazine and had addressed the topic of what constitutes a successful toy show, so the question was fresh in my mind. For me, success at one show involved actually seeing an Arcade Showboat on a dealer's table. The simple joy of looking at a toy that I've only ever viewed as a photo in a book made the long drive to that show entirely worth it—for the disgruntled patron at this particular show, success must have meant something different.

This led to the realization that although toy collectors share a common interest in toys, individual tastes vary to such an extent that arriving at a community consensus as to exactly what makes a toy show successful is a near impossibility. All we can hope to agree on are a few basic principles.

And perhaps those are enough.

It is the common thread that builds a community. Toy collectors share in the unique heritage of playthings that reflect the varied times in which they were created. What was life like for children during World War II? Look at the wooden toys that replaced the pressed steel varieties of just a few years before—how often do you run across the wooden Erector sets produced by A.C. Gilbert during that period, or a wooden Buddy "L" tank like the one featured in the color section of this book? What kind of economic and trading climate did the United States enjoy during the 1950s? Look at the explosion of battery-operated toys imported from Japan, Hong Kong, and China.

Appreciating the toys of another era can lead different generations to appreciate each other, and promoting that kind of understanding can only benefit the hobby and ensure its longevity. I grew up with *The Dukes of Hazzard* not the *Howdy Doody Show*, but if you yell, "Hey kids, what time is it?" you better believe that I know to answer, "It's Howdy Doody time!" Toy shows represent an ideal opportunity to show children not only what it was like for their parents growing up, but their grandparents as well. As those children grow up and develop their own collecting tastes, they become the caretakers of past toys and preserve the hobby for the future.

Acquiring and sharing information is another characteristic of the collecting community. By expressing your interests to others, they know your collecting tastes and are able to look out for pieces that might interest you. At the same time, they develop an appreciation for items that they don't necessarily wish to collect, but recognize as being desirable. Toy shows present an ideal venue for information exchange at the personal level. Dealers are more than willing to share information regarding the toys on their tables and often acquire pieces to sell with their repeat customers in mind. Because dealers are more often than not collectors themselves, they are a wealth of information to those seeking education. After all, the more you know about the toys you seek, the better able you are to make good decisions about their condition and value.

The process of assembling this 11th edition of *O'Brien's Collecting Toys* has been remarkably similar to attending a toy show. I've had the privilege and pleasure of talking to dozens of toy collectors who specialize in specific areas and have been gracious enough to share their expertise within these pages. One person couldn't hope to collect all the toys contained herein, so I am very grateful for their assistance.

The thousands of photographs, updated prices, and improved listings represent 29 toy collecting fields. While you likely don't collect the toys of all 29, the education received from flipping through the chapters is much like a stroll through the aisles of a toy show. The amazing variety presented here is an opportunity to learn more about your collection and the other toys of the past.

What makes for a successful toy show?

For me, success is the active participation in the hobby. The knowledge I bring through the door to a show makes me familiar with even the toys I don't collect and keeps me curious about the toys I've never seen in person. Striking up conversations with dealers allows me to learn even more, and in turn, I'll share what I've learned with other collectors. After more than 20 years of attending toy shows, I have left some empty-handed, but I've never left without an increased appreciation for this hobby and all of those wonderful toys.

What makes a toy show a success for you?

About the 11th Edition

Look at the Contents page and you'll notice several changes. Conversations with collectors over the past year revealed that the title needed to focus more on antique toys and less on their modern counterparts. With this in mind, several chapters were removed including Action Figures, Model Kits, PEZ, and Hot Wheels. All four receive detailed coverage in sister publication *Toys & Prices*, a title that was changed this year to focus on post-World War II toys and Baby Boomer toys. This new focus provided the opportunity to add hundreds of photos not included in the 10th edition and expand chapters to provide better coverage of your favorite toys.

Although I couldn't make all of the changes I wanted with this edition (there is never enough time), I did add several chapters. Returning to the title is an expanded Steam Toys chapter by Richard Leach. Featuring more photos than any previous version of the chapter, this is a bright addition to the title and one that I look forward to expanding in the future. Also returning to the title is Randy Welch's chapter on Ramp Walkers. He updated the listings and prices and provided photos of walkers that this title has never featured before. Welch also constructed a chapter on Mechanical Sparkler and Plunger Toys. No other toy title has such detailed coverage of the whimsical sparklers, and it was a delight to add the chapter. Mark Rich, columnist for *Toy Shop* and *Toy Cars & Models* magazines, reconstructed a chapter on collectible yo-yos that I'm very happy to share with you in this edition.

Several chapters received significant upgrades. The Erector Set chapter now contains a detailed listing of the sets released yearly by the A.C. Gilbert Co. The chapter is certainly a work in progress and it wasn't possible to obtain pricing for each set, so you will find NPF (No Price Found) designations in the value column. Future editions will contain pricing as I continue to research auction results and toy shows as I consult with collectors. I welcome the input of fellow collectors in this process—after all, that's half the fun of working on this book!

The Fisher-Price chapter was overhauled and should prove to be more collector-friendly as well as more complete. Kate Bosson's pricing updates in the Farm Toys chapter are a welcome addition as that chapter proves to be popular among collectors. The Wooden Toys chapter also doubled in size as contributors Jim and Judy Sneed provided interesting company histories, expanded listings, and some wonderful photos. All of these chapters can look forward to even more expansion in the future.

A Note on Value

O'Brien's Collecting Toys has been in print now for more than 25 years. It is a title that has grown with each edition into the premiere resource for collectors of antique toys. But a price guide is only a guide—it's a place to start the process of acquiring new toys for your collection, not the sole determiner of what a toy is worth. As buyers and sellers, *you* determine the value of any given toy. Value is decided ultimately by what a buyer is willing to pay, so do your homework with this value guide and use every available research tool, including the Internet and toy shows, to assess the toys you buy and sell.

Future Editions

This title is constantly being updated and collector input is welcomed and needed to continue its growth. I love to talk toys, so stop me at a show or drop me a line if you have suggestions to improve this book. Any toy information, suggestions, or photos (good quality 35mm prints or slides, please) you'd like to donate to our archives (you will receive photo credit for all photos used in print) may be sent to me at the following address:

O'Brien's Collecting Toys
Krause Publications
700 E. State St.
IOLA, WI 54990
(715) 445-4612
email: obrienk@krause.com

Enjoy your collection and support your local toy shows!

Karen O'Brien
January 2004

HOW TO USE THIS BOOK

This book contains twenty-nine chapters devoted to all types of toys. Listings for toys include the toy name, a description where possible, the year(s) the toy was produced, the company that manufactured the toy, the toy number assigned by the manufacturer, the toy's dimensions, an O'Brien number where applicable, and a value in up to four condition grades.

A note on O'Brien numbers: Richard O'Brien introduced the numbers as a method to catalog various toys. At no time were these numbers found on the actual toys. Collectors have found them useful to distinguish toys over the years and I have included the numbers in parentheses within this edition. The goal of this project was to make the listings as collector-friendly as possible, and the continued inclusion of O'Brien numbers furthers that objective nicely.

Abbreviations

N/A   Not applicable. If n/a appears in a price column, then an item has no value in that condition grade

NPF   No price found. If NPA appears in a price column, then the item's value was not able to be determined.

Condition

Determining the condition of a toy is the single most important factor in assessing its value. The values in this guide are for complete toys without missing parts. It should be noted that this edition is adopting the condition code used by Richard O'Brien in his 8th Edition. The greatest change over the 9th and 10th editions is the definition of C10 condition. The C10 prices in this edition reflect mint toys without their original boxes—boxes add a premium above the C10 price.

CONDITION CODE

C6   Good; evident overall wear, well played with but acceptable to many collectors
C8   Very Good; minor overall wear, very clean
C10   Mint; like new

Note: Mint in Box commands a higher price.
Condition below C6 brings considerably lower prices

Note: Prices in photo captions are listed at C10 condition, whether or not the item pictured is in C10 condition.

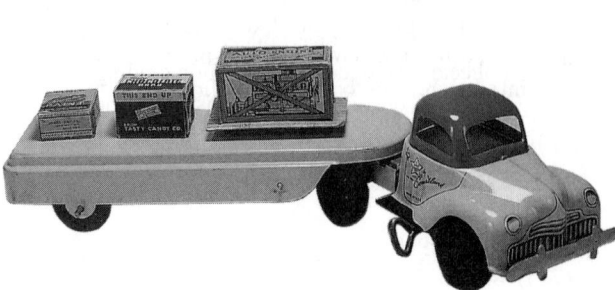

AIRCRAFT

(See also Tin Wind-ups, Comic Characters, Premiums and Paper)

By Perry R. Eichor

The airplane, until about twenty years ago, was one aspect of toy collecting that attracted little interest and even less enthusiasm. Prices of toy airplanes generally reflected this lethargy.

Suddenly, those of us born and raised during 1920-1940 (the golden age of aviation) had the time, the inclination, and means to acquire those objects on which our fantasies were transported during childhood. The scramble began, and demand and prices have been climbing steadily ever since.

Collecting toy aircraft and memorabilia has finally come into its own. As an investment, they seem a good risk and have held their own during the recent economic downturn. Though I find few true collectors who get any joy from acquiring only objects that are guaranteed to appreciate in value. True value lies in the ability of an object to rekindle the fires of our memories and bring to mind those halcyon days of our youth.

Those interested in collecting die-cast toy aircraft can choose from Tootsietoy, Hubley, Erie, Manoil, Barclay, Dinky, Mercury, S.R., Solido, Tekno, C.I.J., and a host of others. Cast iron was used by numerous companies before World War II, including Hubley, Arcade, Dent, and Kilgore to name a few.

Pressed steel seemed to be dominated by Wyandotte and Marx for the smaller types, while Keystone, Kingsbury, and Steelcraft, among others, produced the larger types. Tin is unlimited, and many companies made toy aircraft. Some pre-war types were made by Marx, Strauss, Chein, Kingsbury, Girard, American Flyer, and numerous European manufacturers. Japanese companies, although having produced some very desirable toys prior to World War II, joined the fray in the 1950s. Some of the later Japanese tin types were very accurate representations of actual aircraft, while others resembled aircraft as much as Godzilla resembles Snow White.

Some of the nicest toy aircraft ever produced were the "Gnom" series made by Lehmann in the 1930s. These accurate small tin toys were base on two Heinkel aircraft and variations thereof. They are difficult to find and quite a nice display item.

In addition to the above, there are numerous examples of slush-cast items from Barclay, Kansas Toy and Novelty, Tommy Toy, Ralstoy, Lincoln White Metal, Best, and perhaps the finest examples of the slush-cast

toy industry from C.A. Wood. The Sun and Auburn rubber companies produced some very unique planes but well-preserved and undistorted rubber toy aircraft are very rare.

Some excellent plastic types were produced immediately after World War II and into the 1950s. Some items, such as the P-38, B-25, B-17, and P-40 by Renwal and the B-26 by Hubley, were faithful copies, while others, such as the P-39 by Ideal, are so out of proportion that they lack even the symbiotic charm that often accompanies grotesqueness. Other toy manufacturers of plastic toy aircraft were Thomas, Acme, Premier, Lido, and Reliable.

If one collects toy aircraft, it follows that one wants to display toy aircraft, and they look best on the numerous toy airports depicting structures of the same time period. In addition to airfields and hangars, there were numerous ground support personnel and vehicles. As with other toy collecting fields, related memorabilia begin to encroach into the aircraft collector's acquisitions.

Interest in aviation continues, and the increase in air show attendance, global military action, and quantum leaps in technology including interactive video games, will have a dramatic effect on the interest in things related to flight. Consequently, prices will rise and availability will decrease in inverse proportion to interest.

The introduction of online auctions has affected the prices and knowledge within the hobby. Because of increased knowledge and availability, some items originally considered rare and expensive, were discovered to be in abundance and prices declined. Other items, such as the slush-cast items, found a new popularity and consequently, prices climbed. On the whole, the Internet has added to the hobby. It has educated a growing group of new collectors as to identity, condition grading, and average prices. There are those who disparage the Internet, but it is a fact of life and is here to stay.

However, there will always be room for those of us who were excited during our youth by the sound of a rotary engine in a biplane passing overhead, doing slow rolls among cotton-ball clouds. We all still secretly yearn to fly with our youthful heroes and perform daring feats of aerial combat. How many of you have a leather flight jacket in your closet? I rest my case.

Keep 'em Flying!

Contributors: Capt. Perry R. Eichor, USAF (retired) and Donna Eichor, 703 North Almond Drive, Simpsonville, SC, 29681.

*American Flyer Monoplane, No. 560, c. 1929, 24"
wingspan, $900. Photo courtesy Wilkinson
Collection, Detroit Antique Toy Museum*

*Arcade Arcadia Airport, missing awnings, with two planes. At
right is the Arcade Monocoupe.*

American Flyer ad from the 1929 Playthings
magazine.

A.C. Williams	C6	C8	C10
UX-166, Lindy-type plane, nickeled engine and wheels, cast-iron	75	112	150
UX83, cast iron.............................	100	150	200
UX-99, cast iron	112	170	225
Zeppelin, "Graf Zeppelin", cast iron	150	225	400
Zeppelin, "Graf Zeppelin", cast iron	100	150	200
Zeppelin, "Graf Zeppelin", cast iron	50	75	125
American Flyer	**C6**	**C8**	**C10**
Monoplane, "A.F. Lines Air Service", c. 1929.............................	350	525	900
Spirit of America, c. 1928	200	300	500
Arcade	**C6**	**C8**	**C10**
Airplane, single engine, pressed-steel wing, body resembles Corsair, red and yellow, or blue and yellow, cast-iron.........................	230	345	500
Airplane, twin engine, pressed-steel wing, cast-iron............................	175	265	350
Airplane, tri-motor, pressed-steel props, cast-iron........................	75	125	200

Arcade (Continued)	C6	C8	C10
Airplane, twin engine, "United Boeing", cast iron	75	125	200
Arcadia Airport................................	600	950	1400
Monocoupe......................................	262	395	525
Monocoupe, pull toy, cast iron........	1300	2100	3200
Monocoupe, steel wing, cast iron....	475	750	1000
Monocoupe......................................	200	250	400
Auburn Rubber	**C6**	**C8**	**C10**
Army Pursuit Plane, "US 1X2755" on wings, Curtiss P-37, (AA3)....	20	40	75
Boeing, "Clipper", (AA1)	25	70	115
Consolidated A-11 Light Bomber, (AA2)	25	70	100
Douglas DC2 Transport, (AA4)	40	60	125
Jet, marked "XR577", (AA6)..........	35	52	70
Jet 559, (AA5)	22	33	45
Automatic Toy Co.	**C6**	**C8**	**C10**
Futurmatic Airport..........................	150	225	300
Rocket and Space Ship, friction, w/rubber wheels, sparks, tin litho, 1930s.................................	30	50	75

Arcade Monocoupe, No. 357, 11" wingspan, $3200. Photo courtesy Bertoia Auctions

Barclay Aeroplane, No. 195, $125. Photo courtesy Hank Anton

Top row, left to right: Auburn Rubber Boeing. No. 1548, 8" wingspan, $115; Auburn Rubber Consolidated A-11 Light Bomber, 4" wingspan, $100. Bottom row, left to right: Auburn Rubber Army Pursuit Plane, No. 586, $75; Auburn Rubber Douglas DC2 Transport, $125. Photo courtesy Ed Poole

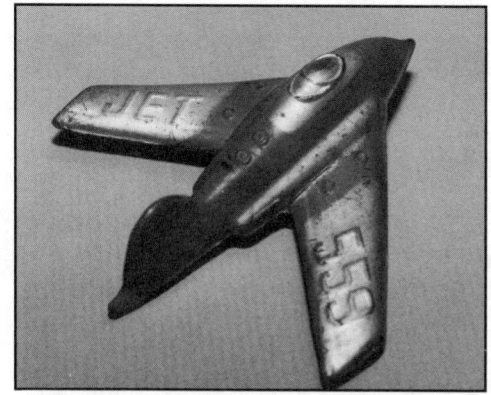

Auburn AA5 "Jet 559." Photo by Max Heiss

Automatic Toy Co. (Continued)	**C6**	**C8**	**C10**
Silver Eagle, wooden wheels, two engine, aluminum, c. 1930s	75	125	250

Barclay	**C6**	**C8**	**C10**
Aeroplane, "U.S. Army," single engine transport, (BA7)...............	20	30	50
Aeroplane, w/Monoplane piggy-backed on it, (BA7a)	50	85	140
Aeroplane, w/clip of bombs attached to it, (BA7b)..................	45	80	125
Altantic Bremen, The, c. 1928, (BA2)...	40	75	100
Dirigible, early to mid-1930, (BA4a)..	30	60	100
Giant Zeppelin, (BA4).....................	20	60	100
Lindy-type Plane, small, (BA10).....	15	20	30
Monoplane, thick-winged, w/over-sized wheels; shown in 1935 Barclay Bros. Catalog, (BA9).....	20	30	45
Monoplane, single engine, (BA1a)...	48	72	95

Barclay (Continued)	**C6**	**C8**	**C10**
Monoplane, single engine, high-wing, Crackerjack size, one-piece, vertical prop, sold w/Aeroplane Carrier and piggy-back on Aeroplane, (BA3)	20	30	40
Rocket Ship, (BA6)	100	150	200
Rocket Ship, (BA5)	100	150	200

Big Bang	**C6**	**C8**	**C10**
Bombing Plane, single barrel, die-cast propeller, cast iron	600	900	1500
Bombing Plane, double barrel, steel propeller, cast iron......................	350	600	800

Buddy "L"	**C6**	**C8**	**C10**
Army Tank Transport Plane, two detachable tanks under wings, tanks have hum motor device, pressed steel, 1941	460	690	925
Monoplane and Catapult Hanger, c. 1930-31	1200	2200	3000
Single high-wing monoplane, c. 1929-31	400	600	800

C.A.W. Novelty Company, Army Pursut Plane No. 37, P-37 Monoplane, 2-7/8"x3-1/2", (CWA12). Photo courtesy Perry Eichor

Big Bang Bombing Plane, No. 11-P, 13" long, $800. Photo courtesy Sotheby's, New York

Buddy "L" Army Tank Transport Plane, No. 959, 1941, 27" wingspan, $925. Photo courtesy Richard MacNary

C.A.W. Novelty Company Army Pursuit Plane, No. 37, 2-7/8" x 3-1/2", $160. Photo courtesy Perry Eichor

Buddy "L" (Continued)	C6	C8	C10
Transport Airplane (Ford), c. 1946	300	450	600
Triple Hangar and three planes, (planes are monocoupes), c. 1931	1700	2700	3750

C.A.W. Novelty Company

Charles A. Wood was known as the "Pioneer Birdman" in Clay Center, Kansas. Master aircraft mechanic, early pilot and aviation booster, his emphasis on aircraft in his toy line reflected his life-long love. Unfortunately his toys have been largely unavailable to collectors.

Wood's line was heavy with miniature airplanes. It was reported he flew his toys to Eastern markets. This could have been true under special circumstances only, for in its best years (over sixty employees and two million toys) the company output would have been too large to ship by air.

In comparing his toys and others, we see that Wood didn't take any shortcuts. He manufactured a Ford Trimotor with the landing gear and outboard motors on struts; pilot's heads showing through open cockpit windows; and a most realistic model

of Ben Howard's famous stunt-plane with "Mr. Mulligan" prominently embossed. Wood's early production had metal disk wheels with painted black "tires." Later toys had rubber or plastic wheels. All aircraft had cast propellers, tapered and rounded wings except for C.A.W. All of his pieces are more models than toys. His replicas of famous aircraft, local airliners, and mail-planes are miniature souvenirs of history.

Because Wood was such an activist a brief biography may be of interest. He was born about 1891, and went to work for Longren Aircraft Mfg. Co. in Topeka, Kansas in 1915. He opened the toy factory in Clay Center in 1925, and was influential in establishing a local airport in a wheat field in 1929. He received his pilot's license, bought a Waco F biplane, erected a Butler hangar, and opened a repair service in 1930. He was active in persuading Midland Air Express and Western Air Express lines to make route stops in Clay Center, which put this county seat on the air map.

In 1938, during National Airmail Week, Wood flew a commemorative from Morganville to Kansas City. One mail sack was delivered to the airfield by a Pony Express horseman. During the war he was an instructor at a naval training center. Later, he owned a Rearwing plane, was a Piper Club dealer, and in 1955, designed and built a monoplane dubbed "Little Monster." He continued to fly until 1976—a grand old man of early aviation.

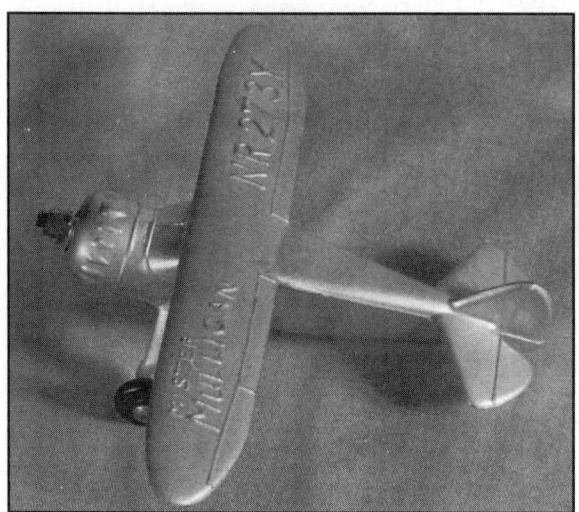

C.A.W. Novelty Company Mister Mulligan Airplane No. 34, c. 1936, 3"x3-1/2", (CWA10). Photo courtesy Perry Eichor

C.A.W. Novelty Company Mister Mulligan Airplane, No. 34, c. 1936 production, 3" x 3-1/2", $400. Photo courtesy Perry Eichor

C.A.W. Novelty Company Monoplane, No. 12, 3-1/8" x 4-3/8", $150. Photo courtesy Gary Franson

Top row, left to right: C.A.W. Novelty Company Monoplane, 3-1/8" x 3-5/8", $175; C.A.W. Novelty Company Sr. Low-wing Monoplane, No. 29, 3-3/4" x 4", $120; C.A.W. Novelty Company Jr. Low-wing Monoplane, No. 28, 3-5/8" x 3-1/2", $70. Bottom row, left to right: C.A.W. Novelty Company Boeing Bomber, No. 36, 2-5/8" x 3-1/2", $120; C.A.W. Novelty Company Army Pursuit Plane, No. 37, 2-7/8" x 3-1/2", $160. Photo courtesy Perry Eichor

C.A.W. Novelty Co.	C6	C8	C10
Army Pursuit Plane, P-37 Monoplane, low-wing, marked "Seversky," under wings is Air Corp mark, "37" and "Made in USA," cowled radial engine, (CWA12) .	60	100	160
Boeing Bomber, low-wing, marked "Boeing," "NC13361" and "Made in USA," bi-motored, three-bladed props, looks like Boeing model 247 airliner, (CWA11)	60	80	120
Jr. low-wing monoplane, Northrop, cowled radial engine, w/two restrooms, six wondows, pilot in open cockpit near tail, (CWA8)	30	50	70

C.A.W. Novelty Co. (Continued)	C6	C8	C10
Mister Mulligan Airplane, high-wing, marked "Mister Mulligan" and "NR273Y," cowled radial engine, two windows, two doors, c. 1936 production, (CWA10)	100	225	400
Monoplane, Ford tri-motor model 4, seven cylinder, radial engines, outboards and landing gear on struts, tail wheel, complex molding, (CWA7)	75	110	150
Monoplane, low-wing cabin or pursuit plane, cowled radial engine, forward cockpit, divided windshield, open windows w/pilot's head inside, (CWA13)	75	125	175

C.A.W. Novelty Company Top row left to right: CWA1, CWA2, CWA8, CWA6; bottom row left to right: CWA5, CWA9, CWA7. Photo courtesy Perry Eichor

C.A.W. Novelty Company Monoplane, 3-1/8" x 3-5/8", $175.

C.A.W. Novelty Company Monoplane, high-wing, 3-5/8" x 3-1/2", $60. Photo courtesy Perry Eichor

C.A.W. Novelty Company Monoplane, small, 2-3/8" x 2-1/2", $40. Photo courtesy Gary Franson

C.A.W. Novelty Co. (Continued)	C6	C8	C10
Monoplane, high-wing, Ford Model, V-12 engine, eight window, two restrooms, crew of two in open cockpit behind wing, tail wheel, (CWA3)	30	40	60
Monoplane, high-wing, Ford model 2?, V-12 engine, eight window, w/two restrooms, closed cockpit in front of wing, tail wheel, (CWA4)	20	40	60
Monoplane, high-wing, Ford model 2?, V-12 engine, eight window, w/two restrooms, crew of two in open cockpit behind wing, tail wheel, stubbier wings, possibly CAW copy, (CWA2b)	40	60	100
Monoplane, large, high-wing Lindy Ryan-type but w/V-8 engine, oversized propeller, five windows and door, probably C.A.W., (CWA14)	20	40	60
Monoplane, large, amphibian, Douglas Dolphin, bi-motored, (CWA6)	60	85	125

C.A.W. Novelty Co. (Continued)	C6	C8	C10
Monoplane, small, high-wing racing-type, V-8 engine, closed cockpit in front of wing, six windows, marked "CAW" and "Pat., appld. for" under tail, (CWA2)	40	60	85
Monoplane, small, high-wing Lindy-type, six-cylinder radial engine, negative dihedral in wings, (CWA1)	20	30	40
Monoplane, small, Amphibian, Douglas Dolphin, bi-motored, (CWA5)	40	60	85
Sr. Low-wing Monoplane, Lockheed or Northrup cowled radial engine, six windows, pilot in open cockpit near tail, tail wheel, (CWA9)	50	75	120

Dent	C6	C8	C10
Air Express, tri-motor, cast iron	2500	4000	7000
Air Express, green, cast iron	750	1400	2000
Airline Monoplane, "?" on fuselage, stripes on rudder, cast aluminum	700	1050	1400

Dent Air Express, 12" wingspan, $2000. Photo courtesy Wilkinson Collection; Detroit Antique Toy Museum

Dent Los Angeles Dirigible, c.1920s, 10-3/4" long, $1700. Photo courtesy Bertoia Auctions

Dent (Continued)	C6	C8	C10
Airline Monoplane, "X5043" cast on rudder, cast iron	750	1000	1500
Ford, tri-motor, "1417" cast on rudder above "Ford", cast iron	2000	3500	6000
Lindy, cast iron	1000	1900	3000
Los Angeles Dirigible, cast iron, c. 1925	450	675	900
Los Angeles Dirigible, c. 1932	150	225	400
Los Angeles Dirigible, cast iron, c. 1925	1000	1500	2000
Los Angeles Dirigible, cast iron, c. 1920s	700	1200	1700
Lucky Boy	100	200	225
Lucky Boy, "X6043" cast on rudder, cast iron	800	1400	2000
Lucky Boy, tri-motor, cast iron	600	900	1500
Lucky Boy Glider, high-wing, cast iron	400	750	1000
Question Mark, tri-motor, "?" on fuselage, cast iron	3500	7500	10,000
Zep Zeppelin, cast iron	150	300	400
Zep Zeppelin, aluminum	70	100	150
Zep Zeppelin, cast iron	125	160	210

Erie	C6	C8	C10
Boeing 247, twin engine, marked "U.S. Army"	25	50	100
Boeing B-17	40	80	125
Northrup Delta, single-engine passenger airliner	40	80	140
Northrup Gamma, single seat, open cockpit	60	90	150
Two-place open cockpit, "U.S. Army" on wings	35	60	80

Gibbs	C6	C8	C10
Biplane, tin tail, aluminum propeller, pull plane, propeller spin, wooden	40	70	200

Girard	C6	C8	C10
High-wing Monoplane, pressed steel	150	500	750
High-wing Monoplane, pressed steel	150	275	500
Whiz Skyfighter Biplane, early	100	200	300

Hubley	C6	C8	C10
302 DO-X Seaplane, high-wing, six engine, cast iron, (H31)	100	200	300
Air Ford, two open cockpits, cast iron, (H38)	150	200	275
Air Ford, (H40)	85	125	170
Airplane, folding wings, retractable landing gear, plastic cockpit, resembles Brewster Buffalo, red and silver w/four-bladed prop in early version, later version was green and yellow w/two-blade prop, die-cast, (H25)	52	78	125
America, largest cast-iron plane made, tri-motor, open cockpit, w/pilot and copilot, cast iron, (H1)	3500	7000	12,000
America, single engine, wire spring drive, w/two pilots in open cockpit, cast iron, (H15)	3000	7500	12,000
American Eagle or Flying Circus, Early—red and silver, four-bladed prop, no airscoop on top of engine cowl, (H21)	75	100	150

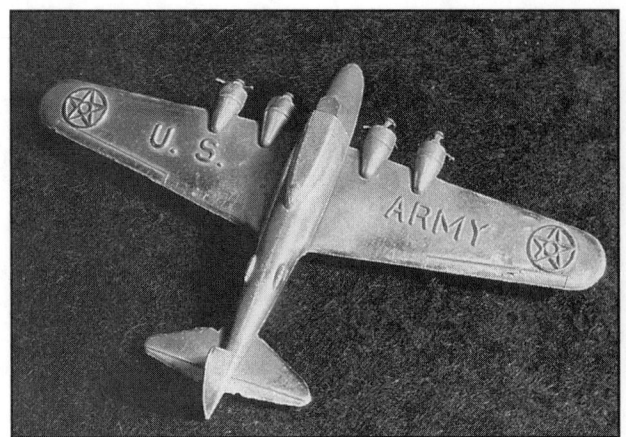

Erie Boeing B-17, $125. Photo courtesy Perry Eichor

Erie Northrup Delta, $140. Photo courtesy Perry Eichor

Erie, Northrop E-2. Photo courtesy Perry Eichor

Erie Boeing 247, $100. Photo courtesy Perry Eichor

Erie Northrup Gamma, $150.

Hubley (Continued)	C6	C8	C10
American Eagle or Flying Circus, Mid—two tone blue, red cowl, large airscoop atop engine cowl, four-bladed prop, (H21)	40	75	125
American Eagle or Flying Circus, Late—orange and yellow, large airscoop, either four- or two-bladed prop, (H21)	20	40	75
Attack Bomber, retractable landing gear, Martin B-26 Marauder copy, plastic, (H19)	75	125	225

Hubley (Continued)	C6	C8	C10
Bell Airacuda XFM-1, red and silver, folding landing gear, movable guns in front of twin pusher engines, three-bladed props, new in 1940, die-cast, (H2)	150	250	425
Bremen, cast iron, (H13)	750	1200	1500
Bremen, cast iron, (H13A)	750	1200	1750
Bremen, marked "Junkers Bremen" on fuselage, open cockpit w/two pilots, prop turned by wheels, cast iron, (H14)	2000	5000	8000
Bremen, aluminum, (H12)	250	500	1000

Hubley, Airacuda, rear view. Photo courtesy Perry Eichor

Hubley Friendship Seaplane, 13" wingspan, $10,000. Photo courtesy Bertoia Auctions

Hubley Bell Airacuda XFM-1, $425. Photo courtesy Perry Eichor

Hubley American Eagle or Flying Circus, $125. Photo courtesy Perry Eichor

Hubley (Continued)	**C6**	**C8**	**C10**
Crusader, twin engine, twinboom, marked, "TAT NC-31", die-cast, (H27)	40	80	120
Delta Wing Jet, folding, retractable landing gear, red and silver plastic cockpit, die-cast, (H26)	30	60	100
DO-X Seaplane, high-wing, six engine, cast iron, (H32)	100	275	425
Friendship Seaplane, marked "Fokker" embossed on fuselage, cast-iron, (H16)	3000	6000	10,000
Giro Plane, nickel-plate rotor, prop and engine, cast iron, (H30)	75	120	200
Hellcat, plastic, (H33)	20	30	40
Jet, single engine, folding wings, retractable landing gear, cast cockpit, either red and silver or blue and silver, die-cast, (H7)	40	60	80
Lindy, cast iron, (H9)	800	1500	2100

Hubley (Continued)	**C6**	**C8**	**C10**
Lindy, prop turns via gear attached to wheel, cast iron, (H10)	1000	2000	4500
Lindy, w/"Spirit of St. Louis" decals, ratchet drive action noise-maker, has wing struts, cast iron, (H11)	1250	3000	5000
Lindy, single engine, cast iron, (H3)	75	100	150
Lindy Glider, cast iron, (H34)	300	700	1200
Lockheed Sirius, marked "Lindy NR-211", (H37)	3000	7000	10,500
Monoplane, low-wing single engine, nickel-plate wings and prop w/various colored body, cast iron, (H28)	50	80	120
Monoplane, low-wing, single-engine, nickel plate wings and prop, cast iron, (H29)	30	50	75
Navy Blimp, (H39)	140	210	280

Hubley, Bell Airacuda. Photo courtesy Roger Johnson

Hubley Attack Bomber, No. 326, 7-7/8" wingspan, $225. Photo courtesy Perry Eichor

Hubley P-38, 12-5/8" wingspan, $200. Photo courtesy Roger Johnson

Hubley Bremen, 6-1/2" wingspan, $1500. Photo courtesy Bertoia Auctions

Hubley (Continued)	**C6**	**C8**	**C10**
P-38, red and silver, retractable landing gear, later versions are yellow and green camouflage, die-cast, (H24)	100	150	200
P-39, "U.S. Army" imprinted on rear horizon stabilizers, tin wings, die-cast and tin, (H20)	30	50	75
P-40, early version was silver and red w/three-bladed prop, later version orange and yellow w/two-bladed prop, die-cast, (H23)	68	100	135
Piper Club, red, also in olive drab L-4 version, (H22)	20	40	60
Question Mark, tri-motor, (H36)	1750	4000	6000
Twin Engine, painted and nickel plate, marked "TAT NC 431", cast iron, (H5)	50	75	120
Twin Engine, silver and red or green, (H6)	30	60	80

Hubley (Continued)	**C6**	**C8**	**C10**
U.S. Army Monoplane, white rubber tires, enclosed in cast fairings, single engine, low-wing, die-cast, (H4)	30	45	70
U.S. Army Monoplane, low-wing, single-engine, folding wheels, silver and red (early versions had red wood hubs w/white rubber tires, cast cockpit may have openings or be cast or solid), die-cast, introduced in 1939, (H17)	65	100	130
U.S. Army Monoplane, low-wing, single-engine, folding wheels, silver and red, folding wheels, "U.S. Army" embossed on horizontal stabilizer, plastic, (H18)	25	45	75
U.S.N. 3-B-4, twin engine, twin vertical stabilizer, retractable landing gear, die-cast, (H8)	60	80	110

Ideal	**C6**	**C8**	**C10**
Electronic Fighter Jet, c. 1959	135	200	270

Left to right: Hubley Hellcat, 9-1/4" wingspan, $40; Hubley U.S. Army Monoplane, 6" wingspan, $75. Photo courtesy Perry Eichor

Hubley Lockheed Sirius, 9" long, $10,500. Photo courtesy Bertoia Auctions

Hubley planes as shown in the December 1929 Butler Bros. catalog.

Hubley Lindy, 10" wingspan, $2100. Photo courtesy Perry Eichor

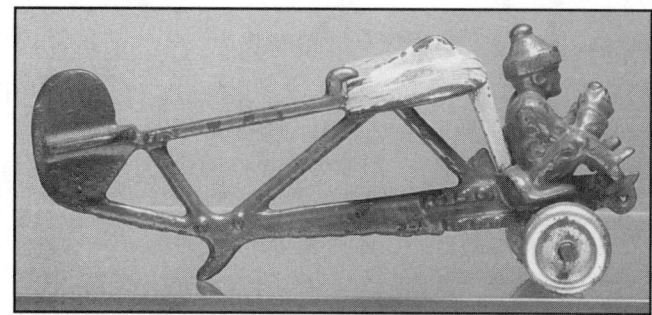

Hubley Lindy Glider, 6-1/4" long, $1200. Photo courtesy Sotheby's, New York

---

CONDITION CODE

C6 Good; evident overall wear, well played with but acceptable to many collectors

C8 Very Good; minor overall wear, very clean

C10 Mint; like new

Note: Mint in Box commands a higher price.
Condition below C6 brings considerably lower prices

Three cockpit variations of the Hubley U.S. Army Monoplane. Photo courtesy Perry Eichor

Left to right: Kansas Toy & Novelty Company Cabin Plane, 3-5/8" x 3", $75; Kansas Toy & Novelty Company Cabin Plane, No. 6, 3-3/4" x 3", $70. Photo courtesy Perry Eichor.

Kansas Toy & Novelty Company Airliner, No. 47, 3-5/8" x 3-1/2", $100. Photo by Al Lane

Kansas Toy Aircraft: KTA6, KTA5. Photo courtesy of Perry Eichor

Kansas Toy & Novelty Company Airliner, No. 45, 2-1/2" x 2-1/2", $100. Photo courtesy Bill Conover

Ideal (Continued)	C6	C8	C10
Globemaster	42	63	85
Helicopter City Play Set	70	105	140
U.S. Navy Rescue Float Plane, wind-up, plastic	32	48	65

Kansas Toy & Novelty Company

The years 1920-1940 were decisive for aviation—it was an era of ferment and growth, and was a time of barnstorming and record-breaking; Lindbergh and Earhart made headlines.

The state of Kansas played a large part in the development of airmail and airlines with its manufacturing centers at Topeka and Wichita (Beach, Boeing, Cessna, Laird, Stearman and others), but the toy industry reflected only dimly the excitement of the era.

Listed below are the aircraft said to have been made by KT&N from 1924 to about 1931, using metal disc or wire wheels. Reproductions from Best Toy and Ralstoy will be found with later wheels. Best Toys' later reproductions will have "Made in the U.S.A."

For a more detailed history of Kansas Toy & Novelty, see their section in the vehicles chapter.

Kansas Toy & Novelty Company	C6	C8	C10
Airliner, "KTN 47," Fokker, similar to No. 45, sometimes referred to as a seaplane, 3-5/8" x 3-1/2", (KYA9)	40	75	100
Airliner, marked "KTN 47," Fokker, sometimes called a seaplane, similar to No. 45, (KTA10)	40	75	100

Kansas Toy & Novelty Company (Continued)	C6	C8	C10
Airliner, Fokker?, high, oval, corrugated wing and tail, nine circular cabin windows, nine rectangular flightdeck windows, six-cylinder radial engine, large tin propeller, (KTA8)	40	60	90
Cabin Plane, similar to No. 6, Air Service dot-in-circle insignia, V-8 engine, cast propeller, (KTA2)	25	50	75
Cabin Plane, small, similar to No. 32, w/o windows and different rudder, or wingtip, (KTA6)	20	30	40
Cabin Plane, small, high, positive dihedral wing, Air Corps star insignia, six cylinder, radial engine, six oval windows, three metal "wire" wheels, large tine or cast propeller, (KTA5)	25	35	50
Cabin Plane, high-wing w/flaring positive dihedral, Army Air Corps star-in-circle insignia, six cylinder, radial engine, pilot head in open cockpit, eight oval windows, cast prop, lacquer finish, also unnumbered version with large tin propeller, (KTA1)	30	50	70

Keystone Airmail Plane, 24" wingspan, $2130. Photo courtesy Calvin L. Chaussee

Kilgore Ford "TAT," 13-1/2" wingspan, $6000. Photo courtesy Bertoia Auctions

Kansas Toy & Novelty Company (Continued)	C6	C8	C10
Cabin Plane, large, Lindy-type, high negative dihedral wing w/large stars, six cylinder radial engine, wheels w/black tires, (KTA4)	30	50	75
Cabin Plane, high-wing, larger "U.S. Mail" version of above, dot-in-two-circles insignia, V-8 engine, cast propeller, white disc wheels w/painted black "tires", (KTA3)	30	40	75
Glider, high oval wing marked "GLIDER," pilot in front, flat lattice fuselage, (KTA11)	20	40	60
Zeppelin, front and rear cabins, three tail planes, mooring loop on nose, rear axle through rear cabin, (KTA7)	50	75	100

Katz Toys	C6	C8	C10
Pathfinder, The, tri-motor monoplane	350	600	1200
Red Arrow, The, single monoplane, pull toy	300	750	1200

Kenton	C6	C8	C10
Air Mail Plane	600	1200	1700
Los Angeles Dirigible	500	750	1050
Pony Blimp, cast iron	125	200	400
United Boeing, twin engine, cast iron	112	168	225

Keystone	C6	C8	C10
Airmail Plane, "NC-263"	500	750	1000
Airmail Plane, marked "NX-265", pressed steel	800	1500	2130
Ride 'Em Mail Plane, marked "NC-273", 1930s	1200	2000	3000
Ride 'Em Riding Plane	400	600	850

Keystone (Continued)	C6	C8	C10
Riding Plane, seat over tail, steering bar over cabin, single wing, high, one engine	500	750	1000
Trimotor, 1920s	900	1400	2200

Kilgore	C6	C8	C10
Ford, tri-motor, "TAT", cast iron	2000	3000	6000
Kilgore Comet Plane, cap-firing	50	100	150
Monocoupe, high-wing	125	200	250
Monoplane, marked "N4," open cockpit, cast iron	125	188	250
Monoplane, high-wing	50	75	100
Monoplane, bullet, open cockpit, cast iron	100	175	275
Sea Gull, high-wing, pusher prop	750	1200	1500
Seagull, high-wing, pusher prop	200	300	400
TAT, twin-engine passenger monoplane	150	250	325
TAT, largest Kilgore plane	2500	4200	7700
Travel Air Mystery, double open cockpits, cast iron	275	400	650

Kingsbury	C6	C8	C10
Biplane, wind-up, pilot	400	750	1000
Monoplane, high-wing, tri-motor, clockwork	500	750	1100
Tin Goose, tri-engine, c. 1930s	600	900	1500
Trans Atlantic Monoplane, painted wind-up, pressed steel, c. 1930	200	300	500
U.S. Airmail biplane, wind-up, pressed steel	200	500	900

Lehmann	C6	C8	C10
Ikarus, tin and paper, early	1200	2000	3000
Shenandoah Dirigible	225	388	750

Kilgore Sea Gull, 8-1/4" wingspan, $1500. Photo courtesy Chic Gast

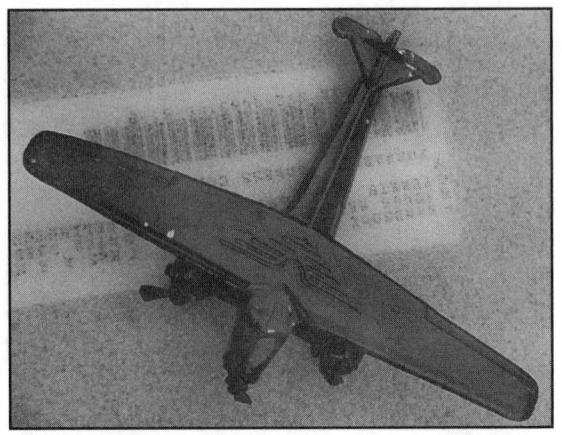

Lincoln White Metal Airplane, 3-1/4" x 4-1/2", $150. Photo by Fred Maxwell

Lehmann (Continued)	C6	C8	C10
Zeppelin, "EPL 2", c. 1907	400	750	1200
Zeppelin, "EPL 1"	400	800	1400

Lincoln White Metal	C6	C8	C10
Airplane, tri-motored, Fokker F-11(?), tapered high-wings w/wings symbol embossed, seven cylinder, radial engines, outboards mounted in wings, unrealistic window patterns, metal wheels, (LWA1)	45	75	100
Airplane, tri-motored, Fokker F-11(?), tapered high-wings w/wings symbol embossed, seven cylinder, radial engines, outboards mounted on landing gear struts, tin propellers, metal wheels, no windows, (LWA2)	80	120	150
Airplane, steamlined, swallow-shaped, pilot, cowled radial engine, tin propeller, would be called batplane today, (LWA4)...	50	80	125
Airplane, streamlined, swallow-shaped, pilot, cowled radial engine, tin propeller, would be called batplane today, (LWA3)	75	120	200

Manoil	C6	C8	C10
Bonanza B-35	30	50	75
Ercoupe	30	50	75
Lockheed F90	30	50	75
Navion	30	50	75

Marx	C6	C8	C10
Air Mail Biplane, four engine, 1930	300	450	800
Air Mail Monoplane, two-engine, 1930	165	248	330

Marx (Continued)	C6	C8	C10
Airplane, light fuselage	100	150	200
Airplane, medium fuselage	100	150	200
Airplane, U.S. Army two-engine, no guns	163	245	325
American Airlines Flagship	155	230	310
Army Bomber, three engine, c. 1935	75	150	250
Astrojet Airport Set, planes, helicopter, etc.	155	230	310
Bomber, sparkling mechanism, camouflaged, four engine, tin litho	60	140	200
Bomber, four engine, drops wooden bombs	80	125	250
City Airport Set	300	500	750
Crop Duster Plane Set	75	125	200
Curtiss Transport, khaki, pressed steel	50	75	100
DC-3 Transport, pressed steel, c. 1939	60	80	120
DC-4 type, four-engine passenger, pressed steel, c. 1930s	60	125	250
DC-6 Transport Plane, plastic	75	120	200
Electric Lighted Radio Aiport, 1930s	200	350	500
F84 Jet Fighter, remote control	68	100	150
Futuristic Airport	212	318	425
Gyroplane	50	80	150
Hangar, tin litho, c. 1941	50	75	100
Little Lindy Aeroplane, friction, 1930s	100	150	200
Lockheed Prop Jet	125	188	250
Mainstream Aiport, c. 1930s	110	165	220

Marx Bomber, 18" wingspan, $200. Photo courtesy Richard MacNary

Marx Bomber, 14-3/4" wingspan, $250. Photo courtesy Perry Eichor

Marx (Continued)	C6	C8	C10
Municipal Airport Hangar, w/plane, early	400	600	800
P35, w/ and w/o wheel skirts, pressed steel	60	90	150
P35-type, two-engine bomber	105	158	225
Pan American, four engine, propeller-driven, also as PAA, pressed steel, 1940	200	300	400
Pan American Super 7 Clipper, also as American Airlines	160	240	320
Piggyback Airplane Set	75	125	150
Pioneer Air Express, high-wing monoplane, tin litho	100	200	300
Skycruiser, two-engine transport plane w/siren and whirling propellers, Stratoliner 700, rubber wheels, c. 1940s	180	300	450
Skycruiser Stratoliner 700, two-engine	50	75	100
Skycruiser Stratoliner 700, four-engine	100	200	400
Sparkling Rocket Fighter, tin litho	37	56	75
Swingtail Flying Tiger Transport	300	450	600
Transport, friction-powered, four-engine w/whirling propellers, tin litho	60	90	200
Trimotor Biplane	60	90	120
Universal Airport, w/two metal planes, c. 1940s	100	175	300
Zeppelin, "Akron" Marx, c. 1930s	100	140	250

Metalcraft	C6	C8	C10
Build-A-Zep, builds twenty-one different 18" zeppelins	250	400	550
Ford, tri-motor	112	162	225
Northrup Alpha Monoplane, marked "PURE the Pure Oil Company"	600	1000	1800
Riding Rocket	100	150	200
Spirit of St. Louis, came as kit	118	175	235

Miscellaneous	C6	C8	C10
Adam Bomb, also "Atom Bomb", wood and metal, c. 1946	50	100	150
Aeroplane, marked "U.S. 256," Air Corps star insignia, metal cast	15	20	25
Aeroplane, two engine, lead (some marked "Fred Greene"), metal cast, c. 1940s	15	25	45
Air Mail Pedal Plane, American National, 1926	3000	5000	9000
Airplane, ride-on, wood	75	100	150
Airplane, single wing, prop behind tail, pilot, open fuselage, early 1900s	300	450	600
Airplane and Pylon, Lionel	300	450	1100
Airplane Kit, "Schoenhut's Airplane Builder", wood	130	200	300
Airport, mechanical airport w/early plastic planes that fly, control tower controls for stunts, crash truck pumps water, airport bus, gasoline truck, T. Cohn Co., tin litho, c. 1940s	100	200	400
Amphibian, two overhead engines, hand-painted, tin wind-up, Bing	1400	2500	3400

Marx DC-6 Transport Plane, $200. Photo courtesy Perry Eichor

Marx Hangar, c.1941, $100. Photo courtesy James Apthorpe

Marx P35, 13-1/2" wingspan, $150. Photo courtesy Perry Eichor

Marx P35-type, 15-7/8" wingspan, $225. Photo courtesy Richard MacNary

Left to right: Marx Trimotor Biplane, 9-1/2" wingspan, $120; Marx Gyroplane, $150. Photo courtesy Perry Eichor

Marx Pan American Super 7 Clipper, 17-1/2" wingspan, $400. Photo courtesy Perry Eichor

Marx Piggyback Airplane Set $150. Photo courtesy Tim Oei

Marx Skycruiser Stratoliner 700, c. 1940s, 18" wingspan, two-engine, $450. Photo courtesy Richard MacNary

Marx Skycruiser Stratoliner 700, four-engine, $400. Photo courtesy Richard MacNary

Miscellaneous (Continued)	C6	C8	C10
Biplane Pedal Plane, two motor	500	900	1800
Cargo Plane, Eldon	20	40	60
Champion Monoplane, high-wing, cast iron	110	150	200
Dirigible, "USN," Tommy Toy, slush lead, 1930s	30	50	75
Erector Biplane, w/electric motor, A.C. Gilbert	200	400	750
Fighter, single engine, four machine guns mounted on wing, tin, c. 1940	30	40	70
Flagship America airplane, metal Ford tri-motor, pressed steel, c. 1930s	175	300	600
Flying Plane, Liberty Playthings, early 1930s	300	600	1000

Miscellaneous (Continued)	C6	C8	C10
Giant Flyer Monoplane, Tip Top, c. 1920s	200	350	500
Helicopter, Army, drive, spinning prop, tin litho	40	70	100
Helicopter, friction, Irwin, c. 1950	30	45	60
Hillclimber Biplane, c. 1917	225	400	750
Jet, USAF, friction powered, tin litho	15	20	35
KD-1 Mak-a-plane, w/rubber wheels, mechanical, all metal, 1940s	40	50	70
Lindy, nickel prop and wheels, cast iron	105	158	210
Lindy-type Plane, North & Judd, cast iron	175	265	350

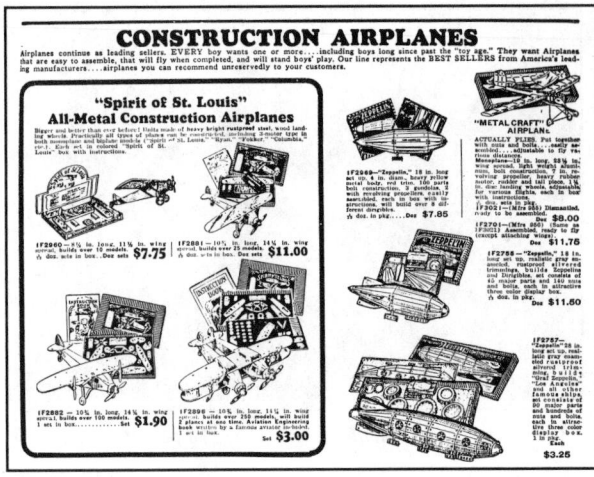

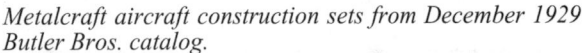

Metalcraft aircraft construction sets from December 1929 Butler Bros. catalog.

Metalcraft Spirit of St. Louis, assembled, 9" long, $235. Photo courtesy Mapes Auctioneers

Miscellaneous (Continued)

	C6	C8	C10
Lindy-type Plane, lead	10	20	30
Luscombe Airplane	30	45	60
Monoplane, high wing, marked "U.S.," single engine, open iron-work body, spool wheel works, prop	200	300	400
Monoplane, two pilots in open cockpit Liberty V-12 engine, cast propeller, eight oval and two round windows, two painted main gear disc wheels, Midwest	25	40	70
Monoplane, Liberty V-12 engine, cast propeller, eight oval and two round windows, ailerons and tail surfaces detailed and three disc wheels w/those black painted "tires"	40	80	120
Monoplane, high-wing, open cockpit and pilot, red, yellow or blue, painted disc wheels, Dayton	300	500	1000
NX-130, high-wing monoplane, Boycraft, pressed steel	350	525	850
Pedal Plane, pursuit plane, 1941	1800	2500	3500
Pyro Jet, plastic	10	15	25
Sky Cruiser, two-motor transport, engines turn w/friction mechanism, tin litho	40	75	100
Spirit of America Aeroplane, pull-toy, steel and litho	45	75	125
Spirit of Columbia, friction, pressed tin	500	750	1000
Spirit of St. Louis, go around tower, two planes, electrical, United Electric, pressed steel	800	1200	1600

Miscellaneous (Continued)

	C6	C8	C10
Spirit of St. Louis, marked "Pat." and " Ancient Art Metal Co., Brooklyn, N.Y.", lead, c. 1927	75	150	200
Swallow Monoplane, high-wing, American National	1200	2000	3000
Theodore Hahn Aeroplane, lead alloy, 1920s	40	80	150
Turner High-wing Monoplane, one engine, 1930s	275	500	900
Turner High-wing Monoplane, pressed steel	350	600	1200
Twin-engine Bomber, B-25?, Metal Cast	20	30	40
Watrous Biplane, single engine, bell toy, pressed steel, c. 1915	200	500	900
Zeppelin, "Goodyear" decals, hatch opens	125	225	350
Zeppelin, "Los Angeles", cast iron	300	750	1500
Zeppelin, "Pony DE107", cast iron	50	100	250
Zeppelin, "U.S. Akron", pot metal, c. 1932	25	40	100
Zeppelin, "ZEP", cast iron	80	120	160
Zeppelin, cast iron	40	60	80
Zeppelin, metal	42	64	85
Zeppelin, pull toy, "Little Giant"	75	200	400
Zeppelin, pull toy, silver, cast iron, c. 1920-30s	60	90	120

Left to right: Ralstoy Pursuit Plane, No. P40, 3" x 3-1/4", $50; Ralstoy Cabin Plane, 3-3/8" x 3-3/8", $75; Ralstoy Cabin Plane, 3-5/8" x 3-1/2", $90. Photo courtesy Perry Eichor

Top row; left to right: Renwal B-17, No. 777, 1944, 9-1/4" wingspan, $125; Renwal P-38, $100. Middle row; left to right: Renwal B-25, c. 1944, 6-3/4" wingspan, $100; Renwal B-29, No. 29, $100; Renwal C54 Transport, $100. Bottom row; left to right: Renwal B-17, No. 17, $60; Renwal P40, $100. Photo courtesy Perry Eichor

Ralstoy	C6	C8	C10
Cabin Plane, small, marked "Ralstoy," wings positive dihedral (see Kansas Toy's No. 32 Small Cabin Plane), (RAA1)	20	30	50
Cabin Plane, slim midwing, cowled radial engine, pilot, tin propeller, underside marked "Scout" and "Made in USA", (RAA5)	40	75	90
Cabin Plane, marked "NC414" and "Ralstoy," midwing, V-12 engine, tin propeller, (RAA2)	30	45	75
Cabin Plane, large, Lindy-type, high-wing, six-cylinder radial engine, metal wheels, (RAA6)	30	40	60
Cabin Plane, high-wing, cowled radial engine, two doors, six windows, marked "Ralstoy" and "Made in USA", (RAA3)	35	55	90
Pursuit Plane, Curtiss "U.S. Army," midwing, Air Corps star-in-circle insignia, V-12 engine, two machine guns, three-bladed propeller, marked "Made in USA" and "Ralstoy" in diamond, (RAA4)	25	35	50

Remco	C6	C8	C10
Flying Boxcar	50	75	100
Kennedy Airport	58	85	115
Whirlybird Helicopter	20	30	40
WWI "Air Aces" Play Set, 1965	138	205	275

Renwal	C6	C8	C10
B-17, small	20	40	60
B-17, plastic, 1944	30	60	125
B-25, plastic, c. 1944	30	60	100
B-29	30	60	100
C54 Transport, large, plastic	40	35	100
DC-4	40	50	100
Martin Mars	40	80	150
P38, plastic	20	40	100
P40, plastic	20	45	100
P47, plastic	20	40	100
PB2Y Flying Boat	20	40	100

Savoye	C6	C8	C10
Blimp, "U.S.N."	30	50	100
Monoplane	30	50	100

Schieble	C6	C8	C10
Biplane, c. 1920s	300	450	600
Ford, tri-motor, steel	500	900	1550

Steelcraft	C6	C8	C10
Akron Blimp, pull toy	125	200	400
Army Scout Plane, green and orange	100	300	500
Army Scout Plane, tri-motor, single high-wing, c. 1920s	400	1500	2500
Army Scout Plane, single engine, high-wing monoplane, c. 1920s	700	1200	2000
Graf Zeppelin, pull toy	300	450	600
Graf Zeppelin, pull toy, pressed steel	250	375	500

Renwal DC-4, 7" wingspan, $100. Photo courtesy James Apthorpe

Renwal Martin Mars, No. 15, $150. Photo courtesy James Apthorpe

Savoye Monoplane, 3-1/2" wingspan, $100. Photo courtesy Al Lane

Savoye Blimp, 4" long, $100. Photo courtesy Al Lane

Steelcraft (Continued)	C6	C8	C10
Lockheed Sirius, pull toy.................	650	1500	2500
Macon Zeppelin..............................	350	525	700
Monoplane, two open cockpits, c. 1930s	250	450	800
NX107, "Little Jim"	550	825	1300
NX130, blue eagles on wings..........	475	700	950
NX130 U.S. Mail Plane, one engine	388	580	775
NX131 U.S. Mail Plane, tri-motor, pull toy	700	1500	2000
Pedal Monoplane, high-wing..........	1500	2500	4000
Pedal Plane "Pursuit", 1940	1000	1700	3000

Strauss	C6	C8	C10
Chicago Dirigible, tin litho..............	125	188	250
Flying Airship, wind-up, aluminum	275	350	550
Graf Zeppelin.................................	240	360	480
Zeppelin, "Graf Zeppelin", aluminum..	175	250	350

Sun Rubber	C6	C8	C10
Dual-Control Plane.........................	25	35	50

Sun Rubber (Continued)	C6	C8	C10
Pursuit Ship, marked "25-P75", c. 1940-41	20	35	50
Transport	40	70	100

Thomas Toys	C6	C8	C10
Defiant, plastic..............................	20	30	40
F-80 Jet Action Rocket Launcher....	20	30	40
Warhawk, plastic	20	30	40

Tootsietoy	C6	C8	C10
Aerodawn, rubber tires, 1928	30	55	100
Aerodawn, metal tires, 1928............	30	60	125
Aerodawn Seaplane........................	30	60	125
Aeroplane whistle tin-litho, Crackerjack..	15	25	40
Air Defense set of ten, die-cast midget series	50	100	150
Airport hangar, two planes, box set.	300	750	1100
Army Cutlass, 1958-60....................	8	16	25
Army DC-4 Transport, 1941	40	75	110
Atlantic Clipper, midget series........	4	8	12
Autogyro, 1934...............................	50	100	150

Schieble Ford, 29-1/2" long, $1550. Photo courtesy Wilkinson Collection, Detroit Antique Toy Museum

Steelcraft Lockheed Sirius, 21-1/2" wingspan, $2500. Photo courtesy Christie's East

Steelcraft NX130 U.S. Mail Plane, $775. Photo courtesy Calvin L. Chaussee

Steelcraft Pan American World Airways Clipper, 26", $300.

Thomas Toys F-80 Jet Action Rocket Launcher, $40. Photo courtesy Islyn Thomas

Left to Right: Thomas Toys Warhawk, 4" long, $40; Thomas Toys Defiant, 4" long, $40.

Steelcraft Army Scout Plane, c. 1920s, 22-1/2" wingspan, $2000. Photo courtesy Continental Hobby House

Wyandotte Airliner, 12-3/4" wingspan, $200. Photo courtesy Perry Eichor

Left to Right: Wyandotte Airacuda, 8-1/2" wingspan, $120; Wyandotte Airliner, $150. Photo courtesy Perry Eichor

Wyandotte China Clipper, No. 207, 13" wingspan, $300. Photo courtesy Wilkinson Collection, Detroit Antique Museum

Wyandotte Gyrocopter, c. 1930s, 12-1/2" wingspan, $300. Photo courtesy Perry Eichor

Tootsietoy (Continued)

	C6	C8	C10
Beechcraft Bonanza, 1948	8	16	25
Bellanca, high tin wing monoplane, 1932	30	60	90
Biplane, open-spoke tires, 1926	60	120	200
Bi-Wing Plane, closed metal tires	25	50	75
Bi-Wing Seaplane	25	50	75
Bleriot Plane, 1910	60	150	250
Boeing 707, 1958	18	35	55
Boeing Stratocruiser, 1951-54	35	70	105
Coast guard Seaplane, 1950	50	125	200
Crusader, twin boom, twin engine, 1937	40	75	125
Curtis P-40 Pursuit, olive	100	250	400
Curtis P-40 Pursuit, silver, 1941	100	250	400
DC-2 TWA, midget series	4	8	12
DC-4, die-cast charm	1	3	5
Delta, two-piece casting	20	40	60

Tootsietoy (Continued)

	C6	C8	C10
Delta, 1954-55	15	25	40
Dive-Bomber Waco Biplane, 1937	50	125	200
F-40 Skyway, 1956-69	7	13	20
F-86 Sabre Jet, single casting, 1956	7	13	20
F-86 Sabre Jet, two-casting body, 1950	8	16	25
F-94 Army Jet, 1956-69	8	16	25
F-94 Starfire Jet, 1956-69	7	13	20
Fly-N-Giro, small-version auto-gyro, 1938	85	200	400
Ford Tri-Motor, 1932	45	85	150
High Wing Monoplane, midget series	5	10	16
High Wing Monoplane, two-color, CJ, tin-litho, early	18	35	55
High Wing Monoplane, Cracker-jack, tin-litho	15	25	40
Hiller Helicopter, 1968-69	15	30	45

Left to right: Wyandotte Crusader, 9-3/4" wingspan, $85; Wyandotte Crusader, 9-3/4" wingspan, $100. Photo courtesy Perry Eichor

Wyandotte Mystery Plane, No. 101, 4-1/2" wingspan, $100. Photo courtesy John Gibson

Wyandotte Stratocruiser, 13" wingspan, $150. Photo courtesy Perry Eichor

Wyandotte Rocket Racer, No. 319, c. 1935, $150. Photo courtesy Brian Seligman

Tootsietoy (Continued)	C6	C8	C10
Lockheed Constellation, 1951	45	90	135
Lockheed Electra twin-engine, 1937	25	50	75
Lockheed Sirius, tin low wing	30	60	90
Low Wing Monoplane, Crackerjack, tin-litho	15	25	40
Navion, 1948-53	10	20	30
Navy Cutlass, 1956-69	7	13	20
P-38, midget series	10	20	30
P-38 Fighter, twin boom, twin engine, 1950	40	75	110
P-39 Fighter, 1947	50	125	200
P-80 Shooting Star, 1948	10	20	30
Panther Jet, two-casting body, 1953-55	15	25	40
Panther Jet, single casting, 1956-69	7	13	20
Piper Club, 1948-52	8	16	25

Tootsietoy (Continued)	C6	C8	C10
Rescue Helicopter, four-blade	8	16	25
Rescue Helicopter, two-blade, 1975-79	6	12	18
Scorpion Helicopter, 1977-79	2	5	8
Sikorsky S-58 Helicopter, 1958-69	30	55	85
Sky fleet, die-cast midget series, set of four	25	50	75
TWA DC-2, 1937	30	60	90
Twin-Engine Convair, twin engine, 1950	35	65	95
U.S. Army Northrup Alpha Pursuit plane, 1936	25	50	75
U.S. Navy Waco C-Model Biplane, 1937	45	85	125
United DC-4 Supre Mainliner, 1941	35	65	95
USN Los Angeles Dirigible, 1937	45	85	125

Wyandotte	C6	C8	C10
Airacuda, twin vertical stabilizers, twin pusher engines, blue or red, pressed steel	50	80	120
Airliner, four-engine, pressed steel	75	125	200
Airliner, two-engine, wooden wheels, WWII-era	75	110	150
Bomber, Army, two-engine, pressed steel	90	135	180
China Clipper	125	200	300
City Airport, American Airlines, two hangars, control tower, etc., lights up	150	250	400
Crusader, twelve-window version	40	75	100
Crusader	35	55	85
Gyrocopter, twin-engine passenger plane, c. 1930s	100	200	300
Military Air Transport	40	60	80
Monoplane, Lockheed Vega, high-wing passenger, single engine, bullet nose	175	265	350
Mystery Plane, twin engine, wings trail backward	30	50	100
Rocket Racer, c. 1935	70	120	150
Stratocruiser	75	120	150
Super Jet	80	120	160
U.S. Navy Seaplane, c. 1941	215	322	430

I.D. Planes

By Franc Isla

Black I.D. planes, as these wartime aircraft models are known to collectors and enthusiasts worldwide, were manufactured of early cellulose-acetate plastic for the U.S. Navy's World War II Recognition Training Program. The vast majority of these 1:72 scale (1 inch equals 6 feet) models were made by the Cruver Company of Chicago and a few were molded by Design Center and Leominster.

They were used to instruct our troops in the vital differences between friendly and enemy aircraft. Painted in flat, non-reflective black lacquer, they are marked on the underside with the aircraft's designation number (and sometimes name), nationality, and the date of model issue. Some of the early-war enemy planes were very speculative as far as proportions and details; these were frequently issued in corrected versions later—that explains the additional issue dates for some.

In addition to those listed here, there was an early-war production of black cardboard punch-out models in the same 1:72 scale. Aircraft models were also produced during the war in 1:43 scale, cast in both plastic and metal. (A limited number of U.S. plastic models were featured as premiums in KIX cereal boxes.) I.D. models of tanks were issued of painted pot metal in 1:36 and 1:08 scales. Ships ere produced in both 1:1200 and 1:500 scale. All are certainly collectable, but beyond the scope of this compilation.

The most complete history of black I.D. models was written by Robert C. Mikesh in the May/June 1984 issue of *FineScale Modeller* in an article entitled, "Recognition Models—The Government-Issue Miniature Air Force."

An estimated 2,000,000+ black I.D. models were manufactured during the WWII period, but because certain aircraft were produced in very small quantities, the same turned out to be true of their I.D. model equivalents, which is why some are extremely rare today.

The newest of the listed models is more than 50 years old. Because many models came home as G.I. souvenirs and were played with as toys, those few still in existence can vary a great deal in condition. They are not easy to find, but the hunt is worthwhile.

As to grading, C10 means no scuffs, no warpage, no "prune-skin," no repainting or, in other words, a brand new 50-year-old airplane. C8 covers models that are very nice—planes should be complete with wheels or floats; free of serious defects like "prune-skin" or missing parts, and not repainted. The C6 grade covers everything else and probably includes the majority of models still in existence. Each model is identified by type and date marked.

*molded by Design Center
** molded by Leominster
All others molded by Cruver

Contributor: Franc Isla, 4122 D'Youville Trace, Atlanta, GA 30341-1433. All photos courtesy of Richard MacNary. A special thanks is still due to master modeler Ray ".43 Magnum" Wheeler of Lilburn, Georgia, for his help in identifying some of the more obscure types listed.

I.D. Planes JR2S-1 (S44) Excalibur, $200. Photo courtesy Richard MacNary

I.D. Planes B-29 Super Fortress, $200. Photo courtesy Richard MacNary

I.D. Planes (United States)	C6	C8	C10
A-20 Havoc, 6/42	25	37	50
A-24 Dauntless, SBD-3, 7-42	15	22	30
A-26 Invader, 2/44	25	37	50
A-29 Hudson (PBO-16), none	25	37	50
A-30 Baltimore, 2/43	25	37	50
A-31 Vengeance, 7/42	15	22	30
A-31 Vengeance, 7/44	15	22	30
A-35 Vengeance, 4/44, rare	25	40	60
AT17 Bobcat, 7/43	30	60	90
B-17 Flying Fortress, 7/42	100	150	200
B-24 Liberator, 7/42	100	150	200
B-25 Mitchell, 7/42	75	100	125
B-26 Marauder, 10/42	50	70	85
B-26 Marauder, none	75	100	125
B-29 Super Fortress, 3/44	100	150	200
B-29 Super Fortress, 9/44	100	150	200
B-29 Super Fortress, none, rare	100	150	200
B-32 Dominator, 12/44	150	200	225
C-46 Commando, 3/43	50	75	100
C-47 Skytrain, 3/43	40	60	80
C-47 Skytrain, 5/43, extremely rare	60	75	100
C-54 Skymaster, 3/43	60	90	120
C60A Lodestar, 3/43	25	38	50
C69 Constellation, 4/44, rare	100	150	200
C78 Bobcat, 6/44	30	45	60
C87 Liberator, 3/44, rare	100	150	200
CG-4A Waco Glider, 6/43	30	45	60
F4F-4 Wildcat, 5/43	15	22	30
F4U-1 Corsair, 3/43	20	30	40
F6F Hellcat, 4/43	15	22	30
GH-1 Nightingale, 5/43, very rare	50	75	100
J2F-4 Duck, 12/42	60	75	90
JR2S-1 (S44) Excalibur, 11/44	100	150	200
JRF OA-09 Goose, 7/43	60	75	90
JRS-1 (S43), 11/42, very rare	75	100	125
L-1 Vigilant, 3/43	25	37	50

I.D. Planes (United States)	C6	C8	C10
L-2 Grasshopper, 7/44	25	37	50
L-4 Grasshopper, 2/43	25	37	50
L-5 Sentinel, 1/44	25	37	50
OS2U (on floats), 2/43	35	50	70
OS2U (on wheels), 2/43	25	37	50
OS2U-1 (on floats), 7/43	40	55	75
P-38 Lightning, 7/42	25	37	50
P-39 Airacobra, 6/42	15	22	30
P-40 Warhawk, 9/42, rare	25	35	50
P-40 Warhawk, 4/44	15	22	30
P-43 Lancer, 5/43	15	22	30
P-47 (D) Thunderbolt, 2/44	15	22	30
P-47 (N) Thunderbolt, 4/45	15	22	30
P-47 Thunderbolt, none	15	22	30
P-47 Thunderbolt, 9/42	15	22	30
P-51 Mustang, 6/42	15	22	30
P-51D Mustang, 4/45	15	22	30
P-61 Black Widow, 2/44	35	50	65
P-63 King Cobra, 5/44	15	22	30
P-80 Shooting Star, 4/45	20	30	40
PB2Y-3 Coronado, 4/43	75	100	150
PBM-3 Mariner, 6/43	50	75	100
PBY-5 Catalina, 5/43	40	60	80
PV-1 (B-39) Ventura, 5/43	25	37	50
PV-2 Harpoon, 5/43, rare	40	55	70
SB2A-2 Buccaneer, 5/43	15	22	30
SB2C-1 Helldiver, 3/43	15	22	30
SB2C-2 Helldiver, 3/43	25	37	50
SB2C-2 Helldiver (floats), 3/43, extremely rare	50	70	100
SB2U-3 Vindicator, 6/43	15	22	30
SB3C-2 Helldiver, 2/45	15	22	30
SNJ-2 Texan, 7/42	15	22	30
SNJ-3 Texan, 7/42	15	22	30
SO3C-1 Seagull (floats), 3/43	30	45	60
SO3C-2 Seagull (wheels), 3/43	25	37	50
SR-10B Reliant, 10/42	25	37	50

I.D. Planes (United States)

	C6	C8	C10
TBD-1 Devastator, 5/43, rare	25	40	60
TBF Avenger, 7/43	20	35	50

I.D. Planes (Japanese)

	C6	C8	C10
(Adam) Naka. 97, 11/42, rare	50	65	85
(Ann) Mitsu. T-98, 7/42	30	45	60
(Babs) Mitsu. T-97, 6/42	40	60	80
(Claude) Mitsu. T-96, 6/42	50	75	100
(Dave) Naka. T-95-NOB, 7/42	25	37	50
(Ida) Mitsu. T-98 ALB, 6/42	30	45	60
(Kate) Naka. T-97, 6/42	15	35	50
(Mary) T-97 ALB, 6/42	30	45	60
(Mavis) Kawa., 11/42, rare	100	150	200
(Nate) "97" Fighter, 9/42	25	37	50
(Nell) Mitsu. T-96, 6/42	25	37	50
(Sally) Mitsu. T-97, 6/42	25	38	50
(Sonia) Mitsu. T-99, 7/42	20	35	60
(Topsy) Mitsu. MC-20, 10/42	25	37	50
(Val) Aichi T-99, 6/42	40	60	80
(Zeke) Mitsu. 00, 9/42	20	30	40
Betty (G4M1), 9/43	50	75	100
Betty (G4M2), 4/45	50	75	100
Dinah (Ki46), 8/44	30	45	60
Emily (H8K2), 3/45	50	75	110
Francis (PIY), 3/45	25	37	50
Frank (Ki84), 5/45	20	30	40
George (NIKI-J), 5/45	15	22	30
Hamp (T-00, Zeke 32), 7/43	20	30	40
Helen (Ki49)	30	45	60
Irving (J1N1), 5/45	30	45	60
Jack (J2M1), 12/44	25	37	50
Jake (E13A), 9/44, rare..................	30	50	75
Jill (B6N), 5/45	15	22	30
Judy (D4Y), 3/45	30	30	40
Lily (Ki48), 9/43	20	30	40
Myrt (C6N), 3/45	15	22	30
Nell (G3M), 1/44, extremely rare....	40	60	80
Nick (Ki45), 8/44	25	37	50
Oscar T-01 (Ki43), 9/43	20	30	40
Paul 14, Exp, 12/44	25	37	50
Pete (F1M2), 6/43.........................	35	50	70
Rufe (A6M2-N), 8/43	40	60	80
Tojo (Ki44), 6/44	15	22	30
Tojo (Ki44), 3/45	20	30	45
Tony (Ki61), 4/45	15	22	30
Val T-99 MK2, 8/43	40	60	80
Zeke 52 (A6M5)*, 12/44	20	30	40

I.D. Planes (German)

	C6	C8	C10
Arado Ar196, 12/43......................	25	37	50

I.D. Planes (German) (Continued)

	C6	C8	C10
Blohm & Voss BV138, 5/44	50	75	100
Blohm & Voss BV222, 2/44, rare ...	100	150	200
Blohm & Voss HA139, 11/42, rare .	100	150	200
DFS 230, 8/43..............................	15	22	30
Dornier DO 172, 9/42....................	25	37	50
Dornier DO 215, 9/42....................	25	37	50
Dornier DO 217E, 8/42	25	37	50
Fi 156 Storch, none, very rare	50	65	90
Focke Wulf 200, 3/44, very rare......	100	150	200
Focke Wulf FW 187, 8/42...............	25	37	50
Focke Wulf FW 189, 5/42...............	25	37	50
Focke Wulf FW 190, 7/42...............	15	22	30
Focke Wulf FW 190, 12/42.............	15	22	30
Focke Wulf FW 200K, 9/42.............	100	150	200
Gotha Go 242, 7/42	25	37	50
Heinkel He 111, 9/42.....................	25	37	50
Heinkel He 112, 7/42.....................	20	30	40
Heinkel He 113, 5/42.....................	25	35	45
Heinkel He 113, 9/42.....................	20	30	40
Heinkel He 115K, 9/42...................	40	60	80
Henschel Hs 126, 10/42.................	25	37	50
Henschel Hs 129, 8/44...................	25	37	50
Junkers Ju 188, 7/44, extremely rare	60	80	100
Junkers Ju 52, 8/42	60	90	120
Junkers Ju 86K, 9/42	25	37	50
Junkers Ju 87B, 8/42	20	35	65
Junkers Ju 88, 9/42	25	37	50
Junkers Ju 90, 9/42	50	70	85
Messers. Me 109E, 7/42	20	30	40
Messers. Me 109F, 7/42	20	30	40
Messers. Me 110, 8/42	25	38	50
Messers. Me 210, 7/43	30	45	60

I.D. Planes (Italian)

	C6	C8	C10
Cantiere Z. 1007, 9/42...................	30	45	60
Cantiere Z. 506B, 9/42..................	65	80	100
Caproni CA.133, 9/42....................	75	100	125
Fiat BR. 20, 6/42..........................	25	38	50
Fiat CR. 42, 9/42..........................	30	45	60
Fiat CR. 42, 1/43, very rare	40	60	80
Fiat G. 50, 8/42............................	20	30	40
Macchi C. 200, 8/42.......................	20	30	40
Macchi MC. 202, 3/43....................	20	30	40
Piaggio P. 32 BIS, 9/42..................	25	38	50
Reggiane Rc. 2000, 9/42.................	20	30	40
Reggiane Re. 2001, 3/43	20	30	40
Savoia Marchetti 79, 9/42..............	50	75	100
Savoia Marchetti 81, 9/42..............	65	80	100
Savoia Marchetti 82, 9/42..............	30	45	60

I.D. Planes Spitfire 9B (10/44), $50; Spitfire (8/42), $50. Photo courtesy Richard MacNary

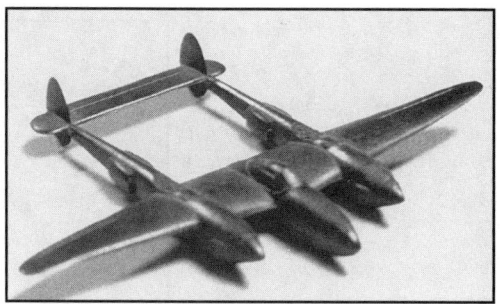

I.D. Planes P-38 Lightning, $50. Photo courtesy Richard MacNary

I.D. Planes (Italian) (Continued)	**C6**	**C8**	**C10**
Savoia Marchetti 84, 4/43	30	45	60
I.D. Planes (Russian)	**C6**	**C8**	**C10**
DB-3F, 4/44	35	60	80
DB-3F, 9/42	25	50	75
I-16, none	15	22	30
I-18 (MiG-3), 2/43	15	22	30
IL-2, 12/43	15	22	30
IL-2, 9/42	15	22	30
MiG-3, 2/44	20	30	40
MiG-3, 8/42	15	22	30
Pe-2, 9/42	15	22	30
SB-3, 11/43	15	22	30
TB-7*, 4/44	25	35	55
I.D. Planes (Netherlands)	**C6**	**C8**	**C10**
Fokker T8W, 11/42, rare	50	75	100
I.D. Planes (British)	**C6**	**C8**	**C10**
Albacore, 8/42	30	45	60
Albemarle, 9/44, very rare	25	50	75
Barracuda, 2/43	15	22	30
Beafighter 1, 9/42	30	40	50
Beafighter 2, 9/42	30	45	60
Beafighter 6, 5/44	35	50	65
Beaufort, 9/42	25	37	50
Beaufort, none, rare	30	45	60
Blenheim IV, 8/42	25	37	50
Boomerang (Aust.), none, very rare	40	60	80
Botha, 8/42	20	35	45
Defiant, 8/42	15	22	30
Firefly, 2/43	15	25	40
Fulmar, 8/42	15	22	30
Halifax, 9/42	75	100	125
Hampden, 8/42	25	37	50
Horsa, 9/44	25	37	50
Hotspur, 6/43	15	22	30
Hurricane, 8/43	15	22	30

I.D. Planes (British) (Continued)	**C6**	**C8**	**C10**
Lancaster, 4/43	75	100	150
Lerwick, 9/42, rare	30	60	75
Lysander, 7/43	25	37	50
Manchester, 8/42	25	37	50
Maryland, 2/43	20	30	45
Mosquito, 3/43	30	45	60
Roc, 8/42	15	22	30
Skua, 8/42	15	22	30
Spitfire, 8/42	25	37	50
Spitfire, 1/44	35	45	60
Spitfire 22, 7/45	25	37	50
Spitfire 9A, 10/44	25	37	50
Spitfire 9B, 10/44	25	37	50
Stirling, 5/42	50	75	100
Sunderland, 9/42	90	120	150
Swordfish, 9/42	40	60	80
Tempest 2, 3/45	15	22	30
Tempest 5, 10/44	20	30	40
Typhoon, 6/43	20	30	40
Walrus, 4/44, very rare	50	75	110
Wellington 2, 9/42	30	45	60
Wellington 3, 9/42	30	45	60
Whirlwind, 8/43	25	37	50
Whitley, 9/42	25	37	50
York, 9/44	50	75	100

Japanese Tin Airplanes

Starting with the birth of aviation, toy manufacturers began making toy replicas of anything that flew—older pusher planes through the Spirit of St. Louis, World War I bi-planes, World War II fighters and bombers, commercial and military jets, and even the Concorde.

The same companies that produced battery-operated tin cars often produced aircraft as well. Here is an easy way to help identify some manufacturers. Asahi Toy Company, "ATC." Alps Shoji Co., "ALPS" on a mountaintop. Bandai, "B." Still in business, Bandai is

I.D. Planes Focke Wulf FW 189, $50. Photo courtesy Richard MacNary

currently known for the popular Power Rangers line. Ichiko marked their toys with the words, "Ichiko Japan." Nomura Toy Ltd., used the initials, "TN" and collectors frequently refer to the toys as TN rather than use the Nomura name. Yonezawa earned a reputation for its high-quality toys and can be identified by the capital "Y" inside a leaf.

Contributor: Ron Smith, 33005 Arlesford, Solon, OH, 44139, 440-248-7066, fax 440-519-0906. Smith has always loved toy cars and planes; he can still show you his first Dinky Toy his aunt bought him at Fred Harvey's Toy Store in Cleveland's Terminal Tower Building. Smith has collected die-cast cars, trucks, and planes, cast-iron toys and plastic promotional cars, but for the past fifteen years he has specialized in tin-plate cars and planes. Smith lives with his wife Joan and their two cats, T-2 and Bogart.

Japanese Tin Airplanes	C6	C8	C10
1930s German, wind-up, Tipp, (A29)	800	1600	2800
American Airlines Boeing 727, battery, "Y" Co., (A39)	100	150	250
American Airlines DC-7, battery, (A37)	200	250	450
American Airlines Electra, battery, Linemar, (A38)	200	300	400
B-29, friction, "Y" Co., (A58)	150	300	500
B-36, friction, "Y" Co., (A59)	400	800	1350
B-45 Tornado, friction, Bandai, (A60)	75	150	225
B-47 USAF, friction, Daiya, (A61)	150	225	325
B50, friction, Bandai, (A14)	40	60	125

Japanese Tin Airplanes	C6	C8	C10
B-50 Superfortress, friction, TCP, (A63)	200	300	400
B-50 USAF, battery, "Y" Co., (A62)	200	300	400
Bluebird Seaplane, friction, S&E, (A13)	100	200	350
Boeing 707, battery, (A40)	200	300	400
Boeing Stratocruiser, friction, T.N., (A41)	350	500	725
Bristol Bulldog, friction, S&E, (A4)	80	150	350
C-120 Pack Plane, friction, (A64)	250	500	950
C-124 Globemaster, friction, "Y" Co., (A65)	350	700	1300
Cessna, friction, T.N., (A1)	100	200	350
Cessna, friction, West German, (A5)	50	75	125
Comet Jetliner, friction, "Y" Co., (A42)	75	150	250
Constellation, friction, Ingap, (A11)	100	200	400
Construction, England, (A28)	125	175	400
De Havilland Comet, wind-up, Rico, (A20)	100	250	500
Disney Comic Plane, friction, Linemar, (A23)	150	300	450
Eastern Constellation, friction, Hadson, (A44)	200	350	500
Eastern Constellation, friction, MSK, (A43)	100	150	250
Eastern DC-7, friction, Bandai, (A45)	200	300	450

Japanese Tin Airplanes, 1930s German, 16" wingspan, $2600. Photo courtesy Ron Smith

Japanese Tin Airplanes, Bluebird Seaplane, 13" wingspan, S & E, $350. Photo courtesy Ron Smith

---

CONDITION CODE

C6   Good; evident overall wear, well played with but acceptable to many collectors

C8   Very Good; minor overall wear, very clean

C10   Mint; like new

Note: Mint in Box commands a higher price. Condition below C6 brings considerably lower prices

---

Japanese Tin Airplanes Bristol Bulldog, 14-1/2" wingspan, S & E, $350. Photo courtesy Ron Smith

Japanese Tin Airplanes, Cessna, 25" wingspan, T.N., $350. Photo courtesy Ron Smith

Japanese Tin Airplanes	C6	C8	C10
F-102 USAF, friction, HTS, (A69)	125	150	225
F-104 Lockheed, friction, "Y" Co., (A70)	125	150	175
F3F Biplane, battery, Cragstan, (A12)	150	250	500
F-80, friction, Bandai, (A22)	40	60	80
F-84 Airforce, battery, Linemar, (A66)	100	150	250

Japanese Tin Airplanes	C6	C8	C10
F-86 Airforce, friction, "J" Co., (A67)	75	125	175
F-94C Starfire, friction, "Y" Co., (A68)	150	300	500
Farman, friction, (A36)	500	900	1400
Fiat CR-42, wind-up, Ingap, (A30)	500	1500	3000
Ford, friction, T.N., (A6)	80	170	350

Japanese Tin Airplanes, Cessna, 12" wingspan, W. Germany, $125. Photo courtesy Ron Smith

Japanese Tin Airplanes, Constellation, 15" wingspan, Ingap, $400. Photo courtesy Ron Smith

Japanese Tin Airplanes, F3F Biplane, 11-1/2" wingspan, Cragstan, $500. Photo courtesy Ron Smith

Japanese Tin Airplanes, Construction, 22" wingspan, England, $400. Photo courtesy Ron Smith

Japanese Tin Airplanes, De Havilland Comet, 13" wingspan, Rico, $500. Photo courtesy Ron Smith

Japanese Tin Airplanes, Farman, 10" wingspan, $1400. Photo courtesy Sotheby's, New York

Japanese Tin Airplanes, Fiat CR-42, 10" wingspan, $3000. Photo courtesy Ron Smith

Japanese Tin Airplanes, Lockheed Sirus, 13" wingspan, $1200. Photo courtesy Tanaka

Japanese Tin Airplanes, Hein, 14" wingspan, $600. Photo courtesy Tanaka

Japanese Tin Airplanes, P-51 Mustang, 10" wingspan, $300. Photo courtesy Ron Smith

Japanese Tin Airplanes	C6	C8	C10
German Biplane, Bar/wind-up, Tipp, (A27)	500	1000	2500
Hein, friction, Bandai, (A32)	200	350	600
Hospital, Tekno, (A26)	400	1000	1600
Jenny Biplane, friction, Haji, (A7)	30	50	100
Jenny Biplane, friction, S&E, (A2)	75	125	250
Lockheed Sirus, friction, (A35)	400	800	1200
Northwest DC-7, friction, "Y" Co., (A50)	100	150	200
Northwest DC-7, friction, Asahi, (A52)	300	600	950
Northwest Orient, battery, "Y" Co., (A51)	300	500	650
P-47 Thunderbolt, friction, HTC, (A18)	75	150	275
P-51 Mustang, friction, HTC, (A17)	100	200	300
Pam Am Jet Clipper, battery, Linemar, (A49)	200	300	425

Japanese Tin Airplanes	C6	C8	C10
Pam Am Stato Clipper, friction, (A48)	225	300	450
Pan Am DC-7, friction, T.N., (A47)	300	600	800
Presidents Plane, battery, (A46)	275	350	600
Ryan Spirit of St. Louis, friction, HTC, (A8)	100	250	500
Sky Bird "Spirit of St. Louis", friction, Bandai, (A15)	50	80	120
Spitfire, friction, HTC, (A16)	80	150	300
Stuka, Dux, (A31)	300	600	1200
TWA Constellation, friction, "Y" Co., (A53)	200	300	600
TWA DC-2, wind-up, (A55)	175	300	425
TWA DC-4, friction, Linemar, (A54)	150	350	475
U.N. Hospital Plane, friction, HTC, (A9)	90	175	350
United DC-7, friction, (A57)	125	250	400

Japanese Tin Airplanes, Hospital Plane, 14" wingspan, Tekno, $1600. Photo courtesy Ron Smith

Japanese Tin Airplanes, P-47 Thunderbolt, 10" wingspan, HTC, $275. Photo courtesy Ron Smith

Japanese Tin Airplanes, WWII Tri-Motor, 9" wingspan, Spain, $550. Photo courtesy Ron Smith

Japanese Tin Airplanes	C6	C8	C10
United DC-7 Mainliner, battery, T.N., (A56)	150	275	350
WWII Fighter, friction, (A10)	80	150	275
WWII Fighter, wind-up, Spain, (A21)	100	200	400
WWII Tri-Motor, wind-up, Spain, (A25)	100	300	550
Zero, friction, Nomura, (A33)	150	275	350
Zero, friction, new issue, (A19)	NPF	NPF	125

Japanese Tin Airplanes, Jenny Biplane, 11-1/2" wingspan, Haji, $100. Photo courtesy Ron Smith

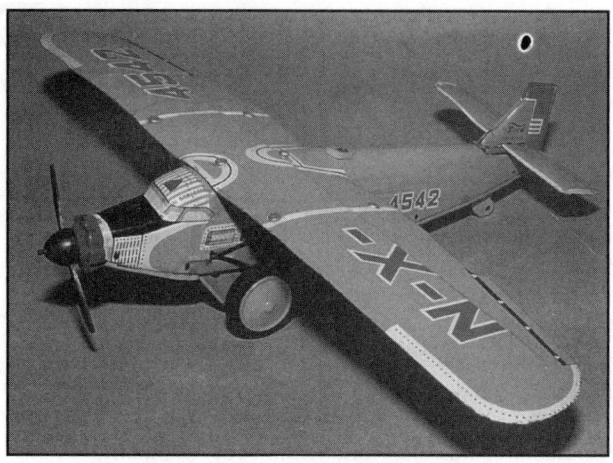

Japanese Tin Airplanes, Ford, 15" wingspan, T.N., $350. Photo courtesy Ron Smith

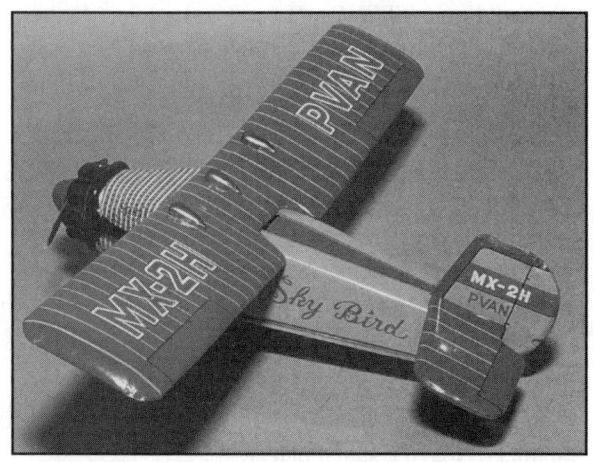

Japanese Tin Airplanes, Sky Bird "Spirit of St. Louis," 9" wingspan, Bandai, $120. Photo courtesy Ron Smith

Japanese Tin Airplanes, WWII Fighter, 8-1/2" wingspan, Spain, $400. Photo courtesy Ron Smith

Japanese Tin Airplanes, WWII Fighter, 14-1/2" wingspan, $275. Photo courtesy Ron Smith

Japanese Tin Airplanes, Zero, 14" wingspan, Nomura, $350. Photo courtesy Tanaka

AMERICAN PAPER TOYS

Paper toys and dolls (also called cut-outs, punchouts and press-outs) have been around since the mid-1600s when they were called Pantins. Dolls as well as forts, planes, and trains, have been produced in paper. Paper toys and doll were extremely popular from the end of the last century to the period after World War II. Almost every type of toy can be found in a paper or cardboard version.

American companies began turning out paper toys by the thousands around 1900. The most popular manufacturer was the McLoughlin Bros. Company, which started out with paper toys in 1857 in New York City. McLoughlin was eventually bought out by Milton Bradley and moved to Springfield, Massachusetts in 1920. McLoughlin/Milton Bradley products included beautifully lithographed covered boxed sets or cardboard figures on wooden stands and sheets of American and foreign soldiers.

During the years 1895 to 1905, almost every major newspaper in America had Sunday Art Supplements, which were paper toys for children. These sheets included a wide range of subjects including armies and navies of the world, historical panoramas, political figures, personalities of the day, and cut-out dolls of celebrities with vast wardrobes. Paper houses and villages were sold by several companies including McLoughlin Bros., Milton Bradley, Built-Rite and Megow. The World War II-era was the golden age of paper toys in the United States.

During the 1940s every conceivable type of toy was available in paper, usually with a patriotic wartime theme. The major paper doll publishers were Merrill and Saalfield and Whitman. They produced paper doll books that were popular with the children of the 1940s through the 1960s.

There are now quite a few books on paper dolls and paper toys, including *Blair Witton: Paper Toys of the World*, Hobby House Press, 1986; *Paper Soldiers* by Edward Ryan, *WWII-Era Paper Toys* by John Matthews, Mary Young has written several books on paper dolls, and Ann Tolstoi Wallach: Paper Dolls, Van Nostrand 1982.

Contributor: Judith Izen, P.O. Box 623 Lexington, MA 02173. Izen is a noted doll and paper doll authority whose paper doll articles have appeared in several publications. Her books include *Collectors Guide to Ideal Dolls* and *Collectors Encyclopedia of Vogue Dolls* (coauthored with Carol Stover).

Abbott

	C6	C8	C10
Blue Feather and Silver Cloud, No. 1356, Native-American dolls, 1940s	25	40	55
Cut-Me-Out Paper Dolls, No. 1358, 1940s	20	30	35
Janet Leigh, No. 1805, 1958	30	55	75
TV Star Time Paper Dolls, No. 1367, c. 1950s	20	25	30

All-Nu

	C6	C8	C10
Decal sheet of soldiers, by Frank Krupp, meant to be attached to heavy cardboard backing, c. 1942	60	75	100
Soldiers, No. 113, nurse, heavy cardboard, c. 1942-43, 5" high	4	5	10
Soldiers, No. 100, officer marching w/sabre, heavy cardboard, c. 1942-43, 5" high	4	5	10
Soldiers, No. 101, marching, slope arms, WWI helmet, heavy cardboard, c. 1942-43, 5" high	4	5	10
Soldiers, No. 102, bugler, campaign cap, heavy cardboard, c. 1942-43, 5" high	4	5	10

All-Nu (Continued)

	C6	C8	C10
Soldiers, No. 103, signalman, WWI helmet, heavy cardboard, c. 1942-43, 5" high	4	5	10
Soldiers, No. 104, officer kneeling w/binoculars, heavy cardboard, c. 1942-43, 5" high	4	5	10
Soldiers, No. 105, kneeling firing rifle w/WWI helmet, heavy cardboard, c. 1942-43, 5" high	4	5	10
Soldiers, No. 106, throwing grenade, WWI helmet, heavy cardboard, c. 1942-43, 5" high	4	5	10
Soldiers, No. 107, fixed bayonet, WWI helmet, heavy cardboard, c. 1942-43, 5" high	4	5	10
Soldiers, No. 108, charging w/gas mask, WWI helmet, heavy cardboard, c. 1942-43, 5" high	4	5	10
Soldiers, No. 109, charging w/rifle, port arms, WWI helmet, heavy cardboard, c. 1942-43, 5" high	4	5	10
Soldiers, No. 110, seated machine gunner, WWI helmet, heavy cardboard, c. 1942-43, 5" high	4	5	10

Artcraft, Tricia Paper Coll, No. 4248, 1969, $245.

Artcraft, Dodie from "My Three Sons" A Paper Doll Book, No. 5115, 1971, $55.

All-Nu (Continued)

	C6	C8	C10
Soldiers, No. 110, seated machine gunner, WWI helmet, heavy cardboard, c. 1942-43, 5" high....	4	5	10
Soldiers, No. 112, General McArthur, heavy cardboard, c. 1942-43, 5" high..........................	12	14	20
Soldiers, No. 155, truck w/soldiers in rear, WWII helmets, heavy cardboard, c. 1942-43, 5" high....	4	5	10
Soldiers, No. 114, two men carrying wounded soldier on stretcher, WWII helmets, heavy cardboard, c. 1942-43, 5" high......................	4	5	10
Soldiers, No. 115, two men firing rifles from prone position, WWII helmets, heavy cardboard, c. 1942-43, 5" high..........................	4	5	10
Soldiers, No. 116, soldier on wireless radio, heavy cardboard, c. 1942-43, 5" high..........................	4	5	10
Soldiers, No. 117, on heavy cardboard, three soldiers w/rifles leaving boat, WWII helmets, heavy cardboard, c. 1942-43, 5" high.....	4	5	10
Soldiers, No. 118, on heavy cardboard, two paratroopers, one w/tommy gun, WWII helmets, heavy cardboard, c. 1942-43, 5" high..	4	5	10

All-Nu (Continued)

	C6	C8	C10
Soldiers, No. 119, on heavy cardboard, ski trooper, heavy cardboard, c. 1942-43, 5" high...........	4	5	10
Soldiers, No. 120, on heavy cardboard, soldier advancing w/rifle, WWII helmet, heavy cardboard, c. 1942-43, 5" high......................	4	5	10
Soldiers, No. 150, on heavy cardboard, three men in jeep, WWI helmets, heavy cardboard, c. 1942-43, 5" high.........................	4	5	10
Soldiers, No. 152, on heavy cardboard, two men manning wheeled AA gun, WWI helmets, heavy cardboard, c. 1942-43, 5" high..	4	5	10
Soldiers, No. 153, on heavy cardboard, tank w/three men, heavy cardboard, c. 1942-43, 5" high .	4	5	10
Soldiers, No. 154, Ambulance, heavy cardboard, c. 1942-43, 5" high	4	5	10
Soldiers, No. 111, flag-bearer, WWI helmet, heavy cardboard, c. 1942-43, 5" high......................	4	5	10

Artcraft

	C6	C8	C10
Dodie from "My Three Sons" A Paper Doll Book, No. 5115, Dodie and Dolly, 1971	30	40	55

Artcraft (Continued)

	C6	C8	C10
Hee Haw, No. 5139, 1971	25	40	45
Julia, No. 5140, includes Diahann Carroll, Julia, Corey, Marie and Earl J. Waggedorn, 1968	25	40	50
Little Women, No. 5127, c. 1970	15	25	35
Lost Horizon, No. 5112, 1973	15	25	30
Partridge Family, The, No. 5137, 1971	30	45	60
Partridge Family, No. 5143, 1972 ...	35	45	55
Susan Dey as Laurie (Partridge Family), fashions by Kate Greenaway, 1972	25	35	45
The Flying Nun, The, No. 4417, 1968, 1969	25	40	50
Tricia Paper Doll, No. 4248, 1969 ..	190	225	245

Artfield

	C6	C8	C10
Nanny and the Professor, No. 4283, 1971	25	35	45

Built-Rite

	C6	C8	C10
No. 0001 Toy Soldiers, WWI helmets, each	2	3	4
No. 0002 Toy Trench	25	45	60
No. 0004 Armored Car	15	20	30
No. 0007 Army Plane Hangar	48	60	70
No. 0007 Private Garage, brick	35	45	55
No. 0008 House, brick	65	80	90
No. 0009 House, stucco and brick...	65	80	90
No. 0010 House, two-story, brick and shingle	65	80	90
No. 0014 Front Line Trench and Soldier Set, w/trench and six WWII soldiers	40	55	60
No. 0015 Commercial Garage	65	80	90
No. 0016 Fort, no ramp	70	90	125
No. 0017 Service Station	65	80	90
No. 0018 Airport	65	80	85
No. 0020 Army Battery set.............	90	125	145
No. 0020 Railroad Tunnel	12	22	27
No. 0022 Army Outpost	45	65	75
No. 0025 Fort, one-ramp	90	120	130
No. 0025A Twenty-six-piece Fort and Soldier Set, same fort as No.25, WWII soldiers, two sandbag foxholes and fiberboard pistol, sold through 1954	120	150	175
No. 0026 United Airlines Airport Hangar	60	75	85
No. 0027 Barn, w/animals	30	45	55
No. 0028 Garage and Super Service Station	70	85	95

Built-Rite (Continued)

	C6	C8	C10
No. 0029 Three Cart Set..................	25	40	45
No. 0033 House, Tudor-type	65	80	90
No. 0033 Lokdwood Dolls, paper dolls, 1940s	25	35	45
No. 0034 House, two-story.............	65	80	90
No. 0035 Modern Doll House	65	80	90
No. 0036 House	65	80	90
No. 0036F Three-room Furnished Doll House	85	95	105
No. 0037 Farm Machinery Set	35	50	60
No. 0045 Living Room Furniture....	45	55	65
No. 0046 Dining Room Furniture ...	45	55	65
No. 0047 Bedroom Furniture	45	55	65
No. 0048 Bathroom Furniture	45	55	65
No. 0049 Kitchen Furniture............	45	55	65
No. 0050 Army Raiders' Victory Unit, twenty-eight pieces, truck, tank, AA gun, jeep, semi-trach and twenty soldiers, WWII	75	90	100
No. 0055 Five Cardboard Miniature Houses	35	55	65
No. 0056 Five Miniature Buildings, church, school, RR station, firehouse and drugstore	35	55	65
No. 0057 Farm Set, eight-piece	40	50	65
No. 0060 Navy Battle Fleet and Coast Artillery Gun	35	60	75
No. 0066 Three-piece Kitchen	30	45	55
No. 0075 Living Room Furniture....	45	55	65
No. 0076 Dining Room Furniture ...	45	55	65
No. 0077 American Ranger Fighters, eight vehicles, WWII soldiers......	80	90	100
No. 0077 Bedroom Furniture	45	55	65
No. 0078 Kitchen Furniture.............	45	55	65
No. 0083 Weapons Carrier..............	15	20	30
No. 0100 A Fortress, w/two ramps, c. 1938	120	155	180
No. 0105 Farm Set, w/twenty plastic animals	35	45	55
No. 0111 Railroad Accessory Set....	25	30	40
No. 0112 American Fighters, includes 100A fortress w/soldiers, cannons, etc., fifty-five pieces, no flag on tower	120	155	180
No. 0115 Doll House, garage set w/car...................	65	80	90
No. 0119 Farm Set.........................	45	65	75
No. 0120 Five-room Suburban Doll House	65	85	90
No. 0127 Large Barn, w/animals.....	30	40	50

Built-Rite (Continued)

	C6	C8	C10
No. 0128 Miniature Village and Scenery set	35	48	60
No. 0148 Train Accessory set	30	40	50
No. 0156 Miniature houses and buildings	55	65	70
No. 0178 Train Accessory set	30	40	50
No. 019 Railroad Station	60	70	80
No. 0201 Twenty-six-piece Guardsman set, two trenches, artillery base, cannon, pistol and WWII soldiers	70	90	120
No. 0202 Train Scenery, twenty-eight pieces	45	65	75
No. 0204F Furnished Country Estate	60	80	90
No. 0210 Railroad Station and Accessories	30	40	50
No. 0212 Station and Railroad Accessories	35	45	55
No. 0245 Miniature Village	35	50	60
No. 0252 Fort Set, twenty-six pieces, No. 25 fort, post-war	110	150	180
No. 0298 Train Accessory set	30	40	50
No. 0300 Stock and Grain Elevator	30	35	45
No. 0375 Station and Railroad Set	30	40	50
No. 0415 House, boxed set w/19"house and garage, twenty-seven pieces of furniture, sedan, baby buggy, shrubbery, etc., c. 1943, 13" x 20"	85	110	135
No. 0459 Five rooms of toy furniture	45	55	65
No. 0460 Pocket-size Series of Miniature Paper Doll Set	15	20	24
No. 0498 Train Accessory Set	25	35	45
No. 0566 Village	40	55	65
No. 1001 Modern Stock Farm	50	60	80
No. 1027 Stock Farm	50	60	80
No. 1033 Doll House	50	65	75
No. 1422 Fort and Soldiers, ninety-four pieces, two-ramp fort	110	145	175
No. 2050 Country Estate, house, bushes, dog, cat, baby buggy	70	90	100
Ranch, over 180 pieces	150	185	200

Colorgraphic

	C6	C8	C10
Young Patriot Invasion Set, No. 500, contains destroyer, amphibian tractor, tank, jeep, anti-tank gun, bomber and diver bomber, boxed set, c. 1944, 10-1/2" x 13"	75	80	95

Colorgraphic (Continued)

	C6	C8	C10
Young Patriot Learn to Know Your Army, No. 350, includes tank, howitzer, jeep, anti-tank gun, bomber, fighter and soldiers, w/shooting guns and dropping bombs, 1943	75	80	95
Young Patriot Learn to Know Your Navy, No. 360, construction set includes battleship, destroyer, aircraft carrier, mosquito boat, submarine, planes and depth charges, w/moveable parts, 1943, 10" x 14"	75	80	95

D.A. Pachter Co.

	C6	C8	C10
Bild-A-Set Constructor Kit, No. 85, Erector-type set of cardboard, boxed, 1943	22	30	35
Bild-A-Set Navy Fighting Fleet, 214 pieces, cardboard ship set, 1943	30	60	100
Bild-A-Set Stock Farm, cardboard construction set, 1943	10	20	30
Bild-A-Set Vought Corsair, No. 253, flying model airplane, 1944	8	16	25

Golden Press

	C6	C8	C10
Career Girls, 1960	20	30	40

Grinnel

	C6	C8	C10
American Family Paper-Doll Book, No. C1002, "Costumes for all the family from 1610 to now"	40	50	75
Mother and Daughter, No. C-1005, by Patrie Winston, includes mother and daughter doll w/two scotties, 1940, 15" mother, 11" daughter	20	35	45
My Paper Doll's Sewing Kit, No. C-1018, by Margot Voight, 1940	15	20	30

Lowe

	C6	C8	C10
8 Ages of Judy, The, No. L1025, by Fern Bisel Peat, Judy as baby and ages one to seven, 1941	40	60	80
Assemble Nine Model Warplanes, w/four model tanks, 1941	55	75	85
Babysitter Paper Dolls, No. 945	15	20	30
Brenda Lee Teenage Celebrity, No. 2785, 1961	40	60	80
Bride Doll Cut-out Book, No. 1043, 1940s	20	30	40
Cinderella Steps Out, No. 1242	25	35	50
Clothes Make a Lady, No. 1029, 1941	20	30	40
Dick the Sailor, No. L1074, c. 1942	20	35	45

Lowe, Glenn Miller, No. 21041, 1942, $200.

Lowe, Model Tanks, No. 1065, 1941, $75.

Lowe (Continued)	**C6**	**C8**	**C10**
Down on The Farm, No. 1056, 1940s	15	20	30
Dr. Kildare and Nurse Susan, No. 2740, 1960s	35	55	70
Fashion Cut-outs, No. 1243, w/Sturdibilt dolls, 1940s	15	20	30
Five Little Peppers, No. L1030, Little Women and Annie three-book set, Lauries, 1941	35	55	75
Glenn Miller, No. 21041, Marion Hutton Turnabout Doll Book, 1942	100	150	200
Harry the Soldier, No. L1074, 1941	45	65	75
House for Sale, No. 9042, 1962	35	45	50
Judy and Jack, Peg and Bill Cut-out Dolls, No. L1024, by Pelagie Doane, 1940	35	45	70
Junior Prom, No. 1042, by Newman, 1942	20	35	45
Model Airplanes, No. 1069, WWII Airplanes, International, 1941	50	65	75
Model Tanks, No. 1065, 1941	50	65	75
Model Tanks Construction Set, No. 1267, boxed, 1942	50	65	75
Model War Planes Construction Set, No. 1266, boxed, 1942	50	65	75
My Very First Paper Doll Book, No. 4732, a Bonnie Book, 1957	10	15	20

Lowe (Continued)	**C6**	**C8**	**C10**
On Guard, No. L535, 1942	40	45	50
Over 80 Turn-About, No. 140, Standup Sailors, 1943	45	55	60
Over 80 Turn-About Standup Sailors, No. 141, 1943	45	55	60
Patience and Prudence, No. 2736, 1958	10	15	20
Playhouse Paper Dolls, No. 1028, designed by Doris and Marion Henderson, 1941	20	30	40
Playtime Pals, No. 1045, 1946	10	15	20
Polly Patchwork and Her Friends, No. 1024, by Pelagie Doane, 1941	20	30	40
Pressed Board Dolls and Their Dresses, No. 1942, boxed set	25	35	45
Rosemary Clooney, No. 1256	40	50	60
Rosemary Clooney, No. 2487, 1958	40	50	60
Sally and Jane, No. 2755, 1964	20	30	40
Sally the Standing Doll, No. 1042, 1940s	20	30	40
Service Kit of America's Armed Forces-On Land-On Sea-In the Air, No. 265, 1942	45	55	60
Square Dance Paper Dolls, No. 968-10, by J. Voelz	15	20	25
The Sue and Tom Cut-out Dolls Book, No. 149, 1946	15	20	25

Lowe, Judy and Jack, Peg and Bill Cut-out Dolls, No. L1024, 1940, $70.

Lowe, House For Sale, No. 9042, 1962, $50.

Lowe (Continued)	**C6**	**C8**	**C10**
Tom the Aviator, No. L1074, c. 1942...	25	35	45
Toni Hair-do Cut-out Dolls, No. 1284, 1950..................................	35	45	60
Toni Hair-Do Dress-Up Dolls, No. 1251..	40	50	60
Toy Models: Warplane and Tank Punch-out, 1941	45	50	65
Turnabouts Dolls Book, The, No. 1048, dolls printed front view on each side, 1940s	25	30	35
TV Tap Stars Paper Dolls, No. 99010...	6	12	25
U.S. Commandos Book, No. 1089, 1943...	45	55	60
United States Soldiers, No. L1063, 1942...	50	55	60
Victory Girls Arlene the Airline Hostess, c. 1940s.......................	35	45	55
Victory Punch-Out Tanks, No. 848, soldiers, sailors, planes, c. 1943..	50	55	60

Magic Wand Co.	**C6**	**C8**	**C10**
Tabitha from "Bewitched" TV show, No. 115-100, baby paper doll, 1960..................................	10	15	25

McLoughlin Bros.	**C6**	**C8**	**C10**
02 Series American Indians, kneeling and standing, c. 1904-1910 ...	2	3	5
02 Series British Highlanders, c. 1904-1910	2	3	5
02 Series U.S. Continentals, c. 1904-1910	2	3	5
02 Series U.S. Infantry in Campaign Uniforms, Spanish-American War, c. 1904-1910	2	3	5
02 Series U.S. Navy, c. 1904-1910 ..	2	3	5
02 Series U.S. Zouaves, c. 1904-1910...	2	3	5
02 Series West Point Cadets, c. 1904-1910	2	3	5
02 Series West Point Cadets, round base, c. 1915............................	2	3	5
100 Soldiers on Parade, second set, c. 1898...	300	350	400
100 Soldiers on Parade, first set, c. 1898...	300	350	400
260 Series Annapolis Cadets, price for each, c. 1889-1895.................	2	3	5
260 Series Bandsmen, various instruments, price for each, c. 1889-1895	3	4	5

Lowe, On Guard, No. L535, 1942, $50.

Lowe, Pressed Board Dolls and Their Dresses, 1942, $45.

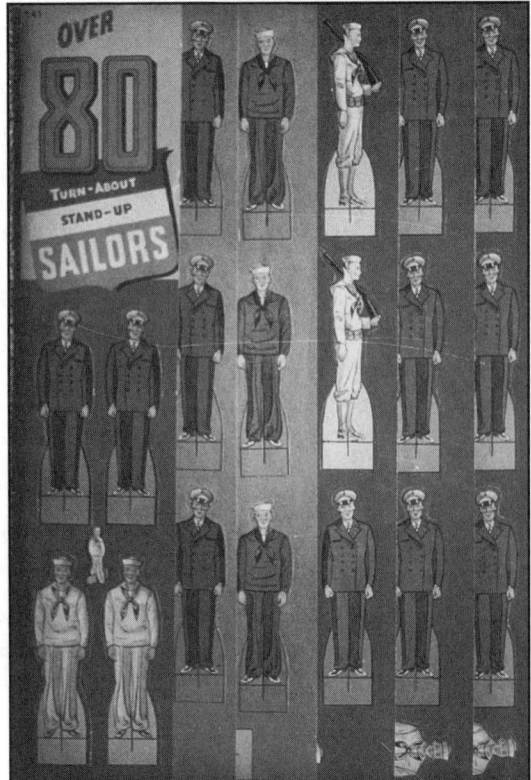

Lowe, Over 80 Turn-About Standup Sailors, No. 141, 1943, $60.

Lowe, Sally the Standing Doll, No. 1042, 1940s, $40.

Lowe, Playhouse Paper Dolls, No. 1028, 1941, $40.

Lowe, Toni Hair-do Cut-out Dolls, No. 1284, 1950, $60.

McLoughlin Bros. (Continued)	C6	C8	C10
260 Series Grenadier Guards, price for each, c. 1889-1895	2	3	5
260 Series Navy— USS Boston, c. 1889-1895	2	3	5
260 Series U.S. Infantry, c. 1889-1895	2	3	5
260 Series U.S. Infantry, c. 1889-1895	2	3	5
260 Series U.S. Regulars, c. 1889-1895	2	3	5
260 Series U.S. Regulars, spiked helmet, price for each, c. 1889-1895	2	3	5
260 Series West Point Cadets, c. 1889-1895	2	3	5
Big-Girl Paper Dolls, No. 707, 1940	20	30	40
Boy Scouts, holding rifles across chests, c. 1915	5	6	7
Brass Band, price for each, 1890	4	5	6
British Infantry Red Coats, w/spiked helmets on small wooden blocks, complete set, c. 1898, 6" high	150	200	250
British Infantry Red Coats, w/spiked helmets on small wooden blocks, price for each, c. 1898, 6" high	4	5	6

McLoughlin Bros. (Continued)	C6	C8	C10
Diane and Daphne the Round About Dolls Book, No. 545, large cut-outs by Campbell, 1937	30	55	65
Dutch Paper Doll, No. 0103, boy of the Village of Vollendam, c. 1910, 10-1/2" x 10-1/2" sheet	18	25	30
Fashion Book of the Round About Dolls, The, by Betty Campbell, eight stand-up dolls plus scissors and pack of paper dolls clothes in package, 1936	35	55	75
Figures, horizontal sheet of ten figures, uncut, c. 1890	35	50	75
Grenadiers, price for each, 1890	3	4	5
Infantry, price for each, c. 1875	3	4	5
Infantry Soldiers, printed, price for each, 1857	3	4	5
Landing Party for USS Texas, printed, sailor, 1898, 5-1/4" high	4	5	6
Little Red School House Kindergarten, The, by Margo Voight, includes two teachers and twenty-three children, 1940	30	45	55
Mounted U.S. Cavalry, Hussar type, charging, several different poses, price for each, c. 1884	3	4	5

McLoughlin Bros., building from New Pretty Village, $18.

The box for New Pretty Village from McLoughlin Bros.

McLoughlin Bros. (Continued)	C6	C8	C10
New Folding Doll House, cardboard w/lithographed paper, boxed set, 1897	400	500	575
New Pretty Village, individual buildings	12	15	18
New Pretty Village Church Set, 1897	90	125	145
New Pretty Village School Set, 1897	90	125	145
Soldiers, No. 4026, seven soldiers plus officer in field uniform, includes Belgium, Italy, France and Britain, price for each, c. 1916, 10-1/2" x 10-1/2"	20	30	40
U.S. Infantry, Spanish-American War, on wooden blocks, price for each, c. 1898, approx. 6" high	4	5	6
U.S. Regulars, glossy series of figures in full dress, c. 1898, 5" high	4	5	6
U.S. Zouaves, Civil War era, blue coats, red baggy trousers on small wooden blocks, c. 1898, 6" high	4	5	6
West Point Cadets, small glossy series, price for each, c. 1898, 4-1/2" high	4	5	6
Winnie's New Wardrobe, No. 555, by Geraldine Cline, 1939	30	32	36
Zouaves, price for each, 1884	3	4	5

Merrill	C6	C8	C10
Alice Faye, No. 4800, 1941	100	150	200
American Beauty Paper Dolls with Dresses Worn by White House First Ladies from 1789-1951, No. 154815, 1951	20	30	40
American Defense Battles Punch-out Book, No. 3430, by George Trimmer, 1940	75	95	105
Ann Blythe, No. 2250-25, 1952	45	55	90
Army Nurse and Doctor Paper Dolls, No. 3425, 1942	32	40	65
Around the Clock with Sue and Dot, No. 1546, 1950s	25	40	50
Babyland, No. 3642, 1955	20	35	45
Becky and Betsy, No. 3452, 1952	20	30	40
Betty Grable, No. 1558, 1951	55	80	125
Big-Little Sister Paper Doll, No. 1549, 1951	25	40	50
Blue Bonnet Paper Dolls, No. 3444, by Florence Salter, 1942	30	55	65
Boarding School Dolls and Clothes, No. 3492, 1942	25	40	55
Bride and Groom, No. 3443, 1949	25	35	50
Bride and Groom, No. 1555, 1949	25	35	50
Bride and Groom Military Wedding Party, No. 3411, set includes sixteen dolls, 1941	40	60	80

McLoughlin Bros., New Pretty Village Church Set, 1897, $145.

Merrill (Continued)	<u>C6</u>	<u>C8</u>	<u>C10</u>
Children in the Shoe, No. 1562, 1949	20	30	40
Coke Crowd, The, No. 3445, eight teens w/costumes, 1946	30	45	65
College Style Paper Dolls, No. 3400, Peter and Patsy, 1941	30	45	65
Cowboy and Cowgirl Cut-outs, No. 3449, 1950	25	40	50
Cowgirl Jill and Cowboy Joe, No. 3459	25	35	45
Dancing Dolls with Famous Costumes, No. 3448, ballet dancers, 1954	20	35	45
Deanna Durbin, No. 3480, 1940	50	100	165
Dolls from Storyland, No. 1554, by Vivian Robbins, 1948	25	40	50
Double Wedding 15 Paper Dolls, No. 3472, 1939	40	65	85
Esther Williams, No. 1563, three dolls, 1950	55	75	110
Family Princess Paper Dolls, No. 1548, 1958	25	40	55
Frontier Fort, No. 257225, 1952	15	25	30
Gene Autry Ranch Cut-out Book, 1940	65	80	90
Girl Pilots of the Ferry Command, No. 4852, 1943	55	75	115
Gone With the Wind, No. 3405, includes five dolls, 1940	200	300	400
Gone With the Wind, No. 3404, includes eighteen dolls, 1940	200	300	400
High School Girls, No. 1551, 1948	40	45	55
Jack and Jill, No. 1561, six dolls and clothes from Storyland, 1962	15	20	30

Merrill (Continued)	<u>C6</u>	<u>C8</u>	<u>C10</u>
Janet Leigh Cut-outs and Coloring Book, No. 2554, 1953	40	55	85
Jeanette MacDonald, No. 3640, 1941	100	150	200
Karen Goes to College!, No. 1564, 1955	20	30	40
Kitty Goes to Kindergarten, No. 1548, 1956	15	25	35
Liberty Belles Paper Doll Book, No. 3477, 1943	25	35	50
Little Ballerina, No. 154215, 1953	20	35	45
Navy Scouts Paper Doll Book, No. 3428, 1942	45	65	85
Our Army and Navy in Action, Cut and Stick, No. 4835, 1942	35	45	50
Paper Doll Family and Their Trailer, No. 3436, 1938	70	80	90
Pert and Pretty, No. 1552, 1948	25	30	50
Pig Tails, No. 344410, 1949	20	30	40
Pilot and Stewardess Airliner Paper Dolls, No. 3423, 1941	25	30	50
Pink Prom Twins, No. 2583, 1956	40	50	65
Pink Wedding, The, No. 1559, 1952	45	55	65
Piper Laurie, No. 2551, 1953	55	65	75
Polly & Playmates, No. 1556, 1951	20	30	40
Sally's Silver Skates, No. 1549, 1956	25	35	45
Stand-Up Dolls Honey and Bunny, No. 3403, 1936	50	60	70

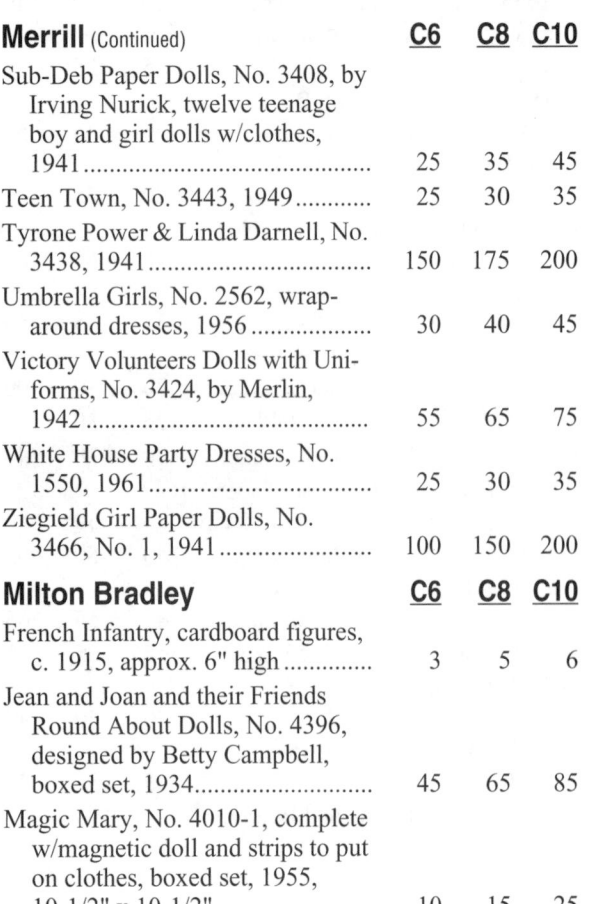

Merrill, Alice Faye, No. 4800, 1941, $200.

Merrill, Betty Grable, No. 1558, 1951, $125.

Merrill (Continued)

	C6	C8	C10
Sub-Deb Paper Dolls, No. 3408, by Irving Nurick, twelve teenage boy and girl dolls w/clothes, 1941	25	35	45
Teen Town, No. 3443, 1949	25	30	35
Tyrone Power & Linda Darnell, No. 3438, 1941	150	175	200
Umbrella Girls, No. 2562, wrap-around dresses, 1956	30	40	45
Victory Volunteers Dolls with Uniforms, No. 3424, by Merlin, 1942	55	65	75
White House Party Dresses, No. 1550, 1961	25	30	35
Ziegield Girl Paper Dolls, No. 3466, No. 1, 1941	100	150	200

Milton Bradley

	C6	C8	C10
French Infantry, cardboard figures, c. 1915, approx. 6" high	3	5	6
Jean and Joan and their Friends Round About Dolls, No. 4396, designed by Betty Campbell, boxed set, 1934	45	65	85
Magic Mary, No. 4010-1, complete w/magnetic doll and strips to put on clothes, boxed set, 1955, 10-1/2" x 10-1/2"	10	15	25

Milton Bradley (Continued)

	C6	C8	C10
Sharp-Shooters, No. 4103, includes two sets of five cardboard soldiers and one officer on stands, boxed, c. 1915	85	100	135
Soldiers Five, No. 4395, five cardboard soldiers, pistol, boxed set, c. 1920	80	100	125
Soldiers on Parade, No. 4518, set of ten	55	80	90

Miscellaneous

	C6	C8	C10
American Beauties Paper Dolls, No. 917, Reuben Lilja & Co., c. 1942	15	20	25
Amos & Andy Cut-out Dolls, cardboard of just Andy, stand-up, 8-1/2" high	5	7	10
Army Air Forces Aircraft Identification, Silhouette Model-Feb., 1:72-scale of Japanese fighter Najajima T-97, A.N.F., 1943, 7" x 11" envelope	16	20	27
Army Ambulance, Handi-Kraft, c. 1942	30	40	48
Around the World with Bob and Barbara, No. 3000, Children's Press, 1946	15	20	30
Betsy McCall Around the World Paper dolls, c. 1962	20	30	40

Merrill, College Style Paper Dolls, No. 3400, 1941, $65.

Merrill, Double Wedding 15 Paper Dolls, No. 3472, 1939, $85.

Merrill, Girl Pilots of the Ferry Command, No. 4852, 1943, $115.

Merrill, Pilot and Stewardess Airliner Paper Dolls, No. 3423, 1941, $50.

Merrill, Esther Williams, No. 1563, 1950, $110.

Merrill, Our Army and Navy in Action, Cut and Stick, No. 4835, 1942, $50.

Miscellaneous (Continued)	C6	C8	C10
Betsy McCall Dress 'n Play Paper Dolls, No. 802, boxed set, Standard/Toycraft/McCall, 1963, 12" x 18"	25	40	50
Betsy McCall Sheets from McCalls magazine	3	5	8
Betsy Ross and Her Friends, No. 224B, boxed set, Platt and Munk, 1963, 7" x 11"	7	10	15
Betty Bonnet Her Family and Friends, by Sheila Young, George W. Jacobs & Co., Phila., 1915 each series includes six sheets and folder; first series	125	150	175
Betty Sue A Cut-out Doll, No. 1010, c. 1940	15	25	35
Binson-Freeman Pre-Flight Trainer, cockpit and how-to-fly course	75	113	150
Birthday Party Stand-up Cut-out Dolls, twenty boys and girls, National Syndicate Displays, Inc., 1944	20	35	45
Brenda Lee, No. 4360, De Journette, 1964, 6-1/2" x 10"	45	55	85
Bridal Doll Book, No. 1818, Watkins-Strathmor, 1963	15	20	30

Miscellaneous (Continued)	C6	C8	C10
Bride and Groom, Western box set, 1982	3	5	8
Camouflage Defense Force, No. 431, heavy cardboard, airplanes, soldiers, anti-aircraft guns all hidden within farm buildings, boxed, Jay Line Mfg. Co., c. 1943	55	75	90
Career Girls Artcraft, No. 4471, 1960s	15	20	30
Colorgraphic Statue-ettes, three-dimensional and stand-up paper dolls of Marine, Soldier, Sailor, Nurse, WAAC and WAVE, boxed, 1943	25	40	50
Comet Model Airplane Co. Die-Cut Glider, containing die-cut U.S. Army fighter, printed in 1942 by the Comet Model Airplane Co., 5-1/2" x 8" sheet	10	15	18
Commando Machine Gun, thin cardboard cut-out makes model over, 1940s, 25" long	18	22	28
Coronation Cut-out Model Book	55	65	70
Coronation Glitter Model Book	25	40	50

Merrill, Paper Doll Family and Their Trailer, No. 3436, 1938, $90.

Merrill, Stand-Up Dolls Honey and Bunny, No. 3403, 1936, $70.

Miscellaneous (Continued)	C6	C8	C10
Crepe Paper Doll Outfit, No. 36, Dennison Manufacturing Company	55	65	110
Dancing Black Baby, Littauer & Bauer, 1895	75	100	150
Davy Crockett Punch-Out Book, No. 1943, 1955	40	65	85
Decalco-Litho Co. Paper Dolls Sheets, 1) woman and girl and nine outfits; 2) woman and girl and ten outfits; 3) two women and seven outfits; price per sheet, c. 1920s, 8" x 10-1/2" sheets	12	18	25
Dennison's Dolls and Dresses, No. 37, c. 1930	55	65	115
Disneyland Park Punch Out, No. 175, 1960	25	35	50
Dress-Up For the New York World's Fair, No. 700, by Judy and Barry Martin, Spertus, 1963	15	20	30
Dress-Up Paper Doll Cut-outs, Reuben Lilja & Co., 1947	10	15	25
Ellen or the Naughty Girl Reclaimed, S & J Fuller, 1811	150	200	250
Fabulous High Fashion Models, No. 2776, Bonnie Brooks/Child Craft, 1958	10	15	20

Miscellaneous (Continued)	C6	C8	C10
Fairy Folk Cut-out Paper Dolls, by Margaret Carlson, Stills & Edwards Co., Inc., 1920s	15	25	35
Fire House P-18, brick firehouse, boxed set, Megow, 1945	35	48	58
Fun Farm, Reed and Associates	8	15	18
Gene Autry Ranch Cut-out Book, 1953	50	70	80
Girls in Uniform Paper Dolls Book, No. L1048, c. 1942	35	65	95
Heavy Cruiser "This is the Navy", Skyline Mfg. Co., c. 1943	20	30	40
Historical Dolls To Cut Out and Dress, No. 226B, includes mother, father and two children of heavy cardboard, plus outfits, boxd set, Platt & Munk, 1961, 7" x 11"	20	30	35
House that Jack Built, house and story's characters w/stands, paper litho, c. 1895	400	500	600
Jaunty Juniors, No. 903, 1946	15	25	35
Junior Bombardier, No. 202, Einson & Freeman Co., 1953	25	35	50
Lettie Lane Paper Family, original house folder and six sheets, George W. Jacobs & Co.; third series, 1909	130	155	180

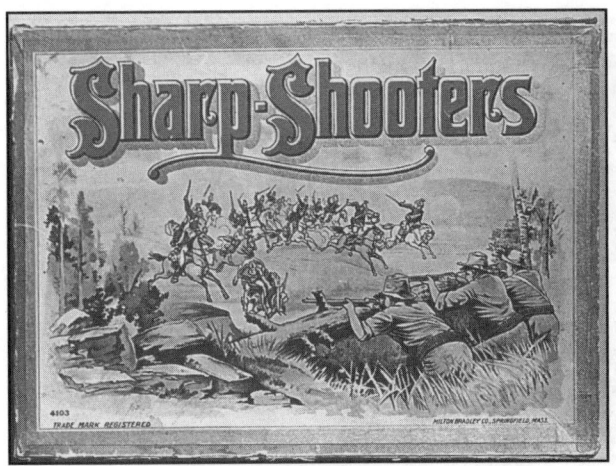

Milton Bradley, Sharp-Shooters box, No. 4103, c. 1915, $135.

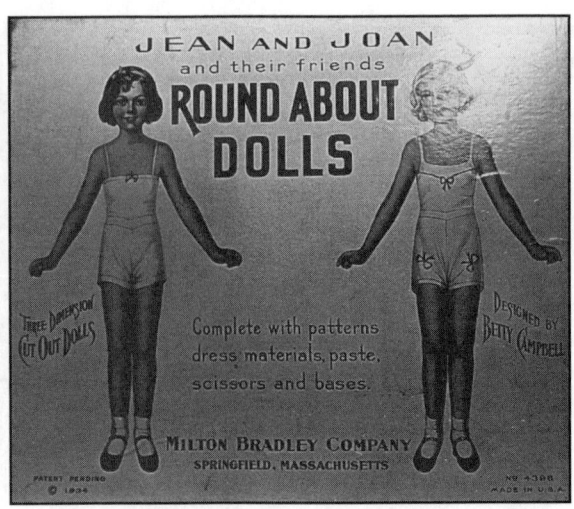

Milton Bradley, Jean and Joan and their Friends Round About Dolls, No. 4396, 1934, $85.

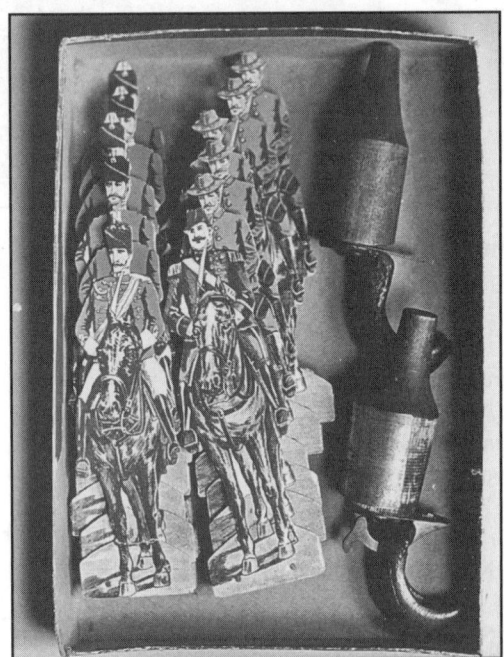

Milton Bradley, Sharp-Shooters, No. 4103, c. 1915, $135.

Betty Bonnet Her Family and Friends, George W. Jacobs & Co., $175.

Bild-A-Set Constructor Kit, No. 85, $35.

Birthday Party Stand-up Cut-out Dolls, National Syndicate Displays, 1944, $45.

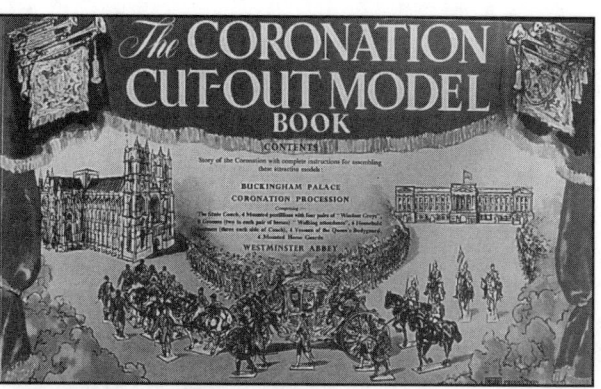

Coronation Cut-out Model Book, $70.

Coronation Glitter Model Book, $50.

Miscellaneous (Continued)	C6	C8	C10
Little Fairy Lightfoot, No. 4, Chandler's Paper Dolls; Brown, Taggard & Chase	150	200	250
Little Friends from History, No. 186, by Muriel Wilhoite, Rand McNally, 1936	25	40	50
Little Golden Paper Dolls, Golden, Hilda Miloche, 1950s	25	35	45
Little Nurse Cut-out Book, No. 909, Reuben H. Lilja and Co., Inc., early 1940s	20	30	40
Look Who I Am!, by Doris Stelberg, w/fifteen costumes, spiral bound, Hart Publishing Co., 1952, 18" doll	15	20	25
Madame Hattie Fashions, No. 908, Reuben Lilja, 1940s	35	45	48
Make Your Own Battle Set Mechanized Force, Electric Corporation of America, 1942	45	50	55

Miscellaneous (Continued)	C6	C8	C10
Maybelle Mercer's Front and Back Dolls, No. 978, w/wrap-around dresses, by Queen Holden	50	75	110
Me and Mimi a Bonnie Story Book Doll, done in the style of the Little Golden Books, a Doll and her Dolly Story Book, plus dolls and their dresses, 1957, 6" x 8"	15	25	35
Mickey and Minnie paper dolls, two figures w/clothes, 1930s, 10"	100	135	175
Model Sports Cars of the World, 10 paper car models by the Wallis Rigby Co., 1954	10	22	35
Our Happy Family Cut-out Sheets, No. D141, Sam'l Gabriel Sons Co., 1928	65	75	90
Our New Home, story by Susan S Popper, pictures by Helen E. Ohrenschall, hardcover book w/six pages of rooms and six gummed pages of people, furniture, etc., Sam'l Gabriel Sons, 1930	80	100	125

Crepe Paper Doll Outfit, No. 36, Dennison Manufacturing Company, $110.

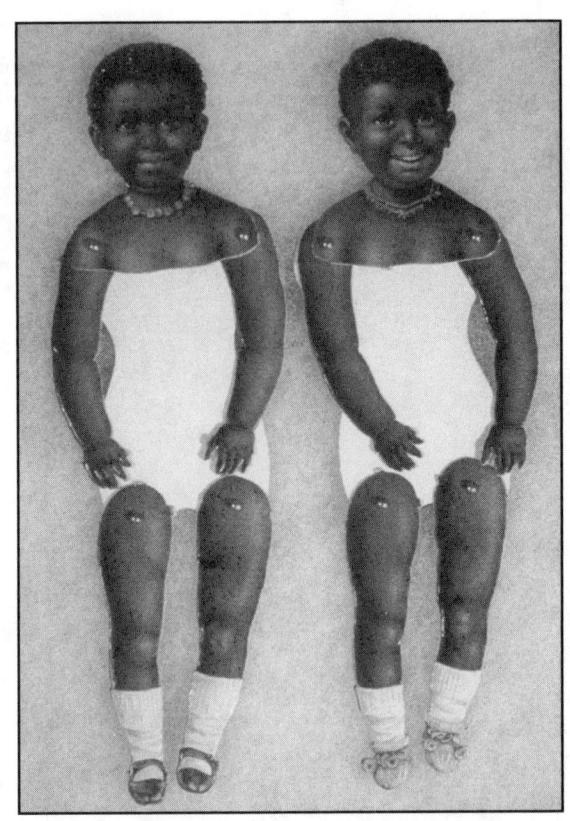

Dancing Black Baby, Littauer & Bauer, 1895, $150.

Miscellaneous (Continued)	C6	C8	C10
Paper Doll Outfit Dresses & Hats, No. 102, American Toy Works, boxed set	50	65	80
Paper Dolls of the Latest Paris Fashions, #4 Little Fairy Lightfoot; Brown, Taggard & Chase	150	200	250
Paper Dolls of the Latest Paris Fashions Brown, #1 Carry with Her Dresses; Brown, Taggard & Chase, 1800s	150	200	250
Patsy, No. 30002, includes Patsy, dog, doghouse, etc., Children's Press, 1946	15	25	35
Patti Page Book of Paper Dolls, 1958	60	70	80
Rap-A-Jap, No. C1, Woodburn Mfg., c. 1943	55	65	72
Ready Cut Village, 1930s	55	70	80
Ricky Nelson Paper Dolls, 1959	35	45	55
Rigby Flying Models of Jet and Rocket Planes, includes ten planes, Garden City Books, 1949	70	80	90

Miscellaneous (Continued)	C6	C8	C10
Rigby's Book of Model Ships, 1953	75	85	90
Rigby's Easier to Build Models of Naval Craft, designed by Wallace Rigby, twenty-four models of warships, twenty-seven pages, includes Battleship North Carolina, aircraft carrier, cruiser and destroyer, 1944, 11-1/2" x 14"	95	120	135
Rigby's Easy to Build Models of Fighting Planes	85	95	115
Rigby's Model Book of Flying Clippers, designed by Wallace Rigby, includes two scale models of Douglas DC-Jet Clipper and Douglas DC-7C, 1947, 11" x 14" book	60	70	80
Rigby's Model Sports Cars of the World "Sportsracer", includes Chevette, Jaguar, Mercedes-Benz, etc., 1954, 18"	60	70	80
Roy Rogers Sticker Fun Book, No. 2161, 1953	22	30	36
Royalty Cut-out Books: A Procession of the Knights of the Garter	55	65	70

Fairy Folk Cut-out Paper Dolls, Stills & Edwards, 1920s, $35.

Jaunty Juniors, No. 903, 1946, $35.

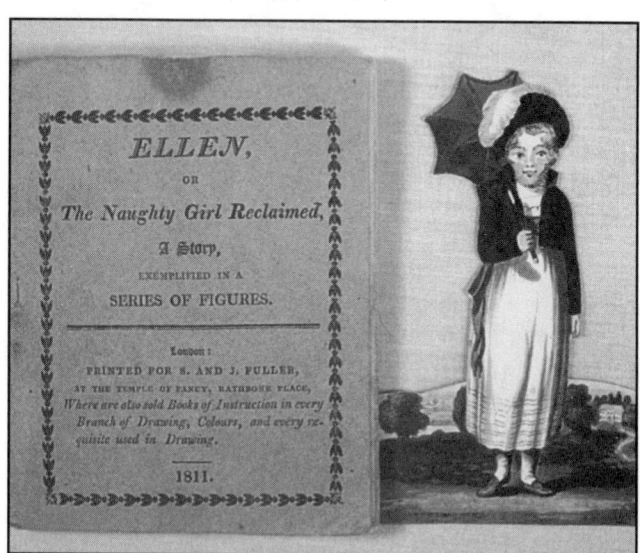

Ellen or the Naughty Girl Reclaimed, S & J Fuller, 1811, $250.

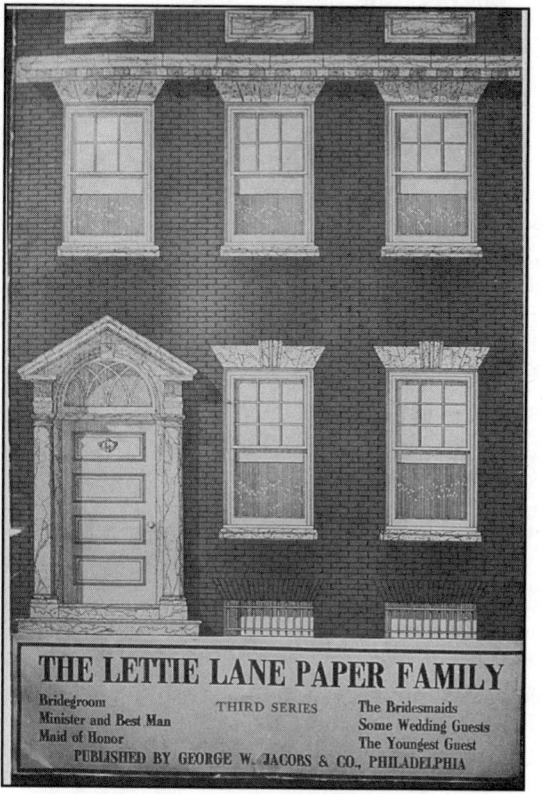

Lettie Lane Paper Family, George W. Jacobs & Co., 1909, $180.

Little Friends from History, No. 186, Rand McNally 1936, $50.

Little Fairy Lightfoot, No. 4, Brown, Taggard & Chase, $250.

Miscellaneous (Continued)

	C6	C8	C10
Royalty Cut-out Books: Trooping the Colour	55	65	70
Ruth Newton's Cut-out Dolls and Animals, includes over eighty pieces to cut out and play with, 1934, 11" x 17"	55	65	75
Second series	100	145	175
Six Movie Starlets, including Anne Nagel, Peggy Moran, Jane Frazee, Anne Gwynne, Helen Parrish and Ann Gillis, 1942	85	100	125
Smash the Axis, Electric Corp. of America, 1943	40	55	60
Soldiers, contains nine press-out soldiers, boxed set, wooden cannon and ammunition, Concord Toy Co., c. 1940, 3-1/2" each	50	60	75
Soldiers, U.S. Infantry in campaign hats, mounted, cardboard, approx. 6" high, each	3	4	5
Soldiers Set, No. 1551, contains five cardboard soldiers, and marbles by J. Pressman and Co., Inc., New York, c. 1940, 4-1/2" each	35	50	60

Miscellaneous (Continued)

	C6	C8	C10
Soldiers—Navy, both officer and sailors on wooden blocks, cardboard, c. 1920, approx. 6" high, each	3	4	5
Soldiers—U.S. Sailor, on wooden blocks, cardboard, approx. 6" high, each	3	4	5
Soldiers—West Point Cadets, cardboard, approx. 6" high, each	4	5	6
Stencils Large and Small, No. 954, by Roy Best, thirty animal punch outs and stencils, w/tiny box of crayons, (Whitman?), c. 1935	15	22	28
Stock Farm set, No. 123, 1,200 die-cut pieces including house, barn, silo, chicken house and tractor, boxed, Concern, c. 1944	45	55	60
Story of Cinderella, The, A Fold-A-Way Toy Book, designed by Will Pente, Reilly & Britton Co., c. 1925	30	45	48
Streamline Flyer, No. 122, contains engine, station, crossing gates, crossing signal, baggage truck, baggage and people, boxed set, Concord Toy Co., c. 1940, 10-3/4" x 13-1/2"	45	55	62

Little Golden Paper Dolls, 1950s, $45.

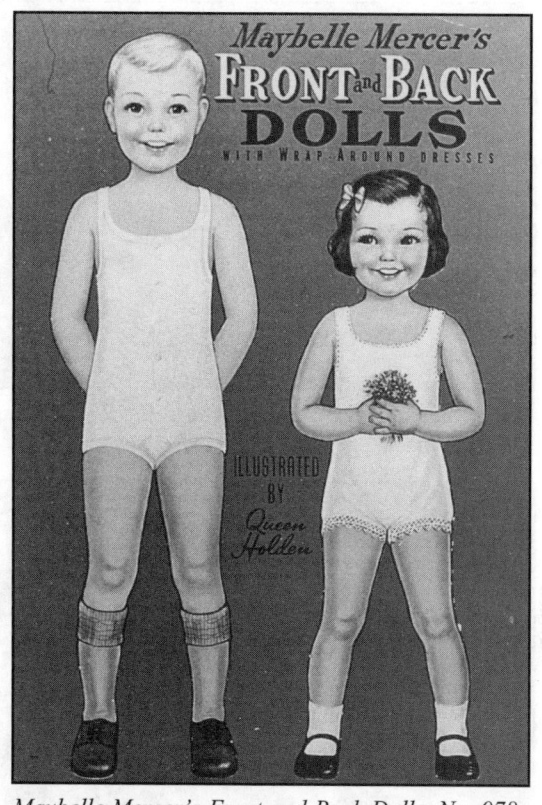

Maybelle Mercer's Front and Back Dolls, No. 978, Queen Holden, $110.

Miscellaneous (Continued)	C6	C8	C10
Swing-A-Plane, model of a Flying Tiger and on a string, by J.L. Schilling Co., 1944	12	18	20
Tammy, includes paper dolls to cut out and dress, illustrated by Ada Salvi, A Little Golden Story Book, 1963	30	40	75
Tarzan of the Apes, figure set, 1933	40	50	55
The Dress-Up Doll Book, No. T-167, Treasure Books, 1953	8	14	20
The Lone Ranger Rides Again Punch-Out Set, makes fences, figures of LR and Tonto, horses and campfire, DeJournette Mfg. Co.	35	45	55
Third series	100	145	175
Three Flying Models of Famous Allied Fighting Planes, by Judd Reed, contains Hell Cat, Spitfire and Stormovik planes, included is "American Ace Spotter," w/turning dial of forty-eight three-view silhouettes of sixteen planes in little windows, 1944, 9" x 12"	30	40	50
Tina and Trudy, No. 1967, by Kathy Lawrence, 1967	20	25	30

Miscellaneous (Continued)	C6	C8	C10
Toby Tyler Circus Playbook Punch-Out, No. 1936, 1959	35	45	55
Toy Town, series of fifty different buildings, boxed set, American Color Type Co., 1916	75	100	125
Treasure Hour Puppet Book—The Rustlers of Rocky Ranch, No. 4, a play of cowboys and Indians in five scenes, cut-out section makes model theater Murray Sales and Service, 1968	20	30	35
U.S. Infantry-Spanish—American War, soldier on small wooden block, approx. 6" high	3	4	5
Walt Disney's Babes in Toyland, No. 10363, Golden Punch-Out Book, 1961	40	45	50
Walt Disney's Jane and Michael from Mary Poppins, No. 1892-6, Watkins/Strathmore, 1963	40	45	50
War Between the States, No. GF152, Golden Press, 1959	55	65	75
War Plane Cut-outs, heavy-stock, eight different scale models, 1943, 10" x 14"	35	40	45

Our Happy Family Cut-out Sheets, No. D141, Sam'l Gabriel Sons Co., 1928, $90.

Paper Doll Outfit Dresses & Hats, No. 102, American Toy Works, $80.

Royalty Cut-out Books: A Procession of the Knights of the Garter, $70.

Paper Dolls of the Latest Paris Fashions, Brown, Taggard & Chase, 1800s, $250.

Ottenheimer	C6	C8	C10
My Fair Lady, No. 2960-2, by Evon Hartman, 1965	25	35	50
New York World's Fair Make a Model, No. 600-50, includes Unisphere, Swiss Ride, N.Y. Port Authority and Heliport, Spertus, 1963	25	30	35

Reed	C6	C8	C10
Model Battleship, c. 1945, 7" x 10"	20	25	30
Model Flat-top, c. 1945	20	25	30
Thrilltown Railroad Pullman Passenger Set, 1943	65	80	90

Saalfield	C6	C8	C10
A Day With Diane, No. 1770, by Laura Bischoff	25	35	45
Air-Hostess, No. 2546, 1947	30	40	50

Saalfield (Continued)	C6	C8	C10
Animal Paper Dolls to Dress, No. 2598, includes bear, monkey, pig and kitten, 1950	15	20	25
Animals to Paint, 1910	10	15	23
Army Cut-outs, No. 245, 1937	55	65	80
Barbara Britton Paper Dolls with Magic Stay-on Costumes, No. 5190, boxed set, 1954	50	65	75
Beautiful Paper Dolls by Betty Campbell, No. 242, has some of same paper dolls as Little Miss Amreica Paper Dolls, 1941	20	35	45
Belle of the Ball Paper Dolls, No. 2702, 1948	20	35	45
Book of Paper Doll Cut-outs, No. 2051, 1927	40	55	65
Bridal Party Paper Dolls, 1963	15	25	35

Soldiers, c. 1940, Concord Toy Co., $75.

Royalty Cut-out Books: Trooping the Colour, $70.

Saalfield, Bridal Party Paper Dolls, 1963, $35.

Saalfield, Really Truly Paper Dolls, No. 453, $45.

Saalfield, Cinderella, No. 1610, 1950, $45.

Saalfield, Claudette Colbert, No. 2451, 1943, $200.

Sallfield, Diana Lynn Paper Dolls, No. 157910, 1953, $65.

Saalfield (Continued)

	C6	C8	C10
Charming Paper Dolls, No. 1357, c. 1960	10	15	25
Cinderella, No. 1610, by Ethel Hays, 1950	25	35	45
Circus Paper Dolls, No. 2610, 1952	10	15	20
Claudette Colbert, No. 2451, 1943	100	150	200
College Chums, No. 719, 1950s	25	35	45
Colonial Paperdolls, No. 1353	25	40	50
Coronation Paper Dolls and Coloring Book, No. 4450, Queen Elizabeth, Prince Philip, young Prince Charles, and Princess Ann, 1953, 10-1/2" x 15" book	50	75	100
Cowboy Cutouts, Platt and Munk, forty cowboys and indians cutouts, c. 1930s, 1937	30	40	55
Date Time, half-size book	4	6	8
Debs and Sub Debs Paper Doll Book, No. 2361, twenty punchouts, 1941	20	35	45
Diana Lynn Paper Dolls, No. 157910, 1953	30	45	65
Donna Reed Paper Dolls, No. 5197, boxed set, 1960, 9" x 12"	50	75	100

Saalfield (Continued)

	C6	C8	C10
Eve Arden Paper Dolls, No. 158510, 1953	40	60	80
Evelyn Rudy—Little Star of Screen and Television, No. 1745, 1958	25	40	50
Family of Paper Dolls, No. 2564, 1947	15	20	30
Fiesta Paper Dolls, No. 2771, 1950s	15	25	35
Fire Fighters in Action, 1938	22	48	52
Four Sisters Paper Dolls, No. 269, 1943	15	20	30
Gigi Perreau, No. 2605, 1951	25	40	55
Gigi Perreau Paper Dolls, No. 1542, 1951	25	40	55
Girl Friend-Boy Friend Paper Dolls, No. 1605, 1955	15	20	30
Gloria Jean Paper Doll Cut-outs, No. 1661, 1940	55	85	115
Good Neighbor Paper Dolls, No. 2487, 1944	10	15	25
Gulliver's Travels Cut-outs, No. 1261, 1939	35	55	75
Hedy Lamarr Paper Dolls, No. 1955	75	115	150
Heidi and Peter, No. 1355, c. 1970	12	15	20
Holiday Paper Dolls, No. 1742, 1950s	10	15	20

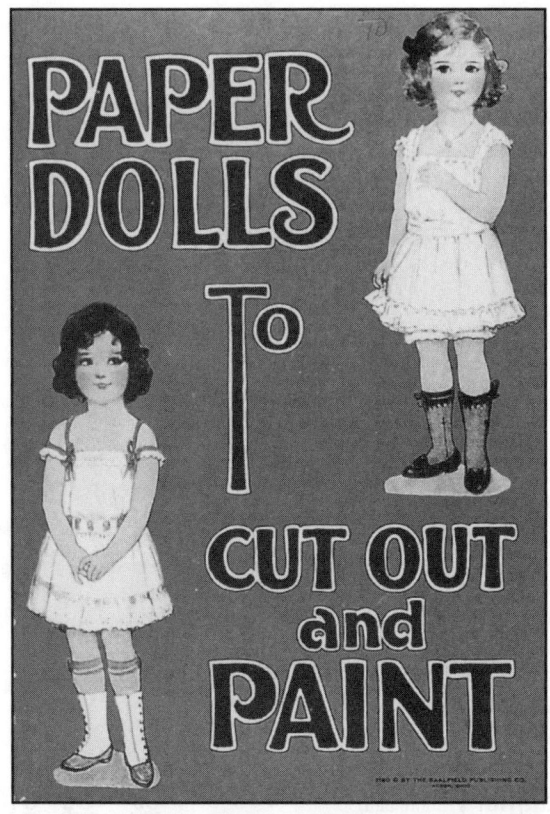

Saalfield, Paper Dolls to Cut Out and Paint, No. 1180, 1920s, $75.

Saalfield, Sheree North, No. 1728, 1957, $65.

Saalfield, Story Princess—Alene Dalton, No. 1727, 1957, $50.

Saalfield, Lots of Little Paper Dolls, No. 1537, 1949, $35.

Saalfield, New Shirley Temple in Paper Dolls, No. 2425, 1942, $150.

Saalfield, Paper Dolls Julia and Marie, No. 1530, 1958, $25.

Saalfield (Continued)

	C6	C8	C10
Hollywood Fashion Dolls, No. 397, twelve male and female dolls plus clothes, 1939	30	45	60
Hollywood Fashions, No. 1535, 1949	25	35	45
Hour of Charm Paper Dolls, No. 2481, women musicians, 1943	55	80	110
Jane Russell, No. 2611, 1955	40	60	80
Judy Paper Doll, No. 1713, 1960s	10	15	20
Julia, includes Julia, Earl J. Waggedorn and Corey, 1969	25	35	50
Lilac Time, No. 1362	20	30	40
Little Ballet Dancers, No. 1743, 1950s?	10	15	20
Little Folks' Friends, No. 156, 1915	15	20	25
Little Friends Paper Dolls, No. 1746, 1950s	10	15	20
Little Miss America Paper Doll Book, No. 2358, fifteen punch-outs by Campbell, 1941	25	35	45
Little Women, No. 1377	25	35	45
Lots of Little Paper Dolls, No. 1537, by Angela Tuite Price, 1949	15	25	35
Lucille Ball Paper Dolls, No. 2475, 1944	55	75	110

Saalfield (Continued)

	C6	C8	C10
Martha Hyer Paper Dolls, No. 4423, 1958	30	45	60
Mary Belle Cut-out Doll, No. 2100, by Fern Bisel Peat, four separate sheets, w/three sheets of clothes, 1934, 17" doll	45	55	70
Mary Martin, No. 2427, 1942	115	160	225
Mini Mod PDs with London Fashions, No. 1348, 1966	20	25	35
Modern Miss in Paper Dolls, No. 2397, by Van Swearingen, 1942	30	40	45
Nancy and Her Dolls with 7 Busy Days of Fun, No. 2478, 1944	15	25	35
New Shirley Temple in Paper Dolls, No. 2425, 1942	65	90	150
Outdoor Paper Dolls, No. 1958, fourteen dolls and four pages of clothes, 1941	15	20	30
Paper Doll Family and Their House, No. 4125, by Florence and Margaret Hoopes, 1934	60	70	75
Paper Doll Playmates, No. 154, nurse and nineteen children, costumes, toys, 1940	25	35	50
Paper Dolls and Their Dollies, No. 1615, by Mary Knight, 1950s	20	30	40

Saalfield, Fiesta Paper Dolls, No. 2771, 1950s, $35.

Saalfield, Paper Dolls of All Nations New York World's Fair, No. 227, 1939, $60.

Saalfield (Continued)	C6	C8	C10
Paper Dolls from Mother Goose, No. 2758, includes Mary, Bo-Peep, Boy Blue, Bobbie Shaftoe, Miss Muffet and Jack Horner, 1957	15	20	30
Paper Dolls Julia and Marie, No. 1530, by Angela Tuite Price, 1958	15	20	25
Paper Dolls of All Nations New York World's Fair, No. 227, 1939	40	50	60
Paper Dolls of Eve Arden, No. 1706, 1956	45	65	85
Paper Dolls to Cut Out and Paint, No. 1180, 1920s	55	65	75
Paper Dolls United We Stand, No. 113, by Margot Voight, six children w/uniforms	60	65	75
Playhouse Paper Dolls, No. 381, 1947	15	20	30
Popular Paper Dolls, No. 1973, 1942	15	20	25
Pre-Teen Paper Dolls, No. 1366, c. 1960s	10	15	20
Pretty as a Picture, No. 2775, 1950s	20	30	40
Prince and Princess Paper Dolls, No. 2706, 1949	20	25	35

Saalfield (Continued)	C6	C8	C10
Quiz Kids Paper Dolls, No. 2430, 1942	100	120	140
Raggedy Ann and Andy, No. 2719, by Ethel Hays, 1953	20	30	40
Raggedy Ann and Andy Paper Dolls, No. 2719-15, 1944	35	45	55
Raggedy Ann and Andy Paper Dolls, No. 2741, by Ethel Hays, 1944	35	45	55
Really Truly Paper Dolls, No. 453	25	35	45
Riders of the West Paper Dolls, No. 2716-15, 1950	10	15	25
Robin Hood and Maid Marian Paper Dolls, No. 1761, 1950s	25	35	45
Rowan & Martin's Laugh-In Punch-Out Paper Doll Book, No. 1325, includes Rowan, Martin, Jo Ann Worley, Arte Johnson, Judy Carne and Goldie Hawn, 1969	30	40	50
Sandra Dee, No. 5511, two dolls and thirty-four costume pieces, boxed, 1959	45	55	65
School Girl Paper Dolls, No. 2400, 1942	20	30	40
Schoolmates, No. 1757, 1950s	5	7	10

Saalfield, Playhouse Paper Dolls, No. 381, 1947, $30.

Stephens Publishing Co., Circus Day, No. 135, 1946, $28.

Saalfield (Continued)	C6	C8	C10
Sheree North, No. 1728, 1957	45	55	65
Skating Party Paper Doll Book, No. 2328, includes seventeen punch-outs, 1941	20	30	40
Smart Paper Dolls, No. 1935, 1940..	15	25	35
Square Dance Paper Dolls, No. 2717, 1950....................................	15	20	25
Stage Door Canteen, No. 2468, 1943..	70	80	90
Star Bright, No. 2797, 1950s	20	30	40
Story Princess—Alene Dalton, No. 1727, 1957..................................	30	40	50
Style Shop Paper Dolls, No. 1516, 1943..	20	25	35
Sweetheart Paper Dolls, No. 2458, 1943..	20	25	30
That Girl Marlo Thomas, No. 1351, 1967..	35	45	55
That Girl Marlo Thomas, No. 1379, 1967..	25	35	45
Tom Corbett Space Cadet Punch-Out Book, No. 4304, 1952, 14" long, 10-1/2" wide......................	40	48	52
Top Notch Paper Dolls, No. 1504, 1948..	20	25	30
Tricia Paper Dolls White House Tour Game, No. 1248, White House stand-up doll of Tricia Nixon and costumes, 1970..	12	23	45

Saalfield (Continued)	C6	C8	C10
Tuesday Weld Paper Dolls, No. 5112, two dolls and fifty-eight costume pieces, boxed, 1960...	40	50	60
Two Little Charmers	3	5	10
Uncle Sam's Little Helpers Paper Dolls, No. 2450, by Ann Kovach, 1943...	35	45	50
Virginia Mayo, No. 4422, 1957..	50	60	70
Walking Paper Dolls Family, No. 1074, 1934..................................	55	65	75
Wedding Day, No. 4246, 1970..	15	20	25
Wedding Day, No. 4458, 1968..	20	25	30

Skyline Mfg.	C6	C8	C10
This is the Navy, No. 501, heavy cruiser, c. 1942	25	35	40
This is the Navy, No. 500A, includes destroyer and PT boat, c. 1942	25	35	40

Stephens Publishing Co.	C6	C8	C10
Cheerleader-Teenage Doll, Mary and Elaine, No. 182, w/four pages of clothes, 1950?	10	15	20
Circus Day, No. 135, by Art Tan-chon, animals, clown, circus cages and wagons, 1946..............	18	22	28

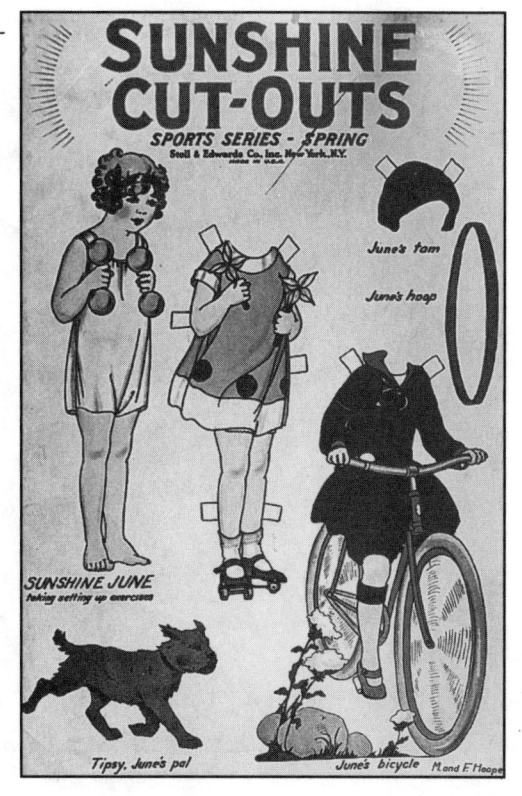

Stroll & Edwards Co., Sunshine Cut-outs Sports Series-Spring, 1926, $90.

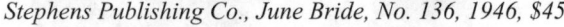

Stephens Publishing Co., June Bride, No. 136, 1946, $45.

Stephens Publishing Co.	C6	C8	C10
Glamour Parade Cut-out Dolls, No. 184, four models and four pages of clothes, 1950s?	10	15	25
June Bride, No. 136, by Art Tanchon, 1946	20	35	45
Movie Starlets Paper Dolls, No. 178, includes Miss Premier, Miss Stardust, Miss Hollywood and Miss Preview plus four pages of costumes, c. 1949	15	20	30
Patty's Party Paper Dolls, No. 175, c. 1950	15	20	30
Playhouse Dolls, No. 1965, four dolls and four pages of clothes, 1949	10	15	25
Scissors Bird Paper Dolls, No. 137, 1946	10	15	20
Six Good Little Dolls, No. 183	13	15	22
Sweetie Pie Twins, No. 166, Jane and Jean, 1949	10	15	25

Stroll & Edwards Co.	C6	C8	C10
Sunshine Cut-outs Sports Series— Spring, four-part foldout, by M. and F. Hoopes, 1926	70	80	90

Toy Factory	C6	C8	C10
Welcome Back, Kotter Sweathogs Paper Dolls, 1977	20	25	35

Watkins-Strathmore	C6	C8	C10
Teen Time, No. 1820, 1963	20	30	40

Whitman	C6	C8	C10
Alice in Wonderland, 1976	5	10	15
Ann and Arthur—Little Paper Doll Books, No. 1146, copyright 1939, 3-1/2" x 7-1/2"	35	40	45
Ava Gardner, No. 119215, 1949, 1952	60	85	125
Baby Brother by Queen Holden, No. 920, 1929	55	85	110
Baby Brother Tender Love, 1977	5	10	15
Baby First Step, No. 1997, (Mattel), 1965	10	15	24
Baby Pat, No. 2072, 1963	10	15	20
Barbie and Ken, No. 4797, boxed set, 1962, 7" x 12"	25	35	55
Barbie and Ken Paper Dolls, No. 1086, 1970	25	30	40
Barbie and Skipper, No. 1957, yachting outfits, 1964	20	30	40
Barbie and Skipper Campsite at Lucky Lake, No. 1836, 1980	7	10	15
Barbie Boutique, No. 1954, 1973	10	15	25

Whitman, Bob Hope and Dorothy Lamour, No. 976, 1942, $250.

Whitman, Cut-out Dolls—Puppies and Kittens, No. 931, 1939, $100.

Whitman (Continued)	**C6**	**C8**	**C10**
Barbie Costume Dolls, No. 1976, 1964	25	35	55
Barbie Doll Cut-Outs, No. 1963, 1962	50	65	85
Beth Ann, No. 1953, 1970	7	10	15
Betsy McCall, No. 4744, 1971	25	35	45
Betty and Joan, Lois and Joan, No. 1015, 1941, 1945	20	30	40
Beverly Hillbillies, The: Jed, Jethro, Granny and Elly May, No. 1955, 1964	35	55	75
Big Invasion Punch-out Book, No. 1936, punch-out of beach landing, 1964	25	35	40
Bob Hope and Dorothy Lamour, No. 976, 1942	100	150	250
Bobby Socks Cut-out Dolls, No. 988, designed by Doris Lane Butler, 1945	20	30	40
Bombers by Schomburg, No. 961, includes B-17, B-25, B-24, Douglas A-20A, short "Stirling", 1943	60	75	100
Book of Airplanes, No. 923, 1930	20	25	30
Brady Bunch, The, No. 1976, 1973.	35	60	90

Whitman (Continued)	**C6**	**C8**	**C10**
Bridal Doll Book, No. 1983, 1978	7	10	15
Bridal Party, No. 1187, set contains five dolls, 1950	20	30	40
Bride and Groom, No. 1957, 1968 ..	10	15	25
Brother and Sister Statuette Dolls, No. 1182-15, heavy cardboard, 1950, 7-1/2" dolls	15	25	30
Buffy and Jody (Family Affair), No. 4764, two magic dolls w/stay-on wardrobes, 1970	30	40	60
Buffy Paper Dolls (Family Affair), No. 1955, 1968	32	45	65
Career Girls, No. 937, w/cloth-like clothes, by Doris Lane Butler, 1944	20	30	40
Charmin' Chatty, No. 1959, 1964 ...	20	30	45
Children From Other Lands, No. 2089, eight cut-out dolls w/native costumes, 1961	10	15	20
Chrissy Paperdoll with Fun Fashions, 1972	10	15	20
Claire McCardell, No. 2067, designer of the American look, 1956	30	45	65

Whitman, Grace Kelly 2 Cut-Out Dolls and Clothes, No. 2049, 1955, $130.

Whitman, Lucille Ball Desi Arnaz Cut-out Dolls with Little Ricky, No. 2116:25, 1953, $125.

Whitman (Continued)	C6	C8	C10
Cloth-Like Clothes for Three Cute Girls, No. 1178:15, flocked clothes, 1949	20	25	35
Connie Francis, No. 1956, 1963	30	45	65
Cradle Crowd, The, No. 1173, four doll babies w/cloth-like clothes, 1948	25	35	50
Crissy & Velvet Paper Dolls, 1971	15	20	25
Crissy Fashion & Hairstyle Boutique, 1970	15	20	25
Crisy Magic Paper Doll, 1972	10	15	20
Cut-out Dolls, No. 983, w/paints and clothes to color, book w/four 17" children and sixteen pages of clothing and sheet of paints by Avis Mac, c. 1930s, 11" x 18"	30	45	65
Cut-out Dolls—Puppies and Kittens, No. 931, 1939	50	75	100
Cyd Charisse, No. 2084, 1956	50	75	100
Cynthia and Bobby Little Paper Doll Books, No. 1146, copyright 1939, 3-1/2" x 7-1/2"	35	40	45
Dodi Paper Doll, No. 1965, 1966	20	25	35

Whitman (Continued)	C6	C8	C10
Dolls that Walk "They Walk-They Dance-They Play", No. 977, two identical girls and two identical boys, designed by Emily Sprague Wurl, 1939	35	50	70
Doris Day, No. 210325, 1952	75	90	125
Dorothy Provine, No. 1964, 1962	35	45	65
Double Date Cut-out Dolls, No. 962, by Elinee Fon Vaughan, 1949	20	30	40
Elizabeth Taylor, No. 973-10, 1950	90	120	160
Eskimo Cut-outs by Milo Winter, No. 1054, 1939	20	35	45
Family Affair, No. 4767, 1968	25	40	55
Family of Paper Dolls, No. 991, by Queen Holden, mother, father, nurse and six kids	55	75	110
Farm Cut-outs by Milo Winter, No. 1054, six pages of heavy paper cut-outs, 1938, 6-1/2" x 10-1/2"	5	25	35

Whitman, Kiddieland Village, No. 2004, c. 1935, $95.

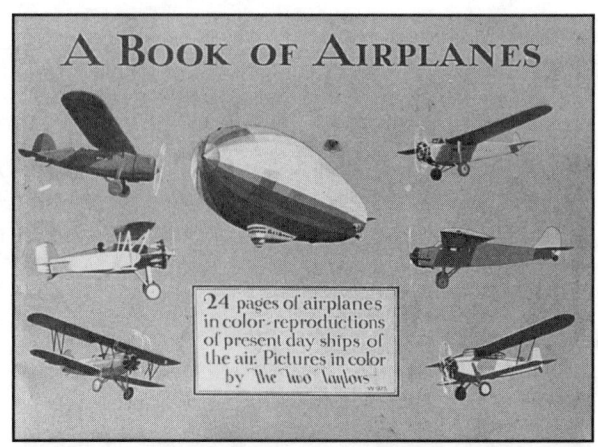

Whitman, Book of Airplanes, No. 923, 1930, $30.

Whitman (Continued)

	C6	C8	C10
Fifteen ABC Blocks to Play and Learn, No. 976, book containing fifteen die-cut blocks to put together, each w/illustrations of nursery rhymes, alphabet letters, animals and numbers on each block, 1933	20	30	40
Fourteen Dogs to Cut Out and Stand Up, No. 935, twelve cardboard punch-out pages of dogs, copyright 1930	25	35	48
Freckles & Sniffles, 1977	3	5	8
Gene Autry Melody Ranch Cut-out dolls, No. 990-10, 1950	45	65	95
Ginghams, The, box sets	3	5	10
Girl Friends Paper Dolls, No. 974, 1944	20	30	40
Grace Kelly, No. 2069, 1956	65	95	150
Grace Kelly 2 Cut-out Dolls and Clothes, No. 2049, 1955	60	95	130
Hair-Do Dolls, No. 991, by Queen Holden, 1948	50	75	100
Hayley Mills "The Moonspinners", No. 1960, 1964	30	50	60
Here Comes the Bride, No. 118915, 1952	25	35	45
Here's the Bride, No. 2109, 1953	25	35	45
Howdy Doody Puppet Show Punchout Book, No. 211129, cardboard puppets may be controlled by strings, includes Howdy, Bluster, Inspector, Dilly Dally, Clarabell and Flubadub, copyright 1952	40	65	80
Howdy Doody Sticker Fun, No. 219525, copyright 1951	25	35	40

Whitman (Continued)

	C6	C8	C10
Howdy Doody Sticker Fun, No. 215825, copyright 1953	25	35	40
Howdy Doody Sticker Fun Circus, No. 2165, copyright 1955	25	35	40
I Love Lucy, No. 2101, Lucille Ball and Desi Arnaz, 1953	55	85	125
It's A Date, No. 1976, 1956	30	40	50
Jimmy & Jane Visit Gene Autry at Melody Ranch, No. 118415, 1951	35	55	70
Joan's Wedding by Florence Sarah Winship, No. 990, clothes designed by Ruth M. Ruhman, 1942	25	35	55
Judy and Dick—little paper doll books, No. 1146, copyright 1939, 3-1/2" x 7-1/2"	35	40	45
June Allyson, No. 119015, 1950, 1952	50	65	85
June Allyson, No. 1173:15, 1953	55	65	85
Kiddieland Village, No. 2004, nine buildings and sixty-five cut-out figures, boxed set, c. 1935, 11-1/2" x 15"	65	80	95
Kitty and Billy—Little Paper Doll Books, No. 1146, copyright 1939, 3-1/2" x 7-1/2"	35	40	45
Lazy Dazy, 1973	3	5	10
Lennon Sisters, No. 1979, 1957	25	35	50
Lennon Sisters, No. 1983, 1961	25	35	50
Little Brothers and Sisters, No. 971:10, includes Tim, Kay Ann and Pete, 1953	10	15	25
Lois and Joan Cut-out Dolls, No. 1015, 1941, 1945	20	30	40

Whitman, Statuette Dolls and Their Clothes, No. 992, 1943, $35.

Whitman, This is Bunny-One of the Five Cut-out Dolly Sisters, 1939, $40.

Whitman, This is Patsy-One of the Five Cut-out Dolly Sisters, 1939, $40.

Whitman (Continued)	C6	C8	C10
Look-a-Like Cut-out Dolls, No. 97210, two mother and daughter pairs of dolls, 1952	15	20	30
Lori Martin in National Velvet, No. 4612, boxed set, 1962, 6" x 11-1/2"	35	45	55
Lucille Ball Desi Arnaz Cut-out Dolls with Little Ricky, No. 2116:25, 1953	86	100	125
Magic Stay-on Dresses, No. 4618	10	15	25
Malibu Skipper, No. 1952, 1973	10	15	25
Margaret O'Brien Paper Dolls, No. 96410	100	135	165
Marge and Gower Champion, 1959	50	75	100
Mary and Joan, No. 1015, 1941, 1945	20	30	40
Mary Jane—A Cut-out Doll, No. 1010, by Florence Winship, w/suitcase for accessories, 1939, 1941	20	35	45

Whitman (Continued)	C6	C8	C10
Mary Lee—A Cut-out Doll, No. 1010, c. 1939	20	35	45
Mary of the WACS—A Young American, No. 1012, by Hilda Miloche and Wilma Kane, 1943	30	40	60
Mary Poppins, No. 1977, 1973	20	35	45
Mexican Cut-outs, No. 1054, by Milo Winter, six pages of people, animals and houses, 1938	30	38	48
Midge—Barbie's Best Friend, 1963	30	45	60
Molly Bee, No. 2091, 1962	20	30	40
Mommy and Me, No. 977:10, 1954	15	20	30
Mouseketeer Cut-outs, No. 1974, 1957	40	60	75
Movie Starlets, No. 960, includes Gail Russell, Diana Lynn, Olga San Juan, Marjorie Reynolds and Joan Caulfield, 1946	35	55	75
Mrs. Beasley Paper Doll Book, No. 1973, (Family Affair), 1970	25	35	50

Whitman (Continued)	C6	C8	C10
Muriel and David—Little Paper Doll Books, No. 1146, copyright 1939, 3-1/2" x 7-1/2"	35	40	45
My Twin Babies with Older Brother and Sister, No. 970, 1940	20	30	45
Nancy and Tommy—Little Paper Doll Books, No. 1146, copyright 1939, 3-1/2" x 7-1/2"	35	40	45
Natalie Wood Paper Dolls, 1958	70	100	130
National Velvet, No. 1958, 1961	30	40	60
Night Before Christmas, No. 948, w/cut-outs	10	15	25
Nineteen Farmyard Animals to Cut Out and Stand Up, No. 935, twelve pages, copyright 1930	35	40	45
Nursery School Dolls, No. 1176, 1953	20	30	40
Oklahoma with Shirley Jones and Gordon MacRae, No. 1954, 1956	45	60	90
One Hundred Soldiers Punch-out Book, No. 999, 1943	55	60	65
Our Nurse Nancy—A Young American, No. 1012, by Hilda Miloche and Wilma Kane, cut-outs, 1943	25	40	55
Our Sailor Bob Doll, w/uniforms, c. 1943, 10"	25	40	50
Our Soldier Jim, No. 3980, designed by Hilda Miloche and Wilma Kane, standup doll w/uniforms, 1943, 10-1/2"	25	40	50
Our WAVE Joan—A Young American, No. 1012, by Hilda Miloche and Wilma Kane, 1943	35	45	55
Paper Doll "Joan" and Paper Doll "Bobby", No. 907, by Queen Holden, 1928	70	85	100
Paper Dolls Peter and Peggy, No. 965, by Dixon, sixty-four pages w/very large punch-outs on front and back, 1935	45	50	55
Pat Boone, No. 1968, 1959	25	35	45
Pat Crowley, No. 2050, 1955	25	35	45
Patsy a Wooden Doll with Dresses, No. 3037, standup cardboard doll w/wood backing, c. 1938, 10"	20	30	40
Patsy Ann and Her Trunk full of Clothes, No. 992, by Queen Holden, 1939	65	85	110
Peter and Peggy, No. 99210, 1950	15	20	25

Whitman (Continued)	C6	C8	C10
Peter and Peggy, Jerry and Joan Paper Dolls, No. 985, by Rachel Taft Dixon, 1935	30	45	60
Photo Fashions, No. 973, 1953	10	15	25
Play Time, No. 210525, 1952	10	15	20
Playmates, No. 99510, 1952	15	20	25
Playthings To Cut Out and Stand Up, No. 934, includes ventriloquist's dummy, floating ships, general's hat, lantern, animals and other moving toys, c. 1935	32	36	45
Pollyana Cut-out Dolls, No. 995, 1941	30	40	50
Portrait Girls, No. 1170, w/cloth-like clothes, designed by Hilda Miloche and Wilma Kane, 1947	35	40	45
Power Models Cut-out Dolls Book, No. 981, six dolls, 1942	65	90	110
Pretty Belles, No. 1966, 1965	7	10	15
Prom Time, No. 2084, two dolls and party clothes, 1962	10	15	20
Queen Holden! Betty and Bob, No. 99110, 1952, 12-1/2"	45	55	65
Queen Holden! Hair-Do Dolls, No. 99110, three dolls, clothes and thirty-one different hair-dos, 1948	55	65	75
Raggedy Ann and Andy, No. 4740, 1968	7	10	15
Raggedy Ann and Andy, No. 1944, 1974	3	5	10
Rock Hudson Paper Dolls, No. 2087, 1957	45	55	65
Roy Rogers and Dale Evans, No. 1186, 1950	55	65	75
Roy Rogers and Dale Evans, No. 1950, 1954	55	65	75
Roy Rogers Cut-out Dolls, No. 995, 1948	60	70	80
Rub-A-Dub Doly, No. 1941, 1977	10	15	20
Sally Ann—A Cut-out Doll, No. 1010, c. 1940	15	25	35
Sandra and Sue Statuette Dolls and their Clothes, No. 1180, by Lee Lunzer, 1948	15	25	35
Sandy and Sue, No. 1956, 1963	10	15	20
Shirley Temple Paper Doll Book, 1976	8	12	18
Skating Stars, No. 2105, 1954	25	35	45

Whitman (Continued)	C6	C8	C10
Snow White and the Seven Dwarfs, No. 970, 1938, 12" x 17"	100	125	150
Snow White and the Seven Dwarfs, No. 1998, c. 1970	15	20	30
Spaceport, U.S.A., 1953	15	20	22
Sports Time, No. 210525, 1952	5	10	15
Statuette Dolls and Their Clothes, No. 998, 1942	20	30	40
Statuette Dolls and Their Clothes, No. 986, two girls and a boy, 1946	15	25	40
Statuette Dolls and Their Clothes, No. 992, two women, 1943	15	25	35
Sunbonnet Sue, No. 2062-29, 1951	15	20	25
Tammy and Her Family, No. 1997, 1964	30	35	45
Tammy and Pepper, No. 1953, 1966	30	35	45
Teen Gal Cut-out Dolls, No. 980, by Hilda Miloche and William Kane, 1943	30	40	50
They Stand Up, No. 932, by Avis Mac, includes five children, 1939, 13" x 18"	40	50	60
Thirty Toy Soldiers, No. 2950, c. 1943	40	50	60
This is Bunny—One of the Five Cut-out Dolly Sisters, 1939	20	30	40
This is Dotty—One of the Five Cut-out Dolly Sisters, 1939	20	30	40
This is Magic—One of the Five Cut-out Dolly Sisters, 1939	20	30	40
This is Patsy—One of the Five Cut-out Dolly Sisters, 1939	20	30	40
This is Peggy—One of the Five Cut-out Dolly Sisters, No. 1002, 1939	20	30	40
Three Bears Cut-out Book, No. 1020, includes Goldilocks and the three bears, copyright 1939	30	40	50
Three Little Girls Who Grew and Grew and This is How They Grew, No. 1176, w/cloth-like clothes, flocked, 1945	25	35	45
Three Little Girls Who Grew and Grew and This is How They Grew, No. 99410, 1945	25	35	45
Three Little Pigs Cut-out Book, No. 1020, includes pigs and Big Bad Wolf, copyright 1939	25	35	45

Whitman (Continued)	C6	C8	C10
Three Sweet Baby Dolls to Cut Out and Dress, No. 975, 1954	10	15	20
Tiny Chatty Twins Paper Dolls, No. 1985, 1963	30	35	40
Transfer Pictures, No. 1085, includes 100 decals, copyright 1939	10	15	18
Trudy Phillips and Her Crowd, No. 2104, 1954	15	20	25
Twenty-two Animals To Cut Out and Stand Up, No. 935, includes rabbits, bears, owls, and squirrels, Copyright 1930	35	45	50
Twiggy Paper Doll, No. 1999, w/Twiggy dress for small girls, 1967	35	45	55
WACS and WAVES, No. 985, 1943	55	65	75
Walt Disney Match and Patch Sticker Fun, includes Mickey Mouse, Donald Duck, Pluto, and Goofy, 1953	15	18	20
Walt Disney Presents Hayley Mills in That Darn Cat, No. 1955, 1965	45	50	55
Walt Disney Sticker Fun Book, 1951	10	12	15
Walt Disney Sticker Fun with Peter Pan, 1952	12	15	18
Walt Disney's Cinderella Paper Dolls, 1965	50	60	75
Walt Disney's Let's Build Disneyland, No. 1986, sets for Adventureland, Frontierland, Tomorrowland and Fantasyland, 1957	25	35	40
Walt Disney's Mary Poppins, No. 1982, 1964	40	45	50
Walt Disney's Pinocchio Doll Cut Outs, No. 925, 1939	75	100	150
Wedding Paper Dolls, No. 1970, 1970	10	15	20
We're a Family Cut-out Dolls, No. 1181, 1954	25	30	35
Whitman Paper Doll Books, No. 3059, four dolls and ten sheets of clothes in folder, 1933	35	40	45
Wispy Walker, 1976	4	7	10
Zoo Cut-outs by Milo Winter, No. 1054, six pages of heavy cut-out animals, 1938	30	38	48

ANIMAL-DRAWN

In this category, the toys generally commanding the highest prices are horse-drawn cast-iron pieces. One reason for the eye-opening prices is that horse-drawn cast-iron toys have considerable value apart for their lure as toys—there is an air of genuine Americana about them, and they are likely to attract the interest of many who otherwise pay no attention to toys (decorators figure largely in this area).

Since prices are often so high, reproductions, whether honest or dishonest, can be a problem. Things

to look for when a reproduction is suspected include a rougher surface than any old toy would have (recastings are invariably rougher), uneven fit of pieces, a blurring of details and "aging" that doesn't have the patina of age. Since at least one company, John Wright (formerly Grey Iron), is still manufacturing turn-of-the-century horse-drawn vehicles—some of them from the original molds—it is wise to become familiar with the field before investing heavily.

Althof, Bergmann	C6	C8	C10
Fruits and Vegetables, 17-1/2" long	5000	7500	10,000
Milk Wagon, 13" long	600	900	1200
Pull Toy, wagon, "Express", 26"	3000	5000	8000
Pure Milk Milk Cart, c. 1880, 14" long	500	750	1000

Arcade	C6	C8	C10
Bakery Wagon, 13" long	300	450	600
Big Six Circus & Wild West Wagon, 14-1/2" long	425	638	850
Cart, horse, driver	100	150	200
Circus Wagon, c. 1917	400	600	800
Coal Car, w/horse	150	225	300
Contractors Dump Wagon, w/two horses and driver, 1930s, 13-1/4"	230	345	460
Contractors Dump Wagon, w/horse team and driver, 14" long	250	375	500
Sulky Plow, w/one horse, 10-1/2"	150	250	350

Barclay	C6	C8	C10
Animal Cage Circus Wagon, c. 1930s, 9-7/8"	30	45	60
Coach, c. 1930s, approx. 10-1/4"	30	45	60
Covered Wagon, "1849," w/oxen, 1930s, 7" long	30	40	55

Bliss	C6	C8	C10
Cinderella Coach, w/two horses and two coach-men, lift off roof, blocks inside tell Cinderella story, 1890, 26" long	1000	3500	5500
Fire Hook and Ladder, 30" long	1500	2500	4000
Fire Hook and Ladder, w/two firemen and two horses, 29" long	2000	3000	4000
Pansy Four-horse Stagecoach, 1890, 31"	1000	1500	2500

Bliss (Continued)	C6	C8	C10
Rough and Ready Fire Engine, w/two horses, 30" long	1600	2700	4000

Carpenter	C6	C8	C10
Cart, w/two horses, 12" long	635	950	1270
Cart, two-wheel, w/one horse and no driver, pat. 1882	250	400	500
Cart, animated, c. 1902, 10-1/2" long	450	675	900
Coal Cart	2000	3000	4000
Delivery Wagon, pat. 1881, 12" long	200	300	400
Doctor's Cart	400	600	800
Dump Cart, w/two horses	350	600	800
Dump Cart, w/one horse, 12"	400	600	800
Fire Patrol, w/two horses, one driver and three figures, 1885, 16-1/2" long	900	1400	1900
Fire Wagon, w/one horse and one fireman	350	500	750
Hook and Ladder, w/two horses, and two firemen in standard helmets, early	800	1200	1600
Hook and Ladder, w/two horses, one driver and rear man, ladders, c. 1883-1890, 26-1/2"	700	1050	1400
Horse and Carriage, 1880, 14" long	750	1000	1500
Horse Cart, w/one horse and two men, c. 1880, 14-1/2" long	800	1200	1600
Ox Cart, w/two oxen, c. 1880-1903, 11" long	400	600	800
Pumper, w/two horses, 18" long	1100	1850	2800
Tally-ho, w/four horses and seven festive riders in coach, 27-1/2"	4000	9500	12,000
Wagon, w/two horses, 10" long	550	850	1300

Althof, Bergmann Milk Wagon, $1200. Photo courtesy Sotheby's, New York

Althof, Bergmann Pull Toy, $8000. Photo courtesy Sotheby's, New York

Bliss Fire Hook and Ladder, $4000. Photo courtesy Wilkinson Collection, Detroit Antique Museum

Converse	C6	C8	C10
Delivery Wagon, w/one horse, c. 1915..	350	525	700
Milk 16 Wagon...............................	70	1100	1700
U.S. Mail 17 Wagon........................	700	1100	1700

Dent	C6	C8	C10
Buckboard, w/rider, one horse.........	125	190	250
Cart, w/horse and driver, 10" long..	125	190	250
Cart, w/lady driver and horse, 11" long..	150	225	300
Contractors Dump Wagon, w/two horses, 15" long...........................	150	225	300
Coupe, w/one horse and driver, 9-3/4"...	125	190	250
Dray, w/two horses and driver.........	550	980	1300
Dump Cart, w/black man and mule...	300	450	600
Fire Engine Pumper, silver w/two horses, 21" long...........................	400	750	1000

Dent (Continued)	C6	C8	C10
Fire Engine Steam Pumper, three horses, 21" long...........................	1000	1700	2400
Fire Hook and Ladder, 27" long......	1000	1700	2400
Fire Patrol, w/three horses, w/driver and six riders, c. 1905, 22" long..	1200	2000	2800
Fire Patrol, w/three horses and firemen figures, 15-1/2" long............	400	1000	2000
Fire Pumper, paint and nickel plate, w/three horses and driver, c. 1908, 15-1/2"..............................	500	800	1100
Fire Snorkle Wagon, w/three horses and driver...................................	500	750	1000
Hansom Cab, w/driver and lady passenger, c. 1905, 14" long.......	700	1150	1600
Hansom Cab, two-wheeled, w/one horse..	175	260	350
Hook and Ladder, w/three horses, extra large.................................	500	1000	1500

Dent Fire Hook and Ladder, $2400. Photo courtesy Christie's East

Carpenter Tally-ho, missing its seven riders, $12,000.

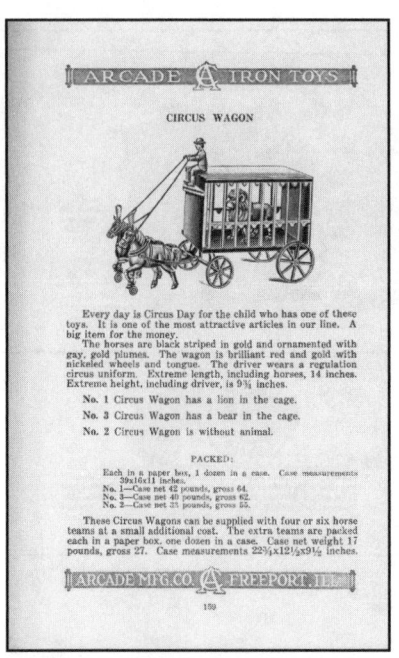

A page from the No. 33 Arcade catalog shows the Arcade Circus Wagon.

Dent (Continued)	C6	C8	C10
Hook and Ladder, mechanized horses, 1915, 14" long	250	400	800
Horse and Cart, low sides	125	190	250
Horse and Cart	150	225	300
Hose Reel, w/figures and three horses, figures, 24" long, 10" horse	1200	2000	2900
Ice Wagon, w/two horses, 12" long.	100	200	300
Ice Wagon, w/one horse, 14" long ..	300	500	750
Ice Wagon, black horse pulling yellow and orange ice wagon, w/driver, c. 1910, 15-1/2"	675	1000	1350
Ladder Wagon, w/four horses, 1890, 43-1/2" long	3000	4500	6500
Ox Cart, stake sides, w/one ox	125	190	250
Ox Wagon, w/driver and two oxen, 16" long	250	500	600
Police Patrol, w/driver, policeman and three horses, 21" long	800	1350	1875
Pony Cart, w/driver and team of horses, stake sides on cart	125	190	250
Pumper, moving horses, 1915, 14-1/2" long	650	1000	1500
Road Car, w/driver in top hat, two seats and one horse, 16" long	450	675	900
Sleigh, w/one horse, c. 1905, 16-1/4"	900	1500	2200
Small Truck Wagon, stake sides	200	300	400
Sulky, w/jockey	150	225	300

Dent (Continued)	C6	C8	C10
Surrey, horse w/wheel attached to one leg	200	300	400
Transfer Wagon, w/two horses, 21" long	450	750	1150
Transfer Wagon, w/driver and two horses, 26" long	500	850	1200
Truck Wagon, w/driver and one horse stake sides, 16" long	200	300	400
Water Tower, w/two horses, c. 1910, 31" long	900	1500	2200

George Brown	C6	C8	C10
Cab, w/driver and one horse, 8-1/2" long	560	840	1120
Cart and Horse, 1880, 7-1/2" long...	200	300	500
Delivery Cart, 12"	1100	1800	2600
Doctor's Buggy, 14" long	650	975	1300
Dog Cart, c. 1870	400	700	1000
Dump Cart, 1885, 8-1/4" long	100	150	200
Dump Cart, back gate lifts out for dumping, 1880, 13"	200	300	400
Eagle Chariot, 1870, 11" long	500	1000	2500
Express Wagon, w/iron wheels, 10-1/2" long	300	450	600
Fine Groceries Cart, w/horse	1250	1875	2500
Gig, w/one horse, 10" long	150	225	300
Gig, 9" long	300	450	600
Goat Coat, 7" long	300	450	600

George Brown Express Wagon, $600. Photo courtesy Sotheby's, New York

George Brown (Continued)

	C6	C8	C10
Grand Central Depot Trolley, w/two horses, 13-1/2" long	600	950	1350
Horse Cart, 1870, 11-1/2" long	125	190	250
Ox Cart, 1880, 9" long....................	500	1000	2000
Peddle Wagon, wheeled horses, driver andawning, c. 1880, 2 20" long..	1000	2500	5000
Rockaway Passenger Cart, w/two horses, 13" long..........................	1850	2500	4500
Sulky, 8-3/4" long..........................	250	375	500
Sulky, clockwork, 13" long	3000	5500	9000
Yankee Notions Peddler Wagon, 16-1/2" long................................	3000	7000	10,000

Gibbs

	C6	C8	C10
Cart and horse, 13" long	150	225	300
Delivery	150	225	300
Dog Cart, boy driver........................	375	560	750
English Pony Cart............................	110	165	220
Gray Beauty Pacers	150	225	300
Groceries The Great Atlantic and Pacific Tea Co. Cart, mule-drawn, 12" long	350	500	1000
Gypsy Wagon	250	375	500
Pacing Joe......................................	175	263	350
Pioneer Wagon	65	100	130
Pony Chariot...................................	165	250	350
Pony Circus Wagon.........................	200	300	400
Pony Pacer, 7" long	115	170	230
Tea Co. Mule Cart...........................	350	500	1000
U.S. Mail Cart................................	300	450	600
Yankee Dump Cart..........................	225	338	450

Harris

	C6	C8	C10
Brownie Shell Cart, 1903	225	340	450
Cart, w/mule driver, 10" long..........	250	500	750
City Truck, w/two horses and driver, 15" long	1200	1900	2700
City Truck, w/one horse and driver	1300	2000	3150
Dog Cart, w/girl driver, 7" long..	275	360	550

Harris (Continued)

	C6	C8	C10
Fire Patrol Wagon, w/driver, three riders and two horses, 19" long..	800	1400	1900
Goat Coat, w/rider, 9-1/2" long	800	1425	1950
Goat Coat, shell-type, w/driver, 5" long..	100	250	350
Hook and Ladder, w/three horses, 19" long...	140	210	280
Transfer Wagon, w/three horses, 1903, 18-1/2" long......................	400	650	850
Wagon, mule, 12" long....................	300	450	600

Hubley

	C6	C8	C10
Brake, four-seat, w/four horses and eight articulated passengers, 28"...	2000	3500	5625
Brake, three-seat, w/two horses, 18" long...	4000	7000	12,500
Brake, three-seat, w/four horses, 18" long.......................................	4200	7300	13,000
Brake, two-seat, w/driver and three women passengers, 16-1/2" long	2500	5000	7500
Brake, two-seat, 16" long	1600	2700	4000
Brougham, w/nickeled, horse and driver, 16" long	300	1000	1500
Brougham, w/top-hatted driver and one horse, 17" long......................	550	850	1300
Cab, w/driver cast in, w/one horse ..	300	500	750
Cab, 14" long.................................	300	500	700
Cane Wagon, 15" long....................	600	900	1200
Cart, w/driver, 5-1/2" long	150	225	300
Cart, w/horse and driver, 8" long..	155	232	310
Cart, w/iron wheels and iron horse, 1910, 10-1/2" long......................	175	265	350
Chariot, 8-3/4" long........................	500	750	1000
Chariot, w/driver and two horses, 9-1/2"..	600	900	1200
Chariot, w/clown and three horses, early, 12-1/2" long......................	800	1200	1600
Chariot Bank, elephant-drawn, 13" long..	650	1100	1600

Gibbs U.S. Mail Cart, No. 27, $600. Photo courtesy Detroit Antique Museum

Gibbs English Pony Cart, No. 40, $220.

A Gibbs advertisement from 1914.

Hubley (Continued)	**C6**	**C8**	**C10**
Coal Wagon, w/mule, 9" long	300	450	600
Coal Wagon, w/two horses, 16"	500	750	1000
Conestoga Wagon, w/cloth canopy, w/two horses, 15" long...............	550	825	1350
Dray Barrel Wagon, w/barrels and barrel ramp, w/driver and two horses, 23" long..........................	1100	1750	2500
Eagle Milk & Cream Wagon, 12" long..	500	750	1000
Essex Trap, driver and horse, 1890, 13" long	500	1500	2500
Fire Patrol, driver, w/four firemen and prancing horse team, 21" long...	700	1100	1500
Fire Patrol, driver, w/four riders, all in standard helmets, 13" long......	750	1200	1750
Fire Pumper, white painted, w/two horses, c. 1906-1910, 19" long.....................................	500	775	1100
Fire Pumper, w/two horses, driver and two firemen, 20" long...........	750	1125	1500
Fire Pumper, w/three horses and driver, c. 1906-1910, 20-1/2" long..	800	1200	1600

Hubley (Continued)	**C6**	**C8**	**C10**
Fire Pumper, w/American eagle, w/two horses, c. 1905-1910, 21" long..	500	1000	1500
Fire Pumper, w/three horses, 22" long..	800	1400	2090
Fire Pumper, w/two horses and driver, c. 1910, 14" long...............	200	400	600
Gig, horse-drawn w/lady driver, 15" long..	350	650	950
Hook and Ladder, w/two horses, 28" long	700	1200	1650
Hook and Ladder, w/eagle on shield on side, w/three horses, 33" long	1000	1700	2450
Hook and Ladder, w/three horses, two firemen and two wooden ladders, c. 1906-1910, 27-3/4" long..	550	850	1300
Hook and Ladder, "126," w/three horses, 33-1/2" long	438	657	875
Hose Reel, w/three horses and driver, c. 1906, 19" long..............	750	1200	1700
Hose Reel, w/one horse and three figures, 13" long........................	500	750	1000

Hubley Brake, $5625. Photo courtesy Sotheby's, New York

Hubley Landau Carriage, 1905, $2800. Photo courtesy Sotheby's, New York

Front to back: Hubley Brake, $7500; Hubley Brake, $12,500. Photo courtesy Sotheby's, New York

Hubley (Continued)	C6	C8	C10
Hose Tower Wagon, c. 1915, 28" long	800	1300	1800
Ice Wagon, w/two black horses pulling green wagon and driver, c. 1906, 15-1/2" long	800	1300	2000
Ice Wagon, 8" long	100	150	200
Ice Wagon, 1920s, 9-1/2"	175	265	350
Ice Wagon, painted, w/driver and horse, 1910, 14"	400	850	1200
Ice Wagon, w/one horse, 15"	800	1300	2000
Ice Wagon, w/two horses and driver, 16-1/2" long	1000	1650	2200
Ice Wagon, w/two horses, 15" long	500	800	1200
Landau Carriage, painted, 1905, 16-1/2" long	1400	2100	2800
Log Wagon, w/two oxen and driver, c. 1905, 15" long	500	750	1100
Log Wagon, w/one horse, 19" long	400	600	800
Milk Cart, 12-1/2" long	425	640	850
Milk Wagon, 5" long	140	210	280

Hubley (Continued)	C6	C8	C10
Monkey Trapeze Circus Mirror Van, 12-1/2" long	500	800	1300
Phaeton, w/one horse	1200	2000	3000
Police Patrol, w/driver and riders, 17-1/2" long	600	950	1430
Police Patrol, w/driver and six cops, 21" long	1000	1600	2200
Police Patrol, w/driver and three riders, early, 13" long	500	750	1000
Roman Chariot, w/three large horses	600	900	1200
Roman Chariot, w/driver and three horses, 16" long	200	300	400
Roman Chariot, w/three small horses	425	637	850
Royal Circus, w/animals, driver and two horses, 15" long	500	1000	1200
Royal Circus Bandwagon, w/eight musicians and driver, 1920, 30"	1500	2250	3000
Royal Circus Bandwagon, w/four horses and seven riders, 22"	1000	2000	3000

Hubley Brake, $4000. Photo courtesy Sotheby's, New York

Hubley Cab, $750. Photo courtesy Sotheby's, New York

Hubley Royal Circus Bear Wagon, $3000. Photo courtesy Sotheby's, New York

Hubley Coal Wagon, $1000. Photo courtesy Sotheby's, New York

Hubley Ice Wagon, $2000. Photo courtesy Sotheby's, New York

Left to right: Hubley Royal Circus Rhino Wagon, $2500. Hubley Royal Circus Tiger Wagon Cage, 1920, $1000. Photo courtesy Sotheby's, New York

Hubley Stanhope Gig, $400. Photo courtesy Sotheby's, New York

Hubley Santa Claus Sleigh, 1910, $1500. Photo courtesy Sotheby's, New York

Hubley Hose Tower Wagon, c. 1915, $1800. Photo courtesy Sotheby's, New York

Hubley Royal Circus Bandwagon, $3000. Photo courtesy Sotheby's, New York

Hubley Police Patrol, $2200. Photo courtesy Sotheby's, New York

Hubley (Continued)	**C6**	**C8**	**C10**
Royal Circus Bandwagon, w/two horses and seven riders, c. 1920, 22-1/2"	1800	2900	4000
Royal Circus Bear Wagon, 15" long	1500	2250	3000
Royal Circus Calliope, 12-3/4" long	1400	2400	3400
Royal Circus Clown on Trapeze Van, oval-mirrored sides, 1920, 16-1/2"	1600	2700	4000
Royal Circus Farmer Van, head revolves and disappears in top of wagon as toy pulled, 1920, 16" long	1700	1850	4250
Royal Circus Giraffe Cage, w/large and small giraffes and driver, 1920, 27" long	3000	5500	9200
Royal Circus Lion Cage, 9"	375	565	750
Royal Circus Lion Wagon, w/rare gray horses and wagon, 15-3/4"	700	1100	1650
Royal Circus Polar Bear Cage, 1920s, 11-3/4" long	600	1000	1375
Royal Circus Rhino Wagon, 16" long	850	1700	2500
Royal Circus Tiger Wagon Cage, w/driver and two tigers, 1920, 16" long	500	750	1000

Hubley (Continued)	**C6**	**C8**	**C10**
Santa Claus Sleigh, early, 17" long	800	1300	2000
Santa Claus Sleigh, w/one reindeer, early, 15" long	1500	2500	4000
Santa Claus Sleigh, w/two reindeer, 1910, 16" long	600	1000	1500
Shell Cart and Horse, 1905, 7" long	250	375	500
Sleigh, w/one horse and woman w/movable arms, early, 14-3/4" long	700	1200	1700
Sleigh, w/one horse, 1900, 15" long	250	375	500
Sleigh, w/two horses, 1910, 15" long	800	1300	2000
Sleigh, painted, w/one horse, 1910, 14-1/2" long	500	800	1200
Spring Wagon, w/horse and driver	200	300	400
Stanhope Gig, 11-1/2"	200	300	400
Sulky, 8-1/2" long	187	280	375
Surrey, two-seat w/driver, woman passenger and two horses, 13-3/4" long	600	900	1200
Surrey, w/two horses and driver, 18"	400	600	800
Surrey, two horses, woman driver, 13-3/4" long	750	1125	1500

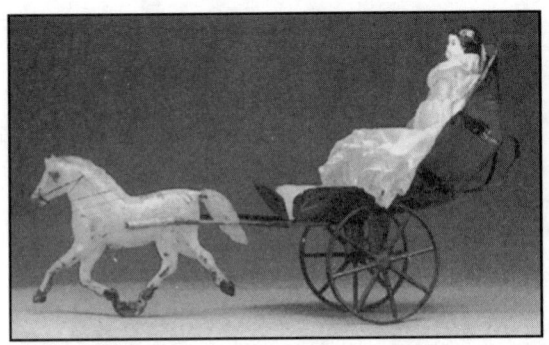

Hull & Stafford Gig, c. 1885, $1500. Photo courtesy Christie's East

Ideal, "Patrol" cast-iron Fire Patrol, 21" long, $2500. Photo courtesy Sotheby's, New York

Hull & Stafford Prospect Park Omnibus, c. 1880, $15,000. Photo courtesy Christie's East

Hubley (Continued)

	C6	C8	C10
Surrey, w/two horses, driver and rider, c. 1900, 12" long	240	360	480
Surrey, clockwork w/brass works, 1894, 9" long	500	1000	1500
Surrey, w/one horse and lady driver, 13-3/4" long	318	475	635
Trotter, w/horse and driver, 1900, 8-3/4" long	200	300	400
Trotter Gig, w/lady driver, 11"	150	225	300
Wagon, w/horse, 12"	150	225	300
Wagon, expandable, w/wood ben, w/two horses and driver, 26"	750	1125	1500

Hull & Stafford

	C6	C8	C10
Dump cart	700	1000	1600
Express Wagon	350	550	750
Gig, w/china doll, c. 1885, 12" long	650	1150	1500
Prospect Park Omnibus, w/two horses and driver, c. 1880, 16-1/2"	5000	10,000	15,000
Wagon, 9" long	800	1400	2000

Ideal

	C6	C8	C10
Fire Department, three horses, 30" long	500	1000	1500
Fire Patrol, marked "Patrol", 21" long	1000	1700	2500
Fire Pumper, two horses, two riders, 20-1/2" long	250	500	750

Ives

	C6	C8	C10
Adams Express, w/two horses, 21"	750	1300	1800
Bandwagon, w/nine passengers, 31-1/2" long	2500	4000	6000
Brewery Wagon, w/two horses, 18-1/2" long	1000	1700	2500
Caisson, w/driver, cannon, rider and two horses, 21" long	1700	3000	4000
Chief Fire Dept., 15-1/2" long	400	700	1000
Coal Dump Cart, w/donkey and black driver	363	545	725
Coal Dump Wagon, w/donkey and black driver	375	560	750
Doctor's Cart, w/two wheels, 10-1/4"	400	600	1000
Dray Wagon, stake sides, w/horse, 15" long	1100	2100	3000
Fast Mail Wagon, w/walking horses, 17" long	750	2000	3500
Fire Patrol, w/one horse, five riders and driver, c. 1890, 19" long	1200	1900	2700
Fire Patrol, w/two horses, driver, and six firemen, c. 1880-1910, 20-1/2"	900	1400	2200
Fire Pumper, w/two horses, 13" long	400	650	900
Gig, driver w/top hat, 1890s, 5-1/2" long	500	750	1000

Ives Hook and Ladder, c. 1890, $2200. Photo courtesy Sotheby's, New York

Ives Hook and Ladder, 34" long, $3700. Photo courtesy Sotheby's, New York

Ives Hook and Ladder, c. 1890, $3600. Photo courtesy Sotheby's, New York

Ives Hansom Cab, $4000. Photo courtesy Bertoia Auctions

Ives Dray Wagon, $3,000. Photo courtesy Sotheby's, New York

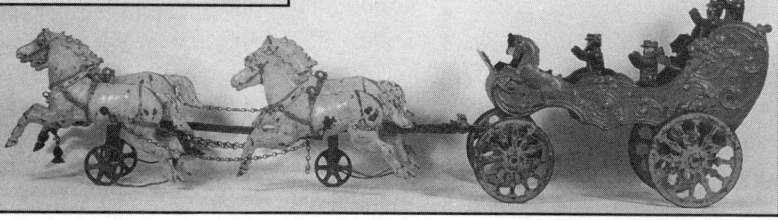

Ives Bandwagon, $6000. Photo courtesy James Maxwell/Virginia Caputo

An early advertisement from Playthings magazine.

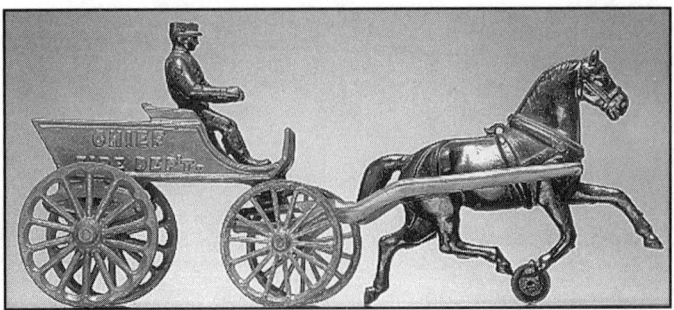

Ives Chief Fire Dept., shown with incorrect driver, $1000. Photo courtesy Sotheby's, New York

Ives Hook and Ladder, c. 1885, $2100. Photo courtesy Christie's East

Ives Fire Patrol, c. 1880-1910, $2200. Photo courtesy Sotheby's, New York

Ives Patrol Fire Wagon, $2050. Photo courtesy Sotheby's, New York

Ives (Continued)	C6	C8	C10
Hansom Cab, w/walking horse, 18" long	1500	2500	4000
Hook and Ladder, w/ladders and pails, No. 45, c. 1885, 28" long	900	1500	2100
Hook and Ladder, w/two horses and two riders, c. 1890, 29" long	900	1400	2200
Hook and Ladder, w/driver and two horses, 34" long	1500	2400	3700
Hook and Ladder, Phoenix, c. 1890, 28" long	1500	2400	3600
Horse Cart, 1870, 10" long	600	950	1400
Horse Cart, w/two horses, 1883, 17-1/2"	750	1200	2500
Hose Reel Wagon, w/driver, rider, and one horse, very low back platform	2000	4000	7000

Ives (Continued)	C6	C8	C10
Hose Reel Wagon, w/one horse and driver, 16" long	600	950	1300
Ox Cart, w/two oxen	400	750	1150
Patrol Fire Wagon, 22" long	800	1350	2050
Phoenix Hose Reel Wagon, w/one horse and driver, c. 1880-1910, 15" long	1600	2400	3200
Phoenix Pumper, w/driver and two horses, 17-1/2" long	950	1600	2300
Phoenix Pumper, clockwork, rarest of Ives pumpers, c. 1890, 19" long	900	1500	2200
Police Patrol Wagon, w/six patrolmen and driver, 1890s, 20-1/2" long	1000	2000	3000

Ives Phoenix Pumper, 17-1/2" long, $2300. Photo courtesy Bertoia Auctions

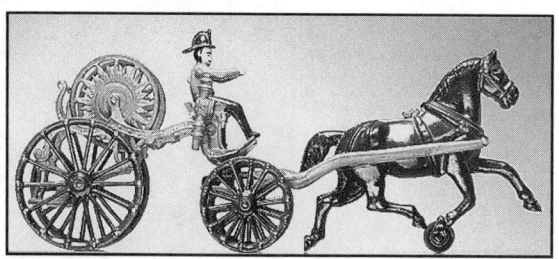

Ives Hose Reel Wagon, $1300. Photo courtesy Sotheby's, New York

Ives Phoenix Pumper, Clockwork, 19" long, $2200. Photo courtesy Bertoia Auctions

Ives Stake Wagon, $800. Photo courtesy Sotheby's, New York

Ives (Continued)

	C6	C8	C10
Pull Toy, walking horse, horse walks by means of wheel mechanism, pulls two-wheeled cart, late 19th century	1800	2800	4000
Pumper, 23" long	2000	3200	4500
Stake Wagon, w/two donkeys, 15-1/2"	400	600	800
Steam Pumper, w/two horses, 20-1/2"	4000	6000	8000
Wagon, w/mules, 1896	600	950	1400

James Fallows

	C6	C8	C10
4th Avenue Streetcar, w/one horse	500	800	1200
Cart, 12" long	500	750	1000
Cart and Horse, 1870, 8-1/2" long	100	200	400
Covered Wagon, scenes on sides, 12"	800	1000	1500
Dump Wart, w/one horse, c. 1890, 16" long	600	1000	1200
Fancy Goods and Toys, 21" long	1750	2625	3500
Fine Groceries Delivery Wagon, 7-1/2" long	1250	1875	2500
Fire Pumper, very early, 24" long	5000	10,000	15,000
Fire Pumper, w/two horses, very early, 18" long	5000	8500	10,000
Horse and Carriage, 1890, 12-1/2" long	500	750	1000
Pure Milk Wagon, 1895, 12-1/2"	800	1200	2000

James Fallows (Continued)

	C6	C8	C10
Streetcar, w/two horses, 10" long	350	500	800
Streetcar, 9" long	400	600	900
Wagon, w/donkey, 10-1/2" long	175	260	350

Kenton

	C6	C8	C10
Aerial Fire Tower, w/three horses and driver, 30" long	800	1400	1900
Ambulance, 2nd Regiment, w/driver and one horse, 15" long	1200	2400	3600
Back to Back Trap, w/driver and woman rider, 12-1/2" long	1100	1900	2750
Bakery Wagon, 1941	325	500	650
Band Wagon, w/musicians, driver and rider on horse	150	225	300
Beer Delivery Wagon, (3.2), w/two horses, driver and ten wooden kegs, 1930s, 14-1/2" long	350	525	700
Beer Wagon, w/driver and two horses, 15" long	500	800	1200
Boar Cart, w/Egyptian driver, c. 1910, 8" long	350	500	750
Cairo Express Egyptian Cart, elephant drawn, 10" long	500	800	1100
Cement Mixer, w/driver and horse, 14" long	350	750	1000
Chariot, 6" long	150	225	300
Chariot, w/comic driver, 1910, 7-1/2" long	250	375	500

Kenton Hook and Ladder, $3200. Photo courtesy Sotheby's, New York

Kenton Milk Wagon, $540. Photo courtesy Sotheby's, New York

Kenton Overland Circus Calliope Wagon, $700. Photo courtesy Sotheby's, New York

Kenton (Continued)

	C6	C8	C10
Chariot, camel-drawn w/clown driver, 11" long	700	1200	1600
Chariot, w/three horses	600	900	1200
Chief Wagon, w/horse and driver, 12-1/4" long..............................	500	800	1500
Circus Cage Wagon, w/two horses, two riders, driver and animal in cage	350	700	1000
City Express Wagon, w/driver and one horses, 17" long	500	750	1045
Coal Cart, w/donkey and black driver	365	550	725
Contractor's Wagon, w/black driver and two horses, 15-1/2" long.......	500	800	1200
Covered Wagon, w/two horses........	130	195	260
Cupid in Horse-drawn Slipper, w/one horse, 10-1/2" long	550	950	1400
Cupid in Slipper, w/one-horse cart, 8-1/2" long.................................	450	800	1100
Delivery Cart, w/donkey	150	225	300
Delivery Wagon, w/driver and two horses, 15" long.........................	250	375	500
Dog Cart, greyhound pulling dog riding in cart, 7" long	250	375	500
Dray, w/two black and white horses pulling green dray w/driver, 13-1/2"..........	300	450	600
Dray, painted, 1930, 14-1/2" long ...	175	265	350

Kenton (Continued)

	C6	C8	C10
Dray, w/two horses pulling a green cart w/driver, late 1940s, 14-3/4" long.....	95	140	190
Dump Wagon, w/two horses, lever releases bottom wagon	250	375	500
Dump Wagon, early 1900s, 10-1/4" long..........	150	225	300
Egyptian Cart, elephant drawn	300	450	600
English Trap, w/two horses, woman and dog, c. 1895, 14" long	1600	2700	4000
Express Wagon, w/horse and driver, 12" long......................	200	300	400
Fire Ladder Wagon, w/front driver only, 12" long.............................	150	225	300
Fire Ladder Wagon, horse drawn, w/drivers front and rear, 17" long.....	135	200	270
Fire Patrol Wagon, w/driver and three riders, 12" long...................	360	535	714
Fire Pumper, w/two horses and driver, 20" long	175	260	350
Fire Pumper, 26-1/2" long..............	600	1000	1400
Fire Wagon, nickel plated wagon, w/two horses, driver, equipment and bell, 23" long	200	300	400
Goat Cart, figure w/large cars, 7" long.........	250	375	500
Gravel Wagon, w/two horses, 13" long.............	150	225	300

Kenton Log Wagon, early 1900s, $1100. Photo courtesy Sotheby's, New York

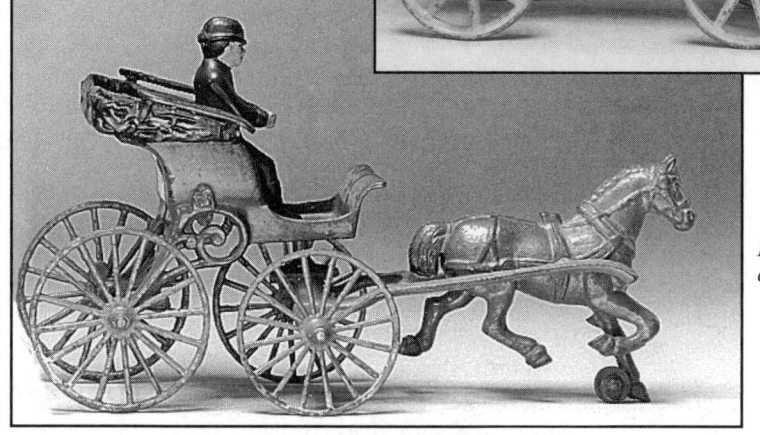

Kenton Spider Phaeton, $2000. Photo courtesy Sotheby's, New York

Kenton (Continued)	C6	C8	C10
Hansom Cab, 12" long	500	750	1000
Hansom Cab, w/top-hatted driver and lady rider	700	1050	1400
Hansom Cab, w/top-hatted driver, 8" long	150	225	300
Hansom Cab, w/figures and horse, 15-1/2" long	300	500	700
Hansom Cab, w/one horse and top-hatted driver, 10" long	1000	1500	2000
Hook and Ladder, w/three horses, 16" long	300	450	650
Hook and Ladder, w/three horses, 17" long	250	375	500
Hook and Ladder, w/three horses, c. 1910, 19" long	150	225	300
Hook and Ladder, w/two horses and driver, 20" long	200	300	400
Hook and Ladder, painted, w/ladders, 1915, 26" long	600	1000	1400
Hook and Ladder, 30" long	1400	2200	3200
Hook and Ladder Wagon, w/two horses and driver, 20" long	250	375	500
Hose Reel, painted, 1920, 13-1/2" long	500	750	1000
Hose Reel, w/two horses, c. 1905, 14-1/2" long	600	900	1200
Ice Wagon, w/two horses and driver, 1920s, 15" long	250	375	500

Kenton (Continued)	C6	C8	C10
Landau, white horse pulling green carriage w/driver, c. 1910, 15" long	600	900	1200
Log Wagon, black man w/two oxen, early 1900s, 15" long	500	800	1100
Log Wagon, w/one horse and driver, 14-1/2" long	425	640	850
Milk Wagon, w/horse and driver, 12-1/2" long	280	420	540
Overland Circus Bandwagon, w/six musicians and driver, 15-3/4"	500	800	1210
Overland Circus Bear Wagon, w/two horses, driver and cage containing cast-iron bears, 1940s, 13"	235	350	470
Overland Circus Calliope Wagon, 14-1/2" long	300	500	700
Ox Cart, 7" long	110	165	220
Ox Cart, 12-1/2" long	385	575	770
Ox Cart, 5" long	100	150	200
Ox Wagon, w/two oxen, 18" long	400	600	800
Patrol, w/two horses, driver and riders, 17" long	650	1100	1500
Patrol Wagon, w/driver and rider, 12" long	275	415	550
PlantationCart, Black driver, mule, 1910, 10" long	500	800	1210

Kenton (Continued)	C6	C8	C10
Police Patrol, w/mule team, 16"	500	750	1000
Pumper, w/three horses, 18" long....	400	600	800
Rabbit pulling two-wheeled cart, 5" long......................................	200	300	500
Rhino Cart, 8" long........................	100	200	300
Sand and Gravel Dump Wagon, w/driver and two horses, 10" long...	180	270	360
Sand and Gravel Dump Wagon, w/driver and two horses, 15" long...	175	260	350
Spider Phaeton, 11-1/2" long..........	850	1350	2000
Stake Wagon, w/two horses and driver w/reins, 15" long..............	83	125	165
Sulky, driver cast to sulky, 6" long......................................	75	112	150
Sulky, w/driver, 7" long	250	375	500
Surrey, w/fringe top, w/driver, passenger and two horses, 1952, 13" long......................................	145	220	290
Surrey, w/one horse, c. 1940, 16" long......................................	150	225	300
Surrey, w/two horses, driver and passenger, 12-1/2"......................	263	395	525
Team of Horses, w/log and black driver	500	750	1000
Transfer Wagon, w/two horses and driver	650	975	1300
Victoria Cab and Horse, w/driver and woman, 15-1/2" long...........	150	225	300
Wagon, w/one-horse and driver, 15" long.....................................	125	190	250
Wagon, w/one horse, 15"	125	190	250
Wagon, w/two horses, 15" long.......	90	135	180
Wagon, w/driver and two horses, 10-1/4".......................................	100	150	200
Water Tower Wagon, driver and two horses, c. 1915, 32" long......	440	660	880

Kingsbury	C6	C8	C10
Dray, w/two horses, 20-1/4" long....	300	450	600
Hook and Ladder, w/two horses, driver and three ladders, 27" long.....................................	600	900	1200
Hook and Ladder, w/three horses and two riders, rubber covers on wheels, 25-1/2"..........................	400	600	800
Ladder Truck, 1900, 13" long	300	450	600

Lancaster	C6	C8	C10
Hook and Ladder, w/three horses and two drivers, 28" long...........	250	375	500

Lancaster (Continued)	C6	C8	C10
Hook and Ladder, w/two horses and two drivers, 28" long..................	200	300	400
Hook and Ladder, w/two horses, 25" long....................................	150	225	300
Surrey, w/one seat, driver and horse, Hubley	150	225	300
Surrey, no driver, Hubley	75	115	150

Mason & Parker	C6	C8	C10
Buckboard, painted, w/one horse, 1910, 31"...................................	500	750	1000
Cart, w/horse, mechanical action from axle, 1910, 13" long...........	500	750	1000

Miscellaneous	C6	C8	C10
Africa, two-wheeled cart with driver being pulled by Ostrich, Lehmann..................................	NPF	NPF	NPF
Bakery Wagon, w/one horse, 13" long......................................	100	200	300
Barnum and Bailey Circus Cage, painted, elephant drawn, 1930, 35" long....................................	400	600	800
Bowery & Central Park Trolley, w/two horses, 28" long...............	1500	2300	3500
Bread and Cakes Wagon, w/driver and tin horse, 12-1/2" long..........	350	525	700
Brewery Wagon, w/two horses and driver, 20-1/2"..............................	350	525	700
Buckboard, w/one horse and driver, 14" long.....................................	200	300	400
Buggy, w/driver, 6-1/2"....................	70	100	140
Buggy, w/cast-iron wheels and horse......................................	40	60	80
Buggy, w/horse, 7" long.................	175	265	350
Cab and Horse, Merriam, 1880, 8-1/2" long..................................	1300	2700	4000
Carriage, w/horse, malleable iron horse w/articulated legs and tail...	300	450	600
Cart, w/one horse, 8" long	200	300	400
Cart, painted, w/one horse, 1890, 15" long....................................	250	500	750
Cart, stake sides, w/one horse, 7" long......................................	150	225	300
Cart, 7" long	125	190	250
Cart, w/woman and prancing horse, 10-1/4" long..............................	500	750	1200
Cart, w/one horse, 9" long	75	115	150
Cart, w/driver and buffalo, 7-1/2" long......................................	400	600	800
Cart, two-wheeled cart pulled by lions, 8" long	125	190	250

Buggy, $350. Photo courtesy Sotheby's, New York

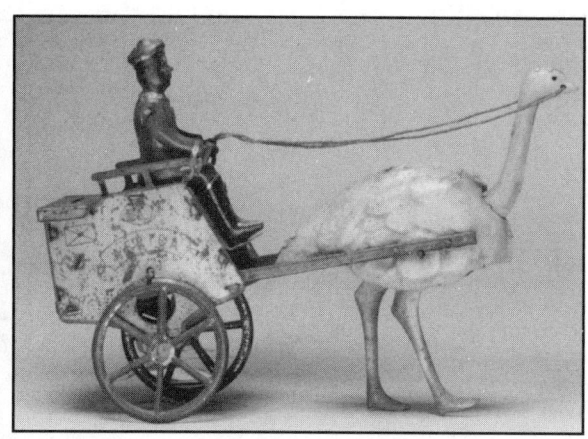

Africa. Photo courtesy Sotheby's, New York

Doctor's Cart, $2000. Photo courtesy Sotheby's, New York

Miscellaneous (Continued)	C6	C8	C10
Cart, two-wheeled cart pulled by bulls	100	150	200
Chariot, drawn by tin horse, 13-1/2" long	125	190	250
Chariot, w/clown and camel	1000	1600	2400
Chief Fire Wagon, w/one horse, 15-1/2" long	350	525	700
Chief's Wagon, "Chief," w/one horse, c. 1915-1920, 12" long	150	225	300
Circus Wagon, w/two horses and lion cage, 9" long	200	300	400
Circus Wagon, contains carved wood bear, 13" long	250	340	500
Coal Wagon, w/driver and coal shovel, 9-1/4"	137	200	275
Conestoga Wagon, w/cloth cover and two horses, 12-1/2" long	50	75	100
Conestoga Wagon, w/walking horses and iron wheels, 18" long	140	210	280
Covered Wagon, w/cloth top, w/one horse and driver, 13" long	170	255	340
Covered Wagon, Indian head litho on side, w/driver and horse	40	60	80
Dispatch Wagon, w/one horse, Chein, 11-1/2" long	90	135	180

Miscellaneous (Continued)	C6	C8	C10
Doctor's Cart, 11" long	850	1450	2000
Dog Cart, baby carriage, c. 1875, 10" long	400	600	800
Donkey Cart, w/driver, Stevens	200	300	400
Donkey Cart, w/iron star wheels, 8" long	300	450	600
Donkey Cart, 8-1/2" long	250	375	500
Dray, w/one black horse pulling dray, 14" long	150	225	300
Dray Wagon, w/driver and two horses, 18" long	250	375	500
Dump Truck, w/one horse	200	300	400
Fine Groceries Wagon, w/two horses, 14" long	400	600	800
Fire Hose Reel, horse-drawn, 6" long	150	225	300
Fire Patrol, w/two horses, three firemen and driver, c. 1910, 19"	1250	1875	2500
Fire Patrol, w/two horses, three firemen and one driver, c. 1890, 20-1/2" long	600	950	1300
Fire Patrol, wagon contains two firemen and driver, drawn by three horses, 17" long	900	1350	1800

Fire Patrol, c. 1890, $1300. Photo courtesy Sotheby's, New York

Dog Cart, c. 1875, $800.

Produce Wagon, $700. Photo courtesy Sotheby's, New York

Donkey Cart, $400. Photo courtesy Sotheby's, New York

Miscellaneous (Continued)	C6	C8	C10
Fire Pumper, w/two horses and driver, 13" long	600	900	1200
Fire Pumper, w/three horses, 14-1/2"	650	1050	1500
Fire Pumper, w/three horses, c. 1910, 17-1/2" long	500	750	1000
Fire Pumper, w/three horses, w/driver, and fireman, c. 1910, 18-1/4" long	425	640	850
Fire Pumper, w/two horses and driver, 19-3/4" long	500	750	1000
Fire Pumper, w/three horses, 11-1/4"	500	750	1000
Friendship 1774 Fire Pumper, w/rubber hose, 16" long	375	565	750
Goat Cart, early, 10-1/2" long	150	225	300
Goat Cart, iron goat and wheels w/tin cart, 7-1/2" long	100	150	200
Golden Pasture Farm Products, Milk & Cream Wagon, painted and stenciled, steering mechanism for child to ride, 1915, 30" long	500	750	1000
Grass Cutter, two-wheeled cart w/two horses and driver	1000	1500	2000
Hansom Cab, w/driver, 9-1/2"	120	188	250

Miscellaneous (Continued)	C6	C8	C10
Hansom Cab, movable legs on horse, 15-1/2" long	175	265	350
Hard and Soft Coal-Coke and Kindlings Dump Cart, 19" long	500	750	1000
Hook and Ladder, w/three horses and driver, 25" long	500	750	1000
Hook and Ladder, w/three horses, two drivers and four ladders, c. 1910-1914, 31-1/4" long	1000	1500	2000
Hook and Ladder, ladder, w/figurines and three horses, 29-1/2" long	750	1125	1500
Hook and Ladder, w/three horses, 25-1/2" long	600	900	1200
Hook and Ladder, w/two horses, 22-3/4" long	1000	1650	2000
Hook and Ladder, w/three horses, two firemen and ladders, 21"	175	265	350
Hook and Ladder, w/two horses, driver and three ladders, 16-1/2" long	150	225	300
Hook and Ladder, w/figures, ladders, unusual hanging horses	250	375	500
Hook and Ladder, w/three horses, driver, 27-1/2" long	750	1125	1500

Miscellaneous (Continued)

	C6	C8	C10
Horse and Cart, on wooden horse, tin cart....................	150	225	300
Horse and Cart, open carriage w/driver in top hat, 5-1/2" long...............	150	225	300
Hose Reel, w/three horses, one driver and fireman, c. 1910-1914, 21"......................	1000	1500	2000
Hose Reel, w/one horse and driver, 11" long..................	1000	1650	2500
Hose Reel, w/one horse and driver, 12" long..................	1000	1650	2500
Hose Reel, w/one horse and driver and cord fire hose, 12-1/2" long..........................	500	750	1000
Hose Reel, w/driver, two horses and man standing on rear bumper, 21" long...................	750	1125	1500
Hose Reel, w/three horses, c. 1910, 19" long...................	600	900	1200
Hose Wagon, w/two firemen, three horses and bell, 21-1/2" long.......	750	1125	1500
Ice Wagon, w/one horse, 12"...........	500	750	1000
Ice Wagon, w/two horses, 12"........	600	900	1200
Klondike Ice Co., New York Wagon, w/two horses, 17-1/2"....	350	525	700
Ladder Wagon, w/two horses and three sections of ladder, w/bell, 25-1/2"..................................	250	375	500
Ladder Wagon, w/two drivers and three horses, four sections of ladder, dart type, 30-1/2" long.........	800	1400	2100
Ladder Wagon, w/two ladders and three galloping horses, 13-1/2"...................................	150	225	300
Log Wagon, w/driver and two oxen, 15-1/4" long................	450	675	900
Mail Cart, horse drawn....................	140	210	280
Mail Wagon, w/two horses, 17"......	175	260	350
Mess Cart, WWI-type, painted, w/two horses.........................	100	150	200
Milk Wagon, painted, goat-drawn, possibly George Brown, 6"........	150	225	300
Milk Wagon, w/driver and one horse, 12-3/4" long....................	200	300	400
Mower, w/two horses and driver, 10" long..................................	150	225	300
National Express Wagon, w/one horse, 15" long.........................	250	375	500
People's Omnibus, w/two horses and driver, c. 1880s-1890s..........	4000	6000	8000
Police Patrol, w/one horse, 12".......	150	225	300

Miscellaneous (Continued)

	C6	C8	C10
Police Patrol Wagon, w/driver, five policemen and two horses, 15" ...	1700	2800	4000
Police Patrol Wagon, w/one horse, figures and driver, 11-1/2" long ..	100	150	200
Produce Wagon, painted, w/one horse, possibly George Brown, 12-1/2" long.........................	350	525	700
Pull Toy, horse and cart w/iron wheels, 11" long.........................	250	375	500
Pull Toy, horse-drawn wagon w/articulated legs, "Borden's Farm Products"	315	470	625
Pull Toy, w/iron wheels, horse pulling water wagon, 7-1/4" long......	125	190	250
Pull Toy, w/iron wheels, horse pulling water wagon, 6-3/4" long......	350	525	700
Pull Toy, horse-drawn carriage, 12"...	150	225	300
Pull Toy, horse and covered delivery wagon, 5-1/4" long...............	150	225	300
Pull Toy, "Dump Cart," horse pulling cart, 7-3/4" long	80	120	160
Pull Toy, "Dry Goods", c. 1860, 26" long......................................	400	600	800
Pull Toy, horse and two-wheeled wagon, 9-1/4" long......................	125	190	250
Pumper, w/three horses and figure, 13" long...............................	300	450	600
Pumper, driver part of casting, w/two horses, 15-1/2" long	200	300	400
Pumper, w/driver and two horses	125	188	250
Santa Claus and Sleigh, two reindeer pulling a white sled containing black-painted Santa Claus..	500	800	1200
Santa Claus and Sleigh, composition Santa and plush reindeer, 25" long.......................................	1500	2250	3000
Sheep, sheep pulling two-wheeled wagon, 8" long	125	200	300
Sheffield Farms Company Wagon, horse w/articulated legs, 21" long...	250	400	650
Spring Wagon, w/driver and horse, 11" long.....................................	150	225	300
Spring Wagon, w/driver and horse, 14-1/2" long...............................	150	250	350
Spring Wagon, w/driver and two horses, 14-1/2" long	150	275	400
Spring Wagon, w/driver and two horses, plus miniature pick, shovel and sledgehammer, 14-1/4" long.....................................	600	900	1200

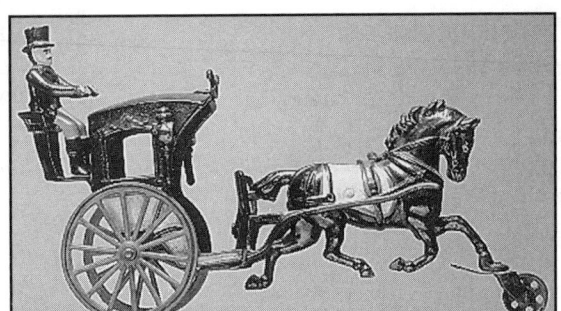

Pratt & Letchworth Hansom Cab, c. 1892, $1800. Photo courtesy Sotheby's, New York

Pratt & Letchworth Surrey, c. 1890, $1100. Photo courtesy Sotheby's, New York

Miscellaneous (Continued)	C6	C8	C10
Spring Wagon, w/two horses, 15" ...	150	225	300
Stagecoach, w/cowboy driver and two horses, 11" long..................	130	195	260
Stagecoach, w/six horses, 27" long .	60	90	120
Stakebed Wagon, w/one horse, 14-3/4" long......................	400	700	1000
Stanley Surrey, w/driver, lady passenger and two horses, 14-3/4" long..............................	100	150	200
Steam Pumper, w/two horses and w/driver, 18" long	600	1000	1500
Steam Pumper, w/driver and two horses, 20-1/2" long	800	1300	2000
Steam Pumper, w/stationary driver, and two horses, 15" long............	500	750	1000
Steam Pumper, w/stationary driver and three horses, 10-1/2" long.....	150	225	300
Steam Pumper, w/stationary driver and two horses, 9-1/4" long.........	100	150	250
Steam Pumper, w/driver and three horses, bell, 17-1/2" long	600	900	1200
Sulky, w/driver, 7-1/4" long...........	150	225	300
Sulky, Williams, c. 1920, 8" long....	150	225	300
Sulky, w/driver, c. 1890s, 8-1/2" long...........................	250	400	550
Sulky, w/horse and rider, cart mounted w/four bells, 6-1/2" long..............................	200	300	400
Sulky Racer, Wolverine..................	55	80	110
Transfer Wagon, w/three horses and driver, wagon bolted to team, 19"...............................	325	488	650
Transfer Wagon, w/driver and two horses, 19-1/2" long	400	600	800
Transfer Wagon, w/two horses, driver, 18" long	300	450	600
Trolley, w/jockey and horse, 6" long..............................	150	225	300

Miscellaneous (Continued)	C6	C8	C10
Trotter, All-Nu, 1941, approx. 4" long..............................	30	45	60
Uncle Sam Eagle Head Chariot, w/two horses, Jones & Bixler..............................	3000	5000	8000
United States Transfer Co. No. 7 Wagon, w/two stuffed horses, 31" long..............................	300	450	600
Wagon, two-wheeled w/driver, 7-1/4" long..............................	100	150	200
Wagon, two-wheeled w/mule and driver, 9-1/2" long	300	450	600
Wagon, two-seater, w/one horse	150	225	300
Wagon and Horse, painted and stenciled, Merriam, 1890, 19-1/2" long..............................	2500	3375	5000

Pratt & Letchworth	C6	C8	C10
Barouche, w/driver and two horses, 17" long..............................	750	1400	2000
Brake, four-seat, w/four horses, driver and seven passengers, 28" long..............................	4000	7000	11,000
Chemical Wagon, w/three horses and driver	3000	6000	9000
Chief's Wagon	1100	1650	2200
City Delivery Wagon, w/driver, barrels and horse, c. 1885..........	1100	1700	2500
Doctor's Cart, w/one horse and driver, 11" long	650	1100	1550
Double Surrey, 15" long.................	450	750	1100
Dray, w/one horse, 1890, 12" long..............................	80	1450	2200
Dray, w/one horse and driver, 14-1/2" long.........................	500	850	1500
Fire Chief's Wagon, w/figure and horse, c. 1885, 12" long..............	700	1100	1500
Gig, w/one horse and one rider, 10-1/2" long.........................	400	600	800
Hansom Cab, c. 1892, 13" long.......	700	1200	1800

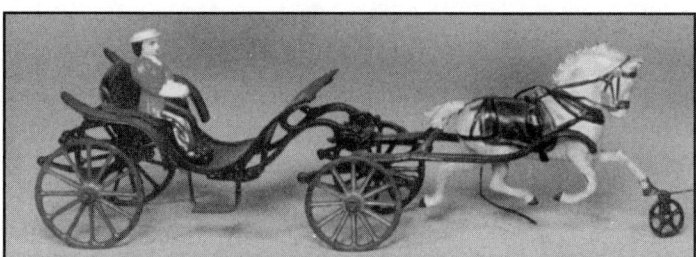

Pratt & Letchworth Pony Phaeton, c. 1892, $1500. Photo courtesy Sotheby's, New York

Reed Band Chariot, $2000. Photo courtesy Christie's East

CONDITION CODE

C6 Good; evident overall wear, well played with but acceptable to many collectors

C8 Very Good; minor overall wear, very clean

C10 Mint; like new

Note: Mint in Box commands a higher price.
Condition below C6 brings considerably lower prices

Pratt & Letchworth (Continued)	C6	C8	C10
Hay Cart, 10-1/2"	500	750	1000
Hose Reel, w/one horse and driver in standard helmet	900	1350	1800
Hose Reel, w/one horse, 14-1/4" long	900	1350	1800
Pony Cart, 11" long	413	620	825
Pony Phaeton, w/driver and one horse, c. 1892, 15-1/4" long	600	1000	1500
Pratt & Letchworth Cart, 10" long	150	225	300
Pumper, w/driver, rider and two horses, 17" long	750	1400	2000
Sulky, 8-1/2" long	700	1200	1820
Sulky, 15" long	550	850	1300
Surrey, rear seat, w/one horse, c. 1890, 15-1/2" long	500	850	1100

Reed	C6	C8	C10
Band Chariot, w/fourteen band members, c. 1895, 28-1/2" long	800	1200	2000
Band Chariot, w/fourteen bandsmen, 28-1/2" long	800	1200	2000
Bowery & Central Park Trolley, w/two horses, 1895, 28" long	1500	2300	3500
Cinderella Coach, twin horse-drawn, auctioned in 1994	NPF	NPF	2760
Mammoth Show Circus Wagon, w/three animals and two trainers, c. 1890, 14" long	1100	1700	2500

Reed (Continued)	C6	C8	C10
Pansy Stage Coach, w/four horses, driver and litho alphabet blocks, 28"	1000	1500	2000

Rich Toys	C6	C8	C10
Borden's Golden Crest Dairy Cart, 18" long	240	360	480
Budweiser Beer Wagon	300	500	800
National Biscuit Company Wagon, w/one horse	400	600	800
Sand and Gravel Wagon, w/driver and two horses, 15" long	150	225	300
Sand and Gravel Wagon, w/driver and two horses, 14-3/4" long	100	150	200
Sand and Gravel Wagon, w/driver, 9-1/2" long	150	225	300
Streetcar, w/two horses, c. 1925, 20" long	600	900	1200

Shimer	C6	C8	C10
Choice Family Groceries Tea, Coffee & Spices, 12-1/2" long	500	800	1200
Ice Wagon, w/driver and two horses, 13" long	375	560	750
Lumber Wagon, w/two horses, 26" long	358	535	715
Patrol, animated, w/black prisoner and five policemen, 21" long	3500	6500	9000
Surrey, woman driver	375	560	750

*Rich Toys Dairy Cart, $480.
Photo courtesy Joe and
Sharon Freed*

*Shimer Choice Family Groceries Tea, Coffee & Spices,
$1200. Photo courtesy Sotheby's, New York*

*Rich Toys Streetcar, No. 59, c. 1925, $1200. Photo courtesy
Wilkinson Collection, Detroit Antique Toy Museum*

Welker & Crosby

	C6	C8	C10
Hose Reel, 13-1/2"	800	1400	1900
Ox Cart, w/two oxen and black driver	600	900	1200

Wilkins Toy Company

	C6	C8	C10
Aerial Fire Wagon, w/three horses and driver, 43" long	2000	3500	5150
Artillery, w/rider on caisson and two horses, seat top lifts off, cannon, c. 1895, 10" long	1000	1500	2000
Boys Express Co. Wagon, w/two horses, 16-1/2" long	700	1200	1600
Broadway Car Line 75 Streetcar, horse-drawn	900	1600	2400
Buckboard	120	180	240
Caisson, horse-drawn, 18"	650	1000	1500
Cane Wagon, w/mule and driver, 11" long	300	450	600
Carriage, w/driver in derby, passenger and one horse	1000	1500	2000
Cart, animated, 6" long	250	375	500
Cart and Horse, 10" long	450	700	1000
Cart and Horse, w/driver, 12"	750	1200	1600

Wilkins Toy Company

	C6	C8	C10
Chariot, w/four horses, 7" long	180	270	360
Chariot, woman driver w/three horses, 10-1/2" long	400	600	800
City Truck, w/two horses and driver	1000	1500	2000
Coal and Wood Wagon	750	1125	1500
Consolidated Street R.R. 712 Streetcar, 14" long	1200	1900	2800
D.P.W. Street Sweeper, w/one horse, brush and driver, 13" long	2000	3200	5700
Delivery Wagon, w/driver and prancing horse team, 21" long	600	900	1200
Doctor's Cart, c. 1900, 10-1/2" long	500	750	1100
Dog Cart, 1890, 7-1/2" long	150	225	300
Dog Cart, w/St. Bernard-type dog and rider in cap, c. 1890, 10-1/2" long	600	950	1400
Donkey Cart, 11" long	237	355	475
Donkey Cart, 13-1/4" long	350	525	700

Wilkins Toy Company "Broadway Car Line 75" Streetcar, $2800. Photo courtesy Wilkinson Collection, Detroit Antique Toy Museum

Wilkins Toy Company Ox Cart, $700. Photo courtesy Sotheby's, New York

Wilkins Toy Company	C6	C8	C10
Dray, w/driver and two mules, 17-1/2" long	600	900	1250
Dray, drawn by two horses, w/driver in derby hat, c. 1910, 20-1/2" long	900	1350	2200
Dray, w/six horses, 16" long	325	500	700
Dray, 15" long	300	450	600
Dray, w/black driver, and one horse, 12" long	500	750	1100
Fire Chief Buggy, w/one horse and rider, 12" long	650	1050	1500
Fire Chief Engine Pumper, w/two horses, 19" long	500	750	1000
Fire Hose Reel, 10-1/2" long	350	550	750
Fire Ladder Truck, w/three horses and two firemen, c. 1910, 20"	415	620	830
Fire Patrol, w/six firemen and three horses, 20" long	500	750	1050
Fire Patrol Wagon, w/firemen, 12" long	450	675	900
Fire Patrol Wagon, w/two horses and two firemen, 20-1/2" long	550	825	1200
Fire Pumper Wagon, w/driver and three horses, 25" long	1800	3200	5000
Fire Pumper Wagon, w/driver and two horses, 20" long	600	900	1200
Fire Pumper Wagon, horizontal chemical tank, w/two horses, 19-1/2" long	1700	2800	4000

Wilkins Toy Company	C6	C8	C10
Fire Pumper Wagon, w/two horses, 18"	1700	2800	4000
Gentlemen's Cart, w/gentlemen driver and white horse, 1900, 10"	300	450	600
Gig, fancy, w/driver, 10"	150	225	300
Goat Cart, driver, c. 1900, 9-1/2" long	900	1350	2200
Groceries Wagon, w/one horse, c. 1900, 13-1/2" long	200	300	400
Hansom Cab, 15" long	600	950	1400
Hook and Ladder, w/two horses and two firemen, 19-1/2" long	385	575	770
Hook and Ladder, w/two horses, ladders and figures; horses sit on pegs	1000	1500	2000
Hook and Ladder, 24" long	700	1100	1700
Hook and Ladder, w/prancing team, 27" long	600	925	1350
Hose Reel, w/two horses and two firemen in standard helmets, 16" long	1500	2500	3500
Hose Reel, w/one horse, c. 1890, 18" long	800	1300	1900
Huckster's Wagon, w/two horses and driver	800	1450	1950
Ice Wagon, 10" long	150	225	300
Landau, w/articulated horses, two coachmen and opening doors, 15-1/4" long	1200	2000	3100

Top row: Wilkins Toy Company Fire Pumper Wagon, $4000; Bottom row; left to right: Wilkins Toy Company Fire Pumper Wagon, $4000; Wilkins Toy Company Hose Reel, $3500. Photo courtesy Christie's East

Wilkins Toy Company Fire Pumper Wagon, with three horses, $5000. Photo courtesy Sotheby's, New York

Wilkins Toy Company Hook and Ladder, $770. Photo courtesy Bertoia Auctions

Wilkins Toy Company	C6	C8	C10
Ox Cart	300	500	700
Panama Earth Mover, w/driver and two horses, 1903, 20" long	400	600	800
Phaeton, w/driver in top hat and gray pony	450	750	1100
Phaeton, w/woman driver, late 1800s, 16" long	1000	2500	4000
Plantation Cart, 1910, 11"	460	690	920
Police Patrol, w/driver, two horses and six policemen, 1911, 20" long	1700	2700	3700
Pony Cart, w/one horse and driver, 7-1/2" long	400	600	800
Pony Cart, w/one horse and driver, 9-1/2" long	500	750	1075

Wilkins Toy Company	C6	C8	C10
Pumper, w/two horses and two firemen	1100	1650	2200
Spring Wagon, w/driver and horses	300	450	600
Stake Wagon, 1907	500	675	1000
Steam Engine, w/two horses and driver, 17" long	600	900	1300
Transfer Wagon, 15" long	500	850	1200
Wagon, w/driver and mule, 9" long	300	450	600
World's Fair Street R.R. 372 Streetcar, w/one horse and six passengers, 15"	900	1600	2400

BANKS

Mechanical Banks

After trains, mechanical banks are perhaps the most avidly pursued of all the toys cataloged in this book. The most collectible remain those that were produced in cast iron from around 1870-1908—over three hundred different types were produced during that period. One factor that adds to their interest is that many were manufactured with an eye toward adults, as well as children (the "Tammany" bank, for instance). As a result, prices are high—and they were high long before any of the other toys in this book were thought of as collector's items. Because of their rarity, several of the banks listed have only auction prices, and these prices may seem astronomical. This was done to demonstrate how high mechanical banks can sell for; please keep in mind that not all mechanical banks will sell for such prices.

With such valuable items the problem of counterfeiting arises, and care is strongly urged in the purchase of any high-priced bank. Counterfeits tend to be rougher, to fit together less smoothly, and to lack the patina or "look" of age.

Still Banks

The same companies that made mechanical banks often made still banks as less-expensive alternatives. Several of the banks can be found in both still and mechanical versions. Companies such as Arcade, Ives, Kenton and Stevens are familiar to still and mechanical bank collectors alike.

Building-shaped banks are perhaps the single largest type of still banks, with others fashioned as animals, people and busts, appliances like safes, clocks, mailboxes, and globes.

One notable class of still banks is the registering bank. Often in the shape of a safe or cash register, these banks typically accept certain coins, such as dimes and nickels. They keep a running tally of deposits and pop open once the bank is filled, typically at $5 or $10. While their delayed reaction mechanism has earned them places in some mechanical collections, they are generally classified as still banks.

As in many other areas of collecting, restoration of banks is strongly discouraged in the marketplace. Unless undertaken by an experienced professional, the restoration of a bank can result in irreparable damage to its collector value.

Contributor: Bertoia Auctions, 2141 DeMarco Dr., Vineland, NJ 08360. Web site: www.bertoiaauctions.com

Bill Bertoia

The following article is reprinted from the May 30, 2003 issue of *Toy Shop Magazine.*

By Sharon Korbeck

One of the most recognizable and revered names in antique toys, Bill Bertoia, died May 6 after a battle with cancer. He was 52.

Bertoia was a recognized authority in the field of antique toys and banks. President of Bertoia Auctions in Vineland, N.J., Bertoia had a long, storied history in collecting, trading and auctioning toys. He also served as an appraiser on PBS's Antiques Roadshow.

"Bill's whole life was about living. He loved what he did," said Andy Ourant, an auctioneer who has worked for Bertoia Auctions for the past six years.

Ourant will serve as the auctioneer May 16-17 for the Bertoia Auctions' Collectors Toys Chest sale. According to Bertoia's brother, Rich, the sale will go on as planned.

"Bill wouldn't want it any other way," Ourant added.

Ourant and his wife, Becky, recently started their own auction company. And Bertoia was completely supportive.

"My whole business is because of Bill Bertoia. I considered him a very close friend.

"I consider he and Noel Barrett [of Carversville, Pa.] the fathers of this type of selling," Ourant said, referring to the practice of using color catalogs to illustrate a variety of antique toys up for sale.

"When the history of the toy collecting hobby is written, Bill Bertoia's name will be at the very top of the list of important contributors. He added incredible energy and so many innovative ideas to the way toys are bought and sold," said Catherine Saunders-Watson, an editor and writer who has covered the antiques and toy industries for 15 years.

"It is an inestimable loss, and I hope the Bertoia family will carry on the tradition he and Jeanne started, which I understand is their intention," she added.

Bertoia was a member of the Mechanical Bank Collectors of America, Antique Toy Collectors of America and Still Bank Collectors of America. His auction house has hosted some of the most prominent bank and toy collections ever assembled, including the legendary Stan Sax collection, Perelman Toy Museum, Hegerty Bank collection, the Atlanta Toy Museum, the Bill Norman collection and, along with others, the largest toy collection ever sold - the Acevedo collection.

Bertoia was born in Buenos Aires, Argentina, in 1950, and he moved with his family to New Jersey. He attended Cumberland County College and Glassboro State College (now Rowan University). He was an avid golfer, skier, fly fisherman, hunter and world traveler.

He is survived by his wife of 25 years, Jeanne (Inferrera) Bertoia of Vineland; daughter, Lauren; son, Michael; father and mother; brother Rich and many nieces and nephews.

Always Did Despise A Mule (Mechanical Banks), J. & E. Stevens, 1879, $2800. Photo courtesy PB Eighty-Four, New York

Artillery, Shepard Hardware, 1892, $2600. Courtesy Christie's East

Bad Accident Mule (Mechanical Banks), J. & E. Stevens, 1880s-90s, $4200. Photo courtesy PB Eighty-Four, New York

Mechanical Banks	C6	C8	C10
Acrobat Bank, 1883, J. & E. Stevens, 5" high	2000	3000	10,500
Alligator in Trough, patented, 1867................................	10,000	20,000	35,000
Always Did Despise A Mule, African-American jockey on mule, 1879, J. & E. Stevens, 10" long................................	800	1200	2800
Always Did Despise A Mule, African-American on bench being kicked by mule, 1897, J. & E. Stevens	800	1200	2800
American Bank Sewing Machine................................	3000	6000	10,000
Artillery Bank, Union Officer w/mortar, firing into fort, 1892, Shepard Hardware.......	500	1100	2600

Mechanical Banks	C6	C8	C10
Astronaut's Bank, gold moon w/rocket on stand, has rings showing orbit of space capsule, ring has astronauts' names—"Shepard, Grissom, Glenn, Carpenter, Schirra, Cooper," little plane up side of rocket shoots money into moon, pot metal, 11" high.....	25	38	50
Atlas Bank	1000	1750	3000
Bad Accident Mule, mule and African-American on two-wheeled cart, 1880s-90s, J. & E. Stevens.............................	850	1500	4200
Bank Teller, The, 1876, J. & E. Stevens	10,000	30,000	96,000
Bear Hugging Tree	450	675	900
Bill E. Grin, 1887, Judd.............	500	900	2200

Boys Stealing Watermelons (Mechanical Banks), $2500. Photo courtesy Christie's East

Boy on Trapeze (Mechanical Banks), J. Barton & Smith, 1891, $6500. Photo courtesy PB Eighty-Four, New York

Boy Scout Camp (Mechanical Banks), J. & E. Stevens, 1912, $12,000. Photo courtesy Sotheby's, New York

Mechanical Banks	C6	C8	C10
Bird on Roof, 1978, J. & E. Stevens	650	1000	2200
Book of Knowledge Reproduction of Original Banks, Artillery Bank; Bulldog Bank; Creedmore; Eagle and Eagles; Jonah & Whale; Magician; Man and Pig; Man milking Cow; Teddy and the Bear; Trick Dog; Trick Pony, Tree Trunk and Buffalo; price for each. Note: The original markings are sometimes filed away from the bottom in an attempt to pass one of these banks off as an original, c. 1950	195	295	390
Boy on Trapeze, 1891, J. Barton & Smith	600	1500	6500
Boy Robbing Bird's Nest, 1906, J. & E. Stevens	1000	3000	10,500
Boy Scout Camp, 1912, J. & E. Stevens	1500	3500	12,000

Mechanical Banks	C6	C8	C10
Boy Stealing Watermelons	750	1500	2500
Bread Winner, 1886, J. & E. Stevens	3500	7000	20,000
Bull & Bear, brass model, 1930s, J. & E. Stevens	800	1200	1800
Bulldog, 1880s, J. & E. Stevens	400	1200	3500
Bulldog, c. 1887, Judd	350	600	1200
Bulldog Savings Bank, 1878, Ives, Blakeslee & Wms	1000	2000	3000
Butting Buffalo	500	800	1800
Butting Goat In Tree Stump, c. 1887, Judd	600	1000	2000
Calamity, three football players, 1905, J. & E. Stevens	3000	8000	35,000
Called Out, 1900	4000	10,000	20,000
Cat and Mouse Bank, 1891, J. & E. Stevens	1000	2200	4200

Circus Bank (Mechanical Banks), Shepard Hardware, 1888, $45,000.

Boy Robbing Bird's Nest (Mechanical Banks), J. & E. Stevens, 1906, $10,500. Photo courtesy Bertoia Auctions

Confectionary (Mechanical Banks), Kyser & Rex, 1881, $8500. Photo courtesy Bill Bertoia Auctions

Dog on Turntable (Mechanical Banks), Judd, 1870s, $1200.

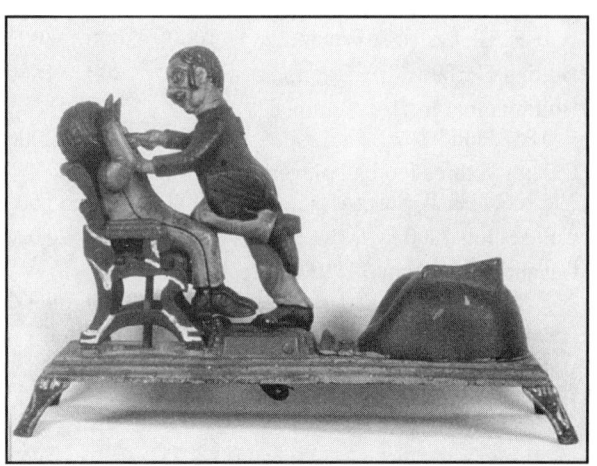

Dentist Bank (Mechanical Banks), J. & E. Stevens, 1880, $9500.

Bulldog (Mechanical Banks), manufacturer unknown. Photo courtesy Sotheby's, New York

Cat and Mouse Bank (Mechanical Banks), J. & E. Stevens, 1891, $4200. Photo courtesy PB Eighty-Four, New York

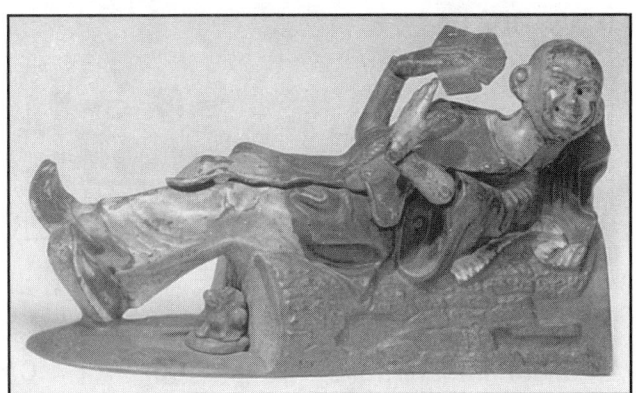

Chinese Reclining (Mechanical Banks), $8800. Photo courtesy Christie's East

Chimpanzee (Mechanical Banks), Kyser & Rex, 1880, $3200. Photo courtesy PB Eighty-Four, New York

Mechanical Banks	C6	C8	C10
Charlie McCarthy, sitting w/legs crossed on top of trunk, drop coin in back and mouth moves, pot metal, copyright 1938, 5-3/4" high ..	75	125	200
Chein Monkey, seated, tips hat when coin dropped in, 5" high	70	105	140
Chief Big Moon, Indian in tee-pee, 1899, J. & E. Stevens	1200	2200	6000
Chimpanzee, red version, 1880, Kyser & Rex	1400	2200	3200

Mechanical Banks	C6	C8	C10
Chinese Reclining, 1882	2900	4300	8800
Circus Bank, 1888, Shepard Hardware..............................	5000	8000	45,000
Circus Ticket Taker, 1830, Judd......................................	550	850	1500
Clown & Harlequin	10,000	30,000	90,000
Clown on Bar	10,000	20,000	70,000
Clown on Globe, 1890, J. & E. Stevens	900	1500	4500
Columbus	300	450	600

Left to right: Clown on Globe (Mechanical Banks), J. & E. Stevens, 1890, $4500; Eagle and Eaglets (Mechanical Banks), J. & E. Stevens, 1883, $1800. Photo courtesy PB Eighty-Four, New York

Cow Kicking (Mechanical Banks), $25,000. Photo courtesy Sotheby's, New York

Creedmore Bank (Mechanical Banks), J. & E. Stevens, 1877, $1500. Photo courtesy Sotheby's, New York

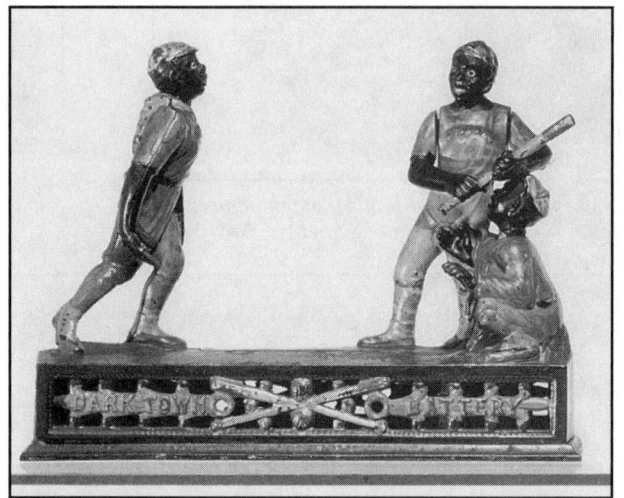

Darktown Battery (Mechanical Banks), J. & E. Stevens, 1888, $8000. Photo courtesy PB Eighty-Four, New York

Mechanical Banks	C6	C8	C10
Confectionary, 1881, Kyser & Rex	2000	4000	8500
Cow Kicking, cow kicks over boy	7500	15,000	25,000
Creedmore Bank, man firing into tree, 1877, J. & E. Stevens, 10" long	600	900	1500
Crowing Rooster, 1937, Keim & Co.	500	800	1200
Dapper Dan, 1910, Marx	300	500	900
Darktown Battery, African-American pitcher and catcher, 1888, J. & E. Stevens	1200	2800	8000
Darky and Cabin, 1885	500	750	1000
Darky and Watermelon, (Foot Ball Bank), Stevens Co., 1888	50,000	100,000	354,500
Darky Football	25,000	75,000	250,000

Mechanical Banks	C6	C8	C10
Dentist Bank, white dentist working on African-American patient, 1880, J. & E. Stevens	2000	5500	9500
Dinah, bust of African-American woman, 1911, J Harper & Co., 6-1/2"	600	900	1450
Ding Dong Bell, 1888	10,000	20,000	74,000
Dog Charges Boy, bronze finish	400	700	1000
Dog on Turntable, 1870s, Judd	400	800	1200
Dog Standing	150	350	500
Eagle and Eaglets, 1883, J. & E. Stevens	600	1200	1800
Elephant, Three Star, trunk flips up to catch coin, 1884, 5" high	300	650	1250

Advertisement for Eagle and Eaglets mechanical banks. Photo courtesy James Maxwell/Virginia Caputo

Darky and Cabin (Mechanical Banks), 1885, $1000. Photo courtesy PB Eighty-Four, New York

Elephant and Clowns (Mechanical Banks), J. & E. Stevens, 1883, $2800. Photo courtesy PB Eighty-Four, New York

Fortune Teller (Mechanical Banks), Nickel, Baumgarter & Co., 1901, $1400. Photo courtesy PB Eighty-Four, New York

Mechanical Banks	C6	C8	C10
Elephant and Clowns, 1883, J. & E. Stevens	600	1200	2800
Elephant Howdah Bank, 1934, Hubley	300	500	1250
Ferris Wheel, Hubley	1000	2000	3000
Fortune Teller, safe, complete w/roll of fortunes, 1901, Nickel, Baumgarter & Co.	500	800	1400
Forty-Niner, The, donkey moves ear and tail	100	225	400
Fowler, sportsman shoots bird, J. & E. Stevens	6500	14,000	20,000

Mechanical Banks	C6	C8	C10
Freedman	50,000	100,000	300,000
Frog and Snake in Pond, in the form of a snake striking at a frog which opens its mouth to receive the coin	3000	4500	6500
Frog on Arched Track	10,000	20,000	35,000
Frog on Lattice, 1870s, J. & E. Stevens	450	675	900
Frog on Rock, 1920s, Kilgore	200	400	11
Frog on Round Base, 1872, J. & E. Stevens	350	550	1000
Frog, Goat and Old Man	1500	3500	6000

Frog and Snake in Pond (Mechanical Banks), $6500. Photo courtesy PB Eighty-Four, New York

Gem, Dog and Building (Mechanical Banks), J. & E. Stevens, 1893, $3000. Photo courtesy PB Eighty-Four, New York

Frogs (Mechanical Banks), J. & E. Stevens, $4000. Photo courtesy PB Eighty-Four, New York

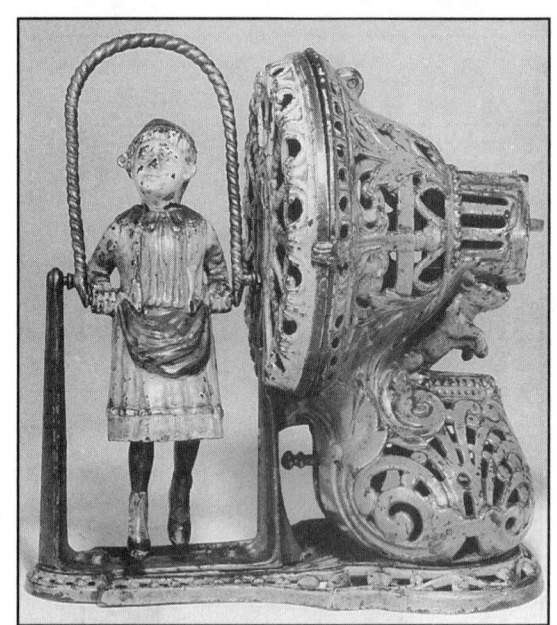

Girl Skipping Rope (Mechanical Banks), J. & E. Stevens, 1890, $45,000. Photo courtesy PB Eighty-Four, New York

Mechanical Banks	C6	C8	C10
Frogs, two, J. & E. Stevens	1200	2400	4000
Gem, Dog and Building, 1893, J. & E. Stevens	600	1200	3000
Giant, holding a club	10,000	15,000	20,000
Girl Skipping Rope, w/key, 1890, J. & E. Stevens	10,000	20,000	45,000
Globe Savings Fund Bank	250	375	500
Guessing Bank, 1877, McLoughlin	1200	2000	3500
Hall's Excelsior Bank, monkey cashier, 1869, J. & E. Stevens	300	600	850

Mechanical Banks	C6	C8	C10
Hall's Lilliput, 1875, J. & E. Stevens	300	600	850
Hen and Chick, Stevens, 1901, J. & E. Stevens	1100	1700	5500
Hindu, 1882, Kyser & Rex	800	1300	1850
Hold the Fort, five-hole, c. 1877	3000	5000	9500
Home Bank building, w/two pillars, teller at window	230	345	460
Horse Race, straight base, 1870, J. & E. Stevens	3500	5500	8000
Humpty Dumpty, 1882, Shepard Hardware	800	2200	4000

Giant (Mechanical Banks), $20,000. Photo courtesy PB Eighty-Four, New York

Mammy Feeding Child (Mechanical Banks), Kyser & Rex, 1884, $6500. Photo courtesy PB Eighty-Four, New York

Hall's Excelsior Bank (Mechanical Banks), J. & E. Stevens, 1869, $850. Photo courtesy PB Eighty-Four, New York

Mason and Hod Carrier, Shepard Hardware, 1887, $7500. Photo courtesy PB Eighty-Four, New York

Home Bank building (Mechanical Banks), $460. Photo courtesy PB Eighty-Four, New York

Mechanical Banks	C6	C8	C10
Independence Hall, 1875, Enterprise Mfg.	350	550	1050
Indian Shooting Bear, 1883, J. & E. Stevens	900	2500	5500
Initiating Bank First Degree, 1880, Mechanical Novelty Works	5000	7000	9000

Mechanical Banks	C6	C8	C10
Jolly Nigger, string tie, England, 1890s	175	300	500
Jolly Nigger, high hat, 1880s, J. Harper & Co., 8" high	250	400	650
Jolly Nigger, moves ears, 1920, Starkie	250	400	650

Humpty Dumpty (Mechanical Banks), Shepard Hardware, 1882, $8000. Photo courtesy PB Eighty-Four, New York

Horse Race (Mechanical Banks), J. & E. Stevens, 1870, $8000. Photo courtesy Christie's East

Initiating Bank First Degree (Mechanical Banks), Mechanical Novelty Works, 1880, $9000.

Jonah and the Whale (Mechanical Banks), Shepard Hardware, 1890s, $5500. Photo courtesy PB Eighty-Four, New York

Mechanical Banks	C6	C8	C10
Jonah and the Whale, Jonah in boat, 1890s, Shepard Hardware	1200	2500	5500
Jonah and Whale, Jonah emerges, 1880s, J. & E. Stevens	12,000	20,000	55,000
Jumbo on Platform	850	1700	2500
Keeping 'Em Flying, dime register	25	37	50
Kick Inn, a mule standing in front of a small building, Presto, 1921, Melvisto Novelty	200	500	900
King Aqua	15,000	30,000	95,000

Mechanical Banks	C6	C8	C10
Leap Frog Bank, two boys and tree, 1891, Shepard Hardware	750	1500	5500
Liberty Bell	200	300	500
Lighthouse Bank, 1891	1200	1800	5500
Lion and Monkeys, 1883, Kyser & Rex	650	1400	4200
Lion Hunter, 1911, J. & E. Stevens	2000	5000	10,000
Little Jocko, 1912, Ferdinand Strauss	500	1200	2200
Little Joe, 1910, J. Harper & Co.	150	350	575
Locomotive	300	600	900
Magic, 1873, J. & E. Stevens	800	1400	2800

Left to right: Lion and Monkeys (Mechanical Banks), Kyser & Rex, 1883, $4200; Indian Shooting Bear (Mechanical Banks), J. & E. Stevens, 1883, $5500. Photo courtesy Sotheby's, New York

Novelty Bank (Mechanical Banks), J. & E. Stevens, 1873, $2250. Photo courtesy Sotheby's, New York

Lion Hunter (Mechanical Banks), J. & E. Stevens, 1911, $10,000. Photo courtesy PB Eighty-Four, New York

Magician Bank (Mechanical Banks), J. & E. Stevens, 1901, $6500. Photo courtesy PB Eighty-Four, New York

Mechanical Banks	C6	C8	C10
Magician Bank, 1901, J. & E. Stevens	2500	3500	6500
Mama Katzenjammer and the Kids, 1908, Kenton, 5-3/4"	3000	5000	7500
Mammy Feeding Child, 1884, Kyser & Rex	3000	4500	6500
Mason and Hod Carrier, 1887, Shepard Hardware	2000	4000	7500
Merry-Go-Round, 1888, Kyser & Rex	7500	11,000	15,000
Meyers No. 84, Jumbo Elephant	100	250	350
Mikado Bank, The, 1886, Kyser & Rex	15,000	25,000	55,000

Mechanical Banks	C6	C8	C10
Money Box Bank, hand-carved on wood base, 10-1/4"	800	1200	1600
Monkey and Coconut, 1886, J. & E. Stevens	350	900	2500
Mosque, 1880s, Judd	600	1400	2600
Mule Bucking, African-American man riding a mule	500	750	1000
Mule Entering Barn, 1880, Kyser & Rex	600	1200	3500
National Bank, 1873, J. & E. Stevens	2000	3500	6000
Naughty Girl Bank, modern	25	50	75
New Bank, brass policeman in building, c. 1875, 4-1/2" long	170	255	340

Mule Bucking (Mechanical Banks), $1000. Photo courtesy Sotheby's, New York

Mule Entering Barn (Mechanical Banks), Kyser & Rex, 1880, $3500. Photo courtesy Sotheby's, New York

New Bank (Mechanical Banks), c. 1875, $340. Photo courtesy Sotheby's, New York

Owl (Mechanical Banks), head turns, J. & E. Stevens, 1880, $900. Photo courtesy PB Eighty-Four, New York

Mechanical Banks	C6	C8	C10
New Creedmore, 1891, J. & E. Stevens	550	950	1850
North Pole, Eskimos and dog sled, J. & E. Stevens	10,000	15,000	25,000
Novelty Bank, house-like bank, 1873, J. & E. Stevens	550	1000	2250

Mechanical Banks	C6	C8	C10
Old Woman in the Shoe, W.S. Reed Co.	50,000	100,000	426,000
Organ Bank, monkey and revolving cat and dog, 1882, Kyser & Rex, 7-1/4" high	500	850	1650

Organ Grinder And Monkey (Mechanical Banks), 1929, $600. Photo courtesy Sotheby's, New York

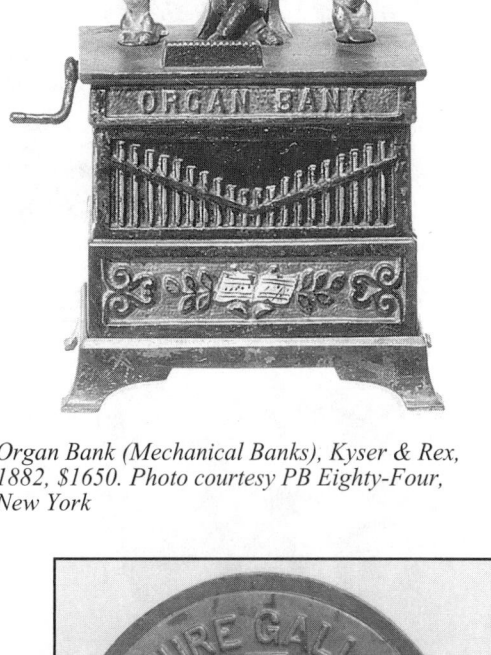

Organ Bank (Mechanical Banks), Kyser & Rex, 1882, $1650. Photo courtesy PB Eighty-Four, New York

Paddy and his Pig, J. & E. Stevens, 1882, $6500. Photo courtesy Garth's Auctions inc.

Picture Gallery (Mechanical Banks), 1885, $20,000. Photo courtesy PB Eighty-Four, New York

Mechanical Banks	C6	C8	C10
Organ Bank, monkey only, 1881, Kyser & Rex	350	500	850
Organ Boy and Girl, monkey flanked by boy and girl holding tambourine, pat. June 13, 1882, 1882, Kyser & Rex	500	850	1650
Organ Grinder And Bear, 1890s, J. & E. Stevens	2300	3500	8500
Organ Grinder And Monkey, 1929	330	485	600
Owl, turns head, 1880, J. & E. Stevens	250	500	900

Mechanical Banks	C6	C8	C10
Owl, slot in book, 1926, Kilgore	350	650	1200
Owl, slot in head, 1926, Kilgore	350	650	1200
Paddy and His Pig, 1882, J. & E. Stevens	900	2500	6500
Panorama Bank, 1882, J. & E. Stevens	2500	4500	6500
Patronize the Blind Man and His Dog, 1878, J. & E. Stevens	2000	3000	4500
Pegleg Beggar, 1875, Judd	750	1200	1700
Pelican, "Boy thumbs nose"	775	1550	2310
Perfection Registering	4500	7000	10,000

Trick Pony (Mechanical Banks), 1885, $4500.

Teddy and The Bear (Mechanical Banks), J. & E. Stevens, 1907, $4500. Photo courtesy PB Eighty-Four, New York

Trick Dog (Mechanical Banks), Hubley, 1888, $2500.

Watchdog Safe (Mechanical Banks), J. & E. Stevens, 1890s, $1250. Photo courtesy Sotheby's, New York

Uncle Remus, Jyser & Rex, 1891, $3500. Photo courtesy Sotheby's, New York

Zoo (Mechanical Banks), Kyser & Rex, 1890s, $2250. Photo courtesy Sotheby's, New York

Patronize the Blind Man and His Dog (Mechanical Banks), J. & E. Stevens, 1878, $4500. Photo courtesy Sotheby's, New York

Professor Pug Frog's Great Bicycle Feat (Mechanical Banks), J. & E. Stevens, 1886, $10,000. Photo courtesy Sotheby's, New York

Tammany Bank (Mechanical Banks), J. & E. Stevens, 1873, $3000. Photo courtesy Sotheby's, New York

Mechanical Banks	C6	C8	C10
Piano, c. 1900, E.M. Roche Co.	250	500	750
Picture Gallery, 1885	4500	7500	20,000
Pig, Bismarck, 1883, J. & E. Stevens	1800	3500	6000
Pig in High Chair, 1887, J. & E. Stevens	350	550	1400
Preacher in Pulpit	30,000	40,000	50,000
Presto, shape of building, 1894, Kyser & Rex	250	525	950
Presto-Mouse on Roof	7500	12,000	17,500
Professor Pug Frog's Great Bicycle Feat, 1886, J. & E. Stevens	1500	3500	10,000
Pump, Bucket	300	700	1000
Punch and Judy, 1884, Shepard Hardware	600	2500	5500

Mechanical Banks	C6	C8	C10
Rabbit, tall	600	1200	2000
Rabbit, small, circular base, Lockwood Mfg	450	850	1250
Rabbit in Cabbage Patch, 1925, Kilgore	200	650	1400
Red Riding Hood, 1880s, W.S. Reed	8500	14,000	18,000
Roller Skating, 1880s, Kyser & Rex	12,000	18,000	45,000
Rooster, 1900s, Kyser & Rex	600	900	1800
Santa Claus at Chimney, 1889, Shepard Hardware	800	1800	5500
See Him Frisk	10,000	20,000	55,000
Shoot the Chute	12,500	17,500	25,000
Speaking Dog Bank, 1885, Shepard Hardware	850	1500	4500

*Pig in High Chair, J. & E. Stevens, $1400.
Photo courtesy Sotheby's, New York*

*Presto Bank, Kyser & Rex, 1894, $950. Photo courtesy
Sotheby's, New York*

*Roller Skating (Mechanical Banks), Kyser & Rex, 1880s,
$45,000. Photo courtesy PB Eighty-Four, New York*

*World's Fair (Mechanical Banks), J. & E. Stevens, 1893,
$2400.*

Mechanical Banks	C6	C8	C10
Springing Cat, lead alloy, sold in 1991, 1882, Charles Bailey	3500	6000	8000
Squirrel and Tree Stump, 1881, Mechanical Novelty Works ..	850	1250	2250
Standing Bear	100	165	220
Strato Bank, pot metal, rocket and planet, 1950s, 8" long.....	10	15	25
Stump Speaker, 1886, Shepard Hardware	850	2200	4500
Tabby, 1887	250	650	1050

Mechanical Banks	C6	C8	C10
Tammany Bank, 1873, J. & E. Stevens, 5-3/4" high	400	800	3000
Tank and Cannon, 1919, Starkie	650	900	1500
Teddy and The Bear, Teddy Roosevelt firing at bear in tree, 1907, J. & E. Stevens	1000	2200	4500
Telephone	150	300	450
Trick Dog, clown w/hoop, dog and barrel w/six-part base, 1888, Hubley	750	1500	2500

Punch and Judy (Mechanical Banks), Shepard Hardware, 1884, $5500. Photo courtesy PB Eighty-Four, New York

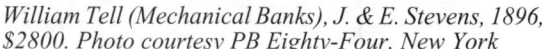

William Tell (Mechanical Banks), J. & E. Stevens, 1896, $2800. Photo courtesy PB Eighty-Four, New York

Tabby (Mechanical Banks), 1887, $1050.

Santa Claus at Chimney (Mechanical Banks), Shepard Hardware, 1889, $5500. Photo courtesy PB Eighty-Four, New York

Speaking Dog Bank (Mechanical Banks), Shepard Hardware, 1885, $4500. Photo courtesy PB Eighty-Four, New York

Stump Speaker (Mechanical Banks), Shepard Hardware, 1886, $4500. Photo courtesy PB Eighty-Four, New York

Pegleg Beggar (Mechanical Banks), Judd, 1875, $1700. Photo courtesy Sotheby's, New York

Uncle Sam (Mechanical Banks), Shepard Hardware, 1886, $9200. Photo courtesy PB Eighty-Four, New York

Mechanical Banks	C6	C8	C10
Trick Dog, clown w/hoop, dark dog and dark barrel, 1929, Hubley	200	450	1000
Trick Pony, 1885, Shepard Hardware	900	1250	4500
Turtle Bank, 1920s, Kilgore	7500	12,000	20,000
U.S. and Spain, 1898, J. & E. Stevens	2000	4500	7500
U.S. Building, boy and dog in windows, J. & E. Stevens ?, 1878	3100	4650	6200
Uncle Remus, 1891, Kyser & Rex	1700	2300	3500
Uncle Sam, bust	300	450	600
Uncle Sam, w/umbrella in left hand, 1886, Shepard Hardware	2000	5000	9200
Uncle Tom, w/lapels, one star, brass base, 1891, Kyser & Rex	250	650	1250
Uncle Tom, w/lapels and one star	250	650	1250

Mechanical Banks	C6	C8	C10
United States Bank, Stevens, 1880, J. & E. Stevens	800	2200	4000
Watchdog Safe, 1890s, J. & E. Stevens	350	675	1250
Weeden's Plantation, 1888, Weeden	750	1250	1850
William Tell, 1896, J. & E. Stevens	600	1250	2800
Wireless Bank, 1926, Hugo Mfg.	350	650	850
Woodpecker	1500	2800	4000
World's Fair, 1893, J. & E. Stevens	850	1250	2400
Zig Zag	40,000	80,000	190,000
Zoo, 1890s, Kyser & Rex	850	1650	2250

Still Banks	C8	C10
$100,000 Money Bag, silver-gray finish, 3-5/8" tall	300	650
1 Pounder Shell Bank, artillery shell, "1 Pounder Bank", 1918, Grey Iron Casting, 8"	25	95

Bear Seated on Log (Still Banks), $950.

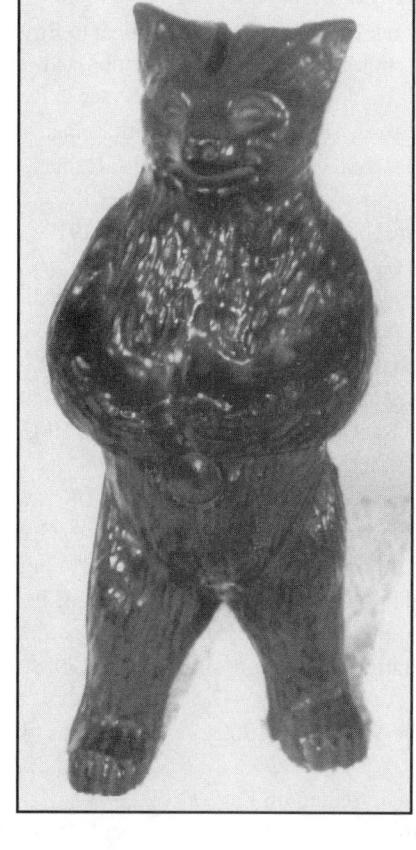

Bear, Begging (Still Banks), A.C. Williams, 1900s, $150.

Still Banks (Continued)	**C8**	**C10**
1876 Bank, Large, building bank w/bronze/copper finish, 1895, Judd, 3-3/8" tall	75	250
1926 Sesquicentennial Bell, 1926, Grey Iron Casting, 3-3/4" x 3-7/8" diameter	75	200
A.A.O.S.M.S. Shriner's Fezm, red fez w/tassle and gold lettering, 1920s, Allen Mfg., 2-3/8"	250	650
Administration Building, unpainted, 1893, Magic Introduction, 5"	250	650
Air Mail Bank on Base, red, 1920, Dent, 6-3/8" tall	375	1400
Alamo, unpainted bronze finish, 1930s, Alamo Iron Works, 1-7/8" tall, 3-3/8" wide	200	450
Alphabet Bank, octagonal, 3-1/2"	1200	3500
Amish Boy, painted, 1970, John Wright, 5" tall	10	65
Amish Boy in White Shirt, blue coveralls, black hat, 1971, John Wright, 5" tall	10	65
Amish Girl, painted, 1970, John Wright, 5" tall	10	65

Still Banks (Continued)	**C8**	**C10**
Andy Gump, Andy sits reading a paper, painted, 1928, Arcade, 4-3/8" tall	500	1200
Apollo, plain, unpainted, 1968, John Wright, 4-1/4"	20	65
Apollo 8, red, white and blue, 1968, John Wright, 4-1/4"	20	75
Apple, painted apple on twig w/leaves, 1882, Kyser & Rex, 5-1/4" tall	600	2400
Arabian Safe, 1882, Kyser & Rex, 4-9/16" x 4-1/4"	100	300
Armoured Car, red car on gold wheels, 1900s, A.C. Williams, 6-3/4" long, 3-3/4" tall	650	3500
Art Deco Elephant, red, 4-3/8" tall	100	225
Aunt Jemima, also called Mammy with Spoon, 1900s, A.C. Williams, 5-7/8"	125	325
Auto, black, red wheels, four passengers, 1910?, A.C. Williams, 5-3/4" long	500	1200
Baby in Cradle, rocking cradle, 1890s, 3-1/4" tall	500	1500
Bank of Columbia, unpainted, "Bank of Columbia", 1800s, Arcade, 4-7/8"	150	375

Still Banks (Continued)

	C8	C10
Bank of England Safe, identical to Egyptian Safe except front is embossed Bank of England, 1882, Kyser & Rex.	350	750
Barrel, 1873, Judd, 2-3/4" tall	100	225
Baseball on Three Bats, 1914, Hubley, 5-1/4"	350	1850
Baseball Player, several colors, 1910s, A.C. Williams, 5-3/4" tall	200	750
Baseball Player, gold, 1909, A.C. Williams, 5-3/4"	100	550
Basket Puzzle Bank, unpainted, 1894, Nicol, 2-3/4" tall, 3-1/2" wide	300	650
Basket Registering Bank, woven, 1902, Chas. A. Braun, 2-7/8" x 3-3/4"	50	125
Basset Hound, bronze finish, 3-1/8"	650	1500
Battleship Maine, "Maine", 1800s, Grey Iron Casting, 5-1/4" tall, 6-5/8" long	650	4500
Battleship Maine, white, 1901, J. & E. Stevens, 6" tall, 10-1/4" long	500	6000
Battleship Oregon, silver finish, 1890s, J. & E. Stevens, 4-7/8" long	200	450
Be Wise Owl, 1900s, A.C. Williams, 4-7/8" x 2-1/2"	150	375
Bear Seated on Log, 7"	400	950
Bear Stealing Pig, painted, 1913, Ober, 5-1/2" tall	400	1000
Bear with Honey Pot, painted, Hubley, 6-1/2" tall	75	175
Bear, Begging, bronze finish, 1900s, A.C. Williams, 5-3/8"	75	150
Beehive Bank, 1882, Kyser & Rex, 2-3/8"	250	500
Beehive Registering Saving Bank, 1891, 5-3/8" x 6-1/2"	200	425
Beehive with Brass Top, unpainted, W.M. Gobielle, 5-1/2" tall on base	350	750
Bethel College Administration Building, 1935, Service Foundry, 2-7/8" x 5-1/4"	175	350
Bicentennial Bell, 1976, 4" x 4"	25	45
Billiken, on square base, bronze finish, red cap, 1909, A.C. Williams, 4-1/4" tall	55	125
Billiken on Throne, 1909, A.C. Williams, 6-1/2" tall	65	175
Billy Bounce, silver painted body, 1900s, Hubley, 4-11/16" tall	375	1200
Billy Possum ("Possum & Taters"), on base "Billy Possum", 1909, J.M. Harper, 3" x 4-3/4"	1200	5500
Bird Bank Building, unpainted cupola building w/bird on top, "Bank New York", 5-7/8"	650	3500

Still Banks (Continued)

	C8	C10
Bird Cage Bank, similar to Crystal Bank No. 926, but glass is replaced by open mesh, 1900s, Arcade, 3-7/8" tall	50	125
Bismark Bank (Pig), "Bismark Bank", 1883, 3-3/8"	100	300
Bismark Pig with Rider, bronze finish, 1880s, 7-1/4" tall, 6-1/2" long	1000	3500
Boss Tweed, 1870s, 3-7/8" tall	1500	3500
Boston State House, painted, 1800s, Smith & Egge, 6-3/4" tall	3000	6000
Boxer Bulldog, seated, bronze finish, 1900s, Hubley, 4-1/2"	125	225
Boy Scout, brown finish, 1910s, A.C. Williams, 5-7/8" tall	50	150
Boy with Large Football, brown, 1914, Hubley, 5-1/8" tall	2000	3200
Buckeye (SBCCA), painted, "Ohio The Buckeye State," "SBCC 1973", 1973, Lou Filler, 3-1/2"	25	100
Buffalo, red, green, or blue, 1929, Arcade, 3" x 4-1/4"	175	300
Buffalo Bank, gold, 1900s, A.C. Williams, 3-1/8" x 4-3/8"	50	175
Buffalo Nickel, 1970s, George Knerr, 3-7/8"	35	100
Building with Belfry, in browns, Kenton, 8" tall	550	4500
Bull on Base, unpainted, 4" tall	200	450
Bull with Long Horns, painted, 3-11/16" tall	50	125
Bulldog, Large, painted, 1960s, John Wright, 6"	25	65
Bulldog, Seated, 1928, Hubley, 3-7/8"	200	400
Bulldog, Standing, painted, 1900s, Arcade, 2-1/4"	250	450
Bungalow Bank, white cottage w/green roof, 1900s, Grey Iron Casting, 3-3/4" x 3"	225	650
Bust of Man, 5"	100	350
Buster Brown & Tige, 1900s, A.C. Williams, 5-1/2"	100	375
Cadet, blue uniform w/gold trim, 1905, Hubley, 5-3/4" tall	300	750
Camel, Kneeling, 1889, Kyser & Rex, 2-1/2" tall, 4-3/4" long	350	1050
Camel, Large, 1900s, A.C. Williams, 7-1/4" x 6-1/4"	200	650
Camel, Small, 1920s, Hubley, 4-3/4" x 3-7/8"	100	225
Camera, 1888, Wrightsville Hardware	1000	5000

Camel, Large (Still Banks), A.C. Williams, 1900s, $650.

Century of Progress Building (Still Banks), Arcade, 1933, $3000.

Still Banks (Continued)	C8	C10
Camera Bank, bronze finish bellows camera on tripod, 1800s, Wrightsville Hardware, 4-5/16" tall	2500	5000
Campbell Kids, 1900s, A.C. Williams, 3-5/16" x 4-1/8"	150	350
Cannon, black cannon on red wheels, 1914, Hubley, 3" tall, 6-7/8" long	2500	5000
Capitalist, The (Everett True), painted, 1913, Ober, 5" tall	1200	2000
Capitol Bank, 1981, Riverside Foundry, 5-1/8"	25	50
Captain Kidd, Kidd stands by tree trunk w/shovel, base reads "Captain Kidd", 1900s, 5-5/8" tall	275	850
Carpenter Safe, 1907, J.M. Harper, 4-3/8"	2500	5000
Cash Register Savings Bank, unpainted, "Cash Register Savings Bank", 1906, Hubley, 4-3/4"	500	750
Cash Register Savings Bank, round face on three claw foot feet, "Cash Register Savings Bank", 1880s, 5-5/8" tall	350	850
Cash Register with Mesh, red finish w/gold-bronze mesh, 1900s, Arcade, 3-3/4" tall	50	125
Castle Bank, Small, 1882, Kyser & Rex, 3" x 2-13/16"	200	650
Cat on Tub, bronze finish, 1920s, A.C. Williams, 4-1/8" tall	100	200
Cat with Ball, 1900s, A.C. Williams, 2-1/2" tall	200	375
Cat with Bow, 1930s, Hubley, 4-1/8"	275	575
Cat with Bow, Seated, brown finish, 1922, Grey iron Casting, 4-3/8" tall	225	475

Still Banks (Continued)	C8	C10
Cat with Bow, Seated, painted, white body, red bow, John Wright, 4-3/8" x 2-7/8"	25	50
Cat with Long Tail, 1910s, Grey Iron Casting, 4-3/8" tall, 6-3/4" long	375	1250
Cat with Soft Hair, Seated, 1900s, Arcade, 4-1/4" x 2-7/8"	85	225
Century of Progress Building, white, "A Century Of Progress" building from Chicago World's Fair, 1933, Arcade, 4-1/2" x 7"	800	3000
Champion Heater, green and black, "Champion", 4-1/8"	125	500
Chanticleer (Rooster), bronze finish, painted face and comb, 1911, 4-5/8"	850	7500
Chicken Feed Bag, "Chicken Feed", 1973, George Knerr, 4-5/8"	35	350
Chipmunk with Nut, black, 4-1/16"	300	950
Church Towers, 6-3/4"	850	1900
Church Window Safe, 1890s, Shimer Toy, 3-1/16"	50	165
City Bank with Chimney, painted, 1870s, 6-3/4" tall	650	3500
City Bank with Crown, 1870's, 5-1/2" tall	600	4500
City Bank with Teller, bronze finish, Judd, 5-1/2"	400	750
Clown, gold and red w/tall curved hat, 1908, A.C. Williams, 6-1/4"	125	250
Clown Bust, painted, 1973, George Knerr, 4-7/8"	100	350
Coca-Cola Bank, red and green w/logo, 3-3/8" tall	600	2200

Still Banks (Continued)

	C8	C10
Coin Registering Bank, w/red doors and dome, 1890, Kyser & Rex, 6-3/4".......	2500	6500
Colonial House with Porch, Large, white, 1900s, A.C. Williams, 4" tall....	100	375
Colonial House with Porch, Small, brown finish w/red, green or gold roof, 1910s, A.C. Williams, 3" tall......	75	250
Columbia, silver finish building bank, Kenton, 4-1/2" tall	600	900
Columbia Bank, unpainted silver finish, 1890s, Kenton, 5-3/4" tall...................	300	700
Columbia Bank, bronze finish, 1890s, Kenton, 8-3/4" tall	600	1000
Columbia Magic Savings Bank, unpainted, "Columbia Magic Savings Bank", 1892, Magic Introduction, 5"	300	700
Columbia Tower, unpainted three-story tower, 1897, Grey Iron Casting, 6-7/8"	450	950
Covered Bridge, white w/red roof, 1960s, John Wright, 2-1/2" tall, 6-1/8" long.....................	35	75
Covered Wagon, unpainted, Wilton Products, 6-5/8" long.....................	10	25
Cow, brown or red finish, 1920, A.C. Williams, 3-3/8" x 5-1/4"	75	550
Crosley Radio, Large, green w/gold highlights, 1930s, Kenton, 5-1/8" tall..	650	1800
Crosley Radio, Small, green, 1930s, Kenton, 4-5/16" tall	150	700
Cross, dark finish, "God Is Love" on base, 9-1/4" tall.................................	750	2200
Crown Bank on Legs, Small, painted, 4-5/8"	600	950
Cupola Bank, painted building w/center roof cupola, 1869, Vermong Novelty Works, 5-1/2" tall	300	1250
Cupola Bank, red and gray, 1872, J. & E. Stevens, 4-1/4" x 3-3/8"	100	850
Cupola Bank, black, 1870s, J. & E. Stevens, 3-1/4" tall	75	425
Cutie Dog, painted, 1914, Hubley, 3-7/8"...	65	175
Czar Safe Combination Bank, door of heavy nickel plate, sides of white plated steel, 1929, Arcade, 3" x 2-1/2" x 2-1/2"...	100	225
Daisy, red safe bank, 1899, Shimer Toy, 2-1/8" tall.................................	50	175

Still Banks (Continued)

	C8	C10
Darkey Sharecropper, toes visible on one foot, 1900s, A.C. Williams, 5-1/2" tall	75	375
Decker's Iowana (Pig), unpainted, 2-5/16"	75	200
Derby, "Pass Around the Hat", 2-5/16"...	100	325
Dime Registering Coin Barrel, unpainted, 1889, Kyser & Rex, 4" x 2-1/2"	125	225
Dime Savings, "Dime Savings", 1899, Shimer Toy, 2-1/2" safe.....................	200	425
Dog, red, green, or blue, 1929, Arcade, 5-1/2" x 3-3/4"	175	350
Dog on Tub, bronze finish, 1920s, A.C. Williams, 4-1/16" x 2" diameter..........	125	200
Dog Smoking Cigar, painted, white body, red bow tie, Hubley, 4-1/4"	450	850
Dolphin Boat Bank, sailor boy in boat holds anchor, 1900s, Grey Iron Casting, 4-1/2" tall............................	500	850
Domed Bank, 1899, A.C. Williams, 3" tall..............	20	95
Domed Mosque Bank, gold/bronze finish, 1900s, Grey Iron Casting, 4-1/4" tall..	85	175
Domed Mosque Bank, bronze finish, 1900s, Grey Iron Casting, 3-1/8" tall ..	65	145
Donkey, red, green, or blue, 1929, Arcade, 4-1/2" x 4-1/2"	110	165
Donkey, black w/red yoke, 3-1/4" tall.....	100	200
Donkey, "I Made St. Louis Famous," gray finish, 1903, Arcade, 4-11/16" tall........	800	1800
Donkey with Blanket, painted, gray w/red blanket, 1930s, Kenton, 3-7/8" tall	450	950
Donkey, Large, painted, 1920s, A.C. Williams, 6-13/16" tall	150	450
Donkey, Small, blue, gold or gray finish, 1910s, Arcade, 4-1/2" tall...................	85	200
Dormer Bank, painted building bank w/red roof, 4-3/4" tall	3500	6000
Double Door, building w/two doors, painted white w/gold highlights, 1900s, A.C. Williams, 5-7/16"	200	425
Doughboy, painted World War I soldier, 1919, Grey Iron Casting, 7" tall	350	850
Dry Sink, dark finish, 1970, John Wright, 3" x 2-3/4"	25	45
Duck, white painted body, 1930s, Hubley, 4-3/4"	150	275
Duck Bank, unpainted, 1900s, A.C. Williams, 4-7/8"	150	275
Duck on Tub, "Save for a Rainy Day", 1930s, Hubley, 5-3/8"	95	450

Boy Scout (Still Banks), A.C. Williams, 1910s, $150.

Dolphin Boat Bank (Still Banks), Grey Iron Casting, 1900s, $850.

Home Savings Bank (Still Banks), Shimer Toy, 1899, $525.

Captain Kidd (Still Banks), 1900s, $850.

Buster Brown & Tige (Still Banks), A.C. Williams, 1900s, $375.

City Bank with Chimney (Still Banks), 1870s, $3500.

Still Banks (Continued)	C8	C10
Duck, Round, painted, yellow body, red beak and top of head, 1930s, Kenton, 4" tall	225	650
Dutch Boy, Grey Iron Casting, 6-3/4" tall	600	850
Dutch Boy, doorstop conversion, 8-1/4" tall	150	275
Dutch Boy on Barrel, 1930s, Hubley, 5-5/8"	75	275
Dutch Girl, bronze finish, Grey Iron Casting, 6-1/2" tall	600	850
Dutch Girl Holding Flowers, painted, iron trap in base, 1930s, Hubley, 5-1/2" tall.	100	275
Eagle Bank Building, painted building w/gold eagle on roof, 9-3/4" tall	450	1250
Eagle with Ball, Building, building w/eagle and ball on roof, 10-3/4" tall..	850	6500
Edison Bust, 1972, Charlotte Blevins, 5-5/16"	35	65
Eggman (Wm. Howard Taft), 1910, Arcade, 4-1/8" tall	850	3000
Egyptian Tomb, safe on base, decorated w/Sphinx and obelisk on front, sides show, pyramid, walled ruins and urn w/flowers, gold, 1882, Kyser & Rex, 6-1/4" square	450	750
Electric Railroad, 1893, Shimer Toy, 8-1/4" long	2500	6000

Still Banks (Continued)	C8	C10
Elephant, "GOP 1936", 1936, Hubley, 3-1/2" tall	750	1200
Elephant on Bench on Tub, 1920s, A.C. Williams, 3-7/8"	125	225
Elephant on Tub, in bronze finish, 1920s, A.C. Williams, 5-3/8"	100	185
Elephant on Tub, Decorated, painted version of No. 483, 1920s, A.C. Williams, 5-3/8"	125	200
Elephant on Wheels, unpainted, 1920s, A.C. Williams, 4" tall	150	300
Elephant Trumpeting, black finish, 1971, John Wright, 7-1/4" tall	15	35
Elephant with Bent Knee, tan finish, 1904, Kenton, 3-1/2"	200	375
Elephant with Chariot, Large, also made w/o chariot, 1900s, Hubley, 4-3/4" tall	2000	3000
Elephant with Chariot, Small, gray elephant, red chariot, yellow wheels, 1906, Hubley, 7" long	1400	2200
Elephant with Howdah, Large, 1900s, A.C. Williams, 4-7/8" x 6-3/8"	65	125
Elephant with Howdah, Large, gold, 1900s, A.C. Williams, 6-3/4"	85	150
Elephant with Howdah, Short Trunk, painted gray w/red belt, 1910, Hubley, 3-3/4" tall	125	275

Columbia Tower (Still Banks), Grey Iron Casting, 1897, $950.

Dutch Girl (Still Banks), Grey Iron Casting, $850.

Still Banks (Continued)	**C8**	**C10**
Elephant with Howdah, Small, 1900s, A.C. Williams, 3-1/2" x 5"	65	125
Elephant with Raised Slot, gray body, gold blanket, 4-1/2" tall	150	350
Elephant with Swivel Trunk, black finish w/gold swivel trunk, 2-1/2"	125	250
Elephant with Tin Chariot, red chariot, 1900s, Wing, 8" long	1000	1600
Elephant with Tucked Trunk, red or green, 1900s, Arcade, 2-3/4" x 4-5/8"	65	125
Elephant with Turned Trunk, Seated, unpainted, 4-1/4"	450	950
Elephant, Circus, painted, w/lavender pants and red dotted white shirt, 1930s, Hubley, 3-7/8"	150	350
Elf, painted, converted doorstop, 10" tall	150	450
English Setter, black, 1970, John Wright, 8-1/2" tall	125	275

Still Banks (Continued)	**C8**	**C10**
Fidelity Safe, Large, green w/gold trim, "Fidelity Safe", 1880, Kyser & Rex, 3-5/8" tall	150	300
Fidelity Trust Vault, Lord Fauntleroy, 1890, Barton Smith Co., 6-1/2" x 5-7/8"	300	650
Fido, painted, white body, black eyes and ears, red collar, 1914, Hubley, 5"	60	225
Fido on Pillow, painted, 1920s, Hubley, 7-3/8" long	100	550
Finial Bank, building bank w/single finial on roof, 1887, Kyser & Rex, 5-3/4" tall, 4-3/8" wide	275	1400
Flags Bank (SBCCA), white pyramid w/color US flags, 1976, Littlestown Hardware, 3-1/4" tall, 6" square	75	125
Flat Iron Building Bank, silver, 1900s, Kenton, 5-1/2" tall	135	350
Floral Safe (National Safe), 1898, J. & E. Stevens, 4-5/8" x 4-1/8"	125	350
Football Player, 1910s, A.C. Williams, 5-7/8" tall	250	550

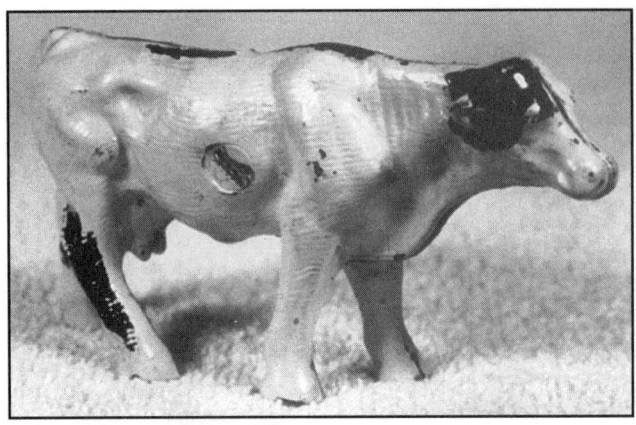

Cow (Still Banks), A.C. Williams, 1920, $550.

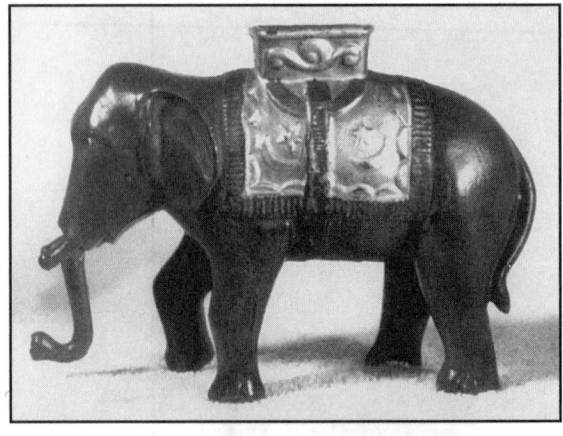

Elephant with Swivel Trunk (Still Banks), $250.

Still Banks (Continued)	**C8**	**C10**
Fort, unpainted bronze finish, 1910s, 4-1/8"	125	275
Four Tower, painted white building w/red roof, 1949, Ohio Foundry Co., 5-3/8"	35	85
Four Tower, unpainted w/gold highlights, J. & E. Stevens, 5-3/4"	125	450
Foxy Grandpa, painted, 1920s, Hubley, 5-1/2" tall	150	375
Frog, deep green finish, 1973, Iron Art, 4-1/8"	75	125
Frowning Face, hanging bank, chin drops below surface level, 5-5/8" tall	850	1750
G.E. Radio Bank, brown cabinet radio on four legs, 1930s, Arcade, 3-3/4" tall	125	325
G.E. Refrigerator, Small, blue, 1930s, Hubley, 3-3/4"	75	225
Gas Pump, red, 5-3/4" tall	275	650
Gem Stove, brown finish, Abendorth Brothers, 4-3/4"	75	175
General Butler, painted head on frog body, 1884, J. & E. Stevens, 6-1/2" tall	1500	3500
General Butler, 1880s, J. & E. Stevens	1800	3500
General Butler, 1880s, J. & E. Stevens	1000	3500
General Pershing Bust, bronze finish, 1918, Grey Iron Casting, 7-3/4" tall	75	175
General Sheridan on Base, General seated on rearing horse, 1910s, Arcade, 6" tall	250	650
George Washington Bust on Safe, 1903, J.M. Harper, 5-7/8" tall	1000	2500

Still Banks (Continued)	**C8**	**C10**
Gettysburg Bank, gray monument w/reclining soldier, 1960, Wilton Products, 4-3/4" x 7-1/4"	75	200
Give Me A Penny, African-American figure in hat, painted, 1900s, Hubley, 5-1/2" tall	200	450
Globe Bank with Eagle, red w/eagle on globe, 1875, Enterprise Mfg., 5-3/4"	125	450
Globe in Wire Arc, painted, spinning globe, red continents, 1900s, Arcade, 4-5/8" tall	125	450
Globe on Arc, red, 1900s, Grey Iron Casting, 5-1/4" tall	100	300
Globe on Claw Feet, Kenton, 6"	175	375
Globe on Hand, bronze finish, 1893, 4"	375	1275
Globe Safe with Hinged Door, 1900s, Kenton, 5"	100	250
Globe Savings Fund Bank, painted "Globe Savings Fund 1888", 1889, Kyser & Rex, 7-1/8"	1800	4000
Gold Eagle, 1970, John Wright, 5-3/4"	5	20
Good Luck Horseshoe, Buster Brown and Tige w/horse inside horseshoe, 1908, Arcade, 4-1/4" x 4-3/4"	150	550
Goose Bank, unpainted, 1920s, Arcade, 3-3/4"	85	175
Graf Zeppelin, silver-gray finish, 1920s, A.C. Williams, 6-5/8" long	85	375
Graf Zeppelin on Wheels, silver pull-toy bank, 1934, A.C. Williams, 7-3/4" long	150	475
Grandpa's Hat, top hat, 2-1/4" tall, 3-7/8" wide	225	450
Grenade with Pin, Bartlett Mayward, 4-1/4"	85	175

Indian with Tomahawk (Still Banks), Hubley, 1900s, $550.

Little Red Riding Hood Safe (Still Banks), J.M. Harper, 1907, $4000.

Still Banks (Continued)	C8	C10
Gunboat, blue hull, white top, twin masts, Kenton, 8-1/2" long	650	1800
Hall Clock, dark finish w/gold highlights, 1923, Arcade, 5-5/8" tall	300	700
Hall Clock, brown finish, paper face, 1900s, Hubley, 5-1/4" tall	275	475
Hall Clock with Cast Face, 1920s, Hubley, 5-3/26" tall	275	425
Hanging Mailbox, green, wall mount mailbox replica, gold lettering, 1920s, A.C. Williams, 5-1/8" tall	65	175
Hanging Mailbox on Platform, red box hangs on post in platform base, 1800s, 7-1/4" tall	650	1500
Hard Hat, white w/red lettering, 1970s, George Knerr, 1-15/16" tall	100	250
Harleysville Bank, white w/gray roof, 1959, Unicast Foundry, 2-5/8" tall, 5-1/4" long	75	225
Hen on Nest, bronze finish w/red highlights, 1900s, 3"	100	1750
High Rise Building, Kenton, 7" tall	200	550
High Rise, Tiered, Kenton, 5-3/4"	125	350
Hippo, bronze w/red highlights, 2" tall, 5-3/16" long	3500	6000
Holstein Cow, black finish, 1910s, Arcade, 2-1/2" tall, 4-5/8" long	125	650

Still Banks (Continued)	C8	C10
Home Bank, dark finish, 1890s, Judd, 4" x 3-1/2"	175	500
Home Bank with Crown, painted, "Home Bank", 1872, J. & E. Stevens, 5-1/4"	475	1400
Home Savings Bank, painted, 9-5/8" tall	175	650
Home Savings Bank, "Property of Peoples Savings Bank, Grand Rapids, Mich.", 10-1/2" painted	175	650
Home Savings Bank, painted, 1899, Shimer Toy, 5-7/8"	150	525
Home Savings Bank with Dog Finial, 1891, J. & E. Stevens, 5-3/4" tall	125	550
Home Savings Bank with Finial, mustard finish, 1891, J. & E. Stevens, 3-1/2" tall	125	375
Honey Bear, silver finish unpainted bear sits eating honey, 2-1/2"	675	1200
Hoover/Curtis Elephant "GOP", ivory finish, 1928, Hubley, 3-3/8"	675	1600
Horse on Tub, Decorated, 1920s, A.C. Williams, 5-5/6"	135	300
Horse, "Beauty", black w/raised letters on side, 1900s, Arcade, 4-1/8" x 4-3/4"	85	175
Horse, Prancing, black w/gray hooves, 1910s, Arcade, 4-1/4" tall	55	150

Still Banks (Continued)

	C8	C10
Horse, Prancing with Belly Band, light bronze finish, 4-1/2"	175	375
Horse, Prancing, Large, bronze finish, 1910s, A.C. Williams, 7-3/16" tall	75	165
Horse, Rearing on large rectangle base, gold bronze horse, on, 1929, Arcade, 7-1/4" x 6-3/4"	125	185
Horse, Rearing on Oval Base, 1920s, A.C. Williams, 5-1/8" x 4-7/8"	95	250
Horse, Rearing on Pebbled Base, gold finish, 7-1/4" x 6-1/2"	85	165
Horseshoe with Mesh, horse head inside horseshoe that forms end of mesh coin cage, bronze finish, A.C. Williams	65	145
Hot Point Electric Stove, white, on legs, 1925, Arcade, 6"	350	1250
House with Basement, painted, 1893, Ohio Foundry Co., 4-5/8" square	850	1800
House with Bay Window, painted, 1874, 5-5/8" tall	900	2200
House with Chimney Slot, painted, 2-7/8" x 2-13/16"	275	850
House with Knight, unpainted "Savings Bank" w/knight figure on roof peak, 7-1/4"	375	950
Hub, 1892, Magic Introduction, 5" x 5-1/4" x 1-5/8"	300	850
Humphrey-Muskie Donkey, pale silver finish, "Humphrey Muskie 68", 1968, 4-1/2" tall	10	35
Humpty Dumpty, painted, white egg, red brick wall, 1930s, 5-1/2" tall	375	850
Humpty Dumpty, Seated, painted, 1974, Edward K. Russel, 5-3/8" tall	75	125
Husky, 1910s, Grey Iron Casting, 5"	200	550
I Made Chicago Famous, Large Pig, 1902, J.M. Harper, 2-5/8" x 5-5/16"	250	550
I Made Chicago Famous, Small Pig, 1902, J.M. Harper, 2-1/8" x 4-1/8"	200	400
Ice Box, white, " Save For Ice", Arcade, 4-1/4" tall	175	650
Independence Hall, deep red/brown finish, Enterprise Mfg., 1875, Enterprise Mfg., 10" tall	450	1150
Independence Hall, mustard building on base w/bell tower, 1875, 8-1/8" tall, 15-1/2" long	1800	3500
Independence Hall Tower, 1876, Enterprise Mfg., 9-1/2"	225	525

Still Banks (Continued)

	C8	C10
Indian Chief Bust, unpainted, 1978, 4-7/8"	35	85
Indian Family, unpainted, 1905, J.M. Harper, 3-5/8" x 5-1/8"	850	2200
Indian Head Penny, 1972, George Knerr, 3-1/4" diam.	35	85
Indian Seated on Log, unpainted, 1970s, A. Ouve, 3-5/8" tall	85	150
Indian with Tomahawk, 1900s, Hubley, 5-7/8"	175	550
Indiana Paddle Wheeler, black w/red trim, 1896, 7-1/8" long	4000	8000
International Eagle on Globe, unpainted, 8" x 8"	1200	2800
Ironmaster's House, unpainted, 1884, Kyser & Rex, 4-1/2"	600	2200
Japanese Safe, 1882, Kyser & Rex, 5-3/8" tall	100	300
Japanese Safe, painted, 1883, Kyser & Rex, 5-1/2" tall	125	375
Jarmulowsky BuildingJarmulowsky Building, bronze finish building bank, J. & E. Stevens, 7-3/4" tall	1200	2800
Jewel Safe, unpainted, 1907, J. & E. Stevens, 5-3/8"	125	350
Junior Cash Register, Small, elaborate cast w/slot at top, 1920s, J. & E. Stevens, 5-1/4" x 4-5/8"	175	375
Kelvinator Bank, white w/grey trim replica refrigerator, No. 832, 1930s, Arcade, 4-1/2" tall	150	375
Key, silver finish skeleton key, 1905, W.J. Somerville, 5-1/2" long	250	650
Key, St. Louis World's Fair, dark finish, 1904, 5-3/4" long	275	700
King Midas, painted, 1930s, Hubley, 4-1/2" tall	1250	2500
Kitty Bank, painted, white body w/blue bow, 1930s, Hubley, 4-3/4" tall	65	150
Kodak Bank, "Kodak Banks", 1905, J. & E. Stevens, 4-1/4" tall, 5" wide	200	450
Labrador Retriever, black finish w/gold collar, 4-1/2"	125	375
Lamb, painted white w/black highlights, 1970, John Wright, 3-1/4" tall	35	75
Lamb, Small, painted white, 3-3/16"	200	375
Laughing Pig, painted, Hubley, 2-1/2"	125	275
Liberty Bell, 1905, J.M. Harper, 3-3/4"	275	550
Liberty Bell with Yoke, antique bronze finish, 1920s, Arcade, 3-1/2"	25	65

Mammy with Hands on Hips (Still Banks), Hubley, 1900s, $400.

Palace (Still Banks), Ives, 1885, $3500.

Still Banks (Continued)	C8	C10
Liberty Bell, Minniature, Penncraft, 3-1/2" x 1-3/4"	20	35
Lighthouse, "Light of the World", 1950s, Lane Art, 9-1/2" tall	125	250
L'il Tot, 1982, Bob Watkins, 5-7/8"	125	175
Limousine, black w/white rubber tires, 1920s, Arcade, 8-1/16" long	750	2500
Limousine, same as No. 1478, but w/steel wheels, 1921, Arcade	1200	2800
Limousine Yellow Cab, repaint of No. 1478, 1921, Arcade	1400	2800
Lincoln High Hat, black finish, "Pass Around the Hat", 1880s, 2-3/8" tall	125	225
Lion on Tub, Decorated, 1920s, A.C. Williams, 5-1/2" tall	125	225
Lion on Tub, Plain, bronze finish, 1920s, A.C. Williams, 7-1/2" tall	100	200
Lion on Tub, Small, brown or green finish, 1920s, A.C. Williams, 4-1/8" tall	85	175
Lion on Wheels, gold, 1920s, A.C. Williams, 4-1/2" x 5-1/2"	145	225
Lion, Ears Up, 1930s, A.C. Williams, 3-5/8" x 4-1/2"	75	125
Lion, Small, 1934, A.C. Williams, 2-1/2" x 3-5/8"	85	150
Lion, Tail Between Legs, 3" x 5-1/4"	85	145

Still Banks (Continued)	C8	C10
Lion, Tail Left, bronze finish, 1910s, Hubley, 3-3/4" tall	100	175
Lion, Tail Right, bronze finish, 1900s, A.C. Williams, 5-1/4" tall	55	150
Lion, Tail Right, 1900s, Arcade, 4" tall	55	100
Lion, tail Right, 1920s, A.C. Williams, 3-1/2" x 4-15/16"	55	100
Little Red Riding Hood Safe, painted, 1907, J.M. Harper, 5-1/16" tall	2000	4000
Log Cabin, painted, 1882, Kyser & Rex, 2-1/2" x 3-1/4"	175	425
Lost Dog, unpainted, 1890s, Judd, 5-3/8"	275	850
Lucky Cabin, painted w/horseshoe over door, 1970, John Wright, 4-1/8" tall	35	65
Mailbox on Legs, Large, green street corner box replica, 1920s, Hubley, 5-1/2" tall	85	225
Mailbox on Legs, Small, green replica street corner mailbox, 1928, Hubley, 3-3/4" tall	35	100
Main Street Trolley with People, bronze finish, 1920s, A.C. Williams, 3" x 6-3/4"	175	475
Main Street Trolley without People, 1920s, A.C. Williams, 6-3/4" long	175	400

Still Banks (Continued)

	C8	C10
Majestic Refrigerator Bank, in red, green or blue w/gold trim, replica of single door fridge on four legs, coin slot in back, w/key lock, 1930s, Arcade, 4-1/2" tall	375	600
Majestic Radio Bank, mahogany finish replica of a floor standing radio on four legs, coin slot in back, w/key, 1930s, Arcade, 4-1/2" tall	125	200
Mammy, doorstop conversion, red dress, white apron, 1970s, 8-1/4" tall	10	25
Mammy with Hands on Hips, red dress, white apron, 1900s, Hubley, 5-1/4" tall	85	400
Man in Barrel, painted, 1890s, J. & E. Stevens, 3-3/4" tall	175	550
Man on Cotton Bale, painted darkie sits on hay bale, red scarf, yellow pants, 1898, U.S. Hardware, 4-7/8" tall	1500	3500
Marietta Silo, gray finish, 5-1/2"	275	850
Marshall Stove, red, 3-7/8"	125	225
Mary & Little Lamb, painted white w/red trim, 1901, 4-3/8" tall	350	1500
Mascot, boy stands on baseball, 1914, Hubley, 5-3/4" tall	850	2400
McKinley/Teddy Elephant, bronze finish, 1900, 2-1/2" tall	650	2200
Mean Standing Bear, Hubley, 5-1/2"	100	225
Mellow Furnace, brown finish, Liberty Toy, 3-9/16" x 3-1/8"	125	225
Mermaid Boat, companion piece to Dolphin, girl in boat holds fish, 1900s, Grey Iron Casting, 4-1/2" tall	350	850
Merry-Go-Round, unpainted, 1920s, Grey Iron Casting, 4-5/8" tall	175	550
Metropolitan Bank, "Metropolitan Bank", 1872, J. & E. Stevens, 5-7/8"	125	275
Mickey Mouse, bookend bank, painted, 1970s, John Wright, 5" x 3-3/4"	85	150
Mickey Mouse, Hands on Hips, painted, 9" tall	125	450
Middy with Clapper, brown finish, 1887, 5-1/4"	150	350
Minuteman, painted, 1905, Hubley, 6" tall	200	650
Model T Ford, black, 1920s, Arcade, 4" tall	650	1250
Moody & Sankey, painted, two oval portraits on front, 1870, Smith & Egge, 5"	800	3500

Still Banks (Continued)

	C8	C10
Mosque, Large, Three-story, 1920s, A.C. Williams, 3-1/2" tall	45	125
Mosque, Small, Two-story, 2-7/8" tall	35	115
Mother Hubbard Safe, 1907, J.M. Harper, 4-1/2" tall	1500	5000
Mulligan Policeman (Keystone Cop), painted, 1900s, A.C. Williams, 5-3/4"	175	400
Multiplying Bank, painted building, 1883, J. & E. Stevens, 6-1/2"	700	3500
Mutt & Jeff, gold, 1900s, A.C. Williams, 4-1/4" x 3-1/2"	75	275
National Safe, heavy nickel plate, combination lock on front, 1929, Arcade, 4-3/4" x 3-3/4" x 3-1/2"	100	200
National Safe, unpainted, 1800s, J. & E. Stevens, 3-3/8" tall	65	125
Nest Egg, bronze finish egg on side, "Horace", 1873, Smith & Egge, 3-3/8" tall on base	450	850
Nesting Doves Safe, bronze finish, 1907, J.M. Harper, 5-1/4"	1500	3500
New Heatrola Bank, green finish w/red trim, 1920s, Kenton, 4-1/2" tall	85	375
Newfoundland Dog, blue or green finish, 1930s, Arcade, 3-5/8" x 5-3/8"	100	225
Newfoundland Dog with Pack, 4-11/16" tall	85	175
Nixe, silver boy in boat, "Nixe", 4-1/2" tall	350	1450
Nixon Bust, 1972, Charlotte Blevins, 5-5/16"	45	85
Nixon/Agnew Elephant, 1968, 2-5/8"	15	35
North Pole Bank, unpainted, "Save Your Casting Money And Freeze It", 1920s, Grey Iron Casting, 4-1/4"	375	775
Oak Stove, unpainted, 1899, Shimer Toy, 2-3/8" tall	125	475
Old Abe with Shield, Eagle, unpainted, 1880, 3-7/8"	450	1300
Old South Church, bronze finish, 10" tall	2000	5000
One Car Garage, painted, 1920s, A.C. Williams, 2-1/2"	125	350
One Story House, 1900s, Grey Iron Casting, 3" tall	65	175
Oregon Gunboat, blue hull, gray guns, black and red stacks, "Oregon", Kenton, 11" long	850	1800
Organ Grinder, painted, Hubley, 6-3/16" x 2-1/8"	125	350

Santa Claus with Tree (Still Banks), Hubley, 1910s, $950.

Rabbit Standing, Large (Still Banks), A.C. Williams, 1908, $325.

Minuteman (Still Banks), Hubley, 1905, $650.

Still Banks (Continued)	**C8**	**C10**
Oriental Boy on Pillow, painted, 1920s, Hubley, 5-1/2" tall	85	200
Oriental Camel, on rockers, 3-3/4" tall	300	875
Ornate Hall Clock, tan finish, paper face, 1900s, Hubley, 5-7/8" tall	200	425
Osborn Pig, "You can bank on the Osborn...", 2" x 4"	100	350
Oscar the Goat, black w/silver hooves and horns, 7-3/4" tall	75	175
Owl, painted, 1930, Vindex Toys, 4-1/4"	75	325
Owl on Stump, red, 3-5/8"	65	125
Ox, painted, Kenton, 4-3/8"	85	150
Palace, 1885, Ives, 8" wide, 7-1/2" tall	850	3500
Park Bank Building, 4-3/8" painted	450	2200
Parlor Stove, gray and black, 6-7/8"	275	425
Parrot on Stump, painted, 6-1/4"	125	450
Pavillion, 1880, Kyser & Rex, 3-1/8" x 3"	225	500
Pay Phone Bank, unpainted, 1926, J. & E. Stevens, 7-3/16"	450	1800

Still Banks (Continued)	**C8**	**C10**
Pearl Street Bank, unpainted, silver finish, 4-1/4"	350	1800
Pelican, painted white, 1930s, Hubley, 4-3/4"	350	1500
Penny Register Pail, unpainted, 1889, Kyser & Rex, 2-3/4"	125	250
Penthouse Building, silver finish, A.C. Williams, 5-7/8" tall	350	850
Peters Weatherbird, Arcade, 4-1/4" tall	750	2500
Phoenix Dime Register Trunk, steamer trunk, 1890, Piaget, 3-3/4" x 5"	125	250
Pig, black, 1929, Arcade, 4"	125	275
Pig, A Christmas Roast, 3-1/4" x 7-1/8"	85	250
Pig, Seated, 1900s, A.C. Williams, 3" x 4-9/16"	35	125
Plymouth Rock 1620, "1620", 3-7/8" long	650	1850
Polar Bear, Begging, white, 1900s, Arcade, 5-1/4"	275	450

Still Banks (Continued)	C8	C10
Policeman Bank, blue w/aluminum finish on gloves and star, gold buttons, black shoes, flesh face and hands, 1930s, Arcade, 5-5/8" tall	250	1000
Policeman Safe, 1907, J.M. Harper, 5-1/4"	1250	4500
Polish Rooster, painted, 5-1/2" tall	850	2200
Pooh Bank, 5" x 4-7/8"	5	15
Possum, silver finish, 1910s, Arcade, 2-3/8" tall, 4-3/8" long	125	575
Postal Savings Mailbox, 1920s, Nicol, 6-3/4"	85	275
Pot Bellied Stove, flat black finish, 1968, George Knerr, 5-3/4" tall	25	65
Potato, "Bank", 1897, Mary A. Martin, 5-1/4" long	850	1650
Presto Bank, silver finish, "Bank", 3-1/4" tall	65	150
Presto Bank, building, silver w/gold dome, 4-1/4" tall	85	175
Presto Bank, silver finish w/gold dome, 1900s, A.C. Williams, 3-5/8" tall	85	175
Presto Trick Bank, red doors and roof, 1892, Kyser & Rex, 4-1/2" tall	250	950
Professor Pug Frog Bank, 1900s, A.C. Williams, 3-1/4"	75	550
Pugdog, Seated, painted, 1889, Kyser & Rex, 3-1/2"	250	475
Puppo, painted bee on body, 1920s, Hubley, 4-7/8" tall	125	250
Puppo on Pillow, painted brown, cream, black, pink, 1920s, Hubley, 5-5/8" x 6"	150	275
Put Money in Thy Purse, change purse, black, 1886, 2-3/4" tall	625	950
Puzzle Try Me, safe, "Puzzle Try Me", 1868, 2-11/16" tall	475	975
Quadrafoil House, Several Makers, 1900s, 3-1/8" tall	125	225
Queen Stove, "Queen" on oven door, 1975, John Wright, 3-3/4" to cook top	25	65
Quilted Lion, bronze finish, 3-3/4" tall, 4-3/4" long	185	450
Rabbit Lying Down, unpainted, 2-1/8" x 5-1/8"	175	575
Rabbit Standing, Large, brown metal finish, 1908, A.C. Williams, 6-1/4" tall	125	325

Still Banks (Continued)	C8	C10
Rabbit with Carrot, painted white, orange and green carrot, 1972, George Knerr, 3-3/8"	85	200
Rabbit, Begging, 1900s, A.C. Williams, 5-1/8"	85	275
Rabbit, Large Seated, painted white w/pink highlights, 1900s, Hubley, 4-5/8" tall	125	375
Rabbit, Small, Seated, gold bronze, 1910s, Arcade, 3-5/8" tall	125	325
Radio Bank, metallic blue, 1928, Hubley, 3-5/16" tall	100	375
Radio Bank with Three Dials, red, 1920s, Kenton, 3" tall, 4-5/8" long	100	350
Radio with Combination Door, metal sides and back, 1930s, Kenton, 4-1/2" red	125	375
Reclining Cow, black, 2-1/8" tall, 4" long	100	400
Recording Bank, 6-5/8" x 4-1/4"	200	575
Red Ball Safe, red ball on base, 3"	175	425
Red Goose Shoes on Base, on pedestal w/base, 1920s, Arcade, 5-1/2"	300	750
Red Goose Shoes on Pedestal, red goose on bronze base, 4-7/16"	175	350
Red Goose Shoes, Squatty, red body, yellow feet, 1920s, Arcade, 4" tall	275	500
Reindeer Bank, red, green, or blue, 1929, Arcade, 6-1/4"h x 6-3/4"l	125	175
Reindeer on Base, 1973, John Wright, 10" x 8"	75	125
Reindeer, Large, bronze finish, 1900s, A.C. Williams, 9-1/2" tall	125	250
Reindeer, Small, bronze finish, A.C. Williams, 6-1/4" tall	75	150
Republic Pig, painted pig in business suit, 1970s, Wilton Products, 7" tall	35	85
Rhesus Monkey, converted doorstop, painted, 8-1/2"	35	125
Rhino, gold, 1910s, Arcade, 2-5/8" tall, 5" long	225	650
Rochester Clock, w/working clock, 5" tall	225	750
Rocking Chair, brown finish, 1898, C.J. Manning, 6-3/4" tall	1500	2750
Rocking Horse, white w/red saddle, "SBCC", 1975, George Knerr, 5-5/8"	350	550
Roller Safe, 1882, Kyser & Rex, 3-11/16" x 2-7/8"	125	245

Rabbit Lying Down (Still Banks), $575.

Tower Bank (Still Banks), Kyser & Rex, 1890, $2200.

Still Banks (Continued)	**C8**	**C10**
Roof Bank, 1887, J. & E. Stevens, 5-1/4" x 3-3/4"	125	450
Roof Bank, 1900s, Grey Iron Casting, 5-1/4"	125	300
Rooster, brown finish, w/red comb and wattle, 1910s, Hubley/Williams, 4-3/4"	125	350
Rooster, black w/red comb, 1910s, Arcade, 4-3/4"	125	400
Rooster, Large, unpainted except for red comb and wattle, 1913, 6-3/4"	550	1250
Rumplestiltskin, 1910s, 6" x 2-1/4"	200	500
Saddle Horse, 1928, Grey Iron Casting, 4-3/8" tall	375	650
Safe Deposit, "Safe Deposit", 1899, Shimer Toy, 3-5/8"	85	150
Safety Locomotive, gray, 1887, 3-1/4" tall	650	2200
Sailor, Medium, 1910s, Hubley, 5-1/4" tall	225	475
San Gabriel Mission, painted, musical building, 4-5/8" x 3-3/4"	2000	7500

Still Banks (Continued)	**C8**	**C10**
Santa Claus, painted w/arms folded in front, 1900s, Hubley, 5-3/4"	450	950
Santa Claus with Tree, w/arms folded in front, tree at back, painted, 1910s, Hubley, 5-3/4"	450	950
Santa with Wire Tree, w/removable ornate tree, 1890s, Ives, 7-1/4" tall	875	1500
Scottie, Seated, black finish, red collar, 1930s, Hubley, 4-7/8" x 6"	125	300
Scrollwork Safe, 1900s, 2-3/4" tall	85	225
Seal on Rock, black, 1900s, Arcade, 3-1/2"	175	500
Security Safe, red door, 1894, 4-1/2" tall	125	275
Security Safe Deposit, 1881, 3-7/8" tall	95	150
Shell Out, conch shell on base, off white, 1882, J. & E. Stevens, 4-3/4" long	225	700
Show Horse, 1973, Lane Art, 5-7/8" tall	75	150

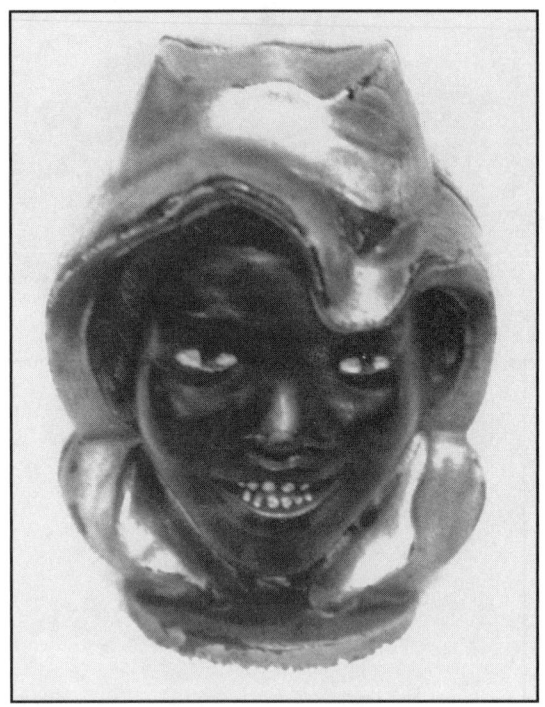

Two-Faced Black Boy, Large (Still Banks), A.C. Williams, 1900s, $350.

Pay Phone (Still Banks), J. & E. Stevens, 1926, $1800.

Still Banks (Continued)	**C8**	**C10**
Six-Sided Building, unpainted, 2-3/8" tall	225	650
Six-Sided Building, Two Story, 3-3/8" tall	100	275
Skyscraper Bank, silver building, four gold posts, 1900s, A.C. Williams, 5-1/2" tall	85	150
Skyscraper Bank, silver building, four gold posts, 1900s, A.C. Williams, 4-3/8" tall	85	125
Skyscraper with Six Posts, silver building, gold posts, 1900s, A.C. Williams, 6-1/2" tall	125	450
Songbird on Stump, bronze finish, 1900s, A.C. Williams, 4-3/4"	300	800
Space Heater with Bird, English, 1890s, Chamberlain & Hill, 6-1/2" tall	175	375
Space Heater with Flowers, English, Far East motif, red finish, 1890s, 6-1/2" tall	175	375
Spaniel, large, painted, 1960s, John Wright, 10-1/2" long	65	125
Spitz, bronze finish, 1928, Grey Iron Casting, 4-1/4"	225	575
Squirrel with Nut, 4-1/8"	425	1250

Still Banks (Continued)	**C8**	**C10**
St. Bernard with Pack, Large, 1900s, A.C. Williams, 5-1/2" x 7-3/4"	125	225
St. Bernard with Pack, Small, 1900s, A.C. Williams, 3-3/4" x 5-1/2"	85	175
Star Safe, 1882, Kyser & Rex, 2-5/8" tall	150	450
State Bank, bronze building bank, 1890s, Kyser & Rex, 5-1/2" tall	125	325
State Bank, bronze finish, 1910s, Arcade, 4-1/8" tall	85	175
State Bank, unpainted building bank, 1890s, Kenton, 3" tall	95	200
State Bank, 1900, Kenton, 8" x 7"	550	1200
State Safe, heavy nickel plate, 1929, Arcade, 4" x 3" x 2-1/2"	85	165
Statue of Liberty, A.C. Williams, 6-3/8" tall	85	125
Statue of Liberty, 1900s, Kenton, 6-1/16" tall	85	125
Statue of Liberty, silver finish w/gold highlights, 1900s, Kenton, 6-3/8" tall	100	175
Statue of Liberty, Large, silver gray finish, gold highlights, 1900s, Kenton, 9-1/2" tall	350	1200

Three Wise Monkeys (Still Banks), A.C. Williams, 1900s, $550.

Pavillion (Still Banks), Kyser & Rex, 1880, $500.

Still Banks (Continued)	C8	C10
Steamboat, brown finish, 1900s, A.C. Williams, 7-5/8" long	125	375
Steamboat with Small Wheels, silver finish, Kenton, 7-7/16" long	175	425
Stop Sign, green w/red and gold highlights, 1920, Dent, 5-5/8" tall	325	1450
Stork Safe, 1907, J.M. Harper, 5-1/2"	850	1750
Street Car, painted, 1891, Grey Iron Casting, 4-1/2" long	250	650
Sun Dial, 1900s, Arcade, 4-5/16" tall	650	2200
Sunbonnet Sue, painted, 1970, 7-1/2"	65	165
Tabernacle Savings, unpainted, Keyless Lock Co., 2-1/4" x 5"	850	1250
Taft-Sherman Bust, one side Smiling Jim, other side Peaceful Bill, 1908, J.M. Harper, 4" tall	1000	2000
Tank Bank 1918, Large, gold finish, 1920s, A.C. Williams, 3" tall x 3-11/16" long	100	200
Tank Bank 1918, Small, gold finish, 1920s, A.C. Williams, 2-3/8" long	65	150
Tank Bank 1919, silver finish, "1919", 3" x 5-1/2"	125	350
Tank Savings Bank, "Tank Savings Bank", 1919, Ferrosteel, 9-1/2" long	175	525
Teddy Bear, 1900, Arcade, 2-1/2" x 3-7/8"	125	350

Still Banks (Continued)	C8	C10
Teddy Bear, gold bronze, 1929, Arcade, 4" x 2-1/2"	100	275
Teddy Roosevelt Bust, 1919, A.C. Williams, 5" tall	175	450
Templetone Radio, red, 1930s, Arcade, 4-1/2"	275	650
Thoroughbred, bronze finish, 1946, Hubley, 5-1/4"	75	150
Three Wise Monkeys, 1900s, A.C. Williams, 3-1/4" tall, 3-1/2" wide	225	550
Time Is Money Clock Bank, alarm clock shaped, gold finish, "Time Is Money", 1910s, A.C. Williams, 3-1/2" tall	125	200
Time Safe, unpainted, E.M. Roche Co., 7" tall, 3-3/4" wide	375	750
Tower, unpainted, 1915, Kenton, 4-1/8"	175	375
Tower Bank, unpainted, brown finish, J.M. Harper, 1900s, J.M. Harper, 9-1/4" tall	175	375
Tower Bank, building w/tower rising from roof, "Tower Bank 1890", 1890, Kyser & Rex, 6-7/8"	1200	2200
Town Hall Bank, red, "Town Hall Bank", 1882, Kyser & Rex, 4-5/8"	375	950
Toy Soldier, painted, "SBCCA", 1982, Laverne A. Worley, 7-1/2" tall	15	65
Treasure Chest, smaller version is No. 928, 1970, John Wright, 2-3/4" x 4"	60	135

Rooster (Still Banks), Arcade, 1910s, $400.

Sailor, Medium (Still Banks), Hubley, 1910s, $475.

Still Banks (Continued)	**C8**	**C10**
Triangular Building, "Bank", 1914, Hubley, 6" tall	325	675
Trick Buffalo, black, 5-1/2" tall	750	1500
Trolley Car, painted, silver, 1900s, Kenton, 5-1/4" long	225	650
Trunk on Dolly, 1890, Piaget, 2-5/8" x 3-9/16"	175	350
Trust Bank, 1800s, J. & E. Stevens, 7-1/4"	1800	3500
Tug Boat, red, pull toy, 5-1/2" long	4500	7500
Turkey, Large, painted wattle, 1900s, A.C. Williams, 4-1/4" x 4"	250	550
Turkey, Small, red head and wattle, 1900s, A.C. Williams, 3-3/8" tall	150	275
Turtle Bank, 1" tall, 3-7/16" long	2000	3500
Two Car Garage, painted, 1920s, A.C. Williams, 2-1/2"	125	350
Two Goats Butting, two goats on tree stump, "Two Kids" on base, J.M. Harper, 4-1/2"	950	2000
Two Story House, brown finish w/red roof, 1930s, A.C. Williams, 3-1/16" tall	75	150
Two-Faced Black Boy, Large, 1900s, A.C. Williams, 4-1/8" tall	125	350
Two-Faced Black Boy, Small, 1900s, A.C. Williams, 3-1/8" x 2-3/4"	85	300

Still Banks (Continued)	**C8**	**C10**
Two-Faced Devil, deep red, 1904, A.C. Williams, 4-1/4" tall	550	1250
Two-Faced Indian, bronze finish w/painted highlights, 1900s, A.C. Williams, 4-5/16" tall	1500	2750
U.S. Bank, Eagle Finial, x green w/gold trim, 1890s, 4-5/16" tall	850	1500
U.S. Mail, silver gray w/red lettering, 1900s, Kenton, 4-3/4" tall	100	375
U.S. Mail, red and green, trimmed in gold, 1929, Arcade, 3-1/2" x 2-3/4" x 1-3/4"	150	300
U.S. Mail Bank with Combination Lock, silver gray w/red lettering, 1903, O.B. Fish, 6-7/8" tall	225	775
U.S. Mail with Eagle, 1930s, Kenton, 4-1/8" x 3-1/2"	85	175
U.S. Mail with Eagle, 1906, Hubley, 4" x 4"	175	325
U.S. Mail, Small, silver or green mail box w/red lettering, 1900s, Kenton, 3-5/8" x 2-3/4"	75	150
U.S. Navy Akron Zeppelin, silver finish, "US Navy Akron", 1930, A.C. Williams, 6-5/8" long	175	500
U.S. Treasury Bank, painted, 1920s, Grey Iron Casting, 3-1/4"	250	475

Yellow Cab (Still Banks), Arcade, 1921, $2400.

World's Fair Administration Building (Still Banks), 1893, $2250.

Still Banks (Continued)	C8	C10
Ulysses S. Grant Bust, 1976, 5-1/2" tall ..	125	250
Ulysses S. Grant Bust on Safe, 1903, J.M. Harper, 5-5/8" tall	1750	3000
Uncle Sam Hat, red, white and blue, George Knerr, 2" x 3"	125	350
United Banking and Trust, Building Bank, bronze finish, A.C. Williams, 3" tall	225	450
Victorian House, unpainted deep gray finish, 1892, J. & E. Stevens, 4-1/2" ...	175	375
Victorian House, gray metallic finish, 3-1/4" tall	150	275
Villa, unpainted except for red finial, 1894, Kyser & Rex, 5-9/16"	375	850
Villa Bank, "1882", 1882, Kyser & Rex, 3-7/8" x 3-3/8"	375	700
Vindex Bulldog, painted, "Vindex Toys", 1931, Vindex Toys, 5-1/4" tall	125	275
Washington Bell with Yoke, red, 1932, Grey Iron Casting, 2-3/4"	125	325
Washington Monument, 1900s, A.C. Williams, 6" tall	150	325
Washington, George, Bust, bronze finish, 1920s, Grey Iron Casting, 8" tall	850	1450
Watch Dog Safe, w/brass handle, dog stands guard on front, 5-1/8"	1850	4000
Water Spaniel with Pack (I Hear a Call), 1900, J.M. Harper, 5-3/8" x 7-7/8"	225	450

Still Banks (Continued)	C8	C10
Weaver Hen, white w/red comb and wattle, "Weaver", 1970s, 6"	20	50
Westside Presbyterian Church, silver finish, 1916, 3-3/4" x 3-5/8"	350	950
Whale of a Bank, "A Whale of a Bank", 1975, George Knerr, 2-3/4" x 5-3/16"	85	200
Whippet on Base, gold finish, 3-1/2" tall	75	125
White City Barrel No. 1 on Cart, unpainted, "White City Puzzle Savings Bank, A Barrel of Money", 1894, Nicol, 5" long	275	475
White City Barrel, Large, silver finish barrel, 1893, Nicol, 5-1/8" tall	175	275
White City Pail, silver finish pail w/handle, 1893, Nicol, 2-5/8" tall	125	225
White City Puzzle Safe No. 10, unpainted, 1893, Nicol, 4-5/8"	125	225
White City Puzzle Safe No. 12, unpainted, 1893, Nicol, 4-7/8"	150	325
White Horse on Base, 1973, George Knerr, 9-1/2" tall	125	225
Wirehaired Terrier, painted, 1920s, Hubley, 4-5/8"	125	275
Wisconsin Beggar Boy, "Help the Crippled Children of Wisconsin", 6-7/8" tall	525	900

Still Banks (Continued)

	C8	C10
Wise Pig, The, painted off-white pig holding plaque, 1930s, Hubley, 6-5/8" tall	85	225
Woolworth Building, 1915, Kenton, 5-3/4" x 1-1/4"	85	150
Woolworth Building, bronze finish, 1915, Kenton, 7-7/8" tall	100	225
Work Horse on Base, painted white, 9" tall	75	125
Work Horse with Flynet, 1910s, Arcade, 4" tall	300	800
World's Fair Administration Building, painted, 1893, 6" x 6"	1400	2250
Yellow Cab, orange and black, rubber tires, 1921, Arcade, 7-7/8" long	1500	2400
York Stove, unpainted, "York Stove", Abendorth Brothers, 4" tall	225	525
Young America, Kyser & Rex, 1882, Kyser & Rex, 4-3/8" x 3-1/8" safe	125	275

Woolworth Building (Still Banks), Kenton, 1915, $225.

BATTERY-OPERATED TOYS

The words "Made in Japan" are the words toy collectors look for in their pursuit of high-quality mechanical tin toys.

Before World War II, these same words were synonymous with cheap, poor quality, drab-looking toys made from recycled materials and ideas. Most of the toys were people-animal-oriented with less emphasis on vehicle, nautical, or aircraft-type toys. They were powered by a spring or a flywheel and didn't last very long or do very much as far as play-value goes. These inexpensive, poor-quality toys kept Japan a third-rate toy-manufacturing nation until after World War II, when Japan's surrender resulted in economic chaos for this industrial nation.

In their quest for economic recovery and to compete in a toy market already dominated by Germany and America, the Japanese knew they had to come up with a new, different and exciting type of toy that would be more desirable than those produced by their competitors.

The Japanese toy designers concentrated their technology on a different type of toy operation. Not satisfied with the limited action and short duration of spring-driven or flywheel propelled toys, the toy engineers developed a small electric motor powered by flashlight batteries. This mini-motor took up less room than other mechanisms, had a longer-running duration, and enabled the toy to perform more functions. This development opened up an entirely new dimension in toy design—it introduced the concept of the battery-operated toy.

The toy designers integrated this new concept into hundreds of automaton-like toys, capable of as many as eight different types of actions in one cycle. These unique toys were an instant hit with the foreign market, especially the United States. These clever, unusual, and high-quality toys made Japan the dominant toy producer and exporter for the next twenty to thirty years.

It should be noted that Japan flooded the market with these ingenious, well-made toys while quality control remained a high priority. These merits were not only apparent in their figural toys, but also in their vehicle line. The Japanese toy makers concentrated on very fine detail and quality, especially in their scale-model passenger cars. Their ultimate goal was to produce toys that looked like the real thing. They succeeded. Their workmanship carried over into their other vehicle lines—motorcycles; emergency and construction vehicles, and novelty (silly) and comic character cars; trucks; and space toys.

No other nation was able to equal (much less surpass) the impetus and determination of the Japanese toy makers until Japan relinquished its domination by redirecting its economy.

Now that they are approaching middle age, it is no wonder that these fine toys remain in great demand today and often command a very high price.

The value of a battery-operated toy depends not only on its desirability, rarity, and complexity, but also very much on its condition. A toy in Mint condition is generally worth twice as much as a toy in Good condition. A toy in Very Good condition will be priced about halfway between Good and Mint.

C-10: Mint. A Mint toy is in the condition in which it was originally issued (perfect) regardless of age. It will also be in perfect mechanical condition, complete with all accessory parts when applicable, and will look brand new. The cloth or fur (plush) covering on some battery toys may reveal some discoloration (yellowing) due to age, but this should not affect its value as a Mint toy as long as it is clean. All toys in this category must be in perfect working condition. The original box in Mint condition will significantly enhance the value.

C-8: Very Good. A battery toy that has seen some use and is starting to show its age is described as Very Good. It will still be in perfect working order, and have all its accessory parts when applicable. It will have some age soiling, but will have no rust or corrosion. Overall, it will have an appearance of freshness and still be highly desirable to the fussy collector.

C-6: Good. The term Good applies to a battery toy that has seen some considerable use, wear and tear, and some age soiling, but is still in perfect working condition with no missing parts or accessories. The wet toys might show some slight surface rust that can be easily removed. A toy in Good condition is still a welcome addition to any toy collection, but will be targeted for upgrading by a piece in better condition.

Any battery toy below the condition of Good will reflect a drastic reduction in value. Toys in good shape, but missing parts, will not lose as much value as those that are severely rusted, corroded, painted over, have parts broken off, or are totally inoperable. These toys in Poor condition are usually collected for their scrap value by the toy repairer and seldom are they worth more than $10.

The key to grading is to use common sense and avoid wishful thinking. Grading the condition of a toy may be difficult at times, and consulting with an expert in the field can help dispel doubts about your judgment or your purchase. (See Collectors & Dealers for more information.)

To keep it in Excellent condition, your prized battery toy needs some tender loving care. If it stops working, you could have frustration, if not a disaster on your hands. The following suggestions should be of some help in avoiding this.

Battery toys, like other mechanical toys, should be operated periodically to keep them loosened up. A lightweight spray lubrication now and then will help considerably if the mechanism is accessible. Do not over lubricate as the excess might stain any cloth or fur covering on the toy.

A quality car wax or polish will keep the lithographed and bare metal parts looking like new, especially on the "wet" toys. Always test an obscure lithographed area to make sure the polish doesn't soften or dissolve the paint. Care should be exercised when polishing metal parts adjoining any cloth or plush covering, as the cleaning substance might stain the coverings. Light surface rust usually disappears with a careful polishing. Nothing can be done for deep rust or corrosion without further ruining the value of the toy. Repainting will only further reduce the value and is not recommended.

Should your battery toy fail to operate, the following steps might be helpful.

1. Make sure it not gunked-up and that no moving parts are binding.

2. Make sure the battery contacts are not dirty or corroded. If they are, clean them with crocus cloth.

Always use fresh batteries!

3. Lightly tap the toy with your finger or **lightly** nudge one of the moving parts while the switch is in the "on" position.

If none of the above steps work, then your toy needs major surgery. This means the toy must be completely torn down, repaired, and reassembled. Most battery toys are repairable as long as they have not been destructively tampered with and no parts are missing or corroded beyond repair. This job is best left to an expert in toy repair, and should never be attempted by one who doesn't know what he or she is doing. Expert repairs will not affect the value of a battery toy as long as the repair is undetectable and the toy looks and functions exactly as it did before the repair. Such repairs are acceptable in toy collecting circles. Expert repairs are expensive, but well worth the investment if it means the difference between a highly-prized Mint toy and one below the grade of Good. An inoperable toy is practically worthless, regardless of condition.

Contributor: Leo Rishty may be reached c/o O'Brien's Collecting Toys, Krause Publications, 700 E. State St., IOLA, WI 54990.

	C6	C8	C10
007 Aston-Martin, includes eject-able passenger, eight actions, Gilbert Co., 1966, 11-1/2" long	210	315	420
007 Secret Agent's Car, (Impala), five actions, Spesco Co. (Joy Toy), 1960s, 15" long	170	255	340
4 Prop Airplane, four actions, Waco Co., 1960s, 17" long, 16-1/4" wingspan	140	210	280
A-B-C Fairy Train, one piece, four actions, MT Co., 1950s, 14-1/2" long	80	95	160
Accordion Bear, six actions, "Y" Co., 1950s, 10-1/2" tall	250	375	500
Accordion Bear, (Flare Toy), five actions, MST Co., 1950s, 9-1/4" high	175	250	350
Accordion Player Bunny, six actions, Alps Co., 1950s, 12" tall, 9" long	250	350	500

	C6	C8	C10
Accordion Player Hobo, with Baby Monkey Playing Cymbals, six actions, Alps Co., 1950s	300	450	600
Acro Chimp Porter, minor toy, Y-M Co., 1960s, 8-1/2" tall	50	75	100
Acrobat Clown, minor toy, Y-M Co., 1960s, 9" tall	60	90	120
Acrobat Robot, three actions, S-H Co., 1970s, 4-1/2" tall	225	338	450
Air Cargo Prop-Jet Airplane, Sea-board World Airlines, five actions, Marx Co., 1960s, 12" long, 14-1/2" wingspan	150	300	425
Air Control Tower, includes detach-able airplane and helicopter, four actions, Bandai Co., 1960s, 11" high, 37" span extended	210	315	450
Air Defense Pom-Pom Gun, five actions, Linemar Co., 1950s, 14" long	115	175	260

	C6	C8	C10
Air Taxi Helicopter, three actions, Haji Co., 1960s	50	75	100
Aircraft Carrier, six actions, Marx Co., 1950s, 20" long	325	500	750
Aircraft Carrier, eight actions, Marx Co., 1950s, 20" long	200	300	400
Aircraft Carrier Forrestal, includes detachable plastic airplane, three actions, Linemar, 1950s, 13-3/4" long	200	300	400
Airport Saucer, four actions, MT Co., 1960s, 8" diameter	100	150	200
Airport Saucer, four actions, S-T Co., 1960s, 9" diameter	100	150	200
All Stars Mr. Baseball Jr., includes eight plastic balls, three actions, rare, K Co., 1950s	500	750	1000
Alley the Exciting New Roaring Stalking Alligator, five actions, Marx Co., 1960s, 17-1/2" long	150	225	300
American Airlines 4 Prop Airliner, four actions, Waco Co., 1960s, 12" long, 16-1/2" wingspan	125	200	250
American Airlines Airliner DC-7, seven actions, Linemar Co., 1960s, 17-1/2" long, 19" wingspan	200	325	450
American Airlines Airliner DC-7 Multiaction, seven actions, Yonezawa Co., 1960s, 21" long, 23-1/2" wingspan	195	285	380
American Airlines DC-7, w/automatic turnover propellers, seven actions, Linemar, c. 1950s, 19" wingspan	250	350	475
American Airlines Electra, , Linemar Co., 1950s, 18" long, 19-1/2" wingspan	175	300	450
American Airlines Flagship Caroline, three actions, Linemar Co., 1950s, 18" long, 19-1/2" wingspan	175	300	400
American Circus Television Truck, includes detachable metal antenna, six actions, rare, Exelo Co., 1950s, 9-1/4" long	600	900	1200
Amphibian Navy Patrol Plane, w/flashing lights, five actions, rare, Alps Co., 1950s, 13" long, 15" wingspan	900	1350	1800
Amtrak Locomotive, minor toy, ST Co., 1960s, 16" long	60	90	120

	C6	C8	C10
Andy Gard Brink's Armored Car-Bank, minor toy, General Molds & Plastics Corp., 1950s, 6-3/4" long	40	60	80
Andy Gard Combat Knight, includes lance, stanchion, three plastic rings, and helmet plume, three actions, General Molds & Plastics Corp., 1960s, 10-1/4" high	50	75	100
Animated Santa on Rotating Globe, five actions, HTC Co., 1950s, 15" high	400	600	800
Animated Squirrel, eight actions, rare, S&E Co., 1950s, 8-1/2" tall	150	225	300
Answer Game Machine Robot, educational toy, eight actions, Ichida Co., 1960s, 14-1/2" tall	400	600	800
Anti-Aircraft Jeep, five actions, K Co., 1950s, 9-1/2" long	100	150	200
Anti-Aircraft Jeep, includes detachable tin radar antenna, six actions, TN Co., 1950s, 11" long	250	375	500
Anti-Aircraft Unit, three electrical actions and three manual actions, Linemar Co., 1950s, 12-1/2" long	150	225	300
Antique Gooney Car, four actions, Alps Co., 1960s, 9" long	100	125	150
Apollo II-American Eagle Lunar Module, includes detachable plastic antenna, seven actions, DSK Co., 1960s, 10" high	250	350	450
Apollo Lunar Module, mostly plastic, four actions, DSK Co., 1970s, 6" high	170	205	240
Apollo Space Ship USA NASA, four actions, MT Co., 1960s, 9" long	100	125	150
Apollo Spacecraft, includes detachable astronaut, four actions, MT Co., 1960s, 10" long	200	300	400
Apollo Super Space Capsule, five actions, S-H Co., 1960s, 9" high	100	150	200
Apollo-X Moon Challenger Rocket, six actions, TN Co., 1960s, 16" long	150	225	300
Armored Attack Set, includes fifteen 2" plastic figures, Marx Co., 1960s, jeep 6-1/4" long and tank 5-1/4" long	150	225	300

Amphibian Navy Patrol Plane, Alps Co., 1950s, $1800. Photo courtesy Don Hultzman and Ron Chojnacki

Atom Rocket 7, M-T Co., 1950s, $250. Photo courtesy Don Hultzman and Ron Chojnacki

	C6	C8	C10
Army Helicopter, Huey by Bell, six actions, TN Co., 1960s, 10-1/2" long	100	150	200
Army Radio Jeep J1490, four actions, Linemar Co., 1950s, 7-1/4" long	75	125	165
Arthur A-Go-Go, includes detachable cymbals and drum set, six actions, Alps Co., 1960s, 10" high	130	200	295
Astro Captain, three actions, rare, Daiya Co., 1960s, 6-1/2" tall	300	450	600
Astro Dog, (looks like Snoopy), two cycles, five actions, "Y" Co., 1960s, 11" high	100	150	200
Astro Dog, three actions, Y-M Co., 1960s, 11" tall	90	135	180
Astrobase, motorized, six actions, Ideal Co., 1960s, 20" high	150	225	300
Atom Motorcycle, five actions, MT Co., 1950s, 11-3/4" long	500	750	1000
Atom Rocket 7, vehicle with fins, four actions, MT Co., 1950s, 9-1/2" long	150	200	250
Atomic Boat, minor toy, Famus Co., 1950s, 15" long	150	225	300
Atomic Fighter Robot, five actions, S-H Co., 1950s, 11" tall	150	200	250

	C6	C8	C10
Atomic Rocket X-1800, three actions, MT Co., 1960s, 9" long	150	225	300
Attacking Martian Robot, seven actions, two cycles, S-H Co., 1950s, 11-1/2" tall	200	250	300
Automated Santa, three actions, Santa Creations Co., c. 1960s, 10-1/4" tall	100	150	200
Automatic Toll Gate, includes 8" tin Valiant, six actions, Sears, 1955, 16" x 17" base	150	225	300
Auto-Top Ferrari Convertible, three actions, Bandai Co., 1960s, 11" long	550	750	1000
B-58 Hustler Jet, four actions, Marx Co., 1950s, 21" long, 12" wingspan	425	650	925
Baby Carriage, includes plastic baby bottle to activate switch, minor toy, TN Co., 1950s, 11-3/4" long, 7" high	60	90	120
Ball Blowing Clown, w/ball, three actions, TN Co., 1950s, 11" tall	200	300	400
Ball Playing Bear, includes five celluloid balls and one umbrella, no marking, six actions, rare, 1940s, 10-1/2" tall	200	300	400
Ball Playing Dog, three actions, Linemar Co., 1950s, 9" high	150	250	300

Arthur A-Go-Go, Alps Co., 1960s, $295.

Bubble Blowing Monkey, Alps Co., 1950s, $225. Photo courtesy Don Hultzman and Ron Chojnacki

	C6	C8	C10
Balloon Blowing Monkey, five actions, w/balloon, Alps Co., 1950s, 11-1/8" tall	150	200	250
Balloon Blowing Teddy Bear, six actions, w/balloon, Alps Co., 1950s, 11-1/8" tall	150	200	250
Balloon Vendor, includes four plastic balloons and tin tray, four actions, "Y" Co., 1960s, 12" tall	150	200	300
Baragon, (Godzilla), three actions, Bullmark Co., 1960s, 10" tall	290	435	580
Barber Bear, five actions, TN Co., 1950s, 9-1/2" tall	300	400	500
Barking Boxer Dog, minor toy, Marx, 1950s, 7" long	45	65	85
Barking Dog, four actions, two cycles, STS Co., 1950s, 7" long, 7" high	50	75	100
Barking Spaniel Dog, minor toy, Marx, 1950s, 7" long	50	75	100
Barney Bear Drummer, five actions, resembles Steiff bear, Alps Co., 1950s, 11" tall	130	195	260
Barnyard Rooster, five actions, Marx, 1950s, 10" high	100	150	200

	C6	C8	C10
Bartender, six actions, TN Co., 1960s, 11-1/2" tall	50	75	100
Batmobile, 1972 National Periodical Publications, three actions, ASC Co., 12" long	250	350	450
Battery Locomotive, three actions, TN Co., 1950s, 10" long	40	60	75
Bear Chef, (Cutey Cook), includes chef hat and tin litho egg, five actions, "Y" Co., 1960s, 9-1/2" tall	200	300	375
Bear Target Game, includes gun, rubber-tipped darts, detachable drum, four actions, MT Co., 1950s, 8-3/4" high and 4" x 5" base	200	300	400
Bear the Cashier, five actions, MT Co., 1950s, 7-1/2" high	200	300	400
Bear the Magician, nine actions, rare, MTS Co., 1950s, 12-1/2" tall	1500	2000	2500
Beauty Parlor Bear, seven actions, rare, S&E Co., 1950s, 9-1/2" high	700	1000	1200
Begging Pubby, six actions, "Y" Co., 1960s, 9" long	40	60	80

Barber Bear, T-N Co., 1950s, $500. Photo courtesy Don Hultzman and Ron Chojnacki

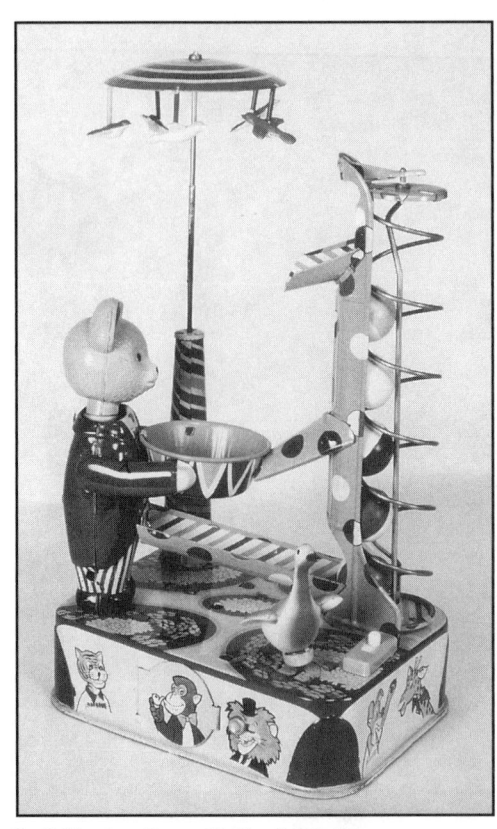

Ball Playing Bear, 1940s, $400. Photo courtesy Don Hultzman and Ron Chojnacki

Beauty Parlor Bear, S&E Co., 1950s, $1200. Photo courtesy Don Hultzman and Ron Chojnacki

Bartender, T-N Co., 1960s, $100.

	C6	C8	C10
Bengali the Exciting New Growling, Prowling Tiger, Linemar Division, from nose to end of tail, three actions, two cycles, Marx Co., 1961, 18-1/2" long	150	250	300
Big Dipper, includes three tin cars, minor toy, Technofix Co., 1960s, 21" long, 11" high	100	150	200
Big Hunter Automatic Gun, three actions, Tada Co., 1950s, 21" long extended	50	75	100
Big John, three actions, Alps Co., 1960s, 12" high	60	90	120
Big John the Indian Chief, five actions, TN Co., c. 1960s, 12-1/2" tall	150	200	250
Big Loo Your Friend from the Moon, includes ball, darts, compass, etc., twelve actions, Marx Co., 1960s, 38" tall	1250	1750	2500
Big Max Robot, four actions, Remco Co., 1958, 8" long, 7" tall	80	125	175
Big Parade, The, includes detachable gun and baton, four actions, Marx Co., 1963, 11-1/2" tall, 15" wide	120	180	240
Big Ring Circus Truck, three actions, MT Co., 1950s, 13" long	140	210	280
Big Shot Cadillac, four actions, rare, TN Co., 1950s, 10" long	200	300	400
Big Wheel Coca Cola Truck, three actions, Taiyo Co., 1970s	100	150	200
Big Wheel Family Camper, three actions, 1970s, 10" long	60	90	120
Big Wheel Ice Cream Truck, three actions, 1970s, 10" long	60	90	120
Biller Train, includes rubber cable track and two hopper cars, a minor toy, rare, TN Co., 1950s, 13" long	70	105	140
Billy Blastoff Space Scout, four actions, Eldon Co., 1960s, 16" long	100	150	200
Billy the Kid Sheriff, four actions, two cycles, "Y" Co., 1950s, 10-1/2" tall	200	300	400
Bimbo the Clown, includes detachable hat, three actions, Alps Co., 1950s, 9-1/4" tall	190	325	400
Bingo Clown, three actions, TN Co., 1950s, 13" tall	200	300	400

	C6	C8	C10
Black Smithy Bear, four actions, rare, TN Co., 1950s, 9" high	200	250	325
Blacksmith Bear, six actions, A-1 Co., 1950s, 9-1/2" tall	200	300	400
Blink-A-Gear-Robot, five actions, S-H Co., 1960s, 14-1/2" tall	400	600	800
Blinky-the-Clown, includes multicolor paper hat, no marking, five actions, 1950s, 10-1/2" tall	300	450	600
Blow-Up-Ball Locomotive, includes celluloid ball, minor toy, MT Co., 1950s, 9-1/2" long	80	120	160
Blushing Willie, four actions, "Y" Co., 1960s, 10" tall	75	100	125
Bobby Drinking Bear, six actions, "Y" Co., 1950s, 10" tall	200	300	400
Bobby the Drumming Bear, four actions, Alps Co., 1950s, 10" tall	175	275	380
Boeing 727 Jet Liner, three actions, "Y" Co., 1960s, 17-1/2" long, 16-1/4" wingspan	140	210	280
Boeing 727 Jet Plane, three actions, MT Co., 1960s, 12-1/2" long, 10-3/8" wingspan	150	225	300
Bomber Pilot, six actions, K-O Co., 1960s, 10-1/2" long, 9" wingspan	190	285	380
Bongo Player, four actions, Alps Co., 1960s, 10" tall	80	120	160
Bongo, Drumming Monkey, includes plastic hat, three actions, Alps Co., 1960s, 9-1/2" high	80	120	160
Bowling Bank, three actions, M.B. Daniel & Co., 1960s, 10" long	100	150	200
Brave Eagle, five actions, TN Co., 1950s, 11" tall	100	150	200
Breakfast Chef, includes plastic egg and coffee maker, minor toy, K Co., 1960s, 8-1/4" tall	100	125	150
Brewster the Rooster, five actions, Marx Co., 1950s, 9-1/2" high	200	250	300
Bristol Bulldog Airplane T-360, four actions—lights, prop spins and stop and go, noise, S&E Co., 12" long, 14-1/2" wingspan	160	240	320
Bruno the Accordion Bear, five actions, "Y" Co., 1950s, 10-1/2" tall	175	250	350
Bubble Blowing Bear, four actions, MT Co., 1950s, 9-1/2" high, 4" x 5" base	150	225	300

Box for Cragstan Crapshooter.

Cragstan Crapshooter (loose), "Y" Co., 1950s, $225.

	C6	C8	C10
Bubble Blowing Boil Over Car, three actions, MT Co., 1950s, 10" long	100	150	200
Bubble Blowing Boy, four actions, "Y" Co., 1950s, 7" high	100	200	300
Bubble Blowing Bunny, four actions, "Y" Co., 1950s, 7" high	100	150	200
Bubble Blowing Dog, three actions, "Y" Co., 1950s, 8" high	100	150	200
Bubble Blowing Kangaroo, three actions, rare, MT Co., 1950s, 9" high (base to tip of ears)	200	300	400
Bubble Blowing Lion, four actions, MT Co., 1950s, 7-1/2" high, 3-1/2" x 7" base	100	150	200
Bubble Blowing Monkey, includes plastic bowl for bubble solution, four actions, Alps Co., 1950s, 10" tall	125	150	225
Bubble Blowing Musician, three actions, "Y" Co., 1950s, 11" tall	300	400	500
Bubble Blowing Popeye, five actions, Linemar Co., 1950s, 11-3/4" tall	1000	1500	2500

	C6	C8	C10
Bubble Blowing Washing Bear, includes plastic washtub, three actions, "Y" Co., 1950s, 8" high	200	275	350
Bubbling Bull, w/plastic bowl, five actions, Linemar Co., 1950s, 6-1/2" long, 8" high	100	150	200
Bulldozer, five actions, TN Co., 1950s, 7-1/2" long	60	80	120
Bulldozer, six actions, MT Co., 1950s, 11" long	70	105	140
Bunny the Cashier, five actions, MT Co., 1950s, 7-1/2" high	150	225	300
Bunny the Magician, includes card-ribbon apparatus for card trick, five actions, Alps Co., 1950s, 14-1/2" tall	400	500	600
Burger Chef, includes chef's hat and tin-litho hamburger, eight actions, "Y" Co., 1950s, 9" tall	175	250	350
Busy Bizzy Friendly Bug, three actions, MT Co., 1950s, 6-1/4" long	60	90	120

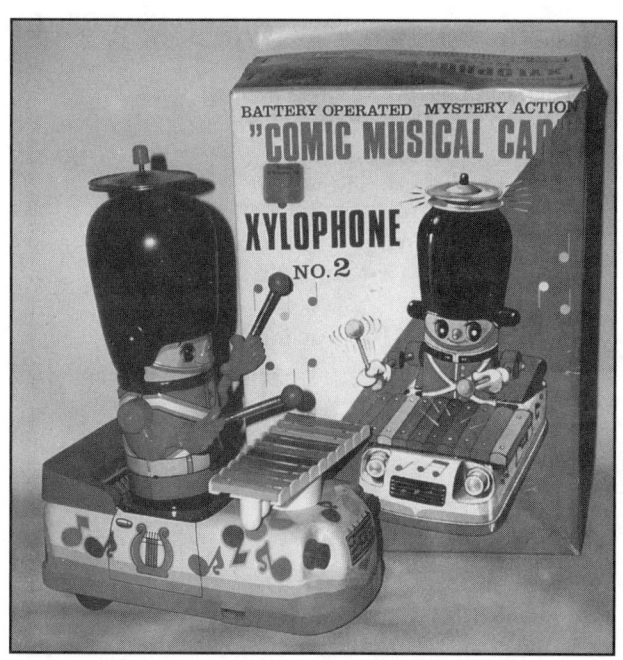

Comic Musical Car, T-N Co., 1960s, $140. Photo courtesy Don Hultzman and Ron Chojnacki

Cragstan Mother Goose, "Y" Co., 1960s, $200. Photo courtesy Don Hultzman and Ron Chojnacki

	C6	C8	C10
Busy Cart Robot, includes plastic wheelbarrow, four actions, S-H Co., c. 1960s, 11" high	200	300	400
Busy Housekeeper, The, four actions, Alps Co., 1950s, 8-1/2" tall	250	350	400
Busy Housekeeper, The (bunny), four actions, Alps Co., 1950s, 10" tall	250	350	400
Busy Secretary, seven actions, Linemar Co., 1950s, 7-1/2" high, 7-1/4" long	175	250	350
Busy Shoe Shining Bear, five actions, Alps Co., 1950s, 10" high	150	200	250
Butt Stompin' Ashtray, includes tin manhole cover, ashtray insert and 4-1/2" high plastic shoe, four actions, Poynter Prod., 1977, 7-1/4" high	40	60	80
Buttons, Puppy with a Brain, also called Buttons the Push Button Pup, eight actions, Marx, 1960s, 12" high	200	300	450
B-Z Porter Baggage Truck, includes three pieces of luggage, minor toy, MT Co., 1950s, 7-1/2" long, 6-1/2" high	150	250	300
B-Z Rabbit, four actions, MT Co., c. 1950s, 7" long	60	90	120

	C6	C8	C10
B-Z Vendor, ice cream cart, three actions, rare, MT Co., 1950s, 7-1/2" long	450	675	900
Cabin Cruiser, three actions, SGK Co., c. 1950s, 21-1/2" long	150	225	300
Cabin Cruiser with Outboard Motor, minor toy, Linemar Co., 1950s, 12" long	100	135	200
Cable Train, four-piece set; minor toy, TN Co., 1940s, 12" long	80	120	160
Cadillac Car, three actions, Ashai Toy Co., 1949, 10" long	150	225	300
Calypso Joe, four actions, rare, Linemar, 1950s, 11" tall	300	400	500
Camera Shooting Bear, includes plastic worms, five actions also called Cine-Bear, Linemar Co., 1950s, 11" tall	450	600	850
Candy Vending Machine Bank, five actions, rare, Wonderful Toy Co., 1950s, 9" high	600	900	1200
Capitol Airlines Viscount, four actions, Linemar, 1950s, 11" long, 14" wingspan	160	240	320
Cappy the Baggage Porter Dog, four actions, Alps Co., 1960s, 12" high, 11" long	150	200	250
Captain Blushwell, six actions, "Y" Co., 1960s, 11" tall	80	120	160

	C6	C8	C10
Captain Hook, includes tin sword and felt hat, three actions, rare, Marusan Co., 1950s, 10-3/4" high	800	1200	1600
Caterpillar, three actions, Alps Co., 1950s, 16" long	90	135	180
Caterpillar Tank M-1, five actions, MT Co., 1950s, 8-1/2" long, 11" long with barrel extended	150	225	300
Central Choo Choo, three actions, MT Co., 1960s, 15" long	40	60	80
Champion Weight Lifter, five actions, Y-M Co., 1960s, 10" tall	150	200	250
Change Man Robot, astronaut, four actions, rare, S-H Co., 1960s, 13-1/4" tall	4000	6000	8000
Chaparral 2F car, five actions, Alps Co., 1960s, 11" long	80	120	160
Charlie the Drumming Clown, includes detachable drum and cymbals, six actions, Alps Co., 1950s, 9-1/2" tall	150	225	300
Charlie Weaver, six actions, TN Co., 1962, 12" tall	75	100	150
Charm the Cobra, three actions, Alps Co., 1960s, 6" high	90	130	175
Chee Chee Chihuahua, five actions, Mego Co., 1960s, 8" high	50	75	100
Chef Cook, includes tin litho egg and hat, five actions, "Y" Co., 1960s, 11-1/2" tall w/hat	150	250	350
Chemical Fire Engine, four actions, HTC Co., 1950s, 10" long	100	150	200
Chief Robotman, four actions, K.O. Co., 1950s, 12" tall	450	675	900
Chimp and Pup Rail Car, four actions, TN Co., 1950s, 8" high	90	135	180
Chimp with Xylophone, includes four records and hammer, minor toy, "Y" Co., 1970s, 12" long, 8" high	100	150	200
Chimpee the One-Man Drummer, includes detachable drum and cymbals, six actions, Alps Co., 1950s, 9" high	70	105	140
Chippy the Chipmunk, (nosetip to tail tip), four actions, Alps Co., 1950s, 12" long	75	120	155
Christmas Time, three actions, rare, Marusan Co., 1950s, 10" high, 7" base diameter	400	600	800

	C6	C8	C10
Cindy the Meowing Cat, (nosetip to tail tip), four actions, two cycles, Tomiyama Co., 1950s, 12" high	50	75	100
Circus Elephant with Blowing Ball and Parasol, includes celluloid ball and tin litho umbrella, three actions, rare, TN Co., 1950s, 9-3/4" high	200	275	350
Circus Fire Engine, four actions, MT Co., 1960s, 11" long	110	175	235
Circus Jet, three actions, TN Co., 1950s, 9" high assembled	90	135	180
Circus Lion, includes whip and flannel carpet w/levers, four actions, two cycles, Rock Valley Toy Co. (Via), 1950s, 11" high	400	550	750
Clancy the Great, includes plastic hat and test coin, three actions, Ideal Toy Co., 1960s, 19-1/2" tall without hat	85	135	200
Climbing Donald Duck On His Friction Fire Engine, four actions, Linemar Co., 1950s, 12" long	400	600	900
Climbing Fireman, includes three tin ladder sections, five actions, T.P.S. Co., 1950s, 24" high assembled	200	300	400
Climbing Linesman, includes three tin pole sections, three actions, rare, T.P.S. Co., 1950s, 24" high when assembled	250	375	500
Clown and Lion, four actions, MT Co., 1960s, 11-3/4" high from base to top of tree	250	375	500
Clown Circus Car, five actions, MT Co., 1960s, 8-1/2" long, 9" high	100	175	235
Clown on Unicycle, three actions, MT Co., 1960s, 10-1/2" high	180	280	375
Clown the Magician, includes card-ribbon apparatus for card trick, six actions, Alps Co., 1950s, 12" tall	250	350	450
Clown Violinist, Seated clown w/cloth outfit holds tin violin, on tin litho base, 1960s, 10-1/2" tall	50	100	150
Clown with Lion, includes spiral apparatus, four actions, TN Co., 1950s, 12" high	200	300	400

Cycling Daddy, Bandai Co., 1960s, $250.

Dancing Merry Chimp, Kuramochi Co. (C-K), 1960s, $200.

	C6	C8	C10
Clowns Bank, The, all plastic, unmarked, minor toy, 1940s, 10" high	80	120	160
Coca-Cola Dispenser Bank, includes four plastic Coke glasses and rubber stopper, minor toy, Linemar Co., 1950s, 9-1/2" tall	450	675	900
Cock-A-Doodle-Doo Rooster, four actions, Mikuni Co., 1950s, 8" high	80	120	160
Colonel Hap Hazard Robot, four actions, Marx Co., 1968, 11-1/4" tall	300	440	600
Combi-O-Mixer, mixer-blender, minor toy, Excelo Co., 1950s, 9" long, 9" high	30	45	60
Comic Hungry Bug, VW auto, five actions, Tora (S-T) Co., 1970s, 7-3/4" long	40	60	80
Comic Musical Car, four actions, TN Co., 1960s, 6" long, 8-1/2" tall	70	105	140
Comic Road Grader, four actions, Bandai Co., 1950s, 9" long	70	105	140
Comic Road Roller, four actions, Bandai Co., 1960s, 9" long	70	105	140

	C6	C8	C10
Coney Island Penny Machine, includes plastic prizes, minor toy, Remco Co., 1950s, 13" high	90	130	300
Coney Island Rocket Ride, four actions, Alps Co., 1950s, 13-1/2" high	300	450	600
Continental Blue Locomotive, four actions, MT Co., 1960s, 12-1/2" long	30	45	60
Corvair Bertone, four actions, Bandai Co., 1970s, 12" long	50	75	100
Cowboy Riding Horse, three actions, TN Co., 1950s, 7" high	70	105	140
Cragstan Astronaut, four actions, Daiya Co., 1950s, 14" tall	400	600	800
Cragstan Beep Beep Greyhound Bus, three actions, Cragstan Co., 1950s, 20" long	150	200	250
Cragstan Biplane 7F18, five actions, TN Co., 1950s, 12" long, 14-3/8" wingspan	300	400	500
Cragstan Biplane 7F7, U.S. Navy, four actions, TN Co., 1950s, 9-1/2" long, 11-1/2" wingspan	200	300	400

	C6	C8	C10
Cragstan Crapshooter, includes pair of small dice, four actions, "Y" Co., 1950s, 9-1/2" tall	125	175	225
Cragstan Crapshooting Monkey, includes pair of small dice, three actions, Alps Co., 1950s, 9" tall	125	175	225
Cragstan Dishwasher Automatic, includes twenty-four-piece dish set, two dish baskets and metal tray, minor toy, Alps Co., 1960s, 9" high	75	100	125
Cragstan Firebird III, three actions, Alps Co., 1950s, 11-1/2" long	400	600	800
Cragstan Flying Plane with Pylon Tower, minor toy, 1950s, plane 8" long, 9-1/2" wingspan, tower 26" high	150	200	250
Cragstan Great Astronaut, five actions, Alps Co., 1960s, 14" tall	500	750	1000
Cragstan Mother Goose, six actions, "Y" Co., 1960s, 8-1/4" high	100	150	200
Cragstan Mr. Robot, four actions, "Y" Co., 1960s, 10-1/2" tall	350	525	700
Cragstan One-Arm Bandit, three actions, includes 3" x 3-1/4" sign, "Y" Co., 1960s, 6-1/4" high	150	200	250
Cragstan Peanut Vendor, includes felt hat, five actions, TN Co., 1950s, 8" tall	180	270	360
Cragstan Playboy, five actions, Cragstan Co., 1960s, 13" high	75	150	200
Cragstan Roulette, A Gambling Man, includes steel ball, chips, tin table, game sheet, five actions, "Y" Co., 1960s, 9" tall	175	250	325
Cragstan Satellite, , Cragstan Co., 1950s, 8" diameter, 5-1/2" high	90	135	180
Cragstan Smoking Jet Plane - U.S.A.F., four actions, TN Co., 1950s, 11-1/2" long, 7-1/2" wingspan	120	180	240
Cragstan Talking Robot, three actions, "Y" Co., 1960s, 10-1/2" tall	400	550	800
Cragstan Telly Bear, six actions, S&E Co., 1950s, 8" high	300	400	500
Cragstan Tootin'-Chugging Locomotive, longest single-piece battery toy made, three actions, Cragstan Co., 1950s, 24" long	70	105	140

	C6	C8	C10
Cragstan Tugboat, three actions, San Co., 1950s, 12-3/4" long	175	250	300
Cragstan Two Gun Sheriff, includes tin hat, five actions, "Y" Co., 1950s, 9-1/2" tall	200	250	325
Cragstan Vertol 1107 Helicopter Soldiers, includes rotors, four actions, TN Co., 1950s, 13-1/2" long	120	180	240
Cragstan Western Locomotive, four actions, Cragstan Co., 1950s, 12" long	60	90	120
Crane Tractor, , SKK Co., 1950s, 7-1/2" long, 11-1/2" high extended	70	105	140
Crawling Baby, minor toy, Linemar Co., 1940s, 11" long, 8-1/2" high	50	75	100
Crazy Car, five actions, Marusan Co., 1950s, 9" long	60	90	120
Cycling Daddy, four actions, Bandai Co., 1960s, 10" high	150	200	250
Cyclist Clown, seven actions, K Co., 1950s, 7" high	200	300	400
Cyclist Clown, six actions, MT Co., 1950s, 6-1/2" high	200	300	400
Cyclist Clown, five actions, Alps Co., 1950s, 9" high	200	300	400
Cymbal Playing Turnover Monkey, three actions, TN Co., 1960s, 8" tall	50	75	100
Daisy the Jolly Drumming Duck, includes detachable drum and cymbals, seven actions, rare, Alps Co., 1950s, 9" high	150	200	275
Dalmatian One-Man Band, includes cymbals and stand, six actions, Alps Co., 1950s, 9" high	120	180	240
Dancing Merry Chimp, five actions, Kuramochi Co. (C-K), 1960s, 11" tall	100	150	200
Dancing Sweethearts, minor toy, TN Co., 1950s, 7" tall	90	135	180
Dandy the Happy Drumming Pup, includes detachable drum and cymbals, six actions, Alps Co., 1950s, 8-1/2" high	85	150	200
Dapper Jigger Dancer, minor toy, Haji Co., 1950s, 12" tall	150	225	300
Dennis the Menace (Playing London Bridge), includes xylophone Rosko, three actions, 1950s, 9" high	175	225	300

Dentist Bear, S&E Co., 1950s, $600. Photo courtesy Don Hultzman and Ron Chojnacki

Cymbal Playing Turnover Monkey, T-N Co., 1960s, $100.

CONDITION CODE

C6 Good; evident overall wear, well played with but acceptable to many collectors

C8 Very Good; minor overall wear, very clean

C10 Mint; like new

Note: Mint in Box commands a higher price. Condition below C6 brings considerably lower prices

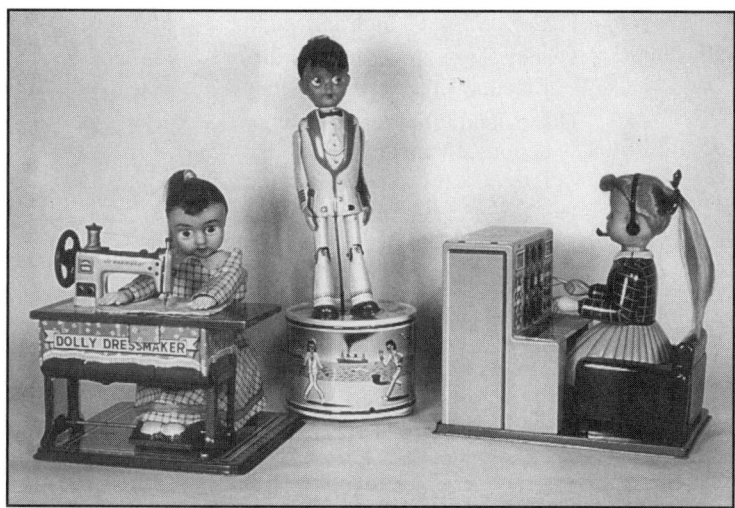

Left to right: Dolly Dressmaker, T-N Co., 1950s, $350, Strutting My Fair Dancer (Dancing Sailor Girl), Haji Co., 1950s, $200; Switchboard Operator, Linemar, 1950s, $1000. Photo courtesy Don Hultzman and Ron Chojnacki

Chef Cook, "Y" Co., 1960s, $350.

Left to right: Dennis the Menace (Playing London Bridge), 1950s, $300; Chimp with Xylophone, "Y" Co., 1970s, $200. Photo courtesy Don Hultzman and Ron Chojnacki

Drinking Captain, S&E Co., 1960s, $200.

	C6	C8	C10
Dentist Bear, includes detachable head, seven actions, S&E Co., 1950s, 9-1/2" tall, 6-3/4" x 4-1/4" base	300	450	600
Desert Patrol Jeep, includes turret gunner, four actions, MT Co., 1960s, 11" long	90	135	180
Destroyer 206 Boat, includes detachable antenna and five depth charges, six actions, "Y" Co., 1950s, 14" long	110	165	220
Diesel Locomotive, minor toy, Cragstan Co., 1950s, 16-1/2" long	30	45	60
Dino Robot, five actions, S-H Co., 1960s, 11" tall	500	750	1000

	C6	C8	C10
Disney Acrobats (Mickey, Donald and Pluto), minor toys, Linemar Co., 1950s, 9" high	300	625	800
Disney Fire Engine, four actions, Linemar Co., 1950s, 11" long	600	800	1000
Disneyland Fire Engine, five actions, Linemar Co., 1950s, 18" long	350	550	750
Docking Rocket, includes plastic radar antenna, six actions, Daiya Co., 1960s, 16" long, 24" extended	100	150	200
Dog Family, four actions, Alps Co., 1960s, 11" long	50	75	100
Dog Sled, four actions, rare, TN Co., 1950s, 14" long	300	450	600

	C6	C8	C10
Dolly Dressmaker, includes cloth sample, Dolly Seamstress on box, ten actions, rare, TN Co., 1950s, 7" high	225	275	350
Donald Duck, four actions, Linemar Co., 1960s, 8" tall	200	300	400
Donald Duck Locomotive, three actions, MT Co., 1970s, 9" long	150	225	300
Donald Duck Trolley, three actions, MT Co., 1960s, 11" high	160	240	320
Douglas C-124 Globe Master, eight actions, Yonezawa Co., c. 1950s, 20-1/2" wingspan, 18" long	300	450	600
Douglas DC-9TWA Jet Plane, four actions, TN Co., 1960s, 14" long, 17" wingspan	100	150	200
Doxie the Dog, five actions, Linemar Co., 1950s, 9" long	20	25	45
Dozo the Steaming Clown, Rosko toys, five actions, TN Co., 1960s, 10" tall	200	300	400
Dream Boat Hot Rod, four actions, TN Co., c. 1950s, 7" long	140	210	280
Drill, includes attachments, minor toy, Linemar Co., 1950s, 6" long	20	30	40
Drinker's Savings Bank, minor toy, Illfelder Co., 1960s, 9" high	90	135	180
Drinking Bear, six actions, Alps Co., c. 1970s, 12" high	75	125	150
Drinking Captain, six actions, S&E Co., 1960s, 12" tall	100	150	200
Drinking Dog, four actions, "Y" Co., 1950s	90	135	180
Drinking Licking Cat, six actions, "Y" Co., 1950s, 10" high, 4" x 4" base	150	200	250
Drum Bear, five actions (walks, lights, beats drum, noise), Alps Co., c. 1950s, 7-3/4" tall	150	225	300
Drum Monkey, three actions, Yada Co., 1970s, 8" high	40	60	80
Drummer Bear, six actions, Alps Co., 1950s, 10" tall	140	210	280
Drumming Mickey Mouse, four actions, rare, Linemar, 1950s, 10" tall	1000	1500	2000
Drumming Polar Bear, three actions, Alps Co., 1960s, 12" tall	100	150	200
Ducky Duckling, four actions, Alps Co., 1960s, 8" high	35	55	85
Dump Truck, seven actions, TN Co., 1960s, 10-1/4" long	60	90	120

	C6	C8	C10
Dynamic Fighter Robot, five actions, Junior Toy Co., 1960s, 10" tall	100	125	150
Earthman-Astronaut, five actions, rare, TN Co., 1950s, 9-1/2" tall	900	1300	1800
El Toro-Cragstan Bullfighter, includes detachable tin matador, four actions, TN Co., 1950s, 9-1/2" long	90	145	200
Electric Powered TV and Radio Station, three actions, Marx, 1950s, 30" long	100	150	200
Electric Remote Control Robot, four actions, rare, MT Co., 1950s, 7-1/2" tall	500	750	1000
Electric Robot, five actions, Marx, 1950s, 14-1/2" tall	300	450	600
Electric School Bus, minor toy, MT Co., 1950s, 9-1/2" long	70	105	140
Electric Vibraphone, three actions, TN Co., 1950s, 7-1/2" long, 5-1/2" high	70	105	140
Electro Special Racer, three actions, Yonezawa Co., 1950s, 10" long	500	750	1000
Electro Train Transcontinental, three pieces, three actions, M Co., 1950s, 20-1/2" long	90	135	180
Electronic Countdown, six actions, Ideal Toy Co., 1959, 24" long	60	90	120
Electronic Fighter Jet 4800, eleven actions, 1950s, 19" long	175	225	275
Electronic Fire House, includes plastic fire engine, minor toy, Banner Co., 1940s, 7" square	70	105	140
Electronic Periscope (Nautilus) Firing Range, three actions, Cragstan, 1950s, 11" high on tripod	100	150	200
Electronic Twin Train Set, includes two three-piece trains, minor toy, Woodhaven Metal Stamping Co., 1950s, 28" long, 11" wide	100	150	200
Engine Robot, four actions, S-H Co., 1960s, 9-1/2" tall	100	150	200
Excavator Robot, four actions, S-H Co., 1960s, 10" tall	200	300	400
Expert Motor Cyclist, five actions, rare, MT Co., 1950s, 12" long	800	1200	1500
F.D. Fire Engine, four actions, Y-M Co., 1960s, 10" long, 12" high when ladder is extended	110	165	220

Left to right: Fighting Spaceman, S-H Co., 1960s, $300; Turn Signal Robot Auto Accessory, T-N Co., 1960s, $320. Photo courtesy Don Hultzman and Ron Chojnacki

Gino the Neapolitan Balloon Blower, Tomiyama Co. (Rosko), 1960s, $250.

	C6	C8	C10
F-101A Voodoo Fighter, minor toy, K-O Co., 1960s, 15" long, 14" wingspan	100	150	200
F-14-A Navy Jet Fighter, six actions, TN Co., 1960s, 13" long, 13" wingspan	200	300	400
Fairyland Loco, locomotive, four actions, Daiya Co., 1950s, 9" long	60	90	120
Farm Truck, five actions, TN Co., 1950s, 9" long	120	180	240
Farm Truck, three actions, Alps Co., 1960s, 11" long	120	180	240

	C6	C8	C10
Feeding Bird Watcher, includes detachable tin branch and bird, five action, rare, Linemar, 1950s, 9" high	300	350	600
Ferris Wheel Truck, four actions, Linemar Co., c. 1950s, 11" long	400	600	800
Fido the Xylophone Player, includes detachable xylophone, six actions (body sways, head turns, arms activate lights and sound), Alps Co., c. 1950s, 8-3/4" high	150	200	250
Fighter (airplane), six actions, K-O Co., 1960s, 10-1/2" long, 9" wingspan	160	240	320

Go-Go Girl, Poynter Prod. Co., 1969, $100. Photo courtesy Don Hultzman and Ron Chojnacki

Gypsy Fortune Teller, Ichida Co., 1950s, $2200. Photo courtesy Don Hultzman and Ron Chojnacki

	C6	C8	C10
Fighter Airplane, four actions, Marx Co., c. 1960s, 7" wingspan..........	75	100	125
Fighter Jet, four actions, Marx Co., c. 1960s, 7" wingspan	75	100	125
Fighting Bull, five actions, Alps Co., 1960s, 9-1/2" long	100	125	150
Fighting Bull, four actions, two cycles, Rock Valley Tech Co., 1970s, 12" long nose to tail tip.................	100	150	200
Fighting Robot, all plastic, four actions, S-H Co., 1970s, 10" tall.................	70	105	140
Fighting Spaceman, five actions, S-H Co., 1960s, 12" tall	150	225	300
Fire Boat, five actions, MT Co., 1950s, 15" long	175	250	350
Fire Chief, three actions, "Y" Co., 1960s, 11-1/4" long	90	135	180
Fire Chief Mystery Action Car, four actions, TN Co., 1960s, 9-3/4" long.............................	130	195	260
Fire Command Car, five actions, TN Co., 1950s	170	255	340
Fire Engine, four actions, Marusan Co., 1950s, 9" long.....................	120	180	240

	C6	C8	C10
Fire Engine, three actions, TN Co. (Electro Toy), 1950s, 9" long, ladder extends 13"......................	150	225	300
Fire Engine, six actions, "Y" Co., 1950s, 12" long, ladder extends 16"....................................	100	150	200
Fire Engine, three actions, S-H Co., c. 1950s, 8" long........................	100	150	200
Fire Patrol Boat, three actions, KKS Co., 1950s, 12" long...................	110	165	220
Fire Tricycle, four actions, TN Co., 1950s, 9-1/2" long	180	270	360
Firebird Racer, four actions, Tomiyama Co., 1950s, 14-1/4" long..	300	450	600
Fishing Bear (also Fishing Panda Bear, Polar Bear, Forest Bear), includes detachable pond, tin fish, six actions, Alps Co., 1950s, 10" high......................	200	300	400
Fishing Bears Bank, six actions, rare, Wonderful Toy Co., 1950s, 9-1/2" tall................	500	750	1000
Flashing Jet-FC-657 Airplane-U.S.A.F. 7452, four actions, Marx Co., 1950s, 7" long, 6" wingspan	100	150	200

	C6	C8	C10
Flashy Jim, minor toy, rare, S.N.K. Co. (Ace), 1950s, 7-3/4" tall	1100	1650	2200
Flashy Ray Space Gun, minor toy, TN Co., 1950s, 18-1/2" long	50	75	100
Flintstone Yacht, , Remco Co., 1961, 17" long	90	145	200
Floating Satellite Target Game, The, includes tin gun, rubber-tipped darts and celluloid ball, 1960s, 8-1/2" high	100	150	200
Flutter Birds, includes detachable pulley assembly, six actions, rare, Alps Co., 1950s, 26-1/2" high when assembled	300	450	600
Flying Dutchman-PH-KLM Airliner, five actions, TN Co., 1950s, 11" long, 14" wingspan ...	100	150	200
Flying Jet Plane-Boeing 747P, five actions, J Toy Co., 1960s, 13" long, 12" wingspan	90	135	180
Flying Platform, includes detachable tin soldier, four actions, rare, Cragstan Co., 1950s, 5-1/2" diameter, 9" high	200	300	400
Flying Tiger Airplane, four actions w/remote control, Marx Co., 1960s, 7" long, 7" wingspan	60	90	120
Ford Model T, includes detachable tin roof, four actions, Nihonkogei Co., 1950s, 10-1/4" long	75	100	150
Ford Mustang 2 x 2, four actions, Wenmac-AMF Co., 1960s, 16" long..................	60	90	120
Ford Skyliner, four actions, TN Co., 1950s, 9" long	100	150	200
Fork Lift Truck, minor toy, MT Co., 1960s, 10-1/4" high	80	120	160
Foto Finish, racehorse, minor toy, MT Co., 1950s, 12" long............	120	180	240
Frankenstein, w/five actions, remote control, Marx Co. (Japan), 1950s, 12" tall................	600	900	1200
Frankenstein Monster, six actions, TN Co., 1960s, 14" tall	150	200	250
Frankie the Rollerskating Monkey, , Alps Co., 1950s, 12" tall	150	225	300
Fred Flintstone Bedrock Band, four actions, Alps Co., 1962, 9-1/2" high........................	500	650	1000
Fred Flintstone on Dino, eight actions, Marx Co. (Japan), 1961, 22" long........................	600	800	1000

	C6	C8	C10
Friendly Jocko My Favorite Pet, includes detachable cymbals, plastic cup, five actions, Alps Co., 1950s, 8" high.....................	110	175	245
Fruit Juice Counter, includes plastic barrel, lid, glasses and tin tray, three actions, K Co., 1960s, 8" long, 8" high.....................	90	135	180
FS-059 Fighter Plane, jet w/prop, five actions, TN Co., 1950s, 11" long, 13" wingspan.....................	170	255	340
Funland Cup Ride, includes six umbrellas, three actions, Sonsco Co., 1960s, 7" tall, 6" x 6" base ..	100	150	200
Galloping Cowboy Savings Bank, minor toy, rare, "Y" Co. (Cragstan), 1950s, 8" high, 6-1/2" long.....................	450	675	900
Gama Mercedes-Benz 220 SE Sedan, three actions, Mignon Co., 1960s, 9" long.....................	150	225	300
Gear Robot, four actions, "Y" Co., 1960s, 10" tall	250	375	500
Gino the Neapolitan Balloon Blower, includes bubble solution plastic tray, five actions, Tomiyama Co. (Rosko), 1960s, 10" tall.....................	150	200	250
Girl with Baby Carriage, three actions, TN Co., 1960s, 8" high.....................	100	150	200
Godzilla, five actions, Bullmark Co., 1960s, 10-1/2" tall	300	450	600
Godzilla Monster, three actions, Marusan Co., 1970s, 11-1/2" tall	150	200	300
Go-Go Girl, (bar toy), minor toy, risqué toy, PG-rated, Poynter Prod. Co., 1969, 15-1/4" tall	60	80	100
Go-Kart, includes control wire w/steering key, minor toy, MT Co., 1960s, 6-1/2" long	90	135	180
Go-Kart, includes detachable head, three actions, Rosko Co., 1950s, 10" long.....................	90	135	180
Golden Gear Robot, five actions, S-H Co., 1960s, 9" tall.....................	300	450	600
Golden Locomotive, minor toy, Nihonkogei Co., 1950s, 10-1/2" long.....................	40	60	80
Golden Roto Robot, five actions, S-H Co., 1960s, 8-1/2" tall	100	150	200
Gomora Monster, includes plastic missiles, four actions, Bullmark Co., 1960s, 8" tall.....................	150	225	300

Haunted House Mystery Bank (Disneyland promotion), Brumberger Co., 1960s, $550. Photo courtesy Don Hultzman and Ron Chojnacki

Hysterical Robot, The (a.k.a. Hysterical Harry and Happy Harry), S-H Co., 1960s, $300. Photo courtesy Don Hultzman and Ron Chojnacki

	C6	C8	C10
Good Time Charlie, seven actions, MT Co., 1960s, 12" tall...............	150	200	250
Gorilla, white or brown, five actions, TN Co., 1950s, 9-1/4" tall...	200	300	400
Go-Stop Benz Racer, three actions, Marusan Co., 1950s, 11" long.....	150	225	300
Grace Ocean Liner, three actions, MT Co., 1950s, 15" long.............	250	375	500
Grandpa Bear, includes rocking chair, five actions, Alps Co., 1950s, 9" tall	225	275	350
Grand-Pa Car, four actions, "Y" Co., 1950s, 9" long.....................	100	125	150
Granpa Panda Bear, five actions, MT Co., 1950s, 9" tall.................	100	175	245
Great Garloo, The, includes chain and medallion, seven actions, Marx Co., 1960s, 23" tall	450	550	750
Green Caterpillar, three actions, Daiva Co., 1950s, 19-1/2" long...	150	250	350
Greyhound Bus, minor toy, KKK. Co., 1950s, 7-1/4" long	90	135	180

	C6	C8	C10
Greyhound Bus Scenicruiser, three actions, I.Y. Metal Toy Co., 1950s, 16" long	90	135	180
Greyhound Bus with Headlights, three actions, Linemar Co., 1950s, 10-1/4" long	100	150	200
Grumman F9F Navy Jet, Cougar, three actions, K Co., 1950s, 11-1/2" long....................................	150	225	300
Guided Missile Launcher, includes plastic missiles, three actions, Irco Co., 1950s, 8" long, 3" tall, 5" wide	110	165	220
Gypsy Fortune Teller, includes twenty fortune cards, five actions, rare, Ichida Co., 1950s, 12" high w/hat, 5-3/4" x 7" base .	1100	1700	2200
Hamburger Chef, includes tin frying pan, hamburger, plastic bottles, three actions, K Co., 1960s, 8" long, 8" high	150	250	350
Handy Hank Mystery Tractor, four actions, TN Co., 1950s, 9" long ..	100	125	150

	C6	C8	C10
Happy Band Trios, seven actions, rare, MT Co., 1970s, 12" high.....	400	600	800
Happy Clown Car, three actions, "Y" Co., 1960s, 6-1/2" long........	100	150	200
Happy Clown Theater, w/Pinocchio-like puppet, three actions, "Y" Co., 1950s, 10" tall	200	300	400
Happy Fiddler Clown, The, includes tin litho violin, four actions, Alps Co., 1950s, 9-1/2" high..............	250	350	450
Happy Miner, three actions, Bandai Co., 1960s, 11" tall.............	110	165	220
Happy 'N' Sad Face Cymbal Clown, five actions, "Y" Co., 1960s, 10" tall	120	180	200
Happy Naughty Chimp, four actions, Daishin Co., 1960s, 9-1/2" high assembled	75	100	150
Happy Plane, three actions, TPS Co., 1960s, 9" long, 10-1/2" wingspan	100	150	200
Happy Santa, three actions, Z Co., 1960s, 11" tall	100	150	200
Happy Santa (walking), five actions, Alps Co., 1950s, 11" tall	150	225	300
Happy Santa One-Man Band, includes cymbals and stand, six actions, Alps Co., 1950s, 9" high	100	185	245
Happy Singing Bird, three actions, MT Co., 1950s, 9" high, bird 3" long, 5-5/8" diameter base	60	90	120
Happy the Clown Puppet Show, w/Pinocchio-like puppet, three actions, "Y" Co., 1960s, 10" tall.	190	285	380
Happy Tractor, four actions, Daiya Co., 1960s, 8" long......................	40	60	80
Happy'n Sad Magic Face Clown, five actions, "Y" Co., 1960s, 10" tall..................	150	225	300
Harbor Queen Boat, minor toy, MT Co., 1950s, 12" long...................	150	225	300
Hasty Chimp, four actions, "Y" Co., 1960s, 9" high.....................	50	75	100
Haunted House Mystery Bank (Disneyland promotion), four actions, Brumberger Co., 1960s, 7-5/8" high..................	300	425	550
Heavy Machine Gun, includes detachable tripod and plastic ammo belt, four actions, TN Co., 1950s, 24" long, 13" high on tripod..................	100	150	200

	C6	C8	C10
Hi Bouncer Moon Scout Robot, includes five plastic balls, five actions, rare, Marx Co., 1968, 11-1/4" tall..................................	450	675	900
High Jinks of the Circus, six actions, TN Co., 1950s, 14" high, extends to 29"............................	350	450	550
Highway Drive, includes tin magnetic car, three actions, TN Co., 1950s, 15-1/2" long.....................	70	105	140
Highway Patrol Jeep, four actions, Daiya Co., 1950s, 10" long	70	105	140
Highway Patrol Police Special, five actions, "Y" Co., 1960s, 11-1/2" long...............................	100	150	200
Highway Skill Driving, three actions, K Co., 1960s, 13" long...............................	70	105	140
Hiller Hornet Helicopter, four actions, Alps Co., 1950s, 12-1/4" long, 15" two-piece metal rotor...	120	180	240
Hippo Chef (Cuty Cook), includes chef hat and tin litho egg, five actions, "Y" Co., 1960s, 10" tall.	150	250	350
H-O Gauge Electric Train Set with Real Smoke, seventeen-piece set, Amico Co., 1960s, 23" long........	70	105	140
Hobo Clown with Accordion (with cymbal-playing monkey), six actions, Alps Co., 1950s, 10-1/2" high..............................	400	500	650
Hole-in-One Bank, includes marked test coin and golfer, no marking, minor toy, 1960s, 8-1/2" long x 3-1/2" wide	70	105	140
Holiday Sink-Stove Combination, includes three-piece pan set, minor toy, TN Co., 1950s, 9" high..............................	40	60	80
Hong Kong Rickshaw, all plastic, made in Hong Kong, 1960s.........	100	200	300
Hoop Zing Girl, minor toy, Linemar Co., 1950s, 11-1/2" tall	115	185	245
Hoopy the Fishing Duck, includes magnetic fish and detachable pond, seven actions, Alps Co., 1950s, 10" high	275	375	525
Hootin' Hollow Haunted House, eight actions, Marx, 1960s, 11" high..............................	600	850	1200
Hooty the Happy Owl, six actions, Alps Co., 1960s, 9" tall	65	100	145
Hot Rod Car, minor toy, TN Co., 1950s, 10" long	160	240	320

Jolly Penguin, T-N Co., 1950s, $200. Photo courtesy Don Hultzman and Ron Chojnacki

Jungle Jumbo, B.C. Co., 1950s, $400. Photo courtesy Don Hultzman and Ron Chojnacki

	C6	C8	C10
Hot Rod Custom 'T' Ford, four actions, Alps Co., 1960s, 10-1/2" long	180	270	360
Hot Rod Limousine, four actions, Alps Co., 1960s, 10-1/2" long	180	270	360
Hungry Baby Bear, six actions, "Y" Co., 1950s, 9-1/2" tall	200	300	400
Hungry Cat, includes tin tray and plastic fish, seven actions, Linemar Co., 1960s, 9" high	250	450	700
Hungry Hound Dog, six actions, "Y" Co., 1950s, 9-1/2" high	200	300	400
Hungry Sheep, three actions, two cycles, MT Co., 1950s, 9" long	100	150	200
Hy Que Monkey, six actions, TN Co., 1960s, 17" tall	150	225	300
Hysterical Robot, The (a.k.a. Hysterical Harry and Happy Harry), seven actions, S-H Co., 1960s, 13-1/2" tall	150	225	300
Ice Cream Baby Bear, three actions, rare, MT Co., 1950s, 9-1/2" high	200	300	400
Ice Cream Truck, five actions, Bandai Co., 1960s, 10-1/2" long	100	150	200
Indian Joe, four actions, Alps Co., 1960s, 12" tall	100	150	175
Indian Signal Choo Choo, four actions, Kanto Toys Co., 1960s, 9-1/2" long	80	120	160
Interceptor, target game, four actions, S&E Co., 1950s, 13" high, 16" wingspan	150	225	300

	C6	C8	C10
Interplanetary Rocket, five actions, "Y" Co., 1960s, 14-3/4" tall	120	180	240
JDN 7673 Sedan-4-door, minor toy and one of the earliest battery-operated toys, rare, Distler Co., 1920s, 14" long	600	800	1000
Jeep, minor toy, Cragstan, 1950s, 5-1/2" long	70	105	140
Jeep USA, minor toy, TKK Co., 1950s, 12-1/2" long	70	105	140
Jet Airport with 4 Jet Airplanes, seven actions, Turnpike Lines (Sears), 1960s, 12-1/2" long	200	275	350
Jet Plane Base, includes crank, seven actions, rare, "Y" Co., 1950s, 7-1/4" x 11" base, plane 9" long, 7" wingspan	450	675	900
Jig-Saw-Matic, minor toy, Z Co., 1950s, 7-1/4" high, 4-1/2" x 8-1/2"	40	60	80
Jocko the Drinking Monkey, includes top hat, four actions, Linemar, 1950s, 11" tall	150	200	250
John's Farm Truck, seven actions, TN Co., 1950s, 9" long	100	150	200
Jo-Jo the Flipping Monkey, minor toy, TN Co. (Illfelder), 1970s, 10" high	35	75	80
Jolly Bambino, includes candy pieces, five actions, Alps Co., 1950s, 9" high	250	350	500
Jolly Bear Peanut Vendor, The, includes felt hat, five actions, TN Co., 1950s, 8" high	250	285	500

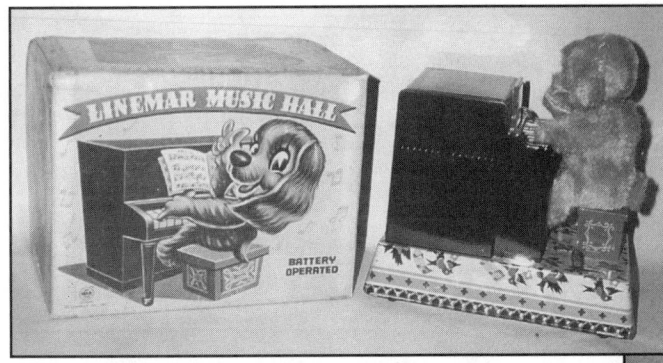

Linemar Music Hall, Linemar Co., 1950s, $200. Photo courtesy Don Hultzman and Ron Chojnacki

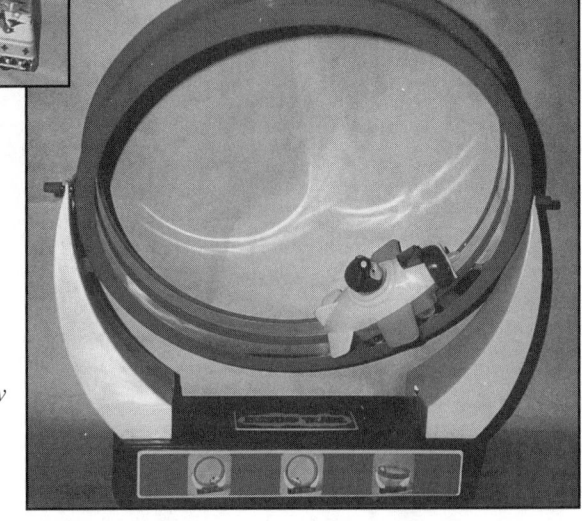

Looping Airplane, "Y" Co. Sears (distributor), 1960s, $80. Photo courtesy Don Hultzman and Ron Chojnacki

	C6	C8	C10
Jolly Bear the Drummer Boy, five actions, K Co., 1950s, 7" tall.......	100	150	200
Jolly Bear with Robin, three actions, rare, MT Co., 1950s, 10" high..	400	600	800
Jolly Daddy, four actions, Marusan Co., 1950s, 8-3/4" tall	165	250	350
Jolly Drummer Chimpy, includes cymbals and stand, six actions, Alps Co., 1950s, 9" high	125	150	175
Jolly Drumming Bear, four actions, TN Co., 1950s, 7" tall	125	150	175
Jolly Penguin, five actions, TN Co., 1950s, 7" tall	100	150	200
Jolly Pianist, five actions, Marusan Co., 1950s, 8" high......................	100	150	200
Jolly Santa on Snow, includes tin skis, four actions, two cycles, Alps Co., 1950s, 12-1/2" tall.......	150	225	300
Josie the Walking Cow, seven actions, two cycles, Daiya Co., 1950s, 14" long, 8-1/2" high	175	225	300
Journey Pup, four actions, remote control, S&E Co., c. 1950s, 7-1/2" long......................................	75	100	125

	C6	C8	C10
Jumbo the Bubble-Blowing Elephant, includes plastic bowl for bubble solution, three actions, "Y" Co., 1950s, 7-1/4" high........	75	110	150
Jungle Elephant, remote control, walks and bellows	100	200	300
Jungle Jumbo, six actions, two cycles, hunter resembles Teddy Roosevelt, B.C. Co., 1950s, 10" high..	200	300	400
Jungle Trio, includes tin litho whistle, eight actions, Linemar, 1950s, 8" high	400	600	800
Jupiter Robot, four actions, Yonezawa Co., 1950s, 12-3/4" tall	150	225	300
Jupiter Rocket Launching Pad, , TN Co., 1960s, 8-1/2" long, 7" high..	200	300	400
K-55 Electric Tractor, three actions, MT Co., c. 1950s, 7" long...........	70	105	140
King Flying Saucer, three actions, K.O. Co., 1960s, 7-1/2" diameter....................................	85	120	150
King Size Fire Engine, three actions, Bandai Co., 1960s, 12-1/2" long......................................	150	225	300

	C6	C8	C10
Kissing Couple, five actions, Ichida Co., 1950s, 10-3/4" long	150	200	300
Kitchen-ette Stove and Sink, no marking, minor toy, includes kitchen utensils and side tray and stoppers, 1940s, 6-1/2" long x 6-3/4" high	50	75	100
Knight in Armor, five actions, rare, MT Co., 1950s, 10" tall	1100	1650	2200
Knight in Armor Target Game, includes crossbow and rubber tipped darts, three actions, MT Co., 1950s, 12" tall	200	300	400
Knitting Grandma, three actions, TN Co., 1950s, 8-1/1" tall	200	300	400
Kooky-Spooky Whistling Tree, w/two color schemes, six actions, Marx Co., 1950s, 14-1/4" tall	550	800	1600
Ladder Fire Engine, five actions, Linemar Co., 1950s, 13" long	170	255	340
Lady Pup Tending Her Garden, five actions, Cragstan Co., 1950s, 8" high	200	275	400
Lambo with Magnetic Trunk and Light, includes two tin logs and trailer, seven actions, rare, Alps Co., 1950s, 16" long w/trailer	260	385	525
Laughing Clown, The, seven actions, S-H Co., 1960s, 14" tall	160	240	320
Lectric Revolver, three actions, Daisy Mfg. Co., 1950s, 11-1/2" long	40	60	80
Leo the Growling Pet Lion with Magic Face Change, three actions, two cycles, Toyiyama Co., 1970s, 9" long	100	150	200
Light House, includes detachable spin-ball tower, five actions, rare, Alps Co., 1950s, 8-1/2" high, 6-3/4" x 6-3/4" base	600	900	1200
Lighted Freight Train, five pieces w/eight-section track, four actions, "Y" Co., 1950s, 25-1/2" long	70	105	140
Lighted Space Vehicle with Floating Satellite, includes celluloid ball, three actions, MT Co., 1960s, 8-1/2" long	175	250	325
Linda Lee Laundromat, washing machine, minor toy, TN Co., 1940s, 6-1/2" high	30	45	60

	C6	C8	C10
Linemar Music Hall, four actions, Linemar Co., 1950s, 8" high, 7-3/4" x 5-1/2" base	100	120	200
Lion, four actions, Linemar Co., 1950s, 9" long	100	150	200
Lion Target Game, includes dart gun and darts, four actions, MT Co., 1950s, 7-1/2" high	120	180	240
Locomotive Continental Blue, four actions, MT Co., 1970s, 13" long	40	60	80
Loop the Loop Clown, minor toy, TN Co., 1960s, 10" high	60	120	175
Looping Airplane, minor toy, "Y" Co. Sears (distributor), 1960s, 14-1/2" high, airplane 5" long	40	60	80
Looping Space Tank, five actions, Daiya Co., 1960s, 8" long	300	450	600
Los Walky-Son, includes detachable rifles and baton, Geyper Co., 1960s, 11-1/2" high, 15" wide	120	180	240
Loser, The (Bar Toy), three actions, Poynter Prod. Co., c. 1971, 13" high	40	60	80
Lost in Space Robot, three actions, Remco Co., 1966, 13" tall	200	300	400
Love-Beetle-Volks, three actions, K.O. Co., 1960s, 10" long	60	90	120
Lucky Crane, includes tin prizes, five actions, rare, MT Co., 1950s, 8-1/1" high	400	600	800
Lucky Locomotive, four actions, Marusan Co., 1950s, 8" long	40	60	80
Lucky Seven Dice-Throwing Monkey, includes plastic straw hat, five dice, two game sheets, twenty chips, five actions, Alps Co., 1960s, 11-1/2" tall	75	100	125
Lufthansa Jet Airplane, three actions, GAMA Co., 1960s, 19-1/2" long, 18-1/2" wingspan	110	165	220
Lunar Captain, five actions, TN Co., 1960s, 13-1/2" long extended	110	165	220
Lunar Loop/Swing and Orbiting Action, three actions, Daiya Co., 1960s, 14" high, 12" diameter-hoop	100	150	200
M-101 Aston-Martin Secret Ejector Car, includes ejectable passenger, six actions, Daiya Co., 1960s, 11" long	200	300	400
Mac the Turtle, five actions, "Y" Co., 1960s, 8" high	85	135	185

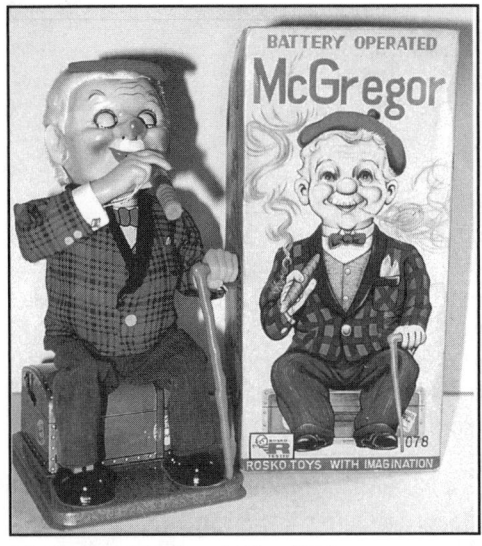

McGregor, T-N Co., 1960s, $300.

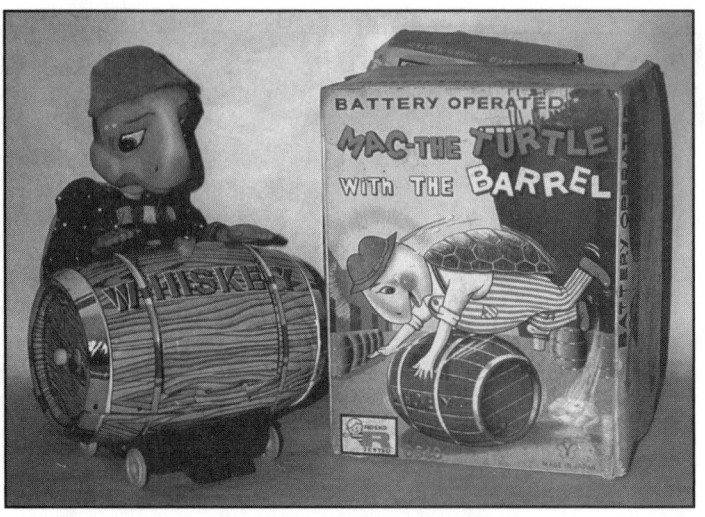

Mac the Turtle, "Y" Co., 1960s, $185. Photo courtesy Don Hultzman and Ron Chojnacki

	C6	C8	C10
Magic Action Bulldozer, three actions, TN Co., 1950s, 9-1/2" long	125	175	225
Magic Color Moon Express, four actions, S-H Co., 1960s, 13" long	100	150	200
Magic Man Clown, five actions, Marusan Co., 1950s, 11" tall	300	400	600
Magic Snowman, includes detachable tin broom, plastic pipe, and styro ball, four actions, MT Co. (Santa Creations), 1950s, 11-1/4" tall	175	225	325
Magnet Rail Moon Orbiter, minor toy, "Y" Co., 1960s, 14" high, 12" diameter	100	125	150
Main Street, three actions, rare, Linemar Co., 1950s, 19-1/2" long	1000	1500	2000
Major Tooty, includes drum and hat, three actions, Alps Co. (R.F.), 1960s, 14" tall	85	130	175
Make Up Bear, four actions, rare, MT Co., 1960s, 9" high	500	750	1000
Mambo the Jolly Drumming Elephant, includes cymbals and stand, six actions, Alps Co., 1950s, 9-1/2" high	125	175	225
Man in Space Astronaut, minor toy, Alps Co., 1960s, 6" tall	100	150	200
Mars Explorer, robot, seven actions, S-H Co., 1950s, 9-1/2" tall	200	300	400
Mars Explorer, astronaut, six actions, S-H Co., 1960s, 10" tall	250	375	500

	C6	C8	C10
Mars King Robot, four actions, S-H Co., 1960s, 9-1/2" tall	210	315	420
Marshal Wild Bill, includes tin cowboy hat, four actions, two cycles, "Y" Co., 1950s, 10-1/2" tall	225	325	425
Martian Robot, four actions, SJM Co., 1970s, 12" tall	75	100	125
Marvelous Car, T-Bird, three actions, TN Co., 1956, 11" long	250	375	500
Marvelous Fire Engine, four actions, "Y" Co., 1960s, 11" long	100	150	200
Marvelous Mike, four actions, Saunders Co., 1950s, 17" long	100	175	245
Maxwell Coffee-Loving Bear, five actions, TN Co., 1960s, 10" tall	150	200	250
McGregor, six actions, TN Co., 1960s, 12" tall when standing	175	225	300
Mechanic Robot, five actions, S-T Co., 1960s, 12" tall	150	225	300
Mechanized Robot, The (Robby), four actions, rare; one of the most recognizable robot toys, it is based on Robby the Robot from The Forbidden Planet, TN Co., 1950s, 13-1/2" tall	750	1000	1250
Mercury Explorer, five actions, T.P.S. Co., 1960s, 8" long	120	180	240
Mercury X-1 Space Saucer, four actions, "Y" Co., 1960s, 8" diameter	100	125	150

	C6	C8	C10
Merry Christmas Santa In His Rockin' Chair, includes detachable tree and stocking, three actions, rare, Alps Co., 1950s, 21" tall assembled	500	750	1000
Merry Ice Cream Truck, five actions, Bandai Co., 1960s, 10-1/2" long	100	150	200
Mew-Mew Walking Cat, three actions, remote control, 1950s	75	125	150
Mexicali Pete-Drum Player, three actions, Alps Co., 1960s, 10-1/2" high	60	90	120
Mickey Mouse and Donald Duck Fire Engine, three actions, MT Co., 1960s, 16" long	400	550	750
Mickey Mouse Locomotive, six actions, MT Co., 1960s, 9" long	200	300	400
Mickey Mouse Melody Railroad, includes four circular rails w/xylophone bars, minor toy, rare, Frankonia Co., 1960s, handcar 6-3/4" long	800	1200	1600
Mickey Mouse on Handcar, three actions, MT Co., 1960s, 9-3/4" long, 7-3/4" high	350	500	650
Mickey Mouse Sand Buggy, four actions, MT Co., 1960s, 11" long	150	225	300
Mickey Mouse Trolley, three actions, MT Co., 1960s, 11" high	150	225	300
Mickey the Magician, includes tin rabbit, four actions, Linemar, 1960s, 10" tall	1000	1500	2500
Mighty Kong, five actions, Marx, 1950s, 11" tall	250	375	500
Mighty Mike the Barbell Lifter Bear, four actions, K Co., 1950s, 10-1/2" tall	150	225	300
Mighty Robot, four actions, K-O Co., 1960s, 11-1/2" tall	900	1350	1800
Military Air Defense Truck, four actions, Linemar Co., 1950s, 15-1/4" long	100	150	200
Military Command Car, five actions, TN Co., 1950s, 11" long	150	225	300
Military Jet Plane, three actions, Marx Co., 1960s, 16" long, 14" wingspan	100	150	200
Military Police Car, six actions, Linemar, 1950s, 8-1/2" long	100	150	200
Million Bus, three actions, rare, KKK Co., 1950s, 12" long	1250	1875	2500
Mimi Poodle with Bone, includes plastic bone, five actions, two cycles, TN Co., 1950s, 11" long, 10" high	50	75	100
Mischievous Monkey, includes tree and monkey, six actions, MT Co., 1950s, 18" tall	200	300	400
Mischievous Monkey with Bulldog, four actions, TN Co., 1950s, 12" high	220	330	440
Miss Friday the Typist, w/removable head, six actions, TN Co., 1950s, 8" tall	200	250	350
Missile Robot Mr. 45, five actions, MT Co., 17-1/2" tall	100	150	200
Mix-ette Mixer, includes mixer stand and bowl, minor toy, KDP Co., 1940s, 9" high when assembled	40	50	75
Mobile Satellite Tracking Station, includes detachable antenna, six actions, "Y" Co., 1960s, 9" long	400	600	800
Mobile Space TV Unit with Trailer, six actions, rare, TN Co., 1960s	500	750	1000
Mod Monster Blushing Frankenstein, five actions, TN Co., 1960s, 13-1/4" tall	200	275	350
Modern Robot, four actions, rare, Yoshiya Co., 1950s, 12" tall	450	675	900
Monkee Mobile, minor toy, ASC Co. (Aoshin Co.), 1967, 12" long	300	450	600
Monkey Handcar, three actions, TN Co., 1950s, 7" high	70	105	140
Monkey on a Picnic, seven actions, Alps Co., 1950s, 9-1/2" high	150	225	300
Monorail Rocket Ship, minor toy, Linemar Co., 1950s, 10" long w/supports and rail rods	175	250	300
Monster Robot, three actions, S-H Co., 1970s, 10" tall	100	125	150
Moon Astronaut, four actions, Daiya Co., 1950s, 9" tall	500	750	1000
Moon Explorer Robot, five actions, rare, Bandai Co., 1960s, 17-1/2" tall (feet to antenna top)	600	900	1200
Moon Explorer Vehicle, five actions, Gakken Co., 1960s, 11" long	150	225	300
Moon Express, Magic Color, three actions, TPS Co., 1950s, 12" long	120	180	240

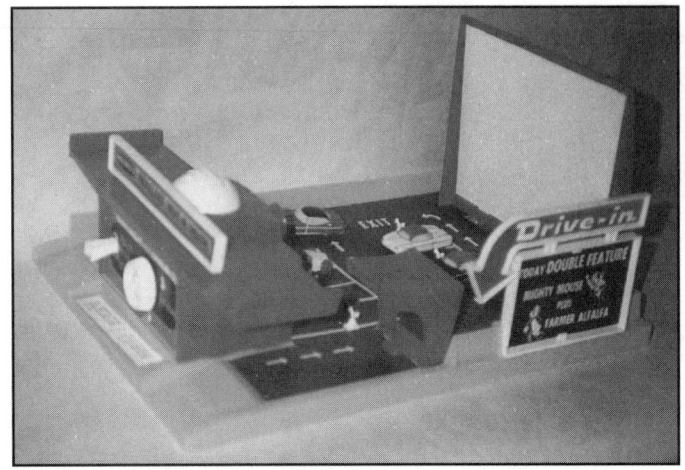

Movieland Drive-In Theater, Remco Co., 1959, $120. Photo courtesy Don Hultzman and Ron Chojnacki

Mr. MacPooch Taking a Walk and Smoking His Pipe, SAN Co., 1950s, $325. Photo courtesy Don Hultzman and Ron Chojnacki

Mr. Mercury Type I (left) and Type II (right), Marx Co., 1960s, $800 each. Photo courtesy Don Hultzman and Ron Chojnacki

	C6	C8	C10
Moon Globe Orbiter, rocket orbits globe, noise, lights, three actions, "Y" Co. (Mego), c. 1960s, 10-1/2" high	100	150	200
Moon Orbiter, includes six sections of track and trestles, minor toy, "Y" Co., 1960s, 4" long	120	180	240
Moon Patrol Space Rover, five actions, Gakken Toy Co., 1960s, 11-1/2" long	175	225	300
Moon Rocket, three actions, rare, "Y" Co., 1950s, 15-1/4" long	400	600	800
Moon Traveler Apollo Z, five actions, TN Co., 1960s, 12" long, 15" extended	120	180	240
Mother Bear Sitting and Knitting in Her Old Rocking Chair, four actions, MT Co., 1950s, 9-1/2" high	225	300	375

	C6	C8	C10
Motorcycle Cop, five actions, Daiya Co., 1950s, 10-1/2" long, 8-1/4" high	500	750	1000
Mountain Cable Car, includes cable, minor toy, Cragstan Co., 1950s, 9" long	60	90	120
Movieland Drive-In Theater, includes six small cars, ad cards, filmstrips, minor toy, Remco Co., 1959, 14" long	60	90	120
Mr. Atom the Electronic Walking Robot, six actions, Advance Doll & Toy Co., 1950s, 17" tall	400	600	800
Mr. Atomic, robot, three actions, rare, Cragstan, 1950s, 11" tall	2500	3750	5000
Mr. Baseball Jr., w/game box, three actions, TN Co., 1950s, 7" high	500	750	1000
Mr. Chief Robot, four actions, K-O Co., 1950s, 12" tall	450	675	900

Musical Jolly Chimp, C-K Co., 1960s, $150.

Picnic Bear, Alps Co., 1950s, $225.

	C6	C8	C10
Mr. Fox, the Magician with the Magical Disappearing Rabbit, includes plastic rabbit, five actions, "Y" Co., 1960s, 9" tall ...	500	750	1000
Mr. Hustler Robot, six actions, Taiyo Co., 1960s, 11" tall	200	300	400
Mr. MacPooch Taking a Walk and Smoking His Pipe, four actions, SAN Co., 1950s, 8" tall	175	225	325
Mr. Magoo Car, includes cloth roof top, five actions, Hubley Co., 1961, 9" long	200	300	400
Mr. Mercury Type I, seven actions, Marx Co., 1960s, 13" tall	400	600	800
Mr. Mercury Type II (lighted), seven actions, Marx Co., 1960s ..	400	600	800
Mr. Robot the Mechanical Brain, three actions, rare, Alps Co., 1950s, 8" tall	600	900	1200

	C6	C8	C10
Mr. Strong Pup Weight-Lifting Dog, five actions, K Co., 1950s, 9" tall	130	195	260
Mr. Traffic Policeman, four actions, A-I Co., 1950s, 14" tall, 6" x 6" base...	175	270	365
Mr. Zerox, four actions, S-H Co., 1960s, 9-1/2" tall	150	225	300
Multi Action Electra Jet KLM Royal Dutch Airlines PH-DSF, three actions, TN Co., 1960s, 14" long, 17" wingspan......................	110	165	220
Mumbo Jumbo, Hawaiian drummer, three actions, Alps Co., 1960s, 9-3/4" high	85	120	160

	C6	C8	C10
Musical Bank Organ Grinder & Monkey, includes test coin and detachable celluloid monkey, four actions, rare, HTC Co., 1950s, 8" tall	500	750	1000
Musical Bear (drum and cymbals), includes detachable tin horn, six actions, Linemar Co., 1950s, 10" tall	200	300	400
Musical Bulldog Playing Piano, four actions, SAN Co., 1950s, 8-1/2" tall, 6" x 9" base	600	900	1200
Musical Cadillac Car, minor toy, Irco Co., 1950s, 9" long	200	300	400
Musical Clown (New Adventures of Clown), three actions, TN Co., 1960s, 9" tall	150	225	300
Musical Comic Jumping Jeep, six actions, Alps Co., 1970s, 12" long	70	105	140
Musical Drummer Robot, three actions, rare, TN Co., 1950s, 8-1/4" tall	4000	6000	8000
Musical Jackal, six actions, rare, Linemar Co., 1950s, 10" tall	150	225	600
Musical Jolly Chimp, five actions, two cycles, C-K Co., 1960s, 10-1/2" high	100	125	150
Musical Marching Bear, includes detachable tin horn, four actions, Alps Co., 1950s, 11" tall	115	170	600
Musical Showboat, includes two detachable smokestacks, minor toy, Gakken Toy Co., 1960s, 13" long	100	150	200
My Fair Dancer, minor toy, Haji Co., 1950s, 10-1/2" tall	100	150	200
Mystery Fire Chief Car, No. 81, three actions, Sanshin Co., 1950s, 9-1/4" long	100	150	200
Mystery Plane, four actions, TN Co., 1950s, 10" long, 10-1/2" wingspan	120	180	240
Mystery Police Car, three actions, TN Co., 1960s, 9-3/4" long, 6" wide, 4" high	100	150	200
NAR Television Truck, includes six film strip inserts, four actions, Linemar Co., 1950s, 12" long	300	450	600
NASA Space Capsule, four actions, 1950s	200	300	400
NBC Television Truck, five actions, Linemar Co., 1950s, 9" long	400	500	750
Neptune Tugboat, four actions, MT Co., 1950s, 15" long, 7" high	90	135	180
New Astronaut Robot, six actions, S-H Co., 1970s, 9-1/2" tall	80	120	160
New Bell Ringer Choo Choo, locomotive, three actions, MT Co., 1960s, 10" long	50	75	100
New Space Capsule, six actions, S-H Co., 1960s, 9" long	120	180	240
News Service Car, four actions, T.P.S. Co., 1960s, 10" long	150	225	300
Non-Stop Robot, three actions, rare, MT Co., 1960s, 15" tall	600	900	1200
Nutty Mad Indian, four actions, Marx, 1960s, 12" tall	150	200	250
Nutty Mads Car (Drincar), three actions, Marx Co., 1960s, 9-1/4" long	175	250	325
Nutty Nibs, includes litho bowl of nuts and steel ball, minor toy, rare, Linemar, 1950s, 11-1/2" tall	700	850	1400
Ol' MacDonald's Farm Truck, includes plastic pig, cow and chicken, four actions, Frankonia, 1960s	100	150	200
Ol' Sleepy Head RIP, seven actions, "Y" Co., 1950s, 9" long.	150	250	320
Old Fashioned Car, four actions, S-H Co., 1950s, 10" long	75	100	125
Old Fashioned Fire Engine, four actions, MT Co., 1950s, 12-1/2" long	120	180	240
Old Fashioned Telephone Bear (?), four actions, MT Co., 1950s, 9-1/2" high	200	250	300
Old Ford Touring Car, four actions, Z Co., 1950s, 10" long	40	60	80
Old Time Automobile, includes detachable tin-litho driver and steering wheel, three actions, "Y" Co., 1950s, 8-3/4" long	100	150	200
Old Timer Car, three actions, Cragston Co., 1950s, 9" long	100	150	200
Oldtimer Automoball, includes celluloid ball, three actions, MT Co., 1950s, 10" long	90	135	180
Oldtimer Sunday Driver, four actions, Daiya Co., 1960s, 9" long	70	105	140
Overland Choo Choo Express Locomotive, minor toy, MT Co., 1950s, 14" long	30	45	60

Piston Action Robot, T-N Co., 1950s, $1800. Photo courtesy Don Hultzman and Ron Chojnacki

Playful Pup in Shoe, "Y" Co., 1960s, $100. Photo courtesy Don Hultzman and Ron Chojnacki

	C6	C8	C10
Overland Stage Coach, four actions, Ichida Co., 1960s, 18" long	100	150	200
P.D. Police Patrol Car (Buick), three actions, Asakusa Toy Co., 1960s, 11-1/2" long	80	120	160
P-51 Mustang Shooting Figher Plane, minor toy, TN Co., 1950s, 9" long, 9" wingspan	90	135	180
Pacific Piping Express Locomotive, four actions, Kanto Toy Co., 1960s, 14" long	40	60	80
Pam Am Sky Taxi Helicopter, three actions, Haji Co., 1960s, 11" long	70	105	140
Pan American World Airways 'Seven Seas' DC-7, five actions, TN Co., 1950s, 15" long, 19" wingspan	200	250	300
Panda Bear, mostly plastic, four actions, MT Co. (Masudaya Co.), 1970s, 10" long	30	45	65
Papa Bear Reading & Drinking in His Old Rocking Chair, four actions, MT Co., 1950s, 10" high	150	225	300

	C6	C8	C10
Passenger Bus, four actions, "Y" Co., 1950s, 16" long	230	345	460
Pat O'Neill, standing, six actions, TN Co., 1960s, 12" tall	150	225	300
Pat the Dog, five actions, two cycles, NGS Co., 1950s, 9-1/2" long	30	45	60
Pat the Roaring Elephant, w/attached baby elephant, four actions, "Y" Co., 1950s, 9" long	150	200	250
Patrol Auto Tricycle, four actions, TN Co., 1960s, 19" long, 7-1/2" high	200	300	400
Patrol Helicopter No. 7, four actions, Bandai Co., 1960s, 11" long	70	105	140
Penguin on Tricycle, three actions, TN Co., 1950s, 6-1/2" high	100	150	200
Pepi Tumbling Monkey, minor toy, Yanoman Toy Co., 1960s, 9-1/2" high	40	60	80
Peppermint Twist Doll, minor toy, Haji Co., 1950s, 12" tall	150	225	300

Space Fighter, S-H Co., 1970s, $175. Photo courtesy Don Hultzman and Ron Chojnacki

Popcorn Eating Bear, M-T Co., 1950s, $250. Photo courtesy Don Hultzman and Ron Chojnacki

	C6	C8	C10
Peppy Puppy, includes tin-litho bone, seven actions, two cycles, "Y" Co., 1950s, 8" long, 6-1/2" high	75	100	125
Pet Turtle, four actions, two cycles, Alps Co., 1960s, 7" long	70	105	140
Pete the Space Man (Walking Mate Series), minor action, Bandai Co., 1960s, 5" tall	60	90	120
Peter the Drumming Rabbit (VIA-Cragstan), five actions, Alps Co., 1950s, 13" tall	150	225	300
Phillips '66' Power Yacht, includes plastic parts for yacht and dock, unmarked, minor toy, 1950s, 18" long	70	105	140
Pick-Up Truck, four actions, TN Co., 10" long	100	150	200
Picnic Bear, w/Coke, Pepsi and generic logo, five actions, Alps Co., 1950s, 10" high	150	175	225

	C6	C8	C10
Picnic Bunny, four actions, Alps Co., 1950s, 10" tall	150	175	225
Picnic Monkey, four actions, STS Co., 1950s, 10" high	150	175	225
Picnic Poodle, four actions, two cycles, STS Co., 1950s, 7" long, 7" high	50	75	100
Pierrot Monkey Cycle, five actions, MT Co., 1950s, 8" long, 10-1/2" high	325	460	650
Piggy Barbecue, includes chef's hat and tin-litho fried egg, five actions, "Y" Co., 1950s, 9-1/2" tall	150	250	350
Piggy Cook, includes chef's hat and tin-litho fried egg, five actions, "Y" Co., 1950s, 9-1/2" tall, 4" x 6" base	150	250	350
Pinkee the Farmer, seven actions, MT Co., 1950s, 9-1/2" long	100	155	200

	C6	C8	C10
Pinky the Clown, includes tin-litho propeller, ball on nose, five actions, rare, Rock Valley Toy Co. (Via), 1950s, 10-1/4" tall.................................	200	300	400
Pinocchio Playing London Bridge, includes xylophone, three actions, TN Co. (Rosko), 1962, 10" tall....................................	150	225	300
Pioneer Covered Wagon, includes detachable canopy and driver, four actions, Ichida Co., 1960s, 14-1/2" long.................................	120	180	240
Pipie the Whale, minor toy, Alps Co., 1950s, 12" long....................	250	325	500
Pistol Pete, includes tin hat, five actions, Marusan Co., 1950s, 10-1/4" high..........................	250	325	500
Piston Action Bulldozer, two cycles, Linemar Co., 1960s, 7-1/2" long................................	90	135	180
Piston Action Robot, resembles Robbie, three actions, TN Co., 1950s, 8-1/4" tall........................	900	1350	1800
Piston Head Robot, three actions, S-H Co., 1960s, 10" tall..................	150	225	300
Piston Robot, four actions, S-H Co., 1960s, 10-1/2" tall....................	110	165	220
Planet Explorer, four actions, S-H Co., 1950s, 9" long......................	150	225	300
Planet Rover, wheeled tank, six actions, J Co., 1960s, 9" long, 6-1/2" high..	140	210	280
Planet 'Y' Space Station, three actions, TN Co., 1960s, 9" diameter..	140	210	280
Playful Pup in Shoe, three actions, "Y" Co., 1960s, 10" long	60	80	100
Playful Puppy, four actions, MT Co., 1950s, 7-3/8" long, 5" high..	100	150	200
Playing Monkey, The, includes detachable hat and tin yo-yo, six actions, S&E Co. (Ahi Brand), 1950s, 10" tall	200	300	400
Pluto, five actions, Linemar Co., 1960s, 10" long	300	450	600
Polar Bear, three actions, Alps Co., 1970s, 8" long	50	75	100
Police Auto Cycle, motorcycle w/plastic driver and remote control, five actions, Bandai Co., 1960s	175	250	325
Police Motorcycle, seven actions, MT Co., 1950s, 11-3/4" long	200	300	400

	C6	C8	C10
Police No. 5 Police Car, four actions, TN Co., 1950s, 9-1/2" long..	90	135	180
Police Patrol Jeep, four actions—lights, bump and go, noise and smoke, TN Co., 1960s, 9-1/4" long..	100	150	200
Pom Pom Tank, five actions, S&E Co., 1950s, 12" long...................	160	240	320
Popcorn Eating Bear, five actions, MT Co., 1950s, 9" high...............	150	200	250
Popcorn Vendor, includes litho umbrella, six actions, S&E Co., 1960s, 8" high, 7" long...............	200	300	400
Popcorn Vendor Truck, three actions, TN Co., 1960s, 9" long ..	150	225	300
Popeye and Rowboat with Moving Oars, three actions, rare, Linemar Co., 1950s, 10" long....................	5000	7500	10,000
Porsche with Visible Engine, three actions, Bandai Co., 1964, 10" long..	90	135	180
Poverty Pup, bank, three actions, Poynter Products Co., 1966, 6" long, 4-1/4" high	60	90	120
Power Shovel, six actions, Alps Co., 1950s, 15" long extended	90	135	180
Pretty Peggy Parrot, six actions, TN Co., 1950s, 11" long....................	250	375	500
Princess the French Poodle, no markings, five actions, 1950s, 9" long, 8" high..............................	40	60	80
Professor Owl, includes two disks, five actions, E-T Co., 1950s, 8" high...	200	300	400
Project Yankee Doodle, includes plastic missiles, rockets and accessories, six actions, Remco Co., 1959, 15" long	60	90	120
Puffy Morris, five actions, uses real cigarette, "Y" Co., 1960s, 10" tall...	150	200	250
Puzzled Puppy, five actions, MT Co., 1950s, 7-1/2" long, 5" high..	100	150	200
Queen of the Sea, inlcudes detachable antenna and flag, four actions, MT Co., 1950s, 21-1/2" long..	300	450	600
R.R. Line Locomotive, four actions, Marx, 1950s, 6-1/2" long	40	60	80
R-35 Robot, five actions, MT Co., 1950s, 7-1/2" tall	300	450	600

	C6	C8	C10
Rabbits and Carriage, The, four actions, S&E Co., 1950s, 10" tall	150	225	300
Racecar #25, three actions, rare, Alps Co., 1950s, 9" long	800	1200	1600
Radar Jeep, four actions, TN Co., 1950s, 11" long	150	225	300
Radar Robot, remote robot w/face control box, three actions, TN Co., 1960s, 9" tall	600	900	1200
Radar Robot, five actions, S-H Co., 1970s, 12" tall	125	150	175
Radar Scope Space Scout, three actions, S-H Co., 1960s, 9-1/4" tall	140	210	280
Radio Rex, includes celluloid dog, minor toy, Elmwood Button Co., 1920s, 5" x 7" dog house	100	150	200
Railroad Hand Car, includes rubber track, minor toy, KDP Co., 1950s, 8" long	90	135	180
Railway Yard Shuttle Train, includes locomotive boxcar and track, three actions, ATC Co., 1950s, 8" long, 28" long track	100	150	200
Ranger Robot, six actions, Daiya Co., 1950s, 11" tall	400	600	800
Ray Gun, machine gun, includes tripod, three actions, TN Co., 1950s, 17-1/2" long	50	75	100
RCA NBC Mobile Color TV Truck, four actions, Yonezawa Co., 1950s, 9" long	400	500	750
Reading Bear, five actions, Alps Co., 1950s, 9" tall	100	175	225
Rembrandt Monkey Artist, five actions, Alps Co., 1950s, 8" high	170	240	365
Reversible Diesel Electric Tractor, minor toy, Marx Co., 1950s	50	75	100
Ricki the Begging Poodle, five actions, Rock Valley Toys (VIA), 1950s, 9" long, 8" high	30	45	60
River Queen Sidewheeler, three actions, MT Co., 1950s, 13-1/2" long	175	225	300
Riverboat, includes detachable tin smokestack, three actions, Marusan Co., 1950s, 12-3/4" long	130	195	260
Road Construction Roller, four actions, Daiya Co., 1950s, 8-1/2" long	60	90	120
Road Grader, three actions, TN Co., 1960s, 12" long	50	75	100

	C6	C8	C10
Road Roller, four actions, MT Co., 1950s, 9" long	60	90	120
Roarin' Jungle Lion, four actions, two cycles, Marx Co., 1950s, 16" long nose to tail tip	200	275	350
Roaring Gorilla Shooting Gallery, includes fold-outtarget box, tin gun, plastic darts, three actions, MT Co., 1950s, 9-1/2" tall	200	300	400
Robby Space Patrol, five actions, rare, TN Co., 1950s, 12-1/2" long	2000	3000	4000
Robert the Robot, three actions, Ideal Toy Co., 1950s, 14" tall	150	200	250
Robert the Robot Mechanical Bulldozer, four actions, rare, Ideal Toy Co., 1950s, 9" long	300	450	600
Robot, minor toy, rare, "Y" Co., 1950s, 6" tall	600	900	1200
Robot, three actions, "Y" Co., 1960s, 10-1/2" tall	400	600	800
Robot 2500, four actions, Durham Industries, 1970s, 10-1/2" tall	60	90	120
Robotank TR-2, four actions, TN Co., 1960s, 5" high	140	210	280
Robotank Z Space Robot, five actions, TN Co., 1960s, 10-1/4" high	300	450	600
Rock 'N' Roll Hotrod (Dreamboat), three actions, TN Co., 1950s, 7" long	150	225	300
Rock 'N' Roll Monkey (three variations), includes plastic hat, five actions, Rosko Co., 1950s, 13" tall	175	250	325
Rocket Express Rocket Ship Monorail, twenty-piece rail and girder set, three actions, Linemar Co., 1950s, 10" long	100	150	200
Rocket Launching Pad, includes tin-litho satellite and rocket, five actions, "Y" Co., 1950s, 8-1/2" high	160	240	320
Rocking Chair Bear, five actions, MT Co., 1950s, 10" high	150	200	250
Rocking Santa, four actions, rare, Alps Co., 1950s, 10" high	300	450	600
Roller Skater, minor toy, Alps Co., 1950s, 12" tall	125	175	225
Rollerskating Clown, minor toy, rare, T.P.S. Co., 1950s, 6" tall	500	750	1000
Romance Car M-841, three actions, M Co., 1950s, 8" long	90	135	180

Santa the Bellringer, Chase Import Co., 1950s, $200. Photo courtesy Don Hultzman and Ron Chojnacki

Shipping Monkey, T-N Co., 1960s, $80. Photo courtesy Don Hultzman and Ron Chojnacki

Shoe Maker Bear, T-N Co., 1960s, $250. Photo courtesy Don Hultzman and Ron Chojnacki

	C6	C8	C10
Rootbeer Counter, includes plastic barrel, glasses, and tin tray, three actions, K Co., 1960s, 8" long, 8" high	100	160	230
Rosko Robot, five actions, Rosko Co., 1950s, 13" tall	500	750	1000
Rotate-O-Matic Super Astronaut, six actions, two cycles, S-H Co., 1960s, 11-1/2" tall	100	150	200
Rover the Poodle Bell Ringer, three actions, two cycles, Alps Co., 1960s, 10-1/2" tall	60	90	120
Roy Rogers Western Telephone, three actions, Ideal Co., 1950s, 9" high	100	150	200
Royal Club in Buggy, pushed by Mama Bear, six actions, S&E Co., 1940s, 8" long, 8" high	140	210	280
Rudy the Robot, four actions, Remco Co., 1968, 16-1/4" tall	110	165	220
Sam the Shaving Man, includes metal mirror, seven actions, Plaything Toy Co., 1960s, 11-1/2" tall	150	225	300
Sammy Wong the Tea Totaler, four actions, TN Co., 1950s, 10" tall	140	200	285
Santa Bank (Trim a Tree), four actions, HTC Co., 1960, 11" high	150	225	300
Santa Claus (Sitting on House), four actions, H.T.C. Co., 1950s, 8" high	150	200	250
Santa Claus Bellringer, five actions, Santa Creations Co., 1950s, 13" tall	100	150	200
Santa Claus on Handcar, three actions, MT Co., 1960s, 10" high	100	140	200
Santa Claus on Scooter, four actions, MT Co., 1960s, 10" high	110	150	200
Santa Claus Phone Bank, includes remote 4-3/4" high pay phone, seven actions, S&E Co., 1950s, 8" high	400	600	800
Santa Claus Stands & Sits, six actions, TN Co., 1960s, 10" tall	150	225	300
Santa Copter, three actions, MT Co., 1960s, 8-1/2" long	150	200	250
Santa Fe Diesel Battery Cable Train with Headlight (two-piece hookup), minor toy, TN Co., 1950s, 13-1/2" long	80	120	160
Santa Sled, four actions, rare, TN Co., 1950s, 14" long	300	450	600

	C6	C8	C10
Santa the Bellringer, electromagnet activated and Blinker bulb, minor toy, Chase Import Co., 1950s, 7" high	100	150	200
Satellite Interceptor, two-piece target set w/two darts and styro ball, minor toy, Linemar Co., 1950s, 6-1/2" long gun-telescope, 5" high blower	200	300	400
Satellite Target Game, includes celluloid ball and special gun, minor toy, S-H Co., 1960s, 8" high, 10-1/2" wide	100	150	200
Saxophone Playing Monkey, four actions, Alps Co., 1950s, 9-1/2" high	200	300	400
School Bus, minor toy, Cragstan, 1950s, 20-1/2" long	70	105	140
Sea Bear #7 Racing Boat, minor toy, Bandai Co., 1950s, 10" long	60	90	120
Seascape Tugboat, three actions, Marx Co., 1950s, 6-1/2" long	50	75	100
Secret Service Action Car (Green Hornet motif), four actions, rare, ASC Co., 1960s, 11" long	400	600	800
Serpent Charmer, four actions, Linemar Co., 1950s, 7" high	175	300	425
Shaggy the Friendly Pup, three actions, Alps Co., 1960s, 8" long	35	45	65
Shaking Classic Car, four actions, TN Co., 1960s, 7" long	75	100	125
Shaking Old-Timer Car, includes plastic driver, four actions, TN Co., 1960s, 9" long	75	100	125
Shark-U-Control Racing Car, all plastic, minor toy, Remco Ind. Inc., 1961, 19" long	80	120	160
Sheriff Car, four actions, TN Co., 1950s, 10" long	100	125	175
Shoe Maker Bear, three actions, TN Co., 1960s, 8-1/2" high	125	200	250
Shoe Shine Bear, five actions, TN Co., 1950s, 9" tall	175	250	325
Shoe Shine Joe, six actions, Alps Co., 1950s, 11" high	175	250	325
Shoe Shine Monkey, five actions, TN Co., 1950s, 9" high	175	250	325
Shoe-Shaking Dog, five actions, MT Co., 1950s, 8" long, 6" tall	50	75	100
Shooting Bear, six actions, SAN Co., 1950s, 10" tall	160	240	320

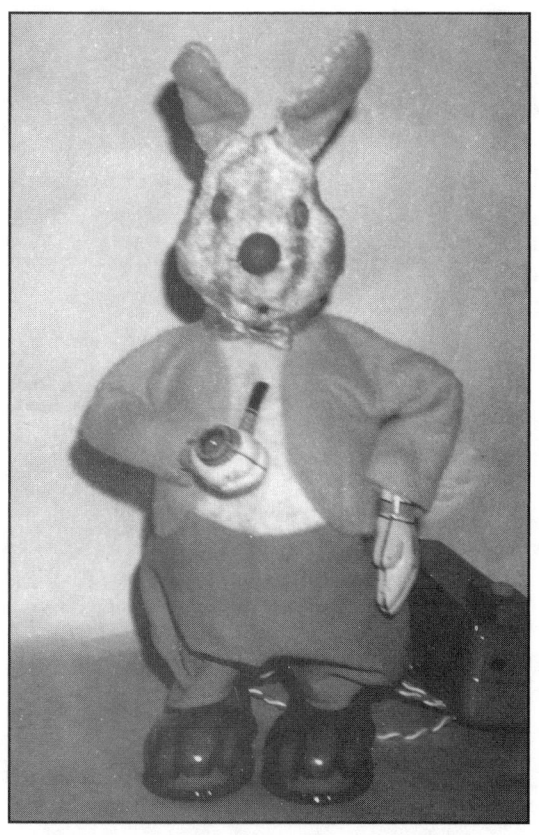

Smoking Bunny, SAN Co., 1950s, $225. Photo courtesy Don Hultzman and Ron Chojnacki

Smoking Elephant, Marusan Co., 1950s, $225. Photo courtesy Don Hultzman and Ron Chojnacki

	C6	C8	C10
Shooting Gorilla, includes tin gun and darts, four actions, MT Co., 1950s, 12" high	200	300	400
Shutterbug, photographer, five actions, TN Co., 1950s, 9" tall	600	800	1000
Shuttling Freight Train, includes locomotive, lumber car, four pieces of track, platform and logs, six actions, Cragstan Co., 1950s, 51" long assembled	150	200	250
Shuttling Train and Freight Yard, includes locomotive, baggage car, two platforms and litho luggage, four actions, Alps Co., 1950s, 11" long, track 51" long	150	200	250
Sight Seeing Bus, four actions, Bandai Co., 1960s, 14-1/2" long	100	150	200
Sight Seeing Bus, minor toy, Yonezawa Co., 1950s, 9" long	140	210	280
Sikorsky Rescue Army Helicopter, four actions, Alps Co., 1950s, 11" long	90	135	180

	C6	C8	C10
Silver Bell Choo Choo, three actions, Kanto Co., 1950s, 12" long	40	60	80
Silver Mountain Express Locomotive, four actions, MT Co., 1960s, 15-3/4" long	50	75	100
Silver Mountain Locomotive, three actions, MT Co., 1950s, 16" long	50	75	100
Silver Ray Secret Weapon Space Scout, six actions, rare, S-H Co., 1960s, 9" tall	750	1075	1500
Silver Streak Locomotive No. 6682, four actions, MT Co., 1950s, 16" long	50	75	100
Sing Tail Cargo Plane Flying Tiger, five actions, TN Co., 1960s, 14" long, 14" wingspan	300	450	600
Singing Bird in Cage, four actions, TN Co., 1950s, 9" high, 4" x 6" rectangular base	100	150	200
Siren Fire Car, four actions, MT Co., 1950s, 9" long	130	195	260
Siren Patrol Car, four actions, MT Co., 1960s, 12-1/2" long	90	135	180

Smoking PaPa Bear, SAN Co., 1950s, $250.

Snake Charmer (and Casey the Trained Cobra), Linemar Co., 1950s, $500. Photo courtesy Don Hultzman and Ron Chojnacki

	C6	C8	C10
Siren Patrol Motorcycle, three actions, MT Co., 1960s, 12" long	300	400	500
Skating Circus Clown, minor toy, rare, T.P.S. Co., 1950s, 6" tall	450	595	800
Skiing Santa, includes tin skis, four actions, MT Co., 1960s, 12" tall	150	225	300
Skipping Monkey, minor toy, TN Co., 1960s, 9-1/2" tall	40	60	80
Sky Patrol Flying Saucer, includes detachable antenna, seven actions, K-O Co., 1950s, 7-1/2" diameter	100	150	200
Sky Patrol Space Cruiser, five actions, TN Co., 1950s, 13" long	150	225	300
Sky Taxi-Panam-Boeing Vertol 107, includes two detachable rotors, three actions, Haji Co., 1970s, 12-3/4" long	120	180	240
Slalom Game, includes plastic skier, minor toy, TN Co., 1960s, 15-1/4" long	100	160	225
Sleeping Baby Bear, includes detachable alarm clock, six actions, 1950s, 9" long	250	350	450
Sleeping Pup, five actions, Alps Co., 1960s, 9" long	45	75	100
Slurpy Pup, four actions, TN Co., 1960s, 6-1/2" long, 4" high	50	75	100

	C6	C8	C10
Smilex Deluxe Coffee Set, includes four sets of cups, saucers, and spoons, plastic, minor toy, "Y" Co., 1950s, 12" high assembled	60	90	120
Smokey the Bear Jeep, four actions, MT Co., 1950s, 10" long	220	330	440
Smoking Bulldozer, four actions, WKC Co., 1960s, 9" long	90	135	180
Smoking Bunny, four actions, SAN Co., 1950s, 10-1/2" tall	125	165	225
Smoking Elephant, four actions, Marusan Co., 1950s, 8-3/4" tall	115	165	225
Smoking Grandpa (in Rocking Chair), Type II-eyes closed, four actions, SAN Co., 1950s, 8" tall	200	300	400
Smoking Grandpa (in Rocking Chair), Type I-eyes open, four actions, SAN Co., 1950s, 8" tall	200	275	350
Smoking Jet Plane, four actions, TN Co., 1950s, 12" long, 11" wing-span	150	225	300
Smoking PaPa Bear, four actions, SAN Co., 1950s, 8" tall	150	200	250
Smoking Pop Locomotive: The General, four actions, SAN Co., 1950s, 10-1/4" long	70	105	140
Smoking Popeye, five actions, rare, Linemar, 1950s, 9" tall	800	1200	1600

Teddy the Artist, "Y" Co., 1950s, $750.

	C6	C8	C10
Smoking Robot, all plastic, four actions, MT Co., 1960s, 10" tall	90	135	180
Smoking Spaceman, six actions, Linemar Co., 1950s, 12" tall	750	1200	1600
Smoking U.S.A.F. Jet, four actions, TN Co., 1950s, 13" long, 12" wingspan	150	225	300
Smoking Volkswagen, four actions, Aoshin Co., 1960s, 10-1/2" long	60	90	120
Smoky Bear, includes detachable tin hat, four actions, SAN Co., 1950s, 9" tall	250	300	500
Smoky Bill on Old-Fashioned Car, four actions, TN Co., 1960s, 9" long	150	200	250
Smoky Joe Fancy Mobile, four actions—smokes, lights, bump and go and noise, TN Co., 1960s, 9" long	150	200	250
Snake Charmer (and Casey the Trained Cobra), four actions, Linemar Co., 1950s, 8" high	250	375	500
Snappy the Dragon, six actions, rare, TN Co., 1960s, 30" long	2000	3000	4000
Sneezing Bear, five actions, Linemar Co., 1950s, 9" high	200	300	400
Snoopie the Non-Fall Dog, three actions, Amico Co., 1960s, 8" long	50	75	100
Snoopy Sniffer, four actions, MT Co., 1960s, 8" long	40	60	80
Somersaulting Pup with Bark, four actions, two cycles, TN Co., 1960s, 9" long	50	75	100
Sonicon Space Rocket, minor toy, MT Co., 1960s, 13" long	250	375	500
Space Capsule, four actions, MT Co., 1960s, 10-1/2" long	150	225	300

	C6	C8	C10
Space Capsule, includes styrofoam saucer and astronaut, four actions, MT Co., 1960s, 10" long	100	150	200
Space Commando Space Station, four actions, TN Co., 1960s, 10" diameter	150	225	300
Space Commando Spaceman, four actions, MT Co., 1960s, 7-3/4" tall	500	750	1000
Space Explorer #1041, six actions, rare, Yonezawa Co., 1960s, 7-3/4" high, extends to 11-1/2" high	600	900	1200
Space Explorer Ship (saucer), six actions, MT Co., 1950s, 11" diameter	100	150	200
Space Fighter, robot, six actions, S-H Co., 1970s, 9" tall	100	150	175
Space Frontier Saturn 5 Rocket, six actions, K-Y Co. (Yoskino Toy Co.), 1960s, 18" long	100	150	200
Space Patrol 3 Saucer, five actions, K-O Co., 1950s, 7-1/2" diameter	100	150	200
Space Patrol Car, four actions, TN Co., 1950s, 9-1/2" long	300	450	600
Space Patrol Car, w/lighting guns, three actions, Linemar Co., 1950s, 9" long	450	675	900
Space Patrol Robot, six actions, S-H Co., 1950s, 11" tall	175	250	300
Space Patrol Rocket, three actions, MT Co., 1970s, 11" long	70	105	140
Space Patrol Snoopy, four actions, MT Co., 1960s, 11" long	125	175	225
Space Patrol Tank, includes detachable tin jet plane, five actions, Cragstan Co., 1950s, 9" long	150	225	300

	C6	C8	C10
Space Patrol Vehicle, three actions, MT Co., 1960s, 9-1/2" long	100	150	200
Space Patrol Vehicle, four actions, K Co., 1950s, 9" long	130	195	260
Space Pioneer Vehicle, three actions, MT Co., 1960s, 12" long...	100	200	300
Space Robot (X-70), five actions, TN Co., 1960s, 12" tall	500	750	1000
Space Robot Car, six actions, rare, Yonezawa Co., 1950s, 9-1/4" long...	1000	1500	2000
Space Robot Trooper, three actions, rare, K-O Co., 1950s, 7-1/2" tall .	500	750	1000
Space Rocket Blue Eagle, , Masuya Toy Co., 1950s, 15" long from tail to probe tip	150	200	250
Space Rocket Solar X, five actions, TN Co., 1960s, 15-1/12" tall	150	225	300
Space Scooter, three actions, MT Co., 1960s, 10-1/2" high, 8" long	100	150	200
Space Scooter, Snoopy or Astro-Dog, three actions, MT Co., 1960s, 8" long	100	150	175
Space Ship, four actions, I.Y. Co., 1950s, 9-1/2" diameter	180	270	360
Space Ship, three actions, MT Co., 1970s, 9" long	90	135	180
Space Ship X-5, four actions, MT Co., 1970s, 8" diameter	75	100	150
Space Ship X-8, four actions, Tada Co., 1960s, 8" long.....................	100	150	200
Space Station, four actions, TN Co., 1950s, 9" diameter.....................	100	150	200
Space Station, five actions, S-H Co., 1950s, 11-3/4" diameter	500	750	1000
Space Tank, four actions, Daiya Co., 1950s, 8" long.....................	120	180	240
Space Tank Robbie Type, four actions, K-O Co., 1960s, 6" long...	2000	3000	4000
Space Tank-M41, includes detachable plastic antenna, four actions, MT Co., 1950s, 9" long...............	100	150	200
Spaceman Robot, four actions, TN Co., 1950s, 9-1/4" tall	400	600	800
Spaceman Robot, three actions, Linemar, 1950s, 7-1/2" tall	350	525	700
Spad XIII S-7 Stunt Biplane, three actions, T.P.S. Co., 1960s, 9" long, 10-3/8" wingspan	200	250	300
Spanking Bear, six actions, Linemar Co., 1950s, 9" high.....................	175	225	350
Sparking Burp Gun, three actions, Mark Co., 1950s, 24" long..........	40	60	80
Sparkling Mike the Robot, three actions, rare, Ace Co., 1950s, 7-1/2" tall	1000	1500	2000
Sparky Savings Bank, electromagnet action, includes 4" long composition dog, minor toy, Byron Co., 1930s, 4" long, 4-1/2" high doghouse	60	90	120
Sparky the Seal, includes celluloid ball, four actions, two cycles, MT Co., 1950s, 6" high, 7" long........	100	150	200
Spirit of 1776, locomotive, five actions, MT Co., 1976, 15-3/4" long..	40	60	80
Sports Car Race Set, includes four plastic race cars, minor toy, T.P.S. Co., 1960s, 8" x 14" base..	80	120	160
SSN-571 Submarine, Skate, minor toy, Marusan Co., 1950s, 16" long w/rudder extended..............	120	180	240
SSN-571 Submarine Nautilus, minor toy, Marusan Co., 1950s, 16" long w/rudder extended	120	180	240
Star Strider Robot, six actions, S-H Co., 1980s, 12" tall......................	110	165	220
Steam Roller, includes tin trailer, four actions, "Y" Co., 1950s, 8" long..	100	150	200
Steam Roller (Road Roller), four actions, TN Co. (Rosko), 1950s, 12" long w/trailer	90	135	180
Steerable Tank, five actions, Linemar Co., 1950s, 9" long...............	60	90	120
Strange Explorer, four actions, DSK Co., 1960s, 7-1/2" long	300	450	600
Strato Jet U.S.A. F., three actions, TN Co., 1950s, 13" long, 14" wingspan	120	180	240
Struttin' Sam, minor toy, Haji Co., 1950s, 10-1/2" tall	300	400	500
Strutting My Fair Dancer (Dancing Sailor Girl), two pieces, minor toy, Haji Co., 1950s, 12" tall.......	100	150	200
Sunbeam Jeep, three actions, Marusan Co., 1940s, 10" long	100	150	200
Sunday Driver, includes detachable driver, four actions, MT Co., 1950s, 10" long	55	90	125
Super Astronaut Robot, five actions, two cycles, S-H Co., 1960s, 11-1/2" tall	150	200	250

Suzette the Eating Monkey, Linemar Co., 1950s, $750. Photo courtesy Don Hultzman and Ron Chojnacki

Swivel-O-Matic Astronaut Robot, S-H Co., 1960s, $200. Photo courtesy Don Hultzman and Ron Chojnacki

	C6	C8	C10
Super Astronaut Robot, four actions, SJM Co., 1960s, 12" tall	150	225	300
Super Giant Robot, six actions, S-H Co., 1960s, 15-1/2" tall	200	300	400
Super Jet, three actions, TN Co., 1950s, 12" long, 8" wingspan	250	375	500
Super Space Capsule, four actions, S-H Co., 1960s, 9" high	100	150	200
Super Space Commander, three actions, S-H Co., 1960s, 10" tall	70	105	140
Super Susie, six actions, Linemar Co., 1950s, 9" high	350	625	700
Surrey Jeep, three actions, TN Co., 1960s, 11" long	90	135	180
Suzette the Eating Monkey, includes tin litho steak, five actions, rare, Linemar Co., 1950s, 8-3/4" high, 7" x 5" base	400	500	750
Suzy-Q Automatic Ironer, four actions, GW Co., 1950s, 7" high	90	135	180
Swingtail Airplane Flying Tigers, seven actions, Marx Co., 1960s, 19-1/2" long, 21" wingspan	300	450	600
Switchboard Operator, four actions, rare, Linemar, 1950s, 7-1/2" high	400	600	1000
Swivel-O-Matic Astronaut Robot, five actions, two cycles, S-H Co., 1960s, 11-1/2" tall	100	150	200

	C6	C8	C10
Talking Parrot (called Pete), six actions, TN Co., 1950s, 18" high	300	400	500
Talking Police Car Mystery Action, three actions, "Y" Co., 1960s, 14" long	70	105	140
Talking Robot, three actions, rare, Yonezawa Co., 1960s, 10-3/4" tall	600	900	1200
Tank 392 U.S. Tank Division, three actions, Marx Co., 1950s, 9-1/2" long	100	125	150
Tank Daisy-Matic, includes darts, five actions, Daisy Mfg. Co., 1965, 8-1/2" long	100	150	200
Tank Daisymatic Rapid Fire Tank, four actions, Daisy Mfg. Co., 1960s, 8" long	120	180	240
Tank M-103, three actions, MT Co., 1950s, 7" long	100	150	200
Tank M-107 U.S. Army, includes four missiles, four actions, "Y" Co., 1950s, 6" long	120	180	240
Tank M-35, three actions, HTC Co., 1950s, 8" long	100	150	200
Tank M-4 Combat Tank, five actions, Taiyo Co., 1960s, 11-1/2" long, 13" w/gun barrel extended	100	150	200

	C6	C8	C10
Tank M-41, four actions, J Co., 1970s, 8-1/4" long	100	150	200
Tank M-48-T, four actions, TN Co., 1960s, 8-1/4" long	100	150	200
Tank M-56, wheel drive, seven actions, MT Co., 1940s, 7-1/2" long	100	150	200
Tank M-81, seven actions, MT Co., 1960s, 8-1/2" long	100	150	200
Tank M-X, five actions, TN Co., 1950s, 8-1/2" long	70	105	140
Tank Robot, five actions, S-H Co., 1960s, 10" tall	300	450	600
Tank T-5, includes detachable radar antenna, three actions, TN Co., 1950s, 8-1/2" long	150	200	250
Tank X-3 (explorer defense), includes six cartridge shells, five actions, Cragstan Co., 1950s, 7-3/4" long	130	195	260
Tank X-75, includes tin gun and darts, three actions, MT Co., 1950s, 9" long	110	165	220
Tarzan, four actions, Marusan Co. (Banner), 1966, 13" tall	500	765	1000
Taxi, yellow cab, five actions, Linemar Co., 1950s, 7-1/2" long	100	150	200
Taxi Cab, five actions, "Y" Co., 1950s, 8-1/2" long	100	150	200
Taxi Cab, four actions, "Y" Co., 1960s, 9" long	100	150	200
Teddy Bear Circus Acrobat, includes detachable bear flyer, three actions, rare, Tomiyana Co., 1950s, 15" high	500	750	1000
Teddy Bear Swing, includes four wire supports and tin sign, three actions, two cycles, TN Co., 1950s, 17" high	300	380	600
Teddy the Artist, includes removable tray and nine patterns, three actions, "Y" Co., 1950s, 8-1/2" high, 5-1/4" x 7" base	400	500	750
Teddy the Boxing Bear, five actions, "Y" Co., 1950s, 9" tall	115	190	240
Teddy the Rhythmical Drummer, three actions, Alps Co., 1960s, 11" tall	100	150	200
Teddy-Go-Kart, four actions, Alps Co., 1960s, 10-1/2" long	100	150	175
Telephone Bear, six actions, Linemar, 1950s, 7-1/2" high	250	350	450

	C6	C8	C10
Telephone Bear Ringing and Talking in His Old Rocking Chair, four actions, MT Co., 1950s, 10" high	250	350	450
Telephone Bunny Ringing and Talking in His Old Rocking Chair, four actions, MT Co., 1950s, 10" high	250	350	450
Television Spaceman, six actions, Alps Co., 1960s, 14-1/2" high to tip of antenna	400	600	825
Television Truck, three actions, Linemar Co., 1950s, 11" long	250	375	500
Thunder Jet Boat, three actions, Bandai Co., 1950s, 9-3/4" long	130	195	260
Tin Man, robot, all plastic, four actions, Remco Industries, Inc., 1960s, 21" tall	100	150	200
Tinkling Trolley, includes two plastic cowcatchers, four actions, two cycles, MT Co., 1950s, 10-1/2" long	150	200	250
Tiny Jeep, minor action, WACO Co., 1950s, 4-1/4" long	30	45	60
Tiny Tank, minor action, WACO Co., 1950s, 4-1/4" long	30	45	60
Tom and Jerry Car, three actions, rare, Rico Co. (Spain), 1960s, 13" long	400	600	800
Tom and Jerry Choo Choo, five actions, MT Co., 1960s, 10-1/4" long	175	225	325
Tom and Jerry Handcar, three actions, MT Co., 1960s, 7-3/4" high, 7-3/4" long	175	250	350
Tom and Jerry Handcar, three actions, MT Co., 1960s, 9-3/4" high, 7-3/4" long	175	250	350
Tom and Jerry Helicopter, three actions, MT Co., 1960s, 9-1/2" long	150	200	300
Tom and Jerry Highway Patrol, three actions, MT Co., 1960s, 8" long	150	200	300
Tom and Jerry Jumping Jeep, three actions, MT Co., 1960s, 9" long	150	200	300
Tom-Tom Indian, four actions, "Y" Co., 1961, 10-1/2" tall	100	150	175
Topo Gigio Playing the Xylophone, three actions, TN Co., 1960s	265	440	525
Torpedo Boat-PT 107, three actions, Linemar, 1950s, 11-1/2" long	110	165	220

Walking Elephant, Linemar Co., 1950s, $200. Photo courtesy Don Hultzman and Ron Chojnacki

X-70 Robot, T-N Co., 1960s, $1000. Photo courtesy Don Hultzman and Ron Chojnacki

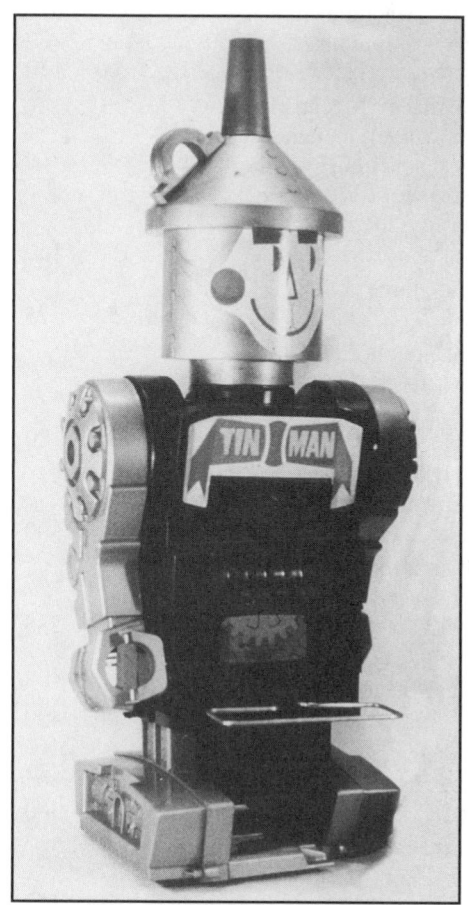

Tin Man, Remco Industries, Inc., 1960s, $200. Photo courtesy Don Hultzman and Ron Chojnacki

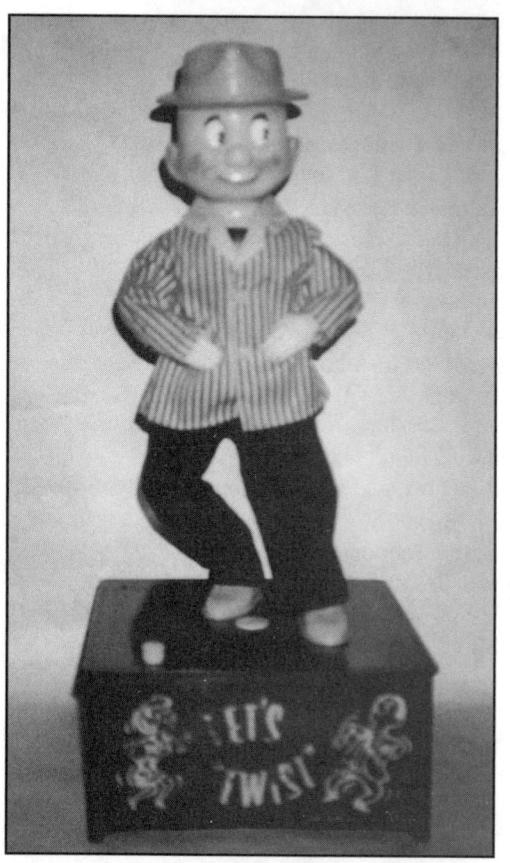

Twist Dancer (Let's Twist), 1960s, $250. Photo courtesy Don Hultzman and Ron Chojnacki

	C6	C8	C10
Tractor, includes litho tin driver, four actions, Showa Co., 1950s, 7-1/2" long............	60	90	120
Tractor, three actions, "Y" Co., 1960s, 6" long	50	75	100
Tractor on Platform, minor toy, TN Co., 1950s, 9" long tractor w/7" trailer long	80	120	160
Train Robot, four actions, rare, MT Co., 1950s, 15-1/2" tall	1500	2250	3000
Traveler Bear, three actions, Linemar Co., 1950s, 8" high...............	100	150	200
Treasure Chest Bank, five actions, two cycles, risqué toy, PG-rated, Illfelder Co., 1960s, 11" tall........	90	135	180
Tric-cycling Clown, five actions, MT Co., 1960s, 12" high.............	350	500	600
Tricky Dog House, four actions, "Y" Co., 1960s, 6-3/4" high, 7-1/4" long, 6-3/4" wide	60	90	120
Trumpet Playing Bunny, four actions, Alps Co., 1950s, 10" high...........................	150	225	300
Trumpet Playing Monkey, includes tin horn, four actions, Alps Co., 1950s, 9" high	150	225	300
Tubby the Turtle, three actions, "Y" Co., 1950s, 7" long.....................	50	75	100
Tugboat, three actions, Marusan Co., 1950s, 13-1/2" long	110	165	220
Tugboat, minor toy, Marx, 1950s, 6-1/2" long.............................	50	75	100
Tumbles the Bear, includes porter's hat, minor toy, Y-M Co. (Yanoman), 1960s, 8-1/2" tall.....	100	150	200
Turn Signal Robot Auto Accessory, five actions, TN Co., 1960s, 11" tall............................	160	240	320
Turn-O-Matic Gun Jeep, five actions, TN Co., 1960s, 10" long	100	150	200
Turntable Xylophone Melody Train, three actions, Cragstan Co., 1960s, 29-1/2" long assembled............................	50	75	100
TWA Multiaction DC-7C Airliner, seven actions, Yonezawa Co., 1960s, 22-1/2" long, 23-1/4" wingspan	200	300	400
Twin Coupled Tram Cars, two cars, minor toy, K Co., 1950s, 11-1/2" long............................	100	150	200

	C6	C8	C10
Twin Racing Cars, three actions, Alps Co., 1950s, 7" long, 10" long w/coupling rod	400	600	800
Twirly Whirly, four actions, Alps Co., 1950s, 13-1/2" high	290	450	600
Twist Dancer (Let's Twist), includes two plastic-rubber rockets, no manufacturer mark, minor toy, 1960s, 15" high	150	200	250
Two Stage Rocket Launching Pad, three actions, TN Co., 1950s, 7" long, 4" wide, 8" high	250	375	500
U.S Navy Pom Pom Gun, four actions, Remco Co., 1950s, 20" long............................	80	120	160
U.S. Air Force Military Airlift Command Jet, four actions, TN Co., 1960s, 14" wingspan............	130	195	260
U.S. Air Force Smoking Jet, three actions—smokes, engine noise and bump and go, rare, TN Co., 1950s, 12" wingspan	200	300	400
U.S. Army Machine Gunner, unmarked, four actions, 1960s, 10" long.........................	100	150	200
U.S. Royal Tire Mechanical Toy (ferris wheel), includes plastic figures, souvenir from the 1964-65 New York World's Fair, minor toy, Ideal, 1964-65, 10" high..........................	100	150	200
UFO-X05, three actions, MT Co., 1970s, 7-1/2" diameter	50	75	100
Union Mountain Cable Lines, Monorail set, minor toy, TN Co., 1950s, 8" long car w/22" x 32" 16-piece oval track	80	120	160
United DC7 Mainliner, five actions, Yonezawa Co., 1950s, 14" wingspan	200	300	400
United Mainliner Stratocruiser, four actions, Linemar, 1950s, 19-1/2" long, 13" wingspan.....................	190	285	380
United States Ocean Liner, three actions, "Y" Co., 1950s, 18-1/2" long..............................	300	450	600
United States Ocean Liner, three actions, Linemar Co., 1950s, 14" long..............................	200	300	400
Universal Machine Gun, three actions, TN Co., 1950s, 14-3/4" long..............................	70	105	140

U.S. Royal Tire Mechanical Toy (ferris wheel), Ideal, 1964-65, $200. Photo courtesy Don Hultzman and Ron Chojnacki

Walking Bear with Xylophone, Linemar Co., 1950s, $400. Photo courtesy Don Hultzman and Ron Chojnacki

	C6	C8	C10
USA NASA Apollo Space Ship, four actions, MT Co., 1960s, 9" long	150	225	300
USA NASA Gemini Space Capsule, includes detachable astronaut, four actions, MT Co., 1960s, 9" long	120	180	240
V.I.P. the Busy Boss, six actions, S&E Co., 1950s, 8" high	250	350	450
Video Robot, three actions, S-H Co., 1960s, 10" tall	150	175	225
Visible Ford Mustang, four actions, Bandai Co., 1960s, 10" long	80	120	160
Vision Robot, five actions, S-H Co., 1960s, 11-3/4" tall	150	225	300
Voice Control Astronaut Base, includes plastic missiles and phonograph records, four actions, Remco Co., 1969, 19" long	90	135	180
Volkswagen, three actions, Bandai Co., 1960s, 10" long	90	135	180
Volkswagen Convertible, three actions, TN Co., 1950s, 9-3/4" long	250	375	500
Volkswagen with Visible Engine, three actions, K.O. Co., 1960s, 7" long	80	120	160
Volkswagen with Visible Engine, three actions, Bandai Co., 1960s, 8" long	90	135	180

	C6	C8	C10
Volkswagen-Elektrik, three actions, Mignon Co., 1950s, 8-1/2" long	70	105	140
Wagon Master, four actions, MT Co., 1960s, 18" long	120	180	240
Walking Bear with Xylophone, seven actions, Linemar Co., 1950s, 10" high	200	300	400
Walking Elephant, three actions, Linemar Co., 1950s, 8-1/2" long	100	150	200
Walking 'Esso' Tiger, four actions, Marx Co., 1950s, 11-1/2" tall	300	400	500
Walking Itchy Dog, five actions, Alps Co., 1950s, 9" long	45	75	100
Warpath Indian, three actions, Alps Co., 1950s, 12" tall	150	200	250
Wash-O-Matic washing machine, includes lid, minor toy, TN Co., 1940s, 5-3/4" high, 4-1/4" diameter	50	75	100
Water Spouting Whale with Flopping Tail, minor toy, KKS Co., 1950s, 13" long	100	150	200
Wester Express, Locomotive, four actions, Kanto Toy Co., 1960s, 14" long	50	75	100
Western Badman Red Gulch Bar, includes three plastic bottles and two plastic glasses, eight actions, MT Co., 1960s, 9-3/4" high	300	450	600

V.I.P. the Busy Boss, S&E Co., 1950s, $450.

	C6	C8	C10		C6	C8	C10
Western Locomotive, four actions, MT Co., 1950s, 10-1/2" long	45	65	80	Worried Mother Duck and Baby, three actions, TN Co., 1950s, 11" long, 7" high...............................	100	150	200
Western Special Locomotive, five actions, MT Co., 1950s, 12" long.................................	50	75	100	X-1800 Space Vehicle, includes detachable plastic antenna, five actions, MT Co., 1960s, 9" long .	140	210	280
Wheel-A-Gear Robot, five actions, Taiyo Co., 1960s, 14" tall	250	375	500	X-7 Space Explorer Ship, four actions, MT Co., 1960s, 7" diameter.................................	100	150	200
Whirlybird Helicopter, three actions, Remco Co., 1960s, 25" long.................................	80	120	160	X-70 Robot, five actions, rare, TN Co., 1960s, 12-1/4" tall	500	750	1000
Whistling Showboat, three actions, MT Co., 1950s, 14" long.............	150	200	250	X-F 160 Jet Airplane, , K-O Co., 1960s, 8" wingspan	80	120	160
WHOH Skyway Patrol Helicopter, four actions, MT Co., 1950s, 18" long.................................	100	150	200	Yeti the Abominable Snowman, four actions, Marx, 1960s, 12" tall..	250	335	500
Wild West Rodeo, includes plastic bowl for bubble solution, five actions, Linemar, 1950s, 6-1/2" long, 8" high..............................	100	150	200	Yo-Yo Clown, includes plastic yo-yo, three actions, Alps Co., 1960s, 9" high	150	200	300
Windy the Elephant, includes celluloid ball and tin litho umbrella, three actions, TN Co., 1950s, 9-3/4" high................................	150	200	250	Yo-Yo Monkey, includes plastic yo-yo, three actions, Alps Co., 1960s, 9" tall	150	200	300
Winner 23, Rocket, includes rubber track, minor action, KDP Co. (Excelo), 1950s, 5-1/2" long	150	225	300	Yo-Yo Monkey, minor toy, Y-M Co., 1960s, 12" tall, spring extension to 32"	100	150	200
Winner of the West Overland Stagecoach with Four Galloping Horses, four actions, Alps Co., 1950s, 18" long	200	300	400	Yummy Yum Kitty, five actions, Alps Co., 1950s, 9-1/2" high.......	170	270	325
Winston the Barking Bulldog, three actions, two cycles, Tomiyama Co., 1950s, 10" long...................	70	105	140	Zero Fighter Plane, three actions, Bandai Co., 1950s, 12-1/2" long, 15" wingspan.............................	150	230	300
				Zoom Motorboat, three actions, K Co., 1950s, 12" long....................	100	150	200
				Zoomer the Robot, three actions, TN Co., 1950s, 8" tall	250	375	500

BB Guns

Spring Air BB guns, sometimes referred to as air rifles, are simple in design and operation. They cannot be pumped up to high pressures and their muzzle velocity is usually in the neighborhood of 400 feet per second. Operation is simple: a one-stroke cocking action compresses a spring and draws a piston back through a cylindrical air chamber. Locked in this position, the BB gun is ready to fire. Meanwhile a BB has been placed in the breech, either manually or by an automatic feed mechanism. When the trigger is pulled the piston is driven forward, forcing the air in the cylinder put through the barrel, driving the BB ahead of this blast of air. Meanwhile a BB has been placed in the breech, either manually or by an automatic feed mechanism.

When the trigger is pulled the piston is driven forward, forcing the air in the cylinder out through the barrel, driving the BB ahead of this blast of air.

A BB gun is not a toy in the traditional sense. If improperly handled it can be dangerous and cause injury. Yet it was conceived, designed, manufactured, and advertised for use by children. Common sense tells us that a BB gun should not be placed in the hands of a child too young to understand its dangers or who has not been properly instructed in its safe use.

Daisy and Markham/King both went into the BB gun business in the late 1880s. Located just across the railroad tracks from one another in Plymouth, Michigan, they were in vigorous competition for years. By the early 1930s, Daisy not only owned King, but the King guns were being produced in the Daisy plant. During that period of about forty years, as many as thirty companies tried their hand at the BB gun business. Few made a great success of it; none have survived. By the 1930s, "Daisy" and "BB Gun" had become pretty much synonymous terms.

Daisy started life as the Iron Windmill Company in 1882. Iron windmills weren't great sellers, and when windmill designer C.J. Hamilton brought in a small prototype BB gun to be considered for manufacture, the board of directors was cool toward the idea. Eventually, it was decided that the little gun would be made as a premium to be given to windmill purchasers. But as Cass Hough, grandson of one of Daisy's founders, said in his 1976 book *It's A Daisy*, "It didn't take long for the tail to begin to wag the dog." A few months later production started in earnest, and the first Daisy was on the market.

The people who were running the Iron Windmill Company didn't realize that their BB gun was only the first of hundreds of models that would be produced over the next century. Neither that first Daisy nor the variations and new models that followed over the next few years were assigned a letter or number designation. Finally, in 1900 Daisy produced a variation with the designation "Model B." The designations such as "first model, second model," etc. are informal terms used by collectors. The BB guns are not so marked. The first Daisy was simply marked "DAISY MFD. BY IRON WIND MILL CO. PLYMOUTH MICH. PAT. APD. FOR." After that, Daisy produced BB guns with names, letters, numbers, or combinations of the same. Their system, or more accurately, lack of system, is confusing to the average collector, and even the advanced collector cannot answer questions about the chronology of Daisy BB guns with absolute certainty every time. Daisy didn't know they were making collectibles, or that anyone would care a hundred years later when a particular model was manufactured. Some guns have no special marking except a name, which may be shared with several models. Some have a single letter or number designation; still others may have a combination of letters and numbers. Many of Daisy's guns form the late 1930s have a number and a model number such as "No. 111 Model 40," in addition to name, in this case, "Red Ryder." A classic case is the No. 50 Golden Eagle of 1936. This out of sequence number was used because the gun was made to commemorate Daisy's 50th Anniversary.

To make it easy for the reader, the Daisy listings have been broken down into several sections. Name-only guns are in the first section. Those identified by a letter (alphabet guns) are next, followed by numbered guns. Guns with a combination of letters and numbers will be listed according to whichever appears first, the letter or the number.

With a few exceptions, the listings are limited to guns made between 1888 and 1942. BB guns made after World War II have not yet aroused much collector interest. That is not to say that none of the postwar guns are collectible or that some collectors do not collect these later models, but most collector interest is focused on the prewar era. This eliminated most of the plastic-stocked guns from this chapter and most of the guns from Daisy's facility at Rogers, Arkansas. Daisy switched to plastic stocks around 1950 and moved to Rogers in 1958.

Like the prices of all collectibles, BB gun prices are somewhat subjective and actual prices paid can vary widely. Many factors have to be considered. Supply and demand, nostalgia, condition, how badly the buyer wants the item, and the thickness of the buyer's wallet are all-important factors in the collectibles game. There is no infallible guide to BB gun values. The prices listed are based upon collecting, buying, and selling BB guns over the past few years and may not reflect prices in every area.

One last word on the listing method used in this book: the term C10 means a piece that is in exac5tly the condition it was in the day it was made. In the case of many BB guns, no such piece will ever be found. Just because it is the best example you have ever seen or heard of does not make it a C10.

There are many contributors to this chapter, far too many to list here, but two deserve mention. Jim E. Thomas of Tulsa Oklahoma has long been my mentor in learning the intricacies of Daisy BB gun chronology. In addition, Bill and Lynn Johnson of Rosamond, California, have been great assistance in sorting out the very early Daisys and Kings. Much of this early information is very obscure. Daisy did not bother to keep complete records of early model changes for production. Bill who has studied the subject for many years and has a fine collection of old Daisy/King ads and other paper was nice enough to go over the evaluations and lend his personal input prior to publication.

Two other important sources of information have been Arni Dunathan's 1971 book, *The American BB Gun*, and *It's A Daisy*, by Cass S. Hough. Hough, grandson of one of Daisy's founders, was mainly responsible for developing the great Daisy character

guns of the 1930s. The Buck Jones, Buzz Barton, and that most famous of all BB guns, the Daisy Red Ryder, were all Hough creations.

Abbreviations used:

LA:	Lever Action
BA:	Break Action
PA:	Pump Action
SS:	Single Shot
RPTR:	Repeater
WDS:	Wood Stock
PLAS:	Plastic Stock
NIC:	Nickel Finish
BLU:	Blued Finish
PNTD:	Painted Finish

Contributor: Jim Buskirk, c/o TGCA, 3009 Oleander Ave., San Marcos, CA 92069. A casual BB gun collector for several years, Buskirk began collecting in earnest 1985, and in 1989 he began publishing The Toy Gun Collectors of America Newsletter, a quarterly magazine for toy gun buffs. His collection of cap guns, BB guns, and related items numbers several hundred pieces and consists of mostly pre-WWII items, and its main focus is the 1930s era. The Daisy Red Rider BB guns are of special interest, and his collection includes what is believed to be the first Red Ryder ever made—a factory prototype that was hand-built on a King Model 5536 frame.

DAISY

Daisy with Names

	C6	C8	C10
1000 Shot Daisy, marked, "1000 Shot Daisy" on top and/or side of frame, LA, RPTR, WDS, NIC, 1903	150	200	300
20th Century, marked, "20th Century," BA, SS, WDS, NIC, w/cast-metal grip frame, 1899	180	210	300
500 Shot Daisy, marked "500 Shot Daisy" on top and/or side of frame, LA, RPTR, WDS, NIC, 1905	150	175	250
Daisy, repeater variation of BA, SS, WDS, NIC, marked "Daisy" in indented rectangle on side of grip frame, also marked "Pat. Aug 13, 1889, July 14, 91, Jan. 21, 92, March 26, 1901," frame is all sheet metal, referred to by collectors as the "20th Century sheet metal," but not so marked, 1901	120	140	200

Daisy with Names (Continued)

	C6	C8	C10
Daisy, BA, SS, WDS, NIC, marked "Daisy" in indented rectangle on side of grip frame, also marked "Pat. Aug 13, 1889, July 14, 91, Jan. 21, 92, March 26, 1901," frame is all sheet metal, referred to by collectors as the "20th Century sheet metal," but not so marked, 1901	125	175	250
Daisy, third model, marked "Daisy Pat May 6, 90," July 14, 91, BA, SS, stock may be wire or wood, NIC, cast-metal grip frame may have checkering, wire stock may have wood insert, 1891	275	375	450
Daisy, second model, marked "Daisy Imp'd Pat May 6, 90," BA, SS, wire stock, NIC, cast-metal grip frame, 1890	300	350	500
Daisy, first model, marked "Daisy Pat Apd For" or "Daisy Pat Aug 13, 89," LA, SS, wire stock, NIC, cast-metal grip frame, 1889	600	800	1000

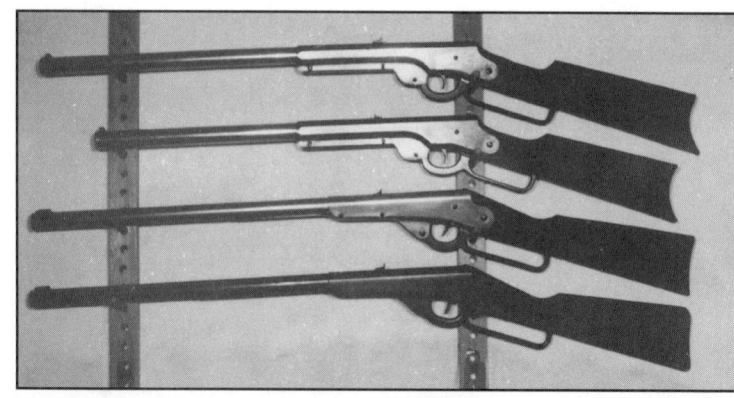

Top to bottom: Daisy 1000 Shot, 1903, $300; Daisy 500 Shot, 1905, $250; two versions of Daisy Model B, 1909, $75-125. Photo courtesy Jim Buskirk

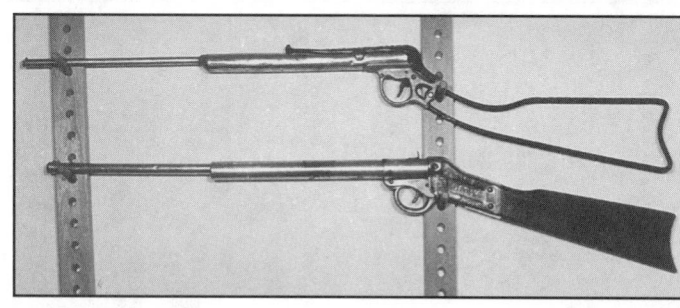

Top to bottom: Daisy, 1889, $1000; Daisy 20th Century, 1899, $300. Photo courtesy Jim Buskirk

Daisy with Names (Continued)

	C6	C8	C10
Sentinel, marked, "Sentinel," BA, SS, WDS, NIC, Daisy's first all sheet metal gun, somewhat streamlined in appearance compared to the earlier guns, semi pistol-grip stock and grip frame, 1899	125	175	225
Sentinel, marked, "Sentinel," BA, RPTR, WDS, NIC, repeater variation, 1899	150	200	250

Daisys with Letter Designations

	C6	C8	C10
Model A, BA, SS, WDS, NIC, 1907	120	140	200
Model A, BA, RPTR, WDS, NIC, 1907	90	105	150
Model B, LA, RPTR, WDS, NIC (500 shot), 1909	75	100	125
Model B, LA, RPTR, WDS, NIC (1000 shot), 1909	75	100	125
Model B, LA, RPTR, WDS, BLU (500 shot), 1909	50	60	75
Model B, LA, RPTR, WDS, BLU (1000 shot), 1909	50	65	85
Model C, BA, RPTR, WDS, NIC, repeater variation (350 shot), 1912	75	125	200
Model C, BA, SS, WDS, NIC, 1910	75	125	200

Daisys with Letter Designations (Continued)

	C6	C8	C10
Model H, LA, RPTR, WDS, NIC (350 or 500 shot), 1914	75	90	150
Model H, LA, RPTR, WDS, BLU (350 or 500 shot), 1914	55	65	90
Model H, LA, SS, WDS, NIC, 1913	75	90	125
Model H, LA, SS, WDS, BLU, 1913	55	65	100

Daisys with Number Designations

	C6	C8	C10
Model 1938, Red Ryder, LA, RPTR, WDS, PNTD, later variation, similar in appearance to the earlier variations, brand may be on left or right side of stock, 1972	25	45	80
Model 21, double barrel, BA, RPTR, PLAS, PNTD, 1968	180	250	350
Number 100, Model 38, BA, SS, WDS, BLU, 1938	30	50	100
Number 101, Model 33, LA, SS, WDS, BLU, 1933	25	40	50
Number 101, Model 36, LA, SS, WDS, BLU, 1936	25	40	50
Number 102, Model 36, LA, RPTR, WDS, NIC, 1936	40	60	100
Number 102, Model 36, LA, RPTR, WDS, BLU (500 shot), 1936	30	45	80

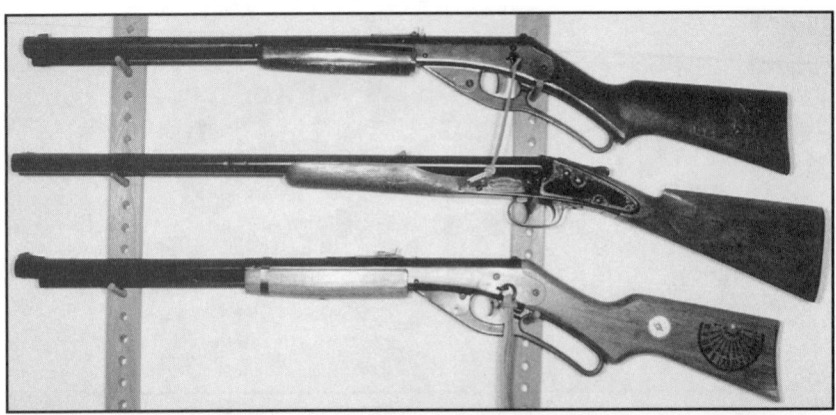

Top to bottom: Daisy Number 111 Model 40 Red Ryder, 1951, $85; Daisy Model 21, 1968, $350. A Christmas Story Red Ryder BB Gun, 1983—due to a screenwriter's error, the Red Ryder was described in the movie as having a compass and sundial in the stock, which it never had. Daisy went along and produced a special prop gun for use in the movie and also produced a limited number of these Red Ryders for sale. Photo courtesy Jim Buskirk

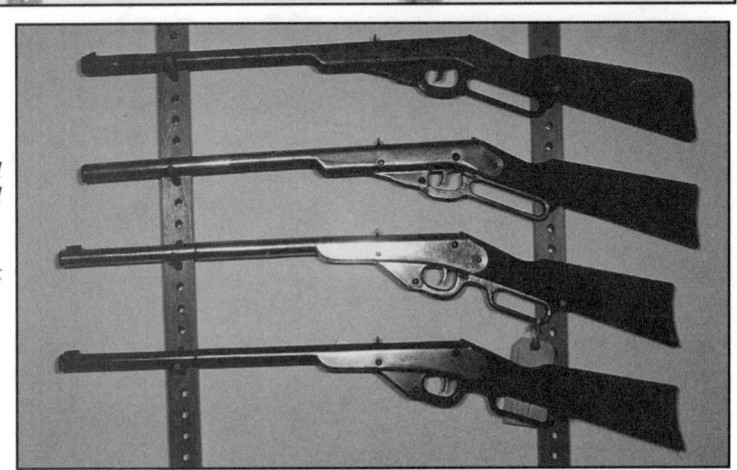

Top to bottom: Daisy Number 101 Model 33, 1933, $50; Daisy Number 102 Model 33, 1933, $50; Daisy Number 12, 1918, $125; Daisy Number 11, 1917, $100. Photo courtesy Jim Buskirk

Daisys with Number Designations (Continued)

	C6	C8	C10
Number 102, Model 33, LA, RPTR, WDS, BLU (500 shot), 1933	20	35	50
Number 103, Model 33, LA, RPTR, WDS, NIC, "Buzz Barton" variation, w/star-shaped Buzz Barton brand on stock, 1934	125	150	225
Number 103, Model 33, LA, RPTR, WDS, NIC, w/rear tube sight, 1933	140	175	250
Number 104, double barrel, BA, RPTR, WDS, BLU, 1938	425	550	700
Number 105, Junior Pump Gun, PA, RPTR, WDS, BLU, 1932	120	140	200
Number 107, Buck Jones Special, PA, RPTR, WDS, BLU, engraved frame, compass and sundial stock, 1934	80	100	140
Number 108, Model 39 Carbine, LA, RPTR, WDS, BLU, 1939	60	85	125
Number 11, LA, RPTR, WDS, BLU, may also have model number (500 shot), 1917	60	75	100

Daisys with Number Designations (Continued)

	C6	C8	C10
Number 11, LA, RPTR, WDS, NIC, may also have model number (500 shot), 1917	80	100	135
Number 111, Model 40, Red Ryder, LA, RPTR, WDS, BLU, w/aluminum cocking lever, 1947	50	75	100
Number 111, Model 40, Red Ryder, LA, RPTR, PLAS, BLU or PNTD, both stock and forestock are plastic, 1951	55	70	85
Number 111, Model 40, Red Ryder, LA, RPTR, WDS, BLU, w/cast-iron cocking lever and copper plated barrel bands, 1940	80	110	175
Number 111, Model 40, Red Ryder, LA, RPTR, WDS, BLU, w/cast-iron cocking lever, 1941	60	90	120
Number 111, Model 40, Red Ryder, LA, RPTR, WDS, BLU, w/plastic forestock, 1950	50	75	100
Number 12, LA, SS, WDS, NIC, may also have model number, 1918	75	90	125

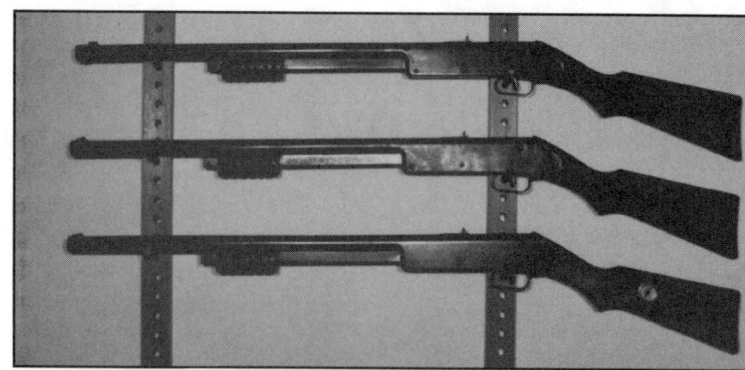

Top to bottom: Markham/King BB Guns Number 5 Pump Gun, 1931, $150; Daisy Number 105 Junior Pump Gun, 1932, $200; Daisy Number 107 Buck Jones Special, 1934, $140. Photo courtesy Jim Buskirk

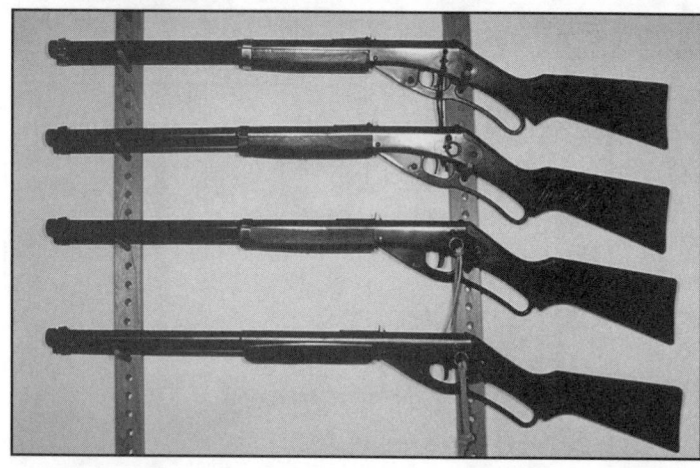

Four examples of the Daisy Number 111 Model 40 Red Red Ryder. Top to bottom: No. 111, Model 40 Red Ryder, copper bands, 1940, $175; No. 111, Model 40 Red Ryder, blued bands, iron lever, 1941, $120; No. 111, Model 40 Red Ryder, blued bands, aluminum lever, 1941, $100; No. 111, Model 40 Red Ryder, wood stock, plastic forearm, 1950, $100. Photo courtesy Jim Buskirk

Daisys with Number Designations (Continued)

	C6	C8	C10
Number 12, LA, SS, WDS, BLU, may also have model number, 1918	55	65	100
Number 140, Defender, LA, RPTR, WDS, BLU, w/long wooden forestock, dummy bolt and bolt handle and sling, 1941	125	150	225
Number 195, Buzz Barton Special, LA, RPTR, WDS, BLU, w/oval Buzz Barton brand on stock, 1932	70	100	175
Number 195, Model 36 Buzz Barton Special, LA, RPTR, WDS, BLU, w/oval Buzz Barton brand on stock, 1936	60	85	160
Number 20, Little Daisy, BA, SS, WDS, NIC, w/no grip frame, 1908	75	90	125
Number 20, Little Daisy, BA, SS, WDS, NIC, two screws in grip frame, 1912	75	90	125
Number 20, Little Daisy, BA, SS, WDS, NIC, w/three rivets in grip frame and "ring" trigger, 1915	70	80	110

Daisys with Number Designations (Continued)

	C6	C8	C10
Number 20, Little Daisy, BA, SS, WDS, BLU, w/three rivets in grip frame and "ring" trigger, 1915	55	65	90
Number 25, pump gun, PA, RPTR, WDS, BLU, w/pistol grip stock, 1925	40	60	85
Number 25, pump gun, PA, RPTR, WDS, BLU, w/straight stock, 1914	50	65	110
Number 25, pump gun, PA, RPTR, WDS, BLU, w/pistol grip stock and engraved frame, 1936	40	60	80
Number 25, BB Gun, Daisy's Centennial Commemorative Model, comes in colorful litho box, w/medallion in stock, 1986	40	60	100
Number 30, LA, RPTR, WDS, BLU, may also have model number (500 shot), 1925	35	50	80
Number 30, LA, RPTR, WDS, NIC, may also have model number (500 shot), 1925	50	65	80

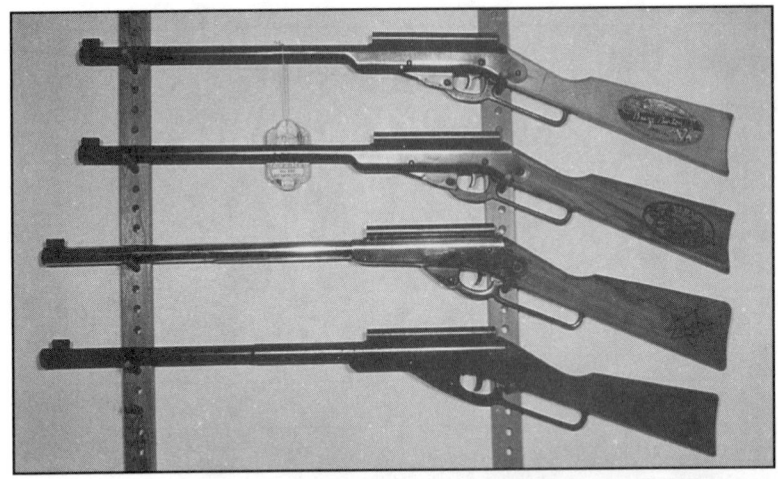

Top to bottom: Daisy Number 195 Model 36 Buzz Barton Special with paper label, 1936, $160; Daisy Number 195 Buzz Barton Special, 1932, $175; Daisy Number 103 Model 33, 1934, $225; Daisy Number 195 Model 36 with Buzz Barton stock brand. Photo courtesy Jim Buskirk

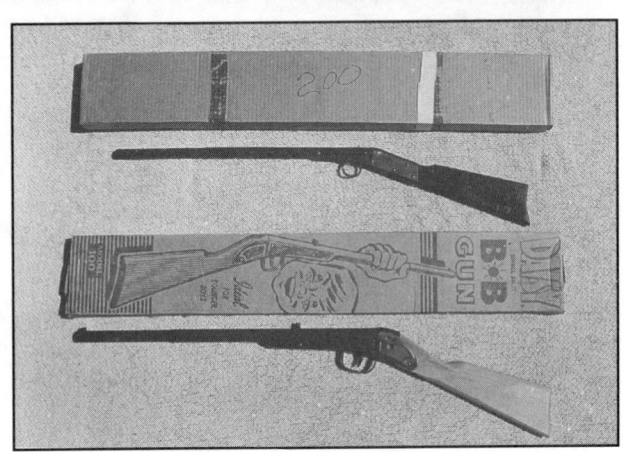

Top to bottom: Daisy Number 20 Little Daisy, 1908, $90-$125; Daisy Number 100 Model 38, 1938, $100 and $50 for the box. Photo courtesy Jim Buskirk

Daisys with Number Designations (Continued)

	C6	C8	C10
Number 3B, LA, RPTR, WDS, black nickel finish, came in colorful lithographed box marked "Daisy Special" (1000 shot), 1914	100	175	250
Number 40, LA, RPTR, WDS, BLU, Daisy's WWII military-styled gun, w/full-length wood stock, sling and bayonet, 1916	175	250	375
Number 50, Golden Eagle, LA, RPTR, WDS, entire gun is copper plated, stock painted black and w/special eagle decal, w/rear tube sight, 1936	100	125	200
Number 94, Red Ryder, LA, RPTR, PLAS, PNTD (1000 shot), 1955	35	50	100

MARKHAM/KING BB GUNS

Markham/King All Wood Guns

	C6	C8	C10
Challenge, under-barrel cast-iron cocking lever, sheet metal trigger guard, single shot, may have no markings, 1887	225	265	375
Chicago, break action, single shot, outside cocking rods on both sides, oval Markham logo on stock, 1888	90	125	175
Junior No. 10, BA, SS, WDS, NIC, 1910	60	70	100
Model C, repeater variation, 1905	50	75	100
Model D, BA, SS, WDS, NIC, grip frame wraps around wrist of stock, streamlined shape without pistol grip stock, 1905	50	75	100
New Chicago No. 24, BA, SS, WDS, BLU, 1923	80	100	150

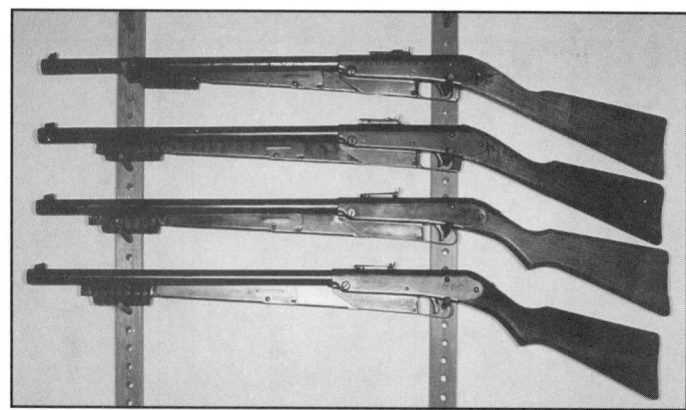

Four different versions of Daisy's Number 25, $80-110. Top to bottom: Early version with shot cocking lever and straight stock; long lever with straight stock; long lever with pistol grip stock; long lever and pistol grip stock with hunting scene stamped on frame. Photo courtesy Jim Buskirk

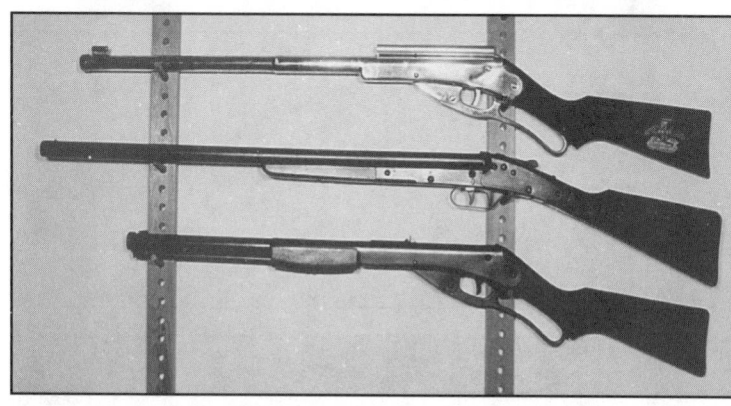

Top to bottom: Daisy No. 50 Golden Eagle, 1936, $200; Daisy No. 104 Double Barrel, 1938, $700; Daisy No. 108 Model 39 Carbine, 1939, $125. Photo courtesy Jim Buskirk

Markham/King All Wood Guns (Continued)	C6	C8	C10
New King, BA, SS, WDS, NIC, stock stained red, pistol grip stock is stamped "New King Patent 483153" in oval logo, 1895	85	125	165
New King, repeater, BA, RPTR, WDS, NIC, repeater variation of the above gun, w/small lever on muzzle cap used to allow a BB to drop into the shot tube, 1896	90	150	200
Number 1, same as "Model D" above, redesignated No. 1 in 1910, 1910	45	60	85
Number 17, BA, SS, WDS, BLU, w/outside cocking rods, 1917	70	95	140
Number 2, same as "Model C" above, redesignated No. 2 in 1910, 1910	45	60	85
Number 21, LA, SS, WDS, NIC, 1916	60	70	100
Number 2136, LA, SS, WDS, BLU, 1936	20	30	50

Markham/King All Wood Guns (Continued)	C6	C8	C10
Number 22, LA, RPTR, WDS, BLU, 1916	60	70	100
Number 2236, LA, RPTR, WDS, BLU (500 shot), 1936	20	30	50
Number 4, LA, RPTR, WDS, NIC, frame w/octagon shape (500 shot), 1908	100	115	175
Number 5, LA, RPTR, WDS, NIC, frame w/octagon shape (1000 shot), 1908	100	115	175
Number 5, Pump Gun, PA, RPTR, WDS, BLU, 1931	75	100	150
Number 55, LA, RPTR, WDS, BLU, may have straight or curved lever (1000 shot), 1921	38	42	60
Number 5533, LA, RPTR, WDS, BLU (1000 shot), 1933	38	42	60
Number 5536, LA, RPTR, WDS, BLU (1000 shot), 1936	45	55	75
Number 5B, LA, RPTR, WDS, BLU, a deluxe variation of the No. 5, came in a lithographed box, 1910	120	140	200

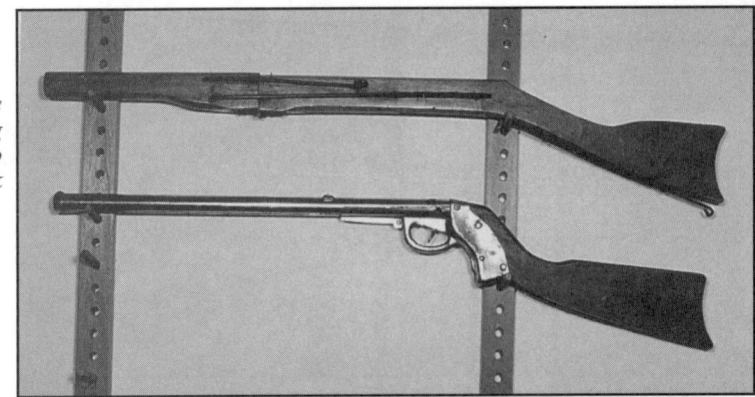

Top to bottom: Markham/King BB Guns Chicago, 1888, $175; Markham/King BB Guns New King, 1895, $165. Photo courtesy Jim Buskirk

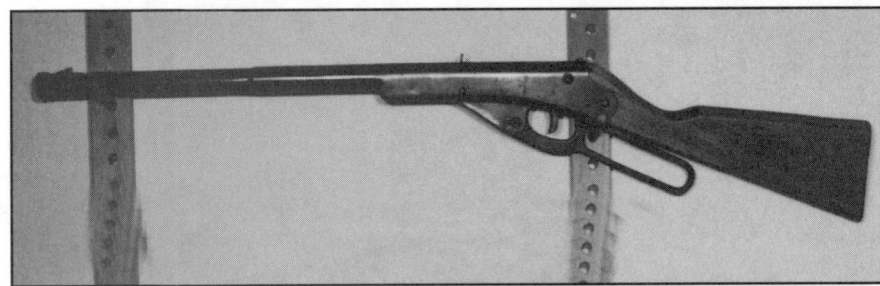

Markham/King BB Guns Number 2236, 1936, $30. Photo courtesy Jim Buskirk

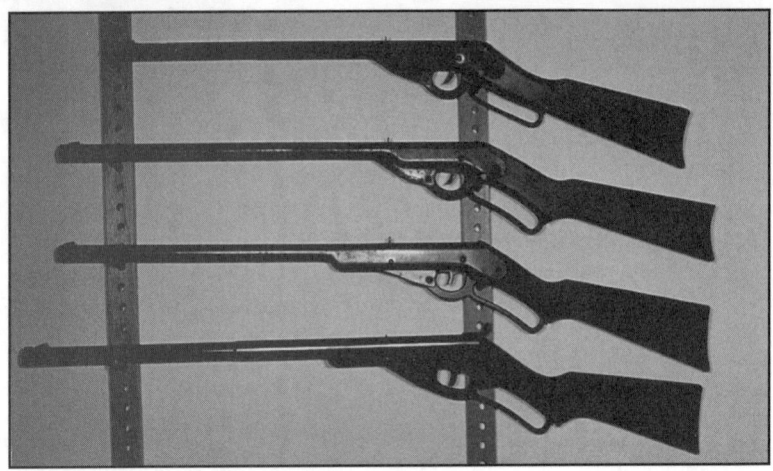

Top to bottom: Markham/King BB Guns Number 21, 1916, $100; Markham/King BB Guns Number 55, 1921, $60; Markham/King BB Guns Number 5533, 1933, $60; Markham/King BB Guns Number 5536, 1936, $75. Photo courtesy Jim Buskirk

BELL TOYS

Are You a Buffalo, Gong Bell Mfg. Co., $1600. Photo courtesy James Maxwell/Virginia Caputo

Cat and Dog, Gong Bell Mfg. Co., $4500. Photo courtesy James Maxwell/Virginia Caputo

	C6	C8	C10
Acrobats Holding Bells, Gong Bell Mfg. Co., 54	310	465	620
Alligator Ridden by Black Boy, N.N. Hill Brass Co., 1910, 5-1/2" long....................................	1000	1700	2300
Alligator Snapping at Teasing Boy, 9-1/4" long..................................	1500	2400	3500
Althof Bergmann, "Chime & Design Patd. May 19th 1874," three soldiers, one w/flag, two w/rifles.......................................	1600	2400	3200
Are You a Buffalo, Gong Bell Mfg. Co.	800	1200	1600
Bear, bounces on air	800	1100	1600
Bear on Tricycle, 4" long	150	225	300
Billy Goat, goat mechanically butts bell, Gong Bell Mfg. Co., 51, 1900, 7-1/2" long..........................	750	1125	1500
Bird and Bell, 6" long.....................	600	900	1200
Boy and Goat, Althof Bergmann, 9" long...	600	900	1200
Boy Scouts, heart-shaped tin wheels, 13-1/2" long	750	1125	1500
Boys Eating Bananas, ...	700	1050	1400
Camel with Rider, Althof Berg- mann, c. 1874, 9" long	1200	2000	2800
Cat and Dog, Gong Bell Mfg. Co.	2000	3200	4500
Cinderella Chariot, 9-1/4" long	425	638	850
Clown, Gong Bell Mfg. Co., 5-3/4" long...	262	393	525

	C6	C8	C10
Clown and Black Man on See-Saw, six color, Watrous, c. 1905, 6-1/2" long.....................................	600	900	1200
Clown and Pig, 1900	325	488	650
Clown Bell-ringers Riding Back to Back on a Mule, ...	1000	1500	2000
Comic Characters, two, three bells, pierced heart wheels....................	700	1125	1400
Daisy, Gong Bell Mfg. Co., 9" long	600	1000	1400
Darky Fishing, Stevens, 8" long......	440	660	880
Ding Dong Bell, Pussy's Not in The Well, Gong Bell Mfg. Co., c. 1880, 9-1/2" long........................	600	925	1235
Dog on Platform, carrying pail in mouth, bell on back, Fallows, 5-1/2" long....................................	425	700	950
Eagle, Gong Bell Mfg. Co., c. 1906, 5-1/4" long....................................	550	850	1200
Elephant & Rider in Howdah, driver on elephant's head, 4-1/2" long...	700	1100	1500
Elephant on Platform, tin elephant w/trunk curled under stands on green platform w/spoked wheels, Fallows, 9" long	425	638	850
Elephant with Bell in Trunk, N.N. Hill Brass Co., c. 1905	700	1050	1400
Elephants on Platform, tin mother and baby elephant on blue plat- form w/spoke wheels. Bell is struck by lever as toy is pulled., Fallows, c. 1882, 6-1/4" long...	600	1200	1800

Daisy, Gong Bell Mfg. Co., 9" long, $1400. Photo courtesy Sotheby's, New York

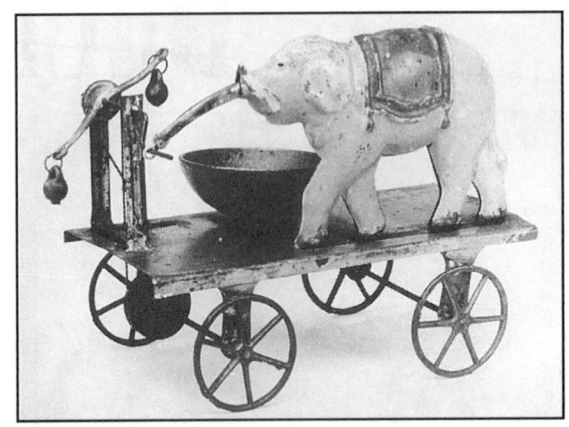

Elephant on Platform, Fallows, 6-3/4" long, $850. Photo courtesy Detroit Antique Toy Museum; courtesy Wilkinson Collection

Evening New Baby Quieter, Stevens, 1890s, 8" long, $2450. Photo courtesy Christie's East

Ding Dong Bell, Pussy's Not in The Well, Gong Bell Mfg. Co., c. 1880, 9-1/2" long, $1235. Photo courtesy Sotheby's, New York

	C6	C8	C10
Eskimo & Bear,	750	1125	1500
Evening New Baby Quieter, man reading paper to baby, Stevens, 1890s, 8" long	1100	1700	2450
Goat, small woman at left leg of goat, either Althof Bergmann or Ives, c. 1890, 7-1/2" high	500	750	1000
Goat, Fallows, 1880, 14"	1100	1650	2200
Goat, Lamb and Girl on Platform, George Brown, early, 11" long	550	850	1200
Goats, two, butting, Gong Bell Mfg. Co.	1200	2000	3000
Hello, Hello Telephone Chimes, w/monkey, Gong Bell Mfg. Co.	2000	3000	4000
Horse and Rider, heart-shaped wheels, 9" long	750	1125	1500

	C6	C8	C10
Horse Drawn Tumbler, single hand-painted tin horse w/red saddle pulls tumbler. Two wheels w/heart-shaped spokes. Bell suspended between the two wheels., Gong Bell Mfg. Co., c. 1885, 7-1/2" long	300	500	750
Hunter and Rabbit, N.N. Hill Brass Co., 1900	750	1125	1500
Jack and Jill on Seesaw, Watrous, 7-1/2" long	440	660	880
Jockey on Horse, early, 7-1/2" long	200	300	400
Jonah and Whale, N.N. Hill Brass Co., 5" long	900	1500	2200
Landing of Columbus, cast-iron, detailed, removable Columbus, ship has wheels and pig figure head, Gong Bell Mfg. Co., c. 1892, 7-1/2" long	525	775	1025

Goat, either Althof Bergmann or Ives, c. 1890, 7-1/2" high, $1000. Photo courtesy PB Eighty-Four, New York

Poodle Dog Bell Ringer with Clown, Gong Bell Mfg. Co., $4200. Photo courtesy James Maxwell/Virginia Caputo

Hello, Hello Telephone Chimes, Gong Bell Mfg. Co., $4000. Photo courtesy James Maxwell/Virginia Caputo

Uncle Sam and the Don (missing bell), Gong Bell Mfg. Co., $4500. Photo courtesy James Maxwell/Virginia Caputo

	C6	C8	C10
Liberty Bell Centennial, Gong Bell Mfg. Co., 8" long	800	1200	1600
Mary and Her Little Lamb, Gong Bell Mfg. Co., 8" long	600	900	1250
Monkey and Coconut, "Monkey Mobile", N.N. Hill Brass Co., 6" long	350	525	700
Monkey and Dog, heart wheels, 7" long	500	750	1000
Monkey and Horse, Gong Bell Mfg. Co., 23	1500	2250	3000
Monkey in Wheeled Chariot, Gong Bell Mfg. Co	2000	3000	4000
Monkey on a Log, Gong Bell Mfg. Co., c. 1900	750	1125	1500
Monkey on a Velocipede, 8" high	1500	2400	3800

	C6	C8	C10
Monkey Riding Elephant, clockwork, Fallows, 10" long	1400	2100	2800
Oriental Clown & Poodle, cloth in hoop, poodle jumps through hoop and back, 44, 1900, 13" long	1250	1875	2500
Pig with Clown Rider, Gong Bell Mfg. Co., 6" long	418	625	835
Poodle Dog Bell Ringer with Clown, Gong Bell Mfg. Co.	1200	2800	4200
Rough Rider, Watrous, early, 6-1/2" long	123	185	245
Sailors, J&E Stevens, 9-3/4" long	NPF	NPF	NPF
Saw the Watermelon, Gong Bell Mfg. Co., 8-1/2" long	1100	1700	2800
Steeplechase, two jockeys on horses, Hubley	600	900	1200

Jonah and Whale, N.N. Hill Brass Co., 5" long, $2200. Photo courtesy James Maxwell/Virginia Caputo

Top row: Saw the Watermelon, Gong Bell Mfg. Co., 8-1/2" long, $2800. Bottom row, left to right: Pig with Clown Rider, Gong Bell Mfg. Co., 6" long, $835; Monkey on a Velocipede, 8" high, $3800.

Monkey and Coconut, N.N. Hill Brass Co., 6" long, $700. Photo courtesy Sotheby's, New York

Landing of Columbus, 7" long, $1025. Photo courtesy Sotheby's, New York

Liberty Bell Centennial, Gong Bell Mfg. Co., 8" long, $1600. Photo courtesy Sotheby's, New York

Monkey and Horse, Gong Bell Mfg. Co., $3000. Photo courtesy James Maxwell/Virginia Caputo

Top row, left to right: Tramp, Gong Bell Mfg. Co., 6" long, $875; Acrobats Holding Bells, Gong Bell Mfg. Co., $620. Bottom Row, left to right: Mary and Her Little Lamb, Gong Bell Mfg. Co., 8" long, $1250; Trick Pony, Gong Bell Mfg. Co., 1893, 8" long, $1350. Photo courtesy Christie's East

Monkey in Wheeled Chariot, Gong Bell Co. (?), $4000. Photo courtesy James Maxwell/Virginia Caputo

Trick Elephant, Gong Bell Mfg. Co., 7-3/4" long, $1600. Photo courtesy James Maxwell/Virginia Caputo

	C6	C8	C10
Tramp, Gong Bell Mfg. Co., 6" long	438	655	875
Trick Elephant, Gong Bell Mfg. Co., 7-3/4" long	800	1200	1600
Trick Pony, "39", Gong Bell Mfg. Co., 1893, 8" long	600	1000	1350
Uncle Sam and The Don, Gong Bell Mfg. Co.	2250	3375	4500
Victory in a Shell-form Chariot, mounted w/bell and eagle	1500	2250	3000

	C6	C8	C10
Watermelon, N.N. Hill Brass Co., c. 1905, 8-1/2" long	600	900	1200
White Horse Pulling Heart-shaped Wheels, Ives, c. 1896, 9-1/2" long	1000	1500	2000
Wild Mule Jack,	750	1125	1500
Young America, Gong Bell Mfg. Co., c. 1880, 6" long	450	675	900

CATALOGS

A.C. Williams, $90.

1932 Arcade Cast Iron Toys catalog No. 40.

	C6	C8	C10
A.C. Williams, 1908	220	330	440
A.C. Williams, value is for each item, 1930	45	68	90
A.C. Williams, 1934	45	68	90
A.J. Fisher, New York, illustrating cap pistols, etc., 1877	18	27	36
Aldens Christmas, 1946	40	60	80
Althoff-Bergmann, 81 pages, 1874	125	275	450
Arcade, 1889	100	150	200
Arcade, 1899	105	158	210
Arcade, 1900	115	172	230
Arcade, 1901	375	562	750
Arcade, 1902-03	85	128	170
Arcade, 1917	500	750	1000
Arcade, 1924	150	225	300
Arcade, 1931	125	188	250
Arcade, Catalog No. 40. As of 1932, over 700,000 booklets "The Tiny Arcadians" and "Fred and Jane with the Tiny Arcadians" had been distributed, 1932	40	80	120

	C6	C8	C10
Arcade, Catalog No. 58, 1940	100	150	225
Auburn Rubber, pre-World War II	50	75	100
Aurora, 1960	27	41	55
Aurora, value is for each item, 1963, 1964	50	75	100
Aurora, value is for each item, 1965, 1967	55	82	110
Aurora, value is for each item, 1971, 1972	17	26	35
Aurora, 1973	27	41	55
Aurora, 1975	25	38	50
Aurora, 1977	22	33	45
Baltimore Price Reducer, illustrated w/toys, games, etc., 1928	15	22	30
Barclay, pre-World War II	200	300	400
Bilt E-Z, 1924	5	8	10
Buddy L, flier, 1926	175	263	350
Buddy L, 1929	275	352	550
Buddy L, Robotoy flier, 1932	125	188	250
Buddy L, 1935	175	262	350
Buddy L, 1940	125	188	250

Fisher-Price, 1966, $50.

1940 Arcade Cast Iron Toys catalog No. 58.

	C6	C8	C10
Buddy L, 1941	135	202	270
Buddy L, value is for each item, 1952, 1953, 1956, 1957, 1959	7	11	15
Buddy L, 1961	22	33	45
Buddy L Jr., 1930	150	225	300
Buffalo Toy, 1939	75	112	150
Butler Bros., tin toys, squeak toys, etc., 1889	30	45	60
Butler Bros., illustrated w/mechanical banks, toys, dolls, etc., 1891	30	45	60
Butler Bros., November, 1899	40	60	80
Butler Bros., June, 1917	70	105	140
Butler Bros., Christmas, 1930	35	52	70
Butler Bros., Christmas, 1931	35	52	70
Butler Bros., value is for each item, 1935, 1936	40	60	80
Butler Bros., Spring, 1941	60	90	120
Carpenter, Francis, 1880s	900	1350	1800
Champion, four pages and cover	150	225	300
Chein, value is for each item, 1956, 1960	50	75	100
Chein, Spring & Summer, 1958	15	30	45
Corgi, value is for each item, 1966, 1967	10	15	20
Daisy, 1975	22	33	45
Dayton, 1929	150	225	300
Dent Hardware Co., Fullerton, Pa., undated	30	45	60

	C6	C8	C10
Dent Hardware Co., forty pages, 1900	40	60	80
Dent Hardware Co., 1905	37	56	75
Dent Hardware Co., 1910	37	56	75
Dent Hardware Co., Fullerton, Pa., 1930	32	48	65
Dinky, 1950s	27	41	55
Dunham, Buckley & Co., New York, toys, etc., 1895	40	60	80
Durable Toy & Novelty, 1920s	10	15	20
Ehrich Bros., New York, illustrations of banks, toys, dolls, etc., 1892	40	60	80
Eldon, autos, 1961	6	9	12
Eldon, boats, 1961	6	9	12
Erector Set, thirty-eight pages, 1938	15	22	30
Ertl, 1974	3	5	6
Eureka Trick & Novelty Co., thirty-two pages, 1875	20	30	40
Ewing Merkle Catalog, 1903	21	35	70
Fisher-Price, 1954	6	9	12
Fisher-Price, 1966	25	38	50
Garton Pedal Cars, 1940	100	150	200
Garton Toy Company, Pedal cars including "Kidillac" models, 1961	20	40	60
Gendron, 1927	600	900	1200
Gilbert, 1966	27	41	55

Late 1950s Dinky catalog.

	C6	C8	C10
Gould, L., Christmas, 1922	125	188	250
Gould, L., 1940	55	83	110
Grey Iron, No. 24, 1920s	115	172	230
Hasbro, 1975	27	41	55
Hasbro, 1987, 1989	20	30	40
Howdy Doody Merchandise, 1955	27	41	55
Hubley, horse-drawn, cast-iron, 1906	25	50	75
Hubley, 1914-15	55	83	110
Hubley, 72 pages, included the rare "Christie Tractor", 1919/20	30	65	110
Hubley, 34 pages, 1928	20	45	70
Hubley, 40 pages, 1932/33	20	40	60
Hubley, 28 pages, 1935	20	40	60
Hubley, Debut year for die-cast "Kiddie-Toy" line, 1936	20	40	60
Hubley, 1939	60	90	120
Hubley, 1966	16	24	32
Hubley, 1969	11	16	22
Hubley, 1974	22	33	45
Ideal, 1973	12	18	25
Ideal, 1976	12	18	25
Ives and Williams, illustrated brochure of cap pistols and animated cap pistols, 18" x 24"	20	30	40
Ives Yachts, Ships and Shipping, twenty-four pages, 1915	50	75	100
Ives, Blakeslee & Williams, two-sided broadside, 1890	70	105	140
JC Penney, Christmas, value is for each item, 1963, 1964, 1965	68	102	135
JC Penney, Christmas, value is for each item, 1966 through 1970	50	75	100

	C6	C8	C10
JC Penney, Christmas, value is for each item, 1971 through 1975	35	52	70
JC Penney, Christmas, value is for each item, 1975 through 1980	27	41	55
Jones & Bixler, 1912	100	150	200
Kenton, Catalogue No. 9, 96 pages, 1913	30	60	100
Kenton, Catalogue No. 16, 108 pages, 1923	30	60	100
Kenton Hardware Co., 112 pages, No. 16, 1920s	70	105	140
Kenton Hardware Co., color illustrations, 1934	50	75	100
Keystone, Debut catalog featuring line of pressed steel toys, 1925	30	60	100
Kilgore, 1977-78	22	33	45
Kingsbury, 1919	55	82	110
Kingsbury, value is for each item, 1920, c. 1925	32	48	65
Kingsbury, small size, 128 pages, 1930s	100	150	200
Kingsbury Toys, motor driven, sixteen pages, 1936	40	60	80
Knapp Electric Toys, No. 35	10	15	20
Knickerbocker, 1961	8	12	17
Lionel Catalog, 1903	21	35	70
Lionel Catalog, 1904	21	35	70
Lionel Catalog, 1905	21	35	70
Lionel Catalog, 1906	21	35	70
Lionel Catalog, 1907	21	35	70
Lionel Catalog, 1908	21	35	70
Lionel Catalog, 1909	21	35	70

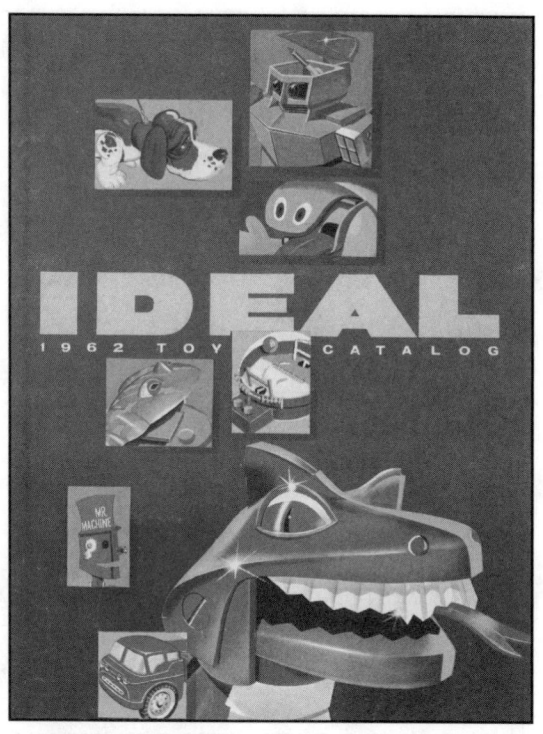

1962 Ideal Toy catalog.

1949-1959 Fisher-Price catalog. This lively catalog included the first appearance of the No. 454 Donald Duck Drummer and the No. 473 Merry Mutt xylophone player.

	C6	C8	C10		C6	C8	C10
Lionel Catalog, 1910	21	35	70	Lionel Catalog, 1935	17	28	55
Lionel Catalog, 1911	21	35	70	Lionel Catalog, 1936	15	24	48
Lionel Catalog, 1912	21	35	70	Lionel Catalog, 1937	11	18	35
Lionel Catalog, small, 1913	15	25	50	Lionel Catalog, 1938	14	23	45
Lionel Catalog, 1913	21	35	70	Lionel Catalog, 1939	11	18	35
Lionel Catalog, 1914	21	35	70	Lionel Catalog, 1940	12	20	40
Lionel Catalog, small, 1914	15	25	50	Lionel Catalog, 1941	14	23	45
Lionel Catalog, 1915	21	35	70	Lionel Catalog, 1942	14	23	45
Lionel Catalog, 1916	21	35	70	Lionel Catalog, 1945	5	8	16
Lionel Catalog, 1917	21	35	70	Lionel Catalog, 1947	20	25	35
Lionel Catalog, 1920	21	35	70	Lionel Catalog, 1948	9	15	30
Lionel Catalog, 1922	21	35	70	Lionel Catalog, 1949	50	80	110
Lionel Catalog, 1923	15	25	50	Lionel Catalog, 1950	25	40	55
Lionel Catalog, 1924	21	35	70	Lionel Catalog, 1951	15	25	35
Lionel Catalog, 1925	21	35	70	Lionel Catalog, 1952	9	15	30
Lionel Catalog, 1926	18	30	60	Lionel Catalog, 1953	7	12	24
Lionel Catalog, 1927	22	38	75	Lionel Catalog, 1954	5	9	17
Lionel Catalog, 1928	22	38	75	Lionel Catalog, 1955	10	15	20
Lionel Catalog, 1929	21	35	70	Lionel Catalog, 1956	5	8	16
Lionel Catalog, 1930	21	35	70	Lionel Catalog, 1957	3	6	11
Lionel Catalog, 1931	21	35	70	Lionel Catalog, 1958	4	6	12
Lionel Catalog, 1932	22	38	75	Lionel Catalog, 1959	4	7	13
Lionel Catalog, 1933	16	28	55	Lionel Catalog, 1960	3	5	10
Lionel Catalog, 1934	15	24	48	Lionel Catalog, 1961	4	6	12

1961 Lionel Train Lines catalog.

Fall 1961 Mattel catalog. This catalog featured a variety of toy guns including the Roll-cap firing Fanner 50 and the Shootin' Shell Fanner.

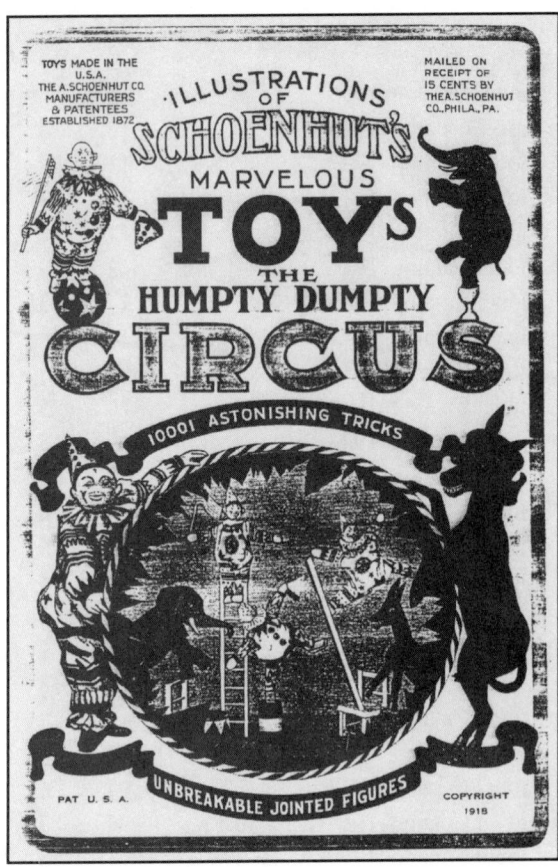

Schoenhut Circus, 1918, $225.

1962 Lionel Train Lines catalog.

Matchbox, 1969, $12.

Matchbox, 1968, $15.

1958 Tonka Toys catalog.

1960 Tonka Toys catalog.

	C6	C8	C10
Lionel Catalog, 1962	3	6	11
Lionel Catalog, 1963	2	3	5
Lionel Catalog, 1964	2	3	5
Lionel Catalog, 1965	1	2	4
Lionel Catalog, 1966	1	2	4
Lionel Catalog, 1968	1	2	4
Lionel Catalog, 1969	1	2	4
ManoilManoil, 1935-39	100	150	200
Marx, thirty-six pages, 1930s	225	338	450
Marx, 1964	125	188	250
Marx, 1966	100	150	200
Marx, 1969	110	165	220
Marx, 1976	12	18	25
Matchbox, 1964	25	38	50
Matchbox, 1965	22	33	45
Matchbox, 1966	15	22	30
Matchbox, 1968	7	11	15
Matchbox, 1969	6	9	12
Matchbox, 1970	4	6	8
Matchbox, 1973	11	16	22

	C6	C8	C10
Matchbox, 1978	13	19	26
Mattel, 1967	150	225	300
McCadden & Bros. Philadelphia, illustrated iron and tin toys, banks, mechanical toys, dolls, games, etc.	50	75	100
Mego, value is for each item, 1967-69 ..	50	75	100
Mickey Mouse Merchandise Catalog, by Kay Kamen Co., eighty pages, hundreds of illustrations of Mickey Mouse items, 1935	300	450	600
Montgomery Ward, Christmas, value is for each item, 1934 through 1940	82	123	165
Montgomery Ward, Christmas, value is for each item, 1941 through 1965	68	102	135
Montgomery Ward, Christmas, value is for each item, 1966 through 1970	50	75	100

1964 Ideal Tammy & Pepper catalog.

1933 Tootsietoys catalog.

	C6	C8	C10
Montgomery Ward, Christmas, value is for each item, 1971 through 1975	35	52	70
Montgomery Ward, Christmas, value is for each item, 1976 through 1980	27	41	55
Montgomery Ward, Christmas, value is for each item, 1981 through 1985	20	30	40
Nicol & Co., illustrating banks, etc., 1895	27	41	55
Ohio Art, 1961	8	12	17
Popsicle Pete Radio News and Premium catalog, early	40	60	80
Popsicle Pete's, four-page gift list, 1949	10	15	20
Pyro, each, 1966, 1967	19	28	38
Pyro, 1970	9	13	18
Rel Toy Boats foldout, 1958	20	30	40
Revell, 1957-58	37	56	75
Revell, 1958-59	25	38	50
Revell, 1969	10	15	20
Schoenhut, 1903	100	150	200
Schoenhut Circus, 1918	112	168	225
Schoenhut Circus, 1928	100	150	200
Schoenhut Humpty Dumpty Circus, (includes other toys), many illustrations, 1915	100	165	220

	C6	C8	C10
Sears, Fall-Winter, 1919	30	45	60
Sears Christmas, 1926	67	100	135
Sears Christmas, 1933	60	90	120
Sears Christmas, each, 1936 through 1940	82	123	175
Sears Christmas, value is for each item, 1941 through 1945	82	123	165
Sears Christmas, each, 1946 through 1950	82	123	165
Sears Christmas, each, 1951 through 1955	82	123	165
Sears Christmas, each, 1956 through 1960	82	123	165
Sears Christmas, each, 1961 through 1965	82	123	165
Sears Christmas, each, 1966 through 1970	60	90	120
Sears Christmas, each, 1971 through 1975	45	68	90
Sears Christmas, each, 1976 through 1980	30	45	60
Selchow & Righter, games and toys, illustrated trains, boats, bell toys, mechanical banks, etc., 1894-95	125	180	250
Selchow & Righter, 108 pages, 1908-1909	80	120	160
Selchow & Righter, 1921	32	48	65

Woolworth's Christmas, 1954, $30.

Woolworth's Christmas, 1952, $30.

	C6	C8	C10
Shure, N., 1940	85	128	170
Smith-Miller, 1954	40	70	100
Spiegel, Christmas, value is for each item, 1941 through 1965	68	102	135
Spiegel, Christmas, value is for each item, 1966 through 1970	50	75	100
Spiegel, Christmas, value is for each item, 1971 through 1975	35	52	70
Spiegel, Christmas, value is for each item, 1976 through 1980	27	41	55
Spiegel, Christmas, value is for each item, 1981 through 1985	20	30	40
Spiegel, Christmas, value is for each item, 1986 through 1990	15	22	30
State Adams & Dearborn Sts., Chicago, illustrated	10	15	20
Steelcraft, forty-four pages, 1934	300	450	600
Steelcraft, 1936	350	525	700
Stern, Carl P., illustrating cap pistols, etc.	15	22	30
Stevens, J.E. Co., No. 51, export	40	60	80
Stevens, J.E. Co., illlustrations of iron toys and mechanical banks, 1906	40	60	80
Strauss, tiny, thiry-two pages, 1926	37	56	75

	C6	C8	C10
Structo Toys, eight pages, 1931	10	15	20
Supplee-Biddle of Philadelphia, 174 pages, many toys, 1930	90	135	180
Thorsen & Cassady, guns, etc., 1894	20	30	40
Tinkertoy, 1926	6	9	12
Tom Mix Premium Catalog, 1936	30	45	60
Toy Yearbook, value is for each item, 1952-53, 1956-57, 1957-58, 1958-59	12	18	25
Transogram, 1949	15	22	30
Vindex, 1932	275	365	550
Walt Disney Character Merchandise, 1930s	250	375	500
Walt Disney Character Merchandise, 1940-41	250	375	500
Western Auto, each, 1960 through 1969	32	48	65
Williams, Charles, 1928	22	33	45
Woolworth's Christmas, 1951	30	45	60
Woolworth's Christmas, 1952	15	22	30
Woolworth's Christmas, 1954	15	22	30
Woolworth's Christmas Catalogs, pre-World War II	30	45	60

COMIC CHARACTERS

(See also American Paper Toys, Mechanical Banks, Battery-Operated Toys, Premiums, Movies, Ramp Walkers, Vehicles-Tootsietoy, and Wood Toys)

Collecting Comic Characters
By John K. Snyder, Jr.

After attending many of the major toy shows and keeping close tabs on the multitude of auctions and dealer inventories, it is clear that the demand for high-grade vintage character toys definitely exceeds the supply. While on the surface it might seem reasonable to expect a drop-off in sales related to the national economy and international events, it just didn't happen. What has happened instead is the now-familiar trend of many sellers pricing mid-grade specimens at high-grade prices. This struggle by retailers has created, in some quarters, the impression of a sluggish market, but accurately priced toys continue to sell in all collector-friendly grades.

While new product has been somewhat negatively affected by world events or the domestic economy, creatively packaged, well-thought-out new toys still have done very well. Top name characters continue to have appeal, and many are finding new audiences.

Perhaps the most important factor in the continuing increase in demand for top-flight items is the tremendous effort that has been put into educating collectors and documenting the history of character toys. This documentation—whether in the multitude of specialty guidebooks, television programs, Internet sites, newspaper and magazine articles, or other media—has created a new awareness of the indispensable history to be found in collecting.

An ongoing education is a necessity to any collector who wants to keep his or her skills sharp, and it remains an essential component of our experience as collectors. Many collectors are involved in organized educational activities such as attending conventions, writing articles, or posting information on Web sites. Others more casually seek new information whenever possible, but just about every serious collector is looking for new chances to learn, as well as for opportunities to educate others.

The involvement of education is not new to toys, though it is something we're just beginning to fully appreciate. Many toys represented—and still represent—adults turning children's playthings into learning devices. Toy cars, trains, tools, telephones, and other objects encouraged children to familiarize themselves with how the adult world worked. This concept may well date to the first toys ever made. Think about it for a moment. While they are playing, laughing, and enjoying their youth, aren't children at least in a way teaching themselves about the adult world? And doesn't our understanding of this enhance our understanding of toys?

Richard Olson, Ph.D. wrote, "It is very important that we realize that all of our diverse collecting interests come together under this generic category of 'toys' and that we share a common field of interest." As he delineated, the term "toys" represents more than 350 categories. One of those categories is comics. Following through on this thought, comics would include political cartoons, newspaper comics, and comic books (they also include more than 100 other sub-categories).

This process is not just limited to collectors recapturing their own childhood, however. A failed school of thought suggests that when the generation an item was produced in passes away, there will no longer be sustained collector interest in that category. What could be further from the truth? If the fact that there are many people enthusiastically collecting The Brownies (the earliest recurring comic characters), Yellow Kid, and Buster Brown doesn't answer that charge, what would? Newly started Mickey Mouse, Donald Duck, Superman, Batman, or Spider-Man collectors would probably be delighted if the toys they dream about were *more* available and *less* expensive than they were previously, but that's just not going to happen.

As other collectors have pointed out, beware of anyone spending a lot of time trying to convince you that the interest in a certain type or area of collecting will fade as a generation passes on; they have either entirely missed the boat or they're trying to buy your collection cheap. Remember, unlike fads that explode onto the scene, fade out, return, and fade out again, the interest in both nostalgia and history is going to expand for the foreseeable future.

Even in the range of current or recently produced toys, there are success stories, and many of those tie directly into the older categories. Dark Horse Comics has received enormous praise for their Classic Comic Character line of Syroco-like figures which included characters from Krazy Kat, Flash Gordon, Terry and the Pirates, and many others.

The Current Market

The market continues to vary based on geographic region and a number of other factors, though the impact of region is decreased by Internet sales and auctions where anyone can bid for an item regardless of location. It cannot be overstated, though, that condition is king. High-grade comic character collectibles still represent one of the best possible avenues of investment. If you have been amazed by some of the record prices realized this past year, just wait until you experience the months and years ahead.

In collecting, time is not the enemy; lack of information is. As our supply of information keeps growing, so will demand.

Contributors: John Fawcett, Fawcett's Toy & Art Museum, P.O. Box 1156, 3506 Route 1, Waldoboro, ME 04572; Phone: (207) 832-7398; Web site: http://home.gwi.net/~fawcetoy; Email: fawcetoy@gwi.net

John K. Snyder Jr. is present of Diamond International Galleries and is a leading expert on comic character collectibles. He serves as a pricing advisor to *Hake's Price Guide to Character Toys*, *The Overstreet Comic Book Price Guide*, *The Overstreet Comic Book Grading Guide*, *The Overstreet Toy Ring Price Guide*, *Tomart's Radio Premiums Price Guide*, Krause Publication's *Radio Premiums Price Guide*, *Toys & Prices*, and the *Original Comic Art Price Guide*. Web site: www.diamondgalleries.com

Alphonse & Gaston

Turn of the 20th Century comic strip pair famous for their overly-courteous retorts, "After you Alphonse," says Gaston. To which, Alphonse replies, "No, no, after you Gaston." Created by Frederick Burr Opper in 1902 for The *New York Journal*, Alphonse & Gaston were a feature for decades before declining to the occasional appearance in Happy Hooligan. Their famous phrases survive to this day.

Alphonse

	C6	C8	C10
Nodder, cast iron, mule pulling wagon, Hubley, 7" long..............	275	475	820
Nodder, in horse-drawn carriage, nodder toys, Hubley, c. 1910, 10-1/2" long......................	500	850	1350
Nodder, cast iron, movable arms and hands in a goat-pulled cart, Hubley, early 1900s, 13-3/4" long, 7-1/2" high	350	475	820
Nodder, cast iron, movable arms and hands, two goats pulling wagon, Hubley, early 1900s, 13-3/4" long, 7-1/2" high.................	220	340	600

Archie

MLJ Comics was formed in 1939 and published various super-hero oriented tales. As filler for the December, 1941 issue #22, MLJ introduced a red-haired teenager named Archie. The enormous success of Archie and his friends pushed the super-hero tales to the background and by 1945, the MLJ logo was removed from the covers in favor of "An Archie magazine," and the company has been known as Archie Comics ever since.

Archie

	C6	C8	C10
Archie and Veronica Jalopy, tin wind-up, w/illustration on side, Spanish, 7"	145	230	375
Archie Hand Puppet, vinyl, Ideal, 1973	25	40	60

Barney Google

King Features debuted Barney Google on June 17, 1919. The strip's popularity soared in 1922 with the introduction of Spark Plug the horse and again in 1934 with the first appearance of hillbilly Snuffy Smith. The powerful combination of the two characters lead to several runs in comic books. Dell Comics (4 books issued in 1942, 1943, 1944, and 1964), Toby Press (4-issues from June 1951 through February 1952), and Charlton Comics (6-issues from March 1970 to January 1971) all produced short-run comic book adaptations.

Barney Google

	C6	C8	C10
Barney Google and Spark Plug Pull Toy, tin litho, Spark Plug in barn	1500	2250	3800
Barney Google and Spark Plug Scooter Race, pull toy, Nifty Toy Co., 1920s, 8" long.....................	3000	5200	7400
Barney Google and Spark Plug Tin Wind-up, Nifty, ...	650	1000	1450
Barney Google Candy Container, glass	150	300	425

Alphonse Nodder, Hubley, $820. Photo courtesy Christie's East

Rudy the Ostrich, Nifty (Barney Google), 1924, $1200.
Photo courtesy James Maxwell/Virginia Caputo

Barney Google (Continued)

	C6	C8	C10
Barney Google Doll, wood, w/composition head and movable arms and legs, Schoenhut, 1922, 9" high..............................	185	375	525
Barney Google Hand Puppet, Gund	45	90	185
Barney Google Riding Spark Plug Paperweight, metal, 3"	80	160	275
Barney Google Tin Wind-up, c. 1923	375	850	1200
Rudy the Ostrich, tin, Nifty, 1924 ..	450	825	1200
Snuffy Smith Hand Puppet, cloth w/rubber head, "King Features", Gund	35	60	95
Spark Plug Candy Container, ...	145	230	375
Spark Plug Doll, stuffed cloth	125	200	350
Spark Plug on Wheels, 3-1/4" high..	225	338	500
Spark Plug Wa-Gee Walker, cloth, felt and metal, wind-up, 9" long..	295	500	750

Batman

Batman first appeared in Detective Comics #27 in May 1939. His popularity has endured through numerous adaptations including radio, television, movie serials, comic books, and feature films. Although Batman collectibles had been around for years, it was the immense international popularity of the mid-1960s television series starring Adam West as Batman that lead to an explosion of Bat-related items, many of which are quite valuable today.

Batman

	C6	C8	C10
Bat Grenade, 1966	50	65	90
Bat Ray, Remco, 1977.....................	25	38	70
Batchute, in box add $300, 1966	30	125	250
Batman Paper Mask, paper, newspaper premium, announced first appearance of Batman newspaper comic, Philadelphia Record Newspaper, 1943	550	1750	2500
Batmobile, No. 267, Corgi	60	125	225
Batmobile, Robin driver, Marx, 4" long..	65	98	160
Batmobile, Batman driver, Marx, 1966	65	100	185

Batman (Continued)

	C6	C8	C10
Bullhorn, Bayshore Ind., 1966	75	150	300
Escape Gun, Lincoln, c. 1966	42	70	135
Flying Batman, inflatable, Ideal, 1966, 12"	10	15	35
Glasses, 1966	4	12	30
Hand Puppet, cloth body	27	60	90
Hand Puppet, vinyl, Ideal, 1965	27	60	90
Helmet and Cape, helmet fits over whole head, Ideal, 1966	145	250	425
Hot Line Batphone, ten different sayings, Marx, 1966	250	375	625
Picture Pistol, Marx, 1966	225	350	550
Play Set, Batman and the Justice League of America playset, eleven pieces including characters and vehicles. This is the most desirable of 1960s Batman toys., Ideal, 1966	1200	4500	10,000
Play Set, small cardboard stand-ups of characters and vehicles, Ideal, 1973	25	50	85
Robin Hand Puppet, Ideal, 1966	70	105	150
Robin Soaky	40	60	150
Soaky	30	40	75
Switch 'N Go Play Set, forty feet of track, 9" plastic Batmobile, figures, etc., Mattel, 1966	150	325	650
Thingmaker Set, on original card, 1960s	250	350	520
Utility Belt, w/belt-radio buckle, on original card, 1960s	50	125	225
Utility Belt Set, Remco, 1979	50	125	225

Beetle Bailey

Mort Walker's Beetle Bailey first appeared on September 4, 1950 in limited circulation (only a dozen or so newspapers) as a lazy college student. By March of 1951, Beetle quit college, enlisted in the Army, and began his adventures at Camp Swampy. Several comic books featured the military misfit and his pals, but Beetle Bailey's true calling seems to be as a daily comic strip. Still popular after more than 50 years, Beetle and friends are featured in more than 1,700 newspapers.

Beetle Bailey

	C6	C8	C10
Beetle Bailey, tin litho, "Pop Up Beetle Bailey", Linemar	180	270	375
Beetle Bailey Figure, vinyl, 3"	8	12	20
Beetle Bailey Hand Puppet, Gund	45	68	100
Beetle Bailey's Camp Swampy Play Set, MPC	115	180	275
Sergeant Snorkel Hand Puppet	37	60	80

Beetle Bailey (Continued)

	C6	C8	C10
Zero Hand Puppet, vinyl and cloth, Gund, 1960s	30	50	80

Blondie

Chic Young (1901-1973) created *Blondie* in 1930 and intended her to follow the pattern of the popular *Polly & Her Pals* strip. Instead, she married Dagwood Bumstead on February 17, 1933 and the rest is comics history. Blondie, Dagwood, their son Alexander (remember when he was called "Baby Dumpling?"), daughter Cookie, and Daisy the dog formed an unbeatable cast. In addition to the continuing comic strip, the hilarious adventures of the Bumstead family were immortalized in virtually every medium. The 1939 feature film, *Blondie*, starring Arthur Lake as Dagwood and Penny Singleton as Blondie was the first of more than two dozen films, and in 1950, they conquered television.

Blondie was also a successful comic book property. McKay published the first issue in the spring of 1947, passed the comic to Harvey in April of 1950, and Charlton published the title from issue #177 in February of 1969 until its final issue, #222 in November, 1976.

Blondie

	C6	C8	C10
Blondie Figure, lead, 1940s, 2-1/2" tall	12	65	135
Blondie Hingees Set, 1944	20	30	50
Blondie Paint Set, American Crayon, 1946	30	110	250
Blondie Paper Cut-Outs, "Blondie's Jalopy", 16" long	1200	2000	2800
Blondie Paper Cut-Outs, No. 982, Whitman, 1940	60	125	210
Blondie Paper Cut-Outs, No. 967, Whitman, 1947	37	65	100
Blondie's Peg Board Set, multi-colored pegs, hammer, cut-outs of Dagwood, Blondie, etc., King Features, 1934, 9" x 15-1/2"	45	150	300
Blondie's Presto Slate, illustration of Blondie and Dagwood and other characters, Presto, 1944, 10" x 13"	20	60	90
Dagwood Aeroplane, "Dagwood's Solo Flight", Marx, 1935	350	575	850
Dagwood and Kids Figures, Dagwood, Alexander, and Cookie - each, King Features, 1944	30	85	150
Dagwood Marionette, wood body w/plastic head, hands, feet and life-like hair, marked "Hazelle's", 1940s, 15"	60	100	200
Dagwood the Driver Crazy Car, Marx, 1935, 8" long	500	850	1250
Puzzle, Featured Funnies, 1930s	50	125	175

Jiggs Jazz Car (Bringing Up Father), Nifty, 1920s, $6000. Photo courtesy Christie's East

Maggie and Jiggs Squeeze Toy (Bringing Up Father), German, c. 1925, $875. Photo courtesy Christie's East

Bringing Up Father

On January 2, 1913, King Features debuted the George McManus strip, *Bringing Up Father*. The story of an Irishman named Jiggs and his family coping with sudden and unexpected wealth struck a chord with the public and the strip took off. Day after day, Jiggs didn't see why his wealth should prevent him from hanging around with his friends to the chagrin of his social ladder-climbing wife, Maggie.

The strip inspired several movies, single-issue Dell comics in 1942 and 1944, a play, and even inspired a restaurateur to change the name of his establishment. James Moore believed himself to be the inspiration for Jiggs' tavern-owner friend, Dinty Moore, because McManus was a frequent patron. He changed the restaurant's name to "Dinty Moore's" and reaped the benefits of the association with *Brining Up Father*. You guessed it, he also created the Dinty Moore line of canned foods.

Bringing Up Father	C6	C8	C10
Bringing Up Father Hingees, 1944,	17	26	35
Jiggs Doll, wood-jointed, Jaymar, 5"	80	120	185
Jiggs Doll, hard plastic, 1960s, 3" high	6	9	20
Jiggs Jazz Car, wind-up, Nifty, 1920s, 6-1/2" long	1200	3200	6000
Jiggs Stick Puppet, 12" high	80	120	180
Maggie and Jiggs, seated on four-wheeled platform, Nifty, 1920s, 8" long	800	1200	1800

Bringing Up Father (Continued)	C6	C8	C10
Maggie and Jiggs Squeeze Toy, tin litho, German, c. 1925, 8"	400	650	875
Maggie and Jiggs Wind-up, Strauss, 1924, 7-1/4" long	800	1225	1800
Maggie Doll, hard plastic, 1960s, 3" high	6	12	25

Buck Rogers

Buck Rogers in the 25th Century A.D. and *Tarzan of the Apes* made their debuts on January 7, 1929. Both characters were veterans of pulp magazines and it was the August, 1928 issue of *Amazing Stories* magazine that brought "Anthony" Rogers to the attention of newspaper syndicator John F. Dille. Featured in the story, "Armageddon 2419 AD," Rogers was a hero that Dille wanted to bring to the comics. He commissioned creator Phillip F. Nowlan to write the stories and Richard Calkins to lend his artistic talents. Dille also suggested a name change to "Buck" Rogers after western film hero Buck Jones.

After a 500-year slumber, Buck awakens to a new future where the world is enslaved. He is quickly recruited into the resistance movement and accompanied by the faithful Wilma Deering and Dr. Huer, they bring freedom to the planet. This was followed by other sci-fi plots and introduced space travel, ray guns, and talking robots to the public. The Buck Rogers strip also inspired the creation of another sci-fi series destined to outlast it—Flash Gordon.

The strip suffered ups and downs after the departures of Nowlan and Calulkins in the 1940s as the succession of writers and artists lacked stability in the story. It was cancelled in

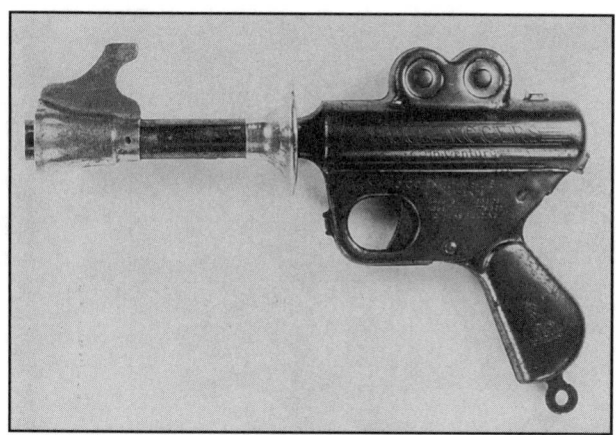

Buck Rogers Rocket Pistol XZ-31, Daisy, 1934, $600. Photo courtesy Hake's Americana and Collectibles

Buck Rogers Atomic Pistol U-235, Daisy, 1946, $600. Photo courtesy Hake's Americana and Collectibles

1967. A revival in the strip coincided with the 1979 feature film and debut of the television series starring Gil Gerard, but success was short-lived and it was cancelled in 1983. The TSR comic book appeared in 1990 and lasted just ten issues.

Buck Rogers

	C6	C8	C10
Atomic Pistol U-235, with box, add $600, Daisy, 1946	150	375	600
Battle Cruiser, two grooved wheels on top to run on string, Tootsietoy, 1937	100	150	275
Casting Set, Junior Caster, Rapaport Bros., 1930s	325	500	850
Chemical Laboratory, large set, Gropper Toys, 1937	800	1250	1850
Chemical Laboratory, small set, Gropper Toys, 1937	600	1000	1400
Disintegrator Pistol, w/box $500, Daisy, 1936	200	390	650
Figure, Tootsietoy, 1-3/4" high	38	90	160
Flash Blast Attack Ship, two grooved wheels on top to run string, Tootsietoy, 1937, 4-1/2" long	225	360	550
Flying Saucer, paper, 1940s	75	112	175
Helmet, leather, Daisy, 1933	300	600	850
Liquid Helium Water Pistol, w/box add $1,200, Daisy, 1936	1050	1250	2350
Pop Pistol, 1930s	125	375	500
Rocket Pistol XZ-31, w/box add $600, Daisy, 1934, 9-1/2" long	132	375	600
Rocket Police Patrol, wind-up, Marx, 1939	800	1300	1800
Rocket Ship, wind-up, Marx, 1934, 12" long	375	650	1000
Rubber Band Gun, 1940, 5" x 10"	50	75	130
Sonic Ray Gun, yellow plastic, with box, 1952	65	185	350

Buck Rogers (Continued)	C6	C8	C10
Stamper Kraft Astral Heroes Set, small, 1930s	30	60	100
Stamper Kraft Print Set, medium size, 1930s	100	200	400
Stamper Kraft Rubber Stamps Set, #4090, 22 different rubber stamps, 1930s	1500	2000	2500
Strato Kite, 1946	37	56	80
Super Sonic Glasses (binoculars), 1953	70	105	150
Super Sonic Ray Gun, w/box	150	225	375
Super-Scope, w/adjustable plastic telescope, Norton-Honer Mfg. Co., 1952, 8-1/2" long	92	138	195
U-238 Atomic Pistol and Holster set, adventure book and coupon, w/box, Daisy, 1946	900	1300	1800
U-238 Atomic Pistol and Holster set, w/box add $600, 1948	425	850	1200
USN Los Angeles, Tootsietoy, 5" long	117	175	250
Venus Duo Destroyer, two grooved wheels on top to run on string, Tootsietoy, 1937	170	255	375
Walkie Talkie, 1950s	110	165	250
Wilma Pistol and Holster Set, small version of Buck Rogers "Pop" pistol, 1930s	210	425	750

Buster Brown and Tige

Richard Outcault's mischievous Buster Brown debuted in the *New York Herald* on May 4, 1902. Accompanied by his dog, Tige, who only spoke to Buster when no one else was around, Buster appealed to all segments of society. His popularity crossed ethnic and economic boundaries, and his beloved misadventures lead to a merchandising blockbuster. Buster Brown shoes appeared at the 1904 World's Fair. In

Buster Brown Seesaw Tin Wind-up, German, $1800. Photo courtesy Christie's East

1906, Outcault switched to the Hearst papers and published the strip without using Buster's name in the title while the *Herald* continued to publish Buster Brown using a series of other writers and artists. Outcault's strip stopped running in 1921 and the Hearst version only lasted until 1911.

Buster Brown and Tige	C6	C8	C10
Buster Brown and Tige, cast iron, Buster in cart pulled by Tige, 7-1/2" long	500	750	1050
Buster Brown and Tige Paper Dolls, w/envelope, dolls, Tige, four suits and hats, and hat for Tige, J. Ottman Lith. Co. N.Y.	150	200	325
Buster Brown and Tige Ring, brass, 1930s	35	50	100
Buster Brown and Tige Tin Wind-up, w/street lamp and bell, c. early 1900s	2000	3500	5800
Buster Brown Doll, 1920s, 23" high	200	325	500
Buster Brown Doll, Ideal, 1929	125	200	275
Buster Brown Figure, lead	20	35	50
Buster Brown Secret Agent Periscope, c. 1950, 20" long	25	50	75
Buster Brown Seesaw Tin Wind-up, w/Buster and Tige, German, 9-1/2"	600	1200	1800
Buster Brown Tin Wind-up, drives horseless carriage, Lehmann	500	900	1500

Captain America

Joe Simon and Jack Kirby brought Captain America to life with the March 1941 issue of Captain America Comics. While World War II raged overseas, kids were fighting the Axis along with Captain America and his sidekick, "Bucky" Barnes. Cap's popularity waned after the war, and the book was cancelled in 1949. A brief return in 1953 failed to generate readership, he remained frozen in time until 1964 when a new team of Marvel heroes called The Avengers discovered Cap frozen in the Artic. He has enjoyed continued success as an Avenger and in his own titles since.

Captain America	C6	C8	C10
Captain America Hand Puppet, 1966	30	50	90
Captain America Jailhouse Lock Set, Larami, 1974	10	15	30
Captain America Utility Set, Remco, 1977	16	30	65

Captain Marvel

The success of Superman (1938) launched a super-hero frenzy and sent publishers scrambling to introduce their own super-powered characters. Fawcett Publications introduced Captain Marvel and his alter ego Billy Batson in the pages of *Whiz Comics* 1940. Artist Charles Clarence (C.C.) Beck and writer Bill Parker crafted a story in which the homeless young Billy follows a stranger in a subway tunnel and discovers the wizard Shazam. The wizard endows Billy with the power to become Captain Marvel upon speaking the word, "Shazam."

Children identifying with the child hero who had the ability to solve problems as an adult began a phenomenon that took the country by storm and earned a lawsuit from DC Comics who thought that the Captain bared too close a resemblance to their Kryptonian hero. In 1941, Captain Marvel received his own title. Adding characters like Captain Marvel Jr. and Mary Marvel gave the book a family feel and readership increased when the *Marvel Family* title was released.

The title suffered as all super hero titles did in the early 1950s and was eventually cancelled in 1953. Fawcett settled their suit with DC Comics, and agreed to never publish Captain Marvel's character again.

Captain Marvel	C6	C8	C10
Billy Batson Magic Box	75	100	175

Buster Brown and Tige, $1050. Photo courtesy Christie's East

Buster Brown and Tige Tin Wind-up, c. early 1900s, $5800. Photo courtesy Christie's East

Captain Marvel (Continued)	C6	C8	C10
Buzz Bomb, ...	20	50	100
Captain Marvel Lightning Racing Cars, four tin wind-up race cars, box turns into race track with fans in the stand, track is held up by metal supports; individual cars are valued at between $450-$500, 1947	2000	3750	5250
Comic Hero Punch-outs, includes two Captain Marvels, Captain Marvel Jr., Bulletman, Bulletgirl, Spy Smasher, Ibis, two Golden Arrows, Minute Man, Freddy Freeman, Mr. Scarlet, Commando Yank, Pinky, Bulletdog, Samuel Lowe, 1942	150	210	300
Flying Captain Marvel, paper, Reed, 1944-47, 7" x 10"	15	25	50
Gun, movie gun w/film	175	263	375
Hoppy the Flying Marvel Bunny, paper, Reed, c. 1944-47	10	20	50
Magic Eyes, Reed, c. 1945	15	35	65
Magic Flute, copyright picture of Captain Marvel on side, on original card, 1946	100	150	185

Captain Marvel (Continued)	C6	C8	C10
Magic Picture, Reed, c. 1944, ...	50	80	110
Porsche Car No. 262, Corgi, 1979	37	56	80
Rocket Raider, Reed, c. 1944-47	15	35	65
Three Flying Marvels, paper, Reed, c. 1944-47	15	35	65
Toss Bag	50	60	85

Dennis the Manace

In October, 1950, Hank Ketcham introduced the world to a mischievous but lovable 5-year-old in the Post-Hall Syndicate newspapers. Dennis the Menace has delighted audiences and spoiled the peaceful retirement hopes of Mr. Wilson for more than fifty years. The death of Hank Ketcham in 2001 hasn't slowed the exploits of Dennis, his adventures reside in the hands of King Features Syndicate under the care of Marcus Hamilton and Ron Ferdinand.

Dennis the Menace	C6	C8	C10
Dennis the Menace Figure, Hall, 1970s, 7" high	42	63	90
Dennis the Menace Squirt Gun Figure, plastic, 1954, 5-1/2" high...	40	60	85

Captain Marvel Buzz Bomb, $100. Photo courtesy Continental Hobby House

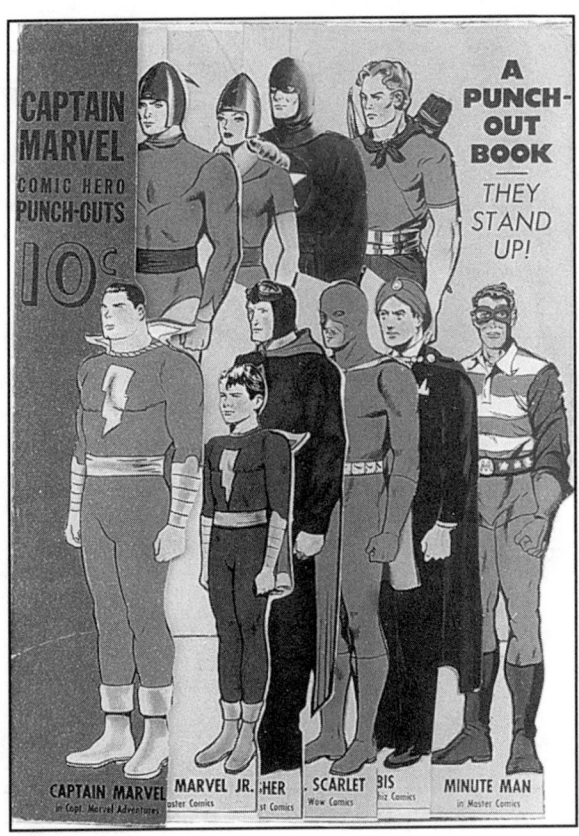

Captain Marvel Comic Hero Punch-outs, Samuel Lowe, 1942, $300. Photo courtesy Bruce Bergstrom-Artman Originals

Dick Tracy

The Chicago Tribune Syndicate debuted the first Dick Tracy comic on October 4, 1931. Chester Gould's unfailingly honest detective and his unprecedented use of violence changed the way the world looked at police-based comics. Tracy's bad guys were memorable for their misshapen physical appearances and the fact that some actually died after facing off against Dick Tracy. The strip's longevity and continued popularity is tied to its willingness to stay with the times and the evolving technology. Tracy has had a two-way wrist radio, a wrist television and now sports a wrist computer. Max Allen Collins took over writing duties when Chester Gould retired in 1977 and the art duties were performed by Rick Fletcher. After Fletcher's death in 1983, Dick Locher assumed the artistic duties and is now teamed with writer Michael Kilian.

Dick Tracy	C6	C8	C10
Air Detective Wings, c. late 1930s	65	80	125
Automatic, w/picture of Eagles, Hubley	90	125	225
B.O. Plenty Holding Sparkle Plenty Tin Wind-up, Marx, mid-1940s	150	270	400
Baby Sparkle Plenty Paper Dolls, No. 1510, Saalfield	35	75	150
Bonny Braids, Ideal, 1951	75	100	125
Bonny Braids Walker, Ideal, 1953	50	75	100

Dick Tracy (Continued)	C6	C8	C10
Braces for Smart Boys and Girls, Deluxe set includes suspenders, magnifying glass, badge, and whistle, Deluxe, 1940s	30	60	100
Click Pistol, No. 36, Marx	110	170	325
Click Pistol, aluminum, No. 78, Marx	45	75	175
Copmobile, plastic, Ideal, 1963	35	52	75
Crime Stoppers Lab, Porter Chem Co., 10" x 12" box	150	225	385
Crimestoppers Set, includes badge, handcuffs, billy club, John Henry	45	68	100
Detective Badge with Secret Compartment, metal, large, leather pouch on back, late 1930s	50	75	175
Detective Fingerprint Set, 1933	100	150	300
Dick Tracy and B.O. Plenty with Crimestopper Whistle and Clue Detector	40	60	80
Dick Tracy Doll, painted composition, mouth moves, 13-1/2" high	275	500	675
Dick Tracy Junior Pinback Button, Parisian Novelty Company, 1930s	75	225	400

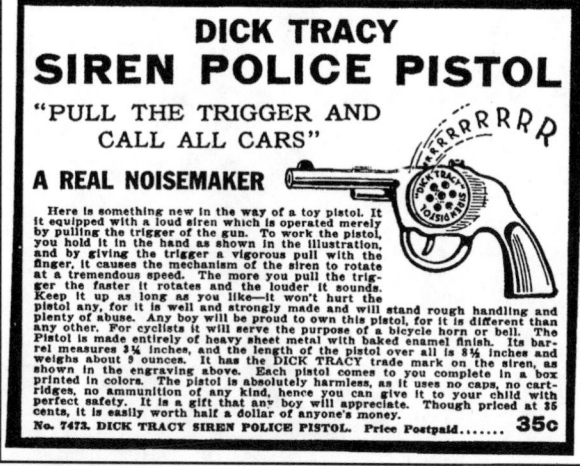

Dick Tracy Riot Car, Marx, c. 1946, $400. Photo courtesy Gary Linden

A newspaper ad for the Dick Tracy Siren Pistol from late 1930s. The pistol is valued at $200.

Dick Tracy Police Station, 1950s, $550. Photo courtesy Ron Chojnacki/Don Hultzman

Dick Tracy (Continued)	C6	C8	C10
Double Target Game, 1941, 9-1/2" square w/8" tin gun and darts......	150	300	425
Electronic Wrist Radio, Remco	35	52	85
G-Man Gun, wind-up, Marx	150	220	300
Hand Puppet, Ideal, 1961	37	56	80
Handcuffs for Junior, No. 700, John Henry Products, c. 1946	50	75	100
Hingee Paper Figures, set of six, 1940s	20	35	50
Inspector General Badge	600	800	1050
Moon Maid's Daughter Doll, w/space helmet, Ideal, 1965, 16-1/2"..	92	150	300
Pen-Lite, 1939	75	85	160
Police Car, remote control, battery operated, (1953 Chevrolet), very rare, Linemar, 1950s	500	1000	1500
Police Car Tin Wind-up, 1949, 7" long..	175	275	400

Dick Tracy (Continued)	C6	C8	C10
Police Station, w/7" long automatic siren car, w/box add $300, 1950s	200	375	550
Power Jet Squad Gun, Mattel, 1962, 28" long..	72	108	160
Riot Car, heavy tin or sheet metal litho, heavy tin or sheetmetal litho, w/friction motor, Marx, 1946, 7-1/2" long........................	125	200	400
Shootin' Shell Snubnose .38 Pistol and Holster	125	175	250
Siren Pistol, red w/blue siren, c. late 1930s	40	90	200
Siren Police Whistle, tin, Marx	40	60	90
Soaky, Colgate-Palmolive, 1965, 10" tall...	15	35	55
Space Coupe, Aurora, 1966	375	650	950
Sparkle Plenty Paper Doll Set, No. 5160, Saalfield, 1948	35	60	110

Sparkle Plenty Washing Machine (Dick Tracy), Kalon Radio Corp., c. 1947, $275. Photo courtesy Lloyd W. Ralston Auctions

Dick Tracy Squad Car No. 1, Marx, $360. Photo courtesy Gary Linden

Dick Tracy Squad Car No.1, Marx, $260. Photo courtesy Gary Linden

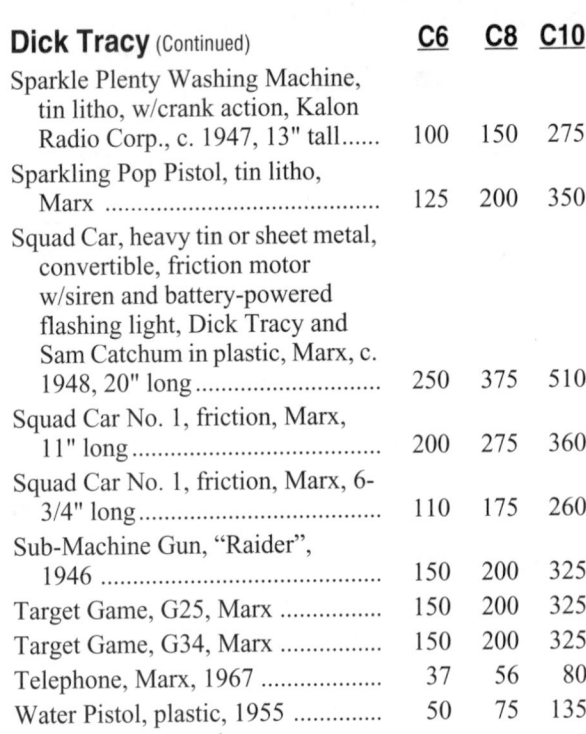

Dick Tracy (Continued)	C6	C8	C10
Sparkle Plenty Washing Machine, tin litho, w/crank action, Kalon Radio Corp., c. 1947, 13" tall......	100	150	275
Sparkling Pop Pistol, tin litho, Marx	125	200	350
Squad Car, heavy tin or sheet metal, convertible, friction motor w/siren and battery-powered flashing light, Dick Tracy and Sam Catchum in plastic, Marx, c. 1948, 20" long	250	375	510
Squad Car No. 1, friction, Marx, 11" long	200	275	360
Squad Car No. 1, friction, Marx, 6-3/4" long	110	175	260
Sub-Machine Gun, "Raider", 1946	150	200	325
Target Game, G25, Marx	150	200	325
Target Game, G34, Marx	150	200	325
Telephone, Marx, 1967	37	56	80
Water Pistol, plastic, 1955	50	75	135

Felix the Cat

Felix the Cat was the brain-child of Otto Messmer. Released in 1919 by the Pat Sullivan Studio, Felix is one of the only characters in this chapter to make his debut in animation rather than a comic stip. He began life in the comics in 1923 and remained there until 1966. His final silent animated comic appeared in 1928. He was revived again in 1936 without success and again in 1960. These comics survive and are still enjoyed today.

Felix the Cat	C6	C8	C10
China Set	80	140	225
Doll, stuffed cloth w/rubber hands, Gund, c. 1950, 15" high	80	130	175
Felix Chases Mice Pull Toy	525	800	1100
Felix on Fire Truck Pull Toy, Gong Bell	110	180	275
Felix on Tricycle Pull Toy, Gong Bell	220	375	550
Felix the Cat and Mickey Mouse Hoop Toy, tin hoop with papier-mâché figures, Spain	NPF	NPF	NPF
Felix the Cat on Scooter, Nifty	600	1000	1600
Figure, cast iron, w/tin umbrella, 2-1/2" high......................................	200	350	520

Felix the Cat on Scooter, Nifty, $1600. Photo courtesy Phillips, New York

Front to Back: Felix the Cat Figure, $520; Felix the Cat Speedy Felix, $2750. Photo courtesy Christie's East

Felix the Cat Figure, c. 1930s, $750. Photo courtesy Christie's East

Felix the Cat (Continued)

	C6	C8	C10
Figure, lead, 2-1/2" high..................	190	285	385
Figure, wood, 12" high....................	275	500	700
Figure, cast iron, Dent, 1923, 2" high..............	180	270	400
Figure, wood, jointed w/rubber head, 1940s, 9" high....................	100	175	325
Figure, composition, c. 1930s, 13" high.............	275	450	750
Nodder, pot-metal, w/Pat Sullivan copyright on bottom of feet, 2" high.............	100	150	285
Pull Car, Borgfeldt, 1925, 12" long.............	300	500	700
Soaky, blue or black version, Colgate-Palmolive, 1965, 11" tall.....	35	52	85

Felix the Cat (Continued)

	C6	C8	C10
Speedy Felix, in car	1000	1700	2750
Squeeze Toy, rubber, Eastern Moulded Products, 6-1/2"....................	75	125	185
Walker, tin wind-up, German	325	500	775

Flash Gordon

On January 7, 1934 Flash Gordon debuted as King Features Syndicate's answer to the successful Buck Rogers strip. Written by Don Moore and brought to life by artist Alex Raymond, Flash Gordon soon became a success and the adventures of Flash, Dale Arden, Doctor Zarkoff and Ming the Merciless were enjoyed until the daily strip was cancelled in 1944. In 1951, Dan Barry revived the daily strip and wrote it for the next four decades. When he retired in 1990, the strip went through the hands of several creators until its 1993 cancellation. Today, it survives as a Sunday strip and is in the creative care of writer/artist Jim Keefe.

Flash Gordon

	C6	C8	C10
Air Ray Pistol, shoots blast of air using rubber diaphragm, 10".......	125	188	310
Arresting Ray, picture of Flash on handle, Marx	133	200	330
Automatic Disintegrator, Hubley ...	200	300	525
Belt, large plastic buckle showing rocket ship flight, 1950s	70	105	160
Casting Set, w/original box, Home Foundry, 1934	600	1000	1350
Jet-propelled Kite	27	41	60
Play Set, Mego	58	87	120
Play Set, die-cast, No. 1793, w/original box, Tootsietoy, 1978	27	41	60
Radio Repeater Clicker Pistol, No. 58, add $250 for box, Marx, 1950s, 10" long	210	325	600
Rocket Fighter, wind-up, Marx, 1939, 12" long	265	500	1000
Signal Pistol, tin litho, No. 74, with box, Marx, 1940s	600	900	1300
Solar Commando, three plastic space men and one ship, 1950s ..	80	100	200
Space Cruiser, 1952	50	80	150
Space Outfit, Esquire Novelty, 1952	90	135	190
Space Target, metal, standup, Alex Raymond illustration, 12" x 14"	100	160	250
Sparkling Battle Rocket, 1969	40	60	90
Strat-O-Wagon, Wyandotte, 9" long..	100	150	225
Two-Way Telephone, Marx, c. 1940	100	150	300
Water Gun, plastic, w/original box add $200, different variant colors, Marx, 7" long	175	325	550

Foxy Grandpa

Foxy Grandpa debuted in The New York Herald in January, 1900 and was the creation of Charles Edward "Bunny" Schultze. The strip moved to the New York American on February 16, 1902. Featuring the adventures of a grandpa causing havoc in the lives of his family, Foxy Grandpa lasted as a daily until 1918. After that, the character survived in Foxy Grandpa Stories, a series of nature tales featuring Grandpa only in the initial panel. Schultze died in 1939 and the series faded into history.

Foxy Grandpa

	C6	C8	C10
Bell Toy, cast iron, vehicle pulled by two boys, 7" long	425	650	1000

Foxy Grandpa (Continued)	C6	C8	C10
Doll, cloth and composition, 17" long..	450	675	1200
Figure, tin, clockwork, German, 8-1/4" high.................................	300	450	700
Foxy Grandpa Button, 1902	25	65	80
Grandpa Riding Donkey Pull Toy, composition, 9" long platform......................................	450	685	1000
Jack-in-the-Box, papier-mâché and paper litho on wood, 1900, 4" square	200	300	425
Nodder, cast iron, in donkey cart, Harirs, 7-1/4" long...................	225	350	550
Nodder, papier-mâché, 1900, 6" tall...	150	210	350
Nodder, cast iron, large-headed Grandpa in cart pulled by donkey, Hubley, c. 1910, 6-1/2"	500	800	1250

Gasoline Alley

The Chicago Tribune Syndicate debuted Frank King's Gasoline Alley in 1918. Gasoline Alley was the first strip in which characters aged at the same pace as readers. Deciding to add a child to the cast in 1921, the baby Skeezix was found on the doorstep of main character Walt Wallet and its popularity soared. King retired in 1959, handing over the strip to Dick Moores, who modernized the characters and continued the strip until his death in 1986. Moores' assistant, Jim Scancarelli took over the strip and continues as its creative force today.

Gasoline Alley

	C6	C8	C10
Gasoline Alley Garage and Auto Racer, tin litho, garage and "Bearcat Racer" car, Girard, 1924	400	750	1200
Mrs. Blossom Doll, oilcloth, Live Long Toys, 17" high....................	100	180	350
Pal Doll, oilcloth, cotton-stuffed, Live Long Toys, 1923	90	140	200
Rachel Doll, cotton-stuffed oilcloth, Live Long Toys, 1923	150	200	350
Skeezix Doll, cotton-stuffed oilcloth, Live Long Toys, 1924, ...	100	150	250
Skeezix Doll, cotton-stuffed oilcloth, as boy, Live Long Toys, 1924	125	175	275
Skeezix Radio, tin litho, Live Long Toys, c. 1924, 5" high	1000	1550	2500
Sunshine X Riding Sparkplug Platform Toy, 9" long......................	1400	2400	3600
Uncle Walt Doll, oilcloth, Live Long Toys, 26" high....................	80	120	170

Andy Gump Roadster (The Gumps), Arcade, $6800. Photo courtesy Christie's East

Gumps, The

Captain Joseph M. Patterson, Chicago Tribune editor responsible for the creation of Little Orphan Annie and Moon Mullins wanted a strip about ordinary folks, or "gumps" as he called them. Sidney Smith wrote and drew the strip that appeared for the first time on February 12, 1917. It introduced Andy Gump, a non-heroic hero and the adventures of his ordinary family. The strip achieved national popularity and was a huge merchandising success. Smith's contract for producing the strip net him a reported $100,000 per year until his unfortunate death in 1935. The strip lasted under other creators until its last appearance on October 17, 1959.

Gumps, The	C6	C8	C10
Andy Gump Dancing Doll, wooden w/tin legs, 9" high	125	188	350
Andy Gump Roadster, cast iron, Old "348" red car, Andy and wheels are nickel plated, no license plate, no crank, Arcade, 1929, 7-1/4" long, 6" tall	650	1500	2400
Andy Gump Roadster, Old "348," red car, Andy in green w/white collar, nickeled tires w/green disc wheels, no license plate, no crank, Arcade, 1929, 7-1/4" long, 6" tall	750	1900	3200
Andy Gump Roadster, Old "348," deluxe version, Andy painted in five colors, red bodied car w/green trim, green disc wheels w/red hubs and white tires, has license plate and crank, Arcade, 1929, 7-1/4" long, 6" high	2000	3500	6800

Gumps, The (Continued)	C6	C8	C10
Chester Gump Cart with Horse, open two-wheel cart w/Chester driving, Arcade, 1920s	280	420	650
Chester Gump Doll, oilcloth, Live Long Toys, c. 1920s, 13" high	150	175	350

Happy Hooligan

Respected cartoonist Frederick Burr Opper joined the staff of Hearst newspapers in 1899 and debuted Happy Hooligan on March 11, 1900. Happy wore a tin can for a hat and was a good-hearted hobo who didn't lament his lot in life. Always a victim of his lack of social status, and frequently the recipient of mayhem in return for his good deeds, Happy was joined in his misadventures by his brother, Gloomy Gus, whose name is still a synonym for a grump. The strip continued until 1932, when Opper's eyesight failed.

Happy Hooligan	C6	C8	C10
Clown Doll, w/bisque face	600	900	1600
Cymbals Player	300	450	700
Doll, bisque face, dressed as clown, 9-1/2" high	700	1200	1750
Donkey Cart, c. 1925, 10" long	240	360	600
Gloomy Gus Figure, cast iron, Harris Toy Co., 1903, 5" tall	150	230	450
Gloomy Gus in Goat Cart, cast iron, 14" long	400	750	1000
Gloomy Gus in Horse Cart, cast iron, Harris, 14" long	1600	2800	3750
Gloomy Gus in Mule Cart, cast iron, Harris	300	450	650

Gloomy Gus in Horse Cart (Happy Hooligan), Harris, $3750. Photo courtesy Christie's East

Happy Hooligan Clown Doll, $1600. Photo courtesy Christie's East

Happy Hooligan in Car (Happy Hooligan), Hill Brass, c. 1903, $5200. Photo courtesy Christie's East

Happy Hooligan in Horse-drawn Wagon, Harris, c. 1905, $4200. Photo courtesy Christie's East

Happy Hooligan (Continued)	C6	C8	C10
Hand Puppet, cast iron and cloth, 9-1/4"..	50	70	150
Happy Hooligan in Car, cast iron, N.N. Hill Brass Co., c. 1903, 5-3/4"..	1400	3400	5200

Happy Hooligan (Continued)	C6	C8	C10
Happy Hooligan in Cart, cast iron, horse-pulled and head nods, Kenton, early 1900s, 10-1/4" long, 7-1/2" high.....................................	700	1200	1800

Happy Hooligan Police Patrol, Kenton, $3600. Photo courtesy James Maxwell/Virginia Caputo

Left to Right: Henry and His Brother Wind-ups, Japanese, $1650; Henry's Mahout on Donkey, $850; Henry on Trapeze Wind-up, $725. Photo courtesy Christie's East

Happy Hooligan (Continued)

	C6	C8	C10
Happy Hooligan in Donkey Cart, wind-up, Ingap Co., 1930s, 6-3/8" long	600	1100	1500
Happy Hooligan in Goat Cart, cast iron, 7-1/2" long	200	350	530
Happy Hooligan in Horse Cart, cast iron, Wilkins, 17" long	500	875	1200
Happy Hooligan in Horse-drawn Wagon, cast iron, w/Gloomy Gus and driver, Harris, c. 1905	1800	3100	4200
Happy Hooligan Jigger, tin litho, dressed as clown, tap dances on drum, wind-up, Kiddies' Metal Toys Co., 9"	750	1200	1500
Happy Hooligan Jigger, w/crank action, Kiddee Metal Toys, 1920s, 10" tall	900	1500	1800
Happy Hooligan on a Ladder,	300	400	600
Happy Hooligan on Donkey, celluloid	325	425	600
Happy Hooligan Walking Toy, wind-up, Chein, 1932, 6" high	400	600	875

Happy Hooligan (Continued)

	C6	C8	C10
Happy on Rabbit Candy Container, composition, 7-1/2"	1000	1500	2100
Police Patrol, Happy hit by cop as Gloomy Gus drives, Kenton	1400	2200	3600
Roly-Poly,	75	100	185

Henry

Carl Anderson's character, Henry, made his debut in the *Saturday Evening Post* on March 19, 1932. The daily newspaper strip began on December 17, 1934 and the Sunday started on March 10, 1935. He was eventually featured in newspapers, magazines, and comic books with his infant-like appearance and non-verbal communication. Anderson passed the daily artistic duties to John Liney and the Sunday duties to Don Trachte in 1942, when arthritis forced him to retire from comics. The daily strip is still being published by King Features Syndicate.

Henry

	C6	C8	C10
Henry and His Brother Wind-ups, celluloid, on wheels, Japanese	700	1100	1650

Humphrey Mobile Tin Wind-up (Joe Palooka), Wyandotte, c. mid-1940s, $650. Photo courtesy Christie's East

Henry on Elephant Wind-up, Japanese, $1700.

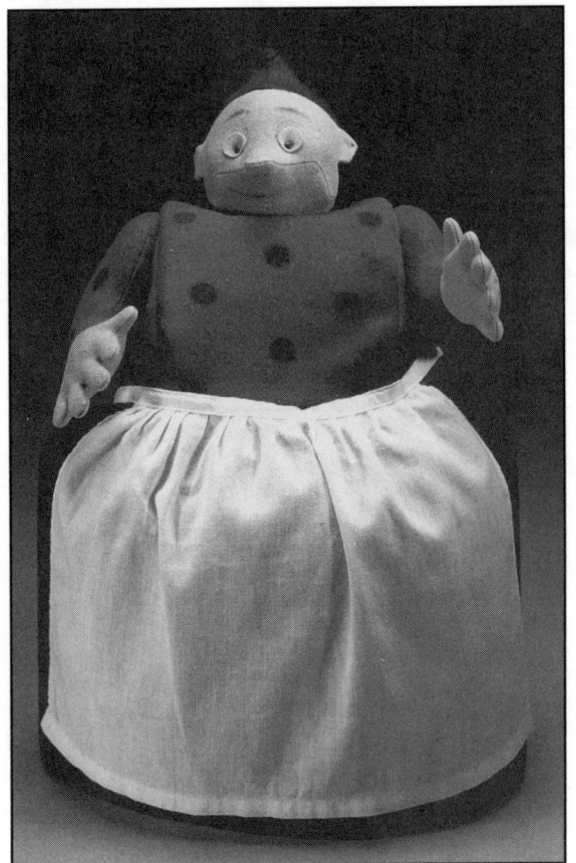

Mama Katzenjammer Doll, Steiff, c. 1908, $2100. Photo courtesy Christie's East

Henry (Continued)

	C6	C8	C10
Henry and his Swan, celluloid mechanical	200	3400	4650
Henry Eating Candy, Linemar, 1950s	500	750	975
Henry on Elephant Wind-up, celluloid and tin, Henry sits on elephant's trunk, w/Mahout, Japanese	700	1150	1700
Henry on Trapeze Wind-up, celluloid	365	525	725
Henry Rubber Squeeze Toy, 1950s, 9-1/2" high	30	50	90
Henry Trapeze Wind-up, part celluloid, Henry, brother and Mahout, Japanese	900	1400	1950
Henry's Mahout on Donkey	450	625	850

Joe Palooka

Sports reporter Ham Fisher was inspired to create Joe Palooka while interviewing a good-natured, but not overly intelligent boxer in 1920. He would shop the character around for almost ten years before it was picked up by the McNaught Syndicate in 1929. The strip's hillbilly setting was a first in comics and would later be used by other strip creators including former Fisher assistant Al Capp in Li'l Abner. Joe Palooka's first film appearance was in 1934, and other serial films followed into the 1950s. The character was also featured in a comic book title from 1945-61, and was among the first characters licensed by Harvey Comics for such use. Mo Leff handled creative duties on the strip until 1955 when he passed it to Tony DiPreta, who was with it until its last appearance in April, 1984.

Joe Palooka

	C6	C8	C10
Championship Belt Buckle, heavy gold-plated brass, buckle shows Palooka w/hands raised in victory, early 1950s	75	100	130
Doll, wood-jointed, 4" high	45	60	110
Doll, wood-jointed, 5-1/2" high	60	85	185
Filmatic, twelve different comic strips	30	50	85
Humphrey Doll, cloth and composition, with tag, pinback and apron, Ideal, 14-1/2" high	225	500	1000

Krazy Kat Platform Toy Tin Wind-up, Nifty, 1920s, $1750. Photo courtesy Christie's East

Joe Palooka (Continued)

	C6	C8	C10
Humphrey Mobile Tin Wind-up, Wyandotte, c. mid-1940s, 7-1/2" high w/smokestack	350	525	650
Joan Palooka Doll, Ideal, 1953	50	75	110
Little Max Speshul Tin Wind-up	3500	5250	7200
Punching Bag, c. 1950	30	45	65

Katzenjammer Kids

Still in syndication after more than 100 years, The Katzenjammer Kids is the longest continuously-running comic strip and was among the first to use sequential panels and word balloons to tell its story. The mischievous adventures of Hans and Fritz (the only characters to have names, the rest were referred to only by their titles) debuted as a Sunday feature on December 12, 1897. Rudolph Dirks gave the boys a loving mother, Mama, oblivious to their destructive nature and after a hiatus to fight in the Spanish-American War, he added the Captain to the cast in 1902 and the over worked truant officer, the Inspector in 1905. Today the Kids are under the creative direction of Hy Eisman.

Katzenjammer Kids

	C6	C8	C10
Katzenjammer Kids Hingees, 1945	16	24	40
Katzenjammer Kids See-Saw Bell Toy, Kenton	900	1550	2100
Mama Katzenjammer Doll, felt, Steiff, c. 1908	700	1250	2100
Mama Spanking Kid, other kid standing, as sailor drives mule cart, Kenton, 1911, 12" long	1050	1850	3600

Krazy Kat

First appearing as a side attraction to The Dingbat Family strip in 1910, the antics of Krazy Kat and Ignatz Mouse received their own strip in 1913. Writer/artist George Herriman gave the strip depth in the character relationships not previously seen in comics and they appealed to a more intellectual audience. The Sunday strip didn't run on the comics page, rather, it ran in the art and drama sections of Hearst newspapers. The appeal to a more sophisticated audience led to a popular appeal shared by no other strips of the time. The strip was handed over to other creators upon the April, 1944 death of George Herriman and as the story goes, William Randolph Hearst noticed the decline in quality of the strip, discovered that Herriman was no longer the creative force behind it, and cancelled the strip. It was the first time a strip was cancelled due to the death of its creator.

Krazy Kat

	C6	C8	C10
Ignatz Figure, jointed wood, Jaymar, 6" high	100	200	300
Krazy Kat Platform Toy Tin Wind-up, Nifty, 1920s, 7-1/2" long	600	1100	1750
Krazy Kat Teacup and Saucer, Chein, 1930s	30	40	80

Li'l Abner

Al Capp, former assistant to Joe Palooka creator Ham Fisher, created one of the most popular comic strips ever printed with 1934's hillbilly adventures of Li'l Abner. Distributed by United Feature Syndicate, the strip's pop culture contributions include the comic strip within a strip, Fearless Fosdick, Capp's Dick Tracy parody, Sadie Hawkins Day, and even new words for the Dogpatch vocabulary like "druthers" and "irregardless." Boldly funny and never afraid to tackle political or cultural topics, Al Capp penned the strip until retiring in 1977.

Li'l Abner

	C6	C8	C10
Daisy Mae and Li'l Abner Paper Dolls, w/Mammy and Pappy Yokum, No. 2360, Saalfield, 1941	75	120	180
Daisy Mae and Li'l Abner Paper Dolls, No. 280, Saalfield, 1942	75	120	200

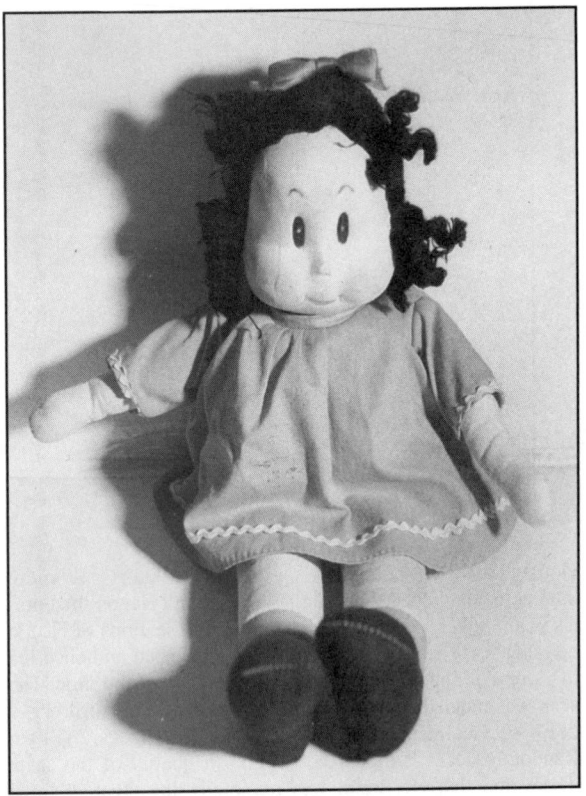

Little Lulu Doll, $300. Photo courtesy Toy Collector News

Little Lulu Doll, Georgene Novelties, $850. Photo courtesy Christie's East

Li'l Abner (Continued)

	C6	C8	C10
Daisy Mae Dogpatch Family Doll, c. 1950s	100	140	275
Daisy Mae Marionette, stringless, National Mask & Puppet Corp., 1940s	70	105	150
Dogpatch Family Doll, c. 1950s	110	165	250
Flyin' Saucer, Brian Specialties, 1962	42	63	100
Li'l Abner and His Dogpatch Band, wind-up, Unique Art, 1945	350	550	750
Li'l Abner Hand Puppet, Baby Barry, 1957	42	63	100
Li'l Abner Stringless Marionette, National Mask & Puppet Corp., 1940s	40	60	90
Lonesome Polecat Rubber Squeak Toy, Reinert, 1950s	50	75	135
Mammy Yokum, Dogpatch Family Doll, Baby Barry Co., 1957	30	60	100
Mammy Yokum Hand Puppet, Baby Barry Co., 1957	42	75	125
Pappy Yokum Doll, Dogpatch Family Doll, Baby Barry Co., 1957	100	150	225
Pappy Yokum Hand Puppet, Baby Barry, 1957	42	63	85

Li'l Abner (Continued)

	C6	C8	C10
Shmoo Doll, vinyl, inflatable, 1940s, 15" high	60	100	200

Little Lulu

First appearing in the *Saturday Evening Post* in 1935, Marjorie Henderson Buell's Little Lulu was a success of magazines, comic books, and animation. Little Lulu appeared as a one-panel cartoon in the *Post* until 1948. She appeared in comic books written by John Stanley and drawn by Irving Tripp regularly until 1984, where she achieved her greatest popularity.

Little Lulu

	C6	C8	C10
Doll, stuffed, Georgene Novelties, 14" high	365	545	850
Doll, felt, 10" high	100	150	300
Doll, w/mask face, M.H. Buell, 1944, 14" high	55	90	150
Shape Book, Whitman, 1971	10	15	30

Little Nemo

Winsor McCay's Little Nemo in Slumberland first appeared in The New York Herald on October 15, 1905. Little Nemo's weekly adventures occurred in a fantasy setting while he was asleep, but halted mid-adventure in the final panel when he

Dr. Primm Rolly Dolly (Little Nemo), Schoenhut, $5200. Photo courtesy Christie's East

Flip Bell Toy (Little Nemo), $875. Photo courtesy Christie's East

CONDITION CODE

C6 Good; evident overall wear, well played with but acceptable to many collectors
C8 Very Good; minor overall wear, very clean
C10 Mint; like new

Note: Mint in Box commands a higher price.
Condition below C6 brings considerably lower prices

awakened. A popular merchandising property, Nemo appeared in books, a play, and even clothing. The strip survived until 1914 and was revived again in the 1920s only to halt in 1927. Noted for its quality of story and art, Little Nemo remains one of the most revered comic strips ever produced.

Little Nemo	C6	C8	C10
Dr. Primm Rolly Dolly, Schoenhut, 11-1/2" high	2700	4200	5200
Flip Bell Toy, cast iron, 6-1/2" long	400	600	875
Little Nemo and Mr. Flip Bell Toy	450	700	1000

Little Orphan Annie

Originally entitled "Little Orphan Otto," Harold Gray's 1924 strip would be retitled by Chicago Tribune Syndicate editor Joseph M. Patterson "Little Orphan Annie." The strip debuted on August 5 and was an instant success despite its message of rags to riches to rags cycle was nothing new. The engrossing stories didn't shy away from the political topics of the day that attracted audiences and kept them coming back day after day. Annie and her dog Sandy were immortalized in a successful radio show that ran for twelve years and a Broadway musical. Gray's death led to several cartoonists taking over duties on the strip, and currently the team of writer Jay Maeder and artist Andrew Pepoy have updated Annie for the new century and continue her spunky self-reliance.

Little Orphan Annie	C6	C8	C10
Annie, Sandy, Daddy, Punjab Hingees, price per set, 1944	20	50	75
Commandos, No. 299, Saalfield, 1943	50	75	150
Little Orphan Annie and Sandy Figures, celluloid	400	600	800
Little Orphan Annie and Sandy Pull Toy, wood, 1930s, 8"	130	195	275

Sandy's Dog House (Little Orphan Annie), Marx, $725. Photo courtesy Christie's East

Sandy with Suitcase in Mouth Tin Wind-up (Little Orphan Annie), $525. Photo courtesy Christie's East

Little Orphan Annie (Continued)	C6	C8	C10
Little Orphan Annie and Sandy Tin Wind-up, two-piece set, Marx, 1930s, 4-1/2" long	450	675	1000
Little Orphan Annie Doll, wood jointed, Jaymar, 5" high	65	100	185
Little Orphan Annie Doll, printed fabric, 1930s, 9-1/2"	100	150	250
Little Orphan Annie Doll, oilcloth, c. 1920s, 16-1/4"	150	200	325
Little Orphan Annie Skipping Rope Tin Wind-up, Marx, 1930s, 5" high	425	638	875
Little Orphan Annie Soaky	14	30	60
Sandy Dog with Magic Tail, Marx, 1930s, 7" long	162	245	385
Sandy Doll, oilcloth, Live Long Toys, c. 1920s, 10-1/2" long	140	210	280
Sandy with Suitcase in Mouth Tin Wind-up	215	350	525
Sandy's Dog House, w/wheeled Sandy, Marx	300	450	725
Stove, 4-3/8" high	62	100	200
Stove, Marx, c. 1930s, 8" high	80	120	225
Water Pistol	90	150	185

Looney Tunes

The long and storied history of Warner Bros. cartoons began with Looney Tunes and a few former Disney employees. Seizing the opportunity to utilize their vast music library in the cartoon format, all early cartoons were required to feature songs that Warner Bros. owned. With Leon Schlesinger acting as middle-man between Warner Bros. and the studio of Hugh Harman and Rudolf Ising, Looney Tunes was born in 1930 and the basic task was to emulate Disney with a character named Bosko. Other characters followed and Porky Pig made his debut in 1935. His success led to many favorite characters that are still popular with children today.

Looney Tunes	C6	C8	C10
Bugs Bunny & Porky Pig Talking Toy, 1940s	95	143	200
Bugs Bunny Hand Puppet, early 1950s	22	33	50
Bugs Bunny Soaky, 10" high	12	20	40
Elmer Fudd Hand Puppet, 1950s	35	52	90
Elmer Fudd Soaky, 1960s, 10" high	18	25	60
Porky Pig Cowboy Tin Wind-up, w/lariat, Marx, 1949, 9" high	325	550	850

Little Orphan Annie Stove, $200. Photo courtesy James Maxwell/Virginia Caputo

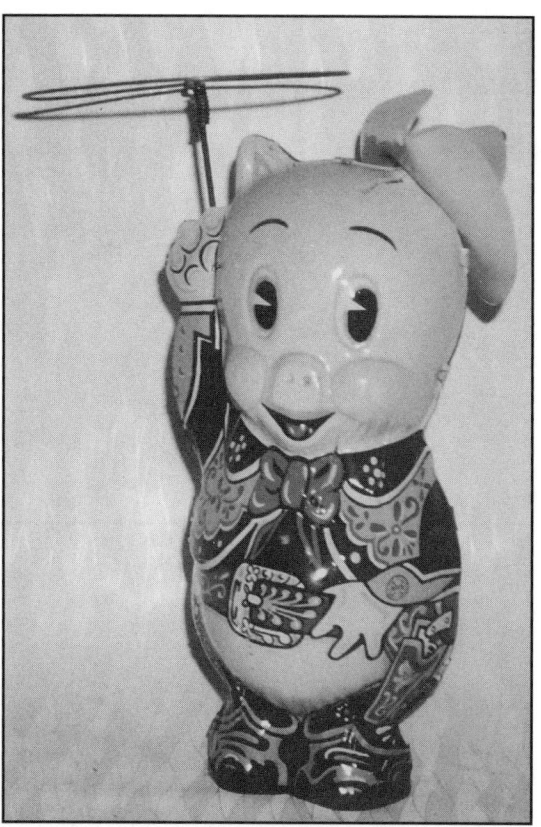

Looney Tunes Porky Pig Cowboy Tin Wind-up, Marx, 1949, $850. Photo courtesy Don Hultzman and Ron Chojnacki

Looney Tunes Porky Pig Tin Wind-up, Marx, 1939, $650. Photo courtesy Detroit Toy Museum, Wilkinson Collection

Looney Tunes (Continued)	C6	C8	C10
Porky Pig Hand Puppet, 1950s, 8" high	30	45	70
Porky Pig Soaky, 1960s, 9" high	20	30	60
Porky Pig SqueezeToy, hollow w/squeaker, has hands behind back, Sun Rubber, c. 1940, 6" high	68	125	200
Porky Pig Tin Wind-up, holding umbrella, raises hat, Marx, 1939, 8"	500	800	1300

Looney Tunes (Continued)	C6	C8	C10
Porky Pig Tin Wind-up, holding umbrella, Marx, 1939, 8-1/2" high	250	375	650
Sylvester, cloth, 1971, 15" high	30	45	70
Sylvester Hand Puppet, early 1950s	50	75	100
Sylvester Soaky	16	24	45
Tweety Bird Soaky	15	25	60
Tweety Bird Squeeze Toy, rubber, 1950s	15	22	50
Wile E. Coyote, Dakin, 1970s	12	20	35

Hi-Way Henry Wind-up, 1920s, $3950.

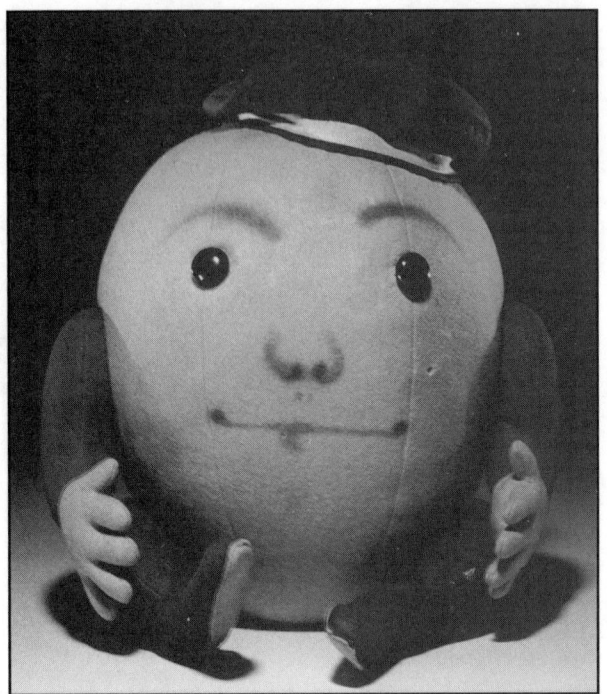

Humpty Dumpty Doll, Steiff, $2000. Photo courtesy Christie's East

Looney Tunes (Continued)

	C6	C8	C10
Yosemite Sam Squeak Toy, Dakin, 1970, 4" high	16	24	35

Mighty Mouse

Originally called Super Mouse, Isadore Klein created an animal version of Superman for the Terrytoons cartoons series. His first cartoon was entitled *The Mouse of Tomorrow*, and was released on October 16, 1942. Upon learning the name was being used on an upcoming comic book, the name was changed to Mighty Mouse and a cartoon legend was born. With Oil Can Harry as the lead villain, and Pearl Pureheart as his female lead, Mighty Mouse was performed in an opera style where dialog was sung instead of spoken. Beloved by multiple generations, Mighty Mouse is a character who will be enjoyed long into the future.

Mighty Mouse

	C6	C8	C10
Mighty Mouse Doll, rubber head w/oilcloth body, 1942, 12" high	400	900	1200
Mighty Mouse Doll, vinyl, 1950	125	160	225
Mighty Mouse Soaky	25	40	75

Miscellaneous

	C6	C8	C10
Alfred E. Neumann Figure, vinyl, Effanbee, 1960	75	188	275

Miscellaneous (Continued)

	C6	C8	C10
Baby Snookums Doll (The Newly-weds), fabric, 5-1/2" high	100	250	450
Boob McNutt Tin Wind-up, Strauss	450	675	1000
Boots and Her Buddies Paper Dolls, No. 2460, Saalfield, 1943	35	50	80
Broom Hilda Figure, Knicker-bocker, c. 1970, 14" high	38	53	75
Comic Strip Rings (Tin), Blondie and Barney Google, includes Phantom, King Features, 1953	10	30	100
Comics Paper Doll Cut-Out Book, page each of Popeye, Katzenjammers, Just Kids, Blondie, Dumb Dora, Annie Rooney, Polly and Her Pals, Saalfield, 1935	150	270	385
Dan Dunn Det. Corps Secret Operative 28 Tin Badge, c. 1930s	35	75	125
Don Winslow Flashlight Gun	70	105	140
Ella Cinders Doll, cloth and composition, 1925, 17" high	100	175	250
Famous Komics Film Viewer, w/three boxes of films, Acme, 1940	150	275	400

Make Your Own Funnies Set, Jaymar Specialty Company, $1300. Photo courtesy Christie's East

Roosevelt Bear on Bicycle, c. 1920, $600. Photo courtesy Detroit Toy Museum, Wilkinson Collection

Sight Seeing Auto 899, Kenton, c. 1910, $7200. Photo courtesy Christie's East

Snowflakes and Swipes Platform Toy, c. 1929, $1950. Photo courtesy Christie's East

Miscellaneous (Continued)

	C6	C8	C10
Favorite Funnies Rubber Print Set, Dick Tracy, Orphan Annie, etc., fourteen stamps, pad, booklet, large size	45	75	125
Harold Teen Ukulele, wood, 1930s, 21"	125	200	250
Herby Doll, oilcloth, 10"	30	60	100
Herman Nodder (Harvey Comics character), rare, Linemar, 1950s, 4-1/2" high	300	500	650
Hi-Way Henry Wind-up, jalopy w/man, woman, laundry above roof, 1920s	1500	2800	3950
Humpty Dumpty Doll, cloth, Steiff, 10" high	700	1200	2000
Jane Arden Paper Dolls, No. 2408, Saalfield, 1942	45	65	125
Komic Kamera, without filmstrips	24	36	48
Komic Kamera, all metal viewer, w/set of five filmstrips, c. mid-1930s	80	120	175
Little King Pull Toy, wood, Jay-Mar, 1938, 4" high	70	110	175
Little Mary Mixup and Her Friend Peggy Paper Dolls, Saalfield, 1922	60	75	110

Miscellaneous (Continued)

	C6	C8	C10
Make Your Own Funnies Set, jointed wooden figures of Pop-eye, Chinaman, Konical Kop, Orphan Annie, Sandy, Kayo, Funny Frog, Comical Mouse and Mon Mullins, price for the set, Jaymar Specialty Company	500	800	1300
Mandrake the Magician Magic Kit, Transogram, 1949	75	125	250
Movie Komics, reels of film for toy viewers, c. 1940s	14	30	50
Nancy Doll (Nancy and Sluggo), stuffed, Georgene Novelties, 14" high	90	175	350
Peter Rabbit Chickmobile	312	500	800
Roosevelt Bear on Bicycle, tin litho, c. 1920, 9" long	225	300	600
Secret Agent X-9 Gun and Billy Club	25	50	100
Sight Seeing Auto 899, cast iron, w/Mama Katzenjammer, Uncle Heine, Alphonse, Gloomy Gus, Happy Hooligan, Kenton, c. 1910, 10-1/2" long	2500	5250	7200
Snowflakes and Swipes Platform Toy, tin litho, c. 1929, 7-1/2" long	800	1350	1950
Terry and the Pirates Hingees, set includes Terry, Flip Corkin, Pat Ryan, Burma, Taffy Tucker, 1944	22	33	65
Western Thrills with Billy The Kid, paper, character from Funny Animals Comics, Reed, c. 1944-47	12	18	30

Miscellaneous (Continued)

	C6	C8	C10
Wonder Woman String Puppet, Madison, 1977	37	56	90

Moon Mullins

Frank Willard's tough-guy character Moon Mullins debuted in the Chicago Tribune Syndicate on June 19, 1923. Blue collar characters were popular in the early 1920s and Moon was intended to rival the success of Barney Google. Moon was a would-be prize fighter of little success who lived in Emmy Schmaltz's boarding house. Other characters included Moon's kid brother Kayo, Mamie the cook and her overly lazy husband, Willie, and Lord Plushbottom, an aristocrat added to the mix to provide a target for social commentary and a decided contrast to the low-born Moon. Fred Johnson became Willard's assistant in 1923 and took over the strip completely in 1958 when Willard died. He remained with Moon and his friends until the strip ceased in 1991, one of the longest creative stints in comic strip history.

Moon Mullins

	C6	C8	C10
Kayo Doll, oilcloth, 9-3/4"	100	150	225
Kayo Doll, wood-jointed, Jaymar, 5" high	56	90	160
Kayo Figure, head swivels, Sun Rubber, c. 1937, 10" high	200	300	450
Moon Mullins and Kayo on Handcar, tin wind-up, Marx, 1930s, 6" long	395	600	900
Moon Mullins and Mamie Face Masks, price for each, 1933	20	30	60
Moon Mullins Doll, wood jointed, Jaymar, 5" high	55	85	150
Moon Mullins Doll, stuffed, Famous Artists Synd., 1930s, 11-1/2" high	55	85	150

Mutt & Jeff

One of the earliest daily strips, Harry "Bud" Fisher's *A. Mutt* debuted in The San Francisco Chronicle on November 15, 1907. The strip's name changed in March 1908 when the tall, lanky Mutt was paired with the short-statured Jeff. Mutt was an easy-going fellow who liked to gamble at the racetrack whenever his wife would allow and Jeff was simply lacking sanity. The pair was a comedy success and "Mutt & Jeff" survives in slang today meaning a tall person paired up with a short one. Fisher's assistant Al Smith began working on the strip in 1932 and took over with Fisher's death in 1954. He stayed until the strip ceased in 1982.

Mutt & Jeff

	C6	C8	C10
Jeff Figure, bendable, 1946	120	180	240
Jeff Stick Puppet, 12" high	40	60	80
Mutt Dancing Doll, wooden	40	60	100
Mutt Doll, composition w/ball joints, felt clothes, 8" high	188	300	475

Mutt & Jeff (Continued)

	C6	C8	C10
Mutt Figure, bendable, 1946	140	210	280

Peanuts

Perhaps the most beloved comic strip of all time, Peanuts was the creative genius of Charles M. Schulz. It debuted in 1950 in the United Feature Syndicate and became the wholesome comic favorite of, let's be honest, the whole world! Good man Charlie Brown, Lucy, the unbelievable Snoopy, Peppermint Patty and the other unforgettable characters are a part of our collective conscious. It branched out into comic books but achieved greater success in animation, and the holiday specials are still television staples. Rather than turn Peanuts (a title that he never really liked) over to another creator, Schulz decided to retire the strip in 1999 when he was 77-years old.

Peanuts

	C6	C8	C10
Charlie Brown Bobbing Head, composition, possibly first Peanuts toy, 1950s	80	120	200
Charlie Brown Figure, plastic jointed, marked "1952"	14	21	40
Lucy Doll, plastic, jointed, marked "1952"	14	21	50
Lucy Squeeze Doll, vinyl, 1950s	15	22	50
Lucy Squeeze Toy, vinyl, 1950s, 8-3/4" high	15	22	50
Lucy Squeeze Toy, 1950s, 7-3/4"	12	18	40
Peanuts Figures: Charlie Brown, Lucy, Linus, Schroeder, Snoopy, Avon, price for each	10	15	30
Schroeder Squeeze Toy, rubber, c. 1960	10	15	50
Snoopy Astronaut Doll, vinyl, 1969, 9-1/2" high	30	50	85
Snoopy Bus, tin litho, 1960s	16	30	50
Snoopy Squeeze Toy, rubber, 1958	25	40	65

Pogo

One of several characters to debut first in comic books and then receive a comic strip was Walt Kelly's Pogo. Dell Comics published the Pogo comic book from 1949-54 after his initial 1941 appearance in *Animal Comics*. Kelly interjected politics into the strip (the comic book refrained from political topics) and remained its creative force until his death in 1973 brought it to an end. It was not picked up by another creative team.

Pogo

	C6	C8	C10
Albert Alligator Figure, plastic, 1969, approx. 5" high ("Duz")	5	11	25
Beauregard Figure, plastic, 1969	7	11	20

Bluto Dippy Dumper Truck (Popeye), $1400. Photo courtesy Christie's East

Popeye Acrobat Tin Wind-up, Marx, $5650. Photo courtesy Christie's East

The Popeye Jeep Doll from the 1930s can range from $900 to $2200. Photo courtesy Christie's East

Popeye and Olive Oyl Sand Toy, T. Cohn, $1000. Photo courtesy James Maxwell/Virginia Caputo

Popeye and Olive Oyl Ball Toss Tin Wind-up, Linemar, c. 1950, $1600. Photo courtesy Christie's East

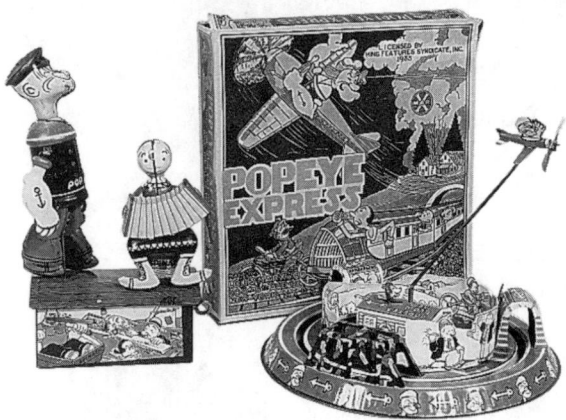

Left to right: Popeye and Olive Oyl Jiggers, Marx, $2400; Popeye Popeye Express, Marx, 1935, $1200.

Popeye and Olive Oyl Slinky Handcar Pull Toy, Linemar, 1950s, $1200. Photo courtesy Christie's East

Pogo (Continued)	C6	C8	C10
Churcy Figure, plastic, 1969, 4-1/2" high	14	21	30
Howland Owl, plastic, 1969, 4-1/2" high	8	10	20
Pogo Figure, plastic, 1969, 4" high	7	11	20
Pogo Pogomobile	200	325	525
Porky Figure, plastic, 1969	7	11	15

Popeye

Popeye first appeared in cartoonist Elzie Segar's *Thimble Theater* on January 17, 1929 when lead characters Castor Oyl and Ham Gravy needed to arrange sea transportation. Popeye was soon an audience favorite and a year later Ham was written out and Popeye was the strip's star. Olive was Castor's sister, Wimpy appeared in 1932 and Swee'Pea joined the fun in 1936. The Thimble Theater title gave way to Popeye in the strip and it was passed to Charles Winner in 1938 after Segar died. In 1958, Forrest Sagendorf assumed creative control and even produced the highly collectible Popeye comic book. He died in 1994 and today the daily strips reprint his work. The Sunday strip is done by Hy Eisman.

Popeye	C6	C8	C10
Bluto Dippy Dumper Truck, celluloid and tin, 9-1/2"	500	800	1400
Bluto on Horse Cart Wind-up, celluloid and tin, 7-1/2"	400	650	1000
Brutus Mask, cardboard, 1940s	40	75	100
Jeep Doll, wood-jointed, 1930s, 7-1/4"	350	525	775
Jeep Doll, wood-jointed, rare, 1930s, 8"	750	1100	1800
Jeep Doll, wood-jointed, rare, 1930s, 6"	425	650	950
Jeep Doll, wood-jointed, 1930s, 14"	800	1400	2200
Juggling Popeye and Olive Oyl, (marked "Linemar"), T.P.S., 1950s, 9-1/2" high	1000	1500	2100
Olive Oyl and Swee' Pea Handcar, Marx, 1930s	240	400	650

Popeye Dippy Dumper Truck, Marx, $1600. Photo courtesy Christie's East

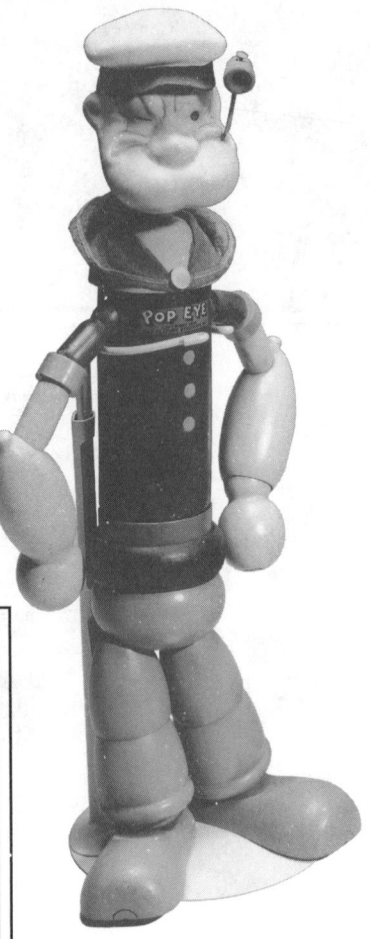

Popeye Doll, $725. Photo courtesy Christie's East

Popeye Doorstop, Hubley, $3200. Photo courtesy Bertoia Auctions

PHOTOS NEEDED

We are always looking for good quality toy images for our archives. Photo quality is our highest consideration and any donated images must be in 35mm print or slide form.

If you can donate photos of toys not pictured here, please contact us at the following address:

O'Brien's Collecting Toys
Krause Publications
700 E. State St.
IOLA, WI 54990
(715) 445-4612
obrienk@krause.com

Popeye (Continued)	C6	C8	C10
Olive Oyl Ballet Dancer, tin, mechanical, Linemar	250	400	675
Olive Oyl Doll, jointed wood, Jaymar, c. 1940s, 5" high	92	150	210
Olive Oyl Figure, cast iron, 2-1/2" high	175	300	425
Olive Oyl Hand Puppet, Gund, c. 1938	60	90	150
Olive Oyl Marionette, Gund, 11"	37	56	90
Olive Oyl Mask, cardboard, 1940s	20	40	70
Olive Oyl Squeeze Toy, rubber, 1950s	90	135	180
Olive Oyl Wind-up, riding tricycle, Linemar, 4"	1400	2200	3250

Popeye (Continued)	C6	C8	C10
Popeye Acrobat Tin Wind-up, tin, Marx	2700	4050	5650
Popeye and Mean Man Mechanical Fighters, rare, Linemar Co., 1950s, 6" long	6000	9200	12,500
Popeye and Olive Oyl Ball Toss Tin Wind-up, Linemar, c. 1950, 19" long	600	1000	1600
Popeye and Olive Oyl Handcar, hollow rubber figures, 6" long	700	1500	2600
Popeye and Olive Oyl Jiggers, Popeye dancing on roof, Olive Oyl Playing Concertina, Marx	900	1600	2400
Popeye and Olive Oyl Sand Toy, tin litho, T. Cohn, 8-1/4" high	450	700	1000

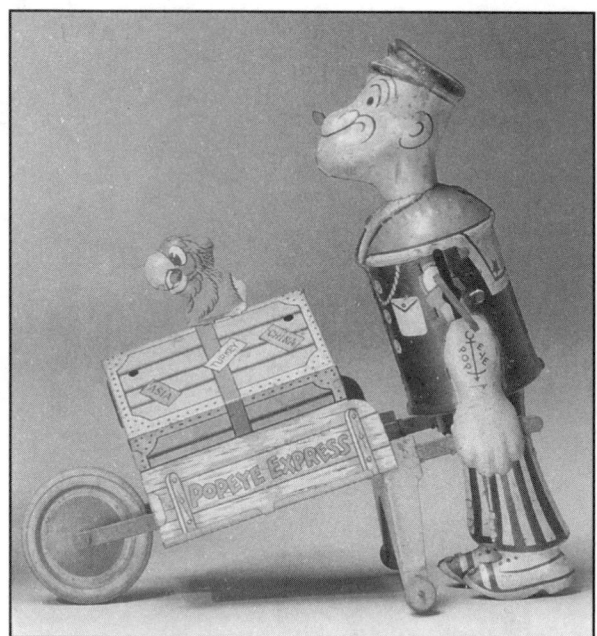

Popeye Express Wind-up, Marx, 1935, $1250. Photo courtesy PB Eighty-Four, New York

Popeye in a Barrel, Chein, $825. Photo courtesy Don Hultzman

Popeye (Continued)	C6	C8	C10
Popeye and Olive Oyl Slinky Hand-car Pull Toy, yellow wheels, red platform, Linemar, 1950s	500	850	1250
Popeye Basketball Player Tin Wind-up, tin litho, yellow backboard w/Olive and Wimpy litho, multi-colored ball, net, Linemar	700	1000	1600
Popeye Bifbat Paddle Toy, 1929	46	85	185
Popeye Bo Lo Paddle, 1929	20	50	110
Popeye Dippy Dumper Truck, Marx	550	1100	1600
Popeye Doll, hard rubber, "Cameo," jointed at neck, hips and shoulders, 14" high...............	115	172	260
Popeye Doll, composition, "Popeye 1935 King Features Syn", 14" high	300	500	725
Popeye Doll, composition, Popeye is rolling up sleeve, 15" high.......	100	150	260

Popeye (Continued)	C6	C8	C10
Popeye Doll, jointed wood body, w/composition head, 8" high.......	90	135	210
Popeye Doll, wood and composition, jointed arms and legs, "1935", 14" high.........................	200	300	425
Popeye Doll, stuffed cloth, Knickerbocker, 1930s, 17" high..............	187	250	450
Popeye Doll, jointed wood, c. 1932, 10-1/4" high................................	225	350	600
Popeye Doll, Chein, c. 1935, 11" high...	293	440	675
Popeye Doll, jointed wood, c. 1935, 11" high......................................	300	450	660
Popeye Doll, stuffed body w/rubber arms and head, Gund, c. 1950s, 20" high...	70	105	160
Popeye Doorstop, cast iron, Hubley, 10" high...	1500	2400	3200
Popeye Drummer, Chein, 7-1/8" high...	550	1000	1500
Popeye Eccentric Plane Wind-up, Marx, 1940, 8" long	375	700	1050

*Popeye in a Barrel Wind-up Walker, Japan, $1650.
Photo courtesy Christie's East*

Popeye Rollerskating, Linemar, $1350.

Popeye (Continued)

	C6	C8	C10
Popeye Express, overhead airplane flies over train, Marx, 1935	500	850	1200
Popeye Express Wind-up, Popeye pushing box w/parrot, Marx, 1935	500	650	1250
Popeye Figure, hollow rubber, dated "1935" on back, 7" high	90	135	210
Popeye Figure, jointed wood, Jaymar, 5" high.................................	68	125	175
Popeye Figure, solid celluloid, 1930s, 4" high	90	160	250
Popeye Figure, cast iron, c. 1930, 3-1/2" high..................................	175	300	450
Popeye Hand Puppet, Gund	20	30	60
Popeye Heavy Hitter Tin Wind-up, Chein, 11-1/2"	2500	4200	6500
Popeye Hingees Paper Punch-outs, No. 102, Reed & Associates, 1945	12	20	40
Popeye in a Barrel, Chein, 7" high ..	350	525	825
Popeye in a Barrel Wind-up Walker, celluloid, Japan, 5-1/2" high...	700	1100	1650
Popeye in a Horsecart, celluloid and tin, Marx, c. 1935, 7-1/2"	1500	2650	4000

Popeye (Continued)

	C6	C8	C10
Popeye in a Rowboat, Hoge, 1935	2500	4200	5850
Popeye Jack-in-the-Box, tin, Popeye pops out of spinach can, mechanical, Mattel	45	75	100
Popeye Jigger Wind-up, Marx, 9-1/2" high..................................	500	850	1300
Popeye Knockout Bank, Straits Mfg. Co., 1935	1000	1500	2350
Popeye Lantern Toy, Linemar, 1950s, 7-1/2" high......................	400	600	800
Popeye Mask, cardboard, 1940s	30	45	75
Popeye Moving Van, tin, friction, Linemar	400	600	875
Popeye on a Tricycle, metal and celluloid, Linemar, ...	370	555	825
Popeye on a Unicycle Wind-up, Linemar, 1950s	600	1000	1400
Popeye One-Man Band, pole with drum and cymbals, rubber Popeye head on top, 1950s, 69" high	100	150	220
Popeye Patrol, Hubley, 8-1/2" long.	2500	4500	6200
Popeye Pirate, click pistol, with box add $300, No. 68, Marx	175	375	600
Popeye Puncher, overhead bag, Chein	2050	4000	6950

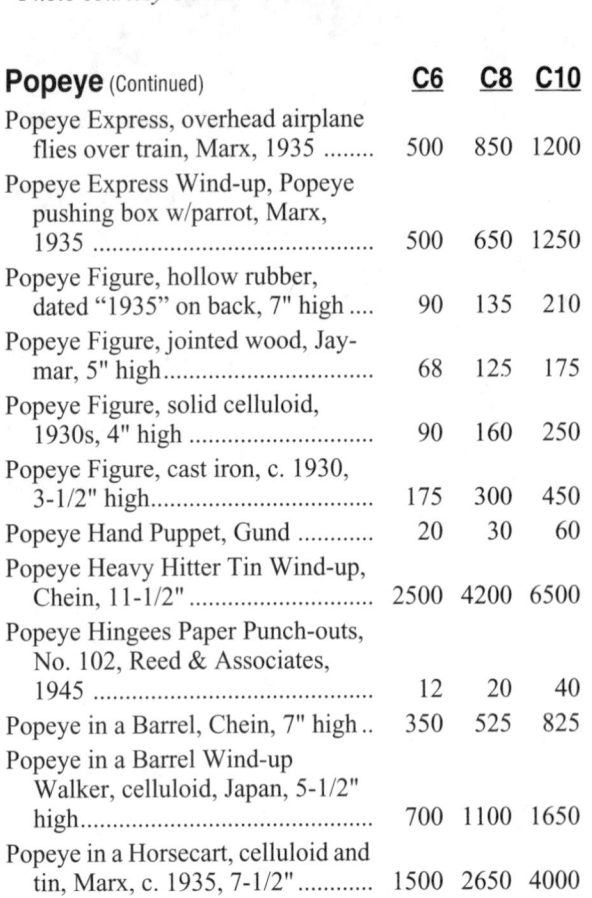

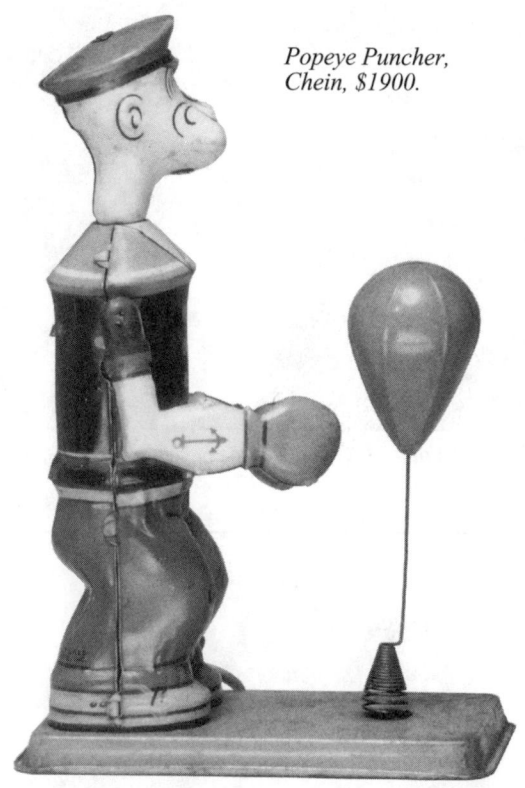

Popeye Puncher, Chein, $1900.

Popeye the Champ, Marx, $3000. Photo courtesy Phillips, New York

Popeye (Continued)	**C6**	**C8**	**C10**
Popeye Puncher, tin and celluloid, w/floor bag, Chein, 1930	800	1450	1900
Popeye Rollerskating, Linemar	550	825	1350
Popeye Roly Poly, celluloid, Japan, 3-1/2"	150	200	350
Popeye Roly Poly Target Game, Knickerbocker, 1958	95	150	250
Popeye Sand Toy, tin litho, teeter-totter, w/Popeye, Swee'Pea, Oyl and Jeep	500	800	1250
Popeye Shadow Boxer, Chein, 1930s, 7" tall	700	1200	1950
Popeye Soaky	22	33	60
Popeye Sparkling Popeye Wind-up, Chein, 1959, 5" long	173	260	360
Popeye Spinach Patrol, Hubley	1400	2500	3800
Popeye Spinach Wagon	1000	1650	2500
Popeye Spinning Olive Oyl in a Chair, Linemar, 1950s, 9" high	800	1400	1950
Popeye Strength Tester, Holgate, 14"	65	98	150
Popeye the Champ, Marx	1100	1900	3000
Popeye the Pilot Wind-up, early version, number "47" on side of plane, Marx, 1930, 8" long	500	900	1350

Popeye (Continued)	**C6**	**C8**	**C10**
Popeye the Pilot Wind-up, later version, "Popeye" on top of left wing, "Pilot" on top of right wing, Marx, 1940, 7" long	490	800	1200
Popeye the Sailor Tin Wind-up, Hoge Mfg. Co., c. 1935	2000	4000	6200
Popeye Transit Co. Truck, Linemar	650	1100	1750
Popeye Tumbling Popeye Wind-up, Linemar, 5" high	450	700	1150
Popeye Turnover Tank Tin Wind-up, Linemar, 1950s, 6" long	360	650	1000
Popeye Walker, plastic walker, Popeye pushing wheelbarrow, Marx, c. 1950s	50	75	125
Popeye Walker Tin Wind-up, Chein, 6-1/2" high	340	525	750
Popeye Whistle Pipe, cardboard bowl w/illustration of Popeye characters, metal stem w/whistle at base, Northwest Products of St. Louis, 3-1/2" long	70	105	150
Popeye Wind-up, Popeye carrying parrots in cages, Marx, 1935, 7-3/4" high	268	450	675

Popeye the Pilot Wind-up, $1350. Photo courtesy Sotheby's, New York

Smitty on a Scooter Tin Wind-up, Marx, c. 1930, $2200. Photo courtesy PB Eighty-Four, New York

Popeye Turnover Tank Tin Wind-up, Linemar, 1950s, $1000. Photo courtesy Don Hultzman

CONDITION CODE

C6   Good; evident overall wear, well played with but acceptable to many collectors
C8   Very Good; minor overall wear, very clean
C10 Mint; like new

Note: Mint in Box commands a higher price.
Condition below C6 brings considerably lower prices

Popeye Thimble Theatre Mystery Playhouse, Harding Products, $3600. Photo courtesy Mapes Auctioneers and Appraisers

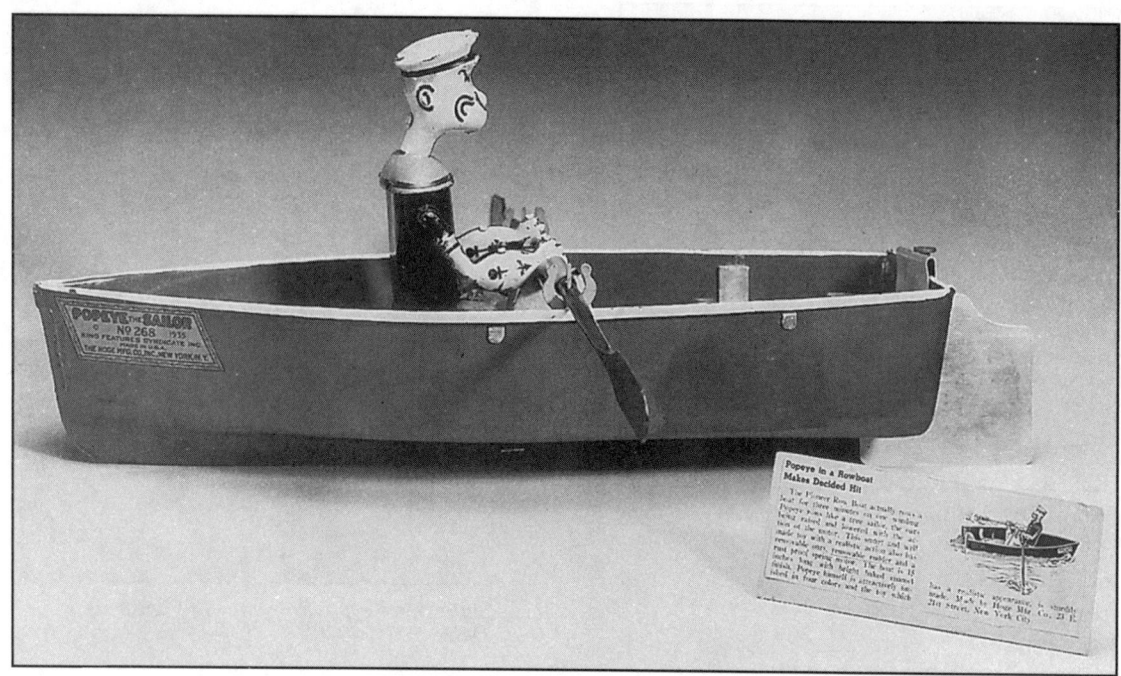

Popeye the Sailor Tin Wind-up, Hoge Mfg. Co., c. 1935, 15-1/2" long, $6200. Photo courtesy Christie's East

Popeye (Continued)

	C6	C8	C10
Popeye Wind-up, celluloid, neck goes up and down, c. 1930, 9" high	475	700	975
Popeye Xylophone Player, American Preschool Co., 1957, 9" long	263	395	650
Popeye Yazoo Pipe, Northwestern Productions, St. Louis, Mo., 1934	80	120	200
Swee'Pea Mask, cardboard, 1940s	10	20	40
Thimble Theatre Mystery Playhouse, composition figures w/wooden shuffle feet (ramp walkers), copyright 1939, "Starring Popeye with Wimpy and Olive Oyl," Philadelphia, 12" x 10" x 3"; individual figures sell for $350 in Mint condition, Harding Products	1500	2500	3600
Wimpy Dippy Dumper	500	800	1200
Wimpy Figure, cast iron, Hubley, 3-1/8" high	175	250	400
Wimpy Figure, jointed wood, "by K.F.S.", 4" high	100	150	260
Wimpy Figure, jointed wood, Jaymar, 5" high	100	150	250
Wimpy Figure, hard plastic, 1960s, 3"	12	18	24
Wimpy Hand Puppet, Gund	29	44	80
Wimpy Mask, cardboard, 1940s,	20	30	60

Popeye (Continued)

	C6	C8	C10
Wimpy Motorcyclist, Linemar	400	700	925
Wimpy Squeeze Toy, rubber, 8" high	60	100	175
Wimpy Tricyclist, Linemar	550	900	1200

Prince Valiant

As a Sunday strip, Prince Valiant debuted on February 13, 1937. The creation of Hal Foster, Valiant's adventures began with the character as a young boy. Today, he is a grandfather but the strip is going strong under the creative direction of John Cullen Murphy.

Prince Valiant

	C6	C8	C10
Prince Valiant Castle Fort, boxed set w/knights, Marx	225	340	450
Prince Valiant Crossbow Pistol Game	22	33	70
Prince Valiant Shield, tin litho	30	45	75
Prince Valiant Sword and Scabbard, tin, Mattel, 1950s	29	45	65

Red Ryder

One of the most widely successful western characters ever to originate in the comic strips, Red Ryder was the creation of Fred Harman. The strip was syndicated by the Newspaper Enterprise Association and debuted on November 6, 1938. Red was joined by a fun cast including girlfriend Beth Wilder, sidekick Little Beaver, bad guy Ace

Superman Rollover Airplane, Marx, 1940s, $2600. Photo courtesy Christie's East

Superman Krypto Raygun with Filmstrips, Daisy, 1939, $2200.

Hanlon, and his faithful horse Thunder. Red Ryder appeared in comic books, on radio, television, in feature films and even became a spokesperson for Daisy BB guns (Daisy still produces the Red Ryder model today). The strip ended in 1964.

Red Ryder

	C6	C8	C10
Little Beaver Archery Set, 1951	30	45	80
Red Ryder Molding Set, 1948	40	75	150
Red Ryder Target Game, 1939	40	110	200

Sad Sack

George Baker, a former Disney employee, used his experiences in the U.S. Army as the basis for his cartoon Sad Sack. First published in *Life* magazine as the winner of a contest, Sad Sack struck a chord with rank-and-file readers when Baker was assigned to *Yank* magazine during World War II. Sad Sack entered comic books as a Harvey property and was turned over to Frank Rhodes in 1953. He left Harvey in 1977 and the title went into a gradual decline. When the Harvey family sold the rights to its characters, Sad Sack was one property they held, so it is unlikely that the title will be revived in the future.

Sad Sack

	C6	C8	C10
Sad Sack Doll, vinyl, 1950, 15-1/2"...	105	170	230
Sad Sack Doll, vinyl w/cloth uniform, Sterling Doll Co., c. 1952, 20" high	70	120	200

Skippy

Skippy was the creation of artist Percy Crosby and appeared in 1923 and was the All-American boy. The character inspired

many toys, dolls and other merchandise and was featured in radio, film, and even Big Little Books. His comic strip was featured in hundreds of newspapers in the 1920s.

Skippy

	C6	C8	C10
Skippy Figure, oilcloth, w/hat, 12" high..	75	100	150
Skippy Figure, celluloid, 5-1/2" high..	150	250	400

Smitty

Walter Berndt created his comic strip about the adventures of an office boy and presented it to Chicago Tribune Syndicate editor Joseph M. Patterson who promptly entitled it, Smitty. A wholesome character with a loving family, Smitty debuted on November 27, 1922, and the Sunday strip appeared on February 25, 1923. The strip enjoyed its half-century tenure and departed in 1973 when Berndt retired.

Smitty

	C6	C8	C10
Smitty Doll, oilcloth, 9-3/4" high....	125	175	225
Smitty on a Scooter Tin Wind-up, Marx, c. 1930, 8" high.................	1100	1800	2200

Smokey Stover

The screwball antics of Bill Holman's Smokey Stover kept the strip in syndication from its debut on March 10, 1935 through its retirement (and Holman's) in 1973. Fireman Smokey drove around in a fire truck called the Foomobile and introduced "foo" into the collective vocabulary of readers. It was distributed by the Chicago Tribune Syndicate.

Superman Tank, Linemar, 1958, $2000. Photo courtesy Christie's East

Smokey Stover

Smokey Stover	C6	C8	C10
Smokey Stover, Hingees, 1944	8	15	35
Smokey Stover Figure, hard plastic, 1960s, 3" high	12	20	50

Spider-Man

Stan Lee's writing and Steve Ditko's art brought Spidey to life in the comic books with 1962's *Amazing Fantasy* #15. His success and enduring popularity cements his place in comic history, but we shouldn't overlook his comic strip, which Stan Lee wrote as of 1977.

Spider-Man	C6	C8	C10
Spider-Man Hand Puppet, Ideal, 1966	42	63	110
Spider-Man Walker Wind-up, Marx, 1966	125	188	250
Spider-Man Webmaker, Chemtoy, 1977	16	25	40

Steve Canyon

Milton Caniff's success with *Terry & the Pirates* opened doors for the creator when he decided to produce *Steve Canyon*. A pilot and adventurer, Steve Canyon debuted in 1947 and was instantly popular with post-WWII America featuring a host of interesting female characters to compliment the strong male lead. By the 1980s, Caniff relied more heavily on the talents of his assistant Richard Rockwell and the strip was retired with Caniff's death in 1988.

Steve Canyon	C6	C8	C10
Steve Canyon Glider Bomb Truck, Ideal	88	132	175
Steve Canyon Jet Helmet, 1959	50	75	125
Steve Canyon Space Goggles, Rock Industries, c. 1950s	25	40	70

Superman

The success of Jerry Siegel and Joe Shuster's character, Superman, in *Action Comics #1* set off a genre of superheroes that still resonates with readers today. The success of the 1938 comic book led to other publications including Superman's own comic strip in 1940.

Superman	C6	C8	C10
2 in 1 Hand Puppet, one side Superman, other Clark, early 1950s	200	300	500
Bendee, Mego, 1973, 5" high..........	22	33	45
City of Metropolis Adventure Set, Corgi, 1979	65	100	150
Colorforms, 1964	25	40	65
Cut-outs, blue or red, No. 177, Saalfield, 1940	750	1850	2400
Figure, composition, Syroco	900	2000	4000
Figure, wood and composition, Ideal, 1940, 13" high..................	600	1000	1400
Flying Toy, Transogram, 1954	68	102	150
Hand Puppet, Ideal, 1965	32	48	64
Krypton Rockets, c. 1939	150	225	350
Kryptonite Rock, 1978	10	15	20
Krypto-Ray Gun, w/seven filmstrips and box, No. 94, Daisy, 1939	750	1350	2200
Movie Viewer, Acme, 1940	333	500	665
Movie Viewer, w/film, Acme, 1947	95	200	375
Movie Viewer, w/film, Acme, 1955	60	90	175
Movie Viewer, Acme, 1965	30	45	60
Play Set, Ideal, 1973	34	51	68
Rollover Airplane, various colors, Marx, 1940s, 6-1/2" long	1000	1500	2600
Rollover Tank, Japan, 1940s, 4" long..	290	450	750
Rollover Tank, silver version, Marx, 1940s, 4" long..................	550	850	1350

Left to right: Toonerville Trolley Powerful Katrinka Tin Wind-up, Lehmann, 1925, $3700; Toonerville Trolley Powerful Katrinka Tin Wind-up, Nifty, 1925, $2600. Photo courtesy Sotheby's, New York

Toonerville Trolley, $600. Photo courtesy Detroit Antique Toy Museum; Wilkinson Collection

Superman (Continued)	C6	C8	C10
Soaky	27	41	80
Superman Button, 1939	35	150	225
Superman Holding Airplane, wind-up, Marx, 1940	800	1750	2650
Superman Tank, tin, battery operated, Linemar, 1958, 10-1/4" long	600	1200	2000
Tricky Trapeze, Kohner, 1966	75	100	150
Water Pistol, in the shape of Superman flying, c. 1950s	35	75	100

Tarzan

The 1912 short story, "Tarzan of the Apes," by Edgar Rice Burroughs led to several novels and in 1929, his own syndicated comic strip. United Features Syndicate launched the first Sunday strip in 1931. Still in Sunday syndication today, Tarzan is authored by artist Eric Battle and writer Alex Simmons.

Tarzan	C6	C8	C10
Dart Board Game Tarzan in the Jungle, large, 1935	130	195	300
Gift Set, figures and truck w/cage trailer, No. 36, Corgi	40	60	80
Mask of Akut the Ape, paper, Northern Paper Mills, 1933	60	90	140
Mask of Numa the Lion, paper, Northern Paper Mills, 1933	60	90	140

Tarzan (Continued)	C6	C8	C10
Mask of Tarzan, paper, Northern Paper Mills, 1933	70	125	250
Target Game Tarzan in the Jungle, battery operated, 1935	140	220	400
Thingmaker Kit, Mattel, 1966	44	66	88

Toonerville Trolley

At a time when kid-based comic strips ran on Sundays only, Fontaine Fox proposed a daily with kid antics as the central theme. In 1908, Chicago Post editor Lew Reilly agreed to run the strip. Originally titled Toonerville Folks, the popularity of The Skipper and his Toonerville Trolley led to the renaming of the strip. The ensemble cast didn't just focus on kids and the audience appreciated the interesting array of Toonerville citizens. The strip ended in 1955, when Fox retired.

Toonerville Trolley	C6	C8	C10
Powerful Katrinka Tin Wind-up, tin, raises and lowers Jimmy in her hand, Nifty, 1925, 6-3/4" high	900	1600	2600
Powerful Katrinka Tin Wind-up, Jimmy in wheelbarrow, Lehmann, 1925, 6-1/2" long..............	1300	2450	3700
Toonerville Candy Container, glass, 3-1/4" long...................................	250	375	550
Toonerville Trolley, wood, includes six people, 7" long......................	125	188	350
Toonerville Trolley, cast iron, Dent	450	675	1000
Toonerville Trolley, aluminum, Dent	357	562	850

Toonerville Trolley, Dent, $1000. Photo courtesy Don Hultzman

Yellow Kid Cap Bomb, $250. Photo courtesy James Maxwell/Virginia Caputo

Toonerville Trolley (Continued)

	C6	C8	C10
Toonerville Trolley, Crackerjack size, 1-7/8" high	275	410	600
Toonerville Trolley, lead, c. 1923	100	150	210
Toonerville Trolley Wind-up, tin, marked "Copyright 1922 by Fontaine Fox," Skipper driving, Nifty, 7-1/2" high	500	750	1200
Toonerville Trolley Wind-up, rare, Strauss, 1921	375	450	650

Toots and Casper

Jimmy Murphy's light-hearted look at family life began in December 1918 when Toots and Casper became one of the early strips syndicated by King Features Syndicate. Joining Toots and Casper in their adventures were their baby Buttercup and dog Spare-Ribs. The strip retired in 1958.

Toots and Casper

	C6	C8	C10
Buttercup & Spareribs, Buttercup beats Spareribs with broom, Nifty, 1920s, 7-1/2" long	700	1200	1600
Buttercup Doll, cloth, 14"	450	700	1000
Buttercup Doll, stuffed cloth, jointed head, arms, legs, c. 1924, 18" high	250	375	500
Buttercup Tin Wind-up, crawls, German, 4-1/4"	650	1100	1750

Uncle Wiggily

Lang Campbell's strip, Uncle Wiggily's Tricks debuted in 1923.

Uncle Wiggily

	C6	C8	C10
Uncle Wiggily Crazy Car, with box, Marx	438	700	1100
Uncle Wiggily Crazy Car, Distler (Germany), c. 1922, 9-1/2" long	2200	4750	6500

Willie the Worm

One of Fawcett's Funny Animals. Made regular appearances in their comic books.

Willie the Worm

	C6	C8	C10
Willie the Worm and Sammy Fish-n Fun	10	15	25
Willie the Worm and Sammy Flying Machine	12	18	30
Willie The Worm and Sammy in Car Trouble, paper, Fawcett Comics characters, Reed, c. 1944-47	10	15	25

Woody Woodpecker

From a supporting character in the 1940 Andy Panda cartoon, *Knock Knock*, Woody found an audience through his distinctive laugh. Woody began his own series with the 1941 cartoon, *The Cracked Nut*.

Woody Woodpecker

	C6	C8	C10
Walter Lantz Ink Stamp Character Set, includes twelve different rubber stamps	12	18	30

Buttercup & Spareribs (Toots and Casper), Nifty, 1920s, $1600. Photo courtesy Christie's East

Uncle Wiggily Crazy Car, Distler (Germany), c. 1922, $6500. Photo courtesy Detroit Antique Toy Museum; Wilkinson Collection

Yellow Kid Figure, $1400; Yellow Kid in Cart being pulled by mule, Kenton, early 1900s, $3000. Photo courtesy Christie's East

Woody Woodpecker (Continued)	C6	C8	C10
Woody Woodpecker Figure, rubber, "Walter Lantz", 6-1/2" high	10	15	25
Woody Woodpecker Hand Puppet, rubber head, cloth body, "W. Lantz", Mattel, 1962	20	30	60
Woody Woodpecker Soaky	20	25	60

Yellow Kid, The

One of the first characters to appear regularly in the comics, Richard Outcault's Yellow Kid debuted in The New York World newspaper as part of the *Hogan's Alley* series in 1895. His oversized ears, bald head, and bright yellow nightshirt (which would later have words written on it) defined the character and set the stage for more characters in the future. He was also one of the first characters to be merchandised to the public.

Yellow Kid	C6	C8	C10
Cap Bomb, cast iron, 1-1/2" high..	100	150	250
Doll, "Design copyrighted 1894 and 1896," Arnold Printworks, 8" high..	250	475	750
Doll, papier-mâché and wood, early 1900s, 11" high	500	900	1500
Figure, cast iron, burlap gown, movable arms, 6-1/2" high..........	600	850	1400
Ladder Toy, 16-1/2" high	700	1200	1500
Yellow Kid Doll, Ideal, 1907	200	500	750
Yellow Kid in Cart, cast iron, he is being pulled by mule, Kenton, early 1900s, 10" long, 6" high.....	900	1650	3000
Yellow Kid in Goat Cart, cast iron, painted, Kenton, 1890, 7-1/2" long..	500	950	1450

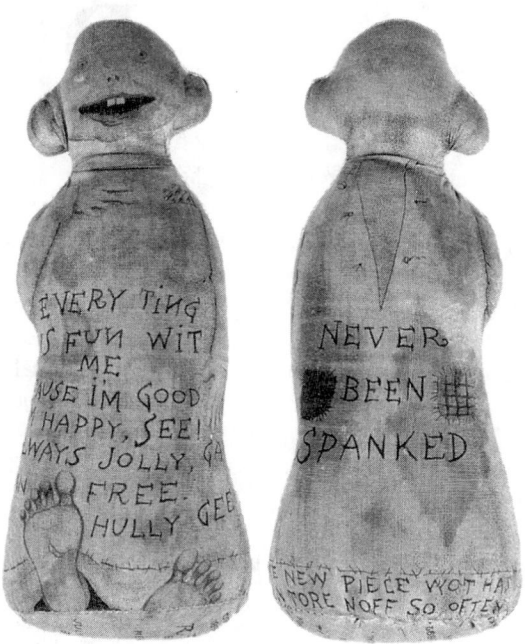

Front and back view of the Yellow Kid Doll, $750. Photo courtesy James Maxwell/Virginia Caputo

Yellow Kid Ladder Toy (missing some figures), $1500. Photo courtesy James Maxwell/Virginia Caputo

Uncle Wiggily, Marx, Crazy Car, $1100. Photo courtesy Sotheby's, New York

DISNEY

(See also Paper, Premiums, Fisher-Price)

Walt Disney was involved in animation as early as 1920, but his first truly notable character was Oswald the Rabbit, introduced in 1927. Disney did not own the rights to Oswald, however, and he eventually fell into the hands of another animator, Walter Lantz. Although Mickey Mouse first appeared in the 1928 short "Plane Crazy," the third Mickey cartoon, "Steamboat Willie," seems to have been the first released (on November 18, 1928). Mickey was a success from then on. Minnie Mouse also appeared in "Steamboat Willie," and Pluto emerged in 1930 but was not known by that name until 1931. Goofy debuted in 1932 and Donald Duck came along in 1934. Mickey Mouse toys were first produced in 1930 and since then the stream of Disneyana (apparently all of it deemed collectible) has been endless.

"I only hope that we don't lose sight of one thing—that it was all started by a mouse." *Walt Disney*

Contributor: John Fawcett, Fawcett's Toy & Art Museum, P.O. Box 1156, 3506 Route 1, Waldoboro, ME 04572; Phone: (207) 832-7398; Web site: http://home.gwi.net/~fawcetoy; Email: fawcetoy@gwi.net

Alice in Wonderland

	C6	C8	C10
Alice in Wonderland Marionette, Peter Puppet	85	128	185
Mad Hatter Doll, Gund	200	300	450
Mad Hatter Puppet	85	130	170
Mad Hatter's Taxi, Linemar, 1950s, 5" long	300	475	650

Babes in Toyland

	C6	C8	C10
Indian on Rollerskates Tin Wind-up, Linemar, 1950s, 6-1/2" tall	100	150	200
Soldier, tin wind-up, Linemar, 1950s, 6-1/2" tall	175	263	350
Wood Officer on Horseback, wheeled, Jaymar	175	263	350
Wood Soldier, w/rifle, Jaymar, 9" high	60	90	120
Wood Soldier, w/cannon, Jaymar	210	315	420

Bambi

	C6	C8	C10
Bambi Soaky	15	30	50
Flower, tin friction, Linemar, 1950s, 3" long	115	172	250
Jumping Bambi, trigger action, Linemar, 1950s, 6" high	250	375	525
Thumper, tin friction, Linemar, 1950s, 3" long	60	110	160
Thumper, Marx, 1950s, 6" high	100	150	225
Thumper Doll, Gund, 1950s, 14" high	38	65	100
Thumper Doll, Gund, early 1940s, 17" high	80	150	200
Thumper Soaky	11	30	50

Bambi (Continued)

	C6	C8	C10
Thumper Squeeze Toy, rubber, Sun Rubber, 7" high	30	50	75

Cinderella

	C6	C8	C10
Cinderella and Prince Dancing Wind-up, plastic, Irwin Co., 1950s, 5" high	65	100	150
Hand Puppet, "1957"	22	33	60
Handcar, Jaq and Gus, 8" long	383	575	775
Soaky, w/movable arms, 1960s	15	30	50
Umbrella Wind-up, spins and dances, Irwin, 4-3/4" high	62	95	140

Davy Crockett

	C6	C8	C10
Alamo Play Set, Marx	250	375	500
Auto-Magic Picture Gun	42	63	85
Badge, "Frontier Marshal", 1950s	27	41	55
Coonskin Hat	22	33	60
Doll, vinyl, Gund, 20" high	60	90	150
Doll, Fortune Toy, 1950s, 8" high	60	90	150
Flying Arrows, balsa wood, to be made into flying arrows, copyright 1955	25	40	65
Frontierland Davy Crockett Outfit, coonskin hat, gun, etc.	70	105	175
Handgun, tin litho, pop-action, 1950s	40	60	100
Play Knife, 1950s	22	40	60
Powder Horn, Daisy	20	30	40
Prairie Wagon, 5" long	26	39	65

Babes in Toyland Soldier, Linemar, 1950s, $350. Photo courtesy Scott Smiles

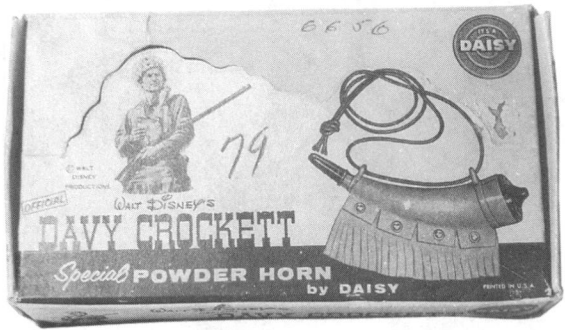

Davy Crockett Powder Horn, Daisy, $40. Photo courtesy Toy Collector News

Davy Crockett (Continued)	C6	C8	C10
Wagon Train, plastic, Marx, 1950s, 14" long	150	225	325

Disneyland	C6	C8	C10
Casey Jr. Disneyland Express, tin and plastic, locomotive, three cars, Marx	73	110	175
Concert Xylophone, Tudor, 18" long	30	45	75
Ferris Wheel Tin Wind-up, Chein, c. late 1956, 17" high	350	525	850
Happy Birthday Carousel, Ross Co., 1950s, 6" high	80	120	200
Jeep, push toy, Marx, 1960s, 10" long	100	150	225
Melody Player, w/four rolls, Chein, 1950s, 7"	95	150	225
Melody Player Extra Paper Rolls, different songs, price for each, 1950s	10	15	20
Play Set, Marx	425	700	950
Roller Coaster, two tin cars, Chein, 1950s, 10" high	250	400	600

Donald Duck	C6	C8	C10
Acrobat, Linemar, 1950s, 8-1/2" high	325	525	750
Band Leader Marionette, Madame Alexander, 1938, 9-1/2" tall	150	250	500

Donald Duck (Continued)	C6	C8	C10
Captain Push Puppet, wood and plastic, Kohner, 1950s	100	150	200
Climbing Fireman Wind-up, Linemar, 1950s, 13-1/2"	300	475	650
Convertible, tin, friction, Linemar, 1950s, 5" long	263	410	575
Crawler Wind-up, celluloid, 9-3/4" long	650	1100	1600
Delivery Tricycle, tin and plastic, Marx, 5"	450	750	100
Dipsy Car, tin car w/plastic Mickey or Donald, Marx, 1950s, 5-1/4" long	385	575	770
Disney Flivver, Linemar, 1950s, 5-1/2" long	300	450	600
Doctor Kit	60	90	150
Doll, composition and cloth, long-billed, in Russian costume, 9" high	1000	1750	2500
Doll, stuffed, long-billed, Knickerbocker, 1930s, 13" high	150	250	400
Doll, composition, long-billed, Knickerbocker, 1930s, 9" high	250	375	500
Doll, long-billed, 1930s, 16" high	75	160	250
Doll, Gund, c. 1949, 13-1/2" high	110	200	300

Disneyland Ferris Wheel Tin Wind-up, Chein, c. late 1956, $850. Photo courtesy Hake's Americana & Collectibles

Disneyland Happy Birthday Carousel, Ross Co., 1950s, $200. Photo courtesy Continental Hobby House

Disneyland Roller Coaster, Chein, 1950s, $600. Photo courtesy Continental Hobby House

Donald Duck (Continued)	C6	C8	C10
Donald Duck and His Nephews, pull-string action, Linemar, 1950s, 5-1/2" high	400	600	800
Donald Duck and His Nephews Wind-up, plastic, Marx, 1950s, 11" long	225	338	450
Donald Duck and Huey, w/voice, string pull toy, Linemar, 1950s, 7" long	500	750	1000
Donald Duck and Pluto in Roadster, Sun Rubber, 1930s, 6-1/2" long	80	120	200
Donald Duck Duet Tin Wind-up, small Donald w/large Goofy, Marx, c. 1945	440	660	950
Donald Duck Figure, Sun Rubber, 10" high	21	32	60
Donald Duck Figure, long billed, Seiberling Rubber, 1930s, 6" high	150	225	350

Donald Duck (Continued)	C6	C8	C10
Donald Duck Figure, celluloid, long billed, Borgfeldt (Japan), 1930s, 5" high	262	395	550
Donald Duck Figure, celluloid, 1940s, 13" high	135	198	300
Donald Duck in His Convertible, friction, Linemar, 1950s, 6" long	275	415	650
Donald Duck Jigger Wind-up, papier-mâché, 11" high	800	1200	1600
Donald Duck Mouseketeers Hat	15	30	50
Donald Duck on Pluto Wind-up, celluloid	1400	2200	3400
Donald Duck on Rocking Horse Wind-up, celluloid and tin, Japan, 3-3/8" long	3000	4500	6200
Donald Duck on Tractor, plastic, friction, Marx, 1950s, 3-1/2" long	120	200	300
Donald Duck on Trapeze, Borgfeldt, 1930s, 9" high	275	362	650

*Donald Duck Climbing Fireman
Wind-up, Linemar, 1950s, $650.
Photo courtesy Don Hultzman*

*Donald Duck Figure, Seiberling Rubber,
1930s, $350. Photo courtesy Hake's
Americana & Collectibles*

Donald Duck (Continued)	**C6**	**C8**	**C10**
Donald Duck Pulled by Pluto, celluloid w/tin cart, long billed, Japan, 1930s	1750	2625	3600
Donald Duck Rail Car, w/Pluto and doghouse, Lionel, 1930s, 10" long	413	625	875
Donald Duck Riding Mule Wind-up, celluloid, long billed, 7-3/4"	850	1400	2000
Donald Duck Roly-Poly, 1940s, 3-3/4"	187	280	400
Donald Duck Rowboat, wood and paper litho, Chad Valley (England), 12-1/4" long	300	450	700
Donald Duck Skier, Linemar	300	550	800
Donald Duck Skier, plastic, Marx, 1940s	375	675	1000
Donald Duck Swimmer Wind-up, celluloid, 6-1/2"	650	1000	1650
Donald Duck Tricycle, w/twirling parasol, M-T Co. (Japan), 1950s, 7-1/2" high	200	375	500
Donald Duck Tricycle Wind-up, Linemar, 1950s, 3-1/2" long	285	450	650

Donald Duck (Continued)	**C6**	**C8**	**C10**
Donald Duck Wind-up, tin, w/umbrella, Linemar, 4" high	300	450	625
Donald Duck Wind-up, "984", Schuco (German), 6" high	158	235	375
Donald Duck Wind-up, hard plastic, Marx, 1960s, 7" high	30	45	75
Donald Duck with Whirling Tail Tin Wind-up, Linemar, 1950s, 5-1/4" high	300	450	600
Donald Duck with Whirling Tail Wind-up, plastic, Marx, 1950s, 6-1/2" high	92	135	185
Donald Duck Zylophone, Tudor, 10" long	55	83	125
Donald Race Car Wind-up, celluloid, Occupied Japan	225	338	500
Donald the Driver, friction car, Linemar, 1950s, 6-1/2" long	225	338	500
Donald the Drummer Wind-up, rocker, Linemar, 1950s, 6" high	250	375	525
Donald the Drummer Wind-up, walker, Linemar, 1950s, 6" high	265	400	530

Donald Duck Doll, $2500. Photo courtesy Christie's East

Donald Duck and His Nephews Wind-up, Marx, 1950s, $450. Photo courtesy Don Hultzman

Donald Duck Duet Tin Wind-up, Marx, c. 1945, $950.

Donald Duck (Continued)	C6	C8	C10
Donald the Drummer Wind-up, Marx, 1950s, 9" tall	275	363	550
Dump Truck, Linemar, 1950s, 5" long	300	450	650
Fire Chief Crazy Car Tin Wind-up, extremely rare, Linemar	700	1500	2000
Huey - Louie - Dewey Locomotive, plastic friction, Marx, 1950s, 3-1/2" long	50	75	120
Rubber Boat, Sun Rubber Co., c. 1940s	40	60	100
Soaky	11	40	65
Straight Shooter, plastic wind-up, 1960s, 6-1/2" high	187	280	450
Teapot, Ohio Art	30	45	75
Tractor, Sun Rubber	112	188	225

Donald Duck (Continued)	C6	C8	C10
Waddler, tin and celluloid, long-billed, "K" Co. (Japan), 1930s, 3-1/4" high	600	900	1200
Waddler, "K" Co., 1930s, 3-1/2" tall	600	900	1200
Walker Wind-up, celluloid, Japan, 3-1/2" high	400	600	825
Washing Machine, M-T Co. (Japan), 1950s, 7-1/2" high	400	600	825

Dumbo	C6	C8	C10
Dumbo Hand Puppet, Gund, c. 1955, 10"	25	38	75
Dumbo Squeeze Doll, vinyl, 1960s, 9"	22	33	60

Donald Duck on Rocking Horse Wind-up, Japan, $6200. Photo courtesy James S. Maxwell and Virginia Caputo

Donald Duck Riding Mule Wind-up, $2000.

Dumbo (Continued)	**C6**	**C8**	**C10**
Dumbo The Acrobatic Elephant Tin Wind-up, Dumbo flips over, Marx, 1941, 4" high	300	450	650
Timothy Mouse Doll, stuffed, Character Novelty, 1942, 17" high	150	225	350

Ferdinand the Bull	**C6**	**C8**	**C10**
Doll, jointed wood, 9"	125	188	300
Ferdinand and Matador Wind-up, tin, Marx, 1938	600	1000	1500
Ferdinand the Bull Wind-up, tail whirls, body shakes, Marx, copyright 1938	212	320	450
Figure, hard rubber, Seiberling, late 1930s, 6" long, 3-1/2" high	102	160	240
Hand Puppet, Crown, 1938	55	82	110
Pull Toy, Hill, 8-3/4" long..............	170	255	340

Goofy	**C6**	**C8**	**C10**
Figure, tin, 1930	400	600	850
Goofy on a Unicycle Wind-up, tin, Linemar, 5-1/2" high	500	750	1100
Goofy the Walking Gardener Wind-up, tin, Marx	482	625	965
Goofy Tricycle Wind-up, Linemar, 1950s, 4" tall	650	975	1300
Goofy with Whirling Tail Wind-up, plastic, Marx, 1950s, 8" high	92	140	185

Goofy (Continued)	**C6**	**C8**	**C10**
Goofy with Whirling Tail Wind-up, Linemar, 1950s, 5" tall...............	300	450	600
Goofy's Disneyland Stock Car Wind-up, Linemar, 1950s, 6" long..	200	300	425
Goofy's Stock Car Wind-up, Linemar, 1950s, 6" long	200	300	425
Soaky	20	30	60

Jiminy Cricket	**C6**	**C8**	**C10**
Doll, latex head, hands and feet w/cloth body, 13" high...............	60	90	150
Doll, felt and cloth, Crown Toy, 14" high..	150	225	325
Doll, felt and cloth, Crown Toy, 15-1/2" high.................................	150	225	325
Doll, cloth body w/rubber head and wooden feet, Gund, 12"...............	22	40	65
Doll, jointed wood, Ideal, 1940, 9" high...	225	375	500
Doll, Knickerbocker, c. 1940, 10" high...	300	450	650
Face Mask, Gillette, 1939...............	25	38	65
Hand Puppet, vinyl and cloth, Gund...	32	48	65
Jiminy Cricket Pushing Bass Fiddle Walkie, Marx........................	15	22	45

Dumbo the Acrobatic Elephant Tin Wind-up, Marx, 1941, $650. Photo courtesy Don Hultzman

Ferdinand and Matador Wind-up, Marx, 1938, $1500. Photo courtesy Don Hultzman

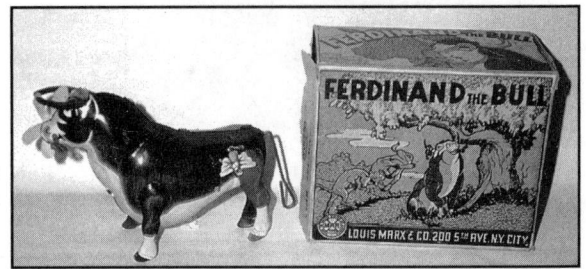

Ferdinand the Bull Wind-up, Marx, copyright 1938, $450. Photo courtesy Don Hultzman

Jiminy Cricket (Continued)	C6	C8	C10
Jiminy Cricket Tin Wind-up, in black tuxedo, top hat has yellow band, Linemar, 1950s, 5-1/2" tall	300	450	650
Soaky	10	30	50

Lady and the Tramp	C6	C8	C10
Si-Am Doll, stuffed w/vinyl face, Gund, c. 1955, 16" high	40	75	100
Tramp Hand Puppet, Gund	35	52	100
Tramp the Dog, friction, Linemar, 1960s, 4" high	90	135	200

Ludwig Von Drake	C6	C8	C10
Ludwig Von Drake Go-Cart, friction, Marx, 1961	158	235	315
Ludwig Von Drake Squeeze Toy, rubber, Dell, c. 1960, 7"	58	90	115
Ludwig Von Drake Talking Doll	50	75	100
Ludwig Von Drake Tin Wind-up, Linemar, 1950s, 6" tall	290	435	580
Professor Von Drake Go Mobile, wind-up, Linemar, 1950s, 6" long	150	225	300

Mickey and Minnie Mouse	C6	C8	C10
Acrobats, Borgfeldt, 1934, 11" high	500	750	1150
Bell Toy, wood and metal, Gong Bell, c. 1933, 10-3/4" long	1050	1575	2200
Drum Set, tin and cardboard, shows Minnie watching Mickey juggle, c. 1940	240	360	525

Mickey and Minnie Mouse	C6	C8	C10
Handcar, red, orange and green, Lionel Co., 1930s, 7" long	650	1100	1900
Mickey and Minnie Mouse on Motorcycle Tin Wind-up	13,000	33,000	65,000
Mickey and Minnie Mouse Playland, celluloid, Japan	3000	5500	10,000
Organ Grinder, depicts Minnie Mouse dancing on organ pushed by Mickey, German	1200	1800	2500
Piano, wooden, grand piano w/decal showing Mickey playing, Minnie listening, c. 1935	200	300	400
Swing Toy, celluloid, w/red and green flag, 11-1/2" tall	420	630	900
Tambourine, heavy paper head, depicts Mickey juggling while Minnie watches, Noble & Cooley Co., 1936, 9"	310	500	750
Tea Set, thirteen pieces, c. 1935	140	210	375

Mickey Mouse	C6	C8	C10
Acrobat, clockwork trapeze w/celluloid Mickey, Japan, 1930s, 9" high	243	365	485
Acrobat, wood, Strombecker, 1950s	45	68	100
Bandleader Doll, black shako, red jacket, this doll was produced in conjunction with Mickey's first color cartoon "The Band Concert", Knickerbocker, 1935, 12" high	650	1200	1850
Banjo, 1930s, 17" long	140	210	300

Goofy the Walking Gardener Wind-up, Marx, $965. Photo courtesy Christie's East

Jiminy Cricket Tin Wind-up, Linemar, 1950s, $650. Photo courtesy Don Hultzman

Mickey Mouse (Continued)	C6	C8	C10
Bank, brass, figure of Mickey Mouse, French	2000	5000	10,000
Bank, cast iron, figure of Mickey Mouse, France, c. 1931	1500	2800	5000
Bubble Buster Gun, cast iron, Mickey standing at gun sight, Kilgore, 6" long	75	150	200
Circus, two wood figures revolving on swinging mechanism, 6/3785, Geo. Borgfeldt, 1931, 11" long	500	850	1300
Clicker, tin litho, Mickey showing teeth while playing violin, c. 1930	90	135	225
Cowboy Mickey Doll, Knickerbocker, 1936, 12" high	2000	5000	8000
Cowboy Mickey Doll, Knickerbocker, c. 1935, 19-1/2" high	1400	3000	4000
Dipsy Car, Linemar, 1950s, 5-1/4" long	300	450	600
Dipsy Car, Mickey, tin car w/plastic, Marx, 1950s, 5-1/4" long	318	475	635
Doll, felt, Mickey has toothy grin, Dean's Rag, 6"	125	200	350

Mickey Mouse (Continued)	C6	C8	C10
Doll, cloth, marked "Walt Disney Mickey Mouse Geo. E. Borgfeldt & Company New York" on bottom of one foot, 11" high	337	505	750
Doll, Borgfeldt, 12" high	625	938	1350
Doll, wooden, w/jointed hands, arms, legs and wire tail, leather ears, first toy made by Borgfeldt of NY, marked "Copyright 1928-1930 by Walter E. Disney", 1930	550	825	1100
Doll, Knickerbocker, 1930s, 12" high	325	488	750
Doll, Knickerbocker, 1935, 22" high	500	750	1150
Doll, felt, dressed in black jacket w/yellow buttons, red pants, bells on toes of yellow shoes, storage space in back, 1950s, 31" high	120	180	240
Doll, felt, Character Co., c. 1939-40, 18" high	70	105	200
Doll, felt, Steiff, early 1930s, 12" high	600	950	1350
Drum, tin, Ohio Art, 6" diameter	130	195	300
Figure, celluloid, w/fat head, 5" high	150	225	300

Ludwig Von Drake Tin Wind-up, Linemar, 1950s, $580. Photo courtesy Don Hultzman

Mickey Mouse Acrobat, Japan, 1930s, $485. Photo courtesy PB Eighty-Four, New York

Mickey Mouse (Continued)

	C6	C8	C10
Figure, wood, w/leather ears, Fen-E-Flex, 5" high	250	375	525
Figure, wood, Fun-E-Flex, 7-1/2" high	300	500	675
Figure, Sun Rubber, 8" high	65	98	150
Figure, rubber, Lakeside Mfg. Co.	80	120	180
Figure, rubber, Dell, 9-1/2" high	50	75	120
Figure, Fun-E-Flex, 1930s, 3-1/2" high	150	225	300
Figure, rubber, Seiberling, 1930s, 3-1/2" high	90	135	240
Figure, cast iron, Mickey Holding Flag, 1930s	140	210	350
Figure, lead, Allied Toys, 1933, 2-1/2" high	70	105	160
Figure, rubber, Sun Rubber, 1940s, 10" high	30	45	75
Figure, wood, w/jointed arms and legs, c. 1933, 8" high	600	900	1300
Figure, celluloid and wood, Mickey on Hobby Horse, c. 1935, 4-1/2"	1050	1800	2500
Figure, rubber, Seiberling, c. 1935, 6" high	150	250	400

Mickey Mouse (Continued)

	C6	C8	C10
Figure, jointed wood, Borgfeldt, early, 7" high	300	450	625
Flute, tin	40	60	100
Gym Toys Acrobats, includes Mickey, Donald, Minnie, price for each, Linemar, 1950s, 8-1/2" high	200	300	400
Handcar, "Santa Car with Mickey Mouse and His Gift Pack," No. 1105, Lionel, 1935	900	1350	2000
Hingees, 1944	25	40	65
Jazz Drummer, finger-activated tin toy, Nifty, 4-3/4" high	1500	2700	4200
Kaleidoscope, 1950s	32	50	80
Marionette, Madame Alexander, 1938, 9-1/2" high	150	250	500
Marionette, Peter Puppet Playthings Co., 1952, 14" tall	55	90	130
Mask, cardboard, c. 1935	60	90	120
Mickey Mouse Bus Lines - Walt Disney Stars, riding toy, Gong Bell, c. 1960, 19-1/2" long	150	225	350

Mickey Mouse Bandleader Doll, Knickerbocker, 1935, $1850. Photo courtesy Don Hultzman

Mickey Mouse Cowboy Mickey Doll, Knickerbocker, c. 1935, $4000. Photo courtesy Christie's East

Mickey Mouse (Continued)	C6	C8	C10
Mickey Mouse Circus Train Set, engine, Mickey in tender, three tin-litho cars (dining, band and circus); set includes large paper circus tent and multiple paper accessories, a composition Mickey "Narker" figures and track, Lionel	1300	2500	5000
Mickey Mouse Express Tin Wind-up, train set, Marx, 1950s, 14" long, base 21" x 13"	700	1100	1700
Mickey Mouse Express Wind-up, Mickey in airplane, Marx, 1950s, 9" diameter	425	638	850
Mickey Mouse Meteor Five-Car Train Tin Wind-up, Marx, 43" long	800	1000	1500
Mickey Mouse Motorcycle, tin friction, Linemar, 1950s, 3-1/2" long	150	225	300
Mickey Mouse Motorcycle, tin friction, Linemar, 1950s, 3" long	200	300	400

Mickey Mouse (Continued)	C6	C8	C10
Mickey Mouse on Handcar Wind-up, basket on back, Japan, 8" long	130	210	300
Mickey Mouse on Tricycle Tin Wind-up, 1940s, 3-1/2" long	450	700	900
Mickey Mouse Pirate Ship, Ideal	138	210	275
Mickey Mouse Racing Car Tin Wind-up, w/Mickey at the wheel, metal or rubber wheels, 1930s, 4" long	400	650	900
Mickey Mouse Rollerskater Wind-up, Linemar, 1950s, 6" high	450	750	1130
Mickey Mouse Trapeze, celluloid, Borgfeldt, 1930s	500	750	1150
Mickey Mouse Trapeze, wood, c. 1930s	34	60	100
Mickey Mouse Tricycle, Linemar, 1950s, 4" tall	500	775	1100
Mickey Mouse Tumbler, pie-eyed, Schuco, 1930s, 4" long	150	225	325
Mickey Mouse Tumbling, Marks Bros., 1947, 8" high	42	63	85

Mickey Mouse Bank, France, c. 1931, $5000. Photo courtesy James S. Maxwell and Virginia Caputo

Mickey Mouse Doll, marked "Walt Disney Mickey Mouse Geo. E. Borgfeldt & Company New York" on bottom of foot, $750. Photo courtesy Hakes Americana & Collectibles

Mickey Mouse (Continued)	C6	C8	C10
Mickey Mouse Wind-up, tin, vibrates, Linemar, 1950s, 5-1/2" high	300	450	600
Mickey Mouse wth Twirling Tail Wind-up, Linemar, 1950s, 5-1/2" high	130	195	275
Mickey Mouse Xylophone Player Tin Wind-up, Linemar, 1950s, 6" high	333	500	665
Mickey on Scooter Tin Wind-up, rare, Linemar, 1950s, 4-1/2" high	350	525	725
Mickey on Unicycle Wind-up, Linemar, 1950s, 5" high	650	975	1300
Mickey Race Car Wind-up, celluloid, Occupied Japan	250	375	500
Mickey the Driver, friction, Marx (Japan), 1950s, 6-1/2" long	400	600	850
Mickey the Magician, battery-operated, Linemar, 10"	500	800	1200

Mickey Mouse (Continued)	C6	C8	C10
Mickey the Musician - I Play the Xylophone Wind-up, Marx, 1950s, 10" high	312	465	625
Mickey Walker, Borgfeldt, 1934, 8" high	2100	3700	5750
Mickey Wouse Waddle Book, Blue Ribbon Book, Inc, 1934	800	2000	6500
Mickey, Minnie and Goofy Sand Pail, tin litho, Ohio Art, 1938	112	168	250
Mickey-in-the-Box, 7" high	260	390	520
Mickey's Delivery Tin Wind-up, tin litho, celluloid head on Pluto, Pluto on tricycle cart, Linemar, 1950s, 5-1/2" long	375	565	750
Mickey's Mousekemovers Wind-up, Linemar, 1950s, 13" long	500	750	1025
Mickey's Service Truck, plastic friction, Marx, 1950s, 3-1/2" long	50	85	150
Mickey's Tractor, Mickey's head turns, Sun Rubber, 1930s, 4-1/2" long	65	100	150

Mickey Mouse Drum, Ohio Art, $300. Photo courtesy Hakes Americana & Collectibles

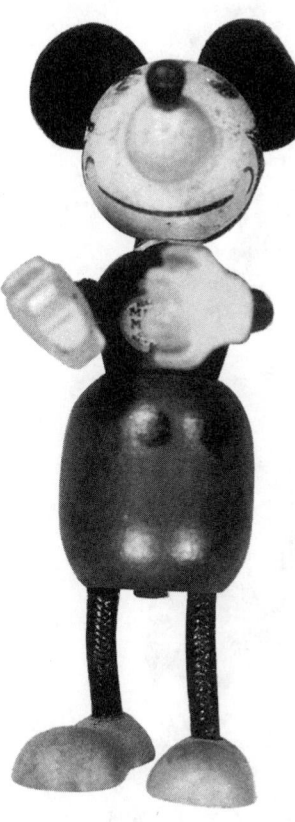

Mickey Mouse Figure, Fun-E-Flex, $675.

CONDITION CODE

C6   Good; evident overall wear, well played with but acceptable to many collectors
C8   Very Good; minor overall wear, very clean
C10 Mint; like new

Note: Mint in Box commands a higher price.
Condition below C6 brings considerably lower prices

Mickey Mouse (Continued)	C6	C8	C10
Movie Fun Optical Toy, Mastercraft, 1950s, 7" x 7" x 5"	150	225	300
Movie Projector, No. E-18, Keystone, 1930s, 10" high	125	210	375
Movie-Jector, 1935	135	200	350
Newsreel, includes three records and five films, Mattel, 9-1/2" high	110	165	225
Parade Roadster, tin litho wind-up, convertible car decorated w/Mickey and other Disney characters, Donald is at the wheel w/Pluto, Mickey and Minnie as passengers, Marx, 1950s, 11-1/4" long	350	525	700
Pencil Box, Dixon Pencil Co., 1930s	110	225	350
Piano, Marks Bros., c. 1935, 10"	1250	2200	3000
Pocket Knife, 1935	40	100	150
Puppet, Gund, 10" high	11	16	35
Puppet, rubber legs and arms, wood body, Pelham, 24" high	40	80	120

Mickey Mouse (Continued)	C6	C8	C10
Puppet, cloth body w/composition head, hands and feet and cloth ears, early 1940s style	175	263	350
Push Puppet, Mickey Mouse Drummer, Kohner, 1950s	100	150	200
Push Puppet, Gabriel, 1977	10	15	30
Race Car, add $250 for box, T.M. Co., 1930s, 3" long	300	450	650
Rocking Mickey Mouse on Pluto Wind-up, Linemar	800	1400	2000
Roly-Poly, celluloid, early, 4" high	187	280	400
Rower, Fun-E-Flex, 10-3/4"	1700	2750	4000
Running Mickey on Pluto Wind-up, celluloid, M-T Co., 1940s, 5-1/2" long	2000	3750	6750
Saxophone Player, 1930s	800	1500	2200
Scooter Jockey Wind-up, plastic, Mavco Co., 1950s, 6" high	400	600	800
Snow Shovel, Mickey and Pluto, shows them building a snowman, 26" long	90	135	225
Soaky	20	40	60

Mickey Mouse Figure, Borgfeldt, early, $625.

Mickey Mouse Handcar, Lionel, 1935, $2000.

Mickey Mouse Bus Lines – Walt Disney Stars, Gong Bell, $350

Mickey Mouse (Continued)	C6	C8	C10
Soda Jerk Hat, felt, shows Mickey from shoulders up saying "have one on me", c. 1930, 5" x 11"	60	90	150
Soldier Set, cardboard soldiers, gun	500	1000	1500
Sparkler Toy, Nifty, 1930s, 5-1/2" tall	325	490	750
Squeeze Toy, w/red shirt and yellow pants, Sun Rubber, 1950	34	51	85
Squeeze Toy, rubber, large size w/clothes, Sun Rubber, 1950	30	45	75
Tea Service, tin, twenty-four pieces, Chein, 1930s	120	225	350
Tool Chest, complete, Hamilton Metal, 1935	170	325	400
Tumbler, Schuco, 4" high	200	300	425
Viewer, w/film of "Brave Little Tailor", 1946	60	90	120
Washboard Set, tin, complete, c. 1935	80	120	175

Mickey Mouse (Continued)	C6	C8	C10
Washing Machine, tin litho, shows two scenes w/Mickey, Minnie, Pluto, Ohio Art Co., 1932 or 1933, 7" high	100	150	220

Mickey Mouse and Donald Duck	C6	C8	C10
Handcar, plastic, wind-up, Marx, 1948	200	300	425
Mickey Mouse and Donald in Fire Truck, Sun Rubber, late 1930s, 6-1/2" long	75	125	200
Mickey Mouse and Donald on Boat, celluloid	1050	1700	2450
Walker, plastic, both on back of alligator, Marx, 1950s	60	90	120

Mickey Mouse Club	C6	C8	C10
Auto-Magic Picture Gun, projects films, 1946	35	52	85
Bow and Arrow Set, c. 1955	20	30	50

Mickey Mouse Circus Train Set (incomplete set), No. 1536, Lionel, $5000. Photo courtesy PB Eighty-Four, New York

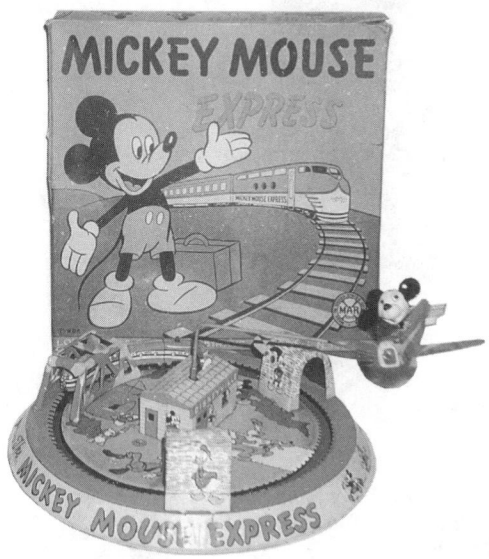

Mickey Mouse Express Wind-up, Marx, 1950s, $850. Photo courtesy Don Hultzman

Mickey Mouse Racing Car Tin Wind-up, 1930s, $900. Photo courtesy PB Eighty-Four, New York

CONDITION CODE

C6	Good; evident overall wear, well played with but acceptable to many collectors
C8	Very Good; minor overall wear, very clean
C10	Mint; like new

Note: Mint in Box commands a higher price. Condition below C6 brings considerably lower prices

Mickey Mouse Club (Continued)

	C6	C8	C10
Mouseketeer Electric TV Story Teller, tin litho, includes TV, record player, records and film reels, T. Cohn, late 1950s............	160	240	320
Mouseketeer Hat, wool and rayon, Benay-Albee, 1950s	5	10	20
Mouseketeer Play Outfit.................	75	112	150
Mouseketeer Soaky	17	35	60
Newreel Projector..........................	68	102	135
Pinback, W.E. Disney, 1928-30	55	110	160
Snap-on Ears, plastic, 1950s............	10	15	20
Television Playhouse Play Set, w/thirty-nine characters, Marx	232	348	465

Minnie Mouse

	C6	C8	C10
Doll, wearing dress and high heels, 1930, 12" high	225	350	500
Doll, cloth, early 1930s, 16" high...	650	975	1300
Figure, wooden, Fun-E-Flex, 4" high...	140	210	300

Minnie Mouse (Continued)

	C6	C8	C10
Figure, cloth, dressed in a red and white polka dot skirt, wearing composition high-heeled shoes, 14-1/2" high.................................	300	450	625
Figure, Fun-E-Flex, 7" high	300	450	625
Figure, celluloid, string tail, 1930s, 6" high	425	638	875
Figure, celluloid, w/fat head, 1930s, 5" high	225	338	475
Figure, wooden, 1930s, 5-1/2" high...	187	286	400
Figure, lead, Allied Toys, 1933, 2-1/2" high.................................	70	105	140
Figure, Sun Rubber, 1940s, 10-1/2" high...	85	125	185
Figure, wooden, jointed, 1940s, 3" high...	200	300	400
Hand Puppet, Peter Puppet Playthings, c. 1952	100	150	200
Marionette, Madame Alexander, 1938, 9-1/2" high......................	150	250	500

Mickey Mouse Tumbler, Schuco, 1930s, $325. Tumbler is atop Mickey Mouse Piano, Marks Bros., c. 1935, $3000. Photo courtesy Christie's East

Mickey Mouse Xylophone Player Tin Wind-up, Linemar, 1950s, $665. Photo courtesy Don Hultzman

Minnie Mouse (Continued)

	C6	C8	C10
Marionette, wood and composition, 1950s, 13"....................................	150	225	300
Mask, cardboard, c. 1935	40	60	80
Minnie Mouse Cowgirl Doll, Knickerbocker, 1936, 18" high ...	470	725	960
Minnie Mouse Knitter Tin Wind-up, Linemar, 1950s, 7" high........	375	600	775
Minnie Mouse Wind-up, hard plastic, Marx, 1960s, 7" high.............	70	105	150
Puppet, wood body w/rubber legs and arms, Pelham, 24" high	195	292	390
Roly-Poly, celluloid, 4"	60	90	120
Tricycle, Linemar, 1950s, 4"	450	675	900
Walker, plastic.................................	20	30	40
Washing Machine, Precision Specialties Inc., 1950	100	150	225

Miscellaneous

	C6	C8	C10
101 Dalmatians, set of six wooden nodders, 1959	125	200	300
Disney Show Boat, plastic, Playworld Toys, 1981	4	10	20
Disney Showboat, large, 1960.........	62	100	150

Miscellaneous (Continued)

	C6	C8	C10
Disneykins, Marx	105	158	210
Elmer Elephant, rubber, w/moveable head, Seiberling	162	243	375
Elmer Elephant Figure, celluloid and string, 1930s, 5".....................	120	180	300
Frontierland Logs, No. 915, Halsam	45	80	120
Johnny Tremain Flintlock Cap Pistol, Marx......................................	60	100	150
Jungle Book Dancing Bear Wind-up, plastic, Marx........................	80	150	200
Nautilus Submarine, (20,000 Leagues Under the Sea)	155	250	375
Oswald the Rabbit, celluloid, crib toy, c. 1927, 6-1/2" long..............	250	400	600
Pecos Bill Wind-up, plastic, Marx, 1950s	200	300	400
Practical Pig, tin litho wind-up, Linemar	260	390	520
Practical Pig Doll, Gund..................	112	180	250

Mickey on Scooter Tin Wind-up, Linemar, 1950s, $725. Photo courtesy Don Hultzman

Mickey Mouse Rower, Fun-E-Flex, $4000. Photo courtesy Christie's East

Mickey the Magician, Linemar, $1200. Photo courtesy Christie's East

Mickey Mouse and Donald Duck Handcar, Marx, 1948, $425. Photo courtesy Don Hultzman

Peter Pan	C6	C8	C10
Captain Hook Hand Puppet, Gund, 1950	17	26	35
Captain Hook Marionette, Peter Puppet Playthings	95	143	190
Peter Pan Figure, Sun Rubber, c. 1952, 9-3/4" high	30	45	75
Peter Pan Jolly Roger Pirate Ship	17	26	35
Peter Pan Marionette, Peter Puppet Playthings, c. 1952	70	105	140
Peter Pan Tea Set, twenty-three pieces, c. 1953	275	363	575
Peter Pan Train Car, 1977	22	33	45
Tinkerbell Hand Puppet, Gund	32	48	65
Wendy Hand Puppet, Gund	14	21	28
Wendy Marionette, 1950s	75	112	150

Pinocchio	C6	C8	C10
Cleo Mask, Gillette, 1939	10	30	50
Cleo the Goldfish Squeeze Toy, Sun Rubber	23	35	60
Donkey Doll, stuffed, Knicker-bocker	95	142	225
Donkey Figure, rubber, Seiberling Rubber, 1940, 4"	70	105	160
Figaro, tin friction toy, Linemar, 1950s, 3" long	70	105	150
Figaro Mask, paper, Gillette, 1939	15	38	50
Gepetto Figure, wood, holding his chin, Multi Products, 1940, 5-1/2"	70	105	140
Gepetto Mask, Gillette, 1939	12	33	45
Jiminy Cricket, 1940	100	200	300

Minnie Mouse Knitter Tin Wind-up, Linemar, 1950s, $775. Photo courtesy Don Hultzman

Pinocchio (Continued)

	C6	C8	C10
Pinocchio, plastic, "Walking Pinocchio", Marx, 1950s	40	60	100
Pinocchio Delivery, Marx	250	375	500
Pinocchio Doll, jointed wood and composition, Ideal, 10-1/2" high.	250	375	525
Pinocchio Doll, jointed wood and composition, Ideal, 12" high	300	450	625
Pinocchio Doll, stuffed, Knickerbocker, 15" high	92	138	200
Pinocchio Doll, jointed, Ideal, 1940, 7-1/2" high	150	225	310
Pinocchio Doll, jointed, c. 1940, 11" high	200	300	420
Pinocchio Doll, jointed, c. 1940, 19-3/4" high	400	600	830
Pinocchio Doll, soft cloth, c. 1940s, 18" high	125	188	275
Pinocchio Figure, rubber, Seiberling, 5-1/2" high	27	41	65
Pinocchio Figure, Ideal, 8" high	132	198	300
Pinocchio Figure, cloth and wood, jointed, Kreuger	160	240	330
Pinocchio Figure, molded wood fiber, Multi Products, 1940, 2-1/2" high	100	150	200

Pinocchio (Continued)

	C6	C8	C10
Pinocchio Figure, molded wood fiber, Multi Products, 1940, 5" high	100	150	200
Pinocchio Hand Puppet, Gund, 1950s	10	15	35
Pinocchio Mask, paper, Gillette, 1939	10	30	50
Pinocchio Soaky	12	30	50
Pinocchio the Acrobat Tin Wind-up, "Watch Him Go!", Marx, 1939	385	575	770
Pinocchio Tin Wind-up, w/moving eyes, Marx, 1939, 8-1/2" high	312	470	650
Pinocchio Tin Wind-up, Linemar Co., 1950s, 5-1/2" tall	350	525	725
Pinocchio Tin Wind-up, w/litho eyes, Marx, c. 1940, 8-1/2" high	300	450	625
Pinocchio Wind-up, wood and papier-mâché, George Borgfeldt, 1940, 10-1/2" high	318	475	700

Pluto

	C6	C8	C10
Begging Rollover Pluto Wind-up, Linemar, 1950s, 6-1/2" long	100	150	200

Disneykins, Marx, $210. Photo courtesy Don Hultzman. Photo by Ron Chojnacki

Elmer Elephant, Seiberling, $375. Photo courtesy Hakes Americana & Collectibles

Pluto (Continued)	**C6**	**C8**	**C10**
Drum Major Tin Wind-up, Linemar, 1950s, 6-1/2" tall................	250	400	600
Figure, wood, Borgfeldt, 6"............	175	263	375
Figure, Seiberling, 7-1/2"...............	65	98	160
Figure, jointed wood, 9".................	250	375	500
Figure, lead, Allied Toys, 1933, 2-1/2" high..........................	60	90	150
Figure, wooden w/bendable legs, c. 1934, 3"...........................	140	210	30
Figure, Seiberling, c. 1935, 4"........	60	90	150
Hand Puppet, Gund, 1950s.............	15	22	50
Marionette, Madame Alexander, 1938, 6" tall..............................	100	150	250
Musical Pluto, plastic, Marx, 1960s, 8" x 8" base	400	600	850
Mysterious Pluto, Marx..................	150	225	325
Playful Pluto & Goofy Wind-up, two-piece set, Linemar, 1950s	800	1300	2000
Pluto in His Sports Car, plastic friction drive, 1950s, 4" long............	50	75	150
Pluto Motorcycle, tin friction, Linemar, 1950s, 3-1/2" long..............	300	450	650

Pluto (Continued)	**C6**	**C8**	**C10**
Pluto on Rockers, wooden, c. 1930s	150	225	325
Pluto Pulling Cart, friction, Linemar, 1950s, 8-1/2" long..............	392	588	785
Pluto Tricycle, Linemar, 1950s, 4" tall...................................	278	415	555
Pluto with Whirling Tail Wind-up, Linemar, 1950s, 4" high.............	235	350	500
Soaky	11	30	50
Squeeze Action Toy with Cable, tin litho, Linemar, 1950s, 4-1/4" tall...................................	200	300	400
Squeeze Toy, rubber, Sun Rubber, 1930s	30	45	75
Squeeze Toy, rubber, in sitting position, 1960s	20	30	50
Watch Me Roll Over Wind-up, Marx, 1939	130	195	300
Wise Pluto Wind-up, Marx, 1939, 8" long......................................	212	318	475
Sleeping Beauty	**C6**	**C8**	**C10**
Sleeping Beauty Hand Puppet, Gund, 1950s	31	50	75

Pecos Bill Wind-up, Marx, 1950s, $400. Photo courtesy Don Hultzman

Donkey Figure (Pinocchio), Seiberling Rubber, 1940, $160.

PHOTOS NEEDED

We are always looking for good quality toy images for our archives. Photo quality is our highest consideration and any donated images must be in 35mm print or slide form.

If you can donate photos of toys not pictured here, please contact us at the following address:

O'Brien's Collecting Toys
Krause Publications
700 E. State St.
IOLA, WI 54990
(715) 445-4612
obrienk@krause.com

Sleeping Beauty (Continued)	C6	C8	C10
Sleeping Beauty Squeeze Toy, sitting w/animals, 6-1/2"	44	66	100

Snow White and The Seven Dwarfs	C6	C8	C10
Bashful Doll, stuffed	60	90	150
Bashful Doll, Ideal, 7" high.............	125	188	275
Bashful Doll, Ideal, 1938, 12" high.	80	120	200
Bashful Figure, Seiberling, 5-3/4" high..	90	135	200
Bashful Figure, lead, Britains, 1-1/2"..	40	60	85
Bashful Marionette, Madame Alexander, 1938, 9-1/2" tall................	100	150	250
Bashful Party Mask, 1937	20	30	50
Doc Doll, composition w/velvet clothes, Knickerbocker, 9" high..	100	150	225
Doc Doll, Ideal, approx. 7" high..	125	188	275

Snow White and The Seven Dwarfs (Continued)	C6	C8	C10
Doc Doll, Ideal, 1938, 12" high..	82	123	190
Doc Figure, lead, Britains, 1-1/2" high..	60	90	120
Doc Figure, Seiberling, 1938, 5-3/4"	50	75	125
Doc Marionette, Madame Alexander, 1938, 9-1/2" tall................	100	150	250
Doc Party Mask, 1937	14	21	50
Dopey and Doc Pull Toy, 14" long..	200	300	425
Dopey Doll, Ideal, 7" high..............	125	188	300
Dopey Doll, composition w/velvet clothes, Knickerbocker, 9" high..	175	263	425
Dopey Doll, Ideal, 1938, 12" high..	150	225	350
Dopey Figure, lead, Britains, 1-1/2"..	40	60	85

Pinocchio, Marx, 1950s, $100. Photo courtesy Ed Hyers Antique Toys

Pinocchio Doll, Ideal, $525.

Snow White and The Seven Dwarfs (Continued)	C6	C8	C10
Dopey Hand Puppet, composition w/bell and buckling belt, Crown Toys, 1938	90	135	225
Dopey Hand Puppet, Gund, 1950s	12	18	35
Dopey Marionette, Madame Alexander, 1938, 9-1/2" tall	100	150	250
Dopey Marionette, Peter Puppet Playthings, c. 1952	80	120	200
Dopey Party Mask, 1937	20	50	75
Dopey Soaky	17	30	50
Dopey Squeeze Toy, rubber, 1950s, 10" high	10	15	35
Dopey Tin Wind-up, Marx, 1938	263	395	575
Grumpy, stuffed w/molded oilcloth face, Ideal, 11-1/2" high	90	135	200
Grumpy Doll, composition w/velvet clothes, Knickerbocker, 9" high	100	150	250
Grumpy Doll, Ideal, 1938, 11" high	80	120	185

Snow White and The Seven Dwarfs (Continued)	C6	C8	C10
Grumpy Figure, Ideal, 7" high	140	210	300
Grumpy Figure, lead, Britains, 1-1/2" high	40	60	100
Grumpy Marionette, Madame Alexander, 1938, 9-1/2" tall	100	150	250
Grumpy Par-T Mask, 1937	10	30	50
Grumpy Squeeze Toy, rubber, 1950s	10	15	35
Happy Doll, Ideal, 7" high	130	195	300
Happy Doll, Ideal, 1938, 12" high	110	165	250
Happy Figure, lead, Britains, 1-1/2"	30	45	85
Happy Figure, Seiberling, 1938, 5-3/4"	60	90	150
Happy Marionette, Madame Alexander, 1938, 9-1/2" high	110	155	250
Happy Party Mask, 1937	40	60	80
Happy Squeeze Toy, rubber, 1950s	10	15	35
Horace Horsecollar Hand Puppet, Gund, c. 1960	17	25	50

Pinocchio Figure, Kreuger, $330. Photo courtesy PB Eighty-Four, New York

A 1940 ad/offer for the Pinocchio Mask by Gillette. Photo courtesy Rex and Richard Grey

Pinocchio Tin Wind-up, Linemar Co., 1950s, $725. Photo courtesy Don Hultzman

Snow White and The Seven Dwarfs (Continued)	C6	C8	C10
Huntsman, Madame Alexander, 1938, 9-1/2" tall	100	150	250
Prince, Madame Alexander, 1938, 9-1/2" tall	100	150	250
Seven Dwarfs Dolls, price for the set, Sieberling, 1938, 5-1/2" high	350	525	850

Snow White and The Seven Dwarfs (Continued)	C6	C8	C10
Seven Dwarfs Puppet-Marionettes, price for the set, Pelham	1500	2250	3500
Seven Dwarfs Squeeze Toy, vinyl, price for each, 1950s, approx. 8"	30	45	75
Sleepy Doll, Ideal, 7" high	125	188	300
Sleepy Doll, Ideal, 1938, 12" high	120	180	300

Mysterious Pluto, Marx, $325. Photo courtesy Don Hultzman

Playful Pluto & Goofy Wind-up, Linemar, 1950s, $2000. Photo courtesy Don Hultzman

Pluto Drum Major Tin Wind-up, Linemar, 1950s, $600. Photo courtesy Don Hultzman

---

PHOTOS NEEDED

We are always looking for good quality toy images for our archives. Photo quality is our highest consideration and any donated images must be in 35mm print or slide form.

If you can donate photos of toys not pictured here, please contact us at the following address:

O'Brien's Collecting Toys
Krause Publications
700 E. State St.
IOLA, WI 54990
(715) 445-4612
obrienk@krause.com

Snow White and The Seven Dwarfs (Continued)	C6	C8	C10
Sleepy Figure, lead, Britains, 1-1/2" high	45	68	100
Sleepy Marionette, Madame Alexander, 1938, 9-1/2" tall	100	150	250
Sleepy Party Mask, 1937	20	35	60
Sneezy Doll, Ideal, 7" high	125	188	300
Sneezy Doll, Ideal, 1938, 12" high	120	180	300
Sneezy Figure, lead, Britains, 1-1/2" high	45	68	100
Sneezy Figure, Seiberling, 1938, 5-1/8" high	60	90	150

Snow White and The Seven Dwarfs (Continued)	C6	C8	C10
Sneezy Marionette, Madame Alexander, 1938, 9-1/2" tall	100	150	250
Sneezy Party Mask, 1937	20	35	60
Sneezy Squeeze Toy, rubber, 1950s	10	15	20
Snow White and the Seven Dwarfs Blocks, set of eighteen w/box	175	263	350
Snow White and the Seven Dwarfs Dining Set, includes dishes, china, with cups, creamer, sugar bowl, plates, 4-1/2" dishes, 6" plate	210	315	420

Pluto Pulling Cart, Linemar, 1950s, $785. Photo courtesy Ed Hayes

Pluto Watch Me Roll Over Wind-up, Marx, 1939, $300.

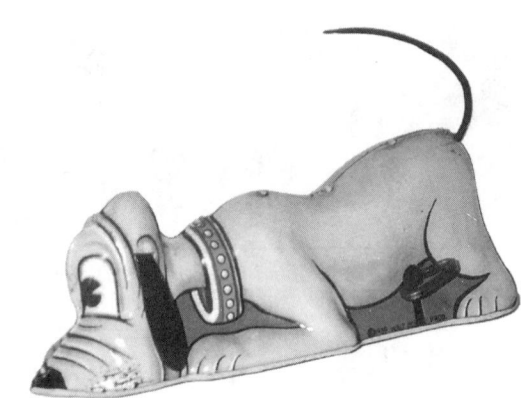

Wise Pluto Wind-up, Marx, 1939, $475. Photo courtesy Don Hultzman

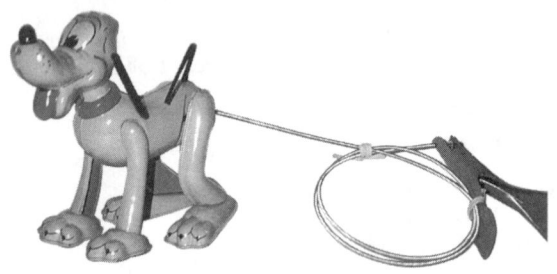

Pluto Squeeze Action Toy with Cable, Linemar, 1950s, $400. Photo courtesy Don Hultzman

Snow White and The Seven Dwarfs (Continued)	C6	C8	C10
Snow White and the Seven Dwarfs Drum, tin litho, 1930s	125	188	275
Snow White and the Seven Dwarfs Figures, each, No. 1654, Britains	20	60	100
Snow White and the Seven Dwarfs Figures, lead, by Lincoln Logs, price for the set	500	850	1200
Snow White and the Seven Dwarfs Musical Top, Chein, 6-1/2" across	110	165	250
Snow White and the Seven Dwarfs Sewing Set, Hasbro	20	30	65
Snow White Doll, Ideal, 1938, 15" high	150	225	350
Snow White Doll, Madame Alexander, 1938, 13" high	120	200	300
Snow White Doll, Knickerbocker, 1940s, 12" high	187	300	425

Snow White and The Seven Dwarfs (Continued)	C6	C8	C10
Snow White Figure, Seiberling, 8-3/4"	250	375	550
Snow White Figure, lead, Britains, 2-1/2"	45	68	125
Snow White Kitchen Set, Wolverine	60	90	150
Snow White Marionette, Madame Alexander, 1938, 9-1/2" tall	150	250	300
Snow White Party Mask	20	30	60
Snow White Sink and Stove, Wolverine	40	60	100
Snow White Soaky	17	30	50
Snow White Washing Machine, Revell Pastics, c. 1950, 7-1/2" high w/wringer	80	120	200
Wicked Witch, Madame Alexander, 1938, 9-1/2" tall	100	150	250
Witch Party Mask	20	30	50

Bashful Doll (Snow White and The Seven Dwarfs), Ideal, 1938, $200.

Doc Doll (Snow White and The Seven Dwarfs), Ideal, 1938, $190.

Dopey Doll (Snow White and The Seven Dwarfs), Ideal, 1938, $350.

Three Little Pigs	C6	C8	C10
Big Bad Wolf, stuffed toy in tux w/carnation, glass eyes, 20" tall..	450	675	1000
Big Bad Wolf and The Three Little Pigs, four-piece set, Linemar, 1950s, 4-1/4" tall	750	1125	1500
Big Bad Wolf Halloween Costume, 4" high	60	90	150
Big Bad Wolf Pinback, celluloid, 1-1/4"...	38	100	150
Three Little Pigs Acrobats, celluloid, Japan	312	465	675
Three Little Pigs Clothes Washer, Chein	102	153	250
Three Little Pigs Drummer, Schuco, 1930s, 4-1/2" tall	175	300	400
Three Little Pigs Figures, wood w/fiber arms and legs, Borgfeldt, c. 1933, 3-1/4" high.....................	120	180	275
Three Little Pigs Flutist, Schuco, 1930s, 4-1/2" tall	175	263	375
Three Little Pigs Par-T Mask, 1933..	40	60	80

Three Little Pigs (Continued)	C6	C8	C10
Three Little Pigs Sand Bucket, 3" tall...	30	45	75
Three Little Pigs Violinist, Schuco, 1930s, 4-1/2" tall	212	318	450
Three Little Pigs Walkers Tin Wind-up, price for each, Linemar	130	195	300

Uncle Scrooge	C6	C8	C10
Uncle Scrooge Hand Puppet, wearing high hat, 1960s	20	50	75
Uncle Scrooge Limousine, w/"$" on back fender	110	185	275
Uncle Scrooge Squeeze Toy Bank, vinyl, c. 1960, 7" high	40	85	125

Walt Disney	C6	C8	C10
Character Carousel, Linemar Co., 1950s, 7" high w/3" characters....	300	450	600
Character T.V. Set, Automatic Toy Co., 1950s, 5" cubic	150	225	300
Friction Delivery Wagon, features Mickey, Donald, Pluto, etc., Linemar, 1950s, 6" long..............	450	675	900

Grumpy Doll (Snow White and The Seven Dwarfs), Ideal, 1938, $185.

Happy Doll (Snow White and The Seven Dwarfs), Ideal, 1938, $250.

Sleepy Doll (Snow White and The Seven Dwarfs), Ideal, 1938, $300.

Walt Disney (Continued)

	C6	C8	C10
Friction Go-Mobile, features Mickey, Pluto, Donald, etc., Marx, 1960s, 6" long	150	225	300
Mechanical Tricycle, features Pluto, Mickey, Donald, etc., Linemar, 1950s, 4" high	200	300	400
Stars Bus, Gong Bell, 19" long	450	675	900
Television Car, Marx, 1950s, 7-1/2" long	275	365	550

Winnie the Pooh

	C6	C8	C10
Eeyore Squeeze Doll, vinyl, 1960s	37	56	100
Piglet Squeeze Doll, vinyl, 1960s	9	16	25

Winnie the Pooh (Continued)

	C6	C8	C10
Tigger Squeeze Doll, 1960s, 9"	9	13	25

Zorro

	C6	C8	C10
Flintlock Pistol, Marx	35	75	125
Hand Puppet, Gund	50	75	100
Hat, hideaway mask and gloves, 1950s	46	70	100
Play Set, Marx	400	600	800
Ring, black top w/"Z" and "Zorro" name	22	40	60
Sword, 1960s, 24" long	5	20	35
Zorro on Rearing Horse, Marx	160	240	320

Sneezy Doll (Snow White and The Seven Dwarfs), Ideal, 1938, $300.

Seven Dwarfs Dolls (Snow White and The Seven Dwarfs), Sieberling, 1938, $850. Photo courtesy Stan Alekna

Snow White Doll (Snow White and The Seven Dwarfs), Ideal, 1938, $350.

Seven Dwarfs Puppet-Marionettes, Pelham, $3500.

A 1938 ad for the Snow White and The Seven Dwarfs figures by Seiberling.

DOLLHOUSES AND MINIATURE FURNITURE

by Marcie and Bob Tubbs

Dollhouses and the miniature furniture and accessories to fit them were originally made not as toys, but to assist in the education of refined young women of the Victorian era. As "pictures of the times" they were designed to be looked at, not played with. They were often made by German toymakers, for the English market. Following the pattern established in the latter part of the 19th century in Europe, U.S. companies like Bliss, McLaughlin, and Converse began making houses of heavy printed cardboard or wood covered with brightly and highly detailed lithographed paper. Furniture was made of cardboard or wood by some of these same manufacturers. After World War I, an ever-growing number of American toymakers entered the dollhouse market. Gottschalk continued to lead the market in Germany, Triang established itself in England, and U.S. companies like Dowst Brothers, Schoenhut, Tynietoy, and Frier Steel manufactured dollhouse of cardboard, wood, and steel. Dowst also made their famous line of metal furniture called Tootsietoy, and Arcade followed suit with cast metal furniture. Until its bankruptcy in 1934, Schoenhut continued its highly collectible line of houses and furniture and Strombecker made its name with a line of wood furniture that was made until the early 1960s. Wood was the furniture of choice in the 1940s, made by companies like Strombecker, Kage, Nancy Forbes, and Donna Lee. Cardboard houses by Built-Rite and Jayline were plentiful.

As WWII ended, consumers had a huge pent-up demand for goods that had been scarce during the War. The peacetime economy boomed as American industry became the supplier to the rest of the war ravaged world. Unlike the Depression years, which had immediately preceded the War, employment surged, as did disposable family income. The American toy industry utilizing materials and mass production techniques developed during the War answered the demands of the Baby Boomers and their parents. Low cost toys were made available through 5&10¢ stores and through the catalogs of Sears and Montgomery Wards.

As suburbia grew, so did the types of miniature dollhouses. Following the prewar trend, houses made of

fiberboard served an upscale toy market. Fiberboard houses were most often silk screened in four colors. The number of colors and the screening method limited the interior and exterior detail. The flat sides and roofs were screwed together, forming sturdy houses capable of withstanding a lot of play. Windows frames of plastic or metal were sometimes inserted in the exterior walls. Hinged wooden doors generally opened and closed, and a few of the houses contained staircases and closets. The houses were roughly scaled 3/4" to 1', making it easy for little hands to rearrange dolls and furniture inside the four to six room houses. Rich Toy, Keystone, DeLuxe Game, and Jayline Toys are the best known of the fiberboard manufactures. Many of these durable homes survive today.

Sheet metal provided postwar toy manufacturers with a more flexible material with which to design houses that copied the styles of the day. The metal walls, floors, and roofs were lithographed with the designs of the interiors and exteriors of the houses, prior to being stamped from large sheets of the thin metal. As time progressed the detail became quite elaborate. Lithography allowed a full range of colors. Perhaps the first of the postwar steel houses, were the two houses produced by National Can Company and marketed under the Playsteel name. In 1948, T. Cohn introduced a now well-recognized house with a red tiled roof. The house had five rooms and an upstairs patio. Each of these earlier houses was scaled 3/4" to 1' and well matched the newly introduced plastic dollhouse furniture. Soon thereafter, Meritoy of Boston introduced an interesting two-story Cape in a smaller scale.

World War II demonstrated the utility of plastic materials, and industries had honed their thermoplastic molding and sheet metal stamping skills. Plastic toys could be made in high-speed processes with minimal need for hand finishing. Toys could be produced in any color of the rainbow as well as in combinations of colors. They were hygienic, and could be formed with amazing details. Dollhouse furniture and accessories could be produced to resemble their real life counterparts. Couches could be made with wood toned bases and brightly colored upholstery. Swings could be made to hold and move little family members. Sewing machines had moving parts as did trash cans, lawn mowers and ironing boards. The toys were aimed at little homemakers eager to be just like their parents.

Renwal, Ideal, and Plasco made a wide range of furniture, while manufacturers like Acme-Thomas, Irwin, and Commonwealth produced numerous accessories that complemented the furniture lines.

In 1950, the market changed dramatically when Louis Marx first introduced a dollhouse packaged with its own furniture, car, four children, and play yard that sold for $3.95. Although Marx produced large and well-detailed dollhouses in its 3/4" scale deluxe and "Marxie Mansion" lines, the majority of its houses were scaled 1/2" to 1'. They ranged in style from two story colonials with or without attached family room to L-shaped ranches and split-levels. Interior lithography changed from time to time, reflecting "modern" decorating trends. The smaller 1/2" scale caught on and dominated the market in the '50s and '60s as companies like Superior and Wolverine, following the Marx example, introduced 1/2" scale houses filled with one piece molded furniture usually from polyethylene, a soft flexible plastic.

Many of the furniture manufacturers produced dollhouse sized dolls to inhabit their houses. For example, Renwal offered a four member hard plastic family, fully jointed to allow them to sit, stand, bend, or kneel. Ideal introduced a now-scarce family from rubber with moveable arms, and in the 1960s introduced a fully poseable family for their *Petite Princess* line. Marx supplied molded dolls in many different poses with their houses and later made families of bendable dolls. Independent dollhouse doll manufacturers like Flagg, Tiny Town, and Twinky produced high quality dolls dressed in cloth outfits to live in the miniature homes. Other U.S. companies like Seiberling, Thomas, and Irwin all produced dolls that added play value to the dollhouses of the era. Foreign manufacturers like Grecon, Dol-Toi, and Erna Meyer made delightful dolls as well.

As in other areas of collecting, online auctions are a good source for dollhouses, miniatures and families, although wonderful finds can still be made at doll and miniature shows, antique shops and flea markets. Prices have continued to rise for the rarer and older pieces, whereas prices for common items have fallen. Condition and rarity continue to be the factors that determine price. A piece of unscratched, unbroken, or unrepaired, plastic toy without melt marks will command a much higher price than a well-played-with piece. Toys with moving parts and opening drawers and cabinet doors are generally priced higher than one-piece toys. Metal houses without rust, fading, bends, scratches, or dents are considered the most desirable, and are priced accordingly.

In recent years, online auctions make foreign toys more accessible, and miniatures and houses from companies like Kleeware, Triang, Mettoy, Eagle, and Reliable are being discovered. Auctions are featuring houses filled with a mix and match of desirable miniature pieces. As collectors fill their houses with furniture, they are turning to dollhouse dolls and accessories like dishes, garden tools, lamps, and paintings to add play value and character to their collections.

Baby Boomer dollhouse collectors can access the Web site for the collectors club, Dollhouse Toys n' Us, www.dollhousetoysnus.org, and learn about joining the organization and receiving the regular mailing of *Dollhouse and Miniatures Newsletter*. Flagg dolls enjoy a very nice dedicated site at www.home.att.net/~flaggdoll/. A number of fine books by Dian Zillner and Patty Cooper, and Charles Donovan and Mary Brett have been published in recent years devoted to a full study of the hobby.

Contributor: Marcie Tubbs began collecting baby boomer dollhouses, dollhouse furniture and figures after purchasing a furnished T. Cohn dollhouse at the Brimfield, MA, antique show a number of years ago. She enjoys collecting and researching the history of the subject. Her focus in recent years has been on dollhouse dolls. She and her husband, Bob, have written a number of magazine articles on dollhouses and their inhabitants. She is always interested in adding unusual examples to her collection, and enjoys hearing from others about the hobby. Marcie can be reached online at cardad@aol.com.

Various Acme/Thomas Toy playground and nursery pieces, clockwise left to right: Baby Carriage ($7); Hammock ($15); Horsehead Stroller ($10); Slide ($10); Single Swing ($12); Dogsled with harness and dog ($40); Express wagon ($10); Horsehead Seesaw ($8); Tommy Horse ($15). Photo courtesy Marcie Tubbs

Toy Companies- A Review
by Marcie and Bob Tubbs

Acme/Thomas Toy

Acme Plastics Manufacturing Co., originally founded in 1935, merged with and became the marketing arm of Thomas Toy Company in 1945. Acme/Thomas never attempted to produce a line of dollhouse furniture with the breadth of Renwal, Ideal Plasco, or Marx, but instead focused on toys with high play value. These pieces were brightly colored nursery and outdoor toys in 3/4" scale that complemented the toys of the other manufacturers. Acme/Thomas also produced a number of dollhouse dolls from the rubber-like Vinylite, which are often found with Baby Boomer plastics. Unfortunately, the chemicals from the Vinylite causes melt marks when the dolls come in contact with hard polystyrene toys. The hard plastic pieces are generally marked either Acme or Thomas along with one or more mold numbers.

Acme/Thomas Toy	C10
Baby Carriage, No. I-139	7
Dogsled with Harness and Dog, No. I-184	40
Double Swing, No. I-154	20
Express Wagon, No. I-144	10
Ferris Wheel, No. I-163	30
Hammock, No. I-166	15
Horsehead Seesaw, No. I-159	8
Horsehead Stroller, No. I-156	10
Horsehead Swing, No. I-154	40
Single Swing, No. I-154	12
Slide, No. I-171	10
Tommy Horse, No. I-179	15
Triple Swing, No. I-154	30

Commonwealth

Commonwealth Plastics Corporation of Leominster, MA, started as a manufacturer of buttons and costume jewelry. It branched into the production of a small line of party favors, nationality dolls and dollhouse accessories that are quite collectible today. The accessories, like the motorized reel-type lawn mower which makes an engine sound when rolled along and the lovebird cage on a stand, accent the furniture of the larger toy manufacturers.

Commonwealth	C10
Birdcage	30
Lamppost with Mailbox	15
Lawn Mower	20
Watering Can and Garden tools	15
Wheelbarrow	8

Flagg Dolls

Flagg dollhouse dolls were introduced in the late 1940's by Sheila and Charles Flagg of Jamaica Plain, MA. They produced the dolls in different scales, including 3/4" and 1" for dollhouse play and 7" and 10 1/2" display dolls. The dolls had one-piece bodies made of flexible, rubber-like plastic. In the 3/4" line, the mother and father dolls were 4 1/2" tall, the children 3 1/2" and the babies, 1 3/4". The faces of early dolls were actually hand painted by Sheila Flagg. She designed the cloth costumes, which are usually stapled to their plastic bodies. Families were sold dressed and undressed. The dolls are not marked. Many extended family members, community helpers, and character dolls were marketed including grandmother and grandfather, mammy, nurse and doctor, teacher, policeman, fireman, postman, preacher, nun, Indians, Pilgrims, cowboys, farmers, wedding parties, and dancers. There was also a line of "Mother Goose" play dolls. The dolls were sold well into the 1980's.

Birdcage, Commonwealth, $30. Photo courtesy Marcie Tubbs

This plastic Garden Furniture from Ideal, valued at $700-$750, is the most highly sought-after Ideal boxed set. The set includes: Patio Umbrella, Plastic Pole, Lawn Bench, Doghouse, Black Scottie Dog, Pool, Birdbath, Circular Lawn Table, Lawn Chair, Picnic Table, Trellis and Lawn Chair. Photo courtesy Marcie Tubbs

Frier Steel

Located in St. Louis MO, Frier Steel made three different models of steel dollhouses in the late 1920's known as the Cozytown Cottage, Cozytown Manor, and Cozytown Mansion. Considered premium toys, the original retail prices ranged between $9.00 and $18.50, quite expensive for the era. The interiors of some models were plain and the company boasted: "You can paper every room yourself." Other models have been found with a silk screened interior.

Ideal

The Ideal Toy & Novelty Co., originator of the "teddy bear", was established in 1903 and became the largest of the postwar American toy and doll manufacturers. Ideal introduced five different lines of dollhouse furniture for Baby Boomers. In 1947, they introduced a line of beautifully detailed 3/4" scale furniture from brightly colored hard plastic. The toys generally are marked with the Ideal trademark and one or more mold numbers. Early boxed sets included room box walls. In later boxed sets, the furniture could be seen through cellophane panels.

The nursery and outdoor pieces tend to bring higher prices today than the more common living, dining, and bedroom pieces. Two different kitchen lines were sold during this period, a standard and the more desirable deluxe version. The slightly larger and more detailed deluxe line also included a dishwasher, a front opening washing machine, and a mangle with a rotating drum. The 3/4" scale furniture was produced until 1952. In 1950 and 1951, Ideal produced a set of furniture known as Young Decorator. The Young Decorator furniture was scaled at almost 1.5" to 1' making it easy to rearrange and play with on a blueprint styled playmat included in each box.

In 1964, Ideal Toy Corporation (the name was changed in 1951) introduced another line of dollhouse furniture in 3/4" to 1' scale. The Petite Princess Fantasy Furniture with real cloth upholstery had glass and metal details and accessories to highlight the plastic furniture. The furniture was too expensive to appeal to the mass toy market, and in 1965 the line was reintroduced as Princess Patti furniture. The materials used to decorate the Princess Patti furniture were not as expensive as the Petite Princess line. With some nod to reality, the Princess Patti line included the, now rare, kitchen, bathroom, and TV set. Much of this Fantasy furniture is found individually packaged in boxes today. Again in 1969, Ideal marketed a vinyl fold-up dollhouse together with plastic furniture made in Hong Kong. The furniture is hallmarked "1969 Ideal."

Ideal	C10
Bed, No. I-0959	10
Birdbath	15
Black Scottie Dog	40
Carpet Sweeper, No. I-1563	15
Chinese Modern Red Dining Table, No. I-0980	25
Circular Lawn Table, No. I-1003	15
Coffee Table	6
Doghouse, No. I-1016	40
Lawn Bench, No. I-1008	12
Lawn Chair, No. I-1018	10
Lawn Lounge Chair, No. I-1115	12
Lawn Mower, No. I-1315	20

Left to right: Sofa, Ideal, $10; Coffee Table, Ideal, $6; Sofa, Renwal, $8; Pedestal End Table, Renwal, $5. Photo courtesy Marcie Tubbs

Young Decorator furniture from Ideal. Left to right: Television, $50; Coffee Table, $10; Torchiere Lamp, $30; Sectional Sofa, individual pieces, $10. Photo courtesy Marcie Tubbs

Left to right: Kiddie Car, Renwal, $35; Tricycle, Renwal, $17. Photo courtesy Marcie Tubbs

Ideal (Continued)	**C10**
Octagonal Sanbox with Pole and Umbrella, No. I-1312	65
Patio Umbrella, No. I-1004	10
Petite Princess, Boudoir Chaise Lounge, No. 44081	15
Petite Princess, Little Princess Royal, Bed, No. 4416-4	25
Petite Princess, Lyre Table with Lamp and Painting, No. 4426-3	18
Petite Princess, Palace Chest with Picture, No. 4420-6	12
Petite Princess, Royal Dressing Table and Stool, No. 4417-2	35
Picnic Table, No. I-1000	20
Plastic Pole	5
Pool, No. I-1060	65
Red Breakfront, No. I-0979	20
Red Buffet, No. I-0983	15
Red Dining Chair with Arms, No. I-0948	12
Red Dining Chair without Arms, No. I-0948	10

Ideal (Continued)	**C10**
Seesaw, No. I-1329	40
Sofa, No. I-0942	10
Trellis, No. I-1012	80
Vaccuum Cleaner, No. I-1559	17
Well Pump, No. I-1084	30
Young Decorator Bathinette, No. I-2082	35
Young Decorator Bathtub, No. I-2172	18
Young Decorator Bed, No. I-2057	15
Young Decorator Blue Bathroom Chair, No. I-2098	12
Young Decorator Buffet, No. I-2034	12
Young Decorator China Cabinet, No. I-2036	18
Young Decorator Coffee Table, No. I-2089	10
Young Decorator Crib, No. I-2109	30
Young Decorator Diaper Pail/Waste Can, No. I-2170	20
Young Decorator Dining Chair, No. I-2045	6
Young Decorator Dining Table, No. I-2040	12
Young Decorator High Chair, No. I-2179	25

Two-story lithographed masonite house with six rooms, fireplace, stairs and closet, 3/4-inch-scle, Keystone, $175. Photo courtesy Marcie Tubbs

Two-story Lithographed Fiberboard with Four Rooms, Front Stoop with Benches, 3/4-inch-scale, Rich, $100. Photo courtesy Marcie Tubbs

Ideal (Continued)

	C10
Young Decorator Kitchen Chair, No. I-2098	10
Young Decorator Kitchen Sink, No. I-2062	45
Young Decorator Kitchen Table, No. I-2100	15
Young Decorator Living Room Sofa Center Curved Section, No. I-2079	10
Young Decorator Living Room Sofa Center Square Section, No. I-2078	10
Young Decorator Living Room Sofa End Section, No. I-2077	10
Young Decorator Nightstand, No. I-2076	10
Young Decorator Playpen, No. I-2108	30
Young Decorator Range, No. I-2052	20
Young Decorator Refrigerator, No. I-2048	18
Young Decorator Sink, No. I-2164	12
Young Decorator Television Set, No. I-2090	50
Young Decorator Toilet, No. I-2168	30
Young Decorator Torchiere Lamp, No. I-2081	30
Young Decorator Tricycle with Bell	30
Young Decorator Vanity, No. I-2086	15
Young Decorator Vanity Stool, No. I-2060	7
Young Decorator Wardrobe, No. I-2084	15

Irwin

Founded by Irwin Cohn in 1925 the company became the largest distributor of plastic toys by the mid 1940s. It consolidated its Fitchburg, MA, and Nashua, NH, manufacturing facilities in Leominster , MA, sometime in the 1960s. In dollhouse toys, the company produced housecleaning and lawn tools and sets of dollhouse dishes. In 1964, Irwin introduced a line of Interior Decorator sets featuring room layouts, furniture, and a family. The colors of the wallpaper, rugs, and upholstery were coordinated with the House and Garden magazine color palette for that year.

Keystone

Among the nicest of the postwar fiberboard homes were those made by Keystone Manufacturing Company of Boston, MA between 1940 and the early 1950s. In the '40s, Keystone shipped their dollhouses already assembled, a big plus for harried parents on Christmas Eve. The Keystone fiberboards generally have three distinct features: a curving staircase, a fireplace, and an upstairs closet. The interior walls often have silk-screened wallpaper and floor designs. The windows are either metal or plastic framed, depending on the age of the house. Unique to Keystone were three "Put-A-Way" houses with one or two extensions that folded back into the house when play was finished. The dollhouses were often marketed with 3/4" scale plastic furniture. Many Keystone houses are marked with the company name and some have a turntable attached to the bottom.

Keystone, 3/4"-scale

	C10
Two-story Lithographed Masonite with Eight Rooms, Double Wing "Put-A-Way"	200
Two-story Lithographed Masonite with Six Room, Single Wing "Put-A-Way"	175
Two-story Lithographed Masonite with Six Rooms, Fireplace, Stairs and Closet	150

Marx Toys

The Louis P. Marx Company became a dominant manufacturer of toys during the postwar era. Founding his toy company in 1917, Louis Marx applied modern mass production methods to the making of toys. The efficiencies he achieved both in manufacturing and marketing made affordable toys with great

Marx 1/2-inch-scale furniture. Left to Right: Milk Bar, $12; Stools, $4 each; Round Table, $4; Kitchen Chairs, $5 each; Ping-Pong Table, $15; Circular Couch, $7; Coffee Table, $7; Piano, $8; Piano Bench, $3; Juke Box, $12. Photo courtesy Marcie Tubbs

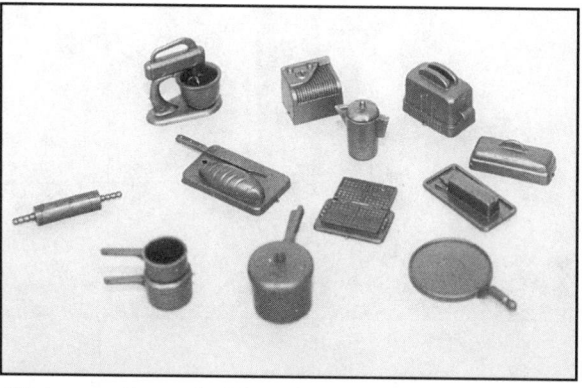

Kitchen appliances by Marx, $3-5, each. Photo courtesy Marcie Tubbs

play value available to all. In 1949, Marx introduced a two story brightly lithographed tin dollhouse filled with six rooms of hard plastic dollhouse furniture. The house and furniture were produced in 1/2" scale. While the detail of the interior was enhanced by the use of four-color lithography, the furniture was of a single color, one-piece construction with no moving parts. During the 25 years that the Marx Company marketed dollhouses, approximately 15 different styles were produced, although there are many decorating and packaging variations of each style as Marx constantly sought appropriate price points for each distribution channel. While the majority of the houses were 1/2" scale, the houses in the 3/4" scale deluxe and Marxie Mansion lines are some of the best of the Baby Boomer dollhouses. The large-scale mansions came in 6 and 7 room versions, electrified and non-electrified, with and without cloth curtains, cornices, awnings, shutters, and doorbells.

As the Marx dollhouses changed over time, so did the furniture packaged with them. The early hard polystyrene pieces were replaced with softer, less breakable polyethylene. Styles for the 1/2" scale furniture included "overstuffed" traditional, French Provincial and contemporary. Furniture and accessories were made for the primary living areas of the houses as well as for laundry rooms, family rooms, patios, gardens, and swimming pools. The hard plastic pieces are often marked with the Marx logo, but the matching soft plastic pieces sometimes are not. In 1964, Marx introduced a beautiful line of plastic furniture known in the United States as Marx Little Hostess and in Canada as Little Miss Deb. The furniture was often multi colored or had gilt detailing and was accompanied by many accessories. In 1976, after the sale of the Marx Company, the line was reintroduced in England as Amanda Ann.

Marx, 3/4"-scale — C10

	C10
Common Items, soft plastic (prices can range between $1 and $3)	3
Kitchen Appliances, Pots and Pans	5
Kitchen Chair, hp	2
Kitchen Table, hp	4
Living Room and Dining Room Boxed Set	60
Refrigerator, hp	4
Sink, hp	4
Stove, hp	4

Marx, Marx Houses — C10

	C10
Colonnade	85

Marx Toys, 1/2"-scale — C10

	C10
Captain's Chair	4
Circular Couch	7
Coffee Table, hard plastic	7
Common Hard Plastic Furniture, price for each	4
Common Soft Plastic Items, price for each	1
Juke Box	12
Kitchen	8
Kitchen Appliances, Pots and Pans, price for each	4
Kitchen Chair	5
Milk Bar	12
Piano	8
Piano Bench	3
Ping-Pong Table	15
Refrigerator	5
Round Table	4
Sink	5
Soft Plastic Furniture	1
Stool	4
Stove	5

Marx Toys, Marx Houses — C10

	C10
L-shaped Ranch with TV Antennae, Cupola, Chimney and Room Divider	100
Split Level with Front and Back Steps, Railings, Fireplace and Chimney	100

Marx Toys, Marx Houses, 1/2"-scale — C10

	C10
Two-story with Attached Breezeway and Rumpus Room	110
Two-story with Disney Nursery and Garage	85
Two-story with Tin Soldier Nursery	50

Marx Toys, Marx Houses, 3/4"-scale — C10

	C10
Colonial Mansion with Florida room	150

Two-story house with attached breezeway and rumpus room, 1/2-inch-scale, Marx, $110. Photo courtesy Marcie Tubbs

Colonial Mansion with Florida room, 3/4-inch-scale, Marx, $150. Photo courtesy Marcie Tubbs

Marx Toys, Marx Little Hostess

	C10
Bench	12
Folding Screen	15
Hamper and Mirror	18
Medicine Cabinet	20
Sink/Vanity Combination	20
Toilet	15
Tub/Shower	20

Meritoy

Among the first of the postwar tin dollhouses is an easily recognized Cape Cod with three dormers produced by Meritoy Corporation of Boston. The six-room house was scaled close to 1/2" to 1', and the furnished versions were sold with either Allied or Kleeware half-scale, hard plastic furniture. The windows were made of a silk-screened sheet of plastic and are hard to find intact today.

Meritoy, 1/2"-scale

	C10
Two-story Cape Cod	120

Mettoy

Mettoy Playthings of the U.K. produced tin toys from the 1930s through the Baby Boomer era. The company produced a number of 1/2" scale tin houses as well as nicely detailed supermarket and hospital playsets. The houses and playsets were packaged with hard plastic accessories and soft plastic figures.

Mettoy

	C10
Two-story 1/2"-scale house	120

Plasco

The Plastic Art Toy Corporation of America produced the Little Homemaker line of dollhouse furniture from 1947 until nearly the end of the Baby Boomer era. The 3/4" scale furniture owed much of it popularity to its affordable price and broad product line. The inside covers of early boxed sets included room like settings. As time progressed Plasco was sold in cellophane window boxes and on blister packs. Later versions of the furniture were cheaply produced and marketed without bases, legs, or headboards. This later furniture is not as highly valued as the older, more detailed pieces. As with many lines of dollhouse furniture, the nursery pieces are among the most prized. Plasco made several dollhouses, all of which are hard to find today.

Plasco

	C10
Bathinette w/lid	30
Club Cahir w/base	7
Coffee Table	7
Crib	20
Fireplace w/book insert	25
Grandfather Clock	12
Highboy	10
Kitchen Pieces w/base	6
Nightstand	3
Sofa w/base	8
Television Set	25
Vanity Chair	3
Wing Chair w/base	7

Two-story Cape Cod, 1/2-inch-scale, Meritoy, $120. Photo courtesy Marcie Tubbs

Left to right: Television Set, Plasco, $25; Grandfather Clock, Plasco, $12. Photo courtesy Marcie Tubbs

Plastic Art Toy Corporation of America (Plasco)

	C10
Bathinette	30
Club Chair	7
Coffee Table	5
Crib	25
Fireplace	15
Grandfather Clock	15
Highboy	10
Nightstand	5
Sofa	10
Television Set	30
Vanity Chair	3
Wing Chair	7

Playsteel

Playsteel was the toy division of National Can Company. Immediately after the war, they introduced two five room tin dollhouses, a two story red roofed, brick and clapboard Colonial and a two story "Buck's County farmhouse" with a fieldstone exterior and blue slate roof. Early on, the houses were packed in boxes that were meant to serve as landscaped yards. The interiors of the two homes were identical. The panes of the windows were cut from the steel of the walls and the front door of the Buck's County house opened. The farmhouse was also packaged with two window boxes that attached to the second-story windows. The 3/4" scale was perfect for the furniture of Renwal, Ideal and Plasco, and mail-order catalogues and dimestores often featured the homes packaged with Renwal.

Playsteel, 3/4"-scale

	C10
Two-story "Bucks County" with Blue Roof	125
Two-story Colonial with Red Roof	125

Reliable

The needs of Canadian Baby Boomers were met nicely by the Reliable Plastics Company, Limited of Toronto. Reliable produced a wide range of hard plastic dollhouse toys. Many of the well-detailed pieces appear to be fashioned after or based upon the molds of Ideal, but others are quite individual in their styling. Most of the 3/4" scale toys are hallmarked.

Reliable

	C10
Bath Tub/Shower	25
Dresser with Mirror	12
Highboy	10
Nightstand	8
Swing Set	20
Table Lamp	15
Twin Bed	12
Vanity Dresser with Mirror	12
Vanity Stool	7

Renwal

Founded in 1939, Renwal is one of the best recognized of the Postwar manufacturers. Besides cars, trucks, and other "boys toys", Renwal produced a wide selection of dollhouse furniture, accessories, and dolls. The toys, made from the hard plastic polystyrene, were approximately scaled 3/4" to 1'. Almost all the pieces were hallmarked with the Renwal name and bear an item number. Introduced in 1945, early Renwal boxed sets contained a cardboard room box for displaying the furniture. Later versions of the furniture had opening drawers and doors. These, together with the later stenciled versions of the toys, bring higher prices today. Renwal stopped producing the furniture in 1956, and eventually the molds were sold. The more common pieces of furniture reappeared in the 1980s marked as made in Hong Kong.

Renwal

	C10
Bathtub, No. T95	7

Renwal (Continued)

	C10
Broom, No. 121	125
Carpet Sweeper with Rollers, No. 116	65
Dresser with Opening Drawer, No. B23	10
Dresser without Opening Drawer, No. B23	5
Dustpan	15
Family Members, price for each, No. 041-44	15
Hamper, No. T98	2
Highboy, No. B85	5
Mop, No. 117	40
Night Stand, No. B84	3
Pedestal End Table, No. L73	5
Scale, No. 010	10
Sewing Machine, No. 089	25
Sink, No. T96	5
Sofa, No. L78	8
Stool, No. 012	11
Toilet, No. T97	10
Trash Can with Flip-Top Lid, No. 064	12
Tricycle, No. 007	17
Twin Bed, No. B81	5
Vaccuum Cleaner, No. 037	20
Vanity Bench, No. L75	2
Vanity with Elaborate Filigree, No. B82	12
Vanity without Elaborate Filigree, No. B82	8

Rich

Rich Toy Manufacturing Co. enjoyed a prominent position among toy manufacturers for a period between 1935 to the early 1960s. Their fiberboard dollhouses, originally designed to match the wooden furniture of companies like Strombecker, worked perfectly with the plastics introduced in 1946. Rich houses can be found in many different styles ranging from 2 room cottages to a curved Art-Deco style. Rich also made a large and small version of a Fairy Castle based on the Coleen Moore dollhouse. Exteriors were generally applied with four-color silk screens. Early models had metal window frames that were replaced by plastic in later models. Interiors were sparsely decorated. Larger houses occasionally had staircases, and the most elaborate had rudimentary lighting and doorbells. Although the houses are rarely marked, they can often be identified by the pine tree design found on the window shutters.

Rich, 1"-scale

	C10
Two-story Lithographed Fiberboard with Six Rooms, Arts and Crafts-style Bungalow	250
Two-story Lithographed Fiberboard with Six Rooms, Interior Staircase	150

Rich, 3/4"-scale

	C10
Two-story Lithographed Fiberboard with Four Rooms, Front Stoop with Benches	100

Strombecker

Incorporated in 1913, the company began making wooden toys in 1919, adding 1" scale dollhouse furniture in 1931 and 3/4" scale furniture in 1934. A line of cardboard houses was marketed, although not manufactured by Strombecker between 1934 and the late 1950s. The dollhouse furniture was produced until the early 1960s.

T. Cohn/Superior

The single patio Spanish styled dollhouse with red tiled roof is among the most recognizable of the Baby Boomer dollhouses. Produced by T. Cohn of Brooklyn, NY, it was introduced in time for the 1948 Christmas season. The house was sold both furnished with furniture made by Plasco or Renwal and in an unfurnished version. The scale matched nicely with the furniture of Renwal and Ideal and the dollhouse is often now found with an eclectic mix of postwar furniture. The windows were made of metal and opened, casement style. T. Cohn continued to market a slightly smaller scaled Superior line through the 1960s, introducing several additional house styles. Houses produced before 1957 were packaged with hard plastic one color furniture marked Superior. After that time, the houses were sold with inferior 1/2" scale soft plastic furniture, reportedly made for Superior by Marx.

T. Cohn/Superior

	C10
Common Hard Plastic Furniture	4
Common Soft Plastic Furniture	1
Patio Bench - 3/4"-scale hard plastic w/tin umbrella and pole	50
Tin Swimming Pool	40

T. Cohn/Superior, T. Cohn Houses

	C10
Modern-style Pastel with Single Patio	75
Spanish-style with Double Patio	80
Three-room Ranch	45

T. Cohn/Superior, T. Cohn Houses, 3/4"-scale

	C10
Spanish-style with Single Patio	100

Tiny Town Dolls

Tiny Town dolls were made in San Francisco, CA, by Alma LeBlanc, formerly an artist with the Nancy Ann Doll Company. Tiny Towns were made in the late 1940s in several different scales. The dolls are flexible with bodies of cloth over wire and limbs of thread wrapped wire Metal shoes, with the name of the doll sometimes stamped on the bottom, are a distinguishing feature. Their felt faces have hand painted features and the dolls are wigged. It is still possible to find a Tiny Town MIB. The doll might have an original wrist tag revealing its name and the company name. Also included in the box was a pamphlet listing available dolls. Some known Tiny Town's are a school set, Mr. & Mrs. Santa Claus, nationalities, a family of four and a series of girl dolls dressed for different activities.

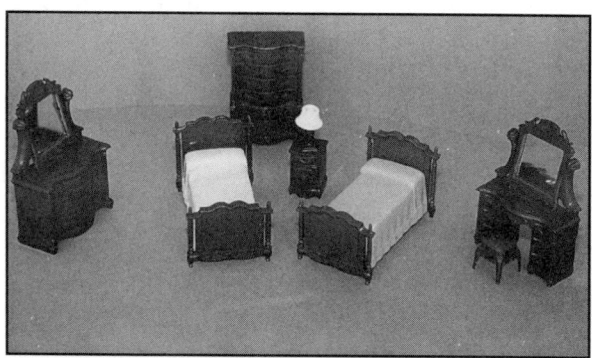

Left to right: Reliable Bedroom set-Dresser with mirror ($12); Highboy ($10); Twin Bed ($12 each); Nightstand ($8); Table Lamp ($15); Vanity Dresser with Mirror ($12); Vanity Stool ($7). Photo courtesy Marcie Tubbs

Left to right: Dresser without opening drawers, Renwal; Twin Bed, Renwal No. B23, $5; Dresser with opening drawers, Renwal No. B23, $10. Photo courtesy Marcie Tubbs

Renwal accessories without original cards. Left to right: Vacuum ($20), Mop ($40), Trash Can with Flip-top Lid ($12), Dustpan ($15), Carpet Sweeper with Rollers ($65) and Broom ($125). Photo courtesy Marcie Tubbs

Left to right: Father, Mother and Brother, Renwal, $15 each. Photo Courtesy Marcie Tubbs

Renwal accessories. Left to right: Stool ($11); Trash can with Flip-top Lid ($12); Dustpan ($15); Scale ($10); Vacuum Cleaner ($20); Broom ($125); Mop ($40); and the Carpet Sweeper with Rollers ($65). Photo courtesy Marcie Tubbs

Left to right: Sewing Machine, Renwal, $25; Sewing Machine, Ideal, $25. Photo courtesy Marcie Tubbs.

Spanish-style house with single patio, 1/2-inch-scale, T. Cohn/Superior, $80. Photo courtesy Marcie Tubbs

Tomy Smaller Homes

In 1980 Tomy introduced a modern dollhouse and complete line of furniture and accessories. Made in Japan from plastic, the furniture also featured fabric upholstery and bed clothes. The furniture was up-to-date and very detailed. The 3/4" scale house was sold unfurnished and each room of furniture and a family was sold separately. Individual accessory packages MOC are highly sought after today.

Tootsietoy (Dowst Manufacturing)

One of the oldest U.S. toy manufacturing companies, Dowst was founded in 1878 by the Dowst brothers. At the turn of the century it began selling cast metal charms and miniatures. In 1922, the company introduced a line of 1/2" scale cast metal enameled dollhouse furniture under the Tootsietoy brand. Dowst also sold the furniture under the "My Dolly's" brand, and Sears and Roebuck offered the furniture under the "Daisy" trademark. A second version of the furniture was introduced in 1930. The company also distributed cardboard houses produced by Wayne Paper Co. under the Tootsietoy and Daisy names. The furniture and houses were produced throughout the 1930s, but did not reappear after WWII.

Twinky Dolls

Originated by Ethel R. Strong of Lynnfield, MA in 1946, "Twinky" dolls are among the most beautiful of all the postwar dollhouse dolls. The original five-member family was molded in hard plastic parts, hand strung and decorated by Ethel Strong. She also designed their costumes and eventually began a cottage industry to help with the production of the hand-sewn clothing. The dolls were a standard 1" scale and were not marked. Over time, this family expanded to include household help, playmates, holiday figures, military, and nationality dolls with intricate costumes. For a short time in 1950, the dolls were sold through the Ohio based dollhouse accessory company, Grandmother Stover's. The dolls were only produced until 1953 and are now very hard to find.

Wolverine

Founded in 1903 by Benjamin Bain of Pittsburgh, PA, the company made a wide range of toys starting in 1920. Between 1972 and 1990 the company produced and sold dollhouses and furniture. A line of 3/4" scale tin lithographed houses was packaged with one-piece molded soft plastic furniture and figures. Later, the company also sold a series of 1" scale fiberboard houses and plastic furniture in its "Rite Scale" line. The company changed its name to Today's Kids in 1986.

ERECTOR SETS

Erector Set collecting is enjoying a renewed popularity. Very few modern toys stimulate the imagination as did the toys of old, and collectors are recognizing the significance of early "educational" toys.

A.C. Gilbert, the inventor of Erector sets, was a 1908 graduate of Yale University, a medical doctor, as well as the winner of the gold medal for the pole vault at the 1908 World Olympics in London. In addition to his many other talents, A.C. Gilbert was an accomplished professional magician and an outgoing, gregarious individual.

Erector went through three development stages. From 1913 to 1923 (Stage I) the sets featured plenty of large, strong girders. Ads showed boys sitting on the bridges built with Erector sets—and it was no exaggeration. After the trauma of World War I and the consequent inflation in the U.S., Erector was redesigned and slimmed down. Girders were smaller, narrower, and lighter, but Gilbert also introduced countless other shapes to make the Erector system more versatile and more capable of building unique and beautiful models. Stage II was born in 1924 and continued on until the advent of Stage III in 1963, the end of the Gilbert company.

A.C. Gilbert ceased to be a major toy producer after 1962. The decline was somewhat agonizing, ending with the purchase of the rights to the famous name "Erector" by Meccano, SA of France, which also acquired Gilbert's old competitor in England.

Rarity

Of about 45 million Erector sets produced, ninety percent probably went to people who didn't take very good care of them. That leaves about 4.5 million fairly nice sets in a good state of preservation, but you should figure that about half of these were thrown out or otherwise disposed of. Now we have about 2.25 million pretty nice Erector sets left.

Where are they? Most of us are inclined towards flea markets and garage sales, but this is probably not your best source. You may get lucky, but in most cases this represents the low end of the market. Many sets form these sources are somewhat "mixed trash." Whether intentional or not, a set may be only fractionally complete and usually will contain a variety of parts from different years mixed together. If you are looking for fine-quality sets in the C10 category, carefully watch for estate auctions, dealers, or buy from established collectors who are continually refining their collections.

Collector Clubs

Many avid collectors are members of the A.C. Gilbert Heritage Society or the Southern California Meccano and Erector Club. Connecting with other knowledgeable collectors is one of the best methods to acquire new sets for your collection.

The A.C. Gilbert Heritage Society may be reached at 1440 Whalley Ave., PMB 252, New Haven. CT 06515. Their Web site is www.acghs.org.

The Southern California Meccano and Erector Club may be reached at P.O. Box 130213, Carlsbad, CA 92013-0213. Their Web site is www.scmec.us.

Value

Keep in mind that unless a set was carefully preserved in a dry climate, there is little chance of acquiring a set that is in truly C10 condition (meaning in the same condition as it left the factory). Standard grading categories are listed below.

C10: 100 percent complete. All parts pinned with the original T-clips; all cardboards present; no rust or white rust; manual present, near perfect, labels near perfect; only the lightest of scratches, parts may show very light cloudy oxidation (dingy).

C8: 98 to 100 percent complete. Some or all cardboards present but may not be all correctly pinned; manual present (may have folded corners); motor must be present and working; less than five percent of the parts may show the very slightest real rust (like in corners, the type that auto chrome polish can easily remove).

C6: 90 to 95 percent complete. Probably no cardboard; motor there and working; acceptable manual, labels may show serious wear; considerable scratching on bottom, some on top; minor dents in metal box; some sign of rust on five to ten percent of parts.

Note

This chapter has received a significant overhaul for this edition. The effort has been to present as complete a listing of Erector sets as possible (though there is still much work to be done), but obtaining accurate values for all of the expanded listings proved problematic and so NPF (No Price Found) appears where no values were available. If you have information to share regarding the sets or their prices, please contact the editor.

Contributors: Contributors to the previous edition included, William Harrison III, Paul Piontkowski, and Francis Usinski.

TYPE I: 1913 TO 1923
(THE ERA OF GIRDERS 1-1/8" WIDE)

1913	C4	C6	C8	C10
Erector No. 00, cardboard box, built 13 models, small instruction sheet......	NPF	NPF	NPF	NPF
Erector No. 01, cardboard box, built 27 models, instruction booklet	150	300	500	700
Erector No. 02, cardboard box, built 39 models, instruction booklet	NPF	NPF	NPF	NPF
Erector No. 03, cardboard box, built 55 models, instruction booklet	NPF	NPF	NPF	NPF
Erector No. 04, cardboard box, built 65 models, instruction booklet, electric motor parts	125	225	350	500
Erector No. 05, cardboard box, built 76 models, instruction booklet, electric motor parts	NPF	NPF	NPF	NPF
Erector No. 06, cardboard box, built 88 models, instruction booklet, electric motor parts, two layers.......	NPF	NPF	NPF	NPF
Erector No. 07, wooden box, built 92 models, instruction booklet, electric motor parts, two layers.....	NPF	NPF	NPF	NPF
Erector No. 08, wooden box, built 100 models, instruction booklet, electric motor parts, three layers...	650	1000	2200	5000

1914	C4	C6	C8	C10
Mysto Erector No. 00, cardboard box, built 69 models, instruction booklet	NPF	NPF	NPF	NPF
Mysto Erector No. 01, cardboard box, built 88 models, instruction booklet	75	125	200	325
Mysto Erector No. 02, cardboard box, built 120 models, instruction booklet	NPF	NPF	NPF	NPF
Mysto Erector No. 03, cardboard box, built 176 models, instruction booklet, two layers	NPF	NPF	NPF	NPF
Mysto Erector No. 04, cardboard box, built 207 models, instruction booklet, electric motor, two layers	65	90	125	180

1914 (Continued)	C4	C6	C8	C10
Mysto Erector No. 05, cardboard box, built 229 models, instruction booklet, electric motor, two layers.	NPF	NPF	NPF	NPF
Mysto Erector No. 06, wooden box, built 264 models, instruction booklet, electric motor, two layers	NPF	NPF	NPF	NPF
Mysto Erector No. 07, wooden box, built 278 models, instruction booklet, electric motor, two layers	NPF	NPF	NPF	NPF
Mysto Erector No. 08, wooden box, built 304 models, instruction booklet, electric motor, three layers	800	1000	1800	4000

1915	C4	C6	C8	C10
Mysto Erector "M" sets, No. 1, 2, and 3 were offered with an electric motor and re-numbered 1M, 2M, and 3M	NPF	NPF	NPF	NPF
Mysto Erector No. 01, cardboard box, built 88 models, instruction booklet	75	125	200	325
Mysto Erector No. 02, cardboard box, built 120 models, instruction booklet	NPF	NPF	NPF	NPF
Mysto Erector No. 03, cardboard box, built 176 models, instruction booklet, two layers	NPF	NPF	NPF	NPF
Mysto Erector No. 04, wooden box, built 207 models, instruction booklet, electric motor, two layers	65	90	125	180
Mysto Erector No. 05, wooden box, built 229 models, instruction booklet, electric motor, two layers	NPF	NPF	NPF	NPF
Mysto Erector No. 06, wooden box, built 264 models, instruction booklet, electric motor, reversable baseplate, two layers	NPF	NPF	NPF	NPF
Mysto Erector No. 07, wooden box, built 278 models, instruction booklet, electric motor, two layers................	NPF	NPF	NPF	NPF

1915 (Continued)	**C4**	**C6**	**C8**	**C10**
Mysto Erector No. 08, wooden box, built 304 models, instruction booklet, electric motor, 1800 parts, three layers	800	1000	1800	4000
Mysto Erector Toy Builder, cardboard box, built 61 models, No. 0 was dropped this was the year's smallest set	NPF	NPF	NPF	NPF

1916-19	**C4**	**C6**	**C8**	**C10**
Gilbert Erector "M" sets, No. 1, 2, and 3 were offered with an electric motor and re-numbered 1M, 2M, and 3M, discontinued after 1916	NPF	NPF	NPF	NPF
Gilbert Erector No. 01, cardboard box, built 111 models, instruction booklet	60	100	150	275
Gilbert Erector No. 02, cardboard box, built 152 models, instruction booklet	NPF	NPF	NPF	NPF
Gilbert Erector No. 03, cardboard box, built 197 models, instruction booklet, two layers	NPF	NPF	NPF	NPF
Gilbert Erector No. 04, wooden box (cardboard in 1919), built 278 models, instruction booklet, electric motor, two layers	80	150	250	400
Gilbert Erector No. 05, wooden box, built 317 models, instruction booklet, electric motor (P58) ...	NPF	NPF	NPF	NPF
Gilbert Erector No. 06, wooden box, built 382 models, instruction booklet, reversable baseplate, two layers	NPF	NPF	NPF	NPF
Gilbert Erector No. 07, wooden box, built 410 models, instruction booklet, two layers	175	275	400	700
Gilbert Erector No. 08, wooden box, built 454 models, instruction booklet, three layers	500	750	900	2500
Gilbert Erector No. 44, wooden box, available 1918 and 1919 only, 2" wide girders, pulley bands and more...........................	NPF	NPF	NPF	NPF

1920	**C4**	**C6**	**C8**	**C10**
Gilbert Erector No. 01, cardboard box, built 111 models, instruction booklet	60	100	150	275
Gilbert Erector No. 02, cardboard box, built 152 models, instruction booklet	NPF	NPF	NPF	NPF
Gilbert Erector No. 03, cardboard box, built 197 models, instruction booklet, two layers	NPF	NPF	NPF	NPF
Gilbert Erector No. 06, wooden box, built 278 models, instruction booklet, electric motor, reverse baseplate, two layers	NPF	NPF	NPF	NPF
Gilbert Erector No. 07, wooden box, built 317 models, instruction booklet, electric motor, two layers	175	275	400	700
Gilbert Erector No. 08, wooden box, built 382 models, instruction booklet, electric motor, two layers	150	225	500	1000
Gilbert Erector No. 10, wooden box, built 410 models, instruction booklet, new electric motor (P73-B), three layer, parts mounted to inside of lid ...	900	1500	2300	5000

1921	**C4**	**C6**	**C8**	**C10**
Gilbert Erector No. 01, cardboard box, built 111 models, instruction booklet	60	100	150	275
Gilbert Erector No. 02, cardboard box, built 152 models, instruction booklet	NPF	NPF	NPF	NPF
Gilbert Erector No. 03, cardboard box, built 197 models, instruction booklet	NPF	NPF	NPF	NPF
Gilbert Erector No. 04, cardboard box, built 278 models, instruction booklet, electric motor parts	80	150	250	400
Gilbert Erector No. 06, wooden box, built 317 models, instruction booklet, electric motor (assembled), two layers w/ cardboard insert tray	NPF	NPF	NPF	NPF

1921 (Continued)	C4	C6	C8	C10
Gilbert Erector No. 07, wooden box, built 382 models, instruction booklet, two layers w/ wooden insert tray	175	275	400	700
Gilbert Erector No. 08, wooden box, built 410 models, instruction booklet, two layers w/ wooden insert tray	150	225	500	1000
Gilbert Erector No. 10, wooden box, built 454 models, instruction booklet, three layers w wooden insert tray and parts mounted to cardboard and attached to lid	900	1500	2300	5000

1922	C4	C6	C8	C10
Gilbert Erector No. 01, cardboard box, built 111 models, instruction booklet	60	100	150	275
Gilbert Erector No. 03, cartboard box, built 197 models, instruction booklet	NPF	NPF	NPF	NPF
Gilbert Erector No. 04, wooden box, built 278 models, instruction booklet, electric motor (assembled), two layers w/ cardboard insert tray	80	150	250	400
Gilbert Erector No. 07, wooden box, built 382 models, instruction booklet, reverse baseplate, two layers w/ wooden insert tray	175	275	400	700
Gilbert Erector No. 08, wooden box, built 410 models, instruction booklet, two layers w/ wooden insert tray	150	225	500	1000
Gilbert Erector No. 10, wooden box, built 454 models, instruction booklet, 110-volt electric motor (P56-G), three layers w/ wooden insert tray and parts mounted to cardboard attached to lid	900	1500	2300	5000

1923	C4	C6	C8	C10
Gilbert Erector No. 01, cardboard box, built 111 models, instruction booklet	NPF	NPF	NPF	NPF

1923 (Continued)	C4	C6	C8	C10
Gilbert Erector No. 03, cardboard box, built 197 models, instruction booklet	NPF	NPF	NPF	NPF
Gilbert Erector No. 04, wooden box, built 278 models, instruction booklet, electric motor	80	150	250	400
Gilbert Erector No. 05, Erector Machinery Outfit, wooden box, unique set with cast-iron and regular Erector parts to build miniature machine shop tools, two layers	NPF	NPF	NPF	NPF
Gilbert Erector No. 07, wooden box, built 382 models, instruction booklet, reverse baseplate, three layers w/ two cardboard insert trays	175	275	400	700
Gilbert Erector No. 08, wooden box, built 410 models, instruction booklet, two layers w/ wooden insert tray	150	225	500	1000
Gilbert Erector No. 10, wooden box, built 454 models, instruction booklet, 110-volt electric motor (P56-G), three layers w/ one wooden insert tray and parts mounted to cardboard attached to lid ..	900	1500	2300	5000

TYPE II: 1924 TO 1962 (THE ERA OF GIRDERS 5/8" WIDE)

1924	C4	C6	C8	C10
Gilbert Erector No. 01, cardboard box, built 278 models, instruction booklet	25	40	60	100
Gilbert Erector No. 03, cardboard box, built 381 models, instruction booklet	NPF	NPF	NPF	NPF
Gilbert Erector No. 04, cardboard box, built 500 models, instruction booklet, two layers, electric motor (P58)	75	120	160	300
Gilbert Erector No. 07, wooden box, built 533 models, instruction booklet, two layers w/ cardboard insert tray, electric motor, Steam Shovel model	125	200	350	500

1924 (Continued)	C4	C6	C8	C10
Gilbert Erector No. 08, wooden box, built 559 models, instruction booklet, two layers w/ wooden insert tray, electric motor, Clamshell	300	500	1100	2500
Gilbert Erector No. 10, wooden box, built 677 models, instruction booklet, three layers w/ wooden insert trays,	500	1200	2500	5000

1925	C4	C6	C8	C10
Gilbert Erector No. 01, cardboard box, built 278 models, instruction booklet, identical to 1924 set	25	40	60	100
Gilbert Erector No. 03, cardboard box, built 381 models, instruction booklet, identical to 1924 set	NPF	NPF	NPF	NPF
Gilbert Erector No. 04, cardboard box, built 500 models, instruction booklet, two layers, electric motor, identical to 1924 set	75	120	160	300
Gilbert Erector No. 07, wooden box, built 533 models, insturction booklet, two layers w/ cardboard insert tray, identical to 1924 set	NPF	NPF	NPF	NPF
Gilbert Erector No. 08, wooden box, built 559 models, same contents as 1924 set, but with less fancy box	300	500	1100	2500
Gilbert Erector No. 10, wooden box, built 677 models, identical to 1924 set	500	1200	2500	5000

1926	C4	C6	C8	C10
Gilbert Erector No. 01, cardboard box, built 278 models, instruction booklet	25	40	60	100
Gilbert Erector No. 03, cardboard box, built 381 models, instruction booklet	NPF	NPF	NPF	NPF
Gilbert Erector No. 04, cardboard box, built 500 models, instruction booklet, two layers w/ cardboard insert tray, electric motor	75	120	160	300

1926 (Continued)	C4	C6	C8	C10
Gilbert Erector No. 07, wooden box, built 533 models, instruction booklet, two layers w/ cardboard insert tray, electric motor, Steam Shovel	125	200	350	500
Gilbert Erector No. 07-1/2, wooden box, built 543 models, instruction booklet, two layers w/ wooden insert tray, White Truck	150	300	500	750
Gilbert Erector No. 08, wooden box, built 570 models, instruction booklet, two layers w/ wooden insert tray, Clamshell	300	500	1100	2500
Gilbert Erector No. 10, wooden box w/ nine drawers, built 700 models, instruction booklet	500	1200	2500	5000

1927	C4	C6	C8	C10
Gilbert Erector No. 01, cardboard box, built 278 models, instruction booklet	NPF	NPF	NPF	NPF
Gilbert Erector No. 03, cardboard box, built 381 models, instruction booklet	NPF	NPF	NPF	NPF
Gilbert Erector No. 04, cardboard box, built 500 models, instruction booklet, two layers w/ cardboard insert tray, electric motor	NPF	NPF	NPF	NPF
Gilbert Erector No. 07, wooden box, built 533 models, instruction booklet, two layers w/ wooden insert tray, electric motor, Steam Shovel	70	130	180	320
Gilbert Erector No. 07-1/2, wooden box, built 554 models, instruction booklet, two layers w/ wooden insert tray, White Truck w/ body	125	200	300	550
Gilbert Erector No. 08, wooden box, built all of the 7-1/2 models, had most Trumodel parts, two layers w/ wooden insert tray	NPF	NPF	NPF	NPF

1927 (Continued)

	C4	C6	C8	C10
Gilbert Erector No. 10, wooden box w/ nine drawers, built more than 700 models, instruction booklet......	1500	2700	4000	6500

1928

	C4	C6	C8	C10
Gilbert Erector No. 01, cardboard box, built 460 models, instruction booklet.....	NPF	NPF	NPF	NPF
Gilbert Erector No. 03, cardboard box, built 562 models, instruction booklet.....	NPF	NPF	NPF	NPF
Gilbert Erector No. 04, cardboard box, built 680 models, instruction booklet, two layers w/ cardboard insert tray, electric motor.	NPF	NPF	NPF	NPF
Gilbert Erector No. 07, wooden box, built 719 models, instruction booklet, two layers w/ cardboard insert tray, Steam Shovel model	70	130	180	320
Gilbert Erector No. 07-1/2, wooden box, built 749 models, instruction booklet, two layers w/ metal tray, White Truck	125	200	300	550
Gilbert Erector No. 08, wooden box, built 827 models, instruction booklet, two insert trays, Tru-model parts, derrick	NPF	NPF	NPF	NPF
Gilbert Erector No. 10, wooden box w/ nine drawers, built 1000 models, instruction booklet, built all models and then some.	1500	2700	4000	6500
Gilbert Erector No. 77, wooden box, built 727models, instruction booklet, two metal insert trays, Steam Shovel, 4 disc wheels	NPF	NPF	NPF	NPF
Gilbert Erector No. A, cardboard box, bult 42 models, large girders	NPF	NPF	NPF	NPF
Gilbert Erector No. B, wooden box, built 54 models, large girders, Ferris Wheel	300	500	750	1000
Gilbert Erector No. C, wooden box, built 19 models, Airplane	NPF	NPF	NPF	NPF

1929

	C4	C6	C8	C10
Gilbert Erector No. 01, cardboard box, built 492 models, instruction booklet.....	NPF	NPF	NPF	NPF
Gilbert Erector No. 03, cardboard box, built 611 models, instruction booklet.....	NPF	NPF	NPF	NPF
Gilbert Erector No. 04, cardboard box, built 733 models, instruction booklet, two layers w/ cardboard insert tray, electric motor.................	NPF	NPF	NPF	NPF
Gilbert Erector No. 06, wooden box, built 765 models, instruction booklet, two layers w/ metal insert tray, Boiler	NPF	NPF	NPF	NPF
Gilbert Erector No. 07, wooden box, built 777 models, instruction booklet, two layers w/ metal insert tray, Steam Shovel..........................	NPF	NPF	NPF	NPF
Gilbert Erector No. 07-1/2, wooden box, built 809 models, instruction booklet, two layers w/ metal insert tray, White Truck ...	NPF	NPF	NPF	NPF
Gilbert Erector No. 08, wooden box, built all No. 7-1/2 models and Zepplin, instruction booklet, two layers w/ metal insert tray	NPF	NPF	NPF	NPF
Gilbert Erector No. 09, wooden box, built all No. 8 models, Mechanical Wonder models, instruction booklet, two insert trays, dividers..................	NPF	NPF	NPF	NPF
Gilbert Erector No. 10, wooden box, built all No. 9 models, Ferris Wheel, instruction booklet, three parts trays	NPF	NPF	NPF	NPF
Gilbert Erector No. A, cardboard box, large girders, instruction booklet, two layers w/ cardboard insert tray	NPF	NPF	NPF	NPF
Gilbert Erector No. B, wooden box, Ferris Wheel, instruction booklet, two layers w/ insert tray	NPF	NPF	NPF	NPF

1929 (Continued)	C4	C6	C8	C10
Gilbert Erector No. C, cardboard box, Airplane models	NPF	NPF	NPF	NPF
Gilbert Erector No. D, cardboard box, Erector Airplane assembled at factory	NPF	NPF	NPF	NPF
Gilbert Erector No. F, Erector Zepplin assembled at factory	600	1200	1800	2600

1930	C4	C6	C8	C10
Gilbert Erector No. 01, cardboard box, built 492 models, instruction booklet	NPF	NPF	NPF	NPF
Gilbert Erector No. 03, cardboard box, built 611 models, instruction booklet	NPF	NPF	NPF	NPF
Gilbert Erector No. 04, cardboard box, built 611 models, instruction booklet, two layers w/ cardboard insert tray, electric motor	NPF	NPF	NPF	NPF
Gilbert Erector No. 06, wooden box, built 765 models, instruction booklet, two layers w/ metal insert tray, Boiler	NPF	NPF	NPF	NPF
Gilbert Erector No. 07, wooden box, built 777 models, instruction booklet, two layers w/ metal insert tray, Steam Shovel	NPF	NPF	NPF	NPF
Gilbert Erector No. 07-1/2, wooden box, built 809 models, instruction booklet, two layers w/ metal insert tray, White Truck	NPF	NPF	NPF	NPF
Gilbert Erector No. 08, wooden box, built all No. 7-1/2 models and Zepplin, instruction booklet, two layers w/ metal insert tray	NPF	NPF	NPF	NPF
Gilbert Erector No. 09, wooden box, built all No. 8 models, Mechanical Wonder models, instruction booklet, two insert trays, dividers	NPF	NPF	NPF	NPF

1930 (Continued)	C4	C6	C8	C10
Gilbert Erector No. 10, wooden box, built all No. 9 models, Ferris Wheel, instruction booklet, three parts trays	NPF	NPF	NPF	NPF
Gilbert Erector No. 45, cardboard box, Airplane set, built 19 Airplane models, instruction booklet	NPF	NPF	NPF	NPF
Gilbert Erector No. 75, cardboard box, "Combination Aircraft and Zepplin," built 22 models, instruction booklet	NPF	NPF	NPF	NPF

1930-1931	C4	C6	C8	C10
Gilbert-Meccano No. 01, cardboard box, built 100 models, instruction booklet	NPF	NPF	NPF	NPF
Gilbert-Meccano No. 03, cardboard box, built 200 models, instruction booklet	NPF	NPF	NPF	NPF
Gilbert-Meccano No. 05, cardboard box, built 300 models, instruction booklet, electric motor	NPF	NPF	NPF	NPF
Gilbert-Meccano No. 110, green wooden box, built car and truck models, 4 black rubber tires, two layers w/ insert tray, instruction booklet	NPF	NPF	NPF	NPF
Gilbert-Meccano No. 115, green wooden box, built 350 models, Ship models, instruction booklet	NPF	NPF	NPF	NPF
Gilbert-Meccano No. 125, green wooden box, built 400 models, Crane and Hoist models, two layers w/ metal insert tray, instruction booklet	NPF	NPF	NPF	NPF
Gilbert-Meccano No. 150, green wooden box, built 500 models, Ferris Wheel, Merry-Go-Round, Crane, instruction booklet	NPF	NPF	NPF	NPF

1931	C4	C6	C8	C10
Gilbert Erector No. 01, cardboard box, built 100 models, instruction booklet	NPF	NPF	NPF	NPF

1931 (Continued)

	C4	C6	C8	C10
Gilbert Erector No. 03, cardboard box, built 200 models, instruction booklet	NPF	NPF	NPF	NPF
Gilbert Erector No. 04, cardboard box, built 300 models, two layers w/ metal insert tray, electric motor, instruction booklet	NPF	NPF	NPF	NPF
Gilbert Erector No. 06, wooden box, built 325 models, two layers w/ metal insert tray, Boiler, instruction booklet..........	NPF	NPF	NPF	NPF
Gilbert Erector No. 07, wooden box, two layers w/ metal insert tray, Steam Shovel, instruction booklet............................	NPF	NPF	NPF	NPF
Gilbert Erector No. 07-1/2, wooden box, built 400 models, two layers w/ metal insert tray, White Truck, instruction booklet	NPF	NPF	NPF	NPF
Gilbert Erector No. 08, wooden box, built all No. 7 models, Hudson Locomotive, two layers w/ metal insert tray, instruction booklet	700	1250	1800	2300
Gilbert Erector No. 08-1/2, wooden box, built all No. 7 models, Hudon Locomotive, Tender, two layers w/ metal insert tray, instruction booklet	800	1200	2500	4000
Gilbert Erector No. 09, wooden box, built 450+ models, Mechanical Wonders, Zepplin, two layers w/ metal insert tray, instruction booklet	600	1200	1800	2600
Gilbert Erector No. 10, wooden box, Ferris Wheel, Zepplin, Steam Shovel, Hudson Locomotive and Tender, White Truck, multi-layers w/ three wooden boxes & two metal insert trays, instruction booklet. Rare and large, Gilbert listed this set as weighing 150 pounds!.............................	NPF	5000	10,000	20,000

1931 (Continued)

	C4	C6	C8	C10
Gilbert Erector No. 45, cardboard box, Airplane set, built 19 Airplane models, instruction booklet	NPF	NPF	NPF	NPF
Gilbert Erector No. 75, cardboard box, "Combination Aircraft and Zepplin," built 22 models, instruction booklet	NPF	NPF	NPF	NPF
Gilbert Erector No. A, wooden box, built Erector Hudson Locomotive, two layers w/ metal insert tray, instruction booklet	600	1100	1600	2000
Gilbert Erector No. B, wooden box, Ferris Wheel, large girders, two layers w/ metal insert tray, instruction booklet	NPF	NPF	NPF	NPF
Gilbert Erector No. D, cardboard box, factory assembled Airplane....................	NPF	NPF	NPF	NPF
Gilbert Erector No. L, cardboard box, factory assembled Erector Hudson Locomotive and Tender ...	NPF	NPF	NPF	NPF
Gilbert Erector No. T, cardboard box, Tender parts, two layers w/ cardboard insert tray, instruction booklet.............................	NPF	NPF	NPF	NPF

1932

	C4	C6	C8	C10
Gilbert Erector No. 01, cardboard box, built 100 models, instruction booklet	NPF	NPF	NPF	NPF
Gilbert Erector No. 03, cardboard box, instruction booklet.............................	NPF	NPF	NPF	NPF
Gilbert Erector No. 04, cardboard box, built 300 models, two layers w/ metal insert tray, electric motor, instruction booklet	NPF	NPF	NPF	NPF
Gilbert Erector No. 06, wooden box, built 325 models, two layers w/ metal insert tray, Boiler, instruction booklet	NPF	NPF	NPF	NPF
Gilbert Erector No. 07, wooden box, two layers w/ metal insert tray, Steam Shovel, instruction booklet.............................	NPF	NPF	NPF	NPF

1932 (Continued)	C4	C6	C8	C10
Gilbert Erector No. 07-1/2, wooden box, built 400 models, two layers w/ metal insert tray, White Truck, instruction booklet	NPF	NPF	NPF	NPF
Gilbert Erector No. 08, wooden box, built all No. 7 models, Hudson Locomotive, two layers w/ metal insert tray, instruction booklet	700	1250	1800	2300
Gilbert Erector No. 08-1/2, wooden box, built all No. 7 models, Hudson Locomotive, Tender, two layers w/ metal insert tray, instruction booklet	800	1200	2500	4000
Gilbert Erector No. 09, wooden box, Mechanical Wonders, Zepplin, two layers w/ metal insert tray, instruction booklet	600	1200	1800	2600
Gilbert Erector No. 10, wooden box, built 500+ models, Ferris Wheel, Zepplin, Steam Shovel, Hudson Locomotive and Tender, White Truck, multi-layers w/ three wooden boxes & two metal insert trays, instruction booklet. 1932 sets were virtually identical to their 1931 counterparts. In 1932, sets No. 7 and up received a 110-volt motor rather than a battery operated one.	NPF	5000	10,000	20,000
Gilbert Erector No. A, wooden box, built Erector Hudson Locomotive, two layers w/ metal insert tray, instruction booklet	600	1100	1600	2000
Gilbert Erector No. B, wooden box, built 58 models, Ferris Wheel, large girders, two layers w/ metal insert tray, instruction booklet	NPF	NPF	NPF	NPF
Gilbert Erector No. T, cardboard box, Tender parts, two layers w/ cardboard insert tray, instruction booklet..............................	NPF	NPF	NPF	NPF

1933	C4	C6	C8	C10
Gilbert Erector No. 01, cardboard box, built 50 models, instruction booklet.....	NPF	NPF	NPF	NPF
Gilbert Erector No. 03, cardboard box, built 75 models, instruction booklet..........................	NPF	NPF	NPF	NPF
Gilbert Erector No. 04, cardboard box, built 100 models, battery-operated motor, two layers w/ insert tray, instruction booklet..............................	NPF	NPF	NPF	NPF
Gilbert Erector No. 06, green metal box, built 150 models, Boiler, 110-volt motor, instruction booklet..........................	90	175	275	500
Gilbert Erector No. 07, red metal box, built 160 models, truck parts, elecro magnet, instruction booklet......................................	125	250	400	600
Gilbert Erector No. 08, wooden box, built all No. 7 models, Hudson Locomotive, two layers w/ metal insert tray, instruction booklet	NPF	NPF	NPF	NPF
Gilbert Erector No. 08-1/2, wooden box, built all No. 8 models, Hudson Locomotive and Tender, two layers w/ metal insert tray, instruction booklet	1000	1500	2600	6000
Gilbert Erector No. A, wooden box, built 14 models, Hudson Locomotive, two layers w/ metal insert tray, instruction booklet..............................	NPF	NPF	NPF	NPF

1934	C4	C6	C8	C10
Gilbert Erector No. 01, cardboard box, built 50 models, instruction booklet.....	NPF	NPF	NPF	NPF
Gilbert Erector No. 03, cardboard box, built 75 models, instruction booklet.....	NPF	NPF	NPF	NPF
Gilbert Erector No. 04, red metal box, built 100 models, battery-operated motor, instruction booklet..........................	NPF	NPF	NPF	NPF

1934 (Continued)

	C4	C6	C8	C10
Gilbert Erector No. 06, green metal box, built 125 models, Boiler, 110-volt motor, instruction booklet	90	175	275	500
Gilbert Erector No. 07, red metal box, built 150 models, electro magnet, instruction booklet	100	200	350	550
Gilbert Erector No. 07-1/2, light blue metal box, built 180 models, automotive set, black rubber tires, instruction booklet	125	250	450	650
Gilbert Erector No. 08, light blue metal box, built all No. 7-1/2 models, Hudson Locomotive and Tender, two instruction booklets ...	1000	1200	2500	4000

1935

	C4	C6	C8	C10
Gilbert Erector No. 01-1/2, cardboard box, instruction boolket	NPF	NPF	NPF	NPF
Gilbert Erector No. 03-1/2, cardboard box, two layers w/ insert tray, some skyscraper parts, instruction booklet..............................	NPF	NPF	NPF	NPF
Gilbert Erector No. 04-1/2, red metal box, two layers w/ two base plate insert trays, skyscraper parts, instruction booklet	NPF	NPF	NPF	NPF
Gilbert Erector No. 06-1/2, green metal box, two layers w/ two base plate insert trays, Boiler, Electric engine, instruction booklet..............................	NPF	225	300	550
Gilbert Erector No. 07-1/2, red metal box, two layers w/ three base plate insert trays, Ferris Wheel, electro magnet, skyscraper parts, instruction booklet..	125	275	400	600
Gilbert Erector No. 08-1/2, blue metal box, two layers w/ three base plate insert trays, Giant Power Plant, truck parts, skyscraper parts, instruction booklet..	150	300	475	700

1935 (Continued)

	C4	C6	C8	C10
Gilbert Erector No. 09-1/2, light blue metal box, built all No. 8-1/2 models, Hudson Locomotive and Tender, two layers w/ insert tray, two instruction booklets	1000	1900	3600	6500
Gilbert Erector No. S, cardboard box, Erector Skyscraper set, included cardboard skyscraper panels, Erector parts..............	NPF	NPF	NPF	NPF

1936

	C4	C6	C8	C10
Gilbert Erector No. 01-1/2, cardboard box, instruction booklet	NPF	NPF	NPF	NPF
Gilbert Erector No. 02-1/2, cardboard box, priced between No. 1-1/2 and No. 3-1/2, instruction booklet...............................	NPF	NPF	NPF	NPF
Gilbert Erector No. 03-1/2, cardboard box, two layers w/ cardboard insert tray, instruction booklet	NPF	NPF	NPF	NPF
Gilbert Erector No. 04-1/2, cardboard box, two layers w/ cardboard insert tray, battery-operated motor, instruction booklet	NPF	NPF	NPF	NPF
Gilbert Erector No. 05-1/2, red metal box, built all No. 4-1/2 models, two layers w/ two base plate insert trays, 110-volt motor, instruction booklet	100	200	275	425
Gilbert Erector No. 07-1/2, blue metal box, two layers w/ two base plate insert trays, Boiler, electric engine, instruction booklet...................	NPF	NPF	NPF	NPF
Gilbert Erector No. 08-1/2, red metal box, two layers w/ three base plate insert trays, Ferris Wheel, electro magnet, instruction booklet.............................	50	85	220	400

1936 (Continued)	C4	C6	C8	C10
Gilbert Erector No. 09-1/2, blue metal box, two layers w/ three base plate insert trays, electric engine, Power Plant, truck parts, instruction booklet	175	335	500	675
Gilbert Erector No. 10-1/2, blue metal box, two layers w/ one large base plate insert tray, built all No. 9-1/2 models, Hudson Locomotive and Tender, two instruction booklets	1000	1500	2900	5800
Gilbert Erector No. S, cardboard box, Erector Skyscraper set, included cardboard skyscraper panels, Erector parts	NPF	NPF	NPF	NPF
Gilbert Erector No. SA, cardboard box, Skyscraper Accessory set, included cardboard skyscraper panels	NPF	NPF	NPF	NPF

1937	C4	C6	C8	C10
Gilbert Erector No. 01-1/2, cardboard box, instruction booklet, same as 1936	NPF	NPF	NPF	NPF
Gilbert Erector No. 02-1/2, cardboard box, priced between No. 1-1/2 and No. 3-1/2, instruction booklet, same as 1936	NPF	NPF	NPF	NPF
Gilbert Erector No. 03-1/2, cardboard box, two layers w/ cardboard insert tray, instruction booklet, same as 1936	NPF	NPF	NPF	NPF
Gilbert Erector No. 04-1/2, cardboard box, two layers w/ cardboard insert tray, battery-operated motor, instruction booklet, same as 1936	NPF	NPF	NPF	NPF
Gilbert Erector No. 05-1/2, red metal box, built all No. 4-1/2 models, two layers w/ two base plate insert trays, 110-volt motor, instruction booklet, same as 1936	NPF	NPF	NPF	NPF

1937 (Continued)	C4	C6	C8	C10
Gilbert Erector No. 07-1/2, blue metal box, two layers w/ two base plate insert trays, Boiler, electric engine, instruction booklet, same as 1936	NPF	NPF	NPF	NPF
Gilbert Erector No. 08-1/2, red metal box, two layers w/ three base plate insert trays, Ferris Wheel, electro magnet, instruction booklet, same as 1936	NPF	NPF	NPF	NPF
Gilbert Erector No. 09-1/2, blue metal box, two layers w/ three base plate insert trays, electric engine, Power Plant, truck parts, instruction booklet, same as 1936	NPF	NPF	NPF	NPF
Gilbert Erector No. 10-1/2, blue metal box, two layers w/ one large base plate insert tray, built all No. 9-1/2 models, Hudson Locomotive and Tender, two instruction booklets, same as 1936	NPF	NPF	NPF	NPF
Gilbert Erector No. S, cardboard box, Erector Skyscraper set, included cardboard skyscraper panels, Erector parts, same as 1936	NPF	NPF	NPF	NPF
Gilbert Erector No. SA, cardboard box, Skyscraper Accessory set, included cardboard skyscraper panels, same as 1936	NPF	NPF	NPF	NPF

1938	C4	C6	C8	C10
Gilbert Erector No. 01-1/2, cardboard box, instruction booklet	NPF	NPF	NPF	NPF
Gilbert Erector No. 02-1/2, cardboard box, instruction booklet	NPF	NPF	NPF	NPF
Gilbert Erector No. 03-1/2, cardboard box, two layers w/ cardboard insert tray, base plates, instruction booklet	NPF	NPF	NPF	NPF

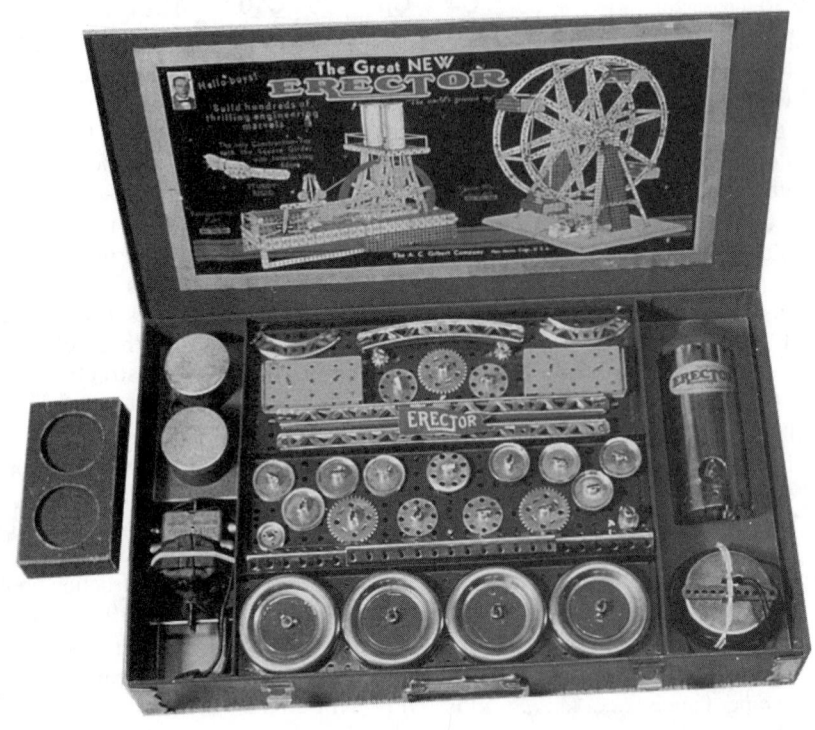

The 1937 #8-1/2, Classis Ferris Wheel Set. Introduced in 1936, the 1937 is valued at $400 in C10 condition. Restored by William S. Harrison III

1938 (Continued)	**C4**	**C6**	**C8**	**C10**
Gilbert Erector No. 04-1/2, cardboard box, two layers w/ cardboard insert tray, base plates, House, wind-up mechanical motor, instruction booklet	NPF	NPF	NPF	NPF
Gilbert Erector No. 05-1/2, red metal box, two layers w/ base plate insert trays, instruction booklet	NPF	NPF	NPF	NPF
Gilbert Erector No. 06-1/2, red metal box, two layers w/ insert tray, electric motor, built Airplane Ride, instruction booklet ..	NPF	NPF	NPF	NPF
Gilbert Erector No. 07-1/2, blue metal box, two layers w/ insert trays, electric motor, Boiler, lights, instruction booklet	NPF	NPF	NPF	NPF
Gilbert Erector No. 08-1/2, red metal box, two layers w/ three base plate insert trays, Ferris Wheel, electro magnet, instruction booklet...............................	NPF	NPF	NPF	NPF

1938 (Continued)	**C4**	**C6**	**C8**	**C10**
Gilbert Erector No. 09-1/2, blue metal box, two layers w/ three base plate insert trays, electric engine, Power Plant, truck parts, instruction booklet	NPF	NPF	NPF	NPF
Gilbert Erector No. 10-1/2, blue metal box, two layers w/ one large base plate insert tray, American Flyer locomotive, instruction manual.......................	750	1000	1500	3300

1939	**C4**	**C6**	**C8**	**C10**
Gilbert Erector No. 01-1/2, cardboard box, instruction booklet, same as 1938	NPF	NPF	NPF	NPF
Gilbert Erector No. 02-1/2, cardboard box, instruction booklet, same as 1938	NPF	NPF	NPF	NPF
Gilbert Erector No. 03-1/2, cardboard box, two layers w/ cardboard insert tray, base plates, instruction booklet, same as 1938	NPF	NPF	NPF	NPF

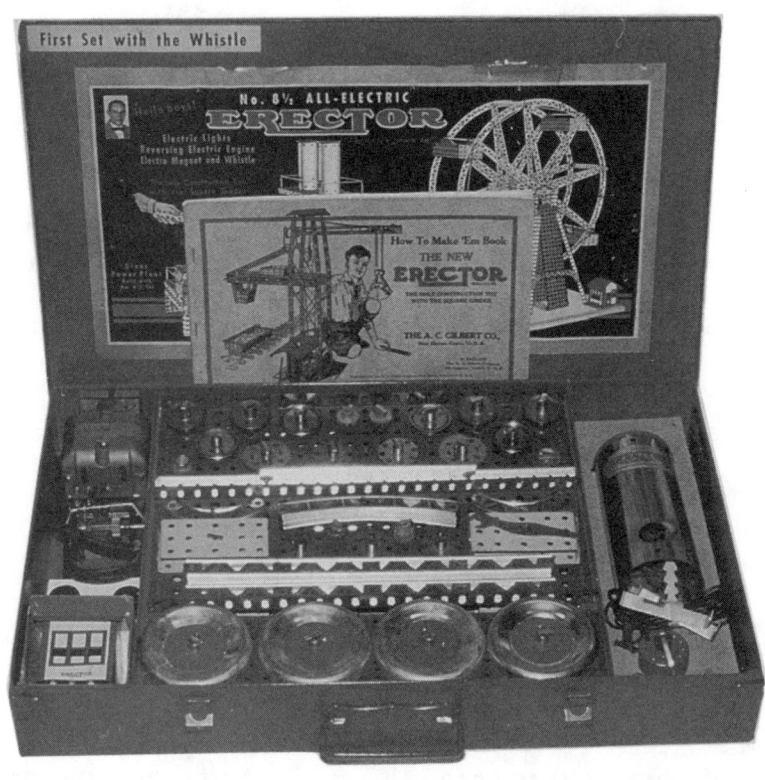

The 1939 #8-1/2, Classic Ferris Wheel Set. This was the first set with a whistle; it was dropped after 1941. Valued at $400 in C10 condition. Restoration by William S. Harrison III

1939 (Continued)	**C4**	**C6**	**C8**	**C10**
Gilbert Erector No. 04-1/2, cardboard box, two layers w/ cardboard insert tray, base plates, House, wind-up mechanical motor, instruction booklet, same as 1938	NPF	NPF	NPF	NPF
Gilbert Erector No. 05-1/2, red metal box, two layers w/ base plate insert trays, instruction booklet, same as 1938	NPF	NPF	NPF	NPF
Gilbert Erector No. 06-1/2, red metal box, two layers w/ insert tray, electric motor, built Airplane Ride, instruction booklet, same as 1938	NPF	NPF	NPF	NPF
Gilbert Erector No. 07-1/2, blue metal box, two layers w/ insert trays, electric motor, Boiler, lights, instruction booklet, same as 1938	NPF	NPF	NPF	NPF

1939 (Continued)	**C4**	**C6**	**C8**	**C10**
Gilbert Erector No. 08-1/2, red metal box, two layers w/ three base plate insert trays, Ferris Wheel, electro magnet, instruction booklet, same as 1938	NPF	NPF	NPF	NPF
Gilbert Erector No. 09-1/2, blue metal box, two layers w/ three base plate insert trays, electric engine, Power Plant, truck parts, instruction booklet, same as 1938	NPF	NPF	NPF	NPF
Gilbert Erector No. 10-1/2, blue metal box, two layers w/ one large base plate insert tray, American Flyer locomotive, instruction booklet, same as 1938	NPF	NPF	NPF	NPF

1940-1942	**C4**	**C6**	**C8**	**C10**
Gilbert Erector No. 01-1/2, cardboard box, instruction booklet	NPF	NPF	NPF	NPF
Gilbert Erector No. 02-1/2, cardboard box, instruction booklet	NPF	NPF	NPF	NPF

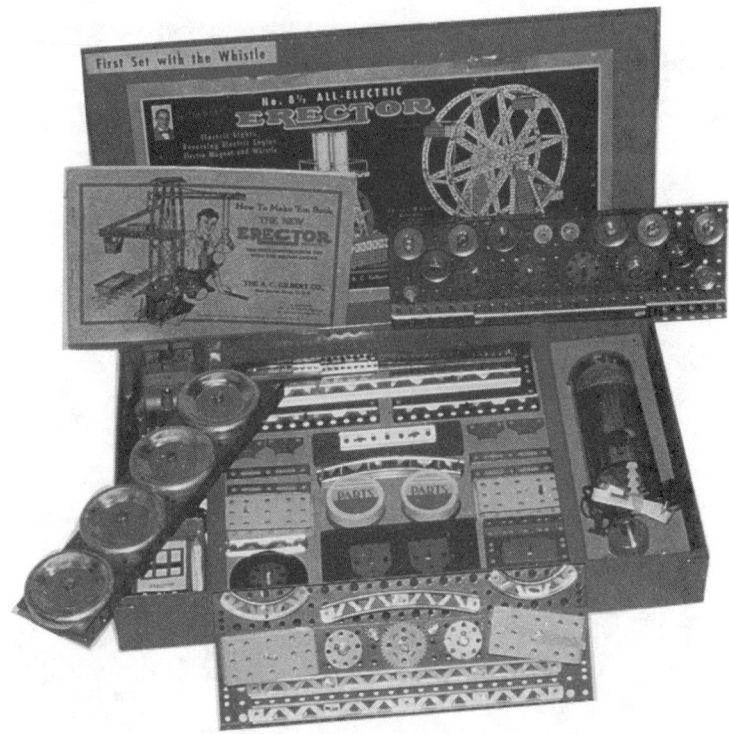

The contents of the 1939 #8-1/2. It should have a large nickel-plated magnet.

1940-1942 (Continued)	C4	C6	C8	C10
Gilbert Erector No. 03-1/2, cardboard box, two layers w/ insert tray, base plates, instruction booklet	NPF	NPF	NPF	NPF
Gilbert Erector No. 04-1/2, cardboard box, two layers w/ cardboard insert tray, House, mechanical motor, base plates, instruction booklet	NPF	NPF	NPF	NPF
Gilbert Erector No. 06-1/2, red metal box, two layers w/ insert tray, Airplane Ride, electric engine, instruction booklet	NPF	NPF	NPF	NPF
Gilbert Erector No. 07-1/2, blue metal box, two layers w/ two base plate insert trays, electric engine, Boiler, instruction booklet	NPF	NPF	NPF	NPF
Gilbert Erector No. 08-1/2, red metal box, two layers w/ three base plate insert trays, Ferris Wheel, electro magnet, lights, instruction booklet	NPF	NPF	NPF	NPF

1940-1942 (Continued)	C4	C6	C8	C10
Gilbert Erector No. 09-1/2, blue metal box, two layers w/ three base plate insert trays, truck parts, Power Plant, Parachute Jump	NPF	NPF	NPF	NPF
Gilbert Erector No. 10-1/2, blue metal box, two layers w/ large base plate insert tray, "Electric Train Set," featured the American Flyer locomotive, Parachute Jump, instruction booklet	NPF	NPF	NPF	NPF

1943-1947	C4	C6	C8	C10
Gilbert Erector No. 01, Erector Junior set produced during World War II, cardboard box, wooden components	NPF	NPF	NPF	NPF
Gilbert Erector No. 03, Erector Junior set produced during World War II, cardboard box, wooden components	NPF	NPF	NPF	NPF

1943-1947 (Continued)	C4	C6	C8	C10
Gilbert Erector No. 05, Erector Junior set produced during World War II, cardboard box, wooden components	NPF	NPF	NPF	NPF

1946	C4	C6	C8	C10
Gilbert Erector No. 02-1/2, cardboard box, instruction booklet	NPF	NPF	NPF	NPF
Gilbert Erector No. 04-1/2, cardboard box, base plates, House, mechanical motor, instruction booklet	NPF	NPF	NPF	NPF
Gilbert Erector No. 06-1/2, cardboard box, two layers w/ cardboard insert tray, Airplane Ride, electric engine, instruction booklet......................................	NPF	NPF	NPF	NPF
Gilbert Erector No. 07-1/2, cardboard box, two layers w/ two cardboard insert trays, Boiler, electric engine, Walking Beam Engine, instruction booklet......................................	NPF	NPF	NPF	NPF
Gilbert Erector No. 08-1/2, red metal box, two layers w/ three base plate insert trays, Ferris Wheel, whistle, electric engine, instruction booklet	NPF	NPF	NPF	NPF
Gilbert Erector No. 09-1/2, blue metal box, two layers w/ three base plate insert trays, truck parts, Power Plant, Parachute Jump, instruction booklet	NPF	NPF	NPF	NPF

1947	C4	C6	C8	C10
Gilbert Erector No. 02-1/2, cardboard box, instruction booklet	NPF	NPF	NPF	NPF
Gilbert Erector No. 04-1/2, cardboard box, two layers w/ cardboard insert tray, base plates, House, mechanical motor, instruction booklet	NPF	NPF	NPF	NPF

1947 (Continued)	C4	C6	C8	C10
Gilbert Erector No. 06-1/2, cardboard box, two layers w/ cardboard insert tray, Airplane Ride, electric engine, instruction booklet......................................	NPF	NPF	NPF	NPF
Gilbert Erector No. 07-1/2, cardboard box, two layers w/ cardboard insert tray, electric engine, Boiler, Walking Beam Engine, instruction booklet	NPF	NPF	NPF	NPF
Gilbert Erector No. 08-1/2, red metal box, two layers w/ three base plate insert trays, Ferris Wheel, electro magnet, lights, instruction booklet	NPF	NPF	NPF	NPF
Gilbert Erector No. 09-1/2, red metal box, two layers w/ three base plate insert trays, truck parts, Power Plant, Parachute Jump, instruction booklet	NPF	NPF	NPF	NPF

1948	C4	C6	C8	C10
Gilbert Erector No. 02-1/2, cardboard box, instruction booklet	NPF	NPF	NPF	NPF
Gilbert Erector No. 04-1/2, cardboard box, two layers w/ cardboard insert tray, base plates, House, mechanical motor, instruction booklet	NPF	NPF	NPF	NPF
Gilbert Erector No. 06-1/2, cardboard box, two layers w/ cardboard insert tray, Airplane Ride, electric engine, instruction booklet......................................	NPF	NPF	NPF	NPF
Gilbert Erector No. 07-1/2, red metal box, two layers w/ two cardboard insert trays, electric engine, Boiler, Walking Beam Engine, instruction booklet......................................	NPF	NPF	NPF	NPF
Gilbert Erector No. 08-1/2, red metal box, two layers w/ three base plate insert trays, Ferris Wheel, electro magnet, lights, instruction booklet	NPF	NPF	NPF	NPF

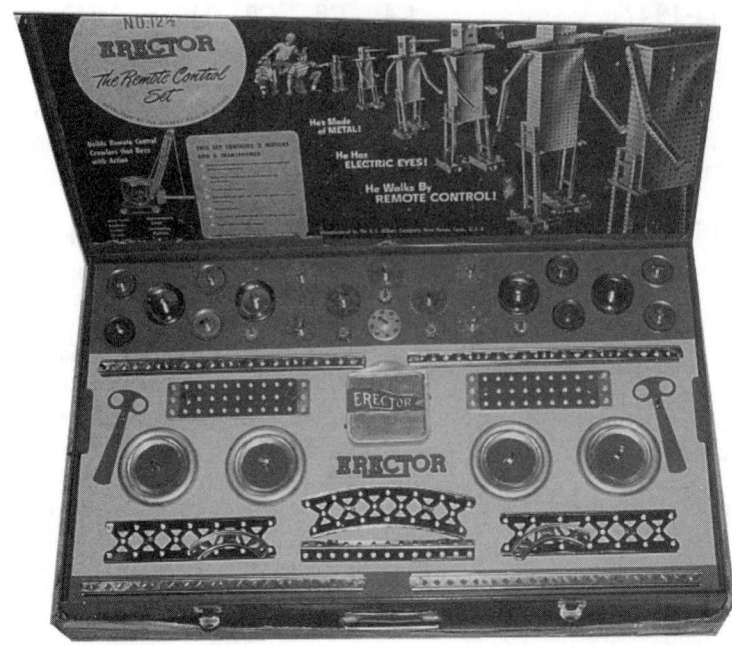

The late 1948 #12-1/2 does not make the Merry-Go-Round or the continuous running parachute jump. In C10 condition the #12-1/2 is valued at $1,500. Restored by William s. Harrison III

1948 (Continued)	C4	C6	C8	C10
Gilbert Erector No. 09-1/2, red metal box, two layers w/ three base plate insert trays, truck parts, Power Plant, Parachute Jump, instruction booklet	NPF	NPF	NPF	NPF
Gilbert Erector No. 12-1/2, red metal box, three layers w/ insert trays, "Remote Control Set," pulleys and treads for Tank and Bulldozer, Mysterious Walking Giant, mechanical motor, instruction booklet.........	350	500	900	1500

1949	C4	C6	C8	C10
Erector No. 05, "Erector Illumination Kit," accessory kit containing colored lights................................	NPF	NPF	NPF	NPF
Erector No. 12-1/2A, "Erector Merry-Go-Round Kit," accessory kit with parts to build Merry-Go-Round model with the No. 9-1/2...........................	NPF	NPF	NPF	NPF
Erector No. IE, "Erector Square Girder Kit," accessory kit containing extra girders, round yellow tube......................	NPF	NPF	NPF	NPF

1949 (Continued)	C4	C6	C8	C10
Gilbert Erector No. 01-1/2, cardboard box, instruction booklet	NPF	NPF	NPF	NPF
Gilbert Erector No. 02-1/2, cardboard box, instruction booklet	NPF	NPF	NPF	NPF
Gilbert Erector No. 04-1/2, cardboard box, two layers w/ cardboard insert tray, base plates, House, mechanical motor, instruction booklet	NPF	NPF	NPF	NPF
Gilbert Erector No. 06-1/2, cardboard box, two layers w/ cardboard insert tray, Airplane Ride, electric engine, instruction booklet......................................	NPF	NPF	NPF	NPF
Gilbert Erector No. 07-1/2, red metal box, two layers w/ two base plate insert trays, Boiler, Walking Beam Engine, instruction booklet...............................	NPF	NPF	NPF	NPF
Gilbert Erector No. 08-1/2, red metal box, two layers w/ three base plate insert trays, Ferris Wheel, lights, electro magnet, Bascule Bridge, instruction booklet..............	NPF	NPF	NPF	NPF

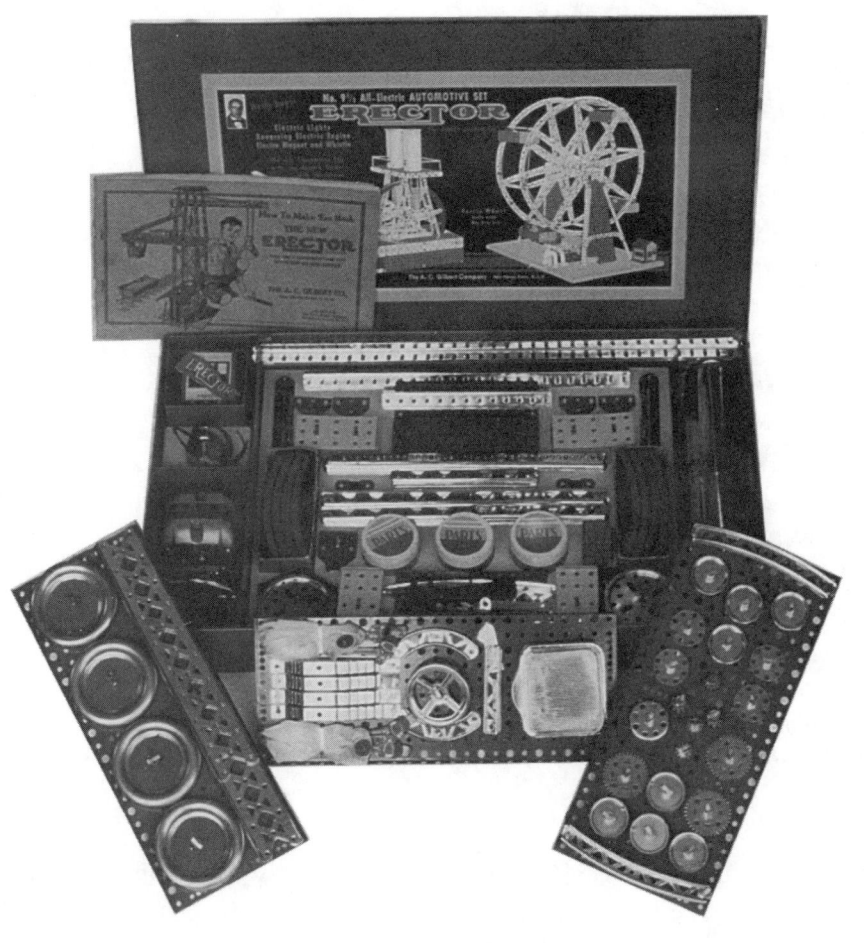

The 1948 #9-1/2 Automotiive set makes the manual control P-jump but not the Merry-Go-Round. In C10 condition the 9-1/2 is valued at $675. Restored by William S. Harrison

1949 (Continued)

	C4	C6	C8	C10
Gilbert Erector No. 091/2, red metal box, two layers w/ three base plate insert trays, truck parts, Parachute Jump, Power Plant, instruction booklet. 1949 was the final year for the 9-1/2.	NPF	NPF	NPF	NPF
Gilbert Erector No. 10-1/2, red metal box, two layers w/ three base plate insert trays, "Amusement Park Set," Parachute Jump, Merry-Go-Round, truck parts, instruction booklet..	150	300	500	800
Gilbert Erector No. 12-1/2, red metal box, three layers w/ insert trays, "Remote Control Set," pulleys and treads for Bulldozer and Tank models, Mysterious Walking Giant, instruction booklet	NPF	NPF	NPF	NPF

1949-1955

	C4	C6	C8	C10
Junior Erector No. 02, Junior Erector set, cardboard box, plastic parts, Windmill, instruction booklet	NPF	NPF	NPF	NPF
Junior Erector No. 04, Junior Erector set, cardboard box, plastic parts, Bridge, Tank, instruction booklet	NPF	NPF	NPF	NPF
Junior Erector No. 10, Junior Erector set, cardboard box, plastic parts, two layers, Ferris Wheel, Merry-Go-Round, instruction booklet	NPF	NPF	NPF	NPF

1950

	C4	C6	C8	C10
Erector No. 05, "Erector Illumnination Kit," accessory kit containing colored lights	NPF	NPF	NPF	NPF

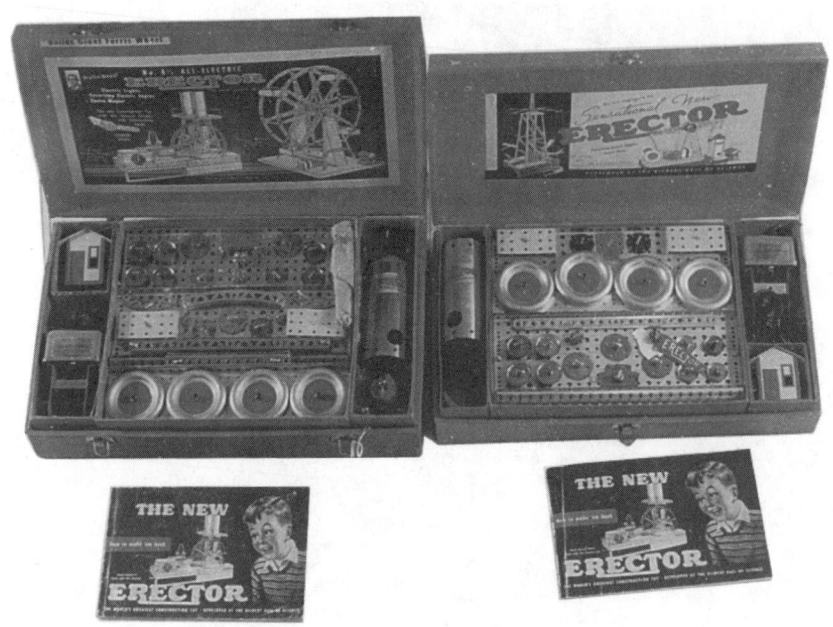

Erector's #8-1/2 (left) and #7-1/2 (right) from 1950 show the heavy cardboard boxes an aluminum baseplates used during the Korean war era. In C10 condition the 8-1/2 is valued at $800 and 7-1/2 at $600. Restored by William S. Harrison III

1950 (Continued)

	C4	C6	C8	C10
Erector No. 06, "Erector Whistle Kit," accessory kit containing whistle and electric controls	NPF	NPF	NPF	NPF
Erector No. 07, "Erector Smoke and Choo-Choo Kit," accessory kit containing smoke and choo-choo noise	NPF	NPF	NPF	NPF
Erector No. IE, "Erector Square Girder Kit," accessory kit containing extra girders, round yellow tube	NPF	NPF	NPF	NPF
Gilbert Erector No. 01-1/2, cardboard box, instruction booklet	NPF	NPF	NPF	NPF
Gilbert Erector No. 02-1/2, cardboard box, instruction booklet	NPF	NPF	NPF	NPF
Gilbert Erector No. 04-1/2, cardboard box, two layers w/ cardboard insert tray, base plates, House, mechanical motor, instruction booklet	NPF	NPF	NPF	NPF

1950 (Continued)

	C4	C6	C8	C10
Gilbert Erector No. 06-1/2, red metal box, two layers w/ cardboard insert tray, electric engine (different from 1949), Airplane Ride, instruction booklet	NPF	NPF	NPF	NPF
Gilbert Erector No. 07-1/2, red metal box, two layers w/ two base plate insert trays, Boiler, Walking Beam Engine, instruction booklet	NPF	NPF	NPF	NPF
Gilbert Erector No. 08-1/2, red metal box, two layers w/ three base plate insert trays, Ferris Wheel, electro magnet, lights, Bascule Bridge, instruction booklet	NPF	NPF	NPF	NPF

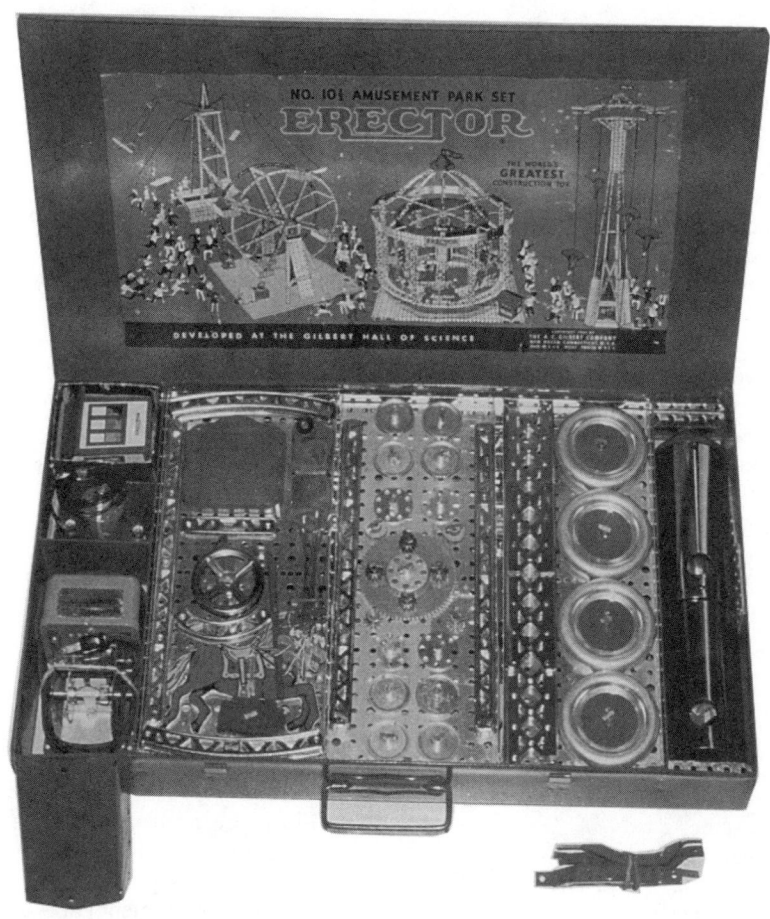

The 1950-51 #10-1/2 Amusement Park set. The Aluminum baseplates and A-47 motor are, once again, due to the Korean War. The #10-1/2 is valued at $800 in C10 condition. Restored by William S. Harrison

1950 (Continued)	C4	C6	C8	C10
Gilbert Erector No. 10-1/2, red metal box, two layers w/ three base plate insert trays, "Amusement Park Set," Parachute Jump, Merry-Go-Round, truck parts, instruction booklet	NPF	NPF	NPF	NPF
Gilbert Erector No. 12-1/2, red metal box, three layers w/ insert trays, "Remote Control Set," pulleys and treads for Bulldozer and Tank, Mysterious Walking Giant, instructin booklet......................................	NPF	NPF	NPF	NPF

1951	C4	C6	C8	C10
Erector No. 05, "Erector Illumination Kit," accessory kit containing colored lights.................................	NPF	NPF	NPF	NPF
Erector No. 06, "Erector Whistle Kit," accessory kit containing whistle and electric controls................	NPF	NPF	NPF	NPF
Erector No. 07, "Erector Smoke and Choo-Choo Kit," accessory kit containing smoke and choo-choo noise	NPF	NPF	NPF	NPF
Gilbert Erector No. 01-1/2, cardboard box, instruction booklet	NPF	NPF	NPF	NPF

1951 (Continued)	C4	C6	C8	C10
Gilbert Erector No. 02-1/2, cardboard box, instruction booklet	NPF	NPF	NPF	NPF
Gilbert Erector No. 04-1/2, cardboard box, two layers w/ cardboard insert tray, House, mechanical motor, base plates, instruction booklet	NPF	NPF	NPF	NPF
Gilbert Erector No. 06-1/2, cardboard box, two layers w/ cardboard insert tray, Airplane Ride, electric engine, instruction booklet	NPF	NPF	NPF	NPF
Gilbert Erector No. 07-1/2, cardboard box, two layers w/ cardboard insert tray, Boiler, Walking Beam Engine, instruction booklet	NPF	NPF	NPF	NPF
Gilbert Erector No. 08-1/2, cardboard box, two layers w/ cardboard insert tray, Ferris Wheel, electro magnet, lights, Bascule Bridge, instruction booklet	NPF	NPF	NPF	NPF
Gilbert Erector No. 10-1/2, red metal box, two layers w/ three base plate insert trays, "Amusement Park Set," Parachute Jump, Merry-Go-Round, truck parts, instruction booklet	NPF	NPF	NPF	NPF

1952	C4	C6	C8	C10
Erector No. 05, "Erector Illumination Kit," accessory kit containing colored lights	NPF	NPF	NPF	NPF
Erector No. 07, "Erector Smoke and Choo-Choo Kit," accessory kit containing smoke and choo-choo noise	NPF	NPF	NPF	NPF
Gilbert Erector No. 01-1/2, cardboard box, instruction booklet, same as 1951	NPF	NPF	NPF	NPF
Gilbert Erector No. 02-1/2, cardboard box, instruction booklet, same as 1951	NPF	NPF	NPF	NPF

1952 (Continued)	C4	C6	C8	C10
Gilbert Erector No. 04-1/2, cardboard box, two layers w/ cardboard insert tray, House, mechanical motor, base plates, instruction booklet, same as 1951	NPF	NPF	NPF	NPF
Gilbert Erector No. 06-1/2, cardboard box, two layers w/ cardboard insert tray, Airplane Ride, electric engine, instruction booklet, same as 1951	NPF	NPF	NPF	NPF
Gilbert Erector No. 07-1/2, cardboard box, two layers w/ cardboard insert tray, Boiler, Walking Beam Engine, instructin booklet, same as 1951	NPF	NPF	NPF	NPF
Gilbert Erector No. 08-1/2, cardboard box, two layers w/ cardboard insert tray, Ferris Wheel, electro magnet, lights, Bascule Bridge, instruction booklet, same as 1951	NPF	NPF	NPF	NPF
Gilbert Erector No. 10-1/2, red metal box, two layers w/ three base plate insert trays, "Amusement Park Set," Parachute Jump, Merry-Go-Round, truck parts, instruction booklet, same as 1951	NPF	NPF	NPF	NPF

1953	C4	C6	C8	C10
Erector No. 07, "Erector Smoke and Choo-Choo Kit," accessory kit containing smoke and choo-choo noise	NPF	NPF	NPF	NPF
Gilbert Erector No. 01-1/2, cardboard box, instruction booklet	NPF	NPF	NPF	NPF
Gilbert Erector No. 02-1/2, cardboard box, instruction booklet	NPF	NPF	NPF	NPF
Gilbert Erector No. 04-1/2, cardboard box, two layers w/ cardboard insert tray, House, mechanical motor, base plates, instruction booklet	NPF	NPF	NPF	NPF

1953 (Continued)	C4	C6	C8	C10
Gilbert Erector No. 06-1/2, cardboard box, two layers w/ cardboard insert tray, Airplane Ride, electric engine, instruction booklet......................	NPF	NPF	NPF	NPF
Gilbert Erector No. 07-1/2, red metal box, two layers w/ two base plate insert trays, Boiler, Walking Beam Engine, instruction booklet.............................	NPF	NPF	NPF	NPF
Gilbert Erector No. 08-1/2, red metal box, two layers w/ three base plate insert trays, Ferris Wheel, electro magnet, lights, Bascule Bridge, instruction booklet......................	NPF	NPF	NPF	NPF
Gilbert Erector No. 10-1/2, red metal box, two layers w/ three base plate insert trays, "Amusement Park Set," Parachute Jump, Merry-Go-Round, truck parts, Power Plant, instruction booklet	NPF	NPF	NPF	NPF

1954	C4	C6	C8	C10
Gilbert Erector No. 01-1/2, cardboard box, instruction booklet, same as 1953	NPF	NPF	NPF	NPF
Gilbert Erector No. 02-1/2, cardboard box, instruction booklet, same as 1953	NPF	NPF	NPF	NPF
Gilbert Erector No. 04-1/2, cardboard box, two layers w/ cardboard insert tray, House, mechanical motor, base plates, instruction booklet, same as 1953	NPF	NPF	NPF	NPF
Gilbert Erector No. 06-1/2, cardboard box, two layers w/ cardboard insert tray, Airplane Ride, electric engine, instruction booklet, same as 1953	NPF	NPF	NPF	NPF
Gilbert Erector No. 07-1/2, red metal box, two layers w/ two base plate insert trays, Boiler, Walking Beam Engine, instruction booklet, same as 1953	NPF	NPF	NPF	NPF

1954 (Continued)	C4	C6	C8	C10
Gilbert Erector No. 08-1/2, red metal box, two layers w/ three base plate insert trays, Ferris Wheel, electro magnet, lights, Bascule Bridge, instruction booklet, same as 1953	NPF	NPF	NPF	NPF
Gilbert Erector No. 10-1/2, red metal box, two layers w/ three base plate insert trays, "Amusement Park Set," Parachute Jump, Merry-Go-Round, truck parts, Power Plant, instruction booklet, same as 1953	NPF	NPF	NPF	NPF

1955	C4	C6	C8	C10
Gilbert Erector No. 01-1/2, cardboard box, instruction booklet	NPF	NPF	NPF	NPF
Gilbert Erector No. 02-1/2, cardboard box, instruction booklet	NPF	NPF	NPF	NPF
Gilbert Erector No. 03-1/2, cardboard box, two layers w/ cardboard insert tray, base plates, instruction booklet.............................	NPF	NPF	NPF	NPF
Gilbert Erector No. 04-1/2, red metal box, two layers w/ two base plate insert trays, House, mechanical motor, instruction booklet	NPF	NPF	NPF	NPF
Gilbert Erector No. 06-1/2, cardboard box, two layers w/ cardboard insert tray, Airplane Ride, electric engine, instruction booklet......................	NPF	NPF	NPF	NPF
Gilbert Erector No. 07-1/2, red metal box, two layers w/ two base plate insert trays, Boiler, Walking Beam Engine, instruction booklet.............................	NPF	NPF	NPF	NPF
Gilbert Erector No. 08-1/2, red metal box, two layers w/ three base plate insert trays, Ferris Wheel, electro magnet, lights, Bascule Bridge, instruction booklet......................	NPF	NPF	NPF	NPF

1955 (Continued)

	C4	C6	C8	C10
Gilbert Erector No. 10-1/2, red metal box, two layers w/ three base plate insert trays, "Amusement Park Set," Parachute Jump, Merry-Go-Round, truck parts, Power Plant, instruction booklet	NPF	NPF	NPF	NPF

1956

	C4	C6	C8	C10
Gilbert Erector No. 01-1/2, cardboard box, instruction booklet, same as 1955	NPF	NPF	NPF	NPF
Gilbert Erector No. 02-1/2, cardboard box, instruction booklet, same as 1955	NPF	NPF	NPF	NPF
Gilbert Erector No. 03-1/2, cardboard box, two layers w/ cardboard insert tray, base plates, instruction booklet, same as 1955	NPF	NPF	NPF	NPF
Gilbert Erector No. 04-1/2, red metal box, two layers w/ two base plate insert trays, House, mechanical motor, instruction booklet, same as 1955	NPF	NPF	NPF	NPF
Gilbert Erector No. 06-1/2, red metal box, two layers w/ two base plate insert trays, Airplane Ride, electric engine, instruction booklet	NPF	NPF	NPF	NPF
Gilbert Erector No. 07-1/2, red metal box, two layers w/ two base plate insert trays, Boiler, Walking Beam Engine, instruction booklet, same as 1955	NPF	NPF	NPF	NPF
Gilbert Erector No. 08-1/2, red metal box, two layers w/ three base plate insert trays, Ferris Wheel, electro magnet, lights, Bascule Bridge, instruction booklet, same as 1955	NPF	NPF	NPF	NPF

1956 (Continued)

	C4	C6	C8	C10
Gilbert Erector No. 10-1/2, red metal box, two layers w/ three base plate insert trays, "Amusement Park Set," Parachute Jump, Merry-Go-Round, truck parts, Power Plant, instruction booklet, same as 1955	NPF	NPF	NPF	NPF
Gilbert Erector No. 12-1/2, red metal box, two layers w/ insert trays, "Master Builder Set," Mysterious Walking Robot, included the "Clamshell" Bucket made by Doepke, instruction booklet	NPF	NPF	NPF	NPF

1957

	C4	C6	C8	C10
Gilbert Erector No. 01-1/2, No. 10010, cardboard box, instruction booklet............................	NPF	NPF	NPF	NPF
Gilbert Erector No. 02-1/2, No. 10020, cardboard box, instruction booklet............................	NPF	NPF	NPF	NPF
Gilbert Erector No. 03-1/2, No. 10030, cardboard box, two layers w/ cardboard insert tray, base plates, instruction booklet	NPF	NPF	NPF	NPF
Gilbert Erector No. 05-1/2, No. 10041, metal lithographed box, two layers w/ two base plate insert trays, Airplane Ride, instruction booklet	20	40	75	125
Gilbert Erector No. 06-1/2, No. 10051, metal lithographed box, two layers w/ two base plate insert trays, Airplane Ride, electric engine, instruction booklet............................	25	55	85	130
Gilbert Erector No. 06-1/2, No. 10046, cardboard box, two layers w/ cardboard insert tray, Airplane Ride, electric engine, instruction booklet	NPF	NPF	NPF	NPF

1957 (Continued)	<u>C4</u>	<u>C6</u>	<u>C8</u>	<u>C10</u>
Gilbert Erector No. 07-1/2, No. 10061, metal lithographed box, two layers w/ two base plate insert trays, Boiler, Walking Beam Engine, instruction booklet.............................	35	70	110	190
Gilbert Erector No. 08-1/2, No. 10071, metal lithographed box, two layers w/ three base plate insert trays, Ferris Wheel, electro magnet, instruction booklet.............................	60	150	225	350
Gilbert Erector No. 100, No. 16010, cardboard box, smallest set offered in 1957, rare	NPF	NPF	NPF	NPF
Gilbert Erector No. 10-1/2, No. 10081, metal lithographed box, two layers w/ three base plate insert trays, "Amusement Park Set," Parachute Jump, Merry-Go-Round, truck parts, Power Plant, instruction booklet	100	200	350	600
Gilbert Erector No. 12-1/2, No. 10091, red metal box, two layers w/ insert trays, "Master Builder Set," Myserious Walking Robot, "Clamshell" Bucket made by Doepke, instruction booklet	NPF	650	900	1500

1958	<u>C4</u>	<u>C6</u>	<u>C8</u>	<u>C10</u>
Gilbert Erector No. 10011, cylindrical cardboard tube, instruction page	NPF	NPF	NPF	NPF
Gilbert Erector No. 10021, cylindrical cardboard tube, instruction page	NPF	NPF	NPF	NPF
Gilbert Erector No. 10026, cardboard box, instruction booklet	NPF	NPF	NPF	NPF
Gilbert Erector No. 10031, cardboard box, base blates, instruction booklet	NPF	NPF	NPF	NPF
Gilbert Erector No. 10041, metal lithographed box, two layers, electric motor, instruction booklet	20	40	75	125

1958 (Continued)	<u>C4</u>	<u>C6</u>	<u>C8</u>	<u>C10</u>
Gilbert Erector No. 10052, metal lithographed box, two layers w/ insert trays, "Rocket Launcher Set," electric engine, Rocket Launcher, instruction booklet.............................	25	55	85	135
Gilbert Erector No. 10062, metal lithographed box, two layers w/ insert trays, Boiler, Walking Beam Engine, instruction booklet......................................	35	70	110	190
Gilbert Erector No. 10072, metal lithographed box, three layers w/ insert trays, "Musical Ferris Wheel Set," eletro magnet, sound effects, Musical Ferris Wheel, instruction booklet	NPF	150	225	400
Gilbert Erector No. 10082, red metal box, two layers w/ three base plate insert trays, "Amusement Park Set," Parachute Jump, Merry-Go-Round, sound effects, Power Plant, two instruction booklets..........	NPF	250	475	750
Gilbert Erector No. 10092, red metal box, two layers w/ insert trays, "Master Builder Set," Mysterious Walking Robot, "Clamshell" Bucket made by Doepke, sound effects, treads, rocket, two instruction booklets.....................	NPF	650	900	1500

1959	<u>C4</u>	<u>C6</u>	<u>C8</u>	<u>C10</u>
Gilbert Erector No. 10011, cylindrical cardboard tube, instruction page	NPF	NPF	NPF	NPF
Gilbert Erector No. 10021, cylindrical cardboard tube, instruction page	NPF	NPF	NPF	NPF
Gilbert Erector No. 10032, cylindrical cardboard tube, base plates, instruction page..........................	NPF	NPF	NPF	NPF
Gilbert Erector No. 10042, metal lithographed box, two layers w/ cardboard insert tray, Radar Scope, instruction booklet	20	40	75	125

1959 (Continued)	C4	C6	C8	C10
Gilbert Erector No. 10053, metal lithographed box, two layers w/ cardboard insert tray, Rocket Launcher, 50th Anniversary set, instruction booklet.....................................	25	55	85	135
Gilbert Erector No. 10063, metal lithographed box, two layers w/ cardboard insert tray, Boiler, Conveyor Belt, instruction booklet.............................	35	70	110	190
Gilbert Erector No. 10073, metal lithographed box, two layers w/ insert trays, sound effects kit, electro magnet, Ferris Wheel (musical), instruction manual..............................	NPF	150	225	400
Gilbert Erector No. 10083, red metal box, two layers w/ insert trays, "Amusement Park Set," sound effects kit, Merry-Go-Round, Parachute Jump, Power Plant, instruction booklet..............................	NPF	250	475	750
Gilbert Erector No. 10093, red metal box, two layers w/ insert trays, "Master Builder Set," Mysterious Walking Robot, "Clamshell" Bucket, sound effects kit, instruction booklet..............................	NPF	650	900	1500
Gilbert Erector No. 18000, cardboard box, one layer, "Space Age Erector," build your own Intercontinental Ballistic Missle or any one of 1001 models according to the box art, instruction booklet	NPF	NPF	NPF	NPF

1960	C4	C6	C8	C10
Gilbert Erector No. 10011, cylindrical cardboard tube, instruction page.......	NPF	NPF	NPF	NPF
Gilbert Erector No. 10021, cylindrical cardboard tube, instruction page.......	NPF	NPF	NPF	NPF

1960 (Continued)	C4	C6	C8	C10
Gilbert Erector No. 10032, cylindrical cardboard tube, base plates, instruction page...........................	NPF	NPF	NPF	NPF
Gilbert Erector No. 10037, cylindrical cardboard tube, remote control, 3-volt motor, instruction page..................................	NPF	NPF	NPF	NPF
Gilbert Erector No. 10042, metal lithographed box, two layers w/ cardboard insert tray, 3-volt motor, instruction booklet	20	40	75	125
Gilbert Erector No. 10053, metal lithographed box, two layers w/ insert trays, Rocket Launcher, Rocket, electric engine, instruction booklet..............................	25	55	85	135
Gilbert Erector No. 10063, metal lithographed box, two layers w/ insert tray, Boiler, Conveyor Belt, instruction booklet	35	70	110	190
Gilbert Erector No. 10074, metal lithographed box, two layers w/ insert trays, Ferris Wheel, electro magnet, no sound effects this year, instruction booklet..............................	80	150	250	350
Gilbert Erector No. 10084, metal lithographed double-sided box, two sides containing parts and insert trays, "Amusement Park Set," Merry-Go-Round, Parachute Jump, Power Plant, instruction booklet .	NPF	250	475	750
Gilbert Erector No. 10094, metal lithographed double-sided box, two sides containing parts and insert trays, "Master Builder Set," Mysterious Walking Robot, "Clamshell" Bucket, treads, instruction booklet	NPF	650	900	1500
Gilbert Erector No. 18010, cylindrical cardboard tube w/ plastic lid, "Space Age Erector," plastic pieces to build rockets, jet planes, instruction sheet	NPF	NPF	NPF	NPF

1960 (Continued)	C4	C6	C8	C10
Gilbert Erector No. 18020, cylindrical cardboard tube w/ plastic lid, "Space Age Erector," larger tube, more plastic pieces than No. 18010	NPF	NPF	NPF	NPF
Gilbert Erector No. 18030, cylindrical cardboard tube w/ plastic lid, "Space Age Erector," larger tube, more plastic pieces than No. 18020	NPF	NPF	NPF	NPF
Gilbert Erector No. 18040, cylindrical cardboard tube w/ plastic lid, "Space Age Erector," larger tube, more plastic pieces than No. 18030	NPF	NPF	NPF	NPF

1961	C4	C6	C8	C10
Gilbert Erector No. 10011, cylindrical cardboard tube, instruction page	NPF	NPF	NPF	NPF
Gilbert Erector No. 10021, cylindrical cardboard tube, instruction page	NPF	NPF	NPF	NPF
Gilbert Erector No. 10032, cylindrical cardboard tube, base plates, instruction page	NPF	NPF	NPF	NPF
Gilbert Erector No. 10042, metal lithographed box, two layers w/ cardboard insert tray, 3-volt motor, instruction booklet	NPF	NPF	NPF	NPF
Gilbert Erector No. 10053, metal lithographed box, two layers w/ insert trays, Rocket Launcher, Rocket, electric engine, instruction booklet	NPF	NPF	NPF	NPF
Gilbert Erector No. 10063, metal lithographed box, two layers w/ insert tray, Boiler, Conveyor Belt, instruction booklet	NPF	NPF	NPF	NPF
Gilbert Erector No. 10074, metal lithographed box, two layers w/ insert trays, Ferris Wheel, electro magnet, instruction booklet	NPF	NPF	NPF	NPF

1961 (Continued)	C4	C6	C8	C10
Gilbert Erector No. 10084, metal lithographed double-sided box, two sides containing parts and insert trays, "Amusement Park Set," Merry-Go-Round, Parachute Jump, Power Plant, instruction booklet	NPF	NPF	NPF	NPF
Gilbert Erector No. 10094, metal lithographed double-sided box, two sides containing parts and insert trays, "Master Builder Set," Mysterious Walking Robot, "Clamshell" Bucket, treads, instruction booklet	NPF	NPF	NPF	NPF
Gilbert Erector No. 18010, cylindrical cardboard tube w/ plastic lid, "Space Age Erector," plastic pieces to build rockets, jet planes, instruction sheet	NPF	NPF	NPF	NPF
Gilbert Erector No. 18020, cylindrical cardboard tube w/ plastic lid, "Space Age Erector," larger tube, more plastic pieces than No. 18010, instruction sheet	NPF	NPF	NPF	NPF
Gilbert Erector No. 18030, cylindrical cardboard tube w/ plastic lid, "Space Age Erector," larger tube more plastic pieces than No. 18020, instruction sheet	NPF	NPF	NPF	NPF
Gilbert Erector No. 18040, cylindrical cardboard tube w/ plastic lid, "Space Age Erector," larger tube, more plastic pieces than No. 18030, instruction sheet	NPF	NPF	NPF	NPF

1962	C4	C6	C8	C10
Gilbert Erector No. 10094, metal lithographed double-sided box, two sides containing parts and insert trays, "Master Builder Set," Myserious Walking Robot, "Clamshell" Bucket, treads, two instruction booklets	NPF	650	900	1500

1962 (Continued)

	C4	C6	C8	C10
Gilbert Erector No. 10161, milk carton container, disc wheels, instruction sheet, rare	NPF	NPF	NPF	NPF
Gilbert Erector No. 10171, milk carton container, base plates, instruction sheet, rare	NPF	NPF	NPF	NPF
Gilbert Erector No. 10181, metal lithographed box, two layers w/ cardboard insert tray, 3-volt motor, instruction booklet	20	40	75	125
Gilbert Erector No. 10201, metal lithographed box, two layers w/ insert trays, 325+ parts, Rocket Launcher, Rocket, electic engine, instruction booklet	25	55	85	135
Gilbert Erector No. 10211, metal lithographed box, two layers w/ insert tray, 375+ parts, "Cape Canaveral Set," Boiler, Conveyor Belt, Cherry Picker, instruction booklet	35	70	110	190
Gilbert Erector No. 10221, metal lithographed box, two layers w/ insert trays, "Lunar Drilling Set," Ferris Wheel, electro magnet, instruction booklet	80	150	250	350
Gilbert Erector No. 10231, metal lithographed double-sided box, two sides containing parts and insert trays, "Astronaut Set," Merry-Go-Round, Power Plant, Parachute Jump, crane, two instruction booklets	NPF	250	475	750

Vital Parts and Accessory Sets

	C4	C6	C8	C10
1E Square Girder Kit, 20-"C," 8-"B," 14-7/8" sc and nt	NPF	NPF	NPF	85
A-48 Mechanical Motor with Key, check for spring slip	NPF	NPF	NPF	40
A-49 Motor and Gearbox, 115 volt AC, running, EXC	NPF	NPF	NPF	40
A-52 Motor, 115 volt AC, running	NPF	NPF	NPF	85
Illumination Kit	NPF	NPF	NPF	150
Musical Parts, comp. reproducer, record, mechanism	NPF	NPF	NPF	200
P-51 Motor and Gearbox, 115 volt AC, running	NPF	NPF	NPF	110
P-55 Motor and Remote Control, 12 volt AC/DC, runs	NPF	NPF	NPF	150
P-56G Motor, 115 volt AC, tapered ends, running	NPF	NPF	NPF	125
P-58 Motor, 6-12 volt AC/DC, "basket case," not running	NPF	NPF	NPF	10
P-58 Motor, "Joe Long" rebuilt	NPF	NPF	NPF	50
Smoke and Choo-Choo Kit, 7-15 volt AC	NPF	NPF	NPF	125

FARM TOYS

By Kate Bossen

Who is a collector?

Farm toys are collected by everyone, from farmers to people who have never stepped foot on a farm. I, myself, did not grow up on a farm. Both sets of my grandparents left the farm during the dust bowl years of the early thirties, yet I am still drawn toward farming. I am not sure if it is the romantic ideal of the family farm or just the lure of big powerful machines. I have always loved machines of any type. I was the one who took all my toys apart and put them back together, usually with some improvements—at least I thought they were improvements. So I am sure I am like many other collectors who think about farming or living in a small town in the American breadbasket—we are living our dreams with our models of farm machinery.

Toys or Models?

Something I have found in America is that we all call what we collect "toys." In speaking with collectors from other countries, they distinguish between toys and models. Toys are designed to be played with and models are meant to be put on the shelf.

In the beginning, farm toys were just that—toys to be played with. It was not until the 1960s and 1970s that anyone really thought about making models for collectors. In the days of traveling salesmen, there were salesmen's samples. These were models used by the salesmen to illustrate the virtues of the product being sold. These were quite intricate and many had working details. These are quite collectible today.

The earliest farm toys were those made by the Wilkins Toy Company of Keene, New Hampshire, in the 1880s. These cast iron toys are hard to find and very expensive. Other manufacturers of cast iron farm toys were Arcade, Vindex, Hubley, Killgore, Kenton, Williams, and Dent.

Cast-iron toys were produced up to World War II in the 1940s. Then with the shortage of metals, toys were produced in Wood and other materials. There were many plastic farm toys made in the 1950s by companies such as Product Miniature, Raphael Lipkin, Monarch Plastics, JoHan, Kaysun Plastics, Alfinson, Atma, Design Fabricators, and Saunders Swader. There are also many rubber farm toys made by Auburn Rubber and Aubrubber.

Fred Ertl Sr. started making sandcast toys in the furnace in the basement of the family home after being laid off after World War II. Other leading manufacturers of diecast and metal farm toys were Eska, Carter Tru-Scale, Slik, Hubley, Lincoln Specialties, Dinky, Lesney, and Ruehl Products. Later, Scale Models and Spec Cast joined the ranks of the many companies producing farm toys and models today.

In the 1960s and 1970s, models were starting to be produced for the collector. At first most were produced by individuals looking to fill gaps in their collections. Ertl started producing collector or limited-edition models in the late seventies. At first most of these collector models produced by Ertl were kept to the toy safety standards of their day. Then in the early 1990s, Ertl introduced its precision line of models. These were models and not farm toys. Now most of the collector editions are models and not toys.

Eska made some of the first pedal tractors produced in the late 1940s. The Ertl Company and then Scale Models followed as the major manufacturers of pedal tractors in the U.S.

Prices

Good: The toy is complete, with no broken parts and has 90 to 95 percent of its original paint.

Excellent: The toy is in mint condition. It does not have any paint chips or scratches. It is complete and has no broken parts.

New in Box: The toy is in its original box and in mint condition. The box is also in excellent condition.

Contributor: Kate Bossen, Bossen Implement, Inc., 300 Washburn Ave., Hwy. 187 South, Lamont, IA, 50650. Phone: (563) 924-2880 Web site: www.bossenimp.com Kate Bossen is also the pricing contributor to the Standard Catalog of Farm Toys (Krause Publications, 2001) and is currently working on pricing for the upcoming second edition of that title.

Case Hay Loader, Vindex, $5200. Photo courtesy Bill Bertoia Auctions

Caterpillar Tractor, No. 6100, Courtland, $450. Photo courtesy Joe and Sharon Freed

Allis-Chalmers

	C6	C8	C10
Pedal Tractor, Model 190, orange, winged decal, Ertl	550	800	1000
Pedal Tractor, Model 190 XT, orange, winged decal, Ertl	450	600	750
Pedal Tractor, Model 200, orange, Ertl	475	650	900
Pedal Tractor, Model 7045, orange and black, Ertl	275	375	450
Pedal Tractor, Model 7080, orange and maroon, Ertl	275	375	550
Pedal Tractor, Model 8070, orange and black, Ertl	275	375	550
Pedal Tractor, Model C, orange, Eska	700	1000	1400
Pedal Tractor, Model CA, orange, Eska	700	1100	1500
Pedal Tractor, Model D14, orange, Eska	675	950	1250
Pedal Tractor, Model D17, orange, with white wheels, Ertl	675	950	1250
Tractor and Dump Trailer, No. 2660, Arcade Manufacturing Company, 1937, 8-1/4" long, AR3A	150	200	300
Tractor and Dump Trailer, No. 2657, Arcade Manufacturing Company, 1937, 12-3/4" long w/trailer, AR3	200	345	460
Tractor and Trailer, No. 2650, Arcade Manufacturing Company, 1936, total length 13" long, AR2	200	300	450

Allis-Chalmers (Continued)

	C6	C8	C10
Tractor Trailer, No. 2650, Arcade Manufacturing Company, 1937, 13" long w/trailer, AR4	250	375	500
Tractor, Model 190	55	115	195
Tractor, Model 7030, maroon engine, Ertl, 1974	95	245	325
Tractor, Model B-112, Ertl	70	110	165
Tractor, Model D-17, Ertl, 1964	145	365	750
Tractor, Model WC, Arcade Manufacturing Company, 1941, 7-3/4" long, AR5	425	675	1000

Avery

	C6	C8	C10
Tractor, very early, Hubley, 4-3/4" long	120	180	240
Tractor, stack, no hood, Arcade Manufacturing Company, 1923, 4-1/2" long, AR17	50	75	110

Case

	C6	C8	C10
Hay Loader, Vindex, 9" long	3000	4500	5200
Manure Spreader, Vindex, 12" long	500	1250	2000
Pedal Tractor, white and orange, Ertl	100	150	250
Pedal Tractor, white and black, Ertl	100	150	250
Pedal Tractor, Agri King, white and orange, Ertl	250	400	500
Pedal Tractor, Agri King 1070, desert tan and orange, Ertl	300	450	550
Pedal Tractor, Model 30 Pleasure King, beige and orange, Ertl	550	700	900

Caterpillar Tractor (Model D6) and Bulldozer, No. 2012, Doepke "Model Toys," $575. Photo courtesy Calvin L. Chausee

Ford Tractor, Farmall, No. 279, Arcade Manufacturing Company, $1100. Photo courtesy Perry Eichor

Case (Continued)

	C6	C8	C10
Pedal Tractor, Model 400, beige and orange, Eska	800	1300	2000
Pedal Tractor, Model 800 Case-O-Matic, beige and orange, Eska	750	950	1500
Pedal Tractor, Model VAC, orange, Eska	500	700	1750
Steam Tractor, No. 71, crew of two, tow-loop, small version of No. 25, Kansas Toy & Novelty Company, 2-1/2" long, KTV54	30	40	60
Steam Tractor, No. 25, crew of two, tow loop, large front, small rear metal open-spoke wheels and flywheel, Kansas Toy & Novelty Company, 3", KTV21	25	40	60
Tractor Plow, Three-bottom, Vindex, 10-1/4" long	1000	2500	3700
Tractor, Model 1070, Golden Demostractor, black hood & yellow cab, Ertl, 1970	225	650	1425
Tractor, Model 800, Johan, 1956-57	125	275	495

Case (Continued)

	C6	C8	C10
Tractor, Model 930, Ertl, 1963	125	275	650
Tractor, Model L, Ertl	42	63	85
Tractor, Model L, Vindex, 6-1/2" long	500	750	1030
Tractor, Model SC, Monarch, 1950s	95	245	435

Caterpillar

	C6	C8	C10
Dozer, Model D-6, Ertl	93	140	195
Dozer, Model D7, die-cast, Reuhl, 1:24-scale	300	475	750
Dozer, Model D7, plastic kit, could be purchased assembled, Reuhl, 1:24-scale	200	375	675
Grader, No. 12, die-cast, Reuhl, 1:24-scale	650	900	1350
Pedal Crawler Model D-4, with blade	2095	2950	NPF
Tractor, No. 271, Arcade Manufacturing Company, 1930, 7-1/2" long, AR30	450	800	1300

Caterpillar (Continued)

	C6	C8	C10
Tractor, No. 266X, Arcade Manufacturing Company, 1931, 3" long, AR33	50	75	100
Tractor, No. 267X, Arcade Manufacturing Company, 1931, 3-7/8" long, AR32	225	325	500
Tractor, No. 268X, Arcade Manufacturing Company, 1931, 5-5/8" long, AR31A	500	800	1350
Tractor, No. 269X, Arcade Manufacturing Company, 1931, 6-7/8" long, AR31	650	1100	1550
Tractor, No. 270Y, later No. 2700Y, Arcade Manufacturing Company, 1936, 7-3/4" long, AR34	750	1250	2200
Tractor, slush lead, Barclay Vehicles, 2-5/8" long, BV72	17	26	35
Tractor, No. 6100, mechanical, w/rubber treads, tin wind-up, Courtland, 6" long, 3" wide, 4-1/2" high	250	350	450
Tractor, w/stack, Savoye Pewter Toy Company, 2-3/4" long, SA19	10	15	20
Tractor, w/cast-iron driver, early, Structo, 8-1/2" long	275	415	550
Tractor, wind-up, Kingsbury, 8-1/2"	225	340	450
Tractor (Model D6) and Bulldozer, No. 2012, Doepke "Model Toys", 15" long	300	450	575
Tractor with Trailer, No. 46, steel treads, heavy spring clockwork motor, Structo	200	300	400
Tractor with Treads, No. 4646, Tootsietoy, 1931	27	41	55
Tractor, Model D-7, Reuhl, Miscellaneous Vehicles	312	468	625
Wheel Tractor, Model DW 10, die-cast, Reuhl, 1:24-scale	325	475	750

David Bradley

	C6	C8	C10
Cultipacker (Disc Harrows?), Auburn Rubber, 4-3/8" long, AI09	22	33	45
Manure Spreader, Auburn Rubber, 4-3/4" long, AI04	20	30	40
Plow, Two Furrow, Auburn Rubber, 4-3/8" long, AI08	20	30	40

Farmall

	C6	C8	C10
Pedal Tractor, Model 560, red with white decal, Eska & Ertl Co.	350	650	1200

Farmall (Continued)

	C6	C8	C10
Pedal Tractor, Model 806, red with white decal, Ertl	300	500	1000
Tractor, Model A, No. 7050, Arcade Manufacturing Company, 1941, 7-1/2" long, AR76	600	1000	1500
Tractor, Model M, No. 7070, Arcade Manufacturing Company, 1941, 7-1/4" long, AR77	300	450	700

Ford

	C6	C8	C10
Backhoe, Model 7500, Ertl	37	56	75
Pedal Tractor, Commander 6000, blue and gray, later style grille and decal, Ertl	800	1100	1500
Pedal Tractor, Commander 6000, blue and gray, early style grille and decal, Ertl	1500	2000	3000
Pedal Tractor, Model 8000, blue, Ertl	175	250	400
Pedal Tractor, Model 900, red and gray, stamped steel fenders, available with two or three bolt axle mounting bracket, Graphic Reproductions	1000	2900	3700
Pedal Tractor, Model 901, red and gray, die cast fenders, bar grille, Graphic Reproductions	1900	2900	3800
Pedal Tractor, Model TW-20, blue, Ertl	125	225	375
Pedal Tractor, Model TW-35, blue, Scale Models	100	225	300
Pedal Tractor, Model TW-5, blue, has dark TW-5 decal with red trim, Ertl	125	225	375
Pedal Tractor, Model TW-5, blue, has light blue TW-5 decal, Ertl	125	225	375
Powermaster, Model 961, Hubley	NPF	NPF	NPF
Tractor, No. 39, Matchbox, 1967	10	15	25
Tractor, No. 46, Matchbox, 1978	5	7	9
Tractor, Farmall, No. 279, Arcade Manufacturing Company, 1929, 6" long, AR78	500	750	1100
Tractor, Model 4000, blue & gray, Hubley, 1963	95	165	325
Tractor, Model 4000, split grille, Ertl, 1965	65	115	250
Tractor, Model 6000, steam boiler in front, Hubley, early 1920s, 4-3/4" long	125	188	250

John Deere Tractor, Model A, Auburn Rubber, $45. Photo courtesy Dave Leopard's book, Rubber Toy Vehicles

Ford (Continued)

	C6	C8	C10
Tractor, Model 6000, Hubley	150	225	300
Tractor, Model 6000 Commander, cast iron, with exhaust & air cleaner, Hubley, 1965	50	105	195
Tractor, Model 6000 Commander, cast iron, Hubley, 1978	25	50	105
Tractor, Model 8000, early, Ertl......	25	40	60
Tractor, Model 8N, plastic, gray w/red engine, Product Miniature, 1948.......................................	115	215	375

Fordson

	C6	C8	C10
Tractor, w/driver, rear wheels larger, visible engine, marked and "Made in USA", Craftoy, 2-1/2" long.......................................	15	30	45
Tractor, cast iron, w/driver, Miscellaneous Vehicles, 5-3/4" long	140	210	280
Tractor, No. 17, driver, horizontal grille pattern, crank, no tow hook, large 1-1/4" and 3/4" metal disk wheels w/four holes in disks, also found w/same size six spoke wheels, Kansas Toy & Novelty Company, 2-7/8" long, KTV17.......................................	25	35	45
Tractor, No. 2730X, rubber wheels, Arcade Manufacturing Company, 1934, 3-1/2" long, AR111 .	75	125	175
Tractor, No. 274, Arcade Manufacturing Company, 1928, 4-3/4" long, AR109	112	190	250
Tractor, No. 273, Arcade Manufacturing Company, 1928, 3-7/8" long, AR110	90	150	200
Tractor, Arcade Manufacturing Company, 1923, 5-3/4" long, AR108	150	225	325

Fordson (Continued)

	C6	C8	C10
Tractor, Model E-27N, Chad Valley, 1950................................	195	450	795
Tractor, Model Major, wind-up, opening hood, Chad Valley, 1930................................	215	375	725

Graham-Bradley

	C6	C8	C10
Tractor, Auburn Rubber, 4-1/2" long, AF09	25	38	50

International

	C6	C8	C10
Backhoe, Ertl..................................	50	75	100

International Harvester

	C6	C8	C10
Cub Tractor, Farmall, plastic, could be purchased assembled, Reuhl, 1:16-scale	175	350	575
Pedal Tractor, Model 1026, red with white decal, Ertl	300	400	800
Pedal Tractor, Model 50, plastic, red and black, Eska	60	125	175
Pedal Tractor, Model 66, red with white decal, Ertl	160	400	500
Pedal Tractor, Model 856, red with white decal, Ertl	300	475	900
Pedal Tractor, Model 86, red with black stripe decal, Ertl.................	175	400	500
Trac-Tractor, No. 277, Arcade Manufacturing Company, 1937, 8-1/4" long, AR218	600	950	1300
Trac-Tractor, No. 7120, Arcade Manufacturing Company, 1941, 7-1/2" long, AR219	1500	2500	3750

International Harvester Farmall

	C6	C8	C10
Pedal Tractor, Model 400, red, Eska..	400	800	1700

International Harvester Farmall (Continued)

	C6	C8	C10
Pedal Tractor, Model 450, red with decal grille, Eska	400	800	1800
Pedal Tractor, Model H, small version, red, open grille, Eska	700	1000	2500
Pedal Tractor, Model H/M, mid size, red, has open grille, Eska	700	1000	1500
Pedal Tractor, Model H/M, mid size, red, closed grille, low steering post, rear seat mounting bracket is about 2-1/2" from the rear of main tractor casting, Eska	700	1000	1500
Pedal Tractor, Model H/M, mid size, red, high steering post, closed grille, Eska	700	1000	1500

International, Farmall, McCormick

	C6	C8	C10
Tractor, Model 1206, No. 436, Ertl, 1966	125	295	835
Tractor, Model 240, Ertl, 1958	215	625	1425
Tractor, Model 400, Ertl, 1955	175	525	1475
Tractor, Model 450, Eska	275	685	1975
Tractor, Model 560, fast hitch, metal rims, Ertl, 1958	125	285	1175
Tractor, Model 806, Ertl, 1964-66	125	275	725
Tractor, Model M, plastic, McCormick decals, Product Miniature, 1946	75	150	365

John Deere

	C6	C8	C10
Bulldozer with Blade, Model 500, Ertl	50	75	100
Bulldozer, Model 440, Ertl	20	30	40
Combine, Model 6600, Ertl	70	105	140
Farm Wagon, w/two horses, Vindex, 7-1/2" long	800	1300	1900
Lanz Tractor, No. 50, Matchbox, 1963	15	25	35
Manure Spreader, horse-drawn, Vindex	500	1100	1800
Pedal Tractor, Model 10, green, three holes in engine compartment, Ertl	300	450	800
Pedal Tractor, Model 10, green, four holes in engine compartment, Ertl	300	450	800
Pedal Tractor, Model 20, green, Ertl	200	300	650
Pedal Tractor, Model 30, green, can be found with metal or plastic front wheel rims, seat and steering wheels, Ertl	175	250	500

John Deere (Continued)

	C6	C8	C10
Pedal Tractor, Model 40, green, Ertl	175	250	450
Pedal Tractor, Model 60, small version, green, Eska	300	550	950
Pedal Tractor, Model 60, large version, green, Eska	400	800	1000
Pedal Tractor, Model 620, green, Eska	325	675	1100
Pedal Tractor, Model 730, green, Eska	300	550	900
Pedal Tractor, Model 730, green, variation in body casting, Eska	400	850	1900
Pedal Tractor, Model A, green, Eska	1000	2000	5500
Pedal Tractor, Model A, red with yellow wheels, block type engine design, Eska	5000	11,000	15,000
Pedal Tractor, Model LGT, green, plastic grille, tin fenders and seat, Ertl	400	700	1000
Thresher, Vindex, 15" long	1500	2800	3900
Tractor Plow, Three-bottom, Vindex, 9" long	900	1400	2400
Tractor, Model 3010, no filters, 3 point hitch, Ertl, 1960	85	175	485
Tractor, Model 3020, many variations, Ertl, 1960s	22	95	235
Tractor, Model 430, w/3 point hitch, Ertl, 1958	395	695	1650
Tractor, Model 620, Ertl, 1956	75	235	845
Tractor, Model A, open, flywheel, cast driver, Ertl, 1946	125	195	650
Tractor, Model A, Auburn Rubber, 5" long, AF01	22	33	45
Tractor, Model A, closed flywheel, cast driver, Ertl, 1947	65	135	550
Tractor, Model B, high post, no driver, Ertl, 1950	85	215	575
Tractor, Model D, Vindex, 6-1/2" long	950	1700	2600

Kubota

	C6	C8	C10
Pedal Tractor, Model M6950, orange, Scale Models	150	225	350

Loadstar

	C6	C8	C10
Grain/Cattle Stake Truck, Ertl	60	90	120

Lorain

	C6	C8	C10
Shovel, Reuhl	700	1250	1900

Massey Ferguson

	C6	C8	C10
Farm Tractor, No. 1011, w/driver, Tootsietoy, 1941, 4" long	200	300	400

Ford Tractor, Farmall, No. 279, Arcade, $1100.

Massey Ferguson (Continued)	**C6**	**C8**	**C10**
Pedal Tractor, Model 390, red, Ertl	150	200	400
Tractor, Model 1080, Ertl, 1970	85	135	255
Tractor, Model 175, metal rims, Ertl, 1965	85	125	235
Massey Harris	**C6**	**C8**	**C10**
Combine, self-propelled, Reuhl, 1951-52	295	545	985
Pedal Tractor, Model 44, small version, red, open grille, Eska	3000	4000	5500
Pedal Tractor, Model 44, large version, red, closed grille, Eska	1200	2200	3100
Tractor, Model 101, cast iron, Hubley, 1939	45	75	135
Tractor, Model 44, 3 point hitch, very detailed, Reuhl, 1954	215	385	795
Tractor, Model 44, w/driver, Slik, 1950	45	135	360
Tractor, Model 44, standard, 8 slots in grille, Lincoln, 1950	95	185	375
Tractor, Model 44, molded in one piece, separate driver, King, 1950	95	195	350
Massey-Harris	**C6**	**C8**	**C10**
Combine, Pull-type, die-cast, made to fit 44 tractor, Reuhl, 1:20-scale	275	400	600
Disc Harrow, die-cast, made to fit 44 tractor, Reuhl, 1:20-scale	175	300	575

Massey-Harris (Continued)	**C6**	**C8**	**C10**
Loader, die-cast, made to fit 44 tractor, Reuhl, 1:20-scale	200	475	675
Roadmaster Wagon, die-cast, made to fit 44 tractor, Reuhl, 1:24-scale	150	275	550
McCormick-Deering	**C6**	**C8**	**C10**
Farmall Tractor, Arcade Manufacturing Company, 1937, 6-1/4" long, AR156	250	400	600
IH Farmall M Tractor, Auburn Rubber, 4" long, AF08	22	33	45
Manure Spreader, cast iron, w/team of horses, Arcade Manufacturing Company, 1930, 14" long	375	560	750
Plow, cast iron, animal drawn, Arcade Manufacturing Company, 1926	175	265	350
Thresher, Arcade Manufacturing Company, 1930, 9-1/2" long, AR158	200	300	400
Thresher, Arcade Manufacturing Company, 1927, 12" long, AR157	300	450	650
Tractor, No. 10-20, Arcade Manufacturing Company, 1925, 6-3/4" long, AR159	400	600	850
Weber Wagon, No. 440, cast iron, w/two horses, Arcade Manufacturing Company, 1927	400	600	800

Minneapolis-Moline

	C6	C8	C10
Tractor, Model R, later style, Auburn Rubber, 1946, 7-1/4" long, AF05	40	60	85
Tractor, Model R, early style, Auburn Rubber, 1940, 7-1/2" long, AF04	40	60	85
Tractor, Model Z, Auburn Rubber, 1938 & 1950, 4" long, AF03	22	33	45

Miscellaneous

	C6	C8	C10
Cattle Truck, Kingsbury, 1930s, 19" long	215	325	450
Cattle Truck, plastic, Hubley, post-war, 12"	85	128	170
Cattle Truck, cast iron, Kenton, c. 1938, 8" long	150	225	325
Combine Harvester, No. 51, Match-box, 1979	4	6	8
Combine, self-propelled, die-cast, made to fit 44 tractor, Reuhl, 1:20-scale	325	475	675
Corn Harvester, No. 702, Arcade Manufacturing Company, 1939, 6-1/2" long, AR56	175	275	400
Corn Harvester, No. 4180, Arcade Manufacturing Company, 1939, 5" long, AR57	130	200	300
Corn Planter, Arcade Manufacturing Company, 1939, 4-1/2" long, AR58	60	90	125
Disk Harrow, No. 62, eight disk on same 1-5/8" wide frame as No. 61, thirteen pieces, includes disks and wheels, four colors, Kansas Toy & Novelty Company, 4" long, KTV47	40	60	80
Disk Harrow, Auburn Rubber, 4-1/2" long, AI11	22	33	45
Farm Cart, mule, black driver, Kenton, 10-1/2" long	375	562	750
Farm Mower, No. 4210X, Arcade Manufacturing Company, 1939, 4" long, AR75	60	90	125
Farm Set, No. 7003, w/Ford Truck and Tractor, Huber StarBox Trailer, and Huber Star Scraper-Raker, Tootsietoy, 1928	135	205	275
Farm Stake, No. 004, Tonka, 1961	85	175	370
Farm Stake and Horse Trailer, No. 735, Tonka, 1962	75	125	225
Farm Stake and Horse Trailer, No. 035, Tonka, 1960	125	180	350
Farm Stake Truck, Tonka, 1957	190	375	480
Farm Stake Truck, No. 004, Tonka, 1958	100	150	300

Miscellaneous (Continued)

	C6	C8	C10
Farm Stake Truck, No. 004, Tonka, 1960	100	200	325
Farm Stake Truck, No. 404, Tonka, 1962	50	95	150
Farm Stake Truck, No. 404, Tonka, 1963	60	90	150
Farm Stake Truck and Horse Trailer, No. 035, Tonka, 1961	100	180	350
Farm Stake with Two-horse Trailer, No. 035, Tonka, 1958, 21-3/4" long	125	250	450
Farm Trailer, No. 286, Arcade Manufacturing Company, 1929, 6-3/8" long, AR229	150	200	325
Farm Trailer, No. 288, Arcade Manufacturing Company, 1929, 4-5/8" long, AR230	50	100	200
Farm Trailer, No. 289, Arcade Manufacturing Company, 1929, 3-3/4" long, AR231	50	100	200
Farm Wagon, w/two horses and driver, Kenton, 15" long	325	490	650
Farm Wagon, w/driver and one horse, early, Kenton, 15" long	300	450	600
Farm Wagon, cast iron, w/two horses and figure, Kenton, 14-1/2" long	500	750	1100
Farm Wagon, w/driver and one horse, Kenton, 14" long	500	750	1100
Farm Wagon, cast iron, w/two horses, 10"	200	300	400
Farm Wagon, cast iron, w/driver and two unusual horses, 14" long	250	375	500
Farm Wagon, cast iron, w/two horses and driver, Arcade Manufacturing Company, 10-3/4" long	463	695	925
Farm Wagon, cast iron and wood, large heavy horses, 25-1/2" long	300	450	600
Farm Wagon, cast iron, w/one horse, Hubley, c. 1915, 12-1/2" long	400	600	800
Farm Wagon and Team, Auburn Rubber	50	70	95
Grain Hauler, Dunwell	50	75	100
Grain Hauler Semi, No. 550, Tonka, 1952, 22-1/4" long	125	180	350
Harrow, Auburn Rubber, 4-1/2" long, AI10	20	30	40
Harvester, open top, Auburn Rubber, 5-1/2" long, AI03	35	50	75

Miscellaneous (Continued)

	C6	C8	C10
Hay Wagon, cast iron, w/driver and one steer, Kyser & Rex, 11-1/2" long	550	850	1300
Hay Wagon, w/two horses, Gibbs, 19" long	100	150	200
Hay Wagon, cast iron, w/driver and two steers, Kyser & Rex, 13" long	700	1200	1700
Livestock Hauler Semi, No. 500, Tonka, 1952, 22-1/4" long	100	150	350
Livestock Transport, Dunwell	90	135	180
Livestock Truck, Tonka, 1955	110	200	350
Livestock Truck, Kilgore, 9" long	500	800	1200
Livestock Truck, Kilgore, 1930s, 7" long	500	700	975
Mechanical Farm Tractor, No. 6000, w/scraper, rear tires are large rubber and front are small rubber tires, tin wind-up, Courtland, 8-3/4" long, 4-3/4" wide, 4-1/2" high	100	150	200
Mechanical Farm Tractor, No. 6050, w/o scraper, rear tires are large rubber and front are small rubber tires, tin wind-up, Courtland, 7-1/2" long, 4-3/4" wide, 4-1/2" high	75	100	150
Mechanical Farm Tractor, No. 6075, w/o scraper, rear tires are large tin litho while the front are small rubber tires, tin wind-up, Courtland, 7-1/2" long, 4-3/4" wide, 4-1/2" high	250	350	450
Mini-Tonka Livestock Van, No. 090, Tonka, 1964, 16" long	50	75	100
No. 63 Freeway Gas Tanker, Matchbox, 1973	10	15	20
Planter, No. 61, marked "KTN No. 61," vee-blade plough w/seed hopper, four pieces includes wheels and three colors, Kansas Toy & Novelty Company, 4" long, KTV46	40	60	80
Plough, No. 63, single blade on same shaft as No. 61, Kansas Toy & Novelty Company, 4" long, KTV48	40	60	80
Plow, cast iron, w/one horse, cast iron, 10-3/4" long	150	225	300
Plow, cast iron, w/one horse and driver, Wilkins Toy Company, 10-1/2"	1200	1900	2800

Miscellaneous (Continued)

	C6	C8	C10
Separtor-Thresher, No. 27, tow hook, auto-type metal open-spoke wheels (not tractor rims), lacquer or enamel, also un-numbered version, Kansas Toy & Novelty Company, 3" long, KTV23	25	40	50
Tipping Farm Trailer, No. 51, Matchbox, 1963	8	10	12
Tractor, "Baby Tractor," friction, marked "patented June 20, 1916", American Metal Toys	100	150	200
Tractor, No. 3560, Oliver, 1941, 7-1/2" long, AR180	500	800	1200
Tractor, has hood, no stack, Arcade Manufacturing Company, 1926, 4-1/2" long, AR18	125	200	325
Tractor, plastic, Ideal, 1948, 4" long	20	30	40
Tractor, No. 250, yellow w/red seat, Tonka, 1963	75	112	150
Tractor, No. 250, Tonka, 1962, 8-5/8" long	50	75	100
Tractor, No. 64, Caterpillar, 1981	3	5	7
Tractor, plastic, Manoil, P-12	12	18	25
Tractor, plain front, Manoil, 73A	12	18	25
Tractor, loop front, Manoil, 73	12	18	25
Tractor, driver in cab, Hubley, 3-1/4" long	100	150	200
Tractor, solid rubber, two dimensional, (part of set), Judy Company, The, 3-1/2" long, JF01	15	20	25
Tractor, No. 4060, black rubber wheels, Arcade Manufacturing Company, 1941, 6-1/4" long, AR223	325	500	700
Tractor, No. 472, Hubley	30	45	60
Tractor, No. 7240, rubber wheels, Arcade Manufacturing Company, 1941, 3-1/8" long, AR227	100	150	200
Tractor, Hubley, 1930s, 5" long	365	545	725
Tractor, Hubley, 9" long	62	93	125
Tractor, No. 7, Barclay Vehicles, late 1920s-early 1930s, BV116	15	22	30
Tractor, No. 42, Barclay Vehicles, 1931, 2-3/16" long, BV128	12	18	25
Tractor, No. 7341, wood wheels, Arcade Manufacturing Company, 1941, 6-1/4" long, AR224	400	600	850

Miscellaneous (Continued)

	C6	C8	C10
Tractor, No. 7200, Arcade Manufacturing Company, 1941, 6-1/2" long, AR222	175	275	400
Tractor, mechanical w/driver, Kingsbury, 8" long	250	375	500
Tractor and Carry-All Trailer, No. 170, w/No. 150 Crane and Clam, Tonka, 1949	200	300	525
Tractor and Carry-All Trailer, No. 120, w/No. 50 Steam Shovel, Tonka, 1949	155	280	475
Tractor and Carry-All Trailer, No. 125, w/No. 100 Steam Shovel, Tonka, 1949	150	250	550
Tractor and Carry-All Trailer, No. 130, Tonka, 1949, 30-1/2" long	100	150	350
Tractor and Cart, tin, w/iron driver, white rubber wheels, Kingsbury, c. 1930s, 11-1/2" long	200	300	400
Tractor and Dump Trailer, No. 7300, Arcade Manufacturing Company, 1941, 15-1/2" long, AR228	600	950	1300
Tractor and Plow, No. 7220, Arcade Manufacturing Company, 1941, tractor 6-1/2" long, overall length 8-3/4", AR104	350	550	850
Tractor and Wagon, No. 333, orange tractor w/black wheels; red wagon w/yellow wheels; originally sold for $.69, Auburn Rubber	40	80	125
Tractor and Wagon 8600, Ertl	44	66	88
Tractor, Heavy Gauge, No. 926, Marx Toy Co.	100	150	200

Oliver

	C6	C8	C10
Pedal Tractor, Model 1800, green with white wheels, plastic grille, Ertl	600	900	1500
Pedal Tractor, Model 1800, keystone decal, metal grille	1800	3100	NPF
Pedal Tractor, Model 1850, green with white wheels, plastic grille, Ertl	550	750	1200
Pedal Tractor, Model 1850, green with white wheels, plastic grille, Ertl	550	750	1200
Pedal Tractor, Model 1855, green with white wheels, plastic grille, Ertl	550	750	1200
Pedal Tractor, Model 88, small version, green with red wheels, w/open grill, Eska	1200	2200	3500

Oliver (Continued)

	C6	C8	C10
Pedal Tractor, Model 88, small version, green with red wheels, w/closed grille, Eska	900	1600	2200
Pedal Tractor, Model 880, green with white wheels, Eska	800	1000	1600
Plow, Arcade Manufacturing Company, 1923, 6-1/2" long, AR176	250	375	550
Plow, No. 4230X, Arcade Manufacturing Company, 1941, 6-1/4" long, AR177	150	2225	300
Row Crop "70" Tractor, Auburn Rubber, 8" long, AF06	45	65	85
Superior Spreader, No. 7140, Arcade Manufacturing Company, 1941, 10-1/4" long, AR178	600	950	1400
Tractor, No. 356, Arcade Manufacturing Company, 1937, 7-1/2" long, AR179	325	500	700
Tractor, Model 1800, No. 604, checkerboard decal, Ertl, 1963	125	275	750
Tractor, Model 55, utility, 3 point hitch, Slik, 1955	245	495	785
Tractor, Model 77, brown driver, Slik, 1948	95	215	435
Tractor, Model 880, solid rubber wheels, Slik, 1958	75	150	375

Reliable

	C6	C8	C10
Front-Lift Seeder, Auburn Rubber, 5" long, AI05	25	35	50

White

	C6	C8	C10
Pedal Tractor, gray, Scale Model	150	225	300

White Oliver

	C6	C8	C10
Pedal Tractor, Model 1855, green with white wheels, plastic grille, Ertl	550	750	1200

Whitewater

	C6	C8	C10
Farm Wagon, w/two horses, Vindex	1400	2400	3700

Wilkins

	C6	C8	C10
Hay dump rake, cast iron, w/driver and horse, Wilkins, 1886	3700	4300	NPF
Hay mower, cast iron, w/driver and pair of horses, Wilkins, 1886	2500	3300	NPF
Hay tedder, cast iron, w/driver and horse, Wilkins, 1886	5500	6200	NPF
Plow, cast iron, 1 bottom w/driver and horse, Wilkins, 1886	3500	4100	NPF

FISHER-PRICE

The Fisher-Price Toy Company began operation on October 1, 1930 in East Aurora, N.Y. Herman Fisher and Irving Price combined their names to title the company. Fisher was a former employee of the FairChild Company (a game manufacturer) and Price previously worked for the Woolworth Company.

As Fisher-Price built its talented work force, the contributions of Helen M. Schelle and Margaret Evans Price were invaluable. Schelle managed the company's early activities and Evans Price was the company's first artist and designer and created the early artwork for the reproduction of color lithography for the toys. The first toy line debuted in 1931. Because pine was abundant and easy to work with, it was the main wood used in the construction of Fisher-Price toys. Heavy cardboard with inserted brass eyelets to prevent wear from spinning axles was also used during the 1930s.

When the U.S. entered World War II, Fisher-Price, like many companies, turned to a different type of manufacturing. Fisher-Prices was set up to create and produce wood products, and this capacity dictated which essential goods they produced for the war. Ship fenders, first-aid kits, cots, bomb crates, and glider ailerons were among the items produced from 1943-1946. The toys of this period were made from scraps of wood, with bells and some metal parts painted instead of plated. Parts from similar toys were interchanged, resulting in odd and sometimes unusual variations.

Experimentation with plastics began in the 1950s as pine became difficult to obtain. Busy Bee was the first toy to successfully incorporate the new material. Plastic was used with increasing frequency in the 1950s due to its ease of molding, durability, and popular bright colors. In the 1960s, plastic took over as the main material used to produce toys.

Herman Fisher resigned as president of the company in 1966, but remained chairman of the board until Quaker Oats acquired Fisher-Price in 1969. Considered one of the oldest and largest toy manufacturers, Fisher-Price still has its main offices at the Girard Avenue address in East Aurora, N.Y.

Opportunities for Collectors

Toy Town USA, a non-profit organization, creates limited-edition (under 5,000) toys manufactured for the Toyfest celebration held in East Aurora each year. This event attracts toy collectors from all over North America and Europe.

The Fisher-Price Collectors Club is a great opportunity for fellow collectors to advance their knowledge, buy, sell, and communicate. The club newsletter, The Gabby Goose, is published three times a year and the club holds a convention in conjunction with Toyfest. For more information contact the Fisher-Price Collector's Club, c/o Jeanne Kennedy, 1840 N. Signal Butte Rd., Mesa, AZ, 85207. Web site: www.fpclub.org. An email address is also available on the Web site.

Assessing Value

The most important factor to consider when assessing the value of a Fisher-Price toy is the paper lithography. Most toys will be found with different degrees of edge wear and are called normal-wear toys. Toys in this condition often fall in a value class of Good/Very Good. When determining condition of a toy other areas consider soiling of the artwork and any fading/color loss. Advanced wear, soiling, or missing lithography classifies the toy as Poor condition.

Paint also contributes to value. Toys with slight paint wear on wheels, bases, and handles are considered Good/Very Good. Missing parts—especially missing lithography—affect the value of a toy. There is no means of replacing lost lithography.

A toy in Mint condition has absolutely no wear or damage. Lithography, paint, wheels, etc., are complete. Boxes—depending on condition, of course—for older Fisher-Price toys may add up to twenty percent to the value of a Mint toy.

Comic character toys and toys displaying company names demand higher prices. Just because a toy features Disney characters, Popeye, or other comic figures does not necessarily imply that a toy is rare. Rarity is based on the number of toys produced over time and the amount still in existence.

Toys that had accessories or figures that were often misplaced will also bring higher values. Often these accessories and/or figures are difficult to locate separately from the toy itself. A toy found mint in the box with accessories will certainly demand a higher price. The Fisher-Price toy prices listed in this guide were established by averaging toy prices taken from toy shows, flea markets, dealers, and collectors.

Contributor: John J. Murray, Box 52, Spring Brook, N.Y. 14140. Murray enjoyed a 30-year career with Fisher-Price and was responsible for color development and model decoration for all Fisher-Price Brands' products. He is currently president of the Toy Town USA Foundation of East Aurora, N.Y., which oversees the Toy Town Museum and the annual ToyFest. He is the co-author with Bruce R. Fox of *Fisher-Price: Historical, Rarity, and Value Guide 1931-Present 3rd Edition*, (Krause Publications, 2002).

Boom-Boom Popeye, No. 491, $1600. Photo courtesy John Murray; photo by Ross MacKearnin

Circus Wagon, No. 156, $1100. Photo courtesy John Murray; photo by Ross MacKearnin

Wooden

	C6	C8	C10
Allie Gator, No. 653, w/ plastic flippers on wooden wheels, 1960	45	140	175
Amusement Park, No. 932, 20-pieces, chair ride, musical merry-go-round, play swing, choo-choo, play people and more, 1963..............	125	310	585
Baby Chick Tandem Cart, No. 50, Easter only, 1953........................	50	75	110
Barky Buddy, No. 150, blue and yellow military uniform, red hat, red wheels, 1934..........................	450	1100	2000
Barky Dog, No. 462, black and white w/ red wheels, 1958...........	110	145	220
Barky Puppy, No. 103, blue wheels, oilcloth ears, pipecleaner and wooden ball tail, 1931	550	1000	2000
Big Bill Pelican, No. 794, opening bill, cardboard fish the first three years of release (add $25 if present), light blue feet, 1961......	95	135	195
Big Performing Circus, No. 250, included nine figures, original retail price was $2.75, 1932	450	900	1800
Blackie Drummer, No. 785, bear in parade uniform strikes bass drum w/ right arm and cymbal w/ left arm, 1939..............................	550	800	1300
Bonny Bunny Wagon, No. 318, Easter release, bunny pulling wagon, light blue wheels, 1959...	30	55	90

Wooden (Continued)

	C6	C8	C10
Boom Boom Popeye, No. 491, Popeye and Sweatpea, two mallets hit litho drum, unpainted wheels, 1937...	600	1100	1600
Bossy Bell, No. 656, bell, light blue wheels, yellow tail and horns, 1959...	50	80	110
Bouncing Bunny Wheelbarrow, No. 727, bell on head, 1939	450	750	1300
Bouncy Racer, No. 8, driver w/ helmet bounces and arms move as pulled, large red plastic wheels, 1960..	40	75	125
Bucky Burro, No. 166, yellow burro that bucks, spring tail, driver w/ sombrero, 1955............................	225	375	495
Buddy Bronc, No. 430, cowboy bounces on horse, 1938...............	275	450	975
Buddy Bullfrog, No. 728, offered w/ checkered pants in last year, croaking noise, jumping action, top hat, 1959...............................	85	120	185
Bunny Basket Cart, No. 303, plastic basket, 1960	30	55	85
Bunny Basket Cart, No. 301, woven basket, 1957	30	45	80
Bunny Bell Cart, No. 604, two mallets strike bell, light blue wheels, cart behind bunny, 1954..............	45	80	160
Bunny Bell Cart, No. 520, two mallets strike bell, yellow wheels, cart in front of bunny, 1941	125	250	550

Bucky Burro, No. 166, $495. Photo courtesy John Murray; photo by Ross MacKearnin

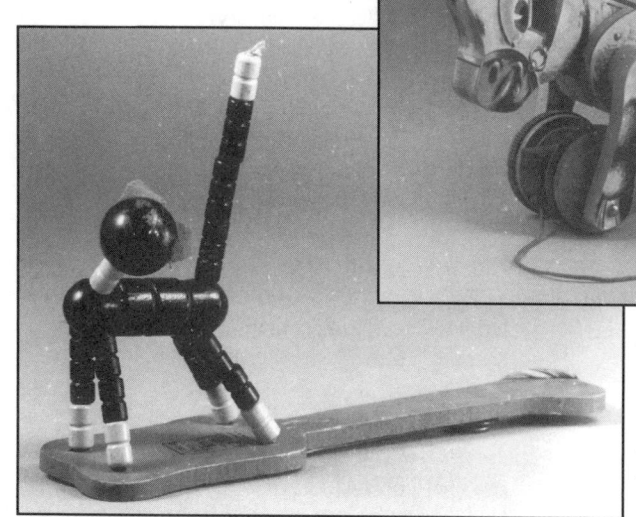

Tailspin Tabby, No. 400, 1931, $1000. Photo courtesy John Murray; photo by Ross MacKearnin

Wooden (Continued)	C6	C8	C10
Bunny Cart, No. 5, white bunny pulls cylindrical cart w/ metal rim, 1948	75	100	165
Bunny Drummer, No. 505, two mallets hit metal bell, yellow cart in front of bunny, red wheels, 1946..	150	225	550
Bunny Drummer, No. 512, two mallets hit painted wood disk or metal bell, yellow wagon in front of bunny, red wheels, 1942	150	225	550
Bunny Egg Cart, No. 404, new for 1949, forerunner of the No. 406 Bunny Cart, 1949	40	95	155
Bunny Egg Cart, No. 28, bunny pulling cart-sides are colorful eggs, dark blue/purple wheels, 1950...	100	160	225
Bunny Engine, No. 703, train w/ bell and bunny engineer, blue w/ yellow wheels, 1954....................	45	85	160
Bunny Push Cart, No. 303, bunny pushes cart, six light blue wheels, 1957..	40	80	120
Bunny Racer, No. 474, yellow and blue "racecar" w/ red wood wheels, wooden axles during WWII, 1942..............................	125	235	475

Wooden (Continued)	C6	C8	C10
Busy Bunny Cart, No. 719, bunny pulls 7" cart, Easter release, 1936..	300	600	1000
Butch the Pup, No. 333, yellow wheels, tail wags, felt ears, 1951..	50	70	110
Buzzy Bee, No. 325, first use of acetate (form of plastic) in a Fisher-Price toy, two spring antennae, 1950	25	45	70
Campbell Kids Farm Truck, No. 845, swayed back and forth, paper vegetable cut-outs, 1954..	145	300	750
Cash Register, No. 972, three numbered coins, plastic keys pop up characters, 1960	55	115	195
Chatter Monk, No. 798, monkey w/ jumping action, wooden hat, vinyl tail, chatter sound, 1957..	85	125	175
Chatter Telephone, No. 747, same as the Talk-Back Telephone of 1961, red plastic handle, blue wheels, wooden wheels through 1966, 1962..............................	30	45	65
Choo-Choo Local, No. 517, push toy, 18" stick, six wheels, steel bell, 1936....................................	350	850	1800

Wooden (Continued)	C6	C8	C10
Chubby Chief, No. 110, elephant on bicycle w/ steel bell, retailed for $1, 1932	450	950	2000
Chuggy Pop-Up, No. 616, red train, yellow wheels, pop-up engineer, metal boiler, realistic sound, 1955	85	125	170
Circus Wagon, No. 156, Ringmaster's arms move up and down and pipes play, blue wheels, 1942	525	750	1100
Concrete Mixer Truck, No. 926, mixing drum rotates and pops, plastic grille, lithographed sides, 1959	150	300	485
Corn Popper, No. 788, push toy, variations of this toy endured through 1990, 1963	15	30	50
Corn Popper, No. 785, red and blue push toy, 1957	35	95	175
Cotton Tail Cart, No. 525, upright bunny pulls red cart, legs rotate, clicking sound, yellow wheels, 1940	150	400	675
Cowboy Chime, No. 700, New version of old Dandy Dobbin, western pony head and litho saddle graphics attached to stick. Metal musical hush chime base had cowboy and indian graphics, 1951	110	285	475
Dandy Dobbin, No. 765, 14-1/2" long, 12-1/4" high, riding horse w/ red seat, green or yellow wheels, braided cord bridle, 1941	285	375	565
Dapper Donald Duck, No. 460, 1936	175	425	650
Dashing Dobbin, No. 742, riding horse, blue or red versions, braided cord bridle, 150lb capacity, 1938	450	650	900
Ding Dong Duckey, No. 724, Easter release, duck's head turned side to side and concealed wires played a tune as pulled, 1949	175	225	425
Dinkey Engine, No. 642, "chug-chug" sound, pistons moved, plastic cowcatcher and cab, 1959	35	50	95
Dizzy Dino, No. 407, Pop-Up Kritters, dinosaur on banjo paddle, pulley system used 50lb test fish line, retailed for $1, 1931	250	400	800

Wooden (Continued)	C6	C8	C10
Dizzy Donkey, No. 433, Pop-Up Kritters, donkey on blue paddle, black ears, 1939	85	130	175
Doc & Dopey Dwarfs, No. 770, each has hammer that hits stump, red wheels, 1938	875	1750	2600
Doctor Doodle, No. 100, styled by Margaret Evans Price, blue wheels, black topcoat and hat, orange bill, 1931	600	950	1500
Doctor Doodle, No. 477, green wheels, waddle, lower bill moves with clicker as quacking sound, 1940	300	450	675
Dogcart Donald, No. 149, Pluto pulls Donald in cart, 1936	600	1400	2500
Doggy Racer, No. 7, black wheels, arms "turned" the steering wheel, 1942	150	300	525
Donald Duck & Nephews, No. 479, w/ two nephews Huey and Louie, red wheels, 1941	425	575	875
Donald Duck Cart, No. 544, swinging arms, concealed voice, blue cart behind Donald in red outfit, red wheels, 1942	275	350	485
Donald Duck Cart, No. 500, unpainted wheels, red cart behind Donald, Easter release, 1937	350	675	1200
Donald Duck Cart, No. 605, orange flip-flop feet, quack-quack sound, flowers litho on blue and yellow cart behind Donald, 1954	125	250	425
Donald Duck Cart, No. 469, red wheels, blue base, Easter release, chick can behind Donald, 1940	200	450	775
Donald Duck Choo-Choo, No. 450, yellow wheels, red base, blue engineer's hat, steel bell, 1942	95	200	325
Donald Duck Choo-Choo, No. 450, yellow wheels, blue base, red engineer's hat, steel bell, 9-1/2" long in 1940, 8-1/2" long in 1941, 1940	300	400	675
Donald Duck Delivery, No. 715, long-billed Donald in front of pink cart w/ blue wheels, 1936	350	750	1100

Doc & Dopey Dwarfs, No. 770, $2600. Photo courtesy John Murray; photo by Ross MacKearnin

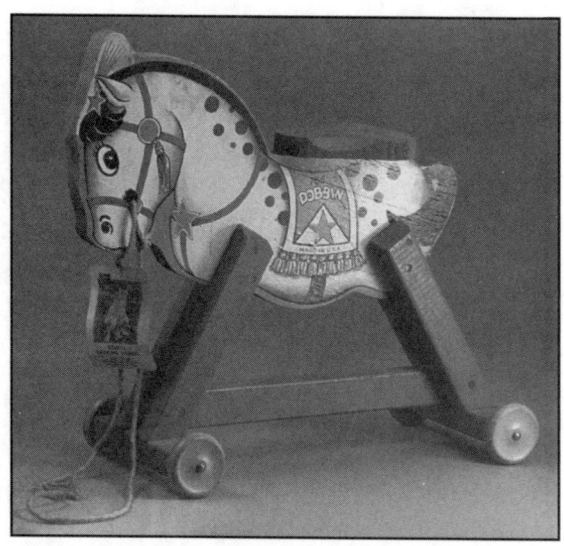

Dandy Dobbin, No. 765, $565. Photo courtesy John Murray; photo by Ross MacKearnin

Ferdinand the Bull, No. 434, $1200. Photo courtesy John Murray; photo by Ross MacKearnin

Donald Duck Drum Major, No. 432/532, $325

Fisher-Price Pony Express, No. 733, $585. Photo courtesy John Murray; photo by Ross MacKearnin

O'BRIEN'S COLLECTING TOYS 11TH EDITION

Wooden (Continued)	C6	C8	C10
Donald Duck Drum Major, No. 550/463, red wheels, green base, Donald holding green baton, 1940	150	350	725
Donald Duck Drum Major, No. 432/532, blue wheels, red base, Donald holding yellow baton, 1948	85	175	325
Donald Duck Drummer, No. 454, two mallets, arms move to strike red drum, red wheels, blue base, 1949	285	325	475
Donald Duck Pop-Up, No. 425, red paddle, rubber bill, oilcloth wings, 1938	325	650	1100
Donald Duck Xylophone, No. 177, red wheels, green base, blue hat (different from No. 185), two arms hold mallets that strike xylophone when pulled, 1946	350	450	675
Donald Duck Xylophone, No. 185, red wheels, blue base, blue hat, two arms hold mallets to strike xylophone when pulled, 1938	475	700	925
Dopey Dwarf, No. 770, blue wheels, red base, two mallets move hit drum when pulled, 1939	350	650	1375
Doughboy Donald, No. 744, 13-3/4" long, soldier outfit, two mortars, Pluto pulling green base w/ red wheels, 1942	550	1000	2375
Drummer Bear, No. 102, yellow wheels, blue base, black hat, 1931	550	1000	2000
Ducky Cart, No. 51, litho yellow duck w/ blue background, red wheels, 1950	45	85	125
Ducky Cart, No. 6, duck pulls cylinder-shaped cart w/ red wheels, 1948	45	85	165
Ducky Daddles, No. 14, yellow duck w/ blue wheels, exclusive for F.W. Woolworth Company, 1941	35	90	165
Ducky Daddles, No. 148, predecessor of Snap Quack, waddle, movable feet, head turns side to side, quacks, 1942	175	300	625
Dumbo Circus Racer, No. 738, rubber arms turned steering wheel, 10-3/4" long,, 1941	450	1000	2000
Easter Bunny, No. 490, pink and white, 1936	125	350	600

Wooden (Continued)	C6	C8	C10
Elsie's Dairy Truck, No. 745, F-P's second advertising toy, based on Borden's Elsie the Cow, truck driven by her son Beau-regard, movable arms struck nickel bell on grille, came with two glass square bottles (add $50 for each bottle), 1948	525	725	975
Farmer in Dell Music Box, No. 763, formerly #764, red crank/handle on side, 1962	30	65	130
Farmer in the Dell Music Box Barn, No. 764, crank, strap, Swiss music box, 1960	25	65	135
Farmer in the Dell TV Radio, No. 166, spring anetnnae, white handle, 1963	25	35	60
Fido Zilo, No. 707, movable arms w/ mallets to strike four nickel keys, red wheels, 1955	90	130	165
Fire Truck, No. 630, red truck w/ yellow grille & ladder, driver bounces and turns when pulled, 1959	35	55	110
Fuzzy Fido, No. 444, spring wire tail, offset green wheels caused waddling, 1941	225	325	450
Gabby Duck, No. 767, blue wheels, yellow duck, orange bill opens, waddling motion, quacks, 1952	55	80	225
Gabby Goofies, No. 777, final version, blue Mama Goofy w/ three ducklings, 1963	20	30	45
Gabby Goofies, No. 775, first version, red Daddy Goofy w/ three ducklings, twirling acetate wings, 1956	40	60	80
Gabby Goose, No. 120, red wheels, sailor suit, concealed voice, 1936	400	750	1100
Galloping Horse & Wagon, No. 737, horse pulling red wagon w/ yellow wheels, 1948	150	325	475
Gold Star Stagecoach, No. 175, two horses pull stagecoach, driver sways side to side, two mail pouches, 1954	285	390	625
Golden Gulch Express, No. 191, red and green train, spring mounted indian on the tender, 1961	110	145	225

Fuzzy Fido, No. 444, $450. Photo courtesy John Murray; photo by Ross MacKearnin

Donald Duck Xylophone, No. 177, $675. Photo courtesy John Murray; photo by Ross MacKearnin

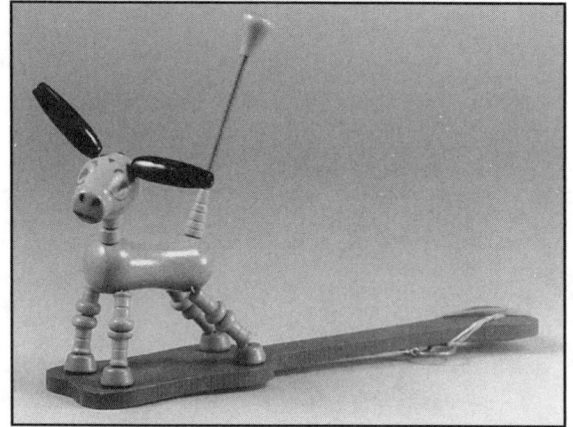

Dizzy Donkey, No. 433, $175. Photo courtesy John Murray; photo by Ross MacKearnin

Squeaky the Clown, No. 777, $475. Photo courtesy John Murray; photo by Ross MacKearnin

Wooden (Continued)	C6	C8	C10
Go'N Back Jumbo, No. 360, Walky-Balky Back-Up Toys, wind up w/ removable key, oilcloth ears, pipecleaner tail, styled by Evans Price, designed by Edward Savage, 1931	450	900	1200
Granny Doodle, No. 101, felt bonnet, orange wheels, orange bill, 1931	600	1000	1500
Granny Doodle & Family, No. 101, duck followed by two baby ducks, green wheels, 1933	650	1500	2000
Happy Helicopter, No. 498, litho teddy bear pilot, yellow wheels and propellers, 1953	150	200	300

Wooden (Continued)	C6	C8	C10
Happy Hippo, No. 151, vinyl ears, spring tail, storage inside for other toys, 1962	115	170	230
Hot Diggety, No. 800, wind up, hat, painted face, heavy metal dancing feet, 1934	600	1200	1800
Howdy Bunny, No. 757, orange "running" legs, green base, red wheels, 1939	300	650	975
Huckleberry Hound Zilo, No. 711, Sears exclusive, 1961	175	475	800
Huffy Puffy Train, No. 999, engine, coal car, cattle car, caboose, yellow wheels, "chug-chug" sound, 1958	110	150	225

Hot Dog Wagon, No. 750, $800. Photo courtesy John Murray; photo by Ross MacKearnin

Donald Duck Choo Choo, No. 450, 1940, $675. Photo courtesy John Murray; photo by Ross MacKearnin

Kriss Kricket, No. 678, $200. Photo courtesy John Murray; photo by Ross MacKearnin

Gold Star Stage Coach, No. 175, $625. Photo courtesy John Murray; photo by Ross MacKearnin

Wooden (Continued)	C6	C8	C10
Humpty Dump Truck, No. 145, big yellow wheels, two characters, 1963	40	90	160
Humpty Dumpty, No. 757, smiling face one side, crying face on the other, bells for hands, could roll along on arms or feet, 1957	265	350	425
Husky Dump Truck, No. 145, big orange tires, two characters, 1961	30	85	140
Jack-n-Jill TV Radio, No. 148, Swiss music box, winding knob, spring aerial, 1959	25	65	110
Jingle Giraffe, No. 472, blue wheels, spring tail, nickeled bell, 1956	150	275	385

Wooden (Continued)	C6	C8	C10
Jolly Jumper, No. 450, red wheels w/ green feet, googly eyes, 1954.	35	60	100
Jolly Jumper, No. 793, green frog, big yellow wheels, mouth opens "croak" sound, 1963	25	50	80
Juggling Jumbo, No. 735, crank pops five colored wooden balls through circular acetate trunk, spring tail, vinyl ears, 1958	235	300	425
Jumbo Jitterbug, No. 422, Pop-Up Kritter, movable trunk & legs, oilcloth ears, blue paddle, 1940 ..	65	150	375
Jumbo Rolo, No. 755, blue elephant pedals tricycle, six colored balls rattle in cage behind tricycle, 1951	235	300	425

Mickey Mouse Choo-Choo, No. 432, $1500. Photo courtesy John Murray; photo by Ross MacKearnin

Looky, Chug, Chug, No. 161, 1953, $375. Photo courtesy John Murray; photo by Ross MacKearnin

Wooden (Continued)	C6	C8	C10
Junior Circus, No. 902, 22-pieces in reusable container, 1963..............	75	350	395
Katy Kackler, No. 140, wings and feet move up and down, "cluck-cluck-squawk" sound, red wheels, first of three versions, 1954....................	80	120	175
Kicking Donkey, No. 175, large rubber ears, red wheels, rope tail, 1937....................	400	850	1300
Kitty Bell, No. 499, cat's arms rotate ball that strikes bell, blue base, yellow wheels, 1950...........	125	170	285
Lady Bug, No. 658, two spring antennae, red shell, "twirp-twirp" sound, 1961	35	70	100
Leo the Drummer, No. 480, red base, yellow wheels, two spring "sticks" to strike drum, 1952....................	235	285	390
Looky Chug-Chug, No. 161, engine and coal car, red wheels, nickel bell, moving pistons, 1949....................	125	225	375
Looky Fire Truck, No. 7, three firemen, moving eyes, nickel bell, red truck w/ yellow wheels, 1950....................	125	160	240
Lop-Ear Looie, No. 415, Pop-Up Kritter, mouse, retailed for 25 cents; paddle in red, blue, yellow or green, 1934....................	225	335	450
Lucky Monk, No. 109, monkey in orange cart w/ blue wheels, felt hat, sound, retailed for $1, 1932....................	350	850	1700

Wooden (Continued)	C6	C8	C10
Merry Mousewife, No. 662, red wheels, sweeps broom, yellow tail and hat, 1962....................	60	90	125
Merry Mutt, No. 473, red base, blue wheels, two nicleled 3" xylophone keys, two spring mallets, 1949....................	85	125	155
Mickey Mouse Band, No. 530, first Disney-themed release, blue base, yellow wheels, Mickey and Pluto, push toy w/ 18" stick, 1935....................	750	1500	2800
Mickey Mouse Choo-Choo, No. 432, blue base, yellow wheels, Mickey w/ long-billed red hat, nickel bell, 1938	750	1125	1500
Mickey Mouse Drummer, No. 476, red base, blue wheels, Mickey's arms move and mallets hit metal-topped drum, 1941	257	350	475
Mickey Mouse Puddle Jumper, No. 310, yellow wheels, car sways, Mickey bounces side to side, 1953....................	125	200	275
Mickey Mouse Safety Patrol, No. 733, Mickey the motorcycle cop pulls cart, yellow wheels, hands swing reading "STOP" and "GO", 1956	265	400	575
Mickey Mouse Xylophone, No. 798, w/out band outfit, 1942	275	500	925
Mickey Mouse Xylophone, No. 798, band outfit, blue base, yellow wheels, 5-key xylophone, arms hold mallets, 1939	575	800	1250

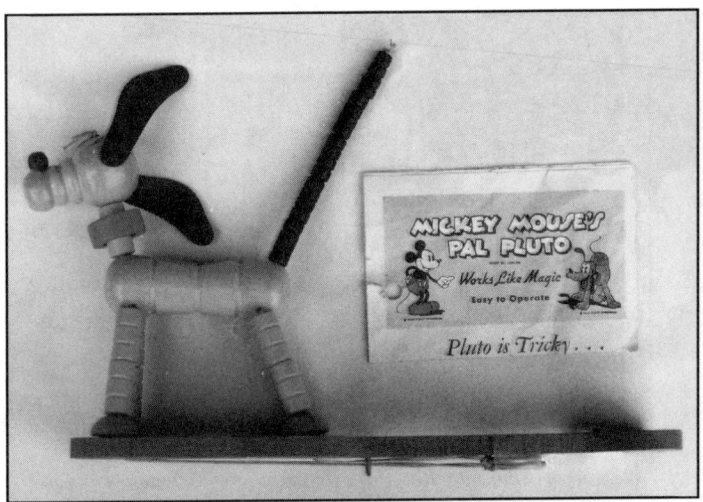

Pluto Pop-Up, No. 440, 1936, $185.

Katy Kackler, No. 140, $175. Photo courtesy John Murray; photo by Ross MacKearnin

Wooden (Continued)	C6	C8	C10
Mickey Mouse Zilo, No. 714, last Sears exclusive xylophone, last Disney pull-toy, Mickey in band outfit, 3 xylophone keys, 1963	165	350	675
Molly Moo-Moo, No. 190, red wheels, head "moo"ves up and down, spring tail, 1956	65	225	400
Moo-oo Cow, No. 155, black and white cow, vinyl ears, pink wheels, spring tail, 1958	125	170	230
Mother Goose, No. 164, orange plastic wheels, blue scarf on head, 1964	NPF	40	75
Mother Goose Music Cart, No. 784, yellow goose pulls red cart, feet flip flop as pulled, 1955	35	70	145
Music Box Sweeper, No. 131, final version, Swiss music box, steel yoke, 1961	40	65	120
Musical Elephant, No. 145, 1948	165	325	700
Musical Push Chime, No. 722, 1950	35	50	125
Musical Sweeper, No. 100, 1950	65	135	235
Musical Sweeper, No. 225, 1953	40	65	160
Musical Tick Tock Clock, No. 997, 1962	25	45	90
Nosey Pup, No. 445, 1956	25	60	95
Patch Pony, No. 616, 1963	20	35	50
Perky Pot, No. 686, 1958	85	110	155

Wooden (Continued)	C6	C8	C10
Peter Bunny Cart, No. 472, 1939	100	235	425
Peter Bunny Engine, No. 721, 1949	150	275	425
Peter Bunny Engine, No. 715, 1941	85	225	475
Peter Pig, No. 479, 1959	35	50	90
Pinky Pig, No. 695, 1958	35	90	140
Pinky Pig, No. 695, first version, wooden eyes, 1956	40	70	110
Pinocchio Express, No. 720, 1939	650	850	1300
Playful Puppy, No. 625, 1961	55	70	100
Playland Express, No. 192, 1962	105	140	195
Plucky Pinocchio, No. 494, 1939	450	725	1100
Pluto Pop-Up, No. 440, 1936	70	135	185
Pony Chime, No. 137, 1962	40	70	95
Pony Express, No. 733, 1941	110	250	585
Poodle Zilo, No. 739, 1962	50	110	185
Pop 'N Ring, No. 809, 1959	40	65	135
Popeye, No. 700, red base, yellow wheels, 1935	700	1750	2500
Popeye Cowboy, No. 705, 1937	700	1650	2300
Popeye Spinach Eater, No. 488, 1939	650	1300	1600
Popeye the Sailor, No. 703, unpainted wheels, arms strike bell attached to steering wheel, green boat-shaped base, 1936	850	1475	2100
Prancing Horses, No. 766, 1937	400	975	1800
Pudgy Pig, No. 478, 1962	40	60	85

Lop-Ear Looie, No. 415, $450. Photo courtesy John Murray; photo by Ross MacKearnin

Mickey Mouse Safety Patrol, No. 733, $575. Photo courtesy Kent M. Comstock

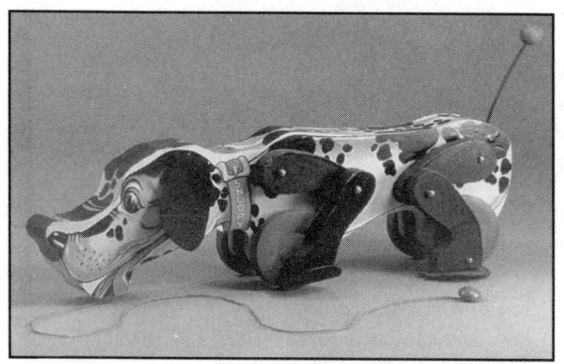

Snoopy Sniffer, No. 180, $235. Photo courtesy John Murray; photo by Ross MacKearnin

CONDITION CODE

C6 Good; evident overall wear, well played with but acceptable to many collectors
C8 Very Good; minor overall wear, very clean
C10 Mint; like new

Note: Mint in Box commands a higher price.
Condition below C6 brings considerably lower prices

Wooden (Continued)	C6	C8	C10
Puffy Engine, No. 444, 1951	50	70	110
Pull-A-Tune Xylophone, No. 870, 1957	45	80	110
Pushy Doddle, No. 507, 1933	550	1350	2000
Pushy Elephant, No. 525, 1934	450	975	1800
Pushy Piggy, No. 500, first push toy, 1932	700	1500	2300
Quacko Duck, No. 300, 1939	60	110	175
Quacky Family, No. 799, 1946	75	130	185
Queen Buzzy Bee, No. 444, 1962	25	45	70
Rabbit Cart, No. 52, 1950	35	70	125
Racing Bunny Cart, No. 723, 1938	150	295	425
Racing Ponies, No. 760, 1936	450	850	1300
Racing Pony, No. 705, 1933	500	1000	1500
Racing Rowboat, No. 730, 1952	235	280	390

Wooden (Continued)	C6	C8	C10
Raggedy Ann & Andy, No. 711, 12" long, green base, red wheels, arms attached to mallet that hits drum between them, 1941	1000	2300	3875
Rattle Ball, No. 682, 1959	20	30	40
Riding Horse, No. 254, 1940	400	625	975
Rock-A-Bye Bunny Cart, No. 788, 1940	175	425	775
Rock-A-Stack, No. 627, 1960	15	40	70
Roller Chime, No. 123, 1953	85	120	155
Rolling Bunny Basket, No. 310, 1961	35	65	110
Rooster Cart, No. 469, 1938	110	325	675
Safety School Bus, No. 990, 1962	80	175	295
Safety School Bus, No. 983, first appearance of "Play Family" figures, 1959	300	450	700
Scotty Dog, No. 710, 1933	350	850	1500

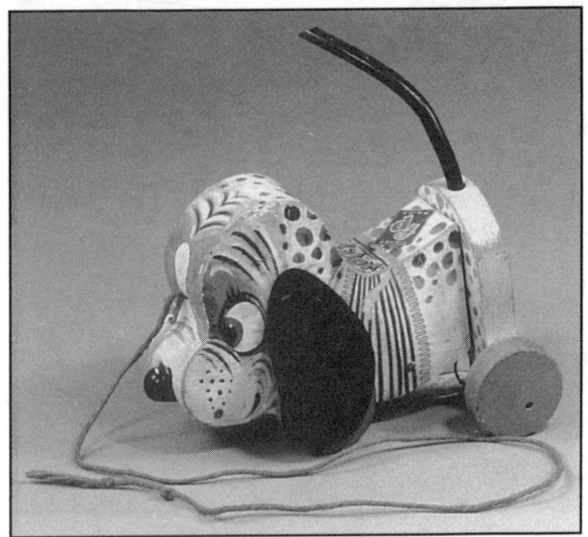

Nosey Pup, No. 445, $95. Photo courtesy John Murray; photo by Ross MacKearnin

Queen Buzzy Bee, No.314, $70. Photo courtesy John Murray; photo by Ross MacKearnin

Wooden (Continued)

	C6	C8	C10
Shaggy Zilo, No. 738, 1960.............	90	120	180
Skipper Sam, No. 155, 1934...........	850	2100	3800
Sleepy Sue (Turtle), No. 495, 1962..	55	75	90
Smokie Engine, No. 642, 1960........	45	70	90
Snoopy Sniffer, No. 180, 1958........	50	115	235
Snoopy Sniffer, No. 180, 1938........	130	290	475
Snorky Fire Engine, No. 168, four fireman figures included, 1960...	185	300	425
Sonny Duck Cart, No. 410, 1941	75	200	425
Space Blazer, No. 750, 1953	375	525	725
Squeaky the Clown, No. 777, 1958..	250	325	475
Stake Truck, No. 649, 1960.............	40	80	160
Streamline Express, No. 215, 1935..	900	1700	2400
Strutter Donald Duck, No. 510, 1941..	125	275	485
Struttin' Donald Duck, No. 900, 1939..	450	975	1500
Sunny Fish, No. 420, 1955	100	200	395
Suzie Seal, No. 460, 1961	25	40	85
Tabby Ding Dong, No. 730, 1939..	350	925	1450
Tailspin Tabby, No. 400, 1931........	225	610	1000
Tailspin Tabby Pop-Up, No. 600, 1947..	145	170	225
Talk-Back Telephone, No. 747, 1961..	75	165	225

Wooden (Continued)

	C6	C8	C10
Talking Donald Duck, No. 765, 1955..	100	140	195
Talky Parrot, No. 698, 1963	145	180	260
Tawny Tiger, No. 654, 1962	115	130	180
Teddy Bear Parade, No. 195, 1938..	850	1400	1750
Teddy Choo-Choo, No. 465, 1937..	200	475	825
Teddy Drummer, No. 775, 1936..	300	695	1400
Teddy Station Wagon, No. 480, 1942..	150	300	475
Teddy Tooter, No. 712, 1957	225	275	395
Teddy Tooter, No. 150, 1940	200	475	985
Teddy Trucker, No. 711, 1949	100	225	395
Teddy Xylophone, No. 752, 1948..	250	300	425
Teddy Zilo, No. 777, 1950	60	130	225
Ten Little Indians TV Radio, No. 159, 1961....................................	25	45	60
This Little Pig, No. 910, 1963........	20	35	50
Thumper Bunny, No. 533, 1942......	225	575	800
Timber Toter, No. 810, 1957...........	50	100	150
Timmy Turtle, No. 150, 1953..........	85	135	180
Tiny Teddy, No. 634, 1955	40	75	110
Tiny Tim, No. 496, 1957.................	35	70	120
Tip-Toe Turtle, No. 773, 1962	30	45	80
Toot Toot Engine, No. 641, 1962....	30	45	85
Tow Truck, No. 615, 1960	45	70	160
Toy Wagon, No. 131, 1951	240	325	450

Super-Jet, No. 415, $225. Photo courtesy John Murray; photo by Ross MacKearnin

Talking Donald Duck, No. 765, $195. Photo courtesy John Murray; photo by Ross MacKearnin

Teddy Bear Zilo, No. 777, $225. Photo courtesy John Murray; photo by Ross MacKearnin

Wooden (Continued)	C6	C8	C10
Trotting Donald Duck, No. 741, 1937	550	825	1800
Tuggy Turtle, No. 139, 1959	95	130	185
Uncle Timmy Turtle, No. 125, 1956	50	120	150
Waggy Woofy, No. 437, 1942	100	185	300
Walt Disney's Carnival, No. 483, 1936	325	850	2400
Walt Disney's Easter Parade, No. 475, 1936	450	1250	2400
Walt Disney's Mickey Mouse, No. 209, 1936	250	400	800
Walt Disney's Pluto-the-Pup, No. 210, 1936	225	450	800

Wooden (Continued)	C6	C8	C10
Whistling Engine, No. 617, 1957	75	115	185
Wiggily Woofer, No. 640, 1957	85	120	185
Winky Blinky Fire Truck, No. 200, 1954	55	110	185
Woodsy-Wee Circus, No. 201, 1931	500	1400	2500
Woofy Wagger, No. 447, 1947	45	140	265
Woofy Wowser, No. 700, 1940	100	325	475
Ziggy Zilo, No. 737, 1958	50	100	185

GUNS

(See also Premiums, Comic Characters)

It can be argued that guns have changed and shaped the course of history in the United States. Throughout every conflict, beginning with the Revolutionary War, guns played a major role in the outcome of battles, both here and abroad. Important in an historical context, guns are a vital and important category of toy collecting. When toys began to be mass-produced after the Civil War, toy guns were among the first to appear on the market. Their success was instantaneous, and toy guns remained among the most popular selling toys through the 1960s.

Although toy guns were patented in the 1850s, they were not manufactured in any quantity until a decade later due to the wartime shortages. These early toy guns were, for the most part, pea shooters and cork poppers and were usually made of wood with metal hardware, although iron and lead types may occasionally be found among them. These early examples are hard to find today and most are known only through their patent drawings. By 1870, inventors, trying to add realism to these toy guns, began using paper caps. This invention had been developed just prior to the Civil War and was known as the Maynard Tape Primer.

The tape primer was originally intended to detonate muzzle-loading arms and closely resembled a roll of modern paper caps. For the first time, toy guns could make a loud noise, yet still be relatively safe and harmless. Naturally this spurred the demand for these new toys and designers worked overtime to create new and appealing guns. Their output was prolific, and today the period from 1870 to 1900 is regarded as the "golden age" of the toy gun—especially the toy cap pistol.

By 1880 the cast-iron cap pistol had become the most popular type of toy gun by far, and the various toy makers—primarily J. & E. Stevens and Ives—were competing among themselves to see who could produce the most unique and appealing designs. A glance at any collection of these early toy pistols will show that realism was secondary to artistic imagination. Many pistols from this period were covered with ornamentation and, in some cases, any resemblance to a real gun was purely coincidental. Leaf-and-scroll designs were the most popular, but pistols can also be found with numerous other designs, including two- and three-dimensional figures, and animated figures. Guns with moving figures, though not as rare as some, are worth much more to a collector than an ordinary-looking pistol from the same period.

Another very desirable pistol from the same era is known as the head pistol. It featured a head, either human or animal, placed at the breech end of the barrel with the mouth open to receive the cap. Over two-dozen varieties of head and animated pistols are known to exist, but are so much in demand that they are seldom offered for sale.

The most popular material used to make these early toy pistols was cast iron, which continued to be used heavily into the twentieth century, until the demands of World War II cut off the supply. Many varieties of old toy guns were, however, made from such diverse materials as paper, wood, steel, tin, lead, rubber, zinc, glass, and even wax. During World War II toy guns were even made of molded sawdust mixed with glue. After the war, a few cast-iron pistols were produced and assembled, using both new and old parts, but the cost proved to be prohibitive, and makers soon turned to less expensive metals such as steel and die-cast zinc. By 1950 most toy pistols were being made of die-cast material and plastic, both of which continue to be used today.

From almost the very beginning, toy gun makers have felt the need to personalize their products; hundreds of different names can be found embossed on these little guns. Some examples that come to mind are Excelsior, Victor, American Bulldog, Acorn, Sun, Boom, Darb, Ace Daisy, Cowboy King, Polo, Triumph, and Terror. Many names were only used once on a particular gun and then dropped, while others have reappeared time and again on different models over the years. This custom of naming toy guns still goes on today; a visit to any toy store will turn up names such as Cowhand, Top Gun Jr., and 007. Many of these names seem to reflect current events or personalities, but the meanings of others have become obscure.

Collectors of toy guns can choose from a large array of models and styles, and because of the tremendous historical popularity of these toys, collectors have the opportunity to acquire interesting and unusual examples at an affordable price. Guns from as far back as the 1920s and 1930s can still be found at flea markets, garage sales, and second-hand stores, often at a price that is only a fraction of what other toys from these same years will sell for.

Contributor: Charles W. Best, 11523 Pine Valley Dr., Franktown, CO 80116. Best is a leading authority on toy weapons and has been collecting them in earnest since 1966. His collection is regarded as one of the finest and most comprehensive in existence, and has one many awards at various gun shows. In addition to writing a number of articles on the subject in such magazines as *Gun Report* and *Antique Toy World*, he is also the author of *Cast-Iron Toy Pistols* and co-author with Sam Logan, of *Cast-Iron Toy Guns and Cap Shooters*, both of which are now out of print.

Note: Measurements given, in general, are from one end of the gun to the other, rather than on a diagonal from grip to muzzle. Dates of manufacturers can vary within five years, though most of the later dates are considerably more accurate.

	C6	C8	C10
.45 Smoker, blows cap smoke, c. 1946	30	45	60
101 Ranch Pistol, cast iron, Hubley, 1930, 11-1/2"	150	200	250
1776-1876 Cap Pistol, cast iron, produced for America's centennial, Stevens, 1876, 5-1/4"	150	225	300
2 in 1 Cap Pistol, cast iron, 9-1/4"	85	125	175
2 Monkeys Animated Cap Pistol, cast iron, maker unknown, monkey hits head against coconut held by another monkey, 1882, 4-1/2"	600	850	1250
25 Jr. Cap Automatic, cast iron, "Made in U.S.A., Patented", Stevens, 1930, 4-1/8"	25	35	50
25-50 Cap Automatic, cast iron, "Oil Moving Parts; Made in U.S.A., Patented," can be fired rapidly w/crank, hole near muzzle holds removable crank, Stevens, 1935	65	90	135
25-50 Cap Automatic, cast iron, "Pat. Appl'd. For, Made in U.S.A.", Stevens, 1928, 4-1/2"	30	45	60
25-50 Cap Automatic, cast iron, "Oil Moving Parts; Made in U.S.A., Patented", Stevens, 1935, 4-1/2"	25	38	50
25-50 Cap Automatic, cast iron, "Made in U.S.A.; Pat, Appld.", Stevens, 1935, 4-1/2"	22	33	45
25-50 Target Automatic, w/silencer-type barrel, "Oil Moving Parts; Made in U.S.A., Patented", Stevens, 1935	150	200	250
49-ER Cap Pistol, cast iron, Stevens, 1940, 9"	150	215	285
5-Star Dart Pistol, steel, Wyandotte	20	25	35
6-Shot, Stevens, 1932, 6-1/4"	50	65	90
6-Shot Cap Pistol, cast iron, "Pat. U.S.A., Jan. 22, 1895", Stevens, 1895, 6-3/4"	200	275	350

	C6	C8	C10
6-Shot Rapid Load Cap Pistol, cast iron, "Made in U.S.A.", Stevens, 1932, 6-1/2"	60	75	100
Ace Cap Pistol, cast iron, Kilgore, 1935, 5" long	25	35	45
Ace Cap Pistol, cast iron, "Made in U.S.A.", Stevens, 1930, 5" long	25	35	45
Acme Automatic, steel cap, repeater, c. 1930	20	30	40
Acorn Pistol, cast iron	75	100	150
Adams Pistol, cast iron, dart or pellet shooting pistol, c. 1890, 5"	325	385	450
Admiral Dewey Cap Bomb, cast iron	150	200	300
Aeromatic Glider Gun, steel automatic, shoots balsa airplanes, c. 1940	50	75	100
Agitator, The, cast iron, cap and torpedo shooter, John Fox, 1908, 8-1/4"	150	220	275
Aim to Save, c. 1909	225	275	400
Air Blaster, plastic, shoots burst of air, Wham-O	40	60	80
Air Raid Warning Signal Pistol	50	75	125
America, Stevens, 1880, 8-3/4"	135	200	275
America Cap Pistol, w/shield, pat. 1873	150	225	300
American Bulldog .22 Blank Shooter, cast iron, second trigger tips barrel to load, handle curves inward, Kenton, 1920, 4-1/2" long	55	75	100
American Bulldog .22 cal. Blank Shooter, cast iron, second trigger tips barrel to load, handle projects outward, Kenton, 1910, 4-1/2" long	50	70	95
American Cap Pistol, cast iron, Kilgore, 1940, 9-5/8"	275	350	450
Army 45 Cap Automatic, cast iron, "Made in U.S.A.", Hubley, 1940, 6-5/8"	65	100	140

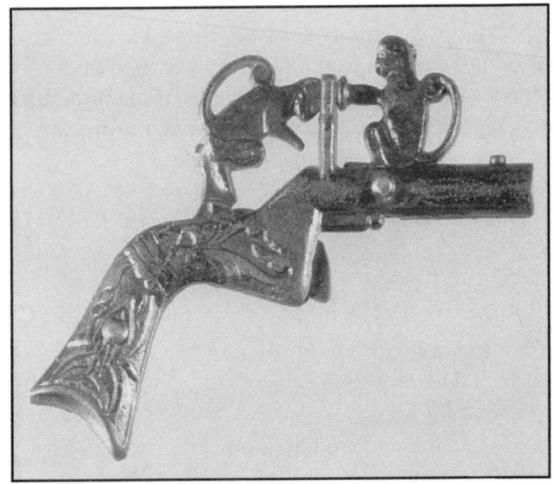

2 Monkeys Animated Cap Pistol, 1882, $1250. Photo courtesy Sotheby's, New York

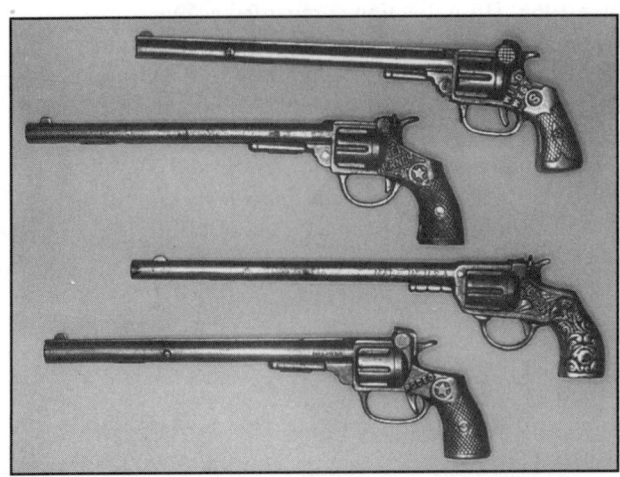

Top to Bottom: Wild West Cap Pistol, Kenton, 1926, $225; 101 Ranch Pistol, 1930, Hubley, $250; Victor Cap Pistol, Stevens, 1924, $250; Rodeo Cap Pistol, Hubley, 1924, $200. Photo courtesy Charles W. Best

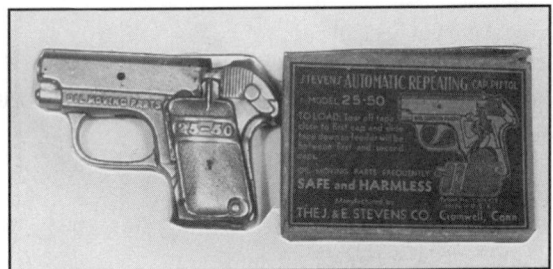

25-50 Cap Automatic, 1935, Stevens, $60. Photo courtesy James S. Maxwell/Virginia Caputo

49-ER Cap Pistol, 1940, Stevens, $285. Photo courtesy Charles W. Best

	C6	C8	C10
Army 45 Cap Automatic, "Made in U.S.A.," die-cast zinc, plastic grips, Hubley, 1940, 6-1/2" long.	35	60	75
Army Cap Pistol, cast iron, 1910.....	40	60	80
Army Pistol, No. 625, tin litho, w/revolving cylinder, Marx.........	30	40	60
Army Sparkling Pop Gun, No. 197, Marx	20	30	45
Astro Ray Signal—Dart gun, plastic, Ohio Art, 1960s, 10"	50	75	100
Atomic Disintegrator Cap Pistol, Hubley	175	305	450
Atomic Flash Space Gun, Chein	40	75	100
Auto Magic Picture Gun, w/film and instructions, projects film onto wall, 1936.........................	100	125	150
Auto Repeating Cap Exploder.........	45	68	90
Automatic Cap Pistol, No. 290, die-cast, Hubley, 6-1/2"....................	30	55	75
Automatic Repeater, No. 40, pressed steel, Wyandotte, 1920s, 7" long	35	55	75

	C6	C8	C10
Automatic Repeater Paper Pop Pistol, No. 74, aluminum, Marx.......	30	35	50
Bang Cap Pistol, cast iron, "Made in U.S.A.", Kilgore, 6" long........	25	38	50
Bang-O Cap Pistol, cast iron, "Made in U.S.A.", Stevens, 1938, 7" long	50	65	100
Banner, cast iron, blank-shooting pistol, Ives, 5".....................	150	200	300
Bell Pistol, Wyandotte.....................	15	25	35
Benjamin Pump Early BB Gun, before 1910	75	112	150
Biff Cap Automatic, cast iron, "Made in U.S.A. Pat. Apld. For", Kenton, 1935, 4-1/2"	40	55	75
Biff Jr. Cap Automatic, cast iron, "Made in U.S.A. Pat. Apld. For", Kenton, 1935, 4-1/8" long...........	30	45	60
Big Bang Pistol, No. 6P, 7-7/8" long...	200	325	450
Big Bang Rifle, No. 21-60, 21-3/16" long...................................	750	2000	3500

6-Shot Cap Pistol, 1895, Stevens, $350. Photo courtesy Charles W. Best

6-Shot, 1932, Stevens, $90.

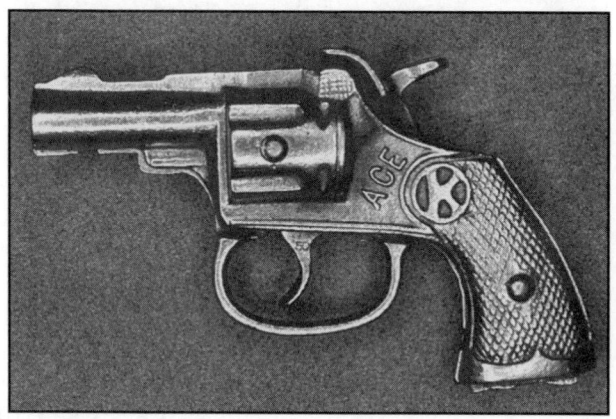

Ace Cap Pistol, 1935, Kilgore, $45. Photo courtesy Charles W. Best

American Bulldog .22 cal. Blank Shooter, 1910, Kenton, $95.

	C6	C8	C10
Big Bill Cap Pistol, cast iron, Kilgore, 1925, 5-1/2" long	25	35	45
Big Bill Cap Pistol, cast iron, large hammer, "Made in U.S.A.", Kilgore, 1935, 4-7/8"	20	30	40
Big Bill Cap Pistol, cast iron, large hammer, "Made in U.S.A.", Kilgore, 1930, 5-3/4"	25	35	45
Big Buster Cap Automatic, cast iron, w/two-piece trigger, "Patd Jul 2 1907, Made in U.S.A.", Kilgore, 1915, 5"	75	120	150
Big Chief Cap Pistol, cast iron, "Made in U.S.A.", Dent, 1930, 3-1/2"	22	25	35
Big Chief Cap Pistol, cast iron, marked w/star and "K", Kilgore, 1935, 6"	22	33	45
Big Chief Cap Pistol, cast iron, Kilgore, 1935, 6" long.................	20	30	45

	C6	C8	C10
Big Clip Cap Pistol, cast iron, "Made in U.S.A.", Stevens, 1930, 6-3/4"..............................	30	40	55
Big Horn Cap Pistol, cast iron, revolving cylinder, Kilgore, 1939, 8-3/8"..............................	175	275	365
Big Injun, hammerless.....................	175	250	350
Big Noise, The, c. 1922...................	45	68	90
Big Scout, 1935	30	45	60
Big Scout, engraved, 1940	30	45	60
Bigger Bang Cap Pistol, cast iron, large hammer, Kilgore, 1930, 6" long...	32	48	65
Billy the Kid Cap Pistol, cast iron, Stevens, 1938, 6-3/4"	75	125	150
Black Jack Cap Pistol, cast iron, long barrel, "Pat. Sept. 11-23", Kenton, 1930, 11"	125	200	250
Blaze Away Dart Pistol, No. G23, Marx	20	30	45

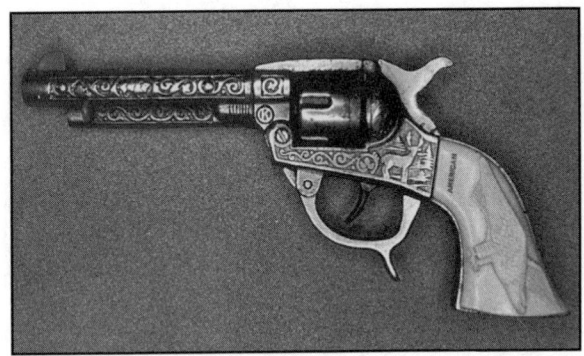

American Cap Pistol, 1940, Kilgore, $450. Photo courtesy Charles W. Best

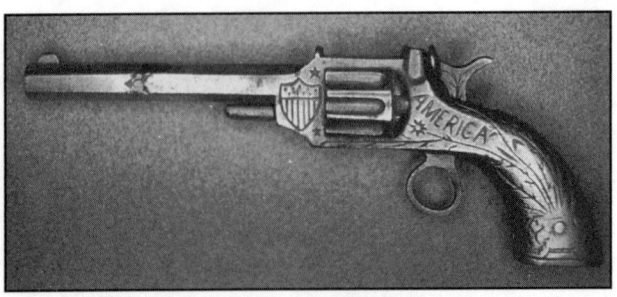

America, 1880, Stevens, $275. Photo courtesy Charles W. Best

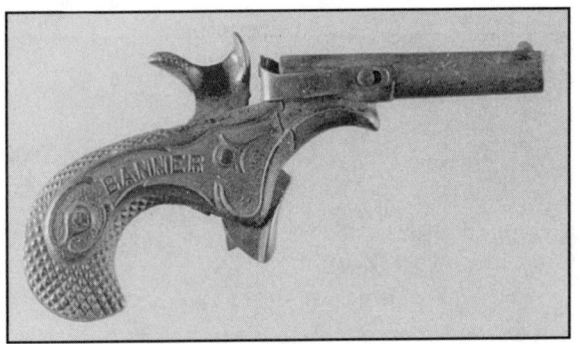

Banner, Ives, $300. Photo courtesy Sotheby's, New York

Army 45 Cap Automatic, 1940. Hubley, $75. Photo courtesy Charles W. Best

	C6	C8	C10
Bob Cap Pistol, cast iron, Kilgore, 1930, 5" long	25	38	50
Bobcat Cap Pistol, die-cast, Kilgore, 1950s, 4-1/4"	20	25	40
Border Patrol, 1940	35	52	70
Border Patrol Cap Automatic, cast iron, Kilgore, 1930, 4-1/4" long	30	40	50
Border Patrol Cap Automatic, cast iron, "Pat. Apld. For, Made in U.S.A.", Kilgore, 1935, 4-1/2" long	30	40	50
Boss Mammoth Cap Pistol, cast iron, Kenton, 1925, 6-1/4"	30	45	60
Boy's Delight Cap Pistol, cast iron, pat. June 1891	225	300	400
Boy's Police Automatic Pop Gun, cardboard, c. 1940s, 8"	15	20	25
Brat Cap Pistol, cast iron	30	45	60
Brevet Depose, Several variations. Breech may also be an animal head. Made in Europe. Fires a percussion cap., 1890, 10-1/4"	300	400	500

	C6	C8	C10
Bronc Cap Pistol, cast iron, "Kenton Made in U.S.A.", Kenton, 1935, 6"	30	45	60
Buc-A-Roo Cap Pistol, cast iron, Kilgore, 1940, 7-3/4"	50	75	100
Buccaneer Flintlock Pistol, fires plastic bullets, Nichols, 1958, 3-1/2"	37	56	75
Buck Pistol, cast iron, Hubley, 1930, 3-1/4"	40	60	90
Buckle Gun, w/bullets, Mattel	48	72	95
Buddy, 1935	25	38	50
Buddy, 1930	25	38	50
Buffalo Bill, cast iron, single shot, Stevens, 1890	200	300	400
Buffalo Bill Cap Pistol, cast iron, long barreled, "Pat. Sept. 11-23", Kenton, 1925, 11-3/8"	150	225	300
Buffalo Bill Cap Pistol, cast iron, "Made in U.S.A.", Stevens, 1940, 7-3/4" long	72	110	145
Buffalo Bill Cap Pistol, cast iron, long barreled, "Pat. Sept. 11-23", Kenton, 1930, 13-1/2"	150	225	300
Buffalo Cap Rifle, Hubley	85	130	175

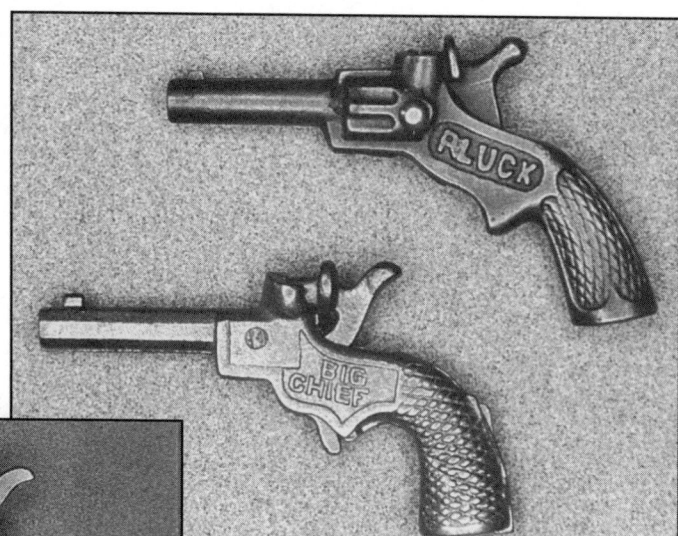

Top to Bottom: Pluck Cap Pistol, Stevens, 1930, $25; Big Chief Cap Pistol, 1930, Dent, $35. Photo courtesy Charles W. Best

Big Horn Cap Pistol, 1939, Kilgore, $365. Photo courtesy Charles W. Best

	C6	C8	C10
Bull Cap Pistol, cast iron, "Pat Appld. For Pat. Mch. 25, '24", Hubley, 1940, 6-1/4"	25	38	50
Bull Dog Cap Pistol, cast iron, "Pat 1,488,046", Hubley, 1935, 6-1/4" long	25	35	45
Bulldog Cap Pistol, cast iron, Kenton, 1923, 5-1/2"	37	56	75
Bulldozer Cap Pistol, cast iron, six-shooter, July 1874	200	275	350
Bulls Eye Safety Pistol, cast iron, flare barrel w/spring, Stevens, 1910, 5-1/2"	100	125	175
Bunker Hill Cap Pistol, cast iron, National, 1925, 5-1/4" long	30	45	60
Burp Gun, aluminum, die-cast and plastic, Mattel, 1956, 13" long	45	68	90
Buster, maker unknown, "Pat. May 28 1901", 6"	175	225	300
Buster Cap Automatic, cast iron, Kilgore, 1910, 5-1/2"	45	68	90
Butting Match Mechanical Pistol, cast iron	300	400	600
Cannon Animated Cap Pistol	250	375	500
Cap Bomb, cast iron, head shape.....	150	200	250

	C6	C8	C10
Cap Bomb, dog's head	150	200	250
Cap Bomb, cast iron, double-faced...	150	200	250
Cap Pistol, cast iron, double-barrel, dated 1880.................................	125	188	250
Cap Pistol, nickel-plated cast iron, marked w/"W" on one side, "S" on other, normal size barrel.........	20	25	30
Cap Pistol, cast iron, six-shot, dated 1895.......................................	150	200	300
Cap Pistol, cast iron, ornate, 1878...	50	75	125
Cap Pistol, cast iron, hammerless w/four revolving triggers, "Pat. Appl'd For", Stevens, 1892, 7-1/4"	250	300	400
Cap Pistol, cast iron, revolving cylinder, 1887	150	200	250
Cap Pistol, steel, repeating, red, Wyandotte, 8" long	15	22	30
Captain Cap Automatic, cast iron, Kilgore, 1940, 4-1/4" long	30	40	50
Cat Animated Cap Pistol, cast iron, Cat hits bottom paw with top paw to fire cap, 4-3/4"	750	900	1250
Cavalier Cap Automatic, cast iron, "Pat. Appld. For, Made in U.S.A.", Kilgore, 1935, 4-1/2"....	35	52	70

Bigger Bang Cap Pistol, 1930, Kilgore, $65. Photo courtesy Charles W. Best

Bulls Eye Safety Pistol, 1910, Stevens, $175.

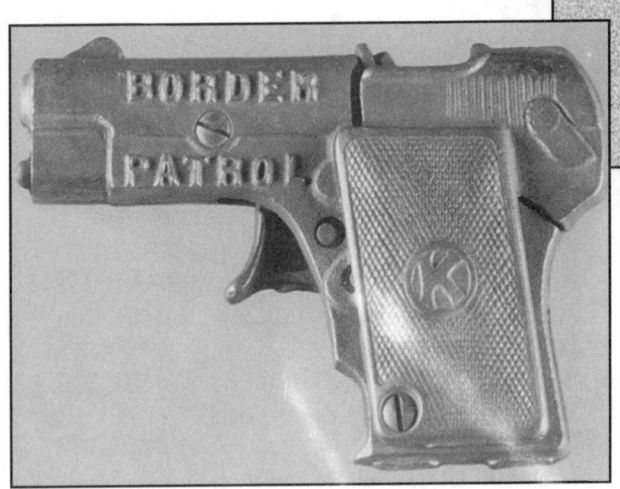

Border Patrol, 1940, $70. Photo courtesy Sotheby's, New York

	C6	C8	C10
Challenge, 1890	150	225	300
Champ Automatic, die-cast, Hubley, 1940, 5"	30	45	60
Chief, 1900-1910	35	45	55
Chief .22 cal. Blank shooter, cast iron, second trigger tips up barrel to load, Kenton, 1915, 6" long	75	100	125
Chief Cap Pistol, aluminum, single shot, Hubley	30	45	60
Chief Cap Pistol, cast iron, "Pat. 1,488,046", Hubley, 1930, 6-1/8"	25	38	50
Chieftain Cap Pistol, cast iron, National, 1920, 11" long	75	112	150
Chinese Must Go Cap Pistol, mechanical	350	450	700
Click Pistol, pressed steel, Marx, approx. 7-3/4" long	15	22	30
Click Pistol, No. 36, tin litho, Marx	15	22	30

	C6	C8	C10
Clicker Pistol, plain black, late 1930s-early 1940s	15	22	30
Clip 50, Bakelite and cast iron, Kilgore, 1940, 4-1/4"	60	90	120
Clip Jr. Cap Pistol, cast iron, Stevens, 1935, 5-1/4"	25	38	50
Clipper Cap Automatic, cast iron, Kilgore, 1935, 4-1/8"	48	72	95
Clown and Mule Pistol, animated	600	800	1500
Clown on a Barrel	500	700	1000
Colt .45, die-cast, Hubley	100	150	200
Colt Cap Pistol, cast iron, "Patented June 17, 1890, Made in U.S.A.", Stevens, 1920, 5-1/2"	50	75	100
Colt Cap Pistol, cast iron, Stevens, 1935, 6-1/2"	30	45	60
Columbia Cap Pistol, cast iron, pat. June 1891	175	250	300

Buster Pistol, unknown maker, $300. Photo courtesy Charles W. Best

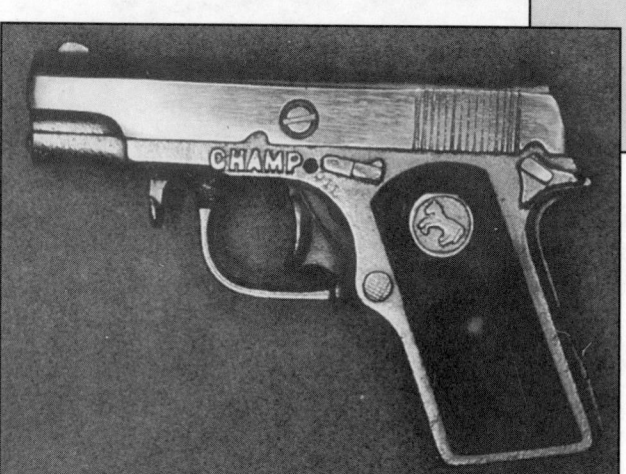

Champ Automatic, 1940, Hubley, $60. Photo courtesy Charles W. Best

Cannon Animated Cap Pistol, $500. Photo courtesy Charles W. Best

	C6	C8	C10
Columbia Cap Pistol, cast iron, 1885	175	250	300
Columbia Cap Pistol, cast iron, Stevens, 1890, 8-3/4"	200	300	400
Columbia Junior, early BB gun	250	375	500
Comet, Stevens, 1885, 5-1/2"	125	200	250
Comet, Stevens, 1925, 7-1/8"	40	60	80
Cop Cap Pistol, cast iron, "Pat. 1,488,046" or "Pat. Mch. 25 '24", Hubley, 1930, 5"	25	35	50
Cork-popper Pistol, spur trigger, Wyandotte	15	20	30
Cork-shooting Rifle, No. 206, Marx	15	20	30
Cork-shooting Rifle, No. 232, steel, double-barrel, Marx	50	75	100
Corn Shooter Cap Pistol	65	90	130
Corporal, maker unknown, 1900, 8-7/8"	75	100	150
Cowboy Cap Pistol, cast iron, "Made in U.S.A.", Stevens, 1935, 3-1/2"	15	22	30

	C6	C8	C10
Cowboy Cap Pistol, cast iron, "Made in U.S.A.", Hubley, 1940, 8"	85	125	175
Cowboy Cap Pistol, cast iron, Ives, 1890, 7-5/8"	125	188	250
Cowboy Cap Pistol, cast iron, long barrel, "Made in U.S.A.", Stevens, 1930	175	263	350
Cowboy King, 1940	175	250	325
Coyote, die-cast, Hubley	40	60	85
Crack, Stevens, 1925, 5"	40	60	80
Cupid, 1900, 5-1/4"	60	85	125
Dagger Derringer, die-cast, Hubley, 1955	45	65	90
Dandy Cap Pistol, cast iron, w/a variety of markings, Hubley, 1935, 5-3/4"	35	52	70
Daniel Boone Wilderness Scout Derringer, Marx	25	38	50
Darb Cap Pistol, cast iron, "Pat. Sept. 11-23", Kenton, 1930, 5-1/2" long	30	45	60

Click Pistol, Marx, $30. Photo courtesy Charles W. Best

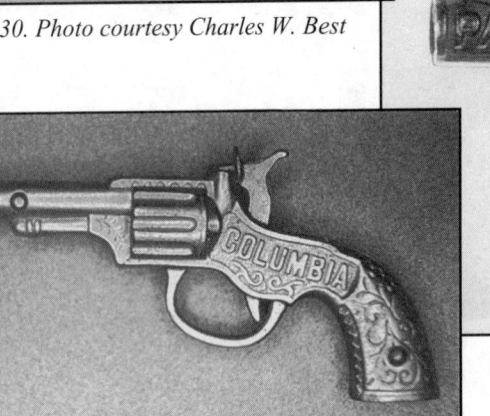

Columbia Cap Pistol, 1890, Stevens, $400. Photo courtesy Charles W. Best

Clown on a Barrel, $1000. Photo courtesy Charles W. Best

	C6	C8	C10
Dart Pistol, Wyandotte, 1950s	27	41	55
Dart Pistol, colorful w/fancy lithographing, Wyandotte	15	20	30
Dead Shot, Stevens, 8-3/4"	125	188	250
Defence, 1896	85	130	175
Demon, cast iron, Made in England, 7-3/8"	275	375	500
Derby Cap Pistol, cast iron, Hubley, 1930, 7"	30	45	60
Desert Patrol Luger & Silencer, Marx, 1960s, 10"	20	25	35
Detroit Cap Pistol, cast iron, 1910, 6-5/8" long...............................	85	110	150
Dick Cap Automatic, cast iron, "Made in U.S.A.", Hubley, 1940, 4-1/8"	30	45	60
Dick Cap Automatic, die-cast, 4-1/4"	20	25	30
Dick Cap Pistol, cast iron, Hubley, 1930, 6"	30	45	60
DIK Cap Pistol, cast iron, "Pat. Sept. 11-23", Kenton, 1935, 4-3/4"	27	41	55

	C6	C8	C10
Dixie, 1888-1890.............................	75	112	150
Dixie Cap Pistol, cast iron, "Made in U.S.A. Pat. Appld. For", Kenton, 1935, 6-1/4"........................	42	63	85
Doc Cap Pistol, cast iron, "Pat. Sept. 11-23", Kenton, 1926, 4-1/2"...	40	50	60
Dolphin Cap Pistol, animated..........	400	600	800
Double-barrel Shotgun, steel and wood, Wyandotte, c. 1935, 25"..	45	65	85
Doughboy Cap Automatic, cast iron, "Made in U.S.A.", Kilgore, 1920, 5"..	45	68	90
Dragnet Detective Special Repeating Revolver Cap Gun, c. 1955...	30	45	65
Duck Cap Pistol, cast iron, animated, 1884, 3-3/4" long.............	2000	2500	4500
Dude Cap Pistol, cast iron w/plastic grips, Kenton, 1941, 6-1/2"........	40	60	80
Dude Pistol, cast iron, "Pat. Mar. 22 '87", Stevens, 1887, 3-1/2"	75	112	150
Eagle, c. 1940	40	60	80

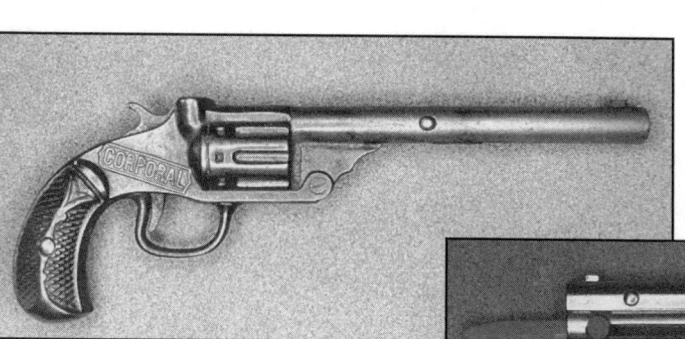

Corporal, 1900, unknown maker, $150. Photo courtesy Charles W. Best

Dagger Derringer, 1955, Hubley, $90. Photo courtesy Charles W. Best

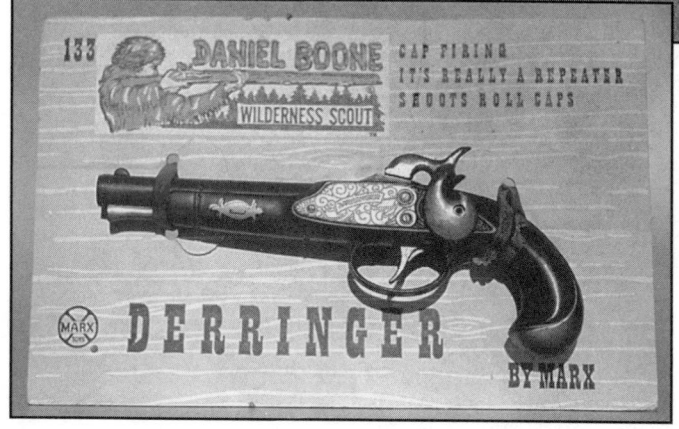

Daniel Boone Wilderness Scout Derringer, Marx, $50. Photo courtesy Gary J. Linden

	C6	C8	C10
Eagle Cap Pistol, cast iron, "Pat. June 17, 1890", Stevens, 1995, 7-1/2"	80	110	150
Echo Cap Pistol, cast iron, six-shooter, wheel under hammer holds caps, Lockwood, 1881	325	400	500
Echo Cap Pistol, cast iron, Stevens, 1920, 4-1/4"	30	40	50
Echo Cap Pistol, cast iron, "Made in U.S.A.", Stevens, 1930, 4-1/2"	30	40	50
Electronic Space Gun, plastic, w/flashlight gun, Remco	37	56	75
Excelsior Cap Pistol, cast iron, "Pat'd Apr. 22, '73", Stevens, 1875, 5-1/4"	100	150	200
Federal Cap Automatic, cast iron, w/removable clip to hold caps, Kilgore, 1940, 4-7/8"	45	70	90

	C6	C8	C10
Federal Cap Pistol, cast iron, "Pat. Dec. 14; Made in U.S.A.", Kilgore, 1920	37	56	75
Federal Cap Pistol, cast iron, Kilgore, 1920, 5-1/2"	25	38	50
Federal No. 2 Cap Pistol, cast iron, Kilgore, 1925, 6-3/8"	60	90	120
Federal-Kilgore No. 1 Cap Pistol, cast iron, Kilgore, 1925, 5-1/4"	25	38	50
Fido, 1910, 4"	50	60	70
Firecracker Pistol, cast iron, w/filigree handle	100	150	200
Firecracker Pistol, iron and brass, five-barrel, 1877	500	800	1200
First No. 1, 1920, 6-3/4"	150	200	250
Flash Cap Pistol, cast iron, "Pat'd", Hubley, 1934, 6-1/4"	45	55	75
Flintlock, No. 280, die-cast, Hubley, 9-1/4"	35	52	70
Flintlock Junior, die-cast, Hubley	20	30	40

Doughboy Cap Automatic, 1920, Kilgore, $90.
Photo courtesy Charles D. Richards

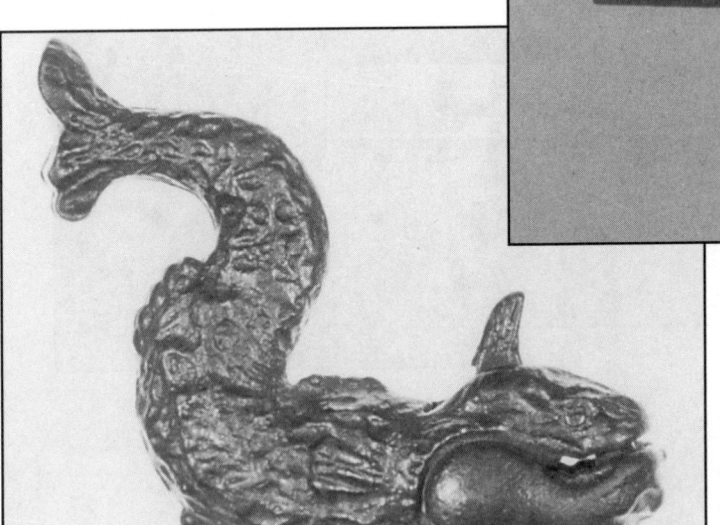

Dolphin Cap Pistol, unknown maker, $800.
Photo courtesy Sotheby's, New York

	C6	C8	C10
Flintlock Midget, die-cast, Hubley..	20	30	40
Flying Saucer Gun, Auburn Rubber, 1964	15	25	30
Forty-five Cap Pistol, The, cast iron, "Made in U.S.A.," unusual shape, National, 1928, 11-1/8"....	75	100	125
Four Way Cap Pistol, cast iron, "Pat. Appld. For," shoots pea or dart, rubber band and cap, Kenton, 1930	150	225	300
Fox Cap Pistol, cast iron, Hubley, 1935, 4-1/2"	30	40	50
Frontier Cap Pistol, cast iron, dog's head a top the barrel facing hammer, "Pat. June 21, 1887 and June 17, 1890", Ives, 1890	200	300	400
Gang Busters Crusade Against Crime Sub-Machine Gun, Marx..	125	188	250
Gem Pistol, cast iron, Stevens, 1900, 3"	30	45	60
Gene Autry Bull's Eye Cap Pistol, cast iron, "Gene Autry" signature on grips, Kenton, 1950s, 6-1/2"	125	188	250
Gene Autry Cap Pistol, "Made in U.S.A. Pat. Appl'd For", Kenton, 1939, 6-1/2"	125	175	250

	C6	C8	C10
Gene Autry Cap Pistol, cast iron, "Made in U.S.A.," red grips, Kenton, 1940, 6-1/2"	125	175	250
Gene Autry Cap Pistol, cast iron, Kenton, 1939, 8-3/8"	150	200	300
Gene Autry Cap Pistol, cast iron, "Made in U.S.A.", Kenton, 1940, 6-1/2"	130	185	275
Gip, 1900	25	38	50
G-Man Automatic Sparkling Pistol, No. 43, aluminum, Marx	65	100	130
G-Man Automatic Sparkling Pistol, No. 44, tin, Marx	65	100	130
G-Man Cap Automatic, Bakelite-framed, Kilgore, 1940, 6"	50	75	100
G-Man Cap Automatic, cast iron, looks like German Luger, removable magazine holds caps, Kilgore, 1935, 6"	75	100	150
G-Man Clicker Pistol, tin, black	25	35	45
G-Man Gun, No. 707, Marx	37	56	75
G-Man Silent Alarm Pistol, No. 54, tin, Marx	25	35	45
G-Man Sparkling Sub-Machine Gun, tin, Marx, 26" long	100	175	250

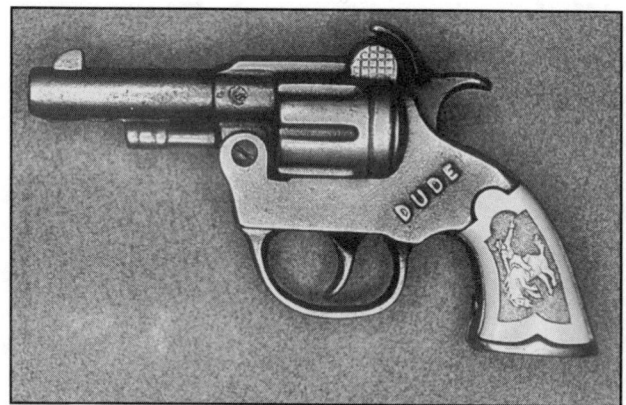

Dude Cap Pistol, 1941, Kenton, $80. Photo courtesy Charles W. Best

Dragnet Detective Special Repeating Revolver Cap Gun, c. 1955, $65. Photo courtesy Hake's Americana & Collectibles

Duck Cap Pistol, 1884, unknown maker, $4500. Photo courtesy Sotheby's, New York

	C6	C8	C10
G-Man Sparkling Tommy Gun, tin litho w/wood stock, Marx, 1936 .	175	275	375
G-Man Wind-Up Machine Gun, tin, miniature, 1940s	20	30	40
G-Man Wind-up Spark Pistol, steel, w/painted finish	60	100	125
G-Man Wind-up Spark Pistol, steel, w/nickel finish and jewels on grip	60	100	125
Go Bang	100	150	200
Guard Cap Pistol, cast iron, "Made in U.S.A.", Kilgore, 1935, 6-1/4"	30	45	60
Hammerless, cast iron, Revolving set of triggers fire several caps, Stevens, 1892	300	375	475
Hanson-Lindsborg K.S. Fire-cracker Pistol, cast iron, "Pat. Appl'd For," fires firecracker, Hanson, 1905, 6-3/8"	75	110	150

	C6	C8	C10
Hawk Automatic Cap Pistol, No. 2343, die-cast, Hubley, 5-3/4"	20	30	40
H-Bar-O Cap Pistol, cast iron, "Made in U.S.A.", Kilgore, 1925, 7-1/2"	60	75	125
Hero Auto Cap Automatic, cast iron, Stevens, 1920, 4-3/4"	45	65	85
Hero Cap Pistol, cast iron, Stevens, 1937, 5-1/4"	25	35	50
Hi-Ho Cap Pistol, cast iron, "Pat. Sept. 11-23", Kenton, 1940, 5-1/8"	35	45	60
Hi-Ho Cap Pistol, cast iron, Kilgore, 1940, 6-1/2"	37	56	75
Hi-Ho Cap Pistol, cast iron, "Made in U.S.A.", Stevens, 1940, 7"	35	45	60
Hi-Ho Cap Pistol, cast iron, "Made in U.S.A.", Stevens, 1940, 7"	37	56	75
Hi-Ranger Cap Pistol, cast iron, Stevens, 1940, 7-3/4"	50	70	90

Federal-Kilgore No. 1 Cap Pistol, 1925, Kilgore, $50. Photo courtesy Sotheby's, New York

Gene Autry Cap Pistol, 1939, Kenton, $250. Photo courtesy Charles W. Best

Top to Bottom: Flintlock, Hubley, $70; Flintlock Jr. Pistol, Hubley, $40; Flintlock Midget Pistol, Hubley, $40. Photo courtesy Charles W. Best

	C6	C8	C10
Hopalong Cassidy Revolver, "Hopalong" on both sides of handle, Wyandotte, 1950s, 9"	200	300	400
Hopalong Cassidy Revolver, with bust of Hopalong, Schmidt, 1950s, 10"	160	225	325
Hub Cap Pistol, cast iron, Hubley, 1940, 6-1/4"	25	38	50
Hustler Pistol, cast iron	55	82	110
Ibex, Stevens, 1895, 4-1/2"	60	90	120
Imperial Cap Pistol, cast iron, Kilgore, 1935, 5-1/4"	60	80	110
Indian Cap Pistol, cast iron, Kenton, 1931, 8-1/8"	60	90	120
Invincible Cap Pistol, cast iron, "Pat. Dec. 14", Kilgore, 1935, 5-1/4"	30	45	60
Invincible New 50 Shot, 1930	30	45	60
Jack Armstrong airplane gun, Daisy, 1936	75	100	150

	C6	C8	C10
Jax Cap Pistol, cast iron, "Pat. Sept. 11-23", Kenton, 1930, 4"	25	35	45
Jet Jr. Space Cap Gun, die-cast, Stevens, 1949, 6-1/2"	110	165	220
Johnnie's Little Gun, detailed, Ives, 1888, 11"	600	1000	1500
Jr. Police Chief Cap Automatic, cast iron, "Made in U.S.A.", Kenton, 1938, 3-7/8"	30	45	60
Jr. Ranger .32 cal., 1925	35	50	65
Jumbo Cap Pistol, cast iron, "Pat. June 17, 1890: Made in U.S.A.", Stevens, 1895, 9-1/2"	110	165	220
Junior Police .32 Cap Pistol, cast iron, "Hubley; Pat'd. 2088891", Hubley, 1940, 5-1/4"	30	45	60
Junior Six-shooter Cap Pistol, cast iron, Kilgore, 1935, 5-1/2"	35	50	65
Just Out Animated Cap Pistol, cast iron, 1880s	1500	3000	5000

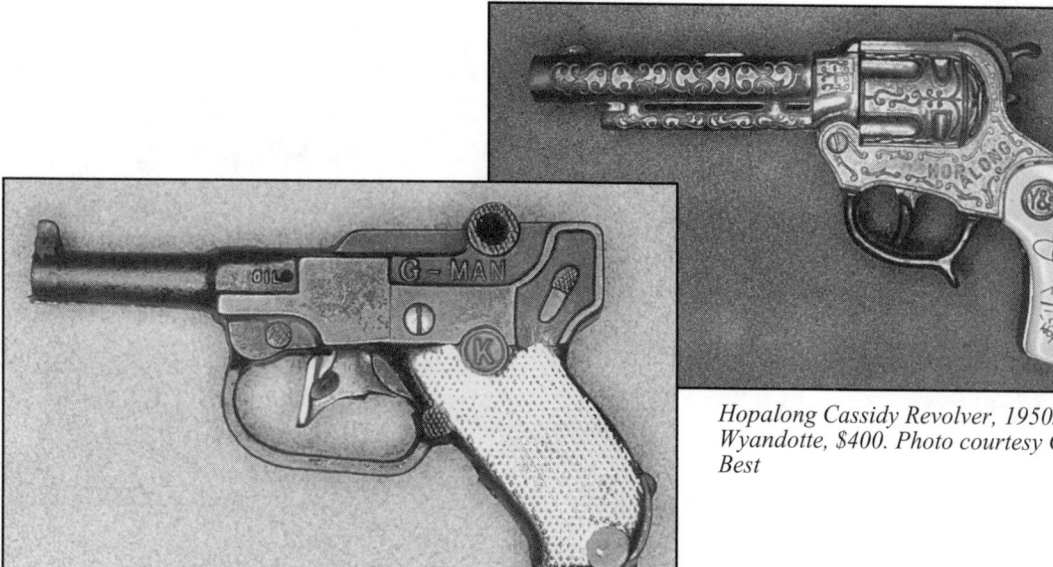

Hopalong Cassidy Revolver, 1950s, Wyandotte, $400. Photo courtesy Charles W. Best

G-Man Cap Automatic, 1935, Kilgore, $150. Photo courtesy Charles W. Best

	C6	C8	C10
Kido Cap Pistol, cast iron, "Kenton Made in U.S.A.", Kenton, 1936, 5-3/8"	25	38	50
Kilgore Cap Pistol, cast iron, Kilgore, 1910, 5"	42	63	85
Kilgore Cap Pistol, cast iron, Kilgore, 1912, 5-1/4"	42	63	85
King Cap Pistol, cast iron, "Made in U.S.A.", Stevens, 1925, 4-3/4"	50	60	75
King Cap Pistol, cast iron, Pat. Aug. 1879	100	150	200
Kit Carson Cap Pistol, cast iron, "Pat. Sept. 11-23", Kenton, 1928, 9"	50	75	100
Las Cap Pistol, cast iron	80	120	160
Lasso 'Em Bill Cap Gun, cast iron, red rubies in handle w/turning cylinder, 1930, 9"	150	225	300
Lawmaker Cap Pistol, cast iron, Kenton, 1941, 8-3/8"	125	175	250
Liberty, 1875	150	200	250
Liberty, tin, ornate, c. 1912	35	52	70
Lightning Express Mechanical Cap Pistol, train slides forward along barrel to explode cap at end, Arcade or Kenton, 1913, 5"	150	225	300
Lion, Ives, 1887, 3-3/4"	175	250	350
Lion, Stevens, 1890, 5-1/4"	175	225	300
Lion Head Cap Pistol, cast iron, Stevens, Pat. 1890, 5-1/4"	175	225	300

	C6	C8	C10
Little Bill Cap Pistol, cast iron, Kilgore, 1925, 5"	30	40	55
Little Chief Firefighter Water Squirt Gun	15	20	25
Lone Eagle Cap Pistol, cast iron, Kilgore, 1929, 5-1/4"	60	100	150
Lone Ranger .45 Flasher Flashlight Pistol, Marx	45	60	85
Lone Ranger Cap Pistol, cast iron, Kilgore, 1938, 8-1/2"	170	255	340
Lone Ranger Click Pistol, Marx, 9"	55	82	110
Lone Ranger Pop Gun, tin, w/picture of Lone Ranger on handles, 1950s	50	60	85
Lone Ranger Sparkling Pop Pistol, No. 096, tin litho, Marx	50	65	100
Lone Ranger Western Gun Collection, six miniature guns mounted on a card w/history of guns on back, c. 1939	85	125	200
Long Boy Cap Pistol, cast iron, "Made in U.S.A.", Kilgore, 1922, 11"	80	120	160
Long Tom Cap Pistol, cast iron, Kilgore, 1939, 10-3/8"	250	375	500
Look Out Cap Pistol, cast iron, dogs head, Stevens, 1890	350	425	500
Luger Water Pistol, plastic, Park Plastics, 1960s, 7"	15	20	25

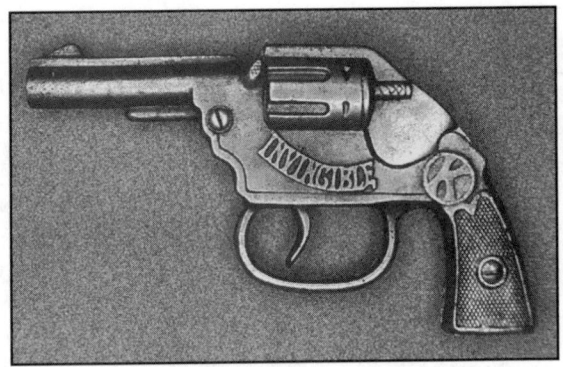

Invincible Cap Pistol, 1935, Kilgore, $60. Photo courtesy Charles W. Best

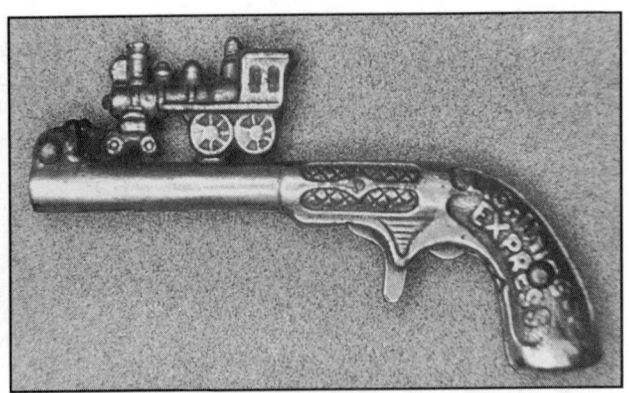

Lightning Express Mechanical Cap Pistol, 1913, Arcade or Kenton, $300. Photo courtesy Charles W. Best

	C6	C8	C10
M&L Water Pistol, die-cast, w/rubber ball	15	20	25
Machine Gun Cap Automatic, cast iron, w/crank, "Ra-Ta-Ta-Tat," caps fired rapidly when the crank is turned, Kilgore, 1938, 5"	150	200	250
Magic .22 cal. Blank Pistol, cast iron, ornate, has second trigger to open barrel for loading, "Pat'd Oct. 17, '99", Kenton, 1900, 6-1/4"	65	100	140
Man from U.N.C.L.E. Cap Gun, Ideal, c. 1965	35	52	70
Marx Miniatures of Famous Guns: Civil War Revolver, Mare's Leg, Tommy Gun, Saddle Rifle, price for each	25	40	55
Mascot Cap Automatic, cast iron, Kilgore, 1936, 3-7/8"	30	40	50
Master Cap Automatic, cast iron, Kilgore, 1930, 4-5/8"	50	60	70
Master Cap Automatic, cast iron, Kilgore, 1922, 4-5/8"	30	40	50
Match-shooting Pistol, cast iron, double-trigger, large, Stephens, PA, 1873	125	188	250
Mauser, The, maker unknown, 1915, 6-3/4"	250	375	500
Me and My Buddy Animated Pistol, steel, w/figure, Wyandotte	55	82	110
Medrick Repeater	75	112	150
Mexican Repeater, cast iron, shoots peas or pellets, 6-1/4"	350	400	450
Mick, 1930	30	40	50
Minute Man Cap Rifle, cast iron, "Pat. Appl'd For, Made in U.S.A.", Kilgore, 1936, 20"	200	300	400

	C6	C8	C10
Mohawk, cast iron, Fires a blank cartridge, has unique echo chamber, 1882, 5-3/4"	450	500	550
Monkey and Coconut Animated Cap Pistol, 1870s-1880s, 4-1/4"	450	650	850
Monkeys Animated Cap Pistol, Lockwood, 1882, 4-1/4"	550	825	1100
Moonface Capshooter, Stevens, c. 1880	500	750	1000
Mordt Cap Pistol, cast iron, maker unknown, 1930, 8"	60	90	120
Mountie Cap Automatic, No. 6, die-cast, Kilgore, 1950, 6"	20	30	40
National Cap Automatic, cast iron, National, 1915, 3-3/4"	35	50	65
National Cap Automatic, cast iron, National, 1925, 4-1/4"	35	45	55
National Cap Automatic, cast iron, "Made in U.S.A.", National, 1925, 5-1/4"	35	45	55
National Cap Pistol, cast iron, National, 1909, 4-7/8"	35	45	55
National Cap Pistol, cast iron, National, 1911, 5"	35	45	55
National Cap Pistol, cast iron, Stevens, 1920, 3-5/8"	35	45	55
National Liquid Pistol, Parker/Stearns, 1900, 4-7/8"	55	82	110
National No. 350 Cap Automatic, cast iron, National, 1928, 5-1/2"	45	55	65
National No. 380 Cap Pistol, cast iron, National, 1930s, 7"	40	55	70
Navy, 1925	35	52	60
Navy, 1878	125	188	250
Navy, 1907	75	112	150

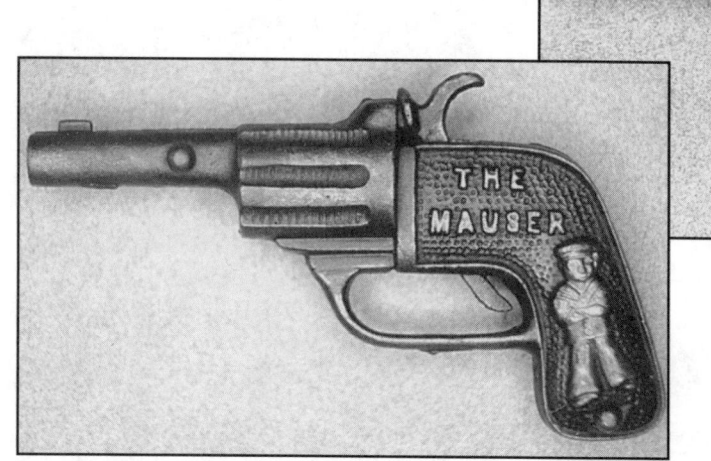

Lion, 1887, Ives, $350. Photo courtesy Charles W. Best

The Mauser, 1915, unknown maker, $500. Photo courtesy Charles W. Best

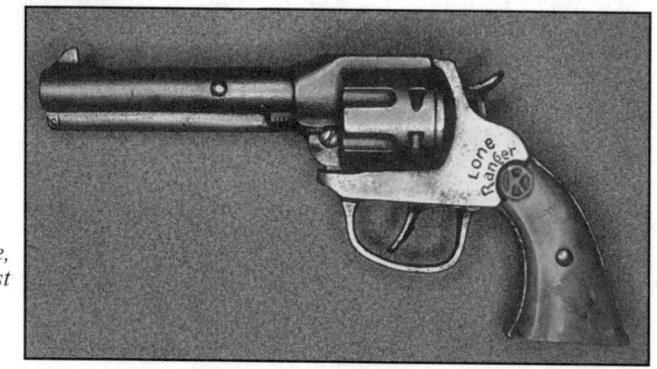

Lone Ranger Cap Pistol, 1938, Kilgore, $340. Photo courtesy Charles W. Best

	C6	C8	C10
Navy Cap Pistol, cast iron, "Pat. Sept. 11-23", Kenton, 1930, 5-1/2"	35	45	55
Navy Double-barrel Cap Pistol	150	225	300
Nemo Cap Pistol, cast iron, maker unknown, 1910, 6-5/8"	60	75	125
New 50-Shot Invincible Cap Pistol, cast iron, Kilgore, 1930, 5-1/2"...	35	50	65
Nigger Head Cap Pistol, cast iron, Ives, 1887, 4-1/2"	400	500	600
No. 500 (like Luger), 1935	55	82	110
Novelty Cap Pistol, cast iron, "Pat. Appl'd For", Stevens, 1885, 5"...	150	225	300
Nu-Matic Paper Buster Gun, Langson Manufacturing Co., 7"	25	35	50
Officer Pistol Cap Automatic, cast iron, modeled after German Luger, Kilgore, 1940, 6"	62	93	125
Official Detective-Type Sub-Machine Gun, No. 2146, Marx ...	60	85	125

	C6	C8	C10
Oh Boy Automatic Cap, "Made in U.S.A.; Pat'd., Aug. 8, 1933," works both as automatic and crank-operated rapid-fire gun, Kilgore, 1933, 4-1/8"	85	128	170
Oh Boy Cap Pistol, iron, "Pat. Sept. 11-23", Kenton, 1930, 5-1/8"	30	35	40
Oh Boy Cap Pistol, cast iron, National, 1922, 5-1/2"	35	45	60
OK Cap Automatic, cast iron, maker unknown, 1935, 3-3/4"	35	45	55
Old Ironsides Cap Pistol, cast iron, 10-3/4"	65	98	130
Our Army Forever	175	263	350
P-38 Steel Clicker Pistol, c. 1945	20	30	40
Padlock Cup Pistol, w/key, Hubley, 4-1/4"	50	90	125
Pal Cap Automatic, cast iron, Kilgore, 1930, 4"	25	35	50
Pal Cap Pistol, cast iron, Kilgore, 1930, 4"	20	30	45

Mick, 1930, unknown maker, $50. Photo courtesy Charles W. Best

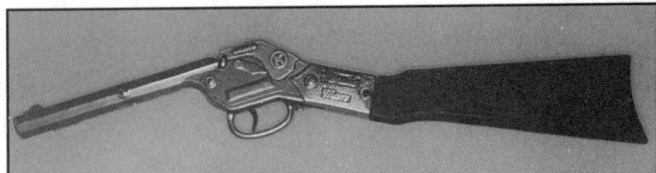

Minute Man Cap Rifle, 1936, Kilgore, $400. Photo courtesy Charles W. Best

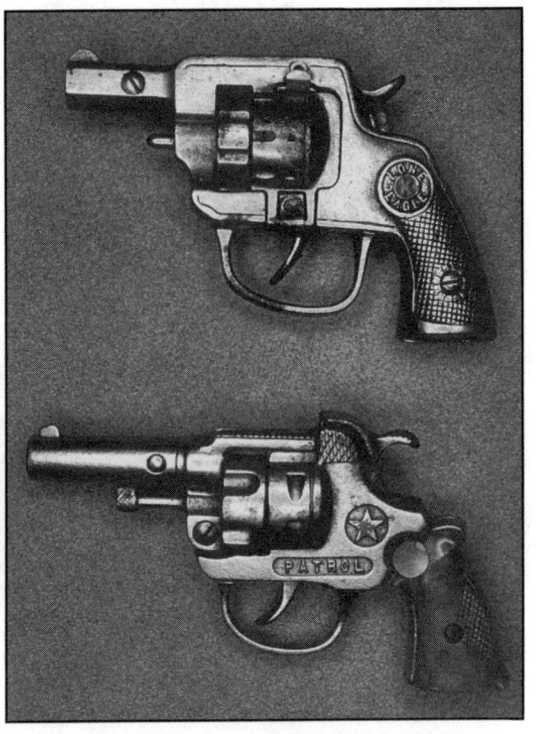

Top to Bottom: Lone Eagle Cap Pistol, 1929, Kilgore, $150; Patrol Cap Pistol, 1939, Hubley, $55. Photo courtesy Charles W. Best

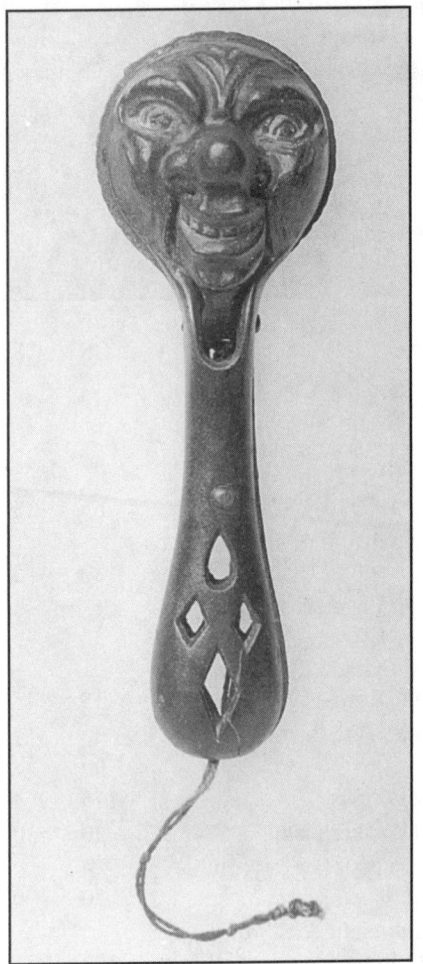

Moonface Capshooter, c. 1880, Stevens, $1000. Photo courtesy Charles W. Best

Monkey and Coconut Animated Cap Pistol, 1870s-1880s, unknown maker, $850. Photo courtesy Charles W. Best

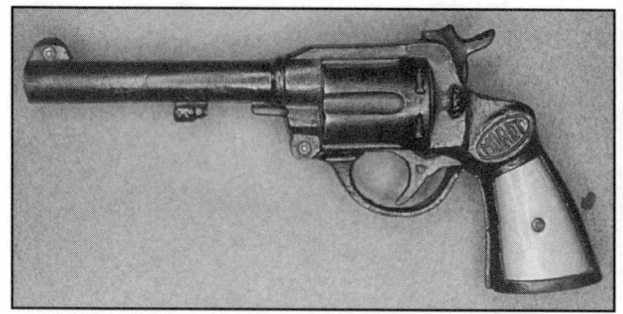

Mordt Cap Pistol, 1930, unknown maker, $120. Photo courtesy Charles W. Best

National Liquid Pistol, 1900, Parker/Stearns, $110. Photo courtesy Charles W. Best

National Cap Automatic, 1925, National, $55. Photo courtesy Sotheby's, New York

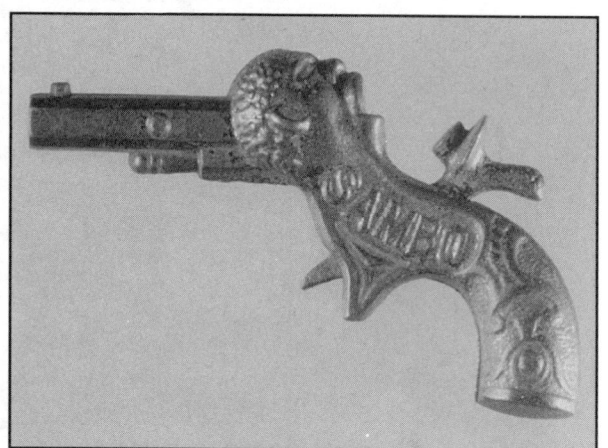

Sambo Cap Pistol, 1887, Ives, $500. Photo courtesy Sotheby's, New York

	C6	C8	C10
Pat Pistol, cast iron, "Pat. Sept. 11-23", Kenton, 1935, 6-1/8"	25	35	45
Patrol Cap Pistol, cast iron, "Made in U.S.A.", Hubley, 1939, 6"	35	45	55
Pawnee Bill, c. 1940	150	200	300
Pea Matic Pea-shooting Repeater, steel	20	25	35
Pea Shooter, pewter, highly embossed handle	35	52	70
Peacemaker Cap Pistol, cast iron, "Made in U.S.A.", Stevens, 1940, 8-1/2"	68	100	135
Peerless, 1905, 5-1/2"	60	90	125
Persuader Cap Pistol, cast iron, "Made in U.S.A., Pat. Appld. For", Kenton, 1939, 6-3/8"	60	90	125
Pet, die-cast, Hubley, 4-1/4"	5	10	15
Ping-Pong Rifle	25	30	35
Pioneer, die-cast, Hubley	60	90	120

	C6	C8	C10
Pirate Cap Pistol, die-cast zinc w/cast-iron hammers and trigger, two-barrel, two hammers that cock, Hubley, 1941, 9-3/8" ..	35	65	90
Pirate Cap Pistol, die-cast zinc, nonfiring, Hubley, 1950	60	90	120
Pistol Packin' Mama, wood w/cardboard sides, four revolving triggers, shoots wooden pegs, c. 1944, 8-1/2"	40	50	75
Pluck Cap Pistol, cast iron, "Made in U.S.A.", Stevens, 1930, 3-1/2"	15	20	25
Pluck Cap Pistol, cast iron, 1895	62	93	125
Police Automatic, 1935	40	60	80
Police Automatic Cap Pistol, steel, 8"	20	30	40
Police Cap Automatic, Bakelite-framed, Kilgore, 1940, 5-1/4"	55	83	110
Police Chief, Kenton, 1938, 4-5/8"	40	50	65

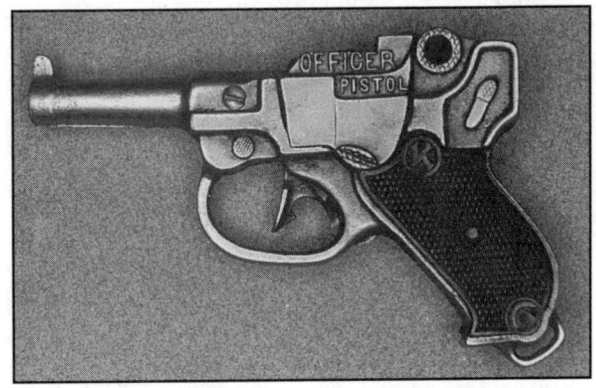

Officer Pistol Cap Automatic, 1940, Kilgore, $125. Photo courtesy Charles W. Best

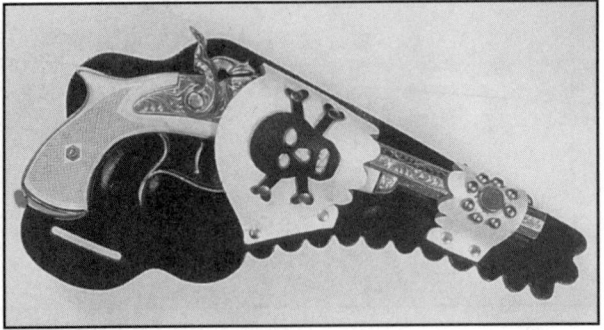

Pirate Cap Pistol with holster, 1950, Hubley, $120. Photo courtesy Charles W. Best

Ad for Langson Manufacturing's Nu-Matic Paper Buster Gun; currently valued at $50, the Numatic originally retailed for 25 cents.

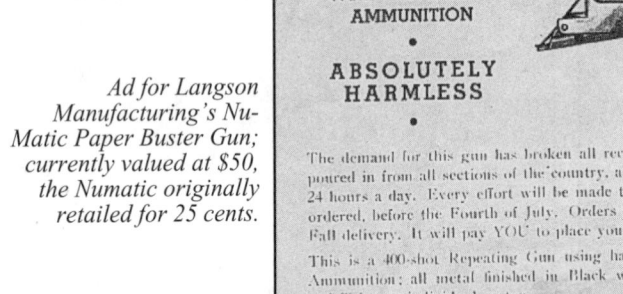

	C6	C8	C10
Police Chief Gun, w/leather shoulder holster set, Wyandotte, c. late 1940s	45	55	75
Polo, Ives, 1878, 6"	75	90	125
Pono Cap Pistol, cast iron, "Pat. Sept. 11-23", Kenton, 1936, 5-1/8"	30	40	50
Pop Gun—Rifle, No. 230, double-barrel, Marx	50	75	100
Powder Keg Cap Bomb, cast iron	85	128	170
Premier Safety, 1914	40	60	85
President Cap Pistol, cast iron, Kilgore, 1925, 8-3/4"	40	60	80
Presto Cap Automatic, cast iron, Kilgore, 1940, 5-1/8"	30	45	60
Private Eye Cap Pistol, Kilgore, 6-1/2"	15	25	35

	C6	C8	C10
Punch and Judy Animated Cap Pistol, cast iron, Punch explodes cap w/nose on Judy's back, Ives, 1880, 5"	550	700	850
Ranger, 1890-1900	80	120	160
Ranger Cap Pistol, cast iron, Kilgore, 1940, 8-1/2"	45	60	85
Ranger Cap Pistol, cast iron, Kilgore, 1939, 8-1/2"	85	130	175
Ranger Cap Pistol, cast iron, Kilgore, 1920, 5-3/8"	50	60	75
Red Ranger Clicker Pistol, steel, black, red "jewel", Wyandotte, c. 1939, 8"	40	60	80
Red Ranger Clicker Pistol, steel, Wyandotte, c. 1941, 8"	30	45	60
Red Ranger Rifle, plastic, Wyandotte	30	50	65

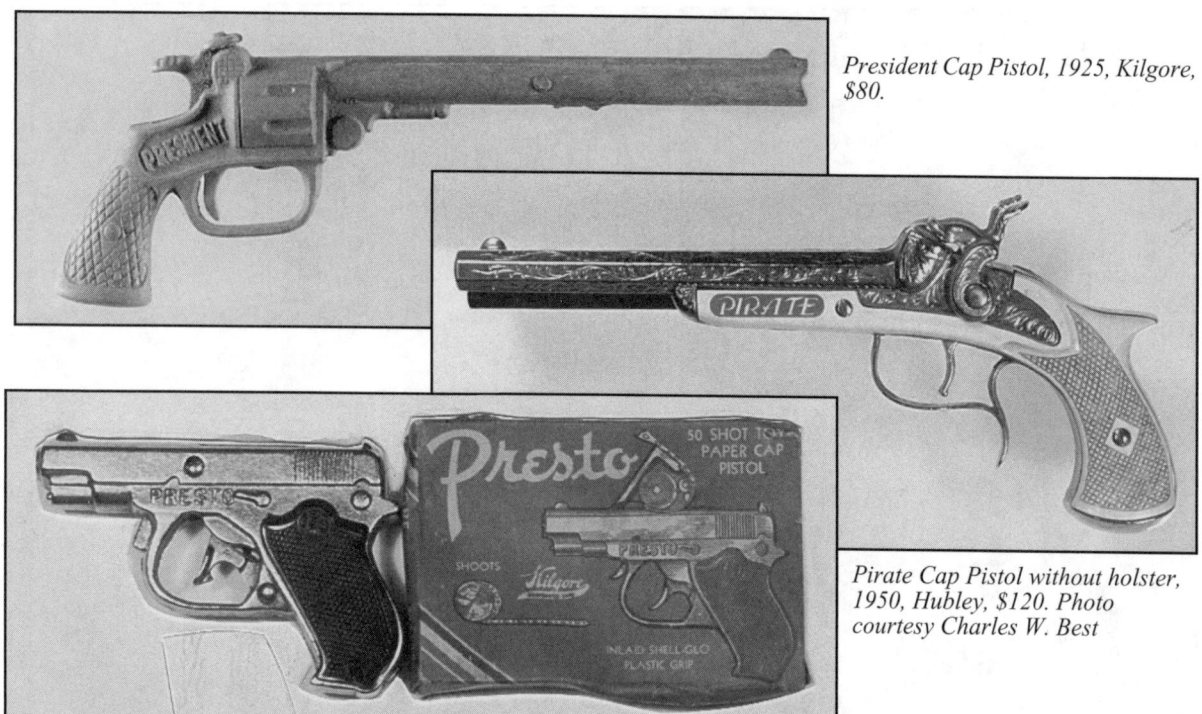

President Cap Pistol, 1925, Kilgore, $80.

Pirate Cap Pistol without holster, 1950, Hubley, $120. Photo courtesy Charles W. Best

Presto Cap Automatic, 1940, Kilgore, $60. Photo courtesy James S. Maxwell/Virginia Caputo

	C6	C8	C10
Red Ranger Six-shooter Repeater, steel w/plastic handles and revolving cyclinder, Wyandotte ..	40	60	75
Remington .36, die-cast, Hubley	50	70	95
Repeating Cap Pistol, No. G375, die-cast, Marx.............................	20	30	40
Rex Cap Automatic, cast iron, Kilgore, 1939, 3-7/8"	35	52	70
Rex Cap Automatic, cast iron, Dent, 1914, 4-1/8"..................................	30	50	65
Rex Mars Planet Patrol X-92 Gun......................................	100	150	200
Rifleman Flip Special Cap Rifle, die-cast plastic, Hubley, 32-1/2"..................................	82	125	165
RIP, c. 1909	75	100	125
Rob Roy, c. 1875	150	225	300
Rocket Ship Space Pistol, Irwin, late 1940s	50	65	90
Rodeo Cap Pistol, cast iron, Hubley, 11-1/4"..................................	125	165	200
Rodeo Cap Pistol, cast iron, Hubley, 1938, 7"..................................	35	55	75
Rotor Fifty Cap Pistol, cast iron, Kilgore, 1930, 6-1/8"	50	70	95

	C6	C8	C10
Roy Rogers Cap Pistol, cast iron, Kilgore, 1940, 10-1/4"	300	450	600
Roy Rogers Cap Pistol, cast iron, Hubley, 1940, 8-1/4"..................	250	375	500
Royal Pistol, cast iron, mechanical cap, "Pat. Apr. 23, '78," fires spring-loaded top that is attached to bottom of the barrel, Iver Johnson, 1878, 4-3/4"..................	400	600	800
S & W Cap Gun, cast iron, 6"	20	25	30
Safety Cap Pistol, cast iron, "Pat. Mch. 25, '24", Hubley, 1924, 5"...	30	40	50
Safety First Cap Automatic, cast iron, "Safe," maker unknown, 1920, 3-3/8".................................	30	45	60
Sambo Cap Pistol, cast iron, "Pat. June 21, 1887," hammer hits head, Ives, 1887, 4-3/8"	250	350	500
Say I Bomb, cast iron	100	130	175
Scout Cap Pistol, cast iron, "Made in U.S.A.", Stevens, 1935, 6-3/4"	35	50	65
Scout Cap Pistol, cast iron, "Pat. June 17, 1890", Stevens, 1890, 7"...	40	60	80

National No. 350 Cap Automatic, 1928, National, $65; National Cap Pistol, 1911, National, $55. Photo courtesy Charles W. Best

Punch and Judy Animated Cap Pistol, 1880, Ives, $850. Photo courtesy Charles W. Best

	C6	C8	C10
Scout Cap Pistol, cast iron, Stevens, 1940, 6-1/8"	35	50	65
Scout Cap Pistol, tin, automatic, 1914..	30	40	50
Scout Jr. Cap Pistol, cast iron, "Made in U.S.A.", Stevens, 1935, 6"	35	50	65
Scoutmaster, Dent, 6-3/4"	65	98	130
Senator Cap Pistol, cast iron, marked w/star and "K", Kilgore, 1925, 7"	50	75	100
Sharpshooter Cap Rifle, Hubley, 37"	75	112	150
Sheriff Cap Pistol, The, cast iron, Stevens, 1940, 8-1/2"	75	125	175
Shoo Fly Cap Pistol, cast iron	100	150	200
Shoot the Hat Mechanical Cap Pistol, cast iron..............................	450	600	750
Shootin' Shell Buckle Gun, Mattel, 1959..	42	63	85
Shotgun, steel, wooden stock, double-barreled, both barrels break down, cock and shoot, 28"	35	52	70

	C6	C8	C10
Siren Signal Pistol, hard plastic, Marx, 1950s	25	35	50
Siren Signal Pistol, tin, Marx, 1940s	30	40	60
Siren Sparkling Pistol, No. 164, tin litho, Marx...................................	50	80	110
Six Shooter Cap Pistol, cast iron w/plastic grips, "Made in U.S.A." on hammer, Kilgore, 1938, 6-1/2"...............................	60	80	100
Six Shooter Cap Pistol, cast iron w/plastic grips, Kilgore, 1935, 6-1/2"...	60	80	100
Six Shooter Cap Pistol, cast iron, Kilgore, 1930, 7"	40	60	80
Six Shooter Cap Pistol, cast iron, Kilgore, 1935, 6-1/2"	40	60	80
Six Shooter Cap Pistol, cast iron, "Made in U.S.A." on hammer, Kilgore, 1938, 6-1/2"	40	60	80
Six-shooter Automatic Cap Pistol, cast iron, (not an automatic), Kilgore, 1934, 6-1/2"	65	85	110

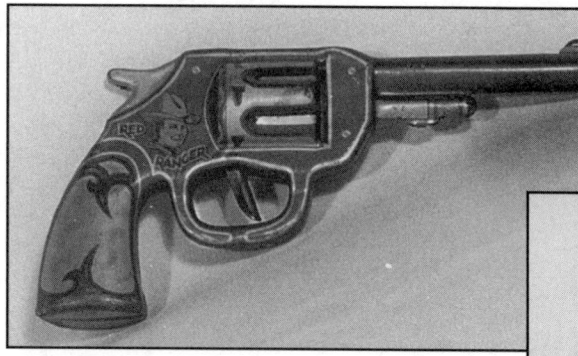

*Red Ranger Clicker Pistol, c. 1941, Wyandotte, $60.
Photo courtesy Charles W. Best*

*The Royal Pistol, 1878, Iver Johnson, $800.
Photo courtesy Charles W. Best*

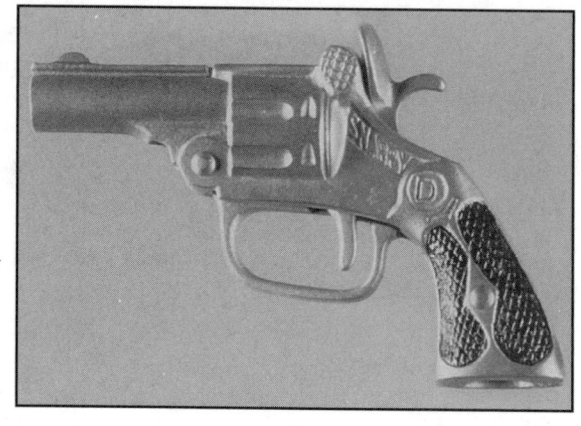

Scout Cap Pistol, 1890, Stevens, $80.

Snappy, 1930, Dent, $60.

	C6	C8	C10
Sliko Cap Pistol, cast iron, "Pat. Sept. 11-23", Kenton, 1930, 6-1/4"	30	45	55
Snappy, Dent, 1930, 5"	35	45	60
Snappy Jack, English, c. 1935	50	65	85
Space Gun, Remco	30	50	65
Space Rocket Gun, plastic, fires two Space Rocket Spheres, M&L, 9"	65	100	150
Sparkling Atom Buster, No. 46, die-cast, Marx	40	60	85
Sparkling Pop Gun, No. 198, Marx	30	45	60
Sparkling Space Gun, Marx	50	75	125
Sparkling Sure Shot	25	35	50

	C6	C8	C10
Spitfire Cap Automatic, cast iron, "Made in U.S.A.", Stevens, 1940, 4-5/8"	40	50	60
Sport, Ives, 1875, 4"	175	263	350
Sport Cap Pistol, cast iron, "Made in U.S.A.", Kilgore, 1930, 7-1/2"	35	50	65
Spud Gun, No. 504, die-cast, Hollywood, Calif., B.J. Cossman	30	45	60
Spud Gun, tin, automatic, c. 1940	25	35	45
Spy Cap Pistol, cast iron, "Made in U.S.A.", Kilgore, 1936, 4-1/4"	30	40	50
Star Cap Pistol, cast iron, Stevens, 1910, 6-1/4"	35	52	70
Star Cap Pistol, pot metal, steer on handle	10	15	20
Stephans, Pat., 1873, 5"	120	180	240

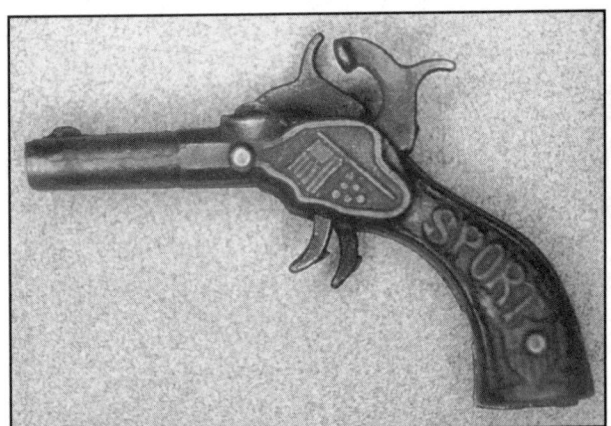

Sport, 1875, Ives, $350. Photo courtesy Charles W. Best

Tip Top Cap Pistol, 1880, Stevens, $225. Photo courtesy Charles W. Best

	C6	C8	C10
Streamline Siren Sparkling Pistol, No. 155, tin litho, Marx	40	60	75
Sun Cap Pistol, cast iron	150	175	200
Super Cap Pistol, cast iron, "Pat. Sept. 11-23", Kenton, 1930, 8-3/4"	45	60	75
Super Nu-Matic Paper Buster Gun	25	35	50
Sure Shot, 1870-1880	150	175	200
Sure Shot Cap Automatic, cast iron, Hubley, 1940, 4-1/4"	35	45	60
Tammany, cast iron, Animal head on barrel, but cap goes behind the head, Ives, 1890	750	850	950
Target Cap Pistol, cast iron, "Pat. 1,488,046", Hubley, 1935, 8"	60	85	125
Targeteer Pistol, Daisy	45	68	90
Teddy Cap Pistol, cast iron, Hubley, 1938, 5-5/8"	35	45	60
Terror, 1925	30	45	60
Terror, cast iron, fires two caps at once, Stevens, 1888, 6-1/2"	225	275	400
Terror Cap Automatic, cast iron, "Pat. Jan 16 '15", Dent, 1915, 4-1/4"	40	60	80
Terror Cap Pistol, cast iron, w/people embossed, 1882	250	350	450
Texan Cap Pistol, cast iron, "Pat. Sept. 11-23", Kenton, 1930, 6-5/8"	45	68	90
Texan Cap Pistol, cast iron, "Pat. No. 1993916", Kenton, 1936, 5-3/4"	60	90	125
Texan Cap Pistol, cast iron, "Made in U.S.A.", Hubley, 1940, 9-1/4"	125	175	225

	C6	C8	C10
Texan Jr. Cap Pistol, cast iron, "Made in U.S.A.", Hubley, 1941, 8-1/8"	100	150	200
Texas Centennial, 1936, 11"	225	338	450
Texas Jack, cast iron, Ives, 1886, 9-3/8"	300	350	500
Thunder-Burp Machine Gun, Mattel, 1960s	40	60	80
Thundergun Rifle, Marx, 36" long	100	150	200
Tiger Cap Pistol, cast iron, Stevens, 1915, 6-3/4"	40	55	70
Tiger Cap Pistol, cast iron, Hubley, 1935, 6-7/8"	35	50	65
Tin Tin Gun, turn crank and it makes noise, Woodhaven Metal Stamping Co., 3 x 5"	20	30	40
Tip Top Cap Pistol, cast iron, Stevens, 1880, 3-1/2"	175	200	225
Trapper Cap Automatic, cast iron, fires only single shot, but roll of caps can be carried in the grip, Kilgore, 1935, 4-1/2"	50	75	100
Triumph, 1878, 5-1/8"	165	225	300
Trooper Cap Pistol, cast iron, Hubley, 1938, 5-1/8"	30	40	50
Trooper Safety Cap Pistol, cast iron, "Pat. Pend; Made in U.S.A.," operates either as straight cap pistol or can be fired w/crank, Kilgore, 1930, 10"	100	150	200
Trooper Safety Cap Pistol, cast iron, Kilgore, 1925, 10-1/4"	75	112	150
Two Time Pistol, cast iron cap and rubber band, "Pat. Appld. For", Kenton, 1930, 9-1/4"	100	150	200
U.S. Navy, 1885, 6-1/2"	75	100	150

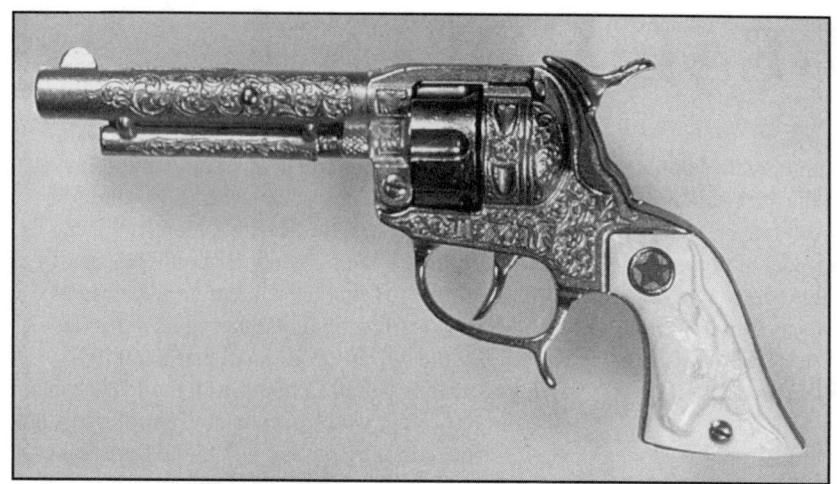

Texan Cap Pistol, 1940, Hubley, $225. Photo courtesy Charles W. Best

	C6	C8	C10
U.S.A. Liquid Pistol Water Pistol, cast iron, "Pat. June 30, 1896", Parker-Stearns, 1896, 4-3/4"	75	100	150
Victor Pistol, cast iron, Stevens, 1924, 12"	150	200	250
Victor Pistol, cast iron, Kenton, 1904, 5"	250	325	400
Villa Cap Pistol, cast iron, "Made in U.S.A.", Dent, 1934, 4-3/4"	40	50	60
Volunteer Cap Pistol, cast iron, "Pat. April 22, '73", Stevens, 1873	125	188	250
War Cap Pistol, cast iron, "Pat. Sept. 11-23", Kenton, 1930, 4-1/4"	35	50	65
Warrior Cap Pistol, cast iron, "Pat. Appld. For, 1926," maker unknown, 1926, 9"	100	125	175
Water Pistol, unmarked, Wyandotte	30	45	60
Water Pistol, No. 41, Wyandotte	30	45	60
Western Cap Pistol, cast iron, "Made in U.S.A.", Kenton, 1939, 7-1/2"	30	45	60
Western Cap Pistol, cast iron w/plastic grips, Kenton, 1931, 7-1/4"	65	98	130
Western Cap Pistol, cast iron, "Pat. Sept. 11-23", Kenton, 1935, 7"	35	48	65
Westo Cap Pistol, cast iron, "Kenton", Kenton, 1936, 7"	40	50	75

	C6	C8	C10
Westo Pistol, cast iron, "Kenton", Kenton, 1938, 7"	40	50	75
Whoopie Cap Pistol, cast iron, Kenton, 1932, 5-7/8"	35	45	60
Wild West Cap Pistol, cast iron, "Made in U.S.A.", National, 1930, 6-1/2"	40	60	75
Wild West Cap Pistol, cast iron, Kenton, 1926, 11-1/2"	125	175	225
Wild West Cap Rifle, w/sight, Marx, 30"	50	75	110
Winner Cap Automatic, cast iron, Hubley, 1940, 4-3/8"	35	45	60
Woodsman Cap Automatic, cast iron, "Patented; Made in U.S.A.", Stevens, 1938, 5-1/4"	60	85	110
Xtra Pistol, cast iron, "Made in U.S.A.", Kenton, 1936, 5"	30	45	55
Yank Cap Pistol, cast iron, 1880	125	175	225
Yankee Cap Pistol, cast iron, Stevens, 1895, 5-1/2"	125	175	225
York Cap Pistol, cast iron, "Pat. Sept. 11-23", Kenton, 1930, 7"	40	55	75
Young Sportsman, wood, c. 1868	75	112	150
Zip Cap Pistol, cast iron, Hubley, 1930, 5"	30	45	55
Zip Cap Pistol, cast iron, Hubley, 1938, 6"	30	45	55
Zulu Cap Pistol, cast iron, w/decoration of African warrior with spear pursuing bird, maker unknown, 1890, 6-5/8"	275	325	375

IDEAL DOLLS

Ideal Toy Corporation produced high quality dolls for over eighty years. Each decade of the 20th century was treated to a wildly popular doll from one of America's largest and oldest manufacturers of dolls and toys. Doll collectors, depending on their age, may remember playing with such Ideal dolls as Flossie Flirt (1920s), Shirley Temple and Betsy Wetsy (1930s), Toni (1940s), Miss Revlon (1950s), Patti Playpal and Tammy (1960s), or Crissy (1970s).

Always an innovator, Ideal used new technology to produce their dolls. Ideal dolls come in materials ranging from cloth, celluloid, composition, hard rubber, latex "magic skin" rubber, hard plastic, injection-molded vinyl, rotation-molded plastic, and blow-molded vinyl. Ideal is responsible for many of the technological breakthroughs in doll manufacturing and holds dozens of patents for innovations such as flirty eyes (eyes that roll from side to side), "ma-ma" voices, "magic skin" latex rubber, and blow-molded vinyl dolls (example Patti Playpal).

Ideal was also a forerunner in licensing—tying in with comic-strip characters, merchandisers, and movie stars to create and promote some of their most memorable dolls. Morris Michtom, founder of Ideal, named a stuffed bear after President Theodore Roosevelt, called it the Teddy Bear, and Ideal was off and running. Ideal was the first American doll maker to tie-in with a cartoon character—the 1907 comic The Yellow Kid. Their first tie-in with a merchandiser was the Uneeda Kid of the National Biscuit Company in 1914. Ideal was the first to strike it big licensing a movie star when they obtained the rights to produce a Shirley Temple doll in 1934. Ideal was a family business owned by the Michoms until the 1980s when it was sold to C.B.S., which subsequently sold it to View-Master, who sold it to Tyco in 1989. The trademark is currently held by the Mattel Toy Corporation and several reproduction Ideal dolls are currently being manufactured.

Many of the Ideal dolls are now very desirable to doll collectors and, since they were mass-produced, affordable. The demand for Ideal dolls has remained consistent through the ups and downs of the toy hobby in recent years. As a result, prices remain steady.

Contributor: Judith Izen, P.O. Box 623, Lexington, MA 02420. Izen is a noted doll and paper doll authority whose paper doll articles have appeared in several publications. Her books include *Collectors Guide to Ideal Dolls* and *Collectors Encyclopedia of Vogue Dolls* (coauthored with Carol Stover) and *American Character Dolls*.

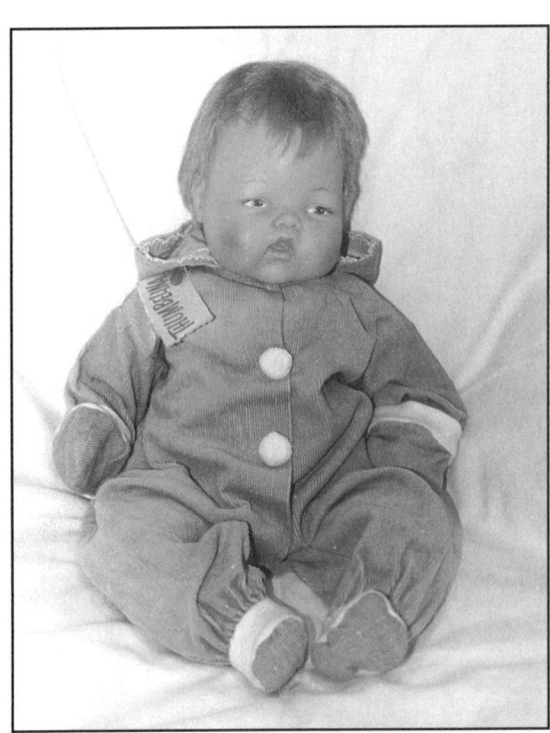

Thumbelina, vinyl doll that wiggles when wound, 1962, 16" tall, $250. Photo courtesy Ellen Cahill

Deanna Durbin, 1938, $600.

Crissy, vinyl doll with hair that grows, 1969, $45. Photo courtesy Susan Mobley

	C10
Addams Family Puppets, The, 1964	65
Angel Babies, 1982	15
Archie Bunker's Grandson, 1976....................	40
Baby Baby-A Handful of Love, 1976	15
Baby Beautiful, 1938.......................................	175
Baby Big Eyes, 1954.......................................	80
Baby Coos, 1948	150
Baby Crissy, 1973	65
Baby Doll, vinyl head and limbs, cloth body, 1950s	100
Baby Dreams, 1975	45
Baby Giggles, 1968	50
Baby Jesus, 1958	125
Baby Kiss-a-Boo, 1981	30
Baby Snooks, 1938...	200
Belly Button Baby, 1971	40
Betsy McCall, 1953..	300
Betsy Wetsy, hard rubber head, 1938	150
Betsy Wetsy, hard plastic head, 1954	150
Betsy Wetsy, all vinyl, 1959	80
Betty Big Girl, 1969	100
Betty Jane, 1940	185

	C10
Big Baby Betsy Wetsy, 1960	100
Bizzie Lizzie, 1971...	45
Blessed Event, 1950	90
Bonnie Baby, 1960..	100
Bonnie Play Pal, 1960	350
Bonny Braids, See Comic Characters	NPF
Bonny Braids Walker, See Comic Characters .	NPF
Boopsie, 1950...	30
Brandi, 1972	60
Brandi & Andy Gibb, 1979	45
Bride, 1939	200
Bridesmaid, 1939	200
Bud, 1965	85
Butterick Designing Set Mannequin, 1953	50
Bye-Bye Baby, 1960	325
Campbell Kids, 1955.......................................	100
Carol Brent, 1961	75
Chew, Chew, Chew Suzy Chew Doll, 1980	35
Chipettes, includes Jeanette, Brittany, Eleanor, 1984..	25
Chipmunks, includes Simon, Alvin, Theodore, 1984..	35

	C10		**C10**
Cinderella, 1938	300	Jim and Dandy, 1985	30
Cinnamon, 1972	70	Jody The Old-fashioned Doll, 1975	30
Clarabelle, 1954	200	Johnny Play Pal, 1960	350
Composition Baby Dolls, 1910-1940s	175	Judy Garland Teen, 1940	600
Country Fashion Crissy Dolls, 1982, 15"	30	Judy Splinters, 1950	200
Cream Puff, 1959	125	Karen and Her Magic Carriage, 1980	35
Cricket, 1971	65	Katie Kachoo, 1966	50
Crissy, 1969	45	Kerry, 1971	60
Cross Patch, 1938	125	Kindles, 1985	20
Crown Princess, 1957	85	Kissy, 1979, 3"	25
Cuddles, 1928	175	Kissy, 1961	125
Daddy's Girl, 1961	1200	Liberty Boy, 1918	250
Deanna Durbin, 1938	600	L'il Honest Abe, 1953	100
Derry Daring, 1975	35	Little Betsy Wetsy, 1957	65
Diana Ross, 1969	300	Little Lost Baby, 1968	65
Dina, 1972	55	Little Miss Revlon, 1959	125
Dodi, 1964	40	Little Wingy, 1953	200
Dorothy Hamill, 1978	35	Little Women, 1984	45
Dracky, 1966	65	Liz, 1962	75
Ducky, 1932	90	Lori Martin, 1961	800
ElectroMan, 1977	45	Magic Hair Crissy, 1977	45
Fantasy Family—Mom, Dad, Boy, and Girl, price for each, 1964	55	Magic Lips, 1955	125
Fashion Flatsy, 1973	45	Magic Skin Baby Doll, 1941	100
Flatsy, 1972	45	Marama, 1940	800
Flexy Dolls, 1939	200	Mary Hartline, 1952	500
Flossie Flirt, 1924	150	Mayfair, 1939	150
Franky, 1966	65	Mera, Queen of Atlantis, 1967	600
Fred Muggs, 1957	70	Mia, 1971	55
Giggles, 1967	65	Mighty Mouse, 1957	60
Ginger, 1938	300	Mini Monsters, 1966	65
Girl Doll, composition, 1910-1940s	175	Miss Curity, 1953	350
Girl Doll, hard plastic, 1950s	200	Miss Ideal, 1961	325
Glamour Misty, 1965	45	Miss Liberty, 1940s	300
Goody Two Shoes, 1965	85	Miss Revlon, 1956	250
Grown Up Pos'n Tammy, 1965	45	Mistress Mary-Quite Contrary, 1938	150
Happi Returns, 1983	25	Mitzi, 1961	150
Hara, 1984	30	My Bottle Baby, 1979	35
Harmony, 1972	50	National Velvet, 1961	800
Harriet Hubbard Ayer, 1953	175	Nursery Tales, 1984	25
Honey Moon, 1965	80	Orange Juice Boy, 1928	150
Honeybunch, 1956	70	Pam's Pram, 1954	40
Honeysuckle, 1956	70	Patti Partridge, 1971	70
IDENITE Dolls, 1936	250	Patti Play Pal, 1959	350
In-A-Minute Thumbelina, 1971	55	Patti Play Pal, 1981	150
Jackie, 1962	900	Patti Playful, 1973	65
Jay J. Armes, 1976	50	Patti Prays, 1957	60
Jelly Belly Dolls, 1982	30	Pattite, 1960	350
		Peggy's Snap-On Magic Wardrobe, 1953	40

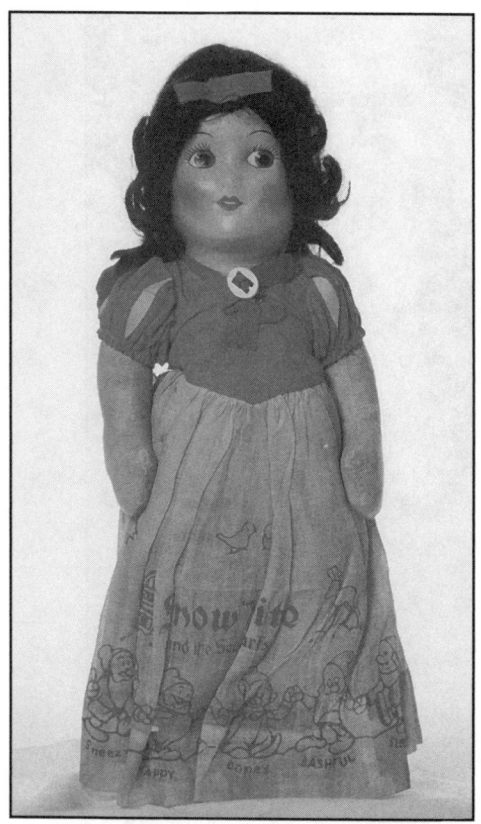

*Snow White, cloth with mask face, 1938, 16"
tall, $300. Photo courtesy Marge Meisinger*

*Patti Playpal, vinyl life-size doll, 1959, 35" tall, $350.
Photo courtesy Betty Hopkins*

	C10
Penny Play Pal, 1959	300
Pepper, 1963	35
Pete and Repete, 1951	45
Peter Playpal, 1960	850
Plassie, 1942	150
Play 'N Jane, 1971	40
Playtex Dryper Baby, 1960	250
Posie, hard plastic, 1954	150
Posie, bendable vinyl, 1969	50
Pos'n Pete, 1965	45
Pos'n Salty, 1965	45
Princess Beatrix, 1938	250
Princess Mary, 1955	175
Queen of the Ice, 1938	150
Raggedy Ann and Andy, the set, 1983	100
Rub-A-Dub Dolly, 1974	35
Ruth, 1953	125
SallyKins, 1934	175
Samantha the Bewitching Doll, 1965	600
Sara Ann, 21"	300
Sara Ann, 1951, 15"	250
Sara Stimson, 1980	40

	C10
Saralee, 1951	300
Saucy Walker, hard plastic, 1953	250
Saucy Walker, vinyl, 1960	200
Shirley Temple, porcelain, 1984	200
Shirley Temple, vinyl, 1960, 36"	1200
Shirley Temple, vinyl, 1984	50
Shirley Temple, vinyl, 1982, 8"	40
Shirley Temple, vinyl, 1974	80
Shirley Temple, vinyl, 1957-61, 12"	200
Shirley Temple, vinyl, 1957-61, 17"	225
Shirley Temple, composition, 1939, 25"	825
Shirley Temple, vinyl, 1957-61, 19"	250
Shirley Temple, composition, 1939, 22"	800
Shirley Temple, composition, 1939, 17"	650
Shirley Temple, composition, 1939, 15"	625
Shirley Temple, composition, 1939, 13"	600
Shirley Temple, composition, 1939, 11"	650
Shirley Temple, 1982, 12"	60
Shirley Temple, composition, 1939, 27"	900
Shirley Temple Baby, 1935	800
Smokey the Bear, 1953	150
Snoozie, 1933	150

Trilby, three-face doll, 1951, 19" tall, $150. Photo courtesy Diane Buck

	C10		C10
Snuggles, 1978	30	Timmy Tumbles, 1977	40
Soldier, 1940s	150	Tiny Tears, vinyl, 1984	35
Soozie Smiles, 1923	125	Tiny Tears, porcelain, 1984	60
Storybook Dolls, 1938	100	Tippy Tumbles, 1977	40
Stretchie, 1973	25	Toni, 1949-53, 14"	300
Suntan Dodi, 1977	30	Toni, 1949-53, 22-1/2"	800
Suntan Eric, 1977	40	Toni Walker, 1954-56, 14"	300
Suntan Tuesday Taylor, 1977	35	Toni Walker, 1954-56, 21"	500
Suzy, 1936	150	Tressy, 1970	70
Suzy Play Pal, 1959	350	Trilby, 1951	150
Tabatha, 1966	500	Tubsy, 1967	50
Talkypot, 1950	90	Tuesday Taylor, 1976	45
Tammy, 1962	45	Twinkle Eyes, 1957	60
Tammy's Dad, 1963	55	Uneeda Kid, 1914	250
Tammy's Mom, 1963	55	Upsy Dazy, 1973	35
Tara, 1976	75	Vampy, 1966	65
Tearie Dearie, 1963	30	Velvet, 1974	40
Ted, 1963	40	Victorian Ladies, 1984, 8"	25
Teddy Bear, porcelain, 1984	80	Victorian Ladies, 1984, 12"	30
Teddy Bear, cloth, 1907	900	Vinyl Doll, all vinyl body, 1955	80
Terry Twist, 1962	150	Wake-Up Thumbelina, 1976	35
Thumbelina, 1961	200	Whoopsie, 1978	45
Tickletoes, 1931	150	Wolfie, 1966	65
Tiffany Taylor, 1974	65	Zu-Zu Kid, 1916	275

LIONEL TRAINS

Lionel is unquestionably the greatest name in the history of toy trains. Founded in 1902 by Joshua Lionel Cowen (born August 25, 1877), it was incorporated as the Lionel Manufacturing Company on March 13.

In his teens Cowen had worked for New York's Acme Electric Lamp Company as a battery-lamp assembler, and he enjoyed experimenting with his spare time. In 1901, Cowen developed what was to become the first Lionel train—a battery-powered "Electric Express." It was originally designed to be used as a showpiece in a shop window. Customers were curious about the Electric Express, and eventually twelve of the showpieces were sold. Cowen was on his way.

In 1902, Cowen added a trolley car to the display, manufactured for him by Massachusetts' Morton E. Converse. At the same time, six barrels were added to the Electric Express. Other accessories in the first 1902 Lionel catalog included a suspension bridge, a track with a switch, a crossover track that allowed a figure-eight layout and a bumper for the end of a track. The Electric Express, like the trolley, could now be powered by batteries or electricity.

By 1909, Lionel was advertising its trains as "The Standard of the World." Cowen had a knack for advertising, and much of Lionel's early success can be attributed to the company's colorful and punchy ad campaigns and catalogs.

The next twenty years saw tremendous growth for Lionel. In 1915, O-gauge cars were introduced, and they eventually became the most popular scale of train. In 1927, Lionel's profits were almost a half-million dollars.

In 1930, the first full year of the Depression, Lionel's profits were down to $82,000, and in 1931 they lost $207,000. The firm temporarily went into receivership in 1934.

That same year the Streamlined Union Pacific diesel M10000 was released. Lionel orchestrated a major publicity campaign timed to coincide with the M10000's release. Sales soared. It was in the fall of this year that Lionel developed the Mickey and Minnie Mouse hand car. It sold more than a quarter million units, and it is very likely the thing saved the company from bankruptcy. By the next year his company was in the black by $154,000.

Standard gauge was discontinued in 1940, and with the interruption of World War II, Lionel's only war years toy was a cardboard train set as the company fulfilled government contracts.

Lionel's postwar line, known by many as the golden years of Lionel train, was introduced by a sixteen-page catalog contained in the November 23, 1946 issue of Liberty magazine. Though competition with American Flyer soon became fierce, Lionel was able to stay ahead. Bakelite and other plastics became prominent, along with such innovations as knuckle couplers, smoke units, a battery-operated diesel horn (1948) and "Mangnetraction" (Magnetized wheels and axles, which gave stronger pulling power) in the 1950s.

However, by the mid 1950s Lionel began to teeter. In 1957, Lionel introduced HO-scale trains, but that year was the last profitable one for the company. Ever sagacious, Cowen retired the next year and sold all of his Lionel stock the following year.

Cowen died at the age of 85 on September 8, 1965.

No. 6804 Flatcar with two gray trucks, $205. Photo courtesy Good Old Days: Photo by Bill Kaufman

1943 Paper Train

	C6	C8	C10
No. 50, Paper Train Set, uncataloged, 1943	90	157	325
No. 224, Paper Locomotive set, steam, paper train, w/original box, uncataloged, 1943	100	150	200
No. 47618, Caboose, paper train, uncataloged, 1943	25	38	50
No. 61100, Boxcar, paper train, uncataloged, 1943	25	38	50

Miscellaneous

	C6	C8	C10
No. 5C, Test Set	1500	2500	4000
No. 5D, Repair Station	800	1400	1900
No. 072, T-Rail, curved track, per section	NPF	2	3
No. HO-349, Turbo Missile Firing Car, HO	30	50	100
No. HO-808, Flatcar, HO, w/tractor	14	23	45
No. HO-850-100, Missile Launching Car, HO	11	19	38
No. 1928, Dealer Display, large cardboard background showing power station, roundhouses, etc.	210	350	700

Pre-WWII (1901-1942)

	C6	C8	C10
No. 5, Trolley, standard, motor car, powered, four wheel, No. 1 Electric-Rapid Transit No. 1, cream body, orange roof, 1906-1910	1200	2000	4000
No. 1, Trolley, standard, motor car, powered, four wheel, white body w/blue roof, marked "No. 1 Electric-Rapid Transit No. 1", 1906-1910	1110	1850	4000
No. 1, Trolley, standard, motor car, four wheel, powered, cream body w/blue roof, "No. 1 Electric-Rapid Transit No. 1", 1906-1910	750	1250	2700
No. 1, Trolley, standard, motor car, four wheel, powered, blue body w/blue roof, marked "No. 1 Electric-Rapid Transit No. 1", 1906-1910	1050	1750	3500
No. 1, Trolley, standard, motor car, four wheel, powered, cream body w/blue roof, marked "No. 1 Electric-Rapid Transit No. 1", 1906-1910	1260	2100	4500
No. 1, Trolley, standard, trailer, non-powered, white body w/blue roof, 1907	1050	1750	3500
No. 1, Trolley, standard, trailer, non-powered, cream body w/blue roof, 1907	1050	1750	3500
No. 1, Bild-A-Motor, O, 1928	150	225	300
No. 1, Bild-A-Motor, small, 1928	75	113	150
No. 00-1, Locomotive, OO, steam, 4-6-4 Hudson full scale three-rail w/either 001T tender without whistle or 001W w/whistle, 1938-42	120	200	400
No. 2, Trolley, standard, motor car, four-wheel, powered, No. 2 Electric-Rapid Transit No. 2 red body, cream windows and doors, 1906-1915	1050	1750	3400

Pre-WWII (1901-1942)

	C6	C8	C10
No. 2, Trolley, standard, motor car, four-wheel, powered, No. 2 Electric-Rapid Transit No. 2 cream body, red windows and doors, 1906-1915	1050	1750	3400
No. 2, Trolley, standard, trailer, non-powered, red body, cream windows and doors, 1906-1915	750	1250	2500
No. 2, Trolley, standard, trailer, non-powered, cream body w/red windows and doors, 1906-1915	750	1250	2500
No. 2, Bild-A-Motor, O, large, 1928	150	250	350
No. 00-2, Locomotive, OO, steam, 4-6-4 Hudson, semi-scale three-rail w/either 002T tender without whistle or OO2W w/whistle, 1938-42	105	175	350
No. 002W, Tender, 4-6-4, steam, w/whistle, 1939	120	200	400
No. 3, Trolley, standard, eight wheel, motor car, powered, No. 3 Electric-Rapid Transit No. 3, light orange body, dark orange roof, 1906-1909	1200	2000	4000
No. 3, Trolley, standard, eight wheel, motor car, powered, No. 3 Electric-Rapid Transit No. 3, cream body, orange roof, 1906-1909	1200	2000	4000
No. 3, Trolley, standard, eight wheel, motor car, powered, No. 3 Electric-Rapid Transit No. 3, dark green body and roof, 1906-1909	1350	2250	4500
No. 3, Trolley, standard, eight-wheel, trailer, non-powered, light orange body, dark orange roof, 1906-1909	1200	2000	4000
No. 00-3, Locomotive, OO, steam, 4-6-4 Hudson semi-scale three-rail w/either 002T Tender without whistle or 002W w/whistle, 1938-1942	120	200	400
No. 4, Trolley, standard, eight-wheel, motor car, green body and roof, powered, double motor, "No. 4 Electric-Rapid Transit No. 4", 1908-1910	2700	4500	7000
No. 4, Trolley, standard, eight-wheel, motor car, cream body and green roof, powered, double motor, "No. 4 Electric-Rapid Transit No. 4", 1908-1910	2700	4500	7000
No. 4, Locomotive, O, 0-4-0, electric, gray, 1928-1932	300	550	1000
No. 4, Locomotive, O, 0-4-0, electric, orange, 1928-1932	270	450	900
No. 4U, Locomotive, O, 0-4-0, electric, orange only, marked "You build it," unassembled and complete w/instructions in original box, 1928	850	1275	1700
No. 00-4, Locomotive, OO, steam, 4-6-4 Hudson semi-scale two-rail w/either 004T Tender without whistle or 004W w/whistle, 1938-1942	120	200	400
No. 5, Locomotive, standard, 0-4-0, steam, no tender, black cab and boiler, red window trim, "Pennsylvania", 1906-1926	900	1500	3000

No. 6 Locomotive, 4-4-0, $1500.
Photo courtesy T.W. Sefton

Pre-WWII (1901-1942)	C6	C8	C10
No. 5, Locomotive, standard, 0-4-0, steam, no tender, black cab and boiler, red window trim, marked "B&ORR", 1906-1926	360	900	1500
No. 5, Locomotive, standard, 0-4-0, steam, no tender, black cab and boiler, red window trim, marked "NYC&HRRR", 1906-1926	780	1300	2600
No. 5, Special Locomotive, standard, 0-4-0, steam, no tender, black cab and boiler, red window trim w/tender, 1910-1911	450	750	1500
No. 6, Locomotive, standard, 4-4-0, steam, w/tender, black cab and boiler, red window trim, marked "Pennsylvania", 1906-1923	705	1175	2350
No. 6, Locomotive, standard, 4-4-0, steam w/tender, black cab and boiler, red window trim, marked "B&ORR", 1906-1923	630	1050	2100
No. 6, Locomotive, standard, 4-4-0, steam w/tender, black cab and boiler, red window trim, marked "NYC&HRRR", 1906-1923	300	500	1000
No. 6, Locomotive, standard, 4-4-0, special, steam, w/tender, black cab and boiler, red window trim, non-lettered, 1908-1909	450	750	1500
No. 7, Locomotive, standard, 4-4-0, steam, brass boiler, nickel cab and tender, 1910-1923	1050	1750	3200
No. 8, Trolley, standard, eight wheel, motor car, powered, cream or dark green, marked "Pay as you enter No. 8", 1908-1909	1170	1950	3900
No. 8, Locomotive, standard, 0-4-0, electric, maroon, 1925-1932	50	100	200
No. 8, Locomotive, standard, 0-4-0, electric, olive, 1925-1932	45	75	150
No. 8, Locomotive, standard, 0-4-0, electric, red, 1925-1932	45	75	150
No. 8, Locomotive, standard, 0-4-0, electric, mojave, 1925-1932	60	100	225
No. 8, Locomotive, standard, 0-4-0, electric, peacock, 1925-1932	75	125	250
No. 8E, Locomotive, standard, 0-4-0, electric, olive, 1926-1932	60	100	200
No. 8E, Locomotive, standard, 0-4-0, electric, red, 1926-1932	80	135	250
No. 8E, Locomotive, standard, 0-4-0, electric, peacock, 1926-1932	110	200	400
No. 8E, Locomotive, standard, 0-4-0, Macy, electric, pea green, cream stripe, 1926-1932	150	250	550

Pre-WWII (1901-1942)	C6	C8	C10
No. 8E, Locomotive, standard, 0-4-0, electric, mojave, 1926-1932	95	162	325
No. 9, Trolley, standardl, eight wheel, motor car, powered, cream or dark green, marked "Pay as you enter No. 9", 1909	2100	3500	6500
No. 9, Locomotive, standard, electric, dark green, 1929	600	1000	2000
No. 9E, Locomotive, standard, 0-4-0, electric, 242, two-tone green, 1928	472	785	1575
No. 9E, Locomotive, standard, 2-4-2, electric, gray, 1931	420	700	1400
No. 9U, Locomotive, standard, electric, orange, assembled, 1928	450	750	1500
No. 9U, Special Locomotive, standard, kit form w/original box, orange, unassembled, 1929	1200	1800	2400
No. 10, Interurban, standard, motor car, powered, maroon or dark green, "Interurban" and "New York Central Lines", 1910	600	1000	2000
No. 10, Interurban, standard, motor car, powered, marked "Interurban," "New York Central Lines," "10 WB&B&A 10", 1910	1500	2500	5000
No. 10, Locomotive, standard, 0-4-0, electric, peacock blue, mojave, gray, 1925-1929	85	140	250
No. 10, Macy Locomotive, standard, 0-4-0, electric, red, 1930	180	350	700
No. 10E, Locomotive, standard, 0-4-0, electric, brown, green frame, 1926-1930	100	175	400
No. 10E, Locomotive, standard, 0-4-0, electric, peacock or gray, 1926-1930	74	122	245
No. 10E, Locomotive, standard, 0-4-0, electric, peacock or red, w/Bild-a-Loco Motor, 1926-1930	158	285	600
No. 10E, Macy Locomotive, standard, 0-4-0, electric, peacock w/orange stripe, uncataloged, 1930	85	140	280
No. 11, Flatcar, standard, 1906-1926	33	55	110
No. 0-11, Switches, O, electric, non-derailing, pair, 1933	50	75	100
No. 0-11-11, Fiber Pins, O, 1937	NPF	NPF	1
No. 12, Gondola, standard, 1906-1911	50	125	300
No. 0-12, Switches, O, electric, 1927	30	50	100
No. 13, Cattle Car, standard, 1906-1911	50	125	300
No. 0-13, Switches, O, panel board set, 1929	25	38	50
No. 14, Boxcar, standard, 1906-1926	60	100	200

No. 7 Locomotive, 4-4-0,
$3500. Photo courtesy
T.W. Sefton

Pre-WWII (1901-1942)

	C6	C8	C10
No. 14, Harmony Boxcar Car Creamery Special, standard, uncataloged, 1920	120	200	400
No. 00-14, Boxcar, OO, yellow and Tuscan, 1938	24	40	80
No. 15, Oil, standard, 1906-1926	48	80	160
No. 00-15, Tank Car, OO, 1938	27	45	90
No. 16, Ballast, standard, dark green, 1906-1926	65	108	215
No. 00-16, Hopper, OO, 1938	66	110	220
No. 17, Caboose, standard, 1906-1926	105	175	350
No. 00-17, Caboose, OO, 1938	25	41	82
No. 18, Pullman, standard, dark olive, marked "Parlor Car" and "New York Central Lines", 1918-1923	210	350	700
No. 18, Pullman, standard, light orange, marked "New York Central Lines", 1916-1917	400	900	1700
No. 18, Pullman, standard, dark olive, marked "New York Central Lines", 1906-1910	360	600	1200
No. 19, Combine, standard, 1906-1927	180	300	600
No. 19, Combine, standard, 1906-1927	300	500	1000
No. 19, Combine, standard, 1906-1927	300	500	1000
No. 190, Observation Car, standard, 1907-1927	180	300	600
No. 190, Observation Car, standard, 1907-1927	300	500	1000
No. 190, Observation Car, standard, 1907-1927	300	500	1000
No. 20, Direct, current shunt resistor, 1906	5	15	25
No. 20, 90 Degrees Crossing, standard, 1909-32	6	9	12
No. 0-20, 90 Degrees Crossing, O, 1915	6	9	12
No. 0-20X, 45 Degrees Crossing, O, 1915	10	15	20
No. 21, Crossing, standard, 1906	4	8	15
No. 21, Switch, standard, w/light, 1915-1925	12	25	40
No. 0-21, Switch, O, w/light, 1915	12	18	25
No. 23, Bumper, standard, red or black, 1906	9	15	25
No. 0-23, Bumper, O, 1915	4	6	8
No. 24, Station, standard, 1906	350	525	700
No. 24, Bulb, eight volt, 1915	NPF	NPF	1
No. 00-24, Boxcar, OO, 1939	20	35	70
No. 25, Station, standard, 1906	375	562	750
No. 25, Bulb, 3-1/2 volt, DC, 1911	NPF	NPF	1
No. 25, Bulb, pear shaped, 1924	NPF	NPF	5

Pre-WWII (1901-1942)

	C6	C8	C10
No. 25, Bumper, standard, cream or black, 1928	20	30	40
No. 0-25, Bumper, O, 1928-1942	17	25	35
No. 00-25, Tank Car, OO, 1939	30	50	100
No. 26, Passenger Foot Bridge, standard, 1906	100	150	200
No. 26, Bulb, 14 volt AC, 1911	NPF	NPF	1
No. 27, Station, standard, 1909	250	375	500
No. 27, Lighting, standard, set for cars, 1911	30	50	75
No. 27, Bulb, 12 volt, red, green or clear, 1927	NPF	NPF	1
No. 27-6, Bulb, 12 volt, clear, 1940	NPF	NPF	1
No. 00-27, Caboose, OO, 1939	21	35	70
No. 28, Bulb, 18 volt, red, green, amber or clear, 1927	NPF	NPF	1
No. 28-3, Bulb, 18 volt, clear, 1939	NPF	NPF	1
No. 28-6, Bulb, 18 volt, red, 1939	NPF	NPF	1
No. 29, Day Coach, standard, dark olive, 1909	600	1200	2500
No. 29, Day Coach, standard, maroon, 1909	300	600	1250
No. 29, Bulb, 3-1/2 volt, 1915	NPF	NPF	1
No. 29-3, Bulb, 18 volt, yellow, 1932	NPF	NPF	1
No. 30, Bulb, 14 volt, 1915	NPF	NPF	1
No. 30, Curved Rubber Roadbed, standard, 1931	3	4	5
No. 0-30, Roadbed, curved, rubber, 1931	3	4	5
No. 31, Combine, standard, orange, brown, green, maroon, 1921-1925	48	80	160
No. 31, Straight Rubber Roadbed, standard, 1931	3	4	5
No. 0-31, Roadbed, O, straight, rubber, 1931	3	4	5
No. 00-31, Track, OO, curved, two-rail, 1939	3	5	6
No. 32, Miniature Figures, standard, set of twelve, 1910	150	225	300
No. 32, Baggage Car, standard, maroon, dark olive, brown, orange, 1921	60	115	200
No. 32, Rubber Roadbed, standard, 90-degree crossing, 1931	3	4	5
No. 32, Track, Super O, straight, 1931	5	10	15
No. 0-32, Roadbed, O, 90-degree crossing, rubber, 1931	3	4	5
No. 00-32, Track, OO, straight, two-rail, 1939	5	10	15

No. 408E Locomotive, $1280.

Pre-WWII (1901-1942)	C6	C8	C10
No. 33, Locomotive, 0-6-0, electric, engine only, dark green, NYC, 1913	240	400	800
No. 33, Locomotive, standard, 0-4-0, electric, dark olive or black, 1913-1924	50	110	200
No. 33, Locomotive, standard, 0-4-0, electric, maroon, 1913-1924	120	200	450
No. 33, Locomotive, standard, 0-4-0, electric, red, 1913-1924	150	250	500
No. 33, Locomotive, standard, 0-4-0, electric, peacock, 1913-1924	150	250	500
No. 33, Locomotive, standard, electric 0-4-0, gray, 1913-1924	60	100	200
No. 33, Rubber Roadbed, standard O, 45-degree crossing, 1931	3	4	5
No. 0-33, Roadbed, standard O, 45-degree crossing, rubber, 1931	3	4	5
No. 0-33, Roadbed, standard O, 45-degree crossing, rubber, 1931	3	4	5
No. 34, Locomotive, standard, 0-6-0, electric, dark green, 1912	175	300	550
No. 34, Locomotive, standard, 0-4-0, electric, dark green, uncataloged, 1913	120	200	400
No. 34, Rubber Roadbed Switch, standard, 1913	3	4	5
No. 0-34, Roadbed Switch, O, rubber, 1931	3	4	5
No. 00-34, Track Connection, OO, for curved track, 1939	3	4	5
No. 35, Lamp Post, gray or silver, 1940	15	25	50
No. 35, Pullman, standard, dark olive, maroon or brown, 1915	21	34	65
No. 35, Pullman, standard, orange, 1915	49	70	150
No. 36, Observation Car, standard, dark olive, maroon or brown, 1912	21	40	80
No. 36, Observation Car, standard, orange, 1912	60	110	225
No. 36RM, Controller, standard, 1937	NPF	2	3
No. 38, Locomotive, standard, 0-4-0, electric, black or gray, 1913-1924	35	100	175

Pre-WWII (1901-1942)	C6	C8	C10
No. 38, Locomotive, standard, 0-4-0, electric, pea green, 1913-1924	96	190	370
No. 38, Locomotive, standard, 0-4-0, electric, red, 1913-1924	150	300	550
No. 38, Locomotive, standard, 0-4-0 electric, brown, 1913-1924	120	200	375
No. 39, Bulb, 12 volt, frosted, 1927	NPF	NPF	1
No. 39-3, Bulb, 12 volt, frosted, 1939	NPF	NPF	1
No. 40, Bulb, 13 volt, 1927	NPF	NPF	1
No. 40-3, Bulb, 8 volt, 1939	NPF	NPF	1
No. 41, Accessory Contactor, 1936	NPF	1	2
No. 42, Locomotive, standard, 0-4-4-0, electric, square body, dark green, 1912	300	650	1200
No. 42, Locomotive, standard, electric, dark green, gray and black, 1913-1923	142	237	500
No. 42, Locomotive, standard, electric, peacock, 1913-1923	825	1375	2750
No. 42, Locomotive, standard, electric, maroon, 1913-1923	300	750	1200
No. 42, Locomotive, standard, electric, mojave, 1913-1923	173	325	650
No. 0-42, Switch, O, manual, single, 1938	12	18	25
No. 43, Bild-A-Motor, standard, gear set, 1929	55	90	130
No. 43, Pleasure Boat, cream, red and white, 1933-1936, 1939-1941	400	600	800
No. 0-43, Bild-A-Motor Gear Set, O, 1929	32	48	64
No. 44, Race Boat, green, white and dark brown, 1935-1936	450	675	800
No. 00-44, Boxcar, OO, 1939	25	42	85
No. 00-44K, Kit, OO, original box, 1939	110	165	220
No. 45/45N/045, Automatic Gateman, green base, creame house, red roof w/cream chimney, 1935-1936, 1937-1942	16	30	65

Pre-WWII (1901-1942)

	C6	C8	C10
No. 00-45, Tank Car, OO, 1939	21	85	70
No. 00-45K, Tank Kit, OO, 1939	100	150	200
No. 46, Bulb, 8 volt, 1936	NPF	NPF	1
No. 46, Single Arm Crossing, cream and green base, lantern on tip of gate, 1939-1942	45	75	150
No. 00-46, Hopper, OO, 1939	25	41	82
No. 00-46K, Hopper Kit, OO, 1939	100	150	200
No. 47, Bulb, 6 volt, 1916	NPF	NPF	1
No. 47, Double Arm Crossing Gates, w/two crossing gates on each side, 1937-1942	70	105	140
No. 47-40, Bulb, 18 volt, red, 1937	NPF	NPF	1
No. 47-73, Bulb, 12 volt, 1942	NPF	NPF	1
No. 00-47, Caboose, OO, 1939	24	40	80
No. 00-47K, Caboose Kit, OO, 1939	100	150	200
No. 48, Bulb, 21 volt, 1936	NPF	NPF	1
No. 48W, Whistle Station, lithographed building, red base housing whistle, 1937-1942	10	18	36
No. 49, Lionel Airport, printed cardboard base w/airplane and controls, 1937-1939	400	800	1200
No. 50, Locomotive, standard, 0-4-0, electric gray, 1924	90	150	300
No. 50, Locomotive, standard, electric, maroon, 1924	105	225	500
No. 50, Locomotive, standard, electric, dark green, 1924	105	175	300
No. 50, Locomotive, standard, electric, mojave, 1924	105	175	300
No. 50, Airplane, 1936	200	400	600
No. 51, Locomotive, standard, 0-4-0, steam, "5 Special", 1912-1923	380	650	1300
No. 51, Airport, printed cardboard base for center control and airplane, 1936-1939	300	450	600
No. 00-51, Track, OO, curved, three-rail, 1939	NPF	1	2
No. 52, Lamp Post, aluminum, 1933	35	52	70
No. 00-52, Track, OO, straight, three-rail, 1939	6	8	10
No. 53, Locomotive, standard, 0-4-0, electric, mojave, maroon, dark olive, 1912-1914	360	600	1200
No. 53, Locomotive, standard, 0-4-0, electric, mojave, maroon, dark olive, 1920	150	250	500
No. 53, Lamp Post, gray, aluminum, mojave, 1931	37	56	75
No. 53-8, Bulb, 18 volt, 1932	NPF	NPF	1
No. 54, Locomotive, standard, 0-4-4-0, electric, square body, brass, 1912	1050	1750	3500
No. 54, Locomotive, standard, 0-4-4-0, electric, brass, single or double motor, 1913-1923	750	1250	2500
No. 54, Lamp Post, double light, dark green, 1929	35	52	70
No. 00-54, Track Connection, OO, for curved track, 1939	NPF	1	2

Pre-WWII (1901-1942)

	C6	C8	C10
No. 55, Bulb, 14 volt, 1924	NPF	NPF	1
No. 55, Airplane, red and silver w/control, 1937-1939	250	375	500
No. 56, Lamp Post, gray, green, mojave, 1925-1949	32	48	65
No. 57, Lamp Post, orange, "Broadway & Main", 1924-1942	25	42	85
No. 57, Lamp Post, orange, "Broadway & Fifth Ave.", 1924-1942	24	40	80
No. 57, Lamp Post, yellow, "Broadway & Main", 1924-1942	30	50	100
No. 57, Lamp Post, orange, "Broadway & 42nd Street", 1924-1942	30	50	100
No. 58, Lamp Post, green, maroon, cream, 1922-1942	14	24	48
No. 59, Lamp Post, green, 1920-1936	15	25	50
No. 59, Lamp Post, olive, 1920-1936	22	37	75
No. 60, Automatic Trip Reverse, standard, 1906	3	5	6
No. 60, Locomotive, standard, 0-4-0, electric, F.A.O. Schwarz Special, uncataloged, 1913	360	600	1200
No. 60, Telegraph Pole, standard, set of six, 1920	66	110	220
No. 0-60, Telegraph Pole, O, set of six, 1929	24	40	80
No. 61, Locomotive, standard, 0-4-4-0, electric, F.A.O. Schwarz Special, uncataloged, 1913	450	750	1500
No. 61, Lamp Post, dark green, maroon, mojave, olive, 1914-1936	15	25	50
No. 00-61, Track, OO, curved, three-rail, 1938	3	5	6
No. 62, Locomotive, standard, 0-4-0, electric, F.A.O. Schwarz Special, uncataloged, 1913	360	600	1200
No. 62, Automatic Reversing Trip, standard, 1914	3	4	5
No. 62, Semaphore, 1920-1932	12	20	40
No. 00-62, Track, OO, straight, three-rail, 1939	3	5	6
No. 63, Semaphore, 1915-1921	30	45	60
No. 63, Lamp Post, double globe, silver, 1933-1942	81	135	270
No. 63-10, Opal Globe, 1933	3	4	5
No. 63-11, Bulb, 18 volt, opal, 1935	NPF	NPF	1
No. 00-63, Track, OO, half-curve, three-rail, 1939	3	5	6
No. 64, Semaphore, 1915-1921	21	35	70
No. 64, Lamp Post, green, 1940-1942	14	24	48
No. 64-15, Bulb, 12 volt, clear, 1940	NPF	NPF	5
No. 64-26, Bulb, 12 volt, opal, 1941	NPF	NPF	5
No. 00-64, Track Connection, curved, three-rail, 1939	5	8	10
No. 65, Semaphore, 1915-1926	30	45	60
No. 65, Whistle Controller, 1935	6	9	12
No. 00-65, Track, OO, half-straight, three-rail, 1939	NPF	1	2
No. 65, Semaphore, 1915-1926	35	52	70

No. 42 Locomotive, electric, $475.

Pre-WWII (1901-1942)	C6	C8	C10
No. 66, Whistle and Reversing Controller, 1936	3	5	6
No. 00-66, Straight, OO, straight, three-rail, 1939	NPF	1	2
No. 67, Lamp Post, 1915-1926	30	50	100
No. 67, Whistle and Reversing Controller, 1936	4	5	7
No. 68, Warning Signal, standard, non-operative, 1926-1939	7	11	14
No. 0-68, Warning Signal, O, 1926-1942	7	11	14
No. 69, Warning Bell, standard, 1921-1935	20	34	68
No. 69-7, Fiber Track Pins, 1933	NPF	NPF	1
No. 69N, Warning Bell, standard/O, 1936-1942	25	38	50
No. 0-69, Warning Bell, O, 1921-1935.	25	38	50
No. 70, Accessory Set, consists of two No. 62, one No. 68 and one No. 59, 1921	75	112	150
No. 00-70, 90 Degree Crossing, OO, three-rail, 1939	8	11	15
No. 71, Telegraph Pole Set, set of six, 1921	54	90	180
No. 071, Telegraph Poles, O, set of six, 1929	63	105	210
No. 00-72, Switches, OO, electric, three rail, pair, 1939	150	225	300
No. 00-72-70, Bulb, O, 12 volt, yellow, 1939	NPF	NPF	1
No. 00-74, Boxcar, OO, two-rail, 1939.	22	38	75
No. 75, Low Bridge Sign, 1921	35	52	70
No. 75, Bulb, 12 volt, 1924	NPF	NPF	1
No. 00-75, Tank Car, OO, two-rail, 1939	21	35	70
No. 76, Block Signal, standard, 1923	25	42	85
No. 76, Warning Bell and Shant, red base, orange roof, black bell fastened to cross gate sign post, similar in appearance to forty-five gateman, no watch man bell inside shanty, 1939-1942	95	143	190
No. 77, Crossing Gate, standard, automatic, 1923-1939	35	52	70

Pre-WWII (1901-1942)	C6	C8	C10
No. 77N, Crossing Gate, standard/O, automatic, 1936-1939	25	38	50
No. 0-77, Automatic Crossing Gate, O, 1923-1939	20	30	40
No. 00-77, Caboose, OO, two-rail, 1939	28	48	95
No. 78, Train Control Block Signal, standard, red base, orange base, 1924	40	60	80
No. 0-78, Train Control Block Signal, O, red or orange base, 1924	45	68	90
No. 79, Flashing Signal, cream or aluminum, 1928-1942	60	90	120
No. 79-23, Bulb, Bulb, 12 volt, red, 1939	NPF	NPF	1
No. 80, Semaphore, standard, 1926-1935	75	112	150
No. 80N, Semaphore, standard, 1926-1942	62	93	125
No. 0-80, Semaphore, O, 1926-1935	50	75	100
No. 80/81, Race Car Set, includes car, driver, eight sections of curve track, 1912-1916	750	1125	1500
No. 81, Rheostat, 1927	7	11	15
No. 00-81, KW Kit, OO, locomotive and tender, three-rail, 1938	600	900	1200
No. 82, Train Control Semaphore, standard, yellow and green, 1927-1935	55	82	110
No. 82N, Train Control Semaphore, standard/O, 1936-1942	92	138	185
No. 0-82, Train Control Semaphore, O, 1927-1935	60	90	120
No. 83, Traffic Crossing Signal, red base, 1935-1942	155	225	310
No. 83, Traffic Crossing Signal, tan base, 1927-1934	155	225	310
No. 00-83, W Locomotive and Tender, OO, three-rail, 1939-1942	180	300	600
No. 84, Racing Cars, 1912	2000	3000	4000
No. 84, Semaphore, standard, 1927-1932	60	90	120
No. 0-84, Semaphore, O, 1928-1932	60	90	120
No. 85, Racing Cars, 1912	2000	3000	4000
No. 85, Telegraph Pole, standard, orange, 1929-1942	15	22	30

Pre-WWII (1901-1942)

	C6	C8	C10
No. 86, Telegraph Poles, standard, set of six, including original box, 1932..	82	138	185
No. 87, Crossing Signal, orange or green base, 1927	105	158	210
No. 88, Rheostat, battery, 1915	7	11	15
No. 88, Direction Controller, 1933	3	4	5
No. 89, Flagstaff and Flag, 1923-1934..	50	75	100
No. 90, Flagstaff and Flag, w/round grass plot, 1927-1942	25	38	50
No. 91, Circuit, automatic, breaker, brown w/red light bulb, 1930-1942 ..	38	56	75
No. 00-91, W Locomotive and Tender, OO, two-rail, 1939......................	180	300	600
No. 92, Floodlight Tower, terra-cotta, green, 1931	90	135	180
No. 92, Floodlight Tower, red, silver, 1931	92	138	185
No. 93, Water Tower, O, green, 1932 ...	20	30	40
No. 93, Water Tower, O, silver, 1932 ...	47	71	95
No. 90-93, W Locomotive, OO, tender, two rail, 1939..............................	180	300	600
No. 94, High Tension Tower, gray, terra-cotta, silver and red, 1932.......	200	300	400
No. 95, Rheostat, 1934	12	18	25
No. 96, Coal Elevator, manual control, 1938-1940	95	132	190
No. 97, Coal Elevator, electric, 1938-1942, 1946-1950	125	188	250
No. 97C, Contactor, 1938....................	5	8	10
No. 0-97, Telegraph Pole Set, O, 1934 .	25	38	50
No. 99, Train Control Block Signal, standard, red or black base, 1932	85	128	170
No. 99N, Train Control Block Signal, standard/O, red or black base, 1936 .	85	128	170
No. 0-99, Train Control Block, O, 1930	75	112	150
No. 100, Locomotive, 2-7/8", 1901.......	100	2000	4200
No. 100, Trolley, standard, motor car, blue or red, marked "100 Electric Rapid Transit 100", 1910	600	1250	2500
No. 100, Bridge Approaches, standard, 1920	20	30	40
No. 101, Summer Trolley, standard, motor car, blue or red, manual, "101 Electric Rapid Transit 101", 1910	600	1200	2400
No. 101, Three Section Bridge, standard, cream and green, 1920............	55	82	110
No. 102, Bridge, standard, four section, 1920	35	52	70
No. 103, Bridge, standard, five section, 1913	80	120	170
No. 104, Tunnel, standard, 1909-1914..	50	75	110
No. 104, Bridge, standard, center span, 1920	15	22	30
No. 105, Bridge, standard, five section, 1911	40	60	80
No. 105, Bridge, standard, three section, 1913	25	38	60
No. 105, Bridge Approaches, O, 1920 ..	7	11	15
No. 106, AC Current Reducer, 110 or 120 volts, 1911	3	4	5
No. 106, Bridge, O, three section, 1920	25	38	50

Pre-WWII (1901-1942)

	C6	C8	C10
No. 107, DC Current Reducer, 110 volts, 1911	10	15	20
No. 107, DC Current Reducer, 220 volts, 1911	10	15	20
No. 108, Battery Rheostat, 1912	3	4	5
No. 108, Bridge, O, four section, 1920 .	48	72	95
No. 109, Tunnel, standard, 1913	50	75	100
No. 109, Bridge, O, five section, 1920..	40	60	80
No. 110, Bridge, O, center span, 1920 ..	15	22	30
No. 111, Trolley, standard, trailer, 1910	600	1000	2000
No. 111, Light Bulb Set, 1920..............	10	15	20
No. 112, Gondola, standard, 1910........	135	225	450
No. 112, Gondola, standard, 1913........	24	40	80
No. 112, Station, standard, cream, 1931-1935......................................	162	243	325
No. 113, Cattle Car, standard, 1912-1926	33	55	100
No. 113, Station, standard, cream, 1931-1934	275	362	550
No. 114, Boxcar, standard, 1912..........	36	60	120
No. 114, Station, standard, cream, 1931-1934	650	1125	1300
No. 115, Station, cream, red or green trim, 1935	215	322	450
No. 116, Ballast, standard, 1910	54	90	180
No. 116, Station, cream, double station, 1935	600	900	1200
No. 117, Caboose, standard, 1912-1926	27	45	90
No. 117, Station, 1936-1942	175	262	350
No. 117, Station, no outside lights, 1936-1942......................................	175	262	350
No. 118, Tunnel, O, 1915-1920............	45	68	90
No. 118L, Tunnel, O, lighted, 1927	40	60	80
No. 119, Tunnel, standard/O, 1915	40	60	80
No. 119L, Tunnel, standard/O, lighted, 1927	50	75	100
No. 120, Tunnel, standard/O, 1915	62	93	125
No. 120L, Tunnel, standard/O, lighted, 1927	67	100	135
No. 121, Special Station, standard, 1909	300	450	600
No. 121x, Station, standard, w/lights, 1917	300	450	600
No. 122, Station, standard, 1920	62	93	125
No. 123, Station, standard, 1920	125	188	250
No. 123, Tunnel, O, curved, 1933	90	135	180
No. 124, Station, standard, 1920	250	375	500
No. 124, Station, standard, 1933	137	207	275
No. 125, Station, standard, 1923	30	45	60
No. 125, Track Template, 1938.............	5	8	10
No. 126, Station, standard, 1923-1936..	135	202	270
No. 127, Station, 1923-1936	117	175	235
No. 128, Tunnel, O, lighted, 1920........	55	83	110
No. 129, Station and Terrace, standard, 1929-1940......................................	800	1200	1600
No. 129, Tunnel, standard/O, lighted, 1920	70	105	140
No. 129, Terrace, standard, 1928	900	1350	1800
No. 130, Tunnel, O, 1920....................	150	225	300

Left to right: No. 57 Boulevard Lamp post with silver lettering, $100; No. 56 Lamp post, $65; No. 53 Lamp post, $75; No. 61 Lamp post, $50; No. 57 Lamp post, $100.

Pre-WWII (1901-1942)

	C6	C8	C10
No. 130L, Tunnel, O, lighted, 1927	125	188	250
No. 131, Corner Elevation, 1924-1928	350	525	700
No. 132, Grass Plot, corner, 1924-1928	200	300	400
No. 133, Grass Plot, heart shaped, 1924-1928	200	300	400
No. 134, Grass Plot, oval, 1924-1928	200	300	400
No. 134, Stop Station, brown w/red roof, 1937-1942	175	263	350
No. 135, Grass Plot, oval, small, 1924-1928	200	300	400
No. 136, Stop Station, lighted, 1937-1942	150	225	300
No. 137, Stop Station, lighted, 1937-1942	112	168	225
No. 140L, Tunnel, standard, lighted, 1927-1932	400	600	800
No. 150, Locomotive, O, electric, 0-4-0, dark green, 1918-1925	60	100	200
No. 152, Locomotive, O, electric, dark gray or dark green, 1917-1927	75	125	250
No. 152, Locomotive, O, light gray, 1917-1927	113	187	375
No. 152, Locomotive, O, peacock or mojave, 1917-1927	135	225	500
No. 152-33, Bulb, O, 12 volt, red, 1940	NPF	NPF	1
No. 153, Locomotive, O, electric, mojave, 1924	60	100	200
No. 153, Locomotive, O, dark green, 1924	60	100	200
No. 153, Locomotive, O, gray, 1924	60	100	200
No. 153C, Contactor, O, 1940	5	8	10
No. 153-23, Bulb, 6 volt, red, 1940	NPF	NPF	1
No. 153-24, Bulb, 6 volt, green, 1940	NPF	NPF	1
No. 153-48, Bulb, 14 volt green, 1940	NPF	NPF	1
No. 153-50, Bulb, 14 volt, red, 1940	NPF	NPF	1
No. 154, Locomotive, O, 0-4-0, electric, dark green, 1917-1923	75	125	250

Pre-WWII (1901-1942)

	C6	C8	C10
No. 154, Highway Signal, O, 1940-1942	19	27	38
No. 154C, Contactor, O, 1940	4	5	7
No. 154-18, Bulb, 12 volt, red, 1942	NPF	NPF	1
No. 155, Freight Shed, yellow base w/maroon roof, 1930-1939, 1940-1942	220	330	440
No. 155, Freight Shed, ivory base w/gray roof, 1930-1942	175	263	350
No. 156, Locomotive, O, 4-4-4, electric, gray, olive, brown, and maroon, 1917-1923	225	425	850
No. 156, Station Platform, O, 1939-1940	52	78	105
No. 156X, Locomotive, O, without pilot trucks, 1923-1924	300	500	1000
No. 156-13, Bulb, 18 volt, clear, 1939	NPF	NPF	1
No. 157, Hand Truck, standard, red, 1930-1932	15	25	50
No. 158, Locomotive, O, 0-4-0, electric, gray, 1919-1923	120	175	300
No. 158, Locomotive, O, 0-4-0, electric, black, 1919-1923	120	190	350
No. 158, Platform Set, lighted, two 156 platforms and one 136 station, w/original box, 1940-1942	165	275	550
No. 159C, Block Signal contractor, 1940	4	5	7
No. 160, Unloading Bin, 1938	NPF	1	2
No. 161, Baggage Truck, standard, green, 1930-1932	30	50	100
No. 162, Dump Truck, standard, red or gray, 1930-1932	28	48	95
No. 163, Freight Accessory, includes two 157 hand track, one 161 baggage car and one dump bin, w/original box, 1930	145	217	290
No. 164, Lumber Loader, 1940-1942	102	170	340
No. 165, Magnetic Crane, 1940-1942	75	125	275
No. 165-53, Bulb, 18 volt, red, 1940	NPF	NPF	1

Pre-WWII (1901-1942)	C6	C8	C10
No. 165C, Controller, 1940	32	48	65
No. 166, Controller, three button, 1938	3	4	5
No. 167X, Whistle Controller, OO, 1940	3	4	5
No. 168, Controller, 1940	3	4	5
No. 169, Uncoupling and Reversing Controller, 1940	NPF	2	5
No. 170, DC Current Reducer, 220 volts, 1914	5	8	12
No. 171, Inverter, DC to AC, 1936	5	8	12
No. 172, Inverter, DC to AC, 220 volts, 1937	5	8	10
No. 180, Pullman, standard, maroon, brown and orange, 1911	50	85	170
No. 180, Trailer Truck, standard, 1915	600	1000	2000
No. 181, Combine, standard, maroon, brown and orange, 1911	60	100	200
No. 182, Observation Car, standard, maroon, brown and orange, 1911	66	110	220
No. 184, Bungalow, lighted, 1923	45	68	90
No. 185, Bungalow, no lights, 1923	40	60	80
No. 186, Bungalow Set, set of five, 1923	300	450	600
No. 186, Log Loading Outfit, log loader, car, bin and uncoupler, 1940	120	200	400
No. 187, Bungalow Set, set of five, 1923	300	450	600
No. 188, Coal Elevator Outfit, 1938	120	200	400
No. 189, Villa, lighted, 1923	162	243	325
No. 191, Villa, lighted, 1923	145	217	290
No. 193, Automatic Accessory Set, O, includes one #69, one #76, one #78, one #77, one #80, 1927-1929	175	263	350
No. 194, Automatic Accessory Set, standard, includes one #69, one #76, one #78, one #77, one #80, 1927-1929	175	263	350
No. 195, Terrace, standard, includes one #191 villa, one #189 villa, one #184 bungalow, one #90 flagpole, two #56 lamp posts, 1927	600	900	1200
No. 196, Accessory Set, standard/O, Includes #127 station, six #60 telegraph poles, #62 semaphore, #68 warning signal, two #58 lamp posts, w/original box, 1927	150	225	300
No. 199, Scenic Railway Set, standard, 1924	120	200	400
No. 200, Gondola, 2-7/8", motorized, auctioned in 1994 in Good to Very Good condition, 1901	1000	1500	300
No. 200, Trolley, standard, trailer, non-powered, 1910	1200	2000	4000
No. 200, Turntable, standard, green and tan, 1928	175	263	350
No. 201, Locomotive, O, 0-6-0, steam, switcher, w/2201 B bell tender, 1940	280	475	950
No. 201, Locomotive, O, 0-6-0, steam, switcher, w/2201 Tender, no bell, 1940	210	350	700

Pre-WWII (1901-1942)	C6	C8	C10
No. 202, Summer Trolley, standard, motor car, marked "202 Electric Rapid Transit 202", 1910	900	1500	3000
No. 203, Locomotive, O, steam, switcher, 0-6-0, no bell, similar to 201, 1940	225	375	750
No. 203, Locomotive, O, 0-4-0, armored, cannon, prewar, oriented locomotive, 1917	690	1150	2300
No. 204, Locomotive, O, 2-4-2, steam, black, uncataloged, 1940-1941	43	72	145
No. 204, Locomotive, O, 2-4-2, steam, gunmetal gray, uncataloged, 1940-1941	67	113	225
No. 205, L.C.L. Merchandise Containers, standard, dark green, each, 1930-1938	75	112	150
No. 208, Tool Set, gray box, includes tools, sledge hammer, pick, rake, shovel and ax, 1934-1942	60	90	120
No. 208, Tool Set, silver box, includes tools, sledge hammer, pick, rake, shovel and ax, 1934-1942	50	75	100
No. 209, Barrels, standard, wooden, set of four, 1934-1942	10	15	20
No. 0-209, Barrels, O, wooden, set of six, 1934-1942	17	26	35
No. 210, Switch, standard, automatic, pair, 1926	15	22	30
No. 211, Flatcar, standard, w/wooden load, 1926-1940	34	57	115
No. 212, Gondola, standard, green and maroon, 1926-1940	45	75	150
No. 212, Gondola, standard, gray, 1926-1940	60	100	200
No. 213, Cattle Car, standard, mojave body w/maroon roof, 1926-1940	200	300	400
No. 213, Cattle Car, standard, terra-cotta, orange body w/pea green roof, 1926-1940	100	200	300
No. 213, Cattle Car, standard, cream body w/maroon roof, 1926-1940	300	450	600
No. 214, Boxcar, standard, terra-cotta, orange body w/green roof, 1926-1940	150	250	350
No. 214, Boxcar, standard, cream body w/orange roof, 1926-1940	100	200	300
No. 214, Boxcar, standard, yellow body w/brown roof, 1926-1940	300	400	500
No. 214R, Refrigerator Car, standard, ivory body w/peacock roof, 1929-1940	300	400	500
No. 214R, Refrigerator Car, standard, white body w/light blue roof, 1929-1940	500	750	1000
No. 215, Tank Car, standard, pea green, 1926-1940	75	125	175
No. 215, Tank Car, standard, ivory, Sunoco decal, 1926-1940	100	200	325
No. 215, Tank Car, standard, silver, Sunoco decal, 1926-1940	200	350	600

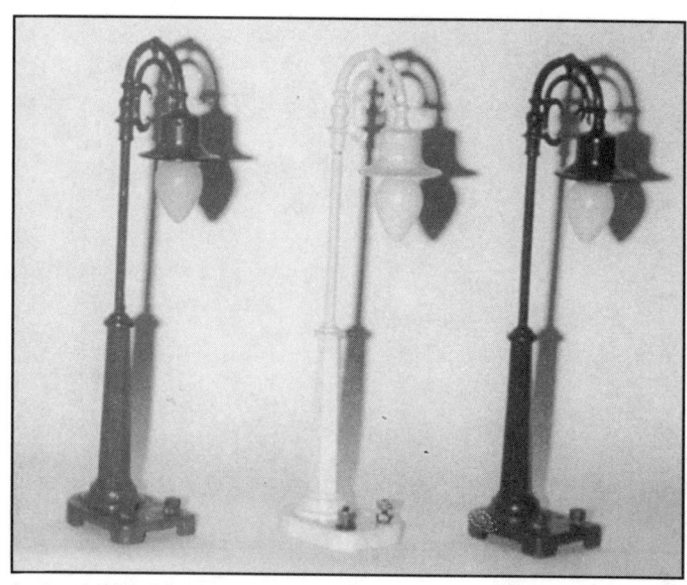

Three version of No. 58 Lamp post, $48. each.

Pre-WWII (1901-1942)	C6	C8	C10
No. 216, Hopper Car, standard, dark green, 1926-1940	100	200	300
No. 217, Lighting Set, standard, for cars, eight volts, 1914	30	50	100
No. 217, Caboose, standard, red and peacock, 1926-1940	69	115	230
No. 217, Caboose, standard, orange and maroon, 1926-1940	90	150	300
No. 218, Dump Car, standard, mojave, 1926-1940	78	130	260
No. 219, Crane, standard, peacock cab, 1926	72	120	240
No. 219, Crane, standard, yellow cab, 1926	115	192	385
No. 219, Crane, standard, white, ivory cab, 1926	135	225	450
No. 220, Floodlight, standard, terra-cotta base, 1931	75	125	250
No. 220, Floodlight, standard, green base, 1931	120	200	400
No. 222, Switches, standard, price per pair, 1926	30	45	60
No. 223, Switches, standard, non-derailing, price per pair, 1932	46	78	155
No. 224/224E, Locomotive, 2-6-2, steam, black w/2224 die-cast tender, 1938-1942	54	90	180
No. 224/224E, Locomotive, 2-6-2, steam, black w/plastic tender, 1938-1942	43	72	145
No. 224/224E, Locomotive, 2-6-2, steam, gunmetal gray w/2224 die-cast tender, 1938-1942	110	183	365
No. 224/224E, Locomotive, 2-6-2, steam, gunmetal gray, w/2689 sheet-metal tender, 1938-1942	66	110	220

Pre-WWII (1901-1942)	C6	C8	C10
No. 224, Paper Train Set, includes: #224 locomotive, #2224 tender, #2812 red gondola, #61100 yellow boxcar w/brown roof, #47618 red caboose, crossing signal, crossing gate, three figures, baggage car, paper track, 1943	300	450	600
No. 225/225 E, Locomotive, O, 2-6-2, steam, black, w/2235, 2265, 2225 or 2245 tenders, 1939-1940	114	190	380
No. 225/225 E, Locomotive, O, 2-6-2, steam, gunmetal gray, 1939-1940	105	175	350
No. 226E, Locomotive, O, 2-6-4, steam, w/2226 tender, 1938-1941	150	250	500
No. 227, Locomotive, O, 0-6-0, steam, switcher scale, w/tender 2227T, marked "8976" under cab window, no bell, 1939	375	625	1250
No. 227, Locomotive, O, w/tender 2227B bell, 1939	378	630	1260
No. 228, Locomotive, O, 0-6-0, steam, switcher scale, similar to 227, w/228T tender, no bell, 1939	325	550	1100
No. 228, Locomotive, O, 0-6-0, steam, w/2228B tender, w/bell, 1939	350	600	1400
No. 229/229E, Locomotive, O, 2-4-2, steam, black, 1939	55	100	180
No. 229/229E, Locomotive, O, steam, gunmetal gray, 1939	35	65	125
No. 230, Locomotive, 0-6-0, steam, switcher scale, 1939	600	1000	2000
No. 231, Locomotive, O, 0-6-0, steam, switcher scale, 1939	600	1000	2000
No. 232, Locomotive, O, 0-6-0, steam, switcher scale, 1940	465	775	1550
No. 233, Locomotive, O, 0-6-0, steam, switcher scale, 1940	600	1000	2000

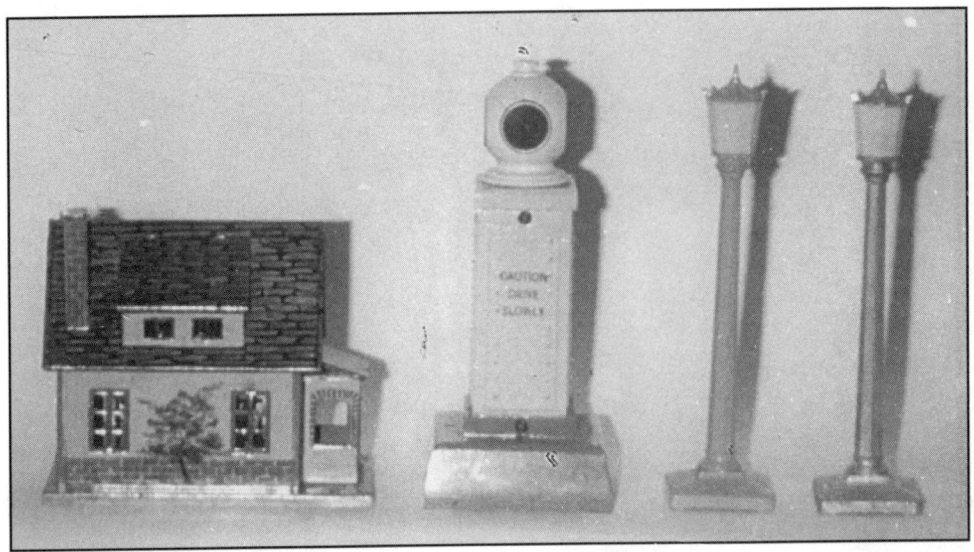

Left to right: No. 184 Bungalow, $90; No. 78 Train Control Block Signal, $80; Two versions of the No. 35 Lamp post, $80, each.

Pre-WWII (1901-1942)	C6	C8	C10
No. 238 or E, Locomotive, O, P.R.R., steam, black or gunmetal gray, torpedo-type, w/222T, 2225W or 265W tender, 1936-1940	113	188	375
No. 248, Locomotive, O, electric, red, orange, dark green and olive, 1926-1932	49	83	165
No. 249 or E, Locomotive, O, steam, gunmetal gray, 1936	80	133	235
No. 249 or E, Locomotive, O, steam, black, 1936	75	150	300
No. 250, Locomotive, O, 0-4-0, N.Y.C., electric, dark green, peacock and orange, 1926	90	150	260
No. 250, Locomotive, O, electric, 0-4-0, orange and terra-cotta, uncataloged, 1934	60	100	225
No. 250E, Locomotive, O, Hiawatha, steam, w/250W, 250WX or 2250W tenders, 1935	450	750	1500
No. 251, Locomotive, O, 0-4-0, NYC, electric, box cab, gray or red cabs, 1925	100	168	335
No. 251E, Locomotive, O, 0-4-0, NYC, electric, box cab, gray or red cabs, 1927	100	168	335
No. 252, Locomotive, O, 0-4-0, NYC, electric, peacock, olive and dark green, 1926	60	100	200
No. 252, Locomotive, O, 0-4-0, NYC, electric, terra-cotta and orange, 1926	75	125	250
No. 252, Locomotive, O, 0-4-0, NYC, electric, maroon, Macy's Special, 1926	120	200	400
No. 252E, Locomotive, O, 0-4-0, electric, terra-cotta or orange, 1933-1935	84	140	280
No. 253, Locomotive, O, 0-4-0, electric, peacock, mojave and dark green, 1924	60	100	200
No. 253, Locomotive, O, 0-4-0, electric, maroon, 1924	150	250	500
No. 253, Locomotive, O, 0-4-0, electric, terra-cotta, 1924	120	200	400

Pre-WWII (1901-1942)	C6	C8	C10
No. 253, Locomotive, O, 0-4-0, electric, red, 1924	135	225	450
No. 253E, Locomotive, O, 0-4-0, electric, green, 1931	125	200	300
No. 253E, Locomotive, O, 0-4-0, electric, terra-cotta, 1931	120	200	325
No. 254, Locomotive, O, 0-4-0, electric, mojave, olive, dark and pea green, 1924	83	138	275
No. 254, Locomotive, O, 0-4-0, electric, apple green, 1924	120	200	400
No. 254, Locomotive, O, 0-4-0, electric, red, 1924	150	250	500
No. 254E, Locomotive, O, 0-4-0, electric, olive green, 1927	60	100	200
No. 254E, Locomotive, O, 0-4-0, electric, apple green, 1927	90	150	275
No. 255E, Locomotive, O, 2-4-2, steam, gunmetal gray w/263W tender, 1935	300	525	1050
No. 256, Locomotive, O, electric, orange, rubber-stamped "Lionel", 1924-1930	150	250	500
No. 256, Locomotive, O, electric, orange, marked "Lionel", 1924-1930	210	350	700
No. 257, Locomotive, O, 0-4-0, steam, w/257T or 259T tender, 1930	90	150	300
No. 258, Locomotive, O, 2-4-0, steam, 1930	75	125	250
No. 258, Locomotive, O, 2-4-2, steam, w/1689T tender, uncataloged, 1941	48	80	160
No. 259, Locomotive, O, 2-4-2, steam, 1932	54	90	180
No. 259E, Locomotive, O, steam, black, 1933	34	73	115
No. 259E, Locomotive, O, steam, gunmetal gray, 1933	48	80	160
No. 260E, Locomotive, O, steam, black, w/260T tender, 1930	150	250	500
No. 260E, Locomotive, O, steam, gunmetal gray, w/263 tender, 1930	180	300	600

Signal No. 153

No. 115 Station, $450. Photo courtesy Steve Hintze

Pre-WWII (1901-1942)	C6	C8	C10
No. 261, Locomotive, O, 2-4-2, steam, w/257T tender, 1931	75	125	250
No. 261E, Locomotive, O, steam, w/261T tender, 1935	84	140	280
No. 262, Locomotive, O, 2-4-2, steam, w/262T tender, 1931	90	150	300
No. 262E, Locomotive, O, 2-4-2, steam, w/262T or 265T tender, 1933	84	140	280
No. 263E, Locomotive, O, 2-4-2, steam, gunmetal gray, 1936	255	425	850
No. 263E, Locomotive, O, 2-4-2, steam, Blue Comet, blue, 1936	240	400	800
No. 264E, Locomotive, O, 2-4-2, Red Comet, steam, streamlined, red, 1935	225	375	750
No. 264E, Locomotive, O, 2-4-2, steam, streamlined, black, 1935	120	200	400
No. 265E, Locomotive, O, 2-4-2, steam, streamlined, black, 1935	87	145	290
No. 265E, Locomotive, O, steam 2-4-2, streamlined, gunmetal gray, 1935	105	175	350
No. 265E, Locomotive, O, 2-4-2, steam, Blue Streak, streamlined, blue, 1935	180	300	600
No. 270, Lighting Set, standard, for two cars, 3-1/2 volt, 1915	40	60	80
No. 270, Bridge, O, maroon or red, 1931	52	78	105
No. 271, Bridge, O, two span, 1931	30	45	60
No. 272, Bridge, O, three span, 1931	60	90	120
No. 280, Bridge, standard, 1931	45	68	90
No. 281, Bridge, standard, two span, 1931	45	68	90
No. 282, Bridge, standard, three span, 1931	50	75	100

Pre-WWII (1901-1942)	C6	C8	C10
No. 289E, Locomotive, O, 2-4-2, steam, streamlined, black, 1689 tender, 1937	52	88	175
No. 289E, Locomotive, O, 2-4-2, steam, streamlined, 1689 tender, gunmetal gray, 1937	45	75	150
No. 300, Trolley, standard, marked "City Hall Park 175", 1901	2100	3500	7000
No. 300, Trolley, standard, trailer, powered, 1910	1080	1800	3600
No. 300, Bridge, standard/O, ivory, green, orange base, marked "Hellgate", 1928	925	1390	1850
No. 300, Bridge, standard/O, white, silver and red base, marked "Hellgate," largest single span bridge Lionel ever made, 1928	810	1350	2700
No. 303, Summer Trolley, standard, motorcar, marked "303 Electric Rapid Transit 303", 1910	1230	2050	4100
No. 309, Trolley, standard, 1901	1500	2000	4250
No. 309, Pullman, standard, blue, apple green, pea green, maroon, light brown, mojave, 1926	43	73	145
No. 310, Track, standard, 1903	5	8	10
No. 310, Baggage Car, standard, blue, apple green, pea green, maroon, light brown, mojave, 1924-1929	40	68	135
No. 310, Baggage Car, standard, blue, apple green, pea green, maroon, light brown, mojave, 1926	54	70	140
No. 312, Observation Car, standard, blue, apple green, pea green, maroon, light brown, mojave, 1926	54	70	140
No. 313, Bascule Bridge, O, gray, 1940-1942	312	468	625

Pre-WWII (1901-1942)

	C6	C8	C10
No. 315-20, Bulb, 12 volt, clear, 1940..	NPF	NPF	1
No. 318, Locomotive, standard, 0-4-0, electric, mojave, pea green, gray, 1924	110	185	370
No. 318, Locomotive, standard, 0-4-0, electric, state brown, 1924	140	238	475
No. 318E, Locomotive, standard, 0-4-0, electric, pea green, mojave, gray, 1926	100	170	340
No. 318E, Locomotive, standard, 0-4-0, electric, state brown, 1926	180	300	600
No. 318E, Locomotive, standard, 0-4-0, electric, black, 1926	240	400	800
No. 319, Pullman, standard, 1924	54	85	170
No. 320, Switch, standard, 1903	20	30	40
No. 320, Baggage Car, standard, 1925..	60	100	200
No. 322, Observation Car, standard, 1924	57	95	190
No. 330, 90 Degrees Crossing, standard, 1903	10	15	20
No. 332, Baggage Car, standard, gray, red, peacock, olive, 1926	28	48	95
No. 332, Baggage Car, standard, beige body w/maroon roof, 1926	90	150	300
No. 332, Macy Baggage Car, standard, uncataloged, 1930	60	100	200
No. 337, Pullman, standard, pea green, olive, red, mojave, 1925	40	65	130
No. 337, Macy Pullman, standard, red, uncataloged, 1930	60	100	200
No. 338, Observation Car, standard, pea green, olive, red, mojave, 1925	33	55	110
No. 338, Macy Observation Car, standard, uncataloged, 1930	60	100	200
No. 339, Pullman, standard, peacock, brown, gray, 1925	27	45	90
No. 339, Pullman, standard, beige body, maroon roof, 1925	90	150	300
No. 339, Macy Pullman, standard, red, uncataloged, 1930	60	100	200
No. 340, Bridge, standard, 1903	175	262	350
No. 341, Observation Car, standard, peacock, brown, gray, 1925	27	45	90
No. 341, Observation Car, standard, beige body, maroon roof, 1925	90	150	300
No. 341, Macy Observation Car, standard, red, uncataloged, 1930	60	100	200
No. 350, Bumper, standard, 1903	25	38	50
No. 380, Elevated Pillars, standard, each, 1903	30	45	60
No. 380, Locomotive, standard, 0-4-0, electric, maroon, 1923	192	320	640
No. 380, Locomotive, standard, 0-4-0, electric, mojave, dark green, 1923	180	300	600
No. 380E, Locomotive, standard, 0-4-0, electric, maroon, 1926	180	300	600
No. 380E, Locomotive, standard, 0-4-0, electric, mojave or dark green, 1926	180	300	600
No. 381, Locomotive, standard, 4-4-4, electric, green body, 1928	1200	2000	4000

Pre-WWII (1901-1942)

	C6	C8	C10
No. 381E, Locomotive, standard, 4-4-4, electric, green body and frame, 1928	1260	2100	4200
No. 381U, Locomotive, standard, electric, kit includes tools, track and original box, 1928	2300	3450	4600
No. 384, Locomotive, standard, 2-4-0, steam, w/384T tender, 1930...	180	300	600
No. 384E, Locomotive, standard, 2-4-0, steam, w/384T tender, 1930	175	293	585
No. 385E, Locomotive, standard, 2-4-2, steam, gunmetal gray w/384T, 385T, 385TW or 385W tender, 1933	295	490	980
No. 390, Locomotive, standard, 2-4-2, steam, w/390T, black, 1929	250	420	840
No. 390E, Locomotive, standard, steam, black, w/tender 390T, 1929	300	500	1000
No. 390E, Locomotive, standard, two-tone blue, w/tender, 1930	420	700	1400
No. 390E, Locomotive, standard, 2-4-2, steam, two-tone green, green or orange stripe, 1929-1931	540	900	1800
No. 392E, Locomotive, standard, 4-4-2, steam, black, 1932	380	630	1260
No. 392E, Locomotive, standard, 4-4-2, steam, gunmetal gray, 1932	495	825	1650
No. 400, Gondola, 2-7/8", trailer, 1901.	720	1200	2400
No. 400E, Locomotive, standard, 4-4-4, steam, w/400T tender, black, 1931-1939	675	1125	2250
No. 400E, Locomotive, standard, 4-4-4, steam, gunmetal gray, w/400T tender, 1931-1939	900	1500	3000
No. 400E, Locomotive, standard, 4-4-4, steam, w/400T tender, blue, 1931-1939	855	1425	2850
No. 402, Locomotive, standard, 0i-4-4-0, electric, mojave, 1923	200	330	660
No. 402E, Locomotive, standard, 0-4-4-0, electric, mojave, 1926	180	300	600
No. 404, Summer Trolley, standard, motor car, 1910	1500	2500	5000
No. 408E, Locomotive, standard, 0-4-4-0, electric, apple green or mojave, 1927	385	640	1280
No. 408E, Locomotive, standard, 0-4-4-0, electric, state brown, 1927	660	1100	2200
No. 408E, Locomotive, standard, 0-4-4-0, electric, green, 1927	1080	1800	3600
No. 412, Pullman, standard, California State Car, light green, 1929	600	1000	2000
No. 412, Pullman, standard, California State Car, light brown, 1929	660	1100	2200
No. 413, Pullman, standard, Colorado State Car, light green, 1929	600	1000	2000
No. 413, Pullman, standard, Colorado State Car, light brown, 1929	660	1100	2200

LIONEL®—NEW IN '56

THE GREATEST VARIETY IN MODEL R. R. EQUIPMENT!

ONLY LIONEL TRAINS HAVE MAGNE-TRACTION

This pamphlet from Lionel shows many new releases for the year of 1956. Top Row: No. 2350, Loco, O, 1956, New Haven, black shell, orange and white striping, $515. Second Row, left to right: No. 3530, GM Generator Car, 1956, O, includes transformer pole, remote searchlight, $220; No. 3424, Operating Brakeman (Tell-Tale) Car Set, 1956, O, blue box car, set of track tips and tell-tales w/poles, $70. Third Row, left to right: No. 3927, Track Cleaner Car, 1956, O, $120; No. 50, Gang Car, 1957, O27, $58; No. 3360, Operating Burro Crane, 1956, O, $230. Bottom Row: No. 400, Budd RDC Car, 1956, O, $270.

CONDITION CODE

C6 Good; evident overall wear, well played with but acceptable to many collectors

C8 Very Good; minor overall wear, very clean

C10 Mint; like new

Note: Mint in Box commands a higher price. Condition below C6 brings considerably lower prices

Pre-WWII (1901-1942)	C6	C8	C10
No. 414, State Car, Illinois, light green, 1930	600	1000	2000
No. 414, State Car, light brown, 1930	660	1100	2200
No. 416, Observation Car, standard, New York State Car, light green, 1929	320	533	1065
No. 416, Observation Car, standard, light brown, 1929	310	515	1030
No. 418, Pullman, standard, mojave, 1923	63	105	210
No. 418, Pullman, standard, apple green, 1923	105	173	345
No. 419, Combine, standard, mojave, 1923	60	100	200
No. 419, Combine, standard, apple green, 1928-1932	130	250	360
No. 420, Pullman, standard, Blue Comet car, light blue body, dark blue roof, marked "Faye", 1930	245	410	820
No. 421, Pullman, standard, Blue Comet car, light blue body, dark blue roof, "Westphal", 1930	245	410	820
No. 422, Observation Car, standard, Blue Comet car, light blue body, dark blue roof, marked "Tempel", 1930	245	410	820
No. 424, Pullman, standard, Stephen Girard set, light green, marked "Liberty Bell", 1931	155	258	515

Pre-WWII (1901-1942)	C6	C8	C10
No. 425, Pullman, standard, Stephen Girard set, light green, 1932	150	272	515
No. 426, Observation Car, standard, Stephen Girard set, light green, "Coral Isle", 1931	150	272	515
No. 428, Pullman, standard, dark green, 1926	90	150	300
No. 428, Pullman, standard, orange, 1926	150	250	500
No. 429, Combine, standard, dark green, 1926	135	225	450
No. 429, Combine, standard, orange, 1926	105	175	350
No. 430, Observation Car, standard, dark green, 1926	90	150	300
No. 430, Observation Car, standard, orange, 1926	105	175	350
No. 431, Diner, standard, mojave, 1927	180	300	600
No. 431, Diner, apple green, orange, dark green, 1928-1929	190	317	635
No. 435, Power Station, 1926	83	138	275
No. 436, Power Station, 1926	95	155	310
No. 437, Signal Tower, green roof, 1926	150	255	510
No. 437, Signal Tower, peacock roof, 1926	125	212	425
No. 437, Signal Tower, orange roof, 1926	180	300	600
No. 438, Signal Tower, orange, red, 1927	200	300	400
No. 438, Signal Tower, white, red, 1927	235	350	470

Pre-WWII (1901-1942)

	C6	C8	C10
No. 439, Panel Board, maroon, 1928 90	135	180
No. 439, Panel Board, red, 1928 100	150	200
No. 439, Panel Board, silver, rare, 1928 150	225	300
No. 0440, Signal Bridge, standard, 1932 235	350	470
No. 440C, Panel Board, 1932-1942 62	93	125
No. 440N, Signal Bridge, O/standard, 1936 175	262	350
No. 441, Weighing Scale Platform, standard, green base, cream building, 1932-1936 300	500	1000
No. 442, Diner, 1938 120	180	240
No. 444, Roundhouse Section, standard, 1932-1935 1700	2550	3400
No. 450, Macy Special Locomotive, O, electric, 0-4-0 red w/black frame, uncataloged, 1930 300	500	1000
No. 455, Electric Range, 1932-1933 700	1100	1500
No. 490, Observation Car, standard, mojave, 1923 75	125	250
No. 490, Observation Car, standard, apple green, 1923 109	180	360
No. 500, Motorized Derrick, standard, 1903 4000	5000	7000
No. 511, Flatcar, standard, dark green, 1927 34	58	115
No. 511, Flatcar, standard, medium green, 1927 30	50	100
No. 512, Gondola, standard, bright green, 1927 36	60	120
No. 512, Gondola, standard, peacock, 1927 22	38	75
No. 513, Cattle Car, standard, 1927 39	65	130
No. 513, Cattle Car, standard, nickel trim, 1927 150	250	500
No. 514, Refrigerator, standard, Lionel ventilated refrigerator, 1927 52	88	175
No. 514, Boxcar, standard, ivory and brown, 1929 57	95	190
No. 514, Boxcar, standard, yellow/brown, 1929 50	85	170
No. 514R, Refrigerator, standard, ivory body, peacock roof, 1929 60	100	200
No. 514R, Refrigerator, standard, nickel trim, 1929 123	208	415
No. 515, Tank Car, standard, Sunoco logo, terra-cotta, ivory and silver, 1927 54	90	180
No. 515, Tank Car, standard, Shell, orange, 1927 240	400	800
No. 516, Hopper, standard, 1928 72	120	240
No. 517, Caboose, standard, red, nickel trim, 1927 30	50	100
No. 517, Caboose, standard, red and black, coal train, nickel trim, 1927 ... 90	150	300
No. 517, Caboose, standard, pea green, 1927 24	40	80
No. 520, Search Light, standard, terra-cotta platform, 1931 50	85	170
No. 520, Search Light, standard, green platform, 1931 75	128	255

Pre-WWII (1901-1942)

	C6	C8	C10
No. 529, Pullman, O, olive green or terra-cotta, 1926	13	21	42
No. 530, Observation Car, O, olive green or terra-cotta, 1926	10	17	35
No. 550, Miniature Figures, set of six, includes original box, 1932	125	188	250
No. 551, Miniature Figure, engineer, 1932	15	22	30
No. 552, Miniature Figure, conductor, 1932	15	22	30
No. 553, Miniature Figure, porter, 1932	15	22	30
No. 554, Miniature Figure, male passenger, 1932	15	22	30
No. 555, Miniature Figure, female passenger, 1932	15	22	30
No. 556, Miniature Figure, red cap, 1932	15	22	30
No. 600, Derrick Trailer, standard, 1903	2000	4500	9000
No. 600, Pullman, O, four wheel, maroon, dark green, brown, 1915	18	30	60
No. 600, Pullman, O, eight wheel, red w/red roof, 1933	54	90	180
No. 600, Pullman, O, light blue w/silver roof, 1933	18	30	60
No. 600, Pullman, O, gray w/red roof, 1933	45	75	150
No. 601, Pullman, O, seven, dark green, 1915	25	42	85
No. 601, Observation Car, O, red w/red roof, 1933	45	75	150
No. 601, Observation Car, O, light blue w/silver roof, 1933	18	30	60
No. 601, Observation Car, O, gray w/red roof, 1933	40	65	130
No. 602, Baggage Car, O, dark green, 1915	21	35	70
No. 602, Baggage Car, red w/red roof, 1933	63	108	215
No. 602, Baggage Car, light blue w/silver roof, 1933	54	90	180
No. 602, Baggage Car, gray w/red roof, 1933	37	63	125
No. 603, Pullman, O, orange, uncataloged, 1921	21	35	70
No. 603, Pullman, O, later, orange, 1920	19	32	64
No. 603, Pullman, O, late, red, green, orange, maroon, 1931	30	50	100
No. 604, Observation Car, O, orange, 1920	24	40	80
No. 604, Observation Car, O, red, green, orange, maroon, 1931	25	43	85
No. 605, Pullman, O, gray, 1925	30	50	100
No. 605, Pullman, O, red, 1925	48	80	160
No. 605, Pullman, O, orange, 1925	48	80	160
No. 605, Pullman, O, olive, 1925	48	80	160
No. 606, Observation Car, O, gray, 1925	48	80	160
No. 606, Observation Car, O, orange, 1925	48	80	160

No. 390 Locomotive

Pre-WWII (1901-1942)	C6	C8	C10
No. 606, Observation Car, O, red, 1925	48	80	160
No. 606, Observation Car, O, olive, 1925	48	80	160
No. 606, Observation Car, O, Macy, uncataloged, 1930	48	80	160
No. 607, Pullman, O, 1926	25	43	85
No. 607, Pullman, O, Macy, uncataloged, 1931	80	135	270
No. 608, Observation Car, O, 1926	25	44	88
No. 608, Observation Car, O, Macy, uncataloged, 1931	90	150	300
No. 609, Pullman, O, uncataloged, 1937	27	45	90
No. 610, Pullman, O, early, 1915	45	78	155
No. 610, Pullman, O, late, 1926	21	35	70
No. 610, Pullman, O, Macy, uncataloged, 1926	24	40	80
No. 611, Observation Car, O, uncataloged, 1937	18	30	60
No. 612, Observation Car, O, early, 1915	40	68	135
No. 612, Observation Car, O, late, 1926	21	35	70
No. 612, Observation Car, O, Macy, 1926	21	35	70
No. 613, Pullman, O, terra-cotta, 1931	85	140	280
No. 613, Pullman, O, blue, Blue Comet set, 1931	180	338	675
No. 613, Pullman, O, red, aluminum roof, 1931	60	100	200
No. 614, Observation Car, O, terra-cotta, 1931	63	105	210
No. 614, Observation Car, O, Blue Comet set, blue, 1931	66	112	225
No. 614, Observation Car, O, red, aluminum roof, 1931	60	100	200
No. 615, Baggage Car, O, terra-cotta, 1933	75	125	250

Pre-WWII (1901-1942)	C6	C8	C10
No. 615, Baggage Car, O, Blue Comet set, blue, 1933	60	100	200
No. 615, Baggage Car, O, red, aluminum roof, 1933	75	125	250
No. 616, E or W Diesel Type Power Car, O, Streamliner, Flying Yankee, black cast frame, chrome shells, 1935	60	105	210
No. 616-13, Bulb, 12 volt, clear, 1935	NPF	NPF	1
No. 616T, Vestibule, O, 1935	12	20	40
No. 617, Coach, O, Streamliner, black and chrome, 1935	24	39	78
No. 617, Coach, O, blue and white, Blue Streak, 1935	36	60	120
No. 618, Observation Car, O, Streamliner, black and chrome, 1935	25	43	85
No. 618, Observation Car, O, Blue Streak, blue and white, 1935	45	75	150
No. 619, Combine, O, Blue Streak, Streamliner, blue and white, 1935	90	150	300
No. 620, Floodlight, O, 1937	30	45	60
No. 629, Pullman, O, four wheel, 1924	20	32	65
No. 629, Pullman, O, eight wheel, uncataloged, 1934	39	65	130
No. 630, Observation Car, O, four wheel, 1924	16	28	55
No. 630, Macy Observation Car, O, four wheel, uncataloged, 1931	24	40	80
No. 630, Observation Car, O, eight wheel, uncataloged, 1934	27	45	90
No. 636W, Diesel Type Power Car, O, U.P., Streamliner, yellow and brown, marked "City of Denver", 1936	42	70	140
No. 636-13, Bulb, 8 volt, clear, 1936	NPF	NPF	1
No. 637, Coach, O, Streamliner, marked "City of Denver", 1936	30	50	100
No. 638, Observation Car, O, Streamliner, yellow and brown, marked "City of Denver", 1936	30	50	100

Pre-WWII (1901-1942)

	C6	C8	C10
No. 651, Flatcar, O, 1935	15	25	50
No. 652, Gondola, O, 1935	16	28	55
No. 653, Hopper, O, 1934	19	33	65
No. 654, Tank Car, O, silver, orange, 1934	15	25	50
No. 655, Boxcar, O, 1934	16	28	55
No. 656, Cattle Car, O, 1935	30	50	100
No. 657, Caboose, O, 1934	10	18	35
No. 659, Dump Car, O, 1935	24	40	80
No. 700, Window Display Set, standard, 1904	NPF	NPF	NPF
No. 700, Locomotive, O, 0-4-0, electric, dark green NYC Lines, 1913-1916	225	375	750
No. 700E, Locomotive, O72, 4-6-4, steam, black, w/700/700W twelve-wheel cast tender, 1937	750	1250	2500
No. 700E250, Display Stand and Track, w/Lionel ID plate, 1938	810	1350	2700
No. 700EWX, Locomotive, O72, steam, black, w/700/700W twelve-wheel cast whistle tender, 1937	1200	2000	4000
No. 700K, Locomotive, O72, 4-6-4, steam kit, gray, six kits all original boxes, 1939	2800	4200	5600
No. 701, Locomotive, 0-4-0, electric, dark green, 1913-1916	270	450	900
No. 703, Locomotive, O, 4-4-4, electric, dark green, 1913-1916	660	1100	2200
No. 706, Locomotive, O, 0-4-0, electric, dark green, 1913-1916	420	700	1400
No. 708, Locomotive, O72, 0-6-0, steam, scale switcher, "8976" cast in boiler front, 1939	900	1500	3000
No. 710, Pullman, O, green, orange, 1924	75	125	250
No. 710, Pullman, O, red, 1924	60	100	200
No. 710, Pullman, O, two-tone blue, 1924	67	112	225
No. 711, Switches, O72, electric, pair, 1935	75	112	150
No. 712, Observation Car, O, green, orange, 1924	72	120	240
No. 712, Observation Car, O, red, 1924	60	100	200
No. 712, Observation Car, O, two-tone blue, 1924	66	110	220
No. 714, Boxcar, O72, 1940	120	200	400
No. 714K, Boxcarcar, O72, kit, new only, 1940	NPF	NPF	1000
No. 715, Tank Car, O72, 1940	120	200	400
No. 715K, Tank Car, O72, kit, new only, 1940	NPF	NPF	1000
No. 716, Hopper, O72, 1940	97	163	325
No. 716K, Hopper, O72, kit, new only, 1940	NPF	NPF	1000
No. 730, 90 Degrees Crossing T-Rail, O72, 1935	15	22	30
No. 731, Switches, O72, electric, T-rail, pair, 1935	175	263	350
No. 752E or W, Streamliner Power Car, O, 1934	140	235	470
No. 752-9, Bulb, 18 volt, clear, 1934	NPF	NPF	1
No. 753, Coach, O, streamliner, 1934	42	70	140

Pre-WWII (1901-1942)

	C6	C8	C10
No. 754, Observation Car, O, streamliner, 1934	42	70	140
No. 760, Pack of Curved Track, sixteen sections, 1935	16	24	32
No. 761, Track, O72, curved, 1934	NPF	1	2
No. 762, Track, O72, straight, 1934	NPF	1	2
No. 762S, Track, O72, straight, insulated, w/lock-on, 1934	NPF	2	3
No. 763E, Locomotive, O, 4-6-4, steam, semi-scale Hudson, black, w/2226WX tender or gunmetal gray 263 or 2263W tender, 1937	555	925	1850
No. 763E, Locomotive, O, 4-6-4, steam, gunmetal gray, w/2226W or 2226WX tender, 1937	720	1200	2400
No. 771, Track, O72, curved, T-rail, 1935	NPF	2	3
No. 772, Track, O72, straight, T-rail, 1935	NPF	2	3
No. 772S, Track, O72, straight, insulated, T-rail, 1940	3	4	5
No. 773, Fish Plate Set, O72, 100 bolts, 100 nuts, fifty fishplates and wrench, 1936	25	38	50
No. 782, Streamliner Front Coach, O72, part of articulated Hiawatha set, gray roof, orange sides and maroon underframe, marked "The Milwaukee Road", 1935	150	250	500
No. 783, Coach, O72, streamliner, part of articulated Hiawatha set, gray roof orange sides and maroon underframe, marked "The Milwaukee Road", 1935	150	250	500
No. 784, Observation Car, O72, streamliner, part of articulated Hiawatha set, gray roof, orange sides and maroon underframe, marked "The Milwaukee Road", 1935	150	250	500
No. 792, Front Coach, O72, streamliner, part of Rail Chief set, w/700E Loco, maroon roof, red sides, red underframe, marked "792 Lionel Lines 792", 1937	150	250	500
No. 793, Coach, O72, streamliner, part of Rail Chief set, marked "793 Lionel Lines 793", 1937	150	250	500
No. 794, Observation Car, O72, streamliner, part of Rail Chief set, maroon roof, red sides, red underframe, marked "794 Lionel Lines 794", 1937	150	250	500
No. 800, Express Motor Car, standard, 1904	1000	2000	4000
No. 800, Boxcar, O, 1915	33	55	110
No. 801, Caboose, O, 1915	19	33	65
No. 802, Stock, O, 1915	21	35	70
No. 803, Hopper, O, dark green, 1923	15	25	50
No. 803, Hopper, O, peacock, 1923	25	43	85
No. 803, Hopper, O, 1929	15	25	50
No. 804, Tank Car, O, early, dark gray, 1923	20	33	65
No. 804, Tank Car, O, terra-cotta, 1923	20	33	65

No. 6-16137 Ford Single Dome Tank Car

Pre-WWII (1901-1942)	C6	C8	C10
No. 804, Tank Car, O, Sunoco, silver, 1923	21	35	70
No. 804, Tank Car, O, 1929	21	35	70
No. 805, Boxcar, O, orange, maroon, 1927	15	25	50
No. 805, Boxcar, O, pea green, orange, 1927	23	38	75
No. 806, Cattle Car, O, 1927	30	50	100
No. 807, Caboose, O, 1927	14	23	45
No. 809, Dump Car, O, 1931	18	30	60
No. 810, Crane, O, 1930-1940	60	100	200
No. 811, Flatcar, O, maroon, 1926	13	21	42
No. 811, Flatcar, O, silver, 1926	40	68	135
No. 812, Gondola, O, 1926	24	40	80
No. 812T, Tool Set, O, 1937	16	24	32
No. 813, Cattle Car, O, 1926	36	60	120
No. 814, Boxcar, O, orange body, brown roof, 1926	30	50	100
No. 814, Boxcar, O, nickel plate, 1926	66	110	220
No. 814R, Refrigerator, O, white body, brown roof, 1929	85	143	285
No. 814R, Refrigerator, O, w/rubber-stamped lettering, 1929	360	600	1200
No. 815, Tank Car, O, aluminum, silver, 1926	57	95	190
No. 815, Tank Car, O, Shell, orange, 1926	40	68	135
No. 816, Hopper, O, red, olive green, 1927	37	63	125
No. 816, Hopper, O, black, 1927	75	125	250
No. 817, Caboose, O, 1926	28	48	95
No. 817, Caboose, O, flat red, brown roof, rubber-stamped lettering, 1926	60	100	200
No. 820, Boxcar, O, orange or maroon, 1915	27	45	90
No. 820, Boxcar, O, dark olive, rubber stamped "ATSF" and "48522", 1915	60	100	200
No. 820, Floodlight, O, terra-cotta base, 1931	45	75	150
No. 820, Floodlight, O, green base, 1931	68	113	225
No. 821, Cattle Car, O, 1915	27	45	90
No. 822, Caboose, O, 1915	22	38	75
No. 831, Flatcar, O, 1927	18	30	60

Pre-WWII (1901-1942)	C6	C8	C10
No. 900, Express Trail Car, 2-7/8", 1904	1000	2000	4500
No. 900, Boxcar, O, ammunition, part of armored train set, 1917	150	250	500
No. 900 or B, Catalog, O, number for 230 and tender, 0-6-0, similar to loco 227, 1939	450	750	1500
No. 901, Gondola, O, gray or maroon, 1919	20	33	65
No. 902, Gondola, O, peacock, 1927	8	13	25
No. 902, Gondola, O, apple green, 1927	8	13	25
No. 910, Grove, eleven trees, 1932	150	225	300
No. 911, Country Estate, 191 villa, shrubbery and trees, 1932	450	675	900
No. 912, Suburban Home, 189 villa, shrubbery and trees, 1932	375	525	750
No. 913, Bungalow, w/garden, flowers and trees, 1932	250	375	500
No. 914, Formal Garden Park, two grass plots, centerpiece, flowering bushes, cream base, 1932	175	268	350
No. 915, Curved Tunnel Mountain, O, large, 1932	200	300	400
No. 916, Tunnel, O, curved, 1932	175	263	350
No. 917, Mountain, medium, 1932	200	300	400
No. 918, Mountain, small, 1932	175	263	350
No. 919, Park Grass, 8 ounces, 1932	9	14	18
No. 920, Scenic Park, small, 1932	2000	3000	4000
No. 921, Scenic Park, large, 1932	1400	2100	2800
No. 921C, Scenic Park, center section, 1932	400	600	800
No. 922, Lamp Terrace, 1932	175	263	350
No. 923, Tunnel, standard, 1933	200	300	400
No. 924, Tunnel, O72, curved, 1935	150	225	300
No. 927, Flag Plot, 1937-1942	40	60	80
No. 1000, Passenger Car, 2-7/8", motorized, 1904	1000	2000	4000
No. 1000, Trolley, standard, trailer, 1910	840	1400	2800
No. 1000, Trailer Truck, standard, 100 series, 1910	840	1400	2800
No. 1007, Platform and Background, O27, 1936	30	45	60
No. 1010, Interurban Trolley, standard, 1910	1750	2625	3500

No. 1625 Locomotive

Pre-WWII (1901-1942)

	C6	C8	C10
No. 1010, Winner Locomotive, O27,, 0-4-0, electric, 1931	30	50	100
No. 1011, Interurban Trolley, standard, motor car, 1910	1050	1750	3500
No. 1011, Winner Pullman, O27, 1931.	9	15	30
No. 1012, Interurban Trolley, standard, 1910	1050	1750	3500
No. 1012, Winner Station Transformer, 1931	22	33	45
No. 1013, Track, O27, curved, 1934	NPF	NPF	1
No. 1013-17, Track Pins, O27, steel, price per dozen, 1938	NPF	1	2
No. 1014, Lockton, O27, 1931	NPF	1	2
No. 1015, Winner Locomotive, O27, 0-4-0, steam, w/1016 tender, black, 1931	30	50	100
No. 1016, Winner Locomotive, w/tender, black, 1931	30	50	100
No. 1017, Winner Transformer Station, 1931	22	34	45
No. 1017, Lionel-Ives Transformer Station, 1933	22	34	45
No. 1018, Track, O27, straight, 1934	NPF	NPF	1
No. 1019, Winner Observation Car, O27, 1931	7	13	25
No. 1019, Track Set, O27, remote control, 1938	5	8	10
No. 1020, Winner Baggage Car, O27, 1931	7	13	25
No. 1021, 90 Degrees Crossing, O27, 1933	1	2	6
No. 1022, Curved Tunnel, O27, 1935	20	30	40
No. 1023, Tunnel, O27, straight, 1934	18	27	35
No. 1024, Switches, O27, manual, price per pair, 1935	5	8	11
No. 1027, Transformer Station, 1934	20	30	40
No. 1028, Transformer, 25 watt, 1935	3	4	5
No. 1029, Transformer, 25 watt, 1936	3	4	5
No. 1030, Winner Locomotive, O27, 0-4-0, electric, orange w/green roof, 1932	30	50	100
No. 1030, Transformer, 40 watt, 1936	4	6	12
No. 1035, Winner Locomotive, O27, 0-4-0, steam, w/1016 tender, 1932	30	50	100
No. 1037, Transformer, 40 watt, 1941	10	15	20
No. 1039, Transformer, 35 watt, 1938	10	15	20
No. 1040, Transformer and Whistle Controller, 60 watt, 1938	12	18	25
No. 1041, Transformer, 60 watt, 1940	12	18	25
No. 1042, Transformer, 75 watt, 1942	12	18	25
No. 1045, Operating Watchman, nickel or brass sign, 1938	25	38	50
No. 1045C, Contactor, 1938	NPF	NPF	1

Pre-WWII (1901-1942)

	C6	C8	C10
No. 1046, Mechanical Gateman and Crossing, 1936	45	68	90
No. 1050, Passenger Car, 2-7/8", trailer, 1905	2000	3500	7500
No. 1100, Summer Trolley, standard, 1911	1050	1750	3500
No. 1100, Trailer Trucks, standard, thirty-five series, 1924	3	5	10
No. 1100, Mickey Mouse Handcar, mechanical, wind-up, orange base, 1935	600	900	1200
No. 1100, Mickey Mouse Handcar, green base, 1935	500	750	1000
No. 1100, Mickey Mouse Handcar, red base, 1935	500	700	900
No. 1101, Trailer Trucks, standard, w/lights, thirty-five series, 1924	3	5	10
No. 1103, Peter Rabbit Handcar, mechanical, wind-up, track operation, 1935	500	700	1000
No. 1103, Peter Rabbit Handcar, floor operation, 1935	500	700	900
No. 1105, Santa Claus Handcar, mechanical, wind-up, green base, 1935	900	1400	1800
No. 1105, Santa Claus Handcar, mechanical, red base, 1935	800	1200	1600
No. 1107, Donald Duck Rail Car, mechanical, wind-up, green roof, 1936	600	900	1200
No. 1107, Donald Duck Rail Car, red roof, 1936	600	900	1200
No. 1121, Switches, O27, electric, remote control, pair, 1937	12	18	25
No. 1200, Trailer Truck, standard, ten series, 1923	4	6	12
No. 1201, Trailer Truck, standard, ten series w/lights, 1923	4	6	12
No. 1229, Transformer, 220 volts, 1938	50	75	100
No. 1230, Transformer, 220 volts, 1938	50	75	100
No. 1239, Transformer, 220 volts, 1941	50	75	100
No. 1241, Transformer, 220 volts, 1941	50	75	100
No. 1300, Trailer Truck, standard, 200 series, 1925	4	6	12
No. 1301, Trailer Truck, standard, 200 series w/lights, 1925	4	6	12
No. 1400, Trailer Truck, standard, 418 series, 1925	5	8	16
No. 1401, Trailer Truck, standard, 418 series w/lights, 1925	5	8	16
No. 1506, L.I. Locomotive, steam, mechanical, 1933	36	60	120

Pre-WWII (1901-1942)	C6	C8	C10
No. 1506, Locomotive Outfit, mechanical, w/1509T Tender, 1515 tank and 1517 caboose, 1935	75	125	250
No. 1506L, Locomotive Outfit, mechanical, w/1502T tender, 1933	36	60	120
No. 1506-8, Bulb, 1-1/2 volt, clear, 1935	NPF	NPF	1
No. 1508, Locomotive Outfit, 0-4-0, mechanical, Vanderbilt-type, w/1509T tender, 1935	81	135	270
No. 1511, Locomotive Outfit, 0-4-0, mechanical, Commodore Vanderbilt-type, black, w/1516 tender, 1936-1937	45	75	150
No. 1511, Locomotive Outfit, 0-4-0, mechanical, red, w/1516 tender, 1936-1937	54	90	180
No. 1512, Winner Gondola, O27, 1931	18	30	60
No. 1512, L.I. Gondola, O27, 1933	18	30	60
No. 1512, Gondola, O27, 1936	18	30	60
No. 1514, Winner Boxcar, O27, 1932	9	15	30
No. 1514, L.I. Boxcar, O27, 1933	7	11	22
No. 1514, Boxcar, O27, 1934	12	21	42
No. 1515, L.I. Tank Car, O27, 1933	11	19	38
No. 1515, Tank Car, O27, 1934	19	32	64
No. 1516T, Tender, O27, 1936	12	21	42
No. 1517, Winner Caboose, O27, 1931	7	11	22
No. 1517, L.I. Caboose, O27, 1933	9	15	30
No. 1517, Caboose, O27, 1931-1937	11	18	36
No. 1520, Animal, 1935	60	100	200
No. 1521, Locomotive Outfit, mechanical, w/1516T tender, 1937	180	300	600
No. 1536, Mickey Mouse Circus Train Outfit, includes cardboard figures, circus facade, tickets and Mickey as barker; train loco 1508, 1509 red, 1536 dinner, 1536 band and 1536 animal car, w/original box, 1935	1500	2500	3500
No. 1550, Switches-mechanical, remote control, price per pair, 1933	20	30	40
No. 1551, 90 Degrees Crossing, mechanical, 1936	2	3	4
No. 1555, 90 Degrees Crossing, mechanical, 1933	3	5	5
No. 1560, Station, mechanical, 1933	15	22	30
No. 1572, Lionel Jr. Telegraph Posts, mechanical, 1934	11	18	36
No. 1573, Lionel Jr. Warning Signal, mechanical, 1934	8	12	16
No. 1574, Lionel Jr. Clock, mechanical, 1934	5	8	16
No. 1588, Locomotive Outfit, 0-4-0, mechanical, torpedo type, w/1588 or 1516 tender, 1936	66	110	220
No. 1630, Pullman, O27, blue sides w/aluminum roof, 1938	20	33	65
No. 1630, Pullman, O27, blue sides w/gray roof, 1938	20	33	65
No. 1631, Observation Car, O27, blue sides w/aluminum roof, 1938	23	39	78
No. 1615E, L.I. Locomotive, O27, 0-4-0, electric, red cab, brown roof, 1933	75	125	250

Pre-WWII (1901-1942)	C6	C8	C10
No. 1661E, L.I. Locomotive, O27, 2-4-0, steam, glossy black, w/1661 Tender, 1933	39	65	130
No. 1662, Locomotive, O27, 0-4-0, steam, switcher, w/2203 tender, 1940	125	205	410
No. 1663, Locomotive, O27, 0-4-0, steam, switcher, 2201 tender, 1940	138	230	460
No. 1664 or E, Locomotive Outfit, O27, 2-4-2, black or gunmetal gray, w/1689T, 1689W, 2666T or 2666W tender, 1938	60	103	205
No. 1666 or E, Locomotive Outfit, O27, 2-4-2, black, w/2666T, 2666W, 2689T, 2689W or 1689W tender, 1938	39	65	130
No. 1666 or E, Locomotive Outfit, O27, 2-4-2, gunmetal gray, w/tender, 1938	36	60	120
No. 1668 or E, Locomotive, O27, steam, black, 2-6-2, w/1689T or 1689W tender, 1937	40	68	135
No. 1668 or E, Locomotive, O27, 2-6-2, steam, gunmetal gray, 1937	42	70	140
No. 1673, Coach, streamliner, mechanical, red, 1936	14	23	45
No. 1674, Pullman, streamliner, mechanical, 1936	14	23	45
No. 1675, Observation Car, streamliner, mechanical, 1936	14	23	45
No. 1677, L.I. Gondola, O27, 1933	12	20	40
No. 1677, Gondola, O27, 1934	12	20	40
No. 1679, L.I. Boxcar, O27, 1933	12	20	40
No. 1679, Boxcar, O27, 1934	8	13	25
No. 1680, L.I. Tank Car, O27, 1933	12	20	40
No. 1680, Tank Car, O27, 1934	13	21	42
No. 1681 or E, Lionel Jr. Locomotive, O27, 2-4-0, steam, black, 1934	42	70	140
No. 1681 or E, Lionel Jr. Locomotive, O27, 2-4-0, steam, red, 1934	48	80	160
No. 1682, L.I. Caboose, O27, 1933	9	15	30
No. 1682, Caboose, O27, 1934	6	10	20
No. 1684, Locomotive, O27, 2-4-2, steam, black, w/1689T, 1688T, 2689T or 2689W tender, 1942	45	78	155
No. 1684, Locomotive, O27, 2-4-2, steam, gunmetal gray, 1942	29	48	95
No. 1685, Pullman, O, Ives transitional car, blue body w/silver roof, four-wheel trucks, uncataloged, 1933	120	200	400
No. 1685, Pullman, O, red body w/maroon roof, four-wheel trucks, uncataloged, 1933	90	150	300
No. 1685, Pullman, O, gray body w/maroon roof, six-wheel trucks, uncataloged, 1933	135	225	450
No. 1686, Baggage Car, O, Ives transitional car, blue body w/silver roof, four-wheel trucks, uncataloged, 1933	120	200	400
No. 1686, Baggage Car, O, red body w/maroon roof, four-wheel trucks, uncataloged, 1933	90	150	300
No. 1686, Baggage Car, O, gray body w/maroon roof, six-wheel trucks, uncataloged, 1933	135	225	450

*No. 250E Locomotive,
Hiawatha, $1500.*

Pre-WWII (1901-1942)

	C6	C8	C10
No. 1687, Observation Car, O, Ives transitional car, blue body w/silver roof, four-wheel trucks, uncataloged, 1933	120	200	400
No. 1687, Observation Car, O, red body w/maroon roof, four-wheel trucks, uncataloged, 1933	90	150	300
No. 1687, Observation Car, O, gray body w/maroon roof, six-wheel trucks, uncataloged, 1933	135	225	450
No. 1688 or E, Locomotive, O27, 2-4-2, steam, black, w/1689T tender, 1936	36	90	120
No. 1688 or E, Locomotive, O27, 2-4-2, steam, gunmetal gray, 1936	60	100	200
No. 1689E, Locomotive, O27, 2-4-2, steam, black, w/1689T tender, 1936.	35	55	110
No. 1689E, Locomotive, O27, 2-4-2, steam, gunmetal gray, 1936	39	65	130
No. 1690, L.I. Pullman, O27, red w/red or brown roof, 1933	15	25	50
No. 1690, Pullman, O27, red, w/red or brown roof, 1934	12	20	40
No. 1691, L.I. Observation Car, O27, red w/red or brown roof, 1933	12	20	40
No. 1691, Observation Car, O27, red w/red or brown roof, 1934	12	20	40
No. 1692, Pullman, O27, peacock body and roof, uncataloged, 1937	12	20	40
No. 1693, Observation Car, O27, peacock body and roof, uncataloged, 1937	12	20	40
No. 1697, Locomotive,Tender and Transformer Outfit, O27, 1937	45	75	150
No. 1698E, Locomotive, Tender and Transformer Outfit, O27, 1936	60	100	200
No. 1699E, Locomotive, Tender and Transformer Outfit, O27, 1936	60	100	200
No. 1700 or E, Power Car, O27, diesel, streamliner, aluminum, red, marked "Lionel Jr.", 1935	66	110	220
No. 1701, Coach, O27, streamliner, aluminum, red or chrome, 1935	36	60	120
No. 1702, Observation Car, O27, streamliner, aluminum, red or chrome, 1935	36	60	120
No. 1703, Front Coach, O27, w/draw-bar, streamliner, 1935	12	20	40

Pre-WWII (1901-1942)

	C6	C8	C10
No. 1717, Gondola, O, orange and tan or yellow and green, uncataloged, 1933	15	25	50
No. 1719, Boxcar, O, peacock w/blue roof, orange doors, yellow and brown, uncataloged, 1933	13	23	45
No. 1722, Caboose, O, orange or red body, uncataloged, 1933	18	30	60
No. 1766, Pullman, standard, 1934	85	142	285
No. 1767, Baggage Car, standard, 1934	90	150	300
No. 1768, Observation Car, standard, 1934	105	175	350
No. 1811, L.I. Pullman, O27, 1933	22	36	72
No. 1811, Pullman, O27, 1934	22	36	72
No. 1812, L.I. Observation Car, O27, 1933	22	36	72
No. 1812, Observation Car, O27, 1934.	22	36	72
No. 1813, L.I. Baggage Car, O27, 1933	18	30	60
No. 1813, Baggage Car, O27, 1934	18	30	60
No. 1816 or W, Power Car, diesel, streamliner, wind-up mechanical, marked "Silver Streak", 1935	42	70	140
No. 1817, Coach, streamliner, mechanical, chrome and orange, 1935	10	16	32
No. 1818, Observation Car, streamliner, mechanical, chrome and orange, 1935	10	16	32
No. 1835E, Locomotive, standard, 2-4-2, steam, w/1835T, 1835TW or 1835W tender, 1934	230	380	760
No. 1910, Locomotive, standard, 0-6-0, electric, dark olive green, marked "New York, New Haven and Hartford", 1910	600	1000	2000
No. 1910, Pullman, standard, dark olive green w/maroon doors, "1910 Pullman 1910," uncataloged, 1910	540	900	1800
No. 1911, Locomotive, standard, 0-4-0, electric, dark olive, 1910	330	550	1100
No. 1911, Locomotive, standard, 0-4-0, electric, maroon, 1910	300	500	1000
No. 1911, Special Locomotive, standard, 0-4-4-0, electric, maroon, marked "New York, New Haven and Hartford" or "New York Central Lines", 1911	420	700	1400
No. 1912, Locomotive, standard, 0-4-4-0, electric, dark olive green, 1910	660	1100	2200
No. 1912, Locomotive, standard, 0-4-4-0, electric, marked "New York, New Haven and Hartford", 1910	720	1200	2400

Pre-WWII (1901-1942)

	C6	C8	C10
No. 1912, Special Locomotive, standard, 0-4-4-0, electric, all brass engine, 1911	1500	2500	5000
No. 1917, Lionel Folder, 1917	8	13	25
No. 1918, Lionel Folder, 1918	8	13	25
No. 1919, Lionel Folder, 1919	8	13	25
No. 1919, Lionel Apology Folder, 1919	13	23	45
No. 1920, Lionel Folder, 1920	8	13	25
No. 1921, Lionel Folder, 1921	8	13	25
No. 1926-3, Lionel-Ives Bulb, 6 volt, 1933	NPF	NPF	1
No. 1930, Winner Folder, 1930	11	21	35
No. 1931, Winner Folder, 1931	11	21	35
No. 1932, Winner Folder, 1932	11	21	35
No. 2200, Summer Trolley, standard, trailer, non-powered, marked "2200 Rapid Transit 2200", 1910	1050	1750	3500
No. 2600, Pullman, O, red body and roof, 1938	60	100	200
No. 2601, Observation Car, O, red body and roof, 1938	60	100	200
No. 2602, Baggage Car, O, red body and roof, 1938	60	100	200
No. 2613, Pullman, O, Blue Comet, two-tone blue, 1938	81	135	270
No. 2613, Pullman, O, green, 1938	84	140	280
No. 2614, Observation Car, O, Blue Comet, two-tone blue, 1938	81	135	270
No. 2614, Observation Car, O, green, 1938	84	140	280
No. 2615, Baggage Car, O, Blue Comet, two-tone blue, 1938	81	135	270
No. 2615, Baggage Car, O, green, 1938	120	200	400
No. 2620, Floodlight, O, red frame on searchlight, 1938	23	38	75
No. 2623, Pullman, O, Irvington, Bakelite, Tuscan brown, 1941	150	250	500
No. 2623, Pullman, O, Manhattan, Bakelite, Tuscan brown, uncataloged, 1941	80	133	265
No. 2624, Pullman, O, Manhattan, Bakelite, Tuscan brown, uncataloged, 1941	240	400	800
No. 2630, Pullman, O, light blue and silver or gray roof, 1938	30	50	100
No. 2631, Observation Car, O, light blue and silver or gray roof, 1938	30	50	100
No. 2640, Pullman, O, light blue w/silver roof, 1938	20	33	65
No. 2640, Pullman, O, green w/dark green roof, 1938	20	33	65
No. 2641, Observation Car, O, light blue w/silver roof, 1938	24	40	80
No. 2641, Observation Car, O, green w/dark green roof, 1938	21	35	70
No. 2642, Pullman, O, light blue w/silver or gray roof, 1941	24	40	80
No. 2643, Observation Car, O, light blue w/silver or gray roof, 1941	15	25	50
No. 2651, Flatcar, O, bright green w/lumber load, 1938	15	25	50
No. 2652, Gondola, O, yellow, 1938	18	30	60

Pre-WWII (1901-1942)

	C6	C8	C10
No. 2652, Gondola, O, brown, 1938	18	30	60
No. 2653, Hopper, O, light green, 1938	15	25	50
No. 2653, Hopper, O, black, 1938	38	62	125
No. 2654, Tank Car, O, aluminum, marked "Sunoco", 1938	20	33	65
No. 2654, Tank Car, O, marked "Shell", 1938	21	35	70
No. 2654, Tank Car, O, light gray, marked "Sunoco", 1938	18	30	60
No. 2655, Boxcar, O, cream body w/maroon roof, 1938	18	30	60
No. 2655, Boxcar, O, cream body w/Tuscan brown roof, 1938	20	34	68
No. 2656, Cattle Car, O, light gray body w/red roof, 1938	38	63	125
No. 2657, Caboose, O, red body w/red roof, 1938	12	20	40
No. 2657, Caboose, O, red body w/brown roof, 1938	9	15	30
No. 2659, Dump Car, O, green, black frame, 1938	12	23	45
No. 2660, Crane, O, red roof, green boom, 1938	27	45	90
No. 2672, Caboose, O27, Pennsylvania N5 type, Tuscan brown, 1942	12	20	40
No. 2677, Gondola, O27, red w/black frame, 1940	11	18	36
No. 2679, Boxcar, O27, yellow w/blue roof, 1938	9	15	30
No. 2679, Boxcar, O27, yellow w/maroon roof, 1938	9	15	30
No. 2680, Tank Car, O27, aluminum, marked "Sunoco", 1938	8	12	25
No. 2680, Tank Car, O27, orange, marked "Shell", 1938	8	12	25
No. 2680, Tank Car, O27, gray, marked "Sunoco", 1938	8	12	25
No. 2682, Caboose, O27, red w/red roof, 1938	7	12	23
No. 2682, Caboose, O27, brown w/brown roof, 1938	7	12	23
No. 2717, Gondola, O, orange and tan, uncataloged, 1938	37	63	125
No. 2719, Boxcar, O, peacock and blue roof, uncataloged, 1938	37	63	125
No. 2722, Caboose, O, red w/maroon roof, uncataloged, 1938	37	63	125
No. 2755, Tank Car, O, gray, marked "Sunoco", 1941	45	75	150
No. 2757, Caboose, O, PRR-N5 type, Tuscan brown, 1941	12	20	40
No. 2758, Boxcar, O, automobile, Tuscan body, marked "Pennsylvania", 1941	21	35	70
No. 2810, Crane, O, yellow cab and red roof, 1938	74	123	245
No. 2811, Flatcar, O, aluminum w/eight logs, 1938	36	60	120
No. 2812, Gondola, O, bright green, 1938	21	35	70
No. 2812, Gondola, O, dark green, 1938	21	35	70
No. 2813, Cattle Car, O, cream body w/maroon roof, 1938	60	100	200

No. 116 Station c. 1932. Photo courtesy T.W. Sefton Collection

Pre-WWII (1901-1942)	C6	C8	C10
No. 2814, Boxcar, O, light yellow body w/maroon roof, 1938	50	83	165
No. 2814, Boxcar, O, orange body w/brown roof, 1938	120	200	400
No. 2814R, Refrigerator, O, white body w/brown roof, 1938	185	325	650
No. 2815, Tank Car, O, silver, Sunoco, 1938	54	90	180
No. 2815, Tank Car, O, orange, Shell, 1938	75	125	250
No. 2816, Hopper, O, red, 1938	60	100	200
No. 2816, Hopper, O, black, white rubber-stamped lettering, 1938	54	90	180
No. 2817, Caboose, O, light red body and roof, 1938	31	53	105
No. 2817, Caboose, O, red, Tuscan roof, white rubber-stamped lettering, 1938	29	48	95
No. 2820, Floodlight, O, two searchlights, green base, plate-stamped lights, 1938	54	88	175
No. 2820, Floodlight, O, green base, cast lights, 1938	90	150	300
No. 2954, Boxcar, O47, Tuscan brown, marked "Pennsylvania", 1940	105	175	350
No. 2955, Tank Car, O72, black, marked "S.U.N.X.", 1940	78	130	260
No. 2956, Hopper, O72, B&O, black, 1940	83	138	275
No. 2957, Caboose, O72, NYC, Tuscan brown, 1940	93	155	310
No. 3300, Summer Trolley, standard, trailer, gold rubber-stamped, 3300 Electric Rapid Transit, 3300, non-powered, 1910	1200	2000	4000
No. 3651, Operating Lumber Car, O, operating, black frame, nickel stakes, w/logs and bin, 1939	13	20	40
No. 3652, Operating Gondola, O, operating, yellow, 1939	25	42	85
No. 3657, Dump Car, silver w/brown bin, 1939	120	200	400

Pre-WWII (1901-1942)	C6	C8	C10
No. 3659, Dump Car, O, operating, black frame, red hopper, 1939	20	33	65
No. 3811, Operating Flatcar, O, black frame w/lumber, 1939	18	30	60
No. 3814, Merchandise Car, O, operating, Tuscan body and roof, discharges five cubes, 1939	48	80	160
No. 3859, Dump Car, O, operating, black, 1938	25	41	82
No. 4400, Summer Trolley, standard, trailer, 1910	1200	2000	4000
Transformer, 40 watt, 1916	20	30	40
Transformer, 50 watt, 1917	13	23	45
Transformer, 75 watt, 1923	13	23	45
Track, standard, curved, 1906	NPF	1	2
Transformer, 75 watt, 1922	15	25	50
Track, standard, curved half section, 1906	NPF	1	2
Track, O, curved, 1915	NPF	NPF	1
Steel Pins, O/standard, dozen, 1937	1	2	2
Track, standard, curved, w/battery connections, 1915	1	2	3
Track, O, curved, w/battery connections, 1915	1	2	3
Track Clip, O, 1937	NPF	NPF	1
Track Clip, standard, 1937	NPF	NPF	1
Track, O, curved w/insulated rails, 1926	NPF	NPF	1
Transformer, 60 watt, 1930	10	15	20
Transformer, 75 watt, 1938	10	15	20
Track, standard, curved racing car-type, 30" dia., 1912	25	38	50
Transformer, 150 watt, 1914	40	60	80
Mechanical Key, square, 1934	3	5	10
Transformer, 75 watt, 1914	10	15	20
Track, standard, curved, racing car-type, 36" dia., 1915	28	42	55
Track, curved, mechanical, 1933	NPF	NPF	1
Track, curved, mechanical, 1933	NPF	NPF	1
Track, straight, mechanical, 1933	NPF	NPF	1
Transformer, 50 watt, 1942	10	15	20

Top row, left to right: No. 341 Observation car, $90; No. 339 Pullman car, $90. Bottom row, left to right: No. 10E Locomotive, $275; No. 332 Baggage car, $95. Photo courtesy PB Eighty-Four, New York

Pre-WWII (1901-1942)

	C6	C8	C10
Track, standard, curved racing car-type 36" diameter, 1912	28	42	55
Transformer, 50 watt, 1915	10	15	20
Transformer, 75 watt, 1939	7	11	14
Transformer, 75 watt, 1939	7	11	14
Bulb, 8 volt, clear, 1939	NPF	NPF	1
Transformer, 100 watt, 1939	25	38	50
Track, O, remote control, 1938	3	4	5
Track, standard, straight, 1906	NPF	1	2
Transformer, 50 watt, 1915	10	15	20
Track, standard, straight half section, 1906	NPF	1	2
Track, O, straight, 1915	NPF	NPF	1
Track, standard, straight w/battery connections, 1915	1	2	3
Track, O, straight, w/battery connections, 1915	1	2	3
Track, curved, insulated, mechanical, 1935	NPF	NPF	1
Track, curved, mechanical, 1935	NPF	NPF	1
Track, standard, straight w/insulated rails, 1926	1	2	3
Track, O, straight w/insulated rails, 1926	NPF	NPF	1
Lockton, standard, 1921	NPF	NPF	1
Transformer, 75 watt, 1915	10	15	20
Lockton, O, 1921	NPF	NPF	1
Transformer, 50 watt, 1933	10	15	20
Lockton, universal, 1937	NPF	NPF	1
Transformer, 150 watt, 1939	55	83	110
Transformer, 75 watt, 1933	5	8	10
Transformer, 250 watt, 1939	80	120	160
Caboose, O72, 1940	165	275	550

Pre-WWII (1901-1942)

	C6	C8	C10
No. 717K, Caboose, O72, kit, new only, 1940	NPF	NPF	500
No. 717-54, Bulb, 18 volt, clear, 1940	NPF	1	NPF
No. 720, 90 Degrees Crossing, O72, 1935	2	5	8
No. 721, Switches, O72, non-electric, pair, 1935	42	70	140

Post-WWII (1945-1969)

	C6	C8	C10
No. 58, Lamp Post, green, maroon, cream, 1946-1950	14	24	48
No. 164, Lumber Loader, 1946-1950	102	170	340
No. 156, Station Platform, O, 1946-1951	52	78	105
No. 0-22, Switches, O, electric, 1946-1949	26	39	125
No. 26, Bumper, O, red, 1948	32	48	65
No. 26, Bumper, O, gray, 1948	65	98	130
No. 27-3, Bulb, 14 volt, clear, 1950	NPF	NPF	1
No. 0-27-C1, Track Clip, O27, 1949	NPF	2	3
No. 30, Water Tank Car, gray support structure, 1947-1950	70	150	250
No. 30, Water Tank Car, black support structure, 1947-1950	125	250	500
No. 31, Track, Super O, curved, 1957	NPF	2	4
No. 33, Half Curve Track, Super O, 1957	NPF	2	4
No. 34, Track, Super O, half, straight, 1957	NPF	2	4
No. 37, Uncoupling Track, Super O, 1957	8	15	20
No. 38, Water Tower, red roof, 1946-1947	225	338	430
No. 38, Water Tower, brown roof, 1946-1947	175	255	450

No. 402E Locomotive 0-4-4-0, $600.

Post-WWII (1945-1969)	C6	C8	C10
No. 38, Accessory Adapter, Super O, 1957	NPF	1	2
No. 39-5, Operating Unit Set, Super O, 1957	3	4	5
No. 39-25, Operating and Upcoupling Set, Super O, 1960	3	4	5
No. HO-039, Track Cleaning Car, HO, 1961	36	60	120
No. 40-25, Four Conductor Cable and Reel, 1950	NPF	1	2
No. 40-50, Three Conductor Cable and Reel, 1960	NPF	1	2
No. 41, Locomotive, O27, army switcher, black shell small motorized unit, 1955	130	150	200
No. 42, Locomotive, O27, Picatinny Arsenal switcher, olive shell, small motorized unit, 1957	135	225	450
No. 43, Power Track, Super O, 1957	NPF	1	2
No. 44, Locomotive, Super O, US Army Missile Launcher, 1959	72	120	240
No. 44-80, Missiles, Super O, four, 1959-1962	2	3	4
No. 45, Locomotive, O, U.S. Marine Missile Launcher, olive shell w/white missiles, 1960-1962	190	225	340
No. 48, Track, Super O, straight, insulated, 1958	4	8	12
No. 49, Track, Super O, curved, insulated, 1958	4	8	12
No. 50, Gang Car, O27, 1954.............	45	55	70
No. HO-050, Gang Car, HO, 1959........	30	50	100
No. 51, Locomotive, O27, Navy switcher, blue shell small motorized unit, 1956-1957.............................	150	190	250
No. 52, Fire Fighting Car, O27, red shell w/man, 1958-1961	165	225	300
No. 53, Snow Plow, O27, DRG, Rio Grande, black and yellow, "a" in Grande backwards, 1957	180	250	330
No. 53, Snow Plow, O27, DRG, Rio Grande, black and yellow, 1957	520	680	900
No. 54, Ballast Tamper, O27, yellow shell, small motorized unit, w/track trips, 1957	100	160	225
No. 55, Tie Ejector, O27, red shell w/wooden track ties, small motorized unit and track trips, 1957-1961 .	72	122	245

Post-WWII (1945-1969)	C6	C8	C10
No. HO-055, Locomotive, HO, M&StL switcher, 1961.................................	30	50	100
No. 55-150, Ties, O27, set of twenty-four, 1957.................................	4	6	8
No. 56, Locomotive, O27, M&StL Mining, red shell, small motorized unit, 1958	250	480	580
No. HO-056, Locomotive, HO, A.E.C. Switcher, 1959...............................	45	75	150
No. 57, Locomotive, O27, A.E.C. Switcher, cream-red shell, small motorized unit, 1959-1960	325	500	750
No. HO-057, Locomotive, HO, U.P. Switcher, 1959...............................	30	50	100
No. 58, Locomotive, O27, rotary snow plow, green shell, 1959-1961	325	450	650
No. 59, Locomotive, U.S. Air Force switcher, white cab, 1962-1963........	300	425	600
No. HO-058, Locomotive, R.I. Switcher, 1960.................................	24	40	80
No. 59, Locomotive, O27, U.S. Air Force Switcher, Minute Man, white shell, 1963	172	288	575
No. HO-59, Locomotive, HO, U.S. Air Force Switcher, 1960........................	30	50	100
No. 60, Trolley, O27, yellow w/red roof, blue lettering, 1955-1958.........	100	150	195
No. 60, Trolley, O27, black lettering, 1955-1958.................................	150	220	300
No. 60, Trolley, O27, moving silhouettes, motor man in front w/direction of movement, 1955-1958...................	135	225	450
No. 60, Trolley, O27, red lettering, rare, 1955-1958.................................	900	1500	3000
No. 61, Ground Lockon, Super O, 1957	NPF	2	4
No. 65, Motorized Hand Car, O27, yellow, two rubber men, small motorized unit, yellow or dark yellow, 1962	135	225	450
No. 68, Executive Inspection Car, red DeSoto, small motorized unit, 1958-1961	200	250	350
No. HO-068, Inspection Car, HO, 1961	30	50	100
No. 69, Motorized Maintenance Car, O27, gray platform, black frame, w/blue man and red danger sign, 1960-1962	175	240	310
No. 70, Lamp Post, yard light, 1949-1950	17	29	58

Aircraft, Bomber, 4-engine in copper color with triangle landing gear, Marx, c. 1941, $250.
Photo courtesy MacNary collection

Japanese Tin Airplanes, Ford friction plane, TN, 15" wingspan, $350.

Aircraft, Mystery Plane No. 101, Wyandotte, 1936-1938, $100.
Photo courtesy John Gibson

Aircraft, Jet 559, Auburn Rubber, $45.
Photo courtesy Max Heiss

Aircraft, Dirigible "Los Angeles," Dent, 10-3/4" long, $1,700.
Photo courtesy Bertoia Auctions

Aircraft, Graf Zeppelin, Steelcraft, 30-1/2" long, $500.
Photo courtesy Tim Oei

Animal-Drawn, Trolley "Prospect Park," Reed, c. 1895, $3,500.
Photo courtesy Christie's East

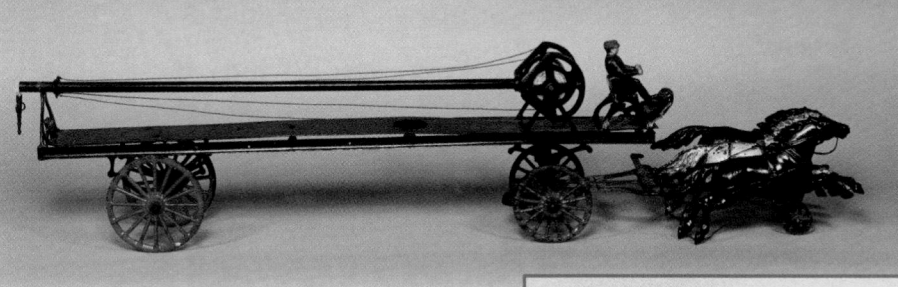

Animal-Drawn, Aerial Fire Wagon, cast iron w/three horses and driver, Wilkins, 43" long, $5,150.
Photo courtesy Bertoia Auctions

Animal-Drawn, Ives, Hansom Cab with walking horse, 18" long, $4,000.
Photo courtesy Bertoia Auctions

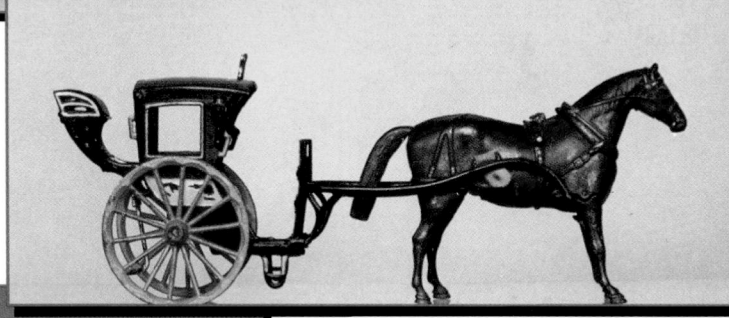

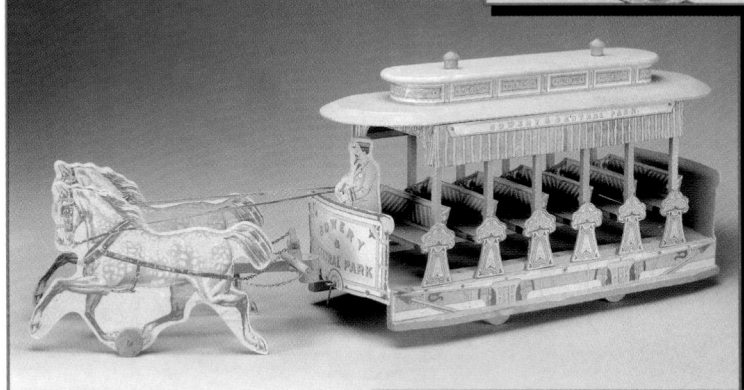

Animal-Drawn, Bowery & Central Park, paper on wood with two horses, Reed, c. 1895, $3,500.
Photo courtesy Christie's East

Animal-Drawn, Royal Circus Lion Cage, Hubley, 15-3/4" long with horses, $750.
Photo courtesy Christie's East

American Paper Toys, Easy to Build Models of Warplanes of the World, 2nd Series, Rigby's, 1940s, $100.
Photo courtesy Ron Bacon

American Paper Toys, Bild-A-Set Fast Freight, complete freight train set, D.A. Prachter Co., 1940s, $45.
Photo courtesy Ron Bacon

American Paper Toys, *Sally and Jane Doll Book*, Lowe, 1964, $65.

American Paper Toys, *Little Women Paper Doll Book*, Saalfield, $45.

Mechanical Banks,
left: Jonah and the
Whale, Shepard
Hardware, $5,500;
right: Chief Big
Moon, J. & E.
Stevens, 1899, $6,000.

Mechanical Banks,
William Tell, J. & E.
Stevens, 1896, $2,800.

Still Banks, City Bank with Chimney,
1870s, $3,500.

Mechanical Banks,
Confectionary, Kyser
& Rex, 1881, $8,500.
*Photo courtesy Bertoia
Auctions*

Mechanical Banks, Germania Exchange Bank, rare, J. & E. Stevens Co., c. 1884, $55,000.

Photo courtesy Bertoia Auctions

Mechanical Banks, Red Riding Hood Bank, J. & E. Stevens Co., c. 1880, $18,000.
Photo courtesy Bertoia Auctions

Mechanical Banks, Preacher in the Pulpit Bank, J. & E. Stevens Co., c. 1876, $50,000.
Photo courtesy Bertoia Auctions

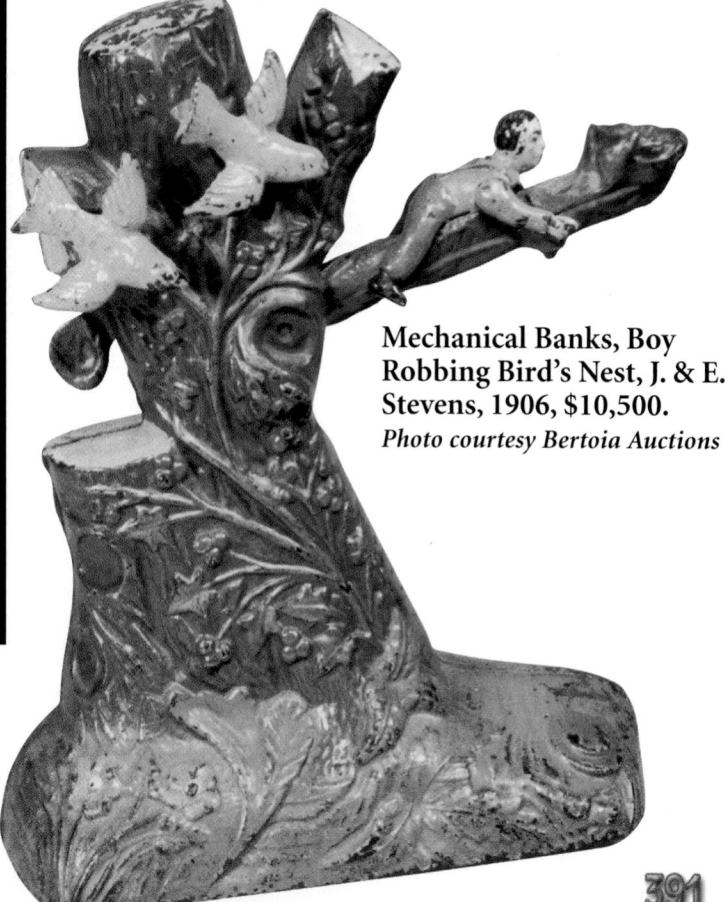

Mechanical Banks, Boy Robbing Bird's Nest, J. & E. Stevens, 1906, $10,500.
Photo courtesy Bertoia Auctions

Mechanical Banks, Chinaman in Boat, made of lead, rare, c. 1880, $42,000.
Photo courtesy Bertoia Auctions

Mechanical Banks, Mikado Bank, Kyser & Rex Co., c. 1886, $55,000.
Photo courtesy Bertoia Auctions

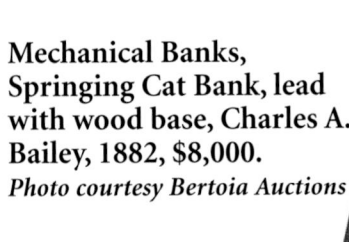

Mechanical Banks, Boy Scout Camp, J. & E. Stevens, 1912, $12,000.
Photo courtesy Bertoia Auctions

Mechanical Banks, Springing Cat Bank, lead with wood base, Charles A. Bailey, 1882, $8,000.
Photo courtesy Bertoia Auctions

Battery-Operated Toys, Cragstan
Crapshooter, "Y" Co., 1950s, $225.

Battery-Operated
Toys, Indian Joe,
Alps Co., 1960s,
$175.

Battery-Operated Toys, Piston Action
Robot, TN Co., 1950s, 8-1/4" tall, $1,800.
Photo courtesy Continental Hobby House

Battery-
Operated Toys,
Bubble
Blowing
Monkey, Alps
Co., 1950s, 10"
tall, $225.
*Photo courtesy
Don Hultzman*

Battery-Operated Toys, Remote Control Missile
Tank, Daisy Matic, $225.
Photo courtesy Darryll Jones

Battery-Operated Toys, Frankonia Road
Sweeper (same as Daisy Matic), $450.
Photo courtesy Darryll Jones

Bell Toys, Monkey and Coconut, N.N. Hill Brass Co., $700.

Bell Toys, Happy Hooligan in Car, two variations, N.N. Hill Brass Co., $900.
Photo courtesy Clint Seeley

Bell Toys, Jonah and the Whale, N.N. Hill Brass Co., cast iron, $2,200.

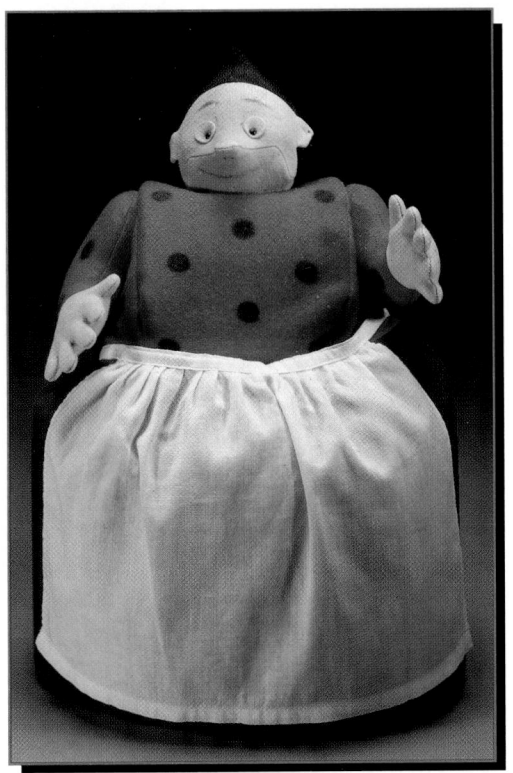

Comic Characters, Flash Gordon Playset, Mego, 1970s, $250.

Comic Characters, Mama Katzenjammer Doll, Steiff, c. 1908, $2,000.
Photo courtesy Christie's East

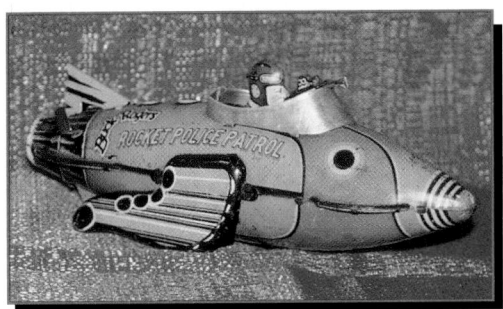

Comic Characters, Buck Rogers Rocket Police Patrol, Marx, 1939, $1,800.

Comic Characters, Dick Tracy Braces for Smart Boys and Girls, 1940s, $100.

Comic Characters, Batman Bat Phone, Marx, 1966, $75.

Disney, Mysterious Pluto, Marx, #1710, $350.

Disney, Babes in Toyland Soldier, tin, Linemar, 1950s, $350.
Photo courtesy Scott Smiles

Disney, Jiminy Cricket tin wind-up, Linemar, 1950s, $650.

Disney, Mickey Mouse the Bandleader doll, baton missing from this photo, Knickerbocker, 1935, $1,850.
Photo courtesy Don Hultzman

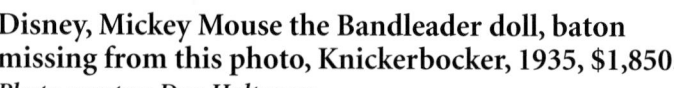

Disneyland Roller Coaster, Chein, 1950s, $600.
Photo courtesy Continental Hobby House

Disney, Rocking Mickey Mouse on Pluto wind-up, Linemar, $2,000.
Photo courtesy Don Hultzman

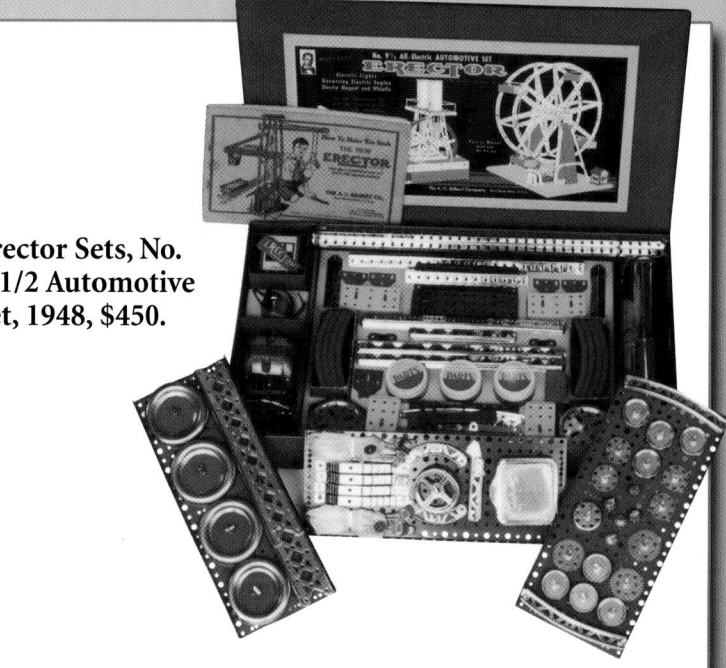

Erector Sets, No. 9-1/2 Automotive Set, 1948, $450.

Erector Sets, No. 10-1/2 Amusement Park Set, 1951, $500.
Photo courtesy A.C. Gilbert Heritage Society

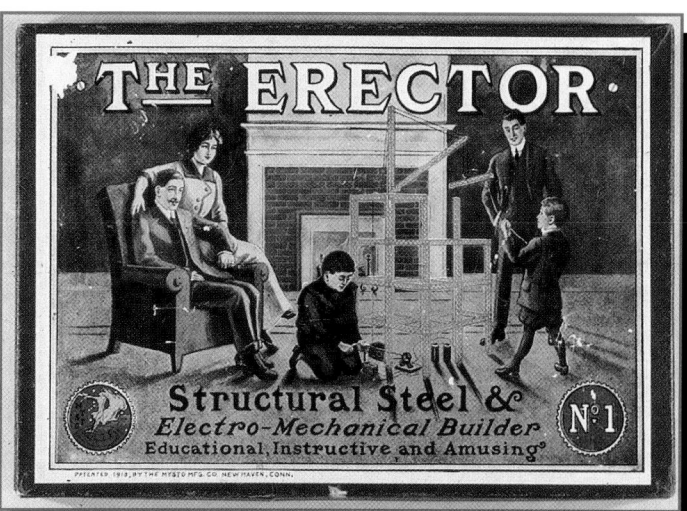

Erector Sets, Erector No. 1, 1913, $400.

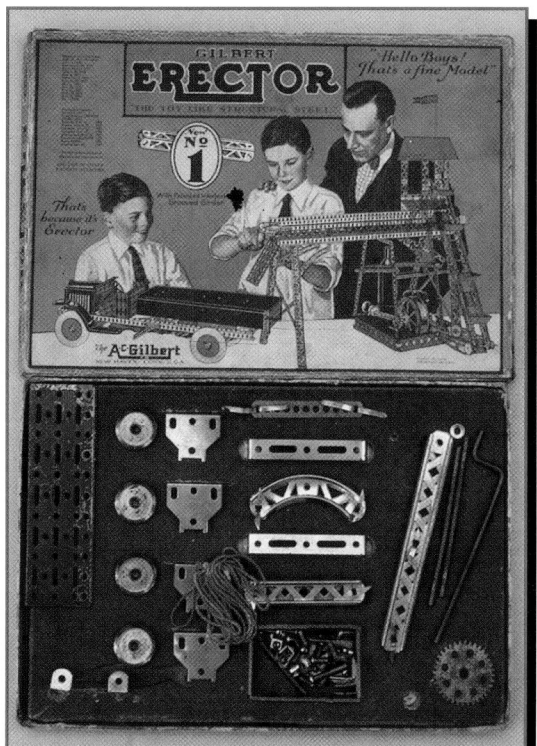

Erector Sets, No. 1, A.C. Gilbert, 1928, $135.

Erector Sets, No. 10062 the Steam Engine set, A.C. Gilbert, 1958, $100.

Fisher-Price, #693 Little Snoopy, 1966, $25.

Fisher-Price, #400-500 Donald Duck Drum Major, 1946, $325.

Fisher-Price, #485 Mickey Mouse Choo Choo, 1949, $245.

Fisher-Price, #799 Quacky Family, with felt beaks and wooden dowels between ducks, 1946, $185.

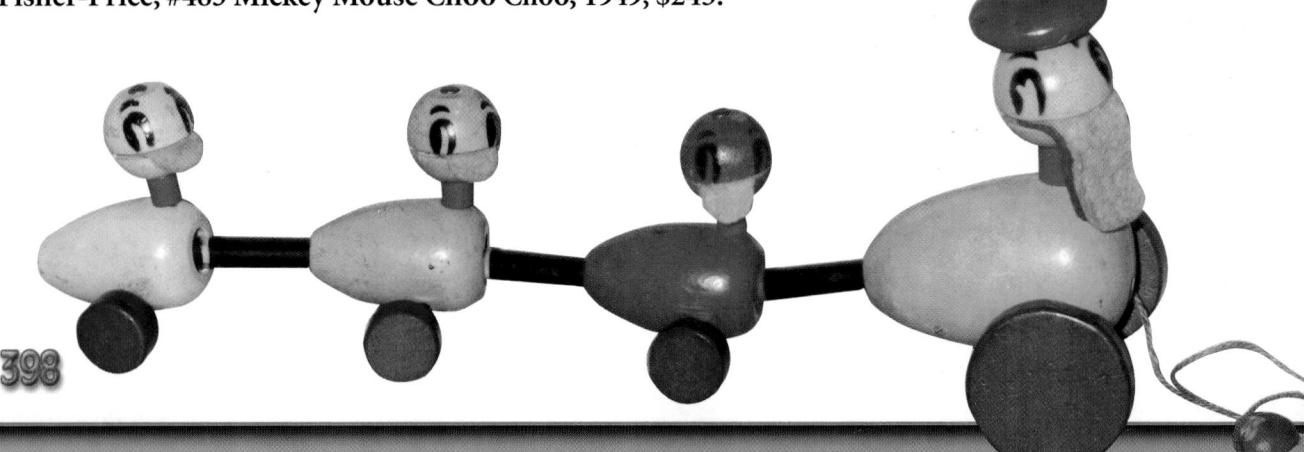

Farm Toys, Arcade, McCormick-Deering tractor, 1925, 6-3/4" long, $850.

Farm Toys, Auburn Rubber, Minneapolis Moline Tractor, #512M, 1950, $100.

Farm Toys, Arcade, cast-iron International Harvester Trac-Tractor, No. 7120, 1941, 7-1/2" long, $3,750.

Farm Toys, Auburn Rubber, Tractor and Wagon, No. 333, $125.

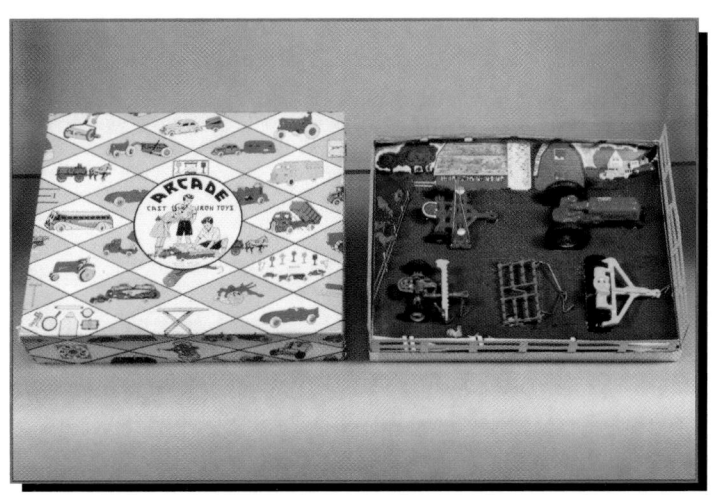

Farm Toys, Arcade, Farm Set in 12" x 15" box, $1,000.

Farm Toys, Arcade, McCormick-Deering Thresher, 1930, 9-1/2" long, $400.

Guns, Big Chief cap pistol, "Made in U.S.A.," Dent, 1930, 3-1/2" long, $35.

Guns, Bigger Bang, Kilgore, 1930, 6" long, $65.
Photo courtesy Charles W. Best

Guns, Hopalong Cassidy cap gun, Wyandotte, 1950, 7-1/2" long, $400.
Photo courtesy Charles W. Best

Guns, Officer Pistol, Kilgore, 1940, 6" long, $125.
Photo courtesy Charles W. Best

Guns, Pirate die-cast cap pistol, Hubley, 1941, 9-3/8" long, $145.
Photo courtesy Charles W. Best

Guns, top to bottom: Tip Top, Stevens, c. 1880, 3-1/2" long, $225; Unmarked, maker unknown, 1878, 3-3/4" long, $125.
Photo courtesy Charles W. Best

Ideal Dolls, Little Miss Revlon, #9105, 1959, $125.

Ideal Dolls, Shirley Temple, composition, 1939, 11", $750.
Photo courtesy McMasters Doll Auctions

Lionel Trains, Top: No. 2332 Virginian engine, $900; Bottom: No. 2331 Virginian engine (variation), $1,500.
Photo courtesy Butterfield & Butterfield Auctions

Lionel Trains, No. 385E locomotive and tender, 1933, $500.

Lionel Trains, No. 384 locomotive and tender, 1930, $600.

Movies, Radio, and Television, Beany & Cecil Leakin' Lena Pound & Pull, 1960s, $110.
Photo courtesy Brad Krewson

Movies, Radio, and Television, Huckleberry Aeroplane, friction, Linemar, 9-1/2" wingspan, 1960s, $900.
Photo courtesy Don Hultzman

Movies, Radio, and Television, James Bond cap pistol with silencer, Lone Star, 1960s, $175.

Movies, Radio and Television, Howdy Doody Official Ranch House Tool Box, Liberty Steel, 1950s, $140.

Movies, Radio, and Television, Hopalong Cassidy Woodburning Set, $65.

Movies, Radio, and Television, Lone Ranger Chuck Wagon Lantern, just add kerosene to this working Dietz lantern, $150.

Schoenhut, Camels, glass-eyed in two styles: left, the Arabian has one hump and an open mouth, $750; right, the Bactrian has two humps, $400.
Photo courtesy Jim and Patsy Carlson

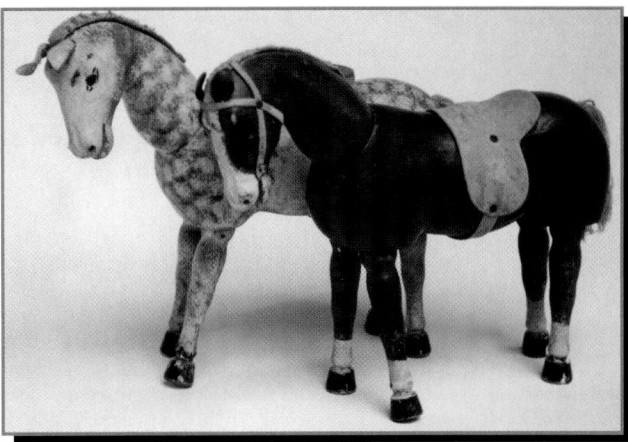

Schoenhut, Horses: left, Dappled White with platform, $275; right, Brown with leather saddle and bridle, $350.
Photo courtesy Jim and Patsy Carlson

Schoenhut, Elephant, glass-eyed with howdah and triangular head dress, $350.
Photo courtesy Jim and Patsy Carlson

Schoenhut, Giraffe, glass-eyed with open mouth inside a flexible cage, $900.
Photo courtesy Jim and Patsy Carlson

Schoenhut, Four bisque-headed Humpty-Dumpty Circus personnel, left to right: Lion Tamer $850; Lady Circus Rider $500; Lady Acrobat $750; Ringmaster $700.
Photo courtesy Jim and Patsy Carlson

Ships, Arcade Showboat,
No. 433, 1920s, $2,500.

Ships, "Sandy Andy" Ferry,
Wolverine, 1930s, $225.

Ships, "Columbus,"
Marklin, c. 1920, $18,000.
Photo courtesy Christie's East

Ships, Viking Ship No. 245,
Renwal, 1955, $150.
Photo courtesy Tim Oei

Soldiers, Naval Officers, left to right: (B55a), (B54a), (B56a); three scarce variations in blue paint, Barclay, $375 each.
Photo courtesy Stan Alekna

Soldiers, #59 Soldier Writing Letter, figure with and without cigarette, (M89), Manoil, $80.
Photo courtesy Stan Alekna

Soldiers, #101 Soldier Jumping with Chute, figure and a variant, (M127), Manoil, $125.
Photo courtesy Stan Alekna

Soldiers, Airplane Mechanic, two variations of (B144) #792, Barclay, $65.
Photo courtesy Stan Alekna

Soldiers, "Tall" Soldier Bomb Thrower, a pair of this super rare figure, (B75), $625.
Photo courtesy Stan Alekna

Tin Wind-Ups, Li'l Abner
and His Dogpatch Band,
Unique Art, 1945, $1,000.

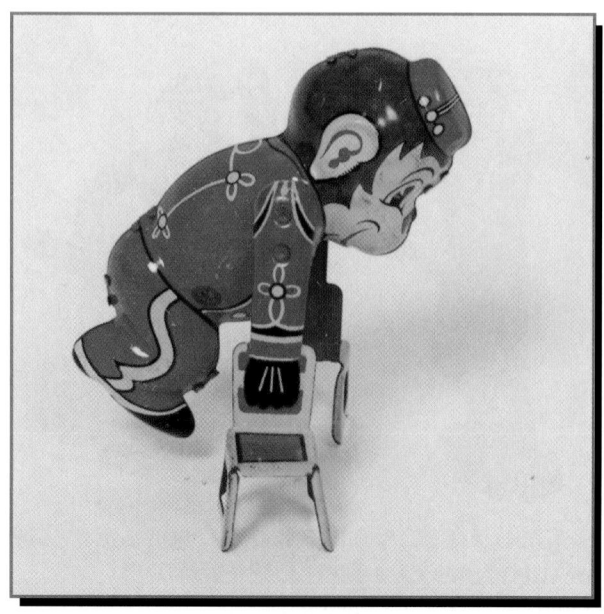

Tin Wind-Ups, Playland
Merry-Go-Round, Chein,
1930s, $800.
Photo courtesy Don Hultzman

Tin Wind-Ups, Red the
Iceman, Marx, 1930s, $600.

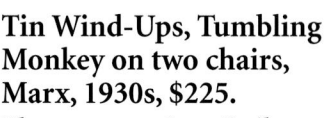

Tin Wind-Ups, Tumbling
Monkey on two chairs,
Marx, 1930s, $225.
Photo courtesy Scott Smiles

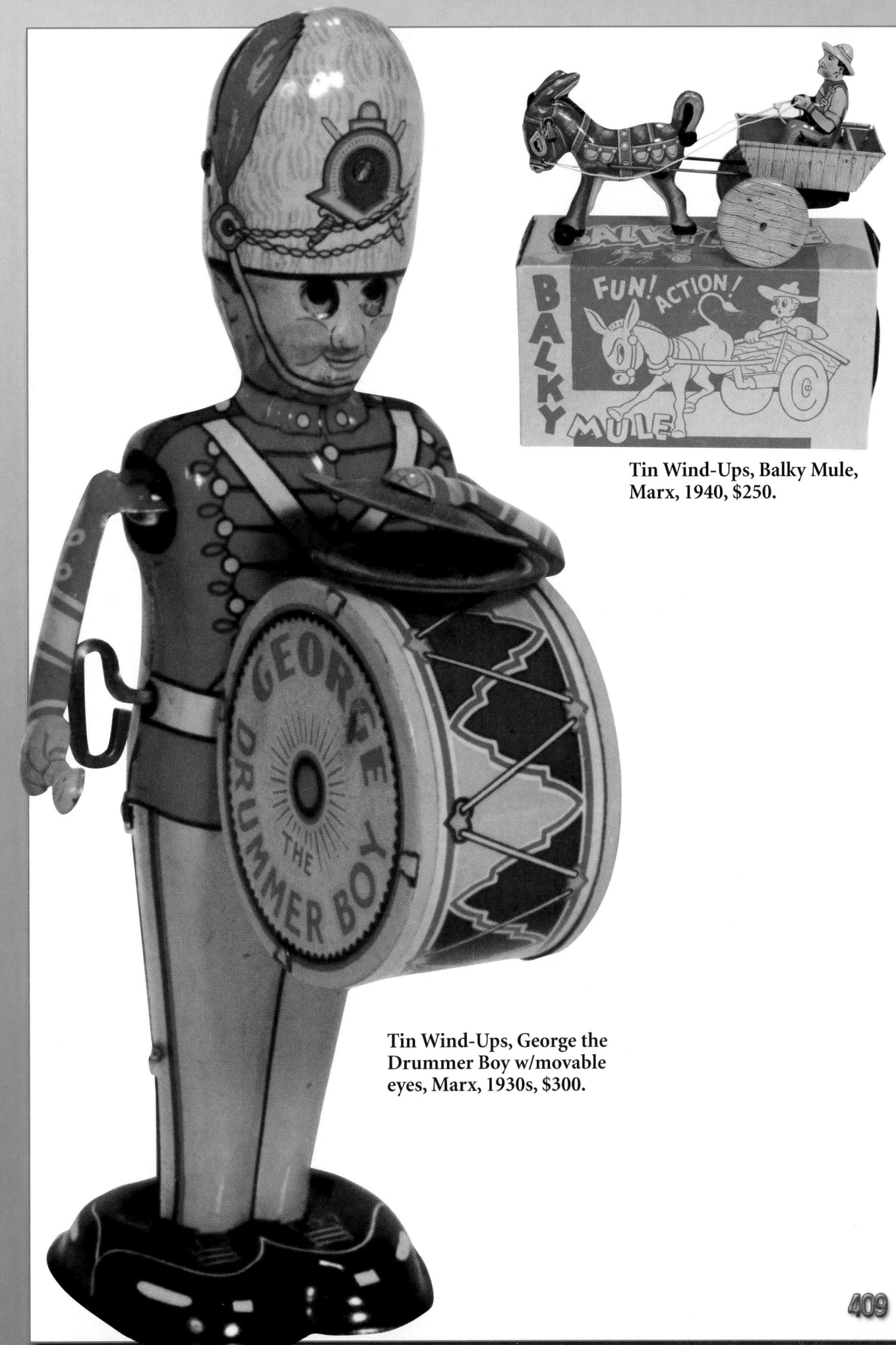

Tin Wind-Ups, Balky Mule,
Marx, 1940, $250.

Tin Wind-Ups, George the
Drummer Boy w/movable
eyes, Marx, 1930s, $300.

Vehicles, A pair of Arcade Mack Ice Trucks, left to right: the 1932 No. 275 (AR147), 10-3/4" long $4,200; the 1930 No. 275 (AR145), 10-5/8" long, $1,200.
Photo courtesy Bertoia Auctions

Vehicles, 1937 International Cabover, Auburn Rubber, 4-1/4" long, $40.

Vehicles, Early 1950s Auburn Rubber cab-forward truck, $45.

Vehicles, Tank Truck, C.A.W. Novelty Co., $60.
Photo courtesy Bob Ackerly

Vehicles, Scarab No. 711,
Buddy "L," 1936-40, 10-1/2"
long, $600.
From the Dick Dance collection

Vehicles, Speed Car No. 103,
Craftoy, $95.
Photo courtesy Perry Eichor

Vehicles, Army Tank No. 362, wood, Buddy "L," 1943, $150.
Photo courtesy Jack Matthews

Vehicles, Japanese Tin Cars,
Cadillac Sedan, Bandai, 12"
$450.
Photo courtesy Ron Smith

Vehicles, Harley-Davidson Motorcycle with Sidecar and two police officers, (HM35), Hubley, $500.
Photo courtesy Kent M. Comstock

Vehicles, No. 500 Mechanical Truck Set, Courtland, $600.
Photo courtesy Joe and Sharon Freed

Vehicles, left to right: Freidag Pickup Truck, 7-1/2" long, $1,000; Freidag Panel Delivery Truck, 7-1/2" long, $3,200.
Photo courtesy Bertoia Auctions

Vehicles, Wrecker Truck with mechanical boom, Girard, 1930s, 10" long, $650.
Photo courtesy John Taylor

Vehicles, Packard Straight Eight, fifteen parts, Hubley, 1929, 11" long, $16,000.
Photo courtesy Bertoia Auctions

Vehicles, Rocket Cycle, Ideal, 6-1/2" long, $200.
Photo courtesy Terry Sells

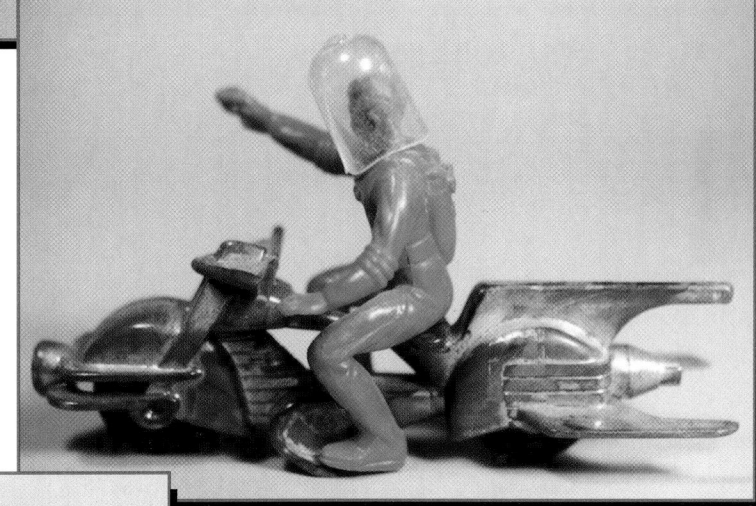

Vehicles, Dump Truck No. 41, Keystone, 1920s, $1,200.
From the Dick Dance collection

Vehicles, Airflow, Kingsbury, c. 1934, $650.
From the Dick Dance collection

Vehicles, Merchants Transfer tin wind-up truck, Marx, 1929, $700.
Photo courtesy Bob Smith

Vehicles, Cadillac four-door sedan, Midgetoy King-Size Series, 4" long, $20.

Vehicles, Pickup truck, Tonka, 1959, $250.
From the Ron O'Brien collection

Vehicles, 1967 Mercury Cougar, Matchbox Regular Wheels, $20.
From the Karen O'Brien collection

Vehicles, Cabover Lowboy with Steam Shovel, Tonka, 1953, $450.
From the Ron O'Brien collection

Vehicles, Tonka Farms Stake Truck and Horse Trailer, Tonka, 1959, $300.
From the Ron O'Brien collection

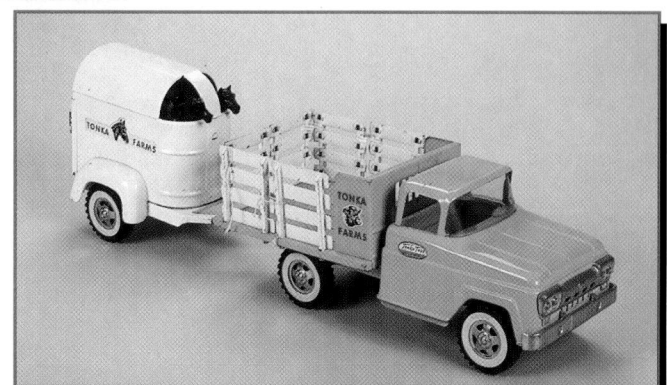

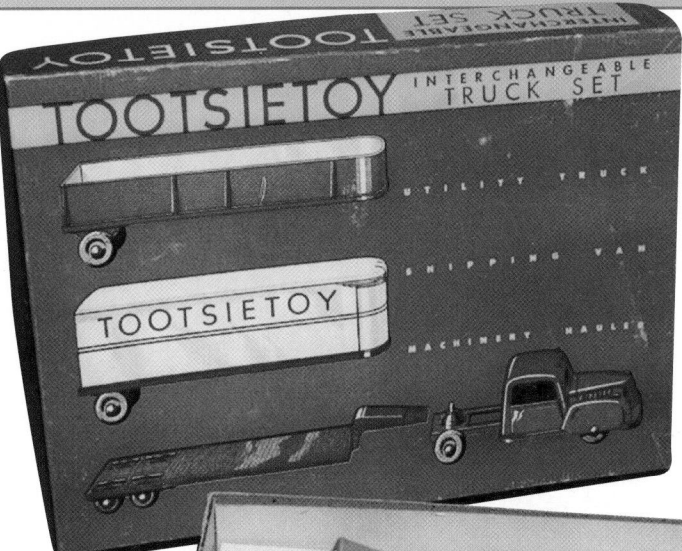

Vehicles, Interchangeable
Truck Set #4900, Tootsietoy,
post-WWII, $125.
Photo courtesy Second Childhood

Vehicles, LaSalle Land Cruiser
#357, Wyandotte, 1936-1939, $190.

Vehicles, Motorcycle with
Removable Cop (VM1),
Vindex, $3,500.
Photo courtesy Kent M. Comstock

415

Wooden Toys, Hustler Toys, left to right: Billy, $125; Watch Dog, $170; Larry, $70; Betty Roll Duck, $30; Pup, $75.
Photo courtesy Jim Sneed

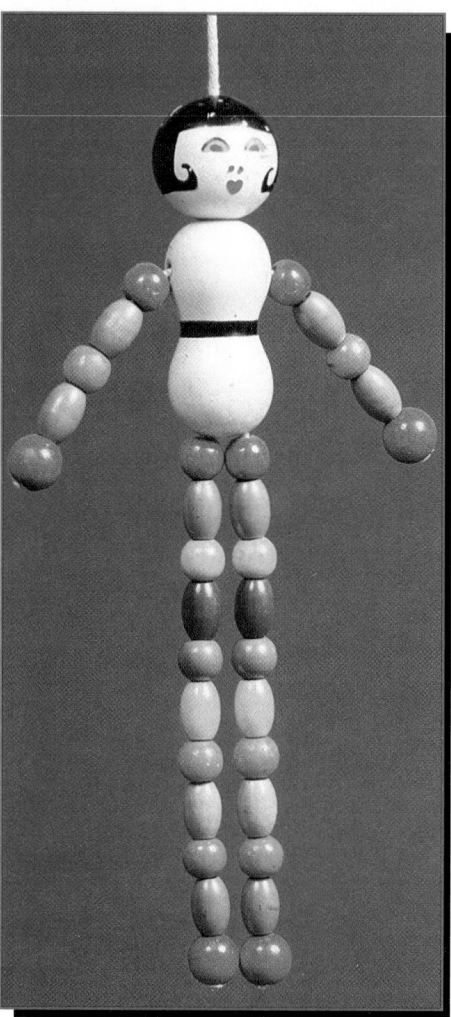

Wooden Toys, TedDoll, Rare Ted Toyler crib toy, $200.
Photo courtesy Jim Sneed

Wooden Toys, TedSoldiers, Ted Toyler soldiers, 10" regular size and 19" giant, $145, and $280.
Photo courtesy Jim Sneed

Wooden Toys, ScareyAnns, left to right: Jack-O-Lantern, New-style sailor, Scary Ann girl, $250, $70, and $70.
Photo courtesy Jim Sneed

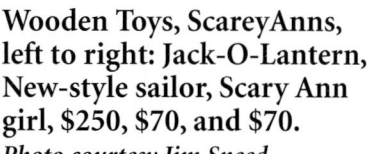

Post-WWII (1945-1969)	C6	C8	C10
No. 71, Lamp Post, crackle gray, 1949-1959 12	15	22	
No. 75, Lamp Set, black plastic, set of two, 1961-1969 17	26	35	
No. 76, Boulevard Lights, green plastic, set of three, 1959-1969 9	12	24	
No. 89, Flag Pole, 1956-1958 22	33	45	
No. 91, Circuit Breaker, brown w/red light, 1957-1960 8	11	12	
No. 92, Circuit Breaker, w/controller, 1959 11	16	23	
No. HO-100, Power Pack, HO, 1961 10	15	20	
No. HO-101, Power Pack, HO, 1961	10	15	20
No. HO-103, Power Pack, HO, 1959	10	15	20
No. HO-103-800, Power Pack, HO, 1961	10	15	20
No. HO-104, Power Pack, HO, 1961	10	15	20
No. 110, Trestle Set, O, twenty-four pieces, 1955-1969	10	15	20
No. HO-110, Trestle Set, HO, 1958	10	15	20
No. 111, Trestle Set, O, ten pieces, 1956-1969	13	17	22
No. 111-100, 2 Piers, O, two pieces, 1960-1963	10	15	20
No. HO-111, Trestle Set, HO, 1959	10	15	20
No. 112, Switch, Super O, w/controls, pair, 1957-1960	42	63	95
No. 114, Newstand, O, w/horn, 1957-1959	52	78	120
No. HO-114, Engine House, HO, w/horn, 1958	50	75	100
No. 115, Station, cream, red or green trim, 1949	155	200	310
No. HO-115, Kit, HO, engine house, 1961	35	52	70
No. HO-117, Engine House, HO, 1959.	45	68	90
No. 118, Newstand, O, w/whistle, 1958	42	63	90
No. HO-118, Engine House, HO, w/whistle, 1958	50	75	100
No. 119, Tunnel, O, 1957	40	60	80
No. HO-119, Tunnel, HO, 1959	7	11	15
No. 120, 90 Degree Crossing, Super O, 1957	8	12	16
No. 121, Tunnel, O, 1959-1966	20	30	40
No. 125, Whistle Station, gray or green base, 1950-1955	22	33	45
No. 128, Newsstand, animated, 1957-1960	85	127	220
No. 130, 60 Degrees Crossing, O, 1957	10	15	20
No. 131, Tunnel, O, curved, 1959-1966	35	53	70
No. 132, Station, O, 1949-1955	45	55	105
No. 133, Station, O, 1957-1966	30	45	85
No. 138, Water Tank, operating, 1953-1957	75	80	145
No. 140, Banjo Signal, O, 1954-1966 ...	25	38	50
No. HO-140, Banjo Signal, HO, 1962 ..	22	33	45
No. 142, Switches, Super O, manual, price per pair, 1957	15	23	30
No. 145, Automatic Gateman, O, 1950-1966	26	32	49
No. 145C, Contactor, O, 1950	6	9	12

Post-WWII (1945-1969)	C6	C8	C10
No. HO-145, Gateman, HO, automatic, 1959	30	45	60
No. HO-245-200, Contactor, HO, 1960	4	5	7
No. 147, Whistle Controller, O, 1961 ...	3	4	5
No. 148, Dwarf Signal, O, 1957	30	45	60
No. 148-100, Double Pole Switch, 1957	4	6	8
No. 150, Telegraph Poles, O, set of six, 1947-1950	19	29	45
No. HO-150, Rectifier, HO, 1958	2	3	4
No. 151, Semaphore, O, 1947-1969	22	35	46
No. 151-51, Bulb, 14 volt, clear, 1950 ..	NPF	NPF	1
No. 152, Crossing Gate, O, 1945-1948 .	21	32	42
No. 153, Block Signal, O, 1945-1969 ...	22	34	45
No. 155, Signal Light, W.M. Bell, 1955-1957	50	75	100
No. 157, Station Platform, O, 1952-1959	37	56	75
No. 161, Mail Pickup Set, O, 1961-1963	35	52	70
No. 163, Block Signal, O, single target, 1961-1963	20	25	38
No. 164-64, Logs, set of five, 1952	NPF	NPF	5
No. 167, Whistle and Reverse Controller, O, 1945	5	8	10
No. 175, Rocket Launcher, O, 1958-1960	105	150	300
No. 175-50, Extra Rockets, O, 1958	10	15	20
No. HO-181, Cab Control, HO, 1958....	7	13	25
No. 182, Magnet Crane, w/165C controller, 1946-1949	110	150	255
No. 192, Railroad Control Tower, 1959-1960	90	135	200
No. 193, Water Tower, 1953-1955	62	93	125
No. 195, Floodlight Tower, 1957-1969.	30	45	60
No. 195-75, Spare Tower Head, add lights and holder for #195 floodlight tower, 1957	10	15	25
No. 196, Smoke Pellets, 100 pellets in bottle/package, price for complete package, 1946	15	25	38
No. 197, Radar Antenna, O, gray w/gray base, 1957-1959	30	53	105
No. 197-75, Replacement Radar Head, 1958	9	15	30
No. HO-197, Radar Antenna, HO, 1958	20	30	40
No. 199, Microwave Tower, 1958-1959	37	56	75
No. 202, Locomotive, O27, UP Alco A diesel, orange w/black lettering, 1957	30	50	100
No. 204, Locomotive, O27, A.T.S.F., Alco AA, diesel, 1957	75	109	150
No. 205, Locomotive, O27, M.P., Alco AA, diesel, 1957	75	120	170
No. 208, Locomotive, O27, A.T.S.F., Alco diesel AA, 1958	78	100	165
No. 209, Locomotive, O27, N.H., Alco AA, diesel, two units, 1958	270	450	900
No. 210, Locomotive, O27, Texas Spec. Alco diesel AA, 1958	110	160	210
No. 211, Locomotive, O27, Texas Spec. Alco AA, diesel, 1962............	80	130	180

No. 42 Locomotive, Picatinny Arsenal

Post-WWII (1945-1969)	C6	C8	C10
No. 212, Locomotive, O27, Alco diesel A, Marine, 1958	90	150	300
No. 212, Locomotive, O27, A.T.S.F. Alco diesel AA, 1964	78	100	150
No. 213, Locomotive, O27, M&StL Alco AA, diesel, 1964	75	125	175
No. 214, Girder Bridge, HO, light or dark gray, 1953-1969	10	20	30
No. HO-214, Girder Bridge, HO, 1958	5	10	15
No. 216, Locomotive, O27, Burlington Alco A, diesel, 1958	100	200	310
No. 216, Locomotive, O27, Minneapolis & St. Louis, Alco diesel A, 1964	75	100	140
No. 217, Locomotive, O27, B&M Alco AB, diesel, 1959	75	100	185
No. 218, Locomotive, O27, A.T.S.F. Alco AA, diesel, 1959	70	100	185
No. 218, Locomotive, O27, A.T.S.F. Alco AB, diesel, 1961	70	100	170
No. 218C, Locomotive, O27, A.T.S.F. Alco B, diesel, 1961	40	50	80
No. 220, Locomotive, O27, A.T.S.F. Alco A, diesel, 1961	75	100	135
No. 221, Locomotive, O27, steam, gray, 1946	48	80	160
No. 221, Locomotive, steam, black, 1946	60	100	200
No. 221, Locomotive, O27, D&RGW Alco A, diesel, 1963	36	60	120
No. 221, Locomotive, O27, A.T.S.F. Alco A, diesel, uncataloged, 1963	175	250	420
No. 221, Locomotive, O27, Alco A, diesel, Marine, uncataloged, 1963	124	207	415
No. HO-226, Truss Bridge, HO, 1961	7	11	14
No. HO-222, Deck Bridge, HO, 1961	10	15	20
No. 223-50, Locomotive, O27, A.B.A.T.S.F. Alco, diesel, 1963	85	125	185
No. 224, Locomotive, O27, Alco AB, diesel, Navy, 1960	100	150	200
No. HO-224, Girder Bridge, HO, 1961	7	11	14
No. 225, Locomotive, O27, C&O Alco A, diesel, 1960	65	100	120
No. 227, Locomotive, O27, C.N. Alco A, diesel, Canadian market distribution, uncataloged, 1960	78	100	160
No. 228, Locomotive, O27, C.N. Alco A, diesel, Canadian market distribution, uncataloged, 1961	70	100	150
No. 229, Locomotive, O27, M&StL Alco A, diesel, 1961	60	90	120
No. 229C, Locomotive, O27, M&StL Alco B, diesel, 1962	40	70	130
No. 229P, Locomotive, O27, M&StL Alco A, diesel, 1962	90	90	120

Post-WWII (1945-1969)	C6	C8	C10
No. 230, Locomotive, O27, C&O Alco A, diesel, 1961	55	80	105
No. 231, Locomotive, O27, R.I. Alco A, diesel, 1961	50	75	110
No. 232, Locomotive, O27, N.H. Alco A, diesel, 1962	65	109	130
No. 233, Locomotive, O27, 2-4-2, steam, w/233W tender, 1961	50	85	105
No. 235, Locomotive, O27, 2-4-2, steam, uncataloged, 1962	80	125	160
No. 236, Locomotive, O27, 2-4-2, steam, 1961	18	30	60
No. 237, Locomotive, O27, steam, 1963	25	35	60
No. 238, Locomotive, O27, steam, 2-4-2, 1963	75	100	130
No. 239, Locomotive, O27, steam, 2-4-2, 1965	65	90	140
No. 241, Locomotive, O27, 2-4-2, steam, uncataloged, 1963	75	125	150
No. 242, Locomotive, O27, steam, 2-4-2, 1962	20	40	60
No. 243, Locomotive, O27, 2-4-2, steam, 1960	70	100	150
No. 244, Locomotive, O27, 2-4-2, steam, 1960	25	30	40
No. 245, Locomotive, O27, 2-4-2, steam, 1959	125	175	250
No. 246, Locomotive, O27, 2-4-2, steam, 1959	25	35	45
No. 247, Locomotive, O27, 2-4-2, B&O, steam, 1959	30	35	65
No. 249, Locomotive, O27, 2-4-2, P.R.R., steam, 1958	20	30	50
No. 250, Locomotive, O27, 2-4-2, P.R.R., steam, 1957	21	35	70
No. 252, Crossing Gate, O, 1950-1962	20	30	40
No. HO-252, Crossing Gate, HO, 1959	20	30	40
No. 253, Automatic Block Sign Signal, O, 1956	30	45	60
No. 256, Freight Shed, 1950-1953	27	41	55
No. 257, Freight Station, w/horn, 1956-1957	32	45	82
No. 260, Bumper, O, 1952	10	15	20
No. 262, Crossing Gate, O, 1962	21	32	42
No. 264, Operating Forklift Platform Assembly, 1957-1960	85	142	285
No. 264-150, Boards, set of twelve, 1957	6	8	10
No. 282, Gantry Crane, O, 1954	72	120	240
No. 299, Code Transmitter Set, 1961-1963	65	80	145
No. HO-300, Lumber Car, HO, operating, 1960	8	14	28
No. HO-301, Dump Car, HO, operating, 1960	12	20	40

Post-WWII (1945-1969)	C6	C8	C10
No. HO-301-16, Cargo Bin, HO, 1960 .	4	5	7
No. 308, Metal Sign Set, O, five piece, 1945-1949	13	20	28
No. 309, Plastic Sign Set, nine piece, 1950-1959	12	19	28
No. 310, Billboard Set, O, billboard and five different inserts, 1950-1968	15	22	30
No. 310R, Billboard, O, racing, 1963 ...	15	22	30
No. 313, Bascule Bridge, silver, 1946-1949	240	375	550
No. 314, Girder Bridge, O, gray, 1946-1950	23	34	45
No. 315, Trestle, O, bridge, illuminated silver, 1946-1947	100	175	250
No. 317, Trestle Bridge, gray, 1950-1956	35	52	70
No. HO-319, Helicopter Car, HO, operating, 1960	16	27	55
No. 321, Trestle Bridge, O, 1958	15	22	30
No. 332, Arch Bridge, O, gray, 1959-1966	20	30	46
No. 334, Operating Dispatching Board, O, 1957-1960	100	150	250
No. HO-337, Giraffe Car, HO, operating, 1961	15	25	50
No. 342, Culvert Loader, O, 1956-1958	115	150	285
No. 345, Automatic Culvert Unloader, O, 1957	165	190	365
No. 348, Manual Culvert Unloader, O, 1966	70	100	185
No. 350, Transfer Table, O, 1957-1960	155	200	350
No. 350-50, Transfer Table Extension, O, 1957-1960	53	88	175
No. 352, Ice Depot, O, red or brown base, 1955-1957	120	160	260
No. 352-55, Ice Blocks, O, set of seven, 1955	10	15	20
No. 353, Trackside Signal, O, 1960-1961	14	25	40
No. 356, Freight Station, O, w/green and orange carts, 1952-1957.............	50	75	110
No. 356-25, Baggage Truck, O, set of two, 1952	9	14	18
No. HO-357, Cop and Hobo Car, HO, 1962	12	20	40
No. 362, Barrel Loader, O, 1952-1957 .	39	65	130
No. 362-78, Barrels, O, set of six, 1952	7	11	15
No. 364, Lumber Loader, O, smooth or crackle gray, 1948-1967	85	100	125
No. 364C, On-Off Switch, 1959	NPF	NPF	15
No. 365, Dispatching Station, O, 1958-1959	70	105	140
No. HO-365, Missile Launching Car, HO, 1962	12	20	40
No. HO-366, Milk Car, HO, operating, 1961	18	30	60
No. HO-370, Sheriff and Outlaw Car, HO, 1962	12	20	40
No. 375, Turntable, O, motorized, 1962-1964	120	185	245
No. 390C, Control Switch, O, 1960	3	6	9

Post-WWII (1945-1969)	C6	C8	C10
No. 394, Rotary Beacon, aluminum, red or green tower frame, 1949-1953	22	33	45
No. 394-10, Bulb, 14 volt, clear, 1951 ..	NPF	NPF	1
No. 394-37, Beacon Cap, 1953	5	10	15
No. 395, Floodlight Tower, four lights, silver tower, 1949-1956....................	25	35	55
No. 395, Floodlight Tower, four lights, green tower, 1949-1956....................	32	48	65
No. 395, Floodlight Tower, four lights, yellow tower, 1949-1956..................	48	80	160
No. 395, Floodlight Tower, four lights, red tower, 1949-1956......................	50	75	85
No. 397, Diesel Type Coal Loader, later model, blue diesel motor cover, 1948-1957	90	100	165
No. 397, Diesel Type Coal Loader, yellow diesel motor cover, 1948-1957 ..	120	200	400
No. 400, Budd RDC Car, O, powered, 1956-1958..	125	150	270
No. 404, Budd RDC Baggage Car, O, powered, 1957-1958............................	165	200	370
No. 410, Billboard Blinker, 1956-1958.	22	35	44
No. HO-410, Suburban Ranch House, HO, 1959	10	15	20
No. HO-411, Figure Set, HO, 1959.......	10	15	20
No. HO-412, Farm Set, HO, 1959.........	10	15	20
No. 413, Countdown Control Panel, 1962	38	50	72
No. HO-413, Railroad Structure Set, HO, 1959	10	15	20
No. HO-414, Village Set, HO, 1959	10	15	20
No. 415, Diesel Fueling Station, 1955-1967	100	150	200
No. 419, Heliport, control tower, 1962 .	125	188	250
No. HO-425, Figure Set, HO, 1962.......	7	11	14
No. HO-430, Tree Assortment, HO, 1959	6	9	12
No. HO-431, Landscape Set, HO, 1959	10	15	20
No. HO-432, Tree Assortment, HO, 1961	7	11	14
No. 443, Missile Launching Platform, 1960-1962	30	45	60
No. 445, Switch Tower, operating, 1952-1957	42	63	85
No. 448, Missile Firing Range Set, 1961-1963	70	75	140
No. 450, Signal Bridge, gray or tan base, 1952-1958..............................	35	52	70
No. 450L, Signal Light Head, 1952	20	25	35
No. 452, Gantry Signal, 1961-1963	65	80	120
No. 455, Oil Derrick, red base, 1950-1954	110	165	220
No. 455, Oil Derrick, green base, 1950-1954	90	135	180
No. 456, Coal Ramp and Hopper Car, 1950-1955..	75	125	250
No. 460, Piggyback Terminal, 1955-1957	75	112	150
No. 460-150, Two Trailers, 1956..........	80	90	100

No. 380E Locomotive 0-4-0, electric, $600.

Post-WWII (1945-1969)	C6	C8	C10
No. 461, Piggyback, w/truck and trailers, most include, "Midge Toy Tractor," red, 1957	300	450	600
No. 462, Derrick Platform Set, 1961-1962	135	165	290
No. 464, Lumber Mill, 1956-1960	87	130	175
No. 464-150, Boards, set of six, 1956	5	10	15
No. 465, Sound Dispatching Station, 1956-1957	75	112	150
No. 470, IRBM Missile Launch, 1959-1962	105	125	155
No. HO-470, Missile Launching Platform, HO, 1960	34	51	68
No. 480-25, Conversion Coupler, 1950	NPF	NPF	4
No. HO-480, Missile Firing Range Set, HO, 1961	7	11	14
No. 494, Rotary Beacon, silver, red, 1954	25	38	50
No. 497, Coaling Station, 1953-1958	100	150	200
No. 520, Locomotive, O27, diesel, eighty ton, original pantograph must not be broken, 1956	60	100	200
No. HO-530, Locomotive, HO, DRGW, diesel F-3 powered A, 1958	20	32	65
No. HO-531, Locomotive, HO, C.M. St. P&P, diesel F-3 powered A, 1958	20	32	65
No. HO-532, Locomotive, HO, diesel F-3 powered A, B&O, 1958	20	32	65
No. HO-533, Locomotive, HO, New Haven, diesel F-3 powered A,, 1958	20	32	65
No. HO-535, Locomotive, HO, Santa Fe, diesel Alco, AB, 1962	20	32	65
No. HO-536, Locomotive, HO, Sante Fe, diesel Alco, 1963	20	32	65
No. HO-537, Locomotive, HO, diesel Alco, AB Santa Fe, 1966	20	32	65
No. HO-540, Locomotive, HO, DRGW, diesel F-3, Dummy B, 1958	15	25	50
No. HO-541, Locomotive, HO, CMST P&P, diesel F-3, Dummy B, 1958	15	25	50
No. HO-550, Locomotive, HO, DRGW, diesel F-3, Dummy A, 1958	15	25	50
No. HO-555, Locomotive, HO, Santa Fe, diesel F-3 powered A, 1963	19	32	64
No. HO-561, Rotary Snowplow, HO, MSTL, 1959	60	100	200
No. HO-564, Locomotive, HO, C&O, diesel Alco, powered A, 1960	19	32	64

Post-WWII (1945-1969)	C6	C8	C10
No. HO-565, Locomotive, HO, Santa Fe, diesel Alco, powered A, 1959	19	32	64
No. HO-566, Locomotive, HO, Texas special, diesel Alco, powered A, 1959	19	32	64
No. HO-567, Locomotive, HO, Alaska, diesel Alco, powered A, 1959	19	32	64
No. HO-568, Locomotive, HO, Union Pacific, diesel Alco, powered A, 1962	19	32	64
No. HO-569, Locomotive, HO, Union Pacific, diesel Alco, powered A, 1963	19	32	64
No. HO-571, Locomotive, HO, PRR, diesel Alco, powered A, 1963	19	32	64
No. HO-576, Locomotive, HO, Texas special, diesel F-3, Dummy B, 1959	19	32	64
No. HO-577, Locomotive, HO, Alaska, diesel F-3, Dummy B, 1959	19	32	64
No. HO-581, Locomotive, HO, PRR, rectifier, 1960	19	32	64
No. HO-586, Locomotive, HO, Texas special, diesel F-3, Dummy A, 1959	15	25	50
No. HO-587, Locomotive, HO, Alaska, diesel F-3, Dummy A, 1959	15	25	50
No. HO-591, Locomotive, HO, New Haven, rectifier, 1959	19	32	64
No. HO-592, Locomotive, HO, Santa Fe, diesel GP9, 1966	19	32	64
No. HO-593, Locomotive, HO, Northern Pacific, diesel GP9, 1963	19	32	64
No. HO-594, Locomotive, HO, Santa Fe, diesel GP9, 1963	19	32	64
No. HO-595, Locomotive, HO, Santa Fe, diesel F-3, Dummy A, 1959	15	25	50
No. HO-596, Locomotive, HO, NYC, diesel GP9, 1959	19	32	64
No. HO-597, Locomotive, HO, Northern Pacific, diesel GP9, 1961	19	32	64
No. HO-598, Locomotive, HO, NYC, diesel GP7, 1961	19	32	64
No. 600, Locomotive, O27, diesel SW2, MKT, 1955	54	90	180
No. 601, Locomotive, O27, diesel, Seaboard, 1956	60	100	200
No. 602, Locomotive, O27, diesel SW2, Seaboard, 1957	62	105	210
No. HO-602, Locomotive, HO, steam, 1960	15	25	50

Post-WWII (1945-1969)	C6	C8	C10
No. HO-605, Locomotive, HO, steam, 1959	20	32	64
No. 610, Locomotive, O27, diesel SW2, Erie, 1955	85	120	160
No. 611, Locomotive, O27, diesel SW2, CNJ, 1957	66	110	220
No. 613, Locomotive, O27, U.P., diesel, SW2, 1958	125	200	415
No. 614, Locomotive, O27, Alaska, diesel, SW2, blue, yellow structure on roof, 1959-1960	65	110	220
No. 616, Locomotive, O27, diesel, SW2, ATSF, 1961	66	110	220
No. 617, Locomotive, O, ATSF, diesel, SW2, black, 1963	90	150	300
No. 621, Locomotive, O27, diesel, SW2, CNJ, 1956	60	75	145
No. 622, Locomotive, diesel, SW2, Santa Fe, black, 1949	150	175	325
No. 623, Locomotive, O, diesel, SW2, ATSF, black, 1952	73	123	245
No. 624, Locomotive, O, diesel, SW2, C&O, blue, yellow stripe, 1952	110	150	270
No. 625, Locomotive, O27, diesel, forty-four ton, LV, 1957	75	120	150
No. HO-625, Locomotive, HO, steam, 1959	27	45	90
No. HO-626, Locomotive, HO, steam, 1963	19	33	65
No. 626, Locomotive, O27, B&O, diesel, forty-four ton, 1957	135	225	450
No. 627, Locomotive, O27, diesel, 45 ton, LV, red body, white stripe, 1956	80	110	145
No. 628, Locomotive, O27, diesel, 45 ton, NP, black w/yellow stripe, 1956	50	83	165
No. 629, Locomotive, O27, Burlington, diesel, forty-four ton, silver, red stripe, 1956	105	175	350
No. 633, Locomotive, O, diesel, SW2, Santa Fe, 1962	100	150	215
No. 634, Locomotive, O, diesel, SW2, Santa Fe, blue body, 1962	18	30	60
No. HO-635, Locomotive, HO, steam, 1961	19	32	65
No. HO-636, Locomotive, HO, steam, 1963	19	33	65
No. 637, Locomotive, Super O, 2-6-4, steam, 2046W tender or 2040W tender, 1959	52	88	175
No. HO-642, Locomotive, HO, steam, 1961	19	33	65
No. HO-643, Locomotive, HO, steam, 1963	19	33	65
No. 645, Locomotive, O27, diesel, SW2, Union Pacific, yellow body, 1963	41	68	135
No. HO-645, Locomotive, HO, steam, 1962	19	33	65
No. 646, Locomotive, O, 4-6-4, steam, 2046W tender, 1954	88	148	295
No. HO-646, Locomotive, HO, steam, 1963	19	33	65
No. HO-647, Locomotive, HO, 1966	19	33	65

Post-WWII (1945-1969)	C6	C8	C10
No. 665, Locomotive, O, 4-6-4, steam, w/6026W or 2046W tender, 1954	100	160	235
No. 671, Locomotive, O, steam, 6-8-6, 671W tender, 1946	70	115	230
No. 671, Locomotive, O, steam, 6-8-6, w/2671 tender, 1946	90	150	300
No. 671-75, Smoke Bulb, 14 volt, 1946	5	10	15
No. 671, R&R Locomotive, O, steam, 671W tender, 1952	75	125	250
No. 675, Locomotive, O, 2-6-2, steam, w/2466W, 2466WX or 6466WX tender, 1947	70	115	230
No. 681, Locomotive, O, 6-8-6, steam, 2671W tender, 1950	78	130	260
No. 682, Locomotive, O, 6-8-6, steam, w/2046W tender, 1954	140	233	465
No. 685, Locomotive, O, 4-6-4, steam, w/6026W tender, 1953	85	142	285
No. 703-10, Smoke Bulb, O, 1946	15	25	30
No. HO-704, Baggage Car, HO, Texas Special, 1959	18	30	60
No. HO-705, Pullman, HO, Texas Special, 1959	18	30	60
No. HO-706, Vista Dome, HO, Texas Special, 1959	18	30	60
No. HO-707, Observation Car, HO, Texas Special, 1959	18	30	60
No. HO-708, Baggage Car, HO, Pennsylvania, 1960	5	10	20
No. HO-709, Vista Dome, HO, Pennsylvania, 1960	8	13	26
No. HO-710, Observation Car, HO, Pennsylvania, 1960	6	10	20
No. HO-711, Baggage Car, HO, Pennsylvania, 1960	6	10	20
No. HO-712, Baggage Car, HO, Santa Fe, 1961	14	22	45
No. HO-713, Pullman, HO, Santa Fe, 1961	14	22	45
No. HO-714, Vista Dome, HO, Santa Fe, 1961	8	13	26
No. HO-715, Observation Car, HO, Santa Fe, 1961	6	10	20
No. 726, Locomotive, O, 2-8-4, steam, w/2426W tender, 1946	200	330	660
No. 726, Locomotive, O, 2-8-4, steam, w/2046W tender, 1946	210	330	385
No. HO-733, Pullman, HO, Santa Fe, 1964	6	10	20
No. HO-735, Observation Car, HO, Santa Fe, 1964	6	10	20
No. 736, Locomotive, O, 2-8-4, steam, w/2046W tender, 1950	250	300	400
No. 746, Locomotive, O, 4-8-4, steam, w/746W tender w/short stripe, marked "Norfolk & Western", 1957.	500	850	1195
No. 746, Locomotive, O, 4-8-4, steam, w/long stripe, 1957	580	900	1500
No. 773, Locomotive, O, 4-6-4 steam, Hudson, w/2426W tender, 1950	700	650	1530
No. 773, Locomotive, 4-6-4, Hudson, w/2046W tender, 1964	455	650	900

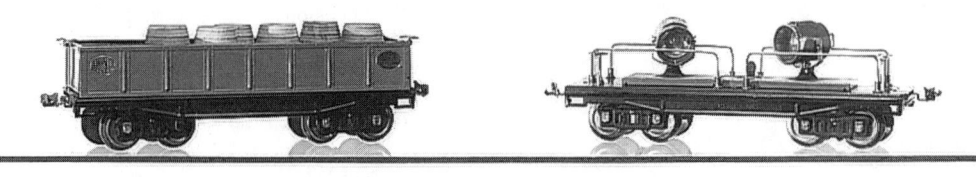

No. 219 Crane. Photo courtesy PB Eighty-Four

Post-WWII (1945-1969)	C6	C8	C10
No. HO-800, Flatcar, HO, w/airplane, 1958	18	30	60
No. HO-801, Flatcar, HO, w/boat, 1958	9	15	30
No. HO-805, AEC Car, HO, w/light, 1959	12	20	40
No. HO-806, Flatcar, HO, w/helicopter, 1959	15	25	50
No. HO-807, Flatcar, HO, w/bulldozer, 1959	14	23	45
No. HO-809, Helium Transport Car, HO, 1961	11	19	38
No. HO-810, Generator Transport Car, HO, 1961	8	13	26
No. HO-811-25, Flat, HO, w/stakes, 1958	6	10	20
No. HO-813, Mercury Capsule Car, HO, 1962	10	16	32
No. HO-814, Auto Transport Car, HO, 1958	15	25	50
No. HO-815, Tank Car, HO, 1958	11	18	35
No. HO-815-50, Tank Car, HO, 1964...	8	13	25
No. HO-815-75, Tank Car, HO, 1963...	8	13	25
No. HO-815-85, Tank Car, HO, 1964...	8	13	25
No. HO-816, Rocket Fuel Tank Car, HO, 1962	8	13	25

Post-WWII (1945-1969)	C6	C8	C10
No. HO-816-50, Rock Fuel Tank Car, HO, 1962	8	13	25
No. HO-817, Caboose, HO, 1958	7	12	24
No. HO-817-150, Caboose, HO, Santa Fe, 1960	6	10	20
No. HO-817-200, Caboose, HO, AEC, 1959	6	10	20
No. HO-817-225, Caboose, HO, Alaska, 1959	6	10	20
No. HO-817-250K, Caboose, HO, Texas Special, 1959	6	10	20
No. HO-817-275, Caboose, HO, New Haven, 1959	6	10	20
No. HO-817-300, Caboose, HO, Southern Pacific, 1959	-6	10	20
No. HO-817-350, Caboose, HO, Rock Island, 1960	6	10	20
No. HO-819-1, Work Caboose, HO, P.R.R., 1958..	8	13	25
No. HO-819-100, Work Caboose, HO, B&M, 1958..	8	13	25
No. HO-819-200, Work Caboose, HO, B&M, 1959..	8	13	25
No. HO-819-225, Work Caboose, HO, Santa Fe, 1960	8	13	25

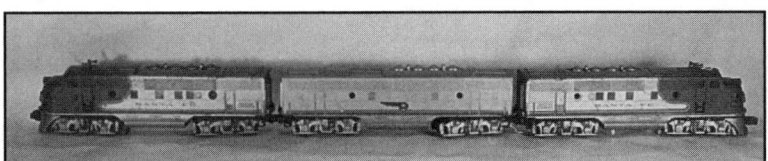

No. 2333 "Santa Fe." Photo by Bill Kaufman, courtesy Good Old Days Store

Post-WWII (1945-1969)	C6	C8	C10
No. HO-819-250, Work Caboose, HO, NP, 1960	8	13	25
No. HO-819-275, Work Caboose, HO, C&O, 1960	8	13	25
No. HO-819-285, Work Caboose, HO, C&O, 1963	8	13	25
No. HO-821, Pipe Car, HO, 1960	8	13	25
No. HO-821-50, Pipe Car, HO, 1964	8	13	25
No. HO-821-100, Pipe Car, HO, 1963	10	16	32
No. HO-823, Twin Missile Car, HO, 1960	21	35	70
No. HO-824, Flatcar, HO, w/two cars, 1958	14	22	45
No. HO-827, Caboose, HO, Lionel, 1961	6	10	20
No. HO-827-50, Caboose, HO, AEC, 1963	6	10	20
No. HO-827-75, Caboose, HO, Lionel, 1963	6	10	20
No. HO-830, Flatcar, HO, w/two vans, 1958	12	20	40
No. HO-834, Poultry Car, HO, 1959	13	21	42
No. HO-836, Hopper, HO, 1961	6	10	20
No. HO-836-60, Hopper, HO, Alaska, 1966	6	10	20
No. HO-836-100, Hopper, HO, Lionel, 1964	6	10	20
No. HO-837, Caboose, HO, M&StL, 1961	5	8	15
No. HO-837-100, Caboose, HO, M&StL, 1963	6	10	20
No. HO-838, Caboose, HO, Lackawanna, 1961	6	10	20
No. HO-840, Caboose, HO, NYC, 1961	6	10	20
No. HO-841, Caboose, HO, 1961	6	10	20
No. HO-841-50, Caboose, HO, Union Pacific, 1962	6	10	20
No. HO-841-175, Caboose, HO, Santa Fe, 1962	6	10	20
No. HO-842, Culvert Pipe Car, HO, 1960	8	12	25
No. HO-845, Gold Bullion Car, HO, 1962	10	16	32
No. HO-847, Exploding Target Car, HO, 1960	6	9	18
No. HO-847-100, Exploding Target Car, HO, 1960	17	29	58
No. HO-850, Missile Launching Car, HO, 1960	11	18	35
No. HO-860, Derrick, HO, 1958	10	16	32
No. HO-861, Timber Transport Car, HO, 1960	6	10	20
No. HO-861-100, Timber Transport Car, HO, 1961	8	13	26
No. HO-862-25, Gondola, HO, 1958	3	5	10
No. HO-863, Rail Truck Car, HO, 1960	8	13	26

Post-WWII (1945-1969)	C6	C8	C10
No. HO-864-1, Boxcar, HO, Seaboard, 1958	6	10	20
No. HO-864-25, Boxcar, HO, NYC, 1958	6	10	20
No. HO-864-50, Boxcar, HO, State of Maine, 1958	6	10	20
No. HO-864-100, Boxcar, HO, New Haven, 1958	6	10	20
No. HO-864-125, Boxcar, HO, Rutland, 1958	6	10	20
No. HO-864-150, Boxcar, HO, M&StL, 1958	6	10	20
No. HO-864-175, Boxcar, HO, Timken, 1958	6	10	20
No. HO-864-200, Boxcar, HO, Monon, 1958	6	10	20
No. HO-864-225, Boxcar, HO, Central of Georgia, 1958	6	10	20
No. HO-864-250, Boxcar, HO, Wabash, 1958	6	10	20
No. HO-864-275, Boxcar, HO, State of Maine, 1962	6	10	20
No. HO-864-300, Boxcar, HO, Alaska, 1959	6	10	20
No. HO-864-325, Boxcar, HO, D.S.S.A., 1959	6	10	20
No. HO-864-350, Boxcar, HO, State of Maine, 1959	9	15	30
No. HO-864-400, Boxcar, HO, B&M, 1960	6	10	20
No. HO-864-700, Boxcar, HO, Santa Fe, 1961	6	10	20
No. HO-864-900, Boxcar, HO, NYC, 1959	6	10	20
No. HO-864-925, Boxcar, HO, NYC, 1964	6	10	20
No. HO-864-935, Boxcar, HO, NYC, 1963	6	10	20
No. HO-865, Gondola, HO, w/canisters, 1958	10	16	32
No. HO-865-225, Gondola, HO, w/scrap iron, 1960	8	13	25
No. HO-865-250, Gondola, HO, w/crates, 1960	8	13	25
No. HO-865-300, Gondola, HO, w/crates, 1963	8	13	25
No. HO-865-350, Gondola, HO, NYC, 1963	6	10	20
No. HO-865-375, Gondola, HO, NYC, 1963	6	10	20
No. HO-865-400, Gondola, HO, NYC w/crates, 1963	6	10	20
No. HO-865-435, Gondola, HO, 1964	6	10	20
No. HO-866-1, Cattle Car, HO, M.K.T., 1958	6	10	20
No. HO-866-25, Cattle Car, HO, Santa Fe, 1958	6	10	20
No. HO-866-200, Circus Car, HO, 1959	10	16	32

No. 68 Executive Inspection Car, 1958-60. Photo by Steve Hintze

Post-WWII (1945-1969)	C6	C8	C10
No. HO-870, Maintenance Car, HO, w/generator, 1959	9	15	30
No. HO-872-1, Reefer, HO, Fruit Growers, 1958	6	10	20
No. HO-872-25, Reefer, HO, Illinois Central, 1958	6	10	20
No. HO-872-50, Reefer, HO, El Capitan, 1958	6	10	20
No. HO-872-200, Reefer, HO, Railway Express, 1959	6	10	20
No. HO-873, Rodeo Car, HO, 1962	6	10	20
No. HO-874, Boxcar, HO, NYC, 1964	15	25	50
No. HO-874-25, Boxcar, HO, NYC, 1965	6	10	20
No. HO-874-60, Boxcar, HO, B&M, 1964	6	10	20
No. HO-875, Flatcar, HO, w/missile, 1959	10	17	34
No. 876, Helios 21 Spaceship, 1965	12	20	40
No. HO-877, Miscellaneous Car, HO, 1958	6	10	20
No. HO-879, Derrick, HO, 1958	8	13	26
No. HO-880, Maintenance Car, HO, w/light, 1959	18	30	60
No. HO-900, Operating Platform, HO, 1960	11	18	36
No. HO-903, Track, HO, straight, 3", 1958	NPF	NPF	1
No. HO-905, Track, HO, straight, 1-1/2", 1958	NPF	NPF	1
No. HO-906, Track, HO, straight, 6", 1968	NPF	NPF	1
No. 909, Smoke Fluid, full bottle, 1957	NPF	NPF	5
No. HO-909, Track, HO, straight, 9", 1958	NPF	NPF	1
No. 920, Scenic Display Set, 1957	57	76	95
No. 920-2, Tunnel Portals, 1958	15	23	30
No. 902-5, Rocks, 1958	NPF	NPF	3
No. 920-8, Lichen, 1958	NPF	NPF	3
No. HO-922, Remote Control Switch, HO, right, 1958	NPF	2	3
No. HO-923, Remote Control Switch, HO, left, 1958	NPF	2	3
No. HO-925, Terminal Track, HO, straight, 1958	NPF	1	2

Post-WWII (1945-1969)	C6	C8	C10
No. HO-925-10, Insulating Clip, HO, 1960	NPF	NPF	1
No. 926, Tube of Lubrication, full, 1955	NPF	NPF	3
No. 927, Lubrication and Maintenance, kit, 1950-1953	10	17	33
No. 927-3, Liquid Track Cleaner, full can, 1955	NPF	NPF	5
No. 928, Maintenance Kit, 1960-1963	31	36	40
No. HO-929, Upcoupling Track, HO, 9", 1958	2	3	4
No. HO-930, 30 Degrees Crossing, HO, 1960	2	3	4
No. HO-939, Uncoupler, HO, 1958	NPF	2	3
No. HO-942, Manual Switch, HO, right, 1958	NPF	2	3
No. 943, Exploding Ammo Dump Car, 1959	20	30	40
No. HO-943, Manual Switch, HO, left, 1958	NPF	2	3
No. 950, Railroad Map, 1958-1966	25	38	50
No. HO-950, Re-railer, HO, 1958	NPF	2	3
No. 951, Farm Set, plastic, thirteen pieces, 1958	8	15	38
No. 952, Figure Set, plastic, thirty pieces, 1958	8	15	34
No. 953, Figure Set, plastic, thirty-two pieces, 1959	8	15	35
No. 954, Swimming Pool and Playground Set, plastic, thirty pieces, 1959	10	15	35
No. 955, Highway Set, plastic, twenty-two pieces, 1958	10	15	30
No. 956, Stockyard, plastic, eighteen pieces, 1959	10	15	30
No. 957, Farm Building and Animal Set, plastic, thirty-five pieces, 1958	10	15	30
No. 958, Vehicles, plastic, twenty-four pieces, 1958	10	20	31
No. 959, Barn Set, plastic, twenty-three pieces, 1958	6	15	33
No. 960, Barn Yard Set, plastic, twenty-nine pieces, 1959	6	15	33
No. HO-960, Bumper Track, HO, 1960	NPF	NPF	1
No. 961, School Set, plastic, thirty-six pieces, 1959	10	15	32

Post-WWII (1945-1969)

Post-WWII (1945-1969)	C6	C8	C10
No. HO-961, Bumper Track, HO, illuminated, 1961	NPF	NPF	1
No. 962, Turnpike Set, plastic, twenty-four pieces, 1958	10	15	38
No. 963, Frontier Set, plastic, eighteen pieces, 1959	10	15	40
No. 964, Factory, plastic, twenty-two pieces, 1959	10	15	50
No. 965, Farm Set, plastic, thirty-six pieces, 1959	13	15	35
No. 966, Firehouse, plastic, forty-five pieces, 1958	13	15	35
No. 967, Post Office, plastic, twenty-five pieces, 1958	10	15	35
No. 968, TV Transmitter, plastic, twenty-eight pieces, 1958	10	15	34
No. 969, Construction Set, plastic, twenty-three pieces, 1960	10	15	30
No. 970, Ticket Booth, cardboard, 1958-1960	65	98	130
No. 971, Box of Lichen, 1959	2	5	10
No. 972, Trees, 1959	2	5	10
No. 973, Landscaping Set, 1959	7	11	15
No. 974, Scenery Set, 1962	11	17	22
No. HO-975, Terminal Track, HO, curved, 1958	1	1	1
No. 980, Ranch Set, plastic, fourteen pieces, 1960	10	15	36
No. 981, Freight Yard Set, plastic, ten pieces, 1960	10	15	34
No. 982, Surburban House, plastic, eighteen pieces, 1960	10	15	34
No. 983, Farm Set, plastic, seven pieces, 1960	10	15	34
No. HO-983, Curved Track, HO, curved, 3", 18" radius, 1958	NPF	NPF	1
No. 984, Railroad Set, plastic, twenty-two pieces, 1961	10	15	30
No. HO-984, Curved Track, HO, 4-1/2", 18" radius, 1958	NPF	NPF	1
No. 985, Freight Area Set, plastic, thirty-two pieces, 1961	13	15	32
No. HO-985, Curved Track, HO, 9", 15" radius, 1958	NPF	NPF	1
No. 986, Farm Set, plastic, twenty pieces, 1962	10	15	33
No. HO-986, Track, HO, curved, 4-1/2", 15" radius, 1958	NPF	NPF	1
No. 987, Town Set, plastic, twenty-four pieces, 1962	10	25	33
No. 988, Railroad Structure, sixteen pieces, 1962	10	25	33
No. HO-989, Track, HO, curved, 9", 18" radius, 1958	NPF	NPF	1
No. HO-990, 90 Degrees Crossing, HO, 1958	3	5	7
No. 1001, Locomotive, O27, 2-4-2, steam, w/1001T tender, 1948	15	25	50
No. 1002, Gondola, O27, 1948	4	7	14
No. 1004, Boxcar, O27, 1948	7	11	22
No. 1005, Tank Car, O27, 1948	4	7	13
No. 1007, Caboose, O27, 1948	3	4	8

Post-WWII (1945-1969)	C6	C8	C10
No. 1008, Uncoupling Track, O27, each, 1957	NPF	NPF	2
No. 1008-50, Automatic Uncoupling Track, O27, each, 1961	NPF	NPF	2
No. 1009, Manumatic Uncoupling Track Set, O27, 1948	5	7	9
No. 1010, Transformer, 35 watt, 1961	8	12	20
No. 1011, Transformer, 15 watt, 1961	8	12	20
No. 1012, Transformer, 35 watt, 1950	7	9	19
No. 1013, Track, O27, curved, half-section, 1968	NPF	NPF	1
No. 1014, Transformer, 40 watt, 1955	10	15	20
No. 1015, Transformer, 45 watt, 1956	8	12	32
No. 1016, Transformer, 35 watt, 1959	6	12	30
No. 1018, Track, O27, straight, half section, 1968	NPF	NPF	1
No. 1020, 90 Degrees Crossing, O27, 1955	1	2	6
No. 1022, Switch, O27, manual, price per pair, 1955	8	12	25
No. 1023, 45 Degree Crossing, O27, each, 1955	1	2	3
No. 1025, Bumper, O27, 1946	6	10	15
No. 1025, Transformer, 45 watt, 1961	12	18	30
No. 1026, Transformer, 25 watt, 1963	5	7	12
No. 1032, Transformer, 90 watt, 1948	30	40	60
No. 1033, Transformer, 90 watt, 1948	40	55	75
No. 1034, Transformer, 75 watt, 1948	28	35	55
No. 1035, Transformer, 60 watt, 1947	12	18	25
No. 1043, Transformer, 60 watt, 1953	10	15	20
No. 1043, Transformer, 50 watt, black, 1953-1957	12	20	35
No. 1043-500FX, Girls Train Transformer, 60 watt, ivory case, 1957	55	75	115
No. 1044, Transformer, 90 watt, 1957	30	40	65
No. 1047, Switchman, w/flat, 1959-1961	50	80	150
No. 1053, Transformer, 60 watt, 1956	30	45	60
No. 1055, Locomotive, O, Alco A diesel, Texas Special, uncataloged, 1960	20	32	65
No. 1060, Locomotive, O27, Scout team, 2-4-2, w/1050T tender, uncataloged, 1960	12	20	30
No. 1061, Locomotive, O27, 2-4-2, steam, w/1061T tender, 1969	12	20	30
No. 1062, Locomotive, O27, 2-4-2, w/1062T tender, 1963	12	19	38
No. 1063, Transformer, 75 watt, 1961	18	25	55
No. 1065, Locomotive, O, Alco A unit only, diesel, Union Pacific, uncataloged, 1961	35	55	90
No. 1066, Locomotive, O, Alco A unit only, diesel, Union Pacific, uncataloged, 1964	50	75	105
No. 1073, Transformer, 60 watt, 1961	20	25	55
No. 1101, Locomotive, O, 2-4-2, steam, 1948	15	25	50
No. 1110, Locomotive, O27, 2-4-2, scout steam, 1949	14	23	45
No. 1120, Locomotive, O27, 2-4-2, scout steam, 1950	15	25	50

No. 414 State Car, $2000.

Post-WWII (1945-1969)

	C6	C8	C10
No. 1122, Switches, O27, remote control, 1952	17	26	35
No. 1122-100, Switch Control, O27, 1957	3	4	5
No. 1122-234, Insulating Pins, O27, 1957	NPF	NPF	1
No. 1122-520, Adapter Kit, O27, 1957.	5	8	10
No. 1130, Locomotive, O27, 2-4-2, steam, w/1130T tender, 1953	16	13	35
No. 1144, Transformer, 75 watt, 1968	22	33	45
No. 1615, Locomotive, O27, 0-4-0, w/1615T tender, switcher, 1955	85	145	200
No. 1625, Locomotive, O27, 0-4-0, steam, switcher, w/1625 tender, 1958	90	150	250
No. 1640-100, Presidential Kit, 1960	80	90	100
No. 1654, Locomotive, O27, 2-4-2, steam, w/1654W tender, 1946	30	50	100
No. 1655, Locomotive, O27, 2-4-2, steam, w/6654W tender, 1945	45	75	150
No. 1656, Locomotive, O27, 0-4-0, steam, switcher, w/6403 tender, 1948	110	185	370
No. 1665, Locomotive, O27, 0-4-0, steam, switcher w/2403B tender, 1946	125	210	420
No. 1862LT, Locomotive, O27, 4-4-0, steam, Civil War, w/1862T tender, marked "General", 1959	100	160	225
No. 1865, Coach, O27, Western & Atlantic, 1959	20	34	68
No. 1866, Baggage Car, O27, Western & Atlantic, 1959	30	50	100
No. 1872, Locomotive, Super O, 4-4-0, steam, w/1872W tender, Civil War, marked "General", 1959	100	200	300
No. 1875, Coach, Super O, Western & Atlantic, 1959	125	150	250
No. 1875W, Coach, Super O, Western & Atlantic, w/whistle, 1959	85	125	200
No. 1876, Baggage Car, Super O, Western & Atlantic, 1959	36	60	120
No. 1877, Flatcar, O27, part of general set, w/six horses, 1959	30	50	80

Post-WWII (1945-1969)

	C6	C8	C10
No. 1882, Locomotive, Super O, steam, Sears production, Civil War General, 4-4-0, also called Halloween General, uncataloged, 1959	200	300	500
No. 1885, Coach, Super O, Sears production, Western & Atlantic, uncataloged, 1959	95	150	275
No. 1887, Flatcar, O27, Sears production, w/six horses, uncataloged, 1959	80	130	180
No. 1946, Lionel Folder, 1946	12	20	40
No. 2016, Locomotive, O27, 2-6-4, steam, w/6026W tender, 1955	60	100	200
No. 2018, Locomotive, O27, 2-6-4, steam, w/6026W tender, 1956	60	85	120
No. 2020, Locomotive, O27, 6-8-6, steam, w/2020W, 2466WX or 6020W tender, 1946	100	140	210
No. 2023, Locomotive, O27, UP Alco AA, diesel, yellow body w/gray roof or silver body w/gray roof, 1950	90	155	310
No. 2023, Color Variation, yellow body w/gray roof and gray nose, 1950	900	1500	3000
No. 2024, Locomotive, O27, Alco A, diesel, C&O, 1969	30	45	80
No. 2025, Locomotive, O27, 2-6-2, steam, w/6466WX or 6466W tender, 1947	70	100	175
No. 2026, Locomotive, O27, 2-6-2, steam, w/6466WX or 6466W tender, 1948	60	80	135
No. 2026-58, Bulb, 18 volt, clear, 1950	NPF	NPF	1
No. 2028, Locomotive, O27, diesel, GP-7 PRR, Tuscan brown, 1955	140	375	500
No. 2029, Locomotive, O, 2-6-4, steam, w/243W tender, 1964	70	90	125
No. 2031, Locomotive, O27, R.I. Alco AA, diesel, black body w/red middle stripe, 1952	150	275	410
No. 2032, Locomotive, O27, Erie Alco AA, diesel, black body w/yellow middle stripe, 1952	125	150	275
No. 2033, Locomotive, O27, U.P. Alco AA, diesel, silver body, 1952	155	200	350
No. 2034, Locomotive, O27, 2-4-2, steam, 1952	36	60	120

No. 1835E 2-4-2 Locomotive and No. 348T tender; No. 1766 Pullman; No. 1767 Baggage; No. 1768 Observation c. 1934-40. Photo courtesy Robert C. Eldred Co. Inc.

Post-WWII (1945-1969)	C6	C8	C10
No. 2035, Locomotive, O27, 2-6-4, steam, w/2466W tender, 1950	65	95	190
No. 2036, Locomotive, O27, 2-6-4, steam, w/6466W tender, 1950	65	90	150
No. 2037, Locomotive, O27, 2-6-4, steam, w/6026W or 6026T tender, 1953	60	90	125
No. 2037-500, Girl's Locomotive, O27, 2-6-4, steam, pink, 1957	360	600	1200
No. 2041, Locomotive, O27, R.I., Alco AA, diesel, black body w/white stripe, 1969	60	85	120
No. 2046, Locomotive, O27, 4-6-4, steam, w/2046W tender, 1950	135	185	270
No. 2055, Locomotive, O27, 4-6-4, steam, w/1025W or 2046W tender, 1953	75	130	220
No. 2056, Locomotive, O27, 4-6-4, steam, w/2046W tender, 1952	105	175	250
No. 2065, Locomotive, O27, 4-6-4, steam, 2046W or 6026W tender, 1954	100	150	225
No. 2240, Locomotive, O27, Wabash F-3 AB, diesel, gray and blue shell, single motor, 1956	400	600	800
No. 2242, Locomotive, O27, New Haven F-3 AB, diesel, checkerboard scheme, silver and black, single motor, 1958	500	800	1200
No. 2243, Locomotive, O27, Santa Fe F-3 AB, diesel, silver shell, red nose, single motor, 1955	300	400	495
No. 2245, Locomotive, O27, Texas Special F-3 AB, diesel red shell, single motor, 1954	300	400	700
No. 2257, Caboose, non-illuminated, w/red plastic smokestack, 1947	175	300	400
No. 2321, Locomotive, O, Lackawanna, diesel, double motor, gray, 1954	300	390	550
No. 2321, Locomotive, O, Lackawanna, diesel, gray w/maroon roof, 1954	400	600	800
No. 2322, Locomotive, O, Virginian, diesel, double motor, yellow w/blue roof, 1965	300	495	635

Post-WWII (1945-1969)	C6	C8	C10
No. 2328, Locomotive, O27, Burlington, diesel, silver shell, 1955	200	300	435
No. 2329, Locomotive, O, Virginian, electric, blue shell w/yellow striping, 1958	315	540	750
No. 2330, Locomotive, O, New Brunswick Green, GG-I, electric, double motor, green w/five gold stripes, 1950	625	900	1550
No. 2331, Locomotive, O, Virginian, diesel, double motor, yellow shell w/black stripe and gold lettering, 1955	720	1150	1400
No. 2331, Locomotive, Virginian, diesel, yellow shell w/blue stripe and yellow lettering, 1955	600	900	1200
No. 2331, Locomotive, Virginian, diesel, yellow w/black roof, 1955	720	1150	1500
No. 2332, Locomotive, New Brunswick GG-I, electric, single motor, green w/five gold stripes, 1947	320	450	880
No. 2332, Locomotive, GG-I, electric, five silver stripes, 1947	900	1400	2000
No. 2332, Locomotive, GG-I, electric, satin black w/five gold or silver stripes, 1947	510	850	1700
No. 2333, Locomotive, O, Santa Fe or NYC F-3 AA, diesel, silver w/red nose, 1948	425	750	1000
No. 2333, Locomotive, O, NYC F-3 AA, diesel, gray, 1948	425	750	1000
No. 2333, Locomotive, O, NYC F-3 AA, diesel, 1948	300	500	1000
No. 2337, Locomotive, O27, Wabash, GP-7, diesel, blue and gray body w/white striping, 1958	110	200	315
No. 2338, Locomotive, O27, Milwaukee Rd. GP-7, diesel, black and orange, 1955	150	200	260
No. 2339, Locomotive, O, Wabash GP-7, diesel, blue and gray w/white striping, 1957	165	210	325

No. 2349 Locomotive, Northern Pacific

Post-WWII (1945-1969)	C6	C8	C10
No. 2340-1, Locomotive, O, GG-1, electric, maroon, double motor, Tuscan brown, w/five stripes, 1955	700	1000	1800
No. 2340-25, Locomotive, O, New Brunswick, GG-1, electric, double motor, green w/five stripes, 1955	650	950	1700
No. 2341, Locomotive, O, Jersey Central, diesel, double motor, orange body w/blue stripe, 1956	950	1300	2000
No. 2343, Locomotive, O, Santa Fe AA, F-3, diesel, double motor, silver w/red nose, 1950	350	400	675
No. 2343C, Locomotive, O, Santa Fe, diesel, 1950	100	200	295
No. 2344, Locomotive, O, NYC F-3 AA, diesel, double motor, gray, 1950	290	400	625
No. 2344C, Locomotive, O, NYC F-3 B, diesel, 1950	120	225	310
No. 2345, Locomotive, O, Western Pacific F-3 AA, diesel, double motor, silver and orange, screen roof, 1952	1100	1400	2075
No. 2345, Locomotive, O, Western Pacific F-3 AA, diesel, louvered roof, 1952	1100	1400	2075
No. 2346, Locomotive, O27, Boston and Maine GP-7, diesel, blue shell, black cab w/white trim, 1965	145	225	320
No. 2347, Locomotive, O27, C&O GP-7, diesel, Sears, blue shell w/yellow lettering, uncataloged, 1962	1350	2250	4500
No. 2348, Locomotive, diesel, GP-9, M.St.L., O27 red shell w/blue roof, 1958	175	275	425
No. 2349, Locomotive, O, diesel, GP-O, Northern Pacific, black shell, red striping w/gold lettering, 1959	200	295	415
No. 2350, Locomotive, O, New Haven, electric, black shell w/orange and white striping, 1956	220	370	515
No. 2351, Locomotive, O, electric, Milwaukee Rd., yellow shell w/black roof and red stripe, 1957	200	350	575
No. 2352, Locomotive, O, diesel, PRR, Tuscan brown, 1958	225	375	615
No. 2353, Locomotive, O, diesel AA, F-3, Santa Fe, double motor, silver w/red nose, 1953	270	400	640
No. 2353C, Locomotive, O, diesel, F-3, Santa Fe, 1954	120	200	400
No. 2354, Locomotive, O, diesel, AA, F-3, NYC, double motor, gray, 1953	270	425	720

Post-WWII (1945-1969)	C6	C8	C10
No. 2354C, Locomotive, O, diesel, B, F-3, NYC, 1954	80	133	265
No. 2355, Locomotive, O, diesel, AA, F-3, Western Pacific, double motor, silver and orange, 1953	800	1300	1900
No. 2356, Locomotive, O, diesel, AA, F-3, Southern RY, double motor, green, 1954	500	1100	1400
No. 2356C, Locomotive, O, diesel, B, F-3, Southern Ry,, 1954	150	250	500
No. 2357, Caboose, O, 1948	12	20	40
No. 2358, Locomotive, O, Great Northern, electric, orange and green shell, yellow stripes, 1959	360	750	1200
No. 2359, Locomotive, O27, B&M GP-9, diesel, blue shell w/black cab and white trim, 1961	185	200	300
No. 2360-1, Locomotive, GG-1, electric, double motor, single stripe, Tuscan brown, decal letters and numbers rubber stamped stripe, 1961	600	1050	1800
No. 2360-1, Locomotive, GG-1, electric, heavy heat stamped letters and numbers, 1961	225	373	745
No. 2360-1, Locomotive, GG-1, electric, light pressed letters and numbers, rubber stamped stripe, 1961	600	1000	2000
No. 2360-10, Locomotive, O, GG-1, electric, double motor, five stripes, Tuscan brown, heat-stamped letter and number, five rubber stamped stripes, 1956	750	1250	2500
No. 2360-25, Locomotive, O, New Brunswick GG-1, electric, double motor, green, heat stamped letters and numbers, five rubber stamped stripes, 1956	575	1000	1300
No. 2363, Locomotive, O, Illinois Central F-3 AB, diesel, double motor, brown shell w/orange stripe and yellow trim, 1955	450	900	1350
No. 2365, Locomotive, O27, C&O GP-7, diesel, blue shell, 1962	135	250	400
No. 2367, Locomotive, O, Wabash F-3 AB, diesel, double motor, gray and blue shell w/white stripe and trim, 1955	400	800	1200
No. 2368, Locomotive, O, B&O F-3 AB, diesel, double motor, blue shell w/black, white and yellow trim, 1956	800	1750	2500
No. 2373, Locomotive, Super O, Canadian Pacific AA F-3, diesel, double motor, gray and maroon w/yellow trim, 1957	950	1500	2100

Post-WWII (1945-1969)

	C6	C8	C10
No. 2378, Locomotive, O, Milwaukee Rd. F-3 AB, diesel, double motor, gray w/orange stripe, 1956	1000	1700	2400
No. 2379, Locomotive, Super O, Rio Grande AB F-3, diesel, double motor, yellow body w/silver roof and stripe, 1957	600	800	1100
No. 2383, Locomotive, Super O, Santa Fe AA, F-3, diesel, double motor, silver w/red nose, 1958	300	500	650
No. 2400, Pullman, O27, Maplewood, green shell w/gray roof and yellow trim, 1948	60	85	150
No. 2401, Observation Car, O27, Hillside, 1948	60	85	150
No. 2402, Pullman, O27, Chatham, 1948	60	85	150
No. 2404, Vista Dome, O27, Santa Fe, aluminum, blue lettering, 1964	30	50	70
No. 2405, Pullman, O27, Santa Fe, aluminum, blue lettering, 1964	30	50	70
No. 2406, Observation Car, Santa Fe, aluminum, blue lettering, 1964	30	50	70
No. 2408, Vista Dome, O27, Santa Fe, aluminum, blue lettering, 1964	35	60	75
No. 2409, Pullman, O27, Santa Fe, aluminum, blue lettering, 1964	35	60	75
No. 2410, Observation Car, Santa Fe, aluminum, blue lettering, 1964	35	60	75
No. 2411, Flatcar, O27, w/load of pipes, gray metal frame, 1946	50	70	90
No. 2412, Vista Dome, O27, silver, blue stripe through windows, illuminated, 1959	35	58	115
No. 2414, Pullman, O27, silver, blue stripe through windows, illuminated, 1959	35	58	115
No. 2416, Observation Car, O27, silver, blue stripe through windows, illuminated, 1959	27	45	90
No. 2419, Wrecker Caboose, O27, DL&W, gray metal frame w/gray cab, 1946	27	45	90
No. 2420, Wrecker Caboose, O, DL&W, w/light, gray metal frame w/gray cab, 1946	40	70	100
No. 2420-20, Bulb, 14 volt-clear, 1946.	NPF	NPF	1
No. 2421, Pullman, O27, aluminum, gray roof w/black stripe, 1950	40	60	95
No. 2421, Pullman, O27, silver roof, no stripe, 1950	40	50	75
No. 2422, Pullman, O27, aluminum, gray roof w/black stripe, 1950	40	60	85
No. 2422, Pullman, O27, silver roof, no stripe, 1950	18	30	60
No. 2423, Observation Car, O27, aluminum, gray roof w/black stripe, 1950.	40	60	100
No. 2423, Observation Car, O27, silver roof, no stripe, 1950	40	50	75
No. 2426, WX Tender, O, 1946	87	145	290
No. 2429, Pullman, O27, aluminum, gray roof w/black stripe, 1952	50	85	120
No. 2429, Pullman, O27, silver roof, no stripe, 1952	50	85	120

Post-WWII (1945-1969)

	C6	C8	C10
No. 2430, Pullman, O27, sheet metal, blue w/silver roof, 1946	20	45	65
No. 2431, Observation Car, O27, sheet metal, blue w/silver roof, 1946	20	45	90
No. 2432, Vista Dome, O27, silver, red lettering reads "Clifton", 1954	24	40	80
No. 2434, Pullman, O27, silver, red lettering reads "Newark", 1954	24	40	80
No. 2435, Pullman, O27, silver, red lettering reads "Elizabeth", 1954	30	40	75
No. 2436, Observation Car, O27, silver, red lettering "Summit", 1954	25	42	85
No. 2436, Observation Car, O27, "Mooseheart", 1954	25	42	85
No. 2440, Pullman, O27, blue w/silver roof, 1946	21	35	70
No. 2440, Pullman, O27, green w/dark green roof, 1946	21	35	70
No. 2441, Observation Car, O27, blue w/silver roof, 1946	21	35	70
No. 2441, Observation Car, O27, green w/dark green roof, 1946	21	35	70
No. 2442, Pullman, O27, sheet metal, brown, 1946	36	60	120
No. 2442, Vista Dome, O27, aluminum, red window stripe, marked "Clifton", 1956	45	75	100
No. 2443, Observation Car, O, sheet metal, brown, 1956	27	45	90
No. 2444, Pullman, O, aluminum, red window stripe, 1956	45	75	140
No. 2452, Gondola, O27, "Pennsylvania", 1945	8	12	25
No. 2452X, Gondola, O27, "Pennsylvania", 1946	11	19	38
No. 2454, Boxcar, O27, "Baby Ruth", 1946	9	15	30
No. 2454, Boxcar, O27, "Pennsylvania", 1946	60	100	160
No. 2456, Hopper, O, Lehigh Valley, 1948	8	14	27
No. 2457, Caboose, O, N5 type, "Pennsylvania", 1945-1947	15	25	50
No. 2458, Boxcar, O, automatic, double door, "Pennsylvania", 1945	20	33	65
No. 2460, Operating Crane, O, Bucyrus Erie, 1946	35	50	85
No. 2461, Transformer Car, O27, metal, gray frame, 1947	36	60	120
No. 2465, Tank Car, O27, double dome, Sunoco logo, 1946	5	10	17
No. 2472, Caboose, O27, N5 type, "Pennsylvania", 1946	10	18	35
No. 2481, Pullman, O27, illuminated, yellow w/red stripes and gray roof, Anniversary Set, 1950	105	150	275
No. 2482, Pullman, O27, illuminated, yellow w/red stripes and gray roof, Anniversary Set, 1950	105	150	275
No. 2483, Observation Car, O27, illuminated, yellow w/red stripes and gray roof, Anniversary Set, 1950	85	125	230

No. 52 Fire Fighting car, $300. Photo courtesy Steve Hintze

Post-WWII (1945-1969)	C6	C8	C10
No. 2521, Observation Car, Super O, "Pres. McKinley," illuminated, extruded aluminum shell, gold stripe, 1962	80	125	180
No. 2522, Vista Dome, Super O, "Pres. Harrison," extruded aluminum shell, illuminated, gold stripe, 1962	80	125	180
No. 2523, Pullman, Super O, "Pres. Garfield," illuminated, extruded aluminum shell, gold stripe, 1962	80	125	185
No. 2530, Baggage Car, O, Railway Express Agency, extruded aluminum shell, large door, 1956	250	400	550
No. 2530, Baggage Car, O, small doors, 1956	125	175	225
No. 2531, Observation Car, O, extruded aluminum shell, illuminated, marked "Silver Dawn", 1952	65	85	110
No. 2532, Vista Dome, O, marked "Silver Range", 1952	65	85	115
No. 2533, Pullman, O, marked "Silver Cloud", 1952	65	85	110
No. 2534, Pullman, O, marked "Silver Bluff", 1952	75	100	140
No. 2541, Observation Car, O, Penn., illuminated, extruded aluminum, brown stripes, marked "Alexander Hamilton", 1955	75	123	245
No. 2542, Vista Dome, O, Penn., marked "Betsy Ross", 1955	75	123	245
No. 2543, Pullman, O, Penn., marked "William Penn", 1955	120	200	400
No. 2544, Pullman, O, Penn., marked "Molly Pitcher", 1955	120	200	400
No. 2550, Budd R.D.C. Mail Baggage Trailer, O, Baltimore and Ohio dummy to match motorized Budd 404, silver shell w/blue lettering, 1957	200	350	575

Post-WWII (1945-1969)	C6	C8	C10
No. 2551, Observation Car, Super O, extruded aluminum shell, illuminated, two brown stripes, top Canadian Pacific, bottom, name of car, "Banff Park", 1957	100	150	265
No. 2552, Vista Dome, Super O, "Skyline 500", 1957	100	150	375
No. 2553, Pullman, Super O, "Blair Manor", 1957	175	250	500
No. 2554, Pullman, Super O, "Graig Manor", 1957	150	225	350
No. 2555, Tank-One-Dome, O, 1945	17	28	55
No. 2559, Budd Car Coach, O, Baltimore & Ohio, silver shell, blue lettering, dummy to match motorized 400 Budd, 1957	150	200	350
No. 2560, Crane, O27, marked "Lionel Lines", 1946	30	50	100
No. 2561, Observation Car, O, extruded aluminum shell, marked "Santa Fe Set, Vista Valley", 1959	100	150	260
No. 2562, Vista Dome, O, marked "Royal Pass", 1959	125	200	310
No. 2563, Pullman, O, marked "Indian Falls", 1959	125	200	310
No. 2625, Pullman, O, Irvington, Bakelite, Tuscan brown, 1946	95	150	220
No. 2625, Pullman, O, Manhattan, 1946	112	188	375
No. 2625, Pullman, O, Madison, 1946	95	175	250
No. 2627, Pullman, O, Madison, Bakelite, Tuscan brown, 1946	95	150	220
No. 2628, Pullman, O, Manhattan, Bakelite, Tuscan brown, 1946	95	150	245
No. 2855, Tank Car, O, one-dome, black, S.U.N.X., 1946	62	103	205
No. 2855, Tank Car, O, gray, 1946	59	98	195
No. 3330, Flatcar, O, w/submarine, 1960	24	40	80
No. 3330-100, Operating Submarine Kit, O27, 1960	100	150	200
No. 3349, Turbo Missile Firing Car, O, 1960	17	28	55

Post-WWII (1945-1969)

	C6	C8	C10
No. 3356, Operating Horse Car, O, w/horses and corral, 1956	40	68	135
No. 3356-2, Operating Horse Car, O, green, car alone, 1956	40	70	100
No. 3356-100, Set of Nine Horses, O, black horses, 1956	6	10	20
No. 3356-150, Horse Corral, O, white fencing, corral only, 1956	52	60	80
No. 3357, Operating Cop and Hobo Car, O, blue boxcar w/hydraulic lift and figures, 1962	30	50	100
No. 3359, Operating Dump Car, O, two gray dump bins, 1955	18	35	55
No. 3360, Operating Burro Crane, O, yellow cab and boom, motorized, including track trips, 1956	150	265	340
No. 3361, Lumber Car, O, operating, 1955	20	30	55
No. 3362, Helium Tank Car, O, operating, green frame, 1961	20	32	64
No. 3364, Log Dump Car, O, operating, green frame, 1966	18	33	65
No. 3366, Circus Car, O, operating, white stock car, nine horses, white, and corral, 1959	125	150	250
No. 3366-100, White Horses, O, set of nine, 1959	9	15	30
No. 3370, Sheriff and Outlaw Car, O, operating, green stock car, 1961	25	43	85
No. 3376, Giraffe Car, O, operating, blue stock car, including track trips, w/teletails and poles, 1960	20	30	55
No. 3376, Giraffe Car, O, operating, green stock car, 1960	36	75	125
No. 3410, Helicopter Launching Car, O, operating, blue flat w/helicopter, 1961	45	80	150
No. 3413-150, Mercury Capsule Launching Car, O, red flat, gray platform, 1961	65	110	175
No. 3419, Helicopter Launching Car, O, operating, blue flat w/helicopter, 1959	40	75	110
No. 3424, Brakeman Car Set, O, operating, blue boxcar, set of track trips and teletails w/poles, 1956	30	50	80
No. 3424-100, Low Bridge Warning Poles, O, w/track clips, set of two, 1956	15	25	30
No. 3428, Mail Car, O, operating, red white and blue boxcar, man dumps mail bag, 1959	48	80	160
No. 3429, U.S.M.C. Helicopter Car, O, olive frame, 1960	200	325	465
No. 3434, Chicken Sweeper Car, O, brown stock car, man at door sweeps back and forth, 1959	50	75	105
No. 3435, Aquarium Car, O, operating, green box w/four clear windows, fish move around on two spindles, 1959	100	175	250
No. 3435, Aquarium Car, O, operating, green boxcar, gold letters marked "Tank 1" and "Tank 2", 1959	400	600	1000

Post-WWII (1945-1969)

	C6	C8	C10
No. 3444, Animated Hobo Gondola, O, red gondola, cop chases hobo around freight load, marked "Erie", 1957	30	45	80
No. 3451, Operating Lumber Car, O, operating, black die-cast base, black platform w/log stacks, 1946	14	23	45
No. 3454, Merchandise Car, O, operating, silver boxcar, discharges five brown cubes, 1946	65	100	130
No. 3456, Hopper Car, O, operating, black, "N&W," drops ore, 1950	17	28	55
No. 3459, Dump Car, O, operating, die-cast frame, black, 1946	24	40	80
No. 3459, Dump Car, O, operating, silver, 1946	93	155	310
No. 3459, Dump Car, O, operating, green, 1946	25	43	85
No. 3460, Piggyback Flatcar, O, red flat w/two trailer containers, 1955	22	45	65
No. 3461, Lumber Car, O, operating, black die-cast frame, 1949	11	25	35
No. 3461, Lumber Car, O, operating, green frame, 1949	17	30	55
No. 3462, Milk Car Set, O, white boxcar, platform, green base, five cans, man discharges cans onto platform, 1947	20	40	55
No. 3462-70, Milk Cans, set of five, 1952	6	8	10
No. 3462P, Milk Car Platform, O, 1952	8	15	75
No. 3464, Boxcar, O, operating, Santa Fe, orange shell, black doors, plunger mechanism opens door w/man, 1949	12	20	40
No. 3464, Boxcar, O, operating, NYC, brown shell, black doors, plunger mechanism opens door w/man, 1952	11	18	35
No. 3469, Dump Car, O, operating, black die-cast frame, 1949	18	30	60
No. 3470, Aerial Target Launching Car, O, blue flatcar, white top shell, blue balloon carriage, batter operation inflates balloons, 1962	30	50	75
No. 3472, Milk Car Set, O27, operating, white boxcar, five cans, man discharges cans onto platform, green base, 1949	20	35	60
No. 3474, Boxcar, O27, operating, W.P., silver box, yellow feather, plunger mechanism, 1952	27	45	90
No. 3482, Milk Car Set, O, operating, white boxcar, man discharges cans onto platform, green base, five cans, 1954	24	40	80
No. 3484, Boxcar, O, operating, Pennsylvania, Tuscan brown, plunger mechanism, 1953	18	35	60
No. 3484-25, Boxcar, O, operating, Santa Fe, orange shell, orange doors, plunger mechanism, 1954	33	60	110
No. 3494, Boxcar, O, operating, NYC Pacemaker, red and gray, red doors, plunger mechanism, 1955	40	75	110

No. 400E Locomotive, $3000.

Post-WWII (1945-1969)	C6	C8	C10
No. 3494-150, Boxcar, O, operating, MP, blue and gray, plunger mechanism, 1956	55	90	120
No. 3494-275, Boxcar, O, operating, B.A.R., State of Maine, red, white and blue, plunger mechanism, 1956	55	90	130
No. 3494-550, Boxcar, O, operating, Monon, maroon shell w/white stripe, plunger mechanism, 1957	125	225	400
No. 3494-625, Boxcar, O, Operating, Soo Line, Tuscan brown, plunger mechanism, 1957	120	210	400
No. 3509, Satellite Car, O, operating, green flat, black and silver satellite, yellow radar scope, manually operated, 1959	22	45	60
No. 3510, Satellite Car, O, operating, red flat, 1959	45	90	155
No. 3512, Fireman and Ladder Car, O, red frame and structure, black ladders, 1959	40	65	130
No. 3512, Fireman and Ladder Car, O, silver ladders, 1959	83	138	275
No. 3519, Automatic Satellite Car, O, remote track operated, 1961	20	30	55
No. 3520, Searchlight, O, gray die-cast frame, orange generator, 1952	30	40	58
No. 3530, G.M. Generator Car, O, blue boxcar w/white markings, transformer pole, remote searchlight, 1956	66	110	220
No. 3535, AEC Security Car, O, red shell, white lettering, gray gun and gray rotating searchlight, one man, 1960	35	80	125
No. 3540, Radar Scanning Car, O, operating, red flat, gray structure, yellow radar scope and silver radar antenna, revolving, 1959	39	85	135
No. 3545, TV Monitor Car, O, operating, black base, blue structure, yellow camera and screen, two men, 1961	53	110	175
No. 3559, Ore Dump Car, O, operating, black die-cast frame, 1946	15	28	45
No. 3562, Barrel Car, O, operating, black, six wood barrels, 1954	75	100	180
No. 3562-25, Barrel Car, O, operating, gray, blue lettering, 1954	25	40	55
No. 3562-25, Barrel Car, O, operating, red lettering, 1954	150	250	500

Post-WWII (1945-1969)	C6	C8	C10
No. 3562-50, Barrel Car, O, operating, yellow, 1955	35	50	85
No. 3562-75, Barrel Car, O, operating, orange, 1958	35	50	92
No. 3619, Reconnaissance Helicopter Car, O, yellow shell, black double door, w/helicopter, 1962	38	63	125
No. 3620, Searchlight, O, gray die-cast frame, orange generator, 1954	25	35	45
No. 3650, Searchlight Extension Car, O, gray die-cast frame, gray generator, remote searchlight w/wire, 1956	40	50	80
No. 3656, Cattle Car, O, operating, orange stock car, set includes car, cattle and corral, white lettering reads "Armour", 1950	35	50	85
No. 3656, Cattle Car, O, operating, black lettering, 1950	120	200	400
No. 3656-34, Cattle Set, O, black, set of nine, 1952	10	15	20
No. 3656-150, Cattle Car Platform, O, green base, ivory fencing, 1952	45	55	75
No. 3662, Operating, O, operating, white shell, brown roof, includes five cans and platform, 1955	30	50	70
No. 3662-79, Milk Cans, O, set of five, 1955	6	9	12
No. 3665, Minuteman Missile Car, O, operating, white shell, blue double door roof, w/missile, 1961	50	80	115
No. 3666, Marine Missile Car, O, operating, Sears, white shell, blue double door roof, w/missile, 1960	170	350	535
No. 3672, Bosco Boxcar, O, operating, yellow shell and brown roof, set includes seven Bosco cans and brown and yellow platform, 1959	120	265	430
No. 3672-79, Bosco Cans, O, brown and yellow, set of seven, 1959	35	75	125
No. 3820, Submarine Car, O, operating, olive, "U.S.M.C.," gray, 1960	120	200	400
No. 3830, Submarine Car, O, operating, blue, marked "Lionel," w/gray submarine, 1960	29	48	95
No. 3854, Merchandise Car, O, operating, Tuscan brown, doors open and eject five merchandise cubes, 1946	200	400	600
No. 3927, Track Cleaner Car, O, orange shell, motor-operated cleaning disk, includes two gray washol containers, 1956	60	80	120

Post-WWII (1945-1969)

	C6	C8	C10
No. 3927-50, Track Cleaner Pads, O, package of twenty-five, 1956	5	10	25
No. 4357, Caboose, O, Pennsylvania N5 type, electronic, metal, green and white, "Electronic Control" decal, red, 1948	68	112	225
No. 4452, Gondola, O, electronic, black, Pennsylvania, 1946	42	75	140
No. 4454, Boxcar, electronic, Baby Ruth, P.R.R., orange w/brown doors, 1946	90	150	300
No. 4457, Caboose, O, electronic, 1946	45	80	165
No. 4671, Locomotive, O, 6-8-0, steam, electronic, 4671W tender, 1946	130	220	315
No. 5100, Roadway, O, straight, 1963 ..	NPF	NPF	1
No. 5101, Roadway, O, straight, 1963 ..	NPF	NPF	1
No. 5102, Railroad and Roadway Crossway, O, 1963	NPF	NPF	1
No. 5103, Roadway, O, straight, w/power connection, 1963	NPF	NPF	1
No. 5104, Lane Change Over, O, 1963 .	NPF	NPF	1
No. 5105, Roadway Intersection, O, 1963	NPF	NPF	1
No. 5106, Inner Roadway, O, curved, 1963	NPF	NPF	1
No. 5107, Inner Roadway, O, curved, 1963	NPF	NPF	1
No. 5108, Outer Roadway, O, curved, 1963	NPF	NPF	1
No. 5109, Outer Roadway, O, curved, 1963	NPF	NPF	1
No. 5150, Banking Set, 1963	5	8	15
No. 5151, Trestle Set, O, 1963	5	8	15
No. 5152, Guard Rail and Flag Set, O, 1963	5	8	15
No. 5154, Electric Lap Counter, O, 1963	5	8	15
No. 5155, Pacesetter Timer, O, 1963	5	8	15
No. 5156-24, Rail Clips, O, 1963	2	3	4
No. 5157-34, Roadway Clips, o, 1963 ..	2	3	4
No. 5158, Barrels, 1963	2	3	4
No. 5159, Lubrication Kit, 1963	3	4	5
No. 5159-50, Lubrication Kit, 1968	3	4	5
No. 5160, Official Viewing Stand, 1963	10	15	20
No. 5163, Maintenance Kit, 1965	3	4	6
No. 5200, Ferrari Racing Car, O, 1963 .	6	9	12
No. 5201, "D" Jaguar Racing Car, O, 1963	6	9	12
No. 5202, Corvette Racing Car, O, 1963	6	9	12
No. 5210, Cooper Racing Car, O, 1963	6	9	12
No. 5211, B.R.M. Racing Car, O, 1963	6	9	12
No. 5222, Cooper Racing Car, O, 1964	6	9	12
No. 5223, Corvette Racing Car, O, 1964	6	9	12
No. 5230, Ferrari Racing Car, O, 1964 .	6	9	12
No. 5231, B.R.M. Racing Car, O, 1964	6	9	12
No. 5232, "D" Jaguar Racing Car, O, 1964	6	9	12
No. 5233, Ford Racing Car, O, 1964	6	9	12
No. 5234, Buick Racing Car, O, 1964 ..	6	9	12
No. 5235, Jaguar XKE Racing Car, O, 1964	6	9	12

Post-WWII (1945-1969)

	C6	C8	C10
No. 5236, Buick Riviera Racing Car, O, 1964	6	9	12
No. 5237, Buick Riviera Racing Car, O, 1964	6	9	12
No. 5238, Ford Racing Car, O, 1964	6	9	12
No. 5239, Ford Convertible Racing Car, O, 1964	7	11	15
No. 5240, Ford Police Racing Car, O, 1964	7	11	15
No. 5242, Conversion Kit, 1966	5	9	18
No. 5300, Racemaster Power Pack, 1963	7	11	15
No. 5302, Racemaster Power Pack, 1965	7	11	15
No. 5304, HO Control Transformer, 1965	5	9	18
No. 5310, Touch-A-Matic Speed Control, 1963	3	6	9
No. 5320, Touch-A-Matic Speed Control, 1963	3	6	9
No. 5321, Touch-A-Matic Speed Control, 1965	3	6	9
No. 5322, Touch-A-Matic Speed Control, 1965	3	6	9
No. 5400, Straight Roadway, HO, 1963	NPF	NPF	1
No. 5401, Straight Roadway, HO, w/power connector, 1963	NPF	NPF	1
No. 5402, Railroad and Roadway Crossing, HO, 1963	NPF	1	2
No. 5403, Roadway Intersection, HO, 1963	NPF	1	2
No. 5404, Lane Change Over, HO, 1963	NPF	1	2
No. 5405, Roadway, HO, curved, 1963	NPF	NPF	1
No. 5406, Roadway, HO, curved, 45 degree, 1963	NPF	NPF	1
No. 5407, Inner Roadway, HO, curved, 90 degree, 1963	NPF	NPF	1
No. 5408, Outer Roadway, HO, curved, 45 degree, 1963	NPF	NPF	1
No. 5409, Inner Roadway, HO, curved, 45 degree, 1963	NPF	NPF	1
No. 5410, Roadway, HO, straight, 1963	NPF	NPF	1
No. 5411, Roadway, HO, straight, 1963	NPF	NPF	1
No. 5412, Roadway, HO, straight, 1963	NPF	NPF	1
No. 5415, Roadway, HO, straight, w/power connection, 1963	NPF	NPF	1
No. 5421, Touch-A-Matic Speed Controller, HO, 1965	5	8	10
No. 5422, Touch-A-Matic Speed Controller, HO, 1965	5	8	10
No. 5425, Loop-the-Loop Kit, HO, 1960	10	15	20
No. 5430, Universal Roadway Kit, HO, 1966	9	14	18
No. 5431, Mystery Route Selector, HO, 1966	5	10	15
No. 5433, Car Lane Controller, HO, 1965	6	9	13
No. 5434, Car Lane Controller, HO, 1965	6	9	13
No. 5450, Trestle Set, HO, 1963	4	6	8

Top row, left to right: No. 514 Refrigerator car, $175; No. 517 Caboose, $300. Middle row, left to right: No. 512 Gondola, $75; No. 515 Tank car, $180; No. 516 Hopper, $240. Bottom row, left to right: No. 390E Locomotive, $1000. Photo courtesy PB Eighty-Four, New York

Post-WWII (1945-1969)	C6	C8	C10
No. 5455, Car Lane Controller, HO, 1966	6	9	13
No. 5457, Relay Kit, HO, 1966	10	15	20
No. 5459, Dump Car, O, operating, electronic, black, "Lionel Lines", 1948	55	115	175
No. 5478, Guard Rail and Flag Set, HO, 1966	10	15	20
No. 5511, Tie-Jector, O, 1958-1961	51	85	170
No. 5531, Buick Riviera Racing Car, HO, 1965	3	5	10
No. 5532, Buick Patrol Racing Car, HO, 1965	3	5	10
No. 5533, Ford Hardtop Racing Car, HO, 1965	3	5	10
No. 5534, Ford Convertible Racing Car, HO, 1965	3	5	10
No. 5535, Ford Police Racing Car, HO, 1965	3	5	10

Post-WWII (1945-1969)	C6	C8	C10
No. 5537, Rolls Royce Racing Car, HO, 1965	3	5	10
No. 5538, Bentley Racing Car, HO, 1965	3	5	10
No. 5539, Jaguar XKE Racing Car, HO, 1965	3	5	10
No. 5540, Car Lane Control Car, HO, Thunderbird, 1965	4	6	12
No. 5541, Car Lane Control Car, HO, Jaguar XKE, 1965	4	6	12
No. 5542, Car Lane Control Car, HO, Thunderbird, 1965	4	6	12
No. 5767-15, Valise Carrying Pack, HO, 1961	8	13	25
No. 6002, Gondola, O27, NYC, 1949 ...	5	9	18
No. 6004, Boxcar, O27, Baby Ruth, P.R.R., 1950	4	7	13
No. 6007, Caboose, O27, Lionel Lines, SP type, 1950	3	5	10

Post-WWII (1945-1969)

	C6	C8	C10
No. 6009, Remote Control Track, O27, 1953	3	5	6
No. 6012, Gondola, O27, black, Lionel, 1955	3	4	8
No. 6014, Boxcar, O27, Air Ex., red, 1951	25	45	75
No. 6014, Boxcar, O27, Air Ex., blue, 1951	15	25	50
No. 6014, Boxcar, O27, Baby Ruth, P.R.R., 1955....................	5	8	10
No. 6014, Boxcar, O27, Frisco, 1957....	4	6	8
No. 6014, Boxcar, O27, Bosco, P.R.R., red or orange body, 1958	5	8	11
No. 6014-85, Boxcar, O27, Frisco, 1969	7	11	22
No. 6014-325, Boxcar, O27, Frisco, 1964	7	11	22
No. 6014-325, Frisco Savings Bank Car, O27, 1963	7	11	22
No. 6014-335, Boxcar, O27, Frisco, 1965	7	11	22
No. 6014-410, Boxcar, O27, Frisco, 1969	7	11	22
No. 6014-150, WIX Boxcar, cream/white, 1959	80	120	175
No. 6015, Tank Car, O27, Sunoco, silver, one dome, 1954	5	8	15
No. 6017, Caboose, O27, Lionel, brown, 1951	3	5	10
No. 6017-50, Caboose, O27, Marine, dark blue, 1958	20	30	55
No. 6017-100, Caboose, B&M, light blue, 1959	15	25	50
No. 6017-100, Caboose, B&M, dark blue, 1959	250	450	800
No. 6017-185, Caboose, O27, ATSF, gray, 1959	10	20	35
No. 6017-200, Caboose, O27, Navy, dark blue, 1960	35	50	85
No. 6017-225, Caboose, O27, ATSF, 1961	25	35	60
No. 6019, Remote Control Track, 1948	3	5	10
No. 6024, Boxcar, O27, Nabisco, 1957	12	20	28
No. 6024, Boxcar, O27, RCA-Whirlpool, red, uncataloged, 1957............	30	50	70
No. 6025, Tank Car, O27, Gulf, orange, 1956	9	15	29
No. 6025, Tank Car, O27, gray, 1956...	11	18	36
No. 6025, Tank Car, O27, black, 1956 .	5	8	15
No. 6027, Caboose, O27, Alaska, blue, 1959	25	45	80
No. 6029, Uncoupling Track Set, 1955.	3	5	6
No. 6032, Gondola, O27, black, "Lionel", 1952	2	4	6
No. 6034, Boxcar, O27, Baby Ruth, P.R.R., 1953....................	8	14	28
No. 6035, Tank Car, O27, gray, single dome, 1950	4	6	8
No. 6037, Caboose, O27, brown, marked "Lionel Lines", 1952	12	20	40
No. 6042, Gondola, O, marked "Lionel," uncataloged, 1959-1964 ...	2	4	7
No. 6044, Boxcar, O27, Airex, light blue, uncataloged, 1959-1960..........	12	20	40

Post-WWII (1945-1969)

	C6	C8	C10
No. 6045, Tank Car, O, green, Cities Service, uncataloged, 1960...............	12	20	35
No. 6047, Caboose, O27, marked "Lionel Lines", 1962	2	4	7
No. 6050, Savings Bank Car, O27, white and green, 1961......................	12	25	35
No. 6050, Savings Bank Car, O27, Libby Tomato Juice, Libby promotional car, uncataloged, 1961	18	30	50
No. 6050-100, Savings Bank Car, O27, Swift's, red, 1963............................	22	38	75
No. 6050-110, Savings Bank Car, O27, Swift's, red, 1962............................	22	38	75
No. 6057, Caboose, O27, Lionel Lines, red, 1959-1962..........................	3	4	10
No. 6057-50, Caboose, O27, H.H., orange, 1962	12	15	25
No. 6058, Caboose, O27, C&O, yellow, 1961	15	25	45
No. 6059-50, Caboose, O27, M&StL, maroon, 1961	8	13	25
No. 6059-60, Caboose, O27, M&StL, shiny or flat red, 1969....................	5	8	15
No. 6062, Gondola, O27, glossy black, 1959	7	12	18
No. 6076, Hopper, O27, A.T.S.F., gray, 1959	10	15	22
No. 6076-75, Hopper, O27, LV, gray or black or red, 1963	6	10	20
No. 6076-100, Hopper, O27, Lionel, 1963	6	10	20
No. 6110, Locomotive, O27, 2-4-2, steam, 1951	15	25	50
No. 6111, Flatcar, O27, w/logs or pipes, 1955	8	13	25
No. 6112, Gondola, O27, w/canisters, blue, marked "Lionel", 1956	3	5	9
No. 6112, Gondola, O27, w/canisters, white, 1956	15	25	50
No. 6112-25, Canisters, O27, white or red, set of four, 1956....................	5	10	15
No. 6119, Work Caboose, O27, 1955 ...	14	23	45
No. 6119-25, Work Caboose, O27, DL&W, 1957	10	15	30
No. 6119-100, Work Caboose, O27, DL&W, 1963	12	24	28
No. 6119-110, Work Caboose, O27, DL&W, 1964	12	24	28
No. 6121, Flatcar, O27, w/pipes, 1956..	5	8	16
No. 6130, Work Caboose, O27, Santa Fe, 1965	10	20	34
No. 6139, Uncoupling Track, O27, remote control, 1963....................	4	6	8
No. 6142, Gondola, O27, w/canisters, 1963	3	5	7
No. 6142-75, Gondola, O27, w/canisters, 1963	3	5	10
No. 6142-100, Gondola, O27, w/canisters, 1964	3	5	10
No. 6142-125, Gondola, O27, 1964	3	5	10
No. 6142-150, Gondola, O27, 1964	3	5	10

No. 217 Caboose, c. 1927-38

Post-WWII (1945-1969)

Post-WWII (1945-1969)	C6	C8	C10
No. 6149, Uncoupling Track, O27, remote control, 1964	3	5	10
No. 6151, Range Patrol, flatcar, cream, orange, yellow, 1958	40	80	120
No. 6157, Caboose, O27, brown, uncataloged, 1960s	3	5	10
No. 6162, Gondola, O27, w/canisters, NYC, red, 1963	17	28	55
No. 6162-25, Gondola, O27, w/canisters, blue, 1959	5	9	12
No. 6162-50, Gondola, O27, w/canisters, Alaska, yellow, 1959	30	50	100
No. 6162-100, Gondola, O27, w/canisters, NYC, 1964	9	16	25
No. 6162-110, Gondola, O27, w/canisters, NYC, 1965	9	16	25
No. 6167, Caboose, O27, Lionel, 1963	4	6	12
No. 6167-50, Caboose, O27, D.R.W., 1963	3	4	5
No. 6167-85, Caboose, O27, U.P., 1969	10	15	30
No. 6167-100, Caboose, O27, Lionel, 1964	3	6	10
No. 6167-125, Caboose, O27, unlettered, 1964	3	6	10
No. 6175, Rocket Car, O27, red and white rocket, red or black frame, 1958	25	50	70
No. 6176, Hopper, O27, yellow, 1964	4	6	12
No. 6176-50, Hopper, O27, L.V., yellow, 1964	3	7	10
No. 6176-75, Hopper, O27, L.V., gray, 1964	3	7	10
No. 6219, Work Caboose, O27, C&O, blue cab, 1960	25	35	75
No. 6220, Locomotive, O27, diesel, SW2, NYC or Santa Fe, black, similar to 622, w/bell, 1949	150	180	360
No. 6250, Locomotive, O27, diesel, SW2, Seaboard, blue and orange, 1954	125	175	315
No. 6257, Caboose, O27, 1948	4	6	12
No. 6257-25, Caboose, O27, uncataloged, 1964	4	7	13
No. 6257-50, Caboose, O27, uncataloged, 1964	3	5	9

Post-WWII (1945-1969)	C6	C8	C10
No. 6257-100, Caboose, O27, 1964	7	10	18
No. 6262, Wheel Car, O, black or red frame w/eight set of wheels, 1956	30	50	65
No. 6264, Forklift Accessory Flatcar, red frame, brown lumber rack, 1957	20	40	55
No. 6311, Flatcar, O, brown, no load, 1955	23	38	75
No. 6315, Tank Car, O, orange, three dome, marked "Gulf", 1956	22	36	72
No. 6315-60, Chemical Car, O, orange, single dome tank, marked "Lionel Lines", 1963	11	19	37
No. 6342, Culvert Car, O, red gondola, w/inclined rake for culvert pipes, 1957	11	18	36
No. 6343, Barrel Ramp Car, O, red, gray ramp, 1961	15	25	47
No. 6346, Covered Hopper, O, Alcoa, silver, 1956	17	28	55
No. 6352, Refrigerator Car, O, for ice depot, Pacific Fruit Express, orange shell, door on roof for deposit of ice blocks, side door discharges, 1955	45	80	110
No. 6356, Stock, O, NYC, yellow, 1954	16	27	53
No. 6357, Caboose, O27, maroon, red, Tuscan brown, 1948	7	11	23
No. 6361, Timber Flatcar, O, green frame w/three lumber branches, 1960	25	50	83
No. 6362, Rail Truck Car, O, orange frame w/three sets of trucks, 1955	20	40	60
No. 6376, Circus Car, O, white stock car, 1956	30	50	80
No. 6401, Flatcar, O, w/two vans, 1965	15	25	50
No. 6402-50, Flatcar, O, w/cable reels, gray frame w/orange reels, 1964	22	38	75
No. 6405, Flatcar, O, w/piggyback van, brown frame w/two trailer vans, 1961	12	25	40
No. 6407, Flatcar, O, w/rocket, red frame, gray supports w/red and white rocket, blue nose, actually a pencil sharpener, 1963	125	300	425

Post-WWII (1945-1969)	C6	C8	C10
No. 6408, Flatcar, O, w/pipes, 1963	10	20	30
No. 6409-25, Flatcar, O, w/pipes, 1963	10	20	30
No. 6411, Flatcar, O27, w/logs, gray die-cast frame, five logs, 1948	11	20	35
No. 6413, Mercury Capsule Car, O, blue frame w/two gray Mercury capsules, 1962	70	110	140
No. 6414, Evans Loader Car, O, red frame, black metal car rack w/four cars, 1961	40	70	100
No. 6414-25, Autos, O, set of four, 1955	55	64	75
No. 6415, Tank Car, O, Sunoco, silver, three dome, 1953	9	15	30
No. 6415-60, Tank Car, O, Sunoco, 1969	9	15	30
No. 6416, Four Boat Loader, O, red frame, black metal boat rack, 1961	80	150	200
No. 6417, Caboose, O, P.R.R., 536417, N5C type, Tuscan brown, 1953	12	20	40
No. 6417, Caboose, O, P.R.R., Lehigh Valley, gray, 1953	50	65	140
No. 6417, Caboose, O, P.R.R., Tuscan, 1953	600	1000	2000
No. 6418, Girder Flatcar, O, depressed center, gray die-cast frame w/two orange girder sections, four sets of trucks, 1955	45	75	100
No. 6419, Wrecker Caboose, O27, DL&W, gray cab, 1948	15	25	45
No. 6419-100, Wrecker Caboose, O27, N&W, light gray cab, 576419, 1954	45	75	135
No. 6420, Wrecker Caboose, O, DL&W, dark gray, die-cast frame w/searchlight, 1949	35	65	105
No. 6424, Twin Auto Car, O, black frame, two autos, 1956	16	30	45
No. 6425, Tank Car, O, Gulf, silver, three dome, 1956	15	25	50
No. 6427, Caboose, O, 64273, Tuscan brown, N5C type, 1954	14	23	45
No. 6427-60, Caboose, O, Virginian, 6427, blue shell, yellow lettering, N5C type, 1958	120	200	400
No. 6427-500, Caboose, O, Girl's train, 57, 6427, blue shell, white lettering, 1957	125	200	350
No. 6428, Boxcar, O, U.S. Mail, red, white and blue, 1960	15	25	45
No. 6429, Wrecker Caboose, O, gray die-cast frame, gray cab, 1963	125	200	310
No. 6430, Flatcar, O, w/piggyback van, red frame w/two trailer vans, 1956	20	40	60
No. 6434, Poultry Car, O, red stock car, gray doors, illuminated, 1958	40	60	80
No. 6436, Hopper, O, N&W, red, 1955	12	20	40
No. 6436-1, Hopper, O, L.V., black, 1956	15	25	50
No. 6436-25, Hopper, O, L.V., maroon, 1956	15	25	50

Post-WWII (1945-1969)	C6	C8	C10
No. 6436-57, Hopper, O, L.V., girl's set, lilac, maroon lettering,, 1957	75	150	225
No. 6436-100, Hopper, O, L.V., 1957	14	24	48
No. 6436-110, Hopper, O, L.V., 1963	23	38	75
No. 6437, Caboose, O, Pennsylvania, N5C, Tuscan brown, 1961	13	23	45
No. 6440, Pullman, O27, green sheet-metal body, dark green roof, 1948	20	30	45
No. 6441, Observation Car, O27, green sheetmetal body, dark green roof, 1948	20	30	45
No. 6442, Pullman, O27, brown sheet-metal body and roof, 1949	20	33	65
No. 6443, Observation Car, O27, brown sheetmetal body and roof, 1949	24	40	80
No. 6445, Fort Knox Gold Car, O, silver w/four clear windows, showing gold bullion, 1961	60	100	140
No. 6446-25, Covered Hopper, O, N&W, gray, 1956	23	38	75
No. 6446-54, Covered Cement, O, N&W, black, 1954	17	28	55
No. 6446-54, Covered Cement, O, N&W, gray, 1954	30	50	100
No. 6447, Caboose, O, N5C type, Tuscan brown, 1963	125	200	350
No. 6448, Expolding Target Range Car, O, red shell, white lettering, 1961	11	20	35
No. 6454, Boxcar, O27, P.R.R., Tuscan brown, 1948	60	130	200
No. 6454, Boxcar, O27, NYC, brown, 1949	15	35	50
No. 6454, Boxcar, O27, Erie, brown, 1950	20	35	55
No. 6454, Boxcar, O27, Erie, SP, 1950	20	35	55
No. 6456, Hopper, O, maroon, black, gray, 1948	6	10	20
No. 6456, Hopper, O, shiny red, yellow letters, 1948	48	80	160
No. 6456, Hopper, O, white letters, 1948	200	350	500
No. 6457, Caboose, O, brown or maroon, SP type, 1949	12	15	28
No. 6460, Crane, O, black cab, 1952	23	40	75
No. 6460, Crane, O, gray cab, 1952	25	40	75
No. 6461, Transformer Car, O27, gray die-cast frame, black transformer, 1949	32	53	105
No. 6462C, Gondola, O, NYC, 1949	4	6	12
No. 6462-25, Gondola, O, NYC, black, bright red, green, 1954	5	8	15
No. 6462-500, Gondola, O, Girl's train, pink, marked "NYC", 1957	65	110	170
No. 6463, Rocket Fuel Tank Car, O, white shell, two dome, red lettering, 1962	23	38	75

No. 6-9438 Ontario Northland Boxcar

Post-WWII (1945-1969)

	C6	C8	C10
No. 6464-1, Boxcar, O, W.P., silver, 1953	35	60	88
No. 6464-25, Boxcar, O, G.N., orange, 1953	35	65	90
No. 6464-50, Boxcar, O, M&StL, maroon, 1953	35	65	90
No. 6464-75, Boxcar, O, R.I., green, 1953	40	65	85
No. 6464-100, Boxcar, W.P., silver w/yellow feather, 1954	60	90	125
No. 6464-100, Boxcar, W.P., orange w/blue feather, 1954	350	600	1000
No. 6464-125, Boxcar, O, red and gray, marked "Pacemaker", 1954	40	80	130
No. 6464-150, Boxcar, O, M.P., blue and gray, 1954	39	80	130
No. 6464-175, Boxcar, O, R.I., silver, 1954	50	85	125
No. 6464-200, Boxcar, O, P.R.R., Tuscan brown, 1954	70	100	140
No. 6464-225, Boxcar, O, S.P., black, 1954	50	75	135
No. 6464-250, Boxcar, O, W.P., orange w/blue feather, 1966	90	150	225
No. 6464-275, Boxcar, O, red, white and blue, marked "State of Maine", 1955	50	75	100
No. 6464-300, Boxcar, O, Rutland, green and yellow, 1955	40	70	125
No. 6464-325, Boxcar, O, B&O, silver and aqua, "Sentinel", 1956	280	450	605
No. 6464-350, Boxcar, O, M.K.T., maroon, 1956	115	205	290
No. 6464-375, Boxcar, O, C.G., maroon and silver, 1956	45	85	120
No. 6464-400, Boxcar, O, B&O, blue and orange, "timesaver", 1956	42	70	140
No. 6464-425, Boxcar, O, N.H., black, 1956	30	50	75
No. 6464-450, Boxcar, O, G.N., olive and orange, 1956	60	100	135
No. 6464-475, Boxcar, O, B&M, blue, 1957	30	45	60
No. 6464-500, Boxcar, O, Timken, yellow and white, 1957	60	100	130
No. 6464-510, Boxcar, O, Girl's train, NYC, lilac, 1957	300	460	620

Post-WWII (1945-1969)

	C6	C8	C10
No. 6464-515, Boxcar, O, Girl's train, M.K.T., yellow, 1957	260	430	600
No. 6464-525, Boxcar, O, M&StL, red, 1957	30	50	77
No. 6464-650, Boxcar, O, D.R.G.W., yellow and silver, 1957	50	90	130
No. 6464-700, Boxcar, O, Santa Fe, red, 1961	50	90	130
No. 6464-725, Boxcar, O, New Haven, black, 1962	30	50	65
No. 6464-825, Boxcar, O, Alaska, blue and yellow, 1959	111	185	370
No. 6464-900, Boxcar, O, NYC, light green, 1960	50	85	120
No. 6465, Tank Car, O27, silver, two dome, marked "Sunoco", 1948	12	20	40
No. 6465, Tank Car, O27, Gulf, black, two dome, 1958	25	50	75
No. 6465, Tank Car, O27, black, Lionel Lines, two dome, 1958	10	20	30
No. 6465, Tank Car, O27, orange, Lionel Lines, two dome, 1958	5	10	15
No. 6465, Tank Car, O27, Cities Service, green, two dome, 1960	12	15	30
No. 6466T W or WX, Tender, O27, 1948	30	50	100
No. 6467, Bulkhead Car, O, red frame, two black bulkheads, 1956	18	35	50
No. 6468, Automobile, O, B&O, blue, double door, 1953	20	40	60
No. 6468, Automobile, O, B&O, brown, 1953	140	215	320
No. 6468-25, Automobile, O, N.H., orange, double door, 1956	25	45	72
No. 6469, Liquefied Gas Tank Car, O, red frame, white cylinder, 1963	75	125	150
No. 6470, Exploding Boxcar, O, red w/white lettering, spring mechanism, 1959	12	28	40
No. 6472, Refrigerator, O, white boxcar, 1950	18	28	38
No. 6473, Horse Transport Car, yellow, two horse heads bob in and out, 1963	10	20	30
No. 6475, Pickle Car, O, Heinz 57, 1960	NPF	NPF	NPF
No. 6475, Pineapple Car, O, Libby, uncataloged, 1960	36	63	125

No. 444 Roundhouse Section, $3400.

Post-WWII (1945-1969)	C6	C8	C10
No. 6476, Hopper, O, red, white letters, 1957	4	10	15
No. 6476-25, Hopper, O, L.V., gray, black letters, 1963	3	5	10
No. 6476-75, Hopper, O, L.V., red, white letters, 1963	4	7	10
No. 6477, Pipe Car, O, red frame, two black bulkheads, w/sidestakes, 1957	24	40	80
No. 6500, Beechcraft Bonanza Transport Car, O, black frame w/red and white plane, 1962	245	425	850
No. 6501, Flatcar, O, w/motor boat, red frame w/white and brown boat, 1962	55	85	120
No. 6502, Flatcar, O, w/girder, blue flat w/orange bridge, 1962	20	40	50
No. 6511, Pipe Car, O, brown or red flat w/three aluminum colored pipes, 1953	15	25	50
No. 6512, Cherry Picker Car, O, black or blue frame, gray ladder support, black ladder w/man, 1962	35	70	105
No. 6517, Caboose, O, bay window, red, marked "Lionel Lines", 1955	30	50	70
No. 6517, Caboose, O, Erie, bay window, red, uncataloged, 1966	180	250	465
No. 6518, Transformer Car, O, gray die-cast frame, four sets of trucks, black transformer, 1956	45	80	120
No. 6519, Allis Chalmers Car, O, orange car, gray reactor, 1958	27	45	90
No. 6520, Operating Searchlight, O, gray die-cast base, green, 1949	132	225	450
No. 6520, Operating Searchlight, O, orange or maroon generator, 1949	25	40	65
No. 6520, Operating Searchlight, O, tan generator, 1949	200	350	500
No. 6530, Fire Prevention Car, O, red shell, white lettering, 1960	40	60	75
No. 6536, Hopper, O, M&StL, red w/white lettering, 1958	20	30	55

Post-WWII (1945-1969)	C6	C8	C10
No. 6544, Missile Firing Car, O, blue frame, gray launch platform, red firing control w/four white rockets, white console, 1960	45	80	110
No. 6555, Tank Car, O, silver, single dome, metal tank, "Sunoco", 1949	18	30	60
No. 6556, Stock, O, M.K.T., Katy, red shell, white lettering and doors, 1958	70	150	240
No. 6557, Smoking Caboose, O, SP-type, Tuscan brown w/smoke unit, liquid type, marked "Lionel", 1958	85	150	250
No. 6560, Crane, O, black frame, gray cab, marked "Bucyrus Erie", 1955	40	50	90
No. 6560, Crane, O, red cab, "Bucyrus Erie", 1955	20	30	55
No. 6560-25, Crane, O, black frame, red cab 6560-25, "Bucyrus Erie", 1961	45	65	110
No. 6561, Cable Car, O, gray die-cast frame w/two orange or gray spools wrapped w/aluminum wire, 1953	20	65	110
No. 6562, Gondola, O, NYC, gray, 1956	14	23	45
No. 6562, Gondola, O, NYC, red, 1956	12	25	35
No. 6562, Gondola, O, NYC, black, 1956	12	25	35
No. 6572, Railway Express Reefer, O, green, 1958	45	70	90
No. 6572, Railway Express Reefer, O, light green, 1958	45	70	90
No. 6630, IRBM Missile Launcher Car, O, black frame, blue ramp, w/red and white missile, 1960	30	70	105
No. 6636, Hopper, O, Alaska, black w/orange lettering, 1959	21	35	70

Post-WWII (1945-1969)	C6	C8	C10
No. 6640, U.S.M.C. Missile Launcher, olive frame, black ramp, w/white missile, 1960	85	150	225
No. 6646, Stock, O, orange shell, black lettering, "Lionel Lines", 1957	17	29	58
No. 6650, IRBM Missile Car, O, red frame, blue support, black ramp w/red and white missile, 1959	28	48	95
No. 6650-80, Missile for 6650-0, five white missiles, 1959	5	8	16
No. 6651, Marine Cannon Car, O, olive frame and cannon w/four cannon loads, uncataloged, 1960	63	110	210
No. 6656, Stock, O, yellow shell, black lettering, 1950	8	13	26
No. 6657, Caboose, O, D.R.G.W., SP type, yellow cab w/silver lower stripe, black lettering, 1957	50	83	165
No. 6660, Flatcar, O, car w/boom, red flat, yellow crane, turn control, 1958	30	55	80
No. 6670, Flatcar, O, car w/derrick, red flat, yellow crane, no turn control, 1959	20	50	70
No. 6672, Refrigerator, O, "Santa Fe," white shell, brown roof, black lettering, 1954	25	50	80
No. 6672, Refrigerator, O, blue lettering, 1954	25	50	70
No. 6736, Hopper, O, Detroit & Mackinac, red shell, white lettering, 1960	17	30	70
No. 6800, Flatcar, O, w/airplane, red frame w/black and yellow plane, 1957	75	125	175
No. 6801, Flatcar, O, w/white boat, red flat, 1957	45	75	110
No. 6801-50, Flatcar, O, w/yellow boat, red flat, 1957	45	75	110
No. 6801-75, Flatcar, O, w/blue boat, red flat, 1957	48	80	160
No. 6802, Flatcar, O, w/bridge, red flat w/black bridge, 1958	14	24	48

Post-WWII (1945-1969)	C6	C8	C10
No. 6803, Flatcar, O, w/tank and sound truck, red frame, two gray vehicles, 1958	70	140	205
No. 6804, Flatcar, O, w/sound truck, red frame, two gray trucks, 1958	70	140	205
No. 6805, Atomic Energy Car, O, red frame, two gray radioactivity containers, lights under containers, 1958	48	80	160
No. 6806, Flatcar, O, w/radar and medical truck, red frame, two gray vehicles, 1958	70	125	175
No. 6807, Flatcar, O, w/duck, amphibian boat, red frame, one gray boat, 1958	60	100	150
No. 6808, Flatcar, O, w/tank and searchlight, red flat w/two gray vehicles, 1958	100	175	250
No. 6809, Flatcar, O, w/medical trucks, red frame, two gray vehicles, 1958	85	155	210
No. 6810, Flatcar, O, w/piggyback van, red frame, one trailer container, "Cooper Jarretting", 1958	18	35	50
No. 6812, Track Maintenance Car, O, red frame, gray, blue or yellow platform, w/two blue men, 1959	33	55	110
No. 6814, First Aid Caboose, O, white frame, cab and tool boxes, two stretchers, oxygen tank and man, marked "Rescue Unit", 1959	37	63	125
No. 6816, Flatcar, O, w/bulldozer, orange bulldozer, red flat, marked "Allis-Chalmers", 1959	200	320	450
No. 6816-100, Bulldozer, O, 1959	75	125	250
No. 6817, Flatcar, O, w/scraper, same as 6816, except bulldozer replaced by scraper, 1959	200	320	425
No. 6817-100, Scraper, O, 1959	27	45	90
No. 6818, Flatcar, O, w/transformer, red frame, black transformer, 1958	25	45	60
No. 6819, Flatcar, O, w/helicopter, red frame w/gray helicopter, 1959	30	50	100

No. 384 Locomotive, $600.

Post-WWII (1945-1969)	C6	C8	C10
No. 6820, Aerial Missile Car, O, blue frame, navy helicopter, 1960	90	150	300
No. 6821, Flatcar, O, w/crates, red frame, tan crates, 1959	20	28	40
No. 6822, Searchlight Car, O, red frame, gray searchlight, black housing w/blue man, 1961	20	30	45
No. 6823, IRBM Missile Car, O, red frame, gray supports, two white missiles, 1959	25	45	75
No. 6824, First Aid Caboose, O, olive frame, cab, tool boxes, w/two stretchers, oxygen tank and man, "Rescue Unit", 1960	63	105	210
No. 6825, Flatcar, O, w/arch bridge, red frame, black bridge, or gray bridge, 1959	20	32	65
No. 6826, Flatcar, O, w/trees, red frame w/bundles of life-like Christmas trees, 1959	50	90	145
No. 6827, Flatcar, O, w/power shovel, black frame, yellow and black steam shovel, 1960	65	100	175
No. 6828, Flatcar, O, w/construction crane, black frame, yellow and black crane, 1960	45	70	140
No. 6828-100, Construction Crane, O, 1960	80	130	180
No. 6830, Submarine Car, O, blue frame, gray sub, marked "U.S. Navy", 1960	50	90	120
Transformer, 90 watt, 1947	40	55	75
Lockton, O, 1947	NPF	NPF	1
Electronic Control Unit, 1946	40	60	80
Electronic Control, instruction booklet, 1946	5	10	15
Transformer, 190 watt, 1950	115	155	195
Lockton, O27, w/light, 1950	10	15	20
Transformer, 125 watt, 1956	105	125	140
Transformer, 110 watt, 1948	48	66	85
Transformer, 135 watt, 1961	55	82	120
Track, O, curved, 1962	NPF	NPF	1
Half Section Curved Track, O, 1966	1	1	1
Steel Pins, O, dozen, 1962	NPF	NPF	1
Straight Track, O, 1962	NPF	NPF	1
Half Section Straight Track, O, 1966	NPF	NPF	1

Post-WWII (1945-1969)	C6	C8	C10
Fiber Pins, O, dozen, 1962	NPF	NPF	1
90 degrees Crossing, O, 1962	4	6	8
Switches, O, remote control, 1962	35	53	70
Transformer, 115 watt, 1953	77	100	145
Uncoupling Track, O, remote control, 1949	8	10	145
Transformer, 150 watt, 1948	98	125	150
Transformer, 250 watt, 1948	140	200	275
Transformer, 275 watt, 1953	177	225	295
No. HO-723, Pullman, HO, Pennsylvania, 1963	6	10	20
No. HO-725, Observation Car, HO, Pennsylvania, 1963	6	10	20
No. 479-1, Lionel Trucks, accompanies 6362, 1955	5	10	15
No. 6014, Boxcar, O27, white body, 1958	35	50	70

No. 6-19212 Pennsylvania Boxcar

Top row, left to right: No. 1107 Donald Duck hand car, $1200; No. 1103 Peter Rabbit hand car, $1000. Bottom row, left to right: No. 110 Mickey Mouse hand car, $1000; No. 1005 Santa Claus hand car, $1800.

MOVIES, RADIO & TELEVISION

Left to Right: Amos & Andy Fresh Air Taxi, cast iron, Dent, $1300; Amos & Andy Tin Wind-ups, without moving eyes, $1800 for the pair; Amos & Andy Fresh Air Taxi tin wind-up, Marx, $1185; Amos & Andy Figures, cast iron, 4-1/4" high, $300; Amos & Andy Figures, chalkware, c. 1930, $800 for the pair.

Addams Family

	C6	C8	C10
Fester Puppet Doll, Ideal, 1964	30	65	80
Gomez Doll, Ideal, 1964	30	65	80
Lurch, Remco	100	150	200
Morticia, Remco, 1964	93	140	195
Morticia Doll, Ideal, 1964	30	60	80
Uncle Fester Hand Puppet, vinyl, 1960s	65	98	130

Amos and Andy

	C6	C8	C10
Amos and Andy in Car, glass, Victory Glass Co., 4-1/2" long	218	327	438
Amos Sparkler	500	750	1050
Amos Tin Wind-up, w/out moving eyes, Marx, 1930, 12" high	450	675	900
Amos Tin Wind-up, w/moving eyes, Marx, 1930, 12" high	493	740	985

Amos and Andy (Continued)

	C6	C8	C10
Andy Panda, plush, Ideal, copyright 1960, 14" high	60	90	120
Andy Tin Wind-up, w/out moving eyes, Marx, 1930s, 12" high	450	675	900
Andy Tin Wind-up, w/moving eyes, Marx, 1930s, 12" high	485	725	970
Dolls, wood jointed, pair, Jaymar, 6" high	300	450	600
Fresh-Air Taxi, tin wind-up, Marx, 1930s, 8" long	500	800	1185
Fresh-Air Taxi, cast iron, Dent, 6" long	600	950	1300

Beany & Cecil

	C6	C8	C10
Beany & Cecil Ge-tar, Cecil's eyes move, Mattel, 1961	78	115	155

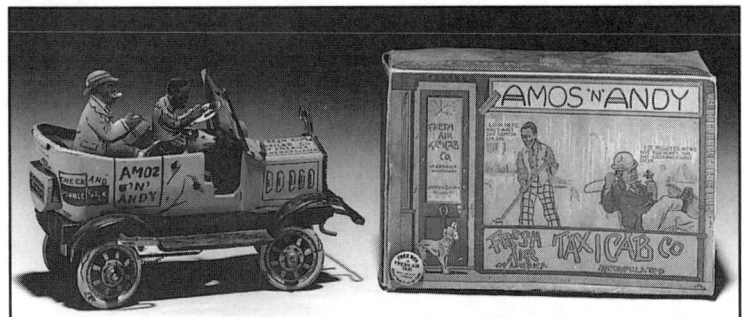

Amos and Andy Fresh-Air Taxi, Marx, 1930s, $1185.

Cecil Music Box, Mattel, 1961, $170.

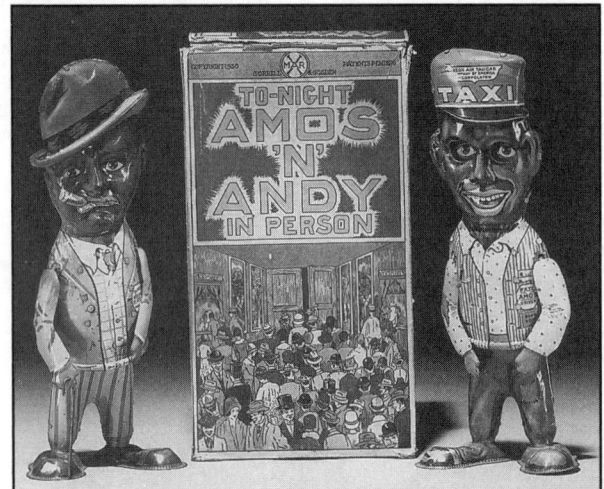

Amos and Andy Tin Wind-up, Marx, with original box, $1800 for the pair.

Left to Right: Betty Boop Doll, c. 1930, $1300; Betty Boop Figure, celluloid, Japanese, $1200. Photo courtesy Christie's

Left to right: Beany & Cecil Ge-tar, Mattel, 1961, $155. Leakin' Lena Pound N' Pull, box (Beany & Cecil) Pressman, 1961, $125. Photo courtesy Brad Krewson

Leakin' Lena Toy Boat (Beany & Cecil), Irwin Toy, 1962, $150. Photo courtesy Brad Kewson

Leakin' Lena Pound N' Pull (Beany & Cecil), Pressman, 1961, $125. Photo courtesy Brad Kewson

Beany & Cecil (Continued)	**C6**	**C8**	**C10**
Beany Doll, talking, Mattel, 1960, 17" high	62	93	125
Beany Doll, non-talking, Mattel, 1960, 15" high	45	68	90
Beany Halloween, Ben Cooper	35	52	70
Beany Hat, w/two propellers	35	52	70
Cecil Doll, non-talking, Mattel, 1960, 24" high	30	45	60
Cecil Doll, talking, Mattel, 1960, 29" high	90	135	180
Cecil Halloween Costume, Ben Cooper	37	56	75
Cecil Hand Puppet, talking, Mattel, 1961	32	48	65
Cecil Music Box, metal, plays show's theme song and Cecil pops up, Mattel, 1961	85	128	170
Cecil Soaky, 1950, 8" high	30	45	60
Colorforms Set, w/box, 1961	60	90	125

Beany & Cecil (Continued)	**C6**	**C8**	**C10**
Dishonest John Hand Puppet, talks, Mattel, 1961	63	95	125
Leakin' Lena Pound N' Pull, wooden, Pressman, 1961	50	75	110
Leakin' Lena Ship, wood, Pressman, 1960s	138	205	275
Leakin' Lena Toy Boat, plastic, Irwin Toy, 1962	75	112	150
Tea Set, six-place settings, Worcester, 1960	36	54	72

Ben Casey	**C6**	**C8**	**C10**
Ben Casey Doll, 1962, 12" high	85	127	170
Ben Casey Play Hospital Set, Transogram	60	90	120

Betty Boop	**C6**	**C8**	**C10**
Acrobat Wind-up, celluloid and metal, Japanese, 1930s	700	1100	1550

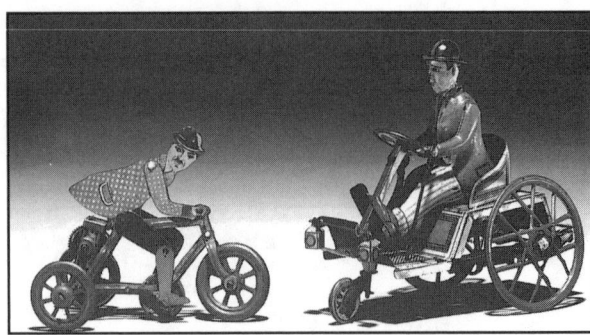

Left to right: Charlie Chaplin Tricycle Rider, 1930, $1800. Charlie Chaplin driving three-wheel vehicle, tin wind-up, Paya, $2200. Photo courtesy Christie's East

Charlie Chaplin Cymbal Player, German, $1400.

Left to Right: Charlie Chaplin tin wind-up with spinning cane, $1800; Charlie Chaplin doll, Boucher, $500; Charlie Chaplin doll, wind-up, Boucher, $2000; Charlie Chaplin Whistler Toy, c. 1920, $2500; Charlie Chaplin squeeze toy, German, $1800; Charlie Chaplin doll, Louis Amberg, c. 1915, $150; Charlie Chaplin Bell Toy, cast iron, c. 1912, $600. Photo courtesy Christie's East

Betty Boop (Continued)

	C6	C8	C10
Betty Boop and Bunny Mechanical Toy	150	225	300
Doll, wood jointed, marked "1931", Jaymar, 3-3/4" high	90	135	180
Doll, wood and composition, jointed, c. 1930, 12" high	550	800	1300
Doll, jointed, 1930s, 9-1/2" tall	240	360	480
Figure, celluloid, head shakes, Japanese, 7" high	600	900	1200

Bozo the Clown

	C6	C8	C10
Bendee, Lakeside, 6" high	10	15	20
Bendem Doll, Knickerbocker, 9" high	11	16	23

Bozo the Clown (Continued)

	C6	C8	C10
Doll, Terrytoons, 1961, 15" high	80	120	160
Doll, talking type, Mattel	45	68	90
Doll, stuffed, Gund, 1970, 14" high	75	112	150
Flexie, Wham-O	8	12	17
Hand Puppet, Capital, 1962	15	22	30
Jumpkin, Kohner, 1960	25	38	50
Periscope, Lido, 1960s	8	12	16
Soaky, 11" high	22	33	44
Soaky	14	21	29
Squeeze Toy, 9"	60	90	120

Captain Kangaroo

	C6	C8	C10
Captain Kangaroo Badge, tin shield, 1960s	20	30	40

Charlie McCarthy and Mortimer Snerd Private Car, Marx, $2265. Photo courtesy Phillips, New York

Charlie McCarthy Drummer Boy tin wind-up, Marx, 1938, $1000. Photo courtesy Don Hultzman. Photo by Ron Chojnacki

Charlie McCarthy Paper Money, front, $5. Photo courtesy Toy Collector News

---

CONDITION CODE

C6 Good; evident overall wear, well played with but acceptable to many collectors
C8 Very Good; minor overall wear, very clean
C10 Mint; like new

Note: Mint in Box commands a higher price.
Condition below C6 brings considerably lower prices

Captain Kangaroo (Continued)

	C6	C8	C10
Captain Kangaroo Doll, talking type, Mattel, 1967, 20" high........	21	32	42
Captain Kangaroo Hand Puppet, 1960s	22	33	45

Casper the Friendly Ghost

	C6	C8	C10
Casper the Talking Ghost, Mattel, 14"	65	98	130
Doll, stuffed w/beanbag body, 1960s, 11"...................................	35	52	70
Hopper, Linemar, 1950s, 5" high	200	300	400
Soaky	16	24	33
Squeak Toy, 8" high	48	72	95
Turnover Tank Tin Wind-up, Linemar...	150	225	300
Video Spaceport Play Set, Superior	250	375	500

Charlie Chaplin

	C6	C8	C10
Bell Toy, cast iron, c. 1912, 9-3/4"...	300	450	600
Bicycle Rider String Toy, c. 1920s	350	525	700
Cymbal Player, tin litho, squeeze action, German, 6-3/4"	700	1050	1400
Dancing Charlie, cardboard............	87	131	175
Doll, "Charlie's Back", Milton Bradley, 1971	35	52	70
Doll, composition and cloth, Louis Amberg, c. 1915, 14" high	75	113	150
Doll, steel, lead and cloth, ball-jointed w/movable arms, legs and feet, Boucher, 7-1/2" high	250	375	500
Figure, celluloid, 4" high.................	900	1350	1800
Figure, composition, marked, "CHAS. CHAPLIN," on base, Mark Hampton Company, 9" high..	350	525	700

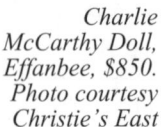

Charlie McCarthy Doll, Effanbee, $850. Photo courtesy Christie's East

Charlie McCarthy Doll, Effanbee, $615. Photo courtesy Christie's East

Charlie Chaplin (Continued)	C6	C8	C10
Squeeze Toy, tin litho metal ball, German, 7-1/4"	900	1350	1800
Squeeze Toy, tin litho, Spanish, c. 1925, 7-3/4" high	900	1350	1800
Tricycle Rider Tin Wind-up, c. 1930, 3-1/2"	900	1350	1800
Walker Wind-up, composition, cloth and metal, 11-1/2" high	500	750	1000
Walker Wind-up, composition, tin and cloth, French, 7" high	450	675	900
Walker Wind-up, composition, cloth and metal, Ferguson Novelty Co., 9" high	1100	1650	2200
Whistler Toy, wood, whistles "How Dry I Am", c. 1920, 13-1/4" high	1250	1875	2500
Wind-up, tips hat, CKO, pre-war, Germany	150	225	300
Wind-up, flat tin litho, tips hat when string is pulled	110	165	220
Wind-up, tin and cloth, Boucher, 8-1/4" high	1000	1500	2000
Wind-up, tin, driving three-wheel vehicle, Paya	1100	1650	2200
Wind-up, tin, Schuco, 1920s	285	428	570
Wind-up, tin, w/spinning cane, 6-3/4" high	900	1350	1800

Charlie McCarthy	C6	C8	C10
Charlie McCarthy and Mortimer Snerd Private Car, Marx	1000	1700	2265
Charlie McCarthy Doll, composition w/moving mouth, 1930s, 13" high	238	357	475
Charlie McCarthy Doll, rubber, Effanbee	45	68	90
Charlie McCarthy Doll, w/moving mouth and summer suit, Effanbee, 20" high	400	600	800
Charlie McCarthy Doll, w/moving mouth and tweed jacket, Effanbee, 20" high	425	638	850
Charlie McCarthy Doll, w/moving mouth, Effanbee, 20" high	308	462	615
Charlie McCarthy in his Benzine Buggy, Marx	463	695	925
Drummer Boy Tin Wind-up, Marx, 1938, 8" high	500	750	1000
Facemask, molded gauze, w/separate monocle	50	75	100
Figure, celluloid, 7-1/2" high	337	455	675
Hand Puppet, composition head, c. 1939	75	112	150
Paper Money	3	4	5
Puppet, cardboard, 1950s, 20" high	45	68	90
Tap Dancer, Marks Bros., 1938	125	188	250

Charlie McCarthy (Continued)

	C6	C8	C10
Ventriloquist Doll, composition w/cloth body, ring pull in back of head activates lower jaw, 14-1/2" tall	600	900	1200
Ventriloquist Doll, Puppet Maker K&S, 33" tall	500	750	1000
Wind-up, tin, marked "Charlie McCarthy" on top hat, c. 1938, 8" high	185	278	370

Chipmunks

	C6	C8	C10
Alvin Chipmunk Soaky	10	15	20
Simon Chipmunk Soaky	11	16	23
Theodore (Chipmunk) Soaky	10	15	20

Chitty Chitty Bang Bang

	C6	C8	C10
Chitty Chitty Bang Bang, Corgi	125	188	250
Dick Van Dyke Doll, talking type, Mattel, 1967	125	188	250

Cisco Kid

	C6	C8	C10
Cisco Kid Broomstick Horse, 1950s	35	53	70
Cisco Kid Neckerchief, w/nickel sombrero slide	50	75	100
Cisco Kid Western Outfit, 1950s	98	145	195

Daniel Boone

	C6	C8	C10
Cannon, Remco, 1964	80	120	160
Canoe, vinyl, 18" long	15	22	30
Crime Lab, includes flashlight, signal gun, badge, handcuffs and fingerprint kit, 1955	90	135	180
Doll, Remco	40	60	80
Los Angeles Police Badge No. 714	10	15	20
Play Set, Grant exclusive, w/box	80	120	160
Police Set, includes gun, handcuffs and badge	35	52	70
Shoulder Holster and Pistol, 1950s	62	93	125
Talking Police Car, Ideal Toys, c. 1954	105	158	210
Water Pistol, No. 714 badge emblazoned on handle, c. 1955	25	38	50
Whistle, black plastic	6	9	12

Dr. Doolittle

	C6	C8	C10
Dr. Doolittle Hand Puppet, talking type, Mattel, 1967	32	48	65
Dr. Doolittle Music Box, Gee-Tar, Mattel, 1967	40	60	80
Dr. Doolittle Pushmi Pullyu, 1965	43	65	87

Flintstones

	C6	C8	C10
Baby Pebbles, Ideal, 1963	65	100	130
Bamm-Bamm Doll, Ideal, 12-1/2" high	39	60	78
Bamm-Bamm Soaky	15	22	30
Barney Rubble Doll, vinyl, 1960, 10" high	36	48	72
Choo Choo Train Tin Wind-up, "Bedrock Express", Marx, 1950s, 13" long	188	280	375
Dino on Tricycle, Linemar, 1962, 4" high	500	750	1000
Dino the Dinosaur, Linemar, 1961, 9" long	188	280	375
Flintstone Flivver, friction type, Marx, 1962, 6-3/4" long	308	460	615
Flintstone Friction Cars, includes Fred, Barney, Wilma, etc., price for each, Linemar, 1962, 4" long	123	185	245
Flintstone Pals Wind-up, Barney and Dino, Linemar, 1962, 8" long	193	290	385
Flintstone Pals Wind-up, Fred on Dino, Linemar, 1962, 8" long	260	390	520
Flintstones Bedrock Express Hand-car Wind-up, play set, Marx, 1962, 22" x 26"	225	338	450
Fred Flintstone Figure, hollow vinyl, 5-3/4" high	37	56	75
Hopping Barney Rubble Wind-up, Marx, 1962, 4" high	200	300	400
Hopping Dino, Linemar, 1962, 4" high	240	360	480
Hopping Fred Flintstone, Linemar, 4" high	200	300	400
Mechanical Shooting Gallery, Marx, 1962, 13" long	48	72	95
Motorized Yacht	375	562	750
Paddy Wagon, Remco, 1961	100	150	200
Pebbles Doll, Ideal, 1964, 16"	75	100	160
Pebbles Doll, jointed, 7" high	60	90	120
Play Set, Marx	205	308	410
Tinykins, Marx	25	NPF	50
Turnover Tank Tin Wind-up, Linemar, 1950s, 4" long	310	465	620
Wilma Tricycle, Marx	240	360	480

Gleason, Jackie

	C6	C8	C10
Jackie Gleason, "Story Stage Theatre", Utopia Enterprises, copyright 1955	123	185	245
Jackie Gleason Bus, "Away, We Go", 13" high	450	675	900

Flintstone Pals wind-up, Marx; Fred (left), $520; Barney (right), $385.

Gleason, Jackie (Continued)	C6	C8	C10
Jackie Gleason Climbing toy...........	62	93	125
Jackie Gleason Doll, 1950s, 30" high..	200	300	400

Green Hornet	C6	C8	C10
Bendee, Lakeside, 1967..................	50	75	100
Car, die-cast, Corgi..........................	192	280	385
Hand Puppet, Ideal	200	300	400
Hat with Flipdown Mask, Arlington Hat Co.	65	98	130
Raft..	175	263	350
Signal Ray, Colorforms, 1966..	300	450	600
Walkie Talkies, Remco	200	300	400

Gulliver's Travels	C6	C8	C10
Gabby Doll, wood-jointed, Ideal, 10-1/2" high..............................	300	450	600
King Little, jointed composition, Ideal, 12"....................................	325	488	650

Gumby	C6	C8	C10
Gumby Bendee Figure....................	11	16	23
Gumby Hand Puppet, Lakeside, 1965..	17	26	35
Gumby Wind-up, dated 1966, 4" high..	50	75	100
Poky Bendee Figure	14	22	29
Poky Hand Puppet, Lakeside, 1965..	24	36	47
Poky Jack-in-the-Box, Lakeside, 1965..	16	24	32

Gumby (Continued)	C6	C8	C10
Poky Wind-up, vinyl, dated 1966, 4" high...	37	56	75

Harold Lloyd	C6	C8	C10
Bell Toy, German, 6-1/2" high........	300	450	600
Donkey Cart, tin litho, Spanish, c. 1929, 9-1/4" long.....................	2200	3300	4500
Funny Face Wind-up Walker, Marx, 1929	400	600	800
Policeman Tin Wind-up, 12" high..	375	562	750
Sparkler, tin litho, German	375	562	750

Hopalong Cassidy	C6	C8	C10
Automatic Television Set, Automatic Toy Co., 1950s, 5" square	150	225	300
Badge, tin, w/insert photo...............	27	41	55
Binoculars, plastic, c. 1950	78	115	155
Compass	105	158	210
Cowboy Outfit	200	300	400
Cowgirl Outfit	125	188	250
Dart Board, depicts stagecoach holdup and target practice, Toy Ent., 1950, 14" x 17"....................	110	165	220
Doll, 1930s-40s, 28" high...............	175	263	350
Field Glasses, metal, 1940.............	85	128	170
Flashlight Gun, plastic, marked w/Hoppy's name on side, 8" long...	30	45	60
Hand Puppet, 1940s........................	200	300	400

Jackie Gleason Bus, $900. Photo courtesy Don Coviello

Left to Right: Harold Lloyd Bell Toy, German, $600; Harold Lloyd Funny Face Walker, Marx, 1929, $800; Harold Lloyd Sparkler, German, $750. Photo courtesy Christie's East

Hopalong Cassidy (Continued)	C6	C8	C10
Hopalong Cassidy Doll, Ideal, 1949	125	175	200
Hop-A-Long Cassidy Tin Wind-up, "Range Rider" rocker base, Marx, 9-1/2" high	315	472	630
Knife, c. mid-1940s, 3-1/2" long	80	120	160
Photo Ring, c. late 1940s	35	52	70
Picture Gun and Theater, Stephens Co., 1939, 12" x 8"	200	300	400
Rocking Horse, Topper	188	282	375
Shooting Gallery, Automatic Toy Co., 1950s, 18" long	170	255	340
Signet Ring, all metal, late 1940s	30	45	60
Spurs, leather and metal	110	165	220
Western Frontier Play Set, w/figures, stagecoach and buildings	300	450	600
Woodburning Set	20	40	65
Zoomerang Gun, shoots paper, Tigrett Enterprises, 1950, 9" long	100	150	200

Howdy Doody	C6	C8	C10
Acrobat Tin Wind-up, Arnold, 1950s	205	308	410
Air-O-Doodle Circus Train Wind-up, Kagran, 1950s, 16" long	90	135	180
Airplane Squeeze Toy, Stahlwood	230	345	460
Clarabelle Clown Squeeze Action Cable, Kagran Corp., Linemar, 1950s, 6-1/2" high	188	280	375

Howdy Doody (Continued)	C6	C8	C10
Clarabelle Clown Wind-up, Kagran Corp., 1950s, 5" high	225	338	450
Clarabelle Hurdy Gurdy, Kagran Corp, FBA Industries, 1950s, 8" long	200	300	400
Clarabelle Marionette, Peter Puppet Playthings, 1950s	140	210	280
Clarabelle Playsuit, Wonderland Costumes	145	220	290
Clarabelle's Horn, 1950s	50	75	100
Dilly-Dally Marionette, Peter Puppet Playthings, 1950s	260	390	520
Flub-A-Dub Figure, plastic, 3-1/2" high	65	98	130
Flub-A-Dub Marionette, early 1950s	225	338	450
Flub-A-Dub Push Puppet, felt and wood, 5" high	50	75	100
Hand Puppets, rubber heads w/cloth bodies	25	38	50
Howdy Doody Doll, Ideal, 1950s, 21" high	225	338	450
Howdy Doody Doll, w/moveable jaws, Goldberger Dolls, 12" high	85	130	170
Howdy Doody Doll, eyes close and mouth opens, w/plastic cloth clothes, 1950s, 7-1/2" high	312	468	625
Howdy Doody Doll, wood-jointed, 13" high	175	263	350
Howdy Doody Doll, wood-jointed, holding NBC microphone, 5-1/2" high	200	300	400

Harold Lloyd Donkey Cart, Spanish, c. 1929, $4500. Photo courtesy Christie's East

Harold Lloyd Sparkler, German, $750. Photo courtesy James S. Maxwell and Virginia Caputo

Hopalong Cassidy Cowboy Outfit, $400. Photo courtesy Barry Goodman

Flub-A-Dub Push Puppet (Howdy Doody), $100.

Li'l Abner and his Dogpatch Band, tin wind-up, Unique, 1945, $750. (See listings in Comic Characters)

Merrymakers, Marx, 1929, $1725. (See listings in Tin Wind-Ups)

Howdy Doody (Continued)	C6	C8	C10
Howdy Doody Marionette, composition head w/wooden arms and legs, 17" high	120	180	240
Howdy Doody Marionette, composition head w/hands and feet, hand-painted features, 1950s, 16" high	145	220	290
Howdy Doody Mask, rubber	12	18	24
Howdy Doody Push Puppet, plastic, w/NBC mike, Kohner, 4" high	85	128	170
Howdy Doody Squeeze Toy, 7" high	75	112	150
Howdy Doody Tin Wind-up, Howdy does jig and Bob Smith sits at piano, Marx, c. 1950, 5-1/2" high	550	825	1100
Howdy Doody Tin Wind-up, Howdy Doody and Bob Smith at the piano, Unique	680	1020	1360
Howdy Doody Tin Wind-up, Howdy plays banjo and moves head, Marx, c. 1950, 5" high	240	360	480
Howdy Doody TV Set, w/paper filmstrips, Lego, 1950s	42	63	85
Howdy Doody Ventriloquist Dummy, 26" high	75	112	150
Howdy-Doody Jeep Wind-up, Marx	200	300	400

Howdy Doody (Continued)	C6	C8	C10
Life Preserver, plastic, shows Howdy, etc., Mr. Bluster, 1950s	21	31	42
Princess SummerFall WinterSpring Marionette, Peter Puppet	125	188	250
Puppet Set, plastic, w/levers in back of head of move mouths, includes Howdy, Bluster, Clarabelle, Princess, Dilly Dally, Tee-Vee Toys, the set	70	105	140
Put-In-Head, similar to Mr. Potato Head, but w/Howdy characters: Howdy, Bluster, Clarabelle, Princess, the set	50	75	100
Ranch House Tool Box, metal box, litho images of Howdy and Claribel, Liberty Steel, 1950s	50	95	140
Sand Forms, molds of Howdy, Bluster, Flub-A-Dub, Clarabelle, w/shovel, 1952	43	65	85
Ukulele, plastic, Emenee, 1950s	55	82	110
Wall Walker Doll, 6" high	27	41	55
Zippy the Chimp Marionette, Peter Puppet Playthings, 1950s	550	800	1200

Huckleberry Hound	C6	C8	C10
Aeroplane, tin friction, "Huckleberry Hound Yogi Bear", Linemar, 1960s, 9-1/2" wingspan	400	650	900
Fireman Squeeze Toy, rubber, 1960s, 9" high	100	150	200

Howdy Doody and Bob Smith at the Piano tin wind-up, Marx, c. 1950, $1100. Photo courtesy PB Eighty-Four, New York

Huckleberry Hound (Continued)	C6	C8	C10
Huckleberry Hound Car Tin Wind-up, tin, Marx, 1962, 4" long	130	195	260
Huckleberry Hound Doll, stuffed, Knickerbocker, 1959, 18" high...............................	27	41	55
Huckleberry Hound Hand Puppet, Knickerbocker, 1959	14	21	28
Huckleberry Hound Hopper Tin Wind-up, Linemar, 1962, 4-1/2" high...................................	200	300	400
Huckleberry Hound Squeeze Toy, rubber, w/top hat, Dell, 1960s, 6" high...................................	22	33	44
Huckleberry Hound Tricycle Wind-up, Linemar, 1961, 4" high	400	600	800

James Bond	C6	C8	C10
007 attache case, includes code book, rifle, bullets, Code-O-Matic, billfold w/money, James Bond business cards and instructions, c. 1965, 11"....................	263	395	525
100 Shot Repeater Cap Pistol with Silencer, from Goldfinger, Lone Star Co., 1961, 9" long.................	88	132	175

James Bond (Continued)	C6	C8	C10
Aston Martin, die-cast, No. 271, Corgi..............................	105	158	210
Aston Martin, die-cast, No. 270, Corgi..............................	98	150	195
Camera...................................	138	205	275
James Bond Hand Puppet, A.C. Gilbert, 1965	140	210	280
Moonraker Shuttlecraft...................	38	57	75

Jetsons	C6	C8	C10
Astro - the Jetsons' Dog Tin Wind-up, Marx, 1963, 5" high	212	318	425
George Jetson Squeeze Action Cable, Marx, 1963, 4" high........	150	225	300
George Jetson Tin Wind-up, Marx, c. 1965, 4" high	190	275	380
Jetson Express Choo Choo Train, wind-up, Marx, 1960s, 13" long...............................	250	375	500
Jetson's Turnover Tank Tin Wind-up, tin wind-up, Linemar............	205	308	410

Laurel and Hardy	C6	C8	C10
Oliver Hardy Bendy Doll, Knickerbocker, 1960, 9" high	27	41	55

Another view of Howdy Doody and Bob Smith at the Piano.

Huckleberry Hound Aeroplane, Linemar, $850. Photo courtesy Don Hultzman. Photo by Ron Chojnacki

CONDITION CODE

C6 Good; evident overall wear, well played with but acceptable to many collectors
C8 Very Good; minor overall wear, very clean
C10 Mint; like new

Note: Mint in Box commands a higher price.
Condition below C6 brings considerably lower prices

Laurel and Hardy (Continued)	C6	C8	C10
Oliver Hardy Hand Puppet, Knickerbocker	25	38	50
Oliver Hardy Roly-Poly, plastic, 10-1/2" high	22	33	44
Oliver Hardy Sparkler, Isla, Spanish	1000	1500	2000
Oliver Hardy Wind-up, Lakeside, 1960s, 5" high	35	52	70
Stan Laurel, wind-up, Lakeside, 1960s, 5" high	35	52	70
Stan Laurel Bendem Doll, Knickerbocker, 1960, 9" high	22	33	45
Stan Laurel Doll, Dean	400	600	800
Stan Laurel Hand Puppet, Knickerbocker	24	36	48

Lone Ranger	C6	C8	C10
Chuck Wagon Lantern, working Dietz kerosene lantern, w/glass dome	75	112	150
Deputy Badge, 1950s	9	13	18

Lone Ranger (Continued)	C6	C8	C10
Double Target Set, includes two-sided target, gun, two darts, Marx, 1939	125	188	250
Hat, white felt w/red trim, marked "Lone Ranger Hi! Yo! Silver!", 1940s	22	33	45
Hat, 1930s	65	98	130
Lone Ranger and Silver Figure, composition, 4-1/2" high	88	132	175
Lone Ranger Bendy, No. 8705, Lakeside, 1967, 6" high	16	24	32
Lone Ranger Doll, composition, Dollcraft, 1938, 20" high	300	450	600
Lone Ranger Flashlight	80	120	160
Lone Ranger Hand Puppet, Ideal, 1966	25	38	50
Lone Ranger Hand Puppet, vinyl head, c. 1956	80	120	160
Lone Ranger Hand Puppet, cloth and vinyl, "Stringless Marionette"	120	180	240

Lone Ranger cap gun and holster set, 1940s, $350. Photo courtesy John Fawcett

Lone Ranger composition 10-1/2" figure by Dollcraft, $600. Photo courtesy John Fawcett

Lone Ranger (Continued)	C6	C8	C10
Lone Ranger Harmonica, Magnus	40	60	80
Lone Ranger Official First-Aid Kit, tin litho, w/contents, 1938	105	158	210
Lone Ranger Official Outfit, M.A. Henry Co., 1942	70	105	140
Lone Ranger Official Outfit, includes mask, jail keys, badge, silver bullet, glow belt, and Lone Ranger buckle, shows Lee Powell and Chief Thundercloud on belt, 1939	62	93	125
Movie Viewer, Lone Ranger Rides Again, 1939	113	170	225
Moviescope Set, includes four films-No. 1 Superman, No. 2 Lone Ranger, No. 3 Lone Ranger, No. 4 Lone Ranger, w/pop-up box, Acme, 1948	72	108	145
Picture Printing set, includes eight rubber stamps, 1939	75	112	150
Play Set, Ranch Set, series 500, Marx	250	375	500
Push Toy, w/wood base, Kohner, 1950s	42	63	85
Rodeo Play Set, w/metal bldgs., plastic figures, etc., Marx, 1950s	200	300	400

Lone Ranger (Continued)	C6	C8	C10
Signal Siren, w/silver bullet secret code, United States Electric Mfg. Co., 1950s	65	98	130
Silver Bullet Knife, 3" long closed	92	138	185
Strongbox, (coin bank), 1938	100	150	200
Target Game, Marx, 1938	52	78	105
Tonto Doll, composition head, hands, feet, Dollcraft, 1938, 20" high	500	750	1000
Tonto Hand Puppet, vinyl head, mid 1950s	48	72	95
Tonto Hand Puppet, Ideal, 1966	21	31	42
Wind-up, on "Range Rider" rocker base, Marx, 1938, 10-1/2" high	350	525	700
Wind-up, on "Range Rider" rocker, chrome version, Marx, 1938, 8-1/2" high from top of lariat	180	270	360
Wind-up, on "Range Rider" rocker, litho version, Marx, 1938, 8-1/2" high from top of lariat	193	290	385

Magilla Gorilla	C6	C8	C10
Magilla Gorilla Doll, Ideal, 8" high	62	93	125
Magilla Gorilla Doll, Ideal, 1960s, 19" high	90	135	180

Jetsons Turnover Tank tin wind-up, Linemar, $410. Photo courtesy Don Hultzman

Jetsons Express Choo Choo Train, Marx, 1960s, $500. Photo courtesy Don Hultzman

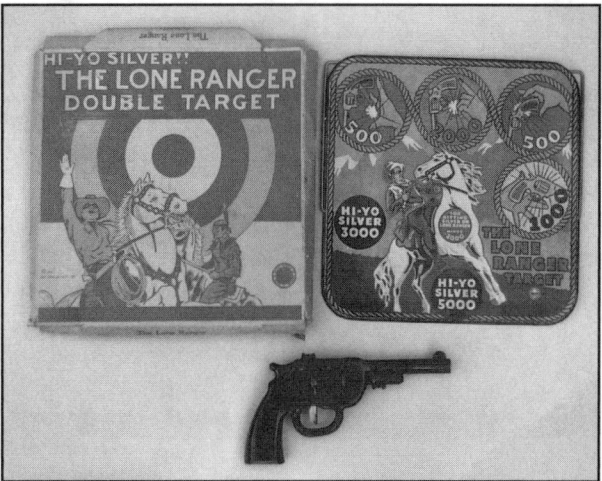

Lone Ranger Double Target set, Marx, 1939, $250. Photo courtesy Charles D. Richards

Lone Ranger and Tonto 20" store dolls by Dollcraft with a 10-1/2" composition Lone Ranger by Dollcraft in front of 1984 Cheerios cereal boxes, $1600 for pair. Photo courtesy John Fawcett

Left to right: Lone Ranger Doll, Dollcraft, 1938, $600; Lone Ranger Tonto Doll, Dollcraft, 1938, $1000. Photo courtesy Christie's East

The Box for Bat Masterson Gun and Holster Set. The complete set, by Carnell, is valued at $275.

Buster Keaton Sparkler, Spanish, c. 1925, $3300. Photo courtesy Christie's East

Magilla Gorilla (Continued)	C6	C8	C10
Magilla Gorilla Hand Puppet, Ideal, 1960s	24	36	48

Miscellaneous	C6	C8	C10
Abbott & Costello, price for each, 1984	30	65	80
Augie Doggie Soaky	27	41	55
Babalooie Doll, vinyl face, Knickerbocker, 14" high	30	45	60
Babalooie Soaky	15	22	30
Baby Huey (Paramount) Hand Puppet, Gund, late 1950s	24	36	48
Baby Sandy Pull Toy, Sandy & Goose, Gong Bell, 12-1/2" long	150	225	300
Bat Masterson Gun and Holster Set, w/cane and vest, Carnell, 1958	138	205	275
Beatles Figures, vinyl, Ringo, John, Paul, George, price for each, Remco, 1964, 5" high	45	68	90
Beatles Soakies, price for each each	62	93	125
Ben Hur Sword, scabbard and shield, Marx, 1959	142	213	285

Miscellaneous (Continued)	C6	C8	C10
Beverly Hillbillies Wind-up Car, Ideal, 1960s	270	405	540
Bob Burns Bazooka, brass kazoo-like toy, metal sliding tube, M.M. Pochapia Toys, 1930s, 13" long not extended	20	30	40
Bob Hope Hand Puppet, c. 1940	32	48	65
Bojangles Dances Again, tin litho and wood, tap button on base and he dances, 1930s	200	300	400
Buck Jones Rangers Chaps	90	135	180
Buffalo Bill Jr. Belt and Buckle, 1950s	25	38	50
Buster Keaton Sparkler, tin litho, w/moving arms and legs, Spanish, c. 1925, 7" high	1650	2475	3300
Captain Gallant Foreign Legion Holster Outfit	80	120	160
Captain Gallant Play Set, Marx	400	600	800
Charley Weaver Nodder	112	188	225
Cheyenne Target Game, Mettoy, 1961	62	93	125

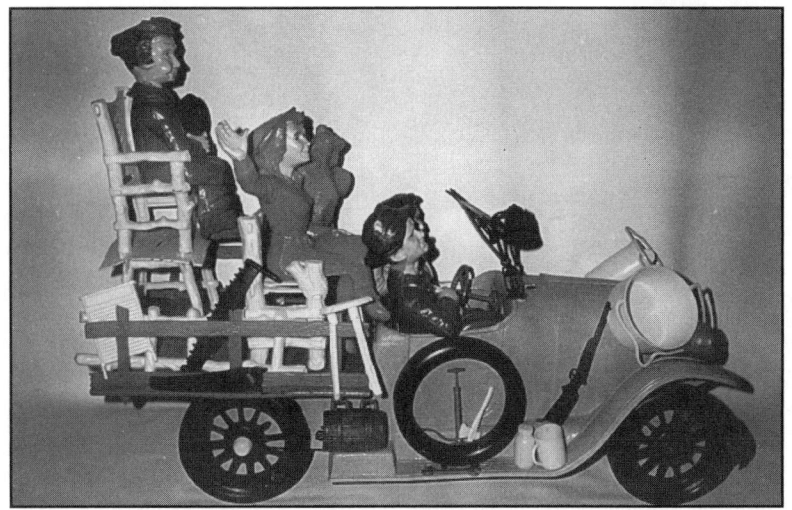

Beverly Hillbillies Wind-up Car, Ideal, 1960s, $540. Photo courtesy Don Hultzman. Photo by Ron Chojnacki.

Miscellaneous (Continued)	**C6**	**C8**	**C10**
Clyde Beatty Hingees Set, 1944	25	38	50
Danny O'Day (Jimmy Nelson) Ventriloquist Doll	40	60	80
Davy Crockett and His Horse, Ideal, 1955	20	35	50
Deputy Dawg Doll, stuffed, Ideal, 1961, 14" high	37	56	75
Deputy Dawg Soaky	15	22	30
Doggie Daddie Doll, vinyl head, Knickerbocker	100	150	200
Ed Wynn Fire Chief, jointed wood, w/ax in hand	80	120	160
Fanny Brice (Baby Snooks) Doll, composition and wire, Ideal, 12" high	125	188	250
Farfel (Jimmy Nelson) Hand Puppet, Juro	85	127	170
Farmer Alfalfa (Terrytoons) Doll, stuffed body w/vinyl head and hands, c. 1950, 17-1/2" high	30	45	60
Flip Wilson Geraldine Doll, talking type, Shindana, 1970	25	38	50
Flying Nun, Hasbro, 1960s, 4-3/4"	25	38	50
Flying Nun Flying Toy, Rayline, 1970	25	38	50
Froggie the Gremlin Squeeze Toy, 10-3/4" high	170	255	340
Froggie the Gremlin Squeeze Toy, 6-1/2" high	34	51	68
Froggie the Gremlin Squeeze Toy, 9-1/4" high	40	60	80

Miscellaneous (Continued)	**C6**	**C8**	**C10**
Froggie the Gremlin Squeeze Toy, hollow rubber, Rempel, 1950s, 5" high	62	93	125
Gangbusters Target Game, Marx	55	83	110
Gene Autry Marionette, 1940s, 18" high	140	210	280
Gene Autry spurs	60	90	120
General Figure, (Wizard of Oz), Mego	45	68	90
Get Smart Spy Purse Kit, Miner Ind., 7" long	30	45	60
Gilligan's Island Floating Island Play Set	88	132	175
Glinda Figure, (Wizard of Oz), Mego, 1972, 8" high	19	28	38
Gomez Hand Puppet, (Addams Family)	70	105	142
Groucho Marx, "Ventriloquist Play Pal,", Goldberger	40	60	80
Gulliver's Travels Boat, wooden, Paramount	110	165	220
Gulliver's Travels Drum, tin, Chein, 1939	25	38	50
Gulliver's Travels Musical top, Chein	30	45	60
Gulliver's Travels Sandpail, tin, Chein	45	68	90
Gumby's Jeep, metal, 1960s, 12"	125	188	250
Gunsmoke Handcuffs and Badge, c. 1952	42	63	85
Henry Fonda Texas Ranger Sheriff Badge, The Deputy, 1951	17	26	35

Miscellaneous (Continued)

	C6	C8	C10
Highway Patrol, "Highway Patrol Car,", Broderick Crawford, 8" long	75	112	150
Highway Patrol Pistol Outfit, includes gun, holster, badge, handcuffs, ID, whistle, etc., Halco, 1956	125	188	250
Hoot Gibson Cowboy Outfit, Wornova Clothes, 1935	70	105	140
Hoot Gibson Lariat	40	60	80
Hoot Gibson Outfit, "Squaw style,", Wornova Clothes, 1930s	60	90	120
Hugh O'Brian-Wyatt Earp, Dodge City Western Town, Marx, 1950s	450	675	900
I Spy Target Set	17	26	35
J. Fred Muggs Hand Puppet (Today show), 1954`	41	62	82
J. Fred Muggs Pull Toy (Today show), Gong Bell	90	135	180
Jackie Coogan ("The Kidd") Walker Tin Wind-up, German, 7" high	800	1200	1600
Jackie Coogan Candy Container, glass, 5" high	800	1200	1600
Jackie Coogan Figure, celluloid, 1920s, 5-1/2" high	130	195	260
Jerry Lewis/Dean Martin Hand Puppet, two-sided	150	225	300
Jerry Mahoney Ventriloquist Dummy	115	173	230
Joe Penner Tin Wind-up, tin wind-up, tips hat, walks, marked "Wanna Buy a Duck?", Marx, c. 1930s, 8" high	350	525	700
Jungle Jim Play Set, Marx	500	800	1100
Kukla & Ollie Puppet theatre, cardboard, 1962	50	75	100
Lambchop Shari Lewis Hand Puppet	18	27	36
Man from U.N.C.L.E. Secret Print Putty, c. 1965	25	38	50
Mary Poppins Hand Puppet, Gund	48	72	95
Matt Dillon (Gunsmoke) badge, U.S. Marshall	9	30	38
Men Into Space Space Helmet, retractable visor, space mike, made of fortiflex	65	98	130
Milton Berle Car, w/two large and two small wheels, "What the Hey," written on car, Marx, 1950s	215	323	430
Mr. Ed Hand Puppet, Mattel, 1962	48	72	95

Miscellaneous (Continued)

	C6	C8	C10
My Favorite Martian, "Martian Magic Tricks," magic set, Gilbert, 1964	115	175	230
Pink Panther Hand Puppet, cloth body, Gund, early	20	30	40
Pinky Lee Doll, vinyl, squeeze and his head pops up, 1950	90	135	180
Pinky Lee Pull Toy, Gong Bell	100	150	200
Quick Draw McGraw, "Quick Draw McGraw Hopper", Linemar, 1962, 4-1/2" high	200	300	400
Quick Draw McGraw, "Animal Airplane", Linemar, 1960s, 8-1/2" long w/9-1/2" wingspan	400	600	800
Quick Draw McGraw, Knickerbocker, 17-1/2" high	105	158	210
Quick Draw McGraw Squeeze Toy, Dell, 9-1/2" high	100	150	200
Ramar of the Jungle Play Set	217	325	435
Rat Patrol Giant Action Battle Set	250	375	500
Rat Patrol Jeep, Marx	200	300	400
Ricochet Rabbit, Ideal	52	78	105
Rifleman (TV) Ranch, Marx	600	1000	1500
Rookies (TV) Official Police Car, Fleetwood, 1975	15	22	30
Rootie Kazootie Doll, Effanbee, 19" high	62	93	125
Rootie Kazootie Marionette, rubber head and hands, wooden shoes, 14" high	90	135	180
Scrappy & Margie Pull Toy, wooden, 13-1/2" long	165	248	330
Scrappy Doll, cloth and composition, (Columbia Pictures), E.D.&T.C. Co., c. 1935, 14-1/2" high	320	480	640
Secret Squirrel Soaky	37	56	75
Sgt. Bilko Holster Set, from CBS TV series "You'll Never Get Rich," contains leather holster and belt w/die-cast Army, arm patch and Sgt. Bilko hat w/Badge, Halco Brand, 1956	100	150	200
Shadow Crimefighter Detection Belt, w/pistol and handcuffs, Madison Ltd., 1978	15	22	30
Shadow Felt Hat, early 1940s	187	280	375
Shirley Temple playhouse	120	180	240
Sneak Facemask, (Gulliver's Travels), molded gauze, 1939	50	75	100

W.C. Fields Doll with moveable mouth, Effanbee, $850. Photo courtesy Christie's East

Scrappy doll, E.D. & T.C. Co., c. 1935, $640. Photo courtesy Christie's East

Jackie Coogan ("The Kidd") Walker Tin Wind-up, German, $1600.

Miscellaneous (Continued)	C6	C8	C10
Soupy Sales Doll, Sunshine Doll Co., 1965, 5" high	90	135	180
Soupy Sales Marionette, Knickerbocker, 1966	37	56	75
Star Trek, Mr. Spock Vulcan Ears, 1976	7	11	15
Tales of the Texas Rangers Deputy Badge	12	18	24
Tarzan Bendy, Mego, 1972	25	38	50
Tennessee Tuxedo Soaky	17	26	35
Three Stooges as part of Jolly Theatre, 1930s	125	188	250
Three Stooges Hand Puppet, includes Moe, Curley, and Larry, price for each, 1959, 9-1/2" high	90	135	180
Tim Holt Litho Target, w/dart gun	70	105	140

Miscellaneous (Continued)	C6	C8	C10
Tim Mix on Tony, Arcor Rubber, 1930s	85	128	170
Tom Mix Rocking Horse, wooden, 1930s	175	263	350
Tom Mix Rodeo Rope, w/box and instructions, 1928	100	150	200
Topo Gigio (Ed Sullivan Show) Nodder	75	112	150
Topo Gigio Airplane, friction	75	112	150
Umbriago (Jimmy Durante) Hand Puppet, American Merchandise, 1945	45	68	90
Untouchable Detective Set, includes gun, holster, etc., Marx	112	168	225
Untouchable Tommy Gun, Marx, 1950s, 23" long	48	72	96
W.C. Fields Doll, w/movable mouth, Effanbee, 19" high	425	638	850
Wagon Train Play Set, Marx	213	320	425

Joe Penner tin wind-up, Marx, c. 1930s, $700. Photo courtesy Sotheby's, New York

Roy Rogers Signal Flashlight, $190. Photo courtesy Gary J. Linden

Miscellaneous (Continued)	C6	C8	C10
Waterfront "Cheryl Ann" Tugboat, (TV series), 1950s, 21"	100	150	200
Wild Bill Hickok and Jingles Holster Set	50	75	100
Wild Bill Hickok Marshal Star Badge, w/picture of Hickok and Jingles in center	42	63	85
Yellow Submarine, Corgi	180	270	360

Mortimer Snerd	C6	C8	C10
Doll, composition and wire, Ideal, 13" high	338	505	675
Figure, celluloid, 5" high	200	300	400
Hand Puppet	75	112	150
Jack-in-the-Box, c. 1930s, 8" high	100	150	200
Teeth, plastic teeth, w/dental wax, c. 1950	15	22	30
Tricky Auto, Marx, 1939	370	555	740
Wind-up, tin, Mortimer's hat tips as he walks, Marx, c. 1939	300	450	600
Wind-up, tin, "Home Town Band", Marx, 1935	450	675	900

Mr. Magoo	C6	C8	C10
Mr. Magoo Doll, Ideal, 1964, 15" high	45	68	90

Mr. Magoo (Continued)	C6	C8	C10
Mr. Magoo Hand Puppet, vinyl, 1962	32	48	65
Mr. Magoo Soaky, 11" high	20	30	40

Munsters	C6	C8	C10
Grandpa Hand Puppet, vinyl, 1960s	93	140	185
Lily Munster Hand Puppet, 1960s	95	140	190
Munster Family Dolls, Ideal, 1966	30	65	80

Munsters, The	C6	C8	C10
Herman Munster Doll, Mattel	88	132	175
Herman Munster Hand Puppet, vinyl, 1960s	95	140	190
Herman Munster Puppet, talking-type	200	300	400

Rin Tin Tin	C6	C8	C10
Rin Tin Tin, Fort Apache Stockade, Marx, 1950s	190	285	380
Rin Tin Tin and Rusty knife, 1950s	60	90	120
Rin Tin Tin Bugle, w/banner	37	56	75
Rin Tin Tin Doll, stuffed, Ideal	37	56	75

Roy Rogers Stage Coach Wagon Train wind-up, 1950s, $160. Photo courtesy Continental Hobby House

Robin Hood	C6	C8	C10
Robin Hood Bow and Arrow Set, Richard Greene, 1956	6	9	12
Robin Hood Money Pouch, w/six foreign coins, 1953-54	20	30	40
Robin Hood Money Pouch, w/fifteen foreign coins	20	30	40
Robin Hood Shield Badge, w/embossed Robin Hood and gem stone, c. 1956	25	38	50

Rocky and Bullwinkle	C6	C8	C10
Rocky the Flying Squirrel Bendee Figure, Wham-O, 1960s	10	15	21
Rocky the Flying Squirrel Hand Puppet	25	38	50
Rocky the Flying Squirrel Soaky	20	30	40

Roy Rogers	C6	C8	C10
Branding Iron Set	40	60	80
Bullet Doll, stuffed, c. 1955	40	60	80
Double R Bar Ranch Play Set, tin litho, ranch house, Marx, 1950s	175	263	350
Mineral City, tin, town includes hotel, music hall, café, bank, barber shop, and trade goods	185	278	370
Nellie Belle Jeep, metal	30	45	60
Pocket Flashlight	37	56	75
Quickshooter Hat with Secret Gun	90	135	180
Ranch Lantern, hurricane-type w/plastic chimney, No. 90, 1950s, 7-3/4" tall	78	115	155
Rodeo Ranch Play Set, Marx	125	188	250
Roy Rogers and Bullet Hobby Horse, N.N. Hill Brass Co., 1950s, 19" long	200	300	400
Roy Rogers and Trigger Pocket Knife	75	112	150
Roy Rogers Bandanna, large	48	72	95

Roy Rogers (Continued)	C6	C8	C10
Roy Rogers Bobbin' Head Doll, 1962, 6" high	90	135	180
Roy Rogers Buckboard, Ideal, 1950s, 16" long	65	98	130
Roy Rogers Fix-it Chuck Wagon, Ideal, 1950s, 13" long	123	185	245
Roy Rogers Fix-it Stagecoach, Ideal, 1950s, 13" long	90	135	180
Roy Rogers Horse Trailer and Jeep, Ideal, 1950s, 15" long	180	270	360
Roy Rogers Stage Coach Wagon Train Wind-up, plastic, 1950s, 14" long	80	120	160
Signal Flashlight	95	140	190
Telescope	40	60	80
Wagon Train, Marx	150	225	300
Western Town Play Set, Marx	125	188	250

Tom Corbett	C6	C8	C10
Cosmic Vision Space Helmet, plastic, one-way vision, early 1950s	207	310	415
Polaris Rocket Ship Wind-up, depicts Tom, Astro and Rogers looking out of cockpit, Marx, 1952, 12" long	300	450	600
Space Academy Set, No. 7000, Marx	238	355	475
Space Cadet 2-Way Space Phone, Zimmerman	80	120	160
Space Cadet Field Glasses, three power, Herald, 5-1/2" long	60	90	120
Space Cadet Flashlight, metal, w/built-in signal siren, U.S. Alite Corp., 7" long	90	135	180
Space Cadet Molding and Coloring Set, Model Craft	55	82	110

Roy Rogers Fix-it Chuck Wagon, Ideal, 1950s, $245.

Tom Corbett (Continued)

	C6	C8	C10
Space Cadet Official Space Pistol, No. 105, Marx	180	270	360
Space Cadet Rifle, Marx	140	210	280
Space Hat, Lee	40	60	80
Space Station	325	490	650
Spurs, metal and leather, 1934	150	225	300
Tom Corbett Official Outfit, Yankiboy	92	138	185
Tom Corbett Space Cadet Atomic Rifle, Marx, 1950s, 24" long	150	225	300
Tom Corbett Space Cadet Official Space Pistol, Rockhill, 1950s, 9-1/2" long	105	158	210

Underdog

	C6	C8	C10
Underdog Doll, small	40	60	80
Underdog Doll, medium	50	75	100
Underdog Doll, large	62	93	125

Universal Monsters

	C6	C8	C10
Creature Soaky	55	83	110
Frankenstein Soaky	55	83	110
Wolfman Soaky	60	90	120

Universal Monters

	C6	C8	C10
Mummy Soaky	60	90	120

Wizard of Oz

	C6	C8	C10
Cowardly Lion Facemask, molded gauze	40	60	80

Wizard of Oz (Continued)

	C6	C8	C10
Dorothy and Toto Figure, Mego	19	28	38
Dorothy Doll, Ideal, 1940	200	300	500
Emerald City Play Set, Mego	80	120	160
Lion Figure, Mego, 1972, 15" long	15	22	30
Mayor Munchkin Figure, Mego	45	68	90
Munchkinland Figures, total of four, price of each	48	72	95
Munchkinland Play Set	65	98	130
Scarecrow Facemask, molded gauze	60	90	120
Scarecrow Figure, Mego, 1972, 8" high	14	21	28
Tinman Facemask, molded gauze	60	90	120
Tinman Figure, Mego, 1972, 8" high	15	22	30
Witch's Castle, Mego	175	262	350
Wizard Figure, Mego, 8" high	8	12	17
Wizard of Oz, four-headed hand puppet, talks, Mattel, c. 1967	105	158	210
Wizard of Oz Masks, set of five, Einson-Freement Co., Inc., 1939	138	205	275
Wizard of Oz Series Dolls, Ideal, 1984	20	30	45

PREMIUMS

Many radio premiums were nearly as free as the wonderful radio shows that advertised them. We did have to pay the electric bill (or our folks did) to run the radio, and to get the offered toys we did have to send in a box top from the sponsor's product.

Sometimes it was only that, a proof of purchase. Orphan Annie and Captain Midnight were particularly generous in responding with gifts for inner labels or inner seals from Ovaltine drink mix. Other times, usually only a dime was required "to handle the cost of handling and mailing." (That's really all it did do—the cost of the premium itself came from the advertising budget.)

The lure of the premium for kids then and for grown-up kids who are now collectors is difficult to explain to those who never lived through the era themselves. The ring or badge was more than the toy itself; it was our tangible link to those magical friends on the other side of the speaker cloth.

Those voices were wonderful out there: the rumbling bass of Brace Beemer as the Lone Ranger; the slightly "country" sound of Curley Bradley as Tom Mix; Bret Morrison, whom we recognized even as children was "sophisticated" as Lamont Cranston (alias The Shadow). But they were bodiless and yes, a bit remote. It was the premium they offered, the same as the one they were using in the story that put us in touch with them.

There were historic precedents for radio premiums. There were pictures of famous actresses in cigarette packages around the turn of the century, and early radio personalities, such as bandleader Vincent Lopez, offered their autographed pictures. Such footnotes to history aside, radio premiums began with Little Orphan Annie in 1931. The plucky little waif from the Sunday comics first gave away sheet music of her theme song ("Who's that little chatterbox with the pretty auburn locks?") and her own photo, but very shortly, she offered a drinking mug that could be used to shake up Ovaltine powder with milk to make something resembling a soda fountain milk shake. The first significant radio premium, it was the only successful one that encouraged further use of the sponsor's product.

Many different models of the shake-up mug were offered by Annie and later by Captain Midnight (on both radio and TV). So successful were the offers, shake-up mugs are not rare or high in value. (The most sought after is the orange and blue, embossed—not decaled—Midnight mug.)

It was two years after Annie came to radio that the fledgling medium developed its classic adventure heroes. In 1933, there appeared the Lone Ranger, Tom Mix, and Jack Armstrong. Unlike Annie, the two Westerners and the All-American Boy were still around until the 1950s, when television began driving out radio drama. In those nearly 20 years, the shows offered hundreds of give-away toys, which inspired similar premiums on dozens of other shows.

Any small toy that could be manufactured inexpensively might turn up as a premium. Those concerned with the great outdoors were popular. We had compasses, pedometers, telescopes, flashlights, pocket knives, signal mirrors, and portable telegraph sets.

Secret decoders and manuals of every size and description had special emblems and tokens. It is these and other paper items that have the greatest dollar value. They were the most easily lost or used up in the rush to adulthood. A Captain Midnight Secret Manual is worth more than the metallic decoder it accompanied.

The rarest paper item is the Lone Ranger Frontier Town, offered about 1947. To complete this model of a Western village, one had to get four different envelopes by mail, then augment this by buying several packages of Cheerios to cut out the model buildings from the packs. The complete set has been known to sell for hundreds of dollars and today might bring $4,000 for a Mint set.

Perhaps the most popular single type of premium was the ring. Rings let the listener show loyalty to the fraternity of his or her favorite hero, but in a less officious and more "grown-up" way than the badge (although they were also highly popular). Besides, the rings looked neat, and many of them could do things— some of them pretty incredible things.

As with radio premiums in general, the Tom Mix show (and Ralston cereal's premium manufacturer, the Robbins Company) blazed the trail with ingenious ring designs. In 1937, Tom Mix Straight Shooters could get a Signet Ring with their own initial on it. (Years later, Captain Midnight would offer a ring that would ink-stamp your initial.) By 1938, Tom had a ring that let you look in a peephole and see a magnified picture of himself and his horse, Tony. (Technology had progressed so much that by the fifties, Straight Arrow offered a similar ring that put your own photo, if supplied, alongside radio's great Indian hero.)

After World War II and the ease in metal rationing, Tom Mix offered a Magnet Ring. His spinning siren whistle ring was neat (but admittedly borrowed in design from Jack Armstrong's 1937 Egyptian Whistle Ring). Tom's Sliding Whistle Ring, which played different musical notes (about 1948), was unique, however. His Look-Around Ring concealed an inner mirror that let you see behind you (sort of), a design rustled for a later Tennessee Jed ring.

The final Tom Mix ring looked attractive, sporting a glowing cat's eye, but the 1949 Tiger-Eye Ring was only lightweight plastic, a far cry from the well-crafted metal rings of a decade earlier. But then, the decade was nearly over, and so was the era, fading in the light of another glowing eye in the living room.

The Shadow's own Glow-in-the-Dark Ring (1939) had a band composed of two sculpted Shadow figures holding up a jagged blue stone—a proxy lump of his sponsor's product, Blue Coal. One of the very few Shadow premiums and the best looking, this ring has sold for $950.

The identical mold for one glowing plastic ring was used for several different radio shows. The band had two crocodiles holding a setting in their mouth. The "stone" was black when it was Jack Armstrong's Dragon Eye Ring in 1940. It was green for "Terry and the Pirates" in the mid-1940s, but it was black for Carey Salt's Shadow ring in 1947 (not the rare Blue Coal model). The setting was red for Buck Roger's Ring of Saturn in 1945. It is black again in the slightly lumpy counterfeit being manufactured today. This ring is one of the handful of premiums of simple enough design to be faked for profit. The best way to authenticate these rings is by the accompanying paper instruction sheets naming the famous character whose prize it is.

These rings are worth whatever you will pay to possess them, as are all radio premiums. A fair average price is $60, with $300 a top price for very rare, complex, and fragile items. Of course, many items are priced much higher. But anybody who is not familiar with the whole field should not pay more, even though $500 or more may be easier to come by today than a dime and a box top were in those days of yesteryear.

Since 1992 there has been a radical change in the prices of radio and early TV premiums (and associated toys). For nearly twenty years there had been no appreciable rise in premium prices. In fact, premium prices had not even kept up with inflation. You could have bought a Tom Mix Magnet Ring for $35 in 1967 and bought the Magnet Ring for the same $35 in 1987. But now there has come a radical change in premium pricing, especially for rings. The Magnet Ring generally bought $150 in 1998.

Part of the reason is the unnatural influence of "investor" types who have manipulated the market, much as they did the old comic book market. The results have been mixed. Prices have risen, but the number of premium collectors and the number of premium objects is far smaller than their counterparts in the comic book field. As a result, most premiums have virtually disappeared from the market. Now is the time to buy, if premiums can be found. They may never be cheaper, and they may never be seen again.

Despite rarity, condition is still very important. No matter how rare, a premium that is battered, defaced or broken is virtually worthless. It may bring a token price of $5.

Stores of premiums newly found in attics no longer seem to be turning up, but older collectors are retiring from occupations and, sadly, selling their collections for needed money. Some die, and survivors sell. These collectors and families know the value of collectibles and sell for top market value. The number of these "retiring" collectors is still fairly small and does not greatly affect the general state of rarity of premiums.

The items connected to once well-known characters (and those still famous) such as the Lone Ranger, Tom Mix, Buck Rogers, Buck Jones, and Gene Autry, have the highest prices. These prices are still on the rise. Even minor and nearly forgotten characters such as Scoop Ward and Speed Gibson are not being given away. Such once well-known characters will generally prevent a button from selling for less than $15, a badge for less than $25 or a ring for under $30.

Rings have a great appeal to many, and are the hottest ticket in the premium market. The rare ones are going up and up. The Shadow Blue Coal Ring, Green Hornet Seal Ring, and Captain Midnight Mystic Sun God have gotten into the thousands of dollars.

Cereal boxes of the sponsors who offered the premiums, especially ones with premium offers on the boxes, have become valuable. Near the top of the line are complete boxes of the nine Lone Ranger Frontier Town Cheerios packs (about $200 each; the backs off the boxes with unassembled model buildings can go for $35). Tom Mix Ralston boxes from the late 1940s-1950s go for up to $400.

A few new authentic premiums have appeared in recent years. Boraxo offered a 20 Mule team model in 1980 (similar to the Death Valley Days original of the 1930s, 1940s, and 1950s); Cheerios offered a Lone Ranger Deputy Kit in 1981 styled after the movie of that year, but similar to earlier offers with mask, badge, etc.

In 1982, Ralston began a limited Tom Mix revival. Premiums offered included a set of four Mix Ralston cereal bowls, a wind-up wrist watch, a Straight Shooters membership kit, a Tom Mix photo, a Mix-in-box miniature comic and an LP recording with old Mix radio episodes and one 1893 episode featuring Curley Bradley. In 1993-94, Ralston again showcased Tom Mix on their boxes, but offered only a chance for the customer to write in their memories of Tom. A full-color box came in 1996.

In 1987, Ovaltine resurrected its original formula in jars and instituted new premiums of their character, Captain Midnight of the Street Squadron. The 1987 premium was a T-shirt, in 1988 a Midnight digital watch was offered, and in 1989 an arm patch was available (apparently the last of the current revival). Dick Tracy premiums, such as the Quaker wrist radio, came with the new movie in 1990. Superman continued his fifth-year-plus association with Kellogg's cereals in 1994, appearing on the box and inside, with a mini-comic book for Kellogg's Cinnamon Mini-Buns. In 2000, Ovaltine offered decoder rings for two proofs of purchase and $2.50. Contrary to popular belief, Ovaltine nor any other radio sponsor has offered a code ring before.

Prices on these are already comparable to older premiums, topped by the Tom Mix watch at $300. The biggest premium news of the early 1990s was the sale of a Superman comic book premium ring for a record of $18,000 and its resale for $43,000. But this event was really a part of the world of incredibly priced Golden Age comic books. In effect, the ring was treated as another rare old comic book, not as the premium ring it was. This astonishing sale only raised the value of a real radio premium, the Superman Crusaders Club ring, from $65 to a less than overwhelming $250. Real radio and TV premiums from broadcast series have broken the $1,000 barrier, with the complete Lone Ranger Frontier Town and rings—Captain Midnight Mystic Sun God, Green Hornet Seal, Shadow Blue Coal, and many others in a new and much changed market.

Contributors: Jim Harmon, 634 South Orchard Dr., Burbank, CA 91506. Harmon is the author of *Radio & TV Premiums; Value and History from Tom Mix to Space Patrol.*

	C6	C8	C10
Admiral Television Studio Give-away, paper punch-out TV Studio and characters, features Sky King, Flight to Mars, Walt Disney's Peter Pan and Three Little Pigs, 1953, 15" x 16"	65	131	262
Amos & Andy Pepsodent Give-away, Amos' Wedding	48	72	95
Amos & Andy Puzzle	55	83	110
Archie Comics Club Button	5	10	20
Aunt Jemima Breakfast Club Badge, metal	12	18	30
Barney Baxter Junior Birdmen of America Wings, metal, c. late 1930s	12	18	25
Bendix Radio, WWII military figures, color photos w/stands—a.) Navy Lt. (jg); b.) Marine 1st Lt. (dress uniform); c.) Coast Guard Commander; d.) Army Air Force officer w/parachute harness; e.) 2nd Lt. W/modern Mae West; f.) Flier w/flying suit; g.) Army Air Force Capt.; h.) Air officer w/fur-lined jacket and helmet; price for each, c. 1944, 5-1/2"	5	10	15
Betty Boop Face Mask, theatre premium, 1931	27	41	63

	C6	C8	C10
Betty Boop Pin, "Roxy Theatre, New York," large	20	30	50
Bobby Benson Code Rule, cardboard decoder, Hecker H-O, 1935	40	75	150
Bobby Benson's Game Circus, 1934	50	97	195
Buck Jones Club Ring	60	110	220
Buck Jones Horseshoe Pin	25	50	100
Buck Jones Jr. Sheriff Badge	25	50	100
Buck Rogers, items given away for Cream of Wheat green triangle (also sold in stores) Buck Rogers Films for Projector	10	15	25
Buck Rogers Badge, enameled	83	125	165
Buck Rogers Chief Explorer Badge	45	90	180
Buck Rogers Flight Commander Whistle Badge	90	175	350
Buck Rogers Girl's Charm Bracelet	83	125	180
Buck Rogers Helmet	200	300	400
Buck Rogers Interplanetary Game	83	125	165
Buck Rogers Knife	83	125	165
Buck Rogers Lead Figures, solid, includes Cocomalt, Buck, Wilma, Killer Kane, price for each	30	60	120

	C6	C8	C10
Buck Rogers Lead Figures, hollow lead, Buck, Wilma, Huer, Robot, Kane, Ardala, price for each, Britains	200	300	400
Buck Rogers Lite Blaster Flashlight	30	60	100
Buck Rogers Morton Salt Punch-O-Bag, 1930s	42	63	85
Buck Rogers Morton Salt Spaceship, came in envelope	83	125	165
Buck Rogers Movie Projector	110	200	400
Buck Rogers Pendant	42	63	100
Buck Rogers Pinback Button, "Buck Rogers in the 25th Century", Whitehead and Hoag, c. 1935	42	63	100
Buck Rogers Printing Set, twelve rubber stamps	48	72	150
Buck Rogers Repeller Ray Ring, seal ring	800	1550	3500
Buck Rogers Ring of Saturn, glows in the dark, w/red stone	250	375	575
Buck Rogers Ring of Saturn Instruction Sheet	63	125	250
Buck Rogers Solar Scouts Badge, all brass color	55	83	110
Buck Rogers Solar Scouts Spaceship Commander Badge, 1936 Cream of Wheat premium	55	83	110
Buck Rogers Solar Scouts Sweater Emblem	1000	2000	4000
Buck Rogers Space Ranger Kit, Sylvania	70	125	250
Buck Rogers Super Dreadnaught, balsa wood	310	625	1250
Buck Rogers Telescope	70	105	140
Buck Rogers Uniform	400	800	1600
Buffalo Bill Bamby Bread Horseshoe Badge, late 1930s	12	18	30
Buffalo Bill Jr. Brass Ring, Buffalo in relief on top, TV premium	30	50	90
Buster Brown Gang (Smilin' Ed) Ring	50	90	165
Buster Brown Gang Tab Pins, assorted, price for each	10	15	25
Butter-Nut Bread Premium, "Sail-Me" glider, c. 1930, 4-1/2" wingspan	6	10	25
Capt. Tim Ivory Club Pin, Ivory Soap, c. 1936	9	13	25
Captain America Sentinel of Liberty Badge	190	375	750

	C6	C8	C10
Captain Franks Air Hawks Ring	70	150	275
Captain Franks Air Hawks Wings, Post's 40% Bran Flakes premium, c. late 1930s	35	50	75
Captain Gallant Medal, w/an animal, c. 1950, dated 1939-1945	17	26	35
Captain Gallant Medal, cross w/GRI, 1950s	17	26	35
Captain Hawk Sky Patrol Propeller Badge, c. late 1930s	15	30	65
Captain Marvel Club Button, five styles	35	70	140
Captain Marvel's Magic Whistle, full-color picture of Captain Marvel on both sides, American Seed Co. ad on the inside, c. 1943, American Seed Co.	27	41	55
Captain Midnight 1941 Manual for Decoder	60	110	225
Captain Midnight 1942 Manual for Decoder	85	160	330
Captain Midnight 1945 Manual for Code-O-Graph	65	90	140
Captain Midnight 1946 Manual for Code-O-Graph	65	90	140
Captain Midnight 1947 Manual for Code-O-Graph	55	65	110
Captain Midnight 1948 Manual for Code-O-Graph	55	65	110
Captain Midnight 1949 Manual for Code-O-Graph	75	110	220
Captain Midnight 1956 Manual for Decoder Badge	125	250	500
Captain Midnight 1957 Manual for Silver Dart Decoder	110	220	335
Captain Midnight 3-Way Mystic Dog Whistle, 1942	25	50	100
Captain Midnight Aerial Torpedo Bomber, 1941	80	100	150
Captain Midnight American Flag Loyalty Badge, 1940	75	150	300
Captain Midnight Code-O-Graph, works as a whistle, 1947	50	100	200
Captain Midnight Code-O-Graph, Key-O-Matic, w/key, 1949	110	135	275
Captain Midnight Code-O-Graph, round, w/mirror, 1948	55	110	225
Captain Midnight Code-O-Graph Badge, w/photo of Captain Midnight, 1942	75	150	300
Captain Midnight Code-O-Graph Decoder Pin, eagle on top, 1941	60	120	225

Buck Rogers Space Ranger Kit, $250. Photo courtesy Toy Collector News

Dick Tracy Badge, "Crime Stoppers," $25. Photo courtesy Jim Harmon

---

CONDITION CODE

C6 Good; evident overall wear, well played with but acceptable to many collectors

C8 Very Good; minor overall wear, very clean

C10 Mint; like new

Note: Mint in Box commands a higher price.
Condition below C6 brings considerably lower prices

	C6	C8	C10
Captain Midnight Code-O-Graph Magnifier, 1945	85	135	175
Captain Midnight Code-O-Graph Mirrormatic, 1946	125	175	250
Captain Midnight Detect-O-Scope, 1941	55	85	150
Captain Midnight Flight Commander Commission, 1956	35	50	100
Captain Midnight Flight Commander Flying Cross, 1942	50	100	200
Captain Midnight Flight Commander Ring, 1941	175	250	500
Captain Midnight Flight Commander Signet Ring, 1957	550	1050	2250
Captain Midnight Flight Patrol Wings Badge, 1942	48	72	95
Captain Midnight Flight Patrol Wings Badge	48	72	95
Captain Midnight Jumping Bean Target, 1939	75	150	300
Captain Midnight Magic Blackout Lite-Ups, 1942	125	250	500

	C6	C8	C10
Captain Midnight Marine Corps Ring, 1942	190	275	550
Captain Midnight Medal, brass, pictures of cast, secret word, spinner, 1940	15	23	30
Captain Midnight MJC-10 Plane Detector, distance finder, 1942	300	600	1200
Captain Midnight Mystic Eye Detector Ring, 1942	135	190	275
Captain Midnight Mystic Sun God Ring, 1946	1200	2250	4400
Captain Midnight Printing Ring, 1948	80	160	350
Captain Midnight Secret Squadron Decoder Badge, gold, 1956	110	165	275
Captain Midnight Secret Squadron Decoder Badge, silver, 1957	85	110	275
Captain Midnight Secret Squadron Insignia Transfer, 1949	20	30	40
Captain Midnight Service Ribbon Pin, 1944	60	115	225
Captain Midnight Spy Scope, 1947	53	80	105

	C6	C8	C10
Captain Midnight Surprise Package, 1942	27	41	55
Captain Midnight Trick and Riddle Book, Skelly Oil premium, sixty-four pages, 1939	15	25	50
Captain Midnight Weather Wings, predicts weather, 1940	42	63	85
Captain Midnight Whirlwind Whistling Ring, 1941	140	280	575
Captain Video Flying Saucer Ring	400	800	1650
Captain Video Rite-O-Lite	50	100	200
Captain Video Rocket Launcher and Ships, 1950s	110	165	220
Captain Video Secret Seal Ring, 1950s	150	325	650
Captain Video Space Fleet Ray Gun, TV premium, Powerhouse, 1952	138	210	275
Captain Video X-9 Rocket Balloon, 1950s	30	45	60
Chandu Boxed Set of Tricks	400	575	800
Chandu the Magician Galloping Coin Trick, 1930s	30	45	60
Chandu the Magician Hindu Cones, 1930s	30	45	60
Charlie McCarthy Puppet Doll, cardboard, Chase & Sanborn mailer, 21" high	25	50	100
Charlie McCarthy Radio Party Game, giveaway by Standard Brands, twenty-one cardboard figures, 1938	25	50	100
Cinnamon Bear Silver Star, annual Christmas show, c. 1940s	35	50	100
Cisco Kid and Pancho Face Masks, price for each, 1953	25	38	50
Cisco Kid Badge, western hat on chain, 1950s	17	26	35
Cisco Kid Cardboard Gun, Harvest Bread giveaway, clicker sounds when handle squeezed, 7" long	20	50	100
Cisco Kid Picture Ring, 1950s	40	75	150
Cisco Kid Secret Compartment Ring	225	450	900
Cisco Kid Triple S Club Kit	25	38	50
Coco Wheats Radio Club Badge, shape of microphone	22	33	45
David Harding Counterspy, Junior Agent Badge	37	56	75
Davy Crockett Goldplated Ring	12	15	25

	C6	C8	C10
Dick Tracy Air Detective Ring	130	375	750
Dick Tracy Badge, "Sergeant"	40	80	160
Dick Tracy Badge, "A Republic Pictures"	50	100	200
Dick Tracy Badge, "Lieutenant"	50	100	200
Dick Tracy Badge, "Inspector General"	200	410	825
Dick Tracy Badge, "Detective," picture of Tracy and Junior	17	25	50
Dick Tracy Badge, "Captain"	100	175	375
Dick Tracy Badge, "Detective Club," secret money pouch in rear	38	75	150
Dick Tracy Badge, "Crime Stoppers"	12	18	25
Dick Tracy Decoder, green, 1948	22	33	45
Dick Tracy Decoder, red, 1948	22	33	45
Dick Tracy Glider Airplane, 1938	40	75	175
Dick Tracy Portrait Ring, enameled	60	200	325
Dick Tracy Secret Compartment Ring	20	40	75
Dick Tracy Secret Service, second year member pin	50	100	200
Dick Tracy Secret Service Patrol Member Pinback, early 1940s	50	100	200
Dick Tracy's Secret Detective Methods & Magic Tricks, 1939 Quaker Oats, sixty-eight pages	30	60	120
Dionne Quints "All Aboard for Shut-Eye Town" Paper Dolls, Palmolive Soap	17	26	35
Don Winslow Decoder Torpedo	875	1750	3500
Don Winslow Honor Badge	75	125	250
Don Winslow Magic Slate Secret Code Book	35	75	150
Don Winslow Ring	350	700	1400
Don Winslow USN Secret Code Book, Oxydol giveaway, sixteen-pages, 1935, 7-3/4" x 4"	40	75	150
Donald Duck Playboard, comics giveaway, 1946, 9" high	50	100	200
Donald Duck Punch-out Figure, Donald Duck bread, c. late 1940s	50	100	200
Elsie the Cow, set of four figural buttons on color illustrated card, Bordon, 1949	11	16	35
Fighting Devil Dogs Ring, w/bulldog head on top, Republic Pictures serial ring, 1938	110	220	425

Dick Tracy Badges, top row, left to right: "Lieutenant," $200; "Captain," $375; bottom row, left to right: "Sergeant," $160; "Inspector General," $825. Photo courtesy Jim Harmon

Top to Bottom: Dick Tracy Secret Compartment Ring, $75; Dick Tracy Portrait Ring, $325.

	C6	C8	C10
Flash Gordon Ring, Post Toasties Corn Flakes, 1949	30	45	65
Fort Apache (Rin Tin Tin) Plastic Ring, TV premium, 1950s...........	15	25	35
Frank Buck Explorer's Sun Watch, post-WWII, offered by Jack Armstrong	53	80	105
Frank Buck Leopard Ring	850	1700	3500
G.E. Punch-out Circus, sixty-five pieces..	65	98	130
G.E. Rodeo Punch-out, sixty-five pieces..	65	98	130
Gabby Hayes Antique Cars, price for set, 1950s	40	80	160
Gabby Hayes Quaker Cannon Ring, 1950s	75	175	350
Gabby Hayes Western Gun Collection, six weapons, six pistols, six rifles, solid non-working, 1950s	37	56	75
Gabby Scoops Junior Press Club Card, Crackajack Comics, 1945..	9	13	25
Gabby Scoops Press Card, Crackajack Comics, 1940-41..................	9	13	25
Gangbusters Pin.............................	25	38	50
G-Man Badge	10	15	20
G-Man Official Signet Ring, metal, radio program premium, 1933-35	35	75	150

	C6	C8	C10
Goofy Playboard, comics giveaway, 1946, 9" high...............................	17	25	35
Green Hornet Secret Compartment Ring, Hornet seal, glows in dark..	450	900	1900
Gun, cardboard, giveaway from Theatorium in Lykens, Penn., Pat'd Dec. 1914 by Lexington, KY, Spots Spec. Co.....................	5	10	15
H.C.B. Club Kit, contains badge, etc., early Cream of Wheat.........	22	33	45
Hop Harrigan Para-Plane, from Grape Nut Flakes plus two code signal blinders, cardboard plane, small parachute w/water container in tail of plane	250	490	975
Hop Harrigan Sun Dial Ring, unmarked.....................................	30	45	75
Hopalong Cassidy Bar 20 Compass Ring...	65	140	275
Hopalong Cassidy Face Ring	50	100	185
Hopalong Cassidy Tin Badge, Post Raisin Bran giveaway, c. 1950s..	17	26	35
Howdy Doody, flexible cardboard figure, Wonder Bread, 8"	32	48	65
Howdy Doody, Princess Winter-Spring SummerFall, cardboard figure, 14"...................................	17	26	35

	C6	C8	C10
Howdy Doody Climber, cardboard, w/string, Welch's Premium, 1950s	37	56	75
Howdy Doody Face Flashlight Ring, 1950s	60	125	250
Howdy Doody Flicker Key chain, three-dimensional picture of Howdy Doody flicks to Poll Parrot (Poll Parrot Shoes), 1950s	15	30	60
Howdy Doody Flicker Ring, flicks from Howdy to Poll Parrot, Poll Parrot premium	15	30	65
Howdy Doody Princess Dancing Puppet, moveable joints, Snickers premium, 1950s, 13"	17	26	35
Howdy Doody Puppet, cardboard, Mars Candy, 1950s, 15" high	37	56	75
I Am A Spy Smasher Button, Fawcett Comics, 1940	25	38	100
Indian Chief Tin Badge, Post Raisin Bran, c. 1950s	4	7	9
Indian Gum Chief's Head Ring, Goudey Gum card premium, silver, 1930s	10	15	20
Jack Armstrong, Secret Norden Bomb Sight, w/three bombs, paper target ships, c. WWII	150	300	650
Jack Armstrong 3-D Viewer, film-strip	63	125	250
Jack Armstrong Big 10 Football Game	45	68	90
Jack Armstrong Crocodile Ring, glows in the dark, green stone	200	425	850
Jack Armstrong Explorer's Telescope	17	25	50
Jack Armstrong Flashlight	15	30	60
Jack Armstrong Hike-O-Meter	25	50	100
Jack Armstrong Magic Answer Box	37	75	150
Jack Armstrong Paper Airplane Models, many different, price per each	17	25	35
Jack Armstrong Paper Airplane Models, many different, reprints, price per each	5	8	10
Jack Armstrong Ped-O-Meter, blue or silver models	25	50	100
Jack Armstrong Secret Egyptian Coder Siren Ring, Wheaties, late 1930s	65	100	150
Jack Armstrong Secret Whistle Code Card for Secret Egyptian Coder Siren Ring	15	20	45

	C6	C8	C10
Jeff Paper Mask, Shell Oil, 1933	10	15	20
Jimmie Allen Colonial Gasoline Flying Cadet Wings, bronze, late 1930s	17	26	35
Jimmie Allen High-Speed Gasoline Flying Cadet Wings, bronze, late 1930s	20	30	40
Jimmie Allen Richfield Hi-Octane Flying Cadet Wings, c. 1930s	20	30	40
Jimmie Allen Richfield Hi-Octane Pilot's Identification Bracelet, metal, late 1930s	21	32	42
Jimmie Allen Skelly Oil Die-cut Airplane Cadet Wings, late 1930s	15	23	30
Jimmie Allen Skelly Oil Flying Cadet Wings, bronze, late 1930s	15	23	30
Joe E. Brown Pin	10	15	20
Junior G-Men Membership Kit, c. mid-1930s	50	100	200
Junior G-Men of America, gold-plated tin badge, late 1930s	22	33	45
Junior Texas Ranger Badge, 1936	17	26	35
Kellogg's Frogmen, add baking soda and they swim underwater, 1950s	10	15	35
Kellogg's Krumbles Around-the-World Paper Dolls, each cutout from box contains boy and girl; includes Italy, Mexico, France and Czechoslovakia, price for each	4	7	9
Kellogg's Nautilus Nuclear Submarine, 1950s	20	40	75
Kellogg's Pep Airplane Carrier, cut-out sheet w/airplane carrier and five planes, 3/4" wingspan, carrier 6-1/2" x 10"	37	56	75
Kellogg's Pep Warplanes, cardboard, price for each, c. 1944	7	11	20
Kellogg's Pep Warplanes, balsa, w/Superman ad on envelope, c. 1945	20	30	45
Little Orphan Annie Necklace, metal enamel figure of Annie on metal chain, c. 1936	63	125	250
Little Orphan Annie Pinback Button, Little Orphan Annie, Member Funny Frosty's Club, mid-1930s	21	32	42

	C6	C8	C10
Little Orphan Annie, Radio Orphan Annie's Secret Society 5th anniversary booklet, 1938	15	30	45
Lone Ranger, brass star badge, A Republic Serial	88	175	350
Lone Ranger Atom Bomb Ring	75	125	175
Lone Ranger Blackout Kit, Kix cereal, glow-in-the-dark material (two pieces), glow-in-the-dark pledge to flag, glow-in-the-dark Lone Ranger Volunteers armband, includes instructions, 1942	52	90	125
Lone Ranger Bond Bread Safety Club Badge, 1938	22	40	50
Lone Ranger Chief Scout Badge, Silvercup Bread, early 1940s	75	112	150
Lone Ranger Clicker Pistol, black, movie giveaway, Lone Ranger on one side and ruby on other, non-moveable silver cylinder, 1939	83	125	200
Lone Ranger Deputy Shield, brass, w/secret compartment	40	60	100
Lone Ranger Flashlight Ring	42	63	95
Lone Ranger Frontier Town, full set	1000	2000	4000
Lone Ranger Glow-in-the-Dark Belt, 1941	85	140	175
Lone Ranger Hi-Yo Silver Pin, 1938	15	30	60
Lone Ranger Kix Air Base, w/cereal box cut-outs, plus map, precursor of Frontier Town	125	250	500
Lone Ranger Lucky Piece, advertises seventeenth anniversary, 1933-50	50	100	200
Lone Ranger Mask, back of black mask promotes a personal appearance by "The Long Ranger and Silver!," one of the last radio premiums, c. 1953 or 1954	20	35	75
Lone Ranger Movie Film Ring, Cheerios, late 1949-50	80	120	175
Lone Ranger Pedometer, Cheerios, 1948	15	23	30
Lone Ranger Rubber Band Gun, cardboard, 1938 Morton Salt giveaway, w/six different targets	100	225	450
Lone Ranger Safety Scout Badge, Silvercup Bread, 1935	22	33	65

	C6	C8	C10
Lone Ranger Secret Compartment Ring, w/picture of Lone Ranger and Silver	135	125	175
Lone Ranger Silver Bullet, secret compartment compass	35	50	100
Lone Ranger Silver Saddle Film Ring, Cheerios, late 1940s	80	115	160
Lone Ranger Silvercup Bread Safety Patrol, metal, silver and blue	25	40	75
Lone Ranger Six-Shooter Ring, gun ring w/plastic and metal gun attached to top, turn wheel and flint sparks	135	190	275
Lone Ranger Victory Corps Badge, Kix Cereal, 1942	32	48	65
Lone Ranger Weather Ring, color square stone on top w/litmus paper, no markings to identify as Lone Ranger	40	60	80
Magic Show Kit, General Mills, 1946	14	21	35
Magician's Book of Cigarette Tricks, Camel Cigarettes, 1933	9	13	30
Major Bowes Home Microphone	30	50	100
Maltex Health Club Pinback Button	4	7	9
Melvin Purvis Junior G-Man Corps Badge, late 1930s	30	40	85
Melvin Purvis Junior G-Man Corps Roving Operative Badge, late 1930s	30	40	85
Melvin Purvis Law and Order Patrol Lieutenant's Secret Operator Badge, mid-1930s	40	60	85
Melvin Purvis Law and Order Patrol Secret Operator Badge, late 1930s	40	60	80
Melvin Purvis Law and Order Ring	55	110	225
Melvin Purvis Secret Operator, Girl's Division	35	50	100
Mickey and Donald's Race to Treasure Island, Standard Oil giveaway, 1939, 12" x 25"	100	150	225
Mickey and Donald's Race to Treasure Island, map of U.S. in full color, Calco Gasoline giveaway, w/stamps, 1939, 20" x 27"	350	500	700
Mickey Mouse Club Pinback Button, "Copyright 1928-30 by W.E. Disney", 1-1/4"	60	185	125

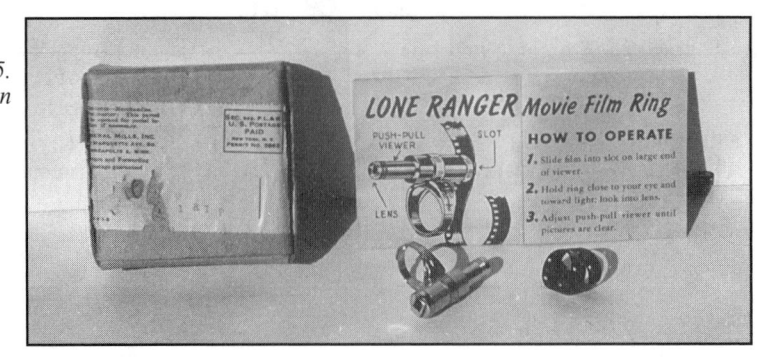

Lone Ranger Movie Film Ring, $175.
Photo courtesy Jim Harmon

	C6	C8	C10
Mickey Mouse Globe Trotters Map, NBC Bread, 1937, 28" x 20"	355	525	715
Mickey Mouse Globe Trotters Map, NBC Bread, w/all pictures pasted on, 28" x 22"	355	525	715
Mickey Mouse Globe Trotters Map, Pevely Milk premium, 1930s	355	525	715
Mickey Mouse Official Money, Mickey Mouse Cones dollar bills, one dollar denomination, each, 1930s	12	18	25
Mickey Mouse Playboard, comics giveaway, 1946, 9" high	27	41	55
Morton Salt "Bat-O-Ball", features The Shadow (cartoon), 1939	62	93	125
Myrt and Marge Recordings, platic, 1930s, 4"	20	30	40
My-T-Fine Grocery Store, folds into a full-color grocery store w/period products on the shelves, shoppers and workers, dated 1930, 8" x 3"	40	75	150
Nabisco Finger Puppet Rings, Slim Chants, horse Humbolt, gun, Prairie Mary, Tagalong Boswell, Cold Deck Charlie, Sam Spiel, price for each	2	3	5
Nabisco Santa Fe Twin Unit Diesel Train, includes engine, train, tracks, grounds, background, 1956	12	18	25
Nabisco Shredded Wheat Nabisco Flying Circus, designed by Wallace Rigby, series of twenty-four, price for each, 1948, 4" x 7" cards	5	8	10
Nabisco Sound-Jet Glider	15	18	25

	C6	C8	C10
Nabisco Trailblazers of America cards, six cards make up horse-drawn van and open van, 1956	5	8	10
Nebbs, The—Detroit Times series No. 27544, (comic strip)	7	11	15
New York World's Fair Children's World G-Man Badge, giveaway, three-color brass badge	30	40	60
Newsboy Brand Soups and Vegetables Official Booster Badge, late 1930s	4	7	9
Pep Pins, Popeye and Olive Oyl, price for each	7	11	15
Pep Pins, Superman	25	35	50
Pep Pins, The Phantom	10	15	25
Pep Pins, Dick Tracy	15	22	30
Pep Pins, Flash Gordon	15	22	30
Pep Pins, Little Orphan Annie	7	11	15
Pep Pins, Felix the Cat	5	8	10
Pep Pins, Others; includes Smitty, Harold Teen, Skeezix, Corky, Pop Jenks, Goofy, Spud, Andy Gump, Gravel Gertie, Punjab, Hans, Kayo, Smilin' Jack, Dagwood, B.O. Plenty, Mr. Bailey, Shadow, Moon Mullins, Flattop, Rip Winkle, Uncle Willie, Emma, Inspector, Chief Brandon, Vitamin Flintheart, Sandy, Uncle Bim, Sundown, Lillums, Tilda, Uncle Walt, Perry Winkle, Judy, Min Gump, Wilmer, Smoky Stover, Daisy, Ma Winkle, Tess Trueheart, Herbie, Mamie, Breezie, Pat Patton, Maggie, Barney Google, Fat Stuff, Chief Brandon, Toots, Nine, etc., average price for each	7	11	20

	C6	C8	C10
Pep Rings, Jack Kramer, Dennis O'Keefe, Burt Lancaster, Sitting Bull, Pocahontas, Pan American Clipper, Douglas F-3D Sky Knight, Republic XF91 Thundercepter, price for each	10	15	20
Pepsodent's Moving Picture Machine, shows Mickey Mouse, Donald Duck, Snow White and Seven Dwarfs, in color	350	500	750
Pillsbury-Farina Complete Tel-A-Phone Set, two holders, mouthpieces, ear phones and fifty feet of line, 1938	30	40	75
Pinocchio Playboard, Disney Comics subscription giveaway, 1946	30	40	60
Popeye the Sailor Man Button, theatre giveaway, copyright 1935, 3/4"	20	25	35
Popsicle Movie Star Coins, aluminum coins, includes Irene Dunne, Clark Gable, Marion Davies, Fredric March, Marie Dressler, Gary Cooper, c. 1930s	5	8	15
Porcelain Enamel & Mfg. Co. West Point Cadet, on card w/Pemco ad on back, 6" figure, 3" x 6" card	2	3	5
Post Cereal Rings, Perry Winkle, Winnie Winkle, Harold Teen, Skeezix, Lillums, Herbie and Smoky Stover, 1948	17	26	35
Post Cereal Rings, Dick Tracy, 1948	20	30	40
Post Grape Nuts Flakes Playing-Filling Station, c. 1950s	5	8	10
Post Grape Nuts Tin Rings, Little King, Phantom, Skeezix, Lillums, Harold Teen	20	30	40
Post Raisin Bran Sheriff Badge	10	15	20
Post Toasties Corn Flakes Comic Rings, Fritz, hans, Tillie the Toiler, Toots and Casper, 1949	17	26	35
Post Toasties Walt Disney Cut-out Figures on Box, Mickey the Traffic Cop, two types of Pinocchio, price for each, 1939	27	41	60
Post's Cereal Junior Detective Club Sergeant Badge, late 1930s	10	15	35

	C6	C8	C10
Post's Explorer Ring, plastic dome, includes compass, sun watch, sunset predictor and star finder, 1947	30	40	60
Radio Orphan Annie 1934 Manual	62	93	125
Radio Orphan Annie 1935 Decoder Manual	62	93	125
Radio Orphan Annie 1935 Decoder Pin	30	40	60
Radio Orphan Annie 1936 Decoder Badge	30	40	60
Radio Orphan Annie 1936 Decoder Manual	62	93	125
Radio Orphan Annie 1937 Decoder Badge	30	50	110
Radio Orphan Annie 1937 Decoder Manual	62	93	125
Radio Orphan Annie 1938 Decoder Badge	40	70	130
Radio Orphan Annie 1938 Decoder Manual	62	93	125
Radio Orphan Annie 1939 Decoder Badge	40	70	130
Radio Orphan Annie 1939 Decoder Manual	62	93	125
Radio Orphan Annie 1940 Decoder Badge	40	70	130
Radio Orphan Annie 1940 Decoder Manual	83	125	165
Radio Orphan Annie 1942 Decoder Manual, w/cardboard decoder	200	350	425
Radio Orphan Annie 3-Way Dog Whistle, 1940	25	50	100
Radio Orphan Annie Altascope Ring, fewer than fifteen known to exist	NPF	NPF	24,000
Radio Orphan Annie Annie and Joe Corntassel Button, 1931	150	300	600
Radio Orphan Annie Associated Membership Pin, 1934	10	25	50
Radio Orphan Annie Bandanna, 1934	20	40	80
Radio Orphan Annie Birthstone Ring, 1935	125	225	550
Radio Orphan Annie Capt. Sparks Aviation Trainer	250	375	500
Radio Orphan Annie Circus Cut-Outs, 1935	150	250	500
Radio Orphan Annie Code Captain Belt and Buckle, 1940	75	150	300
Radio Orphan Annie Code Captain Pin, 1939	25	50	100

	C6	C8	C10
Radio Orphan Annie Foreign Coins, 1937	25	38	50
Radio Orphan Annie Goofy Circus, 1939	188	375	750
Radio Orphan Annie Identification Bracelet, 1935	25	50	100
Radio Orphan Annie Identification Bracelet, 1934	25	50	100
Radio Orphan Annie Identification Tag, 1939	20	35	75
Radio Orphan Annie Magic Transfer Picture, 1937	20	40	85
Radio Orphan Annie Magic Transfer Pictures, 1935	20	40	85
Radio Orphan Annie Mask, 1933	60	80	125
Radio Orphan Annie Mystic Eye Ring, 1939	150	275	550
Radio Orphan Annie Package, includes Whirl-O-Matic Decoder, Whistle Badge, booklet, and order blanks, 1942	125	300	600
Radio Orphan Annie Pin, 1937	17	26	50
Radio Orphan Annie Portrait Ring, ring has head of Annie embossed on top, 1934	50	75	100
Radio Orphan Annie Punch-outs	120	180	240
Radio Orphan Annie Ring, 1934	50	75	100
Radio Orphan Annie Ring, 1935	50	75	100
Radio Orphan Annie Roller Skates, 1938	50	100	200
Radio Orphan Annie School Pin, 1939	20	40	75
Radio Orphan Annie Secret Egyptian Compass and Sundial, 1938	50	75	100
Radio Orphan Annie Secret Guard Clicker, 1942	25	50	100
Radio Orphan Annie Secret Society Silver Star Ring, 1936	100	200	400
Radio Orphan Annie Shake-up Game, 1931	25	50	100
Radio Orphan Annie Signet Ring, 1937	65	130	275
Radio Orphan Annie Silver Star Pin, 1935	48	72	95
Radio Orphan Annie Silver Star Pin, 1934	48	72	95
Radio Orphan Annie Silver Star Ring, 1937	100	200	400
Radio Orphan Annie Silver Star Ring, 1938	100	200	400

	C6	C8	C10
Radio Orphan Annie Treasure Hunt Game, 1933	75	150	300
Radio Orphan Annie Treasure Hunt Game, 1935	75	150	300
Range Rider & Dick West Button, Peter Pan bread, 1950s	37	56	75
Red Ryder Lucky Coin	7	11	15
Renfrew of Mounted Pinback	10	15	20
Rin Tin Tin "Ball-in-the-Hole" Games, sealed coin-size games of Rinty, Rip Masters, Fort Apache, etc., price for each	9	13	18
Rin Tin Tin Ring, plastic, 1950s	20	30	40
Rin Tin Tin Set of Plastic Dinosaurs, radio-TV, 1954	62	93	125
Rin Tin Tin Wonderscope, Telescope-Microscope-Compass w/"Rin Tin Tin" on face, radio-TV, 1954	30	45	100
Rip Masters (Rin Tin Tin) Plastic Rings, 1950s	25	35	45
Rocky Lane's Explorer's Sun Watch, Carnation Milk, 1951	20	40	75
Roy Rogers Branding Iron Ring	80	130	275
Roy Rogers Deputy Badge	10	15	20
Roy Rogers Microscope Ring, Quaker Oats, 1947	65	95	150
Roy Rogers Paint Set, 1950s	12	18	25
Roy Rogers Signal Badge, w/mirror, secret compartment and whistle	40	88	175
Roy Rogers Silver Hat Ring	200	425	850
Roy Rogers Trigger's Lucky Horseshoe, full size, black rubber	12	18	35
Roy Rogers Tuck-A-Way Gun	15	20	40
Scoop Ward News of Youth Official Reporter Badge, Ward's Soft Bun Bread giveaway, late 1930s	10	15	20
Secret Three Badge, w/manual of secret codes	10	15	20
Sgt. Preston Distance Finder	45	65	95
Sgt. Preston Firefighting Set	45	65	95
Sgt. Preston Flashlight, signals has two filters	25	50	100
Sgt. Preston Klondike Land Pouch	25	38	50
Sgt. Preston Klondike Movie Film Viewer	60	120	250
Sgt. Preston Pedometer	15	30	65
Sgt. Preston Police Whistle, nylon cord, brass, 1950	27	41	55

	C6	C8	C10
Sgt. Preston Skinning Knife	125	250	300
Sgt. Preston Totem Pole Set	55	100	200
Sgt. Preston Trail Kit, the most complex of all premiums, rare...	320	475	700
Sgt. Preston Yukon Village	300	450	600
Shadow "Carey Salt" Ring, same as J. Armstrong Crocodile ring w/black stone, (this ring has been counterfeited; original is smoothly circular w/clean-cut design, requires identifying papers for C10 price)..................	300	550	1150
Shadow Ring, Glow in Dark, "blue coal" jewel on white ring	500	740	975
Shield G-Man Club Badge, Pep Comics premium, lithographed celluloid pinback, 1942	35	75	125
Skippy Compass, 1930s?................	10	15	20
Skippy S.S.S.S. Captain, celluloid pinback button, 1930s	12	18	25
Sky Birds Propeller Ring, brass and silver, Goudey Gum premium, 1930s	12	18	25
Sky King Aztec Indian Ring...........	250	500	1000
Sky King Detecto Microscope........	53	78	105
Sky King Detecto Writer	70	105	140
Sky King Electronic Television Ring	110	175	225
Sky King Magni-Glo Ring	110	175	225
Sky King Mystery Picture Ring	60	85	120
Sky King Navajo Indian Ring	135	200	275
Sky King Signal Scope	70	105	140
Sky King Small Plastic Statues, includes Sky King, Penny, Sky King's horse, Sky King's plane, The Songbird, Nabisco give-aways in Wheat Honey and Rice Honey, price for each, 1950s.......	15	22	30
Sky King Stamp Kit........................	48	72	95
Sky King Teleblinker Ring..............	135	200	275
Snow White Game, Tek Toothbrush	35	75	150
Space Patrol Binoculars, c. 1950s	120	175	225
Space Patrol Diplomatic Pouch, contains money, stamps, etc........	138	210	275
Space Patrol Goggles.....................	53	78	105
Space Patrol Jet Glow Code Belt, 1951..	138	210	275
Space Patrol Ring, w/secret powder compartment, c. early 1950s	145	225	300

	C6	C8	C10
Space Patrol Smoke Gun, 1950s	150	225	300
Space Patrol Space Helmet, c. 1950s..	180	270	360
Space Patrol Space Ship, c. 1950s..	88	132	175
Space Patrol Space-O-Phone, 1952..	98	150	195
Speed Gibson's Flying Police Badge, Dreikorn's Bread.............	12	18	25
Staight Arrow Magic Cave Ring, w/original art, 1949	110	150	300
Staight Arrow Puppets and Props, Nabisco radio premium, 1949	30	45	60
Staight Arrow Target Game, litho-graphed tin target board, National Biscuit Company, copy-right on the edge, 10" x 14"	37	56	75
Staight Arrow Tom-Tom, c. early 1950s..	25	50	75
Staight Arrow Wrist Bracelet, w/secret compartment, c. early 1950s..	35	75	150
Straight Arrow Face Ring, c. early 1950s	60	90	125
Sunbrite "Junior Nurse Corps" Brass Badge................................	4	7	9
Sunbrite "Junior Nurse Corps" Pin-back Button, pictures of Dorothy Hart	3	5	7
Superman Crusader Ring.................	140	195	275
Superman Kellogg's Gy Rocket......	50	100	200
Superman Kellogg's Silver Jet Air-plane Ring, plane flies off	80	140	260
Superman Kellogg's Walkie-Talkie	37	56	75
Superman of America Button, pin-back button, 1939 version, 1-3/8"...	20	40	75
Superman Pin, "Read Superman Action Comics Magazine", 1940s..	20	35	75
Superman Planes from Pep Cereal, set of eight, 1948	30	45	60
Superman Premium Club Set, cer-tificate, button and decoder	200	400	800
Superman Tim Club Ring................	3750	7500	15,000
Superman's Secret Code, c. 1939...	24	36	63
Tarzan Gift Statues, Foulds, Tarzan, Jane, Kala, etc., price per set, 1930s...	300	600	1100

Front to Back: Radio Orphan Annie Decoder Manual, 1937, $125; Decoder Badge, 1937, $110. Photo courtesy Jim Harmon

Radio Orphan Annie's Secret Society 1938 Decoder Manual, $125.

Radio Orphan Annie 1939 Decoder Badge, $130. Photo courtesy Jim Harmon

Ad for Roy Rogers Branding Iron Ring on Quaker Oats Box, price for ring $275. Photo courtesy Jim Harmon

Roy Rogers Deputy Badge, $20. Photo courtesy Jim Harmon

Tom Mix Western Movie Viewer, $250. Photo courtesy Jim Harmon

	C6	C8	C10
Tarzan Jungle Map and Treasure Hunt Weston Biscuit, 1933	250	300	600
Tennessee Jed Lariat	37	56	75
Tennessee Jed Look Around Ring, 1940s	130	275	550
Tennessee Jed Paper Gun, c. 1940s	21	32	42
Terry and The Pirates Glow-in-the Dark Ring, crocodiles on sides	40	60	80
Terry and The Pirates Gold Detector Ring	70	95	150
Texas Longhorn Tin Badge, Post Raisin Bran, c. 1950s	4	7	9
The Liberty Gun For Young America - McGrath's Big Store, w/photos of Charlie Chaplin, 7" cardboard	20	30	40
Tom Corbett Decoder, cardboard, 1950s	35	52	70
Tom Corbett Rings, Kellogg's twelve different rings, including-Space Cruiser, Rocket Scout, Space Academy, Space Suit, Space Helmet, Corbett-Space Cadet, Cadet Dress Uniform, Girl's Space Uniform, Parallo-Ray Gun, Strate-Telescope, Sound Ray Gun, price for each, 1950-55	20	30	40

	C6	C8	C10
Tom Corbett Space Cadet Badge, early 1950s	35	75	150
Tom Corbett Space Cadet Belt Buckle Decoder, early 1950s	75	150	300
Tom Mix 1941 Manual	50	80	160
Tom Mix 1944 Manual	50	80	140
Tom Mix 1946 Manual	40	60	115
Tom Mix Airplane and Parachute	100	150	200
Tom Mix Arm Patch, Tom Mix bar on ckeckerboard design, 1933, predominantly blue; 1947, predominantly red; 1983, predominantly black	20	35	75
Tom Mix Badge Ranch Boss	130	263	525
Tom Mix Bag of Marbles	20	30	40
Tom Mix Bandanna, has Tom Mix brand	50	100	200
Tom Mix Baseball	25	38	50
Tom Mix Baseball Bat	25	38	50
Tom Mix Baseball Cap	27	41	55
Tom Mix Belt Buckle with Secret Compartment, belt glows in the dark, offered only on cereal boxes after radio show ended	75	125	250
Tom Mix Blowdart Game	250	300	600
Tom Mix Branding Iron, w/Tom Mix brand	52	78	105
Tom Mix Bullet Flashlight	52	78	105
Tom Mix Bullet Telescope, w/bird-call device, 4" long	35	52	105

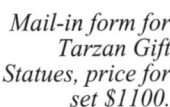

Mail-in form for Tarzan Gift Statues, price for set $1100.

	C6	C8	C10
Tom Mix Catalog of Straight Shooter Premiums, wood gun, black and white sheet w/order form on reverse, desciptions and small pictures of premiums on the front, includes sheepskin vest, rodeo rope, leather cuffs, lucky spinner, etc., 8-1/2" x 11"..	20	30	60
Tom Mix Charm Bracelet, charm steer head, gun, horseman, w/Tom Mix brand	75	150	250
Tom Mix Coloring Book, Ralston, c. 1949	20	30	40
Tom Mix Compass Magnifying Glass, silver color, (originals have "Japan" written on the back; imitations have the words "Comet-Japan" on the back), 1947	45	68	90
Tom Mix Compass Magnifying Glass, brass, 1939......................	50	100	200
Tom Mix Compass Magnifying Glass, plastic, glows in the dark, c. 1948	75	125	150
Tom Mix Cowboy Shirt...................	75	150	300
Tom Mix Cowboy Skirt...................	150	225	300
Tom Mix Cowboy Vest..................	82	125	165
Tom Mix Decoder Badge, moveable six-shooter points to symbols, 1940	110	160	275

	C6	C8	C10
Tom Mix Decoder Buttons Instruction Sheet, Ralston, 1946	20	30	50
Tom Mix Decoder Pin, "Curley Bradley"	15	30	60
Tom Mix Decoder Pins, Tony, Jane, Sheriff, Wash, price for each	20	30	50
Tom Mix Deputy Ring, chewing gum premium, 1934	2000	3500	7500
Tom Mix Glow-in-the-Dark Arrowhead, has compass and magnifying glass, 1946...........................	75	125	150
Tom Mix Gold Ore Badge...............	25	50	100
Tom Mix Good Luck Spinner	27	41	55
Tom Mix Horseshoe Nail Ring, rounded point identifies original, 1933..	25	50	75
Tom Mix Identification Bracelet.....	42	63	85
Tom Mix Initial Ring, 1935	110	175	225
Tom Mix Look-Around Ring, c. 1945..	65	95	150
Tom Mix Lucky Wrist Band, Ralston premium, Tom Mix brand, metal, w/leather strap and buckle, 1936	50	100	200
Tom Mix Magnet Gun and Signal Arrowhead Bracelet, gun and arrowhead glow in the dark........	50	80	165
Tom Mix Magnet Ring, 1945..........	60	80	160

	C6	C8	C10
Tom Mix Makeup Kit, two grease-paint model, plus five grease-paint model	300	450	600
Tom Mix Mask, cardboard	385	580	770
Tom Mix Mystery Picture Ring, w/"look-in" picture of Tom Mix and Tony, viewed through one side of the ring, 1939	175	275	400
Tom Mix Ore Charm, contains genuine gold ore under plastic dome, Ralston, 1940	42	63	85
Tom Mix Parachute, Ralston premium, 1936	75	125	250
Tom Mix Periscope	75	125	250
Tom Mix Postal Telegraph Set, metal, blue, Ralston premium, 1938	45	75	150
Tom Mix Premium Enclosures and Correspondence, many picture postcards, letters on Straight Shooter stationery, etc.; sent out to listeners who wrote to the radio show; these and various coupons, instruction sheets, contest entries are offered by dealers and collectors	20	30	40
Tom Mix Ralston Straight Shooters Pocket Knife, 1940	40	80	175
Tom Mix RCA TV Set, shows photographs or comic strips, brown or reddish model	25	50	75
Tom Mix RCA TV Set, shows photographs or comic strips, gold	75	150	300
Tom Mix Secret Code Manual	25	50	100
Tom Mix Sharpshooters Medal, glows blue in the dark, copy	10	20	40
Tom Mix Sharpshooters Medal, glows green in the dark, original	83	125	165
Tom Mix Sheriff of Dobie County Siren Badge, Ralston, 1946	48	72	115
Tom Mix Signal Arrowhead, made of lucite w/magnifying glass and "whizzer" flute-type whistle, 1949	40	75	150
Tom Mix Signal Flashlight	40	75	150
Tom Mix Signature Ring, pre-WWII	140	200	275
Tom Mix Siren Ring, 1945	75	100	175

	C6	C8	C10
Tom Mix Six-Shooter, wooden, barrel breaks and cartridge drum spins, 1933	60	180	320
Tom Mix Six-Shooter, wooden, barrel spins, 1936	75	150	300
Tom Mix Six-Shooter, wooden, no moving parts, 1939	80	140	275
Tom Mix Spinning Rope, hemp w/wood handle, Ralston, 1936	53	78	105
Tom Mix Spurs, metal, w/plastic glow-in-the-dark rowels	50	100	200
Tom Mix Square and Fair Spinner	37	56	75
Tom Mix Straight Shooters Campaign Medal, silver	42	63	85
Tom Mix Straight Shooters Campaign Medal, gold	42	63	85
Tom Mix Sundial Watch	45	75	150
Tom Mix Telegraph Set, red, uses batteries, 1940	140	210	280
Tom Mix Telephone Set	45	75	175
Tom Mix Telescope, Tom Mix brand on side	45	75	150
Tom Mix Tiger Eye Ring, Ralston, 1949	175	250	325
Tom Mix TM Brand Ring, c. 1933	100	115	160
Tom Mix Western Movie Viewer, shows scenes from Tom Mix films, 1935	75	125	250
Tom Mix Whistle Ring, 1945	75	100	150
Tom Mix Wrangler Badge, Ralston, 1936	40	80	175
Toonerville Trolley Cardboard Village, put out by Coca-Cola	88	132	175
Trigger Button, Post Grape Nut Flakes, 7/8"	12	18	25
Welch's Grape Juice Train, paper engine, box car, passenger car, caboose, price for each	3	5	7
Welch's Grape Juice Train, Complete set	12	18	25
Westinghouse, 1940	10	15	20
Wheaties Jogometer, 1960s	12	18	25
Wheaties Pedometer, late 1940s	10	15	20
Wild Bill Hickok Bunkhouse Set, cut-out pin-ups of Bill, Jingles, guns, ropes, etc.	15	25	50
Wild Bill Hickok Treasure Map and Guide, Kellogg's, 1952	48	72	95

RAMP WALKERS

Ramp walkers—those funny looking characters that waddle down slanted surfaces—are fondly remembered by many aging Baby Boomers. While popular from the 1930s through the 1960s, one of the earliest ramp walkers dates back to the late 1800s. In 1873, Ives patented two versions of a cast-iron elephant walker, one had a pivoting trunk while the other had a fixed trunk with lead feet. While many were manufactured in the United States, wood, cardboard, and composition walkers also came from such exotic locations as Czechoslovakia, Argentina, and Germany.

Louis Marx Co. was the primary manufacturer of plastic walkers during the early 1950s and mid-1960s. The majority were produced in Hong Kong, while a few were made in the United States and sold under either the Marx logo or the Charmore Co., a subsidiary of the Marx Co. Colorful tin lithographed ramps were available for some of the Marx plastic walkers, but most relied on homemade ramps or a weighted string that hung over the end of a table and pulled the toy along. In addition to the United States and Hong Kong, plastic walkers were manufactured in England, Germany, and Argentina. Other manufacturers include, Fun World; Dolls, Inc.; Ohio Art; Educational Toys, a subsidiary of Topper Corp.; and Gantry of England.

The most popular walkers—Wilson Walkies—were made by John Wilson of Watsontown, Pennsylvania. Sold nationwide, most of the two-legged Walkies consisted of an empty cardboard thread body and stood approximately 2-1/4" tall. Walkers produced between 1940 and 1950 are marked with the U.S. Patent number, 2140275 on the bottom of one foot, while earlier versions were marked, "Made in U.S.A. Pat. Pending" or Made in U.S.A. Pat'd 12-18-40."

There are three common sizes of ramp walkers, (a) small, approx. 1-1/2" x 2"; (b) medium, approx. 2-3/4" x 3"; and (c) large, approx. 4" x 5" in size. Most smaller walkers were unpainted, while the medium and larger sizes were either hand painted or spray painted. The recent series of approximately 30 small sized ramp walkers manufactured in China currently sell between $1-5.

Variations

There were some quite interesting variations on the use of walkers. A few are presented here.

The Minnesota Electronics Corp. took the generic pig made by Marx and glued a small magnet in the back end. This was boxed with a plastic children's ring which had a small magnet glued to the top. When the ring was placed near the pig's back end, the opposing forces of the magnets forced the pig to walk along a flat surface. The toy was named Maggie the Magnetic Pig.

Ohio Art produced a plastic farm set named the Walker Farm. This included a bard and a ramp along with seven ramp-walking people and animals pushing interchangeable parts such as a lawnmower, lawn roller, wheelbarrow, and spreader.

The comical Action Target Game by Marx includes a long lithographed tin ramp, a plastic bear ramp walker, a small working plastic rifle, and five wooden bullets. The box was placed behind the ramp as a backdrop. The child would shoot at the bear as it waddled down the ramp. A word key with a picture on it was inserted in to the base of the ramp, the child would then attempt to spell the word for the picture on the key. The letters would march up and down the ramp, and if the word was spelled correctly, Big Bird would pop up with a sign that read, "OK!" If the word was spelled incorrectly, all of the letters would fall down. Additional letters and a ramp extension were available separately.

In 1995, Milton Bradley marketed a children's game named Penguin Shuffle. The game included two sets of like-colored penguins and two ramps that lead down to a slow turning battery-operated wheel. The wheel had five openings into which the penguins fit. The object was to get all three of the same colored penguins into the wheel, the first one to do so wins. If the penguin didn't waddle down the ramp and walk into the opening on the wheel at just the right moment, it fell down a slide and the child had to try again.

Value

The market for Ramp Walkers has changed very little in the last several years. This is good and bad. Although values have not seen steady increases, they also have not suffered significant declines. Because the value of a walker is significantly reduced when the paint is scratched or when there are cracks and breaks, only prices for walkers in Mint condition are listed.

Contributor: Randy Welch, Raven 'Tiques, 27965 Peach Orchard Rd., Easton, MD 21601-8203. Welch began collecting ramp walkers after the purchase of a Huckleberry Hound and Yogi Bear walker at a flea market rekindled childhood memories of marching walkers down his wooden school desk. After discovering there wasn't any reference material available on ramp walkers, Welch began compiling a list and photo collection of over 300 known walkers. His other areas of interest include tin wind-ups and tin lithographed sparklers. He welcomes correspondence from other collectors.

Backing card from the Charmore Co.

Big Band Wolf and Three Little Pigs, Marx, $150.

Donald and Goofy riding a go-cart, Marx, $40.

Argentina (Bakelite Cone and Legs)	C10
Penguin, very similar in size and shape to Wilson	75

Argentina ≈ (Paper Cone and Wood Legs)	C10
China (Gaucho's wife), versions red, blue and green	75
Chinese Man Pushing Tin Cart	90
Clown, w/elephant head pushing tin cart	90
Clown Pushing Tin Cart	90
Gaucho, w/pig head pushing tin cart	90
Gaucho, w/elephant head pushing tin cart	90
Gaucho (Cowboy)	75
Musketeer	75
Policeman	75
School Boy	75

Argentina (Plastic)	C10
Cow Blue (same size as pig)	25
Horse, cream color w/pink legs, similar to Marx.	25

Argentina (Plastic) (Continued)	C10
Pig, blue, similar to Marx only smaller	25

Czechoslovakia (Wood and Composition)	C10
Bird	35
Dog on Four Legs	30
Donald Duck, walks w/front-to-back motion, w/wood ramp	90
Dutch Girl	60
Large Bird, store display	200
Man with Carved Wooden Hat	35
Monkey	35
Pig	20
Policeman	60

Disney (Plastic)	C10
Big Bad Wolf and Mason Pig, Marx	50
Big Bad Wolf and Three Little Pigs, Marx	150
Donald and Goofy Riding a Go-cart, Marx	40
Donald Pulling Three Nephews in a Wagon, Marx	35

Fred Flintstone riding on green Dino, Marx, $75.

Mickey with Pluto hunting, Marx, $40.

Yogi Bear and Huckleberry Hound, Marx, $50.

Top Cat and Benny, Marx, $65.

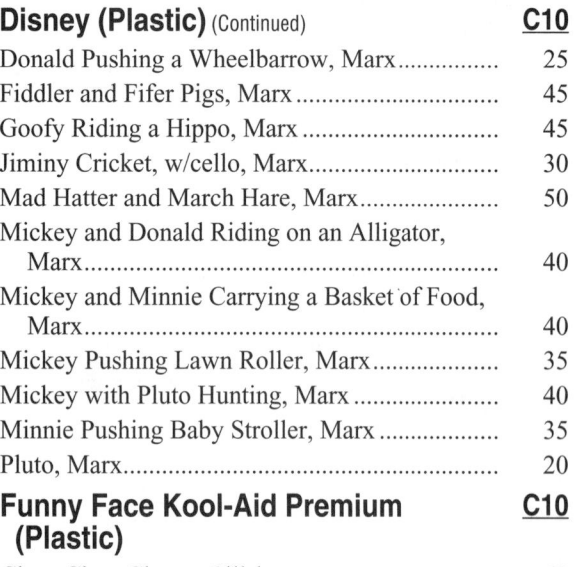

Disney (Plastic) (Continued)   C10

Donald Pushing a Wheelbarrow, Marx	25
Fiddler and Fifer Pigs, Marx	45
Goofy Riding a Hippo, Marx	45
Jiminy Cricket, w/cello, Marx	30
Mad Hatter and March Hare, Marx	50
Mickey and Donald Riding on an Alligator, Marx	40
Mickey and Minnie Carrying a Basket of Food, Marx	40
Mickey Pushing Lawn Roller, Marx	35
Mickey with Pluto Hunting, Marx	40
Minnie Pushing Baby Stroller, Marx	35
Pluto, Marx	20

Funny Face Kool-Aid Premium (Plastic)   C10

Choo-Choo Cherry, Pillsbury	60

Funny Face Kool-Aid Premium (Plastic) (Continued)   C10

Goofy Grape, Pillsbury	60
Jolly Ollie Orange, Pillsbury	60
Root'n Toot'n Raspberry, Pillsbury	60

Germany (Wood and Composition)   C10

Goat	60
Pig	60
Zebra	60

Hanna-Barbera and King Features (Plastic)   C10

Astro, Marx	150
Astro and George Jetson, Marx	90
Astro and Rosey, Marx	95
Fred and Wilma Flintstone Rriding on Dinosaur, Marx	60
Fred Flintstone and Barney, Marx	40

Fred Flintonstone and Barney, Marx, $40.

Astro and Rosey, Marx, $95.

Bunny with carrot on back of dog, Marx, $60.

Monkey carrying bananas, Marx, $60.

	C10
Hanna-Barbera and King Features (Plastic) (Continued)	
Fred Flintstone Riding on Green Dino, Marx	75
Little King and Guard	70
Pebbles Riding on Purple Dino, Marx	75
Popeye Pushing Spinach-can Wheelbarrow, Marx	25
Top Cat and Benny, Marx	65
Yogi Bear and Huckleberry Hound, Marx	50
Irwin (Celluloid)	**C10**
Popeye, 5-3/4" tall	60
Ives (Cast Iron)	**C10**
Elephant, w/lead feet and fixed trunk, pat. 1873	125

	C10
Ives (Cast Iron) (Continued)	
Elephant, w/iron feet and swivel trunk, pat. 1873	125
Large (Plastic)	**C10**
Baby Teeny Toddler Walking Girl, Dolls, Inc.	40
Baby Walk-a-Way baby, Marx	40
Baby Walking baby, cloth dress, w/moving eyes, Marx	40
Baby Walking Baby in Canadian Mountie Uniform, Marx	50
Baby Walking Baby in Pirate Clothes, Marx	50
Cow Milking Cow, Marx	40
Cow Wiz Walking Milking Cow Charmore, Marx	40

Figaro the Cat with ball, Marx, $30.

Left to Right: Frontiersman with dog, Marx, $95; Indian woman pulling baby on travois, Marx, $95.

Popeye and Wimpy, Marx, $65.

Pumpkin head man and woman, Fun World, $100.

Large (Plastic) (Continued)   C10

Double Walking Doll, (boy behind girl), Hong Kong	60
Horse, w/rubber ears and string tail, Marx	30
Horse, Marx	30
Horse with English Rider, Marx	50
Popeye and Wimpy, w/heads on springs, Marx	65
Toni & Vroni (Jack & Jill), w/box, Germany	150

Long John Silvers Premium (Plastic)   C10

Capt. Flint Parrot, green	15
Flash Turtle, green and yellow	15
Quinn Penquin, black and white	15
Sydney Dinosaur, yellow and purple	15
Sylvia Dinosaur, lavender and pink	15

Marx Animals with Riders Series (Plastic)   C10

Ankylosaurus, w/clown	35
Bison, w/native	35
Brontosaurus, w/monkey	35
Hippo, w/native	35
Lion, w/clown	35
Stegosaurus, w/black caveman	35
Triceratops, w/native	35
Zebra, w/native	35

Marx Other (Plastic)   C10

Baseball Player, w/bat and ball, Marx	40
Bear, Marx	20
Boy and Girl Dancing, Marx	45
Bull, Marx	20
Bunnies Carrying Large Carrot	35

Wilson Walkies. Left to right: Indian Chief, $70; Black Mammy, $40; Soldier, $30.

An advertisement for Marx ramp walkers.

Marx Other (Plastic) (Continued)

	C10
Bunny, w/carrot on back of dog, Marx	60
Bunny Pushing Cart, Marx	60
Camel, w/two humps, head bobs up and down	20
Chicks Carrying Large Easter Egg	35
Chilly Willy Penguin on Sled Pulled by Parent, Marx	25
Chinamen Carrying a Duck in a Basket, Marx	30
Chipmunks Carrying Acorns, Marx	35
Chipmunks in Marching Band Playing Drum and Horn, Marx	35
Dachshund Dog, Marx	20
Dairy Cow, Marx	20
Duck, Marx	20
Duck Mama, w/three ducklings, Marx	35
Dutch Boy and Girl, Marx	40
Elephant, Marx	20
Farmer Pushing Wheelbarrow, Marx	30
Figaro the Cat, w/ball, Marx	30
Firemen, Marx	35
Frontiersman, w/dog, Marx	95

Marx Other (Plastic) (Continued)

	C10
Goat	20
Hap and Hop Soldiers, Marx	25
Horse Circus Style, Marx	20
Indian Woman Pulling Baby on Travois, Marx	95
Kangaroo, w/baby in pouch, Marx	25
Maggie the Magnetic Pig, w/box and ring	95
Marty's Market Lady Pushing Shopping Cart, Marx	65
Monkeys Carrying Bananas, Marx	60
Mother Goose, w/goose, Marx	60
Nurse Maid Pushing Baby Stroller, Marx	20
Pig, Marx	20
Pigs, two carrying third in basket, Marx	40
Poodle, Gantoy, England	40
Pumpkin Head Man and Woman, faces on both sides, Fun World	100
Reindeer, Marx	45
Sailors S.S. Shoreleave, Marx	25
Santa, w/white sack, Marx	40
Santa, w/yellow sack, Marx	40

Various Argentinean Walkers. Front row, left to right: Penguin, Bakelite, $75; Chiinese man pushing tin cart, $90; Gaucho with elephant head pushing tin cart, $90; Clown with elephant head, $90; Gaucho with pig head pushing tin cart, $90; Clown pushing tin cart, $90. Back row, left to right: School boy, $75; Musteteer, $75; Gaucho, $75; Policeman, $75; China (Gaucho's wife), in green, red and blue, $75.

Wilson Walkies: Left to right: Penguin, $25; Elephant with four legs, $30; Pig, $40.

Wilson Walkies. Left to right: Little Red Riding Hood, $40; Clown $40; Nurse, $30.

Donald Duck with wood ramp, Czechoslovakia, $90.

Dog with wood ramp, made in Japan for Shackman of New York, $75.

Marx Other (Plastic) (Continued)

	C10
Santa, w/gold open sack, Marx	45
Santa and Mrs. Claus, faces on both sides, Fun World	45
Santa and Snowman, faces on both sides, Fun World	45
Sheriff Facing Outlaw, Marx	65
Spark Plug the Horse, Marx	200
Tin Man Robot Pushing a Cart, Marx	150

Ramps in Box

	C10
Circus Horse, Marx	65
Comical Action Bear, w/long ramp, including gun and bullets, Marx	150
Dick Tracy's Nursemaid Takes Bonny Braids for Stroll, Marx	125

Ramps in Box (Continued)

	C10
Disney Long Ramp, w/generic street scene, Marx	200
Dog, wood w/wood ramp, made in Japan for Shackman of New York	75
Felix Wood Ramp, w/wood walker	1400
Hap and Hop the Dauntless Doughboys, Marx	80
I Like Ike Elephant, Marx	125
Nora the Nursemaid, Marx	75
Plank Ramp (generic), for cow, pig, ducks, bear, etc., Marx	50
S.S. Shoreleave Sailors, Marx	75
Seven Dwarfs, Samco, Italy	800
Slugger the Walking Bat Boy	250

Left: Double Walking Doll with box from Hong Kong. Right: Toni and Vroni with box from Germany. Photo courtesy Randy Welch

Czech Dutch Girl, Bird, Cow, and Monkey. Photo courtesy Randy Welch

Olive Oyl, Whimpy, Donald Duck, and Pinocchio. Photo courtesy Randy Welch

Cast Iron Elephant with Swivel Trunk by Ives, this is one of the first walkers. Photo courtesy Randy Welch

Ramps in Box (Continued)   C10

Street Scene (generic) Short Ramp, for farmer pushing wheelbarrow, etc., Charmore	75

Small (Plastic with Metal Legs)   C10

Cow, head down, Marx	20
Cow, head up, Marx	20
Cowboy on Horse	30
Dog, brown Pluto-like, Marx	20
Donald Duck Pushing Wheelbarrow, Marx	40

Small (Plastic with Metal Legs) (Continued)   C10

Elephant	30
Mexican Cowboy on Horse	30
Mickey and Minnie Mouse, Marx	40
Pluto, Marx	35

Wilson Walkies (Wood and Composition)   C10

Black Mammy	40
Clown	40

Czech Large Bird (store display) and Bird. Photo courtesy Randy Welch

Top Cat and Benny, Marx. Photo courtesy Randy Welch

Celluloid Popeye by Irwin. Photo courtesy Randy Welch

CONDITION CODE

C6 Good; evident overall wear, well played with but acceptable to many collectors

C8 Very Good; minor overall wear, very clean

C10 Mint; like new

Note: Mint in Box commands a higher price.
Condition below C6 brings considerably lower prices

Maggie the Magnetic Pig, Minnesota Electronics Co. Photo courtesy Randy Welch

Tin Man Robot, Marx. Photo courtesy Randy Welch

Slugger the Walking Bat Boy. Photo courtesy Randy Welch

Seven Dwarfs from Samco, Italy. Photo courtesy Randy Welch

Twinkle Toes with box, Doll Art. Co. Photo courtesy Randy Welch

Wilson Walkies (Wood and Composition) (Continued)	C10
Donald Duck	175
Elephant on Four Legs	30
Eskimo	75
Indian Chief	70
Little Red Riding Hood	40
Nurse	30
Olive Oyl	175
Penguin	25
Pig	40

Wilson Walkies (Wood and Composition) (Continued)	C10
Pinocchio	200
Popeye	200
Rabbit	60
Sailor	30
Santa Claus	90
Santa Claus, w/box	150
Soldier	30
Twinkle Toes, w/box, Doll Art Co.	300
Wimpy	175

Advertisement for Marx walking toys. Courtesy Randy Welch

Advertisement for Gravitoys' Mystery Wiz Walkers. Courtesy Randy Welch

SCHOENHUT

The A. Schoenhut Company had a long history of toy manufacturing. Many items were produced, including animals, figures, moving pictures, Palmer Cox Brownies, children's musical instruments and dolls. This section covers some of the items in the Humpty Dumpty Circus.

The Humpty Dumpty items covered in this section span the years of 1903 to 1935. Glass-eyed animals and two-part head personnel, along with other rare examples, are priced higher than painted-eye animals and pressed-head figures produced later. Delevan items are generally priced lower than reduced-size figures.

In the past few years, the toys' popularity among toy collectors and folk art collectors has driven prices up. Particular interest in Teddy Roosevelt's Adventures in Africa series (produced from 1909 to 1911) had led the price increase.

Although this history is not all inclusive, it should help the collector identify age for some animals/figures.

1872	Produced first toy pianos
1903	Began producing Humpty Dumpty Circus items
	Began producing glass-eyed animals, molded/two-part head personnel
1909-11	Produced Teddy Roosevelt figures
1910	Produced bisque head ring master, lady circus rider, lion tamer, lady/gent acrobats
1918	Produced painted-eyed animals, wooden-head personnel
1923	Began producing reduced-size circus
1927	Produced miniature set (donkey, elephant, clown)
1935	Company closed
1950	Nelson Delevan purchased manufacturing rights and produced several figures and animals.

There are a few rules to keep in mind while collecting Schoenhut toys.

Condition determines price.

Mint condition Schoenhut toys are virtually nonexistent. Mint condition means the toy was never played with and demands higher prices. Boxes increase value, and Mint in Box items command a sizeable premium.

Glass-eyed animals, early figures with plaster faces, and rare animals demand high prices.

Bisque-headed figures and molded/two-part head figures generally demand a higher price than carved-face figures.

Condition on the majority of animals and figures found today is between C4 and C7.

Skillful restoration can increase value. Anyone selling an animal or figure with restored sections should indicate where restoration has occurred.

Prices in this guide have not been established for every style of animal and figure.

Because of the importance of condition and the classification for the Schoenhut category of toys, the existing definitions of Schoenhut categories need to be explained.

Rating	Definition
C1	Bits and pieces of Schoenhut toys.
C2	Poor quality with no paint or with a "child's" effort to repaint, or missing a major part. Definitely needs repair.
C3	Fair with no missing major parts but with little paint; moisture/moth/animal damage and soiling. Needs repair.
C4	Good with play wear; soiled/worn clothing, damaged paint/chips, missing leather and/or other attachable parts.
C5	Very good with restored paint, clothes, and/or leather.
C6	Fine with good paint, new or worn leather and minor restorations. Could also have some soiling/wear/color loss and missing minor attached parts.
C7	Very fine with minor wear/color loss and fractional restoration.
C8	Almost perfect with no restoration but may have slight color loss.
C9	Perfect, meaning no damage or color loss of any kind. Almost new.
C10	Mint, meaning never played with and stored under ideal conditions. Factory new.

Note: Restringing is not considered restoration. If the restringing effort is not done properly, however, wood damage can occur and reduce the value of the piece. Additional information on Schoenhut figures or dolls can be obtained by joining the Schoenhut Collectors Club. For a membership application, please contact Pat Girbach, 103 West Huron Street, Ann Arbor, MI 48103.

Contributors: Original list by Jim and Patsy Carlson, 7939 Caberfare Trail, Clarkson, MI 48348-3708. Pricing updates by Keith Kaonis, c/o Antique Doll Collector magazine, 6 Woodside Ave., Ste. 300, Northport, NY 11768, Phone: (888) 800-2588.

Circus Accessories

(Regular and Reduced Size)

These items are most commoonly found in "play wear" condition of C4 to C7 category. Not all accessories have been included.

CIRCUS ACCESSORIES (REGULAR AND REDUCED SIZE)

	C4	C6	C8	C10
Ball, reduced	25	30	40	65
Ball	35	40	50	75
Barrel	5	10	15	20
Chair	2	5	10	15
Flexible Cage	125	250	450	650
Goblet	2	5	7	10
Hoop	30	60	80	110
Horizontal Bar	200	400	650	900
Ladder	2	5	10	15
Pedestal, tall	15	30	60	90
Pedestal, short	10	25	50	75
Table	7	15	30	40
Tent, 24" x 16" (small)	400	800	1500	2000
Tent, 24" x 36" (large)	500	1000	2000	2700
Tent, litho w/panels	1000	2500	4800	7000
Tub	5	10	20	30
Weights, 50/100/200 lbs	75	150	230	325
Whip, 4-1/2" shaft	10	20	60	80
Whip, 5-1/2" shaft	15	25	40	65
Wild Animal Cage Wagon	400	850	1050	1250

Circus Animals: Glass-Eyed and Painted-Eyed (Regular Size)

Prices here are for the animals that are most frequently seen; not all animals have been included. Glass-eyed animals were made from 1903, when A. Schoenhut Company began to produce circus animals and performers, to about 1918. Painted-eyed animals were produced from about 1918 to 1933, when the A. Schoenhut Company closed.

CIRCUS ANIMALS: GLASS-EYED AND PAINTED-EYED (REGULAR SIZE)

	C4	C6	C8	C10
Alligator, painted eyes	175	350	400	450
Alligator, glass eyes	200	450	550	650
Brown Bear, glass eyes	200	425	525	600
Brown Bear, painted eyes	125	250	300	350
Buffalo, painted eyes	200	275	400	500
Buffalo, glass eyes, cloth	350	550	750	900
Buffalo, glass eyes, carved	450	750	1000	1200
Bulldog, glass eyes, carved mane	600	1200	1400	1500
Bulldog, painted eyes	300	500	650	800
Burro, painted eyes	150	350	400	450
Camel, one hump, painted eyes	145	300	350	400
Camel, two hump, glass eyes	450	900	1050	1200
Camel, two hump, painted eyes	225	300	350	400
Camel, one hump, glass eyes	175	400	500	600
Cat, glass eyes	1400	2400	2700	3000
Cat, painted eyes	450	850	1350	1600
Cow, painted eyes	200	400	500	600
Deer, glass eyes	400	950	1100	1400
Deer, painted eyes	250	500	650	800
Donkey, glass eyes	100	175	200	250
Donkey, painted eyes	50	90	110	130
Elephant, glass eyes	100	175	225	300
Elephant, glass eyes w/blanket	200	475	550	600
Elephant, painted eyes	60	110	135	150
Gazelle, glass eyes	750	1500	2300	2750
Gazelle, painted eyes	350	800	1000	1200
Giraffe, glass eyes	225	500	600	700
Giraffe, painted eyes	180	300	350	400
Goat, painted eyes	100	200	250	275
Goat, glass eyes	125	280	325	400
Goose, painted eyes	200	400	525	600
Gorilla, molded ears	1400	3000	3250	3500
Gorilla, leather ears	1400	3000	3300	3750

A group of Schoenhut Humpty Dumpty Circus figures and accessories. Photo courtesy Christie's East

Tent, C8 condition $2000. Photo courtesy Jim and Patsy Carlson

Giraffe with glass eyes and open mouth, C6 condition, $500; Flexible Cage, C6 condition, $675. Photo courtesy Jim and Patsy Carlson

(Continued)	C4	C6	C8	C10	(Continued)	C4	C6	C8	C10
Hippopotamus, glass eyes	225	500	650	750	Monkey, white face	275	600	750	850
Hippopotamus, painted eyes	175	325	400	450	Ostrich, glass eyes	300	700	800	900
Horse, brown, painted eyes	125	250	300	350	Ostrich, painted eyes	200	400	550	650
Horse, white, glass eyes	175	350	400	450	Pig, painted eyes	150	300	350	400
Horse, white, painted eyes	100	200	250	275	Pig, glass eyes	175	500	700	800
Horse, brown, glass eyes	175	350	425	500	Polar Bear, painted eyes	250	600	850	1100
Hyena, glass eyes	2000	4000	5000	6000	Polar Bear, glass eyes	400	1200	1600	2000
Hyena, painted eyes	600	1500	1800	2200	Poodle, glass eyes, carved				
Kangaroo, glass eyes	600	1400	1600	1800	mane	350	800	1050	1200
Kangaroo, painted eyes	200	500	750	1000	Poodle, painted eyes	75	150	175	200
Leopard, painted eyes	225	500	600	700	Rhinoceros, glass eyes	275	600	700	800
Leopard, glass eyes	350	800	1000	1200	Rhinoceros, painted eyes	150	350	450	500
Lion, painted eyes	175	350	450	550	Sea Lion, glass eyes	450	1000	1250	1500
Lion, glass eyes, carved					Sea Lion, painted eyes	250	500	700	800
mane	300	750	1000	1200	Sheep, glass eyes	350	550	650	800
Lion, glass eyes, cloth mane	275	750	900	1000	Sheep, painted eyes	200	375	450	500
Monkey, black face	200	400	500	600	Tiger, painted eyes	175	400	500	600

Left to Right: Tall pedestal, Short pedestal and Tub, all are painted wood with applied printed paper bands; all in C7 condition valued at $90, $75 and $30, respectively. Photo courtesy Jim and Patsy Carlson

Brown Bear with glass eyes in C6 condition, $800. Photo courtesy Jim and Patsy Carlson

Cat, glass eyes, C6 condition, $3000. Photo courtesy Jim and Patsy Carlson

(Continued)	C4	C6	C8	C10
Tiger, glass eyes	400	750	900	1200
Wolf, glass eyes	1000	3250	4250	4750
Wolf, painted eyes	500	1600	1750	1900
Zebra, glass eyes	350	750	1000	1200
Zebra, painted eyes	200	400	500	550
Zebu, painted eyes	400	1000	1250	1500
Zebu, glass eyes	1000	2200	2700	3000

Performers Wooden/Pressed One-Part Head (Regular Size)

The manufacturing sequence for figures was plaster face two-part head/faces, bisque heads, and finally wooden/pressed one-part head. Not all figures have been included.

PERFORMERS WOODEN/PRESSED ONE-PART HEAD (REGULAR SIZE)

	C4	C6	C8	C10
Chinaman	300	600	700	800
Clown	150	275	325	375
Hobo	150	300	350	400
Lady Acrobat	175	325	400	450
Lady Rider	135	275	350	400

(Continued)	C4	C6	C8	C10
Lion Tamer	275	550	650	750
Negro Dude	200	500	600	700
Ring Master	150	325	400	450

Reduced-Size Figures and Animals

Reduced-size figures and animals were first produced around 1927 by the A. Schoenhut Company to appeal to another market and as a last-ditch effort to save the company. Unfortunately, the company closed in 1933.

Not all figures and animals have been included.

REDUCED-SIZE FIGURES AND ANIMALS

Animals, Reduced	C4	C6	C8	C10
Brown Bear	175	325	400	450
Buffalo	175	325	400	450
Camel, two humps	175	325	400	450
Donkey	20	40	50	60
Elephant	35	70	85	100
Giraffe	175	325	400	450
Hippopotamus	175	325	400	450
Horse, white	50	100	125	150
Horse, brown	35	85	110	135

Left to Right: Camel with one hump (Arabian), glass eyes and open mouth, C8 condition, $750; Camel with two humps (Bactrian), glass eyes, carved head and neck showing tool marks, C8 condition, $1200. Photo courtesy Jim and Patsy Carlson

Elephant with glass eyes, blanket and triangular-shaped headdress, the most sought-after of all elephants; C7 condition, $600. Photo courtesy Jim and Patsy Carlson

Gorilla with two-part head and leather ears, C7 condition, $3,750. Photo courtesy Jim and Patsy Carlson

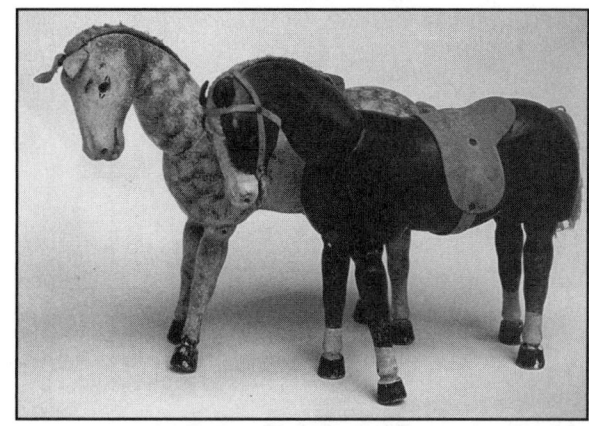

Left to Right: White horse with glass eyes, referred to as "Educated Horse," C8 condition, $450; Brown Horse with glass eyes, leather saddle and bridle, C8 condition, $500. Photo courtesy Jim and Patsy Carlson

Animals, Reduced	C4	C6	C8	C10
Leopard	150	275	325	375
Lion	150	275	325	375
Ostrich	150	350	450	550
Pig	150	350	450	550
Poodle	175	325	400	450
Rhinoceros	175	325	400	450
Tiger	150	275	325	375
Zebra	175	325	400	450

REDUCED-SIZE FIGURES AND ANIMALS

Circus Figures, Reduced	C4	C6	C8	C10
Clown	50	95	110	125

Circus Figures, Reduced (Continued)	C4	C6	C8	C10
Hobo	125	275	325	375
Lady Rider	50	100	120	135
Negro Dude	125	275	325	375
Ring Master	75	120	135	150

Teddy Roosevelt's Adventures in Africa

These figures were produced in low volume from 1909 to 1911 and represent "rare" or "scarce" toys. Some of the animals used as circus play toys were produced with glass eyes until 1918.

Left to Right: Monkey with black face, one-piece molded head, C6 condition, $600; Monkey with white face, C5 condition, $850. Photo courtesy Jim and Patsy Carlson

Wolf, painted eyes, C6 condition $1900. Photo courtesy Jim and Patsy Carlson

Tiger, with glass eyes, full ball-jointed neck and leather ears, C8 condition, $1200. Photo courtesy Jim and Patsy Carlson

Close-up of bisque-head Ringmaster. Photo courtesy Jim and Patsy Carlson

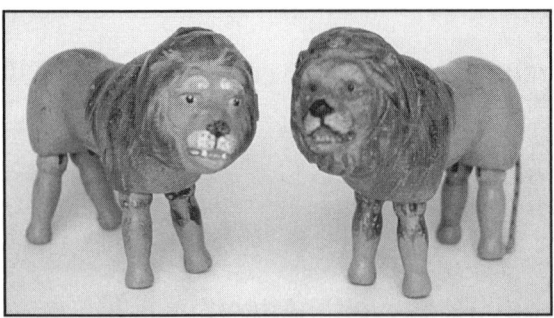

Left to Right: Lion, painted eyes, C8 condition $550; Lion, glass eyes, carved mane, C8 condition, $1,200. Photo courtesy Jim and Patsy Carlson

Lady Rider, C4 condition, $400.

Zebra with glass eyes, closed mouth, head and neck in two sections leather strip mane and cord tail, C7 condition, $1100. Photo courtesy Jim and Patsy Carlson

Chinaman with two-part head, C6 condition, $1,300. Photo courtesy Jim and Patsy Carlson

Clown with two-part head, Dresden "footprint" glued to front of suit and star collar, rare, C7 condition, $700. Photo courtesy Jim and Patsy Carlson

African Chief, C7 condition $800. Photo courtesy Jim and Patsy Carlson

TEDDY ROOSEVELT'S ADVENTURES IN AFRICA

Miscellaneous	C4	C6	C8	C10
Doll House, large	150	225	500	750
Doll House, medium	125	175	375	425
Doll House, small	100	150	250	375
Golfer, Man	125	175	350	425
Golfer, Girl	125	200	375	475
Milk Wagon, horses and driver	1250	2400	3000	4000
Piano, 14" x 10"	30	60	120	175

Miscellaneous (Continued)	C4	C6	C8	C10
Railroad Station, large	125	175	350	475
Roly Poly, Black Clown	200	300	600	850

TEDDY ROOSEVELT'S ADVENTURES IN AFRICA

Teddy Roosevelt Animals	C4	C6	C8	C10
Alligator, glass eyes	100	175	350	475
Camel, glass eyes, one hump, closed mouth	100	150	300	425

Negro Dude, C6 condition $700. Photo courtesy Jim and Patsy Carlson

Left to Right: bisque-head perfomers-Lion Tamer, C6 condition, $750; Lady Rider, C6 condition, $400; Lady Acrobat, C6 condition, $450; Ringmaster, C6 condition, $1600. Photo courtesy Jim and Patsy Carlson

Elephant, with glass eyes, C8 condition $300.

Teddy Roosevelt Animals (Continued)	C4	C6	C8	C10
Deer, glass eyes	200	300	575	875
Elephant, glass eyes	40	70	135	200
Gazelle, glass eyes	400	1000	1600	2400
Giraffe, glass eyes, closed mouth	175	350	475	650
Gorilla, leather ear	1000	1700	2300	3000
Hippopotamus, glass eyes	100	275	550	800
Hyena, glass eyes	1400	1600	2200	3200
Lion, glass eyes, carved mane	300	475	850	1500
Rhinoceros, glass eyes	175	375	600	950
Zebra, glass eyes, closed mouth	175	375	625	950
Zebu, glass eyes	1200	1400	2100	3000

TEDDY ROOSEVELT'S ADVENTURES IN AFRICA

Teddy Roosevelt Figures	C4	C6	C8	C10
African Chief	250	600	700	800
African Drummer	1500	2500	3000	3300
African Native	1300	2200	2500	2800
Arab Chief	1800	2750	3200	3500
Doctor	1800	2750	3200	3500
Naturalist	1800	2750	3200	3500
Photographer (Kermit)	1850	2750	3200	3500
Teddy Roosevelt	1300	2300	2700	3000

SHIPS

(See also Tin Wind-Ups, Paper)

Freighter, 1941, Auburn Rubber, $45.

Warship, c. 1915, Bing, $1100.
Photo courtesy Bertoia Auctions

A.C. Williams

	C6	C8	C10
Speed Boat, cast iron, blue, 4-3/4" long	120	180	240
Speed Boat, cast iron, 5-1/4" long	60	90	120
Speed Boat, cast iron, 4" long	45	68	90
Speed Boat, cast iron, w/rider, 4-3/4" long	120	180	240

Arcade

	C6	C8	C10
Show Boat, cast iron, white ship, words "Show Boat" on side, released to coincide with the premiere of the movie "Show Boat", Arcade, 1929, 11-1/4" long, 3-3/4" high, 3-1/2" wide	600	950	1200

Auburn Rubber

	C6	C8	C10
Battleship, No. 1582, c. 1940, 8-1/4" long	22	33	45
Dreadnaught, extremely rare, 1941, 9-1/8" long	30	50	70
Freighter, 1941, 9-1/4" long	22	33	45
Submarine, c. 1941, 6-1/2" long	20	30	40
Tugboat, plastic	37	56	75

Authenticast

	C6	C8	C10
French Warships, includes Richelieu, Algiers, Fantasque and others, price for each	17	26	35
German Warships, scale models including Narvik, Galster and others, price for each	22	33	44
Japanese Warships, includes Fuso, Kaga, Mogani and others, price for each	17	26	35
U.S. Scale Model Warships, WWII including Iowa, Enterprise, Sims and Farragut and submarine Sarge, each	17	26	35

Bing

	C6	C8	C10
Battleship, tin clockwork, 16"	800	1300	1800
Destroyer, tin clockwork, 22-1/2" long	1500	2400	3500
Ferry, clockwork, 16" long	800	1300	1800
Gunboat, hand-painted tin, 29" long	1800	3000	5500
Ocean Liner, tin keywind, c. 1925, 13-1/2" long	400	650	900
Torpedo Boat, 27-1/2" long	2000	3500	6500
Warship, clockwork, c. 1915, 19" long	500	800	1100

Torpedo Boat, Bing, $6500. Photo courtesy of Bertoia Auctions

Ferry, Bing, $1800. Photo courtesy Bertoia Auctions

Top left: Ocean Liner, tin keywind, c. 1930, Arnold, $900; top right: "Bremen," Falk, $3000; middle left: Merchant Marine ship, Ives, $900; middle right: Oil Tanker, Fleischmann, $1350; bottom left: Ocean Liner, Bing, $900; bottom right: "New York," Ives, $1100. Photo courtesy Christie's East

Dreadnaught, 9-1/8" long, Auburn Rubber, $70. Photo courtesy Dave Leopard from his book Rubber Toy Vehicles

Battleship, Bliss, $4300. Photo courtesy Lloyd Ralston Auctions

"Union Ferry," c. 1900, Bliss, $450. Photo courtesy Bertoia Auctions

"Adirondack," Dent, $2300. Photo courtesy Bertoia Auctions

"New York" battleship, tin, c. 1910, 28" long, Marklin. In 1994, this ship sold for $33,500 at auction. Photo courtesy Christie's East

Vesuvius Gunboat, 25-1/2" long, Bliss, $2800. Photo courtesy Bertoia Auctions

Sidewheeler, "New York," Marklin, $30,000.

Bliss	C6	C8	C10
Admiral gunboat, gun shoots, 20" ...	260	390	520
Battleship, litho and wood, 36"	1800	3000	4300
Battleship New York, paper litho and stained wood, 1890, 36" x 22"	450	675	900
Conqueror, wood and paper litho, 20" long	900	1400	2000
Marguerite Sailing Schooner, 22" long...	350	525	700
Rover Torpedo Boat, paper litho on wood, c. 1896, 20" long	850	1375	1900
St. Louis, litho on wood liner, c. 1895, 34-1/2" long.......................	800	1300	1800
Union Ferry, sidewheel, c. 1900, 24" long	225	375	450
Vesuvius Gunboat, paper litho on wood, 25-1/2" long.....................	1200	2000	2800

Buckman	C6	C8	C10
Steamboat, twin sidewheeler, steam engine, marked "Patented May 7, 1872", 11" long	2000	3500	5000
Steamboat, c. 1872, 11" long...........	1300	2000	3000

Buddy "L"	C6	C8	C10
49 LST, includes tank, 12" long	50	75	100
Tugboat, No. 3000, 1929-30, 28" long..	5000	8500	13,500

Cass	C6	C8	C10
Tugboat, wood, c. WWII?, 15" long..	37	56	75
Yacht, wood, c. WWII?, 15" long..	37	56	75

Chein	C6	C8	C10
Sailboat, wheeled............................	112	168	225
Sailboat, Hercules "Peggy Jane", 23" long..	252	375	505
Speed Boat "Peggy Jane", 14-1/2" long..	115	175	235

Action Submarine, Keystone. Photo courtesy Jack Matthews

49LST, Buddy "L," $100. Photo courtesy Ed Poole

Racing Boat "Baby," Hubley, $120.

Converse	C6	C8	C10
Battleship Indiana, litho on wood, c. 1900, 32" long	650	1100	1600
Battleship Oregon, tin litho and wood, c. 1900	500	750	1000
Dent	**C6**	**C8**	**C10**
Adirondack, cast iron, 15" long	1000	1700	2300
Battleship New York, largest cast-iron boat made, c. 1900, 21"	2000	3200	4350
Eldon	**C6**	**C8**	**C10**
Aircraft Carrier, 22" long	55	83	110
Freighter, 20" long	40	60	80
L.C.T. Landing Craft, 10" long	17	26	35
U.S. Coast Guard Patrol Boat, w/figures, 22"	37	56	75
Fallows	**C6**	**C8**	**C10**
Riverboat "Jumbo", painted tin, w/sidewheel, mechanical walking beam, 1880, 14" long	1000	1500	2000
Volunteer IVL, 16" long	1800	2700	3600
Fleischmann	**C6**	**C8**	**C10**
Battleship	2000	3000	4000
Ocean Liner, painted tin clockwork, 1930, 20-1/2" long	700	1350	1800
Ocean Liner, 7-1/2" long	80	120	160

Fleischmann (Continued)	C6	C8	C10
Ocean Liner, 15-1/2" long	1000	1600	2250
Oil Tanker Esso, 20" long	600	1000	1350
Hubley	**C6**	**C8**	**C10**
Motorboat "Sea Horse", cast iron	1750	2625	3500
Racing Boat "Baby", cast-iron, wheeled, c. 1930, 4-1/2" long	60	90	120
Speed Boat "Baby", cast iron	60	90	120
Ideal	**C6**	**C8**	**C10**
Destroyer, plastic, 15" long	17	28	35
Fireboat, plastic, pumping w/siren, 1955	60	90	120
Houseboat, 5" long	12	18	25
Motorboat, Slo Motion VI, wind-up motorboat, 13" long	60	90	120
Phantom Raider	60	90	120
Pirate Ship, plastic, w/six pirates, 1953	75	112	150
Police Boat, Harbor Police	30	45	60
PT Boat	50	75	100
Scull, cast iron, Varsity Racing, eight rowers w/moving oars, coxswain, c. 1890, 14" long	2000	3000	4000

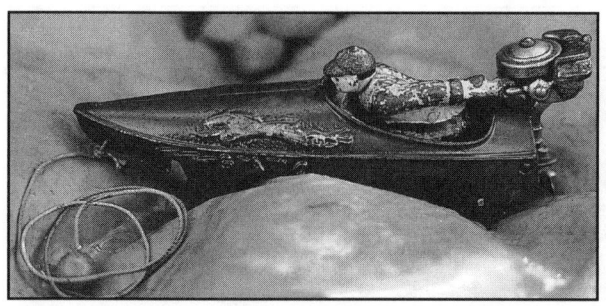

"Sea horse," Hubley, $3500. Photo courtesy Ed Hyers Antique Toys

Destroyer, Ideal, $35. Photo courtesy Toy Collector News

Left to right: "Static," "Penn Yann," Hubley. Photo courtesy Bertoia Auctions

Ideal (Continued)	C6	C8	C10
Submarine, plastic, w/torpedoes, 1950s	20	30	40
Torpedo Boat, plastic, sparking, wind-up, 12" long	50	75	100
Treasure Hunter, plastic	75	112	150

Ives	C6	C8	C10
Merchant Marine Ship, tin keywind, 13" long	450	675	900
Ocean Liner New York, 13" long	500	800	1100
Speed Boat "Miss Liberty", steam-powered, 13-1/2" long	750	1125	1500
Speed Boat "Vim", 10-1/2" long	650	975	1300
Speed Boat "Vixen", 12" long	650	975	1300
Submarine, tin keywind, dives, c. 1910, 10" long	400	600	800
U.S. Merchant Marine Boat, painted pressed tin clockwork, 10-1/2" long	250	375	500

Keystone	C6	C8	C10
Action Submarine	50	75	100
Aircraft Carrier, wooden, 12" long	50	75	100
Battleship, wooden, airplanes take off from a spring on deck of ship, 2' long w/guns	130	195	260

Keystone (Continued)	C6	C8	C10
Battleship, early 1940s, under 2' length	64	96	128
Ferry, wooden, w/two cars and trucks, c. 1930s, 14" long	40	60	80
Fishing Boat, wooden, c. 1940s, 12" long	37	56	75
Racing Sailboat, wood	30	45	60
Radar Rocket Ship	75	112	150

Liberty Playthings

Liberty Playthings was in business in the late 1920s and early 1930s in Niagara Falls, New York. All its toys, which were made of wood and metal, had names related to the word "Liberty," and all had nautical themes. Those advertised in 1929 were No. 2 Tug and Scow. No. 5 Freighter, No. 6 Airplane Carrier, No. 7 Fireboat, No. 8 Destroyer, and No. 22 Seaplane. The Carrier, which in the ad was called "Liberator," sold for $10. The "Libertania" Aircraft Carrier seems to be the same ship, or a slight variation.

Liberty Playthings	C6	C8	C10
Aircraft Carrier, "Libertania," wood and tin litho w/lead planes, 27-3/4" long	250	375	500
Cruiser or Battleship	225	338	450
Destroyer No. 8	225	338	450
Fire Boat, 23"	200	300	400
Runabout, wind-up	155	233	310

Scull, Varsity Racing, Ideal, $4000. Photo courtesy Wilkinson Collection; Detroit Antique Toy Museum

Aircraft Carrier, Keystone, $100.

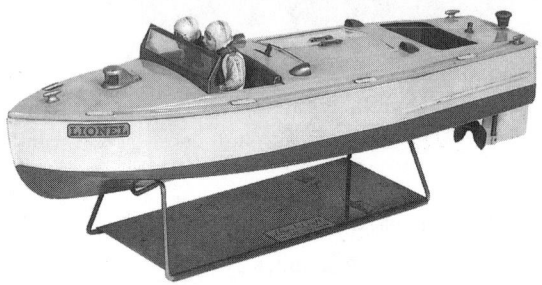

Speedboat, No. 43, wind-up, Lionel, $580. Photo courtesy Phillips New York

Aircraft Carrier "Libertania," Liberty Playthings, $500. Photo courtesy Mapes Auctioneers & Appraisers

Lionel Craft	C6	C8	C10
Speed Boat, No. 44, wind-up...........	750	1100	1700
Speed Boat, No. 43, wind-up...........	290	435	580
Märklin	**C6**	**C8**	**C10**
Battleship, clockwork, 28" long..	2500	4500	9000
Liner "Columbus", tin, electrified, 42" long.....................................	5000	10,000	18,000
Riverboat "Priscilla", 30" long........	5000	10,000	17,600
Sidewheeler "New York", tin and cast iron, w/five lead figures, 19-1/2" long..............................	8000	15,000	30,000
Submarine, tin, clockwork, 9-1/2" long..	288	430	575
Yacht, tin, steam, "Priscilla", 20-1/2" long.....................................	2000	3500	6000
Marx	**C6**	**C8**	**C10**
Luxury Liner "Caribbean", friction, sparkling, 15" long, 3-1/2" tall..	42	63	85
Putt Putt Boat, Mosquito Fleet	55	83	110

Milton-Bradley	C6	C8	C10
Tillicum Battle Fleet, No. 115, c. late 1920s	31	46	62
Tillicum Convoy Set, two destroyers, three freight boats, three ocean liners, two patrol boats, painted wood, c. 1940s, destroyers 5-1/2" long, others about 4-1/2" long.................................	350	525	700
Tillicum Harbor Set........................	20	30	40
Tillicum National Defense Set	40	60	80
Miscellaneous	**C6**	**C8**	**C10**
Adirondack Sidewheeler, cast iron, 13" long......................................	500	750	1000
Admiral Dewey Flagship, paper litho on wood, c. 1900, 30" long.	300	450	600
Admiral Dewey's Flagship from the White Fleet, wood and paper, 6" long...	100	150	200
Aeroplane Carrier, No. 372, Barclay	25	38	50

Miscellaneous (Continued)	C6	C8	C10
Aircraft Carrier, tin litho, "65," large, c. 1950s	50	75	100
Aircraft Carrier, friction, Cragstan, 8-1/2" long	60	90	120
Aircraft Carrier, plastic, Saunders, 12" long	32	48	65
Aircraft Carrier, steel, w/three jet planes that fire rockets, shell or drop bombs, Argo, 6" planes, 36" long	68	102	135
Amazon Sidewheeler, plastic and metal, Atwood Motors, California, c. 1950s	125	188	250
Atomic Submarine, Hasbro	32	48	65
Battleship, pressed steel, Hill-climber, 15" long	200	300	400
Battleship, painted pressed steel, friction, Ohio, 16" long	140	210	280
Battleship, pressed steel, hill climber, 18" long	300	450	600
Battleship, tin friction, c. 1920s, 9-1/2" long	200	300	400
Battleship, plastic, Banner, 4" long	15	22	30
Battleship, glass, candy container, approx. 3" long	60	90	120
Battleship, No. 373, Barclay	27	41	55
Battleship, cast iron, 14-1/2" long	400	600	800
Battleship, friction, Dayton, c. 1920, 16" long	200	300	400
Battleship Admiral, paper litho, 1890, 20" long	600	900	1200
Battleship Missouri, all wood and metal, radio control, w/three electric motors, Sterling "56" scale model	350	525	700
Battleship New York, cast iron, c. 1920s, 20"	375	565	750
Battleship Oregon, paper litho and wood, 25" long	700	1050	1400
Battleship Rover, paper litho and wood, 20" long	600	900	1200
B-LO Submarine, metal, pat. No. 1318048	75	113	150
Boat, tin friction, painted, early	150	225	300
Boat, tin with driver, Hot Air, 9" long	100	150	200

Miscellaneous (Continued)	C6	C8	C10
Boat, wood and brass, wind-up motor concealed within the rudder, controlled from the wheel in the circular cockpit w/a start-stop lever, marked "C.C. Jr", 14-1/2" long	90	135	180
Boat, tin friction, two smokestacks, four lifeboats, 13" long	90	135	180
Boat, tin friction, lithographed	100	150	200
Boat, Kingsbury, 10" long	100	150	200
Boat, cast iron, Freidag, c. 1920s	225	338	450
Boat, tin friction, painted, early	100	150	200
Boat, metal, pull motor	100	150	200
Bremen, tin keywind, Falk, c. 1920, 18" long	1300	2100	3000
Canoe, wood, 6" long	15	22	30
Columbia side paddlewheeler, wood and paper litho, Bradley, c. 1890, 24" long	400	600	800
Destroyer, cast iron, w/wheels, 12" long	1000	1500	2000
Ferry "Ferry Go" Pull Toy, tin litho, w/twin paddlewheels, 14" long	125	185	250
Ferry and Cars, plastic, Pyro, 7" long	25	38	50
Fighting Fire Boat, Knickerbocker, 1950s, 13" long	40	60	80
Gee Whiz speedboat, painted sheet metal, heavy clockwork motor, bronze propeller, Boucher, 25" long	550	825	1000
Gunboat, two guns, two small stacks, two stories above deck, wheeled, friction, 1920s or earlier	300	450	600
Gunboat, tin friction, rocks back and forth on wheels, 10" long	250	375	500
Gunboat, friction, 19" long	400	600	800
Gunboat "Kearsage", cast iron, 13-3/4" long	700	1150	1700
Launch, steam-driven, 18" long	350	525	700
Life Boat, steel, simple design, c. late 1930s, 11" long x 5-1/4" wide	20	30	40
Motorboat, wind-up, Irwin	25	38	50
Motorboat "Sea Wolf", Fleetline, 16" long	112	168	225
Naval Base Play Set, No. 888, Cohn	180	270	360
Navy Gun Boat, cast iron, No. 9B, Big Bang, 8-1/4" long	125	200	250

"Kronzprinz Wilhelm," tin, 37" long, Marklin, offered at auction in 1994. It sold for $23,000. Photo courtesy Christie's East

Speedboat, No. 44 wind-up, Lionel, $1700. Photo courtesy Sotheby's, New York

"Dreadnought," 42" long, handpainted tin, Marklin, 13 brass cannons. Sold for $21,000 in late 1994 in excellent condition, professionally restored. Photo courtesy Bertoia Auctions

Liner, "Columbus," Marklin, $18,000. Photo courtesy Christie's East

"Priscilla" Riverboat, 30" long, Marklin, $17,600. Photo courtesy Bertoia Auctions

U-Boat, tin clockwork, 30" long, Marklin. Photo courtesy Christie's East

"H.M.S. Resolution," tin, 36" long, Marklin. Offered at auction in 1994, it sold for $14,950. Courtesy Christie's East

Top row, left to right: "New Jersey," Orkin, $1,400; "Nevada," Orkin, $1,100. Middle, left to right: "Pennsylvania," Orkin, $1,700; "New Mexico," Orkin, $1,000. Bottom row: "Constitution," Orkin, $1,000. Photo courtesy Christie's East

Battleship Philadelphia, Reed, $880. Photo courtesy Bertoia Auctions

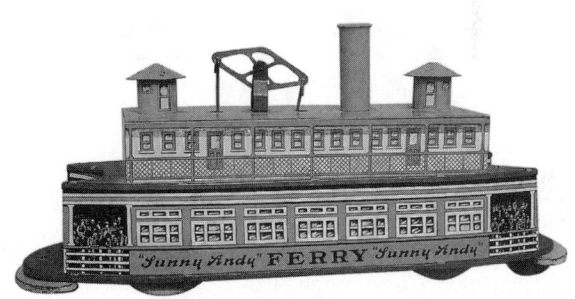

Sandy Andy Ferry, 1930s, Wolverine, $225.

Miscellaneous (Continued)	C6	C8	C10
Navy Ship "Tirpitz", Comet, 19" long	75	112	150
Ocean Liner, tin keywind, Arnold, c. 1930, 11-1/2" long	400	650	900
Pike Steam Launch, Buckman	2500	3800	5500
PT107	30	45	60
Pull For the Shore, litho paper on wood, W.S. Reed	3500	8000	12,000
Riverboat "Columbia", paper and tin litho and wood, working walking beam, c. 1890, 2' long	700	1100	1650
Riverboat "Atlantic", painted and stenciled tin, sidewheel, George Brown, 14" long	2250	3375	4500
Riverboat "Pacific", Althof-Bergmann, 14" long	900	2000	3500
Rowboat, tin, rubber band driver w/man rowing, 9" long	40	60	80

Miscellaneous (Continued)	C6	C8	C10
Rowboat, cast iron, w/four men and oars, mechanical, 9" long	1250	1875	2500
Sea Raider, Payton, 34" long	20	30	40
Shore Patrol, tin, battery operated, 9" long	10	15	20
Showboat, cast iron, 11" long	1000	1500	2000
Showboat, cast iron, Arcade, 1929, 10-3/4" long	500	750	1050
Sidewheeler, cast iron, 10-1/2" long	150	225	300
Sidewheeler, tin, Barmwell-Smith, pat. 1872	2000	3500	5000
Sidewheeler, tin clockwork, 11" long	90	135	180
Sidewheeler, cast iron, approx. 5-1/2" long	100	150	200
Sidewheeler, cast iron, 8" long	188	275	375
Sidewheeler "America", painted tin, c. 1874, 20" long	7000	11,000	18,000

Battleship, 15" long, Hillclimber, $400. Photo courtesy Mapes Auctioneers and Appraisers

Sidewheeler "New Orleans," Wilkins, $1400. Photo courtesy Mapes Auctioneers and Appraisals

Battleship B2, Orkin, $8000. Photo courtesy Sotheby's, New York

Steamship, c. 1885, 19" long, $400. Photo courtesy Mapes Auctions and Appraisals

Miscellaneous (Continued)	C6	C8	C10
Sidewheeler "Betsy", Buffalo Toys, 26" long	350	525	700
Sidewheeler "Constitution" Fallows, 10" long	2000	3000	4000
Sidewheeler "New Orleans", cast iron, c.1895, 10-1/2" long	600	950	1400
Sidewheeler "New York", cast iron, 15" long	500	750	1000
Sidewheeler "Priscilla", paper litho on wood, 37" long	2000	3500	5800
Sidewheeler "Priscilla", cast iron, Dent or Wilkins, approx. 10" long	500	750	1000
Sidewheeler "Puritan", cast iron, 10-1/2" long	480	720	960
Sidewheeler Boat "The Star", tin, height w/stand 21", length 14-1/2"	3500	5200	7000
Sinking Battleship, rubber band torpedo strikes die on ship and sinks it, Walbert Mfg.	250	375	500
Speed Boat, cast iron, Kenton	90	135	180
Speed Boat, wood, rubber band propelled	40	60	80
Speed Boat "Johnson's Sea Horse", cast iron, w/figure, 10-1/2" long	1750	2625	3500

Miscellaneous (Continued)	C6	C8	C10
SS United States, tin friction, 6-1/2" long	50	75	100
Steamboat, live steam, 15" long	300	450	600
Steamboat, tin, self-propelled, 17" long	150	225	300
Steamboat "Dewey", c. 1900, 15-1/2" long	500	750	1000
Steamboat Buckman, No. 55, c. 1870, 19" long	1500	2500	3500
Steamer, litho paper on wood, 39" long, 22-1/2" high	450	675	900
Steamship, alcohol burner, c. 1885, 19" long	200	300	400
Submarine, fires torpedo, 11-1/2" long	12	18	25
Submarine, tin litho, remote controlled, "575", c. 1960	40	60	80
Submarine, tin litho, remote control, automatic	40	60	80
Submarine, lead alloy, No. 79, Manoil	15	22	30
Submarine, steel, 6" long	40	60	80
Submarine and Dreadnought Naval War Toy, torpedo explodes ship, Pat. 4/6/15, Schoenhut	70	105	140
Tanker, Texaco	80	120	160

Showboat, Arcade, 1929, $1050.

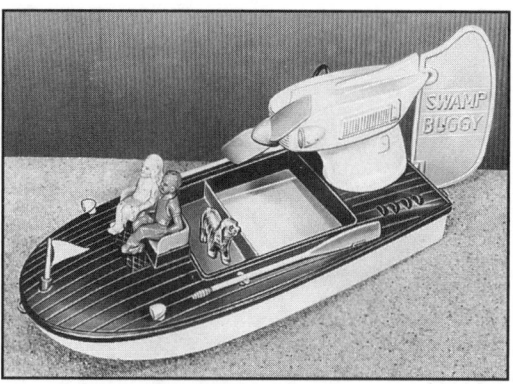

Swamp Buggy, No. 487, Thomas Toys, $25. Photo courtesy Islyn Thomas

Chris-Craft Commuter Yacht, Kilgore, $6000. Photo courtesy Chic Gast

Miscellaneous (Continued)	C6	C8	C10
Turbo Boat, pressed tin, 10-1/2" long	40	60	80
U.S. Naval Base, Superior	60	90	120
U.S. Submarine, painted wood, fires torpedo for target set, 13" long	20	30	40
U.S. Wasp Carrier, wood, storage under deck for planes, 27" long	50	75	100
U.S.S. Narwahl Submarine, lead, 1930s, 7-1/2" long	20	30	40
U.S.S. New Mexico Battleship, lead, 1930s	20	30	40
Warship "Oregon", tin	400	600	800
Yacht, cast iron, Chris-Craft Commuter Yacht, Kilgore, c. 1930, 11" long	2000	3500	6000
Yacht-type Ship, spring wind motor, either Ives or Bing, 28" long	2000	3000	4000

Multiple Products	C6	C8	C10
Patrol Boat, w/radar mast and accessories	27	41	55
Pirate Ship, plastic w/pirates	60	90	125

Orkin

Orkin, of Cambridge, Massachusetts, was founded by Samuel Orkin about the end of World War I. His metal ships were modeled after the real thing. They were big, ranging from about fifteen to thirty-five inches, but relatively inexpensive.

Orkin	C6	C8	C10
Battleship "Constitution", steel key-wind, c. 1914, 25" long	500	750	1000
Battleship "Marcella", 18" long	600	900	1350
Battleship "Nevada", steel, key-wind, c. 1914, 22" long	550	825	1100
Battleship "New Jersey", tin and wood, c. 1920, 35" long	600	900	1400
Battleship "New Mexico", steel, keywind, c. 1914, 25" long	500	750	1000
Battleship "Pennsylvania", steel, keywind, c. 1914, 30" long	700	1100	1700
Battleship "Texas", steel, keywind, 30" long	1000	1800	3800
Battleship B2, pressed steel, 36" long	3000	5000	8000

Orkin Craft

Orkin Craft was owned by the president of the Waterman Pen Company. Manufacturing was done by Calwis Industries Ltd. Of Beverly Hills, California. The pleasure boats sold by the firm were too expensive for the era (the price was in the $15-$20 range), which is probably why they failed about 1935 or 1936. All the boats were motor-driven. Some were all metal, and some had wooden decks.

Orkin Craft	C6	C8	C10
Cabin Cruiser, 30" long	700	1200	1700
Speedboat, clockwork, 29" long	600	1000	1450

Reed	C6	C8	C10
Battleship Philadelphia, paper litho on wood, 30" long	440	660	880

Clipper Ship, c. 1887, Reed, $1200. Photo courtesy Bertoia Auctions

Viking Ship, Renwal, $150. Photo courtesy Islyn Thomas

Speedboat, Orkin Craft, $1450. Photo courtesy Mapes Auctioneers and Appraisers

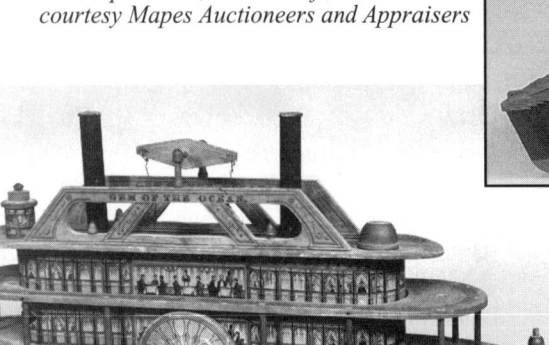

"River Queen," Reed, $880. Photo courtesy Bertoia Auctions

Twin Sidewheeler Steamboat, 11" long, Buckman, $5000. Photo courtesy Wilkinson Collection; Detroit Antique Toy Museum

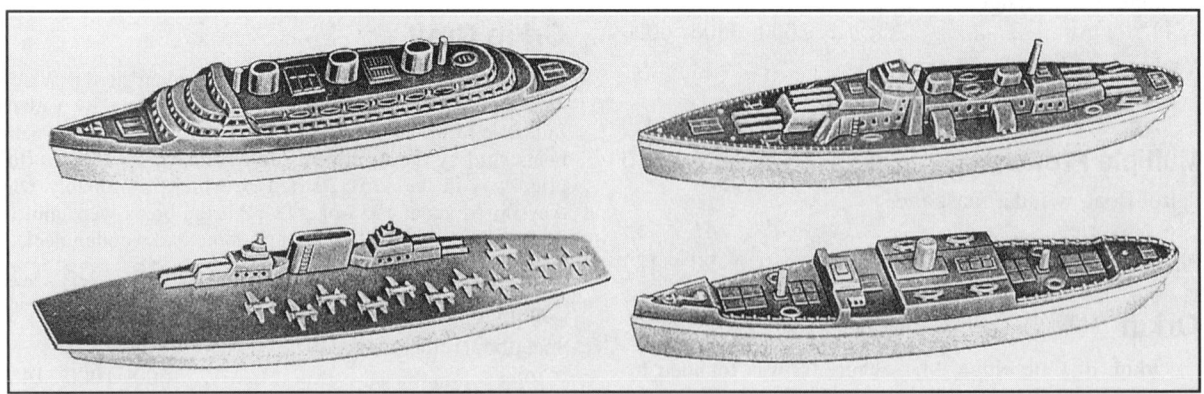

Top left: Queen Mary, $30; top right: Battleship, $35; bottom left: Aircraft Carrier, $25; bottom right: Freighter, $25; all 5-1/2" long, plastic, Thomas Toys.

Panama Canal, Renwal, $215. Photo courtesy Islyn Thomas

National Defense Set, Tillicum, Milton-Bradley, $80. Photo courtesy John D. Matthews

Another view of the Sidewheeler "River Queen," Reed, $880.

Reed (Continued)	C6	C8	C10
Clipper Ship, wood and paper litho, c. 1887, 36" long	550	800	1200
Freighter Ocean Wave, paper litho on wood, w/cargo, c. 1883, 35" long	650	1100	1500
Passenger liner St. Louis, paper litho on wood, 31" long	800	1300	1800
Riverboat "Ocean Queen", litho on wood, 23" long	750	1300	1800
Riverboat "Pilgrim", paper litho, 28-1/2" long	1000	1500	2000
Sidewheeler "River Queen", litho on wood, c. 1895, 25" long	440	660	880
U.S.S. Maine, paper litho on wood	600	900	1200

Remco	C6	C8	C10
Aircraft Carrier "Mighty Matilda", plastic, complete w/all accessories, 35" long	83	125	165

Remco (Continued)	C6	C8	C10
Barracuda Submarine, twenty-three man crew	75	112	150
Battleship Fighting Lady, No. 710, 31" long	115	172	230
Carrier, Mighty Magee Carrier	80	120	160
Roman Warship "Big Caesar", w/figures, 29" long	175	265	350
Roman Warship Gallant Gladiator, 17" long	60	90	120
Showboat Theater	75	112	150

Renwal	C6	C8	C10
Cargo Ship, No. 139, 4" long	4	6	8
Drawbridge Set, w/bridge, twelve cars and boats	50	75	100
Ferry No. 140, 4" long	4	6	8
Ocean Liner	30	45	60
Panama Canal, No. 273, c. 1957, 29" x 11"	108	162	215
Speed Boat, No. 141, 4" long	4	6	8

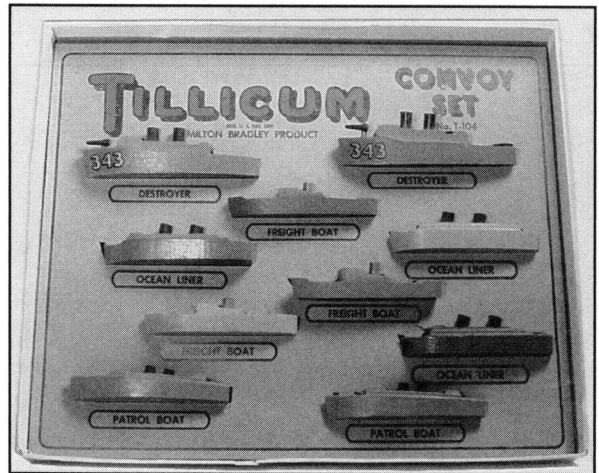

Convoy Set, Tillicum, Milton-Bradley, $700. Photo courtesy John D. Matthews

Battle Fleet, Tillicum, $110. Photo courtesy John D. Matthews

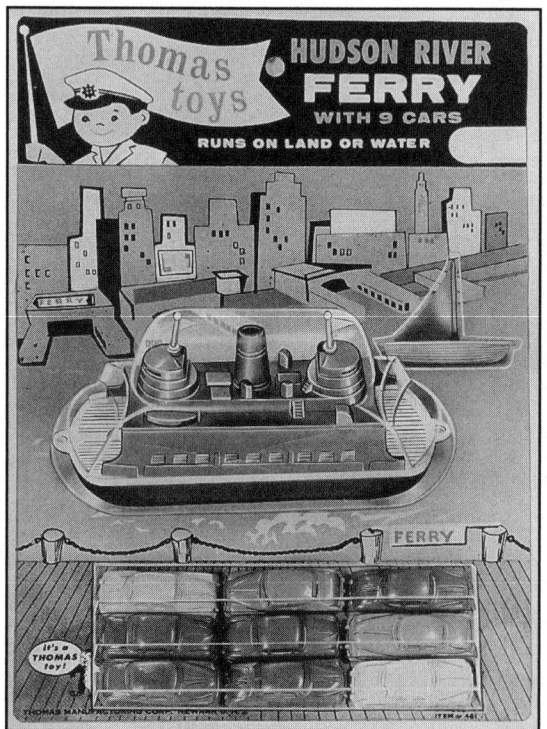

Hudson River Ferry, No. 481, Thomas Toys, $25. Photo courtesy Islyn Thomas

Racing Hydroplane, No. 480, Thomas Toys, $25. Photo courtesy Islyn Thomas

Renwal (Continued)	**C6**	**C8**	**C10**
Tugboat, No. 142, 4" long	4	6	8
Viking Ship, No. 245, 1955, 17" long	55	100	150

Schiebel	**C6**	**C8**	**C10**
Battleship, friction motor, wood stacks and large wood guns and turrets, c. 1920	1250	1875	2500
Battleship, unpowered, c. 1927	1000	1500	2000

Thomas Toys	**C6**	**C8**	**C10**
Aircraft Carrier, plastic, 5-1/2" long	12	18	25
Battleship, plastic, 5-1/2" long	12	18	25
Ferry, Hudson River, plastic, No. 481, w/sailboat, nine cars	12	18	25
Freighter, plastic, 5-1/2" long	12	18	25
Queen Mary, plastic, 5-1/2" long	15	22	30

"Priscilla" Steam Yacht, Marklin. Photo courtesy Christie's East

Top left: No. 1034 Battleship; top right: No. 1036 Carrier; middle left: No. 1035 Cruiser; middle right: No. 1037 Liner; bottom left: No. 127 Destroyer; bottom right: No. 128 Submarine, all Tootsietoy. Photo courtesy Ed Poole

Thomas Toys (Continued)	C6	C8	C10
Racing Hydroplane, plastic, No. 480	12	18	25
Swamp Buggy, plastic, motorized, No. 487	12	18	25
Tugboat, 8-1/4" long	15	22	30

Thomas Toys (Continued)	C6	C8	C10
Weekend Cruise Set, No. 339, w/boat trailer, 4-1/4" car, 4-1/2" boat	22	33	45

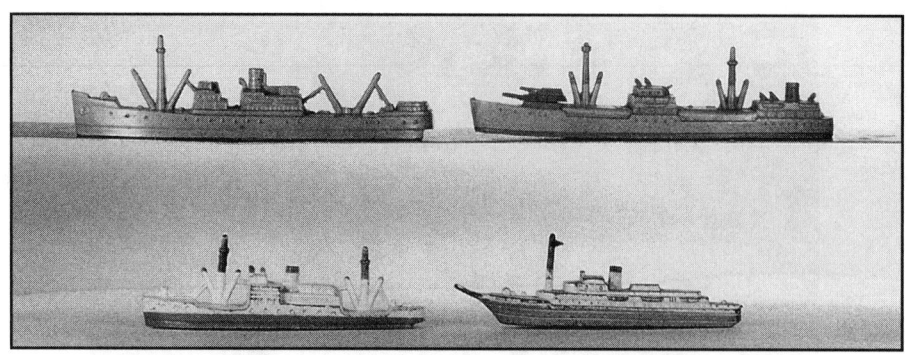

Top left: No. 1037 Transport; top right: No. 1039 Tanker; bottom left: No. 129 Tender; bottom right: No. 130 Yacht, Tootsietoy. Photo courtesy Ed Poole

Tillicum

(see also Milton-Bradley)

	C6	C8	C10
Battle Fleet, four battleships, target, and lighthouse, Tillicum, 1940s	30	60	110

U.S. Hardware

	C6	C8	C10
Rowers, castcast iron, four-man crew and coxswain, large wheels, c. 1890	2000	3500	5200
Rowers, cast iron, eight-man crew and coxswain, large wheels, c. 1890, 14-1/2" long	1800	3000	4200
Scull, nine-man crew, wheeled, 14" long	1600	2400	3200

Wannatoys

	C6	C8	C10
Cruiser	25	38	50
Freighter	25	38	50

Wilkins

	C6	C8	C10
Battleship, cast iron	800	1400	2000
Riverboat, 5-3/4" long	135	205	270
Riverboat, cast iron, 10-1/2" long	450	675	900

Wilkins (Continued)

	C6	C8	C10
Riverboat, cast iron, c. 1910, 7-1/2" long	250	375	500
Riverboat "City of New York", 15" long	800	1400	2035
Riverboat "Puritan", 10-1/2" long	600	1000	1400
Rowers, cast iron, big-wheeled boat, four-man crew and coxswain, c. 1890, 10" long	1250	1875	2500

Wolverine

	C6	C8	C10
Diving Submarine, 13" long	105	158	210
Ferry, tin and wood, Sandy Andy "Ferrygo", 11" long	150	250	350
Ferry, tin litho, "Sandy Andy Ferry", 1930s, 13-1/2" long	100	150	225
Ocean Liner	125	188	250

Wyandotte

	C6	C8	C10
Aircraft Carrier	55	82	110
Pocket Battleship, tin litho, wheeled, 7" long	70	105	140
S.S. America, moves on metal wheels, 1930s, 7" long	50	75	100
U.S.S. Enterprise	80	120	160

SOLDIERS

The price of a toy soldier depends not only on its desirability, but on its condition. Mint condition means the item is in the condition in which it was originally issued—perfect, regardless of age, not the slightest blemish. Needless to say, this is a fairly rare state of affairs, but enough soldiers exist in Mint condition to make it an employable term. Many people, hoping to dispose of toys, are tempted to term them Mint when they are really Near Mint, Very Good, or sometimes even just Good. Inevitably, this can result in unhappiness all around and, not infrequently, in a canceled sale.

Very Good condition indicates a soldier that has obviously seen use. It has signs of wear and aging, but most of its paint remains and, in general, it has a freshness to its appearance that makes it seem attractive and collectible to all but the most discriminating.

Good condition signals a soldier that has seen considerable wear, but has at least one-half to one-third of its original paint, and is basically sound. Collectors will collect it, but they will often not be wholly satisfied with it as an example of their collection, and thus the price is well below that of the same item in Mint condition.

A condition below Good results in another drastic drop in price. Figures with missing parts, although otherwise in Excellent condition, will usually fall into this lower-priced category. At present, a Barclay soldier minus its tin helmet (signaled by a large round hole in the top of its head) is worth about half of what it would otherwise bring. On the cast-iron soldiers, even small spots of rust can seriously lower their price, as can repainting of any of the soldiers. Near Mint, Fine, Very Fine, and similar terms denote conditions between Mint and Very Good, and are priced accordingly.

The key to grading is to avoid wishful thinking. Grading can sometimes be a problem for the uninitiated, but common sense will usually prevail, and when possible, a consultation with an expert in the field can often clear up lingering doubts. A toy in its original box is worth up to ten to twenty percent more if the box is in Mint condition, with the price dropping as condition lessens.

Contributor: Stan Alekna, Toy Soldiers Etcetera, 732 Aspen Lane, Lebanon, PA 17042-9073.

American Metal Toys

Until recently, these 3-1/4-inch dime-store soldiers were attributed to Chicago toy soldier maker J. Edward Jones. Though Jones did make many other figures, research has established that the following were produced by American Metal Toys, Inc. of Chicago. The president of the firm was Royce Reyff (1898-1986) and his equal partner was C. Raymond Pierson. Although the company was formally incorporated on Oct. 24, 1939, it began in 1937 and went out of business in April 1942, when its supply of metal was cut off by the demands of World War II. The sculpting and diemaking were done by Henry Kasselowski.

AMERICAN METAL TOYS

American Metal Toys	C6	C8	C10
Ammunition Carrier, (AM18)	200	300	400
Bugler, (AM25)	78	117	155
Charging, port arms, (AM9)	125	188	250
Cook with Chef's Hat, frying pan, (AM17)	75	112	150
Cowboy Kneeling, with base, rare, (AM33a)	NPF	NPF	NPF
Cowboy Kneeling, (AM33)	40	60	80
Cowboy on Prancing Horse, (AM39)	NPF	NPF	NPF

American Metal Toys	C6	C8	C10
Cowboy on Rearing Horse, firing backward, (AM31)	130	195	260
Cowboy Shooting, on foot, (AM43)	60	70	95
Doctor with Bag, (AM28)	40	60	125
Farmer, (AM37)	9	15	25
Farmer's Wife, (AM38)	9	15	25
Firing Machine Gun on Stump, No. 1 on pocket, (AM10a)	100	150	200
Firing Machine Gun on Stump, (AM10)	40	60	80
Flagbearer, (AM20)	120	180	240
German, charging w/rifle, (AM2)	107	160	215
German, kneeling w/rifle, (AM1)	95	142	190
German, kneeling w/short rifle, (AM1a)	110	165	220
German, prone machine gunner, (AM3)	71	106	143
Grenade Thrower, no weapons, (AM11)	67	100	135

American Metal Toys	C6	C8	C10
Indian Kneeling, shooting, (AM35a)	59	70	85
Indian on Rearing Horse, (AM34)	60	100	200
Indian with Bow, copy of Beton's, (AM35)	NPF	NPF	NPF
Kneeling, firing rifle, no stand, (AM23)	60	90	120
Kneeling, firing shorter rifle, no stand, (AM23a)	75	112	150
Kneeling, firing anti-tank gun, (AM16)	52	78	105
Kneeling, firing anti-tank gun w/barrel brace, "23" on wheel, (AM16a)	50	75	100
Kneeling Horse, probably American Metal, copy of Barlcay's but shorter, (AM42)	NPF	NPF	NPF
Kneeling with AA Gun, (AM8)	60	95	125
Kneeling with Searchlight, "27," "Made in USA" on sides of stanchion, (AM21a)	55	82	110
Kneeling with Searchlight, (AM21)	62	93	125
Knight with Pennant, flat underbase, (AM41)	64	95	128
Marching with Rifle, (AM32)	57	85	115
Motorcyclist, w/machine gun mounted on motorcycle, (AM19)	70	105	140
Nurse with Bag, (AM27)	60	95	175
Observer with Binoculars and Rifle, (AM4)	60	95	125
Officer in Greatcoat, pointing, holding pistol, (AM13)	120	170	275
Prone, firing double-barreled machine gun, (AM15)	78	117	155
Prone, body arched, firing machine gun, (AM24)	60	90	120
Prone with Rifle, trunk upraised, (AM14)	70	105	140
Seated with Phone, (AM22)	60	95	125
Seated with Rifle, (AM12)	60	95	125
Soldier with Gas Mask, plunging rifle down, slightly smaller in size, (AM26)	130	185	275
Soldier with Rifle, gassed or shot in neck, (AM6)	170	255	340
Standing, firing rifle, (AM29)	60	95	125
Stretcher-bearer, (AM7)	80	110	155
Tramp, (AM36)	9	18	25

American Metal Toys	C6	C8	C10
Wire-cutter, prone, (AM5)	225	338	450
Wounded Supine, (AM30)	60	95	125

Auburn Rubber

Auburn (also Aub-Rub'r) was founded in 1913 in Auburn, Indiana, as the Double Fabric Tire Corporation to make auto tubes and tires for Model T Fords. It produced five soldiers in 1935—its first toys. The prototype was a Palace Guard that Auburn president and chief stockholder A.L. Murray obtained in England. The model was taken to a local pattern maker where original molds were made from lead. Sample toys were made and taken to an artist and decorated per Murray's instructions. They immediately caught on when presented to buyers.

The soldiers were molded in 24-inch rubber presses, each containing forty to sixty soldiers. Once trimmed, the soldiers were dipped in a base lacquer and sent down a decorating conveyor where as many as twenty-four women, using small camelhair brushes, added the finishing touches—painting the faces, shoes, belts, buttons, medals, and finally eyes. After drying, each toy was individually wrapped in waxed paper and packaged three dozen to a chip-board carton and twelve dozen to a corrugated carton for shipment. Design of the soldiers was credited to freelance artist Edward McCandlish.

The soldiers sold well from the beginning. Shortly after the first soldiers were introduced, animals and wheeled vehicles (the first was a Cord automobile) were marketed, all successfully. Auburn produced no soldiers during the war and few after it, although it continued to make toys in great quantity. In 1960, the toys portion of Auburn was purchased by the town of Deming, New Mexico, where it remained until it went out of business in 1969.

Auburn's soldiers, all the standard 3-1/4-inch length, went through three stages. The first were frail looking with long, thin bodies; the second, which emerged as early as September 1938, were stockier and larger-headed; and the third, introduced in 1941, were more well-proportioned and realistic. Unlike its competitors, Auburn produced no cowboys, Indians, sailors or civilians, except for baseball and football players and two farm workers. Auburn's infantry came in colors other than brown—the blue were meant to represent U.S. Marines; the white also were sold as Marines. It is thought that some Auburn Ethiopians remain to be discovered.

AUBURN RUBBER

Auburn Rubber	C6	C8	C10
0200 U.S. Infantry Private, (A2)	9	14	23
0202 Bugler, U.S. Infantry, (A4)	13	18	29
0204 U.S. Infantry Officer, (A9)	10	15	26
0206 Stretcher Bearer, (A16)	19	30	42
0208 Wounded Soldier, (A17)	19	30	42
0214 & 218 Foreign Legion Private, (A6)	17	28	40

Auburn Rubber (Continued)	**C6**	**C8**	**C10**
0216 Observer with Binoculars, (A18)	13	18	29
0222 Sniper, crawling, rifle over shoulder, (A20)	45	65	85
0224 Red Cross Doctor, (A14)	22	35	48
0226 Red Cross Nurse, white or khaki uniform (add 25% far kahki figure), (A15)	22	35	48
0230 Machine Gunner, (A13)	9	14	23
0232 Officer on Horse, (A12)	25	35	52
0234 Bomb Thrower, (A21)	30	40	57
0236 Signalman, (A19)	65	110	276
0238 Charging Soldier with Tommy Gun, (A11)	14	19	30
0240 Motorcycle Soldiers with Sidecar, (A24)	34	75	117
0242 Anti-Aircraft Gun, (A22)	19	25	37
0250 Pitcher, (A40)	20	40	59
0252 Batter, (A38)	20	41	60
0254 Catcher, (A41)	20	40	59
0256 Fielder or Baseman, (A39)	21	36	55
0258 Baserunner, (A37)	21	36	55
0260 Lineman, football player, (A45)	21	36	55
0262 Backfieldman, football player, (A44)	20	40	59
0264 Center, football player, (A43)	20	40	59
0266 Passer, football player, (A46)	23	43	62
0268 Carrier, football player, (A42)	23	43	62
0272 Plane Shooter, (A29)	22	35	48
0296 Trench Mortar, (A32)	24	37	50
1546 Motorcycle Cop, blue or khaki as soldier, (A23)	42	59	74
Aircraft Defender, (A25)	30	40	56
Army Docter, khaki uniform, (A14a)	NPF	NPF	NPF
Color Bearer, (A26)	80	125	180
Cowboy, large, on wheeled horse, (A48)	45	70	95
Ethiopian Bugler, only one known, (A7a)	NPF	NPF	NPF
Ethiopian with Shield and Rifle, in robes, only one known, (A7b)	100	200	300
Ethiopian with Shield and Rifle, (A7)	100	200	300
Firing Soldier, (A28)	23	38	57
Foreign Legion, also White Guard officer, (A5)	12	18	24

Auburn Rubber (Continued)	**C6**	**C8**	**C10**
Pilot Running, looking skyward, in pilot helmet and goggles, (A35)	NPF	NPF	NPF
Searchlight, (A31)	22	35	48
Sound Detector, (A30)	19	28	43
Tank Defender, (A33)	24	36	48
Tank Soldier, running w/box, (A34)	19	29	39

Barclay

Barclay Mfg. Co. was the largest manufacturer of toy soldiers in the United States prior to World War II, selling millions of figures annually. The company, named after Barclay Street in West Hoboken, New Jersey, began in 1924 or late 1923, and was owned by Leon Donze (1865-1950) and by Michael Levy (c. 1895-1964). Around 1929, Levy took over the company and turned it into a major manufacturer. It grew from five peoples in 1924 to a pre-war peak of 400 workers and moved several times to increasingly larger quarters.

Barclay's soldiers came in four styles prior to World War II. Soldiers from the first group, probably produced almost from Barclay's beginning, were small with moving arms on the mounted figures. The second group, approximately 3-1/4 inches high, seems to have debuted in 1935. These were designed and sculpted by Barclay employee Frank Krupp and had a separate tin helmet, which was sub-contracted. These figures are rather stiff and are known by collectors as "short stride" because the marching figures' feet are close together. The third style, again by Krupp, also had a separate tin helmet, was more realistic, and is known as "long stride." These were on sale as early as 1936. In 1937 or 1938, a clip was designed to hold on the tin helmets, as the formerly glued-on helmets frequently came off, drawing complaints from the chain stores, such as Woolworth's, that sold Barclay toys. The fourth style was introduced about 1939-1940 when Barclay moved from slush-casting to die-casting its soldiers. It was by freelance artist Olive Kooken (1904-1964) and is known as "cast helmet," as the soldiers featured helmets that were an integral part of the figure.

Barclay's soldiers were made of antimonial lead, consisting of about 13 percent antimony and the rest led. When slush molding was done, only one mold was made of each figure. The lead would be poured into the mold, rocked, and immediately poured out, providing a hollow figure. Later, the diecast molds produced a number of the same figure at the same time.

During World War II, Barclay laid off all but four of its employees and did subcontract work. The company was never as successful after the war `and finally closed down in 1971. Although Barclay assigned numbers to its figures from the beginning for its own records, many of the soldiers themselves bore no number. Figures listed with a question mark after the number are based on the memory of longtime Barclay employee George Fall, whose memory, judged against known Barclay numbers, is accurate, but not infallible.

BARCLAY

1934 and After

	C6	C8	C10
045 Machine Gunner and Driver, (B153)	31	52	76
087 Officer on Horse, in cap, khaki or grey, larger black, grey or brown horse, (B3A)	19	29	40
087? Mounted, in grey cap, intermediate size, (B3)	41	68	86
087? Mounted in colored jacket and cap, might be Chinese or Japanese, (BA)	25	37	49
089 Indian on Horse, on catalog sheet with Ethiopians, (BAC)	27	38	50
089 Indian on Horse, Indian's head turned to right, (B1-1)	35	47	59
089 Indian on Horse, two feathers, (B1a)	31	44	57
090 Cowboy on Horse, (BAD)	27	38	50
090 Cowboy on Horse, variation, no bullets in gunbelt, (B2AA)	25	45	65
090 Cowboy on Horse, variation, thinner bullets in gunbelt, saddle not as long, (B2A)	27	38	50
100 Masked Rider on Horse, facing forward, (B2AAA)	350	525	700
100? Masked Rider with Lasso, horse's tail up, (B2C)	150	225	350
100? Masked Rider with Lasso, horse's tail down, (B2B)	29	49	65
310 Army Motorcyclist, (B93)	34	47	59
310 Army Motorcyclist, post-war, dot eyes or none at all, larger, motor variation, (B93A)	32	45	57
310 Cop on Motorcycle, (B93a)	36	49	61
310 Cop on Motorcycle, head lower, (B93c)	37	50	62
310 Cop on Motorcycle, post-war, dot eyes or none at all, larger, motor variation, (B93B)	36	49	69
310 Motorcyclist, head higher, (B93b)	37	50	62
310 Motorcyclist, larger, markings on cycle, like B93A and B93B but cruder, (B93d)	37	50	62
374 Army Motorcycle, w/sidecar, (B152)	45	65	85
495 Man on Skis, (B190)	16	23	29
496 Girl on Skis, (B191)	16	23	29
497 Man on Sled, (B192)	15	22	28
498 Girl on Sled, (B193)	15	22	28
499 Santa Claus on Sled, (B194)	31	42	55

1934 and After (Continued)

	C6	C8	C10
500 Santa Claus on Lead Skis, (B195)	32	45	58
500 Santa Claus on Skis, no skis poles and no holes for them, (B195a)	75	115	148
510 One Horse Open Sleigh, includes sleigh, horse, seated man and woman, (B198)	51	73	95
530 Man Pulling Children on Sled, (B199)	31	42	65
535 Young Man Putting Skates on Girl Sitting on Bench, (B200)	119	141	175
610 Woman Passenger, w/dog, (B157)	11	19	23
611 Man Passenger, overcoat over arm, (B158)	11	19	23
612 Conductor, (B161)	11	19	23
613 Black Porter, w/whisk broom, (B160)	12	20	25
614 Black Man in Red Cap, w/bags, (B159)	12	20	25
615 Engineer, (B162)	11	19	23
616 Boy, (B163)	10	18	22
617 Girl, (B164)	10	18	22
618 Elderly Woman, (B165)	12	19	23
619 Old Man, (B166)	12	19	23
620 Minister Walking, (B167)	41	62	83
621 Minister Holding Hat, (B168)	11	18	25
621 Newsboy, (B169)	10	18	22
622 Shoeshine Boy, (B170)	19	31	44
623 Detective with Pistol, (B171)	110	147	179
624 Burglar, (B172)	110	147	179
625 Bride, (B173)	11	19	28
626 Groom, (B174)	11	19	28
627 Girl in Rocker, (B175)	10	18	25
628 Boy Skater, (B176)	8	12	20
629 Girl Skater, (B177)	8	12	20
630-1/2 Man and Woman on Park Bench, (B178)	18	29	43
635 Man Speed Skater, (B180)	9	14	22
636 Girl Figure Skater, (B181)	9	14	22
701 Flagbearer, cast helmet, (B7)	11	16	22
701 Flagbearer, Cuban flag variation, painted for ten Woolworth's in Cuba, cast or pot helmet, (B10)	NPF	NPF	NPF

1934 and After (Continued)	C6	C8	C10
701 Flagbearer, tin helmet, long stride, (B6)	16	21	34
701 Flagbearer, tin helmet, short stride, (B5)	12	21	42
701 Machine-Gunner, kneeling, short stride, (B9)	12	18	27
702 Machine-Gunner, kneeling, cast helmet, (B11)	11	17	26
702 Machine-Gunner, kneeling, long stride, (B10)	12	18	27
703 Sniper, kneeling, firing, long stride, tin helmet, (B13)	13	18	25
703 Sniper, kneeling, firing, short stride, (B12)	14	19	26
703 Sniper, kneeling, firing, short stride, shorter rifle, fat portion of gun and thin portion of barrel about equal length, (B12A)	19	29	42
704 Soldier on Parade, shoulder arms, long stride, tin helmet, (B15)	12	19	26
704 Soldier on Parade, shoulder arms, short stride, (B14)	14	21	28
705 Soldier at Attention, actually port arms, (B16)	16	23	31
705 Soldier at Attention, actually port arms, cast helmet, (B17)	14	21	36
706 Soldier, charging, cast helmet, (B21)	11	17	32
706 Soldier, charging, short stride w/shorter rifle, sling around hand, two known, (B18a)	425	638	850
706 Soldier, charging, short stride, (B18)	12	17	32
706 Soldier, charging, long stride, tin helmet, (B20)	55	82	110
706 Soldier, tall, tin helmet, solid puttees, (B19)	325	500	750
707 At Attention, cast helmet, (B22)	13	21	29
707 Sharpshooter, standing, firing, short stride, (B86)	14	21	30
708 Marine Officer, w/sword, cast helmet, (B28)	39	60	85
708 Officer, w/sword, cast helmet, (B27)	36	50	75
708 Officer, w/sword, short stride, (B23)	14	21	30
708 Officer, w/sword, long stride, no chest strap, tin helmet, (B25a)	85	125	250
708 Officer, w/sword, long stride, tin helmet, (B25)	19	31	44

1934 and After (Continued)	C6	C8	C10
709 Bugler, short stride, (B29)	15	22	35
709 Bugler, long stride, tin helmet, (B30)	12	19	32
710 Drummer, long stride, tin helmet, (B32)	19	30	41
710 Drummer, short stride, (B31)	13	19	32
711 Drum Major, long stride, tin helmet, (B34)	14	20	33
711 Drum Major, short stride, (B33)	13	19	32
712 Knight, w/shield, (B156)	11	15	25
712 Knight, w/pennant, (B155)	13	17	27
714 Pirate, (B154)	13	21	38
715 Cowboy, with tin hat brim, badges, stripes painted on vest, (B94A)	NPF	NPF	NPF
715 Cowboy, w/tin hat brim, (B94)	12	17	30
716 Indian Chief, (B48)	9	15	24
717 Indian Brave, rifle across waist, (B47)	10	16	25
718 West Point Cadet, long stride, (B38)	15	20	31
718 West Point Cadet, w/rifle, short stride, (B37)	17	22	33
719 Sailor in White Uniform, in puttees, (B52)	13	18	30
719 Sailor White Uniform, long stride, bell bottoms, (B51)	12	17	29
719 Sailor White Uniform, marching, short stride, (B49)	12	17	29
720 Sailor Blue Uniform, in puttees, (B52a)	13	18	30
720 Sailor Blue Uniform, marching, short stride, (B50)	13	18	30
720 Sailor Blue Uniform, long stride, bell bottoms, (B51a)	15	20	31
721 Naval Officer, long stride, (B56)	17	22	33
721 Naval Officer, short stride, (B55)	12	18	32
721 Naval Officer, short stride, tin top to cap, (B54)	55	80	120
721 Naval Officer in Blue, short stride, tin top to cap, (B54a)	110	200	375
722 Marine, short stride, tin top to cap, (B57)	60	81	120
722 Marine, short stride, (B58)	12	21	38
722 Marine, long stride, (B59)	19	27	40
722 Marine, long stride, white cap (possibly post-war), (B59a)	26	35	47

738 Soldier Bomb Thrower, Barclay, very rare. Photo courtesy Stan Alekna

1934 and After (Continued)

	C6	C8	C10
723 Marine Officer, w/sword, short stride, (B24)	19	29	41
723 Marine Officer, w/sword, long stride, no chest strap, in blue, tin helmet, (B25b)	85	125	275
723 Marine Officer, w/sword, cast helmet, (B26)	51	72	95
724 Ethiopian Soldier, c. 1935-36, (B39)	120	169	277
725 Ethiopian Officer, c. 1935-36, (B40)	135	195	310
726 Italian Soldier, c. 1935-36, (B42)	110	160	241
727 Italian Officer, c. 1935-36, (B41)	110	170	275
728 Machine Gunner Lying Flat, cast helmet, (B62)	13	19	31
728 Machine Gunner Lying Flat, (B61)	14	20	32
728 Machine Gunner Lying Flat, lip of base extends under gun barrel, cast helmet, (B63)	14	20	32
729 Soldier with Binoculars, short binoculars, (B114)	60	80	110

1934 and After (Continued)

	C6	C8	C10
729 Soldier with Binoculars, long binoculars, (B113)	19	25	37
730 Soldier Signal Man with Flag, (B65)	16	24	39
731 Soldier Pigeon Dispatcher, (B66)	17	30	40
732 Soldier Telephone Operator, (B67)	14	20	32
733 Soldier Bullet Feeder, actually a shell, (B68)	12	19	27
734 Soldier Ammunition Carrier, (B69)	14	21	29
735 Soldier Range Finder, (B70)	16	22	34
736 Soldier Sentry, (B71)	16	22	34
737 Soldier Charging Machine Gunner, cast helmet, (B73)	21	36	48
737 Soldier Charging Machine Gunner, tin helmet, (B72)	13	20	28
738 Soldier Bomb Thrower, (B74)	14	21	31
738 Soldier Bomb Thrower, rifle off ground, cast helmet, (B77)	18	30	40

1934 and After (Continued)

	C6	C8	C10
738 Soldier Bomb Thrower, rifle off ground, tin helmet, (B76)	18	30	40
738 Soldier Bomb Thrower, tall, solid puttees, tin helmet, (B75)	325	475	625
739 Soldier Fifer, (B78)	14	21	31
740 Soldier French Horn, (B79)	13	20	30
741 Aviator, (B80)	14	21	31
743 West Point Officer, short stride, (B35)	14	21	31
744 Nurse, hand on hip, (B83)	14	21	31
744 Nurse in Blue, hand on hip, (B83a)	68	90	150
745 Navy Doctor, in white, flat underbase, (B81)	18	30	40
746 Army Doctor, in brown, flat underbase, (B81a)	18	30	40
746 Doctor, in brown, concave base, (B81A&B)	8	12	33
747 Sharpshooter, standing, firing, cast helmet, (B88)	11	18	26
747 Sharpshooter, standing, firing, long stride, tin helmet, (B87)	13	20	30
748 Soldier Running, w/rifle, cast helmet, (B90)	19	26	36
748 Soldier Running, w/rifle, tin helmet, (B89)	20	27	37
749 Soldier Gas Mask, charging w/rifle, tin helmet, (B92)	17	24	34
749 Soldier Gas Mask, charging w/rifle, cast helmet, (B91)	22	34	44
750 Soldier Crawling, (B64)	15	22	32
751 Soldier Sharpshooter, prone position, (B54)	16	23	33
752 Cowboy with Lasso, (B95)	12	19	27
752 Cowboy with Lasso, post-WWII version, lasso goes directly through hands, (B95a)	11	18	26
752 Masked Cowboy with Lasso, (B95A)	14	21	29
753 Cowboy with Two Guns, pointing one, (B96)	12	19	27
754 Indian Chief, tomahawk and shield, (B97)	11	18	26
755 Indian with Bow and Arrow, (B98)	10	17	25
756 Indian Chief, long headdress, may only have been produced post-WWII, (B99)	60	85	105

1934 and After (Continued)

	C6	C8	C10
756 Sailor Flagbearer, long stride, (B53)	22	34	44
757 Indian Brave, standing w/bow and arrow, may only have been produced post-WWII, (B100)	21	29	39
757 Sailor with Signal Flags, (B60)	18	30	40
757 Sailor with Signal Flags, flat underbase, minor variations in cap, (B60a)	20	33	45
758 Camera Man, kneeling, tin helmet, (B101)	22	31	48
759 Soldier Stretcher Bearer, closed hand, (B102a)	15	21	33
759 Soldier Stretcher Bearer, open hand, (B102)	95	125	165
760 Soldier Sitting Eating, (B115)	20	31	40
760 Surgeon, w/strethoscope, (B103)	19	25	38
761 Lying Wounded, tin helmet, (B104)	14	20	32
762 Wounded, sitting, arm in sling, (B85)	18	21	34
763 Raiding, in crouch, tin helmet, (B105)	24	35	50
765 Bayoneting, no bayonet, cast helmet, (B107a)	135	210	325
765 Bayoneting, although no bayonet, thrusting w/gun muzzle, tin helmet, (B107)	41	51	75
766 Clubbing with Rifle, cast helmet, (B109)	75	125	213
766 Clubbing with Rifle, tin helmet, (B108)	32	58	70
767 Advance, raised rifle, tin helmet, (B106)	16	22	35
767 Nurse, kneeling, (B82)	16	22	33
769 Cook, egg-timer, (B110a)	80	125	165
769 Cook, holding roast, (B110)	20	28	40
770 At Mess, typist alone, apparently meant to sit at mess table, (B151A)	14	21	39
771 Peeling Potatoes, (B111)	16	23	31
774 Soldier with AA Gun, cast helmet, (B118)	14	20	32
774 Soldier with AA Gun, tin helmet, (B117)	20	27	37
775 Wounded on Crutches, (B119)	19	40	36

1934 and After (Continued)

	C6	C8	C10
776 Officer Reading Orders, (B116)	19	26	36
776 Standing at Searchlight, high seat, no rivets in front of left foot, (B125)	21	42	68
776 Standing at Searchlight, high seat, two rivets in front of left foot, (B124)	24	33	49
776 Standing at Searchlight, low seat, not connected to searchlight, (B123)	17	23	34
776 Standing at Searchlight, smooth lens, elevation wheel, (B120)	75	125	200
776 Standing at Searchlight, smooth lens, no elevation wheel, (B120a)	75	125	200
776 Standing at Searchlight, ridges along base, ridged lenses, (B121)	28	41	53
776 Standing at Searchlight, smooth base connected to searchlight, no elevation wheel, ridged lenses, (B122)	28	41	53
777 Marching with Pack, cast helmet, (B127)	18	26	45
777 Marching with Pack, tin helmet, (B126)	14	24	35
778 Officer with Gas Mask, cast helmet, (B128)	16	21	32
779 Firing from Behind Wall, cast helmet, (B129)	41	62	78
780 Falling with Rifle, cast helmet, (B130)	24	33	48
781 Digging, cast helmet, (B131)	41	58	70
782 Leaning Out, w/field phone, antenna, cast helmet, (B132)	41	69	88
783 Crouching with Binoculars, cast helmet, (B133)	24	33	42
784 Parachutist Landing, (B134)	16	21	38
785 Skier in Brown, no skis, (B137)	39	61	74
785 Skier in White, w/separate metal skis, meant to be Finn, no left breast pocket, cast helmet, 1940, (B135)	24	36	48
785 Skier in White, no skis, (B136)	16	21	38
787 Diver with Axe, (B135)	350	525	725
788 Soldier Marching with Gun Slung Behind Back, cast helmet, (B140)	20	31	44

1934 and After (Continued)

	C6	C8	C10
789 Soldier Shooting Triple-Barreled Gun, sitting, cast helmet, (B141)	17	24	35
790 Soldier Shooting Anti-Tank Gun, cast helmet, (B145)	18	25	35
791 Soldiers with Mortar, (B143)	26	35	44
792 Airplane Mechanic, prop spins, brace on back of engine bulges, (B144)	29	42	65
793 Soldiers in Boat, cast helmets, (B142)	65	81	98
802 Boy Scout Saluting, (B183)	31	41	59
803 Boy Scout Signaling, (B184)	31	41	59
804 Boy Scout Cooking, (B185)	31	41	59
850 Policeman, arm raised, (B186)	13	19	25
850 Policeman, figure eight base, (B186a)	14	20	26
851 Fireman with Axe, (B187)	20	31	44
852 Fireman with Hose, (B188)	21	32	45
853 Postman, (B189)	9	15	22
951 Soldier Wireless Operator, (B147)	22	39	50
952 Soldier Dispatcher with Dog, (B148)	41	75	98
953 American Legionnaire in Overseas Cap, tall, made for 1937 Legion convention in New York, (B149)	175	285	400
954? American Legionnaire flag-bearer, tall, cloth flag, made for 1937 Legion convention in New York, as above, five known, (B150)	525	875	1500
960 Surgeon and Soldier, (B146)	60	81	121
961 At Typewriter, w/typewriter and table, (B151)	62	81	99
Chinese of Mongolian Rifleman, pronounced right breast pocket, c. 1937, (B46)	90	135	213
Chinese or Mongolian Officer, in steel helmet, c. 1937, (B45)	105	150	275
Fireman with Axe, flat underbase, (B187a)	21	31	45
Japanese, charging w/rifle, c. 1937, (B43)	80	110	160

1934 and After (Continued)

	C6	C8	C10
Japanese Officer, this is the original Ethiopian officer, painted as a Japanese, c. 1937, (B44)	120	165	245
Paint Your Own Army, Set No. 2003, boxed, c. 1934, (BA)	175	250	400
Santa Claus Seated, bag of toys at side, made to ride in sleigh, (B197)	110	165	295
Santa Claus with Holly Sprig, (B196)	50	70	95
West Point Cadet, w/rifle, short stride, w/line-and-dot eyes, white pants, white gloves, (B37a)	20	30	40
West Point Cadet, w/rifle, short stride, but painted as wooden soldier, only four known, (B37)	350	500	750

Barclay Podfoot Series

Made from c. 1950s to 1971, most podfoot soldiers came in khaki and later green. Add fifty percent to the price for a green example.

Barclay Podfoot Series

	C6	C8	C10
081 Two Soldier Crew at Radar Equipment, (B219)	20	30	41
082 Three Soldier Crew at Range Finder, (B220)	23	33	44
083 Two Soldier Crew at Searchlight, (B221)	20	30	41
084 Two Soldier Crew at Mobile Cannon, (B222)	21	31	42
085 Two Soldier Crew at AA Gun, (B223)	21	31	42
187 Officer on Horse, w/pot helmet, (B224)	62	89	121
188 Cowboy on Horse, w/lasso, (B225)	25	35	46
189 Indian on Horse, (B226)	18	28	39
190 Cowboy with Pistol on Horse, (B227)	18	28	39
800 Black Knight with Sword and Shield, (B228)	19	30	42
801 Knight with Red and Blue Shield and Sword, (B229)	19	30	42
802 Knight with Orange and Black Shield and Sword, (B230)	19	30	42
803 Knight with Red and Green Shield and Sword, (B231)	19	30	42
901 Soldier Flag Bearer, (B232)	8	12	24
903 Soldier Sniper, in red, (B233A)	62	81	134

Barclay Podfoot Series

	C6	C8	C10
903 Soldier Sniper, kneeling, (B233)	6	10	19
906 Soldier Charging, (B234A)	7	11	20
906 Soldier Charging, in red, (B234)	62	81	134
908 Soldier Officer, (B235)	8	12	21
908 Soldier Officer, in blue, (B235A)	95	210	375
908 Soldier Officer, in red, (B235B)	62	81	134
909 Soldier Bugler, in red, (B236A)	62	81	134
909 Soldier Bugler, (B236)	9	13	22
919 Sailor White Uniform, (B237)	12	17	28
920 Sailor Blue Uniform, (B238)	12	17	28
922 Marine, (B239)	15	20	31
928 Soldier Machine Gunner Lying Flat, (B240A)	9	13	22
928 Soldier Machine Gunner Lying Flat, in red, (B240)	62	81	134
929 Soldier with Pistol Crawling, (B241)	15	21	31
929 Soldier with Pistol Crawling, in red, (B241A)	62	81	134
937 Soldier Charging Machine Gunner, in red, (B242A)	62	81	134
937 Soldier Charging Machine Gunner, holding tommy gun, (B242)	7	11	20
938 Soldier Bomb Thrower, (B243)	11	17	27
938 Soldier Bomb Thrower, in red, (B243A)	62	81	134
941 Aviator, (B244)	12	16	26
941 Aviator, in red, (B244A)	100	125	175
947 Soldier Marksman, (B245)	5	11	20
947 Soldier Marksman, in red, (B245A)	62	81	134
948 Soldier Running, (B246)	6	12	21
948 Soldier Running, in red, (B246A)	90	110	150
950 Cowboy with Pistol Shooting, (B247)	26	38	50
951 Cowboy with Rifle, (B248)	11	15	23
952 Cowboy with Lasso, (B249)	11	15	23
953 Cowboy with Pistol, upraised, (B250)	11	15	23

Barclay Podfoots in Red. Some collectors believe they were meant to represent the Korean War enemy.

Barclay Podfoot Series	C6	C8	C10
954 Indian with Shield and Tomahawk, (B251)	7	12	19
955 Indian with Rifle, (B252)	16	28	42
956 Indian with Knife and Spear, (B253)	7	12	19
957 Indian with Bow and Arrow, (B254)	7	12	19
960 Soldier Wounded with Crutches, (B255)	18	24	31
960 Soldier Wounded with Crutches, in red, (B255A)	125	160	195
961 Soldier Wounded Head and Arm, (B256)	14	21	28
961 Soldier Wounded Head and Arm, in red, (B256A)	125	160	195
962 Nurse, (B257)	19	31	44
974 Soldier Anti-Aircraft Gunner, in red, (B258A)	62	81	134
974 Soldier Anti-Aircraft Gunner, (B258)	9	13	24
977 Soldier Under Marching Orders, in red, (B259A)	62	81	134
977 Soldier Under Marching Orders, marching, (B259)	7	14	22
988 Soldier Marching with Gun on Back, gun slung over shoulder, (B260)	7	12	19
988 Soldier Marching with Gun on Back, gun slung over shoulder, in red, (B260A)	62	81	134
990 Soldier with Bazooka, (B261)	8	13	20
990 Soldier with Bazooka, in red, (B261A)	62	81	134
991 Soldier Flame Thrower, in red, (B262A)	62	81	134

Barclay Podfoot Series	C6	C8	C10
991 Soldier Flame Thrower, (B262)	8	13	20

HO-scale Figures (1-1/2" tall)	C6	C8	C10
350 Policeman, (B275)	5	8	12
351 Man, (B276)	5	8	12
352 Woman, (B277)	5	8	12
353 Conductor, (B278)	5	8	12
354 Red Cap, (B279)	5	8	12
355 Oiler, (B280)	5	8	12
356 Brakeman, (B281)	5	8	12
357 Engineer, (B282)	5	8	12
358 Porter, (B283)	5	8	12
359 Dining Steward, (B284)	5	9	12
360 Hobo, (B285)	5	8	12
361 Newsboy, (B286)	5	8	12
362 Mailman, (B287)	5	8	12
363 Fireman, (B288)	8	12	20
366 Peg Legged Gateman, (B289)	9	12	21
369 Woman Carrying Baby, (B290)	6	12	16
370 Little Boy, (B291)	5	11	15
371 Little Girl, (B292)	5	11	15
372 Bride, (B293)	10	16	22
373 Groom, (B294)	8	12	22
Advancing with Rifle, (B267)	49	70	105
Bugler, (B264)	49	70	105
Cowboy with Pistol, (B272)	40	65	85
Cowboy with Rifle, (B271)	40	65	85
Firing Bazooka, (B269)	49	70	105
Firing Tommy Gun, (B270)	49	70	105
Flame Thrower	49	70	105

HO-scale Figures (1-1/2" tall) (Continued)

	C6	C8	C10
Indian with Hatchet, (B273)............	40	65	85
Indian with Rifle, (B274)	40	65	85
Marching, slung rifle, (B268).........	49	70	105
Officer with Binoculars, (B265)	49	70	105
Talking on Field Phone, (B266)	49	70	105
Walking Forward, rifle at side, pointing down, (B270A)	49	70	105

Post-War

	C6	C8	C10
723 Marine Officer, w/sword, short stride, in blue, (B24)....................	16	24	32

Post-WWII

	C6	C8	C10
701 Flagbearer, pot helmet, (B201)	16	21	34
703? Kneeling, firing rifle, (B202)	40	65	79
705 Port Arms, (B203)	14	20	31
707 Order Arms, (B204).................	14	20	31
708 Officer with Sword, (B205)......	15	20	31
720 Blue Sailor, (B218a).................	31	43	54
728 Prone Machine Gunner, (B206)	14	20	31
737 Tommy Gunner, (B207)	14	20	31
747 Standing Firing Rifle, (B208)	14	20	31
774 AA Gunner, (B209)	14	20	31
777 Marching at Slope, (B210)	14	20	31
788 Marching, rifle slung, (B211)	14	20	31
789 AA Gunner, (B212)	16	22	36
Bugler, (B215)...............................	50	62	75
Bugler, buttons run down front of uniform, (B215A).......................	52	65	78
Clarinetist, (B216)	50	62	75
Cowboy, two pistols, one in air, (B212a).................................	40	57	65
Drum Major, (B213).......................	50	62	75
Drummer, (B214)	50	62	75
Sailor, white, (B218)	31	43	54
Tubist, (B217)................................	50	62	75

Pre-1934

	C6	C8	C10
087? Mounted Officer, moving arm holding pistol, on cantering horse, (Baa)	37	53	70

Pre-1934 (Continued)

	C6	C8	C10
087? Mounted Officer, moving arm holding sword, on rearing horse, (Ba)..	49	62	75
087? Mounted Officer, moving arm holding bugle, on rearing horse, (Bb)..	49	62	75
186? Cavalryman mounted, no moving parts, modeled on French toy soldier, c. late 1920s-early 1930s, 2-3/4" high, (Bg).............	19	31	40
200 Jockey on Horse, (Bm)............	20	28	38
486 Cavalryman, no moving parts, c. early 1930s, approx. 2-1/4" high, (Bh)	19	31	46
486 Officer on Horse, smaller size, eight known, c. 1931, (Bn).........	12	21	38
500 Santa Claus on Tin Skis............	30	43	56
88? Mounted Cowboy with Lasso, (Bd)	NPF	NPF	NPF
89? Mounted Indian, moving arm holding rifle, (Be).......................	52	76	93
90? Mounted Cowboy, w/moving arm, holding rifle, (Bfa)	49	66	87
90? Mounted Cowboy with Pistol, (Bf)	40	60	80
90? Mounted Indian, moving arm holding pistol, (BeA).................	NPF	NPF	NPF
Baseball Batter, c. 1920s, (Bk)........	78	119	175
Baseball Fielder, c. 1920s, approx. 1-7/8" high, (Bi)	78	119	175
Baseball Pitcher, c. 1920s, (Bj)	78	119	175
Indian Brave on Foot, carrying rifle across stomach, 54 mm, (Bfb)	NPF	NPF	NPF
Indian Chief on Foot, blue and red striped headdress, 54 mm, (Bfa)	NPF	NPF	NPF
Mounted Indian on Rearing Horse, (B1)	20	29	38

Grey Iron

Founded as the Brady Machine Shop in Mount Joy, Pennsylvania in 1840, Grey iron made the only 3-1/4-inch cast-iron soldiers. In 1881, the company was organized as the Gray Iron Casting Company, Ltd., and as early as 1903 it was manufacturing toy banks and stoves, cap pistols, wheeled toys and trains, as well as a number of non-toy items.

On August 14, 1917, the company was granted two patents for their 40mm solid cast-iron soldiers that were approximately three inches tall. Four Revolutionary War soldiers—an infantryman, a foot soldier, a flag bearer, and a mounted officer—may have been introduced earlier, as they are numbered lower, but were not part of the 1933 announcement.

The figures tended to be slight and, while apparently successful, were superseded in July 1936 by Grey iron's "Iron men" series, slightly larger, more robust models that continued to be sold until World War II.

There were at least two designers for the soldiers— Edward Musser and Samuel S. Schmidt. The soldiers were hand-poured and then painted on an assembly line basis, and were initially sold for a dime, while their competitors charged a nickel.

Grey iron is still in business today as the John Wright division of Donsco, and has recently been producing, on an erratic basis, some unpainted soldiers from its old molds.

GREY IRON

Soldiers

	C6	C8	C10
01 Colonial Soldier, (G1)	12	18	35
01A Colonial Foot Officer, (G2)	12	18	35
01B Colonial Color-Bearer, (G3)	275	450	900
01B Colonial Color-Bearer, 1950s version, w/rifle barrel drilled out for flag, (G2)	22	39	72
01MA Colonial Mounted Officer, (G4)	16	28	53
02 Cadet, early version, (G5)	11	19	37
02 Cadet, (G6)	11	19	37
02A Cadet Officer, early, (G7)	11	19	37
02A Cadet Officer, (G8)	11	19	37
03 U.S. Infantry, Shoulder Arms, (G10)	9	15	27
03 U.S. Infantry, Shoulder Arms, early, (G9)	7	13	23
03/1 U.S. Infantry, Port Arms, (G11)	9	15	27
03A U.S. Infantry Officer, early, (G12)	9	15	27
03A U.S. Infantry Officer, (G13)	9	15	27
04 U.S. Infantry, Port Arms, early, (G16)	9	15	27
04/1 U.S. Doughboy Signaling, (G18)	15	27	46
04/2 U.S. Doughboy Combat Trooper, (G19)	12	21	40
04/3 U.S. Doughboy with Range Finder, (G20)	27	52	99
04/4 U.S. Doughboy Ammunition Carrier, (G21)	37	69	130
04/5 U.S. Doughboy Sharpshooter, (G22)	11	18	35
04/6 U.S. Doughboy with Bayonet, (G23)	12	22	41

Soldiers (Continued)	C6	C8	C10
04A U.S. Doughboy Officer with Field Glasses, (G17)	16	25	44
05 U.S. Infantry Charging, early, (G24)	8	12	25
06 U.S. Doughboy, Port Arms, early, (G25)	9	13	26
06 U.S. Doughboy, Shoulder Arms, (G26)	8	12	25
06/1 U.S. Doughboy Charging, (G29)	9	13	26
06/1F Foreign Legion Charging, (G110)	15	29	57
06/2 U.S. Doughboy Sentry, (G30)	11	19	39
06/3 Foreign Legion Bomber, (G111)	19	35	67
06/3 U.S. Doughboy Bomber, crawling, (G31)	12	19	35
06/4 U.S. Doughboy Grenade Thrower, (G32)	16	31	61
06A U.S. Doughboy Officer, (G28)	9	13	26
06A U.S. Doughboy Officer, early, (G27)	9	13	26
06AF Foreign Legion Officer, (G108)	19	34	65
06F Foreign Legion Shoulder Arms, (G109)	18	32	60
07 U.S. Doughboy Charging, early, (G33)	9	15	27
08/F Foreign Legion Cavalryman, (G114)	36	70	125
08A/F Foreign Legion Cavalry Officer, (G113)	36	70	125
08M U.S. Cavalryman, early, (G34)	12	21	41
08M U.S. Cavalryman, (G35)	13	24	47
08MA U.S. Cavalry Officer, early, (G37)	15	28	54
08MA U.S. Cavalry Officer, (G38)	14	27	51
09 U.S. Marine, (G40)	9	16	30
09 U.S. Marine, early, (G39)	10	18	35
10 Royal Canadian Police, early, (G41)	9	15	32
10 Royal Canadian Police, (G42)	12	22	40
11 Indian, w/hatchet, early, (G45)	8	13	24
11 Indian Chief, w/knife, (G46)	11	19	36
11/1 Indian Brave, shielding eyes, (G47)	12	22	40

Soldiers (Continued)

	C6	C8	C10
11/1M Indian Scout Mounted, firing pistol backwards, (G51)	95	175	325
11/2 Chief Attacking, upraised tomahawk, (G48)	34	65	125
11M Indian Mounted, early, (G49)	16	30	58
11M Indian Mounted, lying on horse, (G50)	22	40	78
12 Cowboy, (G53)	10	15	28
12 Cowboy, early, (G52)	9	14	27
12/1 Hold-Up Man, (G54)	12	22	40
12/1M Masked Cowboy Mounted, (G59)	150	265	410
12/2 Cowboy with Lasso, (G55)	18	34	61
12/3 Bandit, surrendering, (G56)	49	84	150
12M Cowboy Mounted, early, (G57)	18	32	60
12M Cowboy Mounted, (G58)	21	39	75
13 U.S. Machine Gunner, (G61)	8	13	24
13 U.S. Machine Gunner, early, (G60)	11	17	36
13/1 U.S. Machine Gunner, (G62)	10	15	28
13F Foreign Legion Machine Gunner, (G112)	19	35	60
14 U.S. Sailor, in blue, early, (G63)	9	16	28
14 U.S. Sailor, in white, early, (G64)	9	16	28
14 U.S. Sailor, in blue, (G65)	9	17	29
14/1W U.S. Sailor Signalman, (G71)	12	23	42
14A U.S. Naval Officer, in blue, (G69)	9	17	29
14A U.S. Naval Officer, early, in blue, (G67)	9	17	30
14AW U.S. Naval Officer, in white, (G70)	9	17	29
14AW U.S. Naval Officer, early, in white, (G68)	9	16	30
14W U.S. Sailor, in white, (G66)	9	17	29
15/1 Boy Scout Saluting, early, (G72)	12	23	42
15/2 Boy Scout Walking, early, (G73)	14	23	42
16/1 Pirate Boy, (G74)	14	26	45
16/2 Pirate Chief, (G75)	12	22	41
16/3 Pirate with Dagger, (G76)	12	22	41
16/4 Pirate with Hook, (G77)	12	22	41
16/5 Pirate with Sword, (G78)	12	22	41

Soldiers (Continued)

	C6	C8	C10
17/1 Legion Drum Major, (G80)	9	17	31
17/1 Legion Drum Major, early, (G79)	18	34	63
17/2 Legion Bugler, (G82)	8	15	29
17/2 Legion Bugler, early, (G81)	9	16	31
17/3 Legion Drummer, early, (G83)	10	18	34
17/3 Legion Drummer, (G84)	9	16	31
17/4 Legion Color Bearer, (G85)	13	23	43
18/1 Ethiopian Tribesman, c. 1936, (G86)	23	42	79
18/2 Ethiopian Chief, (G87)	24	43	84
18/3 Ethiopian Soldier, Shoulder Arms, (G88)	23	42	80
18/3A Ethiopian Officer, (G89)	24	43	84
18/5 Ethiopian Soldier Charging, (G90)	24	43	84
19 Knight in Armor, (G93)	13	25	47
20 Red Cross Doctor, (G94)	13	25	47
21 Stretcher Bearer, (G95)	15	28	52
21 Stretcher with Patient, (G96)	14	26	49
22/1/Wounded Sitting, (G97)	25	48	97
22/2 Wounded on Crutches, (G98)	21	39	77
23 Red Cross Nurse, (G99)	10	19	36
25 Aviator, non-soldier, (G100)	27	49	97
75 Radio Set, Operator and Aerial, (G103)	112	210	410
75 Radio Set, Operator Only, (G103A)	49	74	98
D26 Nurse and Wounded Soldier, (G104)	70	130	240
D27 Doughboy Supporting Wounded Soldier, (G105)	78	148	283
Greek Evzone, (G102)	41	78	153
Italian or English Desert Infantryman, (G91)	75	140	270
Italian or English Desert Officer, (G92)	78	150	280
Ski Trooper, w/original skis, c. 1940, (G101)	25	46	86
U.S. Cavalry Officer, earliest version, (G106)	65	115	220
U.S. Cavalryman, earliest version, (G107)	60	110	215

American Family Series

All American Family figures are approximately 2-1/4-inch high.

American Family at Home

	C6	C8	C10
Boy Flying Kite, w/original kite, (H-3)	10	18	35
Colored Cook, (H-7)	10	19	37
Colored Man Digging, (H-8)	10	18	35
Delivery Boy, (H-10)	8	15	28
Dog, (H-12)	6	10	18
Garageman, (H-9)	8	15	28
Girl Skipping Rope, w/orignal rope, (H-4)	10	18	35
Lawn Seat, (H-13)	5	8	15
Man with Watering Can, (H-1)	8	12	22
Milkman, (H-11)	8	15	22
Old Man Sitting, (H-5)	5	8	15
Old Woman Sitting, (H-6)	5	8	15
Woman with Basket, (H-2)	8	12	22

American Family on the Beach

	C6	C8	C10
Bench, (B-13)	5	8	14
Boy in White Summer Suit, (B-3)	19	37	73
Boy with Ball, (B-8)	19	37	73
Boy with Life Preserver, (B-6)	19	37	73
Girl Catching Ball, (B-9)	19	37	73
Girl in Slacks, (B-4)	19	37	73
Girl with Sand Pail, (B-7)	19	37	73
Life Boat, (B-12)	19	37	73
Life Guard, (B-10)	19	37	73
Life Guard's Chair, (B-11)	19	37	73
Man in Bathing Suit, (B-1)	19	37	73
Old Man Sitting, white suit, (B-5)	19	37	73
Woman in Bathing Suit, (B-2)	19	37	73

American Family on the Farm

	C6	C8	C10
Calf, (F-7)	6	10	18
Cow, (F-6)	6	10	18
Dog, (F-12)	6	10	18
Farmer, (T-1)	7	12	22
Farmer's Wife, (F-2)	7	12	22
Fence, (F-14)	7	12	21

American Family on the Farm (Continued)

	C6	C8	C10
Gate with Post, (F-13)	9	17	32
Girl, (F-3)	7	12	22
Goat, (F-10)	6	10	18
Goose, (F-11)	6	10	18
Hired Man Digging, (F-4)	8	14	24
Horse, (F-5)	6	10	18
Pig, (F-8)	6	10	18
Sheep, (F-9)	6	10	18

American Family on the Ranch

	C6	C8	C10
Boy in Cowboy Suit, (R-4)	19	37	73
Bucking Bronco, (R-8)	19	37	73
Burro, (R-10)	19	37	73
Calf, (R-11)	19	37	73
Colt, (R-9)	19	37	73
Cowboy Rider, (R-2)	19	37	73
Cowboy Squatting, (R-3)	19	37	73
Cowboy with Lasso, (R-1)	19	37	73
Cowgirl Rider, (R-6)	19	37	73
Girl in Riding Suit, (R-5)	19	37	73
Rooster and Chickens, (R-15)	20	38	75
Stallion, (R-7)	19	37	73
Three Ducks, (R-16)	20	38	75

American Family Travels

	C6	C8	C10
Boy in Traveling Suit, (T-3)	6	10	18
Conductor, (T-5)	6	10	18
Engineer, (T-6)	6	10	18
Girl in Traveling Suit, (T-4)	6	10	18
Man in Traveling Suit, (T-1)	6	10	18
Newboy, (T-10)	7	11	20
Old Colored Man Sitting, (T-12)	11	19	35
Policeman, (T-8)	6	10	18
Porter, (T-7)	6	10	18
Postman, (T-9)	6	10	18
Preacher, (T-11)	7	11	20
Seat, (T-13)	5	8	14
Woman in Traveling Costume, (T-2)	6	10	18

This Grey Iron American Family at home set is one of only two known.

Greyklip Armies

	C6	C8	C10
Set 1/Company A, at attention, consists of bugler, officer, flag-bearer, drummer, rifleman (rifleman vallued at C6 $3, C8 $4, C10$5), price for each, (GA)	2	4	6
Set 2/Company B, marching, consists of bugler, officer, flag-bearer, drummer, rifleman (rifleman valued at C6 $3, C8 $4, C10 $6), price for each, (GB)................................	2	4	6
Set 3/Company C, charging, consists of bugler, officer, flag-bearer, drummer, rifleman (C6 $3, C8 $4, C10 $5), price for each, (GC)	2	4	6
Set 4/Troop D, consists of four mounted troopers, one mounted officer with sword on shoulder, price for each, (GD)	3	5	8
Set 5/Aviator Corps, consists of pilot (two of the same figure in set) and plane w/detachable wing, price for set, (GG)	45	85	160
Set 5/Battery E, two-piece set, led by officer from Troop D, second piece is a gun limber w/four horses, several attached soldiers, price for second piece, (GF)........	9	16	30

Greyklip Armies (Continued)

	C6	C8	C10
Set 6/Battery E, consists of shell stack, loader bending, loader standing, gunner, cannon, price for each, shell stack is double, (GE)...	4	7	12
Uncle Sam's Defenders, consists of charging rifleman, machine gunner, charging officer, rifleman at attention, flagbearer, officer saluting, price for each (double the price on saluting officer and ten times the price on flagbearer), (GH)	5	9	16

Manoil

Manoil began production of toy soldiers in 1935. it was in business as early as 1927 under the name Jack Manoil. The company changed its name to Man-O-Lamp Corporation on July 11, 1928 and was owned by Maurice Manoil (1893-1974) and Jack Manoil (1902-1955), two brothers who had emigrated from Romania in the early 1900s. The final name change to Manoil Manufacturing Co., Inc. took place on July 7, 1934.

Manoil advanced into toy making in 1934 manufacturing seven vehicles. The company moved to other addresses as it grew, leaving Manhattan in 1937 for Brooklyn, and moving to Waverly, New York, in June 1940 and employed 225 people at its peak.

With the onset of World War II, Manoil shut down, but resumed production of soldiers in a fine-grained composition (employing sulfur) in January 1944. The pieces were brittle and ultimately unsuccessful, and their manufacture stopped by the end of the year.

After the war, the company introduced several new lines of soldiers, but they were no longer distributed as widely.

In 1953, the firm moved to a smaller location in Waverly, changing its name to Jack Manoil Specialty Company, but went out of business shortly after his death. Jack Manoil and sculptor Walter Baetz were both keenly interested in the company's soldiers and would work late in the night as they collaborated on ideas for them. One of Baetz's continuing concerns was to design the molds so that there were no bubbles. For this reason, many of Manoil's soldiers were redesigned a number of times with sometimes subtle, and sometimes broad, variations.

Manoil's soldiers have a distinctive jauntiness to them, at times veering on caricature, the latter trait becoming more pronounced as the years wore on.

MANOIL

Manoil	C6	C8	C10
007 Flag Bearer, hollow base version, (M1)	50	75	102
007 Flag Bearer, third version, (M2)	18	25	40
007 Flag Bearer, second version, (M3)	15	20	33
008 Parade, stocky version, (M5)	10	20	30
008 Parade, campaign cap straight on head, (M6)	25	35	51
008 Parade, fifth version, (M8)	11	18	26
008 Parade, hollow base version, (M4)	40	65	86
008 Parade, number on back, (M6)	85	105	125
009 Officer, hollow base version, (M9)	50	65	90
009 Officer, second version, (M10)	12	21	33
010 Bugler, hollow base version, (M11)	50	72	97
010 Bugler, second version, (M12)	12	20	32
011 Drummer, hollow base version, (M13)	50	72	97
011 Drummer, stocky version, (M14)	15	30	44
011 Drummer, vertical drum, (M15)	26	42	59
012 Machine Gunner (Prone), no aperture, pack on back, (M20)	14	26	36
012 Machine Gunner (Prone), no aperture between hands and gun, (M19)	11	17	26
012 Machine Gunner (Prone), grass on base, (M16)	16	25	37

Manoil (Continued)	C6	C8	C10
012 Machine Gunner (Prone), flat base, no grass, (M17)	15	22	38
012 Machine Gunner (Prone), spaces under body, (M18)	35	65	90
013 Cadet, hollow base, no buckle on belt, (M21)	36	52	73
013 Cadet, second version, (M22)	14	24	34
014 Sailor, hollow base, (M23)	32	52	74
014 Sailor, in blue, (M23a)	32	52	74
015 Marine, second version, (M26)	14	20	39
015 Marine, hollow base, (M25)	50	72	97
016 Ensign, (M27)	13	20	34
016 Ensign, hollow base, (M27a)	42	65	91
017 Signal Man, hollow base version, (M28)	26	37	58
017 Signal Man, second version, (M29)	24	40	55
018 Cowboy, hollow base version, (M30)	24	40	55
018 Cowboy, second version, (M31)	12	17	29
018A Cowboy with Hands Up, (M32)	13	20	35
018A Cowboy with Hands Up, subtle variation, (M33)	13	21	36
020 Doctor, white, (M34)	13	20	35
020K Doctor, khaki, (M35)	18	28	42
021 Nurse, no hem in skirt, shorter, (M36a)	19	35	53
021 Nurse, (M36)	11	19	31
022 Indian, w/knives, (M38)	13	20	35
022 Indian, w/knives, right toes off base, (M38a)	15	22	37
023 Machine Gunner Sitting, markings under base, (M40)	14	21	36
023 Machine Gunner Sitting, seated on four pillows, bullets feed from ammo box, (M39)	14	21	30
024 Cannon Loader, (M42)	10	19	33
025 Sniper (kneeling), folding rifle, (M44)	140	285	425
025 Sniper (kneeling), longer, thicker rifle, (M46)	14	31	42
025 Sniper (kneeling), short thin rifle, (M45)	15	25	34
026 Sniper, folding rifle, (M47)	140	285	425
026 Sniper, shorter rifle, angle different on underside of rifle, (M48a)	40	55	75

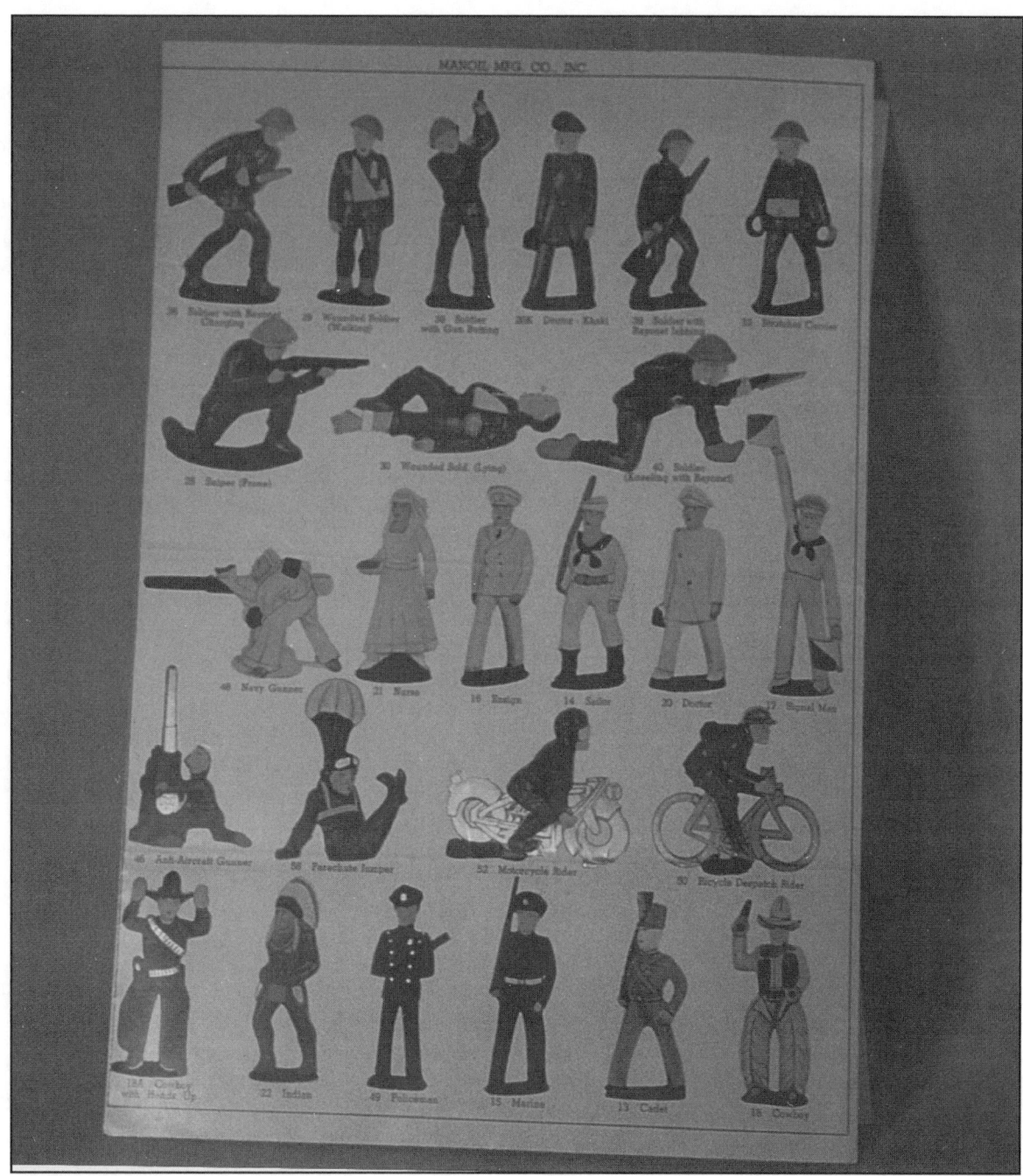

A page from the 1939 Manoil catalog.

Manoil (Continued)	C6	C8	C10
026 Sniper, (M48)	12	26	35
027 Tommy Gunner, bloated version, (M49)	22	32	48
027 Tommy Gunner, second version, (M50)	12	20	36
028 Observer, (M51)	16	29	42
029 Wounded Soldier Walking, (M52)	14	21	36
030 Wounded Soldier Lying, (M53)	10	17	28
030 Wounded Soldier Lying, number on back, shorter head, (M54)	15	21	37
031 Bomb Thrower, three grenades in pouch, (M55)	16	24	36
031 Bomb Thrower, two grenades in pouch, (M56)	17	25	37
032 Stretcher Carrier, medical kit, (M58a)	14	21	33
032 Stretcher Carrier, medical kit, number on back, buttons on uniform, different pockets and collar from above, (M58)	40	80	125
032 Stretcher Carrier, no medical kit, (M57)	13	20	36
033 Sitting Soldier, (M59)	22	32	47
034 Aviator, (M60)	20	35	60
035 Hostess, in green	31	55	79
035 Hostess, in white, (M61)	85	180	275
035 Hostess in Khaki, (M61a)	125	225	300
036 Soldier with Bayonet Charging, (M62)	24	42	65
037 Soldier with Gun Charging, (M63)	30	49	67
038 Soldier with Gun Butting, (M64)	33	52	73
039 Soldier with Bayonet Jabbing, (M65)	30	50	75
040 Soldier Kneeling with Bayonet, (M66)	40	55	80
041 Soldier Crouching with Hand Grenade, (M67)	34	60	80
042 Field Doctor Crawling, (M68)	45	75	90
043 Officer Lying Down, Shooting Revolver, (M69)	28	46	70
044 Crawling Scout with Gun, left leg high when right leg on ground, only three known, (M70)	95	210	300
044 Crawling Scout with Gun, left leg lower, (M71)	27	46	55

Manoil (Continued)	C6	C8	C10
045 Observer with Periscope, (M72)	19	40	58
046 Anti-Aircraft Gunner, barrel of gun drops below arm, (M73)	14	20	36
046 Anti-Aircraft Gunner, barrel of gun ends at arm, (M74)	14	20	36
047 Anti-Aircraft Searchlight, like No. 47 number on back, helmet looks as if it was adapted to look like WWII helmet, (M75b)	21	43	62
047 Anti-Aircraft Searchlight, (M75)	15	21	37
047 Anti-Aircraft Searchlight, w/tin lens, (M75a)	125	200	310
048 Navy Gunner, (M76)	14	24	44
049 Policeman, slightly larger, (M78)	12	24	36
049 Policeman, (M77)	11	20	32
050 Bicycle Dispatch Rider, (M79)	19	30	41
051 Motorized Machine Gunner, (M80)	39	70	93
052 Motorcycle Rider, (M82)	21	39	52
052 Motorcycle Rider, number over rear wheel, grass base, (M81)	28	51	67
053 Sitting Soldier without Gun, (M93)	16	29	42
054 Sitting Soldier Eating, (M84)	26	40	60
055 Sitting Soldier at Table with Phone and Map, (M85)	18	29	57
056 Paymaster, (M86)	75	120	210
057 Camouflage Sharpshooter Lying Down, (M87)	12	22	40
058 Parachute Jumper, (M88)	16	30	61
059 Soldier Writing Letter, smoking cigarette or not smoking versions exist, (M89)	24	48	80
059 Soldier Writing Letter, foot not curled up, pencil is flat, helmet rounder, fuller, (M89a)	26	53	85
060 Cook's Helper with Ladle, helmet looks as if it was adapted to look like WWII helmet, (M91)	49	95	180
060 Cook's Helper with Ladle, normal helmet, (M90)	20	39	68
061 Soldier with Camera, (M92)	28	49	86
062 Soldier with Gas Mask & Gun, (M93)	12	19	37
063 Soldier with Gas Mask with Flare Pistol, (M94)	13	21	40

Manoil (Continued)	<u>C6</u>	<u>C8</u>	<u>C10</u>
064 Soldier Playing Banjo, (M95)...	39	75	136
065 Deep Sea Diver, w/"65" on chest, (M97)	13	20	37
065 Deep Sea Diver, (M96)	13	20	37
066 Soldier with Gun on Parade with Overseas Cap, (M98)	29	49	85
067 Soldier with Gun and Pack Marching, (M99)	11	20	39
068 Soldier Boxing, (M100)	29	54	105
077 Lineman and Telephone Pole, pole comes w/two different-shaped bases, oval or diagonal, (M101)	40	68	125
078 Anti-Tank Gun, wooden wheels, (M104)	25	46	89
078 Anti-Tank Gun, squared shield, (M103)	15	28	55
078 Anti-Tank Gun, round shield, all variations based on Vickers 2.95 mountain gun, (M102)	17	30	57
079 Soldier Marching with Gun Slung at Angle, (M105)	49	93	185
080 Anti-Aircraft Machine Gunner, (M106)	11	19	34
081 Machine Gunner and Helper, aperture between hand and machine gun, (M107)	15	28	52
081 Machine Gunner and Helper, no aperture, (M108)	15	28	52
082 Anti-Aircraft with Range Finder, (M109)	11	19	36
083 Soldier Trench Mortar, (M110)	12	20	38
084 Soldier with Shell, (M111)	15	28	47
085 Aviator Holding Bomb, (M112)	12	22	42
086 Aviator Mechanic with Propeller, away from head, (M113)	165	285	500
086 Aviator Mechanic with Propeller, orange prop, flat lower hand, (M114)	48	88	175
086 Aviator Mechanic with Propeller Orange prop, curved lower hand, (M114b)	48	88	175
086 Aviator Mechanic with Propeller Silver Prop, (M114a)	48	88	175
087 Aviator Carrying Bomb Sight, (M115)	16	30	58
088 Radio Operator Standing, (M116)	26	47	90
089 Radio Operator Lying Down, (M117)	20	38	73

Manoil (Continued)	<u>C6</u>	<u>C8</u>	<u>C10</u>
090 Soldier Digging Trench, (M118)	20	38	72
091 Soldier with Barbed Wire, (M120)	19	36	69
091 Soldier with Barbed Wire, wide-faced version, (M119)	19	36	69
092 Fire Fighter, in gray, (M121)	40	75	140
092 Fire Fighter, in white, (M121a)	38	70	130
093 Soldier on Guard Duty, (M122)	35	60	110
094 Soldier Running with Cannon, thin face, wooden wheels, (M124)	21	40	76
094 Soldier Running with Cannon, marked "Manoil USA," "1," cannon slants to right when looked at from above, (M123)	18	31	58
094 Soldier Running with Cannon, no markings, cannon straight from above, face narrower, (M123a)	21	33	58
099 Finn with Skis, (M125)	31	53	98
100 Finn Machine Gunner, (M126)	27	47	86
101 Soldier Jumping with Chute, (M127)	37	65	120
102 Soldier Jumping with Machine Gun, (M128)	34	63	118
Aviator Holding Bomb, hand variation, (M112a)	15	22	30
Indian, w/hatchet, (M37)	49	90	175
Machine Gunner Sitting, squarer-looking, markings near right leg, (M41)	13	21	36
Sailor, second version, (M24)	10	18	29
Soldier with Camera, thinner arm, (M92a)	32	58	100

MANOIL

Happy Farm Series	<u>C6</u>	<u>C8</u>	<u>C10</u>
41/1 Bench, (M129)	6	10	18
41/10 Farmer Sowing Grain, (M138)	11	18	33
41/11 Man Carrying Sheaves Under Arm, (M139)	11	18	33
41/12 Darky Eating Watermelon, (M142)	32	59	105
41/12 Scarecrow with Top Hat, (M140)	11	18	33

Happy Farm Series (Continued)

	C6	C8	C10
41/13 Farmer Carrying Pumpkin, (M141)	11	18	33
41/15 Scarecrow with Straw Hat, (M143)	11	18	33
41/16 Watchman Blowing Out Lantern, (M144)	12	19	35
41/17 Hod Carrier with Bricks, (M145)	13	25	44
41/18 Man Chopping Wood, (M146)	11	18	33
41/19 Mason Laying Bricks, (M147)	13	25	44
41/2 Girl, (M130)	6	10	18
41/20 Man Dumping Wheel Barrow, (M148)	12	20	50
41/21 Old Man Fixing Shoe, (M149)	15	26	50
41/22 Blacksmith with Wheel, (M150)	11	18	33
41/23 Carpenter Carrying Door, (M151)	21	39	74
41/24 Hound, (M152)	11	18	33
41/25 Carpenter Sawing Lumber, (M153)	11	19	36
41/26 Carpenter with Square, (M154)	21	39	75
41/27 Shepherd with Flute, (M155)	21	39	75
41/28 Lady with Pie, (M156)	11	18	33
41/29 Lady with Child, (M157)	11	18	33
41/3 Young Man, (M131)	6	10	18
41/30 School Teacher, (M158)	17	31	58
41/31 Girl Watering Flowers, (M159)	11	18	33
41/32 Woman Lifting Hen From Nest, (M160)	11	18	33
41/33 Woman with Butter Churn, (M161)	11	18	33
41/34 Woman Laying Out Wash on Grass, (M162)	11	18	33
41/35 Woman Sweeping with Broom, (M163)	11	18	33
41/36 Man Juggling Barrel, (M164)	22	39	76
41/36 Man Juggling Barrel, in khaki, (M164a)	27	49	88
41/37 Man Planting Tree, (M165)	19	35	68
41/38 Girl Picking Berries, (M166)	18	34	67

Happy Farm Series (Continued)

	C6	C8	C10
41/39 Farmer at Water Pump, (M167)	11	18	33
41/4 Man Carrying Sack on Back, (M132)	11	18	33
41/40 Boy Carrying Wood, (M168)	11	18	33
41/41 Stacks of Sheaves, (M169)	11	18	33
41/5 Farmer Pitching Sheaves, (M133)	11	18	33
41/6 Farmer Sharpening Scythe, (M134)	11	18	33
41/7 Blacksmith Making Horseshoes, (M135)	11	18	33
41/8 Farmer Cutting with Scythe, (M136)	11	18	33
41/9 Farmer Cutting Corn, (M137)	11	18	33
Boxed Happy Farm Set, no standard contents, ten pieces, (M169a)	110	225	425

Manoil Composition

	C6	C8	C10
Firing Camouflaged AA Gun, (MC4)	19	39	75
Motorcyclist, minor variation of above, (MC3A)	27	49	95
Motorcyclist, (MC3)	27	49	95
Prone Machine-gunner, (MC1)	19	39	75
Seated Machine-gunner, (MC2)	19	39	75

My Ranch Corral Series

	C6	C8	C10
C01 Fence, (M219)	8	10	18
C02 Large Ranch Fence, gate, (M211)	40	60	75
C12 Blanket Over Fence Section, (M212)	50	70	85
C14 Brahma Bull, (M217)	12	20	29
C18 Small Calf, (M213)	9	13	19
C19 Cow feeding, (M215)	10	18	25
C20 Bull, head turned, (M214)	10	18	25
C22 Horse for Mounted Cowboy, (M221)	15	25	40
C22 Horse for Mounted Cowgirl, (M222)	15	25	40
C23 Cowboy Rider, (M207)	10	18	25
C24 Cowgirl Rider, (M208)	10	18	25
C25 Small Horse, (M220)	12	20	30
C26 Large Cactus, (M218)	15	30	45
C28 Short Cactus, (M216)	15	30	45

My Ranch Corral Series

	C6	C8	C10
C29 Mounted Cowboy, (M209)	35	62	75
C30 Mounted Cowboy Shooting, (M210)...	35	62	75
Small Gate, (M223)	19	30	40

Manoil Postwar

The following were the first new post-World War II series, and were produced only for a limited time. On a trial basis, early production was also sold unpainted.

Post-War

	C6	C8	C10
045/10 At Attention, present arms, (M180).....................................	14	26	48
045/11 Sniper, (M181)	16	28	54
045/12 Tommy Gunner, (M182)...	14	26	48
045/13 Soldier with Bazooka Cannon, some marked "45/18", (M183)...	14	26	48
045/14 Soldier with Shell for Bazooka, some marked "46/14", (M184)...	14	26	48
045/15 General, some "46/15", (M185)...	49	95	180
045/16 Mine Detector, some "46/16", (M186).........................	14	26	48
045/6 Parade, thin, c. late 1945, (M176)...	13	24	45
045/7 Flag Bearer, (M177)	14	27	52
045/8 Parade, (M178).....................	13	24	45
045/9 Combat, (M179)	14	27	52
521 Flag Bearer, all 500s, c. 1950, (M187)...	15	28	53
522 Parade, (M188)	13	24	45
523 Soldier in Poncho, (M189)...	15	28	53
524 Combat, (M190)	15	28	53

Post-War (Continued)

	C6	C8	C10
525 Aviator Holding Bomb, (M191)	16	30	55
526 Observer, (M192)	28	38	48
527 Aircraft Spotter, (M193)..........	28	38	48
528 Soldier with Bazooka, (M194)	28	38	48
529 Motorcycle Rider, (M195)	45	60	70
530 Machine Gunner, lying, (M196)	28	38	48
531 Machine Gunner, sitting, (M197)	28	38	48
532 Sniper, kneeling, (M198)..........	28	38	48
533 Soldier, w/gas mask w/flare pistol, (M199).............................	28	38	48
534 Sniper, (M200)	28	38	48
535 Soldier Throwing Hand Grenade, (M201).............................	28	38	48
536 Anti-Aircraft Gunner, (M202)	28	38	48
537 Soldier, w/tommy gun, (M203)	28	38	48
538 Soldier Firing Up, (M204)	28	38	48
539 Stretcher Bearer, (M205)..........	90	125	150
540 Wounded Soldier, lying, (M206)	100	150	175
Flag Bearer, thin, c. late 1945, (M170)	20	30	40
Machine Gunner Lying, thin, c. late 1945, (M174)	75	100	125
Machine Gunner Sitting, thin, c. late 1945, (M173).......................	65	90	115
Sniper, thin, c. late 1945, (M175)	40	50	60
Tommy Gunner, thin, c. late 1945, (M172)	40	50	60

MECHANICAL SPARKLERS AND PLUNGER TOYS

Mechanical sparklers are fun and colorful tin or plastic hand-held toys, most of which are held between the pointer and middle fingers and operated by depressing a spring-loaded plunger with the thumb. As the plunger is depressed and returned, a round disk holding two cigarette lighter-type flints quickly spins. The flints then grind against a sandpaper plate causing white sparks to be emitted. Most sparklers include two cut-out windows covered with either red and blue or red and green clear pieces of celluloid or plastic. These windows give the illusion of the toy having multi-colored sparks. These toys are more interactive to the user than some other toys of the era such as battery-operated and wind-up toys, which certainly have their own intrigue and appeal.

There are many wonderfully detailed tin lithographed examples of these toys available from the 1920s through the 1950s, especially from Germany and Spain. Tin and plastic versions of sparklers and other plunger toys have been manufactured continuously to the present time from countries including the USA, Japan, France, Australia, Great Britain, Hong Kong, Taiwan, and China. Manufacturers include, Arnold, R.S. La Isla, Ronson, Ranger Steel Products, Chein, Strauss, Domus, Hale Nass, Molto, Mettoy, and many others. Rogelio Sanchis manufactured wonderful sparkler examples in Spain at his castle/home named La Isla. The toys are marked R.S., or La Isla, or both. Several of their character sparklers included moving arms and legs.

Some sparkler and spinner toys have seasonal themes such as the 4th of July, Christmas, and Halloween. Others have comic character themes including, Mickey Mouse, Popeye, Fleix, Amos & Andy, Harold Lloyd, Archie, Stan Laurel, Oliver Hardy, Buster Keaton, and Ed Wynn.

Other variations of the plunger mechanism were used for egg spinners tops, sirens, game spinners, and flying propellers. Egg spinners have four-piece egg or tree shape forms held together with a rubber band, and mounted on top of the round disk. When the plunger is depresses causing the round disk to spin, centrifugal force causes the four egg-shaped pieces to separate, revealing an object on the inside. For example, there are several variations of Christmas tree spinners that have a Santa inside. Another example is a Jack-O-Lantern egg that has a skull on the inside.

Contributor: Randy Welch, Raven 'Tiques, 27965 Peach Orchard Rd., Easton, MD 21601-8203. He encourages correspondence from collectors.

Ronson Pull Cord: Pussy Cat, Round (Large), Archie. Photo courtesy Randy Welch

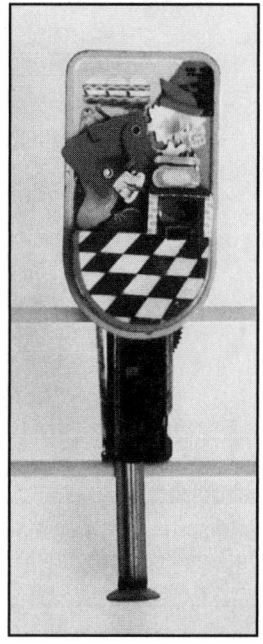

Pop-Up: Man Pushing Duck into Pot. Photo courtesy Randy Welch

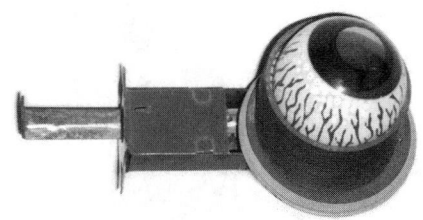

Eye Ball on Spring. Photo courtesy Randy Welch

PLUNGER NON-SPARKLER

Egg Spinners

	C10
Ballerina, tin, w/box, Spain, Molto, 333	60
Chick, tin, w/box, Spain, Molto, 330	60
Chick w/ "push slow" sticker, tin & plastic, Hong Kong	10
Clown, tin, w/box, Spain, Molto, 332	60
Clown w/ "push slow" sticker, tin & plastic, Japan	10
Indian, tin, w/box, Spain, Molto, 334	60
Indian w/ "push slow" sticker, tin & plastic, Japan	10
Santa, plastic	7
Santa, tin, w/box, Spain, Molto, 331	50
Santa w/ "push slow" sticker, tin & plastic, Japan	10
Skull in pumpkin w/ "push slow" sticker, tin & plastic, Japan	10
Uncle Sam, tin, Spain, Molto, 335	60
Witch in pumpkin, plastic, green	7
Witch in pumpkin w/ "push slow" sticker, tin & plastc, black, Hong Kong	7

Miscellaneous

	C10
Disneyland Moviedrome, tin, w/paper rings, United Kingdom	400

Miscellaneous (Continued)

	C10
Eye-ball on spring, tin & celluloid	60
Flying Saucer, tin, with box, flying propeller, Japan, MT	75
Flying Saucer, tin, France	95
Multi-colored Spinning, tin, medium, Western Germany, Arnold	95
Multi-colored Spinning, tin & celluloid, small, Japan	50
Optical Spinning, tin, w/paper pattern disks, Astra	200
Pick-A-Winna, tin, game spinner w/box, United Kingdom, Mettoy	150
Space Race, plastic, USA, Hale Nass	30
Three Children on Carnival Swing, tin & celluloid, Japan	300
Western Game, plastic, on card game spinner, USA, Hale Nass	30

Plunger Sirens

	C10
Baby Face, tin, small, Germany	175
Black Cat, tin, small, Germany	75
Ed Wynn, tin, small, USA	95
Fire Chief, tin, w/box, USA, Ranger, 237B	75
Silver Bicycle Siren, tin, Japan, Royce	60

Disney MovieDrome with paper rings. Photo courtesy Randy Welch

Three Children on Carnival Swing from Japan. Photo courtesy Randy Welch

Left: Airplane with spinning propeller. Right: Airplane (3D). Photo courtesy Randy Welch

Pop-Up Santa from Germany. Photo courtesy Randy Welch

An assortment of Mickey Mouse sparklers. Photo courtesy Randy Welch

*Old Woman.
Photo courtesy Randy Welch*

*An assortment of Sparklers, Spinners, and
Sirens. Photo courtesy Randy Welch*

*Wild Cat Siren by Ranger with box. Photo
courtesy Randy Welch*

*Ranger Sparkler with box. Photo
courtesy Randy Welch*

*Train from Germany. Photo
courtesy Randy Welch*

Plunger Sirens (Continued)

	C10
White Cat, tin, small, Western Germany	75
Wild Cat Siren, tin, w/box, USA, Ranger, 238	100

Plunger w/ Spinning Tops

	C10
Top, tin, globe shape, w/box, Western Germany, VK MNN	150
Tops, tin, 2 globe shape, Japan, Marx	75
Tops, tin, 2 cone shape, US Zone Germany	100

SPARKLERS

Plunger Character Sparkler

	C10
Amos, tin, face shape w/glass eyes, Germany	600
Andy, tin, face shape w/glass eyes, Germany	600
Casper, tin & plastic, Hong Kong	20
Felix, tin, w/short ears, Germany	250
Felix, tin, w/long ears	250

Plunger Character Sparkler (Continued)

	C10
Flash Gordon, tin & plastic, Hong Kong, Ja-Ru, 354	20
Hopalong Cassidy, tin & plastic	150
Howdy Doody, tin & plastic, Hong Kong, Ja-Ru, 2306	20
Jetsons, tin & plastic, Hong Kong, Ja-Ru	20
Mickey Mouse, tin & plastic, Taiwan, Ja-Ru, 378	20
Mickey Mouse, tin, face shape, USA, Nifty	250
Mickey Mouse, tin & plastic, Hong Kong, Strauss	30
Mickey Mouse, tin & plastic, on card, Hong Kong, Strauss, 76/28	30
Mickey Mouse, tin & plastic, castle on card, USA, Chein, 9506	30
Mickey Mouse, plastic, face on card, Hong Kong, 20896	20
Popeye, tin, USA, 1959, Chein	95

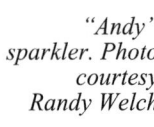

"Andy" sparkler. Photo courtesy Randy Welch

An assortment of Chein Sparkler Boxes. Photo courtesy Randy Welch

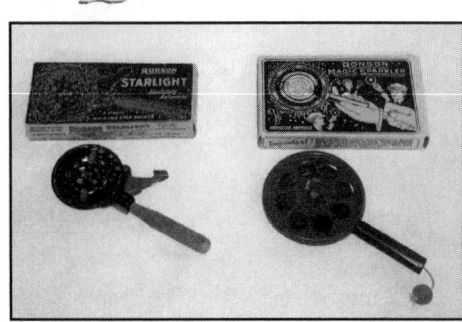

Ronson Starlight with box and Magic Sparkler with its box. Photo courtesy Randy Welch

"Sparkler" store display w/three sparklers. Photo courtesy Randy Welch

Plunger Character Sparkler (Continued)	C10
Popeye, tin, face shape	200

Plunger Insect Sparkler	C10
Bee on Flower, tin, US Zone Germany	75
Butterfly w/celluloid wings, tin, with box, USA, Chein, 164	150
Butterfly w/celluloid wings, tin, Germany...........	50

Plunger Misc. Sparkler	C10
Cat's Meow, tin, w/box, USA, Ranger, 250	75
Clown Face, tin, Germany....................................	75
Gargoyles, plastic, Burger King, China, P-3-10 ..	15
Moon Face, tin..	60
Old Woman, tin, mouth opens, Germany.............	75
Ranger Sparkler, tin, w/box, USA, Ranger	65
Red, White & Blue swirl, tin, on card, USA, Chein, 95	25
Red, White & Blue swirl, tin, w/2 black cats, Hong Kong	20
Red, White & Blue swirl, tin & plastic, w/2 black cats, Japan...	15

Plunger Misc. Sparkler (Continued)	C10
Red, White & Blue swirls, tin, with black cat faces, small, Japan...	25
Red, White & Blue swirls, tin, small, Japan	25
South of the Border, tin & plastic	30
Sparkler Wheel, tin, w/box, Australia, Domus	60
Star Wars Exploding Death Star, plastic, recalled, China, 1996, Applause...........................	15
Stars, tin, various color versions, USA, Chein.....	25
Stars 'N Stripes, tin, red and white swirl on card, USA, Chein, 95	25

Plunger Vehicle Sparkler	C10
Airplane w/Sparking Gun, tin, (3d), Germany	250
Airplane w/Spinning Propeller, tin, Germany	500
Helicopter, tin, (3d), USA, Ranger, 260..............	100
Indian Motorcycle, tin, Germany	800
Jet Copter, tin & plastic, (3d) in box, USA, Ranger, 270	200
Train, tin, new, on card, China, Schylling............	7

Jet Copter with box by Ranger. Photo courtesy Randy Welch

Pick-A-Winna game spinner with box. Photo courtesy Randy Welch

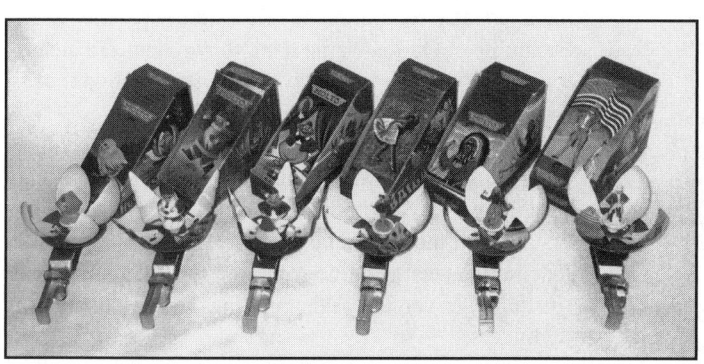

Egg Spinners with boxes from Molto, Spain: Chick, Santa, Clown, Ballerina, Indian, and Uncle Sam

Happy Clown Spinner store display. Photo courtesy Randy Welch

Plunger Vehicle Sparkler (Continued) — C10

	C10
Train, tin, Germany, P.W.	250

Plunger w/ Pop-Up Sparkler — C10

	C10
Chimney Sweep, tin, several variations, Germany, Arnold	95
Clown, tin, Germany	100
Fireman in Burning House Chimney, tin, Japan	90
Man Pushing Duck into Cooking Pot, tin, Germany, Arnold	200
Policeman, tin, France, 3001	50
Santa, tin, Germany	250
Santa in House Chimney, tin, Japan	90

Pull Cord and Side Plunger Sparkler — C10

	C10
Archie, tin, large, (3d), USA, Ronson	175
Magic Sparkler, tin, with box, USA, Ronson	100
Pussy Cat, tin, large, (3d), USA, Ronson	250
Round, tin, large, USA, Ronson	150
Starlight, tin, w/box, side thumb plunger, USA, Ronson	75

Seasonal Sparkler — C10

	C10
Black Cat Face, tin, USA, Chein	60
Halloween Sparkler, plastic, skull on card (3d), Hong Kong	30
Halloween Sparkler, plastic, pumpkin on card (3d), Hong Kong	30
Old Witch, tin, on card (3d), Japan, Ranger, 255.	85
Owl, Cats & Bats design, tin	50
Pumpkin & Bat design, tin, USA, Chein	60
Pumpkin face, tin, USA, Chein	60
Pumpkin in bag, plastic, (3d), China	20
Pumpkin w/hat, plastic, on card, Hong Kong, Fun World	30
Santa Face, tin, (3d), USA, Hale Ness	95
Santa Spinner, plastic, sparkler w/battery operated lights, China	20
Skull in bag, plastic, (3d), Hong Kong, Fun World	20
Trick or Treat, tin, on card, Hong Kong, Creative, 4016	45

STEAM TOYS

By Richard Leach

When I tell people that I collect toy steam engines as a hobby, I usually hear, "What type of trains do you collect?" Then I have to explain that while I have a few live steam locomotives, the majority of my collection consists of stationary live steam toys and related accessories, not just trains. Whenever I say that I collect steam toys, I get a slightly different response, such as, "What is a steam toy?" To clarify, I will try to explain with a brief history of steam toys.

Steam Toy History

Phillip Ely of New York patented the first live steam toy on March 26, 1867. It consisted of a cone-shaped metal container that pivoted on a vertical pointed rod in the center of a small burner. Protruding from the smaller end of the cone was a tube where escaping steam caused the cone to rotate. Just below the steam tube was a small pulley and string belt that gave rotary motion to a small carousal. (See photo of the Ely Thimble model.)

On August 15, 1871, a patent was issued to Russell Frisbie of Cromwell, Conn., for two toy steam engines. Both were made of cast iron and had three legs to support them above a small wicked burner. One had a walking beam to supply power to the flywheel. This model has a very simple but ingenious valve mechanism. The other had a horizontal cylinder and connecting rod that went directly to a crank pin in the flywheel.

Russell worked with J.&E. Stevens Co., also of Cromwell, which also made cast-iron toys and banks. Over the many years that he worked for Stevens, Russell patented several other toys and inventions. It is often asked if he had anything to do with the Frisbee disks of today. The story goes that his family made pie tins that were used by university students as "Frisbees."

Just one month later, on September 19, 1871, Eugene Beggs, who worked in a locomotive shop in Paterson, N.J., filed a patent for a live steam toy locomotive. The Beggs locomotive had a brass horizontal boiler with a black pressed steel body. Beggs also made a deluxe model with a nickel-plated boiler. The boiler was fired by a three-wick alcohol burner that was filled from behind the small, attached coal hopper. It had oscillating brass cylinders, and the rods connected directly to a crank pin in the drive wheels.

Buckman Steam Toys

Kraft & Huffington had been producing toy steam engines during the late 1860s. In 1870, Alexander and Edward Buckman took over their business and started The Buckman Mfg. Co. in Brooklyn, N.Y. Buckman and Huffington have a patent for a small steam engine dated March 28, 1871. Another patent for a steam engine was issued to Alexander Buckman on December 12 of that year. On November 5, 1872, the Buckman brothers also received a patent for a toy paddle wheel steam boat. On that same date, they patented a steam-powered fire pumper that would put out a stream of water measuring 10 to 15 feet.

The Buckman series of Young America steam engines sold very well in the 1870s. The Dollar Steam Engine was a very popular model offered in many toy catalogs of the time. The small vertical boiler oscillating steam engine sold for $1. A $2 engine, really just a larger version of that engine, had two oscillating cylinders.

The Hero engine with its small vertical cylinder was given as a premium for boys selling *The People's Home Journal*. The engine was sent free for two one-year subscriptions at 35¢ each, or could be bought for 25¢ each without the subscription. The three-legged base on the Hero engine was made of cast iron. Later it was made of stamped brass.

The Union Mfg. Co. of Brooklyn, N.Y., took over the Buckman Mfg. Co. prior to 1875. Union made improvements on the Buckman fire pumper, making it look more like an actual model of the fire pumpers of that time. They also made a new series of toy steam boats with lengths of 13," 19," and 26" in length. Both Union and Buckman toys are considered by many collectors as Buckmans.

Youth Companion magazine used several Buckman steam engines as premiums, but the little steamers had no whistle or throttle to control the speed.

Weeden Steam Toys

On September 5, 1884, William N. Weeden of New Bedford, Mass., patented his #1 toy steam engine. The horizontal engine was mounted on a vertical boiler with a screw-type throttle and whistle. The manager of *Youth Companion* was so pleased with this improved model that he ordered 10,000 at a price of $1 each. In the summer of that year, *Youth Companion* listed the new invention as "Weeden's Upright Steam Engine." Today, these early hinged-door steam engines are very rare and quite valuable. The "improved" #1 steam engine had a burner that fit under the boiler, and the door was omitted. By 1890, 100,000 units had been sold.

The #2, an all-brass version of the #1, came out later, but it was never offered by *Youth Companion*. The #2 was offered in *The American Boy* in 1905.

Weeden offered twelve different steam engines in the 1891 catalog, including #1, #3-#7, and double #12. The four favorite engine variations were, Favorite, The Cornish Beam, pumping engine, the Dart Train set, and the side-wheel paddle boat Water Witch. The store window display driven by #1 was very popular at that time and would fetch a very good price now if you were lucky enough to find one.

On July 25, 1891, William Weeden died of diabetes, leaving behind a growing toy business. At the time of his death, Weeden steam toys were advertised by every important periodical and were favorite toys of boys of all ages.

The story didn't end there, however. Due to the management skills of new owner William Ritchie, the company continued to grow over the years. Ritchie had been sales manager at the time of Weeden's passing, so he was very familiar with the operation of the company, which continued to grow and update its offerings.

Just before World War I, Weeden Mfg. Co. introduced a line of toy electric motors, but due to a lack of materials during the war, they were discontinued and never re-established in the post-war period. These motors are now very collectible even though they aren't really steam toys as such. The years from 1910-28 were considered to be Weeden Mfg. Co.'s heyday. By 1922, the company employed about eighty people. William Ritchie died December 20, 1939, and his company stock was inherited by his son, William Barney Ritchie.

William Barney Ritchie began working as his father's assistant at the Weeden plant in 1922. By the time he had a good understanding of the business, the age of steam was coming to an end. In 1942, the U.S. was gearing up for World War II. The toy business did not qualify for an allotment and the factory tools could not be used for the war effort.

Ritchie sold the Weeden Company to National Fireworks, National Play Things, in Watertown, Mass. They purchased the Pairpoint Corp. in March 1943. The new company was named National Pairpoint Co., and Weeden became a division of the company known as Weeden National Play Things.

Weeden National Play Things made at least six models under that name during the 1940s. Four of these models should not be confused with the original Weeden models with the same numbers because they are quite different.

In 1955, Thomas R. Dutcher Jr., who worked for National Fireworks, learned of the now-idle Weeden toy production equipment. He made an offer to buy the leftover equipment and steam engine components that were still being stored. The remains of the once great Weeden Steam Toy Co. sold for a meager $700-$800. Dutcher moved the equipment to Cordova, Tenn., where he had plans of resuming production.

His company, Security Signals Inc., whose main business was the production of fuses, flares, pyrotechnics, and military hardware was seriously considering the production of some of the Weeden toys. At that time they were also awarded a sizable government contract for ordnance needed for the Vietnam War. By mistake, an order was given to clear out the warehouse where all of the Weeden assets were stored. All of the paperwork, records, disks, and special tools from the Weeden Co. were sent to the scrap yard.

Boucher Steam Toys

In 1923, H.E. Boucher bought the Voltamp Co. of Baltimore, Md. Voltamp had been producing several electric toy trains prior to this. The new company was named Boucher Inc. After moving to New York, the company continued to manufacture standard gauge toy trains until 1934. When they started the business, Boucher also produced several live steam boats and power drives for toy boats. They also offered the boats in kit form. Poly-Wog is one of these boats with a twin-cylinder outboard engine powered by a steam boiler in the bow.

The Dolphin, a 36" beam wood boat, with a two-cylinder high-speed steam engine was capable of 10 miles per hour. The Grayling and the Snapper were two other boats that were available as kits or finished and ready to run. These boats needed a lot of heat to fire the boiler and were equipped with a gas-fired blowtorch. The Barracuda was the largest stock boat with a 48" beam and could attain speeds over 12 miles per hour.

These boats sold in kit form with the engine, etc., for $75-$85, or complete ready-to-run kits for $120-$185, depending on the size of the boat. These prices are from a 1925 catalog—a lot of money in those days. With the hard times of the 1930s, another steam toy company came to an end.

Jensen Mfg. Co.

Jensen Mfg. Co. of Jeanetta, Pa., started building steam engines around 1930 and is still in business today. They produce steam engine kits and finished models for hobby shops and novelty catalog sales. They also supply larger steam models and power generating plants to serious collectors and universities.

Jensen models are well built with heavy-duty silver soldered boilers. They are equipped with reversing valves, whistles, etc., and can be heated with electric heaters, solid fuel tablets, or Sterno. The #15 generator with small 3.8-volt lamp comes separately or mounted on a base with the complete power plant. The #100 machine shop consists of five machine tools mounted on a wood base with a lineshaft to connect to any Jensen engine or other power source.

The Atomic Jensen #90 came out around 1960 with an electric heater that looks like an atomic reactor. They only made about twenty-five of these due to the radioactivity scare of that era. This is one that every serious Jensen collector would like to have. Don't worry, there is no plutonium in the reactor!

Metal Ware Co.

Metal Ware Co. in Two Rivers, Wis., made electric kitchen appliances in the early 1920s. They came out with the Empire line of electrically-heated steam engines. They also had a turbine and a hot air or Stirling engine, along with a variety of pumps and accessories.

Metal Ware used electricity to heat the boilers, eliminating the fire hazard from alcohol or kerosene burners, but burns were still caused by hot water or live steam. To please safety-conscious parents, Metal Ware developed three all-electric toy steam engines. The Magnetic engine #B-33 used a magnetic coil in place of the piston and cylinder used on a toy steam engine. It was plugged into a 110-volt electric socket for power. The #B-32 used a 1-1/2-volt telephone battery to energize the magnetic coil. Metal Ware also made a smaller version that used two 1-1/2-volt flashlight batteries for power.

Saf-Toy

In 1947, the Saf-Toy built in Oaklawn, Ill., used the same idea. The company used an electric motor to drive a piston-type air pump that pumped air into a simulated boiler. The compressed air was used to operate a whistle, and the flywheel attached to the motor had plenty of power left over to run other accessories. The original Saf-Toy, which used a tin can for a horizontal boiler, looks much older than the later model made mostly of aluminum castings. Although these electric "steam toys" are actually toy electric motors, you will find quite a few included in steam toy collections of that era.

Other Steam Toy Companies

Several companies came out with steam toys in the post-war era until the early 1950s. They tried to recreate the boom in popularity enjoyed by steam toys before the war, but times were changing and the era of steam was over. Most of these businesses were small and only lasted a few years. Here is a brief listing of these companies.

The Airsol Co. of Neodesha, Kan., built a vertical-boiler steam engine Airsol using one of their aerosol cans as the vertical boiler. These steam engines had a vertical cylinder and a flywheel mounted on the side of the red-painted boiler. There were two models, #301 and #302, that were similar and electrically heated. Airsol also made engines for Dy-Mo and Steam Engine Industries.

American Toy Airship Co. of Mansfield, Ohio, sold the Whizzer steam engine. This little vertical-boiler engine is really a turbine with a fake connecting rod and cylinder arrangement. One model came with an alcohol burner, while the other had prongs for an electric cord like those used on toasters and irons at the time.

Atwood Steamcraft Toys of Montrose, Calif., made plastic hull steam boats and horizontal boiler power units. Congo Launch, Amazon Queen, and Jungle Boat were some of their popular boats, and all were heated with alcohol tablets or sterno.

Harvey Miller Corps. sold the Watt Special, a copper-colored vertical-boiler steam engine with a black base. This engine was manufactured by Specialty Instrument Co. of Pittsburgh, Penn., and was electrically heated.

Marvindustries of Chicago, Ill., produced the Robert Fulton line of steam toys in 1947. There was a vertical-boiler black engine and a silver and gray horizontal. The horizontal engine was heated with electricity.

Major Toy Co. of Detroit and Ecorse, Mich., manufactured the Red Injun vertical boiler steam engine. The red steamer came with spoked or solid flywheels and die-cast or pressed-steel fireboxes. They were heated by alcohol or electricity.

The K.J. Miller Corp. of Chicago, Ill., came out with the Junior Engineer Steam Engine in 1950. Though this steam toy came assembled as a beam-engine model, there were enough extra parts for the young owner to rebuild it as either a horizontal or vertical engine. Included with the toy were three blueprints (each with a picture on the back side) showing how each model could be constructed and how it would look when finished. What a delight for the junior engineer of that day!

References:
American Live Steam & Their Originators, compiled and edited by The Education Committee of The Antique Toy Collectors of America, G. William Holland, Raymond Spong, and Blair Whitton.

The Weeden Manufacturing Co.: It's Men and their Toys, by Hal R. Swann, Jr.

The Toy Engine Collector Quarterly Publication, by Richard Cutler
Contributor: Richard B. Leach has been building steam engines since 1975. He is the author of the *Pictorial Guide to Weeden Steam Toys*. He may be reached at 52938 Jackie Ln., Elkhart, IN 46514-9558. Richard would like to acknowledge the photo contributions of Carl P. Swanstrom from Naperville, Ill., Art Gaier from Versailes, Ohio, and his wife Barbara A. Leach.

Empire Double Boiler B42, c. 1935, $500-$600. Photo courtesy Art Gaier

Frisbie Toy Steam Engine, J. & E. Stevens Co., 1871, $1500-$2000. Photo courtesy Art Gaier

Boucher Poly-Wog boat, steam-powered, 2-cylinder engine, 1925, 24" long, $1000-$1200. Photo courtesy Art Gaier

Empire Accessories, 1939. #40 Water Pump, $100-$200; #48 Swing, $150-$250; Transmission, $150-$250. Photo courtesy Art Gaier

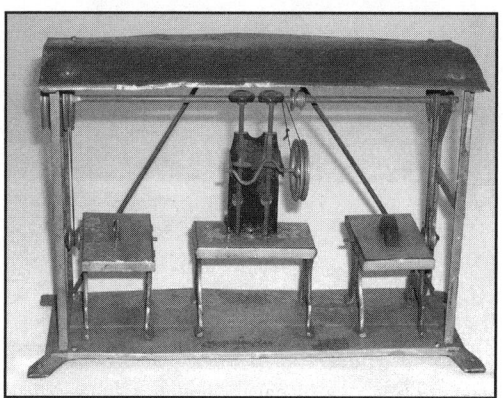

Weeden Workshop #65, 1907-14, $200-$300. Photo courtesy Art Gaier

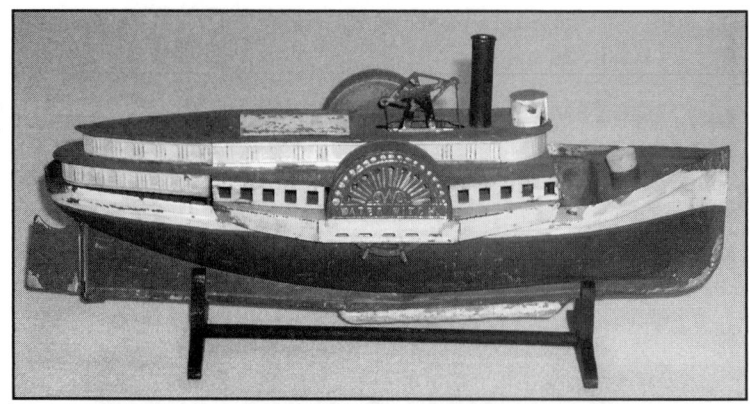

Weeden Water Witch, very rare-only 6 known to exist, 1879-1904, $3000-$5000. Photo courtesy Art Gaier

Weeden #46, 1912, $800-$1000. Photo courtesy Art Gaier

Two Buckman engines, 1885, $400-$500 and $600-$700, respectively. Photo courtesy Art Gaier

Buckman, Holly, 1885, $800-$1200. Photo courtesy Art Gaier

Buckman, 1885, $900-$1100. Photo courtesy Art Gaier

Buckman horizontal, 1885, $600-$700. Photo courtesy Art Gaier

Buckman Workshop, 1885, $2500-$3000. Photo courtesy Richard Leach

Buckman, 1885, $900-$1100. Photo courtesy Art Gaier

Buckman Ajax $300-$400, with Buckman Pump, 1885, $350-$450. Photo courtesy Art Gaier

Buckman horizontal (large), 1885, $700-$800. Photo courtesy Art Gaier

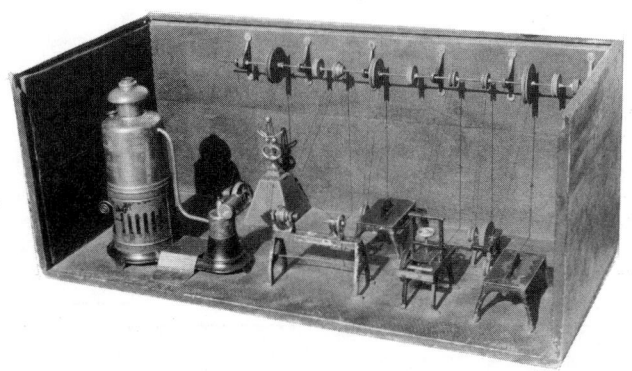

Buckman Workshop, 1885, $2500-$3000. Photo courtesy Richard Leach

Five Buckman steam engines, Left to Right: No. 1, $300; No. 2, $400; No. 3, $400; No. 4, $350; No. 5, $300. Photo courtesy Art Gaier

Four Buckman steam engines, c. 1885. Photo courtesy Art Gaier

The Pioneer Edgar Side Manufacturer Co. Philadelphia, PA, c. 1890s, $1200-$1800. Photo courtesy Art Gaier

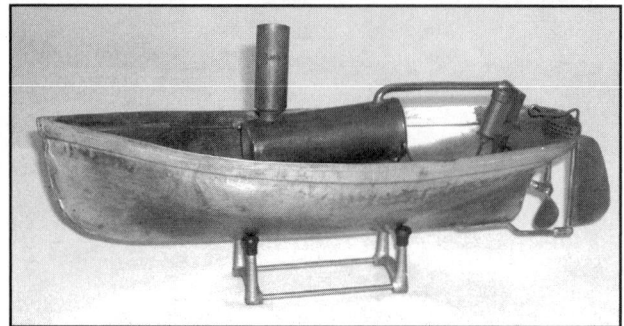

Buckman Boat, 12" long, $750-$850. Photo courtesy Art Gaier

Three Buckman boats. Photo courtesy Art Gaier

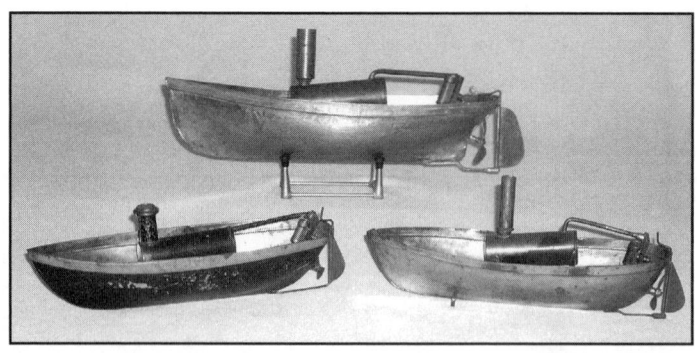

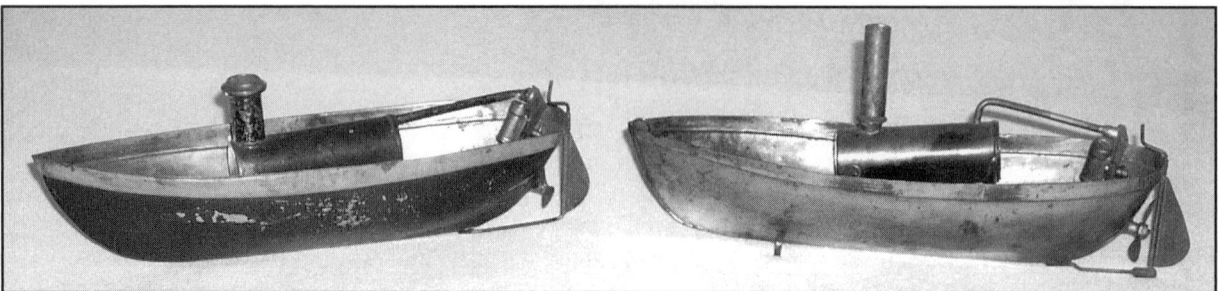

Buckman Boats, 9" long, $500-$600. Photo courtesy Art Gaier

Peerless, c. 1890s, $1200-$1800. Photo courtesy Art Gaier

Jensen #55, this engine is still available, $250-$350. Photo courtesy Art Gaier

Jensen #50, $1200-$1800. Photo courtesy Art Gaier

Weeden Hot Air #22 vertical, 1898-1913, $500-$600. Photo courtesy Art Gaier

Boucher Poly-Wog boat, steam-powered, 2-cylinder engine, 1925, 24" long, $1000-$1200. Photo courtesy Art Gaier

Weeden #312, 1915, $200-$300. Photo courtesy Art Gaier

Weeden, #18, 1901, $800-$1000. Photo courtesy Art Gaier

Weeden #76, 1910-1917, $500-$600. Photo courtesy Art Gaier

Weeden #57, 1916-1920, $300-$400. Photo courtesy Art Gaier

Boucher Engines – Sold complete or as machinist kits. Used in some of Boucher's larger boats; 2-cyl. $250-$350; 4-cyl. $750-$900. Photo courtesy Art Gaier

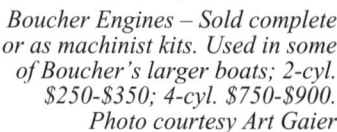

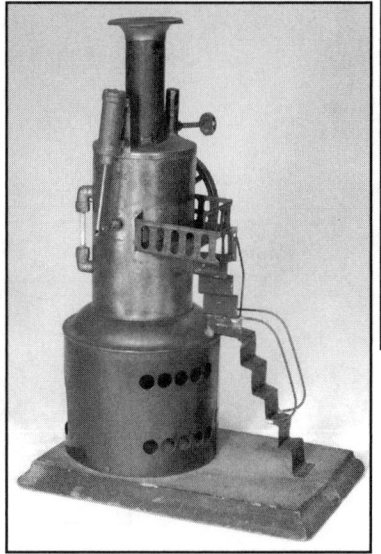

Weeden Boats Torpedo Style; #2 on top, 18" long, 1899-1903, $700-$800; #1 on bottom, 15-1/2" long, 1899-1915, $500-$600. Photo courtesy Art Gaier

Weeden #4B, 1897-1916, $350-$450. Photo courtesy Art Gaier

Weeden #43, stair step, 1903-1916, $250-$400. Photo courtesy Art Gaier

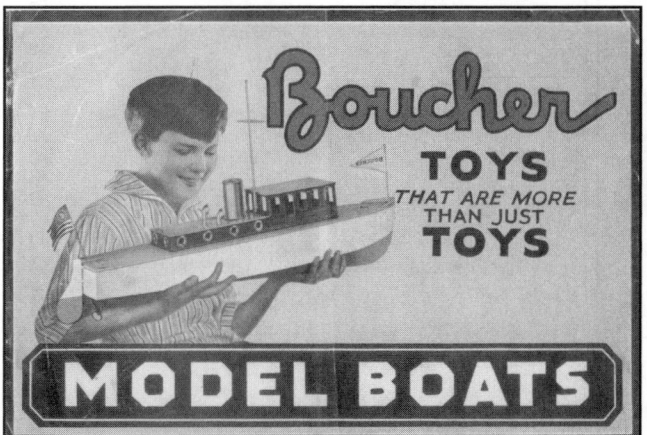

Boucher Poly-Wog boat catalog advertisement, this boat set originally retailed for $22.50 in 1925. Photo courtesy Art Gaier

Weeden Favorite; Engine, 1888-1894, $350-$450; Pump, 1890-1901, $450-$550. Photo courtesy Art Gaier

Weeden Store Display, 1895, $2000-$3000. Photo courtesy Art Gaier

Weeden #12, 1887-1894, $700-$900. Photo courtesy Art Gaier

Weeden Fire Engine, 1895-1915, $2500-$3000.

Empire, #207, 1930s. Photo courtesy Carl Swanstrom

Empire B-30 and accessories. Photo courtesy Carl Swanstrom

Ind-X Electric Steam Engine, #231. Photo courtesy Carl Swanstrom

Robert Fulton horizontal, #211, $50-$125. Photo courtesy Carl Swanstrom

Saf-Toy with Chimney, rear view, #333, 1950, $50-$125 w/box. Photo courtesy Carl Swanstrom

Empire B-30 and accessories. Photo courtesy Carl Swanstrom

Saf-Toy with Chimney, front view, #333, 1950. Photo courtesy Carl Swanstrom

Ind-X Electric Steam Engine, #203. Photo courtesy Carl Swanstrom

Weeden "Dart" steam locomotive and train, $600-$800. Photo courtesy Richard Leach

Watt Special by Harvey Miller, $75-$150. Photo courtesy Carl Swanstrom

Buckman "Bee Hive" steam engine. Photo courtesy Richard Leach

Little Red Injun, Major Toy Co., $50-$125. Photo courtesy Carl Swanstrom

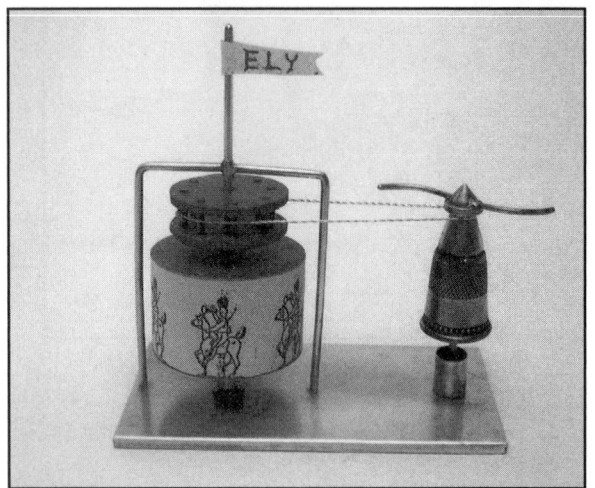

First steam toy with Mini Model thimble boiler, invented by Phillip Ely in 1867.

Thimble steam boiler and steam engine. Photo courtesy Richard Leach

Buckman "Hero" steam engine and box. Photo courtesy Richard Leach

Buckman "Dollar" and "2 Dollar" steam engines. Photo courtesy Richard Leach

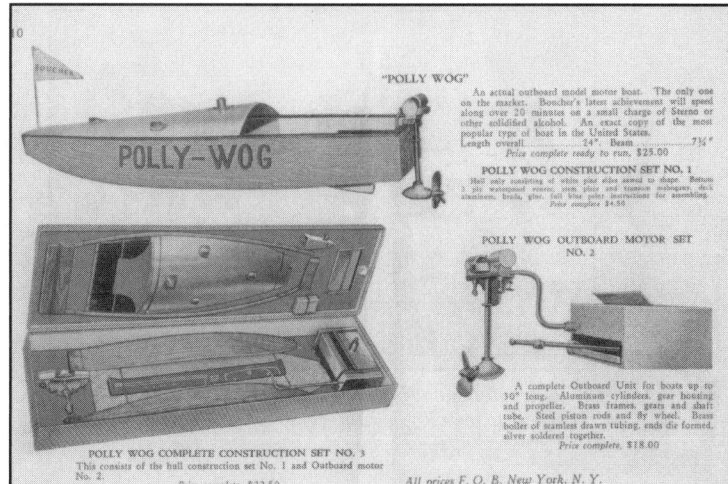

Boucher Poly-Wog boat catalog advertisement, this boat set originally retailed for $22.50 in 1925. Photo courtesy Art Gaier

Mity Mite, Model 303, $50-$100. Photo courtesy Carl Swanstrom

Robert Fulton, #219, Marvin Industries. Photo courtesy Carl Swanstrom

Robert Fulton, vertical, Marvin Industries, $75-$150. Photo courtesy Carl Swanstrom

Dy-Mo, Model 5, Airosol, $50-$100. Photo courtesy Carl Swanstrom

Whizzer, American Toy Airship Co., $75-$125 w/box. Photo courtesy Carl Swanstrom

Airosol Inc. Model 301, 1950, $75-$125. Photo courtesy Carl Swanstrom

Buckman "Hero" steam engines, one with brass legs, one with cast-iron legs. Photo courtesy Richard Leach

Weeden steam engines #7 and #8, $300-$400 each. Photo courtesy Richard Leach

Weeden steam engine #666, electric heated, $150-$250. Photo courtesy Richard Leach

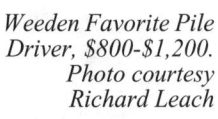

Weeden Favorite Pile Driver, $800-$1,200. Photo courtesy Richard Leach

Weeden steam engine #37 Force Pump, $250-$375. Photo courtesy Richard Leach

PHOTOS NEEDED

We are always looking for good quality toy images for our archives. Photo quality is our highest consideration and any donated images must be in 35mm print or slide form.

If you can donate photos of toys not pictured here, please contact us at the following address:

O'Brien's Collecting Toys
Krause Publications
700 E. State St.
IOLA, WI 54990
(715) 445-4612
obrienk@krause.com

TIN WIND-UPS

The charm and nostalgia of yesterday's tin creations hold a special place in the heart of toy collectors. Those tin toys, made in large numbers mainly before World War II, are among the priciest collectible toys today.

Lithography (later called chromolithography) began with the 1796 experiments of Alois Senefelder allowed for the mass-production of color images on a paper surface. The process had been around for almost 100 years when it was applied to thin sheets of tin to produce children's toys.

Starting in the 1920s, lithographed tin toys began dramatically change toy production, rivaling the popularity of their cast-iron counterparts. American manufacturers could produce these colorful toys more inexpensively than the classic European toys that had dominated the toy market until this time.

With mass production came mass appeal. The advantages of licensing agreements were not lost on toy manufacturers, as new tin mechanical toys based on the popular characters and celebrities of the time became instant hits and remain among today's most desired toys. Newspaper comic strip and Walt Disney characters provided a widely popular subject matter for toy marketers. Among the most well-known makers of mechanical tin toys were Marx, Chein, Lehmann, and Strauss. Others include Courtland, Girard, Ohio Art, Schuco, Unique Art, and Wolverine.

Many of these manufacturers had symbiotic and reciprocal business relationships. Over the years, companies worked together, sub-contracted toy production among themselves, distributed each others' toys, and absorbed other companies. There even appeared to be some pilfering and reproducing of others' ideas.

One of the advantages of lithography was that it allowed old toys to be recycled in many ways. When a character's public appeal began to wane, a new image could be printed on the same body to produce a new toy. Or when a toy company was absorbed by another, older models were dusted off and dressed up with new lithography. Many mechanical tin wind-up toys show up in surprisingly similar versions with another manufacturer's name on them.

A Word on Condition

Remember, the better the condition, the higher the value, especially with tin. When seeking new pieces for your collection, examine the condition of the tin for any rust or worn spots. Also make sure all pieces are there—does that George the Drummer Boy you've found have his mallet and cymbal? Does the toy work? Ask the seller for a demonstration.

Those tin toys with the original box are true treasures and will command a price at a premium above those listed here.

Tin robots have virtually become an endangered species. Those that are on the market generally command premium prices.

Contributor: Scott Smiles is the proprietor of the Antique Toy Information Service. He can be reached at: 157 Yacht Club Way Apt. 112, Hypoluxo, FL 33462, ssmiles@msn.com, (561) 582-6016.

T.P.S. Circus Parade.
Photo by Scott Smiles

Chein Ferris Wheel, 1930s, $525.

Chein Rabbit in Shirt and Pants, c. 1938, $100. Photo courtesy Scott Smiles

Galop Zebra Cart, Lehmann, $550.

Gay '90s Cyclist, Photo by Scott Smiles

Animate Toy Co.

In 1918, this firm was located at East 17th Street in New York City, and its president was L.T. Savage. By 1931 it had moved to 30 North 15th Street in East Orange, New Jersey and employed ten men and forty women. In 1934, the president-vice president was George W. Turnbull and the secretary-treasurer was George H. Webb. Five men and eleven women made up the work force.

Animate Toy Co.	C6	C8	C10
Climbing Tractor, 1929, 9" long	100	150	200
U.S. Baby Tank, pat. 6/20/16, 1918, 2-1/2" long..................................	40	60	80

Automatic Toy Co.	C6	C8	C10
Alpine Express, 1940s	75	112	150
Auto Speedway, c. 1930.................	125	175	225
Cross-Over Trolley Set, 1940s	90	135	180
Dizzy Liz, No. 180, 1940s, 5" long..	125	175	225
Jungle Pete, No. 175, 15" long	100	150	175
Magic Crossroads Track, w/two wind-up cars, c. 1950	130	195	260

Automatic Toy Co. (Continued)	C6	C8	C10
Mystery Alpine Express, 1940s, 20" long, 14" wide, 2" high	100	150	200
Operation Airlift, two plastic planes, 1950s..............................	80	120	160
Rocket Space Ship, No. 305, sparks, 1940s, 8-1/2" long...........	100	150	200
Space Shooting Range, 1950s, 15" long...	150	225	300
Speedway, w/two race cars and garage, 1930s	175	262	350

Chein

Russian immigrant Julius Chein founded his toy company on May 27, 1903. From its start as a producer of small tin toys for F.W. Woolworth's and premium prizes for the new Cracker Jack treat, Chein went on to produce spinning tops during World War I. The wartime boycott on German products, including toys, led to a windfall for the J. Chein Company and the product line expanded to include tin banks, tanks, air guns, cash registers, and even trains. Julius died in April 1926, leaving the company to his wife, Elizabeth. She promptly brought in her brother, Samuel Hoffman, who led the company to new heights of creativity and product diversity. Engineering improvements and licensing agreements resulted in

Man on the Flying Trapeze,
Wyandotte, $200.

T.P.S. "Bear Playing Ball" with box, $375. Photo by Don Hultzman

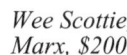

Wee Scottie,
Marx, $200.

Chein Mechanical Frog
Man. Photo by Don
Hultzman

Ride-A-Rocket, Chein, $600.

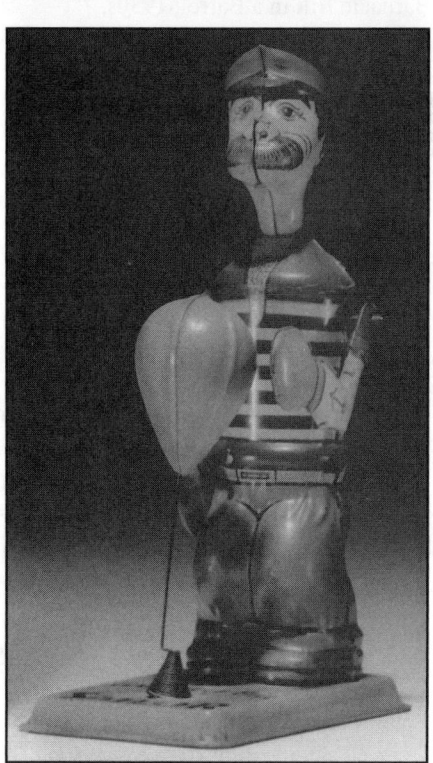

Barnacle Bill the Sailor, Chein, $500.

Chein Roller Coaster, 1938, $500. Photo courtesy Don Hultzman; photo by Ron Chojnacki

Chein Roller Coaster, 1950s, $400. Photo courtesy Don Hultzman; photo by Ron Chojnacki

some of the most memorable tin wind-ups ever produced, including the popular Popeye line of toys.

Chein

	C6	C8	C10
Alligator, w/native on its back, 1930s	150	200	300
Army Drummer, plunger-activated, 1930s, 7" high	125	200	250
Barnacle Bill in a Barrel, 1930s, 7" high	250	350	450
Barnacle Bill the Sailor, punching a bag, 7-1/2"	300	400	500
Barnacle Bill the Sailor, 1930s	250	350	475
Bass Drummer, No. 110, dark shako, light blue pants w/red stripe, red jacket, 1930s, 8-3/4" tall	150	225	300
Bear, w/hat, pants, shirt, bow tie, c. 1938	50	75	100
Cabin Cruiser, 1940s, 9" long	65	98	130
Chick, brightly colored clothes and polka-dot bow tie, 4" high	50	75	100
Chicken Pulling Wheelbarrow, 1930s, 6" x 3-1/2"	50	75	100
Clown, w/umbrella	125	200	275
Clown in Barrel, 1930s, 8" high	300	375	575
Clown Puncher	375	500	625
Dan-Dee Dump Truck	200	300	400
Doughboy, 1920s, 6" high	175	250	325
Drum Major, No. 111, dark shako, light blue pants w/red jacket, 1930s, 8-3/4" high	225	325	425

Chein (Continued)

	C6	C8	C10
Drummer, No. 109, dark shako, light blue pants w/red jacket, 1930s, 8-3/4" tall	100	150	200
Duck, long-beaked, in orange sailor suit, not Donald Duck, but similar, waddles, 1930s, 6" high	125	175	225
Duck, waddles, 1930, 4" high	75	100	125
Ferris Wheel, six compartments, ringing bell, 1930s, 16-1/2" high	275	400	525
Greyhound Bus, 9" long	75	100	125
Handstand Clown, 1940s, 6" high	65	100	125
Indian in Headdress, 1930S, 5-1/2" high	125	175	225
Jumping Rabbit, 1925, 5" long	100	125	150
Marine, hand on belt, 1950s, 6" high	125	150	200
Mark I Cabin Cruiser, 1957, 8-1/2" long	50	75	100
Mechanical Aquaplane, No. 39, boat-like pontoons, no insignia, 1932, 8-1/2" long, 7-1/2" wingspan	200	300	400
Mechanical Aquaplane, post-WWII insignia	150	250	350
Mechanical Aquaplane, pre-WWII insignia	200	300	400
Mechanical Fish, 1940s, 11"	50	75	100
Mechanical Frog Man, 1950s, 11" long	100	150	200
Mechanical Rocket Ride, No. 400, 1950s, 18" high	500	750	1000
Melody Player, No. 135, 4 rolls, 1930s, 6-3/4" high	100	150	200

*Courtland Mfg. Co. Circus Elephant and "Monkeys" Cart, $700.
Photo courtesy Joe and Sharon Freed*

*Lehmann Kadi, 1917-27, $2500. Photo courtesy
Sotheby's, New York*

Chein (Continued)

	C6	C8	C10
Musical Aero Swing, 1940s, 10" high	250	375	500
Navy Frog Man, No. 122, 1950s, 12" long	100	150	200
Pan-Am Clipper, pontoons, 1930s, 11" wingspan	400	600	775
Peggy Jane Boat, 13" long	60	90	120
Penguin in Tuxedo-type Jacket, c. 1940	75	100	125
Pig, 1940s, 4-1/2" high	50	75	100
Playland Merry-Go-Round, 1930s, 9-1/2" high	375	550	675
Playland Whip, No. 340, four bump cars, driver's head wobbles	450	675	850
Rabbit, w/wheelbarrow	75	125	150
Rabbit in Shirt and Pants, c. 1938	50	75	100
Rabbit Pulling Cart	48	72	95
Race Car #52, 1930s, 6-1/2" long	80	120	160
Racer #3, 1920s, 6-1/2" long	150	225	300
Ride-A-Rocket	300	450	600
Rocket Ride, No. 400, four rockets, 18" high, 11" diameter base	400	600	800
Roller Coaster, w/two cars, 1950s	200	300	400
Roller Coaster, w/two cars, 1938	250	375	500
Santa Elf, 1920s, 6" high	220	330	440
Ski Boy, No. 157, 1940s, 7-3/4" long, 5-1/4" tall	125	175	225
Skin Driver, No. 122, 1950s, 12" long	75	100	125
Ski-Ride, No. 320, 19" long	200	300	400
Space Ride, No. 205, 1950s, 10" high	500	750	1000
Space Ride, lever action, 1940s, 9" high	425	650	850

Chein (Continued)

	C6	C8	C10
Spirit of St. Louis Airplane, 1930s, 8" long, 8" wingspan	250	375	500
Taxi, 1920s, 7" long	200	300	400
Toy Town Helicopter, 1950s, 13" long	65	95	120
Turtle, w/native on back	250	375	525
U.S. Army Sergeant, No. 153, 1950s, 5-1/2" high	125	150	175
Walking Pelican, 1930s, 5" high	100	150	200

Courtland Mfg. Co.

	C6	C8	C10
Circus Elephant and "African Lions" Cart, No. 400, 11-5/8" long, 3" wide, 3-1/2" high	250	450	700
Circus Elephant and "Circus Band" Cart, No. 500, 11-5/8" long, 3" wide, 3-1/2" high	350	550	850
Circus Elephant and "Monkeys" Cart, No. 300, 11-5/8" long, 3" wide, 3-1/2" high	250	450	700
Easter Rabbit and Trailer, No. 200, 11-5/8" long, 3" wide, 3-1/2" high	75	125	200
Mechanical Parking Meter and Bank, No. 7500, base 6" x 6", 24-1/2" high	150	225	300
Mechanical Rocking R Ranch See-Saw, No. 8000, 17-3/4" long, 2-1/8" wide, 6" high	125	175	225

Girard

C.G. Wood founded Girard model Works in Girard, Pennsylvania, in 1906 and his son Frank joined the firm a few years after its inception. Originally the company made patterns, models, and special machinery, but in 1918 they began making toys for an unidentified large firm in New York. It was in 1920 that they began making toys under the name Wood's Mechanical Toys. By 1931 Louis Marx was associated with Girard, and during the Depression Marx took over the firm.

Lehmann Express, 1888-1918, $700. Photo courtesy Sotheby's, New York

Woodhaven Tractor, $130. Photo courtesy John Monteleone

The last Girard toys seem to have been produced in 1975, though the firm remained in business until 1980. Many of Marx's toys and Girard's toys are interchangeable.

Girard

	C6	C8	C10
Air Mail Bipane, three-engine	600	900	1200
Airways Express Plane, 13" wing-span	175	275	350
Bi-Wing Monoplane, 1918, 12" long, 14" wingspan (Wood's)	150	225	300
Bus, w/driver, 1930s, 12-1/2" long	200	300	400
Coolie & Pushcart	150	200	275
Farm Boy Walking, w/shovel and rake, (Wood's), 1920, 6"	450	675	900
Fire Chief Siren Coupe, 1930s, 14" long	250	400	525
Flasho the Mechanical Grinder, 1920s	200	250	300
Goble the Gobbling Goose	125	175	250
Man Pushing Wheelbarrow, 1920s, 5-1/2"	225	325	450
Monoplane, high wing, one-engine, 1921-22, 13" long	350	525	700
Monoplane, high wing, one-engine, pilot, 9" long	275	395	550
Pierce-Arrow Coupe, green, orange and cream, c. 1932, 14" long	225	338	450
Race Car #2, 8" long	300	450	600
Railroad Handcar	200	300	400
Spirit of St. Louis, 9" long	400	600	800
Tri-Motor Air Lines, 1920s	175	275	350
Whiz Sky Fighter, biplane, 7" wing-span	300	450	600

Kingsbury

	C6	C8	C10
Ambulance, 7" long	500	750	1000
Artillery Launcher	100	150	200
Biplane, single engine, rubber wheels, c. 1925, 16" long	450	700	950
Bi-Wing Airplane, w/cast-iron pilot, 1918, 16" long, 17" wing-span	400	600	800
Borden's Milk Truck	250	375	500
Convertible, w/rumble seat, electric headlamps, hard rubber wheels, 12-1/2" long	180	270	360
Fireman's Ladder Truck, driver, hard rubber wheels, 23-1/2" long	200	300	400
Monoplane, high wing, single engine, wind-up wheels and spins prop via rubber band, 1930s, 11" long	300	450	600
Roadster, electric headlamps, 12-1/2" long	250	375	500
Station Wagon, 1920s	150	225	300
Streetcar, No. 782, 1930s, 9" long	200	300	400
Transatlantic Air-Go-Round	250	375	500

Lehmann

Founded in 1881 by Ernst Paul Lehmann was located in Brandenburg, Germany. The company produced quality tin toys like the Ikarus plane and Tut Tut auto. After the Soviet occupation of East Germany, the company was moved to Nuremburg, Germany, where they continue to produce toys. The company is perhaps best known today for its line of LGB trains.

Lehmann

	C6	C8	C10
Adam the Porter, 1920s, 9" high	400	800	1200

Rocket Fighter, Marx, c. 1950, $475.

Merrymakers with Marquee, Marx, $1500.

Marx "Butter & Egg Man," $900. Courtesy Scott Smiles. Photo by Mike Adams

Lehmann (Continued)	C6	C8	C10
Aha Delivery Van, No. 550, 1907-1935, 5-1/2" long	500	650	900
Ajax Warrior, No. 659, w/two clubs, 1914-1944	1000	1400	1800
Alabama Coon Jigger, No. 685, 1912	500	700	900
Am Pol, No. 681, Amundsen driving, figure behind w/umbrella, map of North Pole, 1910-1935	1800	2500	3500
Anxious Bride Nanni, No. 470, chauffeur on tricycle, woman in car, 1901-1935	800	1300	2000
Autobus, No. 590, 1907-1945	700	1300	2000
Autohutte Garage, No. 771, 1934-1941, 6" long	450	675	900
Baker & Chimney Sweep, No. 450, 1900-1935	1500	2600	4000
Baldur Limousine, No. 739, 1920-1935, 10" long	700	1100	1800
Balky Mule, 1930s, 7-1/2" long	250	400	650
Berolina Car, 1914	1500	2400	3500
Bucking Bronco, No. 625, Wild West, white horse, 1909-1945, 6-1/2" long	375	575	800
Bucking Bronco, No. 625, Wild West, brown horse, 1909-1945, 6-1/2" long	475	675	900
Climbing Miller, No. 230, cardboard blades, 1890-1945	300	500	675

Lehmann (Continued)	C6	C8	C10
Crawling Beetle, The, No. 431, 1848-1935, 4" long	150	225	300
Crocodile, No. 442, 1948-1945	350	500	600
Dancing Sailor, No. 535, 1904-1948, 7-1/2" high	600	800	1000
Daredevil Zebra Cart, Zikra, No. 752, 1924-1935	400	600	800
Duo, rooster pulling rabbit, 1918-1945	750	1100	1400
Echo Motorcycle, No. 725, 1917-1935, 8-3/4" long	1000	1500	2500
EHE & Co., No. 570, open bed, 1907-1935	325	500	650
EPL I Dirigible, No. 651, 1910-1941	400	600	800
EPL II Dirigible, No. 652, 1912-1958	500	700	1000
Express, No. 140, porter pulling cart, 1888-1918, 6" long	500	600	700
Galop Racer, No. 760, w/garage, 1934-1941	800	1200	1600
Galop Zebra Cart, No. 852, 1954-62	300	450	550
Going to the Fair	1000	1500	2000
Heavy Swell, No. 525, dude-it-up man, 1904-1918	900	1400	2000
Ito Sedan, No. 679, 1914-1935, 6-1/2"	500	700	900

Lehmann Paddy Pig, 1903-1935, $2300. Photo courtesy Sotheby's, New York

Climbing Fireman, Marx, 1950s, $425.

Lehmann (Continued)	C6	C8	C10
Kadi, No. 723, two Chinese men carrying tea chest, 1917-27	1000	1700	2500
Lana Auto, No. 776, 1930-1936......	1200	2000	2800
Lehmann's Autobus 590, No. 590, 1907-1945	1000	1800	2400
Li La Hansom Cab, No. 520, early car w/two excited women passengers, driver in top hat and dog w/turning head, 1903-1935, 5-1/2"	1000	1500	2000
Lo & Li, No. 769, clown and ring master, 1924-38..........................	5000	7500	10,000
Lo Lo, No. 540, early car, driver, 1906-1918	500	750	1100
Lu-Lu Bird......................................	100	150	200
Lu-Lu Delivery Truck, No. 763, 1922-1938, 7-1/4" long	1500	2500	4000
Mandarin, No. 565, two coolies carrying Chinese in sedan chair, 1905-41	1500	2500	4000
Mars Cycle, No. 471, 1901-35	450	675	900
Masuyama, No. 773, coolie pulling rickshaw, 1927-1938...................	800	1400	2000
Mensa Delivery Van, No. 688, 1912-1941	1200	2100	3000
Mikado Family, No. 350, 1894-1918, 6-1/2" long......................	650	1100	1500
Mixtum, No. 775, white driver........	800	1350	1800

Lehmann (Continued)	C6	C8	C10
Mixtum, No. 775, African-American driver...................................	1000	1500	2000
Motor Car Kutsche, 1897-1935, 5-1/2" long.................................	500	750	1000
Na-Ob, No. 680, man driving horse cart, wheels marked w/elf, 1917-1938, 6" long	450	550	650
Naughty Boy, No. 495, 1904-1935 .	800	1300	1800
New Century Cycle, No. 345, 1895-1938, 5" long	400	600	900
Nu-Nu, No. 733, 1924-1938, 4-1/2" long..	600	950	1400
Oh My, No. 690, 10" high	450	650	850
OHO, No. 545, patented 1903, 1906-1916	400	600	800
Onkel	375	562	750
Paak-Paak, No. 645, ducklings in cart pulled by duck, 1910-1935	400	500	600
Paddy Pig, No. 500, 1903-1935, 6" long..	1250	1750	2300
Pao Pao Peacock, 10" long	350	475	600
Performing Sea Lion, The, No. 445, 1899-1935, 7" long.....................	200	300	400
Peter, three-wheeled car	1200	1900	2700
Power Carriage	360	540	720

Lehmann (Continued)

	C6	C8	C10
Quack-Quack, mother duck pulling cart w/three small ducks	300	450	600
Rad-Cycle, c. 1927, 5" long	1000	1600	2000
Rollo Chair	1000	1700	2400
Sedan, No. 765, 1927-41, 5-1/2" long	300	400	550
Skirolf, No. 781, skier, 1930-1941	1200	2200	3000
Taku Battleship, No. 671, 1913-1935	450	650	850
Tap Tap, No. 560, man pushing wheelbarrow, 1907-1945	500	700	900
Terra	800	1100	1500
Tom, No. 385, climbing monkey, 1895-1945, 8" long	150	275	400
Tut-Tut, No. 490, man in car w/horn, 1903-1935, 6-3/4" long..	700	1200	1700
Tyras Walking Dog, No. 432, 1898-1935, 6" long	500	650	850
Uhu, No. 555, amphibious car, 1907-1938	800	1200	1600
Walking Down Broadway, No. 260, strolling couple, 1890-1895	2000	3000	4200
Wild West, No. 625, 1909-1945	400	600	825
Zig Zag, No. 640, 1910-19445, 5" long	900	1400	1900
Zikra, No. 752, 1924-35, 7" long	800	1000	1200
Zulu, No. 721, black man in cart pulled by ostrich, 1918-1938	650	950	1250

Lindstrom

	C6	C8	C10
American Railway Express Truck & Trailer, 16" long	375	550	725
Baby Wee Speedboat, 10-1/2" long	40	60	80
Betty, shako walker, 1930s, 8" tall	175	263	350
Bird	100	150	200
Bumper Car, 6-1/2" long	125	175	225
Dancing Dutch Boy, 1930s, 8" high	125	200	250
Dancing Lassie, shako, 1930s, 8" tall	100	150	200
Delfine 7 Motorboat, c. 1930	175	275	350
Ferry Boat, lithographed, approx. 8-1/4"	100	150	200
Flyer, 14"	100	150	200
Johnny the Dancing Clown, No. 122, 1930s, 8" tall	200	300	400
Katrinka, 1930s, 8" tall	100	150	200

Lindstrom (Continued)

	C6	C8	C10
Mammy, shako walker, 1930s, 8" tall	300	450	600
Miss America Speedboat	125	175	225
Parcel Post No. 2 Truck	200	300	400
Racing Car, 1930s, 6"	175	263	350
Skeeter Bug, bumper car, 1930s, 9" long	100	150	200
Speedboat, 7" long	50	75	100
Speedboat, c. 1950, 18-1/2" long	175	250	325
Sweeping Betty	120	180	240
Sweeping Mammy, No. 1750, shako walker while sweeping, 1930s, 8" tall	212	318	425

Linemar

	C6	C8	C10
Old Jalopy, small, 1950s	150	210	300

Louis Marx Toy Co.

By the 1950s, Louis Marx was the largest manufacturer of toys in the world; his empire included six large factories in the United States and ownership of interest in factories in seven other countries. Marx, born in Brooklyn in 1896, worked for "Toy King" Ferdinand Strauss during his teens, and by the age of twenty his energy and enterprise had made him a director of that company. A falling out with Strauss persuaded Marx to go into business for himself, and in 1921 he and his brother began making their own toys, including some adaptations of items by the now defunct Strauss.

Although Marx made almost every type of toy (with the exception of dolls), his tin wind-up toys are probably the most favored by toy collectors.

Marx Toy Co.

	C6	C8	C10
1st Batt. F.D. Chief's Car, siren, battery headlights, 16"	300	450	600
Acrobatic Marvel, monkey on 13" spring and 7-1/2" rocking base, 1930s	118	175	235
Alligator	75	125	175
Ambulance, w/siren, 1930s, 14-1/2"	350	525	675
Ambulance, "M.D. War Dept.", 1930s	400	600	800
American Tractor, w/implements, 1920s, 10" long	200	300	400
Armored Trucking Co.	150	225	300
Army Dive Bomber No. 482	150	225	275
Army Staff Car, litho steel, 1930s	250	375	475
Army Staff Car, w/flasher and siren, W-601158, 1940s, 11" long	135	200	300
Army Truck, cloth cover, 1930s, 10"	300	425	550
Automatic Car Wash, w/wind-up car, 6"	200	300	400

Daredevil Motor Cop, Unique Art Mfg. Co., $600.

Old Jalopy, Marx, $300.

Auto Speedway, Automatic Toy Co., $225.

Carnival, Wyandotte, $850.

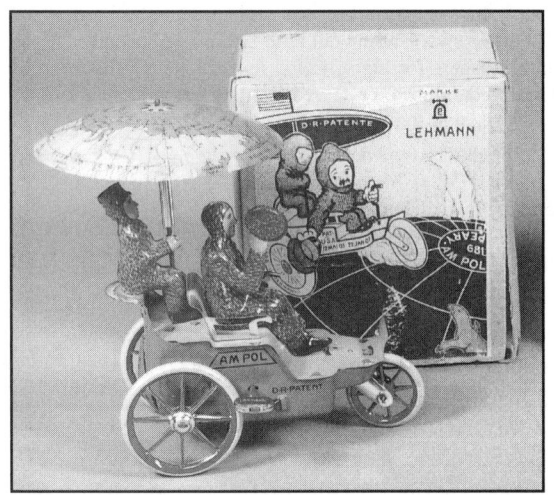

Am Pol, No. 681, 1910-1935, Lehmann, $3500. Photo courtesy Bertoia Auctions

Autobus, No. 590, 1910-1935, Lehmann, $2000. Photo courtesy Bertoia Auctions

CONDITION CODE

C6 Good; evident overall wear, well played with but acceptable to many collectors

C8 Very Good; minor overall wear, very clean

C10 Mint; like new

Note: Mint in Box commands a higher price.
Condition below C6 brings considerably lower prices

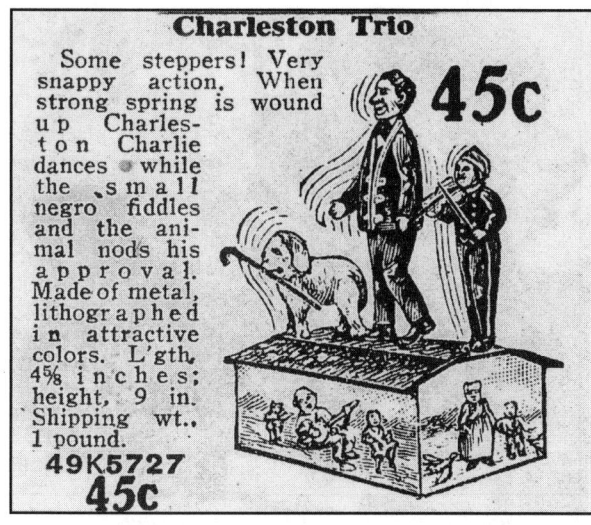

Advertisement for Charleston Trio from the Marx Toy Co.

Advertisement for Chicken Snatcher from the Marx Toy Co.

Marx Toy Co. (Continued)	C6	C8	C10
Automatic Fire House, Fire Chief Car, 7-1/2" long; Volunteer Fire Dept. Garage, 19" long, 1950s, 7-1/2" long, 19" long	200	300	400
Automatic Reversing Road Roller, 1925, 9" long	200	300	400
Balky Mule, 1940, 8-3/4"	125	175	250
Balky Mule, No. 425, 1897-1938, 8" long	350	425	575
Be Bop—The Jivin' Jigger, 1948, 10"	250	325	425
Bear Cyclist, 1930s, 6" long	175	250	325
Beat it the Komikal Kop, 1930s	450	625	775
Big Lizzie Car, early 1930s, 7-1/4".	150	225	300
Big Parade, w/moving vehicles, soldiers, tin airplane, etc., 1929, 24" long	300	475	575
Big Silver, Mack Dump Truck	250	375	500
Big Three Aerial Acrobats, 1920	200	300	400
Boy on Trapeze	100	150	200
Bulldozer Climbing Tractor, caterpillar type, c. 1950s, 10-1/2" long	150	225	300
Bumper Auto, streamlined, large bumpers, front and rear, c. 1939 .	150	225	300
Busy Bridge, vehicles on bridge, 1935	350	525	675
Busy Delivery, Black Pinocchio, 1930s, 9" long, 8" high	675	1000	1200
Busy Miners, includes 2-1/4" tin litho miner's car, 1930s, 16-1/2" long	200	300	375

Marx Toy Co. (Continued)	C6	C8	C10
Busy Parking Station, 1930s, 17" long, w/2" tin race car	200	300	400
Butter & Egg Man, 1930s, 8" high..	500	700	900
Cadillac Coupe, 1931	500	750	1150
Cadillac Roadster, trunk w/tools on luggage carrier, 1930, 13" long...	250	375	500
Car Carrier, three racers, 22-3/4" long	600	900	1500
Careful Johnnie, 1950s, 5-1/2" long	100	150	200
Caterpillar Climbing Tractor, c. 1950s, 10" long	100	150	200
Charleston Trio, one Black adult, Black child dancer and dog, 1921	500	750	950
Climbing, Fighting Tank	125	188	250
Climbing Fireman, 1930s	225	325	425
Climbing Tractor, sparkling, 1960s, 8-1/2" long	125	175	225
Coast Defense, circular, w/three cannon, revolving airplane, 1929	500	750	925
Coast to Coast Greyhound Bus, 1930s	500	850	1200
Coke Coal City Coal Co. Truck	450	700	950
Construction Tractor	300	425	575
Coo Coo Car, 1920s, 7-1/2" long	300	425	550
Cowboy Rider, cowboy w/lariat on dapple or black horse, c. 1941	175	250	350
Crazy Dora nodder head, (also "Dan")	100	150	200
Cross-Country Flyer, Zeppelin and Airplane fly around 18" hangar tower, 1920	400	600	800

Marx Toy Co. Doughboy Tank, $250.

*Echo Motorcycle, No. 725, 1917-35, Lehmann, $2500.
Photo courtesy Kent M. Comstock*

Ito Sedan, No. 679, 1914-35, Lehmann, $900.

Marx Toy Co. (Continued)	C6	C8	C10
Dan Dipsy Car, plastic nodder, 1950s, 5-1/2" long	200	300	400
Dapper Dan Coon Jigger, 1910	500	800	1100
Dare Devil Flyer, new in 1928, 1920s	400	600	800
Daredevil Motor Drome, w/2" wind-up car, 1930s, 5-1/2" high, 9" diameter	100	175	225
Deluxe Delivery Truck, 1950s, 11".	100	150	200
Deluxe Tractor, six wheels, four in treads	250	375	500
Dipsy Doodle Bug Dodgem cars, Dan or Dora, 6" high (pair)	250	375	500
Donkey Pulling Cart, w/rider, 1950s, 10" long	110	165	220
Dora Dipsy Car, plastic nodder, 1950s, 5-1/2" long	100	150	200
Dottie the Driver, 1950s, 6-1/2"	100	150	200
Doughboy Tank, two side turrets, w/top turret, soldier w/gun pops out, 1930, 9-1/4" long	200	275	350
Doughboy Tank, no side turrets	125	175	250
Driver Training Car, 1950s, 6" long	75	110	150
Drive-UR-Self Car, 1950s, 11" long	250	375	500
Dump Truck, 1950s, 13" long	325	425	525

Marx Toy Co. (Continued)	C6	C8	C10
Fire Dept. Chief, c. 1950s, 11" long	150	200	250
Firemen Joe, 1930s, 8" tall	125	200	300
Firewater Boat, 1920, 9" long	350	525	700
Flipo the Jumping Dog, See Me Jump, on hind legs, c. 1940, 3-1/2" x 4"	100	175	250
Flying Fortress 2095 sparkling aeroplane, 1940s	225	350	450
Funny Face, new in 1928	500	750	1000
Funny Flivver, "Whoopie Car with Flappers", 1926, 7-1/2" long	325	500	675
Gee Whiz Auto Racer, four 2" long tin cars, 1930s, 13" diameter	450	700	1000
George the Drummer Boy, No. 881, w/stationary eyes, 1930s, 9" tall	125	175	225
George the Drummer Boy, No. 881, w/moving eyes, 1930s, 9" tall	150	225	300
Giant King Racer, marked "711", c. 1930s	175	250	325
Giant Reversing Tractor Truck, w/tools, "Hauling", c. 1950s, 14" long	150	225	300
G-Man Pursuit Car, 1930s	325	500	675
Golden Goose, hops along pecking at ground, dated July 8, 1924, 1924, 9-1/2" long	100	150	200

Mensa Delivery Van, No. 688, Lehmann, $3000.

Advertisement for the Honeymoon Express from the Marx Toy Co.

Marx Toy Co. Mechanical Speed Racer, 1930s, $200. Photo courtesy Don Hultzman; photo by Ron Chojnacki

Aha Delivery Van, No. 550, Lehmann, $900.

Motor Car Kutsche, 1897-1935, Lehmann, $1000. Photo courtesy Bertoia Auctions

Baker & Chimeny Sweep, Lehmann, $4000. Photo courtesy Kent M. Comstock

Marx Toy Co. Old Jalopy, $350. Photo courtesy Scott Smiles

Advertisement for Pinched Roadster from the Marx Toy Co., c. 1927, $650.

Marx Toy Co. (Continued)	C6	C8	C10
Hauling Tractor Truck, six-wheel ...	200	300	400
Hee-Haw Balky Mule, six-color litho, goes backward, forward and rears, farmer and his dog on seat and five milk cans in cart, 1929, 10-3/4" long	175	275	375
Helicopter Skyport, two plastic copters, 1950s, 9" x 11"	100	150	200
Hey, Hey, the Chicken Snatcher, black holding chicken, dog biting at the seat of his pants, 1926	650	950	1250
Highboy Climbing Tractor, c. 1950s, 10-1/2" long	75	125	150
Highboy Tractor, sparkles, c. 1950s, 10" long	100	150	200
Honeymoon Cottage, 1950s	125	175	250
Honeymoon Express, circling train and plane, 1937, 9-3/8" diameter	125	200	250
Honeymoon Express, 1928	150	225	300
Honeymoon Express, steamlined train on circular track, 1948, 9-3/8"	85	125	175
Hoppo the Waltzing Monkey with Cymbals, 1930s, 9-1/2" high	200	300	400
Jalopy Pickup Truck, 7"	100	125	150
Jazzbo Jim, 1920s, 9" high	275	400	600
Jolly Joe Jeep, plastic helmet, 1950s, 6" long	175	275	350
Joy-Rider 1929, College Boy driver w/bag, wording on car "goes backward, forward, circles and rears" head moves, 8" long	300	425	550
Jumpin' Jeep, c. WWII, 6"	150	225	275

Marx Toy Co. (Continued)	C6	C8	C10
King Racer, 1930s, 8-1/2" long	325	475	600
Let the Drummer Boy Play, 1930s, 8-1/2" high	450	650	825
Light Duty Climbing Tractor, 1930s	150	225	300
Limping Lizzie Car	200	300	400
Looping Plane, No. 382	150	250	350
Looping Plane, No. 182	100	200	300
Lucky Stunt Flyer	200	300	400
Mack Dump Truck, City Coal Co., 1930s, 13" long	350	525	700
Main Street, moving vehicles, traffic cop, etc., 1929	350	525	700
Mammy's Boy, 1930s, 11" tall	500	750	1000
Mechanical Airplane	200	300	400
Mechanical Roadster, 1950s, 11"	125	150	175
Mechanical Speed Racer, 1930s, 9" long	100	150	200
Mechanical Speedway Racer	75	125	175
Mechanical Station Wagon	125	175	225
Mechanical Taxi Cab, 1950s, 11"	75	125	175
Mechanical Tractor, c. 1930s, 6"	100	150	200
Mechanical Tractor with Earth Grader, c. 1950s, 21-1/2" long	100	150	200
Merrymakers, four mice, three in band and one dancer, w/marquee, 1929	800	1300	1500
Merrymakers, four mice, three in band and one dancer, without marquee, has conductor with baton, 1929	600	850	1200

Left to right: Quack Quack, Lehmann, $600. Onkel, Lehmann, $750. Photo courtesy Sotheby's, New York

Mixtum, No. 775, Lehmann, $1800. Photo courtesy Bertoia Auctions

Onkel, Lehmann, $750. Photo courtesy Sotheby's, New York

Left to right: Zig Zag, Lehmann, $1900. Tut Tut, Lehmann, $1700. Photo courtesy Sotheby's, New York

Marx Toy Co. (Continued)	C6	C8	C10
Merrymakers, four mice, three in band and one dancer, without marquee, has violinist, 1929........	750	1000	1400
Midget Climbing Fighting Tank, Pat. No. 1334539, c. 1935, 5-1/2" long.............	70	100	130
Midget Climbing Tractor, c. 1950, 5-1/2" long..............	75	125	150
Midget Racer, 1950s, 6"	50	75	100
Midget Special Race Car No. 2, driver in old headgear and goggles, 1930s, 5" long	75	100	150
Midget Special Race Car No. 7, driver in old headgear and goggles, 1930s, 5" long	75	100	150
Monkey Cyclist, 1930s....................	100	150	200
Moon Creature, (Japan), 1950s, 5-1/2" high......................	100	175	250

Marx Toy Co. (Continued)	C6	C8	C10
Motor Squad, sidecar.......................	225	325	425
Motorcycle Trooper, 1935...............	212	318	425
Mountain Climber, Japan, 1960s, 32" long, 4" car	75	125	175
Mysterious Kitty Kat, 1950s, 8"......	75	125	175
Mystery Police Cycle, 1930s, 4-1/2"...	125	175	250
Mystery Tunnel	50	75	100
Mystic Motorcycle, c. 1930s	150	225	300
New Flivver, 1920s, 7" long............	200	300	400
New Rocket Racer, 1930s, 16"........	200	300	400
New York, circular, w/train and tin airplane, new in 1928, 9-1/2" diameter......................................	600	900	1200
Nodding Goose...............................	75	125	175
North American Van Lines Inc. Long Distance Moving Truck	125	200	250

Marx Toy Co. Sparkling Soldier, $300.

Marx Toy Co. Speed Boy Delivery Motorcycle Delivery, 1930s, $600. Photo courtesy Don Hultzman

Left to right: Mirakomot, No. 1012, Schuco, $600; Motodrill, No. 1006, Schuco, $600.

Marx, "Midget Climbing, Fishing Tank." Courtesy K. Warren Mitchell

G.I. Joe and the K-9 Pups, Unique Art Mfg. Co., $300.

Left to right: Parade Drummer, Marx, 1930s, $800; Tidy Tim the Street Sweeper, Marx, 1933, $750.

Ohio Art Automatic Airport. Photo by Ron Chojnacki. Courtesy Don Hultzman

Synchromatic 5700, Schuco, $1,000. Photo courtesy Christie's East

Marx Toy Co. (Continued)	C6	C8	C10
Old Jalopy, college boys, Yale, Princeton pennants, 1950	250	300	350
Old Jalopy, post-WWII	150	225	300
P.D. Motorcyclist, Pat. No. 2001625, 4" long	165	240	325
P.D. Police motorcycle, w/sidecar, on-off lever, wood wheels, 1930s, 3-1/2" long	175	250	325
Parade Drummer, marked "Let the Drummer Boy Play While You Swing and Sway", 1930s	400	600	800
Parcel Post U.S. Mail, early, 8-1/2" long	225	325	425
Peter Rabbit, eccentric car	300	450	600
Piggy, 4" high	50	75	100
Pike's Peak Mountain Climber, 1930s, 3-1/2" car, 30" long	300	450	600
Pinched Roadster, motorcycle cop in circular track, c. 1927, 9-1/2" x 9-1/2"	325	500	675
Play-Away-Piano, w/songbook, 1930s, 9" x 9"	60	90	120
Police Patrol, motorcycle w/sidecar, 1935	300	450	600
Police Precinct Police Patrol Armored Truck, c. early 1930s, 10-1/2"	1800	2800	3800
Police Siren Motorcycle, 1930s, 8" long	200	300	400
Police Squad, motorcycle cop w/sidecar, 8-1/2" long	300	400	500
Power Snap Caterpillar Climbing Tractor, 1950s, 8" long	75	175	225
Prone WW I Soldier, 1925, 8" long	100	150	200
Racer no. 2, 1930s, 5" long	75	125	150
Racer No. 3, 1930s, 5" long	75	125	150
Racer No. 4, 1930s, 5" long	75	125	150
Racer No. 5, 1930s, 5" long	75	125	150

Marx Toy Co. (Continued)	C6	C8	C10
Racer No. 7, 1930s, 5" long	75	125	150
Racing Car, two-man team, c. 1940, 12"	125	175	225
Racing Car, plastic driver, lithographed, c. 1950, 16" long	125	200	250
Racing Car "27", plastic driver, lithographed, c. 1950	225	300	375
Range Rider, 1940s, 10-1/2" high on rocker base	200	300	400
Range Rider, 1940s, 8-1/2" high	150	225	300
Red Cap Porter	350	550	750
Red Devil Stunt Auto, 1930s, 12" long ramp w/2-1/2" tin racer	150	225	300
Red the Iceman, 1930s	300	450	600
Reversible Coupe, marked "The Marvel Car", c. 1938, 16-3/4" long	250	375	500
Reversing Road Roller	125	200	275
Reversing Tank, 1930s	75	100	125
Reversing Tractor	275	400	500
Rex Mars Planet Patrol, pastel colors, 1950s, 9-1/2" long	250	375	500
Rex Race Car, 1920s	150	225	300
Ride 'Em Cowboy	125	175	225
Ring-A-Ling Circus, early ringmaster and circus animals, pink base	750	1250	1500
Ring-A-Ling Circus, early ringmaster and circus animals, green base	650	1150	1300
Road Roller, w/driver, c. 1930, 8-1/2" long	375	550	725
Rocket Fighter, complete w/tail fin and sparking mechanism, c. 1950s	225	350	475
Rocket Racer, 1930, 16-1/2" long	250	400	475
Rodeo Joe, 1933	200	300	400
Roll Over Cat	75	100	125

Curvo 1000, Schuco, 1950s, $350.

Marx Toy Co. Whoopee Car, 1929, $400. Photo courtesy Scott Smiles; photo by Mark Adams

Marx Toy Co. (Continued)	C6	C8	C10
Roll Over Plane, c. 1920s	150	200	275
Rollover Tank	75	100	125
Rookie Cop, w/siren, 1930s, 8-1/2"	250	350	475
Rookie Pilot, No. 77, c. 1940, 7" long	300	450	600
Rooster Pulling Wagon, 1930s	60	90	120
Royal Bus Line, 10" long	275	400	550
Royal Coupe, 1920s, 9" long	350	525	700
Royal Van Co., reads "We Haul Anywhere", 9" long	275	400	525
Running Scottie, 1940s, 5-1/2" long	70	120	175
Sam, the Gardner, includes six plastic tools, 1950s, 8" tall	125	175	250
Sand and Gravel Truck-Builders Supply Co., 1920	100	125	175
Scenic Express Train Set, c. 1950s	100	150	200
Sheriff Sam & His Whoopee Car, 1960s, 6" long	200	300	400
Single Track Speedway, eight track sections, 1938, 4" long wind-up car	75	125	150
Sky Hawk Airport Tower, No. 333, two planes, tower 7-1/2" high	175	250	350
Skybird Flyer, c. 1927	175	275	375
Skyscraper Go-Round, monoplane, Zeppelin, 1930s, 13-1/2" high	400	600	800

Marx Toy Co. (Continued)	C6	C8	C10
Smoky Sam the Wild Fireman, 1950s, 7"	150	225	300
Snoopy and Gus Hook and Ladder, 8" x 7-1/4"	800	1400	2000
Soap Box Derby Racer No. 3, 5-1/2" long	100	150	200
Soldier, prone, firing rifle, WWI helmet	100	150	200
Space Mobile, (Japan), 1960s, 32" long, 4" long car	125	175	225
Space Satellite with Launching Station, 1950s, 9" x 12" base and plastic accessories	75	125	150
Sparkling Climbing Bulldozer Tractor, later	175	250	325
Sparkling Climbing Fighting Tank, cannon recoils	125	175	250
Sparkling Climbing Tank, 1939	100	150	200
Sparkling Climbing Tractor, 1940s	125	175	225
Sparkling Climbing Tractor, c. 1950s, 8-1/2" long	100	150	200
Sparkling Climbing Tractor and Trailer, c. 1950s, 16" long	150	200	250
Sparkling Heavy Duty Bulldog Tractor with Road Scraper, c. 1950s, 11"	125	175	225
Sparkling Luxury Liner, 1950s, 14" long	75	125	175

Strauss Circus Wagon, containing lion and tamer, $850. Courtesy Sotheby's New York

Marx "Flipo the Jumping Dog," $250. Courtesy Mapes Auctioneers

Marx Toy Co. (Continued)

	C6	C8	C10
Sparkling Mountain Climber Train Set, tin loco and car, 1950s, 9" long	100	150	200
Sparkling Mountain Climber Train Set, 1930s, 11" tall	500	750	1000
Sparkling Rocket Fighter Ship	425	625	825
Sparkling Soldier, crawls, 7-3/4" long	150	225	300
Sparkling Soldier Motorcycle, c. 1940, 11"	400	500	600
Sparkling Space Tank	200	300	400
Sparkling Super Power Tank, c. 1950s, 9-1/2" long	100	150	200
Sparkling Tank, 4" long	100	150	200
Sparkling Tractor, tractor w/plow blade, 1939	150	200	250
Sparkling Tractor and Trailer Set, "Marbrook Farms", c. 1950s, 21" long	100	150	200
Sparkling Turn Over Tank	50	75	100
Sparkling Warship, same as U.S.S. Washington, 14" long	100	150	175
Speed Boy Delivery Motorcycle Delivery, no lights, 1930s, 9-3/4" long	300	400	500
Speed Boy Delivery Motorcycle Delivery, battery-operated light, 1930s, 9-3/4" long	350	500	650
Speed King Racer, 1930s, 16" long	400	600	800

Marx Toy Co. (Continued)

	C6	C8	C10
Speedway Coupe, battery to be inserted for headlights, 8" long	300	450	600
Spic and Span the Hams What Am, drummer and dancer, 1924	1000	1500	2000
Spic Coon Drummer, 1924, 8-1/2" high	900	1400	2000
Streamline Speedway, two wind-up cars w/tin figure-eight track, 1938, 31" long	125	175	250
Streamlined Coupe	225	300	375
Subway Express, w/plastic tunnel, 1954, 9-3/8" diameter	125	175	225
Super Streamline Racer, 1950s, 17" long	125	200	275
Tidy Tim the Street Sweeper, pushing wagon, 1933, 7-1/2" high, 8-1/2" long	350	575	750
Tom Tom Jungle Boy	100	150	200
Toto Acrobat	100	150	200
Tower Aeroplane, 1940s, two 3" tin airplanes, 7-1/2" high	200	300	400
Toy Town Dairy, horsedrawn cart, 1930s, 10-1/2" long	150	225	275
Toyland Farm Products, milk wagon, 1930s, 10-1/2" long	250	375	450
Tractor, early 1940s	105	158	210
Tractor and Trailer, c. 1950s, 16-1/12" long	150	225	300

Marx Toy Co. (Continued)

	C6	C8	C10
Trans-Atlantic Zeppelin, rear propeller, 1930s, 10" long	250	375	500
Tricky Fire Chief, 1925, 4" car on 6" x 10" base	200	300	400
Tricky Motorcycle, non-fail action, 1930s, 4-1/4" long	150	225	300
Tricky Taxi, 4-1/2" long	125	175	225
Tricky Taxi on a Busy Street	200	300	400
Trolley, headlight, bell, 9" long	175	250	325
Tumbling Monkey, on two chairs, 1930s, 5" high	125	175	225
Tumbling Monkey on Trapeze, 1920s, 6" high	100	150	200
Turn Over Tank, No. 3	125	175	225
TWA-U.S. Main-990, c. 1941, 5"	120	180	240
U.S. Army Bomber, two-engine, post-war, 1940s	162	243	325
U.S. Army Fighter Plane, 1940, 8" wingspan	185	280	370
U.S. Mail-TWA Biplane, 1930s, 15" long, 18" wingspan	400	600	800
U.S. Main Truck, 9-1/2" long	425	650	875
U.S.S. Washington Battleship	100	125	150
Vacationland Express	75	100	125
Wacky Taxi	125	175	225
Walking Clancy	400	600	800
Walking Drummer Boy, marked "Let The Drummer Boy Play While You Swing and Sway", c. 1939	350	525	700
Wee Scottie, also called Running Scottie, 5" long	100	150	200
Whoopee Car, laughing cows on wheels, driver looks like cowboy, 1932	200	300	400
Wonder Cyclist, 1930s, 9" high	170	255	340
Xylophonist, 5"	100	150	200
Yellow Cab-LMN 52, 1940s, 6-1/2" long	150	225	300
Zeppelin, 10" long	175	250	325
Zeppelin, 1930s, 27" long	200	300	400
Zeppelin, propeller on front, 1925, 11" long	175	275	375
Zeppelin TransAtlantic, 10" long	150	250	350
Zippo the Climbing Monkey, 1930s, 9-1/2" long	100	150	200

Ohio Art

	C6	C8	C10
Automatic Airport, 1940s, 9" high	90	135	180
Boat, 14" long	80	120	160
Cabin Cruiser, 1950s, 15" long	60	90	120

Ohio Art (Continued)

	C6	C8	C10
Circus Shooting Gallery, 1950s, 12" high, 17" long	60	90	150
Coast Guard Seaplane, 1950s, 10" wingspan	75	125	175
Commando Joe, 1950s, 8" long	125	175	235
Giant Ride Ferris Wheel, 1950s, 16" high	275	375	500
Hot Job Floatplane	100	150	175
Injun Chief, 1950s, 8" long	80	120	160
Jungle Eyes Shooting Gallery, 1950s, 18" long, 14" high	90	135	180
Mechanical Sea Plane	100	150	200
Musical Sail Away Ride	200	300	400
Sea Patrol Seaplane, 10" wingspan	90	135	180
Switch and Dump Train, 1950s, 28" long	100	150	200
Traffic Control, 1950s, 3-1/2" long, base 19" x 13"	60	90	120

Schuco

Schuco was founded in 1912 by Heinrich Muller and Herr Schreyer as Schreyer and Co. They later adoped the name "Schuco" as its trademark. Schuco toys were produced from the 1930s to the 1950s and were marked either "Germany" or "U.S. Zone-Germany." Toys with other markings are reissues.

Schuco

	C6	C8	C10
Akustico 2002, 1940s, 5-1/2" long	100	130	175
Anno 2000, 1940s, 5-1/2" long	80	120	160
Beer Drinker, 1950s, 5-1/2" high	100	150	200
Buick, No. 5311, 9" long	200	300	400
Cadillac DeVille Convertible 5505, 1960s, 11" long	90	135	180
Charly 1005, motorcycle w/driver, 1950s, 3-1/2" long	400	550	700
Clown Juggler, No. 965, 1950s, 5" high	300	450	600
Combination 4003, w/wind-up horn, 1950s, 7-1/2" long	175	263	350
Commando Auto, No. 2000, responds to whistle, 1950s, 5-3/4" long	150	225	300
Curvo 1000, 1950s, 5" long	150	225	350
Dalli 1011, tin car w/plastic driver, 1950s, 6-1/2" long	175	250	325
Disneyland Alweg Monorail, play set, 1950s	300	450	600
Electro Ingenico, No. 5311/61, 1950s, 8-1/2" long car	600	900	1200
Electro Submarine, No. 5552, 1950s, 13" long	100	150	200
Elektro Ingenico 5311, remote control, 1950s, 8-1/2" long	180	270	360

Clown with Umbrella, Chein, $275.

Honeymoon Express, Marx, 1948, $175.

Schuco Examico 4001, 1950s, $175. Photo courtesy Don Hultzman; photo by Ron Chojnacki

Jazzbo Jim The Dancer on the Roof, Strauss, 1910, $700. Photo courtesy Ed Hyers Antique Toys

Midget Special Race Car, No 2, Marx, 1930s, $150.

Schuco (Continued)

	C6	C8	C10
Examico 4001, five-speed BMW, 1950s, 6" long	75	125	175
Fernlenk Auto, No. 3000, part of play set, 1950s, 4-1/4" long	160	240	320
Fex 1111, 1950s, 6" long	100	150	200
Fire Engine, w/remote control, 1950s, 11-1/8" long	1000	1500	2000
Fox and Goose, No. 969, 1950s, 4-1/4" high	800	1200	1600
Gas Station 3054, 1950s, 8" long	60	90	120
Grand Prix Racer 1070, 1950s, 6"	100	150	200
Hegi-Fipsi 110, glider airplane kit, 1950	70	100	150
Hopsa, 1950s, 4" high	120	180	240
Ingenico 5311/56-MK, part of play set, 1950, 8-1/4" long car	500	750	1000
Ingenico 5335 MK, play set, 1950s, 8" long car	700	1050	1400
Jaguar 1250, 1940s, 5-1/2" long	175	250	325
Kommando Anno 2000, 1940s, 5-1/2" long	100	150	200
Latso 3042 Truck, 1950s, 4-1/2"	60	90	120
Magico Alpha Romeo, No. 2010, 1950s, 9-1/2" long	600	900	1200
Magico Auto 2008, responds to blowing, 1950s, 5-1/2" long	300	450	600
Magico Car and Garage, 1950s, 6"	120	180	240
Mercedes 190SL, No. 2095, 1950s, 8"	225	350	450
Mercedes TYP SSK 1928, 1950s, 4" long	100	150	200
Mercer Auto 1225, 1950s, 7-1/2"	100	150	200
Micro Racer 101, Porsche style, 1950s, 3-1/2" long	100	150	200
Micro Racer 102, Indy style, 1950s, 3-1/2" long	100	150	200
Micro Racer 1036, 1950s, 4-1/2"	100	150	200
Micro Racer 1040, 1950s, 4" long	75	112	150
Micro Racer 1041, 1950s, 4" long	75	110	150
Micro Racer 1042, 1950s, 4" long	100	150	200
Micro Racer 1043, 1950s, 4" long	100	150	200
Micro Racer '57 Ford 1045, 1950s, 4" long	100	150	200
Micro Racer Apha Romeo 1048, 1950s, 4" long	100	150	200
Micro Racer Go Kart 1035, 1950s, 4" long	100	150	200
Micro Racer Hot Rod 1036, 1950s, 4" long	90	135	180
Micro Racer Mercedes-Benz 1038, 1950s, 4" long	100	150	200

Schuco (Continued)

	C6	C8	C10
Micro Racer Mercedes-Benz 1044, 1950s, 4" long	110	165	220
Micro Racer Mercer 1036/1, 1950s, 4" long	100	150	200
Micro Racer Porsche 1047, 1950s, 4" long	110	165	220
Micro Racer Rally 1034, eight three-lane tracks, 1950s, 10' 6" long	60	90	120
Micro Racer Stake Truck 1049, 1950s, 4" long	100	150	200
Micro Racer Volkswagen 1046, 1950s, 4" long	100	150	200
Micro Racer Volkswagen Polizei 1039, 1950s, 4" long	100	150	200
Micro-Jet 1030 Thunderjet, 1950s, 5" wingspan, 5-1/2" long	80	120	160
Micro-Jet 1031 Magister 170R, 1950s, 5" wingspan, 5-1/2" long	80	120	160
Micro-Jet 1032 Super Sabre F 100, 1950s, 5" wingspan, 5-1/2" long	90	135	180
Micro-Jet 1033 Douglas F4 D-1, 1950s, 5" wingspan, 5-1/2" long	80	120	160
Mikifex 922, non-fall action mouse, 1950s, 3-1/2" long	40	60	80
Mirakocar 1001, non-fall action, 1950s, 4-1/2" long	75	100	125
Mirakomot 1012, non-fall action, 1950s, 5-1/4" long	300	450	600
Mirako-Peter, No. 1013, rare, 1950s, 5" long	1000	1500	2000
Monkey Car, orange-black, smiling monkey, 1930s, 6" long	1400	2100	2800
Motodrill 1006, circular action, 1950s, 5" long	300	450	600
Motodrill Clown 1007 Motorcycle, composition head, rare, 1950s, 5" long	1000	1500	2000
Mystery Car 1010, non-fall action, 1950s, 5-1/2" long	100	150	200
Patent Motorcar, 1950s, 4-1/2" long	100	150	200
Pick-Pick, No. 905, 1950s, 4-1/2" long	100	150	200
Porsche Formel II-1037, 1950s, 4-1/2" long	80	120	160
Racing Boat 1015, non-fall action, 1950s, 5" long	90	135	180
Radio 4012 Musical Car, 1950s, 6"	200	300	400

Knock-Out Prize Fighters, Strauss, c. 1910, $650.

Finnegan the Baggage Man, Unique, 1930s, $400.

Schuco (Continued)	C6	C8	C10
Sonny 2005, mouse w/balloon in BMW, 1950s, 5-1/4" long	300	450	600
Spirit of St. Louis Plane, Lindbergh figure, rare, 1920s, 4" long	800	1200	1600
Station Car 3118, 1950s, 4-1/2" long	60	90	120
Studio Racer 1050, includes tools, 1950s, 5-1/2" long	125	188	250
Submarine 3007, has some plastic parts, 1950s, 12" long	113	170	225
Synchromatic 5700, resembles Packard Hawk, 1950s, 11" long	500	750	1000
Telesteering 3000 Limo, 1950s, 4" long	75	100	125
Tippy, No. 990, Scotty, 1950s, 4" long	80	120	160
Trip-Trap, dog, 1950s, 7" long	400	600	800
Turn Miki Clown, 1950s, 3-3/4" high	200	300	400
Varianto 3010, two-car play set, 1950s, cars are 4-1/2" long	100	150	200
Varianto 3010 Super, service station, 1950s, w/two 4-1/2" cars	170	225	340
Varianto 3010/0, truck and garage, 1950s, 4-1/2" long	75	100	125
Varianto 3041 Limo, 1950s, 4" long	100	150	200
Varianto 3064, 1950s, 8" long	30	45	60
Varianto Box 3010/30, includes tin garage and 3041 Limo, 1950s, 4-1/2" long	135	200	250
Varianto Bus 3044, 1950s, 4" long	70	105	140
Varianto Electro 3112, truck, 1950s, 4" long	75	100	125
Varianto Electro 3112u, truck, 1950s, 4-1/2" long	75	100	125

Schuco (Continued)	C6	C8	C10
Varianto Lasto, No. 3042, truck, 1950s, 4-1/4" long	80	120	160

Strauss

Ferdinand Strauss emigrated to the United States from Alsace, France. He worked as a toy importer in the early 1900s, and by 1914 had four New York toyshops. When World War I disrupted imports, he began to manufacture toys himself. In 1918 his company was located in East Rutherford, New Jersey, and was staffed by fifty employees. Eventually Strauss was known as "The Founder of the Mechanical Toy Industry in America." Evidently Strauss was wholly or partially out of business in the late 1920s, but later resumed production of wind-ups and other toys until at least 1941-1942. He is also famous for having employed the very young Louis Marx.

Strauss	C6	C8	C10
Air Devil Monoplane	300	450	550
Alabama Coon Jigger, 9-3/4"	375	550	725
Alabama Coon Jigger—Tombo, 1918, 10-1/2" high, 3" x 5" base	400	600	800
Aluminum Flying Airship LA 1017, 1930s, 9" long	275	362	550
Big Show Circus Truck, 9-1/2" long	600	900	1200
Big Trixo Climbing Monkey, 10" long	150	225	300
Billiards Player, 1920s	300	450	600
Black Porter Pulling Wheelbarrow, 6-1/4"	150	225	300
Bus Deluxe, 1920s, 12" long	500	750	1000
Check-A-Cab, 8-1/2" long	500	750	1025
Chicago Zeppelin, 1930s, 9" long	400	600	800
Circus Wagon, containing lion and tamer, no engine compartment, 8-1/2" long	450	650	850

Strauss "Ham and Sam The Minstrel Team, $1150." Photo courtesy Bertoia Auctions

Strauss Alabama Coon Jigger-Tombo, 1918, $800. Photo courtesy Mapes Auctioneers and Appraisers

Strauss Jenny the Balky Mule, 1920s, $450. Photo courtesy Scott Smiles

Bobo the Mechanical Juggling Clown, T.P.S., $700.

Lincoln Tunnel, Unique Art, 1935, $400.

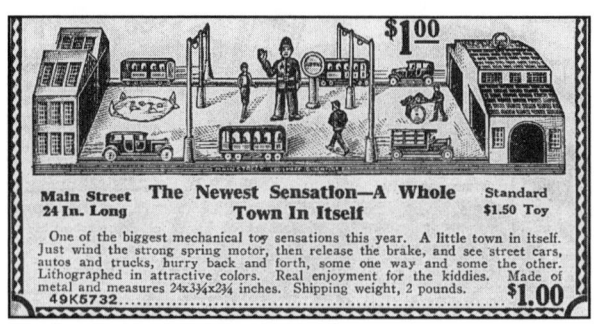

Marx catalog ad for Main Street.

Strauss (Continued)	C6	C8	C10
Circus Wagon, w/engine compartment, 10" long	1100	1700	2500
Dandy Jim, copyright 1921, 1920s	500	700	1000
Dizzie Lizzie	250	375	500
Flying Airship Dirigible	350	500	700
Ham and Sam the Minstrel Team, piano player and banjoist, 1921, 6-1/2" long	600	850	1150
Haul Away Truck, No. 22, dump body	200	350	475
Hooligans Hack	300	450	600
Interstate Double Decker Bus, 1920, 10-1/2" long	500	750	1000
Jackee the Hornpipe Dancer, No. 51, 8-1/2" long	500	800	1150
Jazzbo Jim the Dancer on the Roof, 1910, 10" high	350	500	700
Jenny the Balky Mule, No. 55, six-color litho, goes backward, forward and rears, farmer holding extended tin grain pail from his seat in front of mule's face to keep him moving, vegetables in cart, 1920s, 10" long	250	350	450
Jitney Bus, 1920s, 9-1/4" long	225	350	425
Jocko the Golfer, 1920s	300	400	500
Knock-Out Prize Fighters, No. 52, c. 1910, 7" high	350	500	650
Kraka Jack Car, 1920s, 5-1/2" long	250	350	450
Leaping Lena	300	450	550
Long Haulage Truck	350	525	700
Lux-A-Cab, 8-1/2" long	500	800	1200
Mailplane, 1930s	225	350	475
Miami Sea Sled, 1920s, w/4" dinghy attached, 10" long	250	375	500
Monkey Driving Three-wheel Cart Bulled by Bulldog, 1930s, 4-1/2" high	280	420	560
Old Jalopy, The, w/four college kids	100	150	200
Play Golf, 1920s, 7" x 12" base w/5" high golfer	300	500	750
Red Flash Racer	400	550	750
Red-Cap Porter, porter pushing a large trunk	300	450	600
Rollo Chair, black man pushing boardwalk chair, marked "Stock, DRGM, December 6, 1921"	500	800	1200
Santee Claus, in sleigh w/two reindeer, 1921, 6" high	1000	1500	2000

Strauss (Continued)	C6	C8	C10
Speedwagon	200	300	400
Standard Oil Truck, "73"	300	400	500
Tip Top Dump Truck	500	750	1050
Tip Top Man with Wheelbarrow	80	120	160
Tip Top Porter, No. 40, 1920s, 6" long	275	400	525
Tippy Canoe	175	250	350
Tom Twist, 1920s, 8-1/2" tall	450	675	900
Travel Chiks, chickens on railroad car, 1930s	400	550	725
Trikauto, No. 53	200	300	450
Water Sprinkle Truck	450	675	900
What's It? Car, No. 53, 1925, 9-1/2" long	500	700	900
Yell-O Taxi, 8-1/2" long	400	600	800

T.P.S.

T.P.S. is the trademark of Toplay, Ltd., founded in 1956 and noted for its most unusual and unique mechanical toys. More T.P.S. toys are listed in the Battery-Operated section.

T.P.S.	C6	C8	C10
Animal Barber Shop, 1950s, 5" high	300	400	500
Animals Playland, 1950s, 9-1/4"	200	275	350
Ball Playing Giraffe, 1950s, 8-1/2" tall	200	300	400
Bear Golfer, 1950s, assembled 7-1/2" long	175	225	300
Bear Playing Ball, 1950s, 19" long, 4" high	250	300	375
Big League Hockey Player, 1950s, 6" tall	275	375	475
Bo Bo the Juggling Clown, 1950s, 6"	400	500	700
Bouncing Ball Dolly, 1950s, 5-1/4" tall	125	150	175
Bunny Family Parade, 1950s, 13"	100	125	150
Busy Choo Choo, 1950s, 5-1/2" x 9-1/4" base, w/2-1/4" tin locomotive	75	100	125
Busy Mouse, 1950s, 6" x 9" base, w/3-1/4" tin mouse	75	100	125
Calypso Joe, 1950s, 6" tall	300	400	500
Candy Loving Canine, 1950s, 5-1/2" high	125	150	200
Champ on Ice—Bear Skater Trio, rare, 1960s, 9" long	500	700	900
Circus Acrobatic Seal and Ball, 1950s, 5" high	100	125	150
Circus Bugler, w/trombone, 1950s, 7" tall	325	425	525

Micro Racer 1040, Schuco, $150. Photo courtesy Don Hultzman

Piggy, Marx, $100. Photo courtesy Scott Smiles

T.P.S. Big League Hockey Player, 1950s, $475. Photo courtesy Don Hultzman

T.P.S. (Continued)	C6	C8	C10
Circus Clown and Monkey, 1950s, 5" high	150	225	300
Circus Clown on Ball, 1950s, 5-1/2" high	150	225	300
Circus Cyclist, 1950s, 6-1/2" tall	450	600	750
Circus Parade, 1950s, 11-1/2" long	175	275	375
Circus Parade—Juggling Duck and Friends, 1950s, 9" long	150	225	300
Circus Seal, w/plastic ball on nose, 1960s, 6-1/2" high	75	100	125
Cleo Clown—The Dogs, 1950s, 4-1/2" high	200	300	400
Climbing Panda, 1970s, 6" high	40	60	80
Climbing Pirate, string climber, 1960s, 6" long	125	175	225
Climbo the Climbing Clown, string climber, 1960s, 6" long	175	225	275
Clown Jalopy Cycle, friction, 1960s, 9" long	325	425	525

T.P.S. (Continued)	C6	C8	C10
Clown Juggler with Ball, 1950s, 6" tall	300	400	500
Clown Juggler with Monkey, 1950s, 9-1/2" tall	450	650	850
Clown Making the Lion Jump Thru the Flaming Hoop, 1960s, 4-1/2"	175	250	325
Clown on Rollerskates, 1950s, 5-3/4" tall	175	250	300
Clown Trainer and His Acrobatic Dog, 1960s, 4-1/2" high	150	225	300
Cock-A-Doodle, 1960s, 8" long	50	75	100
Combat Tank on Battle Front, 1960s, 6-1/4" x 15" base, w/2-1/4" tank	125	175	200
Comical Clara, 1960s, 5-1/2" tall	300	375	450
Coney Island Scooter, 1960s, 10" square w/2-1/2" bumper car	175	225	275
Dancing Couple, 1960s, 5-1/2" tall	100	125	150
Dreamland Airport, 1960s, 6-1/2" x 12" base w/3-1/2" tin helicopter	125	150	175

T.P.S. Jolly Wiggling Snake, 1960s, $175. Photo courtesy Don Hultzman; photo by Ron Chojnacki

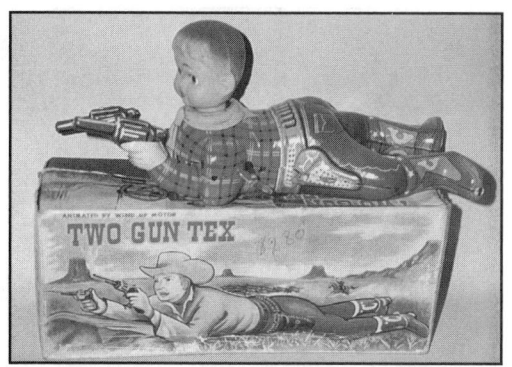

T.P.S. Two Gun Tex, $375. Photo courtesy Don Hultzman; photo by Ron Chojnacki

T.P.S. Happy Skaters, 1950s, $425. Photo courtesy Don Hultzman; photo by Ron Chojnacki

T.P.S. (Continued)	C6	C8	C10
Drive Tester, 1960s, 7" x 10-1/2" base and two 2" cars	150	200	250
Duck Amphibious Taxi, 1960s, 6-1/2" long, 4-3/8" high	400	500	600
Duck Family Parade, 1950s, 12" long	100	125	150
Duck the Mailman, Turn-N-Go action, 1960s, 4-1/2" high	400	450	500
Educational Pet Pooch, 1960s, 4" high	100	150	200
Fairyland Taxi, similar to "Wagon Fantasyland", 1950s, 11" long	200	250	350
Family Giraffe Loco, locomotive w/three cars called "Kiddy," "Mammy," and "Pappy", 1960s, 11" long	150	225	300
Fishing Bear, 1950s, 7-1/2" high	175	225	275
Fishing Monkey on Whale, 1950s, 9" long	250	325	400
Flying Birds with Voice, includes two birds, 1960s, 4" diameter base	150	175	225
Gay 90s Cyclist, 1950s, 7" high	225	300	350
Girl Skipping Rope, 1960s, 12" long, 6" high	150	225	300

T.P.S. (Continued)	C6	C8	C10
Girl with Chickens, 1960s, 6" tall, 5" long	250	325	400
Happy Caterpillar, 1950s, 13" long	60	90	120
Happy Hippo, gray, 1950s	375	500	650
Happy Hippo, brown, 1950s, 5-1/2" long	300	400	500
Happy Skaters, rabbit w/solid pants, 1950s	250	325	425
Happy Skaters, bears, 1950s, 6-1/2" tall	225	300	375
Happy Skaters, monkey, 1950s, 5-1/2" tall	225	350	450
Happy Skaters, rabbit w/plaid pants, 1950s, 5-1/2" tall	300	350	400
Happy the Violinist, striped pants and black shoes, 1950s, 9" tall	150	200	275
Happy the Violinist, bowtie, red jacket and red shoes	250	325	450
Hockey Player, 1950s, 6" tall	175	250	325
Hungry Whale, No. 1960s, 1950s, w/3" long small whale or fish, 5" long	50	75	100
Joe the Acrobat, clown, 1950s, 5-1/2" high	400	525	650

T.P.S. Juggling Clown with Apples, 1950s, $650. Photo courtesy Don Hultzman; photo by Ron Chojnacki

T.P.S. Pango-Pango with box, $325. Photo by Scott Smiles

T.P.S. (Continued)	C6	C8	C10
Joe the Xylophone Player, 1950s, 5" tall	300	375	450
Jolly Wiggling Snake, 1960s, 7-1/2" long	100	125	175
Juggling Clown with Apples, 1950s, 8-1/2" tall	400	500	650
Ladder Truck, 1950s, 2" tin fire engine on 5-1/2" x 9-1/4" base	80	120	160
Lady Bug & Tortoise with Babies, 1960s, 7" long	60	90	120
Lady Bug Family Parade, 1950s, 12" long	50	75	100
Lucky Monkey Playing Billiards, includes plastic balls, 1960s, 6" long	225	275	350
Magic Choo Choo, 1960s, 5-1/2" x 9-1/4" base w/2-1/4" tin locomotive	75	100	125
Magic Circus, includes tin seal and monkey, 1960s, 6" high	125	150	175
Magic Cross Road, 1960s, 5-1/2" x 9-1/4" base w/2-1/4" tin locomotive	75	100	125
Magic Tunnel, 1960s, 6" x 9" base w/2" tin "Dreamland Bus"	125	175	225
Mama Kangaroo with Playful Baby in Her Pouch, 1960s, 6" tall	125	175	225
Midget Lady Bug, 1960s, 7-1/2" tall	50	75	100
Missile Robot, 1960s, 6" high	80	120	160
Monkey Basketball Player, 1960s, 7" high	200	275	350

T.P.S. (Continued)	C6	C8	C10
Monkey Golfer, 1960s, assembled 7-1/2" long	200	225	250
Monkey on Whale, 1950s, 4" long, 3-3/4" high	250	400	500
Mountain Climber, string climber, 1960s, 6-1/2" long	175	225	300
Mounted Cavalryman with Cannon, 1960s, 5-1/2" high, w/2-1/2" long tin cannon	275	350	425
Mouse Race Cat, 1960s, 10" x 10"	100	125	150
Mr. Caterpillar, 1960s, 12" long	100	125	150
Oscar the Seal, w/ball on nose, 1950s, 6-1/2" high	125	150	175
Oscar the Seal, w/flour-bladed plastic propeller on nose, 1950s	100	125	150
Pango Pango, 1950s, 6" tall	175	250	325
Performing Seal and Monkey with Fish, 1960s, 4-1/2" tall	300	425	575
Plane the Loop Pilot, w/remote control, 1950s, 6" high	150	225	300
Playland Scooter, 1960s, 6" x 9" base w/2" tin car	100	125	175
Police Patrol, 1950s, 5-1/2" x 9-1/2" base and 2" tin police car	80	120	160
Pop Eye Pete, 1960s, 5-1/2" tall	275	375	475
Pussy Cat Chasing Butterfly, 1960s, 4-1/2" high	150	200	250
Rabbit and Bear Playing Ball, 1950s, 19" long, 5" high	200	300	400
Samson the Strongman, 1960s, 6" tall	500	625	750
Satellite Fleet, 1960s, 12" long	150	225	300

T.P.S. Lady Bug & Tortoise With Babies, $120. Photo courtesy Don Hultzman; photo by Ron Chojnacki

T.P.S. Lucky Monkey Playing Billiards, $3530. Photo courtesy Don Hultzman; photo by Ron Chojnacki

Capitol Hill Racer, Unique, 1930s, 17-1/2" long, $200.

Wyandotte "Ducky Ducklings." Photo courtesy Don Hultzman; photo by Ron Chojnacki

T.P.S. Happy the Violinist, 1950s, $275. Photo courtesy Don Hultzman; photo by Ron Chojnacki

T.P.S. Mounted Cavalryman with Cannon, 1960s, $425. Photo courtesy Don Hultzman

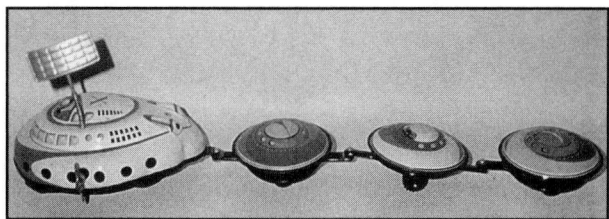

T.P.S. Satellite Fleet, 1960s, $300. Photo courtesy Don Hultzman

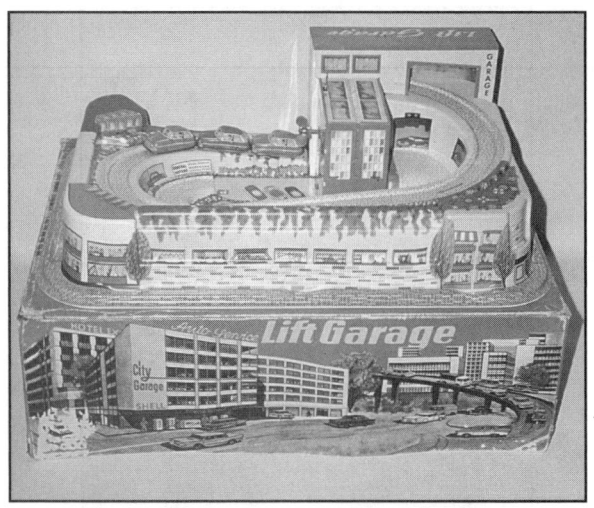

Technofix Lift Garage No. 308, 1950s, $300. Photo courtesy Don Hultzman.

Technofix Cable Car No. 375, 1950s, $375. Photo courtesy Don Hultzman

Technofix Trick Motorcycle, 1950s, $550. Photo courtesy Don Hultzman; photo by Ron Chojnacki

T.P.S. (Continued)	C6	C8	C10
Seal and Monkey with Fish, rare, 1950s, 5" high, 4" long	250	375	450
Shuttle Zoo Train, 1960s, 5-1/2" x 9-1/4" base and two-piece tin train	100	125	175
Skating Chef, African American, 1950s, 6"	325	450	525
Skating Chef, white, 1950s, 6"tall	200	275	350
Skip Rope Animals, 1960s, 8" long	125	150	175
Skippy the Tricky Cyclist, 1950s, 6" tall	150	225	300
Slim the Seal and Friends, w/four-bladed propeller on nose, 1960s, 10" long	300	400	500
Sports Car Race, w/four plastic racers, 1960s, 8" x 14" base	100	150	200
Susie the Ostrich, rare, 1960s, 5-1/2" high	500	700	900
Susy Bouncing Ball, 1960s, 5-1/2" tall	100	125	150

T.P.S. (Continued)	C6	C8	C10
Take-off Airport, 1960s, 5-1/2" x 9-1/2" base w/3" tin airplane	125	150	200
Tippy Toy Train, gravity action, 1960s, 6" diameter, 4" high	60	90	120
Touchdown Pete, 1950s, 5" tall	225	325	425
Tricycle Tot, 1960s, 5-1/2" long	125	175	225
Trombone Player, black hair, 1950s, 5-1/4" tall	200	250	300
Tumbling Chimp, 1950s, 4-1/2"	150	225	300
Two Gun Tex, 11" long	200	300	375
Violinist, 1950s, 5-1/4" tall	175	225	300
Wagon Fantasyland, 1960s, 11" long	200	250	350
World Champion Auto Racer, 1960s, 5-1/2" x 9-1/2" base, 2-1/4" tin car	100	125	150

Technofix

The Technofix Co., founded in Nuremberg, Germany, by Gebruder Einfalt, was engaged in German military technology during World War II. After the war, Technofix diverted its

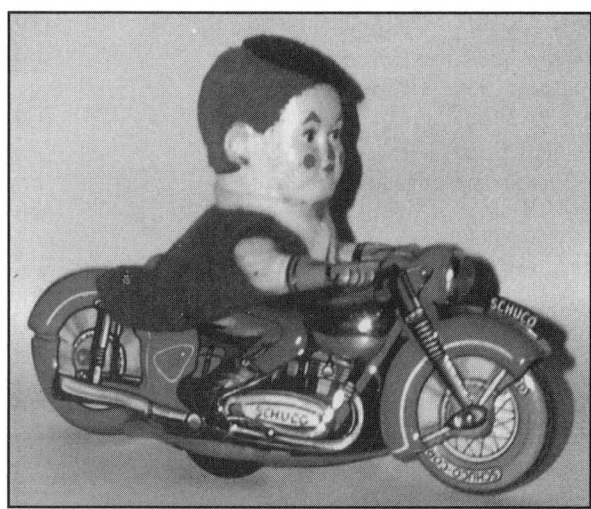

Motordrill Clown 1007, Schuco, $2000. Photo courtesy Don Hultzman

Unique Art Mfg. Co., Rodeo Joe Crazy Car, $325.

G.I. Joe and His Jouncing Jeep, Unique, $350.

Wyandotte Hoky-Poky, $275. Photo courtesy Scott Smiles

expertise to toy manufacturing. Among their toys were impressively large, three-dimensional, platform toys. These colorful items were made from stamped tin blanks and highlighted with delicate relief features that duplicated realistic outdoor-recreational themes. In the late 1950s vacuform plastic took the place of tin, and, as a result, quality declined and sales dropped. Later, many Technofix toys carried the Ohio Art trademark.

Technofix	C6	C8	C10
Alpine Express No. 300, (Ohio Art No. 614), 1950s, 6-1/2" x 32" long extended, two 3" tin cars.....	125	175	225
Cable Car No. 303, 1950s, 7-3/4" x 18-1/2" long, two 1-3/4" long tin cars	225	300	375
Coney Island No. 290, 1950s, 14" x 21" long, two 3" long tin cars......	125	175	250

Technofix (Continued)	C6	C8	C10
Grand Prix, 1950s, 14" x 21" long, three 3" tin cars	150	200	275
Holiday Camp No. 304, 1950s, 9" x 28-1/2" long, two 3-1/2" cars	350	550	750
International Airways No. 309, 1950s, 9" x 28" base, 5" long plastic jet airplane	300	450	600
Lift Garage No. 308, 1950s, 10-1/2" x 15" long base, three 1-3/4" tin cars	100	200	300
Motorcycle and Sidecar No. 225, 1950s, 7" long, 4-3/4" high	200	300	400
Mystic Station No. 306, 1950s, 17" x 8" base........	100	125	150
Rallye, plastic base and four tin cars, 1950s, 15" x 18"	300	450	600
Rocket Express, includes two tin cars, 1950s, 14-3/4" long...........	225	350	450

Technofix (Continued)

	C6	C8	C10
Silver Mine Express, 1950s, 23" x 6" base, w/3" long tin car	100	150	225
Toboggan No. 290, 1950s, 14" x 21" long base, two 3-1/2" tin cars	150	225	300
Touchdown Chimp, 1950s, 3-1/2" high..............	150	200	275
Traffic Control, 1950s, 13" x 19" long base, three 3-1/2" tin cars....	50	75	100
Traffic Crossing with Police Control, 1950s, two 3" tin cars	100	150	200
Trick Motorcycle, 1950s, 7" long....	275	425	550

Unique Art Mfg. Co.

Unique Art Mfg. Co. began producing toys in 1916 when it introduced its Merry Juggler and Charlie Chaplin. In 1931 it was located at Waverly and Peshine Avenues in Newark, New Jersey. Its president was Wm. Marbe. In a 1946-1947 directory the address was 200 Waverly Avenue in Newark, and the president was Samuel Burger.

Unique Art Mfg. Co.

	C6	C8	C10
Artie the Clown in his Crazy Car	300	400	500
Bombo the Monk, two-piece, 1930s, tree 9-1/2" high, monkey 5-1/2" long....................	125	150	225
Capitol Hill Racer, 1930s, 17-1/2" long, w/2" racing car	100	150	200
Casey the Cop, early.....................	600	800	1000
Dandy Jim Dancer, 1921	500	700	900
Daredevil Motor Cop, 1940s, 8-1/2" long....................	300	450	600
Finnegan, w/cardboard luggage, 1930s, 14" long	200	300	400
Flying Circus, elephant supports flying plane and flying clown	450	650	850
G.I. Joe and His Jouncing Jeep, post-WWII, 7"...........................	175	250	350
G.I. Joe and the K-9 Pups, c. 1941, 9" high	150	225	300
Gertie the Galloping Goose, 1930s, 9-1/2" long	145	175	225
Hee Haw donkey Pulling Milk Cart, red cart w/yellow wheels, 1950s, 10" long	150	225	300
Hillbilly Express, three pieces, 1930s, 3-1/4" tin locomotive, 18" long	100	150	200
Hobo Train, dog biting pants of hobo atop train, 1920s, 8-1/2".....	300	450	650
Hott an' Tott Musical Band, 1920s	500	750	1000

Unique Art Mfg. Co. (Continued)

	C6	C8	C10
Jazzbo Jim—The Dancer on the Roof, 1920s, 10" high, base 5" x 3" x 3"	250	375	500
Kiddy Cyclist, steers figure-eight pattern and rings bell, 1930s, 8-3/4" tall........................	275	425	550
Kid-Go-Round Plastic Horsemen and Boat	150	225	300
Krazy Kar, new in 1921	300	450	600
Li'l Abner and His Dogpatch Band, tin litho, Abner in red jacket w/green pants, 1945	500	750	1000
Lincoln Tunnel, moving vehicles, cop, 1935, 24" long	200	300	400
Motorcycle Cop, 1930s, 9" long......	300	400	500
Musical Sail-way Carousel, w/three kids in spinning plastic boats, 9" tall.................	175	250	350
Pecking Goose, Witch and Cat........	350	525	700
Rap and Tap, boxers in ring, 1921 ..	500	750	1000
Rodeo Joe Crazy Car......................	150	225	325
Rollover Motorcycle Cop, 1935......	300	400	500
Sky Rangers Plane and Zeppelin, revolving from tower, 1933	200	300	400

Wolverine

	C6	C8	C10
Acrobat, 1940s.............................	125	175	225
Acrobatic Monkeys, No. 810, 1930s, 10" diameter base	200	300	400
Autolift, includes 2-1/2" tin car w/four sections of track, 1930s, 10-1/4" high................	225	300	400
Drum Major, No. 27, pat. 1892546, 1930s, 13-5/8" tall on rectangular 4-1/2" x 6-1/2" base	150	250	350
Drummer Boy, 1930s, 14" high.......	150	250	300
Farm Wagon, 1950s, 10" long........	30	40	50
Jet Roller Coaster and Small Car, 21" long extended....................	175	250	325
Loop-A-Loop, includes small car No. 30, 1930s, 19"......................	200	275	350
Luxury Liner..................................	100	150	200
Mechanical Man on the Flying Trapeze, 1930s, 8-1/2" high............	125	200	275
Merry-Go-Round, No. 31, includes four tin-litho flags, 1930s, 11" diameter, 12" high	275	400	525
Neck & Neck, horse-racing game, 1940s, 36" long	75	100	125
Pontiac Mystery Car.......................	100	150	200
S.S. Wolverine, 14-1/2" long..........	100	150	200

Unique Art Mfg. Co. Kiddy Cyclist, 1930s, $550.
Photo courtesy Scott Smiles

Rollover Cat, Marx, $125.

Wolverine (Continued)

	C6	C8	C10
Sandy Andy Caterpillar Tractor-Trailer, 21" long	500	750	1000
Sandy Andy Circus, dancing toy	150	225	300
Sandy Andy Tank, 14" long	100	150	200
Zilotone, w/six interchangeable records, 1930s	425	575	750

Woodhaven

Research has established that in the 1930s Herman Joerger bought Animate Toy, and about the same time, Ranger Toys. He sold the business to his son, Herman, Jr., who in turn sold it to his son, Kurt. The firm made toys until at least 1939. It was located in Woodhaven, New York, and is now called Woodhaven Telesis Corporation, making sheet metal parts to order.

Woodhaven

	C6	C8	C10
Robot Bus with the Mechanical Brain, 1940s, 13-1/2" long	78	115	155
Tractor, marked "1916" but produced and sold much later	65	100	130

Wyandotte

	C6	C8	C10
Acrobatic Monkeys, 1930s	200	300	400
Carnival, 16" x 11"	425	650	850
Carousel, 5-1/4" high	150	225	300
Chicken Pulling Chick in Cart, 7-1/2" long	75	100	125
Duck Pulling Tin Easter cart, litho, wooden wheels, 15" long	50	75	100

Wyandotte (Continued)

	C6	C8	C10
Ducky Ducklings	100	125	150
Hoky-Poky, handcar w/two clowns	200	300	400
Man on the Flying Trapeze, 1930s, 9" high	100	150	200
Mechanical Handcar, 1935, 6-1/2" long	200	300	400
Red Ranger Ride 'Em Cowboy, No. 515, 6-1/2" high	150	225	300

Yone

Yone was a Japanese manufacturer of tin wind-up and friction toys in the early to mid-1960s.

Yone

	C6	C8	C10
Bears Seesaw	130	195	260
Chef, Japanese, c. 1960s	90	135	180
Grandpa at Farm, Japanese, man sitting on stump, green base, red and white house w/ umbrella, c. 1960s, 4" tall	45	90	135
No Fishing, Mouse version, Japanese, green base, c. 1960s, 4" tall	50	85	125
Pirate, Japanese, c. 1960s	115	172	230
Soldier, Japanese, c. 1960s	100	150	200

VEHICLES

Modern man has always had a love affair with machines that move. Partial evidence of this is the amazing number of toy vehicles that have been produced in the twentieth century. In fact, it could be reasonably argued that toy vehicles are collected more than any other type of toy.

With the dawn of the modern industrial age, the mass production of full-size automobiles and their toy counterparts seemed to go hand-in-hand. As cars rolled off the assembly lines, their miniature replicas were not far behind.

The earliest toy automobiles came along soon after their big daddy originals in the late nineteenth century and were produced in cast iron. But it wasn't until World War I that toy production really began to hit its stride.

The Early Days

Firms such as Arcade and Hubley are among the most well-known and sought-after manufacturers of early cast-iron vehicles.

Cars, trucks, and buses produced by Arcade Manufacturing of Freeport, Ill. are highly valued to toy vehicle collectors. Arcade actually began producing toys in the late 1800s, but it wasn't until around 1920 when the company reportedly issued its first toy vehicle, a replica of a Chicago Yellow Cab. After that came more realistic models of actual cars, trucks, and buses. The company's slogan was, "They Look Real."

Hubley is another name associated with quality toy vehicles. This Pennsylvania company began manufacturing cast-iron toys in the 1890s, mostly horse-drawn wagons, trains, and guns. By the 1930s, Hubley was producing the cast-iron cars that became their most well-known products. Many were patterned after actual automobiles of the day, while others were apparently looser interpretations of reality. Some of the Hubley vehicles also included company names, and some of the most interesting pieces had separate nickel-plated grilles.

One of the more skilled makers of smaller-scale, cast-iron vehicles was A.C. Williams. The Ohio company began producing toys in the late 1800s. The smaller cars and airplanes produced by A.C. Williams were intended for the five-and-dime market of the time. Williams' toys are difficult for the novice collector to identify since the toys bear no markings.

Steel Takes Over

One of the most famous manufacturers of toy cars and trucks was Buddy "L." Theses large pressed-steel toys were not the kind of toys bought for display or quiet play on the living room floor. These were big trucks (around two feet long) designed for tough play.

Buddy "L" toys grew out of the Moline Pressed Steel company of Moline, Ill. The company was named for the son of the company's owner, reportedly for whom the first toys were produced. The Buddy "L" toys most sought by collectors were produced in the 1920s and 1930s and were of very heavy-duty construction. Starting in the early 1930s, the company began to use lighter-weight materials.

The Buddy "L" name has remained, but its post World War II toys are not considered in the same league as its early issues, which command high collector prices today.

Buddy "L" is best remembered for its heavy-duty trucks, but another name that was synonymous with trucks was Smith-Miller. Founded by Bob Smith and Matt Miller, the company specialized in "famous trucks in miniature." Smith-Miller was later known as Miller-Ironson Corporation, but it is more commonly referred to as Smitty Toys. They produced large cast-metal and aluminum trucks.

Because of their outstanding quality, some of the Mack trucks made by Smith-Miller are very highly regarded among toy collectors. The Smith-Miller name continues today, with new limited-edition trucks produced for collectors.

Wyandotte is another company associated with pressed steel vehicles. Known as either Wyandotte Toys or All Metal Products, this Michigan Company produced several large steel vehicles with baked enamel finishes in the 1930s. Not all Wyandotte toys are marked, which tends to cause some confusion among collectors, but the vehicles can often be identified by their art-deco styling and wooden wheels.

Another company that produced large steel toys was Structo. The company originally produced metal construction sets, but eventually developed a line of vehicles in the 1920s.

Slush Molds

Slush casting was a process simple enough to be done in tiny factories and even in home industries during the Depression. A few large manufacturers made toys in this way—most notably Barclay, Manoil,

Savoye, Kansas Toy and Novelty, and others, but many were made by anonymous, small, unidentifiable, local operations using molds made and marketed by a few firms. Many slush-cast toys are of very little value today, but there are exceptions. Foremost among these were dealer promotional replicas of real cars made by Banthrico and National Products. Other very accurate and detailed slush models, similar in size and scale to the contemporary Tootsietoys, can be valuable. Most notable among these are certain nicely cast models of the Reo Victoria, Packard, Chrysler Imperial, Cord coupe (late 1920s), Buick and Model A Ford. Lincoln White Metal Works produced these and others made with an extra mold part resulting in detailed radiator grilles. Tommy Toy made other small accurate replicas with the names cast on the door sides.

Rubber Toy Vehicles

The Auburn Rubber Company of Auburn, Ind., was not the first to introduce rubber toys to the American market, but it was no doubt the largest and had the greatest impact on the toy field. After introducing some toy soldiers in 1935, Auburn brought out its first vehicle in 1936—a beautiful coffin-nosed Cord sedan. Today the Auburn Cord is one of the most highly prized rubber toys and is seldom seen offered for sale.

Auburn followed the Cord with a wealth of vehicles, including trucks, farm tractors and implements, motorcycles, racers, fire engines, military vehicles, aircraft, ships, and trains. It seems that 1952 was Auburn's last year of marketing rubber toys exclusively. The 1953 Auburn catalog contained a vinyl motorcycle, believed to be the company's first vinyl toy. By 1955, the toy line was mostly vinyl with a few rubber varieties hanging on. The 1956 catalog was exclusively vinyl, except for two rubber fire engines, the last rubber toys to be marketed by Auburn.

The Sun Rubber Company of Barberton, Ohio, was the second largest producer of rubber toys. Like Auburn, it produced a full line of toys in addition to vehicles, including dolls, balls, and baby squeak toys. Sun Rubber's 1936 catalog contains a large selection of cars, trucks, and racers. In later years, the company added a few airplanes and military. Among the most famous of the Sun Rubber vehicles are the Walt Disney characters—Mickey Mouse and Donald Duck driving a tractor, fire truck, roadster, or airplane. By 1955, Sun's catalog line largely consisted of athletic balls, and the Disney toys were included as the only vehicle toys.

Auburn and Sun made the vast majority of rubber toys we see today, but there was a significant number of rubber toys made by other companies, mostly prior to World War II. Several companies from the rubber industry produced rubber toy vehicles, including Firestone, Seiberling, Barr, and Rainbow. All of the Rainbow, Barr, and Seiberling toys appear to have been made from 1935-1936, or at least based on real cars from those years. Most of the Seiberling or Barr toys are 1935 Fords; the Firestone toys include a 1935 Ford, a 1936 Ford, and a 1939 Mercury. Rainbow's vehicles seem to be based on the 1935 Oldsmobile. Some of these toys were mass-marketed through dime stores, just like Auburn and Sun toys, although some were sold or given away at expositions and exhibits. All of the Firestone toys seem to be marked with some significant event, like the Texas Centennial in 1936.

Many rubber toys were produced as promotional items for the automobile industry and are not marked to indicate who manufactured them. A number of Chrysler, DeSoto, Dodge, and Plymouth promotionals were produced during the mid-1930s and are highly prized as collectibles.

A few rubber vehicles were produced as very inexpensive toys, perhaps sold in sets, and can take the form of either a solid rubber or hollow vehicle. These toys often had the wheels molded into the body, so they could not turn. Many of these solid rubber toys are two-dimensional and are referred to as "flat" toys. Although they were originally sold as inexpensive toys, they are actively sought by collectors and constitute a small, but important, segment of the field.

Die-Cast

Other popularly collected vehicles are smaller die-cast models, generally measuring three to six inches long. Probably the leading producer of this type of toy was Tootsietoy.

Although few toys were produced by Tootsietoy before 1920, it was during the 1920s when the name Tootsietoy began to appear regularly. By the 1930s, the company was producing a wide line of toys, many of which are highly prized by collectors today. Tootsietoy's Federal vans from the 1920s are among the most sought-after toys, particularly those with company logos.

Being mass produced and economically priced, Tootsietoys were widely available in the five-and-dime arena. The success of those products no doubt led to several competitors.

One of the competitors was Barclay, which also produced die-cast vehicles, although most were generally considered to be of lesser quality than Tootsietoys. The first Barclay vehicles had metal tires, but in the mid-1930s, white rubber tires on wooden axles were introduced. Metal axles soon replaced the wood, and black tires replaced white after World War II.

Another competitor soon emerged from Europe—Dinky Toys were manufactured from 1933 through the

1970s in England and France. These vehicles were high-quality die-cast, at least until the mid-1960s, generally in 1:43 scale.

Another competitor in this classification of small die-cast vehicles is Corgi, which came on the scene in the late 1950s. Corgi was the trade name for the die-cast toys produced by England's Mettoy Company.

One of the best-known series of toy cars today is Matchbox. These die-cast beauties are roughly three-inches in length. However, Lesney (the company that produced them) did manufacture several larger scale cars before it began the Matchbox line. Some of these early Lesney vehicles are valued up to $2,000 each.

Matchbox vehicles were immensely popular; so much so that in the United States, Mattel introduced a similar line called Hot Wheels. The California-based company gave its cars a California-type appeal, focusing on colorful hot rods that appealed to youngsters.

In the head-to-head battle that followed, Lesney at one time was producing 5.5 million toys a week.

Eventually Lesney lost the battle and went into receivership. Matchbox was restructured and sold twice, eventually landing with Tyco Toys. In 1996, Mattel purchased Tyco, bringing Matchbox cars into the Hot Wheels family.

Tips on Grading

Demand and desirability are affected by a number of factors, one of which is nostalgia. As a guide to other factors affecting desirability, there are a few broad, easy clues. Accuracy of scale and proportion, the use of many different cast parts, cast-in or decal logos and details and hand-painting (by the original maker and not by some later child or collector) all enhance the value. In most cases, a four-inch roadster with a separate chassis, separate nickel-plated radiator and headlights, and a separate cast figure will be worth much more than a two-piece vehicle with the halves riveted together. While any imperfections or scratches always lessen a vehicle's value, such things are more likely to deflate prices on vehicles such as Hot Wheels or Matchbox cars. On the latter two, any defect will bring the value down about twenty-five percent.

Reproductions are usually easy to spot once one has gained a little experience. They are usually held together by a long screw, which is threaded all the way to the head. Only a few genuinely old toys are assembled with a screw rather than a long peaned rivet, and the few screws used often had only about a quarter-inch threaded at the tip (the Hubley Packard is an important exception). Modern axles are usually a hollow rolled piece of sheet metal, much like a shear pin, though a few are rods with threaded ends and sheet metal acorn nuts. The castings themselves are the most dependable giveaway but require a little experience. The old castings are thinner, lighter, and smoother, the modern ones being gritty, thick, and coarse of detail.

Streamline Coupe, No. 30, Airflow, V-pattern grille, C.A.W. Novelty Company, $32.

C.A.W. Novelty Tank Truck, semi-trialer, two-tanks, $60.

C.A.W. Novelty Company Tank Truck, 3-3/16" long, $45. Photo courtesy Gary Franson

Wonder Special, No. 33, Airflow coupe, C.A.W. Novelty Company, $32.

Tank, A.C. Williams, 4" long, $145.

Coupe, 1930, cast iron, A.C. Williams, 6-3/4" long, $310.

A.C. Williams Sedan with interchangeable body, 1931, $700.

CONDITION CODE

C6 Good; evident overall wear, well played with but acceptable to many collectors
C8 Very Good; minor overall wear, very clean
C10 Mint; like new

Note: Mint in Box commands a higher price.
Condition below C6 brings considerably lower prices

A.C. Williams

A.C. Williams was founded in 1886 when Adam Clark Williams bought the J.W. Williams Company from his father. After a fire in 1893, the firm moved from Chagrin Falls, Ohio, to Ravenna. Toy production began about this time. Small cast-iron toys were Williams' specialty, with banks, cars, and aircraft predominant. A.C. Williams retired in 1919, but the firm continued to make toys until 1938, after which it continued in business in a non-toy capacity. Williams marked few, if any, of its toys. Two clues to A.C. Williams toy are turned steel hubs and starred axle peens.

A.C. Williams

	C6	C8	C10
Car, four-casting nickeled radiator car, 4" long	80	125	165
Car Carrier, w/three Austins, 1920, 12-1/2" long	450	675	900
Coupe, two-piece body, 1936, 3" long	95	145	190
Coupe, cast iron, rumble seat, side mounts, rubber tires, 1930, 6-3/4" long	165	225	325
Delivery Van, 8" long	350	525	700
Dump Truck, 6-1/4" long	195	292	390
Laundry Truck, 8" long	400	600	800
Lincoln Touring Car, 7" long	325	470	640
Mack Gas Tank Truck, 7-1/4" long	350	525	700
Mack Gas Tank Truck, 3-3/4" long	125	185	250
Mack Gas Tank Truck, 5-1/8" long	100	150	200

A.C. Williams (Continued)

	C6	C8	C10
Mack Stake Truck, 3-1/2"	45	68	90
Mack Stake Truck, 4-1/4"	80	120	160
Mack Stake Truck, 5-1/8"	112	170	225
Mack Stake Truck, 7" long	150	225	300
Mack Stake Truck, 8-1/2"	200	325	450
Mack Truck, 4-3/4" long	95	140	190
Mack Truck, 6-3/4" long	100	150	200
Mack Truck, 3-1/2" long	45	68	90
Model T Coupe, 6" long	180	275	375
Moving & Storage Truck, 3-1/2" long	112	168	225
Racer, boattailed, 6-1/2" long	275	425	600
Sedan, cast iron, interchangeable body, c. 1931, 6-3/4" long	350	525	700
Sedan, 5" long	75	112	150
Sedan, cast iron, streamlined rear fender, c. 1930, 6-1/2" long	175	265	355
Stake Truck, "C to C Co.," two pieces, 7" long	200	300	400
Steam Roller, 1930s, 5-1/2"	95	145	190
Studebaker, two-tone sedan, c. 1933-34, approx. 4" long	110	165	220
Tank, 4" long	73	110	145
Taxi, 5-3/4" long	175	275	380
Touring Car, cast iron, 9-1/2" long	475	712	950

Arcade Manufacturing Company Austin Stake Truck, (AR15), 1932, $300. Photo courtesy Rod Carnahan

Arcade Manufacturing Company Double-Decker Bus, (AR24), $950. Photo courtesy Southeby's, New York

C-5 Cattle Liner, All American Toy Company, 38" long, $1,150.

D-3 Dyna-Dump, All American Toy Company, 20" long, $590.

A.C. Williams (Continued)

	C6	C8	C10
Touring Car, w/driver, 5"	100	150	200
Willys Knight, cast iron, w/driver, 1920s, 8" long	120	180	240
Wrecker, 6-1/2" long	250	375	550

All American Toy Company

All American was founded by Clay Steinke in Salem, Oregon, in 1948. It continued until 1955, with its location in the Jorgenson Building on Ferry Street. At its peak, it employed forty-two people. In total, it sold 26,000 toys. And despite the formidable 1950 price of $20, All American's most popular toy was the Timber Toter. Collectors should note that toy vehicles made by All American had air-horn steering and Goodyear tires.

Patrick Russell purchased All American Toy Company in 1992. Available now are parts and new limited edition vehicles.

All American Toy Company

	C6	C8	C10
C-5 Cattle Liner, 38" long	500	800	1150
CL-8 Cargo Liner, 38" long	470	705	940
D-3 Dyna-Dump, 20" long	295	445	590
Hay Feed and Grain	275	410	550
HD-7 Play-Dozer, 9" long	338	505	675
HH-9 Heavy Hauler, 38" long	475	710	950
L-2 Timber Toter, w/logs, 38" extended length	275	415	625
LJ-4 Timber Toter, Jr., w/lumber, 20" long	212	318	425
MS Midget Skagit, battery-powered, 18" long	300	450	600
S-1 Scoop-A-Veyor, 16" long	237	355	475

American Metal Toys

	C6	C8	C10
Mack Truck, "Giant", 26-1/2" long	800	1400	2000
Packard Coupe, steerable front wheels, 54" long	3000	5000	7000
Pedal Car, Velie	1600	2500	3400
Pedal Car, dump truck, "Juvenile Auto," red and yellow, 57" long	2000	3500	5000
Tank, throwing flame, flame touching hull	40	60	80
Tank, throwing flame, flame not touching hull	45	67	90
Tank, throwing flame	60	90	120
Tank, "22" on side	50	75	100

Arcade

In 1869, a foundry in Freeport, Illinois, was organized as a two-man partnership under the name of Novelty Iron and Brass Foundry. It was dissolved in 1885 when a new, larger factory was incorporated under the name of Arcade Manufacturing Co.

Arcade made industrial castings and household items, but no toys. After a disastrous fire in 1892 and management changes in 1893, toys began to appear in its catalog, and by the early 1900s, and by the early 19000s the line had become so extensive that a fifty-page catalog was issued showing a large line of notions and novelties, small stoves, banks, and a few trains, including a pile-driver. But it was not until an enterprising young lawyer married the daughter of one of the officers and joined the firm in 1919 that the firm rapidly became one of the major makers of cast-iron toys.

Struck by the large numbers of Yellow Cabs in the streets of Chicago, the young man approached the Yellow Cab Com-

Motorcycle and rider, "Champion," 4-3/4" long, on left, 7" long on right, Champion, $300.

Left to right: Arcade Manufacturing Company A.C.F. Bus, 1927, 11-1/2" long, $4100; Arcade Manufacturing Company Yellow Parlor Coach Bus, 1926, 13" long, $2200. Photo courtesy Bertoia Auctions

pany with a novel proposition: in return for the sole right to make replicas of the cab, the Yellow Cab Company would have the exclusive right to use the toy in its advertising. Success was instantaneous.

In the booming 1920s, the company's sales swelled so much that a new and larger plant was built in 1927. Two years later, the stock market crash heralded the Great Depression, and hard times hit the small car business just as it did the large ones.

Cheap competition and dwindling demand for toys costing more than a dime had brought the company to the brink of bankruptcy by 1933. Management gave the firm new life with an exclusive arrangement to provide souvenir replicas of the fairground buses made by G.M.C. for the Chicago Century of Progress.

As with most toy companies, Arcade stopped making toys during World War II.

After the war, the company returned to making industrial and household hardware and a few toys, but cheaper toys eclipsed the more expensive cast-iron toys. In 1946, the firm was sold to the Rockwell Manufacturing Co. of Pittsburgh. Arcade is no longer in business. Arcade toys were meant to be played with and are extremely rare in Mint condition. The year listed is the year the toy was introduced.

Contributor: Michael W. Curran, Illinois Antiques, P.O. Box 545, Hampton, IL 61256, 309-496-9426.

Arcade Manufacturing Company

	C6	C8	C10
A.C.F. Bus, 1927, 11-1/2" long (AR1)	1700	2700	4100
Ambulance, No. 187, 1932, 7-3/4" long (AR6)	400	700	1200
Ambulance, No. 188, 1932, 6" long (AR7)	370	550	740
Ambulance, white-painted version of No. 2620 Chevolet Panel Delivery Truck, 4" long (AR8)	350	575	800
Anthony Dump Truck, 1927, 8-1/8" long (AR9)	1000	1700	2750
Austin Autocrat Road Roller, No. 291, 1928, 7" long (AR10)	300	475	675
Austin Delivery Truck, No. 173, 1932, 3-3/4" long (AR11)	50	75	100

Arcade Manufacturing Company (Continued)

	C6	C8	C10
Austin Racer, No. 175X, 1932, 3-3/4" long (AR12)	50	90	135
Austin Roadster, No. 174, 1932, 3-3/4" long (AR13)	125	200	275
Austin Roll-A-Plane, 8" long (AR14)	500	900	1400
Austin Stake Truck, No. 176X, 1932, 3-3/4" long (AR15)	125	200	300
Austin Wrecker, No. 177X, 1932, 3-3/4" long (AR16)	125	200	300
Borden's Milk Bottle Truck, No. 2640X, 1936, 6-1/4" long (AR19)	1000	1600	2400
Brinks Express Truck, 1932, 11-3/4" long (AR20)	8000	15,000	20,000
Buick Opera Coupe, 1927, 8-1/2" long (AR21)	2500	4400	6250
Buick Sedan, 1927, 8-1/2" long (AR22)	1500	2500	4000
Bus, No. 316X, Double-Decker, 1929, 8-1/2" long (AR23)	400	600	900
Bus, No. 317, Double-Decker, "Chicago Motor Coach" stamp, 1936, 8-1/4" long (AR24)	400	675	950
Car Carrier, No. 238, Ford AA truck w/5" Ford Model A cars or three 6" Ford Model A cars, 1930, 24-1/2" long (AR26)	2000	3500	5000
Car Carrier, No. 296, Ford AA truck carries all options of 5" and 6" Ford Model A cars and trucks, 1932, 24-1/2" long (AR25)	2000	3500	5000
Car Transport, No. 2977, holds two sedans and two trucks, 1937, 11-1/2" long (AR28)	427	640	900

Arcade Manufacturing Company, left to right: International Stake Truck No. 3090, (AR128), 1936, $2300; International Stake Truck No. 7090, (AR130), 1941, $2100. Photo courtesy Bertoia Auctions

Arcade Manufacturing Company Mack High Dump, (AR141), 1931, $2300. Photo courtesy Bertoia Auctions

Arcade Manufacturing Company Ladder Truck, (AR132), 1936, $1000. Photo courtesy Bertoia Auctions

Arcade Manufacturing Company Austin Autocrat Road Roller, (AR10), 1928, $675. Photo courtesy David W. Mapes, Inc.

Left to right: Mack Ice Truck, Arcade, 1932, No. 257, 10-3/4" long, $4,000; Mack Ice Truck, Arcade, 1930, No. 257, $1,000.

Arcade Manufacturing Company Buick Opera Coupe, (AR21), 1927, $6250.

Arcade Manufacturing Company Austin Roll-A-Plane, (AR14), $1400. Photo courtesy Bertoia Auctions

Champion Panel Delivery, 7-3/4" long, $990. Photo courtesy Bill Bertoia Auctions

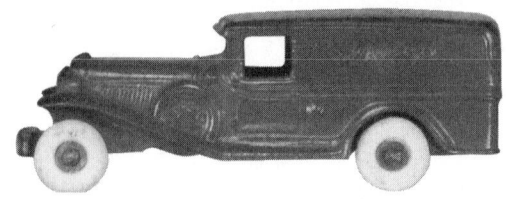

Century of Progress Bus, Arcade, 1933, No. 3220, $350.

Arcade Manufacturing Company Brinks Express Truck, 1932, 11-3/4" long, $20,000. Photo courtesy Bertoia Auctions

Arcade Manufacturing Company left to right: Chevrolet Sedan, (AR44A), $2200; Chevrolet Sedan, (AR44), $2200. Photo courtesy Bertoia Auctions

Arcade Manufacturing Company Chevrolet Superior Sedan, 1925, 7" long, $1050. Photo courtesy Bertoia Auctions

Arcade Manufacturing Company Checker Cab, No. 157, 1932, 9-1/4" long, $62,000. Photo courtesy Bertoia Auctions

Arcade Manufacturing Company (Continued)	C6	C8	C10
Car Transport, No. 3107, came w/two No. 1501 sedans, No. 1502 stake truck and No. 1503 wrecker, 1937, 18-1/2" long (AR27)	900	1350	1800
Carry Car Truck and Trailer Set, No. 2970, carries three Austins, 1934, 14-1/4" long (AR29)	650	1000	1650
Century of Progress Bus, No. 3210, 1933, 12" long (AR36)	200	325	450
Century of Progress Bus, No. 3220, 1933, 10-1/2" long (AR37)	175	275	425
Century of Progress Bus, No. 3230, 1933, 7-5/8" long (AR38)	100	175	250
Century of Progress Bus, No. 3250, 1933, 14-1/2" long (AR35)	250	375	525
Century of Progress Yellow Cab, 6-3/4" long (AR38B)	1000	2000	3200

Arcade Manufacturing Company (Continued)	C6	C8	C10
Checker Cab, No. 157, came w/and w/o "Checker" on visor, 1932, 9-1/4" long (AR40)	15,000	20,000	62,000
Chevrolet Coupe, No. 121X, 1929, 8-1/4" long (AR41)	700	1200	1800
Chevrolet Coupe, No. 1150X, rumble seat, 1934, 4-3/8" long (AR42)	150	250	350
Chevrolet Panel Delivery Truck, No. 2620X, 1936, 4" long (AR43)	125	175	275
Chevrolet Sedan, No. 122X, 1929, 8-1/4" long (AR44)	900	1500	2200
Chevrolet Sedan, No. 1170X, 1934, 4-1/4" long (AR45)	70	110	180
Chevrolet Stake Truck, 1925, 9" long (AR46)	950	1650	2500
Chevrolet Stake Truck, No. 2610, 1936, 4-1/4" long (AR47)	90	120	200

Arcade Manufacturing Company Chevrolet Coupe, No. 121X, 1929, 8-1/4" long, $1800. Photo courtesy Virginia Caputo

Arcade Manufacturing Company Chevrolet Utility Coupe, 1925, (AR51), $1950. Photo courtesy Bertoia Auctions

Arcade Manufacturing Company Coupe (AR60), $1750. Photo courtesy Bertoia Auctions

Arcade Manufacturing Company Century of Progress Yellow Taxi Cabs, 6-1/2" and 4-1/2" long. Photo courtesy John Innuzzi

Arcade, Fageol Bus, 1925, $800.

Arcade Manufacturing Company (Continued)	C6	C8	C10
Chevrolet Superior Roadster, 1925, 7" long (AR48)	1000	1700	2500
Chevrolet Superior Sedan, 1925, 7" long (AR49)	450	700	1050
Chevrolet Superior Touring Car, 1925, 7" long (AR50)	700	1250	2000
Chevrolet Utility Coupe, 1925, 7" long (AR51)	750	1300	1950
Chevrolet Wrecker Truck, No. 2630X, 1936, 4-1/4" long (AR52)	150	225	325
Chief Fire Chief Coupe, No. 1230, 1934, 6-3/4" long (AR53)	1500	2500	3500
Chief Fire Chief Coupe, No. 1240, 1934, 5" long (AR54)	500	800	1400
Coast to Coast GMC Transcontinental Bus, No. 4378X, 1937, 9" long (AR55)	200	325	475

Arcade Manufacturing Company (Continued)	C6	C8	C10
Coupe, "1922" on spare tire, 9" long (AR59)	1500	2500	4000
Coupe, No. 109, no Arcade markings, rumble seat opens, 1932, 6" long (AR61)	300	450	650
Coupe, no 1922 date on spare (AR60)	850	1250	1750
Deluxe Sedan, No. 1590X, same as Yellow Cab No. 1590Y, but w/top lights and sun roof ground off, 1941, 8-1/2" long (AR62)	500	825	1250
DeSoto Sedan, No. 1460X, 1936, 4" long (AR63)	150	225	325
Double Decker Bus, No. 3180, 1939, 8" long (AR64)	425	625	900
Dump Truck, No. 2320, 1936, 4-1/2" long (AR65)	90	130	200
Dump Truck, No. 3910X, 1941, 7" long (AR66)	300	450	600

Arcade Manufacturing Company Chevrolet Superior Touring Car, 1925, 7" long, $2000. Photo courtesy Bertoia Auctions

Arcade Manufacturing Company DeSoto Sedan, (AR63), 1936, $325. Photo courtesy Bertoia Auctions

Arcade Manufacturing Company Double Decker Bus, 1939, 8" long, $900. Photo courtesy Bertoia Auctions

Arcade Manufacturing Company Express Truck, (AR69), 1929, $1000. Photo courtesy Bertoia Auctions

Arcade Manufacturing Company Fire Engine, No. 6990, 1941, 13-1/2" long, $1650. Photo courtesy Bertoia Auctions

Arcade Manufacturing Company Fire Trailer Truck, No. 1940, 1934, 16-1/4" long, $1200. Photo courtesy Bertoia Auctions

Arcade Manufacturing Company Ford Dump Truck, No. 219X, 1929, 7-1/2" long, $700. Photo courtesy Bertoia Auctions

Fire Trailer Truck, Arcade, 1934, No. 1940, $1,200.

Arcade Manufacturing Company Ford Express Truck, (AR92), 1929, $2400. Photo courtesy Bertoia Auctions

Arcade Manufacturing Company Ford Model A Coupe, (AR162), 1928, $1400. Photo courtesy Bertoia Auctions

Arcade Manufacturing Company Ford Model T Coupe, (AR88), 1924, $750. Photo courtesy Bertoia Auctions

Arcade Manufacturing Company Greyhound Lines Great Lakes Exposition, No. 436, 1936, 6-3/4" long, $725. Photo courtesy John Gibson

Arcade Manufacturing Company (Continued)	C6	C8	C10
Dump Truck, driver, no cab, 1923, 7" long (AR68)	450	650	1000
Dump Truck Trailer, No. 234, 1931, 12-7/8" long (AR67)	850	1450	2250
Express Truck, No. 214X, 1929, 5" long (AR71)	150	250	400
Express Truck, No. 207X, 1929, 8" long (AR69)	450	650	1000
Express Truck, No. 209X, 1929, 6" long (AR70)	200	300	500
Fageol Bus, 1925, 12" long (AR72)	375	550	800
Fageol Bus, 5" long (AR74A)	80	150	300
Fageol Bus, 8" long (AR74)	325	525	750
Fire Chief Car, 1941, 5-5/8" long (AR78A)	160	300	450
Fire Engine, pumper, 1923, 7-1/2" long (AR79)	225	375	525
Fire Engine, No. 1740, pumper, 1936, 9" long (AR80)	475	775	1250
Fire Engine, No. 2340, 1936, 4-1/2" long (AR82)	90	150	250
Fire Engine, No. 6990, 1941, 13-1/2" long (AR83)	700	1150	1650
Fire Ladder Truck, No. 1820, 1936, 7" long (AR84)	200	300	450

Arcade Manufacturing Company (Continued)	C6	C8	C10
Fire Trailer Truck, No. 1940, 1934, 16-1/4" long (AR85)	600	900	1200
Ford Coupe, No. 1610X, rumble seat opens, 1934, 6-3/4" long (AR89)	200	350	500
Ford Dump Truck, No. 219X, 1929, 7-1/2" long (AR91)	285	425	700
Ford Express Truck, No. 210X, 1929, 8-1/4" long (AR92)	1000	1650	2400
Ford Model A Coupe, No. 106, rumble seat, 1928, 6-3/4" long (AR162)	550	950	1400
Ford Model A Coupe, No. 116X, rumble seat, 1928, 5" long (AR161)	300	450	550
Ford Model A Coupe, No. 113X, 1928, 4-1/8" long (AR163)	200	300	400
Ford Model A Fordor, No. 207, 1928, 6-3/4" long (AR164)	350	500	750
Ford Model A Tudor, No. 108, 1928, 6-3/4" long (AR165)	550	850	1200
Ford Model A Wrecker, No. 215, w/"weaver" host, 1929 (AR106)	550	850	1400
Ford Model A Wrecker, No. 218, 1930, 4-1/2" long)	125	200	300

Arcade Manufacturing Company, Color variations of the Greyhound Lines Bus, (AR113), 1937, $400. Photo courtesy Bertoia Auctions

Arcade Manufacturing Company International Delivery Truck, (AR119), 1936, $4200. Photo courtesy Bertoia Auctions

Arcade Manufacturing Company Greyhound Cruiser Coach Bus, No. 4400, 1941, 9-1/8" long, $450. Photo courtesy Sotheby's, New York

Arcade Manufacturing Company Ford Model T Touring Car Bank, (AR103), 1923, $2250. Photo courtesy Bertoia Auctions

Arcade Manufacturing Company (Continued)	C6	C8	C10
Ford Model T Coupe, 1923, 6" long (AR87)	175	300	450
Ford Model T Coupe, 1924, 6-1/2" long (AR88)	290	435	750
Ford Model T Fordor Sedan, removable chauffeur, 1924, 6-1/2" long (AR93)	250	350	650
Ford Model T Sedan, center door, 1923, 6-1/2" long (AR94)	325	490	650
Ford Model T Stake Truck, No. 2010X, 1934, 7" long (AR101)	300	600	950
Ford Model T Stake Truck, 1925, 8-3/4" long (AR99)	800	1100	1600
Ford Model T Stake Truck, 1927, 9" long (AR100)	750	1000	1750
Ford Model T Stake Truck, 1927, 5-3/4" long (AR167)	175	250	350
Ford Model T Touring Car, 1923, 6-1/2" long (AR102)	450	650	900
Ford Model T Touring Car Bank, 1923, 6-1/2" long (AR103)	1000	1500	2250

Arcade Manufacturing Company (Continued)	C6	C8	C10
Ford Model T Tudor, No. 118, 1928, 5" long)	350	550	700
Ford Model T Wrecker, 1927, 11" long (AR168)	700	1200	2000
Ford Sedan, No. 1620X, 1933, 6-7/8" long (AR95)	350	600	850
Ford Sedan, "Century of Progress", 1934, 6-7/8" long (AR96)	900	1500	2500
Ford Sedan, "Century of Progress", 1934, 4-3/4" long (AR97A)	200	600	900
Ford Sedan with Trailer, No. 1970, "Covered Wagon", 1937, 12" long, trailer 5-1/2" long (AR98)	650	1200	1700
Ford Truck, cab, one ton, 1923, 8-1/2" long (AR105)	800	1000	1700
Ford Tudor, 1937, 5-1/4" long)	550	950	1500
Greyhound Cruiser Coach Bus, No. 4400, 1941, 9-1/8" long (AR112)	200	325	450
Greyhound Lines Bus, No. 3850 SP, 1937, 7-3/4" long (AR113)	175	275	400
Greyhound Lines Bus, GMC, one-piece casting, 1933, 6")	100	200	300

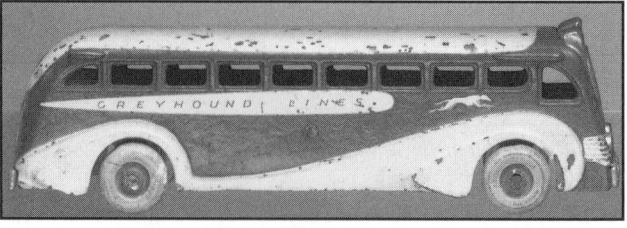

Greyhound Super Coach, Arcade, 1937, No. 4380, $750.

Arcade Manufacturing Company Ice Truck, (AR117), 1941, $575. Photo courtesy Bertoia Auctions

Arcade Manufacturing Company Ford Model T Touring Car, 1923, 6-1/2" long, $900. Photo courtesy Bertoia Auctions

Arcade Manufacturing Company Ford Model T Fordor Sedan, 1924, 6-1/2" long, $650. Photo courtesy Bertoia Auctions

Arcade Manufacturing Company (Continued)

	C6	C8	C10
Greyhound Lines Great Lakes Exposition, No. 437, 1936, 11" long (AR114)	450	700	1000
Greyhound Lines Great Lakes Exposition, No. 436, 1936, 6-3/4" long (AR115)	350	475	725
Greyhound Super Coach, No. 4380, 1937, 9" long (AR116)	275	425	600
Ice Truck, No. 1933, circa 1941, 6-3/4" long (AR117)	275	375	575
International Delivery Truck, No. 3020, 1936, 9-1/2" long (AR119)	1800	2900	4200
International Delivery Truck, No. 226, 1932, 9-3/4" long (AR118)	500	800	1300
International Dump Truck, No. 7100, 1941, 11-1/8" long (AR124)	600	900	1400
International Dump Truck, No. 236-0, 1931, 10-3/4" long (AR120)	750	1200	1800
International Dump Truck, No. 3710, 1937, 9-1/2" long (AR122)	450	700	1000
International Dump Truck, No. 3030, 1936, 10-1/2" long (AR121)	1000	1600	2350

Arcade Manufacturing Company (Continued)

	C6	C8	C10
International Dump Truck, No. 1670, chassis and dump box are steel, 1940, 11-5/8" long (AR123)	650	1000	1650
International Pickup Truck, No. 7000, 1941, 9-1/2" long (AR126)	500	750	1100
International Stake Truck, No. 237-0, 1931, 12" long (AR127)	700	1100	1700
International Stake Truck, No. 3090, 1936, 12" long (AR128)	900	1500	2300
International Stake Truck, No. 2600, 1937, 9-1/2" long (AR129)	850	1450	2800
International Stake Truck, No. 7090, 1941, 11-1/2" long (AR130)	950	1450	2100
International Wrecker, No. 1650, wrecker crane body and crane are steel, 1940, 13" long (AR131)	500	800	1200
Ladder Truck, No. 1700, w/ladders, 1936, 12-1/2" long (AR132)	475	725	1000
Ladder Truck, No. 2350, 1936, 4-3/4" long (AR133)	90	150	200
Mack Bus, No. 318, 1929, 13-1/4" long (AR134)	950	1500	3000

Buddy "L" No. 5429, Merry-Go-Round. Courtesy Thomas G. Nefos, Federal Shipping Network

Riding Academy, No. 5455 Truck, with three horses, Buddy "L," $300.

Mister Buddy Ice Cream Van, 1964-65, Buddy "L," $275.

Buddy "L," No. 711, "Scarab." Courtesy Heinz Mueller, Continental Hobby House. (Bumpers missing in photo.)

Arcade Manufacturing Company (Continued)	C6	C8	C10
Mack Cement Mixer, drum revolves, 1931, 6-11/16" long (AR135)	700	900	1200
Mack Chemical Truck, fire ladder truck, 1929, 15" long (AR137)	800	1500	2000
Mack Chemical Truck, No. 245R, fire engine, has ladders, 1928, 15" long (AR136)	2000	3500	5500
Mack Chemical Truck, fire engine w/ladders, 1929, 10" long (AR138)	425	625	1000
Mack Dump Truck, 1925, 12" long (AR139)	1400	2400	3400
Mack Dump Truck, No. 248X, 1929, 8-1/2" long (AR140)	600	950	1600
Mack Fire Apparatus Truck, No. 242, ladder truck, 1929, 21" long (AR143)	850	1200	1600
Mack High Dump Truck, No. 244X, 1931, 10" long (AR141)	900	1600	2300
Mack High Dump Truck, No. 259X, 1931, 8-1/2" long (AR142)	700	1150	1700

Arcade Manufacturing Company (Continued)	C6	C8	C10
Mack Hoist Truck, No. 198, 1932, body 8" long (AR144)	900	1500	2200
Mack Ice Truck, No. 257, w/driver, glass "ice" and tongs, 1930, 10-5/8" long (AR145)	375	600	1200
Mack Ice Truck, No. 226, 1931, 8-1/2" long (AR146)	450	675	950
Mack Ice Truck, No. 257, w/driver, glass "ice" and tongs, 1932, 10-3/4" long (AR147)	1600	2800	4200
Mack Side Dump Truck, No. 1960, 1932, 9" long (AR148)	1200	2000	2800
Mack Stake Truck, No. 246X, 1929, 12" long (AR149)	1100	1900	2800
Mack Stake Truck, No. 253, 1929, 8-3/4" long (AR150)	950	1500	2250
Mack Tank Truck, No. 241, sheet metal tank, marked "Gasoline" and "Mack", 1930, 13" long (AR154)	1100	1900	2800
Mack Tank Truck, "American Gasoline", 1925, 13-1/4" long (AR152)	1200	1850	2800

Arcade Manufacturing Company International Delivery Truck, No. 226, 1932, 9-3/4" long, $1300. Photo courtesy Bertoia Auctions

Arcade Manufacturing Company International Dump Truck, (AR122), 1937, $1000. Photo courtesy Bertoia Auctions

Arcade Manufacturing Company International Stake Truck, (AR129), 1937, $2800. Photo courtesy Bertoia Auctions

Arcade Manufacturing Company International Dump Truck, No. 1670, 1940, 11-5/8" long, $1650. Photo courtesy Tim Oei

Arcade Manufacturing Company (Continued)	C6	C8	C10
Mack Tank Truck, "Lubrite", 1925, 13-1/4" long (AR153)	1200	1800	2800
Mack Tank Truck, 1925, 13-1/4" long (AR151)	1000	1600	2800
Mack Wrecker, No. 255, 1930, 12-1/2" long (AR155)	1900	3200	4700
Mullins Red Cap Auto Trailer)	225	338	450
Nash Coupe, 1934, 4-1/2" long)	250	400	650
Nash Panel Delivery, 1934, 4")	150	250	400
Nash Wrecker, 1936, 4-1/2" long (AR169)	225	400	575
National Trailways Bus, No. 3870, 1937, 9-1/4" long (AR170)	750	1300	1800
New York World's Fair Bus, No. 3750, 1939, 7" long (AR173)	150	200	325
New York World's Fair Bus, No. 3770, 1939, 8-1/2" long (AR172)	300	450	675
New York World's Fair Bus, No. 3780, 1939, 10-1/2" long (AR171)	450	650	950

Arcade Manufacturing Company (Continued)	C6	C8	C10
New York World's Fair Tractor-Train, No. 7290, w/three cars, 1939 (AR175)	450	675	900
New York World's Fair Tractor-Train, No. 7270, tractor and one car, 1939, tractor 3-1/4" long, car 4-1/4" long (AR174)	200	350	525
Pierce Silver Arrow, 1934, 7-1/4" long)	300	450	750
Plymouth Coupe, No. 1340, 1933, 4-3/4" long (AR181)	400	800	1100
Plymouth Sedan, No. 1330, 1933, 4-3/4" long (AR182)	350	550	775
Plymouth Stake Truck, No. 1840, 1933, 4-3/4" long (AR183)	250	325	450
Plymouth Wrecker, No. 1830, 1933, 4-3/4" long (AR184)	175	250	350
Pontiac Sedan, 1935, 6-1/2" long (AR186)	350	525	800

Arcade Manufacturing Company Mack Tank Truck, 1925, 13-1/4" long, $2800. Photo courtesy Bertoia Auctions

Arcade Manufacturing Company Mack Chemical Truck, (AR136), 1928, $5500. Photo courtesy Bertoia Auctions

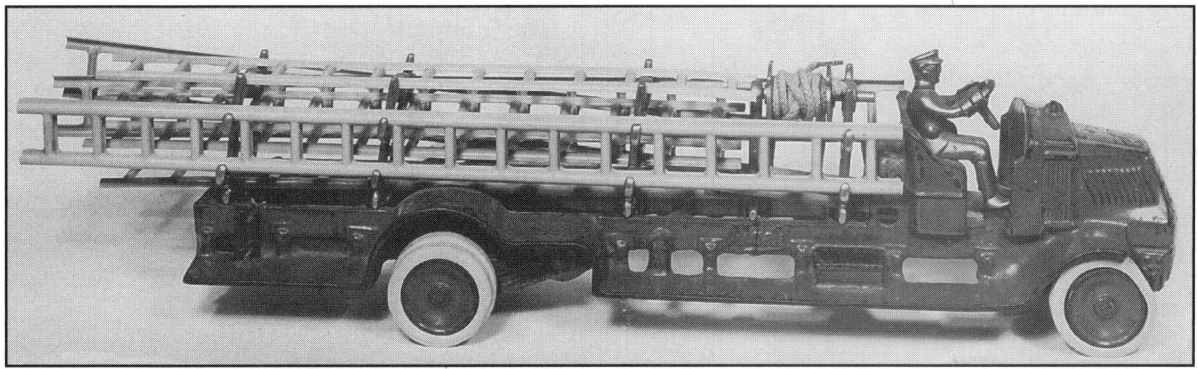

Mack Fire Apparatus Ladder Truck, Arcade, 1929, No. 242, $2,000.

Arcade Manufacturing Company (Continued)	C6	C8	C10
Pontiac Sedan, No. 1350, 1935, 4-1/4" long (AR185)	150	250	375
Pontiac Stake Truck, No. 2390, 1935, 6-1/4" long (AR187)	300	450	650
Pontiac Stake Truck, No. 2780, 1936, 4-1/4" long (AR188)	150	250	350
Pontiac Wrecker, No. 2000, 1936, 4-1/4" long (AR189)	125	188	250
Racer, No. 1457, 1937, 5-3/4" long (AR196)	100	150	225
Racer, pre-1923, 7-3/4" long (AR190)	400	600	850
Racer, No. 140, plastic or celluloid windshield, 1932, 10-1/2" long (AR193)	4000	9000	11,500
Racer, No. 137, 1932, 5-5/8" long (AR194)	120	180	240
Racer, No. 138, 1931, 6-3/4" long (AR192)	200	300	450
Racer, No. 139, Bullet Racer, 1931, 7-5/8" long (AR191)	950	1500	2300
Red Baby Dump Truck, No. 2, 1923, 10-3/4" long (AR197)	600	900	1500

Arcade Manufacturing Company (Continued)	C6	C8	C10
Red Baby Dump Truck, No. 1, 1923, 10-3/4" long (AR198)	600	900	1500
Red Baby Weaver Wrecker, 1929, 12" long (AR199)	900	1500	2300
Reo Coupe, 1931, 7-1/2" (AR201)	1000	1700	3000
Reo Coupe, No. 1247, 1932, 9-3/8" long (AR200)	1000	2000	3000
Sand Loading Shovel, No. 298 later No. 299, 1932 (AR202)	500	800	1250
Scraper, No. 287, 1929, 8-1/4" long (AR203)	50	100	200
Sedan, No. 1501X, 1937, 4-3/4" long (AR204)	90	150	200
Sedan and Trailer, No. 1497X, 1937, car 5-5/8" long, trailer 2-1/2" long (AR205)	300	500	900
Side Dump Trailer, No. 290, fastens to trucks or tractors, 1932, 7" long (AR206)	100	200	350
Stake Trailer Truck, No. 233, 1931, 11-5/16" long (AR208)	325	550	750
Stake Truck, No. 208, no Arcade markings, 1932, 6" long (AR211)	300	500	750

Mack Tank Truck, Arcade, 1925, 13-1/4" long, $2,800.

Arcade Manufacturing Company Reo Coupe, No. 1247, 1932, 9-3/8" long, $3000. Photo courtesy Harris Auctions

A.C. Williams Racer, $525. Photo courtesy Bertoia Auctions

Arcade Manufacturing Company Red Baby Weaver Wrecker, 1929, 12" long, $2300. Photo courtesy Bertoia Auctions

Arcade Manufacturing Company (Continued)	C6	C8	C10
Stake Truck, No. 1502, 1937, 4-1/4" long (AR212)	125	200	300
Stake Truck, No. 213, 1929, 5" long (AR210)	125	200	300
Stake Truck, No. 208X, 1929, 6" long (AR209)	220	330	475
Steam Shovel, No. 292, Industrial Derrick, 1932, body 6" long (AR213)	750	1125	1600
Tandem Disc Harrow, No. 704, 1939, 6-3/4" long (AR214)	60	90	150
Tank, No. 400, Army, 1937, 8" long (AR215)	600	950	1500
Tank, No. 3960, shoots, 1941, 4" long (AR216)	200	300	450
Texas Centennial Bus, 1936, 10-3/4" long (AR217)	1500	2500	4000
Transport Trailer Truck, No. 1800, 1934, 7-1/2" long (AR232)	385	580	770
Two-Wheeled Jack, No. 216, 1932, 5-1/2" long (AR234)	50	100	150
W&K Truck Trailer, 1923, 8-1/2" long (AR233)	100	150	225

Arcade Manufacturing Company (Continued)	C6	C8	C10
White Bus, No. 319, 1928, 13-1/4" long (AR235)	2800	5500	7750
White Delivery Truck, No. 252X, 1929, 8-1/4" long (AR236)	2000	3800	6250
White Dump Truck, No. 249, 1929, 11-1/2" long (AR238)	8000	15,000	23,000
White Moving Van, No. 251, 1929, 13-1/2" long (AR237)	4000	9000	13,000
White Tank Truck, No. 254, "Gasoline", 1931, 14-1/8" long (AR240)	1000	1500	2200
Wrecker, No. 217, 1929, body 8" long (AR241)	450	700	1100
Wrecker, No. 225, no Arcade markings, 1932 (AR242)	500	850	1350
Wrecker, No. 2020, 1934, 7" long (AR243)	600	950	1500
Wrecker, No. 1493, 1937, 6-1/2" long (AR244)	150	250	350
Wrecker, No. 1503, 1937, 4-3/4" long (AR245)	100	150	200
Wrecker, No. 3900, 1941, 8-1/2" long (AR246)	90	135	200

Arcade Manufacturing Company National Trailways Bus, No. 3870, 1937, 9-1/4" long, $1800. Photo courtesy Bob Smith

Arcade Manufacturing Company Red Baby Dump Truck, No. 2, 1923, 10-3/4" long, $1500.

Arcade Manufacturing Company Yellow Cab Bank, 1923, 8" long, $1500. Photo courtesy Bertoia Auctions

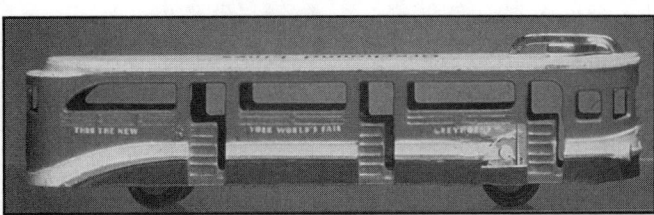

New York World's Fair Bus, Arcade, 1939, No. 3780, $900.

Left to right: Stake Truck, Arcade, 1929, No. 213, $325; International Dump Truck, Arcade, 1931, No. 236-0, $1,750.

Arcade, "Yellow Cab," 9" long, c. 1928. Courtesy Mapes Auctioneers & Apprasiers

Arcade Manufacturing Company Yellow Cab, (AR256), 1941, $600. Photo courtesy Sotheby's, New York

Arcade Manufacturing Company Austin Wrecker, No. 177X, 1932, 3-3/4" long, $300.

Arcade Manufacturing Company Yellow Cab Panel Delivery Truck, (AR259), 1925, $2700. Photo courtesy Bertoia Auctions

Arcade Manufacturing Company Yellow Cab, (AR258), 1927, $9200. Photo courtesy Bertoia Auctions

Arcade Manufacturing Company White Bus, No. 319, 1928, 13-1/4" long, $7750. Photo courtesy Bertoia Auctions

Arcade Manufacturing Company Yellow Coach Double-Decker Bus, (AR260), 1925, $4800. Photo courtesy Bertoia Auctions

Auburn Rubber, A pair of 1937 International Cab-over trucks, $45 each.

Arcade Manufacturing Company Yellow Parlor Coach Bus variation as a Pennsylvania Rapid Transit, (AR261), 1926, $3000. Photo courtesy Bertoia Auctions

Arcade Manufacturing Company Yellow Parlow Coach, (AR262), 1926, $750. Photo courtesy Sotheby's, New York

Arcade Manufacturing Company (Continued)	C6	C8	C10
Yellow Baby Dump Truck, 1923, 10-1/2" long (AR246A)	600	1050	1650
Yellow Baby Wrecker, 1929, 12" long (AR247)	650	1100	1600
Yellow Cab, No. 1580Y, 1936, 8-1/4" long (AR255)	1700	2800	4250
Yellow Cab, No. 1590Y, 1941, 8-1/2" long (AR256)	225	300	600
Yellow Cab, No. 1350, 1935, 4-1/4" long)	200	300	450
Yellow Cab, No. 1, 1927, 9" long (AR248)	600	900	1500
Yellow Cab, No. 2, 1922, 8" long (AR249)	500	800	1200
Yellow Cab, No. 2, 1925, 8" long (AR252)	600	900	1400
Yellow Cab, No. 3, 1925, 5-1/4" long (AR253)	500	800	1200

Arcade Manufacturing Company (Continued)	C6	C8	C10
Yellow Cab, No. 5, 1927, 8-1/2" long (AR251)	500	800	1000
Yellow Cab, Ford Sedan, 1934, 6-7/8" long (AR254)	1300	2000	3000
Yellow Cab Bank, 1923, 8" long (AR257)	700	1100	1500
Yellow Cab Bank, "Flat Top", 1927 (AR258)	1800	4500	9200
Yellow Cab Panel Delivery Truck, w/driver, 1925, 8-1/4" long (AR259)	1000	1700	2700
Yellow Coach Double-Decker Bus, 1925, 14" long (AR260)	1750	3250	4800
Yellow Parlor Coach Bus, 1926, 9-1/2" long (AR262)	325	550	750
Yellow Parlor Coach Bus, 1926, 13" long (AR261)	800	1400	2200

Arcade Manufacturing Company Yellow Cab, No. 1, 1927, 9" long, $1500. Photo courtesy Sotheby's, New York

Auburn Rubber 1936 Cord, (AA01), $150. Photo courtesy Max Heiss

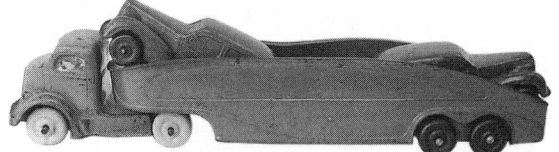

Auburn AT14. Photo by Dave Leopard.

Auburn Rubber '37 Olds, 4-1/2" long, $50. Photo courtesy Dave Leopard's book, Rubber Toy Vehicles

Auburn Rubber

For more than twenty years, American kids and moms loved rubber toys—children thought they were fun, and moms liked the fact that these toys wouldn't scratch furniture and floors. Then, almost as suddenly as they appeared on the market, the toys disappeared.

The Auburn Rubber Company of Auburn, Indiana, was not the first to introduce rubber toys to the American market, but it was no doubt the largest and had the greatest impact on the toy market. After producing toy soldiers in 1935, Auburn introduced its first vehicle in 1936—a beautiful coffin-nosed Cord sedan. Today, the Auburn Cord is one of the most prized rubber toys and is seldom seen for sale.

Auburn followed the Cord with a wealth of vehicles, including trucks, farm tractors and implements, motorcycles, racers, fire engines, military vehicles, aircraft, ships, and trains. The following listing consists of approximately ninety varieties of Auburn Rubber vehicles.

According to catalogs, 1952 was the final year Auburn rubber exclusively marketed rubber vehicles. By 1955, Auburn's line was mostly vinyl with a few rubber toys left in the line. What appears to be the last rubber toys to be marketed by Auburn were two fore engines shown in the 1956 catalog.

Auburn continued in the toy business in Auburn, Indiana, and later, Deming, New Mexico, until going out of business in 1969.

Note: The numbers in parenthesis coincide with the numbers in Dave Leopard's book, Rubber Toy Vehicles.

Contributor: Dave Leopard, 2507 Feather Run Trail, West Columbia, SC 29169-4915. Leopard, a retired United States Air Force Colonel now employed by the state of South Carolina, is a collector of small, American-made toy cars and trucks. He is considered an expert on the subject of rubber toys and self-published Rubber Toy Vehicles, a definitive work in this field.

Auburn Rubber	C6	C8	C10
'35 Ford, two-door slantback sedan, 4" long, (AA09)	27	41	55
'35 Ford Coupe, 4" long, (AA08)	27	41	55
'36 Cord, four-door coffin-nose sedan, w/rounded bumper, minor variations, 6" long	25	35	50
'36 Cord, four-door coffin-nose sedan, 6" long, (AA01)	65	100	150
'37 International Cabover Stake Truck, "US Army" decal, khaki, 5-3/8" long, (AT01A)	30	40	55
'37 International Cabover Stake Truck, 3-3/4" long, (AT05)	20	30	40
'37 International Cabover Stake Truck, 4-1/4" long, (AT03)	20	30	40
'37 International Cabover Stake Truck, 5-3/8" long, (AT01)	22	55	45
'37 International Cabover Stake Truck, milk version, 4-1/4" long, (AT07)	60	80	100

Auburn Rubber (Continued)

	C6	C8	C10
'37 International Cabover Stake Truck, khaki, w/rounded bumper, minor variations, 4-1/4" long, (AT04) 20	30	40	
'37 International Cabover Stake Truck, khaki, 4-1/4" long, (AT03A) 20	30	40	
'37 Olds, four-door sedan, 4-1/2" long, (AA02) 25	35	50	
'38 GMC Cab/Open Squared-off Trailer, 9" long, (AT15) 42	63	85	
'38 GMC Carry Car Auto Transport, 11-1/2" long, (AT14) 50	70	110	
'38 Olds, four-door sedan, 5-3/4" long, (AA03) 30	50	70	
'39 Plymouth, two-door trunk back sedan, 4-1/4" long, (AA12) 25	35	50	
'40 Olds, four-door sedan, fender skirts, 6" long, (AA05) 25	38	50	
'40 Olds, four-door sedan, open fenders, 6" long, (AA04)	27	41	59
'46 Lincoln convertible, two-door, round headlights, 4-1/2" long, (AA13)	20	30	40
'46 Lincoln convertible, two-door square headlights, 4-1/2" long, (AA13)	20	30	40
'47 Chevy Cab Forward Box Truck, 5-3/4" long, (AT11)	22	33	45
'48 Buick, two-door sedanette, fastback, 7-1/4" long, (AA06)	40	70	100
'50 Cadillac, four-door sedan, 7-1/4" long, (AA10)	40	60	100
'50 Pickup Truck, open fenders, 4-1/2" long, (AT12c)	20	30	40
'50 Pickup Truck, fender skirts, 4-1/2" long, (AT13c)	20	30	40
Ahrens-Fox Fire Engine, 5-1/2" long, (AE01)	75	112	150
Cab-Forward Box Truck, smooth sides, futuristic, 5-1/2" long, (AT09)	22	33	45
Cabover Box Truck, smooth sides, futuristic, 4-1/8" long, (AT10)	20	30	40
Carry Car Transport (Updated), cab changed, trailer same, 11-3/4" long, (AT16)	45	65	95
Fire Engine, hose and ladders, c. 1940s, 7-3/4" long, (AE02)	27	41	55
Fire Engine, ladders, no hose, c. 1940s, 7-3/4" long, (AE04)	27	41	55
Late 40s Futuristic Sedan, fin down back, 5" long, (AA15)	20	30	40

Auburn Rubber (Continued)

	C6	C8	C10
Open Racer, short, boattail, 6-1/2" long, (AR04)	30	45	60
Open Racer, V-6, low fin, 10-1/2" long, (AR02)	45	65	85
Open Racer, V-6, high fin, 10-1/2" long, (AR01)	55	82	110
Open Racer, short, tapered tail, large tires, 10-1/2" long, (AR03)	40	60	80
Open Racer, no fenders, low fin, long back, 5-1/4" long, (AR08)	20	30	40
Open Racer, boattail, no side pipes, 4-3/4" long, (AR09)	25	35	50
Open Racer, boattail, 4-3/4" long, (AR05)	30	45	60
Open Racer, small fin, 6-1/4" long, (AR06)	30	45	60
Pumper, boiler, c. 1940s, 7-3/4" long, (AE03)	27	41	55
Side-Cutter Sickle Bar Mower, David Bradley, 3-3/4" long, (AI07)	20	30	40
Tank, Marmon-Harrington, 3-1/4" long, (AM02)	20	30	40
Tank, Marmon-Harrington, 4-1/2" long, (AM01)	25	35	50
Trailer, two wheel, Graham-Bradley, 5-3/4" long, (AI01)	22	33	45
Trailer, four wheel, Graham-Bradley, 4-3/4" long, (AI02)	22	33	45

Banner

Emanuel M. Pressner and Bernard Schiller founded banner in 1944. Pressner had been a toy importer, and in 1938, he bought interest in Columbia Protektosite, which cast Beton's plastic toy soldiers. Schiller was eventually edged out.

In 1950, Banner moved from 150 Buckner Blvd., Bronx, New York, to 80 Beckwith Ave., Paterson, New Jersey, where it remained.

Banner manufactured small plastic cars and trucks and specialized in plastic tea sets and metallic plastic forks, knives, and spoons. Banner used "off-falls"—blanks formed when holes were cut in steel for car windows and television tubes—to produce their stamped-steel toys.

The company, which at its peak had up to 200 employees, went into Chapter 11 bankruptcy in 1965. They rebounded for a few years, only to sold in 1967 to Tal-Cap, a toy conglomerate in Minnesota.

Contributor: John Taylor, P.O. Box 63, Nolensville, TN 37135-0063.

Banner

	C6	C8	C10
Aeriel Ladder Fire Truck, No. 1143, pressed metal wheels, 20" Long..	125	175	250

Auburn Rubber '38 GMC Cab/Open Squared-off Trailer, 9" long, $85. Photo courtesy Dave Leopard's book, Rubber Toy Vehicles

Auburn Rubber 1948 Buick, 7-1/4" long, $100. Photo courtesy Dave Loepard's book, Rubber Toy Vehicles

Auburn Rubber Cabover Box Truck, futuristic, $40. Photo courtesy Dave Leopard's book, Rubber Toy Vehicles

Banner (Continued)	C6	C8	C10
American Express Truck, tin, 11-1/2" long	150	225	300
American Express Truck, tin, 10" long	75	150	225
American Express Van	50	75	100
Army Ambulance, tin and plastic, 6" long	12	25	40
Auto Transport, wooden wheels, 1940s, 16" long	100	175	250
Car Transport, w/two cars, lithographed trailer, 16" long	125	200	275
Carnation Milk Van	163	245	325
Circus Train, pulled by tractor, 1949	NPF	NPF	NPF
Cross Country Express, rubber tires, late 1940s-early 1950s, 12" long	125	200	275
Dodge, plastic, 1950, 4" long	8	15	25
Dump Truck, plastic, 5-1/4" long	10	15	20
Fair Lawn Dairy Truck, pressed metal wheels, 1940, 11-1/2" long	125	175	250
Garbage Truck, plastic, Ford, 1954, 4" long	8	15	30

Banner (Continued)	C6	C8	C10
Grocery Service Truck, pressed metal wheels, 13" long	125	200	275
Hi-Way Emergency Truck, w/tools and two spare tires, 1940, 12" long	150	225	325
International Harvester Metro 1950 Van, plastic, 4" long	8	12	25
Jewel Tea Van	175	275	375
Kellog's Express Truck, six wheels, pressed metal wheels, dual metal axles, 1940, 13" long	250	400	550
LaFrance Fire Truck, plastic, 1950, 4" long	8	12	25
North American Van Lines Truck and Trailer, 15" long	100	175	225
Sand and Gravel Dump Truck, No. 1142, pressed metal wheels, red cab and frame, "Sand-Gravel-" litho on sides of dump, 13" long	100	175	225
Service Station, cardboard, w/three plastic trucks, c. late 1940s-early 1950s	22	35	50
Side Dump Truck, plastic, 1950s, 5-1/4" long	10	20	30
Stake Truck, plastic, GMC, 4" long	12	18	25

Auburn Rubber, three versions of the 1937 International Cabover Stake truck, $45 each. Photo courtesy Dave Leopard from his book, Rubber Toy Vehicles.

Auburn Rubber '37 International Cabover Stake Truck, 4-1/4" long, $100. Photo courtesy Dave Leopard's book, Rubber Toy Vehicles

Auburn Rubber, left to right: 1940 Oldsmobile, (AA05), $50; 1940 Oldsmobile, (AA04), $60.

'38 Olds, four-door sedan, Auburn Rubber, $60, Photo from Rubber Toy Vehicles *by Dave Leopard*

Auburn Rubber '50 Cadillac, 7-1/4" long, $100. Photo courtesy Dave Leopard's book, Rubber Toy Vehicles

Auburn Rubber '47 Chevy Cab Forward Box Truck, 5-3/4" long, $45. Photo courtesy Dave Leopard's Rubber Toy Vehicles

Auburn Rubber, left to right: 1946 Lincoln Continental w/square headlights, $40; 1946 Lincoln Continental w/round headlights, $40

Pumper, c. 1940s, Boiler, Auburn Rubber, $55. Photo from Rubber Toy Vehicles *by Dave Leopard*

Auburn Rubber '39 Plymouth, 4-1/4" long, $50. Photo courtesy Dave Leopard's book, Rubber Toy Vehicles

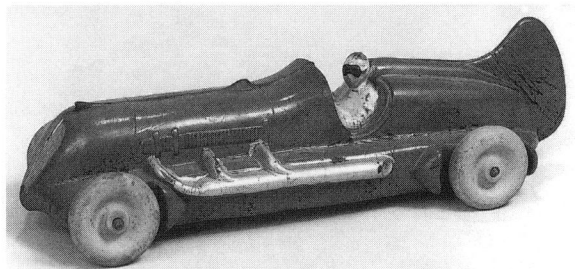

Auburn Rubber Open Racer, 10-1/2" long, $110. Photo courtesy Dave Leopard's book, Rubber Toy Vehicles

Auburn Rubber Cab-Forward Box Truck, 5-1/2" long, $45. Photo courtesy Dave Leopard's book, Rubber Toy Vehicles

Auburn Rubber Trailer, 4-3/4" long, $45. Photo courtesy Dave Leopard's book, Rubber Toy Vehicles

Banner (Continued)	C6	C8	C10
Station Wagon, plastic, Oldsmobile, 1948, 4" long	16	24	32
Tanker, plastic, 7" long	15	22	30
Toy Truck Van, 9" long	75	112	150
Tractor, plastic, wheelhorse, 3" long	14	21	28
Trailer Steamshovel, 6-3/4" long	15	25	35
Wonder Bread Truck, tin litho, c. 1950s, 11" long	75	125	175
Wonder Bread Truck, tin lithographed, 11" long	75	125	175

Barclay

Barclay, named after Barclay Street in West Hoboken, New Jersey, began in 1924 or late 1923, and was owned by partners Leon Donze (1865-1950) and by Michael Levy (c.1895-1964). In 1929, Levy took over the company and turned it into a major toy manufacturer. Under his guidance it grew from five employees to a prewar peak of 400 workers and moved several times to increasingly larger quarters.

While known for its toy soldiers, Barclay was the largest producer of lead-alloy vehicles in the 1930s and early 1940s. The most popular vehicle was the No. 53 racer.

World War II was a difficult time for all toy manufacturers and Barclay was no exception. Forced to lay off all but four of its employees, Barclay moved in the direction of subcontract work. Unfortunately, the firm was never able to regain its prewar success and closed its doors in 1971.

Barclay Vehicles	C6	C8	C10
Ambulance, No. 194, small cross, 3-1/2" long (BV1)	26	39	52
Ambulance, No. 50, 5" long (BV3).	55	82	110
Ambulance, No. 194, large cross, 3-1/2" long (BV2)	20	30	40
Anti-Aircraft Gun Truck, No. 48, one man, 4" long (BV19)	22	33	45
Anti-Aircraft Gun Truck, No. 48, two men, 4" long (BV20)	16	24	32
Anti-Aircraft Gun Truck, No. 198, shown in 1931 Barclay catalog, 3-1/8" long (BV16)	20	30	40
Armored Army Truck, No. 152, 2-7/8" long (BV6)	8	13	17
Army Oil Truck, c. 1968, approx. 2" long (BV106)	9	13	18
Army Tank Truck, No. 197, c. 1935-36, 3-1/8" long (BV7)	11	16	22
Army Tractor, (Minneapolis-Moline "Jeep"), 2-3/4" long (BV9)	14	21	28
Army Truck, open bed, c. 1968, approx. 2" long (BV105)	7	11	15
Army Truck with Anti-Aircraft Gun, No. 151, 2-1/2" long (BV5)	10	15	21

Banner Grocery Service Truck, 13" long, $275. Photo courtesy Bob Smith

Banner Aerial Ladder Fire Truck, 20" long, $250. Photo courtesy John Taylor

Banner Hi-Way Emergency Truck, 12" long, $325. Photo courtesy John Taylor

Barclay Vehicles (Continued)

	C6	C8	C10
Army Truck with Gun, No. 151, 2-3/4" long (BV4)	13	19	27
Auburn Speeder, No. 58, c. 1931 (BV139)	17	26	35
Austin Coupe, No. 43, c. 1931, 2" long (BV10)	30	45	60
Auto Transport Set, No. 330, two 1950s cars, 4-1/2" long (BV11)	36	55	73
Beer Truck, No. 376, w/wood barrels, c. 1940, 4" long (BV12)	27	41	55
Beer Truck, No. 377, w/barrels (BV13)	35	52	70
Buick Sedan, 1929, 3" long (BV118)	27	41	55
Build and Paint Set, No. 2004, truck, coupe, sedan, parts, paints, early (BV90)	180	270	360
Bus, futuristic, "Made in U.S.A.", 3" long (BV14)	34	51	68
Bus, Coast to Coast, No. 405, two-piece, "Barclay Toy", 2-7/8" long (BV24)	42	63	85
Cannon Car, battery-powered headlight, first appeared in 1935 catalog, 3-1/2" long (BV18)	80	130	225
Cannon Car, gunner low, 3-5/16" long (BV15)	13	21	27
Cannon Car, slight casting differences from headlight version, 3-1/4" long (BV17)	19	28	38

Barclay Vehicles (Continued)

	C6	C8	C10
Cannon Truck, moveable cannon, 4" long (BV83)	37	56	75
Cannon Truck, w/moveable cannon, 4" long (BV21)	20	30	40
Car Carrier, two small cars, early 1930s (BV114)	25	38	50
Chief Police Car, approx. 2" long (BV97)	5	8	10
Chrysler Airflow, c. 1936, 4" long (BV23)	30	45	60
Chrysler Airflow Sedan, No. 1703, large, 1935 (BV127)	17	26	35
Convertible, w/vacationers (BV88)	50	75	100
Cord Front Drive Coupe, No. 40, c. 1931, 3-5/8" long (BV31)	25	38	50
Coupe, removable spare tire, 1935, 4-1/2" long (BV146)	30	45	60
Coupe, 1934, 4-1/4" long (BV27)	40	60	80
Coupe, two-piece, "Barclay Toy", 1930s, 2-7/8" long (BV28)	42	63	85
Coupe, No. 361, Streamline (BV112)	17	26	35
Coupe, No. 301, Streamline, 3-1/4" long (BV123)	50	75	100
Coupe, "Made in U.S.A.", 1930s, 3" long (BV25)	12	18	25
Coupe, c. 1935, 2-1/2" long (BV26)	50	75	100
Coupe, No. 51, c. 1931, 2-3/16" long (BV132)	17	26	35
Coupe, 200 series (?), cast rear tire, c. 1935, 3-1/8" long (BV145)	21	31	42

Banner Trailer Steamshovel, 6-3/4" long, $35.

Barclay Vehicles Streamline Sedan, No. 302, c. 1936, 3-1/8" long, $50.

Barclay Vehicles Coupe, 1930s, 3" long, $25.

Barclay Vehicles (Continued)	C6	C8	C10
Delivery Truck, No. 206, "Bakery Fine Cake Pies", c. 1934, 3-1/8" long (BV131)	70	105	140
Delivery Truck, No. 309, 2-15/16" long (BV33)	15	23	30
Delivery Truck, No. 309, c. 1936, 3-1/2" long (BV136)	12	18	25
DeSoto Airflow, 1935, 5-3/16" long (BV113)	17	26	35
Double Decker Bus, 4" long (BV34)	60	90	120
Double Decker Bus, No. 56, c. 1931, 3-1/4" long (BV138)	22	33	45
Double Transport Set, No. 440, four cars on upper and lower racks, hinged for unloading, 1939-1963, 4-1/2" long (BV157)	72	109	145
Dump Truck, c. 1960s, approx. 2" long (BV94)	7	11	15
Dump Truck, spring action, ratchet, 1935, 4" long (BV147)	20	30	40
Express Stack Truck, 1930s, 2-15/16" long (BV37)	30	45	60
Field Kitchen, 2-1/4" long (BV39)	35	52	70
Fire Engine, No. 390?, moveable ladder, c. 1950s (BV38)	15	22	30
Fire Engine, No. 209, c. 1934, 3-1/8" long (BV134)	25	38	50
Fire Engine, No. 41, two firemen, black metal wheels, 1930s, 2-3/4" long (BV40)	17	26	35
Fire Engine, French-looking, 4" long (BV41)	17	26	35
Fire Truck, No. 210, c. 1934, 3-1/8" long (BV133)	25	38	50

Barclay Vehicles (Continued)	C6	C8	C10
Fire Truck, No. 368, "Fire Dept. No. 99", 1930s, 5-3/4" long (BV126)	20	30	40
Fire Truck, No. 50, c. 1931, 2-3/8" long (BV137)	22	33	45
Ford, 1931, 2-1/4" long (BV42)	15	22	30
Gas Truck, 200 series, four tanks on top, c. 1935, 3" long (BV144A)	25	38	50
Gasoline Truck, small, three tank on top, c. 1931, 2-5/16" long (BV144)	30	45	60
Golden Arrow Racer, 1930s, 4-1/2" long (BV43)	20	30	40
Hook and Ladder, No. 208, 1935, 3" long (BV122)	16	24	32
Hospital Truck, c. 1968, 2" long (BV104)	9	13	18
Imperial Chrysler Coupe, No. 39, c. 1931 (BV129)	15	22	30
Log Truck, c. 1960s, approx. 2" long (BV93)	7	11	15
Mack Pickup Truck, 3-1/2" long (BV44)	15	22	30
Milk & Cream Truck, No. 377, stamped, white rubber tires, 3-5/8" long (BV45)	81	122	163
Milk Truck, No. 377, black rubber tires, 3-5/8" long (BV45A)	22	33	45
Milk Truck, No. 567, in shape of bottle (BV84)	162	243	325
Milk Van Truck, bottle on side, 2-7/8" long (BV85)	20	30	41
Motorcycle with Flat Rider, No. 55, full-dimensional sidecar, 2-3/4" long (BV46)	47	70	95

Banner American Express Truck, 10" long, $225. Photo courtesy Bob Smith

Banner Car Transport, 16" long, $275. Photo courtesy John Taylor

Banner Sand and Gravel Dump Truck, No. 1142, 13" long, $225. Photo courtesy John Taylor

Banner Wonder Bread Truck, 11" long, $175. Photo courtesy Harvey K. Rainess

Banner Kellog's Express Truck, 1940, 13" long, $550. Photo courtesy John Taylor

Banner Cross Country Express Truck, 12" long, $275. Photo courtesy John Taylor

Banner Fair Lawn Dairy Truck, 11-1/2" long, $250. Photo courtesy John Taylor

Banner Dump Trucks, plastic, 1950s, 5-1/4" long, $35 each. Photo courtesy Bob and Alice Wagner

Barclay Vehicles Build and Paint Set, No. 2004, early, $360. Photo courtesy Perry Eichor

Barclay Vehicles Double Transport Set, No. 440, 1939-1963, 4-1/2" long, $145. Photo courtesy Craig Clark

Barclay Vehicles Moving Truck (three different trucks show decal variants), c. 1960s, approx. 2" long, $18. Photo courtesy Stan Alekna

Barclay Vehicles (Continued)	C6	C8	C10
Moving Truck, c. 1960s, approx. 2" long (BV161)	8	13	18
Officer's Car, w/megaphone on top, 2-1/2" long (BV86)	22	33	44
Oil Truck, c. 1960s, approx. 2" long (BV99)	9	13	18
Oil-Fuel Truck, No. 308, c. 1936, 3-9/16" long (BV47)	12	18	25
Open Coupe with Driver in Cab, early 1930s (BV110)	15	22	30
Parcel Delivery Truck, No. 45, 1930s, 3-5/8" long (BV48)	65	98	130
Pepsi-Cola Truck, 1960s, 2" long (BV100)	9	13	18
Police Car, 2" long (BV96)	5	8	10
Police Car, No. 317, 3-5/8" long (BV49A)	15	22	30
Race Car, open, driver, 4" long (BV150)	70	105	140
Race Car, 3" long (BV50)	12	18	24
Racer, two passengers, 4-1/4" long (BV54)	55	82	110
Racer, No. 306, 1936 (BV120)	15	22	30
Racer, No. 303, streamline, 4-3/8" long (BV121)	15	22	30
Racer, No. 53, 1920s-30s, approx. 2" long (BV53)	24	36	48
Racer, No. 5, 1931 (BV130)	15	22	30
Racer, closed cockpit, c. 1939, 7" long (BV52)	30	45	60
Racer, closed cockpit, 5-1/2" long (BV51)	17	26	35

Barclay Vehicles (Continued)	C6	C8	C10
Racer with Tail Fin, "Made in U.S.A.", 3-1/2" long (BV55)	17	26	35
Racing Car, c. 1968, approx. 2" long (BV95)	5	8	10
Racing Car, no fenders, c. 1968, approx. 2" long (BV101)	5	8	10
Racing Car, large, raised exhaust pipe, driver, appeared in the 1935 catalog (BV149)	17	26	35
Racing Car, No. 37, large, 1930s, 14-1/4" long (BV115)	16	24	32
Renault Tank, No. 47, c. 1937, 4" long (BV56)	22	33	45
Searchlight Truck, second version (BV57A)	87	130	175
Searchlight Truck, white rubber tires, c. 1940, 4-1/16" long (BV57)	87	130	175
Sedan, No. 311, c. 1936 (BV135)	21	32	43
Sedan, two-door, 1960s, 1-5/8" long (BV108)	2	3	5
Sedan, two-door, rubber wheels, c. 1935, 3-1/8" long (BV59)	37	56	75
Sedan, No. 362, streamline, large, 1935 (BV125)	41	61	82
Sedan, c. 1934 (BV140)	37	56	75
Sedan, four-door, possibly a Chrysler, c. 1936, 5" long (BV58)	17	26	35
Sedan, No. 401, two-piece, two-door, "Barclay Toy", 1930s, 2-7/8" long (BV60)	42	63	85

Barclay Vehicles Convertible, $100.

Left to right: Barclay Vehicles Cord Front Drive Coupe, No. 40, c. 1931, 3-5/8" long, $50; Parcel Delivery Truck, No. 45, 1930s, 3-5/8" long, $130; Golden Arrow Racer, 1930s, 4-1/2" long, $40.

Barclay Vehicles Sedan and Tourist Trailer, 1930s, 6-1/2" long, $70.

Barclay Oil Truck, (BV99), several decal variations, $18 each. Photo courtesy Stan Alekna

Left to right: No. 302 Steamline Car, c. 1936, $50; Delivery Truck, No. 309; Fire Engine, French-looking, $35.

Barclay Racer, (BV54), 4-1/4" long, $110. Photo courtesy Evelyn Besser; photo by Bill Kaufman

Barclay Vehicles (Continued)	C6	C8	C10
Sedan and Tourist Trailer, "Made in U.S.A.", 1930s, 6-1/2" long (BV61)	35	52	70
Side Dump, 1-1/2" long (BV87)	7	11	15
Silver Arrow Race Car, 5-1/2" long (BV62)	22	33	45
Sport Coupe, removable spare tire, 1935, 2-7/8" long (BV148)	32	48	65
Stake Truck, 1935, 4-3/8" long (BV151)	36	54	72
Stake Truck, No. 207, 1935 catalog, 3-1/8" long (BV124)	39	58	78
Station Wagon, No. 404, two-piece, "Barclay Toy", 1930s, 2-15/16" long (BV63)	37	56	75
Steam Shovel, no number, known as Panama Shovel, built w/Mack truck chassis with steam engine body with tin shovel hinged on a derrick, w/driver, metal disc wheels, vertical hood louvers, no windshield, 4" x 1-3/4")	150	250	500
Steam-Roller, No. 44, traction type, c. 1931, 3-1/4" long (BV64)	30	45	60

Barclay Vehicles (Continued)	C6	C8	C10
Streamline Coupe, Large, No. 363, appeared in 1935 catalog, 6-7/8" long (BV143)	45	68	90
Streamline Coupe, Large, 1930s (BV143)	15	22	30
Streamline Sedan, No. 302, c. 1936, 3-1/8" long (BV32)	25	38	50
Tank, based on U.S. M2 light tank, 2-1/4" long (BV70)	20	31	41
Tank, "4562," one man in turret, 3-7/8" long (BV66)	17	26	35
Tank, "4562," two men in turret, 3-7/8" long (BV67)	NPF	NPF	NPF
Tank T41, 4-1/2" long (BV68)	15	22	30
Taxi, No. 318, 3-1/4" long (BV71A)	50	75	100
Taxi, c. 1940s, 3-1/4" long (BV71)	14	21	28
Tow Car, No. 205, appeared in 1935 catalog, 3-1/16" long (BV141)	20	30	40
Tow Truck, No. 312, "Towing," appeared in 1936 catalog, 3-3/8" long (BV119)	17	26	35

Barclay Vehicles Tow Car, No. 205, 3-1/16" long,
$40.

*Barclay Vehicles
Steam Shovel, 4" x
1-3/4", $500.
Photo courtesy
Fred Maxwell*

Barclay Vehicles Oil Truck with Yoo-Hoo, Pepsi-Cola
Truck and Coca-Cola decals, c. 1960s, approx. 2" long,
$18. Photo courtesy Stan Alekna

Barr Rubber '35 Ford Panel Truck/Ambulance, 4-1/4" long,
$55. Photo courtesy Dave Leopard's book, Rubber Toy
Vehicles

Barclay Vehicles (Continued)

	C6	C8	C10
Tow Truck, No. 1105, "Towing Service," large (BV117)	82	124	175
Tractor, No. 203, peg hitch, 2-1/8" long (BV109)	11	16	22
Trailer Truck variously "Railway Express", or w/other moving company name, c. 1950s (BV74)	5	8	10
Transport Set, No. 330, w/two cars, 1960s, 4-1/2" long (BV75)	25	40	75
Transport Set, two car, 4-3/4" long (BV152)	42	63	85
Truck, "Esso Gas", 1930s, 5" long (BV111)	20	30	40
U.S. Army Truck, wire or peg hitch, white rubber wheels, 2-1/2" long (BV77)	12	18	25
U.S. Army Truck, c. 1968, 2" long (BV103)	7	11	15
U.S. Army Truck, No. 204, no hitch, red wood hubs, 2-1/2" long (BV76)	19	28	38
U.S. Mail Truck, 1960s, 2" long (BV91)	10	17	24
U.S. Motor Unit Truck, three versions-no hitch, wire hitch, peg hitch, white rubber tires, c. 1940, 3-1/4" long (BV78)	17	26	35

Barclay Vehicles (Continued)

	C6	C8	C10
Van, "White Horse" van (some have sticker reading "Welcome I.C.MA. Compliments the White Motor Co."), approx. 03" long (BV156)	55	82	110
Van, no number, embossed "Moving Van," horizontal grille pattern, no windshield, vertical stripes on van body, metal disc wheels, dual rear axles, 4")	100	150	200
Vintage Car, approx. 2" long (BV98)	15	22	30
Volkswagen, 1960s, approx. 2" long (BV102)	12	18	24
Wheel-A-Rific speedway track, two lead racers, black rubber wheels, 10' of plastic track, c. 1970 (BV79)	17	26	35
Wrecker, No. 403, two piece, "Barclay Toy", 1930s, 2-7/8" long (BV82)	42	63	85
Wrecker, No. 46, c. 1931, 3-1/2" long (BV80)	22	33	45

Barr Rubber

Barr Rubber was located in Sandusky, Ohio. The following list and code numbers in parentheses was compiled by Dave Leopard. Vehicles are broken down by type.

Contributor: Dave Leopard, 2507 Feather Run Trail, West Columbia, SC 29169-4915.

Left to right: '35 Ford Stake Body Truck, Barr, $4155; '35 Ford Army Truck, Barr, $65. Photo from Rubber Toy Vehicles by Dave Leopard

Left to right: Barr Rubber '35 Ford Two-door Slantback Sedan, 4" long, $55; '35 Ford Coupe, 4" long, $55. Photo courtesy Dave Leopard's book, Rubber Toy Vehicles

Left to right: Police car, Beaut $20; Taxi, Mfg. Co., $20.

Best Toy & Novelty Factory Cab Unit, No. 101, 3-1/4" long, $80.

Barr Rubber

	C6	C8	C10
'35 Ford Army Truck, 4-3/4" long (BT03)	32	48	65
'35 Ford Coupe, 4" long (BA01)	27	41	55
'35 Ford Panel Truck/Ambulance, 4-1/4" long (BT02)	27	41	55
'35 Ford Stake Body Truck, 4-3/4" long (BT01)	27	41	55
'35 Ford Two-door Slantback Sedan, 4" long (BA02)	27	41	55

Beaut Mfg. Co.

Beaut Mfg. Co., North Bergen, New Jersey, was founded in 1946 by Eugene Buhler and Irving Reader (former machinist and salesman, respectively) for Barclay Mfg. Co. The company put out five toys—a taxicab, a police car, a fire engine, a sedan, and a child's wagon. The company was successful at first, selling to Woolworth's and many overseas buyers. Beaut ceased toy-making activities around 1950 because of competition from the plastic toys, although they continued until 1982 as a general machine shop.

Beaut Mfg. Co.

	C6	C8	C10
Fire Car, No. 4, approx. 3-3/4" long	10	15	20
Police Car, approx. 3-3/4" long	10	15	20
Sedan, approx. 3-3/4" long	10	15	20
Taxi, approx. 3-3/4" long	10	15	20

Best Toy & Novelty Factory

Best Toy, founded by John M. Best in Manhattan, Kansas, during the 1930s, started as a family hobby for Best's children, relatives, friends, and neighbors. From a hobby it grew into a respectable business, supplying toy distributors and dime stores. After several years of operation it was sold in 1939 to Ralstoy, a Ralston, Nebraska, company. Best toys are still found in today's toy markets.

At this point we are not certain when Best started or what number in the series was his first molding. In 1933, Best took over production from the toy line of Kansas Toy & Novelty of Clifton, Kansas. It's not known whether he introduced any new patterns, although with his experience it is likely that he did. Regardless, it was an important chapter in the story of those wandering molds. Best Toy & Novelty, along with the Kansas Toy molds, were acquired by Ralstoy, of Ralston, Nebraska, in 1939.

Best Toy reproductions can usually be distinguished by the rubber wheels and the marking "Made in the U.S.A." However, some of their toys used the metal wheels of the Kansas Toy originals or the later wood hubs with rubber tires. It is also possible that Best modified or rebuilt his molds to create variations.

For more information, see O'Brien's Collecting Toy Cars & Trucks.

Contributors: Fred Maxwell. Maxwell, a collector and occasional author, has been collecting antique aircraft and vehicle toys for over twenty-five years. He founded the Auto Collectors Club twenty-five years ago to promote interest in the central Atlantic states region.

Perry R. Eichor, 703 North Almond Drive, Simpsonville, SC 29681. Captain Eichor has been collecting aircraft toys since he was a young officer in the Air Force; his twenty-one years as Air Force officer only served to deepen his interest in the subject. Today when he is not collecting, researching, or writing about aeronautical toys, he works as a criminal justice administrator as well as an appraiser and auctioneer.

*Champion Mack Dump Truck, c. 1930s, 7" long, $365.
Photo courtesy Harry Wolf; Detroit Antique Toy Museum*

Champion Wrecker, 7-1/2" long, $615.

Best Toy & Novelty Factory	C6	C8	C10
Cab Unit, No. 101, International (?), sleeper cab, slanted grille, hood cap, Motometer or ornament, two open windows, rare, 3-1/4" long (BEV15)	40	60	80
Coupe, Pontiac (?), streamlined, hood cap, Motometer or ornament, rearmount, 4" long (BEV13)	25	45	70
Coupe, Dodge (?), chopped top, Brewster-like heart-shaped grille, hood cap, Motometer or ornament, long streamlined front fenders, 3-3/4" long (BEV6)	20	30	40
Coupe, apparently same car as No. 91, grid pattern grille, two open windows, 3-1/2" long (BEV10)	20	45	50
Coupe, No. 93, Cadillac?, Streamlined, hood similar to No. 91, grid pattern grille, two open windows, hard rubber wheels, 3-5/8" long (BEV7)	16	24	32
Coupe, No. 98 (BEV12)	15	30	40
Oil Transport, No. 102, streamlined "Gasoline" semi-trailer to No. 101, four tanks, four storage compartments, total length of cab-trailer, 6-3/4", 4" long (BEV16)	47	70	95
Racer, No. 85, record car w/large square fin, driver, hood cap, Motometer or ornament, vertical grille pattern, twelve exhaust ports, wooden hubs, rubber tires, 4" long (BEV1)	10	15	20

Best Toy & Novelty Factory	C6	C8	C10
Racer, No. 97, Bluebird record car, driver, large fin, twelve exhaust port, faired, hard rubber wheels, 4-1/2" long (BEV11)	10	15	20
Sedan, No. 87, Brewster (?) (BEV3)	15	25	35
Sedan, No. 94, two door, airflow, similar to No. 90, four open windows, taxi lamp on roof, 4-1/2" long (BEV8)	35	45	70
Sedan, No. 90, two door, airflow, hood reaches front bumper w/no grille, four open windows, hard rubber wheels, 3-1/2" long (BEV4)	25	40	70
Sedan, No. 91, Cadillac (?), two door airflow, high style vee grille, faired front fenders, 3-1/2" long (BEV5)	25	40	70
Sedan, No. 95, two door, airflow, similar to No. 94 w/three headlamps, four open windows, trunk, hard rubber wheels, Chrysler-Briggs show car (?), 3-1/2" long)	30	40	55
Sedan, No. 95, two door, airflow, similar to No. 94, w/three headlamps, four open windows, trunk, hard rubber wheels, w/"Police Dept." shield on doors, centered headlamp may be a siren, one version has "Police" painted on roof, 3-1/2" long (BEV9b)	35	45	60
Sedan, No. 100, Pontiac, streamlined, two door, hood open, horizontal grille pattern, four open windows, trunk, 4" long (BEV14)	20	30	40

Left to right: Best Toy & Novelty Racer, No. 76; Racer, No. 85, 4" long, $20. Photo courtesy Perry Eichor

Buddy "L" Army Signal Corps Truck, 12" long, $300. Photo courtesy Calvin L. Chaussee

Best Toy & Novelty Factory

	C6	C8	C10
Sedan, No. 86, Lincoln (?), two-door fastback, clanted grille w/grid pattern, horizontal hood louvers, divided windshield, rear wheel skirts, 4" long (BEV2)	20	30	50

Buddy "L"

Buddy "L" toys, named after owner Fred Ludahl's son, Buddy, were first manufactured by the Moline Pressed Steel Company of Moline, Illinois in 1921. Lundahl started the company eight years earlier in order to manufacture car and truck parts. The toys, originally made as special items for his son, caught the attention of other children and their fathers.

Buddy "L" toys are large, averaging twenty-one to twenty-six inches in length. The original toys were made of heavy steel and could support a grown man's weight, but lighter material was adopted in the 1930s. Wooden toys were produced during World War II when steel was in short supply.

Lundahl relinquished control of the company to J.W. Bettendorf in 1930 and died later that year. The name of the company has changed many times over the years, yet it continues to make toys at the present time.

Because the early Buddy "L" toys were almost indestructible, fifty percent of the items found are either rusty or have been repainted, which lowers the value considerably.

Contributor: John Taylor, P.O. Box 63, Nolensville, TN 37135-0063. 11th Edition pricing contributor Mark Rich, P.O. Box 971, Stevens Point, WI 54481. Email: mark.rich@sff.net

Buddy "L" Construction Equipment

	C6	C8	C10
Aerial Tramway, No. 360, 1929-30, 33-1/2"	1500	2400	3700
Concrete Mixer, No. 280, 1926-30, 17-3/4"	500	750	1000
Dredge, No. 270, (Clamshell), 1926-30, 19"	800	1200	1500
Heavy Shovel, No. 220AB, (on Treads), 1929-30, 14" tall	2500	4000	7000
Heavy Steam Shovel, No. 220A, 1929-30, 17" tall	400	600	800
Hoisting Tower, No. 350, 1929-31, 29" tall	500	900	1250
Large Derrick, No. 241, 1922-31	275	375	600

Buddy "L" Construction Equipment (Continued)

	C6	C8	C10
Mixer, No. 280A, (on Treads), 1929-31, 15-1/2" long	2500	3800	5200
Overhead Crane, No. 250, 1924-27, 46" long	800	1500	2300
Pile Driver, No. 260, 1926-28, 22-1/2" high	800	1700	2500
Road Roller, No. 290, 1929-31, 20" long	1300	2400	3500
Sand Loader, No. 230, 1925-31, 18" high	175	250	350
Sand Screener, No. 300, 1929-30	700	1100	1700
Small Derrick, No. 240, 1922-31, 21-1/2" tall	300	450	625
Steam Shovel, No. 220, 1921-31, 25-1/2" tall	250	375	600
Tractor Dredge, No. 270A, (on Treads), 1929-30, 21" long	2500	5000	8000
Traveling Crane, No. 250A, 1928-30	800	1600	2300
Trencher, No. 400, 1928-31, 24" long	1800	2700	4200

Buddy "L" Fire Trucks

	C6	C8	C10
Aerial Ladder, No. 205B, w/three ladders, 1926-30, 30" long	900	1800	2800
Hook & Ladder, No. 205, 1923-32, 26" long	900	1800	2800
Insurance Patrol, No. 205C, 1925-30	1500	2500	3500
Pumper, No. 205A, 1925-30	1000	1800	3000
Pumper, No. 205AB, (Working), 1930-31	1000	1800	2500
Water Tower Truck, No. 205D, (Working), 1929-32, 36-1/2" long	2000	4000	6000

Buddy "L" Large Trucks

	C6	C8	C10
Auto Wrecker, No. 209, 1928-31	1750	2750	4500
Baggage Truck, No. 203B, 1927-32, 26" long	1500	3000	4500

Buddy "L" Army Tank No. 362, wood, 1943, $150. Photo courtesy Jack Matthews

Automatic Tail-Gate Loader with steering handle, Buddy "L," $350.

Buddy "L" Baby Ruth/Butterfinger Curtiss Candies Tandem Truck, late 1930s, $2000. Photo courtesy John Taylor

Buddy "L" Concrete Mixer No. 832, 1950-51, $575. Photo courtesy Bertoia Auctions

Buddy "L" Large Trucks	C6	C8	C10
Coach, No. 208, light green motorbus w/gold stripes, 1928-31, 28-1/2" long	2000	3000	4800
Coal Truck, No. 202, 1926-32, 26" long	3700	7500	11,500
Dump Truck, No. 201, (Ratchet), 1923-29, 25"	500	750	1250
Express Truck, No. 200, 1921-31, 23-1/2" long	1000	1600	2500
Hydraulic Dump Truck, No. 201A, 1926-31	700	1400	2100
Ice Truck, No. 207, w/ "ice" and canvas tarp, 1926-31, 26" long	600	1200	1900
Lumber Truck, No. 203A, 1925-30, 24" long	1500	2500	4000
Moving Van, No. 204, 1924-30	750	1250	2000
Oil Truck, No. 206A, 1925-30, 23" long	900	1500	2200
Railway Express, No. 204A, 1926-31, 25"	1000	1600	2500
Sand & Gravel Truck, No. 202A, 1926-32, 25" long	1500	2500	3500
Stake Truck, No. 203, 1921-24, 1926-28, 24-1/2" long	850	1650	2500
Street Sprinkler Truck, No. 206, 206B, 1924-31, 26" long	1200	1800	3200

Buddy "L" Model T Series	C6	C8	C10
Flivver Coupe, No. 210B, 1924-30	400	700	1200
Flivver Roadster, No. 210A, 1924-26	500	750	1250
Flivver Truck, No. 210, 1924-30	900	1400	1900
Ford Dump Cart, No. 211, 1926-30	800	1550	2750
Ford Dump Truck, No. 211A, 1926-30	1100	1700	2650
Ford Express Truck, No. 212, 1927-30	1400	2300	3225
One-Ton Ford Delivery Truck, No. 212A, 1927-30	2000	3500	5000

Buddy "L" Post-1932	C6	C8	C10
Allied Van Lines, No. 910, 21" long	600	1000	1500
Allied Van Lines Moving Van, No. 366, 31" long	340	600	950
Army Signal Corps Truck, 1941-42, 12" long	140	225	300
Army Tank, 1943, 13" long	50	95	150
Army Transport Truck, six-spoke wheels, 1954-57, 17" long	225	350	475
Army Truck, c. 1940	150	200	300
Army Truck, No. 506, 20-1/2" long	150	200	300
Army Truck	100	150	200

Buddy "L" top to bottom: Hydraulic Dump Truck, No. 201A, 1926-29, $800; Dump Truck No. 201, chain-drive dump mechanism, 1923-29, $600. Photo courtesy Tim Oei

Buddy "L" Hose Truck No. 38, 1933, $325. Photo courtesy Joe and Sharon Freed

Buddy "L" Post-1932	C6	C8	C10
Automatic Tail-Gate Loader, w/steering handle	200	325	475
Baby Ruth/Butterfinger Curtiss Candies Tandem Truck, International-style cab, late 1930s-40s, 29" long	750	1500	2000
Baggage Truck, No. 11, 1933, 26-1/2" long	225	350	550
Baggage Truck, 1940s, 17"	95	150	200
Big Show Circus Truck, No. 484, 1947, 25-1/2" long	750	1000	1500
City Baggage Dray, No. 439, 1934-37, 19" long	400	800	1200
City Baggage Dray, No. 839, 1938, 20-3/4" long	125	200	325
Coca-Cola Truck, No. 5536, 1955-56, 15" long	200	350	400
Coca-Cola Truck, No. 5426, 1960-61, 15" long	150	250	400
Coca-Cola Truck, No. 5646, 1957-59	200	300	450
Concrete Mixer, No. 832, w/motor sound, 1950-51, 10-3/4" long	250	400	575
Concrete Mixer with Truck, No. 54, 1937, 34-1/2" long	300	200	450
Country Squire Station Wagon, No. 53051, 1963-64, 15" long	100	150	250
Curtiss Candy Truck	275	500	650
Dairy Truck, No. 2002, (Junior Line), 1930-32, 24" long	1100	1800	2700
Dandy Digger, No. 33 and 2025, 1931-37, 27" long	75	100	150
Delivery Truck, No. 803, Deluxe Rider, 1945-48, 22-3/4" long	225	400	650
Double Hydraulic Self-Loader-N-Dump Truck, No. 5892, 1956-57, 29" long	75	125	225

Buddy "L" Post-1932	C6	C8	C10
Dump Truck, No. 434, 1936, 20" long	225	325	425
Dump Truck, No. 634, 1948, 22-1/2" long	150	250	375
Emergency Auto Wrecker, No. 3317	100	200	275
Engine, No. 29, 1933-34, 25-1/2" long	200	250	525
Excavator Truck and Shovel Set, No. 948, 1940, 27-1/2" long	275	400	600
Express Trailer Truck, No. 35, 1933-34, 23-3/4" long	475	650	950
Fast Delivery Truck, No. 3313	100	150	225
Fire Chief's Car with Siren, No. 483, 1949, 19-1/2" long	475	750	1100
Fire Ladder Truck, semi, rounded trailer fenders, 1960	100	150	200
Greyhound Bus, winds up, 1938-40, 16-1/2" long	300	325	500
Greyhound Bus with Bell, No. 481, 1948-49, 18-1/2" long	450	675	1000
Hi-Lift Scoop-A-Dump	75	112	150
Hook and Ladder Truck, No. 859, 21-1/2" long	250	375	550
Hose Truck, No. 38, 1933, 21-3/4" long	125	225	325
Hydraulic Aerial Truck, No. 27, 1933-34, 40" long w/ladders down	800	1000	1400
Hydraulic DumpTruck, No. 10, 1933-34, 24-3/4" long	300	500	600
Ice Truck, No. 12, 1933-34, 26-1/2" long	600	1000	1750
International Delivery Truck, No. 51, 1935, 24-1/2" long	200	300	500
Merry-Go-Round Truck, No. 5429	75	125	200

C.A.W. DeSoto Sedan, (CWV9), $60. Photo courtesy Perry Eichor

C.A.W. Novelty Company Overland Bus, 3-3/4" long, $50. Photo courtesy Gary Franson

C.A.W. Novelty Company Dump Truck, 3-1/8" long, $40.

C.A.W. Novelty Company Sport Roadster, 3-1/2" long, $50. Photo courtesy Gary Franson

Fuel Tanker, Ford? Truck, cab with driver inside, 3-3/4" long, C.A.W. Novelty Company, $40.

Buddy "L" Post-1932	C6	C8	C10
Mister Buddy Ice Cream Van, 1964-65, 11-1/2" long	125	200	325
Railway Express Truck, No. 480, 1947, 16-1/4" long	300	450	700
Railway Express Truck, Baby Ruth/Butterfinger tandem, 1935, 23" long	1000	1700	2750
Railway Express Truck, No. 763, 1952, 25" long	600	1000	2000
Ride-N-Dump Truck	200	300	450
Riding Academy Truck, No. 5455, w/three horses, 18-1/2" long	65	85	125
Robotoy Dump Truck with driver, operates on remote control, 21-5/8" long	500	1000	1250
Sand & Gravel Truck, No. 3312, 13-1/2"	100	150	225

Buddy "L" Post-1932	C6	C8	C10
Scarab, No. 211, no wind-up mechanism, 1941, 10-1/2" long	200	300	400
Scarab, No. 711, wind-up, 1936-40, 10-1/2"	250	400	600
Service Truck, No. 5409, 1960	120	180	300
Shell Truck, 13-1/2" long	175	275	400
Siren Pull-n-Ride, No. 3722, 1953	100	160	240
Steam Shovel, No. 30, mechanical, 1935, 17-1/2" long, 13-1/2" high	175	275	400
Steam Shovel and International Truck, No. 16, 1937, 29-1/2" long, 36" extended	150	250	375
Steam Shovel on Treads, No. 2005, (Junior Line), 1930-32, 24" long	300	450	700

Buddy "L" Emergency Auto Wrecker, 11-1/2" long, $250. Photo courtesy Calvin L. Chaussee

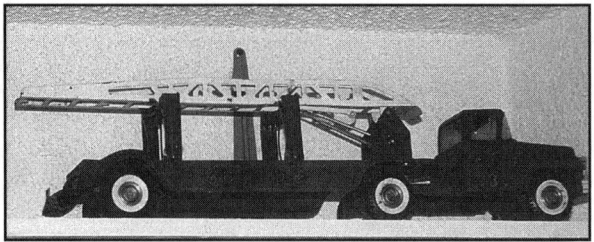

Buddy "L" Fire Ladder Truck, $200. Photo courtesy Calvin L. Chaussee

Buddy "L" Flivver Roadster No. 210A, 1924-26, $1250. Photo courtesy Harry Wolf, Detroit Antique Toy Museum

Buddy "L" Steam Shovel No. 220, 1923-29, $400. Photo courtesy Joe and Sharon Freed

Buddy "L" Post-1932	C6	C8	C10
Tank Truck, No. 438, "Shell", 1935, 19-1/4" long	450	750	1200
Tank Truck, No. 938, 1941, 21-1/2" long	200	300	450
Texaco Tanker, No. 5603, promo sold at gas stations, 25" long	150	225	300
Traveling Zoo, No. 5420, 1965-66	100	175	250
Utility Delivery Truck, No. 946, 1941-42, 25" long	75	125	200
Victory Jeep and Cannon, No. 353	100	150	250
Water Tower, No. 28, 1936	1250	2250	3500
Wrecker, No. 3667, "Repair-It", 1953, 24" long	150	225	300
Wrecker, No. 937, two-tone slant, 1939, 25-1/4" long	150	250	350
Wrecker, No. W37, 1939, 25-1/4" long	150	225	300

Buddy "L" Post-1932	C6	C8	C10
Wrecker, No. 503, 1940, 1941-42, 19-1/4" long	175	275	375
Wrecker, No. 437, 1934-37, 24" long	375	527	750
Wrecker, No. 13, 1933-37, 31" long	850	1500	3000
Wrecker, No. 37, 1933, 24" long	200	350	450
Wrigley's Spearmint Railway Express Agency Truck, No. 953, 1940, 24" long	800	1350	2250
Wrigley's Spearmint Railway Express Truck, No. 435, headlights light up, 1935, 23-1/8" long	700	1400	2200

C.A.W. Novelty Company

Charles A. Wood, founder of C.A.W. Novelty Company, not only ran a substantial operation, but made some of the finest replica toys in the slush-mold industry. Founded about 1925,

Buddy "L" Wrigley's Spearmint Railway Express Truck (Post-1932), No. 435, 1935, 23 1/8" long, $2200.

Buddy "L" Texaco Tanker Truck, promo truck sold at gas stations, $300.

C.A.W. Air Drive Coach, (CWV5), $60. Photo courtesy Fred Maxwell

C.A.W. Novelty Company New Design Racer, No. 38, 3-3/8" long, $50.

Wood's company was active until about 1940, when lead casting came to a halt due to World War II.

All of Wood's output showed artistry, ingenuity, and meticulous craftsmanship. The toys are smooth and crisp, with detailed moldings and extra touches such as open windshields and multiple colors. Early products had metal disk wheels with painted black tires or metal-spoked wheels. Other details included open v-shaped, divided windshields; drivers inside cabs; and tri-motored aircraft with the outboard engines mounted on the landing gear struts. Wood once told a reporter that it sometimes took three or four years to make a mold—just one example of how much pride Wood took in his work.

Charles Wood was born in 1891. He lived and worked in Topeka, Kansas, and in nearby Clifton before moving to Clay Center. He was known for his civic boisterism and good works. After he helped establish the local airport, he built and operated his own aircraft maintenance hangar. A master machinist, he produced all of his toy molds, production tools, toy parts, and even plastic wheels.

The C & H Mfg. Co., formed in 1940 by Rod Hemphill, the last C.A.W. employee, and Howard Clevenger, made toys using original C.A.W. molds. These reproductions are heavier than C.A.W.'s and have black rubber wheels.

The seldom found C.A.W. trademark consists of unique, lead blind hubs fitted over a wire axle. They are sometimes found with ordinary axles piercing the hubs.

Contributors: Fred Maxwell, 4722 N. 33 St., Arlington, VA 22207. Perry R. Eichor, 703 North Almond Drive, Simpsonville, SC 29681.

C.A.W. Novelty Company	C6	C8	C10
Air Drive Coach, No. 25, blimp-like bus w/fin and rear propellor drive, twelve open windows, white soft rubber disc wheels w/unique fitted hubs with cap hidden axles, there is also a version w/o propellor, 3-7/8" long (CWV5)	30	45	60
DeSoto Sedan, No. 32, airflow, divided windshield, BOW, horizontal louvers, vertical grille pattern, hood cap, white soft rubber wheels, 3-7/8" long (CWV9)	40	50	60
Dump Truck, no number, Ford (?), hinged dump body, divided open windshield, two open windows, horizontal grille, metal disc wheels, 3-1/8" long (CWV13)	20	30	40
Fuel Tanker, Ford (?), cab w/driver inside, no windshield, horizontal grille pattern, three tanks, hose compartment, metal open-spoke wheels, 3-3/4" long (CWV4)	40	60	80

C.A.W. Novelty Company

	C6	C8	C10
New Design Racer, No. 38, streamlined coupe, rounded tail, driver visible through two oval open windows, hood cap loop (string-pull?), white soft rubber wheels w/hubs, 3-3/8" long (CWV10)	30	40	50
Overland Bus, no number, Fageol (?), Yellow line (?) tour bus, horizontal grille pattern, no headlamps, twelve windows, shallow observer deck, metal disc wheels, left sidemounted spare, 3-3/4" long (CWV3)	20	40	50
Racer, No. 39, transparent winshield, Indy FWD two-man racer, vee-shaped vertical grille, dual exhausts, boattail, unique hubs as on No. 25 (also WRW), not complete if divided plastic windshield is missing, 3" long (CWV11)	25	50	75
Sport Roadster, Buick?, no windshield, plain grille, vertical louvers, rearmount spare tire/wheel, right sidemounted spare, metal disc wheels, also version w/metal-spoked wheels, 3-1/2" long (CWV2)	30	40	50
Sport Roadster, open Buick, driver w/cap (gilt or silver), no windshield, horizontal grille, vertical louvers, no headlamps, rearmount, metal disc wheels, 3-1/2" long (CWV1)	30	45	60
Streamline Coupe, No. 30, Airflow, vee pattern grille, hood cap, four open windows, small rear fin, small winged design on rear-wheel skirts, metal disc wheel also white soft rubber wheels, bottom pan goes over rear axle, 3" long (CWV6)	25	50	75
Tank Truck, no number, gasoline semi-trailer, two tanks, cab w/divided windsheild and open windows shows it is part of a set (CWV15)	30	40	60
Tank Truck, no number, Ford (?), three fuel tanks, hinged dump body, divided open windshield, two open window, horizontal grille pattern, metal disc wheels, unusual body connected by rear axle, 3-3/16" long (CWV14)	25	35	45

C.A.W. Novelty Company

	C6	C8	C10
Three Auto Set, No. 40, includes: (a) Midget coupe racer, no number, horizontal grille pattern, horizontal hood louvers, divided open windshield, two open windows, two colored body ventilators, 2-1/16" long; (b) Midget racer, no number, gilt driver, vertical hood louvers, horizontal grille pattern, metal disc wheels (easily confused w/ Barclay No. 53), 2-1/8" long; (c) Austin Bantam, no number, two-door sedanette, five open windows, hood louvers, plain grille, rearmount spare tire/wheel, metal disc wheels (easily confused w/other makers' Bantams), 2" long; value per each (CWV12)	20	30	40
Wonder Special, No. 33, airflow coupe, three windshield companion to No. 30 Streamline Coupe, vertical grille, four open windows, white soft rubber wheels, front wheel skirts, pan goes over front axle, 3-3/8" long (CWV7)	25	50	75
Wonder Special, No. 33, airflow coupe, three-wheeled companion to No. 30 above, vertical grille pattern,, four open windows, white soft rubber wheels, front wheel skirts, pan goes over front axle, 3-3/8" long (CWV7)	25	50	75

Champion

	C6	C8	C10
Car, four casting nickeled radiator car, approx. 4" long	175	262	350
Coupe, Reo type, 7-1/2" long	212	318	425
Gas and Motor Oil Truck, cast iron, c. 1930s, 8" long	380	570	760
Mack Dump Truck, c. 1930s, 7" long	183	275	365
Mack Stake Truck, c. 1930, 4-1/2" long	90	135	180
Mack Stake Truck, 7-1/2" long	175	265	350
Motorcycle and rider, "Champion", 4-3/4" long	150	225	300
Panel Delivery, 7-3/4" long	495	745	990
Policeman on Motorcycle, rubber tires, 7" long	235	355	470

Chein Hercules Coal Truck, $1600.

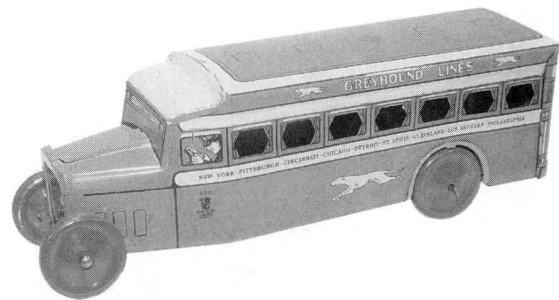

Chein Greyhound Lines push toy, 9" long, $400. Photo courtesy Bob Smith

Chein Hercules Crane, 1925, 23" long, $550. Photo courtesy Bob Smith

Chein Hercules Fire Pumper, No. 650, 1926, 18" long, $1600.

Champion

	C6	C8	C10
Race Car, cast iron, removable driver, 6" long	150	225	300
Race Car, c. 1930s, 9" long	250	375	500
Race Car, w/two riders, 5-1/2"	125	188	250
Sedan, 5-1/4" long	112	188	225
Wrecker, cast iron, "Champion", 7-1/2" long	308	463	615

Chein

Chein (pronounced chain) was founded in 1903 by Julius Chein. The New Jersey company specialized in lithographed metal toys, the majority of them mechanical. In 1918, it was located at 310 Passaic Ave., in Harrison, New Jersey, with 250 employees. In 1934, it had 147 employees. In a 1946-1947 directory, it listed 148 male and 132 female employees. Chein made toys until 1979, and is still in business today in Burlington, New Jersey.

Chein Hercules "C" Cab Mack Trucks

Chein introduced the Hercules series with vehicles in 1925, the first model being the Dump Truck. It was made entirely out of lightweight stamped steel (heavy-gauge tin). Chein made at least fourteen different Hercules models, the smallest being seventeen inches long and stretching to thirty inches (with the C-Cab Bull Dog Mack mobile clam truck, including boom). These toys generally retailed between one

dollar and one dollar and twenty-five cents. They were manufactured until the middle 1930s.

Contributor: Bob Smith, the Village Smith, 62 West Ave., Fairport, NY 14450-2102.

Chein

	C6	C8	C10
Army Truck, tin, cannon on back, early, 8-1/2" long	135	202	270
Dan-Dee Dump Truck, wind-up	200	300	500
Greyhound Bus, wind-up, 9" long	120	200	400
Hercules Coal Truck, black cab, chassis, green bed, tin coal chute, chute door opens, 20" long	550	900	1600
Hercules Crane, 1925, 23" long	225	300	550
Hercules Fire Pumper, No. 650, 1926, 18" long	650	1150	1600
Hercules Mack Army Truck, brown w/canvas cover, 19-3/4" long	450	750	1500
Hercules Mack Crane Truck, No. 1100, 18" long	750	1250	1800
Hercules Mack Dump Truck, black cab, chassis, red dump body, tailgate opens, 20" long	350	650	375
Hercules Mack Motor Express, tin litho, black cab, orange stake bed, 19-1/2" long	550	900	1450

Chein Hercules Mack Crane Truck, No. 1100, 18" long, $1800. Photo courtesy Bob Smith

Chein Hercules Racer No. 8, 20" long, $2200.

Chein Hercules Ready-Mix Concrete Truck, 17" long, $2000.

Chein Hercules Roadster, 18" long, $1200.

Chein (Continued)	C6	C8	C10
Hercules Mack Oil Tanker Truck, black and orange, c. 1928, 19" long	600	1100	1700
Hercules Racer No. 8, w/driver, spare tire mounted on rear, red w/yellow trim, 20" long	700	1500	2200
Hercules Ready-Mix Concrete Truck, deluxe model, orange and black, lithographed, rotating drum, 17" long	750	1300	2000
Hercules Roadster, red and black, rumble seat, luggage rack, 18" long	475	800	1200
Hercules Royal Blue Line Pullman Bus, 18" long	500	750	1350
Hercules Wrecker Truck, open cab, 18" long	500	750	1350
Junior Oil Tank Truck, 1920s, 8-1/2" long	125	250	475
Junior Truck, 1920s	125	225	400
Limosine, tin wind-up, 1930s, 7" long	225	375	550
Mack Army Truck, open bed, 8-1/2" long	200	300	450

Chein (Continued)	C6	C8	C10
Mack Ice Truck, 8-1/2" long	225	325	550
Mack Moving and Storage Van	400	650	750
Playland Whip, No. 340, four bump 'em cars, wind-up	400	600	800
Racer No. 3, wind-up, 1920s, 6-1/2" long	150	250	350
Racer No. 52, tin wind-up, 6-1/2" long	90	150	275
Rapid Delivery Truck, No. 10, tin wind-up	275	425	600
Roadster, tin lithographed, 1925, 8-1/2" long	250	475	675
Sedan, tin wind-up, six-window, c. 1920s, 8-1/2" long	250	475	675
Taxi, wind-up, 1920s, 7" long	185	325	450
Touring Car, tin litho, 7" long	250	375	500
Truck, "Junior Oil Tank", 1920s, 8-1/2" long	62	93	125
Woodie Sedan, tin wind-up, 5-1/4" long	48	72	95
Woodie Station Wagon, wind-up	100	150	200

Chein Hercules Mack Dump Truck, 20" long, $375.

*Chein Mack Tanker Truck, 19" long, c. 1928.
Courtesy Phillips New York*

*Hercules Mack, Motor Express, 19-1/2" long,
Chein, $1,060.*

*Chein Hercules Wrecker Truck, 18" long, $1350.
Photo courtesy Bob Smith*

Converse

Beginning in 1878, Converse helped make Winchendon, Massachusetts, "Toy Town U.S.A." It made wooden, tin, and steel toys and was felled in 1934 by the Depression. It was originally owned by Morton E. Converse.

Converse	C6	C8	C10
Auto with fringe on top, pressed steel, three-seat, painted, clockwork, rubber tires, 1905	600	900	1200
Fire Engine Ladder Truck, bell, wooden headlight, 1915, 10" long...	1250	1875	2500
Parcel Post Van, 1920s, 15" long...	1500	2500	3700
Pick-up Truck, very early, open cab	500	750	1100
Roadster, wind-up, open cab, 1908, 15-1/2" long..............................	1100	1600	3000
Touring Auto, pressed steel, canvas roof, 1910	900	1400	2300
Transitional Taxi, clockwork, 10-1/2" long.....................................	525	770	1200

Cor-Cor

According to Margaret E. Holland (as reported by Ross Hermann in the July 27, 1992 *Antique News*), the granddaughter of Cor-Cor founder Louis A. Corcoran, this Washington, Indiana, firm began no 21st Street in 1925, then expanded to East 3rd and Vantress. After a fire, Cor-Cor built its final plant on Front Street. At this latter location the company changed its name to Corcoran Metal Products. At its height, the firm employed up to 590 people. Corcoran retired in 1941 because of failing health, and died in 1945. His toys are marked " Cor-Cor" on the wheels.

Cor-Cor	C6	C8	C10
Airflow, wind-up, electric lights, 16" long.......................................	1000	1700	2265
Bus, 23" long	425	638	850
Dump Truck, dumps back or side to side, 23" long.............................	225	338	450
Graham Paige Sedan, electric, 20" long...	900	1450	1950
Van, painted metal, c. 1928, 23" long...	363	445	725

Bus, "Royal Blue Line Coast to Coast Service," Champion, $1,280.

Chein Mack Ice Truck, 8-1/2" long, $550. Photo courtesy Bob Smith

Chein Racer No. 52, $275. Photo courtesy Bob Smith

Chein Sedan, 8-1/2" long, $675. Photo courtesy Bob Smith

List originally compiled by Joe and Sharon Freed.

Courtland	C6	C8	C10
Checker Cab Car, No. 4000, green and yellow, tin wind-up, 7-1/4" long, 3-1/4" wide, 2-3/4" high..............................	200	225	350
Checker Cab Car, No. 4000, green and white, 7-1/4" long, 3-1/4" wide, 2-3/4" high......................	200	225	350
City Meat Market Delivery Sedan, No. 4000, tin wind-up, 7-1/4" long, 3-1/4" wide, 2-3/4" high.....	75	150	175
Country Produce Pickup, No. 4500, tin wind-up, 7-1/4" long, 3-1/4" wide, 2-3/4" high......................	75	125	175
Courtland Side Dump Tractor-Trailer, No. 1200, 13" long, 3" wide, 3-1/4" high......................	100	150	200
Courtland Tractor-Trailer, same tractor as No. 2000 except marked, "Loft-Fresh Candies"	350	550	850
Dump Truck, w/dual rear wheels, 10-1/2" long, 3" wide, 3-3/8" high..............................	250	350	475
Easter Greetings Rabbit Truck, No. 800, 9" long	325	525	750

Courtland (Continued)	C6	C8	C10
Express and Hauling Truck, No. 900, 1946, 9" long, 3" wide, 2-3/4" high.....................................	100	175	275
Express Service Pickup, No. 4500, tin wind-up, 7-1/4" long, 3-1/4" wide, 2-3/4" high......................	75	125	175
FBI Riot Squad Car, No. 4050, similar to No. 7600 FBI Riot Squad Car......................................	100	125	150
FBI Riot Squad Car, No. 7600, 7-1/4" long, 3-1/4" wide, 2-3/4" high.....................................	100	150	200
Fire Chief Car, No. 4000, red and white, tin wind-up, 7-1/4" long, 3-1/4" wide, 2-3/4" high..............	100	125	175
Fire Chief Car, No. 4000, red, tin wind-up, 7-1/4" long, 3-1/4" wide, 2-3/4" high......................	100	125	150
Fire Department with Automatic Darage Door, No. 9050, nonpowered fire chief car w/the Courtland Toy Co., Phila. Pa., markings,, 7-3/4" x 10-1/8" x 6-3/4"	75	125	175
Fire Patrol No. 2 Truck, No. 900, 1946, L 9", W 3", H 2-3/4"	100	175	275

Chein Rapid Delivery, No. 10, $600. Photo courtesy Bob Smith

Chein Woodie Sedan tin wind-up with Chein Garage, Sedan priced at $95. Photo courtesy of Dave Leopard

Top to bottom: Cor-Cor Graham Paige Sedan, $1950; Sturditoy "Sturditoy Oil Company" truck, $2500; Buddy "L" Ice Truck, $1750. Photo courtesy Christie's East

Courtland Checker Cab Car, No. 4000, 7-1/4" long, 3-1/4" high, $350.

Courtland City Meat Market Delivery Sedan, No. 4000, 7-1/4" long, 3-1/4" wide, 2-3/4" high, $175.

Courtland (Continued)	C6	C8	C10
Ice Cream Truck, No. 900, 1946, 9" long, 3" wide, 2-3/4" high	125	200	300
Log Truck Tractor-Trailer, No. 620, 1946, 13" long, 3" wide, 3-1/4" high.................	150	225	350
Mechanical Automatic Ladder Fire Truck, No. 1400, tin wind-up, 9" long, 3" wide, 2-3/4" high	175	250	350
Mechanical Black Diamond Coal Truck, No. 5100, tin wind-up, 10-1/2" wide, 3" wide, 3-3/8" high..............................	150	225	300

Courtland (Continued)	C6	C8	C10
Mechanical Chromed Trimmed Tow Truck, No. 8500, tow boom shows detail, tin wind-up, 8" long, 3-1/4" wide, 3-1/2" high.....	75	175	225
Mechanical Chromed Trimmed Tow Truck, No. 8500, tow boom is solid color, tin wind-up, 8" long, 3-1/4" wide, 3-1/2" high.....	175	300	350
Mechanical Combination Steam Shovel Carried by Low-boy Tractor-trailer, No. 5300, tin wind-up, 15-1/2" long, 3-7/8" wide, 10-1/2" high......................	350	550	775

Open Van Tractor-Trailer, 1946, No. 600, Courtland, $300.

Easter Greetings Rabbit Truck, No. 800, Courtland, $750.

Courtland Mechanical Black Diamond Coal Truck, No. 5100, 10-1/2" wide, 3" wide, 3-3/8" high, $300. Photo courtesy Joe and Sharon Freed

Courtland Mechanical Gasoline Trailer Truck, $325.

Courtland (Continued)	C6	C8	C10
Mechanical Dump Truck, No. 3100, tin wind-up, 7" long, 3" wide, 3-1/4" high	65	100	135
Mechanical Dump Truck, No. 1600, tin wind-up, 7" long, 3" wide, 2-3/4" high	65	100	135
Mechanical Emergency Rescue Squad Tractor-Trailer, tin wind-up, 13" long, 3" wide, 3-1/4" high	150	200	250
Mechanical ESSO Gasoline Tractor-Trailer, No. 2000, tin wind-up, 13" long, 3" wide, 3-1/4" high	250	350	450
Mechanical Express and Hauling Truck, No. 1300, tin wind-up, 9" long, 3" wide, 2-3/4" high	125	200	275
Mechanical Fire Chief Car, No. 7000, w/siren, tin wind-up, 7-1/4" long, 3-1/4" wide, 2-3/4" high	150	200	250
Mechanical Fire Chief Car with Siren, No. 7500, 7-1/4" long, 3-1/4" wide, 3-1/4" high	150	200	250
Mechanical Fire Patrol No. 2 Truck, No. 1300, tin wind-up, 9" long, 3" wide, 2-3/4" high	125	200	275
Mechanical Freight Haulers Tractor-Trailer, No. 2600, tin wind-up, 13" long, 3" high, 3-1/4" wide	150	250	325

Courtland (Continued)	C6	C8	C10
Mechanical Gasoline Tractor-Trailer, No. 2000, tin wind-up, 13" long, 3" wide, 3-1/4" high	150	250	325
Mechanical Gulf Gasoline Tractor-Trailer, No. 3875, 13" long, 3" wide, 3-1/4" high	225	350	475
Mechanical Heavy Duty Sand and Gravel Tractor-Trailer, No. 2375, tin wind-up, 13" long, 3" wide, 3-1/4" high	175	225	275
Mechanical Hook and Ladder Tractor-Trailer, No. 2100, tin wind-up, 13" long, 3" wide, 3-1/4" high	100	150	175
Mechanical Ice Cream Scooter, No. 6500, tin wind-up, 6-1/2" long, 3" wide, 4-1/2" high	200	300	400
Mechanical Ice Cream Truck, No. 1300, tin wind-up, 9" long, 3" wide, 2-3/4" high	150	200	250
Mechanical Lawn Mower, No. 21, tin wind-up, 12" wide, 29" high, 5" wheels	65	85	110
Mechanical Lawn Mower, No. 20, tin wind-up, 11-1/4" wide, 29" high, 5" wheels	65	85	110
Mechanical Lawn Mower, No. 15, tin wind-up, 8-1/4" wide, 24" high, 3" wheels	50	75	100

Courtland Friction-Powered Vehicle No. 4000 Fire Chief Car, red & white, with red plastic bubble on hood. Photo courtesy Joe and Sharon Freed

Courtland Mechanical Emergency Rescue Sqaud Tractor-Trailer, 13" long, 3" wide, 3-1/4" high, $250.

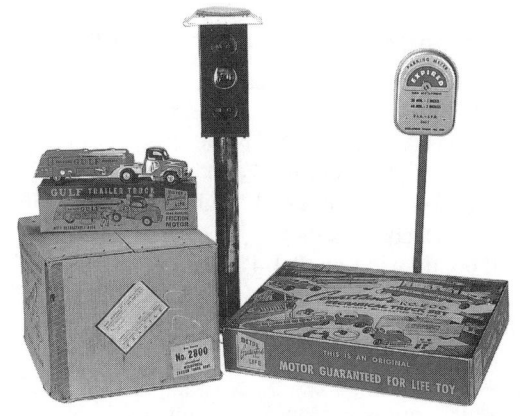

Courtland, Gulf Gas Truck No. 3875 on top of an unopened wholesale case; Traffic Signal No. 7800; Mechanical Truck Set No. 500; Parking Meter No. 7500. Photo courtesy Joe and Sharon Freed

Courtland Mechanical Fire Chief Car, No. 7000, 7-1/4" long, 3-1/4" wide, 2-3/4" high, $250. Photo courtesy Joe and Sharon Freed

Courtland (Continued)	C6	C8	C10
Mechanical Logging Tractor-Trailer, No. 2200, tin wind-up, 13" long, 3" wide, 3-1/4" high	150	200	250
Mechanical Military Gun Car, painted gun shield, 7-1/2" long, 3-1/4" wide, 2-1/2" high..............	100	175	200
Mechanical Military Gun Car, lithographed gun shield, 7-1/2" long, 3-1/4" wide, 2-1/2" high..............	100	175	250
Mechanical Milk Tractor-Trailer, No. 2050, "American Dairies", tin wind-up. Note: 1951 catalog shows Milk Trailer markings that read the same as above except "Approved" is used in the place of "Vitamin D." This variation is not known to have been produced, 13" long, 3" wide, 3-1/4" high..............	150	250	325
Mechanical Moving and Storage Truck, No. 1300, tin wind-up, 9" long, 3" wide, 2-3/4" high	175	250	375

Courtland (Continued)	C6	C8	C10
Mechanical Moving and Storage Truck, w/No. 130 litho on the sides of the truck bed, tin wind-up..............	175	250	375
Mechanical No. 51 Steam Shovel, No. 5200, tin wind-up, 15-1/2" long, 3-3/4" wide, 9-1/2" high.....	150	200	250
Mechanical Open Van Tractor-Trailer, No. 2350, tin wind-up, 13" long, 3" wide, 3-1/4" high	75	125	175
Mechanical Open Van Tractor-Trailer, No. 2300, tin wind-up, 13" long, 3" wide, 3-1/4" high..............	75	125	175
Mechanical Operation No. 51 Crane Turck, No. 5000, tin wind-up, 13" long, 3-5/8" wide, 5" high..............	225	325	400
Mechanical Power Lawn Mower, No. 25, tin wind-up, 12" wide, 29" high, 5-3/4" wheels..............	75	100	125

Courtland Non-Powered Vehicle No. 620 Log Truck, Photo courtesy Joe and Sharon Freed

Courtland Fire Department w/ automatic garage door, $175.

Courtland (Continued)	C6	C8	C10
Mechanical Road Roller Truck, No. 3000, tin wind-up, 9" long, 3" wide, 3-1/4" high	250	350	450
Mechanical Road Roller Truck, No. 1500, tin wind-up, 9" long, 3" wide, 3-1/4" high	250	350	450
Mechanical Side Tipper Tractor-Trailer, No. 2700, tin wind-up, 13" long, 3" high, 3-1/4" wide	200	300	375
Mechanical Side Tipper Tractor-Trailer, No. 3900, "Black Diamond Coal Company-340," tin wind-up, 13" long, 3" high, 3-1/4" wide	300	400	500
Mechanical Stake Bed Truck, No. 3200, tin wind-up, 7" long, 3" wide, 3-1/4" high	125	150	175
Mechanical State Police Car, No. 7500, w/siren, tin wind-up, 7-1/4" long, 3-1/4" wide, 2-3/4" high	165	225	275
Mechanical State Police Car with Siren, No. 7500, 7-1/4" long, 3-1/4" wide, 2-3/4" high	150	200	250
Mechanical Three-piece Train Set, No. 2259000, 24" long, 2-1/4" wide, 3-1/4" high	100	150	200
Mechanical Tractor, w/tin wheels, w/o scraper, 7-1/2" long, 4-3/4" wide, 4-1/2" high	250	350	450
Mechanical Trailer Tow Truck, No. 2400, tin wind-up, 13" long, 3" wide, 3-1/4" high	225	325	400
Mechanical Trailer-Truck, No. 1200, tin wind-up, 13" long, 3" wide, 3-1/4" high	200	250	375
Mechanical Truck Set, No. 500, w/box, includes four trucks: Nos. 2000, 2100, 2200, 2300	150	300	600

Courtland (Continued)	C6	C8	C10
Mechanical Truck Terminal Set, No. 600, two trucks	450	750	1100
Modern Bakery Delivery Sedan, No. 4000, tin wind-up, 7-1/4" long, 3-1/4" wide, 2-3/4" high	100	150	175
Modern Decorators Pickup, No. 4500, tin wind-up, 7-1/4" long, 3-1/4" wide, 2-3/4" high	100	125	150
Moving and Storage Truck, No. 900, 1946, 9" long, 3" wide, 2-3/4" high	150	225	350
Open Van Tractor-Trailer, No. 600, 1946, 13" long, 3" wide, 3-1/4" high	100	150	200
Pop-Up Ladder Fire Truck, No. 5450, 13" long, 3" wide, 3-1/4" high	250	350	450
Private Garage with Automatic Door, No. 9075, nonpowered car w/Courtland Toy Co., Phila. Pa. Markings, 7-3/4" x 10-1/8" x 6-3/4"	75	125	175
Side Dump Tractor-Trailer, No. 610, 1946, 13" long, 3" wide, 3-1/4" high	100	150	200
Side Dump Tractor-Trailer, No. 700, 1946, 13" long, 3" wide, 3-1/4" high	100	150	200
Space Rocket Patrol Car, No. 4060, 1952, 7-1/4" long, 3-1/4" wide, 2-3/4" high	150	200	250
Woody Sedan, No. 4000, blue and tan, stamped "A Walt Reach Toy by Courtland Toy Co. Philadelphia, PA. Made in U.S.A.", 7-1/4" long, 3-1/4" wide, 2-3/4" high	65	75	100

Courtland Mechanical Heavy Duty Sand and Gravel Tractor-Trailer, No. 2375, 13" long, 3" wide, 3-1/4" high, $275.

Courtland Mechanical Hook and Ladder Tractor-Trailer, No. 2100, 13" long, 3" wide, 3-1/4" high, $175.

Courtland Mechanical Ice Cream Truck, No. 1300, $250. Photo courtesy Joe and Sharon Freed

Courtland Mechanical Logging Tractor-Trailer, No. 2200, 13" long, 3" wide, 3-1/4" high, $250.

Courtland (Continued)	**C6**	**C8**	**C10**
Woody Sedan, No. 4000, red and tan, marked stamped "A Walt Reach Toy by Courtland Toy Co. Philadelphia, PA. Made in U.S.A.", 7-1/4" long, 3-1/4" wide, 2-3/4" high	65	75	100

Craftoys

Craftoys, a small Oklahoma, Nebraska, firm, had a brief career casting slush-mold vehicles before World War II when the need for lead brought the pot metal era to a long halt. Craftoys acquired some of the molds when Ralstoy was reorganizing in 1940.

Contributor: Fred Maxwell, 4722 N. 33 St., Arlington, VA 22207. Perry R. Eichor, 703 North Almond Drive, Simpsonville, SC 29681.

Craftoy	**C6**	**C8**	**C10**
Cement Mixer, No. 78, two open windows, "Made in USA", 3-3/4"	8	12	16
Fire Truck, No. 101, hose truck or insurance patrol, four open windows, 4-1/2" long	40	60	80

Craftoy (Continued)	**C6**	**C8**	**C10**
Freight Train, No. 3600, "Locomotive, 0-6-4, 4-1/2", "KT&N RR," "Made in USA," price per car, 16-1/2", cars 3-1/4", caboose 2-3/4"	6	9	12
Oil Truck, No. 104, 1938 International, tanker, COE, two open windows, marked "Gas" and "Oil", 3-3/4" long	45	70	80
Racer, No. 81, Miller FWD Indy, marked "Made in USA", 4-1/2" long	20	40	60
Racer, No. 100, Indy type, driver, removable tine hood, rounded nose, available as reproduction, 4-1/2" long	20	40	60
Racer, no number, Indy type, driver, removable tin hood, slanted nose, available as reproduction, 3-3/4" long	30	40	60
Racer, No. 81, Miller FWD Indy racer, "Made in USA", 4-1/2"	10	15	20

Courtland Mechanical Road Roller Truck, No. 3000, 9" long, 3" wide, 3-1/4" high, $450.

Courtland Mechanical Tractor w/tin wheels, No. 6075, $450. Photo courtesy Joe and Sharon Freed

Courtland Mechanical Truck Set, No. 500, $600. Photo courtesy Joe and Sharon Freed

Courtland Mechanical Truck Terminal Set, No. 600, $1100. Photo courtesy Joe and Sharon Freed

Craftoy (Continued)

	C6	C8	C10
Sedan, No. 92, streamlined two-door sedan, four open windows, screen pattern grille, 4" long	20	40	60
Speed Car, No. 103, streamlined closed racer, body trimmed in fantasy streamlines, available as reproduction, 4-1/4" long	45	70	95
Station Wagon, No. 105, stream-lined, four open windows, 3-3/4" long	NPF	NPF	NPF
Tanker, No. 102, International K-Line (?), semi-trailer, two open windows, marked "Gasoline", 6-3/4" long	40	60	80
Tractor, No. 17, "Fordson," "Made in USA," farm tractor, driver, rear wheels larger, visible engine, 2-1/2"	8	12	16

Dayton Friction Works

	C6	C8	C10
Armored Car, flywheel drive, red and gold, 1909, 11"	250	450	600
Coal and Ice Truck, friction, c. 1920	200	300	400
Coupe, tine friction, 17" long	500	650	900
Coupe, c. 1920, 12-1/2" long	600	900	1200
Coupe, 1928, 12"	450	675	900
Dayton Friction, rubber tires, 1920s, 14-1/4" long	250	375	500
Dump Truck	200	300	400
Fire Ladder Truck, 18" long	275	365	550
Fire Pumper, flywheel drive, white/gold, 1909, 14-3/4" long	500	750	1000
Ladder Truck, 1920s	350	525	700
Touring Car, unpowered, 13-1/2" long	350	525	700
Touring Car, friction motor, 13-1/2" long	500	750	1000

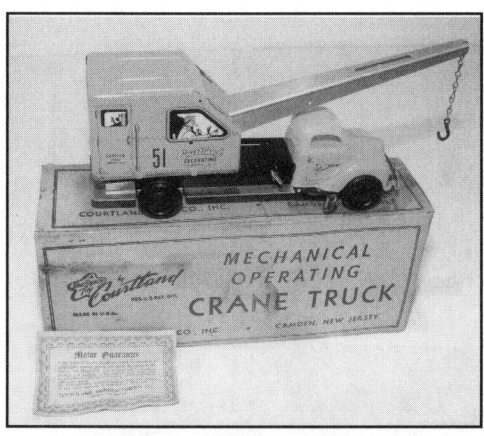

Left to right: Courtland Mechanical Fire Patrol Truck, No. 2, $275; Courtland Mechanical Moving and Storage Truck, No. 130, $375.

Courtland Mechanical Operating Crane Truck, No. 51, $400. Photo courtesy Bob Smith

Courtland Pop-Up Ladder Fire Truck, No. 5450, 13" long, 3" wide, 3-1/4" high, $450.

Dayton Friction Works

	C6	C8	C10
Touring Car, seven passenger, open, w/driver, flywheel drive, red and gold, patent date April 2, 1909, 13-1/4" long	150	225	300

Dent Hardware Company

Dent, of Fullerton, Pennsylvania, was in business from 1895-1973. Henry H. Dent, with four partners, was the owner. Dent is known for particularly fine castings in its vehicles. It was also one of the first manufacturers to try (with little success) aluminum toys in the 1920s. Toys seem to have been phased out during the Depression. Dent toys are difficult to identify due to the fact that few, if any, of its toys are marked.

Dent Hardware Company

	C6	C8	C10
American Oil Co. Truck, 10-1/2" long	800	1250	1750
Bus, 6-1/4" long	350	500	750
Bus, 10-1/2" long	500	800	900
Bus Line, 9" long	450	600	1250
Coast to Coast Bus, 7-1/2" long	125	175	275
Coast to Coast Bus, 10" long	300	450	650
Coast to Coast Bus, c. 1925, 15" long	1100	1700	2500
Contractors Mack Dump, open cab, 10-1/2" long	100	2000	3000
Coupe, 5" long	125	175	250
Express J & B Stakebed Truck, driver, 1915, 14-1/2" long	500	800	1250
Fire Ladder Truck, w/driver, 8-1/2" long	400	625	925

Dent Hardware Company

	C6	C8	C10
Fire Truck, w/ladder and men, 18" long	800	1250	1900
Fire Truck, 7" long	125	500	325
Freeman's Dairy Truck, sliding doors, milkman, 6" long	650	1150	1750
Hose Reeler, w/men, large	450	700	1100
Interurban Bus, 9" long	225	350	550
Ladder Truck, two drivers, 10" long	225	350	550
LaSalle, 4-1/2" long	425	700	975
Mack Dump Truck, iron wheels, c. 1925, 4-1/2" long	50	75	125
Model T Sedan, two door, iron wheels, c. 1925	125	187	250
Patrol, c. 1920s, 6-1/2" long	125	187	250
Police Patrol, 8-3/4" long	700	1125	1650
Public Service Bus, c. 1926, 13-1/2" long	1750	3000	4750
Sedan, spare tire, has stop and go light, full bumpers on front, 7-1/2"	900	1350	1800
Steam Roller, 6" long	40	70	90
Touring Car, driver and passenger, 12" long	450	700	1100
Valley View Dairy, 8" long	500	900	1500
Yellow Cab, approx. 7-3/4" long	800	1250	1800

Dinky

Dinky toys were first made in England in 1932 under the name "Modeled Miniatures," and later "Meccano Miniatures," and in 1934, "Dinky," which in England means, "fetching."

Space Rocket Patrol Car, No. 4060, 1952, Courtland, $250.

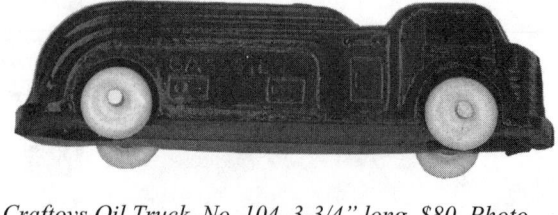

Craftoys Oil Truck, No. 104, 3-3/4" long, $80. Photo courtesy Fred Maxwell

Craftoys Speed Car, No. 103, 4-1/4" long, $85. Photo courtesy Perry Eichor

Top to Bottom: Craftoys Racer, No. 100, 4-1/2" long, $60; Craftoys Racer, 3-3/4" long, $60. Photo courtesy Perry Eichor

Craftoys Tanker, No. 102, 6-3/4" long, $80. Photo courtesy Ferd Zegel

Dinky	C6	C8	C10
1948 Plymouth Station Wagon, No. 027f	75	150	200
1968 Pontiac RCMP Police Car, No. 252	40	80	100
45 Vauxhall Victor, No. 045	15	20	40
Alvis, No. 038d	115	160	225
AN Simca Bailly, No. 033	55	110	150
Austin Devon, No. 151	17	26	35
Austin Taxi, No. 254	45	85	110
Austin Taxi, No. 241	25	40	50
Beach Buggy, No. 227	15	20	40
Bedford Dump, No. 267	30	45	75
Bentley, No. 036b	95	145	190
Coventry Fork Lift, No. 014c	35	75	100
Dodge Fire Rescue, No. 267	30	45	75
Double Decker Bus, No. 029c	75	115	150
Estate Car, No. 344	30	40	60
Euclid Truck, No. 097	15	20	40
Ferrari Racer, No. 023h	15	20	40
Flat Truck, No. 025c	85	125	175
Ford Consul Corsair, No. 130	40	55	90
Ford Escort, No. 168	15	25	50
Ford Sedan, No. 170, 1950	35	55	75

Dinky (Continued)	C6	C8	C10
Ford Taurus, No. 154	17	26	35
Fordson Truck, No. 030r	40	60	80
Hudson Hornet Sedan, No. 174	65	115	155
Humber, No. 036c, 1936	100	150	200
Jaguar XK 120, No. 157	65	130	165
Lagonda, No. 038c	95	150	195
Leyland Tractor, No. 308	30	40	60
Lincoln Zephyr, No. 039c	140	225	275
Matra 630, No. 200	15	20	40
Morris Mini, No. 197	55	110	145
Panhard Esso, No. 032c/576	60	90	120
Plymouth, No. 137, 1963	50	75	95
Plymouth Rally, No. 201, 1976	15	20	40
Riley 4DS, No. 040a	90	130	175
Rolls Royce Phantom V, No. 198	40	80	105
Rover, No. 036d	85	127	170
Royal Mail Van, No. 034	40	55	90
Studebaker Land Cruiser, No. 172	55	80	110
Telephone Service Truck, No. 261	65	130	165
Thunderbird 2 Space, No. 106	45	95	125
Triumph 2000, No. 135	20	30	40
Triumph Purdey, No. 112	40	55	85

*Dayton Friction Works Armored Car, 1909, 11",
$600. Photo courtesy Bob Smith*

*Dayton Friction Works Touring Car. Photo courtesy
OEI Enterprises Ltd.*

Dayton Friction Works Coupe, 17" long, $900.

Dayton Fire Pumper Truck, c. 1909, $1000.

*Touring Car, open, dated 1909, friction motor, with
driver, Dayton Friction Works, $500.*

Dinky (Continued)	C6	C8	C10
Triumph TR7 Leyland, No. 207	15	20	40
Triumph Vitesse, No. 134	30	42	65
Volkswagen MBD, No. 181	50	100	135

Doepke "Model Toys"

Charles Wm. Doepke Mfg. Co., Inc., also known as
Doepke, was located in Rossmoyne, Ohio. Each of their toys
was an authorized replica of the actual vehicle, right down to
the decals. The exception was the manufacturer's own model
Toys design. Doepke "Model Toys" advertised their toys as
outlasting all others—three to one.

Of the Doepke "Model Toys" that were mass produced,
several had variations in their basic construction. Usually
these changes were an elimination of the more intricate operating procedures and had little or no effect on the toys overall
appearance.

Doepke accepted orders to make models of actual vehicles
for various companies, but the toys with the most allure, play-
ability, feasible mass production design, and greatest enter-
tainment value were mass produced. The others, those that
would not withstand rough handling by young hands or were
too expensive, were only manufactured in low numbers,
sometimes only one. This is no doubt the explanation for the
number gaps between the marketed items.

At the end of World War II, Doepke hit the market with
five models, the first in a line of heavy-duty metal operating
replicas employing metal tread or authentic miniature tires.
The tires were either Goodyear or Firestone, with authentic
tread and name and tire sizes. The first five numbers in the toy
series were 2000, 2001, 2002, 2006, 2007. Following is a list
of Doepke vehicles.

Doepke "Model Toys"	C6	C8	C10
Adams Diesel Road Grader, No. 2006, 26" long	210	295	395

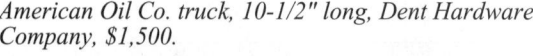

American Oil Co. truck, 10-1/2" long, Dent Hardware Company, $1,500.

Police Patrol, 8-3/4" long, Dent Hardware Company, $1,500.

Dent Coast to Coast Bus, c. 1925, 15" long, $2500. Photo courtesy Bertoia Auctions

Dent Hardware Company Freeman's Dairy Truck, 6" long, $1750.

Touring Car, driver and passenger, 12" long, Dent Hardware Company, $710.

Doepke "Model Toys"	C6	C8	C10
American LaFrance Aerial Ladder Fire Truck, No. 2014, 23" long ...	290	375	450
American LaFrance Aerial Ladder Truck, No. 2008	245	325	400
American LaFrance Improved Aeriel Searchlight Truck, No. 2023, 1955..................................	950	1650	2100
American LaFrance Pumper Fire Truck, No. 2020, 18" long...........	200	300	400
Barber-Greene High-capacity Bucket Loader, No. 2001, tracks, 13" high..	430	510	625
Barber-Greene Mobile, No. 2013, high-capacity bucket loader, wheels, 22" long..........................	325	400	525
Clark Airport Tractor and Baggage Trailers, No. 2015	375	450	550
Euclid Earth Hauler Truck, No. 2009, 27" long............................	250	300	400

Doepke "Model Toys"	C6	C8	C10
Heiliner Earth Scraper, No. 2011, 29" long..................................	295	300	375
Jaeger Concrete Mixer, No. 2002, 15" long..................................	225	310	450
Jaguar, No. 2018, 1955....................	450	550	650
MG, No. 2015, 1954, 15" long........	360	450	525
Unit Mobile Crane, No. 2007, 11-1/2" long..................................	225	300	400
Wooldridge H.D. Earth Hauler, No. 2000, 25" long............................	225	300	425

Dunwell

Dunwell was the trade name given to its toys by Metal Products Co. of Clifton, New Jersey. Its trucks seem to have been sold from 1953-1958. Dunwell vehicles resemble the Tonka line, and are rare.

Dunwell	C6	C8	C10
Auto Transport	162	243	325

Public Service Bus, c. 1926, 13-1/2" long, Dent Hardware Company, $2,400.

Valley View Dairy, 8" long, Dent Hardware Company, $1,500.

Doepke Barber-Greene Mobile bucket loader, No. 2013, $525.

Doepke Adams Diesel Road Grader, No. 2006, $395. Photo courtesy Calvin L. Chaussee

Dunwell (Continued)	C6	C8	C10
Dump Truck	100	150	200
Log Truck	110	165	220
Red Star Express Lines Truck	300	450	600
Snowcrop Refrigerator Semi	350	525	700
Steel Carrier Co. Semi	17	255	340
Wrecker	168	254	335

Dyna-Model Products Company

Dyna-Models Products Co. may have pioneered the scale model industry of today's markets with their "Syna-Mo" brand of HO toys. They produced pot-metal toys, identified by their method of assembling body parts (clamping axles between small posts) and by the standardized appearance of the undersides of the whole line.

Produced in the 1930s, and perhaps into the postwar era, the toys were made by a coarse die-casting process. The earlier vintage cars were made in two to five parts, exclusive of wheels and axles, to be pinned, clamped, or glued together, including body, frame, steering wheel, top and windshield. Some were packaged as kits with instructions printed on the box. The toys were factory painted in as many as four colors.

Contributors: Fred Maxwell, 4722 N. 33 St., Arlington, VA 22207. Perry R. Eichor, 703 North Almond Drive, Simpsonville, SC 29681.

Dyna-Model Products Company	C6	C8	C10
Convertible, Cadillac two-door Sedan, late 1930s, 2-3/8" (D16)	6	9	12

Dyna-Model Products Company (Continued)	C6	C8	C10
Delivery Van, Pontiac, open windshield and door windows, late 1930s, 2-3/8" (D21)	4	6	8
Dump Truck, open windows, hinged body w/realistic load of coal, three-piece, two colors, dual rear wheels, 2-3/4" (D24)	6	9	12
Limousine, Cadillac, open windows, late 1930s, 2-1/2" (D20)	9	6	12
Pickup Truck, GMC?, one-piece, open windows, one color, 1930s, 2" (D25)	4	6	8
Pickup Truck, Mack?, "US Army," Air Corps star decals, two-piece body, two colors, late 1930s, 2" (D26)	4	6	8
Pickup Truck, GMC?, open windows, spoked wheels, two-piece, three colors, late 1930s, 2-1/2" (D22)	4	6	8
R-26 HO Buick Convertible 55c, open, two-door sedan, top down, one-piece body, solid cast windshield, disc wheels, late 1930s, 2-3/8" (D13)	6	9	12
R-26 HO Surrey, horseless carriage, tiller steering, three colors, three-piece body, kit, 1-3/4" (D1)	4	6	8

No. 2008 American LaFrance Aerial Ladder Truck, Doepke, $400.

Catalog page featuring the Doepke American LaFrance Aerial Ladder Truck No. 2008.

No. 2002 Jaeger Concrete Mixer, Doepke, $280.

Doepke American LaFrance Improved Aerial Search Light Truck, No. 2023, 1955, $2100.

Dyna-Model Products Company (Continued)	C6	C8	C10
R-61 HO Model T Ford 1914 Touring with Top, one-piece body, top up, three colors, "cut plastic windshield to fit, darken edges w/ink or paint and glue top and windshield in place, in slots provided", 1-5/8" (D6)	4	6	8
Roadster, Packard, top up, rumble seat, one-piece body, glued windshield, spoked wheels, three colors, 2" (D9)	6	9	12
Roadster, 1920s Packard convertible, top down, rumble seat, one-piece body, glued windshield, spoked wheels, three colors, 2" (D8)	6	9	12
Roadster, Buick (?), open, right-hand steering, four-piece, three colors, 1-7/8" (D4)	4	6	8
Roadster, Model A Ford (?) top down, open rumble seat, disc wheels, one-piece body, unpainted, 2" (D11)	2	3	4

Dyna-Model Products Company (Continued)	C6	C8	C10
Sedan, Buick two-door airflow, open windshield and windows, 2-3/8" (D14)	6	9	12
Sedan, Cadillac two-door, open windshield and windows, late 1930s, 2-3/8" (D17)	6	9	12
Sedan, Pontiac four-door airflow, open windshield and windows including rear, 2-3/8" (D19)	6	9	12
Sedan, Buick, open windshield and windows, two colors, 1930s, 2" (D12)	4	6	8
Speedster, Antique Mercer, right-hand steering, four colors, three-piece, 2" (D3)	4	6	8
Taxi, Cadillac sedan, open windshield and windows including rear, two colors, late 1930s, 2-3/8" (D18)	6	9	12
Taxi, Buick sedan, open windshield and windows, two colors, late 1930s, 2-3/8" (D15)	6	9	12

No. 2009 Euclid Earth Hauler Truck, Doepke, $300.

No. 2011 Heiliner Earth Scraper, Doepke, $380.

Dyna-Model Products Company (Continued)

	C6	C8	C10
Touring, Packard, top down, rumble seat, one-piece body, glued windshield, spoked wheels, three colors, 2" (D10)	6	9	12
Touring Car, 1914 Ford, top down cast in one-piece body, glued windshield, three colors, 1-3/4" (D7)	4	6	8
Touring Car, Stanley Steamer, open tonneau, right-hand steering, four colors, four-piece, 2" (D2)	4	6	8
Touring Car, realistic folded top attachable w/hinge pins, left hand steering, five-piece, two colors, 1-7/8" (D5)	4	6	8
Truck, Mack (?), tarpaulin-covered, two-piece body, 2" (D27)	4	6	8
Wrecker, GMC (?), open windows, three-piece, four colors, late 1930s, 2-3/4" (D23)	6	9	12

Erie (Parker White Metal)

According to James Apthrope, Erie toys were made by Parker White Metal Company, which apparently began in Erie, Pennsylvania, but moved to Fairview in the early 1960s. However, according to company officials, the firm made toys only prior to World War II. It printed no catalogs.

Contributor: Dave Leopard, 2507 Feather Run Trail, West Columbia, SC 29169-4915.

Erie

	C6	C8	C10
Cabover Truck, tailgate, updated, c. 1937, 3-1/4" long (EV16)	20	25	35
Cabover Truck, no tailgate, c. 1937, 3-1/4" (EV15)	20	25	35

Erie (Continued)

	C6	C8	C10
Champion Coal Truck, 1935, 5" long	40	55	95
Coupe, futuristic, no chassis, c. 1939, 4-1/4" long (EV19)	30	40	50
Ford Ice Truck, "Pure Ice Co.", 1935, 5" long (EV13)	50	65	85
Ford Pickup Truck, high sides, small rear window, 1935, 5" long (EV12)	40	55	70
Ford Pickup Truck, low sides, painted, 1935, 5" long (EV09)	45	60	75
Ford Pickup Truck, high sides, large rear window, 1935, 5" long (EV11)	40	55	70
Ford Pickup Truck, low sides, plated, 1935, 5" long (EV10)	45	60	80
Ford Tow Truck, "Servel Body", 1935, 5" long (EV14)	50	65	80
Lincoln Zephyr Sedan, painted, 1936, 5-1/2" long (EV01)	40	50	70
Lincoln Zephyr Sedan, plated, 1936, 3-1/2" long (EV04)	35	40	55
Lincoln Zephyr Sedan, painted, 1936, 3-1/2" long (EV03)	25	30	40
Lincoln Zephyr Sedan, plated, 1936, 5-1/2" long (EV02)	45	55	75
Packard Roadster, plated, 1936, 3-1/2" long (EV08)	35	40	50
Packard Roadster, painted, 1936, 3-1/2" long (EV07)	25	30	40
Packard Roadster, plated, 1936, 6" long (EV06)	50	70	100
Packard Roadster, painted, 1936, 6" long (EV05)	45	65	95

Erie (Continued)

	C6	C8	C10
Sedan, futuristic, fin on trunk, no chassis, c. 1939, 4-1/4" long (EV18)	30	35	50
Sedan, sharknose, no chassis, c. 1939, 4-1/4" long (EV20)	30	35	50
Tow Truck, no chassis, c. 1939, 4-1/4" long (EV17)	30	40	50

Ertl

Ertl was begun by Fred Ertl Sr., in 1945, working out of his Dubuque, Iowa, home. As business expanded, the firm moved to Dyersville, Iowa. Ertl learned about using sand molds in his native Germany; very early in the company's history, he began working directly from the original blueprints to make his toy tractors, trucks, and other wheeled toys. Ertl's specialty is farm toys, with rights obtained from such manufacturers as International Harvester and John Deere. Today, Ertl is the largest manufacturer of toy-farm equipment in the world; in addition, it makes a number of other toys, such as cars, trucks, and airplanes.

Ertl was purchased by Racing Champions in 1998 and now goes by the name Racing Champions-Ertl.

Ertl

	C6	C8	C10
Conoco Tanker	75	120	175
Ertl Van Lines Pup Trailer, white	100	150	225
Fleetstar Dump Truck, ten wheel, red	125	185	250
Fleetstar Hi-side Dump Truck, red and white	125	185	250
Fleetstar Ten-wheel Dump Truck, red	85	128	170
Fleetstar Tilt Bed, green	125	185	250
GE Truck, white	15	22	30
GMC Dump	100	150	200
Hydraulic Dump Truck, No. 1645	20	30	40
International Dump	100	150	200
International Scout, maroon or blue	85	135	195
Iron Horse Van	35	52	70
Loadstar Box Van, lavender and white	200	375	575
Loadstar Dump Truck	132	198	265
Loadstar Tilt Bed, green/gray	85	128	170
Loadstar Tow Truck, white/red	100	150	200
Mary Kay Cosmetics Trailer Truck	75	112	150
Mobile Tanker	42	63	85
Tilt Bed	92	138	185
Transtar Rowe Furniture Truck	27	41	55
Transtar Texaco Tanker	45	68	90
Velveeta Semi	25	38	50

Firestone

The following list and the numbers in parentheses, was compiled by David Leopard.

Firestone

	C6	C8	C10
'35 Ford Two-door Humpback Sedan, 4-7/8" long (FA02)	75	100	150
'36 Ford Two-door Humpback Sedan, 4-7/8" long (FA03)	75	100	150
'39 Mercury Fastback Four-door Sedan, 4-3/4" long (FA01)	100	125	165

Freidag

	C6	C8	C10
Bus, 6-3/4" long	225	338	450
Coupe, 5-3/4" long	290	435	580
Double-Decker Bus, 9-1/4" long	850	1400	2100
Panel Delivery Truck, 7-1/2" long	1200	2200	3200
Pickup Truck, driver molded into window, 7-1/2" long	500	750	1000
Racer, driver and passenger, 6-1/2" long	550	900	1300
Roadster, w/driver and passenger, 6-1/2" long	400	600	800

Girard

Girard Model Works was founded by C.G. Wood in 1906, in Girard, Pennsylvania. His son Frank was soon made a partner. In 1918, they began making mechanical toys for an unidentified New York firm. In 1920, they sold them under their name "Wood's Mechanical Toys." The business eventually passed into other hands and had 1,000 employees in 1931. During the Depression, Girard laid off its salesman, Louis Marx, who stalled Girard customers as he tried to get a plant of his own is business. Since Marx was better known to buyers than the people at Girard, he emerged triumphant, and in 1934, Marx took over the firm. Girard remained in business until 1980.

Girard

	C6	C8	C10
Coupe, battery-operated headlights, 14" long	350	525	700
Fire Chief Car, 15" long	260	300	400
Fire Chief Siren Coupe, wind-up, 14" long	275	450	600
Fire Truck, 1920s, 12" long	50	75	100
Pierce-Arrow Coupe, wind-up, green, orange and cream, 1932, 14" long	250	350	500
Pump Truck, battery-operated, headlights, 10" long	100	150	200
Roadster, electrified, 14-1/2" long	212	318	425
Side Dump, 11-1/2" long	150	225	300
Stake Truck, electric, headlights, 10" long	150	225	300
Tank Truck, 11-1/2" long	92	138	185
Touring Bus, c. 1920, 12" long	150	225	300
Truck with Trailer, 1930s, 17" long	100	150	200

No. 2001 Barber-Greene high-capacity loader, Doepke, $380.

Doepke Unit Mobile Crane, No. 2007, $400. Photo courtesy Calvin L. Chaussee

Doepke Wooldridge H.D. Earth Hauler, No. 2000, 25" long, $425. Photo courtesy Calvin L. Chaussee

Dunwell Log Truck, $220. Photo courtesy Tim Oei

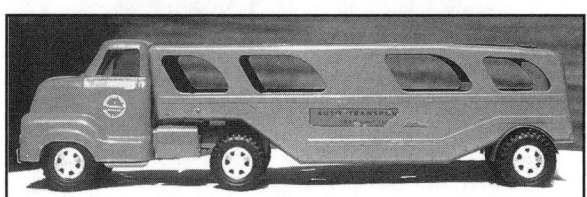

Dunwell Auto Transport, $325. Photo courtesy Roy Bonjour

Dunwell Red Star Express Lines Truck, $600. Photo courtesy Tim Oei

Dunwell Steel Carrier Co. Semi, $340. Photo courtesy Tim Oei

No. 2018 Jaguar, 1955, Doepke, $590.

Dyna-Model Products Company. Top Row, left to right: Sedan, 2-3/8", $12; Limousine, late 1930s, 2-1/2", $12; Sedan, 1930s, 2", $8; Sedan, late 1930s, 2-3/8", $12. Middle Row, left to right: Taxi, Buick, late 1930s, 2-3/8", $12; Taxi, Cadillac, late 1930s, 2-3/8", $12; Delivery Van, late 1930s, 2-3/8", $8. Bottom Row, left to right: Pickup Truck, late 1930s, 2-1/2", $8; Wrecker, late 1930s, 2-3/4", $12; Dump Truck, 2-3/4", $12.

Erie Champion Coal Truck, 1935, 5" long, $95. Photo courtesy John Taylor

Ertl Ertl Van Lines Pup Trailer, $225.

Ertl Fleetstar Hi-Side Dump Truck, $250.

Ertl Fleetstar Dump Truck, $250.

Girard (Continued)	C6	C8	C10
Wrecker Truck, mechanical boom, 1930s, 10" long	275	450	650

Grey Iron	C6	C8	C10
Convertible Midget, 1-1/2"	20	30	40
Coupe Midget, 1-1/2" long	20	30	40
Delivery Truck, Midget, 1-1/2" long	20	30	40
Ford Coupe, 8-3/8" long	475	715	950
Racer, Midget, 1-1/2" long	20	30	40
Sedan, 1927, 9" long	1000	1500	2000
Sedan Midget, older, 1-1/2" long	20	30	40
Sedan Midget, airflow type, 1-1/2" long	20	30	40

Hess Promotional Toys

The Hess Service Stations first staked a claim in the toy world in the mid-1960s, collaborating with Louis Marx Co., in producing a $1.29 Christmastime toy that would promote the East-coast service station chain. The B-Line Mack Tanker, with battery-operated lights, inaugurated a series that would become the mainstay of the collecting world. Hess released a new model yearly, usually a tanker truck or tractor-trailer. It varied the line in 1966 with the Voyager tanker ship, in 1970 with an American LaFrance fire pumper truck, and in 1980 with the GMC Motorhome Training Van. Emergency vehicles returned in 1986, and became a mainstay of the lineup into the 1990s. Race-car transporters became part of the line in 1988. Since collectors emphasize Mint-In-Box toys almost to the exclusion of played-with toys, the following prices are for C10 examples.

Hess

	C6	C8	C10
1964-5 B-Line Mack Tanker Truck, white trailer, made in Hong Kong	NPF	NPF	2000
1966 Voyager Tanker Ship, made in Hong Kong	NPF	NPF	2400
1967 Tanker Truck, green and white trailer, red velvet box, made in United States	NPF	NPF	2400
1968-69 Tanker Truck, green and white trailer, made in Hong Kong	NPF	NPF	650
1969 Tanker Truck, Amerada Hess, made in Hong Kong, never sold to the general public **replica alert**	NPF	NPF	2500
1970 Pumper Fire Truck, Amerada Hess, made in Hong Kong by marx	NPF	NPF	695
1971 Pumper Fire Truck, red, made in Hong Kong by Marx, marked "Season's Greetings"	NPF	NPF	3000
1972-4 Amerada Hess Tanker Truck, split window, (reissue of 1968 model)	NPF	NPF	350
1975 Tractor-Box Trailer, w/oil barrels, paper labels, made in both Hong Kong and United States	NPF	NPF	200
1976 Tractor-Box Trailer, w/oil barrels, no labels, made in Hong Kong	NPF	NPF	200
1977 Tanker Truck, large rear label, made in Hong Kong	NPF	NPF	150
1978-79 Tanker Truck, small rear label, made in Hong Kong	NPF	NPF	95
1980 GMC Training Van, made in Hong Kong	NPF	NPF	250
1982-83 "First Hess Truck" '34 Chevy Tanker, made in Hong Kong	NPF	NPF	65
1983-85 "First Hess Truck" '34 Chevy Tanker Bank, made in Hong Kong	NPF	NPF	65
1984-85 Tanker Truck Bank	NPF	NPF	65
1986 Ladder Truck, made in Hong Kong	NPF	NPF	75
1987 Tractor-Box Trailer Bank, w/oil barrels, made in Hong kong and China	NPF	NPF	50
1988 Race Car Transporter, made in Hong Kong	NPF	NPF	50
1989 Ladder Fire Truck, white, made in Hong Kong	NPF	NPF	35
1990 Tanker Truck, w/"Hess 1990" license plate, made in China	NPF	NPF	30

Hess (Continued)

	C6	C8	C10
1991 Race Car Transporter, made in China	NPF	NPF	50
1992 Tractor-Box Trailer, w/window down and Porsche, made in China	NPF	NPF	35
1993 Patrol Car, white and green w/siren	NPF	NPF	20
1993 Tanker Truck, limited edition "New Premium Diesel," not sold to general public, given as gift to bulk diesel fuel dealers	NPF	NPF	1500
1994 Fire Rescue Pickup Truck	NPF	NPF	15
1995 Helicopter Transporter	NPF	NPF	35
1996 Emergency Ladder Truck	NPF	NPF	25
1997 Tractor-Box Trailer, w/two race cars	NPF	NPF	25
1998 Mini Hess Tanker Truck	NPF	NPF	30
1999 Flatbed Truck with Space Shuttle and Satellite	NPF	NPF	30
2000 Fire Truck, w/working headlights and taillights	NPF	NPF	20

Hubley

The Hubley Manufacturing Company was founded in 1892 by John Hubley. It made iron toys from the start at its plant in Lancaster, Pennsylvania. In the beginning, all toys were cast iron, and some early toys included coal ranges, circus wagons, and mechanical banks. Hubley's cast-iron toys were popular almost from the start, and have long been collector's items because they were well-made and attractive. By 1940, however, the cast-iron toy, due to the increased cost of freight and foreign competition, was slowly becoming a thing of the past. At this time, when Hubley was the largest producer of cast-iron toys and cap pistols in the world, it began to introduce die-cast zinc alloy toys.

After World War II, Hubley manufactured 9,763,610 toys and 11,184,878 cap pistols, about ten times the amount of toys and pistols it produced in 1930, but with a line of toys eighty percent smaller than in 1930. It is the combination of the relative scarcity (and multiplicity) of the older, plus the preference by collectors for cast-iron over die-cast zinc alloy and plastic toys that makes the prewar the most attractive to collectors. Hubley was acquired by Gabriel Industries in late 1965.

Hubley

	C6	C8	C10
Air Compass Truck, c. 1950s, 7" long	50	75	100
Airflow-type Car, "Hubley U.S.A.," c. 1937, approx. 3-1/2" long	20	30	40
Army Motor Truck, No. 807, w/driver, 15" long	1100	1700	2500
Auto, Chevy?, 1922, 9" long	400	650	1000
Auto, 6-1/2" long	80	120	160
Auto, black plastic wheels, c. 1950s	12	18	25

Freidag Double-Decker Bus, 9-1/4" long, $2100. Photo courtesy Bertoia Auctions

Left to Right: Freidag Panel Delivery Truck, 7-1/2" long, $3200; Freidag Pickup Truck, 7-1/2" long, $1000.

Girard Fire Chief Siren Coupe, 14" long, $600.

Freidag Roadster, 6-1/2" long, $800. Photo courtesy Bertoia Auctions

Hubley (Continued)	C6	C8	C10
Auto Carrier, w/three cars and one pickup truck, c. 1939, 10" long ...	262	395	525
Auto Express, 9"	900	1450	2000
Auto Transport, marked "Hubley Transport", 13" long	125	188	250
Bell Telephone Truck, tools and ladders, 8-1/4" long	425	638	850
Bell Telephone Truck, w/derrick and windlass, auger, trailer w/10" pole, three digging tools, and two loose ladders, 1931, 10"	550	950	1300
Bell Telephone Truck, 1940s, 12-1/2" long	75	115	150
Bell Telephone Truck, 3-3/4" long..	150	225	300
Bell Telephone Truck, 5-1/4" long..	200	320	450
Bell Telephone Truck, 7" long	600	1000	1400
Bell Telephone Truck, just ladders as equipment, 13" long	250	375	500
Bell Telephone Truck, implements, 9" long	600	1000	1400
Bell Telephone Truck, post-WWII, 24" long	87	130	175
Bell Telephone Truck, w/tools, 12" long	500	800	1100
Black & White Cab, 1920s	1200	2000	3000
Bulldozer, front scoop, rubber treads, c. 1950, 10-1/4"	80	100	155
Bulldozer, 12"	150	225	300

Hubley (Continued)	C6	C8	C10
Bus, rubber wheels, c. 1938, 5-1/2" long	50	75	100
Bus, 1930s, 8" long	60	90	120
Bus, futuristic type, c. 1935, 3-1/2" long	50	75	100
Bus, "Coast to Coast", 1927, 13" long	1000	1600	2200
Cadillac, 7" long	40	60	80
Car and House Trailer, No. 2278 and No. 2279, c. 1939	150	225	300
Cement Mixer, 18" long	400	600	800
Cement Mixer, 8"	2000	3000	6500
Cement Mixer, Jaeger	475	715	950
Champion Stake Truck, white rubber tires, 1930s, 8-1/2" long	140	210	280
Chemical Truck, w/ladders, 13" long	200	300	400
Chevrolet 1932 Coupe Kit	25	38	50
Chevrolet 1932 Phaeton kit, 1960s..	40	60	80
Chevrolet 1932 Roadster kit, 1960s	25	38	50
Chrysler Airflow, electrified, white rubber tires on wood hubs, 8" long	900	1200	2000
Chrysler Airflow, take-apart body, 6-3/4" long	390	450	700
Chrysler Airflow, take-apart body, 4-1/2" long	117	175	250

Girard Stake Truck, electric headlights, 10", $300. Photo courtesy Charles Jackson

Girard Pierce-Arrow Coupe, 1932, 14" long, $500.

Girard Wrecker Truck, 1930s, 10" long, $600.

Grey Iron Midget Vehicles, $40, each. Photo courtesy Stan Alekna

Hess 1966 Voyager Tanker Ship, $2400. Photo courtesy John and Suzanne Adivari

Hubley (Continued)	C6	C8	C10
Chrysler Airflow Racing Car, c. 1938	100	150	200
Coal Truck, c. 1922, 9-1/2" long	438	655	875
Coal Truck, w/driver, 16-3/4" long	1200	1800	2500
Compressor Truck, Ingersoll Rand, 8-1/4" long	2500	4500	7000
Corvette, 13-1/2" long	255	380	510
Coupe Roadster, rumble seat, rubber tires, 11" long	200	290	390
Coupe, 1933 Ford	140	210	280
Crane, wooden wheels, 1940s	67	100	135
Crash Car, three-wheel motorcycle, chrome wheels, 11-1/2" long	2400	4200	6365
Crash Car, white rubber tires, c. 1937, 4-3/4" long	100	150	200
Delivery Van, 1932, 4-1/2" long	700	1300	1800
Digger, Mack, general, 10" long	450	700	1000

Hubley (Continued)	C6	C8	C10
Duesenberg Town Car, build-it model, 9" long	30	45	60
Dump Truck, 5-1/2" long	87	130	175
Dump Truck, c. 1938, 7-1/2" long	295	442	590
Dump Truck, Mack, six tires, 1930s, 10-3/4" long	1000	1800	2800
Fire Engine, No. 526, c. 1936, 10-1/2" long	175	263	350
Fire Engine, white rubber tires w/wooden rims, c. 1941	112	168	225
Fire Engine Pumper, driver, boiler-tender, black rubber tires, c. 1920, 12-1/2" long	350	525	700
Fire Engine Pumper, No. 504, early	350	525	700
Fire Ladder Truck, early, 7-1/2" long	130	195	260
Fire Ladder Truck, 19-1/2" long	600	950	1450

Hess 1972-74 Amerada Hess Tanker Truck, $350. Photo courtesy John and Suzanne Adivari

Hess 1975 Tractor-Box Trailer, $200. Photo courtesy John and Suzanne Adivari

Hess 1968-69 Tanker Truck, $650.

Hess 1991 Race Car Transporter, $50.

Hubley (Continued)	C6	C8	C10
Fire Ladder Truck, two wood ladders, c. 1920, 15-1/2" long	300	450	600
Fire Ladder Truck, early, 8-1/2"	350	525	700
Fire Truck, 5" long	120	180	240
Fire Truck, w/searchlight, white rubber tires w/wooden rims	55	82	110
Flatbed Truck, No. 506, all metal	118	177	235
Ford Coupe, 1936	40	60	80
Ford Model A Coupe Kit, 1960s	25	38	50
Ford Model A Phaeton Kit, 1960s	32	48	65
Ford Model A Pickup Kit, 1960s	32	48	65
Ford Model A Station Wagon Kit, 1960s	37	56	75
Ford Model A Town Car Kit, 1960s	32	48	65
Ford Model A Victoria Kit, 1960s	40	60	80
Fordson Front-End Loader, early 1930s, 9" long	800	1400	2000
Hook & Ladder Truck, No. 463	28	42	56
Hook & Ladder Truck, 19-1/2" long	200	300	400
Huber Road Roller, tractor-like, 7-3/4" long	257	385	515

Hubley (Continued)	C6	C8	C10
Huber Road Roller, 8" long	450	680	950
Huber Road Roller, 13" long	25	3850	5000
Huber Road Roller, 15" long	2500	3700	6000
Huber Road Roller, 4-1/2" long	110	165	220
Hubley Life Saver Truck, small hole in rear	400	600	800
Hubley Road Grader, 12" long	60	90	120
Jaguar Roadster, 7-1/2"	55	82	110
Kiddie Toy Dump Truck, plastic cab w/metal dump, 8" long	50	75	150
Kiddie Toy Dump Truck, No. 510 series	125	188	250
Kiddie Toy MGTD Roadster, No. 432, 6" long	110	165	220
Kiddie Toy Motorcycle, 5" long	15	22	30
Kiddie Toy Patrol Stake Truck, c. 1937	30	40	55
Kiddie Toy Racer, No. 457, rubber tires, 6-1/2" long	46	69	92
Kiddie Toy Taxi, No. 5, marked "Taxi"	7	12	25
Ladder Truck, late 1930s, 5" long	45	68	90

Hess 1976 Tractor Box Truck, $200. Photo courtesy Thomas Nefos

Hess 1977 Tanker Truck, "Fuel Oils," $150.

Hess 1983 "First Hess Truck" 1934 Chevy Tanker, $65.

Hess 1984 Tanker Truck, $65.

Hubley (Continued)	C6	C8	C10
Ladder Truck, Terraplane front, 1930s, 6" long	312	468	625
Ladder Truck, c. 1940, 13-1/2" long	350	525	700
Ladder Truck, 1930s, 10" long	110	165	225
Life Saver Truck, hole in rear is large enough to hold pack of Life Savers, c. 1930, 4-1/4" long	675	1100	1650
Limousine, six-door, 1920s, 7" long	165	250	330
Lincoln Zephyr, 7-1/4" long	240	360	480
Lincoln Zephyr and House Trailer, 14" overall	400	600	800
Log Truck, No. 469	55	83	110
Log Truck, w/five chained logs, black rubber tires, approx. 19" long	138	205	275
Low Boy Truck, trailer, tractor	200	300	400
Mack Dump Truck, w/driver, 11-1/2" long	650	1100	1600

Hubley (Continued)	C6	C8	C10
Mack Gasoline Truck, 10-3/4" long	800	1350	1800
Mack Truck Steam Shovel-Digger, nickel wheels and scoop, c. 1920, 7" long	1300	2200	3200
Merchants Delivery, 1920s, 6" long	400	600	800
MG, 9" long	60	90	120
MG, 5-3/4" long	55	82	110
Milk Cream Truck, embossed "Milk Cream," white rubber tires, 1930s, 3-1/2" long	265	395	525
Model T Coupe, 4" long	100	150	200
Monarch Tractor, 5-1/2" long	600	900	1200
Motor Express Tractor and Trailer, 500 series, black rubber tires, approx. 19" long	95	143	190
Motorcycle, "Harley-Davidson," civilian rider, 6-1/4" long	382	575	775

Hess 1971 Pumper Fire Truck, $3000. Photo courtesy John and Suzanne Adivari

Hess 1980 GMC Training Van, $250. Photo courtesy John and Suzanne Adivari

Hess 1989 Ladder Fire Truck, $35.

Hess 1987 Tractor-Box Trailer Truck, $50. Photo courtesy Thomas G. Nefos

Hubley (Continued)	C6	C8	C10
Motorcycle, "U.S. Air Mail", 9-1/2" long	1100	2000	2700
Motorcycle, armored, w/sidecar and removable riders, 9" long	1200	2000	2750
Motorcycle, Harley-Davidson, Police, w/sidecar and rider, 5-1/4" long (HM35)	250	350	500
Motorcycle, Harley-Davidson, w/policeman, swivel head, small wheels near feet, 1930s, 7-1/4" long	700	1200	1600
Motorcycle, Harley-Davidson, w/policeman, white rubber wheels, 5-1/2" long	275	363	550
Motorcycle, Indian, policeman rider, nickel-plated cylinder, 9-1/4" long	800	1300	1800
Motorcycle, Parcel Post Delivery, w/two-wheel cart, 9-1/4" long	1300	2200	2900

Hubley (Continued)	C6	C8	C10
Motorcycle, policeman, "Cop", 1920s, 4" long	50	75	100
Motorcycle, two-cylinder Indian, w/sidecar, two cops, 9" long	600	900	1200
Motorcycle, has light in front and place for battery, 6" long	300	450	600
Motorcycle "Traffic Car", four cyclinder Indian w/stake sides on two-wheel cart, 11-1/2" long	1500	2500	3500
Motorcycle and Rider, 4" long	110	165	220
Motorcycle Hill Climber, No. 649, 1936, 6-3/4" long	400	600	800
Motorcycle with Removable Cop, "Made in USA", c. mid-1930s, 4-1/4" long	60	90	120
Motorcycle with Sidecar, battery-operated headlight, cop driver, passenger, 8" long	1150	1900	2650

Hess 1990 Tanker Truck, $30.

Hess 1992 Tractor Box Truck, $35.

Hess 1993 Tanker Truck, $1500. Photo courtesy John and Suzanne Adivari

Hess 1982-83 "First Hess Truck," $65.

Hubley (Continued)	C6	C8	C10
Motorcycle with Sidecar, No. 46-F, two removable policemen, 8-1/2" long..............	700	1200	1600
Motorized Steam Pumper, c. 1930s, 4" long.........................	50	75	100
Nite Coach, went on Nucar carrier, 1930s, 3-1/2" long......................	30	45	60
Nu-Car Transport with Trailer, four cars, 17" long..............................	NPF	NPF	NPF
Packard, fifteen parts, straight eight, 1929, 11" long...........................	6000	12,000	16,000
Packard, "Phaeton" kit, 1930...........	50	75	100
Packard Roadster Kit......................	50	75	100
Panama Digger, Mack, 13" long	800	1400	2100
Panama Digger, 9-1/2" long............	800	1300	1800
Panama Digger, 3-1/2" long............	162	243	325
Parcel Post Motorcycle and Sidecar, Harley-Davidson, 9-1/2"	1600	2800	4000

Hubley (Continued)	C6	C8	C10
Patrol, driver, policeman, 15-1/2" long..	1400	2100	2800
Pipe Truck, No. 803, c. 1950s, 9-1/2" long......................................	35	52	70
Power Shovel, 14"	105	160	210
Pumper, c. late 1930s	115	175	230
Pumper, Terraplane front, 1930s, 6-1/4" long......................................	150	225	300
Racer, black rubber tires, 4" long....	80	120	160
Racer, marked "1790", 5"................	100	150	200
Racer, 6-1/2" long...........................	48	72	95
Racer, driver, rubber tires, 8"	250	375	500
Racer, driver, large tail fin, 7" long .	165	248	330
Racer, exhaust stacks, white rubber tires, wodden hubs, tail fins, marked "1791" on driver and "2233" on cast iron, 6" long........	150	200	250

Hess 1964 B-Line Mack Tanker, $2000. Photo courtesy Thomas Nefos

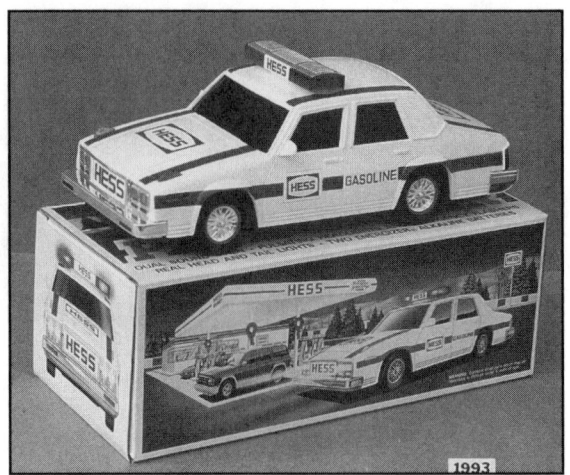

Hess 1993 Patrol Car, $20.

Hess 1970 Pumper Fire Truck, $695. Photo courtesy Thomas Nefos

Hess 1967 Tanker Truck, red velvet box, $2400.

Hess 1986 Ladder Truck, $75.

Hess 1988 Race Car Transporter, $50.

Hubley Coal Truck, c. 1922, 9-1/2" long, $875. Photo courtesy Christie's East

Hubley Compressor Truck, 8-1/4" long, $7000. Photo courtesy Bertoia Auctions

Hubley Crane, wooden wheels, 1940s, $135. Photo courtesy Harvey Rainess

Hubley Corvette, 13-1/2" long, $510.

Hubley (Continued)	C6	C8	C10
Racer, two passengers, 1930s, 5-1/2" long	130	195	260
Racer, animated exhaust stacks, driver, 8" long	600	1000	1400
Racer No. 1, 8" long	250	375	500
Racer No. 22, 7-3/8" long	100	150	200
Racer No. 5, hood opens, painted and nickeled iron and aluminum, 9-1/2" long	900	1600	2300
Racer No. 629, 1936, 6-3/4" long	145	225	290
Railway Express Truck, rubber tires, 5" long	150	225	300
Road Roller, w/driver, late 1920s, 8" long	300	450	600
Road Scraper, No. 481	60	90	120
Say it with Flowers, 10-1/2" long	6000	12,000	18,000
Sedan, two-door, rubber wheels, looks like Ford, c. 1938, 3-1/2"	70	105	140
Sedan, 1920, 7" long	100	150	200
Sedan, 7" long	150	225	300

Hubley (Continued)	C6	C8	C10
Service Car, 4-1/4" long	60	90	120
Service Car, including wheels, 5" long	200	300	400
Sport Car, No. 485	70	105	140
Stake Bed Struck, marked "10 ton", 7" long	300	525	700
Stake Bed Truck, white cab w/blue bed, 12" long	NPF	NPF	NPF
Stake Bed Truck, 3-1/2" long	25	38	50
Stake Bed Truck, 7" long	100	150	200
Stake Truck, c. late 1930s	165	250	330
Stake Truck, No. 614, c. 1930s	75	115	150
Stake Truck with Trailer, No. 927, two-piece, 21" long	100	150	200
Stake-type Truck, No. 452, black, rubber tires, post WWII	55	82	110
Station Wagon, c. 1940s, 1950s, 8-1/2" long	75	112	150
Steam Roller, 5" long	100	150	200

Hubley Bell Telephone Truck, 5-1/4" long, $450.

Hubley Chrysler Airflow, 4-1/2", $200.

Hubley Bus, "Coast to Coast," 1927, 13" long, $2200. Photo courtesy Bertoia Auctions

Hubley Chrysler Airflow, 8" long, $2000.

Hubley Ladder Truck, 13-1/2", c. 1940, $700. Photo courtesy Tim Oei

Hubley Bell Telephone Trucks, 3"; 3-3/4"; 5-1/4", $450; 8"; 8-1/4", $850; 9", $1400. Photo courtesy Bertoia Auctions.

Hubley Motorcycle, armored, 9", $2750.
Photo courtesy Bertoia Auctions

Hubley Motorcycle with Sidecar, $1000.

Hubley Motorcycle, Harley-Davidson, $775.

Hubley Motorcycle, Harley-Davidson, 7-1/4", $1600.
Photo courtesy Mapes Auctioneers and Appraisers

Hubley (Continued)	C6	C8	C10
Steam Shovel, "General", 15" long .	450	700	1000
Steam Shovel, "General", 7" long ...	240	360	580
Steam Shovel, "General," rubber tires on hubs, 9" long..................	375	565	750
Streetsweeper, "The Elgin", 1931, 8" long	1550	2800	4400
Studebaker Roadster, frame and body separate...............................	300	450	600
Studebaker Touring Car	325	518	650
Telephone Truck............................	25	40	50
Touring Auto, chauffeur and rider, 1915, 9-1/2" long.......................	700	1300	1750
Tow Truck, c. 1930s, 8-3/4" long....	180	270	360

Hubley (Continued)	C6	C8	C10
Tractor Loader, No. 501, 1950s, 11" long...............................	80	115	155
Tractor Trailer and Road Scraper, No. 506........................	100	150	200
Trailer Truck, c. 1936-38	100	150	200
Transitional Fire Patrol, driver, fire-men, 1920, 12"	800	1300	2000
Truck, "5 Ton Truck," eight wooden barrels, c. 1920, 17" long...............................	700	1150	1800
Truck, Milk Cream Truck, cast iron, white rubber tires, 1930s, 3-1/2".	400	600	800

Hubley Delivery Van, 1932, 4-1/2" long, $1800.

Hubley Fire Ladder Truck, 7-1/2" long, $260. Photo courtesy Rod Carnahan

Hubley Flatbed Truck, No. 506, $235. Photo courtesy Harvey Raines

Hubley Huber Road Roller, 4-1/2", $220. Photo courtesy Bertoia Auctions

Hubley Merchants Delivery, 1920s, 6" long, $800.

Hubley Kiddie Toy Dump Truck, 8" long, $150.

Hubley Kiddie Toy Motorcycle, 5" long, $30. Photo courtesy Kent M. Comstock

Hubley Life Saver Truck, c. 1930, 4-1/4" long, $1650. Photo courtesy Bertoia Auctions

Hubley Mack Gasoline Truck, 10-3/4" long, $1800. Photo courtesy Bertoia Auctions

Hubley Merchants Delivery, 1920s, 6" long, $800. Photo courtesy Bertoia Auctions

Hubley Milk Cream Truck, 1930s, 3-1/2" long, $525. Photo courtesy Mapes Auctioneers and Appraisers

Hubley (Continued)	C6	C8	C10
Truck, "Borden's Milk Cream," deluxe version, clicker, rubber tires, 7-1/2"	2000	3500	5500
Truck, "Borden's Milk Cream," standard version, 6" long	475	720	950
Truck and Trailer, No. 2287, "Motor Express", 8" long	162	243	325
Woody Station Wagon, take-a-part, 5" long	275	420	560
Wrecker, 3-1/2"	32	48	65
Wrecker, 4-3/4" long	115	175	250
Wrecker, white wheels on large hubs, c. 1940, 6" long	65	98	130
Wrecker, chrome wheels, service car	45	70	100
Wrecker, rubber wheels, 1930, 4-1/2" long	65	100	150
Wrecker, white wheels on large hubs, 1940, 6" long	100	150	200
Wrecking Truck, rubber tires, 1930, 7-1/2" long	150	225	300
Yellow Cab, c. 1939, 8" long	650	1150	1600
Yellow Cab, 1920, 7-3/4" long	550	850	1200

Ideal	C6	C8	C10
American LaFrance Fire Truck	75	110	145

Ideal (Continued)	C6	C8	C10
Barracuda Coupe, 1964, 4" long	15	25	30
Cadillac, four-door, 1948, 4" long	25	40	50
Car Trailer, four cars, 27" long	40	60	80
Car Trailer, c. 1945, 3" long	20	30	40
Cattle Truck, 13" long	25	38	50
Corvette	50	75	100
Dream Car Convertible, 16" long	200	300	400
Dump Truck, 5-3/4" long	21	32	42
FBI Car, No. 3072, talking	NPF	NPF	NPF
Fix-it Convertible	65	100	130
Ford Sunliner, friction, 9"	90	135	175
Ice Cream Truck, 15" long	45	65	90
Ice Cream Truck, 1948-54, 5-1/2" long	30	60	100
Jaguar Roadster, 6" long	35	50	70
Jeep, 1945	40	60	80
Mercedes Sedan, 9" long	35	50	70
Pickup Truck, Ford, 1940, 4" long	20	30	40
Pickup Truck, American, 1948, 4" long	6	10	14
Rocket Cycle, gold cycle, green plastic astronaut w/clear plastic helmet riding, his right arm is raised, 6-1/2" long	100	150	200
Rolls Royce, 8" long	12	18	25

Hubley Motorcycle and Rider, 4", $220.

Hubley Motorcycle Hill Climber, No. 649, $1936, 6-3/4", $800.

Hubley Motorcycle, Indian, Policeman, 9-1/4", $1800. Photo by Kent Comstock

Hubley Parcel Post Delivery, 9-1/4", $2900.

Ideal (Continued)

	C6	C8	C10
Sanitation Truck, 5-1/2" long	20	35	50
Scooter, 4" long	NPF	NPF	NPF
Sedan, 9-1/4" long	20	35	50
Semi, 12" long	35	50	70
Shell Oil Truck, 12-1/2" long	25	38	50
Steam Shovel, 7-1/2" long	22	33	45
Tow Truck, 17" long	50	75	100
Truck, "Television Repair"	50	75	100
Turbo-Jet Car, No. 4867	60	90	120
XP-600 Fix-It Car of Tomorrow, 16" long	85	128	170

Jane Francis Toys

Jane Francis Toys operated in Wilkinsburg Pennsylvania, from 1942-1946 and in Somerset, Pennsylvania, from 1947-1949. Starting as a stuffed toy maker, the company introduced a line of die-cast cars in 1945. the last Jane Francis toys were manufactured in 1949.

Jane Francis Toys

	C6	C8	C10
Gulf Service Station, eight pieces	400	575	750
Gulf Truck, No. 447, tin cover, 5" long (JF05)	30	45	75
Pickup Truck, No. 447, 5" long (JF03)	20	25	30
Pickup Truck, No. 347, 5" long (JF02)	20	25	30
Pickup Truck, 6-1/2" long (JF01)	30	40	50
Sedan, fastback, futuristic, w/wind-up motor, 6-1/2" long (JF07)	30	40	50
Sedan, fastback, futuristic, 6-1/2" long (JF06)	25	30	40
Service Station, "Gulf Truck Service," Jane Francis	500	750	1000
Tow Truck, No. 447, 5" long (JF04)	30	40	65

Hubley Packard, 1929, 11" long, $16,000. Photo courtesy Bertoia Auctions

Hubley Panama Digger, Mack, 13", $2100. Photo courtesy Joe and Sharon Freed

Hubley Racer No. 5, 9-1/2" long, $2300. Photo courtesy Christie's East

Hubley Racer, 5", $200. Photo courtesy Bill Kaufman

Japanese Tin Vehicles

Tin toy cars have been manufactured since the first horse-less carriages roamed the streets of the United States and Europe. They ranged in size and price from the tiny one-inch penny toy to the twenty-eight-inch Eldorado that sold for ten dollars. Although there are German, Spanish, and French toy cars listed here, this chapter concentrates on the 1950s—the Golden Era of Japanese tin toy cars. These examples are popular today and prices continue to rise.

Contributor: Ron Smith, 33005 Arlesford, Solon, OH, 44139, 440-248-7066, fax 440-519-0906. Smith has always loved toy cars and planes; he can still show you the his first Dinky toy his aunt bought him at Fred Harvey's Toy Store in Cleveland's Terminal Tower Building. Smith has collected die-cast cars, trucks, and planes, cast-iron toys, and plastic pro-motional cars, but for the past fifteen years he has specialized in tin-plate cars and planes. Smith lives in Ohio with his wife Joan and their two cats, T-2 and Bogart.

Japanese Tin Cars	C6	C8	C10
Agajanian Racer No. 98, 1950s, "Y" Co., friction, 18" (J286)	500	1000	2000
Aston-Martin DB5 (James Bond), 1960s, Gilbert, friction, 11-1/2" (J1)	75	150	350

Japanese Tin Cars (Continued)	C6	C8	C10
Aston-Martin DB6, 1960s, Asahi Toy Co., friction, 11" (J2)	200	400	600
Atom Car, 1950s, Yonezawa, 17" (J284)	200	400	900
Atom Jet Car, 1950s, "Y" Co., friction, 30" (J283)	300	500	1100
Austin Healey 100 Six Convertible, 1959, Bandai, friction, 8" (J2B)	50	100	200
Austin Healey 100 Six Coupe, 1959, Bandai, friction, 8" (J2A)	50	100	200
BMW 600 Isetta, 1950, Bandai, friction, 9" (J16)	150	300	500
BMW Isetta (three wheels), 1950, Bandai, friction, 6-1/2" (J17)	75	125	200
Buick, 1959, Ichiko, battery-op/friction, 12" (J9)	100	275	350
Buick, 1960, Ichiko, friction, 17-1/2" (J10)	150	300	800
Buick, 1953, Marusan, friction, 7" (J3)	50	100	200
Buick, 1959, T.N., friction, 11" (J8)	90	150	300
Buick, 1961, T.N., friction, 11" (J11)	100	150	250

*Hubley Motorcycle Policeman, "Cop," 4", $100.
Photo courtesy Mapes Auctioneers and Appraisers*

Hubley Motorcycle with Sidecar, 8", $2650.

*Hubley Motorcycle, U.S. Air Mail, 9-1/2", $2700. Photo
courtesy Bertoia Auctions*

*Hubley Motorcycle "Traffic Car," 11-1/2", $3500. Photo
courtesy Bertoia Auctions*

*Hubley Motorcycle two-cylinder Indian, 9", $2750.
Photo courtesy Kent Comstock*

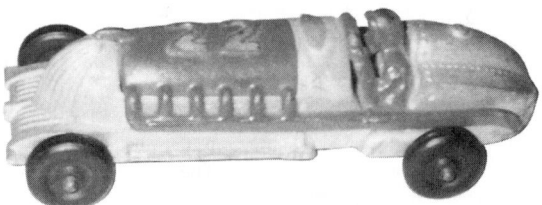

*Hubley Racer No. 22, 7-3/8" long, $200. Photo courtesy
Rod Carnahan*

Hubley "5 Ton Truck," c. 1920, 17" long, $1800.

Hubley Streetsweeper, 1931, 8" long, $4400.

Hubley Railway Express Truck, 5" long, $300.

Japanese Tin Cars (Continued)	C6	C8	C10
Buick Century, 1958, Bandai, friction, 8" (J7)	80	100	150
Buick Century, 1958, Yonezawa, friction, 12" (J6)	400	650	1500
Buick Emergency Car, 1961, T.N., friction, 14" (J12)	50	95	125
Buick Futuristic LeSabre, 1950s, Yonezawa, friction, 7-1/2" (J276)	200	300	500
Buick LeSabre, 1966, Asahi Toy Co., friction, 19" (J14)	100	150	300
Buick Roadmaster, 1955, Yoshiya, friction, 11" (J5)	125	250	500
Buick Sportswagon, 1968, Asakusa, friction, 15" (J15)	150	200	300
Buick Station Wagon, 1954, unknown manufacturer, battery-op, 8" (J4)	75	150	200
Buick Wildcat, 1963, Ichiko, friction, 15" (J13)	200	400	800
Cadillac, 1965, Asahi Toy Co., friction, 17" (J32)	125	250	425
Cadillac, 1967, K.O., friction, 10-1/2" (J34)	100	150	250
Cadillac, 1962, Yonezawa, friction, 22" (J30)	100	250	350
Cadillac, 1960, Yonezawa, friction, 18" (J27)	100	150	300
Cadillac, 1950, Marusan, friction, 11" (J19)	300	500	850
Cadillac, 1965, Ichiko, friction, 22" (J33)	300	400	600
Cadillac, 1954, Gama, friction, 12" (J22)	100	200	450

Japanese Tin Cars (Continued)	C6	C8	C10
Cadillac, 1963, Bandai, friction, 17" (J31)	100	200	350
Cadillac, 1960s, Bandai, friction, 17" (J26)	125	175	375
Cadillac, 1952, T.N., battery-op, 13" (J21)	100	250	500
Cadillac, 1950, Marusan, battery-op, 11" (J18)	400	800	1800
Cadillac, 1954, Joustra, battery-op, 12" (J23)	100	200	450
Cadillac, 1967, unknown manufacturer, friction, 10-3/4" (J35)	75	100	125
Cadillac, 1952, Alps, friction, 11-1/2" (J20)	250	400	800
Cadillac 60, 1961, unknown manufacturer, friction, 9" (J28)	95	125	150
Cadillac Convertible, 1959, Bandai, friction, 12" (J25)	50	100	185
Cadillac El Dorado, 1967, Ichiko, friction, 28" (J36)	200	400	800
Cadillac Fleetwood, 1961, SSS, friction, 17-1/2" (J29)	100	200	350
Cadillac Sedan, 1959, Bandai, friction, 12" (J24)	50	100	185
Champion No. 15 Racer, 1950, German, friction, 18" (J289)	500	750	1500
Champion No. 42 Racer, 1950, German, friction, 18" (J288)	500	750	1500
Champion No. 98 Racer, 1950s, "Y" Co., friction, 18" (J287)	500	800	1100
Chevrolet, 1960, Marusan, friction, 11-1/2" (J60)	200	400	800
Chevrolet, 1954, Marusan, friction, 11" (J49)	300	800	1500

Hubley Road Roller, late 1920s, 8" long, $600. Photo courtesy Mapes Auctioneers and Appraisers

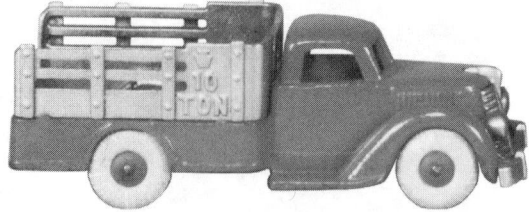

Hubley Stake Bed Struck, 7" long, $700. Photo courtesy Bertoia Auctions

Hubley Station Wagon, c. 1940s-1950s, 8-1/2", $150.

Hubley Tractor Loader, No. 501, 1950s, 11", $155.

From left: Hubley "General" Steam Shovel, 9", $750; Arcade Mack Hoist Truck, No. 198, 1932, 8", (AR144), $2200; Hubley "General" Steam Shovel, 7", $580. Photo courtesy Bertoia Auctions

Hubley Wrecker, 1940, 6" long, $200. Photo courtesy Mapes Auctioneers and Appraisers

Hubley Yellow Cab, 1920, 7-3/4" long, $1200. Photo courtesy Sotheby's, New York

Ideal Rocket Cycle, 6-1/2" long, $200. Photo courtesy Terry Sells

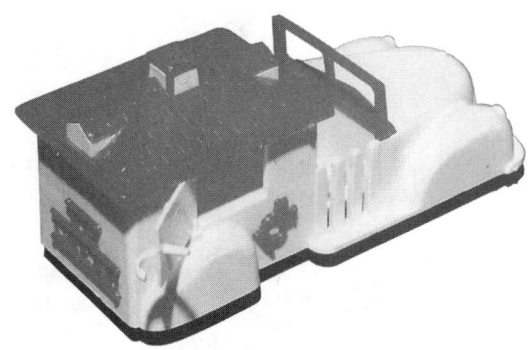

Ideal Ice Cream Truck, 1948-54, 5-1/2" long, $100. Photo courtesy Bob and Alice Wagner

Japanese Tin Cars (Continued)	C6	C8	C10
Chevrolet, 1962, unknown manu-facturer, friction, 11" (J65)..........	125	250	350
Chevrolet, 1955, Marusan, battery-op, 10-3/4" (J50)	300	800	1500
Chevrolet Camaro, 1967, Taiyo, friction, 9-1/2" (J45)..................	10	20	25
Chevrolet Camaro, 1967, Modern Toys, friction, 11" (J47)	25	50	75
Chevrolet Camaro, 1967, T.N., bat-tery-op, 14" (J46)	100	150	300
Chevrolet Camaro Rusher, 1971, Taiyo, battery-op, 9-1/2" (J48)....	10	20	25
Chevrolet Convertible, 1956, Ban-dai, friction, 9-1/2" (J53).............	100	150	225
Chevrolet Convertible, 1958, Ban-dai, friction, 8" (J56)	60	125	275
Chevrolet Corvair, 1963, Bandai, friction, 8" (J44)	50	65	125
Chevrolet Corvair, 1960s, Bandai, friction, 8" (J43)	30	50	80
Chevrolet Corvette, 1964, Ichida, battery-op, 12" (J41)	150	225	350
Chevrolet Corvette, 1958, Yon-ezawa, friction, 9-1/2" (J38)........	200	300	600
Chevrolet Corvette, 1965, Bandai, friction, 8" (J40)	50	75	125
Chevrolet Corvette, 1968, Taiyo, battery-op, 9-1/2" (J42)	20	40	80
Chevrolet Corvette, 1953, Bandai, friction, 7" (J37)	100	200	400
Chevrolet Corvette, 1962, Bandai, friction, 8" (J39)	50	75	150
Chevrolet Impala, 1963, Bandai (?), friction, 18" (J66)	200	300	400
Chevrolet Impala Convertible, 1961, Bandai, friction, 11" (J63).	100	150	300

Japanese Tin Cars (Continued)	C6	C8	C10
Chevrolet Impala Sedan, 1961, Bandai, friction, 11" (J62)...........	100	150	300
Chevrolet Pickup, 1956, Bandai, friction, 9-1/2" (J52)...................	75	125	175
Chevrolet Pickup Truck, 1958, Bandai, friction, 8" (J55).............	50	65	90
Chevrolet Red Cross Ambulance, 1958, Bandai, friction, 8" (J54)...	20	50	100
Chevrolet Secret Agent, 1962, unknown manufacturer, battery-op, 14" (J64)................................	50	75	150
Chevrolet Sedan, 1958, Bandai, friction, 8" (J58)	75	125	175
Chevrolet Sedan/Convert-ible/Wagon, 1959, SY, friction, 11-1/2" (J59)	200	400	800
Chevrolet Station Wagon, 1956, Bandai, friction, 9-1/2" (J51)	60	120	180
Chevrolet Station Wagon, 1958, Bandai, friction, 8" (J57).............	50	65	125
Chrysler, 1958, unknown manufac-turer, battery-op, 13" (J73)..........	300	400	800
Chrysler, 1955, Yonezawa, fric-tion, 8" (J71)...............................	100	200	300
Chrysler, 1953, Yonezawa, fric-tion, 10" (J70B)	100	225	350
Chrysler, 1950, Guntherman, fric-tion, 11" (J70).............................	100	400	800
Chrysler Imperial, 1962, Asahi Toy Co., friction, black, red (white: add 20% to value), 16" (J77).......	600	1200	2200
Chrysler Imperial Convertible, 1959, Bandai, friction, 8" (J74)...	50	100	175
Chrysler Imperial Sedan, 1959, Bandai, friction, 8" (J75).............	50	100	175
Chrysler New Yorker, 1957, Alps, friction, 14" (J72)	500	700	1500

Ideal Talking FBI car, $150. Photo courtesy Tim Oei

Ideal Scooter, $30.

Ideal Turbo-Jet Car, No. 4867, $120. Photo courtesy Tim Oei

Japanese Tin Cars (Continued)	C6	C8	C10
Chrysler Valiant, 1960, Bandai, friction, 8" (J76)	20	30	60
Citroen 2 CV, 1960, Daiya, friction, 8" (J69A)	100	150	250
Citroen DS 19 Convertible, 1960, Bandai, friction, 12" (J67)	300	600	900
Citroen DS 19 Sedan, 1960, Bandai, friction, 12" (J68)	300	600	900
Citroen DS 19 Station Wagon, 1960, Bandai, friction, 12" (J69)	300	600	900
Corvair Bertone, 1963, Bandai, battery-op, 12" (J277)	75	150	250
Daihatsu Auto Tricycle, 1950s, Nomura, friction, 11" (J275)	100	150	350
Daihatsu Midget, 1950, Kokyu Shokai, friction, 5" (J270)	75	100	250
Daihatsu Midget, 1950s, Yonezawa, friction, 7" (J269)	75	100	250
Datsun Bluebird 1200, 1960s, Bandai, friction, 8" (J79)	60	100	200

Japanese Tin Cars (Continued)	C6	C8	C10
DeSoto, 1930s, Masudaya, friction, 8" (J81)	300	400	800
Divco Dugans Bakery Truck, 1950s, friction, 7-1/2" (J80)	200	400	500
DKW 1000 Convertible, 1960, Bandai, friction, 8" (J78)	90	125	250
Dodge Pickup, 1959, unknown manufacturer, friction, 18-1/2" (J84)	350	500	1200
Dodge Sedan, 1958, T.N., friction, 11" (J82)	300	400	800
Dodge Truck, 1959, unknown manufacturer, friction, 24" (J83)	350	500	1000
Dodge Yellow Cab, 1968, T.N., friction, 12" (J85)	100	200	500
Dream Car, "Y" Co., friction, 17" (J278A)	600	800	1500
Dream Car Buick Phantom, 1950s, Tipp & Co., friction, 12" (J278)	300	400	800
Dream Car Firebird III, 1960s, Alps, friction, 11" (J279)	100	200	400

Ideal Jeep, 1945, $80. Photo courtesy Terry Sells

Ideal Sanitation Truck, 5-1/2" long, $50. Photo courtesy Terry Sells

Ideal Steam Shovel, 7-1/2" long, $45. Photo courtesy Dave Leopard

Ideal Cattle Truck, 13" long, $50. Photo courtesy Terry Sells

Ideal Rolls Royce, 8" long, $25. Photo courtesy Ron Fink

Ideal Sedan, plastic, 9-1/4", $50.

Ideal XP-600 Fix-It Car of Tomorrow, 16" long, $170. Photo courtesy Terry Sells

Japanese Tin Vehicles, 1950s, Agajanian Racer No. 98, 18", $2000. Photo courtesy Ron Smith

Japanese Tin Vehicles, 1950s Mazda Auto Tricycle, 8", $250. Photo courtesy Ron Smith

Japanese Tin Vehicles, 1955 Ford Convertible, 12", $700. Photo courtesy Ron Smith

Japanese Tin Vehicles, 1959 Lincoln Continental Mark III Convertible, 12", $175. Photo courtesy Ron Smith

Japanese Tin Cars (Continued)	C6	C8	C10
Edsel, 1958, Yonezawa, friction, 10-1/2" (J92)	300	600	1200
Edsel Ambulance, 1958, Haji, friction, 11" (J88)	200	250	400
Edsel Convertible/Sedan, 1958, Haji, friction, 10-1/2" (J86)	300	500	1000
Edsel Hardtop, 1958, Asahi, friction, 10-3/4" (J91)	100	200	350
Edsel Hardtop, 1958, Toy Nomura, friction, 8-1/2" (J90)	100	150	250
Edsel Station Wagon, 1958, T.N., friction, 11" (J89)	150	200	300
Edsel Wagon, 1958, Haji, friction, 10-1/2" (J87)	200	300	600
Electrospecial No. 21, "Y" Co., battery-op, 10" (J290)	300	600	1200
Ferrari, 1958, Bandai, battery-op, 11" (J148)	90	150	350
Ferrari 250 G. Convertible, 1957, A.T.C., friction, 9-1/2" (J147)	150	300	750
Ferrari Super America Conventible, 1960s, Bandai, friction, 12" (J150)	100	200	350
Ferrari Super America Coupe, 1960, Bandai, friction, 12" (J149)	100	200	350

Japanese Tin Cars (Continued)	C6	C8	C10
Fiat 600 Sedan, 1960s, Bandai, friction, 8" (J151)	50	70	100
Ford, 1960, Haji, friction, 11" (J119)	125	200	350
Ford Ambulance, 1955, Bandai, friction, 12" (J98)	150	200	250
Ford Convertible, 1956, Haji, friction, 11-1/2" (J102)	400	600	900
Ford Convertible, 1964, Rico, friction, 17" (J124)	200	300	400
Ford Convertible, 1955, Bandai, friction, 12" (J100)	200	400	700
Ford Country Sedan, 1962, Asahi, friction, 12" (J121)	200	350	700
Ford Country Sedan, 1961, Bandai, friction, 10-1/2" (J120)	125	150	250
Ford Country Squire Station Wagon, 1958, Bandai, friction, 8" (J112)	60	80	125
Ford Fairlane Hardtop/Convertible, 1958, Bandai, friction, 8" (J113)	60	80	125
Ford Fairlane Hardtop/Convertible, 1958, Sankei Gangu, friction, 9" (J114)	90	115	125
Ford Fairlane Sedan, 1957, Ichiko, friction, 10" (J105)	100	200	300

Japanese Tin Vehicles, 1959 Buick, 12", $350. Photo courtesy Ron Smith

Japanese Tin Vehicles, 1959 Cadillac Convertible, 12", $185. Photo courtesy Ron Smith

Japanese Tin Vehicles, 1960s Rambler Rebel Station Wagon, 12", $150. Photo courtesy Ron Smith

Japanese Tin Vehicles, 1960s Volkswagon Convertible, 11", $200. Photo courtesy Ron Smith

Japanese Tin Cars (Continued)	C6	C8	C10
Ford Fairlane Skyliner, 1959, Sankei Gangu, friction, 9" (J115)	90	115	125
Ford Falcon, 1960s, Bandai, friction, 8" (J118)	20	30	50
Ford Galaxie Hardtop, 1965, MT, friction, 11" (J125)	125	150	300
Ford Good Humor Ice Cream Truck, 1950, KTS, Japan, friction, 10-3/4" (J95)	100	400	800
Ford GT, 1960s, Bandai, battery-op, 10" (J146)	65	85	125
Ford Gyron, 1960, Ichida, battery-op, 11" (J280)	75	150	250
Ford Hardtop, 1964, Ichiko, friction, 13" (J122)	200	450	700
Ford Hardtop, 1956, Yonezawa, friction, 12" (J101)	300	500	950
Ford Hardtop, 1964, Rico, friction, 17" (J123)	200	300	400
Ford Hardtop, 1957, T.N., friction, 12" (J106)	100	200	300
Ford Mustang, 1967, Bandai, battery-op, 13" (J144)	45	65	100
Ford Mustang (FBI), 1965, Bandai, friction, 11" (J141)	100	200	400
Ford Mustang Convertible, 1965, Yonezawa, battery-op, 13-1/2" (J142)	90	125	200

Japanese Tin Cars (Continued)	C6	C8	C10
Ford Mustang Fastback, 1965, Bandai, friction, 11" (J139)	45	65	90
Ford Mustang Fastback, 1966, T.N., friction, 17" (J143)	120	200	325
Ford Mustang Hardtop/Convertible, 1965, Bandai, friction/battery-op, 11" (J140)	75	125	150
Ford Panel Truck, 1955, Bandai, friction, "Standard Coffee", 12"	600	800	1500
Ford Panel Truck, 1957, Bandai, friction, "Standard Coffee", 12"	600	900	1800
Ford Panel Truck, 1955, Bandai, "Flowers," friction, 12" (J99)	200	400	600
Ford Pickup, 1955, Bandai, friction, 12" (J96)	150	250	300
Ford Retractable, 1959, T.N., friction, 11" (J117)	80	100	165
Ford Retractable Top, 1958, K. Japan, friction, 10" (J110)	80	100	165
Ford Retractable Top, 1958, T.N., battery-op, 11" (J111)	80	100	165
Ford Sedan, 1956, Marusan, friction, 13" (J103)	500	1000	3000
Ford Sedan, 1949, Guntherman, wind-up, 11" (J93)	150	300	400
Ford Sedan, 1951, Guntherman, wind-up, 11" (J94)	150	300	400

Japanese Tin Vehicles, 1961 Chevrolet Impala Convertible, 11", $300. Photo courtesy Ron Smith

Japanese Tin Vehicles, 1961 Plymouth T.V. Car, 12", $700. Photo courtesy Ron Smith

Japanese Tin Cars (Continued)	C6	C8	C10
Ford Sedan/Convert-ible/Wagon/Pickup, 1957, Joustra, friction, 12" (J107)	200	250	300
Ford Sedan/Convert-ible/Wagon/Pickup, 1957, Bandai, friction, 12" (J108)	200	250	300
Ford Station Wagon, 1955, Bandai, friction, 12" (J97)	150	250	300
Ford Station Wagon, 1959, T.N., friction, 12" (J116)	100	150	200
Ford Station Wagon, 1957, Nomura, friction, 7-1/2" (J109)	60	80	100
Ford Taunus 17M, 1960s, Bandai, friction, 8" (J145)	20	40	60
Ford Thunderbird, 1956, T.N., friction, 11" (J127)	200	300	400
Ford Thunderbird, 1964, Ichiko, friction, 16" (J137)	100	200	400
Ford Thunderbird, 1955, Bandai, friction, 7" (J126A)	75	100	150
Ford Thunderbird, 1956, T.N., battery-op, 11" (J129)	200	300	400
Ford Thunderbird Convertible, 1964, Asahi, friction, 12-1/2" (J135)	150	200	400
Ford Thunderbird Convertible, 1959, Bandai, friction, 8" (J131)	50	80	125
Ford Thunderbird Hardtop, 1965, Bandai, friction, 10-3/4" (J138)	60	90	175
Ford Thunderbird Hardtop, 1964, Asahi, friction, 12" (J136)	150	200	400
Ford Thunderbird Hardtop Clear Top, 1956, T.N., friction, 11" (J128)	200	300	400
Ford Thunderbird Retractable, 1963, Yonezawa, battery-op, 11" (J134)	80	150	200

Japanese Tin Cars (Continued)	C6	C8	C10
Ford Thunderbird Retractable, 1961, Yonezawa, battery-op, remote control, 11" (J132)	80	150	200
Ford Thunderbird Retractable, 1962, Yonezawa, battery-op, 11" (J133)	80	150	200
Ford Thunderbird Sedan, 1959, Bandai, friction, 8" (J130)	50	80	125
Ford Torino, 1968, S.T., friction, 16" (J126)	175	300	600
Ford Wagon, 1956, Nomura, friction, 10-1/2" (J104)	100	150	300
GM's Gas Turbine Powered Firebird II, 1956, Ashahi, friction, 8-1/2" (J281)	100	200	400
International Cement Mixer, 1950s, SSS, friction, 19" (J152)	300	600	1000
International Grain Hauler, 1950s, SSS, friction, 23" (J153)	300	600	1000
Jaguar 3.4 Convertible, 1960s, Bandai, friction, 8" (J160)	50	60	135
Jaguar 3.4 Sedan, 1960s, Bandai, friction, 8" (J159)	50	60	135
Jaguar XK 140, 1960s, Bandai, friction, 9-1/2" (J157)	75	125	225
Jaguar XK150 Hardtop Convertible, 1960, Bandai, friction, 9-1/2" (J154)	75	125	225
Jaguar XKE, 1960s, Bandai, battery-op, 10" (J158)	90	125	200
Jaguar XKE Convertible, 1960s, T.T., friction, 10-1/2" (J155)	75	100	250
Jaguar XKE Coupe, 1960s, Lendolet Auto, friction, 10-1/2" (J156)	75	100	125
Jaguar XKE120, 1965, Alps, friction, 6-1/2" (J161)	90	150	350

Japanese Tin Cars (Continued)	C6	C8	C10
Land Rover "88" Station Wagon, 1960s, Bandai, friction, 8" (J171)	30	40	80
Lincoln, 1954, unknown manufacturer, friction, 12" (J162)	175	275	375
Lincoln, 1956, Ichiko, friction, 16-1/2" (J165)	150	250	375
Lincoln, 1964, unknown manufacturer, friction, 10-1/2" (J169)	90	175	275
Lincoln Continental Mark II, 1956, Linemar, friction, 12" (J164)	600	1200	2500
Lincoln Continental Mark III Convertible, 1959, Bandai, friction, 12" (J166)	90	125	175
Lincoln Continental Mark III Sedan, 1959, Bandai, friction, 12" (J167)	90	125	175
Lincoln Hardtop/Convertible, 1960, Yonezawa, friction, 11" (J168)	100	150	300
Lincoln Sedan, 1955, Yonezawa, friction, 12" (J163)	250	600	1200
Lotus Elite, 1950s, Bandai, friction, 8-1/2" (J170)	25	35	60
Mazda Auto Tricycle, 1950s, Bandai, friction, 8" (J274)	75	125	250
Mazda Auto Tricycle K360, 1950s, Bandai, friction, 6"	75	125	250
Mercedes, 1960s, Ichiko, friction, 12-1/2" (J175)	100	150	175
Mercedes Limousine, 1950s, Tipp & Co., friction, 14" (J172)	500	800	1000
Mercedes-Benz, 1962, SSS, battery-op, 12" (J190)	150	200	300
Mercedes-Benz, 1970, Ichiko, friction, 24" (J191)	125	150	200
Mercedes-Benz 219 Convertible, 1960s, Bandai, friction, 8" (J177)	50	80	120
Mercedes-Benz 219 Sedan, 1960s, Bandai, friction, 8" (J176)	50	80	120
Mercedes-Benz 230 SL, 1960s, Yanoman, battery-op, 14-1/2" (J180)	125	155	185
Mercedes-Benz 230 SL, 1960s, Alps, battery, 10" (J179)	65	75	95
Mercedes-Benz 230 SL, 1960s, Modern Toys, battery-op, 15" (J178)	175	210	250
Mercedes-Benz 250 S, 1960s, Daiya, friction, 14" (J182)	110	155	175
Mercedes-Benz 250 SE, 1960s, Ichiko, battery-op, 13" (J181)	110	140	185
Mercedes-Benz 300 SL, 1950s, T.N., battery-op, 11" (J183)	125	150	200

Japanese Tin Cars (Continued)	C6	C8	C10
Mercedes-Benz 300 SL, 1950s, KS, battery-op, 7" (J184)	45	65	85
Mercedes-Benz 300 SL, 1950s, Cragstan, battery-op, 9" (J185)	65	95	125
Mercedes-Benz 300 SL, 1950s, Bandai, friction, 8" (J186)	65	95	150
Mercedes-Benz 300 SL, 1957, Marusan, friction, 8-1/2" (J187)	100	200	300
Mercedes-Benz 600, 1960s, unknown manufacturer, friction, 10" (J188)	95	125	175
Mercedes-Benz Racer, 1950s, Linemar, friction, 9-1/2" (J173)	95	150	185
Mercedes-Benz Racer W196, 1950s, Marusan, battery-op, 10" (J174)	150	200	400
Mercedes-Benz Taxi, 1960s, Bandai, battery-op, 10" (J189)	75	100	125
Mercury Cougar Hardtop, 1967, Asakusa Toys, friction, 15" (J197)	200	400	800
Mercury Cougar Hardtop, 1967, Taiyo, battery-op, 10" (J196)	25	45	90
Mercury Hardtop, 1954, Rock Valley Toys, battery-op, 9-1/2" (J192)	100	150	250
Mercury Hardtop, 1956, Alps, friction, 9-1/2" (J193)	600	800	1400
Mercury Hardtop, 1958, Yonezawa, friction, 11-1/2" (J195)	250	325	400
Mercury Station Wagon, 1958, Bandai, friction, 8" (J194)	60	80	100
Messerschmitt Four-wheel Convertible, 1960s, Bandai, friction, 8" (J204)	200	250	450
Messerschmitt Four-wheel Sedan, 1960s, Bandai, friction, 8" (J205)	200	250	450
MG Magnette Mark III Convertible, 1960s, Bandai, friction, 8" (J203)	95	125	165
MG Magnette Mark III Sedan, 1960s, Bandai, friction, 8" (J202)	95	125	165
MG TD, 1954, SSS, friction, 6-1/2" (J199)	35	65	80
MG TF, 1955, Bandai, friction, 8" (J200)	95	125	150
MG TF, 1952, unknown manufacturer, friction, 8-1/2" (J198)	50	75	100
MGA, 1957, A.T.C., friction, 10" (J201)	175	250	500
Midget Special No. 6, "Y" Co., friction, 7" (J291)	300	500	1000

Japanese Tin Cars (Continued)	C6	C8	C10
Mitsubishi Auto Tricycle, 1950s, Bandai, friction, 11" (J272)........	100	150	300
Mitsubishi Auto Tricycle Leo, 1950s, Bandai, friction, 5" (J271)	75	150	300
Nash, 1950s, MSK, battery-op, 8" (J206).............	40	70	90
Nash Ambassador, 1956, Sankei Gangu, friction, 8" (J207)	100	125	150
Oldsmobile, 1952, "Y" Co., friction, 11" (J207A).....................	150	350	500
Oldsmobile Convertible, 1961, Yonezawa, friction, 12" (J214) ...	75	125	200
Oldsmobile Sedan, 1959, Ichiko, friction, 12-1/2" (J213)...............	75	125	175
Oldsmobile Sedan, 1956, Ichiko/Kanto, friction, 10-1/2" (J208)........	200	400	600
Oldsmobile Sedan, 1958, A.T.C., friction, 12" (J210)	200	300	400
Oldsmobile Sedan, 1958, "Y" Co., friction, 16" (J212)	300	400	700
Oldsmobile Super 88 Sedan, 1958, A.T.C., friction, 13" (J211)	250	325	425
Oldsmobile Super 88 Sedan, 1956, Masudaya, friction, 16" (J209)....	200	300	500
Oldsmobile Toronado, 1966, Bandai, battery-op, 11" (J215)..........	65	110	150
Oldsmobile Toronado, 1968, Ichiko, friction, 17-1/2" (J216) ...	300	400	500
Opel Sedan, 1950s, Yonezawa, battery-op, 11-1/2" (J217)...............	70	90	150
Orient Auto Tricycle, 1950s, Yonezawa, friction, 9" (J273)	75	150	300
Packard Convertible/Sedan, 1953, Alps, friction, 16" (J222)............	500	800	1600
Packard Hawk Convertible, 1957, Schuco, battery-op, 10-3/4" (J223)..........	300	400	900
Plymouth Convertible, 1959, A.T.C., friction, 10-1/2" (J229)...	250	400	600
Plymouth Fury, 1958, Bandai, friction, 8" (J227)............	75	90	165
Plymouth Fury Hardtop, 1964, Kusama, friction, 10" (J223).......	30	60	90
Plymouth Fury Hardtop, 1957, "Y" Co., friction, 11-1/2" (J226)........	300	400	600
Plymouth Hardtop, 1956, unknown manufacturer, friction, 8-1/2" (J224)...........	150	200	400
Plymouth Hardtop, 1956, Alps, battery-op, 12" (J225)	300	400	600
Plymouth Hardtop, 1959, A.T.C., friction, 10-1/2" (J228)...............	200	400	600

Japanese Tin Cars (Continued)	C6	C8	C10
Plymouth Sedan, 1961, Ichiko, friction, 12" (J230).....................	150	300	550
Plymouth Station Wagon, 1961, Ichiko, friction, 12" (J231)..........	150	250	500
Plymouth T.V. Car, 1961, Ichiko, battery-op, 12" (J232)	125	350	700
Pontiac, 1954, Minister, Minister, friction, 11" (J218A)	10	20	30
Pontiac Dream Car, 1950s, Mitsubishi, friction, 10" (J282)	100	200	600
Pontiac Firebird, 1967, Bandai, w/wipers, battery-op, 9-1/2" (J221)	40	55	100
Pontiac Firebird, 1967, Akasura, friction, 15-1/2" (J219)...............	200	400	900
Pontiac Firebird, 1967, Bandai, friction, 10" (J220)....................	30	55	100
Pontiac Star Chief, 1954, Asahi, friction, 11" (J218)	250	350	700
Porsche 911, 1960, Bandai, battery-op, 10" (J234).....................	65	95	125
Porsche Speedster, 1950s, Distler, battery-op, 10-1/2" (J235)...........	200	300	600
Rambler Rebel Station Wagon, 1960s, Bandai, friction, 12" (J240)	60	90	150
Record Racer NSU, 1950s, Bandai, friction, 18" (J285)	100	150	300
Renault, 1960, Bandai, friction, 7-1/2" (J241).....................	95	150	200
Rolls Royce, 1960s, Bandai, w/electric lights, battery-op, 12" (J238)	150	300	600
Rolls Royce, 1960, T.N., friction, 10-1/2" (J239)	200	300	500
Rolls Royce Silver Coupe Convertible, 1960, Bandai, friction, 12" (J236)	100	150	300
Rolls Royce Silver Coupe Sedan, 1960s, Bandai, friction, 12" (J237)	100	150	250
Saab 93B, 1960s, Bandai, friction, 7" (J244).....................	50	70	90
Studebaker, 1954, Yoshiva, friction, 9" (J243).....................	150	200	375
Studebaker Avanti, 1960s, Bandai, friction, 8" (J242)	125	175	350
Subaru 360, 1960s, Bandai, friction, 7" (J245)	100	225	450
Toyopet Crown, 1960s, Bandai, friction, 9" (J248)	100	200	400
Toyota, 1960s, Ichiko, friction, 16" (J249)	75	100	150

Kansas Toy & Novelty Truck, No.20, 3-1/8" long, $80. Photo courtesy Fred Maxwell

Kansas Toy & Novelty Warehouse Tractor, No. 48, 3" long, $50. Photo courtesy Fred Maxwell

Japanese Tin Cars (Continued)	C6	C8	C10
Toyota 2000 GT, 1967, A.T.C., friction, 15" (J250)	125	250	350
Triumph TR-3 Convertible, 1960s, Bandai, friction, 8" (J246)	50	80	175
Triumph TR-3 Coupe, 1960s, Bandai, friction, 8" (J247)	50	80	175
Vespa, 1960s, Bandai, friction, 9" (J251)	80	125	200
Volkswagen, 1960s, Bandai, battery-op, 10-1/2" (J263)	25	50	75
Volkswagen, 1960s, Bandai, friction, 8" (J262)	25	45	60
Volkswagen, 1960s, Bandai, battery-op, 11" (J264)	25	50	75
Volkswagen Bus, 1960s, Bandai, friction, 8" (J255)	50	60	100
Volkswagen Bus, 1960s, A.T.C., friction, 12" (J253)	125	175	350
Volkswagen Bus, 1950s, Tipp & Co., battery-op, 9" (J257)	250	375	450
Volkswagen Bus, 1960s, Bandai, battery-op/friction, 9-1/2" (J256)	75	125	200
Volkswagen Convertible, 1960s, Bandai, battery-op, 7-1/2" (J259)	40	60	80
Volkswagen Convertible, 1960s, Bandai, battery-op, 11" (J260)	110	145	200
Volkswagen Convertible, 1960s, Taiyo, battery-op, 10-1/2" (J261)	25	40	80
Volkswagen Convertible, 1950, T.N., friction, 9-1/2" (J258)	100	150	225
Volkswagen Karmann-Ghia, 1960, Bandai, friction, 7" (J252)	100	150	300
Volkswagen Pickup Truck, 1960s, Bandai, friction, 8" (J254)	50	60	100
Volkswagen with or without Sun Roof, 1960s, Bandai, friction, 15" (J265)	60	90	125

Japanese Tin Cars (Continued)	C6	C8	C10
Volvo, 1950s, Sweden, wind-up, 11" (J265A)	600	1000	2000
Willys Jeep FC-150 Pickup, 1960s, T.N. Toy Nomura, friction, 11" (J266)	50	75	95
Zuendapp Janus, 1950s, Bandai, friction, 8" (J267)	200	400	700

Judy Company, The	C6	C8	C10
Pickup Truck, two dimensional, (part of set), 5-1/4" long (JT01)	15	20	25
Sedan, two dimensional, (part of set), 5-1/4" long (JA01)	15	20	25

Kansas Toy & Novelty Company

Arthur Haynes, an auto mechanic, began molding toys in Clifton, Kansas, shed for local stores in 1923. With clever hands and an artist's eye, he charmed his friends and local townspeople with his bright-colored toys. He made his patterns from advertising pictures, from local vehicles, and probably from other makes of toys, such as Tootsietoy. He made his own production tools. His range was diverse, for he made miniatures of aircraft, autos, trains, farm equipment, zeppelin, and a few animals, novelties, and charms.

Haynes believed that he invented the hollow casting of metal toys, so he must have started with solid toys. One day he dropped his full mold, spilling its hot metal. To his delight he had a perfect, hollow toy vehicle, with promise savings of metal and shipping costs.

This was a town enterprise from the beginning. Jess Foster, news editor, helped with alloy mixtures; Mr. Hadsell, Union Pacific agent, suggested they send samples to Woolworth's in New York. Clayton D. Young, a traveling salesman, saw the toys, joined the company, and built a profitable business with the chain stores, including Kress, Kresge, and Sears-Roebuck; he later became a partner. At its peak of international sales in the late 1920s, the firm employed as many as sixty-five in two shifts during the Christmas-order season.

During its good years, Kansas Toy & Novelty created more designs and produced more toys than any producer of white-metal toys except Barclay. Young withdrew his share and

Kenton Ambulance, 7" long, $1800. Photo courtesy Sotheby's, New York

Kenton Bus, 9-1/2", $1500. Photo courtesy Sotheby's New York

retired around 1930. With the loss of these assets and the onset of the Depression, the company went downhill. George Hoeffer reorganized the company and moved the factory down the road, but this effort lasted only a few months. An era was coming to an end. This later history is scanty, but there is evidence that Haynes was having problems. Perhaps he had always overreached, for looking back at the diversity of his toys and novelties, it is remarkable from a few mechanics in a small Midwest town.

Contributors: Fred Maxwell, 4722 N. 33 St., Arlington, VA 22207. Perry R. Eichor, 703 North Almond Drive, Simpsonville, SC 29681.

KANSAS TOY & NOVELTY COMPANY

	C6	C8	C10
Coupe, No. 8, convertible, landau iron, vertical hood louvers, horizontal grille pattern, windshield visor, string-pull knob in handcrank area, rearmount spare tire/wheel, metal simulated wire wheels, no hood cap, motometer or hood ornament, no headlamps, enamel finish, also un-numbered versions w/"Chrysler," headlamps and hood cap, motometer or hood ornament, or metal disc solid spokes, 3-1/8" long (KTV7)	20	30	40
Coupe, No. 66, streamlined three-wheeler, six open windows, metal simulated wire wheels, 3-1/2" long (KTV51)	60	80	100
Coupe, convertible, landau iron, vertical hood louvers, horizontal grille pattern, windshield visor, string-pull knob in handcrank area, metal disc solid spokes, lacquer, 2-7/8"	30	45	60

	C6	C8	C10
Coupe, crude, slant roof, shallow rear body, no fenders, hood similar to first racer above, lacquer; possibly the first "hoopie" or stripdown made?, rare, 3-1/8" long (KTV4)	32	48	64
Coupe, No. 35, convertible, landau iron, vertical hood louvers, horizontal grille pattern, hood cap, motometer or hood ornament, rearmount spare tire/wheel, metal simulated wire wheels, also an un-numbered version, 2-1/4" long (KTV26)	20	30	40
Dirt Tumble, No. 64, adjustable dumping scoop, 1-1/2" wide on same frame as No. 62, six pieces, four colors, 4" long (KTV49)	50	75	100
Dump Truck, No. 42, Ford?, driver, no cab, diamond emblem on hinged body, horizontal grille pattern, string-pull knob in handcrank area, metal simulated wire wheels, 3-1/2" (KTV33)	30	45	60
Indy Racer, No. 10, driver, boattail, exhaust right, vertical hood louvers, horizontal grille pattern, hood cap, motometer or hood ornament, string-pull knob in handcrank area, metal open-spoke wheels or metal simulated wire wheels, also un-numbered version, 3-1/8" (KTV14)	20	30	40
Locomotive-Tender, No. 36, "KT & N RR," six metal open-spoke wheels, four metal disc wheels, 0-6-4, 4-3/8" long (KTV27)	20	30	40

	C6	C8	C10
Midget Racer, No. 31, driver, torpedo tail, vertical hood louvers, horizontal grille pattern, hood cap, motometer or hood ornament, metal simulated wire wheels, lacquer, also un-numbered version, 2-1/8" (KTV24) ...	14	21	28
Midget Racer, No. 67, driver, torpedo-tail, vertical hood louvers, horizontal grille pattern, hood cap, motometer or hood ornament, metal disc wheels, smaller version of No. 31, also an un-numbered version, 1-1/2" long (KTV52)	25	45	55
Midget Racer, no driver, torpedo tail, hood cap, motometer or hood ornament, string-pull knob in handcrank area, vertical hood louvers, horizontal grille pattern, 5/8" metal disc wheels w/simulated lug nuts, lacquer finish, 3" long (KTV1)	20	30	40
Midget Racer, no number, torpedo tail, w/driver, plain metal disc wheels, lacquer; easily confused w/another maker's copy, 3" long (KTV2)	70	105	140
Overland Bus, "Fageol," nine male passengers, driver and "baggage" cast-on windows, horizontal grille pattern, rearmount spare tire/wheel, metal disc wheels, also an un-numbered version w/various family passengers on windows, 3-1/2" (KTV13)	35	50	70
Overland Bus, No. 9, "Fageol," solid windows, 3-1/2" long (KTV12)	25	35	45
Racer, No. 46, 1929 Golden Arrow record car, driver, large tail fin, metal simulated wire wheels, 2-7/8" long (KTV35)	25	35	45
Roadster, No. 14, open, "Chrysler," solid windshield, plain grille, hood cap, motometer or hood ornament, vertical hood louvers, string-pull knob in handcrank area, rearmount spare tire/wheel, metal disc, solid spokes, 3-1/8" long (KTV15)	20	30	45

	C6	C8	C10
Roadster, No. 54, Buick, driver w/cap, rumble seat, external trunk, plain hood and grille, no headlamps, sidemounted spare, metal simulated wire wheels, also an un-numbered version, 2-3/8" long (KTV39)	30	50	70
Roadster, No. 54, Buick, driver w/cap, rumble seat, external trunk, plain hood and grille, no headlamps, no trunk, sidemounted spare, metal simulated wire wheels, also an un-numbered version, 2-1/4" long (KTV40)	60	75	100
Roadster, no number, hood ornament, vertical hood louvers, string-pull knob in handcrank area, rearmount spare tire/wheel, metal disc wheels with solid spokes, horizontal grille pattern, w/open rumble seat, might not be Kansas Toy 7 Novelty (KTV16).	NPF	NPF	NPF
Sedan, No. 60, 1930 Reo Royale? or Chrysler two-door Brougham, plain hood, vee-vertical grille pattern, square rear deck, metal disc wheels, metal disc wheels, sidemounted spare, also an un-numbered version w/metal simulated wire wheels and metal simulated wire wheels, sidemounted spare, 3-1/2" (KTV45)	30	45	60
Sedan, "Chevrolet," six windows, landau iron, windshield visor, vertical hood louvers, string-pull knob in handcrank area, rearmount spare tire/wheel, metal simulated wire wheels, 2-7/8" long (KTV10)	20	30	40
Sedanette, No. 58, Austin Bantam, unique fighting cock on door panels, four open windows, horizontal hood louvers, vertical grille pattern, rearmount spare tire/wheel, mettal simulated wire wheels, three piece molded grille, 2-1/4" long (KTV43)	25	35	45
Steam Road Roller, No. 43, driver, string-pull knob in handcrank area, boiler, wooden rollers, 3-1/4" (KTV34)	30	45	60

	C6	C8	C10
Tour Bus, No. 59, 1928 Pickwick COE double-deck night-coach, screen grille, larger version of No. 49 above, also an un-numbered version-w/dual wheels, 3-3/8" long (KTV44)	75	125	150
Truck, No. 20, Ford (?), solid windshield, two open windows, three tanks, vertical hood louvers, horizontal grille pattern, rear faucet, metal simulated wire wheels, versions w/ and w/o driver, also an un-numbered version, 3-1/8" long (KTV20)	40	60	80
Warehouse Tractor, No. 48, "Caterpillar," "Whoopee," driver, vertical hood louvers, horizontal grille pattern, hood cap, motometer or hood ornament, string-pull knob in handcrank area, tow loop, metal simulated wire wheels, also an un-numbered version, 3" long (KTV36)	25	38	50

Kansas Toy Transitional Vehicles

	C6	C8	C10
Army Tank, No. 74, marked "US Army" two gun turret, olive drab color, a different tank than No. 74 listed earlier, 2-1/4" (KTV61)	NPF	NPF	NPF
Concrete Mixer, No. 78, truck w/water tank and mixing barrel, vertical grille pattern, horizontal hood louvers, wooden hubs, rubber tires; found both w/ and w/o bottom pan; sometimes called a fuel tanker, 3-3/4" long (KTV65)	NPF	NPF	NPF
Coupe, No. 80, convertible, top up, landau iron, two open windows, vertical grille pattern, external trunk, HRDW w/metal disc wheels, sidemounted spare (a different sidemount casting), 3-1/2" long (KTV68)	NPF	NPF	NPF
Coupe, No. 80, convertible, top up, landau iron, two open windows, vertical grille pattern, external trunk, metal simulated wire wheels, w/metal simulated wire wheels, sidemounted spare, three-piece molded grille, 3-1/2" long (KTV67)	30	45	60

Kansas Toy Transitional Vehicles

	C6	C8	C10
Coupe, No. 75, Graham-like (Tootsietoy), vertical grille pattern, sidemounted spare, external trunk, wooden hubs, rubber tires, 1933 issue, 4-1/4" long (KTV62)	NPF	NPF	NPF
Indy Racer, No. 83, FWD, driver, vertical grille pattern, horizontal hood louvers, right exhaust, wooden hubs, rubber tires, 4-5/8" long (KTV71)	NPF	NPF	NPF
Racer, No. 81, Miller FWD, driver, eight cylinder right exhaust, horizontal grille pattern, wooden hubs, rubber tires, 1933 issue, 4" long (KTV69)	NPF	NPF	NPF
Racer, No. 76, Auburn speedster, low driver, headrest fairing, string-pull knob in handcrank area, horizontal grille pattern, slanted louvers, large oval fin, kickplates, wooden hubs, rubber tires, 4-1/4" long (KTV63)	25	38	50
Roadster, No. 77, open short Duesenberg, windshield down, driver, vertical grille pattern, slanted louvers, sidemounted spare, external trunk, 4" long (KTV64)	25	38	50
Sedan, No. 84, DeSoto (?) Airflow, four open windows, hood cap, motometer or hood ornament, horizontal grille pattern, horizontal hood louvers, 1934 issue, 3-5/8" long (KTV72)	NPF	NPF	NPF
Sedan, No. 82, Pierce-Arrow Silver Arrow fastback, six open windows, three-piece molded grille, 4" long (KTV70)	NPF	NPF	NPF
Sedan, No. 79, two-door, Graham-like, four open windows, vertical grille pattern, horizontal hood louvers, rearmount spare tire/wheel, wooden hubs, rubber tires w/five removable tires, found both w/ and w/o bottom pan, 4-1/4" long (KTV66)	20	30	40

Kenton

Kenton Lock Manufacturing Co., was incorporated in May 1890, in Kenton, Ohio. In November of 1894, it became the Kenton Hardware Manufacturing Co. Around this period, it began producing toys. In 1903, it brought out its first toy vehicle line, calling them the Red Devils, since most cars in those days were painted red. The firm was a guild. In 1930, L.S.

Kenton Dump Wagon, 9-3/4" long, $1000. Photo courtesy Sothey's, New York

Kenton Overland Circus Cage Truck, 7-1/2" long, $2000.

Bixler, of Jones & Bixler, was its president. Cast iron was its material.

Kenton	C6	C8	C10
Ambulance, 7" long	700	1200	1800
Army Motor Truck 807, 14" long ...	600	950	1400
Auto, early, 6" long	250	400	650
Boattail Cut-Down Speedster, 1910, 7" long	120	180	260
Buckeye Ditcher, 9" long	500	750	1200
Bus, "Coast-to-Coast"	350	525	700
Bus, 1920s, 10-3/4" long	375	525	750
Bus, 8" long	325	500	700
Bus, double-decker, 1920, 7-1/4" long	1100	1650	2200
Bus, double-decker, 1920s, 6" long.	312	470	625
Bus, double-decker, 9-1/2"	650	1050	1550
Cement Mixer, Jaeger, 8" long	1100	1700	2500
Cement Mixer, 7" long	423	635	845
Cement Mixer, Jaeger, 6-1/2" long .	365	545	730
Cement Mixer, Jaeger, 9" long	1000	2000	3000
Circus Truck, 10" long	1300	2000	2700
Coal Dump Truck, 8-1/2" long	300	450	600
Coupe, 1926, 10" long	3000	5500	9500
Coupe, 5" long	230	345	460
Coupe, 6-1/2" long	425	638	850
Coupe, 8" long	700	1100	1600
Dump Truck, 6" long	340	500	675
Dump Wagon, "Contractors", 9-3/4" long	500	750	1000
Emergency Truck, black rubber tires, c. 1930s	180	270	360
Fire Apparatus Truck	400	600	800
Fire Pump Truck, early w/driver, 10" long	220	330	440
Fire Pumper, w/gong, c. 1920s, 18" long	350	525	700
Fire Pumper, 1920s, 14-1/2" long ...	800	1200	1600

Kenton (Continued)	C6	C8	C10
Fire Truck, w/pumper, 15" long	1200	2000	2800
Franklin, air-cooled, 8-1/2"	1300	1950	2600
Hose Truck, open cab, green, driver, rider, hose, ladders, c. 1920s, 6-3/4" long	285	430	570
Hose Truck, 9" long	500	750	1050
Ice Truck, tongs and glass ice, 7-1/2" long	1000	2000	3000
Ladder Truck, 17-1/4" long	750	1200	1700
Ladder Truck, approx. 7-1/2" long..	300	450	600
Ladder Truck, pressed-steel ladders, 16" long	500	850	1100
Overland Circus, w/lion, 9" long	800	1300	2000
Overland Circus Cage Truck, w/driver, 7-1/2" long	800	1300	2000
Patrol Wagon, marked "Patrol" on side, w/driver and three fireman, c. 1920s-30s, 9" long	650	1100	1600
Phaeton Touring Car, 12" long	350	562	700
Pickwick Nite Coach, 14" long	1500	2500	3800
Pontiac, 4-1/2" long	250	400	525
Racer, early, 7-1/2" long	175	262	350
Racer, early, 9" long	600	1000	1400
Red Devil, w/driver, 6" long	200	300	400
Road Grader, nickel-plated movable blade, rubber tires, 7-1/2" long	212	318	425
Road Roller, "Galion Master", 7" long	150	225	300
Roadster, driver, c. 1908, 6" long....	300	450	600
Runabout Auto, 1900, 5" long	170	255	340
Runabout Auto, w/driver, 1908, 6-1/2" long	700	1050	1400
Sedan, take-apart body, late 1930s, 7" long	1200	2000	2800
Sedan, 4" long	110	165	225
Sprinkler Truck, early, 8"	425	638	850

*Kenton Runabout Auto, 1908, 6-1/2" long,
$1400. Photo courtesy Christie's East*

*Keystone Dump Truck, No. 41, 26-1/2" long, $1100. Photo
courtesy Joe and Sharon Freed*

*Kenton Stake Truck, 9-1/8" long, $1250. Photo courtesy
Bill Bertoia Auctions*

*Kenton Touring Car, No. 1923, 9" long, $1300. Photo
courtesy Bill Bertoia Auctions*

Kenton (Continued)

	C6	C8	C10
Stake Truck, "Speed", c. 1927, 5-1/2" long	410	615	825
Stake Truck, "Speed", 9/1/8" long	450	850	1250
Stake Truck, 6" long	235	352	470
Steam Roller, "Galion Master", 6-1/2" long	225	340	450
Steam Shovel, Marion, 7-1/4"	600	900	1200
Tank, 2-1/2" long	80	120	160
Touring Car, open, driver and passenger, 8-1/2" long	650	975	1300
Touring Car, No. 1923, open, w/driver and passenger, 9" long	650	975	1300
Tow Auto, 1920s, 9-1/2" long	1100	1800	2700
Yellow Cab, 1950s, 6-3/8" long	470	705	940

Keystone

Keystone of Boston had an odd assortment of products—movie projectors, steel trucks, wooden boats and pressed-wood forts and garages. Founded in 1922 or 1923 by Chester Rimmer and Author Jackson, it was first located in a small shop in Malden, Massachusetts, under the name Jacrim. The name was a combination of parts of both partner's last names. Rimmer retired in 2958, and sold out to various companies. The address in Boston was 288 A Street.

Keystone

	C6	C8	C10
Aerial Ladder, No. 79, 30-1/2" long	700	1100	1550

Keystone (Continued)

	C6	C8	C10
Ambulance, No. 73, military, 27" long	800	1400	1950
American Railway Express, No. 43, 26" long	1000	1700	2500
Chemical Pump Engine, No. 57, 27-1/2" long	1000	1550	2100
Dump Truck, No. 41, 26-1/2" long	500	750	1100
Fire Truck, No. 52, 27-1/2" long	645	1000	1300
Fire Truck, No. 49, 27-1/2" long	700	1000	2100
Hydraulic Dump Truck, No. 62, 26" long	500	800	1100
Koaster Truck, No. 54, w/skids, hoist cable, windlass, 26" long when skids retracted	800	1300	1800
Koaster Truck, No. 55, w/o skids and windlass	500	720	1000
Moving Van, No. 58, 26" long	750	1300	1850
Police Patrol, No. 51, 27-1/2" long	800	1400	1900
Riding Steam Roller, No. 60	300	450	600
Sprinkler Truck, No. 53, tank 12" long	1000	1600	2400
Steam Shovel, No. 47, 34-1/2" long when arm is extended	250	375	500
Steam Shovel, No. 46, 26" long when arm is extended	425	650	800
Truck Loader, No. 44, 17-3/4" high	500	800	1100

Keystone American Railway Express, No. 43, 26" long, $2500. Photo courtesy Joe and Sharon Freed

Keystone Fire Truck, No. 49, 27-1/2" long, $2100. Photo courtesy Joe and Sharon Freed

Kilgore "Fire Chief" Sedan, plastic, 1937, $45. Photo courtesy Dave Leopard

Keystone Moving Van, No. 58, 26" long, $1850. Photo courtesy Mapes Auctioneers and Appraisers

Keystone (Continued)	C6	C8	C10
U.S. Army Truck, No. 48, 26" long	500	800	1200
U.S. Mail Truck, No. 45, 26" long ..	900	1450	2100
Water Pump Tower, No. 56, 29" long	700	1100	1600
Wrecking Car, No. 78, 27" long	850	1400	1950

Kilgore

Kilgore, of Westerville, Ohio, appears to have begun toy making in the 1920s. Its toys were cast iron and low priced, with cap pistols its most popular line. But it also did well with a number of attractive trucks, fire engines, and cars as well as scattered aircraft and ships. Some subsidiary manufacturing was done in Lancaster, Pennsylvania, and Canada. In 1937, Kilgore began making plastic cars, trucks, planes, and buses, and later added plastic cap pistols, placing it among the first companies to produce plastic toys. Kilgore remained in business until 1978.

Kilgore	C6	C8	C10
Auto, "LF 1300A," w/driver	180	270	360
Bus, advertised in 1937, 4" long	20	25	30
Convertible, w/rumble seat, w/driver, early 1930s, 7" long	160	240	320
Coupe, streamlined, advertised in 1937, 4" long	25	35	45
Double-Decker Bus, c. 1930, 6" long	450	675	900
Dump Truck, 1930s, 7" long	175	265	350

Kilgore (Continued)	C6	C8	C10
Dump Truck, c. 1934, 5-3/4" long...	160	240	320
Dump Truck, c. 1934, 8-1/2" long...	450	675	900
Fire Chief Sedan, advertised in 1937, 4" long	25	35	45
Fire Truck, w/ladders, 1929, 6-3/4" long	190	285	375
Motorcycle, single rider, 4"	115	175	250
Motorcycle, "Special Delivery", 4-1/4" long	150	225	350
Police Car, 1937, 4"	25	35	45
Pontiac, 1930, 10"	1200	1800	2700
Roadster, driver, rumble seat, 6" long	250	375	500
Roadster, Pierce-Arrow, take-apart body, 6-1/8" long	250	375	500
Sedan, 3-1/4" long	70	100	150
Sedan, Packard Luxury, take-apart body, 8-1/4" long	800	1400	1600
Stutz Roadster, thirteen parts	1200	1800	2700
Taxi, 4" long	25	35	45
Truck, "Toy Town Delivery", 6-1/8" long	445	668	890
Truck, "Arctic Ice Cream Truck", 8" long	800	1300	1800
Truck, "Arctic Ice Cream Truck", 9" long	500	750	1000

Kingsbury Airflow, pressed steel, rubber tires, c. 1934, 14", $620.

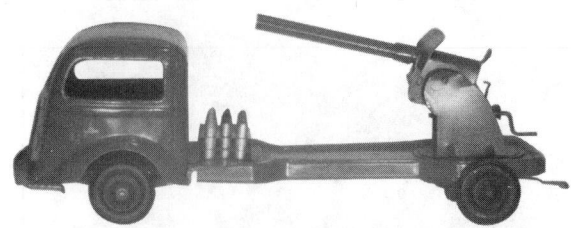

Kingsbury Cannon Truck, 1939, 15", $275.

Kingsbury Ladder Truck, pressed steel wind-up, No. 225, 1930s, 15", $475. Photo courtesy John Taylor

Kingsbury Greyhound Bus, windup, 18", c. 1937, $550. Photo courtesy Richard MacNary

Kilgore (Continued)	C6	C8	C10
Truck, "Express," advertised in 1937, 4" long	25	35	45

Kingsbury

Kingsbury had its origins in 1886 in Keene, New Hampshire. Its owner was Harry T. Kingsbury, who bought the Wilkins Toy Co., apparently not phasing out that firm's name until 1919. Steel and spring motors characterized Kingsbury's toys, with cars, fire engines, farm equipment, and racing cars its primary output. Kingsbury is still in business, but gave up toy production in 1942.

Kingsbury	C6	C8	C10
Aerial Ladder Truck, wind-up, ladder rises automatically to height of 38" when the truck runs into any obstruction, fireman on ladder climbs up and down by turning crank at base of ladder, c. 1905	450	700	1000
Aerial Ladder Truck, wind-up, ladder rises automatically to height of 38" when the truck runs into any obstruction, fireman on ladder climbs up and down by turning crank at base of ladder, c. 1941, 24" long	250	375	625
Airflow, rubber tires, c. 1934, 14" long	350	475	650
Airflow, clockwork, 14" long	500	750	1200

Kingsbury (Continued)	C6	C8	C10
Auto, wind-up, very early, 9-3/4" long	325	525	750
Bluebird Racer, 18" long	1000	1500	2100
Brougham Sedan, wind-up, 13" long	1100	1700	2425
Bus, 18" long	400	590	800
Cannon Truck, very early, clockwork, 11" long	225	325	450
Cannon Truck, wind-up, c. 1939, 15" long	125	190	275
Car, wind-up, curved dash, driver, 9" long	225	340	450
DeSoto, wind-up, c. 1938, 14-1/2" long	225	350	450
Dump Truck, w/driver, 10" long	450	675	900
Dump Truck, clockwork, early 1930s, 16" long	350	525	700
Fire Chief Coupe, 1930s, 14" long	325	450	675
Fire Pumper, clockwork, very early, 11" long	365	550	750
Fire Pumper, 1920s, 23" long	600	800	1200
Fire Truck, 18" long	250	375	500
Ford Sedan & House Trailer, 1937, 23" long	450	675	900
Golden Arrow Racer, 20" long	600	1000	1375
Greyhound Bus, wind-up, 18" long	275	400	550
Ladder Truck, driver, 22" long	200	300	400
Ladder Truck, c. 1930, 35" long	1200	2100	3100

Lincoln Bus, 3-1/2", $65. Photo courtesy Bob Ackerly

Lincoln Coupe, 4-1/2", $80. Photo courtesy Fred Zegel

Lincoln White Metal Works Fire Engine Pumper, 3-3/4" long, $125. Photo courtesy Perry Eichor

Lincoln White Metal Works, Top: Tanker Truck, 3-3/4" long, $100. Photo courtesy Fred Maxwell. Bottom: Railroad, Streamline, 4-1/2" long, $140. Photo courtesy Perry Eichor

Kingsbury (Continued)	**C6**	**C8**	**C10**
Ladder Truck, No. 225, wind-up, 1930s, 15" long	275	375	475
Ladder Wagon Fire Truck, rubber tires, 23-1/2" long	165	250	330
Lincoln Zephyr and Travel Trailer, 1936, 22-1/2" long	325	500	700
Phaeton Auto, rubber slip tires, 1900, 9-1/2" long	1400	2700	3500
Rack Truck, wind-up, 16" long	350	525	700
Roadster, No. 242, electric head-lights, spring motor, luggage rack, 13" long	375	565	750
Sunbeam Racer, red w/rubber tires on steel wheels, clockwork motor, 19" long	800	1300	1725
Transit Truck, 1930s, 19" long	100	150	200
Truck, w/C cap, 10" long	175	265	350
Truck with Crane, 1930s, 20" long	175	300	500
Wrecker, wind-up, 13" long	1000	1600	2300
Wrecker, wind-up, late 1920s, 14" long	550	750	950

Lansing Slik Toys

Lansing Slik Toys were made in Lansing, Iowa, and sometimes bear the name "Kipp," in addition to the "Lansing" and "Slik-Toy" trademarks. Most Slik-toys are made of aluminum in a single casting, but some were made of hard plastic. It seems that all Slik-Toys have a four-digit number beginning with "9." If a toy bears such a number, even if it has no other markings, it is almost surely a Slik-Toy.

Contributor: Dave Leopard, 2507 Feather Run Trail, West Columbia, SC 29169-4915.

Lansing Slik-Toys	**C6**	**C8**	**C10**
Fire Truck, No. 9700, 3-1/2" long	25	35	45
Fire Truck, No. 9706, 4" long	20	25	30
Fire Truck, No. 9606, 6" long	20	30	40
Metro Van, No. 9618, 5" long	25	30	40
Open Stake Truck, No. 9602, 7" long	23	35	50
Pickup Truck, No. 9601, 7" long	25	35	50
Pickup Truck, No. 9605, 6" long	20	30	40
Pickup Truck, No. 9703, 4" long	20	25	35
Roadster, No. 9701, 3-1/2" long	25	35	45
Sedan, No. 9702, 1949 Buick, 4" long	20	25	35
Sedan, No. 9600, fastback, 7" long	30	45	60
Sedan, No. 9604, four-door, 6" long	20	30	40
Sedan, No. 9600, fastback, taxi version, 7" long	30	45	60
Stake Truck, No. 9616, 6" long	25	30	40
Stakebody Truck, No. 9500, 11" long	45	60	75
Station Wagon, No. 9704, 4" long	20	25	35
Tank Truck, No. 9603, 7" long	40	50	60
Tank Truck, No. 9607, 6" long	20	30	40
Tank Truck, No. 9705, 4" long	20	25	35
Tractor/Trailer Rig, No. 9613, flat-bed trailer, 8" long	25	35	50

Lincoln White Metal Works Wrecker, 3-1/2" long, $80. Photo courtesy Perry Eichor

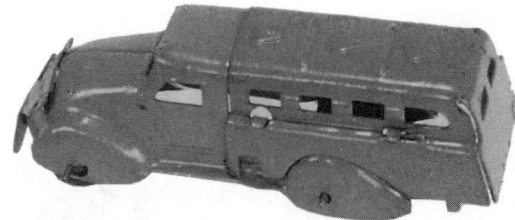

Marx Bus, 1940, 4-1/2" long, $180. Photo courtesy Richard MacNary

Marx Toy City Sanitation Dept. Help Keep Your City Clean Truck Train, c. 1940, 12-3/4" long, $350. Photo courtesy Calvin L. Chaussee

Marx Brake Kar, $210. Photo courtesy Continental Hobby House

Marx Toy Coca-Cola Truck, 10-1/2" long, $350. Photo courtesy Terry Sells

Lansing Slik-Toys (Continued)	C6	C8	C10
Tractor/Trailer Rig, No. 9611, grain trailer, 8" long	25	35	50
Tractor/Trailer Rig, log trailer, 8" long	25	35	50
Tractor/Trailer Rig, No. 9610, milk tanker, 8" long	30	40	55
Wrecker, No. 9617, 5" long	20	25	35

Lincoln White Metal Works

This company, located in Lincoln, Nebraska, was formed by Clayton E. Stevenson, the manufacturer of many high-quality slush-mold vehicles. Stevenson made toys out of his home for many years, and, as a salesman for Western Diecasting Co., even sold molds to Kansas Toy & Novelty Company, Tip Top Toy Co., and others. His specialty was the three-piece mold, there is even some speculation that he was the inventor of this complex mold.

Stevenson's was a remarkably long toy-making career, about fifteen years, through the Great Depression. An auto mechanic, Stevenson was born in 1896 and raised in Axtell, Kansas. He and his wife, Esther, moved to Lincoln in 1931 where they began selling toys in his name. His new business grew rapidly, and he made upwards if 800,000 toys in three

months. As his business grew, he moved to a larger facility at 2204 Y Street and in 1935 the company address was listed as 3433 J Street.

Lincoln White Metal Works toys were sold across the United States at Woolworths, Kress, Kresge, and Schwartz Paper Co. stores, some were even abroad.

After nine years of production, the factory was sold in 1940 due to shortages of lead and rubber and the rising costs of labor. It is not certain who acquired the remaining molds and inventory, although many indicators point to Ralstoy.

A variety of toys were made, including airplanes, midget racers, larger speed sedans, small coupes, tri-motor plane models, and miniature sawmills. Most range in size from three to seven inches in length. Stevenson designed his molds using photographs from magazines as guides. The midget racer was based on a Miller special, and the sedan is a replica of the front-drive Cord. A Nash was the basis for Lincoln White Metal's coupe.

Lincoln White Metal toys had a few distinct characteristics—early toys had metal wheels and tin propellers with pattern-bottomed pans; later toys had rubber wheels. These distinctions can assist collectors in identifying their toys.

The following list of cars is incomplete because of the rarity of these cars.

Marx Toy Coca-Cola Truck Shelf Sidecases, 1950s, $450. Photo courtesy Don Hultzman

Contributors: Fred Maxwell, 4722 N. 33 St., Arlington, VA 22207. Perry R. Eichor, 703 North Almond Drive, Simpsonville, SC 29681.

Marx Toy Dump Truck, c. 1940, 4-1/2" long, $140. Photo courtesy Bob Smith

Lincoln White Metal Works	C6	C8	C10
Brougham, Graham?, vertical vee-grille, SM, four open windows, T, from three-piece mold, 3-1/2" long (LWV21)	40	60	80
Bus, Overland, hood cap, ornament or Motormeter, horizontal grille pattern, ten open windows, 3-1/2" long (LWV27)	25	40	65
Coupe, slanted hood, rearmount hub for rubber tire, slanted grille (see Tootsie Graham), 4-1/2" long (LWV19)	40	60	80
Fire Engine, steam pumper, two-man crew, hose real compartment, hood cap, ornament or Motormeter, 3-1/4" long (LWV12)	25	50	75
Fire Engine Pumper, w/fireman on rear step, Graham-like grille, fenders faired bumper to bumper, patterned pan, sides embossed "Patrol 79," marked "Made in USA", 3-3/4" long (LWV9)	75	100	125
Railcar, Streamline, marked "Union Pacific" with shield symbol, two open windows in cab, eighteen open windows in passenger section, hidden rubber wheels, patterned pan, marked "Made in USA", 4-1/2" long	80	110	140
Sedan, DeSoto (?), two-door, hood cap, ornament or Motometer, horizontal grille pattern, four open windows, sreamlined airflow rear (LWV35)	40	60	80

Lincoln White Metal Works	C6	C8	C10
Sedan, Pierce-Arrow Silver Arrow, vertical vee-grille, headlamps and front fenders faired, six open windows, divided windshield, plain pan, 3-1/2" long (LWV5)	40	60	80
Speed Car, A V-12 version of Bluebird w/triangular fin, Lincoln?, 4-5/8" long (LWV4)	60	90	120
Speed Car, Bluebird record car, driver, V-8 engine w/intake ports, triangular fin w/wing design, 4" long (LWV3)	55	85	110
Stake Truck, slanted grille w/horizontal patten, divided windshield, two open windows, open stakes, rounded pan, 3-1/2" long (LWV22)	20	30	40
Tanker Truck, COE, two open windows, eight companrtments, patterned pan, marked "Made in the USA", 3-3/4" long (LWV10)	60	80	100
Wrecker, high style w/chopped top, Graham-like grille, two open windows, fenders faired bumper to bumper, solid crane w/grid pattern marked "Made in the USA", 3-1/2" long (LWV8)	40	60	80

Lindstrom

The Lindstrom Tool & Toy Company made wind-up toys of light pressed steel, as well as tin. Located in Bridgeport, Connecticut, and Lindstrom began making toy cars about 1913. It seems to have ceased production in the 1940s.

Lindstrom	C6	C8	C10
Cabin Racer	12	18	25
Lumber Truck, No. 160, steerable front wheels, w/driver, 10" long	125	187	250
Racer, 2-3/4" long	10	15	20
Steam Roller, No. 181, mechanical, 12" long	50	75	100

Marx Toy Easter Dump Truck, late 1930s, 6" long, $300. Photo courtesy John Taylor

Marx Toy Magnetic Crane Truck, 1940s, 8-1/2" long, $850. Photo courtesy Bob Smith

Marx Power Grader, No. 1759, 17-1/2", $80.

Marx Willys Jeep, steel, $180. Photo courtesy Richard Jansen

Marx Pepsi-Cola Truck, 1950s, 11", $200.

Marx Merchants Transfer Truck, tin wind-up, 1929, 10", $700.

CONDITION CODE

C6   Good; evident overall wear, well played with but acceptable to many collectors

C8   Very Good; minor overall wear, very clean

C10 Mint; like new

Note: Mint in Box commands a higher price.
Condition below C6 brings considerably lower prices

Manoil

Manoil was owned by two brothers, Jack and Maurice Manoil. Its sole sculptor was Walter Baetz, the man responsible for Manoil's seven early vehicles, which were Manoil's first toys, debuting in 1934. The firm, originally located in Manhattan, then Brooklyn, and finally in Waverly, New York, closed down about 1955.

	C6	C8	C10
Armored Car with Anti-Aircraft Gun (75)	27	41	55
Armored Car with Anti-Tank Gun (74)	22	33	45
Armored Car with Siren, siren cast separately (75A)	25	38	50
Armored Car with Siren, siren cast w/vehicle (75A)	34	51	68
Chemical Truck (104)	11	16	23
Coupe, futuristic (702)	70	100	135
Five Barrel Gun on Wheels (105)	12	18	25
Gasoline Truck (103)	10	15	20
Large Shell on Truck (96)	11	16	22
Pontoon on Wheels (97)	22	33	45
Roadster, futuristic, Pat. No. 95791 (704)	54	80	100
Rocket, futuristic bus-like vehicle, Pat. No. 95793 (706)	60	90	120
Sedan, futuristic (701)	50	75	100
Sedan, futuristic (700)	60	85	115
Sedan, futuristic, Pat. No. 95792 (705)	45	68	98
Shell Carrier with Soldier on Shell Box (71A)	10	15	20
Shell Carrier with Soldier on Shell Box, has loop (71)	12	18	24
Soup Kitchen, large number (70)	9	15	20
Soup Kitchen, small number (70A)	9	13	18
Tank (95)	11	16	22
Torpedo on Wheels (98)	10	15	20
Water Wagon, large number (72)	10	15	20
Wrecker, futuristic (703)	80	120	160

Manoil Plastic Vehicles

	C6	C8	C10
Dump Cart (P-13)	12	18	25
Pick-Up (P-9)	12	18	25
Road Scraper (P-11)	12	18	25
Roadster (P-7)	12	18	25
Sedan (P-8)	12	18	25
Towing Truck (P-10)	12	18	25

Manoil Post-War Vehicles

	C6	C8	C10
Aerial Ladder (711)	200	300	400
Bus (713)	12	18	24

Manoil Post-War Vehicles

	C6	C8	C10
Commerical Truck (715)	10	15	20
Convertible (718)	10	15	20
Convertible, hard top (717)	25	38	50
Fire Engine (709)	18	28	38
Oil Tanker (710)	13	20	27
Pumper (712)	200	300	400
Ranch Wagon (720)	10	15	20
Roadster, vertical radiator (708A)	50	75	100
Roadster, horizontal radiator (708)	27	41	54
Sedan (716)	10	15	20
Sedan (707)	31	46	62
Sport Car (719)	10	15	20
Towing Truck (714)	10	15	20

Marx

By the 1950s, Louis Marx Toy Co. was the largest manufacturer of toys in the world—six large factories in the United States and ownership of interest in factories in seven other countries.

Marx, born in Brooklyn in 1896, was working for the so-called toy king Ferdinand Strauss when he was in his teens. By the age of twenty, his energy and enterprise had made him a director of that company. A falling out with Strauss persuaded him to go into business for himself. In 1921, he and his brother began making their own toys, including some adaptations of items by the now-defunct Strauss. Marx's watchword seems to have been quality at the lowest possible price, and he was such a favorite with toy buyers that he had virtually no need for salesmen or advertising.

Marx made virtually every type of toy, with the exception of dolls. In April 1972, he sold his company to the Quaker Oats Company, who, in 1976, sold it to Europe's largest toy manufacturer, Dunbee-Combex-Marx. The company went into bankruptcy in 1980. Marx died in 1982, at the age of 85.

In 1982, American Plastics bought much of the Marx assets; in 1990, it began producing toys from the original molds. Marx eventually ended up in the hands of Jay Horowitz, the current president. Horowitz produces Marx action figures based on the original molds and has licensed Jim and Debby Flynn to produce new tin-lithographed trains. For more information on Marx trains, see O'Brien's Collecting Toy Trains.

Contributors: Michael W. Curran, Heritage America Company, P.O. Box 545, Hampton, IL 61256, 309-496-9426. John Taylor, P.O. Box 63, Nolensville, TN 37135-0063.

Marx Toy Co.

	C6	C8	C10
Air Force Truck, No. 3290, "Air Defense Group," ride'm toy, 32"	125	190	250
Air Force Truck, canvas top, 20"	105	158	210
Ambulance, "M.D. War Dept.," two-tone green, 1930s, 14" long	270	530	800
Ambulance, No. 8500, 1930s, 14" long	200	325	500
Ambulance, No. 8600, 1930s, 14" long	240	360	480

*Marx Doughboy Tank, tin wind up, c. 1930, $450.
Photo courtesy Harvey K. Rainess*

Marx Nutty Mad Cars, c. 1965, 4" long, $300.

Marx Toy Co. (Continued)	C6	C8	C10
American Railroad Express Agency Inc., Truck Train, open cab, early 1930s, 7" long	150	300	450
American Truck Co. Moving Truck, No. 65, friction	65	98	130
Army Corps of Engineers, canvas top, 20" long	125	190	250
Army Jeep with Searchlight Trailer	100	150	250
Army Staff Car, friction, 9".............	12	18	25
Arrow Special Delivery Truck, 1940s, 13" long	125	175	225
Auto Transport, w/two tin litho cars, 1950s, 34" long	175	205	350
Brake Kar, w/screeching noise	50	100	150
Bud Bowman's Milk Express Truck	175	250	350
Bus, 1940, 4-1/2" long....................	90	135	180
Candy Truck, "Fanny Farmer"	42	83	125
Cannon Truck, "Big Shot," fires cap-loaded missile, 22" long	18	36	55
Car Carrier, Big Boss, 42" long......	90	135	180
Car Carrier, No. T-50447B, "Auto Transwalk", 1930s truck w/three cars	200	300	400
Chief-Fire Dept. No. 1, friction drive, c. 1948..............................	90	135	180
City Sanitation Dept. Help Keep Your City Clean Truck Train, c. 1940, 12-3/4" long.....................	150	250	350
Cloverdale Farms Milk Truck, 11-1/2" long....................................	100	150	200
Cloverdale Farms Milk Truck	135	202	270
Coal Truck, electric motor and lights, early	280	420	565

Marx Toy Co. (Continued)	C6	C8	C10
Coast to Coast Delivery Truck, 1930s, 6" long	75	100	150
Coca-Cola Truck, Linemar, friction, 3" long.................................	25	50	75
Coca-Cola Truck, Sprite decal, late 1940s to early 1950s, 20" long....	280	570	880
Coca-Cola Truck, 10-1/2" long	175	263	350
Coca-Cola Truck Shelf Sidecases, shelf sidecase, 1950s	200	300	450
Cord Convertible, 11" long	250	375	500
Corvette Coupe, friction, 8"	7	33	50
Crane, Lumar Contractors	35	69	105
Cunningham Drug Stores Truck, scarce, 1950s	30	45	75
Curtiss Candy Truck.......................	17	33	50
Dairy Stake Truck, No. E-271, three-color, c. 1941	100	150	200
Delivery Truck, Pet Shop, 1950s, 10"..	80	120	160
Deluxe Coupe, wind-up, electric lights, 15" long	450	650	950
Deluxe Delivery Truck, 13" long	100	175	225
Deluxe Delivery Truck	100	175	225
Dump Truck, No. 1084....................	30	45	60
Dump Truck, No. T751, two-color, c. 1930s	85	130	175
Dump Truck, No. 695B, 17" long ...	50	100	150
Dump Truck, Lumar Contractors, 1940s, 17-1/2" long....................	35	69	105
Dump Truck, c. 1940, 4-1/2" long...	50	95	140
Easter Dump Truck, late 1930s, 6" long...	150	225	300
Easter Stake Truck, w/coal chute, 1940, 7" long	162	243	325

Marx Toy Co. (Continued)	C6	C8	C10
Easter Stake Truck, 1938, 10-1/2" long	190	275	380
Electrically Lighted Truck and Trailer Set Truck and Trailer, No. T-5715, c. 1930s, 15"	150	225	300
Falcon, w/plastic bubble top, black rubber tires, 20" long	85	165	250
Fire Truck, friction, 25" long	225	338	450
Fix-It Jaguar, 12" long	25	50	75
Gang Buster Car, No. 7200, 1930s, 14" long	550	825	1100
Gold Star Transfer Company Trailer Truck	150	225	325
Grader, Lumar Power, 16" long	17	33	50
Gravel Mixer, 1940s	150	225	325
Gravel Truck, 9" long	43	86	130
Gravel Truck, 13" long	50	75	150
High-Boy Climbing Tractor, No. 950, 10-1/2" long	100	150	200
Hi-Way Express Truck	65	125	190
Hydraulic Dump	75	100	150
Ice Truck, w/tongs and ice	275	400	525
Lazy-Day Dairy Farm Truck and Trailer, 22" long	50	75	150
Lifesavers Truck, 9-1/2" long	75	100	150
Lonesome Pine Trailer and Convertible Sedan, 1930s, 13" long	350	525	700
Lumar Scoop-A-Dump, 20" long	50	100	150
Machinery Moving Truck, No. 1016	275	400	550
Magnetic Crane Truck, 1940s, 8-1/2" long	100	150	275
Mammoth Truck Train, No. T-50-12345, truck w/five trailers, c. 1930s	175	262	350
Marx Doughboy Tank, World War II pot helmet, c. 1950	130	195	260
Mechanical Coupe, wind-up, 1933, 8" long	275	400	575
Merchants Transfer Truck, wind-up, 1929, 10" long	275	400	700
Mystery Taxi, press down to operate, c. 1930s	100	150	275
Navy Jeep, No. 1078	65	98	130
Navy Jeep with Searchlight Trailer	100	150	200
Nutty Mad Cars, friction, price for each, c. 1965, 4" long	150	225	300
Panel Wagon	40	60	80
Pepsi-Cola Truck, 1950s, 11" long	50	125	200
Pickup Truck, electric lights, 11" long	100	175	225

Marx Toy Co. (Continued)	C6	C8	C10
Power Grader, No. 1759, black or white wheels, 17-1/2" long	15	30	45
Pure Milk Dairy Truck, w/glass bottles, tin wheels, c. 1940	100	200	300
REA Express Truck, No. 1021	325	488	650
Road Grader, heavy-duty	50	75	125
Roadster, convertible, 1930s, 11" long	200	300	400
Rocker Dump, No. 1752, 17-1/2"	110	165	220
Sand & Gravel Dump Truck, 1940s, 10" long	60	90	120
Searchlight Truck	150	225	300
Siren Fire Chief, "F.D. 1st. Batt.", c. 1930, 15" long	375	550	750
Siren Police Car, No. 8300, 1930s, 14" long	200	300	400
Sparkling Hot Rod Racer, wind-up, 1950s, 8" long	40	60	75
Sports Coupe, 1930s, 15" long	200	300	400
Stake Truck	165	250	350
Stake Truck, c. 1941, 15" long	42	83	125
Steam Shovel, Lumar Contractors	15	30	45
Trailer and Convertible Sedan, Lonesome Pine, 1930s, 19" long	465	700	950
Tricky Taxi, friction, 4-1/2"	75	120	160
Truck, No. 4488, Guided Missile	220	330	440
Truck, Sinclair Fuel	200	325	475
Truck, Grocery, 1950s, 14-1/2"	62	93	125
U.S. Army Truck with Searchlight Trailer, 1950s, 27" total length	150	200	300
U.S. Mail Truck, 14" long	125	188	250
U.S. Navy Jeep with Searchlight Trailer, 1950s, 21" total length	140	200	275
Willys Jeep, hood opens, windshield folds down, c. 1938, 12"	90	135	180
Willys Jeep and Trailer, c. 1940s	133	200	265
Willys Jeepster, wind-up	75	112	150
Wrecker, "Cities Service," Linemar, 4-1/2"	65	100	130
Wrecker and Convertible, "Fix-All," set	125	188	250
Wrecker Truck, No. T-16, c. 1930s	150	225	300
Wrecker Truck, 1920s, 10" long	100	150	200

Matchbox

Matchbox Toy grew out of a company begun in 1947 by two Navy friends, Leslie Smith and Rodney Smith (no relation). Manufacturing toys was not even planned at this point. On June 19, 1947, the two partners combined portions of their first names, and the name Lesney was born. In 1948, Lesney Products produced their first toy, a 4-1/2-inch Aveling Barford Road Roller. Encouraged by brisk sales, three other toys were produced that year—a 4-1/2-inch Caterpillar Bulldozer, a 3-

1/8-inch Caterpillar Tractor, and a 3-3/4-inch Cement Mixer. It was decided to package the toys in a matchbox-type box, and thereafter the toys would be known as Matchbox. Value on these early Lesney toys today is near $1,000.

These small vehicles quickly became very popular. These first small vehicles had metal wheels, but were shortly changed to plastic. These early wheels are known to collectors as regular wheels, not to be confused with the Superfast wheels that were introduced in 1969.

It is not uncommon to find slight color and style variations for the same vehicle. These variations were often due to paint or part shortages, and are now highly sought-after by collectors.

The year 1956 saw the introduction of the Models of Yesteryear line. The king-size line was first developed and marketed in 1957, and was known as Major Packs. Matchbox toys were first marketed in the United States in 1958; by the early 1960s, they became a household standard. The year 1993 marked the 40th anniversary of Matchbox toys, and these small vehicles are rapidly gaining popularity and value among collectors. Listed are all of the basic models and some important variations.

Contributor: Reid Covey, Box 2D Highmarket Rd., Constableville, NY 13325, email: Sullivan@northnet.org.

Matchbox

	C6	C8	C10
No. 01 Aveling Barford Road Roller, 1964	17	26	39
No. 01 Diesel Road Roller, 1953	20	40	90
No. 01 Dodge Challenger, 1976	4	6	8
No. 01 Mercedes Benz Lorry, 1968	6	11	18
No. 01 Mod Rod, 1971	8	12	20
No. 02 Dumper, 1953	25	40	90
No. 02 Hot Rod Jeep, 1971	5	7	12
No. 02 Hovercraft, 1976	5	7	12
No. 02 Mercedes Trailer, 1968	5	10	15
No. 02 Muir-Hill Dumper, 1962	10	15	25
No. 03 Bedford Ton Tipper, 1961	10	15	20
No. 03 Cement Mixer, 1953	25	35	50
No. 03 Mercedes Benz Ambulance, 1968	7	15	20
No. 03 Monteverdi Hai, 1973	5	8	15
No. 03 Porsche Turbo, 1978	5	10	15
No. 04 '57 Chevy, 1981	5	10	15
No. 04 Gruesome Twosome, 1971	3	6	10
No. 04 Massey Harris Tractor, 1954	25	45	80
No. 04 Pontiac Firebird, 1976	5	10	15
No. 04 Stake Truck, 1967	10	20	30
No. 04 Triumph Motorcycle and Sidecar, 1959	25	45	80
No. 05 London Bus, 1954	20	30	65
No. 05 Lotus European Sports Car, 1969	10	20	25
No. 05 Seafire, 1976	3	7	10
No. 05 U.S. Mail Truck, 1981	5	10	15

Matchbox (Continued)

	C6	C8	C10
No. 06 Euclid Ten-Wheel Quarry, 1964	20	30	50
No. 06 Ford Pickup, 1969	8	15	20
No. 06 Mercedes Tourer, 1974	5	8	12
No. 06 Quarry Truck, 1955	20	35	75
No. 07 Ford Anglia, 1961	15	25	35
No. 07 Ford Refuse Truck, 1967	7	10	15
No. 07 Hairy Hustler, 1971	5	8	12
No. 07 Horse Drawn Milk Cart, 1955	25	40	80
No. 07 VW Golf, 1976	4	6	9
No. 08 Caterpillar Tractor, 1955	25	40	75
No. 08 De Tomaso Pantera, 1975	15	22	35
No. 08 Ford Mustang Fastback, 1966	10	15	25
No. 08 Wildcat Dragster, 1971	7	12	16
No. 09 Boat and Trailer, 1967	5	10	15
No. 09 Dennis Fire Engine, 1955	20	35	75
No. 09 Ford Escort RS2000, 1978	3	5	7
No. 09 Javelin, 1972	5	9	11
No. 09 Merryweather Marquis Fire Engine, 1959	20	25	35
No. 10 Mechanical Horse and Trailer, 1955	30	45	75
No. 10 Pipe Truck, 1967	10	15	20
No. 10 Piston Popper, 1973	5	10	15
No. 10 Plymouth "Gran Fury" Police Car, 1980	3	4	7
No. 10 Sugar Container Truck, 1961	25	35	75
No. 11 Car Transporter, 1977	5	8	10
No. 11 Flying Bug, 1972	5	10	15
No. 11 Jumbo Crane, Taylor, 1964	7	12	17
No. 11 Petrol Tanker, Esso decal, 1955	25	35	75
No. 11 Petrol Tanker, green body, no number on bottom	140	200	350
No. 11 Scaffolding Truck, Mercedes, 1969	10	15	25
No. 12 Big Bull, 1975	5	8	11
No. 12 Citroen CX, 1981	5	7	12
No. 12 Land Rover, 1953	15	25	40
No. 12 Safari Land Rover, 1965	11	18	30
No. 12 Setra Coach, 1971	7	10	15
No. 13 Baja Buggy, 1971	8	10	15
No. 13 Bedford Wreck Truck, 1955	25	35	65
No. 13 Dodge Wreck Truck, BP Label, yellow cab, green body, 1961	18	23	35

Matchbox No. 09 Merryweather Marquis Fire Engine, 1959, $35. Photo courtesy Gary Linden

Matchbox No. 12 Land Rover, 1953, $40. Photo courtesy Gary Linden

Matchbox No. 14 Bedford Lomas Ambulance, $60. Photo courtesy Gary Linden

Matchbox No. 25 Bedford Dunlop Van, 1956, $55. Photo courtesy Gary Linden

Matchbox No. 19 MG Midget Sports Car, 1955, $75. Photo courtesy Gary Linden

Matchbox (Continued)	C6	C8	C10
No. 13 Dodge Wreck Truck, green cab, yellow body (rare)	300	490	750
No. 13 Snorkel Fire Engine, 1977	4	5	6
No. 13 Thames Wreck Truck, MB Garages, 1959	10	25	50
No. 14 Bedford Lomas Ambulance.	20	40	60
No. 14 Daimler Ambulance, 1955	15	25	40
No. 14 Iso Grifo Sports Car, 1968	5	10	15
No. 14 Mini Ha Ha, 1975	5	10	15
No. 15 Dennis Refuse Truck, 1963 .	15	20	30
No. 15 Fork Lift Truck, 1972	5	7	11
No. 15 Prime Mover, 1955	25	35	50
No. 15 Volkswagen 1500 Saloon, 1968	8	17	27
No. 16 Badger, 1974	5	8	13
No. 16 Case Tractor Bulldozer, 1969	6	11	18
No. 16 Low-Loading Trailer, six wheels, 1955	15	20	40
No. 16 Low-Loading Trailer, eight wheels, 1955	20	25	45
No. 16 Pontiac, 1981	2	4	6

Matchbox (Continued)	C6	C8	C10
No. 16 Scammel Mountaineer Dump with Plow, 1961	15	25	35
No. 17 Austin Taxi, 1960	25	45	70
No. 17 Bedford Removal Van, 1955	35	65	110
No. 17 Eight-Wheel Tipper "Hoveringham", 1964	7	15	25
No. 17 Horse Box "Ergomatic Cab", 1969	5	8	15
No. 17 Londoner, 1973	10	15	20
No. 18 Caterpillar Bulldozer, 1955 .	20	24	46
No. 18 Field Car, 1969	7	10	20
No. 18 Field Car, green plastic tires (rare)	55	100	165
No. 18 Hondarora, 1975	5	10	20
No. 19 Aston-Martin F.I., 1961	30	45	100
No. 19 Cement Truck, 1976	5	7	9
No. 19 Lotus Racing Car, 1965	6	8	15
No. 19 MG Midget Sports Car, 1955	25	45	75
No. 19 MGA Sports Car, 1959	30	50	100
No. 19 Road Dragster, 1971	4	6	10
No. 20 E.R.F. Lorry Truck, 1955	30	50	75

Matchbox (Continued)	C6	C8	C10
No. 20 Lamborghini Marzel, 1969 ..	8	10	15
No. 20 Police Patrol, 1975	4	6	10
No. 20 Taxi Cab, Chevrolet Impala, 1965	15	25	35
No. 21 Commer Milk Truck, 1961 ..	30	49	58
No. 21 Foden Concrete Truck, 1969	8	12	18
No. 21 Long Distance Coach "London to Glasgow", 1955	24	39	55
No. 21 Road Roller, 1973	6	8	14
No. 22 Blaze Buster, 1975	4	6	10
No. 22 Freeman Inter City Commuter, 1970	6	9	14
No. 22 Pontiac "Grand Prix" Sports Coupe, 1964	10	15	25
No. 22 Vauxhall Cresta, 1955	35	45	55
No. 23 Atlas, 1975	5	7	12
No. 23 Caravan Trailer, 1956	10	15	20
No. 23 House Trailer Caravan, 1967	15	20	35
No. 23 Volkswagen Camper, 1970 ..	5	10	15
No. 24 Diesel Shunter, 1979	3	5	7
No. 24 Excavator, 1956	15	20	30
No. 24 Rolls Royce Silver Shadow, 1967	5	15	25
No. 24 Team Matchbox, 1973	8	13	19
No. 25 B.P. Tanker, 1960	10	15	25
No. 25 Bedford Dunlop Van, 1956 .	20	30	55
No. 25 Flat Car & Container, 1979 .	3	5	7
No. 25 Ford Cortina G.T., 1968	5	10	15
No. 25 Mod Tractor, 1972	10	15	20
No. 25 Volkswagen 1200 Sedan, 1958	40	60	100
No. 26 Big Banger, 1972	4	6	9
No. 26 GMC Tipper Truck, 1968	5	10	15
No. 26 Ready Mix Concrete Truck, 1956	18	26	36
No. 26 Site Dumper, 1976	3	5	8
No. 27 Bedford Low-Loader, 1956 .	30	40	75
No. 27 Bedford Low-Loader, metal wheels (rare)	200	300	415
No. 27 Cadillac Sedan, 1960	35	45	75
No. 27 Lamborghini Countach, 1974	5	7	10
No. 27 Mercedes Benz 230SL, 1965	10	15	22
No. 28 Bedford Compressor Truck, 1956	20	35	50
No. 28 Lincoln Continental, 1980 ...	10	15	20
No. 28 Mack Dump Truck, 1968	5	10	15
No. 28 Mack Ten Jaguar, 1964	35	40	75

Matchbox (Continued)	C6	C8	C10
No. 28 Stoat, 1974	5	10	20
No. 28 Thames Compressor Truck, 1959	20	30	60
No. 29 Austin A55 Cambridge, 1961	20	30	50
No. 29 Bedford Milk Delivery Van, 1956	20	30	50
No. 29 Fire Pumper Truck, 1965	10	20	30
No. 29 Racing Mini, 1971	5	10	15
No. 29 Shovel Nose Tractor, 1976 ..	5	10	15
No. 30 Articulated Truck, 1981	4	6	8
No. 30 Beach Buggy, 1971	5	10	15
No. 30 Favin Crane, eight-wheel, 1965	11	16	25
No. 30 Ford Perfect with Towbar, 1956	30	42	55
No. 30 German Crane Truck, 1961 .	25	39	50
No. 30 Swamp Rat, 1977	4	6	8
No. 31 Caravan, 1977	4	6	8
No. 31 Ford Customline Station Wagon, 1956	25	40	90
No. 31 Ford Fairlane Station Wagon, 1959	25	40	90
No. 31 Lincoln Continental, 1964 ...	10	15	20
No. 31 Volks Dragon, 1971	5	7	10
No. 32 Excavator, 1981	10	15	25
No. 32 Jaguar XK 140 Coupe, 1956	25	40	75
No. 32 Leyland Tanker, 1968	16	24	34
No. 33 Datsun 126X, 1973	5	8	12
No. 33 Ford Zephyr 6 MKIII, 1963 .	20	25	40
No. 33 Ford Zodiac MKII, 1956	25	35	50
No. 33 Lamborghini Muira P400, 1969	10	15	25
No. 33 Police Motorcyclist, 1977	4	6	8
No. 34 Chevy Pro Stocker, 1981	2	4	6
No. 34 Formula 1 Racing Car, 1971	7	11	15
No. 34 Vantastic, 1976	4	7	15
No. 34 Volkswagen Camper, 1961 .	14	21	35
No. 34 Volkswagen Microvan Matchbox Express, 1956	30	44	75
No. 35 Fandango, 1975	5	7	10
No. 35 Marschall Horse Box, 1956 .	40	65	90
No. 35 Merryweather Marquis Fire Engine, 1970	5	10	14
No. 35 Sno-Trac Tractor, 1961	15	20	35
No. 36 Austin A50, w/towbar, 1956	20	30	40
No. 36 Formula 5000, 1975	4	6	8
No. 36 Hot Rod Draguar, 1971	5	8	20
No. 36 Lambretta and Sidecar, 1960	30	55	75
No. 36 Opel Diplomant, 1966	8	13	20

Matchbox No. 28 Bedford Compressor Truck, 1956, $50. Photo courtesy Gary Linden

Matchbox No. 36 Lambretta and Sidecar, 1960, $75.

Matchbox No. 37 Coca-Cola Truck, 1956, $100.

Matchbox No. 38 Darrier Refuse Collector, $75. Photo courtesy Gary Linden

Matchbox No. 46 Morris Minor 1000, 1957, $80. Photo courtesy Gary Linden

Matchbox (Continued)	C6	C8	C10
No. 36 Refuse Truck, 1981..............	3	5	8
No. 37 Cattle Truck, Dodge, 1967 ..	10	15	20
No. 37 Coca-Cola Truck, 1956........	45	62	100
No. 37 Skip Truck, 1976	4	6	8
No. 37 Soopa Coopa, 1973.............	5	7	11
No. 38 Armored Jeep, 1976.............	5	10	15
No. 38 Camper, 1981......................	3	5	7
No. 38 Darrier Refuse Collector......	25	40	75
No. 38 Honda Motorcycle with Trailer, 1968................	11	16	22
No. 38 Stingeroo, 1973....................	6	8	11
No. 38 Vauxhall Estate, 1963..........	11	20	27
No. 39 Clipper, 1973	6	8	12
No. 39 Ford Zodiac Convertible, 1956................	30	40	95
No. 39 Pontiac Convertible, 1962 ...	35	51	65
No. 39 Rolls-Royce Silver Shadow MKII................	4	6	8
No. 40 Bedford Seven-Ton Tipper, 1956................	25	35	65
No. 40 Guildsman, 1971..................	5	8	12
No. 40 Hay Trailer, 1967.................	4	8	12
No. 40 Horse Box, 1977	4	6	8

Matchbox (Continued)	C6	C8	C10
No. 40 Leyland "Royal Tiger" Coach/Long Distance, 1961........	11	18	26
No. 41 "D" Type Jaguar Racing Car, 1956................	80	115	150
No. 41 Ambulance, 1978.................	4	6	8
No. 41 Ford G.T. 40, Sports Racer, 1965................	14	21	30
No. 41 Siva Spyder, 1972................	5	10	15
No. 42 Bedford "Evening News" Van, 1956................	30	45	60
No. 42 Container Truck, 1977........	4	6	8
No. 42 Iron Fairy Crane, 1969	7	11	18
No. 42 Iron Fairy Crane, spoke wheels, 1970................	30	45	60
No. 42 Studebaker Lark Wagonaire, 1965................	10	20	30
No. 42 Tyre Fryer, 1972..................	5	10	15
No. 43 Aveling-Barford Shovel, 1962................	10	20	30
No. 43 Dragon Wheels, 1972	5	7	10
No. 43 Hillman Minx, 1957	30	45	75
No. 43 Pony Trailer, 1968..............	10	15	20
No. 43 Steam Loco, 1978...............	4	6	8

Matchbox (Continued)	C6	C8	C10
No. 44 Boss Mustang, 1972	3	5	8
No. 44 Passenger Coach, 1978	3	5	7
No. 44 Refrigerator Truck, GMC, 1967	10	15	20
No. 44 Rolls-Royce Silver Cloud, 1957	20	30	50
No. 45 BMW, 1976	5	8	11
No. 45 Ford Corsair with Green Boat, 1959	11	15	20
No. 45 Ford Group Six, 1970	6	9	11
No. 45 Vauxhall Victor, 1957	15	25	40
No. 46 Mercedes-Benz 300SE, 1968	6	11	16
No. 46 Morris Minor 1000, 1957	35	50	80
No. 46 Pickfords Removal Van, 1960	20	35	60
No. 46 Stretcha Fetcha, 1972	5	9	15
No. 47 Beach Hopper, 1973	5	7	10
No. 47 Daf Tipper Container Truck, 1968	8	12	16
No. 47 Neilson Ice Cream Van, 1963	30	46	60
No. 47 Pannier Loco, 1980	3	5	7
No. 47 Trojan Brooke Bond Van, 1957	30	55	75
No. 48 Dodge Dumper Truck, 1967	11	16	25
No. 48 Pi-Eyed Piper, 1973	4	6	10
No. 48 Sambron Jack Lift, 1977	4	6	8
No. 48 Sports Boat & Trailer, 1957	30	40	80
No. 49 Army Half Track MKIII, 1958	20	30	55
No. 49 Chop Suey, 1973	10	15	20
No. 49 Chop Suey, chrome handle bar	30	45	70
No. 49 Crane Truck, 1976	3	5	8
No. 49 Mercedes Unimog Truck, 1967	11	18	24
No. 50 Articulated Truck, 1973	6	11	16
No. 50 Commer Pickup Truck, 1958	20	30	50
No. 50 Ford Kennel Truck, 1969	10	15	20
No. 50 Harley Davidson Motorcycle, 1981	2	3	5
No. 51 Albion Truck "Portland Cement", 1958	15	25	35
No. 51 Citroen SM, 1972	5	7	10
No. 51 Eight-Wheel Tipper Truck, 1969	10	15	20
No. 52 BRM Racing Car, 1965	10	15	20
No. 52 Dodge Charger MKIII, 1970	5	10	15
No. 52 Maserati 4 CLT, 1958	35	45	65

Matchbox (Continued)	C6	C8	C10
No. 52 Police Launch, 1976	3	5	7
No. 53 Aston-Martin DB2/4, 1959	19	26	35
No. 53 C.J. 6 Jeep, 1977	4	6	8
No. 53 Ford Zodiac MKIV, 1968	10	15	20
No. 53 Mercedes-Benz 220SE, 1968	15	25	40
No. 53 Tanzara, 1972	3	7	10
No. 54 Army Saracen Personnel Carrier, 1959	20	30	50
No. 54 Cadillac Ambulance, 1965	16	25	35
No. 54 Ford Capri, 1971	4	7	9
No. 54 Mobile Home, 1981	3	5	7
No. 54 Personnel Carrier, 1976	5	7	10
No. 55 D.U.K.W., Army Amphibian, 1959	25	35	65
No. 55 Ford Cortina, 1980	5	9	11
No. 55 Ford Police Car, 1963	50	75	100
No. 55 Hell Raiser, 1975	4	6	8
No. 55 Mercury Parkland Police Car, 1969	15	20	25
No. 55 Mercury Police Car, Station Wagon, 1970	5	10	15
No. 56 BMC 1800 Pininfarina, 1970	7	10	15
No. 56 Fiat 1500, 1965	9	12	20
No. 56 Hi Trailer, 1975	5	10	15
No. 56 London Trolley Bus, 1959	35	45	80
No. 56 Mercedes 450SEL, 1980	4	6	8
No. 57 Chevrolet Impala, 1966	25	35	50
No. 57 Eccles Caravan, 1970	5	10	15
No. 57 Wild Life Truck, 1973	7	9	15
No. 57 Wolseley 1500, 1959	20	25	35
No. 58 British European Airways Coach, 1959	25	35	75
No. 58 DAF Girder Truck, 1968	9	12	16
No. 58 Drott Excavator, 1963	25	30	55
No. 58 Faun Dumper, 1976	5	9	15
No. 58 Woosh-N-Push, 1972	5	10	15
No. 59 Fire Chief Car, 1966	35	45	80
No. 59 Ford "Singer" Van, 1959	45	60	100
No. 59 Ford Fairlane Fire Car, 1964	30	45	90
No. 59 Planet Scout, 1975	15	20	30
No. 59 Porsche 928, 1981	5	7	9
No. 60 Holden Pickup, 1977	8	11	15
No. 60 Lotus Super Seven, 1971	6	9	12
No. 60 Morris Omnitruck J2 Pickup	17	26	35
No. 60 Truck with Site Office, 1967	10	15	20
No. 61 Alvis Stalwart, 1967	20	30	45
No. 61 Blue Shark, 1971	4	6	10

Matchbox No. 49 Army Half Track MKIII, $41. Photo courtesy Gary Linden

Matchbox No. 55 Ford Police Car, 1963, $100. Photo courtesy Gary Linden

Matchbox No. 59 Ford "Singer" Van, 1959, $100. Photo courtesy Gary Linden

Metalcraft left to right: Coca-Cola truck, 11" long, $1000; Heinz Truck, 12" long, $425.

Metalcraft Waldorf Lager Stake Truck with sweetheart grille, $900. Photo courtesy Bob Smith

Matchbox (Continued)	C6	C8	C10
No. 61 Military Scout Car, Ferret, 1959	20	25	35
No. 61 Wreck Truck, 1978	3	5	7
No. 62 Chevrolet Corvette, 1980	2	4	6
No. 62 General Army Lorry, 1959	20	25	30
No. 62 Mercury Cougar, 1969	10	15	20
No. 62 Rat Rod Dragster, 1971	5	10	15
No. 62 Renault 17 TL, 1974	5	7	15
No. 62 TV Service Van, 1964	30	50	65
No. 63 Airport Fire Fighting Crash Tender, 1964	15	25	35
No. 63 Army Ambulance, 1959	25	40	50
No. 63 Dodge Crane Truck, 1968	10	14	20
No. 64 Fire Chief Car, 1976	3	5	8
No. 64 MG 1100, 1966	8	12	16
No. 64 Scammell Army Wreck Truck, 1959	20	35	50
No. 64 Slingshot Dragster, 1971	5	9	15
No. 65 Airport Coach, 1977	5	10	20
No. 65 Claas Combine Harvester, 1968	10	15	20

Matchbox (Continued)	C6	C8	C10
No. 65 Jaguar 3.4 Litre Saloon, 1959	15	20	30
No. 65 Saab Sonnet, 1973	5	8	10
No. 66 Citroen DS19, 1959	20	30	50
No. 66 Ford Transit, 1977	5	10	20
No. 66 Greyhound Bus, 1967	20	30	40
No. 66 Harley Davidson Motorcycle and Sidecar, 1963	50	75	125
No. 66 Mazda RX500, 1972	5	8	10
No. 67 "Saladin" Armored Car, 1959	20	30	40
No. 67 Datsun 260Z, 1978	4	6	8
No. 67 Hot Rocker, 1973	4	6	9
No. 67 Volkswagen 1600 T.L., 1968	10	15	20
No. 68 Army Austin MKII Radio Truck, 1959	15	20	30
No. 68 Cosmobile, 1975	8	10	15
No. 68 Mercedes Coach, 1965	20	25	40
No. 68 Porsche 910, 1970	7	10	15
No. 69 Chevrolet Van, 1980	12	18	26

Matchbox (Continued)

	C6	C8	C10
No. 69 Commer 30 Cwt. Van "Nestle's", 1959	25	40	50
No. 69 Hatra Tractor Shovel, 1965	20	25	40
No. 69 Rolls-Royce Silver Shadow, 1970	10	20	25
No. 69 Turbo Fury, 1973	6	8	12
No. 69 Wells Fargo Security, 1978	5	10	15
No. 70 Atkinson Grit-Spreading Truck, 1965	10	15	20
No. 70 Dodge Dragster, 1971	7	11	16
No. 70 Ferrari, 1981	2	3	6
No. 70 Ford Thames Estate Car, 1959	20	30	40
No. 70 S.P. Gun, 1977	3	6	10
No. 71 Army Water Truck, 1959	15	25	50
No. 71 Cattle Truck, 1976	4	6	10
No. 71 Ford Heavy Wreck Truck, amber windows, light and white bumper	20	30	40
No. 71 Ford Heavy Wreck Truck, 1968	10	20	35
No. 71 Jeep Pickup Truck, 1964	20	40	55
No. 71 Jumbo Jet, 1973	3	5	10
No. 72 Bomag Road Roller, 1980	4	6	10
No. 72 Fordson Tractor, Power Major, 1959	20	30	45
No. 72 Hovercraft SRN6, 1972	4	8	10
No. 72 Standard Jeep, 1967	10	15	20
No. 73 Ferrari Racing Car, 1963	15	27	36
No. 73 Mercury Station Wagon, Commuter, 1969	10	15	20
No. 73 Model "A" Ford, 1981	4	6	8
No. 73 RAF Ten-Ton Pressure Refueler Tanker, 1959	22	32	45
No. 73 Weasel, 1974	5	10	15
No. 74 Cougar Villager, 1978	4	6	8
No. 74 Daimler Bus, 1966	15	20	30
No. 74 Mobile Refreshment Bar, Canteen, 1959	24	40	55
No. 74 Toe Joe, 1972	4	6	10
No. 75 Alfa Carabo, 1971	6	9	13
No. 75 Ferrari Berlinetta, 1965	11	16	22
No. 75 Ford Thunderbird, 1959	50	75	125
No. 75 Helicopter, 1976	4	6	9

Models of Yesteryear

	C6	C8	C10
Y-01 1911 Model "T" Ford, 1964	14	22	30
Y-01 1925 Allchin 7 N.H.P. Traction Engine, 1955	25	35	45
Y-01 1936 Jaguar SS100, 1977	14	22	32

Models of Yesteryear

	C6	C8	C10
Y-02 1911 "B" Type London Bus, 1955	50	75	100
Y-02 1911 Renault Two-Seater, 1963	10	20	30
Y-02 Prince Henry Vauxhall, 1970	10	15	25
Y-03 1907 London "E" Class Tramcar, 1955	55	90	115
Y-03 1910 Benz Limousine, 1965	10	25	30
Y-03 1934 Riley MPH, 1972	10	15	20
Y-04 1905 Shank-Mason Horse-Drawn Fire Engine, 1960	75	100	125
Y-04 1909 Opel Coupe, 1966	15	30	45
Y-04 1930 Dusenberg Model J, 1976	15	25	35
Y-04 Sentinel Steam Wagon, 1955	55	75	100
Y-05 1907 Peugeot, 1968	17	29	36
Y-05 1927 Talbot Van, 1978	20	30	40
Y-05 1929 LeMans Bentley, 1955	50	65	90
Y-05 1929 Supercharged 4-1/2 Litre Bentley, 1960	16	25	33
Y-06 1913 Cadillac, 1967	15	20	30
Y-06 1916 A.E.C. "Y" type Lorry Truck, 1955	25	30	45
Y-06 1920 Rolls-Royce Fire Engine, 1978	18	29	44
Y-06 1926 Type "35" Bugatti, 1961	22	33	44
Y-07 1912 Rolls-Royce, 1967	25	39	48
Y-07 1913 Mercer Raceabout Sportcar, 1961	25	35	45
Y-07 1914 4-Ton Leyland, 1955	30	40	50
Y-08 1914 Stutz Roadster, 1968	15	20	30
Y-08 1914 Sunbeam Motorcycle with sidecar, 1962	20	35	45
Y-08 1926 Morris Cowley "Bullnose", 1955	40	50	60
Y-08 1945 MC TC Sports Car, 1978	7	11	15
Y-09 1912 Simplex, 1967	25	41	56
Y-09 1924 Fowler "Big Lion" Showman Engine, 1955	30	40	55
Y-10 1906 Rolls-Royce Silver Cloud, 1968	12	17	25
Y-10 1908 Grand Prix Mercedes Racing Car, 1957	40	60	80
Y-10 1928 Mercedes-Benz 36/220, 1963	24	38	50
Y-11 1912 Packard Landaulet, 1963	19	29	37
Y-11 1920 Aveling and Porter Steam Roller, 1957	39	57	76
Y-11 1938 Lagonda Drophead Coupe, 1972	15	22	32

Models of Yesteryear

	C6	C8	C10
Y-12 1899 Horse-Bus, London, 1957	81	113	150
Y-12 1909 Thomas Flyabout, 1967.	22	33	44
Y-12 1912 Model "T" Ford, 1979	12	19	25
Y-13 1862 American 4-4-0 Locomotive	33	49	66
Y-13 1911 Daimler, 1965	17	26	32
Y-13 1918 Crossley Truck, 1972	20	33	40
Y-14 1903 Duke of Connaught Locomotive, 1957	85	122	159
Y-14 1911 Maxwell Roadster, 1965	25	38	54
Y-14 1931 Stutz Bearcat, 1972	10	15	20
Y-15 1907 Rolls-Royce "Silver Ghost", 1960	20	35	45
Y-15 1930 Packard Victoria, 1969	10	15	25
Y-16 1904 Spyker Veteran Auto, 1961	30	45	60
Y-16 1928 Mercedes SS, 1971	10	15	25
Y-17 1938 Hispano Suiza, 1972	11	15	25
Y-18 1937 Cord 812, 1979	8	10	12
Y-19 1935 Auburn 851, 1980	5	8	11
Y-20 1938 Mercedes 540K, 1981	6	8	10
Y-21 1929 Woody Wagon, 1981	7	12	20

Metal Cast Products Company

Metal Cast Products was formed when S. Sachs was reorganized in 1925. The producer of slush molds for small businesses and hobbyists, Metal Cast's molds were used by so many different franchises it is difficult to identify the actual makers unless they engraved their names on the model. One such maker was Fred Green Toys. Metal Cast's objective was to offer any or all support materials and services to slush-mold entrepreneurs.

A variety of wheels may be found on Metal Cast vehicles—metal disk wheels, metal spoke wheels, wood wheels with rubber tires, and white or black rubber wheels.

Contributors: Fred Maxwell, 4722 N. 33 St., Arlington, VA 22207. Perry R. Eichor, 703 North Almond Drive, Simpsonville, SC 29681.

Metal Cast Products Company

	C6	C8	C10
Fire Engine, similar to No. 65 w/o watercannon, Metal Cast Products Company, 3-3/8"	6	10	14
Fire Engine, No. 61, hook and ladder truck, crew of two, Metal Cast Products Company, 4-1/2"	25	50	60
Open Rack Truck, No. 01-04, COE cab, stake semi-trailer, Metal Cast Products Company, 6"	15	25	35
Packard Convertible, No. 41, two-door, top down, Metal Cast Products Company, 5-1/4"	20	30	40

Metal Cast Products Company (Continued)

	C6	C8	C10
Streamline Sedan, No. 60, rubber tires, DeSoto? Airflow, eight open windows, spoke wheels, Metal Cast Products Company, 4"	20	30	40
Tank Truck, No. 01-03, same COE cab, semi-fuel tanker, "FRED GREEN TOYS," "Made in U.S.A.", Metal Cast Products Company, 6"	20	30	40
War Tank, No. 08, early heavy Sherman Tank, Metal Cast Products Company, 4"	30	50	65

Metalcraft

Metalcraft of St. Louis, Missouri, began producing its pressed-steel trucks in 1931. About a million were sold, most as advertising toys. In 1937, defeated by the Depression, Metalcraft closed. According to a collector-researcher, Al Korte was the designer of all of the firm's trucks, and worked there from 1931-1936.

Contributor: John Taylor, P.O. Box 63, Nolensville, TN 37135-0063.

Metalcraft

	C6	C8	C10
Acme Stores Truck, heart-shaped grille, 1935, 13" long	200	300	500
Bunte Candies Truck, 1933, 12-1/2" long	NPF	NPF	450
Clover Farm Stores Truck	450	675	900
Coca-Cola Truck, ten bottles in racks, "Every Bottle Sterilized", c. 1928, 11" long	450	650	875
Coca-Cola Truck, ten bottles in rack, "Every Bottle Sterilized," rubber tires, early 1930s, 11" long	450	700	1000
Coca-Cola Truck, ten bottles, long nose, stamped metal, late 1930s, 12" long	450	675	1000
CW Coffee Dump Truck, 1928, 11" long	225	400	525
CW Coffee Wrecker, 11-1/2"	350	525	700
Decker's Iowana Truck, heart-shaped grille, 1935	500	700	1000
Delivery Truck Van, 1928, 11" long	200	300	450
Drink Smile Truck, w/electric lights and spare tire, 1933, 12-1/2" long	300	450	650
Goodrich Silvertone Tires Wrecker, w/three spare tires, 1931, 12" long	225	375	450
Heinz Truck, spare tire, electric lights, "Baked Beans," "Bottled Vinegar," "Rice Flakes", c. 1932, 12" long	250	350	425

Metalcraft Coca-Cola truck, 1928, 11" long, $1000. Photo courtesy R.W. Cannahan

Metalcraft Plee-Zing Quailty Products, 1928, 11" long, $500. Photo courtesy Mapes Auctioneers and Appraisers

Metalcraft (Continued)

	C6	C8	C10
Kroger Food Express Truck, open w/food packages, 10" long	300	450	600
Kroger Food Express Truck, closed, 1929, 11" long	325	450	650
Krug Bakery Truck, 1933, 12-1/2" long	450	675	935
Machinery Hauling Truck, 14-1/2" long	500	700	900
Meadow Gold Butter Truck, battery-operated lights, 1935, 13" long	425	552	750
Plee-Zing Quality Products, 1928, 11" long	250	375	500
Pure Oil Truck, 1935	500	700	1100
Sand-Gravel Dump Truck, No. 150, 1928, 11" long	175	275	375
Shell Motor Oil Truck, eight barrels, 1933, 12" long	325	600	900
St. Louis Truck, c. 1930, 11" long	250	400	550
Steam Shovel, No. 4, 8"	115	150	200
Sunshine Biscuits Truck, 1933, 12-1/2"	250	400	550
Towing & Repairs, 1928, 11-1/2"	250	425	550
Toy Town Grocery	275	425	550
Waldorf Lager, white	400	600	900
Waldorf Logan Truck, heart-shaped grille, 1935	300	500	700
Werks Tag Soap Truck	300	450	600
Weston's Biscuits	250	375	500
White King Delivery Truck, 12" long	300	400	500

Metal Masters

	C6	C8	C10
Bus, c. 1938, 7-1/4" long (MM02)	25	38	50
Fire Truck, removable ladders, c. 1940, 10" long (MM12)	50	65	85

Metal Masters (Continued)

	C6	C8	C10
Fire Truck, ladders, wind-up motors, c. 1940, 10" long (MM13)	60	90	120
Fire Truck, version of pickup, c. 1938, 7" long (MM04)	35	55	75
Jeep, c. 1947, 5-1/2" long (MM06)	20	30	55
Pickup Truck, c. 1938, 7" long (MM03)	25	38	50
Roadster, c. 1938, 7" long (MM01)	25	38	50
Station Wagon, wind-up motor, c. 1940, 8-1/2" (MM08)	45	55	75
Station Wagon, ambulance version, c. 1940, 8-1/2" (MM09)	45	55	75
Station Wagon, c. 1940, 8-1/2" (MM07)	40	55	65
Tow Truck, wind-up motor, c. 1940, 10" long (MM11)	55	80	110
Tow Truck, "ABC Towing Service", c. 1940, 10" long (MM10)	50	75	100
Tow Truck, version of pickup, c. 1938, 7" long (MM05)	35	45	50

Contributor: 11th Edition pricing contributor Mark Rich, P.O. Box 971, Stevens Point, WI 54481. Email: mark.rich@sff.net

MIDGETOY

Chevrolet Tractor-Trailer Series, 8" Vehicles	C6	C8	C10
Auto Transporter with Loading Ramp, 1962	12	20	27
Hook and Ladder Aerial Fire Truck, 1963	12	20	30
Kenworth Sleeper Cab, 1980	2	4	8
Oil Tanker, "Midgetoy Oil Co."	12	20	30
Oil Tanker Trailer, 1962	12	20	30
Shipping Van, "Midgetoy Van Lines, Inc."	12	20	30
Shipping Van Trailer, 1962	12	20	30

Jumbo Series, 6" Vehicles

	C6	C8	C10
American La France Pumper Truck, black rubber tires	11	18	27
Cadillac Four-Door Convertible, black rubber tires	10	17	25
Mobile Artillery, black rubber tires, 1957	10	17	25
Oil Tanker, black rubber tires, 1957	10	17	25
Oil Tanker, "Midgetoy Oil Co."	10	17	25
Scenicruiser Bus, late version, "Midgetoy Bus Line"	NPF	NPF	NPF
Scenicruiser Bus, black rubber tires, late 1950s	12	20	30
Utility Truck	10	17	25

Junior Series, 2-1/2" to 3-1/2" Vehicles

	C6	C8	C10
American LaFrance Pumper, open cab, black rubber tires, late 1950s	6	9	13
Army Amphibious "Battle Bug", 1949?	8	14	22
Army Howitzer, black plastic tires	2	5	7
Army Howitzer, black plastic tires, 1949?	2	5	7
Army Jeep, black rubber tires, 1950	4	7	10
Cadillac Convertible, black rubber tires, 1949	6	11	17
Corvette Convertible, black rubber tires, late 1950s	5	8	10
Ford Hot Rod, br, 2-1/2"	5	8	12
Ford V-8 Hot Rod, black rubber tires, 1948	8	14	22
Ford V-8 Hot Rod, black plastic tires	5	9	12
Ford Wrecker Truck, black rubber tires, late 1950s	5	8	12
Greyhound Bus, black rubber tires, 1955	6	10	15
MG Sports Roadster, black rubber tires, 1958	6	9	13
Open Cockpit Indy Curtis Craft Race Car, black rubber tires, 1950	8	14	22
Sunbeam Racer, black plastic tires	5	8	12
Sunbeam Racer, black rubber tires, 1950	8	14	22
Volkswagen Beetle, black plastic tires, 1960	6	9	15

King-Size Series, 4" Vehicles

	C6	C8	C10
American La France Pumper, black rubber tires, early 1950s	8	14	22

King-Size Series, 4" Vehicles (Continued)

	C6	C8	C10
Army Half-Track, black rubber tires, late 1950s	8	15	20
Army Personnel Carrier, black rubber tires, late 1950s	8	15	20
Army Tank, black rubber tires, late 1940s or early 1950s	8	15	20
Cadillac Four-door Sedan, military, black rubber tires	8	13	18
Cadillac Four-door Sedan, black rubber tires, late 1950s	10	15	20
Cadillac Two-door Coupe, black rubber tires, early 1950s	11	18	24
Chrysler-style Convertible Roadster, black rubber tires	10	16	22
Ford Pickup Truck, black rubber tires, late 1950s	10	16	22
Ford Pickup Truck, black rubber tires, early 1950s	13	20	26
Oil Tanker Truck, military, black rubber tires	10	15	20
Oil Tanker Truck, black rubber tires, late 1950s	12	18	24
Van-style Streamlined Ambulance, Red-Cross, black rubber tires, late 1950s	8	12	16
Van-style Streamlined Station Wagon, black rubber tires, late 1950s	8	12	16

New Junior Series (1970), 2-1/2" to 3" Vehicles

	C6	C8	C10
'68 Corvette L88 Stingray, 1971	2	3	4
Cadillac Ambulance, 1971	5	8	12
Ford 1971 Pickup Truck	2	4	5
Ford Mark IV, 1971	2	4	5
Ford Mustang	1	2	3
Ford Ranchero Pickup	2	3	4
Ford Torino, 1971	1	2	3
Ford Torino Fire Chief Car, 1971	2	4	6
Ford Torino Police Car, 1971	2	4	6
Ford Wrecker Truck, 1971	3	5	7
Jaguar XKE, 1971	3	5	8

Pee-Wee Series (1969), 2" Mini Vehicles

	C6	C8	C10
American LaFrance Fire Truck	1	2	3
Jeep, race cars, sports cars and hot rods	NPF	1	2
MG Sports Roadster	1	2	3

Midgetoy Oil Tanker "Midgetoy Oil Co.," 1963, $30. Photo courtesy Thomas G. Nefos

Midgetoy Cadillac, black rubber tires, 1950s, $20.

Rainbow 1935 Oldsmobile Coupe, $70. Photo courtesy Dave Leopard

Rainbow 1935 Studebaker Stake Side Pickup, $85. Photo courtesy Dave Leopard

Sets

	C6	C8	C10
1860 Western Train, "Train That Won the West," black plastic tires	8	14	25
1860 Western Train	6	12	25
1920 Passenger Train, black plastic tires	8	14	25
1920 Passenger Train	6	12	25
1940 Diesel Train	6	12	25
1940 Diesel Train, late version, "Amtrak," black plastic tires	8	14	25
1950 Freight Train, black plastic tires	8	14	25
1950 Freight Train	6	12	25
Dixie Chargers, three-car set, 1981 .	5	8	12
Interchangeable Truck Set	12	25	45

Neff-Moon Toy Company

William Moon and Charles Neff owned Neff-Moon, of Sandusky, Ohio. Production of its pressed-steel toys began in 1923. The firm, which was located above a grocery, was apparently an early victim of the Depression.

Neff-Moon Toy Company	C6	C8	C10
Groceries Van	300	450	600
Taxi, 12" long	350	525	700
Tow Truck, c. 1925, 16" long	200	300	400

Nylint

The Nylint Tool and Manufacturing Company was formed in 1937 by Bernard C. Klint and David Nyberg (thus its name) in Rockford, Illinois. Toy production began in the spring of 1946. Since 1951, the firm concentrated on the production of heavy-duty scale reproductions, in steel, of earth-moving equipment and over-the-road trucks. Nylint closed in 2000

Contributor: Jeff Hubbard, 1480 39th Street SW, Naples, FL 34117-5365.

Exclusives

	C6	C8	C10
Admiral TV Van, No. 5802, Ford Econoline with decals on both sides and all doors; special premium available through Admiral TV delaers, very rare, 1966	75	325	650
Big Dig Shovel, No. SR1100, Sears exclusive; orange and black, all steel except for rubber tracks; later versions (non-exclusives) available in orange yellow and black while track wheels were yellow plastic, 1964-65	50	140	275
Chase and Sanborne Stake Truck, No. 4501, same as No. 4500 but with coffee boxes (add 75 percent premium if present), 1964 ...	75	175	350
Culligan Water Van, No. 5803, dark blue Ford Econoline with white top and Culligan decals on sides and doors; very rare, 1966	75	275	550

Exclusives (Continued)

	C6	C8	C10
Gambles Stores Pickup, No. 8001, white Ford Econoline with green top, 1966	75	175	350
Hertz Rental Truck, No. 8401, same as No. 8400 but exclusive to Sears; yellow cab, black base, silver cargo box, Hertz decals; rare, 1967	85	250	500
JC Penney Wrecker, No. 6001, light blue Ford Econoline Wrecker with white boom; available only form the JC Penney's wishbook, 1966	75	250	500
Lawn and Garden Set, No. SR1200/5439, Sears exclusive, 1964-65	50	175	350
Michigan Shovel (crane), No. 2201, redesigned version (made to look like Tonka mobile crane); clam-shell bucket; this toy continued with number changes until the mid-1980s, 1966-73	50	150	300
Mobile Home Trailer, No. 6602, dark blue cab with white top, no extras, large "N" logo on cab doors, 1966	75	325	650
Mobile Home Trailer, No. 6603, American Transit Mobile Home Movers and other variations, 1964-66	100	350	700
Mobile Home Trailer, No. 6601, aqua blue or turquoise with white or light tan top, 27 pieces of furniture, one-piece grille/bumper on front, round "6601" decal on cab doors, 1965	75	300	600
Philco Radio Camper, No. 5302	75	325	650
Telescopic Crane, No. 2500, green with white boom for 1959 NY Toy Fair (won award for toy of the year); rare, 1957-60	150	225	450
Trailblazer Camper, No. 5301, green and white Econoline camper, 1969-72	35	65	125
Truck and Haul-It Trailer, No. 9401, rare; knock-off of U-Haul Trailer with similar decals, 1969.	50	175	350
Twin Hopper Dump Truck, No. 1420, Sears exclusive; yellow semi tractor pulling two hopper dump trailers, black dump doors and operating levers, 1967	125	225	450
U-Haul Van, No. 5801, orange Ford Econoline, white U-Haul decals, 1966-67	50	200	400

Exclusives (Continued)

	C6	C8	C10
U-Haul Van Set, No. SR1000/5465, Sears exclusive; orange and white Ford Pickup, U-Haul Van (closed type), and trailer with race car, 1962	75	200	400
Western Auto Econoline Pickup, No. 5201, rare, 1964	75	225	450

Regular Issue

	C6	C8	C10
Aerial Ladder Fire Truck, No. 1210, red with white ladders and black handwheels; Nylint's first large fire truck, 1968-74	75	140	275
Aerial Ladder Fire Truck, No. 1211, second version of No. 1210 (less steel), 1975-	50	100	200
Airport Courtesy Van, No. 6900, Ford Econoline Van, yellow with Holiday Inn decals on sides and doors; rare, 1964, 12" long	75	350	700
Amazing Car, No. 600, wind-up; green or blue; box commands a premium (contains operating instructions), 1946-49	75	150	300
Amazing Car, No. 600, wind-up; red; box commands a premium (contains operating instructions), 1946-49	50	125	250
Ambulance, No. 6700, white Ford Econoline Van with red crosses on sides and doors; included stretcher, interior seats, red flasher light, 1964-67, 12" long	50	150	300
American Oil Emergency Truck, No. 6000, red Ford Econoline Wrecker, white boom, with or without American Oil decals, 1963-69, 11-1/4" long	50	150	300
Army Ambulance, No. 7300, olive drab Ford Econoline Van, stretcher, red cross decals on sides and doors, red flasher light on top, 1965, 12" long	50	175	350
Backhoe, No. 1310, yellow backhoe on rubber crawler tracks with black base, 1968-73	75	140	275
Beach Buggy, No. 2310, 1969-72	25	40	75
Big Dig, No. 1100, regular version	50	115	225
Big Dig, No. 1101, re-design of No. SR1100 to look like Tonka's Mighty Cranes; orange, yellow and black with yellow plastic track wheels, 1967-70	50	100	200

Regular Issue (Continued)	C6	C8	C10
Big Haul Dump, No. 9200, yellow and black, reminiscent of Tonka's Mighty Dump Truck, 1966-68	45	125	250
Big Haul Dump, No. 9201, same as No. 9200 but larger wheels, 1969-72	45	125	250
Bobcat Loader, No. 2070, yellow and black trim, 1970-	35	65	125
Boysen Paints Stake Truck, No. 4502, same as No. 4500, 1964	75	200	400
Bronco Bobcat, No. 2410, dark red Bronco with white top and larger wheels, 1969-72	35	85	175
Bronco Petmobile, No. 1710, dark blue Ford Bronco, white plastic cage for dogs, 1968-70s	40	115	225
Bronco Police Car, No. 1610, white Ford Bronco with lights and black trim, 1968	35	75	150
Bulldozer, No. 4200, orange with towbar instead of winch (1967-70); yellow with towbar (1971-72), 1967-72	50	125	250
Bulldozer, No. 4200, all yellow with rear chain winch (1961-65); yellow with orange winch (1967-70); black plastic motor, 1961-70	50	150	300
Camper Pickup, No. 4400, red Ford pickup truck with two-piece front grille/bumper, white topper camper, two green air mattresses, 1961-63, 13-1/2" long	50	125	250
Car Carrier, No. 8900, yellow car carrier; three cars (1967-68); two cars (1969-77); several color variations for cars, 1967-77	50	150	300
Construction Four-Wheel Platform Dump, No. 4600, 15-3/4" long	100	150	225
Construction Set, No. 5700, orange No. 5000 Dump and Cement Mixer with yellow drum, Econoline Pickup Truck and Open Stake Trailer; rare, 1962-64	100	300	600
Countdown Rocket Launcher, No. 3500, three rockets (Atlas, Jupiter, Thor) in various colors; gray gantry crane, dark blue base with yellow, black, or red countdown dial; last Nylint toy from the 1950s and second plastic toy, 1959-61, 21" long	50	125	250

Regular Issue (Continued)	C6	C8	C10
Custom Camper Econoline Pickup Truck, No. 5300, aqua green truck and plastic camper with opening windows and rear door, slide-out steps under rear door, 1962-66, 12-1/2" long	50	125	250
Custom Camper on Pickup Truck with Boat, No. 5400, with red and green sailboat on trailer, 1962-65, 23-1/2" long	75	175	350
Deliverall, No. 1000, wind-up; three-wheeled scooter with large cargo box; white, yellow, red, blue and black; rare, 1946-51, 10" long	100	300	600
Dump Truck, No. 5100, red truck, yellow dump box, two-piece grille/bumper (1962-64); red/yellow truck, one-piece grille/bumper (1965); light green truck, white dump box, one-piece grille/bumper (1966), 1962-66, 13-1/2"	50	140	275
Dump Truck with Cement Mixer, No. 5000, yellow truck with round decal on doors and two-piece front grille/bumper (1962-64); yellow/green truck with special decal on mixer (1965); yellow body, green dump box, large N logo decal on doors (1966); cement mixer is always yellow, 1962-66, 20-1/2" long	75	200	400
Econoline Pickup Truck, No. 5200, dual headlights (1962); teardrop headlights (1963-72); red/white truck (1962-65); yellow with black roof (1966-72), 1962-72, 11-1/4" long	50	125	250
Electronic Cannon Truck, No. 2400, with yellow radar antenna and four rockets, 1957-59, 22-1/2" long	75	150	300
Electronic Cannon Truck, No. 2400, no radar antenna; four red/black-tipped rockets; Nylint's second battery-operated toy, 1956	75	150	300
Elevating Scraper, No. 2010, two-wheel tractor with large earthmover with rubber belt, pan scraper trailer (looked like a Caterpillar earthmover), 1969-73	75	200	400

Ralston Toy & Novelty Army Tank, $75. Photo courtesy Ed Poole

Renwal Cement Mixer Truck, No. 56, 1948, 7-1/2" long, $125.

Savoye Pewter Toy Pickup Truck, No. SA22, $40.

Savoye Pewter Tank Car Set, (SA20), $80.

Regular Issue (Continued)	C6	C8	C10
Elgin Street Sweeper, No. 2300, battery-operated version, closed cab; yellow cab roof, red/yellow body (1956); red cab roof, yellow body (1957), 1956-57	50	175	350
Elgin Street Sweeper, No. 1100, wind-up; yellow with red and black highlights, white plastic driver; bottom and side brooms rotate, 1950-52, 8-1/4" long	50	175	350
Farm Set, No. 9900, one of four farm sets made by Nylint; included light blue and white Ford Bronco, Ford Econoline Pickup, Stake Truck and trailer, 1968-71	75	175	350
Farm Set, No. 5600, with light blue/white No. 4500 Stake Truck, light blue/white No. 5200 Econoline Pickup Truck and other assorted pieces, 1962-64	75	175	350
Ford Bronco, No. 8200, listed in the 1965 catalog as a Roustabout but was changed to a Bornco right after the catalog was printed, 1965-69, 12-1/2" long	50	140	275

Regular Issue (Continued)	C6	C8	C10
Ford Econoline Van, No. 5800, purple with white decals; dark pink or maroon (1964 only), 1963-64, 12" long	50	175	350
Ford Pickup & U-Haul Box Trailer, No. 4100, orange pickup, white cab roof, orange trailer with white/cream top and opening rear door; trucks made before 1965 have two-piece front grille (trucks from 1965-66 with one-piece front grille/bumper and I-beam suspension), 1961-66	75	175	350
Ford Platform Tilt Truck, No. 3900, metallic blue, white cab roof with tilt cab, narrow side panels on rear bed, 1960, 15-3/4" long	75	175	350
Ford Rapid Delivery Truck, No. 3600, dark blue cabover Ford truck with white stake racks and working lift gate, tilt cab with motor; first Nylint toy of 1960s, 1960-62, 18-1/4" long	75	175	300
Ford Sales & Service, No. 3800, aqua green with utility rack and ladder, 1960-61, 13-5/8" long	50	175	350

Regular Issue (Continued)	C6	C8	C10
Ford Speedway Truck with Racer, No. 4000, dark tan pickup with white top and trailer and race car, 1960-63, 24-3/4" long	75	140	275
Ford U-Haul Rental Fleet, No. 4300, includes orange Ford pickup, orange U-Haul van and orange U-Haul open trailer; pickup has two-piece front grille bumper (1961-64), one-piece bumper and I-beam suspension (1965), 1960s	75	225	450
Fun on Farm Econoline Truck Set, No. 7100, 29 piecesFord Econoline Pickup with farm family, farming items, plus small cans of paint to customize your farm family, 1964-65, 11-1/4" long	50	175	350
Grader-Loader, No. 3000, first version with remote bucket release (1959 only); yellow, black bucket; first Nylint construction toy to have plastic tractor wheels (to keep shipping weight low), 1959-62, 23-3/4" long	75	150	300
Guided Missile Carrier, No. 2800, first version (1958), non-firing missiles, 1958-59, 15-1/2" long	75	125	250
Guided Missile Carrier, No. 2800, later version (through 1960), firing cone of missiles, side-mounted forklift with red/yellow pallet, white missile with red fins and red nose cone, 1958-59	75	125	250
Happy Acres Truck with Horses, No. 4700, same as No. 4500 but red truck with white stakes, large picture decal on doors, 1961-63, 14" long	75	150	300
Happy Ranchers Set, No. 7200, Stake Truck with Open Stake Trailer, both light blue and white, 1964	75	175	350
Highway Emergency Unit Truck, No. 3400, large cabover Ford wrecker, white with red cab roof, red dolly and wrecker boom; later versions without boom hoist (only hook hoist); with whitewall tires and tilt cab with motor (1963 only), 1959-63, 18-5/8" long (3400)	50	150	300
Hopper Dump, No. 1410, regular single-trailer version; yellow with black dump doors, 1968-69.	75	150	300

Regular Issue (Continued)	C6	C8	C10
Horse Van Semi Truck, No. 6300, brownish-gold truck, white doors, decals, four horses and ponies; two-piece grille/bumper on front (1963-64); one-piece grille/bumper (1965-67); light blue and white truck (1967 only), 1963-67, 23-1/2"	50	175	350
Hot Rod, No. 1910, 1969-72	25	40	75
Hydraulic Big Haul Dump Truck, No. 9801, orange and black, new tires, 1969-73	35	140	275
Hydraulic Big Haul Dump Truck, No. 9800, orange and black, 1967-68	35	140	275
Hydraulic Dump, No. 4600, same as No. 2700 but orange with yellow/black decals, front grille guard in yellow/black, hollow plastic wheels, 1961-66	50	125	250
Hydraulic Dump Truck, No. 6100, beige truck with red dump box; two-piece grille/bumper (1963-64); one-piece grille bumper (1965-70), 1963-70	75	150	300
Jalopy, No. 6800, Ford hot rod in red with white top or light blue with white top (1964); also No. 6801 with seats, available in same colors as 1964 version (1965-68); No. 6802 purple and white (1969-71); No. 6803 neon green top and purple body (1972-78), 1964-78, 9-5/8" long	25	150	300
Jumbo Street Roller, No. 2050, roller in front, wheels in back; large red roller in front and red operator's cab (1971); yellow and black (1972-77), 1971-77	50	100	200
Jungle Wagon, No. 9000, two-tone green Ford Econoline with cages to transport wild animals, 1966-72	45	140	275
Junior Jack Hammer, No. 2900, with air compressor package that connected to toy with 4' rubber hose; Nylint's first plastic toy; red/black jackhammer, yellow/red/black compressor box, 1958-59, 19-1/2" long	50	125	250
Kennel Truck, No. 6200, pink Ford Econoline, plastic dog cage in back, 12 dogs (12 different breeds); paper band around cage featuring the dog breeds on it (1964 only), 1963-69, 11-1/2" long	175	265	525

Seiberling Rubber 1935 Ford 2-dr Sedan, $55. Photo courtesy Dave Leopard

Sharon Pierce Arrow-type Sedan, No. 10S, $150. Photo courtesy Perry Eichor

Sharon Racer, spring loaded. Photo courtesy Perry Eichor

Regular Issue (Continued)	C6	C8	C10
Lawn and Garden Set, No. 1200, new number; same as No. 7000, 1965	50	125	250
Lawn and Garden Set, No. 7000, dark green Econoline Pickup with white roof; included lawn mower and other garden equipment, 1964	50	150	300
Lift Truck (fork lift), No. 700, red and yellow; box commands a premium (contains operating instructions), 1946-49	75	125	250
Lift Truck (fork lift), No. 700, green and yellow; box commands a premium (contains operating instructions), 1946-49	75	140	275
Michigan Shovel (crane), No. 2200, 10 wheels, clamshell bucket, single headlights, grille plate, steering (1955-56); six wheels, single or dual headlights, embossed front grille or grille plate (1956-60); no steering, grille sticker (1961-63); magnet added to bucket but only drop-down outriggers (1964-65); only Nylint toy to have real rubber tires through its first 10 years, 1955-65, 31-1/2" long	50	150	300
Missile Launcher, No. 2600, orange, white radar antenna, white missiles with black tips, 1959	100	175	350

Regular Issue (Continued)	C6	C8	C10
Missile Launcher, No. 2600, blue-gray, white radar antenna, white missiles with black tips, 1957-60, 31-1/2" long	50	125	250
Mobile Home Semi Truck, No. 6600, aqua blue cab with white or light tan roof, nine pieces of furniture, two-piece grille/bumper on front, round "6600" decal on cab doors, 1964, 30" long	75	300	600
Payloader, No. 1600, dark green, 1958	50	175	350
Payloader, No. 1600, light green and yellow, 1956-58	50	175	350
Payloader, No. 6500, red and yellow, 1963-66	50	100	200
Payloader, No. 1600, red and yellow, 1951-55, 18" long	50	175	350
Payloader, No. 1600, yellow, 1958	50	175	350
Payloader, No. 1600, tan, 1951	50	175	350
Payloader Tractor-Shovel, No. 3100, first version yellow with levers in cab (1959 only); red/yellow with levers in cab (1959-60); without levers (1961-62); less than 1,300 made, replica of Hough machine; all toys had steel track base and rubber tracks, 1959-62, 17-5/8" long	75	175	350

Smith-Miller B Mack Orange Dump, $2800. Photo courtesy Tim Oei

Smith-Miller GMC Drive-O Steerable Dump, 1946, $925. Photo courtesy Bob Smith

Smith-Miller GMC Bank of America, $500.

Smith-Miller Bekins Van No. 406, $650.

Regular Issue (Continued)	C6	C8	C10
Pepsi Delivery Truck, No. 5500, red, white and blue Ford C-600 truck with decals, six cases of Pepsi and hand truck, 1962-67, 16-1/2"	50	225	450
Platform Dump Truck, No. 3900, yellow, white cab roof, narrow side panels on rear bed; last truck to feature tilt cab, 1961	75	175	350
Pony Farm Van Set, No. 8000, white Ford Econoline Pick,up, green cab top, large green/white Pony Farm decal on sides, four ponies, 11-1/4" long	75	175	350
Power & Light Lineman Truck, No. 3200, yellow cab and flasher light, orange trailer, black rear hoist with tools, rope, yellow spool of wire, two stained poles; orange with yellow cab and flasher light, orange trailer, yellow wire spool, 1959-61, 35-3/4" long	75	175	350

Regular Issue (Continued)	C6	C8	C10
Power & Light Posthole Digger Truck, No. 3300, orange, yellow cab roof, orange trailer, yellow posthole assembly and tool box cover, plastic tools, four wooden phone poles, 1959-61, 35-3/4" long	75	175	350
Power Pony, No. 900, light tan, black, yellow; three-wheeled pony performed tricks; rare, 1949	100	250	500
Pumpmobile, No. 1200, wind-up; Howdy Doody cowboy-like figure (unlicensed), yellow, red and blue, 1950-52, 8-5/8" long	100	300	600
Race Team, No. 5900, Ford Econoline with race car (white and other colors) and red trailer, 1963-66	50	175	350
Race Team, No. 7800, white Econoline Pickup, red trailer, white race car, 1965-69	50	150	300
Race Team, No. 9600, Ford Econline Pikup and trailer with race car, red and white, 1967-69	40	140	275

Regular Issue (Continued)	C6	C8	C10
Ranch Truck, No. 4500, light blue Ford stake truck, two-piece front grille/bumper, white stake racks, round decals on doors, 1961-64, 14" long	50	100	200
Road Grader, No. 1400, first version; small wheels and steel grille plate; orange, 1951, 19-1/4" long	75	125	250
Road Grader, No. 1400, second version; larger 3-3/4" wheels and grille plate; orange, 1952-53	50	175	350
Road Grader, No. 7900, yellow and black, 1965-68, 15" long	25	100	200
Road Grader, No. 1400, third version; embossed grille, large 3-3/4" wheels; orange (1954-55), yellow (1956-58), 1954-58	50	175	350
Road Grader, No. 7910, yellow with larger wheels, 1969	40	65	125
Safari Hunt Set, No. 8800, Ford Bronco with white top, cage trailer with wild animals; cage has door, trailer has slide-out ramp and winch for loading, 1966-71	75	200	400
Scootscycle/Servicecycle, No. 800, wind-up; red, blue, yellow or black; rare, 1946-51, 7-1/4" long	75	225	450
Speed Swing Loader, No. 2000, orange or yellow; by Pettibone-Mulliken Co. orange and black (1955), yellow and black (1956-58), 1955-58, 19" long	50	125	250
Sportsman Set, No. 9700, truck with boat and trailer; white and other colors, 1967-69	50	140	275
Sportster, No. 9500, pink Ford Bronco, 1967-69	45	140	275
Stake Pickup Truck, No. 9100, light blue and white Ford Econoline stake truck, 1966-69	35	125	250
Street Sprinkler Truck, No. 3700, white tank truck, operating nozzles on front bumper, tilt cab, 1960-61, 18" long	75	175	350
Suburban Fire Department Set, No. 7408, red Ford Econoline Pumper Fire Truck, Fire Rescue Econoline Van, Fire Chief's Bronco; Rescue Van and Fire Chief's Bronco available only in this set, 1966-70	75	225	450

Regular Issue (Continued)	C6	C8	C10
Suburban Fire Pumper, No. 8100, Ford Econoline Pumper fire Truck with water cannon; a garden hose could be connected to the cannon to shoot water; hard to find in good condition since the pressure from the garden hose usually blew up the truck, 1965-70, 12-1/2" long	50	150	300
Telescopic Crane, No. 2500, red with yellow boom, four-wheel steering, extendable boom, 1957-60	100	150	300
Texaco Service Van, No. 8300, red Ford Econoline Van, white decals, red flasher light, 1965, 12" long	50	200	400
Tin Lizzy Hot Rod Pickup, No. 9300, red and other colors, 1967-72	35	100	200
Tournadozer, No. 2100, orange with black seat and motor; first version with larger 4-7/16" wheels (1956), 1956-59, 20" long	75	150	300
Tournahauler, No. 1700, third version; dark green embossed grille, 1954-55	50	125	250
Tournahauler, No. 1700, second version dark green with grille plate, 1953-54	50	125	250
Tournahauler, No. 1700, first version; yellow, 1953	100	200	400
Tournahauler, No. 1700, fourth version; light green, 1956	50	125	250
Tournahopper, No. 1500, second version; embossed front, 3-3/4" wheels; yellow (1954-55), orange (1956). After 1953, these are replicas of Letourneau-Westinghouse machines, 1954-56	75	175	350
Tournahopper, No. 1500, first version; grille plate on front of closed tractor; yellow with black decals; replica of a R.G. Letourneau machine, 1952-53, 22-1/2" long	75	175	350
Tournaractor, No. 1900, yellow and black with 4-7/16" wheels; by J.D. Adams, 1954-55, 14-3/4" long	50	175	350
Tournarocker, No. 1300, second version; closed cab, no driver, grille plate on front, larger 3-3/4" wheels; all yellow; also by R.G. Letourneau, 1953-54, 18" long	75	125	250

Regular Issue (Continued)

	C6	C8	C10
Tournarocker, No. 1300, first version; open tractor w/driver; orange (1951) or mustard yellow (1952); scale model of a machine by R. G. Letourneau, 1951-52, 18" long	50	150	300
Tournarocker, No. 1300, third version; embossed grille details, larger 3-3/4" wheels; all yellow (1955), orange and yellow (1956-57); also by R.G. Letourneau, 1955-57	75	125	250
Traveloader, No. 1800, first version with smaller blades on front feeder belt (1953); second version with larger blades (1954-55); both versions orange with black decals, black belts on front feeder, black rear conveyor belt, 1953-55, 30" long	75	125	250
Truck and Horse Trailer, No. 8700, Ford Bronco, two-axle horse trailer with yellow top, 1966-70	50	145	285
Truck and U-Haul Trailer, No. 9400, Ford Econoline Pickup and open trailer, orange and white, 1967-68	50	140	275
Twister Exploration Car, No. 1810, yellow and black; Nylint's version of Tonka's Crater Crawler, 1969-73	25	100	200
U-Haul Cube Van, No. 8400, five-ton cube van, 1966-67, 22" long	75	175	350
U-Haul Truck, No. 8411, Chevy, 1975	100	125	175
U-Haul Truck & Trailer, No. 8410, 1974, 22" long	100	150	200
U-Haul Van, No. 4900, open trailer, orange and cream, U-Haul decals, 1961, 9" long	50	100	200
U-Haul Van, No. 4800, closed trailer, orange and cream, U-Haul decals, 1961, 8" long	50	100	200
Uranium Hauler, No. 2700, olive drab hydraulic bumper, yellow/black front guard, 1958-59, 22-1/2" long	50	125	250
Vacationer Set, No. 8600, blue and white Ford Bronco and camper trailer, 1966-70	50	150	300

Pyro

Pyro began in 1939 in Pyro Park, Union City, New Jersey. The owner was William Lester. At its height, the company had 400 employees.

Pyro	C6	C8	C10
Car, 9" long	235	352	470
City Builders Truck, 5-1/2" long	NPF	NPF	NPF
Coca-Cola Truck, 5-1/2" long	75	112	150
Design-A-Car Set, builds fourteen models	35	55	75
Ice & Coal Truck, 5-1/2" long	NPF	NPF	NPF
Race Car, 4" long	20	30	40
Range Patrol Truck	15	20	25
Road Roller	12	18	25
U.S. Army Truck	9	13	20
U.S. Navy Truck	10	15	20
U.S.M.C. Truck	10	15	20

Rainbow

Contributor: Dave Leopard, 2507 Feather Run Trail, West Columbia, SC 29169-4915.

Rainbow	C6	C8	C10
'35 Oldsmobile Coupe, 3-3/4"	35	55	70
'35 Oldsmobile Four-door Sedan, 5" long	50	75	100
'35 Oldsmobile Four-door Sedan, 3-1/4" long	35	55	75
'35 Studebaker (?) Stake Side Pickup, 5-1/4" long	45	65	85
Open Racer, tapered tail, 4" long	25	38	50

Ralston Toy & Novelty Co. (Ralstoy)

Ralston Toy & Novelty Co., also known as Ralstoy, was formed in July of 1939, by Dr. Felix Despecher, former Mayor of Ralston, Nebraska, A.M. Erickson, and Henry C. Nestor. These three men acquired the molds of Best Toy Co. of Manhattan, Kansas, and the surviving molds of Kansas Toy Co. Included in the acquisition were the temporary services of John M. Best, his molder, Conrad Morsch, and about 140 molds from these pioneering slush-mold companies. Located in a building formerly occupied by the American Legion, they continued a low-cost toy line that had been familiar to collectors since Kansas toy was founded in 1923.

With the death of founder Despecherin in 1940, the young company was forced into reorganization. Lawyer Paul Massey took over control, but was forced to give up the use of pot metal items due to the need for lead during World War II. To survive, Ralstoy turned to making wooden toys, including a replica of an Army Jeep, selling almost two million through dime stores such as Woolworths and Kresge. Other wooden toys included an Army tank and a Navy PT boat.

After World War II, Ralstoy turned to die-cast toys and novelties. As the business expanded it moved to 5707 So. 77th St., where it is today producing a well-known line of promotional trucks under Art Massey.

Ralstoy did label a few of its toys. The bottom pans, introduced by Best Toy, provided a surface to emboss with "Ralstoy" and "Made in the USA." Unlike other slush-mold toys, wheels are not a good clue.

Contributors: Fred Maxwell, 4722 N. 33 St., Arlington, VA 22207. Perry R. Eichor, 703 North Almond Drive, Simpsonville, SC 29681.

Ralston Toy & Novelty Company (Ralstoy)

	C6	C8	C10
Army Jeep, WWII issue (RAV10) ..	20	30	40
Army Tank, "USA W356," "Ralstoy" on bottom, WWII issue (RAV11)	37	56	75
Army Tank, "US Army," two-gun turret, entirely different tank than Kansas Toy No. 74, 74, 2-1/4" (RAV3)	13	20	26
Army Tank, "US Army," two gun-turret, larger version of No. 74 above, also version w/black rubber wheels, wood grooved 3/4" track-laying wheels, 107, 3-1/8" (RAV7)	13	20	26
Ford Tractor, w/trailer, overall, 1948, 9" long	30	45	60
Gun Truck, Large, "US Army Anti-Aircraft Unit," three axle carrier, AA gun, searchlight and crew of three, 5-5/8" (RAV6)	28	42	56
Mayflower Moving Van	20	30	40
Railway (?) Gun, version of No. 23 muzzle-loading cannon on wheeled platform w/hook and loop connectors, perhaps addition to No. 3600 toy train, 108, 3-1/4"	12	18	25
Sedan, large, "2R," Cadillac?, "Ralstoy," "Made in USA," four open vent windows, divided open windshield, three open rear windows, long fenders, rear-wheel skirts, bumper guard, black rubber wheels, early postwar issue (?), 5-5/8" (RAV12)	37	56	75
Tanker Truck, "Ralstoy," International (?) Sleeper cab, two open windows, vertical grille w/"Gasoline" semi-trailer, "No. 102," four tanks, storage compartments, 102, entire length: 6-3/4" sleeper cab length: 3-3/8" (RAV4)	30	45	60
Transporter, large, "Ralstoy" cab unit in RAV4 above, steel semi-trailer w/No. 74 tank, No. 34 muzzle-loading cannon and No. 32 aircraft, olive drab color, not known if Ralstoy issued them as a set (some stamped No. 108, some No. 101), 9" (RAV5)	40	60	80

Renwal

The Renwal Manufacturing company, founded in 1939 by either Irving Rosenblum or Irving Lawner (accounts vary), began by manufacturing a glass knife, later to be replaced by a plastic knife. It was this plastic knife that lead to the production of plastic toys in 1945.

Chein purchased Rewal's tooling when Renwal went out of business in the 1970s, Chein, in turn, sold them to Revell.

Renwal

	C6	C8	C10
Cadillac Convertible, No. 174, w/driver, top goes up and down, 1953, 5-1/2" long	20	30	50
Cement Mixer Truck, No. 56, mixer revolves, rear cap comes off, tank rises, 1948, 7-1/2"	62	93	125
Coal-Coke Dump Truck, w/driver. Doors open, body raises, 1948, 7-1/2" long	50	75	100
Convertible Sedan, No. 39, w/driver, doors open, top slides back, trunk opens, 1948, 6-1/2" ..	30	45	60
Fire Truck, No. 57, w/three fireman, 1948, 7" long, 8" high when ladder extended	48	72	95
Gasoline Truck, No. 8008, 1955, 6" long	30	40	55
Gasoline Truck, No. 49, w/driver....	50	75	100
Racer, No. 173, w/driver, 9-1/2"	85	128	170
Sedan, two door, No. 90, w/driver, doors and trunk open, 1949, 6-1/2" long	45	60	85
Steam Shovel Truck, No. 86, w/truck driver and cran operator, doors open, cab swings, shovel can be raised, 1949, 19" long	45	70	90
TV Truck, No. 260, w/camera, mike, working spotlight, 18" long	75	112	150

Rubber Vehicles (Unknown Manufacturers)

The following list, with its number codes, was compiled by Dave Leopard. Vehicles are broken down by types. The gaps in numbering indicate vehicles that have been identified since the list was compiled.

Contributor: Dave Leopard, 2507 Feather Run Trail, West Columbia, SC 29169-4915.

Rubber Vehicles (Unknown Manufacturers)

	C6	C8	C10
'35 Chrysler Two-door Airflow Sedan, 5-1/8" long (UA08)	60	80	115
'35 DeSoto Four-door Airflow Sedan, 5" long (UA06)	60	80	115
'36 Plymouth Four-door Trunk-back Sedan, 4-7/8" long (UA09).	75	115	150

Rubber Vehicles (Unknown Manufacturers)

	C6	C8	C10
'37 Plymouth Four-door Trunkback Sedan, 4-7/8" long (UA10).	75	115	150
'46 Nash Two-door Fastback Sedan, hollow, molded tires, 4" long (UA11)	12	18	25
Open Racer, V-8, solid, large tires on wood hubs, 4" long (UA02)	25	40	60
Open Racer, left side header pipes, 3-1/2" long (UA01)	20	35	50

Savoye Pewter Toy Company

Savoye was incorporated August 1930. In 1931, Savoye Pewter Toy Co., manufacturer of pewter toys (pewter was often the word used for lead alloy or pot metal) was listed in a directory at 69m Paterson Plank Road in North Bergen, New Jersey, with six male and three female employees. The names of the owners may have been Selma and Joseph Wigh. In 1934, at the same address, the workforce was seven males and two females. Slush-mold toys were probably its only product. Savoye was in the 1936 phonebook, but not in the February 1937 directory.

Collectors identify vehicle toys as Savoye if they have a somewhat coarse appearance, heavy slush-molded body, and white rubber tires on oversized red wooden hubs that are smooth on the outside surface (no axle showing); but whether this is simply lore is not known at present. The son of one of the owners of Tommy Toy Co. thinks some Savoye-looking vehicles were made Tommy Toy. If so, it's possible Savoye sold its molds to nearby Tommy Toy.

Contributors: Fred Maxwell, 4722 N. 33 St., Arlington, VA 22207. Perry R. Eichor, 703 North Almond Drive, Simpsonville, SC 29681.

Savoye Pewter Toy Company	C6	C8	C10
Bus, Heavy 5th Ave. Sight-Seeing, open overhanging upper deck, twelve open windows, gilt or silver trim, 4-3/4" (SA7)	62	93	125
Bus, Cross-Country, partial upper deck, twelve open windows, rearmount spare, 3-3/8" (SA8)	20	30	40
Coupe, (Graham like), two open windows, silver vertical grille, vertical louvers, 3-3/8" long (SA3)	20	30	40
Coupe, similar to above, slanted louvers, fantasy grille and large black rubber wheels, 3-3/8" long (SA4)	14	21	28
Fire Truck, driver and steersman w/high style gilt helmets, bell on hood, two glued ladders, oversized wheel wells w/oversized tires, 4-1/4" long (SA15)	30	50	70

Savoye Pewter Toy Company (Continued)	C6	C8	C10
Milk Grade A Van, two open windows, sidemounts, 3-1/4" long (SA5)	20	30	40
Moving Van, six wheels, 3-7/8" long	105	158	210
Pickup Truck, No. SA22	20	30	40
Roadster, (reminiscent of Tootsietoy Graham), driver, open rumble seat, silver vertical grille, vertical louvers, 3-1/2" long (SA1)	20	35	50
Tank Car Set, tow cab: 3-1/4", two tank cars: 3-1/2"; marked "Oil" "Cap. 80000" (RR type), not known whether Savoye sold these as a set; no known Savoye train, either, overall length: 10-1/4" (SA20)	40	60	80
Truck, stake body, 4-1/2" long (SA11)	12	18	24
Truck, heavy "Beer Truck," six wood barrels set in cast depressions, 4-3/8" long (SA10)	40	60	80
Van, "Police Patrol," policeman on rear step, six open windows, gilt trim, sidemounts, 4" long (SA6)	30	50	75

Schieble Toy & Novelty Co.

William E. Schieble was a partner in D.P. Clark & Co. for nearly ten years. In 1909, after some disagreements with Clark, he broke up the partnership and became the sole owner. At this time, Schieble changed the name of the company to Schieble Toy & Novelty. Things went well during the 1920s, but as did many manufacturing companies, Schieble declared bankruptcy in 1931.

Contributor: Bob Smith, The Village Smith, 62 West Ave., Fairport, NY 14450-2102.

Schieble Toy and Novelty	C6	C8	C10
Fire Ladder Truck, w/small driver, flywheel drive, white and red, 1909, 21-1/2" long	300	450	650
Fire Ladder Truck, 1920s, 20" long	325	475	650
Fire Ladder Truck, large drive, flywheel drive, white and red, 1909, 21-1/2" long	400	600	800
Fire Truck, flywheel drive, red and gold, 1917, 11-1/2" long	300	450	650
Mack Semi Dump truck, chein look-a-like, c. 1925, 22" long	425	700	900
Racer, team, steel wind-up, c. 1910, 12" long	450	675	900
Roadster, spare tire on back, 18-1/4" long	400	600	850

Schieble Toy and Novelty

	C6	C8	C10
Sedan, 17" long	500	775	850
Touring Car, c. 1909, 14" long	375	575	725

Seiberling Rubber

	C6	C8	C10
'35 Ford two-door slantback sedan, 4" long (GA2)	27	41	55
'35 Ford two-door slantback sedan, 5" long (GA1)	32	48	65

Sharon

Founded in 1933 on the campus of Eastern Mennonite School (what is now Eastern Mennonite University) in Harrisburg, Virginia, Sharon was, at the time, the only maker of cast aluminum toys in the United States.

Started by Earnest G. Gehman, A.D. Wenger, and E.C. Shank, the company was designed to give employment to students attending school during rough financial times. Jacob N. Brubaker, a Lancaster County, Pennsylvania minister who was also a designer for Hubley, designed the toys.

Sharon was forced out of business in late 1934 because the National Recovery Administration regulations forced the company to sell their products at a price not competitive with other toys.

Because Brubaker was the designer, many of the toys are mistaken as Hubley, but each Sharon toy is unique unto itself, and only the method of construction was similar. Besides cars and trucks, Sharon also produced numerous novelty items and developed a design for a streamlined train to be constructed from Campbell's Soup cans. Unfortunately Campbell's rejected the idea.

For some time, the toys have been mistakenly labeled as "Sharron" with an extra R, but an examination of actual documents from the company show the name to be Sharon.

Most vehicles were sold with a paper tag that read, "This is a Genuine Cast Aluminum Toy light—Strong—durable." The other side read, "Cast Aluminum Toys, Will not CRUSH if accidentally stepped on. Will not BREAK when dropped on cement. Will not INJURE little toes, polished floors. Will not CUT—no sharp or jagged edges. Will not RUST—so will not stain clothes."

One of their prototypes was a long cast aluminum racer with a very powerful barrel spring, that when compressed would propel the racer across the floor. There is no record of it ever being put into production.

Contributors: Perry R. Eichor, 703 North Almond Drive, Simpsonville, SC 29681. Dave Leopard, 2507 Feather Run Trail, West Columbia, SC 29169-4915.

Sharon

	C6	C8	C10
Mack Dump Truck, No. 13SD, side-dump, 4" long	100	175	250
Open Racer, 6" long (SV003)	80	100	130
Pierce Arrow-type Sedan, No. 20S	75	125	200
Pierce Arrow-type Sedan, No. 10S	50	100	150
Pierce Arrow-type Silver Arrow, 1933, 6" long (SV001)	125	175	225

Sharon (Continued)

	C6	C8	C10
Racer, No. 11R, two-man, twelve cylinder, 5-3/4" long	75	145	225
Racer, unnumbered, spring loaded, 12" long	NPF	NPF	NPF
Rohr, 1934, 5" long (SV002)	100	150	200
Trolley Car (SV004)	NPF	NPF	NPF

Smith-Miller

Smith-Miller trucks entered an already competitive market in 1945. These cast-metal and aluminum trucks, produced in Santa Monica, California, should have failed—who would've thought that a new toy vehicle company could compete with such toy giants as Buddy "L," Structo, Marx, and Hubley? Despite the stiff competition, Smith-Miller Toys stayed on the market for a full ten years, outclassing virtually all toy trucks.

Their first trucks had two different classes, expensive replicas or smaller, no-name trucks that looked like half-breed Fords. During their last year they changed their profile from Mack Trucks to Auto-Car diesels with opening doors and working steering wheels.

Smith-Miller is once again in operation using original and new parts.

Contributor: John Taylor, P.O. Box 63, Nolensville, TN 37135-0063.

Smith-Miller Toys

	C6	C8	C10
Aerial Ladder Semi, No. 410, six-wheel tractor and four-wheel trailer, "SMFD", 36" long	450	850	1500
Arden Milk Truck, No. 204-A, twelve milk cans, four cases, four wheels, 14" long	350	550	800
B Mack Jr. Fire Truck, warning light, battery-operated, four wheels	1400	2650	3950
B Mack Orange Dump, ten wheels	950	1850	2800
B Mack P.I.E., eighteen wheels	400	625	850
Bekins Van, No. 406, six-wheel tractor and four-wheel trailer, 29" long	325	495	750
Bekins Vanliner, No. 208-B, fourteen wheels, 22-1/2" long	325	500	850
Blue Diamond, No. 408, ten-wheel dump truck, 18-1/2" long	650	1100	1600
B-Mack Lumber Truck, No. 404, 19"	375	560	750
Chevy Bekins Van, fourteen wheels, plain tires, hubcaps, 1945-46	200	300	400
Chevy Coca-Cola, four wheels, plain tires, early, 1945-46	450	675	900
Chevy Flatbed Tractor-Trailer, fourteen wheels, unpainted wood trailer, plain tires, hub caps, early, 1945	200	300	450

Smith-Miller Toys (Continued)

	C6	C8	C10
Chevy Milk Truck, four wheels, plain tires, hub caps, early, 1945-46	300	500	950
Coca-Cola Truck, No. 206-C, sixteen Coca-Cola cases, four wheels, 14" long	450	675	900
Coca-Cola Truck, twenty-four plastic bottles in six cases, four wheels, 1954-55	275	400	550
Dump Truck, No. 402, 11-1/2"	250	350	500
Ford Bekins Van, fourteen-wheeler, plain tires, hub, possibly earliest Smith-Miller, 1944	350	450	650
Ford Coca-Cola, four wheels, wood soda cases, early, 1944	600	1000	1400
GMC Bank of America, No. 404-B, lock and key, four wheels	200	400	500
GMC Be Mac T-Trailer, fourteen wheel, 1949	265	350	650
GMC Coca-Cola, No. 306-C, four wheels, sixteen Coca-Cola cases	425	875	1925
GMC Drive-O Steerable Dump, six wheels, cable w/hand control, 1946	325	550	925
GMC Furniture Mart Pickup, four wheels	250	350	500
GMC Heinz Grocery Truck	200	300	400
GMC Hi-Way Freighter Tractor-Trailer, No. 310-H, fourteen wheels	250	350	500
GMC Kraft Foods, No. 304-K, four wheels	275	475	550
GMC Lumber Tractor-Trailer, No. 406-L, fourteen wheels, eight timbers	250	350	500
GMC Lyon Van Tractor-Trailer, No. 308-V, fourteen wheels	375	575	800
GMC Lyon Van Tractor-Trailer, No. 407-V, ten wheels	350	500	700
GMC Machinery Hauler, No. 408-H, thirteen wheels	300	450	600
GMC Machinery Hauler, ten wheeler	200	300	450
GMC Marshall Field & Company Tractor-Trailer, ten-wheel T-Trailer	400	650	1000
GMC Material Truck, No. 402-M, four barrels, two timbers	250	350	500
GMC Materials Truck, No. 302-M, four barrels, three timbers	250	350	500
GMC Mobilgas Tanker, No. 409-G, fourteen wheels, two hoses	270	400	750
GMC P.I.E., No. 412-P, fourteen wheels	250	375	500

Smith-Miller Toys (Continued)

	C6	C8	C10
GMC P.I.E. Tractor-Trailer, No. 312-P	300	450	600
GMC Peoples First National Bank and Trust Company armored Truck, lock and key, 1951	225	400	525
GMC Rack Truck, No. 303-R, six wheels	250	350	500
GMC Rack Truck, No. 403-R, six wheels	225	380	550
GMC Redwood Logger Tractor-Trailer, No. 307-L, three logs	500	800	1100
GMC Rexall Drug, four wheels	475	815	1550
GMC Searchlight Truck, "Hollywood Film Ad" w/trailer, 1953	550	900	1600
GMC Silver Streak Express Tractor-Trailer, No. 311-E, fourteen wheels	212	318	425
GMC Silver Streak Tractor-Trailer, No. 411-E, fourteen wheels	185	350	475
GMC Super Cargo Tractor-Trailer, No. 309-S, fourteen wheels, ten barrels	250	350	500
GMC Transcontinental Tractor-Trailer, No. 410-F, 14 wheels	250	350	550
GMC Triton Oil, No. 405-T, six wheels, three drums	250	400	500
GMC Triton Oil, No. 305-T, three drums	175	263	350
GMC U.S. Treasury Truck, armored truck, w/lock and key, 1952	250	375	500
GMC Wrecker, No. 301-W, four-wheeler	250	350	500
GMC Wrecker, No. 401-W, six wheels	350	525	700
Heinz Grocery Truck, No. 203-H, six wheels, 14" long	250	400	675
L Mack Aerial Ladder, "SMFD," eight wheels	440	660	880
L Mack Army Materials Truck, three barrels, two boards, one large crate, one small crate, ten wheels	460	690	925
L Mack Army Personnel Carrier, ten wheels	460	690	925
L Mack Bekins Van, all white, ten wheels	750	1200	1800
L Mack Blue Diamond Dump, ten wheels	800	1300	1800
L Mack International Paper Co., ten wheels	700	1000	2100
L Mack Lyon Van, six wheels	550	875	1200

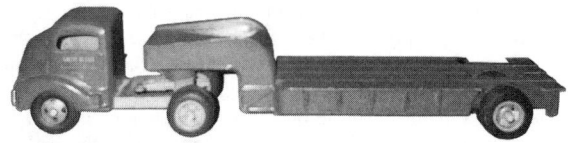

Smith-Miller GMC Machinery Hauler, $450. Photo courtesy Ray Funk

Smith-Miller GMC P.I.E. Tractor-Trailer, $600.

Smith-Miller L Mack Arial Ladder, "SMFD," $880. Photo courtesy Frank Knapp

Smith-Miller Toys (Continued)	C6	C8	C10
L Mack Material Truck, two barrels, six timbers, six wheels.........	350	550	750
L Mack Merchandise Van, six wheels..........................	475	775	1200
L Mack Merchandise Van and Trailer, twelve wheels	850	1400	2500
L Mack Mobil Tandem Tanker, twelve wheels	800	1300	1800
L Mack Orange Hydraulic Dump, ten wheels..................................	750	1650	2950
L Mack Orange Material Truck, three barrels, two boards, one large crate, one small, ten wheels	650	950	1200
L Mack P.I.E., fourteen wheels	450	800	1050
L Mack Sibley's Van, six wheels, rare..	600	900	1500
L Mack Tandem Timber, eighteen or twenty-four timbers, six wheels..	420	630	950
L Mack Telephone Truck, six wheels..	600	1000	1400
L Mack West Coast Transport, six wheels..	800	1300	1800
Lumber Trailer, No. 404-T, 17"	200	300	400
Lumber Truck, No. 201-L, sixty boards, six wheels, 14" long........	300	400	550

Smith-Miller Toys (Continued)	C6	C8	C10
Material Truck, No. 202-M, three barrels, three cases, eighteen boards, four wheels, 14" long......	450	675	900
MIC Aerial Ladder	375	565	750
MIC Fruehauf Road Star Tractor-Trailer, fourteen wheels	400	600	950
MIC House Trailer	380	550	750
MIC Hydraulic Dump, ten wheels ..	500	850	1250
MIC Lift-O-Matic, two barrels, six wheels..	500	800	1100
MIC Lincoln Capri (for MIC House Trailer), steerable	425	700	950
MIC P.I.E. Tractor-Trailer, fourteen wheels..	375	600	850
MIC Teamsters Hydraulic Dump, ten wheels..................................	500	850	1250
MIC Teamsters Tractor-Trailer, fourteen wheels	750	1100	1700
MIC Tow Truck, "Official Tow Car," six wheels	500	800	1200
MIC Tow Truck, unpainted, polished, six wheels	400	775	1025
MIC Tractor-Trailer, polished aluminum trailer, no decals, fourteen wheels..................................	375	600	850
NEC Lumber Truck, nine timbers, six wheels	600	1000	1450

Smith-Miller Toys (Continued)

	C6	C8	C10
Oil Truck, No. 205-P, four drums, six wheels, 14" long	275	415	550
Red Ball, No. 212-R, fourteen wheels, 23-1/2" long	250	350	500
Scoop Dump, No. 403, 14" long	275	325	550
Searchlight Truck, No. 407, "Hollywood Film ad", 18-1/2" long	800	1500	2500
Silver Streak, No. 405, six-wheel tractor, 28" long	170	255	440
Stake Truck, No. 210-S, fourteen wheels, 23-1/2" long	250	375	500
Sunkist Special, No. 211-L, fourteen wheels, 23-1/2" long	250	350	500
Timber Giant, No. 209-T, three logs, fourteen wheels, 23-1/2" long	260	350	550
Tow Truck, No. 401, 15" long	350	550	800

Steelcraft

	C6	C8	C10
Army Truck, Mack, c. 1930, 22" long	650	1000	1450
Bloomindale's Delivery Truck, 25" long	450	600	900
City Delivery Truck	300	425	575
City Fire Dept. Ladder Truck, early	500	800	1200
City Milk Co. Truck, 18" long	400	600	800
Coca-Cola Truck, twelve bottles on side	400	600	800
Cream Crest Truck, 18" long	270	400	550
Dump Truck, Mack, 26" long	450	700	1300
Dump Truck, Airflow	1500	2500	3500
Fire Truck, 25" long	750	1100	1500
Fro-Joy Ice Cream Truck, c. 1930s	400	600	800
GMC Scissor Dump Truck	550	850	1400
Inter City Bus, 24" long	500	800	1100
Little Jim Fire Truck	600	900	1200
Little Jim Mack Dump Truck, red and black, c. 1928	600	900	1400
Model T Roadster Pedal Car, license No. 65-287, 50" long	450	675	900
New York Trucking Co., Headlights work, 1930, 23-1/4" long	800	1100	1400
Railway Express Truck, 26" long	1100	1600	2600
Road Roller, 16-1/2" long	250	350	475
Sheffield Farms Truck, 1930s, 21" long	500	800	1300
Shell Motor Oil Truck, w/oil barrels	300	450	600
Steam Shovel, 26" long	225	350	450
Tank Truck, 25-1/2" long	650	1100	1500
U.S. Mail Truck, c. 1928, 27-1/4" long	1150	1725	2300

Structo

Structo of Freeport, Illinois, was founded in 1908, by brothers Louis and Edward Strohacker, and C.C. Thompson. They initially manufactured Erector Construction Kits, and in 1919 they started making toy vehicles. In 1935, J.G. Cokey bought a majority of the business, and when he died in 1975, the toy patents and designs were taken over by the Ertl Company.

Contributor: Randy Prasse, 916 Hayes Avenue, Racine, WI 53405, 414-637-0620.

Structo

	C6	C8	C10
Aerial Fire Truck, No. 902, 1950s	100	150	200
Aerial Fire Truck, red, conventional Studebaker-style front, rotating ladder base, two ladders, 1936-38, 28" long	40	600	800
Aerial Fire Truck, No. 305, red/yellow, three yellow 18-inch ladders, raising hood, 1940, 29-1/2" long	200	400	600
Aerial Truck Rider, No. 301, red/yellow, same as 1940 model No. 403, 1941, 29-1/2" long	250	500	750
Aerial Truck Rider, No. 403, red/yellow, same as No. 305 only with seat in back on trailer, raising hood, 1940, 29-1/2" long	250	500	750
Air Mail Transport, No. 421, green, tractor/trailer, white balloon tires, "Air Mail Transport" decals, 1927-29, 24" long	300	500	800
Ambulance, No. 416, green, white balloon tires, canvas side skirts on rear sides, scarce, 1927-32, 17" long	300	600	800
Army Searchlight Unit, No. 207, plastic light and generator, battery-operated, rubber tires, rotating searchlight, 1941, 16" long	200	400	700
Army Tank, No. 103, green, 10 wooden wheels, turret with machine gun, makes sound when cranked, 1939-40, 12-3/4" long	150	300	500
Army Tank, No. 102, green, same as previous years but with black metal wheel guards and fenders, 1941, 12-1/2" long	150	300	500
Army Truck, No. 203, green, canvas cover over rear troop area, raising hood, 1940-41, 21-3/4" long	250	500	750
Army Truck, No. 415, green, white balloon tires, canvas cover over rear troop seating area, 1927-32, 17" long	200	400	700

Structo (Continued)

	C6	C8	C10
Army Truck, No. 252, green, w/canvas cover over rear troop area, 1939, 22-1/4" long	250	500	750
Auto Transport Trailer, No. 706, w/cars, 1953-54	115	175	250
Barrel Truck, No. 609, early 1950s	115	175	225
Barrel Truck, No. 811, wind-up, early to mid-1950s	115	175	225
Bearcat Auto, No. 10, red, kit car with windshield, 1919-23, 16" long	500	800	1200
Bearcat Racer, clockwork, 12-1/4" long	400	600	800
Bed set, No. 108, faux maple finish, side by side or stackable, fits 20" dolls, 1940-41, 20" long	75	125	150
Bing-It Game, No. 102, red/yellow, like full-size carnival bell-ringing game, "Show Your Strength," rare, 1939, 18-1/2" long	200	300	400
Camper, w/cloth top, 12" long	55	82	110
Caterpillar, No. 44, green/red, pre-assembled "Ready Built" w/two-wheel trailer, "Structo" embossed, 1924-26, 11-1/2" long	200	400	600
Caterpillar, No. 44, green/red, pre-assembled "Ready Built," w/two-wheel trailer, 1922-23, 11-1/2" long	200	400	600
Caterpillar, No. 44, green/red, pre-assembled "Ready Built," w/disk harrow, 1920-21, 11-1/2" long	200	400	600
Cattle Trailer, No. 708, 1950s	100	125	175
Cement Mixer, 1950s, 20" long	100	150	350
Chain Tread Climbing Tank, No. 58, green, large tank with steel tracks, scarce, 1930-32, 12-1/2" long	500	800	1500
Communications Center Truck, 21" long	175	265	350
Contractor's Sand Unit, No. 410, red/gray, three-piece set includes No. 107 Sand Loader and No. 200 Dump, small hand shovel, 1941, 15-3/4" long	300	500	700
Contractor's Truck, No. 42, orange, pre-assembled "Ready Built", 1922-26, 12" long	600	800	1000
Coupe, convertible, 1920s	350	545	760
Delivery Truck, electric lights	150	225	300

Structo (Continued)

	C6	C8	C10
Deluxe Auto, No. 12, orange, kit car with windshield, convertible top bonnet and spare tire on rear, 1919-26, 16" long	600	1000	1500
Deluxe Auto, No. 20, orange, same as No. 12 only in assembled form, 1924-26, 16" long	600	1000	1500
Doll House Furniture, No. 104, green/yellow/blue, chairs, table and davenport, 1939	100	150	200
Dump Rider, blue, seat in rear of toy, wooden-handled steering mechanism through roof, 1936-38, 18" long	300	500	700
Dump Truck, early, Mack type	200	300	400
Dump Truck, orange/black, C-cab style, 1933-35, 23-1/2" long	250	500	750
Dump Truck, No. 200, red/yellow, box raises automatically, raising hood, 1940-41, 21" long	200	400	600
Dump Truck, No. 404, black/red, pull toy with no motor, large white balloon tires, 1924-26, 14-1/2" long	200	400	600
Dump Truck, green, C-cab style, 1933-35, 23-1/2" long	250	500	750
Dump Truck, yellow/red, four hard rubber wheels with plated caps, spring-loaded dump box, 1936-38, 24" long	300	500	700
Dump Truck, No. 250, red/yellow, two-tone truck with manual lift handle, 1939, 23" long	200	400	600
Evening Ledger Truck, yellow, aka the Popeye Truck, unknown production term, extremely rare, 1933-35, 22" long	1500	2500	4000
Excavator, No. 57, black/orange, steam shovel with steel Caterpillar-style tracks, scarce, 1927-32, 29" long	600	800	1200
Express Truck, red/white, stubby Studebaker-style front, hard rubber tires with steel caps, 1936-38, 18" long	700	1000	1500
Fire Dept. Emergency Patrol Truck, red bubble light, 1950s, 12" long	55	82	110
Fire Insurance Patrol, No. 407, red, white balloon tries, open rear with bench seats and brass bell, 1927-29, 18" long	200	400	600
Fire Insurance Patrol, No. 424, red, white balloon tires, open rear with bench seats and brass bell, 1930-32, 18" long	200	400	600

Smith-Miller MIC Tow Truck, $1200. Photo courtesy Tim Oei

Smith-Miller Silver Streak No. 405, (Structo crane behind) $440.

Smith-Miller GMC Mobilgas Tanker No. 409-G, $750. Photo courtesy Tim Oei

Structo (Continued)	C6	C8	C10
Fire Patrol, No. 321, red/yellow, two ladders, two extinguishers and fireman's axe, raising hood, 1940, 26" long	200	400	600
Fire Patrol, No. 301, red, two ladders, two extinguishers and fireman's axe, 1939, 26" long	200	400	600
Fire Patrol, No. 205, red/yellow, two ladders, raising hood, 1940, 26-1/2" long	200	400	600
Four-Wheel Dump, yellow/red, stubby Studebaker-style front, hard rubber tires with steel caps, 1936-38, 18" long	600	900	1200
Garbage Truck, "Sanitation Dept."	110	160	225
Garbage Truck, 21" long	75	115	175
Gasoline Truck, No. 866, wind-up, steerable front axle, Structo 66 decals, red cab w/red body, early 1950s, 13-1/2" long	150	200	300
Gasoline Truck, No. 912, 1950s, 13" long	75	112	150
Giant Dump Truck, No. 21, red, same as No. 14 only in assembled form, 1924-26, 18" long	700	1200	1700
Giant Dump Truck, No. 14, red, kit truck with dumping box mechanism, 1919-26, 18" long	700	1200	1700

Structo (Continued)	C6	C8	C10
Giant Grab Bucket, No. 111, green/red, with clam bucket, 1924-26, 21-1/4" long	100	200	300
Giant Grab Bucket, No. 111, green/yellow/blue, with clam bucket; no yellow (1930-32), 1927-32, 21-1/4" long	150	250	400
Giant Grab Bucket, No. 66, red/green, smaller version of No. 111, 1927-32, 14" long	100	200	300
Giant Steam Shovel, No. 110, black/orange, with scoop shovel bucket, 1927-32, 22-1/2" long	150	250	400
Giant Steam Shovel, No. 110, black/orange, with scoop shovel bucket, 1924-26, 21-1/4" long	150	250	400
Grab Bucket, No. 52, black/red, with clam bucket, 1924-26, 13" long	100	200	400
Grain Trailer, No. 704, early and mid-1950s	115	175	225
Guided Missile Launcher, No. 906, w/plastic launcher, missiles made of wood and vinyl, 1950s, 13" long	70	105	140
Guided Missile Launching Truck, truck metal, plastic missiles, rubber tires	60	75	110

Structo (Continued)

	C6	C8	C10
High Wheel Tractor, No. 11, green/red, kit tractor with one red trailer, 1919-26, 10" long (16" long overall)	500	900	1500
High Wheel Tractor, No. 19, green/red, same as No. 11 only in assembled form, 1924-26, 10" long	500	900	1500
Hi-Lift Dump, No. 844, wind-up, early 1950s	110	165	220
Hi-Way Transport, No. 404, blue/yellow, same as 1919 model No. 401 with blue and yellow paint scheme, raising hood, 1940-41, 30-1/2" long	200	400	600
Hi-Way Transport, orange, stubby Studebaker-style front, hard rubber tires with steel caps, 1936-38, 18" long	600	900	1200
Hi-Way Transport, yellow/green, stubby Studebaker-style front, hard rubber tires with steel caps, 1936-38, 18" long	600	900	1200
Hi-Way Transport, No. 401, red/white two-tone with diagonal paint line on side of trailer, 1939, 32-1/2" long	200	400	600
Hook and Ladder, No. 205, red/yellow, two ladders, raising hood, 1941, 26-1/2" long	200	400	600
Hook and Ladder, red, black hard rubber tires, hose reel and four ladders on sides, brass bell, 1933-35, 25" long	250	500	700
Hook and Ladder, No. 251, red, two ladders, 1939, 26" long	200	400	600
Hook and Ladder, No. 406, red, white balloon tires, hose reel and four ladders on sides, brass bell, 1927-32, 24" long	250	500	750
Ladder Rider, red, seat in rear of toy, wooden-handled steering mechanism through roof, 1936-38, 22" long	300	500	700
Ladder Truck, 1950s	95	150	225
Lawn Furniture set, No. 104, red, four pieces including chairs, table and davenport; green (1941), 1940-41	100	150	200
Lift Crane, No. 114, black/red, with lift hook on chain, 1924-26, 13" long	100	200	300
Machinery Hauler, 1940s	120	180	240

Structo (Continued)

	C6	C8	C10
Machinery Truck, No. 607, early 1950s	125	195	250
Motor Express Stake Truck, No. 601, also known as Freeport Motor Express Truck, early 1950s	55	83	110
Motor Transport, No. 420, blue, tractor/trailer, white balloon tires, "Motor Dispatch" decals, 1927-32, 24" long	300	500	800
Moving Van, No. 410, orange, black balloon tires with red center hubs, enclosed rear, 1927-29, 17" long	200	400	700
Moving Van, No. 427, open cab, orange, black balloon tires with red center hubs, enclosed rear, 1930-32, 17" long	200	400	700
Overland Freight Trailer, No. 704, early 1950s	100	150	200
Package Delivery, No. 603, early 1950s	100	160	200
Packard Dump Truck, No. 405, red, white balloon tires, also included w/No. 56 Sand Sifter set, 1927-32, 17-1/2" long	200	400	600
Pickup Truck, 13" long	90	135	180
Pile Driver, No. 122, green/red, similar to No. 65 and No. 68 but w/vertical pile driver mechanism, scarce, 1927-32, 14" high	200	400	600
Police Patrol, No. 409, black, white balloon tires, enclose rear paddy wagon appearance, 1927-29, 17" long	200	400	700
Police Patrol, No. 426, blue, white balloon tires, enclosed rear, paddy wagon appearance, 1930-32, 17" long	200	400	700
Police Patrol, No. 320, blue, automatic ringing gong, two bench seats in open back, raising hood, 1940, 23" long	250	500	750
Porch Furniture, No. 106, red/green, three pieces including chairs and glider swing, 1940	100	150	200
Pumping Fire Engine, No. 605, red, operable water tank with pump, hose and reel, two ladders on sides, 1940, 26" long	200	400	700
Pumping Fire Engine, No. 601, red, operable water tank w/pump, hose and reel, two ladders on sides, 1939, 26" long	200	400	700

Smith-Miller Coca-Cola Truck No. 206-C, $900. Photo courtesy R.L. MacNary

Smith-Miller L Mack Army Materials Truck, $925.

Steelcraft Fro-Joy Ice Cream Truck, c. 1933, $800. Photo courtesy John Taylor

Steelcraft City Fire Department Ladder Truck, $1200. Photo courtesy Tim Oei

Structo (Continued)

	C6	C8	C10
Pumping Fire Engine, red, operable water tank, pump and hose, two ladders on sides, 1933-35, 21" long	300	600	800
Pumping Fire Engine, No. 449, red, operable water tank, pump and hose, two ladders on sides, 1927-32, 21" long	200	400	700
Racing Auto, No. 8, green, kit car, 1919-26, 16" long	600	1000	1500
Racing Auto, No. 17, green, same as No. 8 only in assembled form, 1924-26, 16" long	600	1000	1500
Refrigerator, No. 105, white, battery-operated light when door opened, rare, 1940-41, 14" long	100	175	250
Renault Tank, clockwork, green w/red turret	260	400	520
Roadster, clockwork, 1920s, 16" long	600	1000	1400
Roadster, No. 40, red, pre-assembled "Ready Built", 1920-26, 10-1/2" long	400	800	1000

Structo (Continued)

	C6	C8	C10
Sand Elevator and Bin, No. 107, red/yellow, two pieces, nine sand buckets attached to crank-operated chain, four wheels; red/black (1941), 1940-41	150	300	400
Sand Loader, No. 51, black/red, winding elevator track w/sand buckets, 1924-32, 13" high	200	300	400
Sand Sifter set, No. 56, black/red, complete with sand sifter operation, sold with No. 405 Dump Truck, scarce, 1927-29, 72" long	400	800	1200
Sand Sifter set, No. 56, black/red, complete sand sifter operation with No. 405 Dump truck, scarce, 1930-32, 72" long	200	300	400
Shovel Dump, No. 605, also known as Structo Excavating Company, early 1950s	100	150	200
Six-Wheel Dump, orange/black, stubby Studebaker-style front, hard rubber tires with steel caps, 1936-38, 18" long	600	900	1200

Structo (Continued)

	C6	C8	C10
Small Steam Shovel, No. 50, green/red, vertical boiler tank and smoke stack, 1924-26, 13-3/4" long..........................	150	250	350
Speed Wagon, No. 425, orange, black balloon tires, open truck box with drop-down tailgate, scarce, 1930-32, 17" long...........	300	500	700
Speed Wagon, No. 408, green, white balloon tires, open truck box w/drop-down tailgate, scarce, 1927-29, 17" long...........	300	500	700
Stake Delivery Truck, No. 310, red/white, removable stakes, raising hood, 1940, 25" long.......	300	500	800
Stake Truck, C-cab style, orange/green, working lights, 1933-35, 21-12" long..................	300	700	1200
Stake Truck, No. 254, red/yellow two-tone truck with removable plated stakes, 1939, 22-1/2" long..................................	250	500	750
Stake Truck, No. 204, yellow/red, removable sakes, raising hood; blue/yellow (1941), 1940-41, 21-3/4" long.............................	250	500	750
Stake Wagon Truck, black/red, C-cab style, 1933-35, 21-1/2" long..................................	250	500	750
Standard Rider, red, seat in rear of toy, wooden-handled steering mechanism through roof, 1936-38, 18" long......................	300	500	700
Station Wagon, No. 206, shown in catalog but excluded from the 1941 line, 1941...........................	NPF	NPF	NPF
Steam Shovel, No. 100, blue/yellow/black, crank controls; no blue (1940), 1939-41, 21" x 18"..	100	150	250
Steam Shovel, 16"..........................	57	87	115
Steam Shovel, 14" x 11".................	75	150	200
Steam Shovel, No. 65, black/red, smaller version of No. 110, 1927-32, 18-3/4" long................	100	200	300
Steam Shovel, No. 112, green/red, with scoop shovel bucket, 1924-26, 14-1/2" long.........................	100	200	300
Steel Cargo Trailer, No. 702, early to mid-1950s.............................	125	175	225
Straight Truck, white, black hard rubber tires with painted whitewalls, 1933-35, 22" long	250	500	700
Tank, olive drab w/orange turret, ten metal wheels, 12-1/2"............	300	450	600

Structo (Continued)

	C6	C8	C10
Tank, No. 48, 11" long	225	338	450
Telephone Bank, No. 101, black/orange/red, bell rings when coin is deposited; only black (1940), 1939-41, 10-1/2" long.....	75	125	200
Tractor and Grader, No. 61, large blue/orange crawler with green pull-behind grader, scarce, 1930-32, 30" long.................................	600	1000	1800
Tractor and Sand Trailer, No. 45, black/orange, same as No. 44 but with three trailers, 1927-29, 16" long....................................	400	600	800
Tractor and Sand Trailer, No. 44, black/orange, similar to old version of No. 44 with high seat and cast nickel-plated driver, 1927-29, 16" long.................................	300	500	700
Tractor and Trailer, No. 402, green/red, pull toy with no motor, 1924-26, 17-1/2" long......	200	400	600
Tractor and Trailer, No. 39, green/red, one-piece tractor and cab, solid black wheels, wind-up motor, 1924-26, 13" long...........	200	400	700
Tractor Train, No. 45, green/red, same as No. 44 but with three trailers, 1924-26, 28-1/2" long	300	500	700
Tractor, Trailer and Scraper, No. 46, blue, crawler with red four-wheel wagon and gray two-wheel scraper, 1930-32, 23-1/2" long.................................	200	500	700
Transport Trailer, No. 700, early 1950s	90	135	180
Transport Unit, No. 505, red/white, three piece set, same as 1939 model No. 500, raising hood; red/gray (1941), 1940-41, 35" long	300	600	800
Transport Unit, No. 500, three-piece set with tractor and same trailers as No. 300 and No. 401 sets, 1939, 32-1/2" long...............	300	600	800
Trench Digger Truck, black/yellow, conventional Studebaker-style front, chain-operated crane, 1936-38, 26" long......................	500	700	1000
Truck, "Structo Telephone Co.", 1948, 12" long.............................	38	56	75
Truck and Steam Shovel, yellow/blue, stubby Studebaker-style front, hard rubber tires with steel caps, 1936-38, 18" long	700	1000	1500

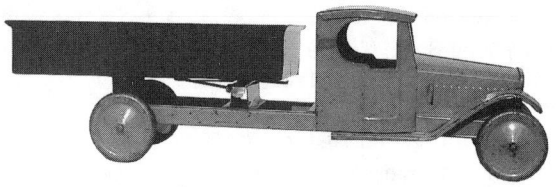

Steelcraft Little Jim Mack Dump Truck, $1400. Photo courtesy John Taylor

Sun Rubber 1934 DeSoto Airflow, (SA02), $50. Photo courtesy Dave Leopard

Sun Rubber left to right: Ambulance (ST07), $50; Coupe, 1936, (SA01), $50. Photo courtesy Bob and Alice Wagner

Sun Rubber Open Racer No. 505, (SR01), $50. Photo courtesy Dave Leopard

Structo (Continued)	C6	C8	C10
Truck and Trailer, No. 300, blue/yellow two-tone tractor and stake trailer, automatic coupling system, 1939, 25-1/2" long	250	500	750
Truck Assortment, No. 317, blue Dump Truck, Stake Truck, Lumber Truck, heavy gauge metal, rubber wheels, original box folds to form garage, price per set, 1920s, each 9" long, 3-1/2" wide, 3-1/2" tall....................................	175	250	400
Truck/Steam Shovel, No. 400, orange/black, flatbed truck with steam shovel on back, 1939, 28" long...............................	300	500	700
Truck/Steam Shovel, No. 402, yellow/black, flatbed truck with Steam Shovel on back, includes ramp, raising hood, 1940, 32" long...............................	300	500	750
Truck/Steam Shovel, No. 402, yellow/black, flatbed truck with Steam Shovel on back, includes ramp, raising hood, 1941, 32" long...............................	200	400	600
U.S. Mail Truck, No. 428, green, black balloon tires w/red center hubs, enclosed rear with lattice, 1930-32, 17" long......................	200	400	700

Structo (Continued)	C6	C8	C10
U.S. Mail Truck, No. 411, green, black balloon tires with red center hubs, enclosed rear with lattice, 1927-29, 17" long................	200	400	700
Van, No. 300, open top, red/gray, open grain-hauler style trailer with tailgate, 1941, 25-1/2" long..............................	300	500	800
Whippet Tank, No. 48, heavy spring clockwork motor, may read "Patented 1920," green/red, pre-assembled "Ready Built" (1922-26); also yellow, with gun on turret (1927-29); only green/red with gun (1930-32), 1922-32, 12" long......................	200	400	600
Wrecker, "Toyland Garage"............	50	75	125
Wrecker, No. 822, "Toyland Garage," wind-up, early to mid-1950s	100	135	200
Wrecker, No. 201, blue/white, tow arm with crank-operated tow chain and hood, raising hood; blue/yellow (1941), 1940-41, 21-1/4" long....................................	250	500	750
Wrecker, No. 253, blue/white two-tone truck with manual crank tow arm and winch, 1939, 22" long ...	300	600	800

Structto (Continued)

	C6	C8	C10
Wrecking Auto, No. 115, red/black, with tow arm and winch mechanism, 1924-26, 16-1/2" long	200	400	600
Yuba Tractor, No. 16, black/red, kit tractor with steel tracks and one red trailer, 1920-23, 13-1/2" long (20" long overall)	80	1200	1800

Sturditoy

The Sturdy Corporation of Providence and Pawtucket, Rhode Island, manufactured its steel toy trucks from about 1929-1933.

Sturditoy

	C6	C8	C10
Ambulance, open cab, c. 1929, 26" long	2000	3500	5000
American Railway Express Truck, c. 1920s, 26" long	1000	1800	2750
Coal Dump Truck, 1920s, 25" long	1200	2000	2900
Dump Truck, 1920s, 26-1/2"	600	950	1300
Dump Truck, 1920s, 25" long	800	1300	1900
Pumper, c. 1930, 26" long	1100	1800	2500
Sturditory Oil Company Truck, c. 1929, 27" long	1100	1800	2500
Traveling Store, 26" long	1800	2900	4200
U.S. Mail Screenside Truck	1200	2500	3500
Water Tower	1500	2500	3500
Wells Fargo Armored truck, c. 1927, 24" long	2200	3700	5500
Wrecker, 30" long	1000	1650	2750

Sun Rubber

Sun Rubber of Barberton, Ohio, was founded in 1923. Toy making started in 1924 and vehicles were introduced in April 1935. The owner was Tom W. Smith Jr.

Contributor: Dave Leopard, 2507 Feather Run Trail, West Columbia, SC 29169-4915.

Sun Rubber

	C6	C8	C10
'34 DeSoto Airflow, No. 500, four-door sedan, 4" long (SA02)	25	35	50
'40 Dodge, No. 12001, four-door sedan, 4-1/2" long (SA03)	25	35	50
Ambulance, No. 12006, late 1930s, 3-3/4" long (ST07)	25	35	50
Art Deco Housetrailer, No. 1025, fits Teardrop Sedan, 4-3/8" long (SA05)	60	80	250
Coupe, No. 515, external exhaust pipes, 1936, 4" long (SA01)	25	35	50
Open Racer, No. 505, two drivers, 1936, 4-3/8" long (SR01)	25	35	50

Sun Rubber (Continued)

	C6	C8	C10
Open Racer, No. 12012, boattail, "Super" racer, 6-3/4" long (SR03)	30	45	65
Open Racer, No. 1000, full fenders on rear, 1936, 6-1/2" long (SR02)	40	60	80
Pickup Truck, No. 510, stake sides, streamlined, 4-1/2" long (ST01)	25	35	55
Scout Car, No. 12014, four gunners, 1946, 6" long (SM02)	45	65	100
Tank, No. 12015, revolving turret and gunner, 1946, 6" long (SM01)	50	75	100
Teardrop Sedan, No. 1010, c. 1936, 5-1/2" long (SA04)	25	40	65
Town Car, No. 1015, Brewster-type limo, exposed driver, 5-3/8" (SA06)	40	60	95
Tractor/Trailer, No. 12013, one piece, three axles, futuristic, 5-1/8" long (ST03)	25	35	55
Truck, No. 1005, open, stake side, streamlined, 5-1/4" (ST02)	35	45	55
Truck, No. 12111, open, "Master," futuristic, 5-5/8" long	25	35	55
Truck, No. 12003, open, futuristic, 4-1/2" long (ST04)	25	35	50
White Bus, No. 520, streamlined, 1936, 4-1/2" long (ST07)	20	30	50
Woody Station Wagon, No. 12007, mid-1930s, 3-3/4" long (SA07)	20	30	50

Thomas Toys

Thomas Toys was founded by Islyn Thomas in 1944. Located at 80 Clinton Street, Newark, New Jersey, at its peak had 350 employees. The company's first toys were plastic jeeps, planes, and vinyl dolls. Thomas sold the firm to Banner in 1960.

Thomas Toys

	C6	C8	C10
Buick Torpedo Sedan, No. 133, 11" long	20	30	40
Harley-Davidson, w/removable rider, 3" long	75	112	150
Jeep with Trailer, w/yellow driver wearing GI helmet, 1954, 8-3/8" long	14	16	18
Loudspeaker Van, No. 140, 4" long	20	25	30
Wrecker, 4-1/2" long	12	18	24

Tip-Top-Toy Co.

Tip-Top toys were realistic, crisply detailed, and often unique. Wheels were either metal disks or Tootsietoy-like with lug bolts, metal hubs with rubber tires and rubber wheels.

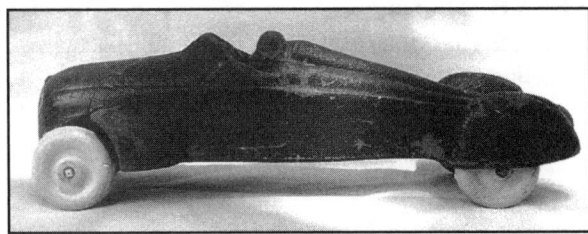

Sun Rubber Open Racer No. 1000, (SR02), $80. Photo courtesy Dave Leopard

Sun Rubber Pickup Truck No. 510, (ST01), $55. Photo courtesy Dave Leopard

Sun Rubber Teardrop Sedan No. 1010, (SA04), $65. Photo courtesy Dave Leopard

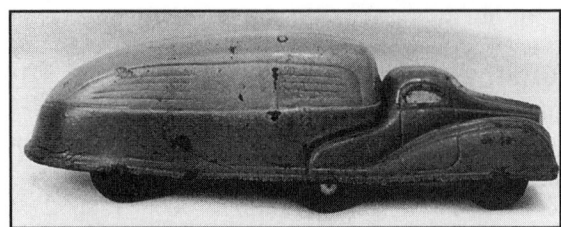

Sun Rubber Tractor Trailer No. 12013, (ST03), $55. Photo courtesy Dave Leopard

This progression helps to date the issues. Windshields and windows were open. Except where noted, cars and trucks were without bumpers.

Contributors: Fred Maxwell, 4722 N. 33 St., Arlington, VA 22207. Perry R. Eichor, 703 North Almond Drive, Simpsonville, SC 29681.

Tip Top Toy Co.

	C6	C8	C10
1923 Dodge (?) Coupe, 1923 Dodge, 3-1/8" (TTTV01)	16	24	32
Overland Bus, thirteen windows, 3-3/8" long (TTTV05)	25	40	60
Stake Truck, four- or six-wheel versions, body cast separately and fastened to chassis, 4-5/8" long (TTTV13)	75	100	125
Tow Truck, 3-5/16" long	16	24	32

Toledo Metal Wheel Company

The Toledo Metal Wheel Company was located in Toledo, Ohio, during the early and late 1920s. it manufactured a large range of pedal cars, as well as toy trucks. Its trade name for its products was "Blue Streak."

Toledo Metal Wheel Company

	C6	C8	C10
Bull Dog Coal Truck, No. 50, 25" long	800	1350	1875
Bull Dog Dump Truck, No. 46, 26-1/2" long	600	1000	1475
Bull Dog Moving Van, No. 48, 26" long	550	1050	1550

Toledo Metal Wheel Company (Continued)

	C6	C8	C10
Bull Dog Sprinkler Truck, No. 47, 27-1/2" long	600	1100	1510
Bull Dog Truck, No. 45, open cab, 26" long	500	1000	1500
Fire Pumper Pedal Car, red, painted, 59" long	1250	1875	2500

Tommy Toy

Tommy Toy, 131 Palisade Ave., Union City, New Jersey, had its first sale on Nov. 13, 1935. Its principal owners were Dr. Albert Greene and Charles E. Weldon. It seems to have gone out of business between August 1938 and May 1939.

Some Tommy Toy vehicles resemble Metal Cast, Savoye, and other maker's vehicles. However, since slush molds tend to change hands, production of a vehicle by one company would not preclude later manufacture of the same toy by another company. American Alloy is known to have produced copies of Tommy Toy's soldiers, using new molds. The only vehicle known to bear the Tommy Toy trademark is the No. 810 Cord.

Tommy Toy

	C6	C8	C10
Aerial Ladder Truck, (like Savoye), late 1920s type (TTV1)	20	30	40
Airflow-type Auto, like Savoye, c. 1935 (TTV2)	32	48	65
Ambulance, like Kansas Toy, late 1920s-early 1930s type (TTV3)	16	24	32
Cannon Truck, like Barclay; Barclay's had wooden hubs, mid-1930s (TTV5)	17	25	34

Tommy Toy (Continued)

	C6	C8	C10
Convertible, 1935 Oldsmobile, w/driver, mid-to-late 1930s (TTV7)	10	15	20
Convertible, no driver, mid to late 1930s (TTV6)	18	27	36
Cord, No. 810, 1935 (TTV8)	40	60	80
Coupe, Packard, mid-1930s (TTV21)	17	26	35
Delivery Truck, "Delivery Deluxe," like Savoye, late 1930s (TTV9)	18	27	36
Double-Decker Bus, closed top, early 1930s (TTV10)	16	24	32
Double-Decker Bus, open top, extended hood, like Savoye, late 1920s (TTV11)	35	52	70
Double-Decker Bus, open top, no hood, like Barclay, late 1930s (TTV12)	16	24	32
Dump Truck, resembles Kansas Toy, Best Toy, Manhattan Toys, late 1930s (TTV13)	16	24	32
Ladder Truck, mid-1930s (TTV15)	20	30	40
Police Patrol, solid windows, late 1920s-early 1930s type (TTV23)	35	52	70
Police Patrol, open windows, late 1920s-early 1930s type (TTV22)	70	105	140
Pumper, large, red hubs, late 1930s (TTV25)	11	16	22
Pumper, mid-1930s (TTV24)	12	18	25
Pumper, small, late 1930s (TTV26)	8	12	16
Racing Car, large, c. mid-1930s (TTV27)	16	24	32
Racing Car, small, c. mid-1930s (TTV28)	12	18	25
Sedan, four-door, c. 1935 (TTV29)	17	26	35
Sedan Towing "Tourist" Trailer, c. 1936-37 (TTV30)	40	60	100
Towing Car Coupe, like Savoye, early 1930s type (TTV31)	16	24	32
Truck, "General Trucking", late 1930s (TTV14)	12	18	25
Truck, "Milk Truck," grilled window, c. late 1930s (TTV17)	20	30	40
Truck, "Milk Truck," smooth window, c. late 1930s (TTV18)	20	30	40
Truck, "Milk", late 1930s (TTV16)	20	30	40
Truck, "Oil," "Cap 80000" (like Metal Cast, which has different capacity number), attaches to Tommy Toy Towing Car Coupe, 1930s (TTV20)	8	12	16

Tommy Toy (Continued)

	C6	C8	C10
Truck, "Beer Truck," w/wooden barrels, late 1930s (TTV4)	14	21	28
Wrecker, late 1930s (TTV33)	10	15	20

Tonka

Tonka was incorporated in Mound, Minnesota, in September 1946. The firm had secured the tooling for the steam shovel and crane and clam from Streator Industries, which had unsuccessfully introduced these toys at the 1946 Toy Fair. In 1948, Tonka introduced a forklift with trailer, and in 1949 premiered its line of trucks, including a dump and a wrecker.

Contributors: Original list by Don & Barb DeSalle and John Taylor. Current pricing by Mark Rich, P.O. Box 971, Stevens Point, WI 54481, email: mark.rich@sff.net. 11th Edition pricing contributor Mark Rich, P.O. Box 971, Stevens Point, WI 54481. Email: mark.rich@sff.net

1947

	C6	C8	C10
Crane and Clam, No. 150, 1947, 24" long	135	200	350
Steam Shovel, No. 050, 1947, 20-3/4" long	135	200	350

1948

	C6	C8	C10
Power Lift Truck and Trailer, No. 200, 1948	200	350	600

1949

	C6	C8	C10
Dump Truck, No. 180, 1949, 12" long	100	175	375
Steam Shovel Deluxe, No. 100, 1949, 22" long	100	250	400
Tonka Toy Transport Van, No. 140, 1949, 22-1/4" long	150	300	500
Wrecker Truck, No. 250, 1949, 12-1/2" long	125	250	375

1950

	C6	C8	C10
Steel Carrier Semi, No. 145, 1950, 22" long	125	200	350
Utility Hauler, No. 175, 1950, 12" long	100	150	300

1951

	C6	C8	C10
Allied Van Lines Semi, No. 400, 1951, 23-1/2" long	175	260	400

1953

	C6	C8	C10
Green Giant Transport Semi, No. 650, 1953, 22-1/4" long	150	300	500
Logger Semi, No. 575, wood flat bed, 1953	125	180	350
Logger Semi, No. 575, 1953, 22-1/4"	125	180	350

Sun Rubber Truck No. 12003, (ST04), $50, and No. 12111, (ST05), $60. Photo courtesy Dave Leopard

Sun Rubber Truck No. 1005, (ST02), $55. Photo courtesy Dave Leopard

Tonka Toy Transport Van, No. 140, 1949, $500. Photo courtesy Calvin L. Chaussee

Tonka Dump Truck, No. 180, 1956, 13" long, $350. Photo courtesy Don and Barb DeSalle

1953 (Continued)	C6	C8	C10
Road Grader, No. 600, 1953, 17" long	50	75	100
Trailer Fleet Set, No. 675, two tractors, five interchangeable trailers, price per set, 1953	450	680	975
Wrecker, 1953	125	200	350

1954	C6	C8	C10
Aerial Ladder Semi Fire Truck, No. 700, 1954, 32-1/2" long	175	260	450
Carnation Milk Step Van, No. 750, 1954, 11-3/4" long	200	400	600
Minute Maid Delivery Van, No. 725, 1954, 14-1/2" long	250	575	950
Parcel Delivery Van, No. 750, 1954, 11-3/4" long	200	300	500
Pick-Up Truck, No. 580, 1954	125	188	250
Road Builder Set, No. 775, five-piece set, Road Grader, semi, T&T crane, and dump truck, 1954	350	525	900
Star Kist Van, No. 725, 1954, 14-1/2"	250	575	950
Steel Carrier Truck, No. 145, 1954	100	185	380
Utility Truck, 1954	110	275	425
Wrecker, 1954	100	300	500

1955	C6	C8	C10
Aerial Ladder Truck, 1955, 32-1/2" long	100	300	450

1955 (Continued)	C6	C8	C10
Allied Van Lines, No. 400-5, 1955, 23-3/4" long	100	200	300
Carnation Milk Delivery Van, No. 750, 1955, 11-3/4" long	200	400	600
Dump, red cab, green dump body, 1955, 13" long	100	150	350
Freighter, 1955	90	135	280
Grader, No. 600, 1955, 17" long	75	125	200
Green Giant Transport, No. 650-5, tractor-trailer, white cab and van trailer, 1955, 12-/34" long	155	350	600
Lowboy and Shovel, 1955	150	300	450
Lumber Truck, No. 850, six wheels, 1955, 18-3/4" long	175	260	400
Minute Maid Orange Juice Van, No. 725, 1955, 14-1/2" long	275	650	950
Pick-Up Truck, No. 880, 1955	125	280	450
Rescue Van, 1955	200	450	800
Stake Truck, No. 860, six wheels, 1955	175	360	500
Trailer, No. 065, stake side, 1955	30	45	60
Wrecker, 1955, 12-3/4" long	100	150	200

1956	C6	C8	C10
Aerial Ladder, No. 700, 1956, 32-1/2" long	150	300	450
Aerial Sand Loader Set, No. 992, includes Loader and Dump Truck, 1956	225	338	450

1956 (Continued)

	C6	C8	C10
Dump Truck, No. 180, red body, green dump, 1956, 13" long........	100	150	350
Farm Stake Truck, No. 991, 1956, 13" long.....................................	150	250	460
Green Giant Transport, No. 650-6, tractor-trailer, white cab and van trailer, 1956, 12-3/4" long...........	155	350	600
Hi-Way Dump Truck, No. 980, 1956, 13" long............................	130	280	395
Lumber Truck, No. 998, 1956, 18-3/4" long.....................................	80	120	160
Pick-Up Truck, No. 880, 1956, 12-3/4"..	150	350	650
Pumper, No. 950, 1956, 17" long....	120	230	350
Rescue Squad Truck, white, delivery van design, sliding side doors, opening rear doors, part of Tonka Fire Department set in 1956; No. 024 in 1957, 1956, 12" long..	130	260	400
Road Grader, No. 600, 1956, 17" long..	75	125	200
Sand Loader Set, No. 994, includes Loader and Dump Truck, 1956 ...	20	230	350
Shovel and Carry-All (Loboy), No. 120, 1956, 33" long total.............	188	280	475
Suburban Pumper, No. 990, 1956, 17"..	175	262	350
Wrecker, No. 996, white, AAA, rare, 1956, 12" long....................	390	525	800

1957

	C6	C8	C10
Big Mike Dual Hydraulic Dump Truck, 1957, 14" long	325	595	1000
Gasoline Truck, 1957, 15" long.......	350	525	1000
Hydraulic Aerial Ladder Truck, 1957, 32" long............................	200	300	500
Parcel Delivery Van, 1957, 12" long.......................................	120	230	350
Pick-Up with Stake Trailer, 1957, 20-1/2" long................................	150	250	400
Stake Trailer, 1957, 8-1/2" long	15	30	45
Stock Rack Truck with Animals, 1957, 16-1/4" long.....................	175	365	650
Three-in-One Hi-Way Service Truck, w/two snowblades, 1957, 13" long..	275	400	700
Thunderbird Express Semi, No. 034, 1957, 24" long................	150	400	600
Wrecker, 1957, 12-1/2" long	100	300	500

1958

	C6	C8	C10
Big Mike Dual Hydraulic Dump Truck with Snow Plow, No. 045, 1958..	375	675	1000
Deluxe Sportsman with Boat Trailer, No. 034, 1958, 22-3/4" long..	150	325	750
Dump Truck, No. 006, 1958, 13-1/2" long......................................	100	150	300
Gasoline Truck, No. 033, hinged back door, hose and nozzle, 1958	350	500	900
Hi-Way Service Truck, No. 041, 1958..	100	200	400
Hydraulic Aerial Ladder, No. 048, 1958, 32-1/2" long.....................	100	250	450
Hydraulic Dump Truck, No. 020, 1958, 13-1/2" long.....................	125	175	275
Livestock Van, No. 036, 1958........	175	250	450
Nationwide Moving Van, No. 039, 1958, 24-1/2" long.....................	250	475	800
Pick-Up Truck, No. 002, blue, 1958, 12-3/4" long.....................	100	150	300
Pick-Up with Stake Trailer and Animal, No. 028, 1958, 20-1/4" long..	125	175	275
Road Grader, No. 012, 1958, 17" long..	75	112	150
Shovel & Carry-All Trailer, No. 043, 1958....................................	200	300	500
Sportsman Pick-Up with Topper, No. 005, 1958, 12-3/4" long........	150	225	450
Sportsman Truck with Box Trailer, No. 029, 1958..............................	150	225	400
Stock Rack Truck, No. 032, white cab, 1958	100	200	300
Suburban Pumper, No. 046, 1958, 17-1/4" long..................................	175	225	450
Thunderbird Express, No. 037, white, 1958..................................	150	300	400
Utility Truck, No. 003, 1958	100	150	300
Wrecker Truck, No. 018, 1958, 13-1/4" long......................................	100	250	450

1959

	C6	C8	C10
Air Express, No. 016, 1959	350	425	700
Boat Transport, No. 041, 1959, 38"	175	263	350
Car Carrier, No. 040, 1959	85	128	170
Deluxe Sportsman, No. 022, blue pick-up with white cab roof, boat trailer, 1959, 22-1/4" long...........	150	325	500
Dragline, No. 014, 1959, 20" long ..	100	175	375
Dragline & Trailer, No. 044, 1959, 26-1/4" long..................................	150	275	400

1959 (Continued)	C6	C8	C10
Hydraulic Land Rover, No. 042, 1959, 15" long	350	525	700
Sanitary Truck, square back, 1959	450	700	1000
Service Truck, No. 001, blue, aluminum ladder, 1959, 12-3/4" long	100	150	350
Sportsman, No. 005, 1959	100	175	350
Tandem Air Express, No. 036, w/trailer, 1959, 24-3/4" long	225	338	450
Tandem Platform Stake, No. 030, 1959, 28-1/4" long	240	450	800

1960	C6	C8	C10
Aerial Ladder, No. 048, 1960	125	250	350
Boat Transport, No. 041, 1960, 38" long	250	450	850
Bulldozer, No. 100, plated roller wheels only in 1960, 1960, 8-7/8"	75	125	200
Car Carrier, No. 040, 1960	100	225	450
Cement Mixer, No. 120, 1960, 15-1/2" long	100	150	300
Deluxe Fisherman, No. 130, also new boat and trailer, 1960	150	350	550
Deluxe Sportsman, No. 022, 1960	100	250	400
Dump Truck, No. 006, 1960, 13-1/2" long	75	125	290
Fisherman Pick-Up with Sportsman Cover, No. 110, 1960, 14" long	100	175	375
Hydraulic Dump, No. 020, 1960	75	150	375
Logger, No. 008, 1960	150	225	300
Lowboy & Bulldozer, No. 125, 1960, 26-1/4" long	190	375	675
Mobile Dragline, No. 135, 1960	100	250	450
Pick-Up, No. 002, 1960	100	200	300
Pick-Up and Trailer, No. 028, 1960	100	150	300
Power Boom Loader, No. 115, 1960 only, 1960, 18-1/2" long	300	650	1000
Rescue Squad, No. 105, 1960, 13-3/4" long	100	250	450
Sanitary Truck, No. 140, 1960	350	550	900
Service Truck, No. 001, 1960	100	150	350
Sportsman, No. 005, tan, white boat, 1960	70	135	200
Surburban Pumper, No. 046, 1960	100	250	350
Tanker, No. 145, first Tonka w/major use of plastic, 1960, 28" long	100	250	450
Thunderbird Express, No. 037, orange, white cab roof, 1960	150	350	550
Tonka Ford Falcon, from set, 1960	50	75	100

1960 (Continued)	C6	C8	C10
Tonka Jolly Green Giant Special, white, green stake racks, 1960	150	300	450
Tonka Standard Oil Company Wrecker Special, 1960	200	400	600
Wrecker, No. 018, white sidewalls, 1960	150	225	300

1961	C6	C8	C10
Aerial Ladder, No. 048, 1961, 32-1/2" long	125	200	450
Allied Van, No. 039, 1961, 24-1/2" long	120	250	450
Boat Service Truck, No. 117, 1961 only, 1961, 23-1/2" long	100	250	450
Boat Transport Truck, No. 041, 1961, 28" long	150	300	650
Car Carrier, No. 040, 1961, 29" long	100	250	450
Cement Mixer, No. 120, 1961, 15-1/2" long	100	150	300
Deluxe Fisherman, No. 130, red and white with boat, 1961, 27-3/4" long	150	350	550
Deluxe Sportsman, No. 022, turquoise and white with motorboat, 1961, 22-1/4" long	100	200	450
Dragline, No. 014, yellow, 1961, 18" long	100	150	250
Dump Truck, No. 006, 1961, 13-1/2" long	75	100	250
Dump Truck with Sandloader, No. 116, 1961, 23-1/4" long	100	175	395
Giant Dozer, No. 118, 1961, 12-1/2" long	70	100	250
Grading Service Truck, Trailer and bulldozer, No. 134, 1961, 25-1/2" long	100	150	350
Houseboat Set, No. 136, 1961, 29" long total	200	400	800
Hydraulic Dump, No. 020, 1961, 13-1/2" long	75	110	250
Mobile Clam, No. 142, 1961, 27-1/4" long	100	250	450
Mobile Dragline, No. 135, 1961	100	250	450
Pick-Up, No. 002, 1961, 12-1/4" long	100	190	320
Road Grader, No. 012, yellow, 1961, 17" long	75	100	200
Sportsman, No. 005, 1961, 12-3/4" long	100	150	375
Tanker, No. 145, 1961, 28" long	100	250	350
Wrecker, No. 018, 1961, 13-1/4" long	100	250	400

1962

	C6	C8	C10
Aerial Ladder, No. 1348, 1962.......	100	150	350
Airlines Luggage Service, No. 420, 1962, 16-5/8" long......................	100	250	400
Allied Van, No. 739, 1962..............	125	250	350
Bulldozer, No. 300, 1962	50	75	100
Camper, No. 530, 1962, 14" long....	75	150	250
Car Carrier, No. 840, 1962..............	100	150	300
Cement Mixer, No. 620, 1962........	85	150	300
Dozer Packer, No. 524, Packer has eleven tires, sold only in 1962, 1962, 18-1/4" long.......................	100	250	400
Dragline, No. 514, 1962	150	225	300
Dump Truck, No. 406, 1962...........	75	150	275
Dump Truck and Sand Loader, No. 616, 1962.................................	100	200	300
Giant Dozer, No. 618, 1962.............	100	150	200
Grading Service Truck, No. 834, green and yellow dump, green bulldozer, yellow trailer, 1962	12	250	350
Hyraulic Dump, No. 520, 1962	75	100	220
Jeep Dispatcher, No. 200, 1962, 9-3/4" long..................................	20	40	60
Jeep Runabout, Trailer and Boat, No. 516, 1962, 25-5/8" long........	75	175	350
Jeep Surrey, No. 350, fringe top, 1962, 10-1/2" long...................	42	83	175
Jeep Universal, No. 249, 1962........	75	125	175
Jet Delivery Truck, No. 410, 1962 only, 1962, 14" long....................	200	350	850
Loader, No. 402, yellow and green, 1962..	40	60	80
Mobile Clam, No. 942, 1962..........	100	150	320
Pick-Up, No. 302, 1962...................	95	150	250
Pick-Up and Trailer, No. 528, 1962	50	75	150
Pumper Truck, No. 926, 1962........	100	150	300
Road Grader, No. 512, 1962............	45	68	90
Serv-I-Car, No. 201, white, 1961, 9-1/8" long..................................	75	125	200
Sportsman, No. 405, 1962	75	100	200
Stake Pick-Up, No. 308, 1962, 12-5/8" long..................................	40	80	120
Utility Dump, No. 301, rervised Golf Club Tractor, 1961 only, 1962, 12-1/2" long.....................	100	150	300
Wrecker, No. 518, 1962, 14-12" long...	50	100	150

1963

	C6	C8	C10
Aerial Ladder Truck, No. 1348, 1963...	100	150	200
Airport Service Set, No. 2100, 1963	150	225	300

1963 (Continued)

	C6	C8	C10
Allied Van, No. 739, 1963	118	175	235
Back Hoe, No. 422, 1963, 17-1/8" long..	100	175	350
Bulldozer, No. 300, 1963	55	82	110
Camper, No. 530, 1963	25	38	50
Car Carrier, No. 840, 1963	42	63	85
Cement Mixer, No. 620, 1963........	75	125	175
Dozer Packer, No. 524, yellow, 1963...	200	300	400
Dragline, No. 514, 1963	60	90	120
Dump Truck, No. 406, 1963...........	45	68	90
Dump Truck and Sand Loader, No. 616, yellow, 1963......................	100	150	235
Giant Dozer, No. 536, 1963	110	160	225
Hydraulic Dump Truck, No. 520, 1963...	45	68	90
Jeep Pumper, No. 425, 1963, 10-3/4" long..................................	100	175	400
Jeep Runabout, No. 516, Trailer and Boat, 1963	75	150	300
Jeep Surrey, No. 350, 1963	50	75	100
Loader, No. 352, 1963....................	40	60	80
Military Jeep Universal, No. 251, 1963, 10-1/2" long.....................	25	38	50
Mini-Tonka Camper, No. 070, 1963, 9-5/8" long.....................	10	20	30
Mini-Tonka Dump, No. 060, 1963, 9-3/4" long..................	10	20	30
Mini-Tonka Jeep Pick-Up, No. 050, 1963, 9-1/4" long..................	10	20	30
Mini-Tonka Stake Truck, No. 056, 1963, 9-1/4" long..................	10	20	30
Mini-Tonka Wrecker, No. 068, 1963, 9-1/2" long.....................	13	26	40
Mobile Clam, No. 942, 1963...........	75	112	150
Pick-Up, No. 302, 1963....................	35	52	70
Pumper, No. 926, 1963....................	60	90	120
Ramp Hoist, No. 640, red and white, 1963, 19-1/4" long...........	175	350	550
Servi-I-Car, No. 201, 1963	55	82	110
Stake Pick-Up, No. 308, 1963.........	50	95	150
Stake Pick-Up and Horse Trailer, No. 625, 1963, 21-3/4" long overall......................................	75	125	175
Style-Side Pick-Up, No. 354, 1963, 14" long....................................	40	60	125
Terminal Train, No. 720, fifteen suitcases, 1963, 33-5/8" long total.......................................	105	175	300
Trencher & Loboy, No. 1001, 1963, 28-1/2" long.............................	75	112	150
Wrecker, No. 518, 1963	45	75	150

1964

	C6	C8	C10
Aerial Ladder, No. 998, two auxiliary ladders, 1964	50	75	100
Allied Van Lines, No. 739, black knob on door, 1964	75	125	175
Dump Truck, No. 315, 1964, 13-1/2"	40	60	90
Dump Truck and Sandloader, No. 616, orange and yellow, 1964	75	125	175
Jeep & Horse Trailer, No. 525, two horses, 1964, 19-1/4" long total	45	68	135
Jeep Commander, No. 304, canvas top, 1964, 10-1/2" long	30	50	75
Jeep Pumper, No. 425, black steering wheel, 1964	100	150	275
Jeep Wrecker, No. 375, 1964, 11"	40	85	125
Mighty Tonka Dump Truck, No. 900, 1964	20	40	60
Military Jeep and Box Trailer, No. 384, 1964, 19-3/8" overall	50	75	150
Military Jeep Universal, No. 251, 1964	35	55	75
Military Tractor, No. 250, black seat, 1964	55	70	100
Mini-Tonka Car Carrier, No. 096, two cars, 1964, 18-1/2" long	20	40	60
Mini-Tonka Mixer, No. 077, 1964, 9"	10	20	30
Mini-Tonka Van, No. 086, 1964, 16"	17	33	50
Mobile Clam, No. 942, yellow, 1964	50	75	100
Ramp Hoist, No. 640, park green and white, very rare, 1964	300	650	900
Stake Pick-Up & Trailer, No. 504, 1964, 21-5/8" long	50	75	185
Stake Truck, No. 404, red, 1964	70	120	170
Troop Carrier, No. 380, 1964, 14"	70	100	150

Tootsietoy

Tootsietoy is one of the best-known names in the world of toy collecting, and for good reason.

The toys, products of a Chicago concern that now has a century of manufacturing behind it, have long appealed to parents because of their cheap price, and to kids because of their high play value. The Tootsietoy line through the years has included toy cars, trucks, trains, dollhouse furniture, airplanes, and toy soldiers. During the company's heyday, roughly from the 1930s-1960s, a person would have had to search long and hard to find a child with no knowledge of the trademark.

Dowst and Company stated in 1876 in the publishing trade, and moved into manufacturing after the 1893 Columbian World Exposition in Chicago, where the new die-cast technology was introduced to the public. By then, named Dowst Brothers, the company released its first die-cast-body, free-axle toy car in 1911, the generic Limousine. The first specific-model car, the Model T Ford touring car, followed in 1914. The name Tootsietoy was adopted in the early 1920s and was registered in 1924 as the company's trademark.

Theodore Dowst, who joined the firm in 1906, is generally seen as the guiding force behind the growth of toy production at Dowst Brothers. He remained with the company even after its purchase by Nathan Shure in 1926, until 1945. for most collectors, the toys of the Ted Dowst period are the most noteworthy.

High points in the world of Tootsietoy collecting include the 1933 graham series, notable for its use of three-piece construction, with separately die-cast bodies, chassis, and radiator grilles, and the 1935 LaSalles, which used four-piece construction, adding a casting for the rear bumpers. Collectors also avidly seek the 1932-1933 Funnies series cars, which featured such comic figures as Andy Gump, Uncle Walt, and Moon Mullins.

Interest seems to be growing in the various advertising toys Tootsietoy produced through the years, ranging from the 1932 Wrigley's Railroad Express truck to more recent U-Haul and Coast-To-Coast vehicles. Collector demand for postwar toys remains stable at a fairly low level; and it may not grow stronger at any time soon, given the heavy contemporary interest in detailed scale models as opposed to made-for-play toys. On the other hand, interest in the post-Vietnam toys is inching upward, reflecting the maturing of the later Baby Boomers.

Contributors: Mark Rich, P.O. Box 971, Stevens Point, WI 54481. Rich is a toy collector and writer. A columnist for *Toy Shop* and *Toy Cars & Models*, he is also the author of 100 Greatest Baby Boomer Toys (Krause Publications). John Gibson, 9713 Pleasant Gate Lane Potomac, MD 20854. 11th Edition pricing contributor Mark Rich, P.O. Box 971, Stevens Point, WI 54481. Email: mark.rich@sff.net

Miniature Ships

	C6	C8	C10
Aero Carrier, No. 1620	4	6	8
Aircraft Carrier, No. 1036, 6" long	14	21	28
Battleship, No. 4519	8	12	16
Battleship, No. 1638	4	6	8
Battleship, No. 0196	4	6	8
Cruiser, No. 1612	3	4	6
Cruiser, No. 1035, 5-1/2" long	15	20	25
Destroyer, No. 1619	3	4	6
Destroyer, No. 0127, 4" long	9	12	15
Destroyer, No. 1613	3	4	6
Fleet, No. 1405, nine-piece carded battleship assortment: USS Idaho, USS Indiana, USS Tennessee, USS Texas, USS New Mexico, USS Maryland, USS Arizona, USS New York, USS Pennsylvania, 1941	50	75	100
Freighter, No. 1038, 5-1/2" long	15	20	25
Naval Defense, No. 1408, fourteen-piece carded assortment, 1941	70	105	140

Miniature Ships (Continued)

	C6	C8	C10
Sea Champions, No. 1811, five-piece carded set contains two No. 1638 battleships, one No. 1618 submarine, one No. 1619 destroyer, and one No. 1620 aero carrier, 1946	30	45	60
Speedboat, No. 4539....................	2	3	4
Submarine, No. 1614, smaller	2	3	4
Submarine, No. 1618....................	3	4	6
Submarine, No. 0128, 4" long	9	12	15
Tanker, No. 1039, 5-1/2" long........	15	20	25
Tender, No. 0129, 4" long	10	15	20
Transport, No. 1037, 6" long	15	20	25
Tugboat, No. 4538.........................	2	3	4
Yacht, No. 0130, 4" long	18	24	30

Postwar

	C6	C8	C10
1907 Stanley Steamer Runabout	8	12	18
1912 Ford Model T Touring Car.....	8	12	18
1919 Stutz Bearcat, 1919................	8	12	18
1921 Mack Dump Truck	10	15	25
1929 Ford Model A Coupe	8	12	18
'31 Ford B Hot Rod, 1961, 3" long .	8	12	20
'37 Inernational Wagon, woodie sides, orange, green or red, black tires, 3" long	15	30	45
'38 Buick Y Experimental Convert-ible, 4" long..............................	20	30	40
'40 Ford Special Deluxe Convert-ible, 1960, 6" long......................	20	30	40
'40 Ford V-8 Hot Rod, 1960, 6" long...	15	22	30
'41 Buick Special, fastback hardtop, two-door, 4" long	12	23	35
'41 Chrysler Windsor Convertible, 4" long.....................................	20	30	40
'41 International Army Ambulance, 4" long.....................................	24	34	50
'41 International K1 Panel Truck, 4" long.....................................	22	32	45
'41 White Army Half Track, 4" long...	10	16	25
'42 Chrysler Thunderbolt Rocket Roadster, 6" long.........................	13	26	40
'46 International K11 Oil Tanker, Standard, 6" long........................	25	35	55
'46 International K11 Oil Tanker, Sinclair, 6" long..........................	12	23	35
'46 International K11 Oil Tanker, Texaco, 6" long	25	40	65
'46 International K11 Oil Tanker, Shell, 6" long.............................	25	40	65

Postwar (Continued)

	C6	C8	C10
'47 Buick Estate Sagon, woodie sides, painted features, 6" long....	25	50	75
'47 Chevrolet Fleetmaster Coupe, 4" long.....................................	13	19	25
'47 Diamond T Stakeside Truck, 6" long..	17	33	50
'47 Futuristic Pickup, 4" long.........	22	32	45
'47 GMC 3751 Greyhound Diesel Bus, blue and silver, 6" long	15	30	45
'47 Kaiser Sedan, 6" long...............	28	37	50
'47 Mack L-Line Dump Truck, 6" long..	14	25	35
'47 Mack L-Line Fire Pumper, 6" long..	35	55	70
'47 Mack L-Line Stake Truck, 6" long..	22	32	45
'47 Mack L-Line Wrecker, 6" long .	20	30	40
'47 Offenhauser Race Car, 4" long .	13	19	25
'47 Offenhauser Race Car, on trailer, 4" long	15	22	30
'47 Studebaker Champion Coupe, rare, 3" long.............................	25	35	55
'48 Buick Super Estate Wagon, 6" long..	27	42	65
'48 Cadillac 60 Special Four-door Sedan, 6" long	18	26	35
'48 Diamond T Bottle Truck, open storage shelves in rear, 6" long ...	25	50	75
'48 Willys Jeepster, 3" long	10	15	20
'49 American La France Pumper, 3" long..	10	15	25
'49 Buick Roadmaster Four-door Sedan, 6" long	22	34	45
'49 Chevrolet Panel Truck, 4" long.	8	17	25
'49 Ford Custom Convertible, 3" long...	10	15	25
'49 Ford Custom Four-door Sedan, 3" long	10	15	25
'49 Ford F1 Pickup, 3" long	10	15	25
'49 Ford F6 Oil Tanker, Texaco, 6" long..	25	35	55
'49 Ford F6 Oil Tanker, 4" long......	13	19	25
'49 Ford F6 Oil Tanker, Shell, 6" long..	25	35	55
'49 Ford F6 Oil Tanker, Sinclair, 6" long..	25	35	55
'49 Ford F6 Oil Tanker, Standard, 6" long.......................................	25	35	55
'49 Ford F6 Stake Truck, 4" long....	15	22	30
'49 Indianapolis No. 3 Race Car, 3" long..	10	15	25

Tonka Steel Carrier, No. 0145, 1954, $380.

Tonka Minute Maid Delivery Van, No. 725, 1954, $950.

Tonka Pickup Truck, No. 880, 1956, $650.

Tonka Hi-Way Dump Truck, No. 980, 1956, $400.

Tonka Suburban Pumper, No. 046, 1958, $450. Photo courtesy Harvey K. Rainess

Tonka Pickup and Trailer, No. 028, 1960, $300.

PHOTOS NEEDED

We are always looking for good quality toy images for our archives. Photo quality is our highest consideration and any donated images must be in 35mm print or slide form.

If you can donate photos of toys not pictured here, please contact us at the following address:

O'Brien's Collecting Toys
Krause Publications
700 E. State St.
IOLA, WI 54990
(715) 445-4612
obrienk@krause.com

Postwar (Continued)	C6	C8	C10
'49 Mercury Fire Chief Sedan, 4" long	22	32	45
'49 Mercury Four-door Sedan, 4" long	15	24	35
'49 Oldsmobile 88 Convertible, 4" long	20	30	40
'49 Twin Coach Bus, 3" long	12	21	30
'50 Chevrolet Army Ambulance, 4" long	15	24	35
'50 Chevrolet Deluxe Panel Truck, 3" long	10	15	25
'50 Chevrolet Fleetline Deluxe Two-door Sedan, 3" long	10	15	25
'50 Chrysler Windsor Convertible, 6" long	70	95	125
'50 Civilian Jeep, 3" long	5	7	14
'50 Dodge Pickup, 4" long	15	22	30
'50 Jeep CJ3 Army, 4" long	9	15	22
'50 Plymouth Special Deluxe Four-door Sedan, 3" long	10	15	25
'50 Pontiac Cheftain Deluxe Coupe Sedan, 4" long	20	30	40
'50 Pontiac Fire Chief Chieftain Sedan, 4" long	22	32	45
'51 Buick Le Sabre Experimental Roadster, 6" long	25	38	55
'52 Ford Mainline Four-door Sedan, 3" long	12	21	32
'52 Lincoln Capri Two-door Hard-top, 6" long	28	37	50
'52 Mercury Custom Four-door Sedan, 4" long	15	22	30
'53 Chrysler New Yorker Four-door Sedan, 6" long	18	28	45
'54 Buick Century Estate Wagon, 6" long	20	34	45
'54 Buick Special Experimental Coupe, 6" long	23	38	50
'54 Cadillac 62 Four-door Sedan, 6" long	20	30	40
'54 Ford Ranch Wagon, 4" long	15	24	35
'54 Ford Ranch Wagon, 3" long	8	12	20
'54 Jaguar XK120 Roadster, 3" long	8	12	20
'54 MG Roadster, 3" long	8	12	20
'54 MG Roadster, 6" long	10	20	30
'54 Nash Metropolitan Convert-ible, 3" long	32	50	70
'54 Volkswagen 113, 6" long	10	20	30
'54-55 Chevrolet Corvette Road-ster, 4" long	15	22	30

Postwar (Continued)	C6	C8	C10
'55 Chevrolet Bel Air Four-door Sedan, 3" long	8	12	20
'55 Ford C600 Oil Tanker, 3" long	8	12	20
'55 Ford Customline V-8 Two-door Sedan, 3" long	8	12	20
'55 Ford Thunderbird Coupe, 3" long	7	11	18
'55 Ford Thunderbird Coupe, 4" long	20	30	40
'55 Mack B-Line Cement Mixer, axle-driven drum, 6" long	30	40	55
'55 Mack B-Line Cement Mixer, 6" long	22	32	45
'55 Mack B-Line Stake Truck, w/"Tootsietoy" tin cover, 1958, 6" long	50	75	100
'55 Oldsmobile 98 Holiday Two-door Hardtop, 4" long	15	24	35
'56 Austin-Healey 100-5 Roadster, 6" long	20	30	40
'56 Caterpillar Bulldozer, 6" long	23	38	50
'56 Caterpillar Road Scraper, 6" long	18	26	35
'56 Chevrolet Cameo Pickup, 4" long	13	19	25
'56 Dodge D100 Panel Truck, 6" long	18	35	55
'56 Ferrari Racer, 6" long	18	28	45
'56 Jaguar XK140 Coupe, 6" long	8	17	25
'56 Lancia Racer, 6" long	18	27	45
'56 Mercedes 190SL Coupe, 6" long	10	20	30
'56 Packard Patrician Four-door Sedan, 6" long	12	23	35
'56 Porsche Spyder Roadster, 6" long	10	20	30
'56 Triumph TR3 Roadster, 3" long	4	8	12
'57 Ford F100 Styleside Pickup, 3" long	5	7	14
'57 Ford Fairlane 500 Convertible, 3" long	6	12	18
'57 GMC Greyhound Scenicruiser Bus, 6" long	10	20	30
'57 Jaguar Type D, 3" long	8	12	20
'57 Plymouth Belvedere Two-door Hardtop, 3" long	8	12	20
'59 Ford Country Sedan Station Wagon, 6" long	10	20	30
'59 Oldsmobile Dynamic 88 Con-vertible, 6" long	14	25	35
'59 Pontiac Star Chief Four-door Sedan, 4" long	10	16	25

Postwar (Continued)	C6	C8	C10
'60 Chevrolet El Camino Pickup, 6" long	12	22	30
'60 Chevrolet El Camino Pickup with Camper and Boat, 6" long	17	32	50
'60 Chrysler Windsor Convertible, 4" long	5	11	16
'60 Ford Country Sedan Station Wagon, 3" long	8	12	20
'60 Ford Falcon Two-door Sedan, 3" long	5	8	15
'60 International Metro Van, rare, 6" long	100	125	150
'60 Jeep CJ5, 6" long	9	18	25
'60 Jeep CJ5 with Snow Plow, 6" long	25	35	55
'60 Rambler Super Cross-Country Wagon, 4" long	15	24	35
'60 Studebaker Lark Custom Convertible, 3" long	9	16	22
'60 Volkswagen Bug, 3" long	7	11	18
'62 Ford C600 Oil Tanker Truck, 6" long	20	30	40
'62 Ford Country Sedan Station Wagon, 6" long	8	18	25
'62 Ford Econoline Pickup, 6" long	8	17	25
'69 Ford LTD Two-door Hardtop, last of the larger-size die-cast Tootsietoys, 4" long	13	19	25
American La France Aerial Ladder Truck	5	8	12
American La France Ladder Truck	4	6	10
Army Cannon, four-wheel, 4" long	10	15	25
Army Cannon, six-wheel, 4" long	12	21	30
Auto Transport, plastic trailer, scaled to match 6" long series	24	32	45
Auto Transport, 1960, scaled to match 6" long series	30	42	65
Auto Transport, metal trailer, 1962, scaled to match 6" long series	42	65	85
Auto Transport, 1965, scaled to match 6" long series	50	75	125
Auto Transport Semi-Cab and Trailer	12	17	25
Auto Transporter, scaled to match 6" long series	30	42	55
Boat Transport, scaled to match 6" long series	24	32	45
Boat Transport, scaled to match 6" long series	28	40	60
Cadillac	8	15	20
Cement Truck	6	8	12

Postwar (Continued)	C6	C8	C10
Coast to Coast Shipping Semi-cab and Van	12	17	25
Dump Truck	13	26	40
Dump Truck	6	8	12
Ford Sunliner Convertible with Boat Trailer	10	18	30
Ford Sunliner Convertible with Midget RacerTrailer	12	22	35
Ford Wrecker Truck	10	15	22
Heavy Duty Hydraulic Crane	8	12	17
Hood and Ladder, 1954, scaled to match 6" long series	35	55	75
Hook and Ladder, scaled to match 6" long series	50	75	125
Hook and Ladder, scaled to match 6" long series	28	40	60
Log Hauler, scaled to match 6" long series	45	70	100
Log Hauler, scaled to match 6" long series	35	55	75
Log Hauler, scaled to match 6" long series	28	40	60
Logging Semi-cab and Trailer	6	8	12
Machinery Hauler, scaled to match 6" long series	30	42	55
Machinery Hauler, scaled to match 6" long series	45	70	100
Machinery Hauler, scaled to match 6" long series	28	40	60
Machinery Hauler, scaled to match 6" long series	25	35	55
Machinery Hauler, scaled to match 6" long series	35	55	75
Metro Van, Sunnydale Milk	32	50	70
Metro Van, Railway Express	18	35	55
Metro Van, US Mail	18	35	55
Mobil Semi-cab and Tanker	10	15	20
Oil Tanker, scaled to match 6" long series	32	50	70
Oil Tanker, Mobil, scaled to match 6" long series	28	40	60
Oil Tanker, Tootsietoy Line, scaled to match 6" long series	40	60	80
Oil Tanker, scaled to match 6" long series	45	70	100
Oil Tanker, Tootsietoy Line, scaled to match 6" long series	50	75	125
Pipe Truck, scaled to match 6" long series	28	40	60
Pipe Truck, scaled to match 6" long series	35	55	75

Tonka Cement Mixer, No. 620, 1962, $300.

Tonka Pickup, No. 302, 1962, $250.

Tonka Sanitary Truck, No. 140, 1960, this truck was retired in early 1961 and is considered rare, $900. Photo courtesy Patrick O'Neil

Tonka Trencher and Loboy, No. 1001, 1963, $150.

Postwar (Continued)	C6	C8	C10
Rambler Station Wagon with U-Haul Trailer	10	18	30
Retaurant Trailer, 6"	32	50	70
Shell, No. 1009, black tire versions.	25	50	75
Shipping Semi-cab and Van	6	8	12
Shipping Van, scaled to match 6" long series	28	40	60
Shipping Van, Tootsietoy Trucking, scaled to match 6" long series	27	37	50
Shipping Van, Dean Van Lines, plastic trailer, scaled to match 6" long series	40	60	80
Shipping Van, Tootsietoy Coast to Coast, scaled to match 6" long series	37	57	80
Shipping Van, Tootsietoy Line, scaled to match 6" long series	32	50	75
Shuttle Truck, 1967	2	3	4
Sinclair, No. 1007, black tire versions	25	50	75
Stake Truck, closed sides, scaled to match 6" long series	28	40	60
Stake Truck, closed sides, scaled to match 6" long series	35	55	75

Postwar (Continued)	C6	C8	C10
Stake Truck, open sides, scaled to match 6" long series	50	70	115
Standard, No. 1006, black tire versions	25	50	75
Texaco, No. 1008, black tire versions	25	50	75
Township School Bus	13	26	40
U-Haul Trailer, 3" long	4	6	8
U-Haul Trailer, 4" long	5	10	15
Utility Truck, scaled to match 6" long series	27	37	50
Utility Truck, scaled to match 6" long series	25	35	55

Prewar	C6	C8	C10
'34 Convertible Coupe, No. 0114, wood hubs	40	60	80
'34 Convertible Sedan, No. 0115, wood hubs	40	60	80
'34 Coupe, No. 0112, wood hubs	33	49	65
'34 Sedan, No. 0111, wood hubs	30	45	60
'34 Wrecker, No. 0113, wood hubs.	38	56	75
'35 Convertible Coupe, No. 0114, white rubber tires	30	45	60

Prewar (Continued)	C6	C8	C10
'35 Convertible Sedan, No. 0115, white rubber tires	30	45	60
'35 Coupe, No. 0112, white rubber tires	18	26	35
'35 Roadster, No. 0116	23	34	45
'35 Roadster Fire Chief Car, No. 0117	50	75	100
'35 Sedan, No. 0111, white rubber tires	15	23	30
'35 Wrecker, No. 0113, white rubber tires	33	49	65
'38 Ford Paneled Station Wagon, No. 0239, white rubber tires, 3" long	20	40	60
A&P Trailer Truck, No. 4670, 1929	100	150	200
American Railway Express Trailer Truck, No. 4670, 1929	115	170	225
Andy Gump Roadster, No. 5101, mechanical	225	340	450
Andy Gump Roadster, No. 5101	175	265	350
Anti-Aircraft Gun Army Truck, No. 4643, 1931	25	38	50
Armored Car, No. 1667	6	9	12
Armored Car, No. 4635, 1938, 4" long	33	50	65
Army Ambulance, No. 0809	75	110	150
Army Long-Range Cannon, No. 4642, 1931	13	18	25
Army Supply Truck, No. 4634, 1939, 4" long	33	50	65
Army Tank, No. 1666	4	6	8
Auburn Torpedo Roadster, No. 1016	15	30	45
Auto Transport, No. 0198, one-piece cab, three '35 Fords	125	200	275
Auto Transport, trailer holds three 1940s Buicks in tilted position, 1941	275	415	550
Auto Transport, No. 0198, two-piece cab, three '35 Fords	150	250	350
Auto Transport Four-car Hauler, No. 0190, w/101-103 Buicks and 109 Ford, 1933	115	170	225
Auto Transport Three-car Hauler, No. 0190, w/101-103 Buicks, 1931	105	140	175
Bakery, No. 4631	50	80	105
Bild-A-Car Coupe, four wheels	65	95	130
Bild-A-Car Roadster, four wheels	85	130	175
Bild-A-Car Sedan, four wheels	65	95	130
Bluebird Dayton Racer, No. 0110, 1932	25	40	55

Prewar (Continued)	C6	C8	C10
Bluebird Dayton Record Car, No. 4666, 1932, 4" long	30	45	55
Boattail Roadster, No. 0233, 3" long	15	20	30
Boxed Set, No. 0510, (eight-piece)	75	100	150
Boxed Set, No. 0510, (ten-piece)	90	130	175
Boxed Set, No. 0610, (twelve-piece, 1941?)	100	150	200
Briggs-Lincoln prototype, No. 0716, "Doodlebug"	75	95	125
Buick Brougham, No. 6003	28	41	55
Buick Coupe, No. 6002	28	41	55
Buick Coupe, No. 4636, 1924	23	34	45
Buick Marquette Coupe, No. 0101/4656, 1931	10	15	20
Buick Marquette Roadster, No. 0102, 1932?	13	19	25
Buick Marquette Sedan, No. 0103/4657, 1931	10	15	20
Buick Roadmaster Touring Coupe, No. 0232, 3" long	15	20	30
Buick Roadster, No. 6001	30	45	60
Buick Screenside Delivery Truck, No. 6006	35	53	70
Buick Sedan, No. 6004	28	41	55
Buick Touring Car, No. 6005	50	75	100
Buick Touring Car, No. 4641, 1925	28	42	55
Bus, No. 1628	6	9	12
Cadillac Brougham, No. 6103	40	60	80
Cadillac coupe, No. 6102	40	60	80
Cadillac Roadster, No. 6101	40	60	80
Cadillac Screenside Delivery Truck, No. 6106	48	71	95
Cadillac Sedan, No. 6104	40	60	80
Cadillac Touring Car, No. 6105	60	90	120
Caterpillar Tractor, No. 0108, w/tread, 1932	23	34	45
Chevrolet Brougham, No. 6203	33	50	65
Chevrolet Coupe, No. 6202	33	50	65
Chevrolet Roadster, No. 6201	33	50	65
Chevrolet Screenside Delivery Truck, No. 6206	35	53	70
Chevrolet Sedan, No. 6204	33	50	65
Chevrolet Touring Car, No. 6205	55	83	110
Chevy Coupe, No. 0231, 3" long	15	20	30
City Fuel Company Coal Truck, No. 0804, four-wheel, 1937	60	95	130
City Fuel Company Coal Truck, No. 0804, ten-wheel, 1933	75	115	150
Coal Truck, No. 4639, 1925, revised 1928	23	34	45

Tonka Troop Carrier in box, No. 380, 1964, $150.

Vindex Motorcycle with Removable Cop, 9", $3500. Photo courtesy Kent M. Comstock

Vindex Power Shovel "P&H," $8000.

Prewar (Continued)	C6	C8	C10
Commercial Tire & Supply Co. Van	112	168	225
Commerical Tire & Supply Co. Van	75	110	150
Contractor Set, No. 0191, w/Mack AC hauling three spoke-wheeled tipper trailers, 1933	105	140	175
Convertible Coupe, No. 0614, six wheels	80	120	160
Convertible Coupe, No. 0714	125	205	265
Convertible Coupe, No. 0514, five wheels	120	160	200
Convertible Sedan, No. 0515, five wheels	80	120	160
Convertible Sedan, No. 0615, six wheels	80	120	160
Convertible Sedan, No. 0715	125	205	265
Coupe, No. 0612, six wheels	72	110	145
Coupe, No. 0712	115	180	240
Coupe, No. 0512, five wheels	70	110	145
Delivery Motorcycle, No. 0807, (1933 adaped from 5103)	85	125	175
Delivery Van, No. 1635	6	9	12
DeSoto Airflow Sedan, No. 1631	5	7	10
DeSoto Airflow Sedan, No. 0118, 1935, 3" long	27	40	55

Prewar (Continued)	C6	C8	C10
Domaco Tank Semi-Trailer, No. 0802, one-piece cab, 1933	60	90	120
Domaco Tank Semi-Trailer, No. 0802, two-piece cab	90	120	150
Express Stake Semi-Trailer, No. 0801, one-piece cab, 1933	55	80	105
Express Stake Semi-Trailer, No. 0801, two-piece cab	80	105	135
Fageol Safety Coach, No. 4651, 1927	30	45	65
Fire Engine, No. 1634	7	10	14
Florist, No. 4635, rarest in series	95	175	225
Ford Model A Coupe, No. 4655, 1928	20	30	40
Ford Model A Delivery Van, "US Mail," sold in sets only, 1931	38	56	75
Ford Model A Sedan, No. 4665, 1929	20	30	40
Ford Model T Pickup, No. 4610, 1916	35	50	70
Ford Model T Tourer, No. 4570, 1914	35	50	65
Ford Pickup Truck, No. 0121, 1936, 3" long	18	26	35

Prewar (Continued)	C6	C8	C10
Ford Stake Truck, No. 0109, 1932 ..	20	30	40
GMC Box Truck, No. 0234, 3" long	15	20	30
Greyhound Bus, No. 1045, w/tin bottom	20	40	60
Grocery, No. 4630	35	55	85
High Wing Monoplane, No. 0107, w/prop, tin wings, 1932..............	35	55	70
Hook & Ladder Fire Engine, No. 4652, 1927.....................................	39	52	75
Hook and Ladder, No. 1040	35	50	70
Hook and Ladder Fire engine, No. 0236, 3" long	15	30	45
Hose Car, No. 1041	35	55	75
Hose Wagon Fire Engine, No. 0238, 3" long	20	30	40
Huber Star Farm Tractor, No. 4654, 1927	40	65	95
Insurance Patrol, No. 1042, w/ladder and rear fireman	35	55	75
Insurance Patrol, No. 1042, open end..	30	45	60
Insurance Patrol Fire Engine, No. 0237, 3" long	15	25	35
Interchangeable Truck Set, No. 0170, 1925-31	50	75	125
Kayo Ice Wagon, No. 5105, mechanical.................................	240	320	400
Kayo Ice Wagon, No. 5105	150	225	300
LaSalle Sedan, No. 0230, 3" long ...	15	20	30
Laundry, No. 4633...........................	45	65	95
Lewis's, No. 0123...........................	195	260	325
Limousine, No. 4528, 1911	24	32	40
Long Distance Hauling, No. 0803, Semi-Trailer, 1933	85	130	175
Low Wing Monoplane, No. 0106, w/prop, tin wings, 1932..............	35	55	70
Mack Insurance Patrol Fire truck, No. 0104/4658, 1931...................	25	35	45
Mack Tank Truck, No. 0105, 1932 .	25	40	55
Market, No. 4632............................	35	60	75
McLeans, No. 0123	280	380	475
Milk, No. 4634, most common in series..	25	40	55
Miller & Rhoads, No. 0123	300	400	500
Moon Mullins Police Wagon, No. 5104, mechanical......................	225	340	450
Moon Mullins Police Wagon, No. 5104..	175	265	350
No-Name Brougham, No. 6-03	55	83	110
No-Name Coupe, No. 6-02.............	55	83	110
No-Name Roadster, No. 6-01	55	83	110

Prewar (Continued)	C6	C8	C10
No-Name Screenside Delivery Truck, No. 6-06..........................	42	83	125
No-Name Sedan, No. 6-04	55	83	110
No-Name Touring Car, No. 6-05	75	113	150
Oil Tank Truck, No. 0235, 3" long..	13	26	40
Oil Tank truck, No. 0120, 1936, 3" long..	23	34	45
Oldsmobile Brougham, No. 6303....	35	53	70
Oldsmobile Coupe, No. 6302	35	53	70
Oldsmobile Roadster, No. 6301	38	55	75
Oldsmobile Screenside Delivery Truck, No. 6306	45	68	90
Oldsmobile Sedan, No. 6304...........	35	53	70
Oldsmobile Touring Car, No. 6305.	55	83	110
Overland Bus Lines, No. 4680, 1929......................................	45	65	95
Paneled Station Wagon, No. 1046, white tires, 1940, 4" long	43	64	85
Racer, No. 1630...............................	5	7	10
Racer with Driver, No. 0023, 1927 .	35	60	80
Railway Express Co., Wrigley's Gum, No. 0810, one-piece cab, 1935..	70	105	150
Railway Express Co., Wrigley's Gum, No. 0810, two-piece cab....	75	115	165
Renault Tank with treads, No. 4647, 1931, 3" long..............................	18	36	55
Roadster, No. 0611, six wheels	120	160	200
Roadster, No. 0511, five wheels......	80	125	165
Roamer House Trailer, No. 1044, w/door and tin bottom, 1937	130	260	400
Searchlight Army Truck, No. 4644, 1931	65	95	130
Sedan, No. 0513, five wheels	70	110	145
Sedan, No. 4629, "Yellow Cab", 1923..	15	25	60
Sedan, No. 0713	115	180	240
Sedan, No. 0613, six wheels............	70	110	145
Shepards, No. 0123	285	380	475
Small Ford Sedan or Coupe 111 or 112, and Camping Trailer, No. 1043, 1937...................................	35	53	70
Smitty Motorcycle, No. 5103, mechanical	225	340	450
Smitty Motorcycle, No. 5103	175	265	350
Special Delivery, No. 0123	30	40	55
Stake Truck, No. 4638, 1925, revised 1928	23	34	45
Steamroller, No. 4648, 1931, 3" long..	65	95	125
Tank Truck, No. 4640, 1925, revised 1928	23	34	45

Prewar (Continued)

	C6	C8	C10
Tootsietoy Dairy Delivery Van, No. 0808	120	160	200
Tootsietoy Dairy Semi-Trailer, No. 0805, dual tires, 1933	70	105	140
Tootsietoy Dairy Semi-Trailer, No. 0805, single tires	60	90	120
Tootsietoy Dairy Tanker, No. 0192, one-piece cab, three trailers, 1935	75	115	150
Tootsietoy Dairy Tanker, No. 0192, two-piece cab, three trailers, 1933	120	160	200
Torpedo Coupe, No. 1017	15	30	45
Torpedo Cross-Country "Greyhound" Bus, No. 1026/1045	25	55	80
Torpedo Pickup truck, No. 1019	20	30	40
Torpedo Sedan, No. 1018	20	30	40
Torpedo Wrecker, No. 1027	23	34	45
Towncar, No. 0616, six wheels	75	110	150
Towncar, No. 0516, five wheels	88	130	175
Trans-America Bus, No. 1045, sold only in sets, 1941	90	130	175
Uncle Walt Roadster, No. 5102	175	265	350
Uncle Walt Roadster, No. 5102, mechanical	225	340	450
Uncle Willie Rowboat, No. 5106	135	210	275
Uncle Willie Rowboat, No. 5106, mechanical	240	320	400
US Mail Air Mail Service, No. 4645, 1931	35	55	75
Water Tower Fire Engine, No. 4653, 1927	38	56	75
Wieboldt's, No. 0123	285	380	475
Wrecker, No. 6016, wind-up version	350	525	700
Wrecker, No. 0806	75	110	150
Wrecker, No. 6016	150	230	350
Wrecker, No. 1629	7	10	14
Wrigley GMC Box Truck, No. 1010, 1940, 4" long	55	80	110
Zephyr, No. 6015	165	245	325
Zephyr, No. 6015, wind-up version	240	365	485
Zephyr and Roamer House Trailer, No. 0180, wind-up	660	880	1100
Zephyr and Roamer House Trailer, No. 0180	555	740	925
Zephyr Railcar, No. 1632	7	10	14

Turner, John C.

Contributor: Bob Smith, the Village Smith, 62 West Ave., Fairport, NY 14450-2102.

Turner

	C6	C8	C10
Ahrens Fox Ladder Truck, 15" long	500	750	1080

Turner (Continued)

	C6	C8	C10
Bulldog Mack Dump Truck, red and green, 23" long	325	600	875
Crane, 22" long	300	450	600
Dump Truck, Dodge, 28" long	200	325	450
Dump Truck, friction, c. early 1930s, 15-1/2" long	625	1000	1500
Dump Truck, C-cab, 22" long	400	600	800
Dump Truck, 26" long	415	620	800
Fire Engine Pumper, 15" long	750	1400	1800
Hook and Ladder, c. 1930s, 15" long	225	338	450
Lincoln Sedan, 26" long	2000	3500	5000
Packard (?) Roadster, friction, 26" long	900	1500	2200
Packard Roadster, 1920s, 16-1/2" long	600	950	1300
Speedster, c. late 1920s, early 1930s, 17" long	500	750	1000
Steam Shovel	75	125	150
Water Truck with Copper Tank	150	225	300

Vindex

Contributor (motorcycles): Kent M. Comstock, 532 Pleasant St., Ashland, OH, 44805, 419, 289, 3308, 800-443-TOYS.

Vindex

	C6	C8	C10
Coast to Coast Bus, c. 1929, 12" long	1250	1875	2500
Motorcycle with Package Truck, "Henderson PDQ Delivery," w/removable blue rider, red or green, 9" long (VM3)	1800	2500	3500
Motorcycle with Removable Cop, "Henderson," red or green, 9" long (VM1)	1800	2500	3500
Motorcycle with Sidecar, two removable cops, "Henderson," red or green, 9" long (VM2)	1200	1800	3000
P&H Power shovel, wheels in caterpillar base, handle revolves rig, 12", 17" extended	2700	4100	8000
Racer No. 2, c. 1920s, 11-1/2" long	1000	1600	2500

Wilkins Toy Company

Wilkins, of Keene, New Hampshire, was begun by James S. Wilkins as the Triumph Wringer Company. But the tiny model Wilkins produced to promote his product proved so intriguing to prospective customers and their children, that requests for them poured in. The real thing was quickly forgotten as Wilkins turned to toy making. Its toys were generally cast iron and steel. The firm was acquired in 1894 by Kingsbury, which is still in business, though now as a tool and die maker.

Wolverine Mystery Trailer, 27" long, $400. Photo courtesy Calvin L. Chaussee

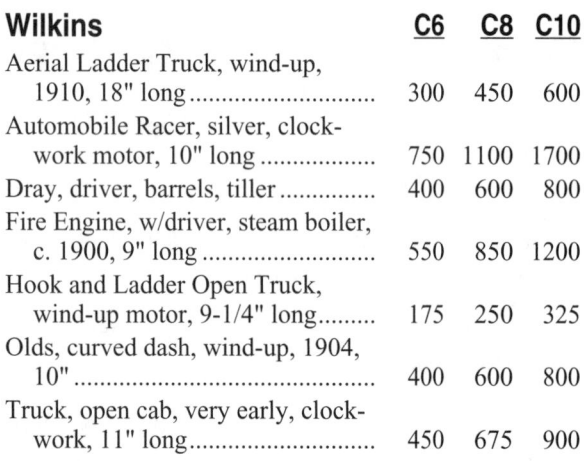

Wyandotte Bus, No. 377, 1936-40, 6-3/8" long, $115. Photo courtesy Brian Seligman

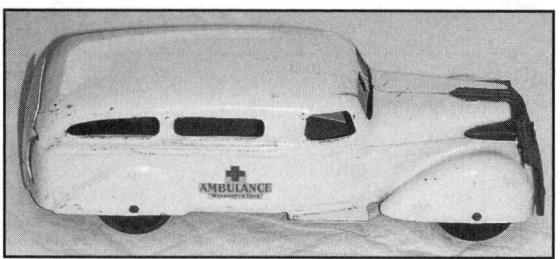

Wyandotte Ambulance, No. 340, 1936-38, 11-1/4" long, $125. Photo courtesy Brian Seligman

Wyandotte Coupe, two-door, 1933, 8-1/4" long, $135.

Wilkins

	C6	C8	C10
Aerial Ladder Truck, wind-up, 1910, 18" long	300	450	600
Automobile Racer, silver, clockwork motor, 10" long	750	1100	1700
Dray, driver, barrels, tiller	400	600	800
Fire Engine, w/driver, steam boiler, c. 1900, 9" long	550	850	1200
Hook and Ladder Open Truck, wind-up motor, 9-1/4" long	175	250	325
Olds, curved dash, wind-up, 1904, 10"	400	600	800
Truck, open cab, very early, clockwork, 11" long	450	675	900

Wolverine

Wolverine, of Pittsburgh, Pennsylvania was founded in 1903 by B.F. Bain. The company got its name from Bain's Michigan hometown. In later years, Wolverine became a subsidiary of Spang Industries. In 1970, it moved to Boonville, Arkansas. The Sandy Andy, in all its variations, was probably Wolverine's most successful and famous toy.

Wolverine	C6	C8	C10
Dump Truck, white, 12"	55	85	110
Mystery Car, press down to make car move, c. 1938, 13" long	150	225	300

Wolverine (Continued)	C6	C8	C10
Mystery Car and Trailer, press down to operate, 27" long	200	300	400
Mystery Taxi	200	300	400
Speeding Bus, driver and occupants, marked "5 Via Main St" and "19302," press down on rear to move, 14" long	100	150	200
U.S.A. Transport Army Truck	150	225	300
White Mustang Dump Truck, 14" long	75	115	150

Wyandotte

Wyandotte was formed in the fall of 1921 with toy pistols being its main product. But by 1935 the Wyandotte, Michigan, firm became known for its simple, streamlined, Art Deco steel cars and trucks with wooden wheels. During World War II, Wyandotte made clips for the M-1 rifle and after the war moved the company to Piqua, Ohio.

In an attempt to diversify, it bought Hafner Train line, but went out of business in '965. Wyandotte's heavy-gauge steel toys with bakes enamel finish also include aircraft, doll buggies, musical toys, wagons, and games.

Wyandotte	C6	C8	C10
Air Speed Coupe, No. 309, flat grille, white rubber tires, 1934-37, 6" long	70	85	110

Wyandotte Circus Truck, No. 503, 1936, 19-1/4" long, $1200. Photo courtesy Brian Seligman

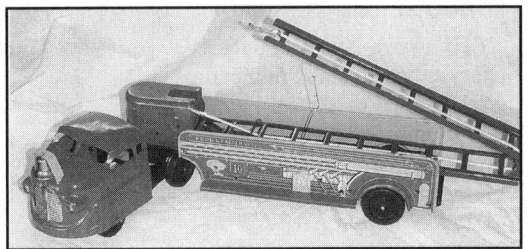

Wyandotte Fire Truck No. 1004, 1940-41, 27-1/2" long, $250. Photo courtesy Brian Seligman

Wyandotte Indy Racer, 7" long, $125. Photo courtesy Brian Seligman

Wyandotte Lumber Truck/Log Hauler, 1952, 10-1/4" long, $105. Photo courtesy Brian Seligman

Wyandotte (Continued)

	C6	C8	C10
Air Speed Coupe, No. 309, flat grille, white rubber tires, 1934-37, 6" long	70	85	110
Ambulance, long nose, black wood wheels, marked "Ambulance" stamped on side, opening rear hatch, 1939, 11-1/4" long	65	85	125
Ambulance, No. 340, long nose, black wood wheels, w/"Ambulance" and "Wyandotte Toys" decals, opening rear hatch, 1936-38, 11-1/4" long	65	85	125
Ambulance, No. 379, rooster comb, white rubber tires, four side ports, "Ambulance" stamped on top, surface mounted grille, 1938, 6-3/8" long	40	65	110
Ambulance, No. 224, flat nose, black wood wheels, side ports, inset front grille, 1939, 6-3/8" long	35	50	105
Ambulance, long nose, black rubber tires, friction, "Ambulance and Red Cross," stretcher, 1952, 6-1/2" long	70	85	105

Wyandotte (Continued)

	C6	C8	C10
Ambulance, No. 817, long nose, black rubber tires, friction motor and siren, marked "Ambulance" and "Red Cross," stretcher, opening rear doors, 1952-53, 9-1/2" long	35	50	120
Army Jeep, No. 368, wood, black wood wheels, marked "Jeep", 1942, 9" long	20	40	90
Army Truck, long nose, black rubber tires, "Army Engineer Corp. No. 42," canvas cloth top, 1941, 17-1/2" long	60	90	140
Army Truck, No. 1006, long nose, black rubber tires, "Army Engineers Corps," canvas cloth top, 1940-41, 21" long	65	95	155
Army Truck, No. 433, long nose, black rubber tires, marked "Army Supply Corp.," canvas cloth top, 1941, 11-3/4" long	45	75	125
Army Truck, No. 214, black wood wheels, marked "Army Supply," all wood construction, 1941-42, 9-1/2" long	35	55	95

Wyandotte (Continued)

	C6	C8	C10
Auto Transport, No. 130, open eye, checker board, black rubber tires, lithographed cab and trailer, w/four cars, marked "Transmobile Jr.," "Transcontinental Auto Freight Lines," and "I.C.C. 2034 / LT.WT. 6800 / CAPY 9000", 1953, 12-5/8" long	50	70	145
Auto Transport, cab over, red cab, includes four plastic cars, 1940s-50s, 9-1/2" long	30	40	85
Auto Transport, No. 455, cab over, black rubber tires, plastic cab and lithographed trailer, marked "#455" "Auto Transport," "Wt.714," "Cap.4," and "Tires.90-20", 1952, 10" long	35	50	95
Auto Transport, cab over, black rubber tires, plastic cab, marked "Wyandotte" or "Auto Transport" on the side, 1952, 10-1/4" long	50	70	145
Auto Transport, cab over, black rubber tires, lithographed cab and trailer, marked "Car A Van Lines" and "Automotive Transport", includes three 5-1/2" Cadillacs, loading ramp, 1956-57, 22-1/2" long	45	70	115
Auto Transport, No. 1104, cab over, pressed metal wheels, red and yellow lithographed cab w/red and yellow trailer and four "Cadillac" cars, ramp for upper cars and tailgate lowers for lower cars, "Auto Transport", 1952-53, 22" long	55	75	155
Auto Transport, shaded windshield, yellow wood wheels, green cab and black trailer w/four vehicles, electric lights, 1932, 21-5/8" long	85	175	300
Auto Transport, No. 482, cab over, black rubber tires, "Haul A Car," includes four plastic cars, 1950s, 8-3/4" long	20	45	85
Baggage Truck, long nose, black rubber tires, marked "Baggage," w/freight cart, 1941, 11-3/4" long	45	75	115
Baggage Truck, shark nose, black metal wheels, marked "Baggage", 1953, 11-1/2" long	40	70	135

Wyandotte (Continued)

	C6	C8	C10
Bank Truck (also called Bus Bank), No. 375, rooster comb, black wood wheels, green, red and orange, four portholes on each side, 1936-40, 6-3/8" long	40	65	115
Bread Truck, panel van, white plastic wheels, marked "Silvercup Bread," friction, 1952, 4-7/8" long	45	75	105
Bus, No. 377, rooster comb, black wood wheels or white rubber tires, green, red, orange and yellow, eight windows on each side and rear panel w/two windows and embossed spare tire, sealed chassis, 1936-40, 6-3/8" long	40	70	115
Bus, No. 233, cab over, black wood wheels, blue, same window and rear panel design as No. 377, but different nose w/inset grille design, open chassis, 1939, 6-3/8" long	40	70	115
Cadillac, plastic wheels, many colors, used on auto transports, 1952-54, 5-5/8" long	30	50	95
Cadillac, No. 3100, "true scale," black rubber tires w/white hubs, plastic, friction motor, many colors, 1955, 8-3/4" long	95	120	150
Cadillac, plastic wheels, many colors, 1954, 3" long	30	50	95
Cement Mixer, cab over, black rubber tires, "Cement Mixer / Sell / Rent," may have had attached mixer, 1940-50, 5" long	20	40	65
Cement Truck, No. 239, cab over, black rubber tires, attached mixer, 1952, 8-1/2" long	20	40	55
Circus Truck, long nose, two-piece, red cab and lithographed double trailers w/swing down rear ramps, reads "Greatest Show On Earth," cardboard animals on metal stands, w/long nose-style cab, scarce, 1941, 19-1/4" long	250	850	1300
Circus Truck, No. 503, rooster comb, embossed wood wheels, two-piece, red cab and lithographed double trailers w/swing down rear ramps, reads "Greatest Show On Earth," cardboard animals on metal stands, 1936, 19-1/4" long	200	750	1200

Wyandotte (Continued)

	C6	C8	C10
Coal Truck, No. 444, shark nose, yellow metal wheels, front scoop, lithographed dump bed w/tailgate, marked "COAL," "FUEL and SUPPLY CO.," and "444", 1949, 13" long	50	130	225
Contractor Truck, No. 434C, long nose, black wood wheels, marked "Contractor Truck", 1941, 11-1/4" long	45	70	105
Convertible, No. 650 (No. 651 w/wind-up motor), sportman's covertible, black rubber tires, retractable top, woody look sides, license plate "WY650", 1947-48, 12" long	165	190	235
Convertible, No. 102, white rubber tires w/white wood wheels, also part of the garage set (1938-40), 1936-40, 4-3/8" long	10	45	65
Cord and Trailer Set, No. 363, black wood wheels, rear door opens in trailer, 1938-39, 23-1/2" long	100	300	575
Cord Convertible, No. 384, black rubber tires, "Fire Dept.," brass bell, wind-up motor w/attached key, 1939, 17-3/8" long	125	325	575
Cord Convertible, No. 601, "Fire Dept.," brass bell, Zephyr motor, 1938-39, 17-1/4" long	100	300	525
Cord Convertible, marked "Fire Dept.," Zephyr motor, hood mounted brass bell, 1938, 13-3/8" long	125	300	425
Coupe, two-door, shaded windshield, white rubber tires, electric lights, 1933, 8-1/4" long	55	100	135
Coupe, two-door, shaded windshield, yellow wood wheels, rumble seat, 1932, 8-1/4" long	55	95	135
Coupe, two-door, shaded windshield, white rubber tires w/red hubs, no light, 1933, 8-1/4" long.	60	115	175
Coupe, two-door, No. 103, long nose, white rubber tires or white wood wheels, car also came w/two car garage set, 1936-40, 4-3/8" long	10	45	75
Dairy/Milk Truck, No. 805, panel van, black rubber tires, "Sunshine Dairy," friction, 1952, 4-7/8" long	20	35	95

Wyandotte (Continued)

	C6	C8	C10
Dairy/Milk Truck, No. 4002, red plastic wheels, w/two crates of milk, marked "Sunshine Dairy," "Milk," and "Cream," box reads "Early Bird Milk Wagon and Horse", 1952, 7-1/2" long	50	80	115
Delivery Truck, No. 345, long nose, black wood wheels, opening rear door, green, red, grey and yellow, "City Delivery" stamped on side, 1938-39, 11-3/8" long	60	75	120
Delivery Truck, No. 353, panel van, black rubber tires, "Toy Town Delivery" and "Super Service," lithographed grille and dashboard, opening side and rear doors, 1952, 11-1/2" long	50	75	110
Delivery Van, No. 120, open eye, black rubber tires, lithographed cab and body, cab w/rear van body, "Express Delivery Service," "Local," "National," and "I.C.C. 120/Cap. 4500/WT. 3250", 1954, 9-7/8" long	35	60	95
Delivery Van, sleepy eye, black rubber tires, 1949, 12" long	30	55	85
Diaper Delivery Truck, No. 805, panel van, black rubber tires, marked "Dy-Dee Wash," and "Stork," friction, 1952, 4-7/8" long	20	35	95
Dump Truck, No. 222, cab over, black plastic wheels, 1939-41, 6" long	20	35	70
Dump Truck, No. E318, rooster comb, black wood wheels, Easter Style, pink cab and purple dump body w/chicken stamped on sides, 1937-38, 6" long	40	60	105
Dump Truck, shaded windshield, white rubber tires w/red hubs, electric lights, 1933-34, 15" long	55	95	165
Dump Truck, No. 343E, long nose, black wood wheels, w/5-1/4", wheelbarrow, 1938-41, 11-1/4" long	60	80	110
Dump Truck, shaded windshield, embossed wood wheels, 1933, 7" long	50	70	100
Dump Truck, No. 318, long nose, black wood wheels, 1938, 6" long	35	55	85

Wyandotte (Continued)

	C6	C8	C10
Dump Truck, No. 318, rooster comb, white rubber tires, red, green and orange, 1934-37, 6" long	40	65	70
Dump Truck, No. 159, cab over, black rubber tires, 1952, 5-1/2" long	20	35	65
Dump Truck, cab over, black rubber tires, late 1940s-50s, 5" long	25	45	65
Dump Truck, No. 315, shaded windshield, white rubber tires, w/grille, green or red, 1934-36, 5-1/4" long	40	65	85
Dump Truck, No. 315, shaded windshield, white rubber tires, without grille, green or red, 1934-36, 4-7/8" long	40	65	85
Dump Truck, shaded windshield, yellow wood wheels, 1932, 5-5/8" long	20	35	75
Dump Truck, No. 352, cab over, yellow metal wheels, tailgate, 1952, 11" long	50	65	105
Earth Mover, black rubber tires, orange, "Heavy Duty," operable rear dump, front scoop, plastic engine and smoke stack, "Highway Engineers", 1952-55, 20-1/2" long	55	85	105
Electric Conveyor, No. 402, black rubber tires, 1955, 41-1/2" long	40	65	190
Fire Truck, No. 157, cab over, black rubber tires, 1952, 5-1/2" long	65	80	110
Fire Truck, No. 1021, cab over, black rubber tires, lithographed trailer, toolbox w/tools, "Hook and Ladder" and "1", 1955-56, 24" long	60	110	225
Fire Truck, No. 1004, cab over, six black wood wheels, "Hook and Ladder No. 10," 29" expanding ladder, hood bell, 1940-41, 27-1/2" long	65	125	250
Fire Truck, No. 156, long nose, black rubber tires, friction, siren and ladder, 1952, 7-1/2" long	30	45	60
Fire Truck, No. 150, square cab, white plastic wheels, red w/white ladders, "W" on wheels, 1952, 6-1/4" long	20	35	70
Fire Truck, No. 308R, open cab, white rubber tires, red body w/three green ladders, 1932, 6" long	65	80	110

Wyandotte (Continued)

	C6	C8	C10
Fire Truck, No. 818, long nose, black rubber tires, friction motor and siren, marked "Fire Dept. Rescue Squad," stretcher, opening rear doors, 0952-53, 9-1/2" long	35	50	105
Garage Set, No. 4000, plastic single door garage w/two 2-3/16" plastic cars, on back of each is imprinted, 1952, 2-3/4" x 2-1/2".	50	75	135
Garbage Truck, No. 332, cab over/square cab, black rubber tires, dump action and rear loading sliding gate, marked "Metropolitan Department of Public Service" and "Help Keep our City Clean", 1956-57, 17" long	70	110	140
Gardener's Truck, No. 121, cab over/checker board, metal wheels w/black rubber tires, marked "Gardening," "Ferry's Seeds," "Fill," "Dirt," "Trees," "Shrubs" decal, wheelbarrow and round nose shovel, 1953, 10-1/4" long	50	75	110
Ice Cream Cart, sliding lid and bell, 1953, 4-1/2" long	30	50	100
Ice Truck, No. 432, long nose, black rubber tires, one ice cube and one pair ice tongs, ink stamped "Toy Town Ice Co.", 1941, 11-3/4" long	45	70	120
Ice Truck, No. 432, long nose, lithographed body, marked "Toy Town Ice Co." and "Crystal Clear", 1941, 11-3/4" long	45	70	120
Ice Truck, No. 432, shark nose, yellow metal wheels, lithographed body, "Toy Town Ice Co.," "Crystal Clear" and "23", 1949, 12" long	45	70	120
Ice Truck, No. 348, long nose, black wood wheels, two ice cubes and one pair of ice tongs, 1938-39, 11-1/2" long	45	70	120
Ice Truck, No. 123, sleepy eye/checker board, lithographed metal wheels, lithographed body, marked "Igloo Ice Company," one ice cube and one pair of ice tongs, 1954, 10-1/4" long	50	75	110
Indy Racer, black rubber tires, lithographed body w/attached head of driver, marked "Wyandotte" and "7," also "Jet Streak" version, 7" long	45	65	125

Wyandotte (Continued)

	C6	C8	C10
La Salle Land Cruiser, No. 357, white rubber tires, 1936-39, 15" long	65	125	190
La Salle Land Cruiser, No. 385, white rubber tires, hood opens, electric lights, 1939, 15" long	115	225	340
Lumber Truck/Log Hauler, No. 176, cab over, black rubber tires, six logs included, 1952, 9-1/4" long	45	60	85
Lumber Truck/Log Hauler, sleepy eye, black and white metal wheels, lithographed cab, flat bed has four plastic posts, marked "Lumber Supply," four logs included, 1952, 10-1/4" long	45	60	105
Medical Truck, No. 430, long nose, black wood wheels, reads "Medical Corps" w/Red Cross on side of canvas cloth top, 1940-41, 11-3/4" long	70	100	135
Oil/Gas Tanker, rooster comb, white rubber tires, four embossed portholes on each side, rear panel w/two windows and embossed tire (like bus), open chassis, 1939, 6-3/8" long	30	55	105
Oil/Gas Tanker, No. 376, rooster comb, white rubber tires, four embossed top hatches and fold down rear hatch, sealed chassis, 1936-38, 6-3/8" long	30	55	110
Oil/Gas Tanker, No. 225, rooster comb, black wood wheels, four embossed top hatches and fold down rear hatch, sealed chassis, 1939, 6-3/8" long	30	55	110
Pickup Truck, No. 155, black rubber tires, 1952, 5-1/2" long	10	40	65
Pickup Truck, black rubber tires, 1950s, 7-7/8" long	10	40	65
Racer, boattail, yellow wood wheels, red w/electric lights, 1933, 8-5/8" long	75	150	225
Racer, boattail, No. 333, white rubber tires, green and red, electric lights, 1934, 8-5/8" long	65	130	195
Racer, boattail, No. 310, white rubber tires, green and red, 193-34, 5-7/8" long	40	60	110
Railway Express Truck, cab over, yellow metal wheels, plastic cab and lithographed body, "Nation-Wide" "Air-Rail Service", late 1940s-52, 11" long	60	90	135

Wyandotte (Continued)

	C6	C8	C10
Railway Express Truck, cab over, black rubber tires, REA lithographed, "Nation Wide," "Air, Rail Service" and "Railway Express Agency", late 1940s-52, 12-1/2" long	60	90	135
Railway Express Truck, cab over, black rubber tires, "Wyandotte Toys" and REA lithographed on each side, late 1940s, 6-1/2" long	35	50	85
Riding Truck, No. 356, rooster comb, black rubber tires, 1935-36, 16-1/4" long	50	85	155
Riding Truck, No. 1704, square cab, black rubber tires, fire truck w/electric spot light and siren, 1952-56, 32-1/2" long	75	105	150
Riding Truck, No. 1705, square cab, black rubber tires on metal wheels, "Towing Service Car," wrecker boom w/chain operated winch, 1956-57, 32-1/2" long	75	105	145
Road Roller, No. 905, multi-color, friction motor, "Construction", 1952, 6-1/2" long	20	40	85
Rocket Racer, No. 319, white rubber tires or black wood wheels, wood rear wheel, 1935-36, 6-1/4" long	60	75	135
Sand Loader And Dump Truck, No. 401, cab over/checker board, black rubber tires, sand loader w/string operated dump hoist, "Wyandotte" on side of truck and "Wyandotte Construction Company" on side of sand loader, 1954-56, 10-3/4" long truck; 10-5/8" tall sand loader	85	125	195
Sedan, No. 311, windshield overhang, white rubber tires, w/grille, trunk mounted rear spare, 1934-37, 4-1/2" long	57	112	170
Sedan with Travel Trailer, No. 346, long nose and trailer, white rubber tires or black wood wheels, opening rear trailer door, 1938, 11-3/4" long	60	140	225
Sedan, four door, No. 425, pressed metal wheels, touring sedan (Nash style), 1939, 11" long	65	105	205
Sedan, four door, No. 344, long nose, lithographed metal wheels w/black rubber tires, enclosed chassis, 1938, 9" long	65	80	120

Wyandotte (Continued)	C6	C8	C10
Sedan, four door, rounded windshield, white rubber tires, 1934, 6-1/2" long	30	50	85
Sedan, four door, No. 316, long nose, white rubber tires, 1938, 6" long	30	50	85
Sedan, four door, No. 311, rounded windshield, white rubber tires, without grille, trunk mounted rear spare, 1934-37, 4-1/2" long..	35	60	95
Sedan, four door, No. 311, no tires, embossed at license plate is "yand," used on small car carriers, 1950s, 2-1/4" long	35	50	70
Sedan, four door, long nose, wood wheels, 1938, 9-1/8" long	65	80	120
Semi-Tractor Trailer, cab over, black rubber tires, "Wyandotte Van Lines," "Coast to Coast" and "Moving Packing Storage", 1953, 7-3/4" long	50	70	105
Semi-Tractor Trailer, No. 390, cab over, black rubber tires, "Wyandotte Express Co", 1939-41, 17-3/8" long	50	75	125
Semi-Tractor Trailer, cab over, black rubber tires, "Valley Farms Livestock Produce", 1953, 8-1/2" long	50	70	105
Soap Box Derby Racer, soap box racer, early red version w/red wood wheels and attached driver helmet, "Soap Box Derby" and "Thunderbird 226", 1941, 6" long	90	195	260
Soap Box Derby Racer, No. 226, soap box racer, red version w/red wood wheels and blue version w/black wood wheels, marked "Soap Box Derby" and "Thunderbird 226", 1941, 6" long	75	150	195
Speedster, No. 378, black wood wheels, without lithographed driver and passenger, 1937-38, 6-3/4" long	40	80	150
Speedster, No. 603, black wood wheels, pull back spring motor, 1937, 10" long	60	100	165
Speedster, No. 378, black wood wheels, w/lithographed driver and passenger, 1937-38, 6-3/4" long	50	100	200
Speedster, black wood wheels, pull back spring motor, cord-like roof over cockpit, 1938, 10" long	65	105	175

Wyandotte (Continued)	C6	C8	C10
Stake Truck, No. 352, shaded windshield, wood wheels, w/ and without electric lights, 1933-34, 15" long	60	95	150
Stake Truck, No. 426, cab over, metal wheels, 1940-45, 12-1/4" long	40	65	105
Stake Truck, No. 314, shaded windshield, white rubber tires, without grille, green or red, 1933, 4-5/8" long	40	65	85
Stake Truck, No. 314, shaded windshield, white rubber tires, w/grille, green or red, 1934, 5-1/4" long	40	65	85
Stake Truck, cab over, black rubber tires, late 1940s-50s, 5" long	35	60	75
Stake Truck, No. 317, rooster comb, white rubber tires, black wood wheels, 1934-37, 5-5/8" long	40	55	75
Stake Truck, long nose, black wood wheels, 1940-41, 12-1/4" long	50	75	105
Steam Shovel, black rubber tires, "Wyandotte Construction Company," also came w/lithographed body and "Sturdy Construction" on side, early 1950s, 7" x 4" body, 12" boom, 6-1/2" x 3-7"/8 chassis	35	55	95
Tow Truck, No. 237, cab over, black rubber tires, 152, 6" long	45	60	75
Tow Truck, sleepy eye, lithographed metal wheels, "Wyandotte Automobile Society," "Towing and Repairs" and "Towing Service Nite and Day," rear crank operated hoist, 1953, 9" long	45	70	110
Tow Truck, No. 365, long nose, black rubber tires, lithographed grille, "Service + Wrecker," "Toy Town Only 24 hr Service", 1941, 17-1/2" long	50	90	140
Tow Truck, No. 1005, long nose, black rubber tires on wood hubs, "AAA Service", 1940, 22-1/2" long	50	90	140
Tow Truck, No. 1005, long nose, black rubber tires on wood hubs, marked w/a "W", 1941, 22-1/2" long	50	90	140
Tow Truck, cab over, black rubber tires, "Wrecker Service", late 1952, 5-1/4" long	45	60	75

Wyandotte Semi-Tractor Trailer, 1953, 7-3/4" long, $105. Photo courtesy Brian Seligman

Wyandotte Tow Truck, 1953, 9" long, $110. Photo courtesy Brian Seligman

Wyandotte (Continued)	C6	C8	C10
Tractor Trailer, cab over, black rubber tires, "Produce Van," "Refrigerated Cargo" and "Coast to Coast", 1953, 7-3/4" long........	30	60	90
Tractor Trailer, No. 390, cab over, black rubber tires, "Green Valley Stock Ranch," lithographed cab marked w/"Wyandotte" and "W" in a dot on cab, 1950s, 17-1/2" long.............................	80	95	165
Winch Truck w/Removable Steam Shovel, cab over, black rubber tires, plastic motor, rubber exhaust pipe, sliding rear ramp, removable crane, 1953, 22" long	80	100	145

Wyandotte (Continued)	C6	C8	C10
Winch Truck w/Removable Steam Shovel, open eye, black rubber tires, on red plastic hubs, tractor and flatbed w/treaded steam shovel, tool box w/tools behind cab, 1954, 22-1/2" long...............	50	75	145
Winch Truck with Removable Steam Shovel, wide face, black rubber tires, "Wyandotte Construction Co." on side of removable crane, 1949-53, 23" long	85	105	145
Winch Truck with Removable Steam Shovel, No. 2001, cab over/open eye, black rubber tires, steam shovel on tracks, 1952, 22" long.............................	80	100	140

WOODEN TOYS

Toy companies did not use plastic, or manmade material for toys of this type until the late 1930s, so items covered in this chapter are from the period 1920 through 1940.

Made primarily of wood, they were shaped by a simple turning on a lathe or by jigsaw. Their form rises from combining these simple shapes using nails, glue, rubber cords, and springs in clever ways to achieve amusing actions when played with by a child.

The wooden characters were often mounted on metal platforms to make pull toys. Workers then painted the toys primarily with the aid of stencils and stamps.

Hundreds of companies made these types of toys. Some of the important makers of these popular toys include—The Toy Tinkers of Evanston, Illinois; Rich Made Toys of Sterling, Illinois; Hyker Toy Co. of Highland Park, Illinois, and the Toy-Kraft Co. of Wooster, Ohio.

All photos for this chapter are courtesy Jim and Judy Sneed.

Contributors: Jim and Judy Sneed, Hollywood, South Carolina. The Sneeds began collecting wooden pull toys about five years ago and now have a collection of over 150 of these toys. They maintain a Web site at www.oldwoodtoys.com where information seekers may find photos, company histories, want lists, and price guides. They can be contacted through this Web site.

Hustler Toy Company

In 1920, the Frantz Manufacturing Company of Sterling, Illinois began making toys. These early toys were marked "Frantz" and included the very popular baseball and football games.

In 1924, responding to rumors that Frantz was getting out of the hardware business, he created the Hustler Toy Company as a subsidiary. Toys of this transition period can be found with a Hustler decal over a Frantz logo. In the late 1920s, they took over the Toylander Corporation, a toy manufacturer in Sterling, Illinois. Some of the goose pull toy and possibly other toys are marked Hustler, while others are marked Toylander.

The chief designer was Clare A. Wetzel, and his name appears on almost all Frantz and Hustler patents.

Hustler Toy Company made wood toys well into the 1930s and seemed to have stopped by 1939. After that, the hustler name appears only on metal strap-on roller skates until about 1970. Frantz Manufacturing is still in business making bearings and steel balls in Sterling, Illinois.

A C6 grade indicates noticeable playwear, but still an attractive sample. A C9 grade indicates a sample that has not seen play but may have one or more handling or storage flaws such as a paint chip, but is otherwise indistinguishable from new. Mint pieces are almost impossible to find and command premium prices, especially with their original boxes. Names and spellings are those of the Hustler Toy Co.

Hustler Toy Company

	C6	C9
Action Builder, canister full of parts, 12" high canister	50	90
Aerorace Shooter, airplane game, 8" x 15"	NPF	NPF
Auto Caravan Truck, w/four trailers, 8" long	60	100
Auto Transport Truck, w/four autos, 21" long	150	280

Hustler Toy Company (Continued)

	C6	C9
Aviator Clown Riding Torpedo Airplane	80	180
Baby Hustler Crib Doll, girl, 6"	25	65
Baseball, lithographed playing surface w/pegs	100	175
Beads, glass jars, three sizes	25	45
Beads, metal cans, three sizes	45	70
Bell-Hop, black bell hop, bags, 8"	85	190
Betty Roll Duck, three-wheel, ivory or yellow	25	45
Betty Roll Duck, four-wheel, fixed ivory, blue, or pink	25	45
Big Joe Hustler, giant version of Joe Hustler	NPF	NPF
Big Pete Hustler, giant version of Peter Hustler, 23"	NPF	NPF
Big Sambo, giant version of Sambo Hustler	NPF	NPF
Bildkraft Erector, set-type	NPF	NPF
Billy Hustler, dog pulling wagon and driver, 15"	75	125
Block Engine, colorful blocks, cylinders, 10"	NPF	NPF
Bobby Beach Duck, green or yellow flat base, duck head	25	45
Camel, w/blanket walker, 11" long	40	85
Circus Pony, push-pull toy, bell on back, 13"	55	110
Circus Train, loco and four circus wagons, 30"	NPF	NPF
Clown Car, clown driving jalopy, from patent	NPF	NPF

Betty Roll Duck, Hustler Doll Co., $75.

Hustler Twins, Hustler, $150.

Hustler Toy Company (Continued)	C6	C9
Color Boat, colored funnels on boat, 12" long.....................................	40	85
Crew, four oarsmen in boat, 10"	45	90
Doc, black base, old style auto, 14"	90	180
Doc, green base, newer syled auto, 14".....	90	180
Doc Stork, stork on delivery bike, 14"	NPF	NPF
Doll Carriage, giant horse, wagon, 18"..	NPF	NPF
Dolly Tinkle Hustler, push toy, doll w/bell, 21"..	NPF	NPF
Duck Duck, w/litho wagon, 13"	50	90
Ducky Racer, duck driving car, 12"	150	325
Easter Bunny Bunny, w/egg box on back, 8"..	NPF	NPF
Elephant, walker, red, hard rubber feet, 11" long..	45	80
Elephant and Trainer, trainer and elephant, 14"...	NPF	NPF
Elephant Parade, elephant and baby elephant, 14"..	NPF	NPF
Floaty Duck, duck on water, bucket, 12"...	NPF	NPF
Football, lithographed field and stadium...	90	165
Fran-zell Walking-Barking Dog, black and white dog, collar,, 8"	35	70
Gardener, driver and horse, large wagon, 23"..	130	270
Golf Game, golfer puts into tray, 18"........	NPF	NPF
Hiram Hustler, farmer driving horse, 11" long...	90	150
Horse Shoe Players, two players w/rings ..	45	80

Hustler Toy Company (Continued)	C6	C9
Jack Rabbit, rabbit holding carrot, 12"	NPF	NPF
Jimmie Mouse, mouse driving red auto, 11"	250	400
Joe Hustler, litho bucket, four wheels, 11"	90	170
Joe Hustler Transfer, wood, bucket, four wheels, 11"...	80	150
Jungle Pals, red lion driven by dog	125	280
Kids, Joe and Pete on tricycle wagon, 14"...	75	180
Kitty, cat pushing ball, 11" long...............	NPF	NPF
Larry Hustler, boy riding horse, 8"	40	90
Limber Jack, man on truck pushing with hands, 15"..	150	280
Movie in Felt, animal show play set..........	NPF	NPF
Nok-Out Bench, mallet and blocks, 12"...	15	35
Peppy Pup, roll over pup, hand control.....	50	90
Peter Hustler, litho bucket, tricycle, 11" ...	90	170
Peter Hustler Transfer, wood bucket, tricycle, 11"	85	150
Play-Learn, letters and pictures learning game	NPF	NPF
Poncho Hustler, clown, dog riding mule, 17"...	125	225
Pup, Hustler walking barking dog, 8"	35	75
Pup with Blanket, pup with blanket on back, 8"	NPF	NPF
Questor, fortune telling game, 9" x 14".....	NPF	NPF
Racer, race horse and jockey, 8" high	90	180

Mexican Man, possibly Jaymar, $50.

Denny Dimwit, 1948, $350.

*Pete the Pup, Cameo Doll Co., 12",
$275.*

Hustler Toy Company (Continued)	C6	C9
Rastus and Rachel, two characters, dog, mule drawn, 20"	225	400
Red Cap, white face porter, 8"	NPF	NPF
Ring Toss, girl, numbered balls, 15"	60	90
Rolls-right, rights itself	15	25
Sam Hustler Transfer, man driving mule, 21"	NPF	NPF
Sambo Hustler, black driver, horse head, 11"	85	135
San Duck, duck head with bucket, 15"	50	90
San Fish, fish with bucket on back, 16"	NPF	NPF
Sand Box, shovel, box, 6" x 10"	30	65
Sand Cart, shovel, cart, 7" x 11"	35	55
Sand Sprinkler, sand sprinker system, shovel, 14"	NPF	NPF
Scotty Hustler, dog barks at frog, 14"	NPF	NPF
Speed Boat, man and two children in boat, 12"	NPF	NPF
Surf-rider, man on surf board, 8"	NPF	NPF
Swimmer, arms on wheels, 9"	34	90
Target Game, cowboy on target, dart gun, 28"	NPF	NPF
Terry Hustler, push-pull toy, walking dog, 11"	55	90
Tulip Peg Board, teaching tool	25	50
Twins, two dancing girls, green base, 7"	75	150

Rich Toys	C6	C9
Borden's Dairy Wagon, wagon is marked "Borden's Dairy"	200	450
Budweiser Wagon, three horses pulling Bud Wagon	350	800
Dutch Maid, girl jumping rope	100	190
Horse and Jockey, The, gallops when pulled	80	160
Large Model Monoplane, propeller and rudder move, 17"	NPF	NPF
Old Dutch Mill, The, fan rotates	80	150
Old Missouri, mule pulls green wagon	NPF	NPF
Our Drummer Boy, soldier marches and beats drum	NPF	NPF
Pat and Pup, dog with red jacket	60	110
Rich Line Train, The, steam engine and two open cars	NPF	NPF

Scarey Anns	C6	C9
Black Face Girl, Known as Picaninny, 5-1/2"	70	110
Black Face Man, rare, 5-1/2"	NPF	NPF
Chinese Girl, rare, 5-1/2"	NPF	NPF
Chinese Man, rare, 5-1/2"	NPF	NPF
Clown, w/lever operating hat and nose, 5-1/2"	80	110
Clown, no mechanism, 5-1/2"	50	80

Scarey Anns (Continued)

	C6	C9
Donkey, ears move, for Democratic Party, 5-1/2"	NPF	NPF
Elephant, trunk moves, for Republican Party, 5-1/2"	NPF	NPF
Grandfather, beard wiggles, rare, 5-1/2"	NPF	NPF
Mexican Man, lever operates nose and sombrero, 5-1/2"	100	250
Policeman, blue suit, 5-1/2"	NPF	NPF
Pumpkin Man, Halloween, Jack-O-Lantern head, 5-1/2"	180	250
Sailor, old style flat hat; hat and nose move, 5-1/2"	25	70
Sailor, new style white hat; hat and nose move, 5-1/2"	25	70
White Face Girl, very rare 2" size	NPF	NPF
White Face Girl, most common, flowers on dress, 5-1/2"	25	70

The Ted Toy-lers

The Ted Toy-lers began toy production in 1925 in New Bedford, Massachusetts. The founder and chief designer was Edwin V. Babbit of Fairhaven, Massachusetts.

The Ted Toy-lers (also spelled Toylers) reached its peak in about 1928 shipping more than 50,000 toys a week all over the world. In 1929, International Toy Company took over, or merged with The Ted Toy-lers. Toy labels of this period say "The Ted Toylers, an International Toy Co." At this time, probable to increase sales, the company made smaller and cheaper versions of its best-selling toys. For example, oilcloth belts and hat plumes were replaced with painted representations. In 1930, The Ted Toy-lers ceased operations and Edwin V. Babbit started a new toy company making dollhouses.

Their toys were of the highest quality, made of birch wood, and painted with a durable lacquer. Early toys used braided cord for arms and legs, but in 1927, springs or wires running through wooden arm and leg beads replaced the cords.

Toys marked International Toys were produced in 1929, and possibly 1928 and 1930.

A C6 grade indicates noticeable play wear, but still an attractive sample. A C9 grade indicates a sample that has not seen play, but may have one or more handling or storage flaws such as a paint chip, but is otherwise indistinguishable from new. Mint pieces are almost impossible to find and command premium prices, especially with their original boxes. Names and spellings are those of the Ted Toylers. Toys are pull toys unless otherwise described.

Ted Toy-lers, The

	C6	C9
Acrobat klown, beaded legs, four wheels	95	170
Acrobat klown, corded legs, three wheel	85	180
Aeroplane, white plane, two heads, pull toy, 16"	125	225

Ted Toy-lers, The (Continued)

	C6	C9
Blue Sailor Doll, corded arms and legs, 6"	35	70
Continental Soldier, 3-point hat, rare	150	250
Dapple Horse, black and white horse, beaded legs, 5"	50	125
Galloping Jockey, dapple horse bifurcated horse legs	60	135
Galloping Jockey, dapple horse, 7"	75	155
Galloping Jockey, black horse, 7"	60	145
Giant Galloping Jockey, klown on dapple horse, 13-1/2"	150	350
Giant Horse, black and white, beaded legs, 11"	100	210
Giant Klown Doll, yellow suit, beaded arms legs, 17"	85	180
Giant Marching Soldier, wood rifle, red body, yellow legs, 19"	125	280
Giant Roaring Racer, yellow race car, two heads, 17-1/2"	100	225
Giant Soldier Doll, red suit, beaded arms legs, 16" high	100	170
Giant Ted Toy Express, two horses pulling wagon, 20"	NPF	NPF
Giant Walking Sailor Doll, blue suit, beaded arms legs, 19"	90	150
Hobby, corded arms and wood stick legs	90	190
Hobby, beaded arms and legs	90	190
Locomotive, red and yellow, 7" long	35	90
Marching Lady Soldier, known only from head and body	NPF	NPF
Marching Soldier, cord arms, 10"	65	135
Marching Soldier, beaded arms	75	145
Marching Soldier Squad, five marching soldiers, 11"	250	550
Racer, one head, 5" long	20	50
Racing Jockeys, two horses w/jockeys, 6"	45	85
Red Soldier Doll, beaded arms, red suit, 8" high	35	75
Roaring Racer, yellow race, two drivers	80	155
Sailboat, two sails, two heads, 12" long	NPF	NPF
Sea Skooter, catamaran boat, two heads, 13"	NPF	NPF
Ted Toy Army Bowling Game, w/five 8" soldiers	180	350
Ted Toy Express, two horses pulling wagon, 12"	60	125
Toy Crafter, builder set in 4" x 10" x 2" box	35	65
Train Loco, w/three cars, 28" long	100	185

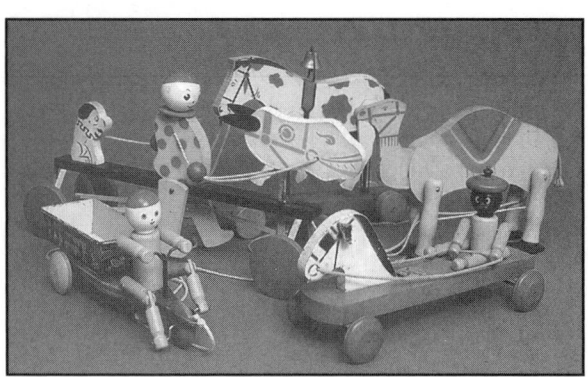

Hustler Toys from left – Pete, $120; Poncho, $180; Circus Pony, 110; Sambo, $250; Camel, $85.

Hustler Toys from left – Billy, $125; Watch Dog, $170; Larry, $70; Betty Roll Duck, $30; Pup, $75.

Hustler Poncho, $200.

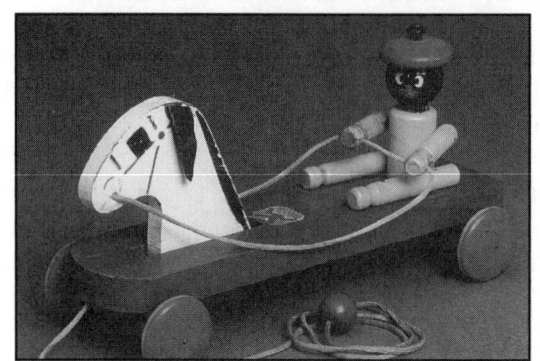

Hustler Sambo, $250.

Hustler Twins with its original box. $210.

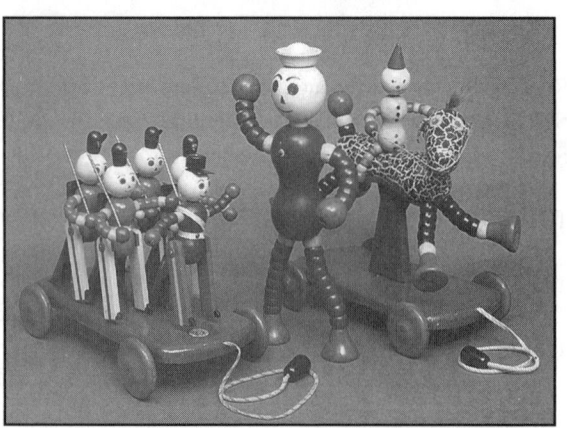

Giant Ted Toylers from left – Marching Squad, $550; Sailor, $100; Galloping Jockey, $350.

Reed Circus, $2000.

Punch and Judy Theater, $650.

Soldiers on Horses, possibly Reed, $300.

Ted Toy-lers, The (Continued)

	C6	C9
Waddling Duck, yellow duck, metal legs and tail, 6"	25	65
Waddling Duck, waddling duck pull toy..	65	110
Walking Sailor, beaded arms, wood legs ..	60	120
Walking Sailor, cord arms and legs..........	55	100
White Sailor Doll, corded arms and legs, 6"	35	80
Yellow Klown Doll, beaded arms and legs, 7"..	55	90

The Toy Kraft Co.

The Toy Kraft Co. of Wooster, Ohio, began toy making in 1916 and continued until 1950. Early toys made were of high quality, but by the 1940s, the line was cheapened by the introduction of cardboard materials.

Today, a Wooster company is reproducing a few of Toy Kraft's early toys.

Toy Kraft Co., The

	C6	C9
Bunny and Wagon, bunny pulling wagon	90	180
Bunny Duck Cart, Bunny pushing two ducks cart	NPF	NPF
Bunny Team and Wagon, two bunnies pulling wagon...	NPF	NPF

Toy Kraft Co., The (Continued)

	C6	C9
Circus Horse and Rider, flat rider on horse pull toy	NPF	NPF
Circus Wagon, w/various animals.............	110	225
Ducky Cart, two ducks pulling wagon	NPF	NPF
Elephant, pull toy, 11-1/2" x 9".................	55	100
Elephant Push Cart, elephant pushing cart..	NPF	NPF
Flower Wheelbarrow, cart w/blue flower on side	NPF	NPF
Lion, pull toy, 10-1/4" x 12"	55	100
Mother Goose, pull toy, 11-1/2" x 7"	45	95
Pup, dog pull toy	55	100
Puss-in-boots Cart, pulling cart, 1933..	NPF	NPF

CONDITION CODE

C6 Good; evident overall wear, well played with but acceptable to many collectors

C8 Very Good; minor overall wear, very clean

C10 Mint; like new

Note: Mint in Box commands a higher price.
Condition below C6 brings considerably lower prices

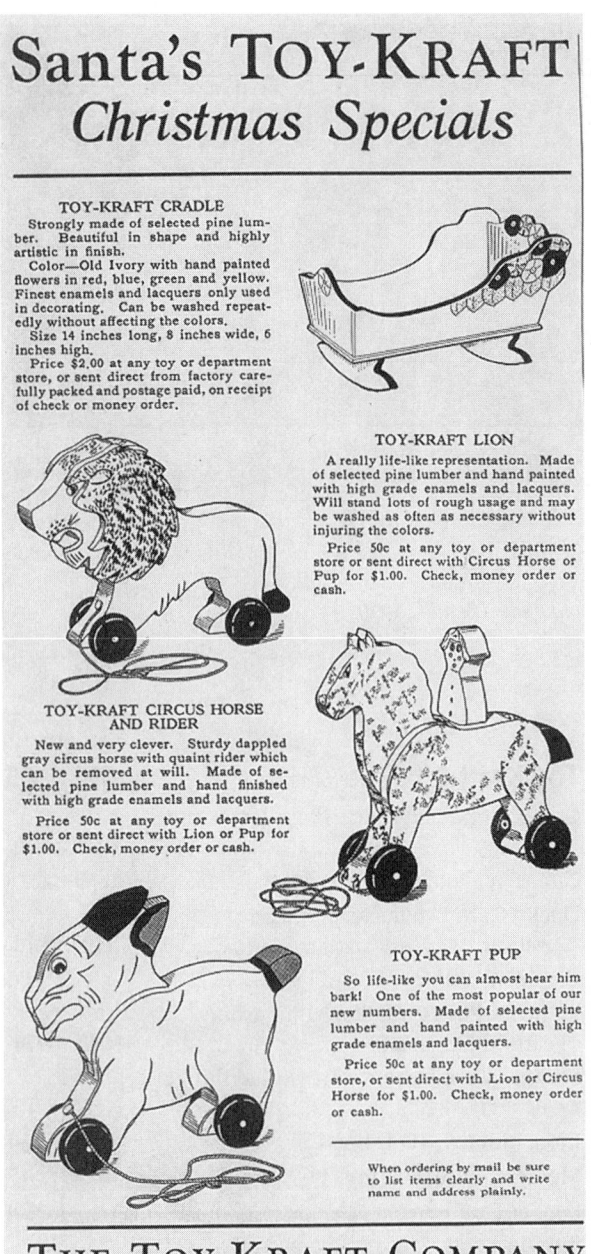

Santa's TOY-KRAFT
Christmas Specials

TOY-KRAFT CRADLE

Strongly made of selected pine lumber. Beautiful in shape and highly artistic in finish.

Color—Old Ivory with hand painted flowers in red, blue, green and yellow. Finest enamels and lacquers only used in decorating. Can be washed repeatedly without affecting the colors.

Size 14 inches long, 8 inches wide, 6 inches high.

Price $2.00 at any toy or department store, or sent direct from factory carefully packed and postage paid, on receipt of check or money order.

TOY-KRAFT LION

A really life-like representation. Made of selected pine lumber and hand painted with high grade enamels and lacquers. Will stand lots of rough usage and may be washed as often as necessary without injuring the colors.

Price 50c at any toy or department store or sent direct with Circus Horse or Pup for $1.00. Check, money order or cash.

TOY-KRAFT CIRCUS HORSE AND RIDER

New and very clever. Sturdy dappled gray circus horse with quaint rider which can be removed at will. Made of selected pine lumber and hand finished with high grade enamels and lacquers.

Price 50c at any toy or department store or sent direct with Lion or Pup for $1.00. Check, money order or cash.

TOY-KRAFT PUP

So life-like you can almost hear him bark! One of the most popular of our new numbers. Made of selected pine lumber and hand painted with high grade enamels and lacquers.

Price 50c at any toy or department store, or sent direct with Lion or Circus Horse for $1.00. Check, money order or cash.

When ordering by mail be sure to list items clearly and write name and address plainly.

THE TOY-KRAFT COMPANY
FACTORY AND STUDIOS, WOOSTER, OHIO

1926 Toy-Kraft ad.

HYKER TOYS
"Real Playthings"

The HYKER TURTLE

❡ Here is the latest and greatest sensation in an animated, land and water toy. The legs and tail move back and forth while the head moves in and out as it is pulled along. This toy can be used anywhere, and when pulled through the water it floats, dives and swims around giving every resemblance of a real live turtle. It is the only toy of its kind on the market.

❡ The Hyker Turtle is 9 inches in diameter, made of solid wood, beautifully decorated in life-like colors, water proof Duco enamel. It is capable of sustaining 180 pounds and a child can stand on the Turtle and can be pulled along without harm to the toy.

❡ Every Hyker Toy is made in the best possible manner, and the four different toys are packed in individual cartons, beautifully printed in colors, which enable the dealer to make a splendid display of different numbers. The sales possibilities of these toys are simply amazing, and before long "HYKER" will be a household word with the children.

❡ We have a very attractive proposition for you and can show you where you can cash in big with the Hyker line. Just mail the coupon on the reverse side of this page for full particulars about these rapid selling toys.

Huber-Sweet Manufacturing Co.
Highland Park, Illinois

Printed in U. S. A.

Hyker Toy Company 1920s toy advertisement.

Ted Toyler soldiers, 10 inch regular size and 19 inch giant.

Scarey Anns from left – Jack-O-Lantern, New style sailor, Scary Ann girl.

Scarey Ann Mexican, $300.

The Toy Kraft Co. 1920s ad.

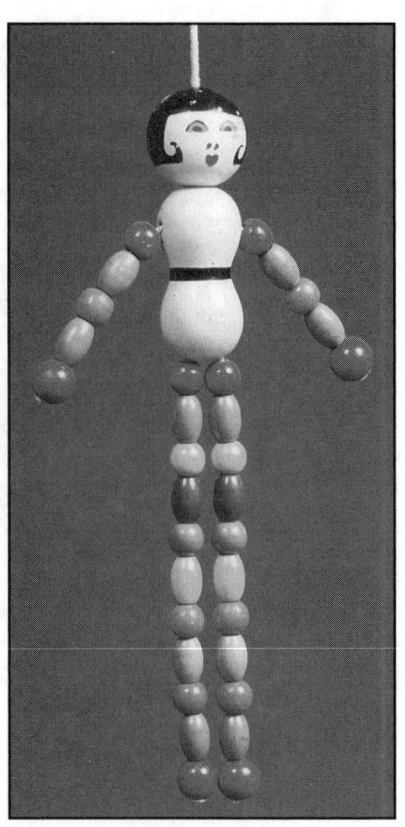

*Rare Ted Toyler
Continental Soldier, $250.*

*Rare Ted Toyler
crib toy, $200.*

Toy Kraft pull toys ad from 1920s.

YO-YOS

Delve back into the misty reaches of history and you'll find yo-yos. If you don't believe me, page through the Oxford English Dictionary to the word "bandalore," the yo-yo term of a prior age. According to the venerable OED, the bandalore even back in the early 1800s was regarded as the toy of a bygone era.

It may have originated in ancient Greece, ancient Egypt, or even the Phillippines, where the items were not toys but weapons of the hunt. The yo-yo of today, however, is most definitely a toy. It is one, moreover, that toy collectors are finding of increased interest.

Yo-yo collecting has become an important toy-collecting activity in the last few decades. While many collectors focus on the higher visibility and higher value yo-yos bearing such names as Flores, Duncan, or Cheerio, the number of other manufacturers that made these toys must be immense. In the post-World War II period of the late 1940s alone, at least a dozen companies were issuing "Yo-Yo Tops." Among them,

for many collectors, only the name of Donald F. Duncan would be familiar. Yet also making yo-yos were A.E. Beck Mfg. Co. of Herrick, Ill.; Corey Games of Boston; Jerome Gropper Co., Nadel & Sons, and F.W. Peterson Co. of New York City; Kaysons Novelty Co. and Pyramid Novelty Co., of Brooklyn; Lawrence Specialty Mfg. Co. of Lawrence, Mass.; Ponham Mfg. Co. of Riverside, R.I.; and The Sock-It Co., of High Point, N.C. One of these smaller companies is introduced below.

Please note that prices remain highly volatile. Poorer condition yo-yos will usually command considerably less than Mint examples, no matter the rarity.

Contributor: Mark Rich, P.O. Box 971, Stevens Point, WI 54481. Rich is a collector, dealer, and free-lance writer.

CAYO MANUFACTURING COMPANY

	C6	C8	C10
Musical Ka-Yo, tin whistler, 1930s	67	132	200
Whistling Ka-Yo, tin whistler	50	100	150

CHEERIO TOYS AND GAMES INC.

	C6	C8	C10
Cheerio Yo-Yo, Kitchener Buttons, Ltd., wood, decal, 1920s-40s	75	115	150
Glitter Spin, wood, four jewels each side, foil decal, 1947	50	100	150
Glitter Spin, wood, die-stamped, four jewels each side, 1950s	42	83	125
No. 25 Tournament Practice Return Tops, wood, foil decal, 1940s-50s	17	33	50
No. 33 Beginners, wood, die-stamped, 1950s	15	30	45
No. 54 Special Yo-Yo, wood	25	37	50
No. 55 Beginner's Return Tops, wood, foil decal	22	43	65
Official Pro 99, wood, foil decal	22	43	65
Tournament Practice 99, wood, foil decal	30	60	90

CHICO TOYS COMPANY

	C6	C8	C10
Olympic Tournament Yo-Yo Tops, wood, foil decal	15	30	45

	C6	C8	C10
Super Deluxe, wood, die-stamped plus label	12	23	35
Super Tournament Tops, wood, label	12	23	35
Superb Junior Top, wood, die-stamped, five stars above "Chico"	12	23	35

DONALD F. DUNCAN INC.

Duncan Advertising Yo-Yos

	C6	C8	C10
7-Up, wood, die-stamped, 1950s	7	15	22
Bosco Bear, wood, die-stamped, 1950s	7	15	22
Chrysler Corp, wood, die-stamped, 1950s	10	20	30
Coca-Cola, wood, die-stamped, 1950s	12	23	35
Dr. Pepper, wood, die-stamped, 1950s	10	20	30
Kist Beverages, wood, die-stamped, 1950s	8	17	25
Whirlpool, wood, die-stamped, 1950s	8	17	25

Duncan Butterfly Yo-Yos

	C6	C8	C10
Duncan Expert Award, wood, metal-fleck paint, die-stamped w/eagle, late 1950s	15	30	45

O'BRIEN'S COLLECTING TOYS 11TH EDITION

Chico Superb Standard Top, $35.

Duncan Beg, Yo-Yo, wood, $30.

Duncan Butterfly Yo-Yos	C6	C8	C10
Duncan Flat Top Return Tops, wood, die-stamped, 1950s...........	25	50	75

Duncan Plastic Yo-Yos	C6	C8	C10
Duncan Autograph Yo-Yo, sperical, late 1950s	15	30	45

Duncan Tin-Litho Yo-Yos	C6	C8	C10
Genuine Duncan Rainbow Yo-Yo, separate inside yo-yo..................	170	330	500
Genuine Duncan Whistling Yo-Yo, No. 88, in various geometric patterns/colors, 1930s........................	93	185	280
Genuine Duncan Whistling Yo-Yo Tops, solid color, 1940s	25	50	75
O-Boy Duncan Whistling Yo-Yo, 1930s	150	300	450

Duncan Wood Yo-Yos	C6	C8	C10
Duncan Autograph Yo-Yo, late 1950s	20	32	45
Duncan Award Yo-Yo, yellow, Mr. Yo-Yo on label, 5"diameter, 1950s	33	65	100
Duncan Beginners Yo-Yo, Man's head die-stamped........................	8	16	24
Duncan Chief Yo-Yo Return Tops, No. 44, foil label w/Indian, 1950s	25	50	75

Duncan Wood Yo-Yos	C6	C8	C10
Duncan Eagle Yo-Yo Return Tops, No. 999, oversized, paper label, 1950s	33	65	100
Duncan Expert Award Yo-Yo, pearlessence paint, 1950s.............	15	30	45
Duncan Jeweled Pearlessence Tournament Yo-Yo Return Tops........	17	33	50
Duncan Jeweled Super Yo-Yo	22	43	65
Duncan Jeweled Tournament Yo-Yo Tops, No. 77, Mr. Yo-Yo decal, fluorescent paint, 1950s	25	37	50
Duncan Junior Yo-Yo, die-stamped, late 1950s	8	17	25
Duncan Litening Yo-Yo Return Tops, crackle paint, foil label, 1950s	25	50	75
Duncan Master Tops, die-stamped with "Mr. Yo-Yo"	12	23	35
Duncan O-Boy Junior, 1930s	15	30	45
Duncan O-Boy Yo-Yo, silver stamped, "Pat Pend.", 1930s	17	33	50
Duncan Pearlessence Tournament Yo-Yo Return Tops, No. 888, late 1950s	15	30	45
Duncan Rainbow Tournament Yo-Yo Return Tops, die-stamped, 1950s	12	23	35

Duncan Wood Yo-Yos

	C6	C8	C10
Duncan Rainbow Yo-Yo Return Tops, No. 77, foil label, late 1950s	17	33	50
Duncan Satellite Yo-Yo, die-stamped w/stars, 1960s	12	23	35
Duncan Small Fry, 1960s	10	20	30
Duncan Special 44 Yo-Yo Tops, 1950s	12	23	35
Duncan Spin Master, 1960s	12	23	35
Duncan Suede Tournament Yo-Yo Tops, flock covering, 1950s	15	30	45
Duncan Super Tournament Yo-Yo Return Tops, No. 77, 1950s	15	30	45
Duncan Super Yo-Yo Practice Return Tops, late 1950s	17	33	50
Duncan Super Yo-Yo Tournament Tops, No. 77, 1950s-60s	12	23	35
Duncan Tournament Yo-Yo, pennent logo, four jewels, 1960s	15	30	45
Duncan Tournament Yo-Yo, die-stamped pennant logo	8	17	25
Duncan Yo-Yo Champion, pearl-essence paint, silver foil sticker w/eagle, late 1950s	33	65	100
Duncarn Yo-Yo Return Toops, M1 Satellite, die-stamped, 1960s	12	23	35
Duncarn Yo-Yo Return Toops, M1 Satellite, whistling model, 1960s	13	26	40
Genuine Duncan Beginner's Yo-Yo, No. 33 and No. 44, junior size, 1940s-50s	8	17	25
Genuine Duncan Beginner's Yo-Yo Tops, No. 44, die-stamped	12	23	35
Genuine Duncan Jeweled Yo-Yo, die-stamped, five jewels	25	50	75
Genuine Duncan Jeweled Yo-Yo Tops, full sized, die-stamped	12	23	35
Genuine Duncan Junior Yo-Yo Tops, No. 33, die-stamped, 1930s	12	23	35
Genuine Duncan Tournament Yo-Yo Tops, No. 77, die-stamped, 1930s	12	23	35
Genuine Duncan Tournament Yo-Yo Tops, air-brushed stripe, 1930s	42	70	95
Genuine Duncan Tournament Yo-Yo Tops, No. 77, crackle paint, decal	195	320	425
Genuine Duncan Tournament Yo-Yo Tops, die-stamped, 1940s	8	19	30

Duncan Wood Yo-Yos

	C6	C8	C10
Genuine Duncan Tournament Yo-Yo Tops, foil decal, 1930s	17	33	50
Genuine Duncan Tournament Yo-Yo Tops, yellow label, 1940s	15	30	45
Genuine Duncan Yo-Yo Tournament Tops, No. 77, Mr. Yo-Yo on yellow decal, oversized version, 1940s	32	63	95
Genuine Duncan Yo-Yo Tournament Tops, No. 77, Mr. Yo-Yo on yellow decal, 1940s	15	30	45
Luck-EJA-DO Contest Tops, four-leaf clover logo, 1950s	17	33	50
O-Boy Duncan Yo-Yo, die-stamped, 1930s	15	30	45
Oboy Yo-Yo, 1929	32	55	75
Seattle Space Needle Duncan Yo-Yo Return Tops, each half resembles the topof Seattle's Space Needle, two-tone paint, "Seattlite" and "Space Needle", 1962	270	530	800

FLI-BACK COMPANY, INC.

	C6	C8	C10
Fli-Back 45, 55 or 65 Yo-Yo, wood, die-stamped	7	16	25
Fli-Back Tops, wood, die-stamped, no eagle	7	13	20
Fli-Back Tops, wood, die-stamped, w/eagle	7	13	20
Orbit Away, wood, butterfly	8	17	25

FLORES, AKA THE YO-YO MANUFACTURING COMPANY

	C6	C8	C10
Flores Yo-Yo, wood, black paper sticker	150	300	450
Flores Yo-Yo, wood, "Pat. Pend.," regular or junior size	150	300	450
Genuine Flores Yo-Yo, wood, stamped	130	260	400
Original Flores Yo-Yo Tops, wood, oversize	15	30	45

GOODY MANUFACTURING COMPANY

	C6	C8	C10
Genuine Goody Atomic Filipino Twirler, wood	32	55	75
Genuine Goody Champion Filipino Twirler, wood, three jewels	25	50	75

Bosco Bear, wood, die-stamped, 1950s, $20.

'56 Chevrolet, wood, $50.

	C6	C8	C10
Genuine Goody Master Filipino Twirler, wood, w/jewel, "Master" w/3 stars on one side; "Genuine Goody Filipino Twirler" on other; see-through axle	62	122	185
Genuine Goody Master Filipino Twirler, wood	22	43	65
Genuine Goody Winner Filipino Twirler, wood, w/jewel	32	55	75
Goody Joy-O-Top, wood	20	40	60
Goody Rainbow Filipino Twirler, wood, seven jewels	33	65	100

THE SOCK-IT CO., INC.

	C6	C8	C10
Fli-Back, wood	7	15	22
Space Whirler, wood, satalliet-like spaceship decal	8	17	25
Whirl-King, wood	7	15	22

Duncan Gen. Beg. Yo-Yo Tops, wood, 1930s, $35.

WANTED: Pop Culture & Nostalgia

Ted Hake established Hake's Americana in 1967 and today the firm is America's leading telephone and internet bid auction house specializing in nostalgia and popular culture collectibles. Each year Hake's buys and sells 20,000 one of a kind collectibles. Hundreds of thousands of dollars are spent annually to purchase material in over 100 different categories to supply the thousands of worldwide customers who subscribe to five annual auctions. As Hake's has an exclusive worldwide clientele, we pay a high percentage of our anticipated retail to ensure a constant supply of quality collectibles for our customers.

Pin-Back Buttons: Political and Non-Political

Our personal favorite for over 30 years. We buy buttons that relate to every category. Defects like stain, scratches and splits greatly reduce value. Here are specific offers assuming no damage whatsoever. Send photocopies

Political

Pre-1896 lapel badges showing candidates on tin or cardboard photos	usually $100+
McKinley & Hobart on bicycle	3,000
McKinley showing factory & dinner pati	1,500
McKinley or Bryan on hobby horse	2,500
McKinley or Bryan "Eclipse" buttons	500+
Teddy Roosevelt shown with Fairbanks	usually 50+
Teddy Roosevelt shown with Johnson	1,000
James Cox 1920 picture buttons	any 100+
Cox and Franklin Roosevelt BOTH PICTURES	10,000
Truman picture on 8-ball design	4,000
Most pre-1932 picture buttons	at least 15
Votes for women & other political causes	10

Non-Political

Product advertising with pictures, pre 1920	usually $10
Farm equipment with pictures	usually 20
Mickey Mouse or Donald Duck 1930s	usually 75
Elvis Presley 1950s fan club	100
Cowboys - Tom Mix, Hoppy, Roy, Gene	usually 10
Santa Claus 1930s or earlier	usually 35
Lindbergh & early aviation	usually 15
Wonder Woman 1940s	500
Flash or U.S. Jones 1940s	ea. 500
Yellow Kid numbered series	ea. 20
Kellogg's Pep comic characters	ea. 5
Thousands of others - send photocopies	

WANTED ITEMS

Advertising: Ad figures representing Speedy Alka-Seltzer $150, Mr. Peanut wood jointed $100, Reddy Kilowatt $75+, Charlie The Tuna $15, hundreds of others. Also paper or objects from early years of famous American Companies.

Artist: From $10 for simple items to $1,000+ for original art by artists such as Disney, Vernon Grant, George Herriman, Winsor McCay, Maxfield Parrish, Richard Outcault and other comic character artists.

Autographs: Letters or signed photos of famous people like Marilyn Monroe $2,000, John Kennedy $1,000, Walt Disney $1,000 and hundreds of others.

Aviation About anything from 1940s or earlier for real or toy airplanes or airships. World War II ID models $25+, Lindbergh toys or games $50+, Zeppelin souvenirs $25+.

Baseball: Any World Series or All-Star items like programs or press pins, up to $1,000+ for early items, Hartland 1960s plastic figures $75, bobbing head 1960s figures $25+. Nearly anything 1960s or earlier has some value.

Beatles Any character merchandise from the 1960s such as toy guitar $150, record cases $75, lunch box $100+, also Yellow Submarine. Gum cards not wanted.

Bicycles Lapel studs or buttons from 1900 era each $5, League of American Wheelmen items $20+, medals for 1900 era meetings or races $25+, high wheel items, most $50+.

Big Little Books All titles, for excellent condition $10.

Black Americana: Mechanical toys, most $100+, salt and pepper sets, most $20+, Martin Luther King signed photo $400.

Boy Scouts: Large calendars pre-1950 $25, most pinback buttons pre-1950 $10, many other items.

Boxing: Joe Louis clock or lamp $100, pre-1930s cards, each $3, famous fight program $20+.

Captain Action: Boxed figures or accessories $100+, loose figures $75, complete outfits $50+.

Cars 1960s or earlier promotional toy models, most $50, 1930s or earlier wind-ups most $100+.

Cels: Most Disney 1950-60 $100+, Disney 1940s most $500, also many non-Disney $100+.

Comic Characters: Almost anything depicting comic or cartoon characters from the 1970s or earlier is of interest. Prices range from $3 for Flintstone jelly glasses to $2,000 for Mickey Mouse 1930s radio.

Cowboys: All items wanted for movie and TV cowboys. Most popular are Tom Mix, Hopalong Cassidy, Roy Rogers. Prices range from $400 for Tom Mix movie posters to $75 for Bonanza lunch boxes.

Cracker Jack: Any pre-1950 paper or metal item, each $10. Not wanted-plastic items or presidential coins. Items must have company name or "C.J. Co."

Dixie Lids: Any clean condition lid, at least $3. Any 8 x 10" premium picture $5+.

Dolls: Any related to specific character or real person. Elvis 1950s $1,000, Mickey or Minnie Mouse 1930s $200+, Roy Rogers or Hopalong Cassidy 1950s many others $100+.

Elvis: All items from 1956-60s era, Gum cards $3 each, toy guitar $250, wallet $100, photo ring $100, much more.

Expositions: Most pre 1970 exposition material is collected. Many items are in $5-10 range. Exception: 1939 radio $400, 1933 lamp $100, many others $25+.

Fire Most pinback buttons or ribbon badges, pre 1930, $5-10.

GI Joe: Only want 1960-1970s large size figures and accessories. Boxed American soldiers $100+, Foreign soldiers $200+, most unboxed figures $50-100, boxed or packaged accessories, many $100+. Loose pieces also purchased.

Gum Cards: All non-baseball cards from 1960s and earlier. Many sets $100+, many individual cards $2 each.

Lunch Boxes: Metal boxes wanted from 1960s and earlier. Mickey Mouse 1930s $500, Underdog $500, Jetsons $400, Paladin $200, many others $100+.

Mirrors: Celluloid covered advertising pocket mirrors usually 2 1/2" or smaller. Colorful pictures add value. Most $25, rarities $100+.

Movies: Posters, lobby cards, games, figural objects related to pre-1950 famous stars and movies, Wizard of Oz or Gone With The Wind 1939 buttons, each $100, posters for original release of classic films, many $500+.

Pin-Ups: Calendars by Varga $50, card decks many $25+, Playboy first issue $500, paper items by Elvgren or Moran, many $10+.

Presidential Campaigns: Snuff boxes $500+, ribbons with portraits, most $75+, cardboard or tintype photo badges, most $100+, pin-back buttons with pictures 1896-1932 $15 each, All types of pre-1964 material wanted.

Pulp Magazines: $10-15 for titles like Weird Tales, Doc Savage, G-8, The Spider, The Shadow, Spicy Detective, many others.

Radio & Cereal Premiums: Wanted all giveaways like rings, decoders, maps, club manuals for shows like Tom Mix, Orphan Annie, Dick Tracy, The Shadow, Green Hornet, Tarzan, Space Patrol, Buck Rogers, Howdy Doody and many more. Buck Rogers knife $500, Lone Ranger 6-Gun ring $50, Orphan Annie decoder $20, Captain Marvel statuette $3,000, Superman 1940s contest ring $5,000+, hundreds more worth $25-500.

Robots: Most from 1960s or earlier such as Lost In Space $200, Mr. Atomic $5,000, many $200+.

Television: Most items related to shows from 1948 - early 1970s. First TV Guide $300, Howdy Doody wood doll $250, Hopalong Cassidy cap gun $100, most board games pre-1970, $20+, most lunch boxes pre-1970 $35, dolls, many $75+, much more.

Toys: All types from 1960s and earlier. Comic character windups 1930s, most $200+, battery toys 1960s boxed, many $100+, Marx playsets complete, many $200+, Aurora monster or character model kits 1960s unbuilt, many $100, much more.

World War II: Homefront or anti-axis items, Douglas MacArthur, Remember Pearl Harbor, V for Victory, Prefer figural objects but much paper (and posters) also of interest. Paying $1,000 each for arcade games with anti-axis themes.

Prices for undamaged items paid by:

Hake's Americana & Collectibles
P.O. Box 1444   Dept. 625
York, PA 17405

e-mail:hake@hakes.com
fax (717) 852-0344
(717) 848-1333 M-F 10-5 Eastern

All inquiries answered. Send photos or photo copies. From those we can usually make a tentative offer. Note any defects. If interested, we will provide shipping instructions. Payment is made immediately upon receipt of item, subject to revision only if the item's condition is less than anticipated when the tentative offer was made.

O'BRIEN'S

Collecting

TOYS

11th Edition

Edited By Karen O'Brien

©2004

Published by

krause publications
An F+W Publications Company

700 East State Street • Iola, WI 54990-0001
715-445-2214 • 888-457-2873
www.krause.com

Our toll-free number to place an order or obtain a free catalog is 800-258-0929.

Library of Congress Catalog Number: 99-61890

ISBN: 0-87349-652-3

Edited by Karen O'Brien
Designed by Wendy Wendt

Printed in the United States of America

On the Cover

Front Cover

Mechanized Robot, battery-operated. Photo courtesy Christie's East
A.C. Williams Lincoln Touring Car, 9-3/4" long. Photo courtesy Bertoia Auctions
Schoenhut Tiger, Style 1, glass-eyed. Photo courtesy Jim and Patsy Carlson
Bliss "St. Louis," c. 1895. Photo courtesy Christie's East

Spine

Hubley Motorcycle, cast-iron with light, (HM17). Photo courtesy Max Heiss

Back Cover

Uncle Sam Mechanical Bank, Shepard Hardware, 1886. Photo courtesy Bertoia Auctions
Charlie McCarthy Strike up the Band tin wind up, Marx. Photo courtesy Don Hultzman
Lionel Train, No. 420 Pullman "Faye." Photo courtesy Bertoia Auctions